DATE DUE

J - Z

ENCYCLOPEDIA
OF BUSINESS

J-Z
VOLUME 2

John G. Maurer

Joel M. Shulman

Marcia L. Ruwe

Richard C. Becherer

ENCYCLOPEDIA
OF BUSINESS

Gale Research

An ITP Information/Reference Group Company

Changing the Way the World Learns

NEW YORK • LONDON • BONN • BOSTON • DETROIT
MADRID • MELBOURNE • MEXICO CITY • PARIS
SINGAPORE • TOKYO • TORONTO • WASHINGTON
ALBANY NY • BELMONT CA • CINCINNATI OH

Riverside Community College
Library
SEP '96 4800 Magnolia Avenue
Riverside, California 92506

r, John G. Maurer, Marcia L. Ruwe, Joel M. Shulman, *Managing Editors*

Gale Research Staff:

Jane Cousins Malonis, *Editor/Project Coordinator*

Shawn Brennan, Donnna Craft, Deborah S. Fennell, Carol T. Gaffke, Jeff Lehman, Susan Boyles Martin, Kimberley A. McGrath, Bradley J. Morgan, Terrance W. Peck, Stefanie Scarlett, Lia Watson, *Contributing Editors*

Donald P. Boyden, *Managing Editor*

Glenn Wolfe, *Fact Checker*

Marlene Hurst, *Permissions Supervisor*
Margaret McAvoy-Amato, *Permissions Assistant*

Mary Beth Trimper, *Production Director*
Pamela Galbreath, *Art Director*
Tracey Rowens, *Graphic Designer*

Benita L. Spight, *Data Entry Services Manager*
Gwendolyn Tucker, *Data Entry Supervisor*
Lysandra Davis and Elizabeth Pilette, *Data Entry Associates*

Since this page cannot legibly accommodate all copyright notices,
the acknowledgements constitute an extension of the copyright notice.

Library of Congress Cataloging-in-Publication Data
Encyclopedia of business / John G. Maurer . . . [et al.], editors. — 1st ed.
    p.   cm.
    Includes bibliographical references and index.
    ISBN 0-8103-9187-2
    1. Business—Encyclopedia.   2. Commerce—Encyclopedia.
3. Finance—Encyclopedia.   4. North America—Commerce—
Encyclopedia.   5. Finance—North America—Encyclopedia.
    I. Maurer, John G., 1937–   .

HF1001.E466 1995
650′.103—dc20   95-33676
                                                            CIP

 The paper used in this publication meets the minimum requirements of American National Standard for Information Sciences—Permanence Paper for Printed Library Materials, ANSI Z39.48-1984.

ISBN 0-8103-9187-2 (set), ISBN 0-8103-9188-0 (V1), ISBN 0-8103-9189-9 (V2)

Printed in the United States of America

I(T)P™ Gale Research, an International Thompson Publishing Company.
ITP logo is a trademark under license.

10 9 8 7 6 5 4 3 2 1

CONTENTS

J - Z
VOLUME 2

ENCYCLOPEDIA
OF BUSINESS

J

JAPAN, DOING BUSINESS IN

Japan's position as an economic superpower is the all the more remarkable when one considers that it is an island nation where 70 percent of the land remains covered by forests and fields. Although agriculture remains essential to Japan's economy, Japan's rapid industrialization over the past three decades has created a permanent shift away from an agricultural economy to one where **innovation** in **manufacturing**, global finance, and high technology has advantageously positioned the country for the next century. Indeed, as the *Economist* noted in March 1993, "Japan's post-war economic performance is unsurpassed in the history of the world."

HISTORY

International trading through Japan flourished during both the Kamakura (1192-1333) and Muromachi periods (1338-1573), but by 1633 the nation became isolated, banned Christianity, and sought to develop a strong culture unique from its Asian neighbors. The current period of Modernization began in 1854 when a peace and amity agreement was signed between the United States and Japan, although peace between the two countries would last for only a half century.

In the early part of the twientieth century, Japan built a modern railway (1872) but found that further modernization was delayed during wars with the Chinese (1894), Russians (1904), and Germany (1914). Much of Tokyo was destroyed in a catastrophic earthquake in 1923, and a major bank crisis caused finan-cial chaos in 1927, two years before the infamous 1929 stock market crash in the United States.

In the 1930s, Japan, which invaded China and had already occupied Korea, pursued rapid militarization. In 1940, with Germany determined to conquer Europe, Japan signed the Tripartite Pact with Germany and Italy. On December 7, 1941, the Japanese attacked American troops at Pearl Harbor, thus igniting the Pacific War, a costly excursion in terms of loss of life for both sides and an embarrassment for the Japanese when they were forced to surrender under the terms of the Potsdam agreement. In 1946 the country accepted a new constitution, promising democracy and less antagonistic relations with the world community.

By the late 1940s, Japan was transforming its manufacturing infrastructure from military to consumer applications, and the government, working with only a few select corporations, later hired prominent management theorists such as W. Edwards Deming to advise them on strategic planning. A strong relationship between government and industry was necessary to create a centrally planned economy that could thrust Japan into becoming a dominant international power. Various companies followed one successful model: always make decisions at the local level with input by teams of workers, design products that are functional and price competitive, and then invest and distribute abroad. By the 1960s, the Japanese were exporting high-quality, low-cost electronic goods to Europe and the United States, triggering a massive influx of capital as well as a trade surplus unsurpassed in human history.

As a result of wide consumer interest in Japanese appliances, automobiles, and other products, the Japanese government encouraged additional investment in **research and development** to maintain economic momentum; in 1990, for instance, the Japanese invested 25.4 percent of their **gross national product (GNP)** in plants and new equipment versus just 9.3 for Americans. This factor, combined with just-in-time delivery practices that reduce inventories, allowed the Japanese to generate such a cash surplus that leading companies were able to negotiate well-publicized investments in real estate and manufacturing plants throughout the United States, Canada, and Europe in the early 1990s.

GENERAL OVERVIEW

With just over 125 million citizens residing in 40 million households, Japan finds that the majority of its population and economic power is concentrated in its major cities, principally in Tokyo, Yokohama and Osaka. Today, Japan's vibrant economy generates 15.6 percent of the world's GNP, second only to the 26.3 percent generated by the United States. Japan's principal stock exchange, the Nikkei, trades shares in many of the world's leading corporations, including Sony, Matsushita, Toyota, and NEC.

DILIGENT EFFORT IS EXPECTED. Workers are typically recruited immediately out of college, which explains why Japanese students study longer than any other society—families demand academic excellence to ensure entry to prestigious institutions such as Tokyo University or Rikkyo University. Once hired, a young engineer or scientist can expect an excellent starting salary and stable employment, although much is expected in return: it is not uncommon for Japanese managers to work from 7 a.m. to 10 p.m.; to demonstrate loyalty to their employer very few Japanese take more than one week of vacation a year. Both at and after work, the Japanese bow to their superiors and are considered subservient; they demonstrate their respect both in addressing their supervisor and in agreeing to any task assigned to them. After work, many Japanese men will spend another hour or two drinking and socializing, meaning that they arrive home by midnight, just before the trains close for the evening.

Japanese workers must retire at the age of 55, although the government is trying to raise that age limit because so many workers are needed to fill both important and menial positions in a variety of industries.

THE KEIREITSU. The American business landscape is dominated by healthy competition and an entrepreneurial spirit that encourages hundreds of thousands of Americans to open their own businesses each year. In the United States, the role of the federal government is largely restricted to issues such as worker and consumer safety, interstate transportation, and environmental measures. In Japan, however, the relationship between government and business is so close that it is often referred to as incestuous.

Although 99 percent of all Japanese companies employ fewer than 300 employees, the reality of Japan lies with the remaining 1 percent of companies that dominate more than 90 percent of the nation's entire economic output. The nation's five largest companies—Toyota, Nippon Telegraph & Telephone Corp., Fuji Bank, Sumitomo Bank, and Sanwa Bank—are leading members of a unique collection of companies that often own pieces of one another through a confusing maze of stock ownership, joint partnerships and alliance agreements that are commonly referred to as the keiretsu. For instance, Hitachi has 688 subsidiaries, Mitsubishi has 459, Honda has 352 and Toshiba 215. Many of these firms routinely design and produce products together, invest in one another and have executives sit on each other's **board of directors**.

The members of the keiretsu are powerful global competitors who benefit from unparalleled access to the various Japanese government ministries that can grant or deny favorable treatment in terms of government loans and grants, permission to export under favorable ''exception'' rules, and other uniquely Japanese favors. Using this access, the Japanese have gained about a third of the American automobile market and 80 percent of the world television manufacturing market, with equally impressive gains in semiconductor, aerospace, and computer software technologies.

According to Professor Charles J. McMillan of York University in Canada, the keiretsu continues to grow in influence each year. ''Toyota's cash hoard, for instance, would enable it to buy, at open market rates, Ford and Chrysler combined, with spare cash. . . . The fact that Japan in this decade will outspend the U.S.—an economy twice its size—in absolute terms, both in private sector research and development and in new plants and equipment, with a primary targeting of investments to new products, services and associated infrastructure, stems in part from Japan's keiretsu structure of organization and management.''

Almost every major multinational business that has sought access to the lucrative Japanese market, from Motorola to Nabisco to Intel, has found that the power and influence of the keiretsu can be overwhelming and that only patience, moderate pressure and occasional retaliatory threats may work.

Many companies seeking to export to Japan report that the Ministry of International Trade and Industry (MITI) provides unfair advantages to Japanese firms while denying access to the marketplace by foreign competitors. Further, Japanese companies possess a major advantage over their international competitors: they spend freely to secure political favors and special treatment in foreign markets.

AN ENVIABLE RECORD

The following statistics illustrate the growing influence of the Japanese in the arena of global business:

- The ten largest banks in the world are owned and managed by the Japanese

- The three largest circulation newspapers in the world are based in Tokyo

- Japan produces more crude steel than any other country in the free world

- One out of three cars purchased every day in the world is Japanese, constituting about 20 percent of the country's exports

- Japan is the world's leading ship builder in terms of tonnage

- Japan's unemployment rate has remained at about a third of that of the United States in recent years

- Over 20 percent of all pharmaceuticals sold in the world are made by Japanese companies, second only to those based in the United States

- Japan's unit labor costs are low compared to the other major industrialized countries

TAXES

Like workers everywhere, the Japanese feel that their tax burden is unduly harsh: the combination of income, corporate, inheritance, liquor, and other **taxes** have increased sharply in recent years. When the Japanese refer to taxes, they combine the income and social security "insurance" tax to create what is called a "tax burden rate" that is an average of 27.8 percent of all incomes, compared with 26.1 percent in the United States and 40.6 percent in Great Britain. The tax burden rate is causing some alarm among policy makers because Japan's birth rate is the second lowest in the industrialized world, creating a situation in which the number of workers over 60 years of age is growing at about 10 percent a year with fewer and fewer younger workers to support their health, retirement, and living needs.

WOMEN RELEGATED TO SERVICE POSITIONS

A highly successful educational and social indoctrination program begins with preschool children who are repeatedly reminded that work is an obligation that leads to a more productive nation, stable family, and productive society. Individualism is discouraged in school and social settings in favor of a team approach that stresses learning and solving problems, a methodology which is successfully and actively applied later in industry.

Today, women comprise 38.6 percent of workers in all industries, a figure that has increased by about 2 percent per year. Although the overwhelming majority of executive and managerial positions are dominated by men, Japanese women have noted with considerable interest the successful inroads made by American and European women into industry and are increasingly demanding equal pay, benefits, and status. Although the Japanese government claims that equality in the workplace is assured, this is far more rhetoric than reality. Indeed, the majority of women are engaged in retail sales, cleaning, and junior level administrative positions.

COMMUNICATIONS

American companies seeking to expand to Japan often find that establishing and maintaining a presence is hampered by the high cost of communication as well as a series of regulatory barriers that prevent competition. Nippon Telegraph & Telephone Corp. has a virtual monopoly on telecommunication services, although three companies compete as long distance carriers. In April 1994 the Japanese government agreed to allow multinational carriers, such as American-based Motorola, Inc., to more fully compete for Japan's lucrative cellular telephone market. Although local telephone calls are comparatively inexpensive (about ten cents per minute from a pay phone), a three-minute call from Japan to the United States costs about five times more than calls generated from the United States to Japan.

Foreign corporations seeking access to the lucrative Japanese market often find that marketing in Japan offers several unique characteristics. There are Japanese marketing groups, such as Tokyu or Dai-ichi Kikaku, that can assist an American company in promoting its products and services, but most American companies turn to **joint venture** agencies that have some Western orientation, such as McCann-Erickson Hakuhodo. Japanese expert Jackson Huddleston estimated that about 50 percent of all mass media advertising is controlled by one omnipresent company, Dentsu, which purchases all television prime time at the beginning of each year and then sells each slot to the highest bidder. Such influence is virtually unheard of in Europe or North and South America. Most newspapers will only accept advertising placed through an advertising agency and almost never negotiate with an advertiser directly. Commercials on television, whether advanced by Coca-Cola or Sony, are short (typically 15 seconds) but may be repeated several times in one hour.

The Japanese are prolific readers, due in part to the typical three hours that workers in Japan spend each day on subways traveling to and from work. Magazines, trade journals, lengthy comic books for adults, and novels are commonly seen reading material. There is considerable advertising on subways and billboards, but most commercials on the radio are concentrated in the early morning and late night hours when workers are home.

Direct marketing (such as mail and coupons) so common and successful in North America, is just emerging in Japanese marketing. Some companies such as KFC (Kentucky Fried Chicken) have enjoyed considerable success by distributing coupons for their ''lunch boxes'' sold on the street to noontime workers, but other companies, such as Lands End and Victoria's Secret, are just beginning to tap the huge potential market for mail orders. American Express Co., which spent a decade trying to determine the best route to invade the Japanese credit card market, is considered by many experts to be the most successful enterprise at direct marketing in Japan. **Market research**, including the use of demographic surveys and **focus groups**, is not as well refined as in the United States, largely because the Japanese are a homogenous people with fewer ethnic and social differences than Europeans or Americans.

On the other hand, Japanese-based consumer-oriented companies employ a wide variety of marketing techniques, ranging from hawkers at department stores who use loud bullhorns to encourage customers to enter, to scores of young people who give away tissue paper and candy with advertising at subway stations and major intersections.

Although one might assume that a modern society such as Japan offers instant access to computers and databases, access to personal computers and databases is still largely reserved for corporate managers; the situation is actually acute at many libraries and research institutions where students may wait for hours to secure access to on-line databases or certain reading rooms. Although some government researchers and corporate managers have access to the **Internet**, cable television and interactive programs such as Prodigy and CompuServe will not be widely available for several years.

TRADE SURPLUS

Japan holds an envious position among industrialized nations, having a trade surplus that exceeded $103 billion in 1994—meaning that the nation exported $103 billion more than it imported. Nearly 80 percent of all exports consist of automobile and electronic products.

This is remarkable for a nation that boasts virtually no natural resources: petroleum, construction products, many foods, and chemicals needed for manufacturing are all imported. Although many reasons exist for this healthy surplus, two reasons dominate. First, the economic and political influence of major corporations in the execution of national policies is unparalleled in the democratic world, allowing companies such as Sony and Matsushita to receive considerable tax and economic incentives. Second, the nation imposes complex barriers to American and European imported goods, thus forcing Japanese consumers to purchase only from domestic concerns. In addition, a shortage of workers in Japan is compelling many leading companies to import lower-level workers from South Korea, the Philippines, and other Asian nations.

Japan's economic miracle has been fueled by a spending increase in research and development (R&D) by the government and leading companies totaling 1,064 percent over the past 21 years; the *Asahi Shimbun* newspaper reports that information processing is currently the leading research field. Other leading categories of Japanese R&D include aerospace development, marine development, and environmental controls.

JAPANESE WORKERS AT HOME

The Japanese family faces new challenges in the midst of an acute labor shortage. With one of the lowest birth rates in the world, the Japanese find increasing strain between a culture in which a woman is encouraged to remain at home and serve the needs of her family and powerful industrial corporations that need female workers to fill critical service (rarely managerial) positions. Thus, more women are entering the **workforce** and demanding equality in salary and benefit packages. Ancillary industries such as day care are proliferating, both on-site within corporations and in local communities.

The typical Japanese home is only about one-fourth the size of an American home since space is at a premium and the costs of real estate are astronomical. According to the Japanese Management and Coordination Agency, the average monthly income in Japan in 1994 was about 564,000 yen (or U.S. $57,000); this figure appears to many Americans to be astronomical, but the cost of living in Japan is about ten times higher than that in the United States. For instance, a movie ticket in Tokyo costs about $17, a loaf of bread $4, a silk tie $120, and a cup of coffee about $5.

The Japanese home, although theoretically managed by the male head of household, survives because of the incredible burdens assumed by the female who must concurrently serve as wife, mother, banker, teacher, and chores manager. These roles take place in a global environment in which professional women seek more assistance, but Japanese men appear unwilling to spend more time at home raising their children, an issue that is causing widespread public debate.

A pressured lifestyle at work and at home is triggering dramatic changes in the health profile of the Japanese: according to the Ministry of Health and Welfare, cancer has been the leading cause of death since 1981, triggered in part due to widespread smoking by both young people and adults. In addition, the Japanese diet has quickly adopted fast food and snacks (leading causes of cardiovascular disease), bringing to Japan a condition largely unheard of half a century ago.

Although many Japanese workers claim to be religious, most do not attend services regularly, and the vast majority of Japanese believe in both Buddhism and Shintoism concurrently or at different stages of their life.

PROBLEMS AND CHALLENGES

Like every major industrialized country, Japan faces its share of business challenges. Although petroleum prices have remained stable worldwide in recent years, Japan imports 99.7 percent of its oil, a fact that could lead to considerable domestic disarray in the event of a Middle East war or embargo. In addition, land reform is desperately needed; farmers argue that they cannot sell their land because of tax and zoning regulations. In addition, corruption in the form of tax evasion, bribery, and payoffs by corporations to government officials have dominated the headlines in recent years, leading to the resignations of dozens of high-ranking officials, including two prime ministers in 1993-94.

In lobbying for a permanent seat on the United Nations Security Council, Japan is seeking a broader geopolitical role as the twenty-first century approaches. The Japanese, however, have been widely criticized in business and diplomatic circles for their comparatively small contributions to peacekeeping and philanthropic campaigns for disaster victims worldwide. In addition, suspicions about Japanese expansionist intentions continue to linger throughout Southeast Asia, five decades after the conclusion of World War II. Such sentiments were ignited on May 4, 1994 when Minister of Justice Shigeto Nagano tried to justify Japan's expansionist role in World War II in a newspaper interview. As a result of numerous international protests, he resigned four days later. Japan increasingly realizes that the ramifications of such negative public relations can be severe upon business and diplomacy if not immediately squelched.

[Laurence Barton]

FURTHER READING:

Choate, Pat. *Agents of Influence.* Knopf, 1990.

Choate, Pat. ''Political Advantage: Japan's Campaign for America.'' *Harvard Business Review.* September-October, 1990, pp. 87-103.

Drucker, Peter F. ''The End of Japan, Inc.?'' *Foreign Affairs.* Spring, 1993, pp. 10-15.

McMillan, Charles J. ''Japan's Contributions to Managerial Development.'' *Business & the Contemporary World.* Winter, 1992, pp. 21-33.

Rosenblatt, Alfred, and Tekla S. Perry. ''Formula for Competitiveness.'' *IEEE Spectrum.* June, 1991, pp. 49-62.

JAPANESE MANAGEMENT TECHNIQUES

Key elements of Japanese **management** techniques include in-house training of managers, consensual and decentralized decision-making, extensive use of quality control circles, and carefully codified work standards. Emphasis is placed on creating harmonious relations among managers and between managers and workers. Compared with the United States, Japanese management is less rigidly hierarchical and more closely integrated with a firm's production processes. Lifetime employment and seniority-based earnings and advancement systems encourage managers and workers alike to take a long-term interest in their firm.

The education of managers in Japan largely takes place on an informal basis within firms. The percentage of Japanese chief executives who have attended university is high, similar to the United States and western Europe. However, very few Japanese executives have attended graduate schools when compared to their counterparts in the U.S. and western Europe. In fact, only one Japanese university offers a degree similar to an MBA, a key credential for managers in the United States.

Formal education for managers is also not well developed at the undergraduate level. Undergraduate education is not viewed by firms as a means of attaining business skills, and firms base their hiring decisions less on a recruit's knowledge than on general attributes such as character and ambition. Firms do not hire recruits to fill specific occupations. Rather, recruits are expected to be malleable, identifying with the general interests of the firm rather than with their specific role within it. The mentor system is widely used in the early training of management recruits and involves middle-level and senior managers serving as teachers and role models.

The emphasis on in-house education is related to the lifetime employment system, in which management recruits are hired each April following university graduation and typically stay with a firm until retirement. The lifetime employment system makes it probable that a firm will benefit from its training investment and also enables it to develop long-range plans for training each recruit.

Management training is based on regular rotation through a broad range of a firm's operations. Management recruits also frequently begin their careers as ordinary workers on a production line. The pattern of regular rotation enables managers to develop a detailed understanding of a number of varied operations, and thus over time to attain a rich general knowledge of the firm.

Linked with the lifetime employment system is the seniority-based salary and promotion system. It results in both higher average age and lesser variance by age of top executives in Japan. Compared to the United States and western Europe, for example, relatively few company presidents in Japan are under age 50. Taken together, these factors provide top Japanese executives with unsurpassed experience regarding their firms' operations.

Japanese managers typically take a more long-term interest in their firms than do their American counterparts, partly a result of the lifetime employment and seniority-based income and advancement systems. In the United States, managers are typically compensated on the basis of their divisions' performance. This bonus system is not used for Japanese managers, as it is considered detrimental to developing a long-term perspective and an interest in the firm as a whole.

The long-term view of Japanese managers is also based on sources of **finance**. While American firms rely heavily on the stockmarket, Japanese firms rely more on borrowing from banks and generally have much higher debt to equity ratios. Consequently, Japanese managers are under less pressure to maximize short-term earnings. By contrast, publicly-held firms in the U.S. are compelled by the Security and Exchange Commission to report earnings on a quarterly basis. In general, Japanese firms are more likely to focus on productivity, growth, and market share, whereas U.S. firms are more inclined to focus on profitability.

While directors from outside a company are common in the United States, they are rare in Japan. The **decision-making** process in Japanese firms is highly decentralized. In publicly-held corporations in the U.S., power is concentrated in a board of directors, with each director having one vote. In Japan, by contrast, both middle- and top-level managers serve as directors. Japanese directors typically retain production line responsibilities. For example, in the early-1970s, 14 of Hitachi's 20 directors were engineers.

This represents another facet of the strong production orientation of Japanese management.

THE RINGI SYSTEM

The traditional decision-making process in Japanese firms is referred to as the Ringi system. The system involves the circulation of a proposal to all managers in the firm who are affected by the decision. Proposals are generally initiated by middle-level managers, though they may also come from top executives. In the latter case, an executive will generally give his idea to his subordinates and let them introduce it. Managers from different departments in the firm hold meetings and try to reach an informal consensus on the matter. Only after this consensus is reached will the formal document, or "Ringi-sho," be circulated for approval by the responsible managers.

The Ringi system requires long lead times, and is thus problematic in a crisis. Certain elements of the system have changed and some Japanese firms make little use of it. Nonetheless, one of its underlying principles remains prevalent. That is, when a decision proves beneficial, the middle-level managers who initially advocated it receive credit; when a decision proves unsuccessful, responsibility is taken by top-level executives. This principle is designed to promote aggressiveness in younger managers. In his article "Decision Making—Eastern and Western Style," Kaufman summarizes the "four primary advantages" of the Ringi system as follows: "Fewer aspects of the decision are overlooked; the trauma that accompanies change is reduced; participants feel committed to implementing a decision they have helped to formulate; and far bolder decisions can be made."

ENTERPRISE UNIONS

One of the distinctive characteristics of labor-management relations in Japan is the enterprise union, which is organized around a single plant. Consequently, workers in any company may be organized across several enterprise unions. Enterprise unions generally belong to a larger federation, but the balance of power is at the at the local level. Japanese unions are distinct not only because of their highly decentralized nature, but because they represent both white- and blue-collar workers, with union membership open to managers up to the section chief level. That upper-level managers typically have moved through union ranks and may have served as union officials is suggestive of the generally less antagonistic labor-management relationship in Japan. Combined with the relatively narrow income gap between managers and workers and the willingness of manager recruits to work on production lines as part of their training, the open membership policies of Japanese unions contributes to an atmosphere in which work is defined more in relation to the firm than to occupation or class.

Union membership is generally associated with lifetime employment guarantees. Membership varies widely by firm size, and relatively few workers in firms with fewer than 100 employees receive lifetime employment guarantees. Nonetheless, in large firms the lifetime employment system creates an environment in which workers are less likely to feel threatened by technical change. As a consequence, changes in the production process are likely to be undertaken by management and workers on a cooperative basis. More generally, since semiannual bonuses and annual wage negotiations are based on a firm's competitive strength, workers have a large stake in the long-term success of their firm.

QUALITY CIRCLES

The extensive use of **quality circles** is another of the distinguishing characteristics of Japanese management. The development of quality circles in Japan in the early-1960s was inspired by the lectures of American statisticians W. Edwards Deming and J.M. Juran, in which they discussed the development of wartime industrial standards in the United States. Noting that American management had typically given line managers and engineers about 85 percent of responsibility for quality control and only about 15 percent to workers, Deming and Juran argued that these proportions should be reversed. Production processes should be designed with quality control in mind, and all those within a firm, from workers to top management, should be familiar with statistical control techniques and undergo continuous education on quality control. In general, Deming and Juran argued, quality control should focus on prevention, with the ultimate goal being improving the production process until no defective parts or products are produced.

In Japan, quality circles consist of groups of about 10 workers who meet weekly, often on their own time. The groups typically include foremen, who usually serve as circle leaders. Quality circles focus on concrete aspects of the operations with which they are directly involved, using tables and graphs as statistical representations of actual production. In one common format, problems are categorized by materials, manpower, methods, and machines.

Quality circles provide a means by which workers are encouraged to participate in company affairs and by which management may benefit from worker suggestions. Employee suggestions play an important role in Japan, and two associations, The Japanese Association of Suggestion Systems and The Japan Human Relations Association, were developed to improve the process. These associations reported that in fiscal year 1980, changes resulting from employee suggestions created benefits of $10 billion for Japanese firms and monetary rewards of $4 billion for Japanese workers.

SCIENTIFIC MANAGEMENT

Japanese management techniques have been strongly influenced by the tenets of scientific management. As with quality control circles, scientific management originated in the United States, only to be more systematically adopted in Japan. The pioneering figure of scientific management is Frederick W. Taylor (1856-1915). Taylor is best known for his time and motion studies of workers as part of an effort to optimize and standardize work effort, but he also argued for a system of bonuses to workers based on productivity. These ideas were implemented by Japanese firms as early as 1908, and a translation of his *Principles of Scientific Management* sold two million copies in Japan.

In the post-World War II years, the use of semiannual bonuses for workers and carefully codified work standards became standard management practices in Japan. Consistent with the Japanese emphasis on teamwork, bonuses are generally allotted to a work group rather than an individual worker. Scientific management emphasizes the role of management in the production process. This is reflected in the more hands-on approach of management training in Japan, as well as the relatively high share of managers directly involved with production processes.

As with managers, Japanese industrial engineers are more directly involved with production processes than their counterparts in the United States. In his book *The Japanese Industrial System*, McMillan summarizes the position of Japanese industrial engineers as follows: "Almost all Japanese companies treat engineers as blue-collar workers, despite their higher pay. Company uniforms are usually identical, salaries are paid monthly with semiannual bonuses, and wages are linked to company seniority. Engineers work hand in hand with blue-collar assembly workers, and industrial and design engineers as well as cost accountants are available for specialized assistance to QC [quality control] circles." In addition, Japan produces up to three times as many engineers per year as the United States. Japan's emphasis on production-oriented engineering is consistent with its dominant competitive strategy in the post-war years: to focus on the development of improved processes rather than new products.

Large Japanese firms are typically widely diversified across industries. Thus, process innovations, such as just-in-time production, are readily applicable across a broad range of industries. Such diversification not only enables a firm to spread risk but also to accommodate government plans in which industries are classified by their long-term growth prospects.

SEE ALSO: Japanese Manufacturing Techniques

[David Kucera]

FURTHER READING:

Beale, David. *Driven by Nissan? A Critical Guide to the New Management Technique.* Lawrence and Wishart, 1994.

"Changes Ahead for Japanese Management." *Economic World.* August 1993.

Gordon, Donald. *Japanese Management in America and Britain: Revelation or Requiem for Western Industrial Democracy.* Avebury, 1988.

Kawamura, Shigekuni. "Japanese Management Style." *Japan and the World Economy.* 5(3), 1993.

Lam, Alice. *Women and Japanese Management.* Routledge, 1992.

Lorriman, John, and Takashi Kenjo. *Japan's Winning Margins: Management, Training, and Education.* Oxford University Press, 1994.

"Management: Japan Keeps up the Pressure." *Financial Times London.* October 6, 1993.

Park, Sung-Jo ed. *Managerial Efficiency in Competition and Cooperation: Japanese, West- and East-European Strategies and Perspectives.* Westview Press, 1992.

Sato, Ryuzo. *The Chrysanthemum and the Eagle: The Future of U.S.-Japan Relations.* New York University Press, 1994.

JAPANESE MANUFACTURING TECHNIQUES

The widely hailed Japanese system of production originated at Toyota just after World War II. The system is often referred to as the Toyota production system, the core of which is just-in-time production. The pioneers of the system were Taiichi Ohno, a former vice president of Toyota, and Shigeo Shingo, a consultant for Toyota. In his book *A Study of the Toyota Production System from an Industrial Engineering Viewpoint*, Shigeo Shingo described the "Basic Features of the Toyota Production System" as follows:

- Targets cost reduction via the elimination of waste.

- Eliminates overproduction through the notion of non-stock and achieves labor cost reduction via minimal manpower.

- Reduces production cycles drastically through the use of the SMED (Single-Minute Exchange of Die) system to achieve non-stock by carrying out small lot production.

- Thinks of demand in terms of order-based production.

The driving force behind the Japanese system of production is waste elimination, and the system itself is a wide-ranging set of principles and practices designed to achieve this. The type of waste on which the system is particularly focused is that resulting from overproduction, whether of finished products or parts and subassemblies making up finished products. The ideal is to produce without the accumulation of product inventory, which requires that products be produced "just in time" for delivery and in just the right number. In this sense, overproduction is defined to include not only products that exceed sales or orders, the conventional sense of overproduction, but also products that match the desired quantity but are produced too early. The ideal of eliminating parts inventories requires in turn that parts be available "just in time" for any given operation in the production process and also in just the right number.

One of the principles underlying the drive towards waste elimination in the Toyota production system is that prices are taken as a market-determined given and not as a mark-up over costs. Under this principle, increases in costs are not passed on to the consumer in the form of higher prices. As a corollary, the only way for a firm to increase profitability is by lowering costs. At the same time, cost reductions enabled Toyota to expand its market by lowering prices.

One of the means by which waste is reduced in the Japanese system is by carefully defining those elements of the **manufacturing** process that add value and those that do not, with the aim of minimizing, and if possible eliminating, the latter. Value-adding operations are defined as those that transform a material's shape or quality. Non-value-adding operations include transporting and inspecting materials and waiting out delays. These include not only the larger aspects of such operations, such as running a forklift in the case of transporting materials, but also such detailed actions within the manufacturing process as moving a part from one hand to the other, also classified as transporting.

Regarding transport, emphasis is placed on designing the layout of machinery to eliminate the distances between consecutive operations in a production process. Minimizing transportation distances is particularly important in just-in-time production, for the emphasis on stockless flows means that fewer parts are transported at a time. Regarding inspection, electronic sensor systems and methods for simplifying the production process have been implemented with the aim of eliminating the need for inspection by eliminating defects. When defects do occur, sensor systems shut down a machine, assuring that a defective part will not continue down a production line and cause further problems. Delays are particularly damaging in just-in-time production, since buffer stocks of materials are generally not kept on hand. Delays have been minimized in part through the reduction of defective parts and in part through elaborate control systems, such as computerized inventory control and the tracking of all parts through every stage of the production process.

In his book *The Toyota Production System*, Toyota's former vice president Taiichi Ohno described the origins of the system as follows: "The Toyota production system evolved out of need. Certain restrictions in the marketplace required the production of small quantities of many varieties under conditions of low demand, a fate the Japanese automobile industry faced in the postwar period." In the United States in the same period, the large scale and rapid growth of the market made it viable to produce a large number of identical models (excepting color variations) over long production runs, without the changeover in tooling that different models required. These autos were not built to individual order but with the reasonable expectation that they would be sold quickly enough.

What distinguishes the Toyota production system from mass production is not the number of automobiles produced, but rather that a greater number of models or model types (e.g., four-doors, two-doors, wagons) are produced in a given span of time. It was only via small-lot production that automobiles could be produced to order in a timely fashion and that the need for inventories could thereby be eliminated. Just-in-time production doesn't just minimize the costs associated with inventory storage. It also offers a marketing advantage, since it dramatically lessens the delivery time of made-to-order products. Whereas the delivery time of a made-to-order American automobile was once three to six months, a made-to-order Toyota could be delivered anywhere in Japan within ten days.

The Japanese system of production required a key technical development, without which small-lot production would not be viable. This development involved radically reduced tool and die changeover times. Different tools and dies are required to impart different shapes to parts for different products. For example, in shaping a body part for an automobile, the stamping die which forms the end of a stamping press arm must be changed for different models for which the part is not interchangeable. Similarly, a machining operation typically requires that a part be held in place with jigs or fixtures, which often differ for parts produced for different automobile models. These rapid changeover techniques are collectively referred to as SMED, for single-minute exchange of die.

In 1970, it took Toyota four hours to change a die for a 1000-ton stamping press. Within a half year, this time was reduced to one and a half hours. Shortly thereafter, top Toyota management requested that changeover times be reduced to three minutes, which was regarded by many within the firm as unrealistic. Nonetheless, this goal was attained in 1971.

Similar improvements were made throughout the plant making use of two methods: improving fastening mechanisms and eliminating adjustability of machine tools. Dies are typically fastened with a set of bolts. In the old system, these bolts needed to be completely removed to change dies. The most time-consuming element of this arrangement was lining up bolts when attaching a new die. Under the new system, U-shaped washers and slotted bolt holes in dies made it possible to simply loosen bolts for changeovers. In other cases, bolts were eliminated altogether. For example, stamping die-sets for smaller presses were developed that could simply be pushed on and pulled off without tools, enabling changeovers in 15 seconds. Regarding adjustability of machine tools, since machine tool manufacturers do not know which settings a manufacturer will require, they produce machines that are infinitely adjustable. Eliminating the adjustability of machine tools requires that a tool be fitted with a constraining fixture. This limits the tools to function in a number of settings, each setting for a different part, rather than over an infinitely variable range.

The development of these rapid changeover techniques enabled the viability of extremely short production runs. For example, if three model types were produced at a plant, one might be produced in the early morning, the second until early afternoon, and the third until a shift's end. Production runs could be cut shorter yet, so that if total daily orders were for 1000 of type A, 2000 of type B, and 3000 of type C, these types might be produced in cycles of one of A, two of B, and three of C throughout the day. Since daily orders for finished products are for a mixture of product types, it is only by means of such short production runs that no inventories will accumulate.

The Japanese system of production as developed at Toyota employs relatively high ratios of machinery to output and machines per worker. The large number of machines operated by each laborer was made possible by electronic sensory control of automated machinery, which enabled machinery to perform an operation without being monitored by a worker. This is referred to as "autonomation." In the event of a failed operation, such machinery automatically shuts down and the type of problem is electronically indicated on a panel. When a breakdown occurs, emphasis is placed not on getting the machine up and running as quickly as possible, but on correcting the root of the problem in an effort to assure that it does not recur.

The high number of machines per worker also required the development of new worker safety systems. Older safety systems require that a machine be actuated with two switches by each of a worker's hands. This minimized the possibility of injury. At Toyota, this problem was addressed by a system of switches that allowed a machine to begin operations only after a worker had moved to an adjacent machine. Toyota estimated that such multi-machine handling resulted in 20 to 30 percent increases in labor productivity.

The Japanese system of production is designed to accommodate relatively low levels of capacity utilization and operating rates of machinery. This distinguishes it from typical mass production techniques, in which greater emphasis is placed on running at full capacity. The Japanese system is justified by its originators on the basis of the substantially higher cost per hour of idle labor versus idle machinery and is related to multi-machine handling.

In the Japanese view, the relative costs of labor versus machinery make it preferable to have a machine complete an operation and sit idle until a worker reactivates it than for a worker to wait for a machine to complete its operation. Higher levels of production are met by raising the operating rates of machinery, increasing the number of workers, and having a worker operate fewer machines. In this sense, the ability to readily vary output to accommodate just-in-time deliveries requires a great deal of flexibility in the labor force. In Japan, union workers typically work alongside non-union temporary workers who are readily available upon demand. Shifts are also scheduled with four-hour breaks between them, so that increases in demand of up to 50 percent can be met immediately through overtime work. A great deal of emphasis is also placed on simplifying the operation of a machine, so that a temporary worker can be fully trained within three days.

The desire for stockless production flows is complicated when machines with high operating capacities work alongside machines with low operating capacities. Balances can generally be achieved by lowering operating rates of high capacity machines. Nonetheless, given the variations that inevitably occur in a production process, a relay system was devised to facilitate the smooth flow of operations. This involves workers at any work station helping workers at any adjacent work station who fall behind. The relay system thus requires that a worker typically be trained to operate three types of machinery. Waiting time resulting from machines with different operating capacities can also be eliminated by having two workers continually cycle around three such machines. Continual flow of operations can also be maintained by having a single worker simultaneously perform two operations on a continual basis. As an example, a worker loads a part into a press, and while the pressing operation is being performed, the worker performs a spot-welding operation. This system of simultaneous operation was an area of considerable study at Toyota during the 1980s.

Maintaining a continual flow of operations is also facilitated by the establishment of time standards for any given operation. These standards are determined by careful observation of a worker performing an operation, as well as by feedback from workers themselves. The optimal method for performing an operation is noted in detail on standard operating charts. Foremen are responsible for seeing that all operations are performed to standard. Though standard operations are codified in detail, it is also expected of foremen that standards undergo continual reevaluation and improvement.

A number of a product's parts, as well as the raw materials to produce all parts, are the same regardless of model types. For automobiles, this might include the frame and certain body parts. Made-to-order considerations thus can not determine the quantities of such parts and materials required over a longer time frame. Consequently the Japanese production system makes use of market research and forecasting to estimate more general production requirements. Estimated production numbers are typically relayed throughout the plant and to the plant's suppliers two months before production. These numbers are firmed up one month before production and are used to plan detailed weekly and daily schedules.

The integration of longer-term considerations with short-term made-to-order considerations provides the just-in-time system with one of its central planning challenges. This integration is achieved by daily adaptation of production schedules to made-to-order requirements. Actual production is based on orders for finished products (called a pull system, as orders pull the production process). Therefore, it is essential that information on orders be continually relayed to all upstream aspects of the production process in order to meet just-in-time requirements. This flow of information is maintained by what is called the "kanban" system. Kanbans are cards that are sent from workers of one process to those of an adjacent process containing information on the number of parts required.

As Toyota developed its production system, the firms with which it contracted for parts complained that Toyota's desire to produce without stocks meant that the suppliers would have to absorb the costs of stocking parts. Toyota's suppliers were slow to implement just-in-time production methods in their factories. Consequently the system of synchronizing orders for automobiles with orders for parts from suppliers took ten years to achieve after Toyota had implemented the system in its own facilities. Once the system was in place, however, Toyota's suppliers were also able to achieve lower costs and greater profitability.

After the oil crisis of 1973, Japanese manufacturing techniques diffused throughout a wide range of industries in Japan. During the 1980s, just-in-time techniques were also implemented by U.S. producers, among them Ford Motor Co., General Motors Corp., and Westinghouse.

SEE ALSO: Japanese Management Techniques

[David Kucera]

FURTHER READING:

Beale, David. *Driven by Nissan? A Critical Guide to the New Management Technique.* Lawrence and Wishhart, 1994.

Lorriman, John and Takashi Kenjo. *Japan's Winning Margins.* Oxford University Press, 1994.

McMillan, Charles. *The Japanese Industrial System.* Walter de Gruyter, 1984.

Monden, Yasuhiro. *Applying Just-in-Time: The American/Japanese Experience.* Industrial Engineering and Management Press, 1985.

Monden, Yasuhiro. *Toyota Production System: An Integrated Approach to Just-in-Time.* Industrial Engineering and Management Press, 1993.

Ohno, Taiichi. *Toyota Production System: Beyond Large-Scale Production.* Productivity Press, 1988.

Park, Sung-Jo (ed.). *Managerial Efficiency in Competition and Cooperation: Japanese, West- and East-European Strategies and Perspectives.* Westview Press, 1992.

Schonberger, Richard J. *Japanese Manufacturing Techniques: Nine Hidden Lessons in Simplicity.* The Free Press, 1982.

Sato, Ryuzo. *The Chrysanthemum and the Eagle: The Future of U.S.-Japan Relations.* New York University Press, 1994.

Shingo, Shigeo. *A Study of the Toyota Production System From an Industrial Engineering Viewpoint.* Productivity Press, 1989.

Sugimori, Y. et al. "Toyota Production System and Kanban System, Materialization of Just-in-Time and Respect-for-Humanity," *International Journal of Production Research.* 15(6), 1977, pp. 553-564.

JOINT OPERATING AGREEMENT

When two or more companies agree to combine some of their operations as a means of sharing costs and reducing operating expenses, they enter into a joint operating agreement (JOA). Benefits involve cost savings and **economies of scale**. Joint operating agreements enable the participating companies to operate with fewer employees; eliminate duplicate facilities, equipment, and functions; and save through bulk purchases of supplies and materials.

Joint operating agreements typically take one of two forms. In some cases a **joint venture** is formed. The companies involved in the JOA form a third company that is jointly owned. The joint venture is capitalized by the participating companies and managed by a board of directors consisting of executives from, or individuals selected by, each of the participating companies. If all of the companies contribute equal amounts of capital, they generally share equally in ownership and profits of the joint venture.

The second form of a joint operating agreement involves an operating partnership. One of the companies acts as the operating partner for the other firms, providing shared services on a contract basis. Secondary partners may contribute facilities, equipments, cash, and other items to the operating partner. Under this type of joint operating agreement, no third-party joint venture is created.

JOAs should be distinguished from mergers. In the case of **mergers and acquisitions**, ownership is combined in the new corporate entity. When one company merges with another, the result is single ownership. In the case of joint operating agreements, the two or more companies involved remain separately owned.

Joint operating agreements do not necessarily involve antitrust violations. It is only when joint operating agreements involve price fixing, market allocation, and **profit sharing** that they violate the **antitrust laws** of the United States. JOAs that are limited to combined operations for the purpose of cost savings and economies of scale are permitted.

In some cases special legislation has been passed by Congress to provide antitrust exemptions for joint operating agreements in specific industries. In 1970 Congress passed the Newspaper Preservation Act, which granted antitrust exemption to joint operating agreements established by two daily newspapers that competed in the same geographic markets.

JOAS IN THE NEWSPAPER INDUSTRY

Perhaps the most widely known, discussed, and analyzed JOAs are those involving newspapers. The first-known JOA between two competing newspaper was formed in 1933 in Albuquerque, New Mexico. Three other newspaper JOAs were established in the 1930s, four in the 1940s, 16 in the 1950s, and four in the 1960s. In 1965 the U.S. Department of Justice challenged the JOA between the *Star* and *Citizen* in Tucson, Arizona, on the grounds that it violated federal antitrust laws. In 1969 the U.S. Supreme Court upheld that challenge.

The Newspaper Preservation Act (NPA) was passed by Congress as a result of extensive lobbying on the part of the newspaper industry. Under the NPA, antitrust exemption was granted to JOAs established by competing newspapers. That meant that under an approved JOA, which included all JOAs currently in existence, newspapers could engage in antitrust practices such as price fixing, profit pooling, and market allocation.

Under the NPA, newspapers that desired to establish new JOAs needed to obtain approval from the attorney general of the United States and the U.S. Department of Justice. In order for a newspaper JOA to be approved, one of the newspapers must be failing. Among the criteria that are considered when determining whether or not a newspaper is failing, are degree of market share disparity between the two newspapers, a downward circulation spiral, and the extent of the failing newspaper's financial losses.

Some newspaper JOAs were not affected by the NPA. These included newspapers in different geographic markets that established centralized facilities to handle operations. Joint newspaper monopolies, where a single company owns two newspapers in a single geographic market, were also not affected by the NPA. In addition there were joint operations that did not violate antitrust laws. For example, newspapers are allowed to combine advertising and circulation operations. They may share printing and production facilities. They may also merge administrative functions, such as accounting and human resources. These types of joint operations do not require an antitrust exemption.

Essentially two factors make it difficult for more than one daily newspaper to publish successfully in a single market. One is that economies of scale heavily favor the larger of the two newspapers. Secondly, many advertisers place ads only in the largest circulating newspapers in any one market, making it difficult for smaller newspapers to compete with larger ones for advertising dollars. Newspaper JOAs offer a way to reduce the high costs associated with newspaper production and distribution as well as the marketing and promotion costs associated with commercial competition.

Following passage of the NPA, two newspaper JOAs were created in the 1970s, three in the 1980s, and several have been established in the 1990s. While newspaper JOAs are designed to preserve editorial competition between two daily newspapers in a single market, whether or not they have been successful has remained a matter of controversy. As has been noted several types of joint operations do not require antitrust exemptions, and the benefit of granting specific antitrust exemptions has been questioned by some experts. In addition other market forces appear to be at work against struggling newspapers. These include the growth of television viewing and overall declining readerships for many newspapers. Many newspaper JOAs have been dissolved, resulting in only one daily newspaper serving a particular geographic market.

[David Bianco]

FURTHER READING:

Busterna, John C., and Robert G. Picard. *Joint Operating Agreements: The Newspaper Preservation Act and Its Application.* Ablex, 1993.

JOINT VENTURES

Joint ventures are domestic or international enterprises involving two or more companies joining temporarily to undertake a particular project. They have grown in popularity in recent years—predictions suggest that joint ventures will grow at the rate of 22 percent annually throughout the 1990s. Certainly, not all of them will be successful, since the failure rate of joint ventures is 70 percent. Nonetheless, companies persist in initiating them for a variety of reasons.

REASONS FOR JOINT VENTURES

Joint ventures may involve companies in one country or in two or more. International joint ventures in particular are becoming more popular, especially in capital-intensive industries such as oil and gas exploration, mineral extraction, and metals processing. The basic reason is simple: to save money. For example, just to start a mining operation in the United States in 1984, a company would have had to spend one to two billion dollars. Few companies then (or now) could finance such an expenditure on their own, so joint ventures became more attractive as a way to share risks and costs and create scale economies.

Another factor that contributed to the expansion in joint ventures in the past few decades was the cost involved for capital-intensive industries in continuing their operations. Companies in these industries depend heavily on advances in technology to reduce costs. By pooling their money and personnel, companies enhanced chances of developing advanced technological methods that would reduce exploration and production costs and increase profits. Joint ventures became an ideal method of doing business for such industries.

Joint ventures between American and international companies are increasingly common. Estimates for 1994 suggested that approximately 20 percent of American companies' direct investments, i.e., the establishment of operating facilities in a foreign country, were in joint ventures. Ideally, the partners contribute approximately equal amounts of resources and capital into each business. The word "approximately" is important in foreign joint ventures, since some countries, such as China, will not allow outside companies to own the majority of a domestic business (although they do encourage joint ventures). In some countries, joint ventures are the only way companies can engage in foreign business. For instance, Mexico requires that all foreign firms investing there have Mexican joint venture partners. In addition to government regulations, other reasons for multinational joint ventures include cutting the costs of doing business, sharing risks, and acquiring technological information and management expertise from other companies.

Joint ventures are also very helpful to some companies in gaining access to foreign markets. Neither party may really be interested in the primary project, but they participate simply to gain access to a new market. Such projects generally represent a direct investment, which is sometimes limited by laws in different countries. One of the aims of a partner in a joint venture is to have a majority interest in it. That way, it maintains control over a project. This explains why some countries do not permit outside companies to hold majority interests in their domestic business ventures.

Companies seeking to cut the costs of doing business see joint ventures as a way to save money. In effect, they are sharing the risks should a particular project fail. For example, if two oil companies wish to produce a new drilling platform to search for oil in swamps or ocean areas, and neither one can finance the project on its own, they might join forces. That way, they are sharing the costs of the projects and reducing their individual risk should they find no oil. That is a decided advantage to many business people.

TYPES OF JOINT VENTURES

Joint ventures fall into several categories. Among them are equity-based operations that benefit foreign and/or local private interests, groups of interests, or members of the general public. There are also non-equity joint ventures, also known as cooperative agreements, in which the parties seek technical service arrangements, franchise and brand use agreements, management contracts or rental agreements, or one-time contracts, e.g., for construction projects. Quite often, non-equity joint ventures are used simply to provide access for the participants into foreign markets.

Equity type arrangements involve two sides: one that provides the capital, and one that receives it. Since there is money involved, there are also inherent risks, particularly with equity ventures launched in less developed countries. The biggest risk is that the business will fail and the money invested will be lost. There is also the risk that some foreign governments will nationalize certain industries in order to protect their own domestic interests. For example, the Chilean government nationalized its copper industry in the 1960s to prevent foreign companies from gaining control over the ore. In 1988, Peru took over Perulac, a local milk producer owned by Nestle, because of a national milk shortage. However, such risks are (or should be) included in both the cost of doing business and in joint venture participants' contingency planning.

Participants do not always furnish capital as part of their joint venture commitments. There are, for example, non-equity arrangements in which some companies are more in need of technical services or technological expertise than they are capital. They may want to modernize operations or start new production operations. Thus, they limit partners' participation to technical assistance. Such arrangements often include some funding as well, albeit limited.

There is also a growing involvement in **franchising** joint ventures. American companies such as McDonald's, Coca-Cola Co., and Stained Glass Overlay have opened foreign franchise operations at an increasing rate. The emergence of new markets such as China and Vietnam have made such operations lucrative and have attracted more and more businesses to joint venture participation. A logical extension of franchising and brand use agreements is the need for managerial expertise. Consequently, companies in well-developed countries form joint ventures with businesses in emerging countries in which they provide management expertise through contractual agreements. Such arrangements benefit both parties immeasurably, which is one of the goals of joint ventures.

Not all joint ventures involve private companies—some include government agencies. This is most common in less developed countries, but there are notable exceptions. For example, the British and French governments combined their resources in conjunction with privately owned firms to develop a supersonic transport (SST) intended to revolutionize transatlantic flying between the two countries and the United States. The project did not realize its financial goals. The flights were too expensive for average flyers, costing as much as $3,368 one way between London and Washington D.C. As a result, most flights were discontinued, although some between European and New York City still exist. Such are the risks of joint ventures, whether they involve private business or government agencies.

Generally, joint venture participants in the private sector furnish the capital, resources, and management and technological expertise involved in the operation. In less developed countries, however, government agencies are often active in business enterprises. They may provide or arrange for funding; own or manage certain industries, such as utility companies and airlines; or act as agents in attracting foreign investment or participation in businesses. They are no less active than privately-held businesses in joint ventures, however. The rules for all participants remain the same, and strategies do not change.

JOINT VENTURE STRATEGIES

Businesses should not engage in joint ventures without adequate planning and **strategy**. They cannot afford to, since the ultimate goal of joint ventures is the same as it is for any type of business operation: to make a profit for the owners and shareholders. A successful company in any type of business is often recruited heavily for participation in joint ventures. Thus, they can pick and choose in which partnerships they would like to engage, if any. They follow certain ground rules, which have been developed over they years as joint ventures have grown in popularity.

For example, experience dictates that both parties in a joint venture should know exactly what they wish to derive from their partnership. There must be an agreement before the partnership becomes a reality. There must also be a firm commitment on the part of each member. One of the leading causes for the failure of joint ventures is that some participants do not reveal their true intentions in the partnerships. For example, some private companies in advanced countries have formed partnerships with militant governments to supply technological expertise and develop products such as chemicals or nuclear reactors to be used for allegedly peaceful purposes. They learned later that the products were used for military purposes. Such results can be detrimental to the companies involved and adversely affect their bottom lines and reputations.

Businesses should form joint ventures with experienced partners. If the partners do not have approximately equal experience, one can take advantage of the other, which can lead to failure. Joint ventures do not survive when one participant takes advantage of another. Nor do they survive if companies jump into them without testing the partnership first.

Partners in joint ventures would often be better off participating in small projects as a way to test one another instead of launching into one large enterprise without an adequate feeling out process. This is especially true when companies with different structures, corporate cultures, and strategic plans work together. Such differences are difficult to overcome and frequently lead to failure. That is why a ''courtship'' is beneficial to joint venture participants.

WHY JOINT VENTURES FAIL

Joint ventures fail for many reasons. In addition to those mentioned above, other factors include: disappearing markets, lagging technology, partner's inability to honor the contract, cultural differences interfering with progress, or government involvement creating uncertainty. However, many of these reasons can be eliminated with careful planning.

Inconsistent government interference is a difficult problem to overcome. For example, the United States government has long maintained restrictions against exporting certain technologies to selected foreign countries, such as those utilized to produce jet engines and computers. These restrictions place American companies at a competitive disadvantage, since other countries do not place similar constraints on their businesses. Thus, American companies are unable to engage in certain joint ventures.

Companies that engage in military-oriented joint ventures are often subject to unanticipated risks. The federal government may allocate funds for the production of certain weapons, sign contracts with manufacturers, and then discontinue the project due to changing needs, budget restrictions, or election results. Such government actions are a common risk in defense-oriented joint ventures. They introduce an element of insecurity into the projects, which is something that partners try to avoid as much as possible.

Another problem with joint ventures concerns the issue of management. The managers of one company may be more adept at decision making than their counterparts at the other company. This can lead to friction and a lack of cooperation. Projects are doomed to failure if there is not a well-defined decision-making process in place that is predicated on mutual goals and strategies.

For example, if two auto manufacturing companies engage in a joint venture, it is imperative that they be similar in their structures and approach to business. If one company relies heavily on nonunionized workers who operate in an autonomous team-building environment, and the other comprises a unionized workforce oriented toward assembly line production in which workers specialize in narrow tasks, the chances of success are poor. The workers at the first plant would be prone to making decisions and solving problems on their own, which would reduce the levels of bureaucracy needed to manage production. Conversely, the workers at the second plant would likely defer to higher-level managers to make decisions. The differences would be difficult to overcome and would lead to higher costs and slower production. While the differences could be alleviated through planning before the actual manufacturing process began, the time expended might lead to technology gaps and other impediments to earning a profit. Most companies engaging in joint ventures would prefer not to deal with such problems after a project was implemented. Rather, they aim to eliminate them through careful planning. Doing so increases profits in the long run, which is one of the many benefits of successful joint ventures.

BENEFITS OF JOINT VENTURES

Among the most significant benefits derived from joint ventures is that partners save money and reduce their risks through capital and resource sharing. Joint ventures give smaller companies the chance to work with larger ones to develop, manufacture, and market new products. They also give companies of all sizes the opportunity to increase sales, gain access to wider markets, and enhance technological capabilities through research and development (R&D) underwritten by more than one party. In fact, funding for R&D today is often provided by government agencies in a myriad of countries operating under all types of economies, ranging from capitalist to socialist and hybrid. That is particularly true in the United States.

Until recently, U.S. companies were reluctant to engage in **research and development** partnerships, and government agencies tried not to become involved in business development. However, with the emergence of countries that feature technologically advanced industries (such as electronics or computer microchips) supported extensively by government funding, American companies have become more willing to participate in joint ventures. Likewise, the U.S. government, along with state governments, has become more generous with its financial suport.

Government's increased involvement in the private business environment has created more opportunities for companies to engage in domestic and international joint ventures, although they are still legally limited in what they can do and where they can operate. Nonetheless, more and more companies are involving themselves in joint ventures, and the trend is to increase their participation, since the advantages outweigh the disadvantages.

DISADVANTAGES OF JOINT VENTURES

The disadvantages of joint ventures include: potential financial losses if a project fails, expropriation or nationalization, disagreements among partners, and less-than-anticipated results. For instance, in the 1980s, American Motors Corp., which has since been acquired by Chrysler Corp., entered a joint venture with the Chinese government to produce Jeeps in Beijing. The Chinese government, which did not allow joint ventures before 1980, created many complications that prevented American Motors from operating efficiently. The result was greatly reduced profits for American Motors.

THE FUTURE OF JOINT VENTURES

It is almost certain that the number of joint ventures will continue to increase in the near future. More and more companies are adopting the joint venture approach as a part of their growth strategies, particularly in the international arena.

It is no secret that different companies in different countries excel in certain types of business. That explains in part why foreign companies are attracted to one another. They benefit mutually by combining their technological and monetary resources. Thus, international joint ventures are becoming the norm

rather than the exception—and in more industries than ever before.

Joint ventures may grow in importance so much in the next few years that many companies could lose their national identities. There will be a growth in multinational corporations to the point where joint ventures will be virtually unrecognizable. In fact, some companies, especially those in capital-intensive industries, have already lost sight of the fact that they engage constantly in joint ventures because they have become so commonplace. That is evidence that joint ventures are—and will continue to be—a successful way of doing business in an ever-expanding global economy.

[Arthur G. Sharp]

FURTHER READING:

Friedmann, Wolfgang G., and George Kalmanoff, eds., *Joint International Business Ventures*. New York: Columbia University Press, 1961.

Hall, R. Duane, *The International Joint Venture*. New York: Praeger Publishers, 1984.

Harrigan, Kathryn Rudie, *Managing for Joint Venture Success*. Lexington MA: Lexington Books, 1986.

Harrigan, Kathryn Rudie, *Strategies for Joint Venture*. Lexington MA: Lexington Books, 1985.

Lynch, Robert Porter, *The Practical Guide to Joint Ventures & Corporate Alliances*. New York: John Wiley and Sons, 1989.

JUNK BONDS

Junk bonds are corporate debt securities of comparatively high credit risk, as indicated by ratings lower than Baa3 by Moody's Investors Service or lower than BBB- by Standard & Poor's. This usually excludes obligations that are convertible to equity securities, although the bonds may have other equity-related options (such as warrants) attached to them. Junk bonds are also known as high yield, noninvestment-grade, below-investment-grade, less-than-investment-grade, or speculative-grade bonds.

HISTORY

The term "junk bonds" dates to the 1920s, apparently originating as traders' jargon. Financial scholar Harold G. Fraine employed the less pejorative label, "high yield bonds," as early as 1937, but noninvestment grade debt received little attention outside a small circle of professional specialists prior to the mid-1980s. For a few years during that period, high yield bonds were employed extensively in the financing of **mergers and acquisitions**, including two controversial variants—**leveraged buyouts** (LBOs) and hostile **takeovers**. Junk bonds, by virtue of their name

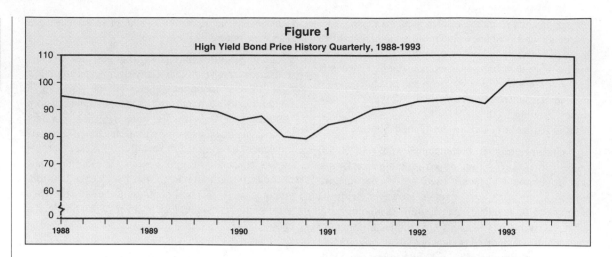

Figure 1
High Yield Bond Price History Quarterly, 1988-1993

alone, became convenient targets for critics of the merger and acquisition boom and its perceived excesses. Public awareness continued to grow as a number of excessively debt-laden LBOs collapsed, causing default rates to surge and high yield bond prices to plummet in 1989-1990 (see Figure 1).

Notwithstanding the sudden notoriety they achieved in the 1980s, high yield bonds by then had been a fixture of the capital markets for several decades. During the 1920s, noninvestment grade paper accounted for 15 percent to 20 percent of total corporate bond issuance. Additionally, "fallen angels," i.e., bonds originally issued with investment grade ratings but subsequently downgraded, offered an attractive niche for a few investors and market-makers.

Demand for higher-risk, higher-return debt remained limited, however, until the establishment of several new **mutual funds** specializing in the high risk sector, beginning in 1969-1970. The assets of these funds grew dramatically during the bond bull market of 1975-76. At the same time, the supply of lower-rated issues shrank through upgrading and refinancing. Investment banks responded by stepping up new issues from the modest level observed in the early 1970s. By the late 1980s, annual primary volume exceeded $30 billion.

Although Drexel Burnham Lambert was not the first underwriter to capitalize on this market opportunity, it did become the dominant player in junk markets. Under the leadership of Michael Milken, Drexel's high yield operation accounted for nearly half of all underwriting volume during the 1980s. As the decade ended, Milken was first dislodged from the firm and then convicted of several counts of securities law violations. Drexel went bankrupt during the high yield market's severe slump in 1990, apparently a victim of excessive concentration in a single line of business and a precarious capital structure. Supporters contended, however, that Milken and Drexel had been undone by a vendetta of entrenched corporate manag-

ers and government regulators, who supposedly felt threatened by the freer access to capital that junk bonds provided.

By 1991, the high yield market was healthy once again. Total returns remained strong for the next few years (see Figure 2), aided by declining **interest rates** and the rehabilitation of many distressed issuers. The use of proceeds in new offerings shifted from mergers and acquisitions to more conventional corporate purposes. Replacement of shorter-term bank borrowings and older, higher-cost public high yield debt were frequently observed applications of funds. Another notable change was the increased prominence of issuers from outside the United States.

ADVANTAGES AND DISADVANTAGES

Junk bonds offer corporations several distinct advantages over other types of financing. They avoid the equity dilution that can result from the issuance of new common shares. In addition, high yield bonds can be a less costly source of funds on an aftertax basis than equity. Compared to private debt (whether in the form of commercial bank loans or private placements with insurance companies or other financial institutions), high yield bonds generally impose less stringent restrictive covenants on the issuer. Furthermore, longer maturities are available in the high yield market than the commercial banks offer.

An offsetting disadvantage, vis-a-vis equity financing, is the higher level of fixed charges that results from issuing high yield debt. For privately owned companies that would not otherwise have to comply with **Securities and Exchange Commission** registration and financial reporting requirements, floating public noninvestment grade bonds in lieu of private debt entails incremental expenses. Also, such companies may not wish, for competitive reasons, to disclose as much information about their operations as high yield bond issuance necessitates.

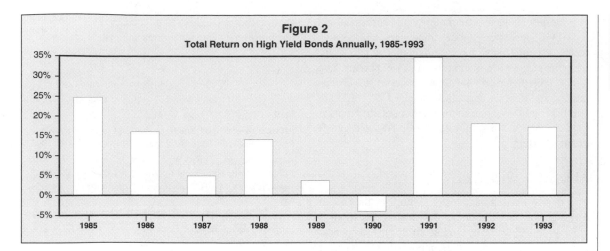

Figure 2
Total Return on High Yield Bonds Annually, 1985-1993

The substantial fixed charge requirement created by issuing noninvestment grade bonds makes them best suited to well-established companies with fairly predictable levels of cash flow. Accordingly, high technology industries, which are characterized by potentially wide swings in earnings and which generate only modest amounts of cash from **depreciation**, account for a minor portion of high yield issuance. Equity and convertible bonds have been the more appropriate vehicle for such classes of issuers.

In other respects, however, noninvestment grade debt has proved adaptable to the borrower's needs, as well as to market conditions. For example, zero-coupon (or deferred-interest) bonds meet the requirements of companies that expect to be large net users of cash in the near term, but substantial cash generators in the future. Zero-coupon instruments pay no cash coupons, but instead are offered at a discount, with the appreciation to par at maturity providing the investor's return. Uneven or unpredictable cash generation patterns can also be accommodated by allowing the coupon rate to vary with the general level of interest rates or with the price of a specified commodity.

From the investor's viewpoint, high yield bonds provide both **income** and potential for **capital gains**. The latter tends to be limited by early redemption provisions, which allow issues to retire the obligations prior to maturity, at modest premiums to par. Significant appreciation may occur, however, in bonds trading at steep discounts to par, reflecting either credit deterioration or a rise in the general level of interest rates since issuance.

Noninvestment grade bond funds generally emphasize the income feature. They ordinarily offer small investors higher yields than they can earn on alternatives such as savings accounts, certificates of deposit, money market funds or investment-grade bonds. In addition, high yield funds provide a diversification benefit, otherwise impractical for an investor of modest means to achieve. By holding portfolios of many different issues, a fund cushions the investor against possible default or underperformance of individual securities.

WHO USES JUNK BONDS?

Other types of mutual funds also invest in high yield bonds. Medium-quality corporate bonds funds are typically permitted, by the provisions of their prospectuses, to allocate a portion of their assets to securities rated lower than Baa3/BBB-. This latitude enables the funds to raise the overall yield on their portfolios. Another category of high yield investor includes "asset allocation funds," which achieve diversification by combining noninvestment grade holdings with other fixed income investments such as foreign bonds or mortgage-backed securities. Some equity mutual fund managers participate in the high yield market as well. Their objectives include speculating in specific issues and increasing the income in their funds during periods in which the stock market offers little potential for capital gains.

Life insurance companies represent a major market for high yield bonds, which they hold in conjunction with a variety of other fixed-income investments. Some states limit the percentage of assets that insurers can allocate to bonds rated less than investment grade. In all states, reserving requirements of the National Association of Insurance Commissioners effectively establish ceilings on the ownership of high yield debt, while also generally skewing such ownership to the better-quality portion of the market.

Pension funds face few specific restrictions on their high yield investments, but historically have been cautious in their involvement. The upheavals of the late 1980s left many plan sponsors wary of the sector. Additionally, the pension funds' overseers often perceived no clearcut role for a debt/equity hybrid in asset allocation schemes generally divided into "equity," "debt," and "alternative" categories.

Despite extensive marketing and educational efforts by underwriters, money managers, and consultants, pension funds have remained comparatively underdeveloped as a market for high yield bonds. The funds nevertheless own vast amounts of noninvestment grade debt in portfolios managed by corporate bond specialists who, like the medium-quality mutual fund managers, are authorized to dip below Triple-B to some extent.

ARE THEY WORTH IT?

For all classes of investors who bear the risk of owning high yield bonds, the central question is whether the rewards represent sufficient compensation. Properly speaking, the analysis should consider not only potential losses through default, but also the risks related to illiquidity in the secondary market, redemptions prior to maturity, and fluctuations in the general level of interest rates.

Arthur Stone Dewing effectively launched the high yield debate in 1926, citing slightly earlier studies that covered bond returns back to 1900. Dewing argued that lower-rated issues had proved to be superior investments, providing higher returns—net of default losses and price declines—than top-quality bonds. In a theme that was to reappear frequently in later years, Dewing suggested that most investors irrationally despised and therefore undervalued lower-rated issues, allowing more level-headed individuals to profit at their expense. Fraine, in contrast, argued that the supposedly superior returns on high yield bonds were illusions arising from period-specific changes in interest rates and risk premiums. Later, Milken took Dewing's side in the debate. He frequently cited the work of W. Braddock Hickman, who was actually more reserved in his conclusions than many subsequent high yield enthusiasts believed.

None of these observers addressed risk in the sense in which contemporary financial theory defines it. Marshall E. Blume and Donald B. Keim made an important advance by considering the variance of returns. They found high yield bond returns to have higher returns and less variance than long-term U.S. Treasury bonds. Blume and Keim hypothesized, however, that the anomaly would disappear if the results were controlled for differences in maturity. Kevin Maloney, Richard Rogalski and Lakshmi Shyam-Sunder further challenged the alleged undervaluation of high yield bonds. They noted that the upside (limited by earlier redemption provisions) was less than the downside (a 100 percent loss), a disparity for which rational investors would require additional compensation. On balance, the evidence points to a generally correct valuation of high yield bonds relative to their fully elaborated risk. The securities represent neither a bargain, as alleged by their advocates, nor an inferior investment, as the critics maintain.

[Martin S. Fridson]

FURTHER READING:

Alcaly, Roger. "The Golden Age of Junk." *New York Review of Books.* May 26, 1994, pp. 28-24.

Altman, Edward I., ed. *The High Yield Debt Market: Investment Performance and Economic Impact.* Dow Jones-Irwin, 1990.

Asquith, Paul A., David W. Mullins, Jr., and Eric D. Wolff. "Original Issue High Yield Bonds: Aging Analysis of Defaults, Exchanges and Calls." *The Journal of Finance.* September, 1989, pp. 923-952.

Becketti, Sean. "The Truth About Junk Bonds." *Economic Review.* Federal Reserve Bank of Kansas City. July/August 1990, pp. 45-54.

Blume, Marshall E., and Donald B. Keim. "The Risk and Return of Low-Grade Bonds: An Update." *Financial Analysts Journal.* September/October, 1991, pp. 85-89.

Cornell, Bradford, and Kevin Green. "The Investment Performance of Low-Grade Bond Funds." *The Journal of Finance.* March, 1991, pp. 29-48.

Dewing, Arthur Stone. *The Financial Policy of Corporations.* Rev. ed. HarperCollins, 1926.

Fabozzi, Frank J., ed. *The New High-Yield Debt Market: A Handbook for Portfolio Managers and Analysts.* HarperCollins, 1990.

Fons, Jerome S. "The Default Premium and Corporate Bond Experience." *The Journal of Finance.* March, 1987, pp. 81-97.

Fraine, Harold G. "Superiority of High-Yield Bonds Not Substantiated by 1927-1936 Performance." *Annalist.* October, 1937, pp. 533, 547.

Fraine, Harold G., and Robert H. Mills. "Effects of Defaults and Credit Deterioration on Yields of Corporate Bonds." *The Journal of Finance.* September, 1961, pp. 423-434.

Fridson, Martin S. *High Yield Bonds: Identifying Value and Assessing Risk of Speculative Grade Securities.* Probus Publishing Company, 1989.

Fridson, Martin S. "What Went Wrong with the Highly Leveraged Deals? (Or, All Variety of Agency Costs)." *The Journal of Applied Corporate Finance.* Fall, 1991, pp. 57-67.

Hickman, W. Braddock. *Corporate Bond Quality and Investor Experience.* Princeton University Press, 1958.

Jefferis, Richard H., Jr. "The High-Yield Debt Market: 1980-1990." *Economic Commentary.* Federal Reserve Bank of Cleveland. April 1, 1990, pp. 1-6.

Maloney, Kevin J., Richard J. Rogalski, and Lakshmi Shyam-Sunder. "An Explanation for the Junk Bond Risk/Return Puzzle." *Working Paper.* The Amos Tuck School of Business Administration, December, 1992.

Odean, Kathleen. *High Steppers, Fallen Angels, and Lollipops.* Henry Holt and Company, 1988.

Lederman, Jess, and Michael P. Sullivan, eds. *The New High Yield Bond Market: Investment Opportunities, Strategies and Analysis.* Probus Publishing Company, 1993.

Shulman, Joel, Mark Bayless, and Kelly Price. "The Influence of Marketability on the Yield Premium of Speculative Grade Debt." *Financial Management.* Autumn, 1993, pp. 132-141.

Yago, Glenn. *Junk Bonds: How High Yield Securities Restructured Corporate America.* Oxford University Press, 1991.

K

KOREA, DOING BUSINESS IN THE REPUBLIC OF

The Republic of Korea (South Korea) has been among the fastest-developing economies in the industrialized world. South Korea's 1993 **gross national product** was approximately $294.5 billion, with a consistent annual growth rate of more than 8 percent since the early 1960s. The South Korean general business climate thus continues to remain among the most favorable in the world.

The success of South Korea's economy is all the more noteworthy since South Korea has very few natural resources and is among the most densely populated of nations. South Korea is an extremely crowded country. The entire nation—including Chefu Island in the East China Sea—is only 38,316 square miles, an area that would fit easily into the state of Kentucky. Crowded into this area are more than 42 million people, well over ten times Kentucky's population.

The extreme population density is made even more a factor by the fact that 80 percent of the country is heavily mountainous, providing difficulties for farming and transportation. These rugged regions remain relatively sparsely populated. By contrast (and in part as a result), roughly three-fourths of the country's people live in urban areas. Indeed, nearly one in every four South Koreans lives in the capital city of Seoul—which has a population of just under 11 million people. Chief among the other major cities are Pusan (with just under 4 million people); Taegu (2.2 million), and Inch'on, Kwangju, and Taejon, each with well over 1 million people.

The Republic of Korea consists of roughly the lower 45 percent of the Korean Peninsula in northeastern Asia. At its furthest point, South Korea comes within less than 50 miles from Japan's Tsushima Islands in the Strait of Korea, and within approximately 120 miles of the main Japanese island of Honshu. Dividing the peninsula about 600 miles from the tip to the north is the approximately 150-mile long demilitarized zone (DMZ) that has separated the Republic of Korea from the hostile Democratic People's Republic of Korea (communist North Korea).

HISTORY OF SOUTH KOREA

Korea has a long and ancient history. The region was inhabited as early as 3000 B.C. The state of Chosen, occupying a major portion of the peninsula, was well established by the fourth century B.C. During the first century B.C., the numerous tribes of Korea centralized into three kingdoms. By the late seventh century A.D. the three kingdoms had united through a series of wars under the kingdom of Silla which lasted roughly until the late eighth century A.D. During this period, both Buddhism and Confucianism took firm root in Korea and the foundation of much of modern Korean culture was laid. By the early ninth century A.D., Silla weakened by provincial rebellions, again divided into three—a period known as the Later Three Kingdoms. These three kingdoms were again reunited under the Koryo dynasty in A.D. 935. It was this dynasty that gave the country its English name. Four centuries later, following internal reforms, the Koryo dynasty was supplanted by the Yi dynasty which ruled Korea through 26 monarchs from its founding in 1392 until the Japanese conquest of Korea in 1910. Korea was liberated from Japan by Allied forces following World War II.

In 1948, Korea was divided into a communist North and a noncommunist South. The Korean War broke out in 1950 after North Korea invaded South Korea in an attempt to reunify the country. The war—never officially ended—established a cease-fire and a demilitarized zone that has divided the two Koreas since 1953. In 1991 North and South Korea set up their first commercial relations, but continuing tensions in the 1990s regarding the development of nuclear weapons in North Korea and the death in July 1994 of Kim Il Sung (the first and until his death only chairman of the North Korean Communist Party) have lent a degree of political instability to the peninsula as a whole.

POLITICAL AND ECONOMIC STRUCTURES

South Korea is a republic. The Constitutional Referendum of 1980 established what is generally called the Fifth Republic. The basic model for the republic is the U.S. tripartite system of government with a separate executive branch led by a president, a legislative branch in the form of the National Assembly, and a judiciary branch with a supreme court. While the Republic of Korea is a democracy, the Democratic Justice Party (formerly the Democratic Republican Party) has held power since it was established in 1963. Trends toward a greater freedom in election results were seen in the December 1992 election. In that election—following a series of scandals connecting government, military and major business leaders—South Korea elected to the presidency Kim Young Sam—an outspoken dissident with no previous ties to the military.

The government of South Korea has had and continues to have a strong influence on business development in the nation. Beginning in the 1960s the government of South Korea began to formulate an industrial policy by which it established target industries and even target companies. These target industries and companies received special aid from the government to help nurture their growth. Under both Presidents Park Chung Hee and Chun Doo-Hwan, five-year plans were established to ensure the economic well-being of these companies through subsidies, tax relief, and protective tariffs. These policies contributed in part to the subsequent success of the Korean giant trading companies or *chaebols*.

THE CHAEBOL

South Korean business is dominated by a collection of industrial groups whose corporate organization is unique to Korea. These industrial groups are known as *chaebols*. Richard M. Steers, Yoo Keum Shin, and Gerardo R. Ungson defined the Korean *chaebol* as "a financial clique consisting of varied corporate enterprises engaged in diverse businesses and typically owned and controlled by one or two interrelated family groups." Steers, Shin, and Ungson indicated that there are six main characteristics of the *chaebol*: (1) family control and **management**, (2) paternalistic leadership, (3) centralized planning and coordination, (4) an entrepreneurial orientation, (5) close business-government relations, and (6) strong school ties in hiring policies.

Currently there are roughly 50 *chaebols* in Korea of varying strength and size. Over 60 percent of South Korea's gross national product (GNP) comes from the largest five of these: Samsung, Hyundai, Lucky-Goldstar, Daewoo, and Sunkyong.

Chaebols, like the Japanese *keiretsu*, consist of numerous companies tied together by internal affiliations, shared boards, and family connections. This federation of interrelated companies is often difficult to understand in the Americas and Europe since no counterparts exist in those regions.

For example, Samsung, the largest *chaebol*, consists of over 30 individual enterprises, each of which would be considered an independent company in the United States. Some of these Samsung "firms" are publicly held and others are privately held. The enterprises themselves cover an enormous array of industrial areas ranging from Samsung Electronics (the second-largest semiconductor manufacturer worldwide) to insurance companies (Samsung Life Insurance; Ankuk Fire & Marine Insurance); from shipbuilding to petrochemicals, and so on.

The other *chaebols* are similar in organization both in the number of affiliated companies and in the diverse sectors in which their affiliated firms are involved. Thus Lucky-Gold Star consists of nearly 40 firms ranging from consumer electronics to financial services to oil refineries. The Hyundai group consists of over 25 member companies ranging from automobile to elevator manufacturing. Daewoo has over 20 firms in its family of companies—ranging from overseas construction projects to heavy equipment manufacturing and personal computer production.

CONDUCTING BUSINESS IN KOREA

LANGUAGE. Korean, the language of Korea, is limited to Korea and has few cognates with Western languages. As a result, many Korean business people are accustomed to Westerners being unable to speak Korean. English is spoken by many educated Koreans, and due to favorable ties to the United States both in trade and militarily, the use of English is often well-received. Nonetheless, the businessperson unable to understand Korean is at a severe disadvantage in Korea. As Boye DeMente observed, the businessperson "who does not learn Korean is greatly limited in both his professional and social contacts in Korea. Those who cannot communicate at all in Korean are severely handicapped in their ability to relate to and participate in life outside the confines of the foreign community and world of international business."

Korean itself as a language has several factors affecting translation into Western languages. For example, the language reinforces hierarchical differences which are untranslatable. The businessperson unable to understand Korean therefore misses both subtle clues to levels of respect directed toward him or her, and the hierarchy established among the Koreans with whom the business is conducted.

Koreans also share the same family names in numbers virtually inconceivable in Western languages. Fifty percent of all Koreans share the same family names: Pak or Park, Lee, Choi, and Kim. The need to memorize a business partner's full name, therefore, becomes a necessity. This situation takes on even more importance when one considers the importance of family ties in hiring in many Korean companies.

GENDER ROLES. Gender roles remain traditionally differentiated along Confucian lines in Korea. Korean women, consequently, are rarely in positions of importance in government or business. Increasingly, Korean women are receiving employment in Western companies, although their role in interacting with Korean men in Korea remains subject to socially learned value systems. Western women are also subject to these traditional attitudes as well, although significantly less so than are Korean women. To some extent, as more and more Western businesswomen play an active role in Korean business with foreigners, they are afforded what amounts to a third gender status outside of the traditional male-female dichotomy.

CONTEXTING. Korea is what is called a high-context culture. As a result, Koreans place a strong emphasis on how a message is said rather than on just the words used. Messages are understood in terms of the full context of the communicators' relationship with one another. This particularly affects the importance for social etiquette and formality in official situations (including business meetings) and creates an emphasis on face-saving.

As a direct consequence of the high-context nature of Korean communication, it is necessary to build a personal relationship in conducting business with Koreans. Without the context of that personal relationship, little if any substantive communication can take place, and necessary levels of trust are inadequate to undertake most business arrangements.

As in most high-context cultures, Korean behavior is more likely to be governed by individual interpretation and the need to save face rather than on external rules and regulations. As a result, in Korea, personal understandings are more binding than contracts. Indeed, contracts in Korea are often seen as the beginning of a relationship that can be modified as the business progresses. This contrasts with the view of low-context cultures (such as the United States) in which the contract is viewed as not subject to change.

Finally, in high-context societies, understood or unofficial rules are often as (or even more) important than written rules. This holds true even in relations with government officials. These unwritten rules, called *naekyu* in Korean, are subject to the context of the situation to which they are applied. As a result, *naekyu* may be employed in some instances and overlooked in others, depending on the context of the individuals involved and of the situation particular to the incident at hand.

STATUS AND AUTHORITY CONCEPTION. Status differences are strongly recognized in Korea. These differences are reinforced through language and traditional Confucianist views of authority as well as such factors as place of education, rank in the organization, and family wealth. Acknowledging differences in rank, showing respect for titles and other symbols of authority, and acting appropriately to one's own social class are important in conducting business in Korea. Foreigners, including those from ostensibly egalitarian societies, are not exempt from these standards, although most foreign business executives are perceived as belonging to the upper-middle or higher class.

NONVERBAL COMMUNICATION. Because face-saving is so important and because contexting is so high, considerable emphasis is placed on nonverbal cues in Korean business communication. *Nunch'i* or the reading of facial expression is particularly important to determine negative reactions or reservations regarding a proposal. This is because the fear of making another person lose face in Korea makes most Korean businesspeople very hesitant about openly saying something disagreeable or unpleasant.

LEGAL CONSIDERATIONS. The framework of Korea's modern legal system was laid out under the Japanese occupation of the first part of the twentieth century. Like Japan, South Korea follows the civil and commercial codes of Continental Europe. As with other civil codes in Japan and Europe, Korea's civil code is comprised of general legal principles and is subject to considerably more interpretation by courts than the case law system of common law practice in the United States. Unlike older civil code countries, however, South Korea's post-occupation Civil Code was officially only put into place in 1960. This poses additional difficulties. As Kyu Wha Lee noted, "Korean courts and lawyers must interpret the laws based on only some 30 years of modern Korean legal history and a sparse body of either case decisions or commentaries by legal scholars." As a result, as Lee concluded, "from an American viewpoint, it may create an impression of too little predictability in the interpretation of laws."

Additionally, as with many high-context cultures, Korean laws are not as strictly consistent or enforceable as in low-context cultures. This is reinforced by the Confucian tradition in which lawsuits are generally brought as a last resort; most conflicts are expected to be resolved outside of the courts. As DeMente pointed out, "Lawyers in Korea do not look upon themselves as owing their primary allegiance to a client ... they put the welfare of Korean society in general (and by extension, the country itself) above the interests of their clients." Lawyers in Korea are peacemakers and maintainers of harmony rather than client advocates.

CONCLUSION

The Republic of Korea maintains consulates and trade advisories in most Western nations. Many West-ern nations additionally maintain chambers of commerce and trade consulates in South Korea. The Republic of Korea's Ministry of Trade and Industry maintains a Korean Trade Promotion arm (KOTRA) and the Korean Chamber of Commerce and Industry, both useful to foreign business involved in South Korea. Finally, many other organizations exist that can help the new business in Korea, such as the non-profit Korean-American Business Institute (KABI). These organizations may be contacted for a more thorough follow-up to this brief introduction.

SEE ALSO: Cross-Cultural/International Communication

[David A. Victor]

FURTHER READING:

DeMente, Boye. *Korean Etiquette & Ethics in Business*. Lincolnwood, Illinois: NTC Business Books, 1988.

Lee, Kyu Wha. "International Business Negotiations in Korea." In *The ABA Guide to International Business Negotiations*, edited by J. R. Silkenat, and J. M. Aresty. Chicago: American Bar Association, 1994, pp. 157-63.

Steers, Richard M., Yoo Keun Shin, and Gerardo R. Ungson. *The* Chaebol: *Korea's New Industrial Might*. New York: Harper & Row/Ballinger, 1989.

Victor, David A. *International Business Communication*. New York: HarperCollins, 1992.

L

LABELING

SEE: Packaging

LABOR ECONOMICS

According to the MIT *Dictionary of Modern Economics* labor economics is the branch of economics that analyzes "the study of the nature and determinants of pay and employment." Particular emphasis is put on the role played by social institutions and different types of market structures that jointly determine the pattern and mobility or speed of adjustment in the labor market where human labor inputs are bought and sold.

With regard to their speed of adjustment, labor markets are relatively slow in comparison to those markets for nonlabor inputs and **commodities**. For reasons best attributed to human behavior, worker movement from relatively low-wage areas to high-wage locations is sluggish. Worker retraining aimed at eliminating wage differentials also requires a substantial amount of time, which is generally not the case for other nonlabor inputs and commodities. As a result, the duration of wage differentials has tended to outlast those of other price differentials.

Another prominent distinction is drawn between internal and external labor markets. Internal labor markets refer to the determinants of pay and employment within a firm, while external labor markets refer

to the determinants of pay and employment between firms or within and across industries. Many labor economists place substantial theoretical weight on these distinctions when trying to explain how labor markets work. As to the question of which type is more efficient or inefficient in the allocation of labor however, unanimity has been absent.

GENERAL OVERVIEW

Almost from its inception (and especially during the post-World War II period), the analytical scope of labor economics mushroomed far outside the domain of traditional economics, making it a difficult field to define in strict economic sense. Many labor economics specialists caution that the word "labor" should not be understood as exclusively linked to the discipline of "economics." Instead, they advocate a more interdisciplinary approach that draws critically from insights provided by the disciplines of sociology, political science, psychology, and organizational theory and behavior. As a result, labor economics has concerned itself with a large range of topics, including race and gender discrimination; labor-management relations; demographic economics; personal or social expenditures on education, medical care, and training, referred to as human capital investments; and a multitude of issues surrounding behavior in the workplace, a subject area germane to industrial and human relations schools.

During the last two decades of the twentieth century labor economics has been preoccupied with the problem of understanding and reversing a general economic productivity slowdown in the United States. As a proposed solution, a majority of labor economists and concerned others have recommended the widespread implementation of a "new" set of nonadversarial, democratic workplace industrial relations called labor-management cooperation schemes. Largely influenced by ideas gleaned from producer cooperative theory, future workplace relations under these schemes will be designed to "empower" workers in all facets of a firm's activities.

To solicit their participation in these new schemes, workers have been promised more than a token voice in shaping company policy, along with the right to exercise higher-level decision making responsibilities formerly reserved for upper management. Labor-management schemes are also supposed to substantially reduce overall unit labor costs by eliminating management surveillance designed to detect on-the-job shirking. On the other hand, workers are expected to forego a rigid job classification system, and corresponding wage structure, and agree in turn to a more flexible job assignment environment. The compelling argument is that worker satisfaction and motivation will increase with the challenge of learning and mastering new jobs, as opposed to the older environment of routine jobs that tended to lower morale over time. For unionized workplaces, this also means eliminating the traditional grievance procedures handled by elected union representatives in favor of nonelected joint labor-management committees that no longer have the option of turning to outside arbitrators to settle disputes.

Labor-management cooperation schemes are theoretically designed to flatten decision making so as to improve communication and spread technical knowledge without supervisory surveillance. Workers, imbued with a greater sense of self-determined voice and responsibility, should come to associate their own work efforts with their firm's success, from which individual or team rates of pay will be calculated. The influence of a more flexible job structure conducted according to democratic principles was expected to impart a long-term positive influence on productivity, but there have been problems after cooperation schemes were implemented. Because this new set of workplace relations often blurs the established, legally recognized separation between worker and management functions, a legal question has developed concerning whether these new type of relations are tantamount to "company unions," which are illegal under the National Labor Relations Act. Unions and management continue to struggle with this new environment.

TWO PREVAILING THEORIES

Up until the period of the Great Depression and World War II, the study of labor economics was confined to the dominant orthodox framework of pure neoclassical economic theory. Analytical concepts familiar to micro and macroeconomists were the guiding precepts. A fundamental theoretical conclusion emerged which held that in a labor market where the competitive forces of supply and demand operated, a uniform industry-wide wage would prevail for laborers with similar skill or occupational characteristics. Any aberrations were thought to be short-lived and generally dismissed. This established theory remained unquestioned until a comprehensive empirical research project conducted by the War Labor Board yielded primarily opposite conclusions. It found that wage rates for similar occupations varied greatly within and across many of the same labor markets. The most ironic finding of the report involved unions. According to established theory, the forces of free competition were thought to be least active in unionized labor markets, which represented the antithesis of neoclassical free competition. The study showed that, in reality, it was only these unionized markets that anything approaching a uniform industry wage prevailed. Faced with this split between reality and theory, post-war labor economics developed into two schools of thought. The orthodox neoclassical school continued to push ahead with the development of theoretical models, while the institutionalist school conducted empirical research whose results typically clashed with the prevailing conclusions reached by theorists. The following sections will explore the history of the theoretical movement and then detail the key institutionalist beliefs.

HISTORY OF THE THEORETICAL SCHOOL

Labor economics as a separate branch of economics emerged out of the political turmoil swirling around two major theoretical traditions and their competing theories of wage determination. On one side stood classical political economy, on the other neoclassical or marginalist political economy. In general, answers to two key questions divide the two traditions. First, do capitalist market forces function to guarantee that workers will receive their "fair share" of the output they generate? Second, if not, is it possible through collective/union efforts to gain a larger share, given the constraints imposed by capitalist market forces?

Classical political economy, which flourished and dominated the field of economic theory and analysis from the eighteenth century until the middle of the nineteenth, would have answered no to the first question and, under certain conditions, yes to the second. Major contributors to the development of classical political economy include Adam Smith (1723-90), David Ricardo (1772-1823), and Karl Marx (1818-83); they brought the field to its highest development. Marx developed his labor theory of value and exploitation to demonstrate how workers received only a portion of their product, with the remainder forming an economic surplus appropriated by capitalists for the maintenance of their consumption and investment activities.

For reasons more political than economic, neoclassical theory displaced classical political economy in the 1870s. It has remained the dominant framework for conducting formal economic analysis ever since. The works of utilitarian social philosopher Jeremy Bentham (1748-1832), were highly influential in the formation of early neoclassical economics. Bentham maintained that all human motivation could be reduced to a single principal: the individual's desire to maximize utility or satisfaction. Contrary to the class conflict conclusions reached by classical political economy, **utilitarianism** espoused an economic doctrine of class harmony where the satisfaction of individual preferences informed all economic decisions. The appeal to class harmony resided in the "rational" notion that if capitalists and workers were brought to understand that they each received only a portion of what they had jointly created, then social justice would prevail. Several early attempts at constructing an economic theory of value and exchange on the basis of a utilitarian approach failed. Only with the separate publication of economic texts by William Stanley Jevons (1835-82) and Carl Menger in 1871, and by Leon Walras three year later, did neoclassical theory emerge as an internally coherent theoretical tradition. A short time later, the work of Alfred Marshall (1842-1924) provided additional support of neoclassical theory.

Neoclassical wage theory developed in response to Marx's critique and in reaction to a burgeoning, often hostile, trade union movement. Its overriding concern was to affirm that capitalist market forces were capable of paying workers their "rightful share" of the net product. With that in mind, John Bates Clark's influential book, *The Distribution of Wealth*, did just that. In his book, Clark argued that workers received wages that were equivalent to the value of their marginal labor product. From there, it followed that wage differentials simply reflected individual differences in skill and ability and the nonmonetary advantages and disadvantages between numerous jobs. Any of the factors that caused the productivity of labor to increase, thus shifting the demand curve for labor upwards, would be met with appropriate wage increases. Clark and other neoclassical labor economists concluded that Marx was wrong and that unions were unnecessary. In fact, they argued that successful union strategies that raised wages above the value of their marginal product would have a negative effect by lowering employment within unionized sectors while increasing the labor supply and lowering wages in nonunion sectors.

By the mid-1940s, neoclassical economists felt secure within their long-run equilibrium interpretation of wage determinants. At that time, however, empirical economists attempting to reconcile real-life labor market phenomena with neoclassical theory encountered unsettling data. When confronted by a growing number of studies suggesting flaws in their theories, neoclassical economists reacted by simply developing several ad hoc explanations to account for these exceptions. Empirical economists, on the other hand, found themselves shunning theoretical models constructed to guide them in their research. Without any theoretical structure to inform their work, they also resorted to ad hoc explanations. As a result a growing schism emerged within labor economics between theory and practice.

INSTITUTIONALIST LABOR ECONOMISTS

In order to address the widening gulf between theory and reality, a new breed of "Institutionalist" labor economists arose at the end of World War II. Recognition of four major economic developments largely explained why this happened. First, the disturbing impact of the Great Depression rattled every branch of economics related to the theories of pure competition and general equilibrium. Second, the publication of John Maynard Keynes's (1883-1946) *General Theory* and its insightful analysis of effective demand posed intriguing questions that were difficult to reconcile with standard neoclassical theory. Third, industrial unions were being formed at an unprecedented pace. Fourth, the development of the theory of imperfect competition in the 1930s seemed better suited to account for the fact that labor and capital markets reflected very large powerful bargaining units that were fewer in number, as opposed to the very large number of small powerless markets assumed by the neoclassical theory of perfect competition.

One of the earliest postwar institutionalists to attempt to explain interindustry wage differentials based on real economic conditions was John Dunlop. In 1948, he proposed four reasons for their existence: unequal productivity levels; the proportion of labor to total costs; the relative degree or absence of competitive product market pressures; and an industry's changing skill and occupational composition of the workforce. Similar institutionalist studies soon followed. Though their points of emphasis varied, all those studies significantly departed from the prevailing neoclassical theory of perfect competition tied to marginal productivity.

Not content to sit on the sidelines, upholders of neoclassical orthodoxy criticized institutionalist theory on methodological grounds. Institutionalist theory, they claimed, was overly dependent on short- as opposed to long-run determinations. Institutionalists replied that orthodox neoclassical theory had yet to explain the widespread and persistent pattern of interindustry wage differentials between workers with nearly identical productivity characteristics, an undeniable fact uncovered repeatedly by institutionalist research.

Neoclassical theory appeared to be vindicated with the publication in 1964 of Gary Becker's book on human capital theory. Becker's human capital approach, for which he was awarded a Nobel Prize in economics in 1993, argued that workers could upgrade their economic status if they made the rational individual choice to invest in more education and skill training. Once completed, their marginal productivity would increase and competitive pressures within the labor market would operate to raise their income. If they chose to do otherwise, it signalled that they somehow preferred the existing distribution of wages and were willing to live with its consequences, no matter how inequitable. Armed with human capital theory, confident neoclassical labor economists entered the realm of empirical research intent on explaining the persistence of inter- and intra-industry differentials among workers with identical productive characteristics. They anticipated the restoration of marginal productivity theory to its former prominence, arguing that wage differentials simply reflected individual differences in skill and effort, hence productivity. Liberal economists also jumped on the bandwagon, viewing human capital theory as a means for justifying larger government expenditures on training programs for the poor and disadvantaged.

Not long after the rise of human capital theory, real problems turned its promises into empty ones. Despite human capital-inspired government programs, the continued fragmentation of the economy into low- and high-wage sectors proved intractable, as did wage differentials between black and white, and male and female workers. According to the logic of human capital theory, the economy's competitive pressures should have operated to eliminate those discriminatory forces, yet with the passage of time they had grown more pronounced. Closer empirical scrutiny of human capital theory raised serious questions concerning the use of average years of schooling as the critical variable used to explain wage differentials. Other factors such as large-scale manufacturing, on-the-job training, and reliance upon studies that separated production from skilled workers offered more credible explanations.

The early 1970s saw another institutionalist theoretical upsurge intended to explain the persistence of race and gender wage discrimination and the growth of a newly emergent "working poor" category. Reviving and building upon a previous institutionalist concept of internal labor markets (ILMS), two "new institutionalist" labor economists, Peter Doeringer and Michael Piore (1942–), led the effort to tackle those issues. They emphasized two major theoretical

issues pertinent to ILMS theory: the growth of job-specific skill training and the notion of a modern "dual economy." In support of their job-specific skill approach, they argued that the development of large manufacturing firms provided the impetus for stable internal labor markets. So structured, firms could minimize the rising costs associated with skill training and worker turnover. Being somewhat sheltered from competitive external labor market pressures, firms could developed mutually beneficial internal job ladders. These would allow experienced workers to reap seniority benefits, be more inclined to stay within the firm, and train new workers.

Advancing a more detailed version of the dual economy approach first put forward by Robert Averits in 1968, Piore and Doeringer also argued that the labor market was divided into a primary and secondary market. Jobs in primary markets were distinguished by sophisticated technologies, skilled and semi-skilled labor, high wages, good working conditions, chances for advancement, employment stability, fairness, and due process in the administration of work rules. On the other hand, jobs in the secondary markets were subject to external competitive pressures; lacked technological sophistication; were performed by unskilled labor; and featured low wages, little or no fringe benefits, high labor turnover, absenteeism and tardiness, higher levels of petty theft, little chance of advancement, and typically autocratic and capricious supervisors.

Proponents of ILMS argued that the existence of dual labor markets, especially its primary component, did not fit well within the orthodox model of pure competition determining wages. The idea that labor mobility would lead to a reduction in wage differentials was flawed, if not altogether wrong, because of the discriminatory barriers that faced blacks and women. When it came to the subject of unions however, Piore and Doeringer's ILMS model encountered difficulty in explaining how supposedly secondary labor markets were able to transform themselves into primary markets through unionizing efforts. Nor were they ever able, like older institutionalist labor economists, to ultimately reject the overriding authority of marginal productivity theory.

In the more liberal academic environment of the 1970s, radical and Marxian ideas began to spread in labor economics. Drawing upon a rich historical legacy of industrial organization under capitalism, Harry Braverman's groundbreaking 1974 publication, *Labor and Monopoly Capital*, painstakingly detailed the de-skilling effects of modern capitalism. Consistent with Karl Marx, Braverman argued that this course was undertaken so that capitalist-inspired management could take control of the labor process away from skilled workers in order to raise the level of exploitation. Influenced by Braverman, many radicals took issue with the assumed connection between highly capital intensive, modern technology, and the high skill levels said to be found in the high-wage primary labor markets, which was a primary part of the dual labor market theory. Others rejected the harmonious view of the labor process held by the new institutionalist school, especially when frequent strikes and productivity slowdowns, seemed to indicate a lack of harmony. Most radical labor market theorists did not so much reject new institutionalist reasoning, however. Instead, they insisted that dual market structures arose from class struggle over the internal organization of the labor processes. They called this labor segmentation theory.

Though essentially restatements of imperfect competition theories from the 1930s, the new Marxist and radical versions of monopoly capital were advanced to explain how market power served to prop up long-standing, above average rates of profit. These rates were considered to be the sustaining lifeblood separating high-wage, primary markets from low-wage secondary markets. Interestingly, while reviving the importance of class struggle (once the centerpiece of classical political economy), most radicals were either ignorant of, or rejected outright, Marx's theory of the law of value. Marx considered this law as absolutely critical—it held the key to understanding the objective limits of a theory of inter- and intra-industry profit and wage differentials tied to his dynamic theory of capitalist accumulation. With the lone exception of Howard Botwinick's contribution, *Persistent Inequalities*, no radical or Marxian work in labor economics has systematically broken away from the underpinnings of neoclassical theory, in either its perfect or imperfect versions, to formulate a theory of wage differentials consistent with Marx's law of value.

Leftist criticisms of radical segmentation theory were several. On theoretical grounds, it was argued that segmentation theory was overly dependent upon ad hoc explanations and lacked theoretical clarity. Even results from empirical studies were contradictory, indicating that overall patterns of working class division and segmentation were broadly diffused, tending to transcend neatly compartmentalized boundaries. This was true not only for the United States, but especially in Europe where significant numbers of immigrants gained entrance into primary labor markets in Germany, France, and Italy instead of entering the secondary markets as segmentation theory would have expected. Moreover, when it came to the historical development of dual economic structures, more attention was paid to capitalist motivations than to workers, especially unionized ones.

Beginning in the late 1970s, primary sector industries such as the automobile and steel industries suffered hug losses and went through periods of labor upheaval. In response to falling profit rates, that were once virtually guaranteed by near monopoly power, former primary market high-wage firms were behaving much like secondary ones. Tactics included forcing concessions in wage and working conditions, threatening to or actually relocating firms to low-wage areas, defeating strikes through the use of scab labor as permanent striker replacements, actively lobbying for passage of trade pacts that threatened high wages, and instituting two-tier wage packages for the same job.

Faced with these difficulties and criticisms, many radical labor economists unceremoniously abandoned ship. Indeed, by the 1990s, many leading radical proponents were no longer touting class struggle as a determinant factor. They had instead joined forces with the orthodox consensus on the need for joint labor-management schemes designed to counter the slowdown in productivity.

A NEW THEORY DEVELOPS

As the twentieth century comes to a close, a development called "efficiency wage theory" is gaining popularity. Efficiency wage theory was initiated by neoclassically-oriented labor economists who acknowledge the failure of their traditional competitive framework to explain persistent real-world inter- and intra-industry wage differentials for workers with identical productive characteristics, as well as its inability to account for the growth of chronic unemployment. Efficiency wage theory has elicited considerable unanimity among the previously feuding groups of radical, institutional, and orthodox neoclassical labor economists.

Though many different versions abound, the central premise of efficiency wage theory is that the payment of wage rates above the assumed market equilibrium wage will result in a profit maximizing outcome and permit capitalist firms to minimize total unit labor costs. Accordingly, above-equilibrium wage rates are thought to induce: increased effort/productivity and a reduction in worker shirking; reduced turnover costs; perceived greater costs of being fired; improved worker morale; the attraction and retention of better quality personnel.

In the long-run, if all firms pursue a similar higher-than-equilibrium wage strategy, unemployment will result. And neither is there reason for firms to lower wages, since this will slacken worker effort and increase unit labor costs. Depending then on the conditions unique to each industry or firm, different levels of efficiency wages will be necessary so that workers with identical productive characteristics will not receive the same wage. With this logic in mind, orthodox labor economists apparently have a plausible answer to the puzzling question of how above-equilibrium wage firms manage to survive in a competitive economy.

[Daniel E. King]

FURTHER READING:

Becker, Gary. *Human Capital*. University of Chicago Press, 1964.

Botwinick, Howard. *Persistent Inequalities: Wage Disparity Under Capitalist Competition*. Princeton University Press, 1994.

Braverman, Harry. *Labor and Monopoly Capital*. Monthly Review Press, 1974.

Clark, John Bates. *The Distribution of Wealth: A Theory of Wages, Interest and Profit*. Kelly and Millman, 1956.

Doeringer, Peter B., and Michael J. Piore. *Internal Labor Markets and Manpower Analysis*. Heath Lexington Books, 1971.

Dunlop, John T. "Productivity and the Wage Structure." *Income, Employment and Public Policy*. W.W. Norton, 1948.

Gordon, David M., Richard Edwards, and Michael Reich. *Segmented Work, Divided Workers*. Cambridge University Press, 1982.

Hicks, John R. *The Theory of Wages*. 1st ed. Macmillan, 1932.

Katz, Lawrence F. "Efficiency Wage Theories: A Partial Evaluation." *NBER Macroeconomics Annual*. MIT Press, 1986.

Kaufman, Bruce E. *How Labor Markets Work*. Lexington Books, 1988.

McNulty, Paul J. *The Origins and Development of Labor Economics*. MIT Press, 1980.

LABOR FORCE

SEE: Human Capital; Multicultural Work Force; Workforce

LABOR LAW AND LEGISLATION

According to *The Encyclopedic Dictionary of Economics* the concept of labor law and legislation refers to "A general term for legislation that partly or wholly relates to matters of **employment** and the activities of employers and workers in relation to one another." To a great extent this definition masks the highly partisan political forces standing for and against the passage of labor law legislation. For more than a century a virtual state of siege had existed between labor and employers. Not until 1935, when meaningful labor law was passed acknowledging the legal rights of independent union organizations, did a climate of relative industrial calm prevail.

To the current day, labor law and legislation remains a highly contentious and divisive issue, with neither side finding the status quo to their liking. Such partisanship has traditionally not confined itself only to the workplace but also permeates numerous areas of civil society such as academia, the legal profession, the courts, management associations, major media, and editorial boards, and religious groups.

When discussing labor law a critical distinction can be made regarding laws that are binding only on organized labor and those that apply to labor as whole, whether organized or not. For instance certain sections in the **Taft-Hartley Act** apply specifically to organized labor while sections of the Social Security Act of 1935 are enforced for all employees. In most, but not all instances, organized labor in the twentieth century has endorsed legislation aimed at covering all employees regardless of their organizational status. For example, organized labor has played an instrumental role in proposing, endorsing, and defending legislation meant to improve the general public welfare. These include: social security, Medicare and Medicaid, unemployment compensation, education funding, mine safety and health laws, black lung disability funds, parental leave, universal single-payer **health insurance**, **occupational safety and health laws**, minimum wage laws, **civil rights legislation**, and progressive tax law.

LABOR LAW REVIEW

Prior to the passage of comprehensive federal labor law legislation in the twentieth century, U.S. labor relations were regulated by state law. Laws governing labor relations were largely handled by state courts on a case by case basis. In legal terminology such a process of judicial decision making is referred to as "common law." On the other hand, laws made by state legislative bodies or administrative agencies are referred to as "statutory laws." Throughout most of the nineteenth century, common law rulings were upheld whenever they came into conflict with statutory decisions. Frequently any action taken on the part of workers to form a union was meet with judicial hostility. Acting on an employer's request, judges were quick to issue labor injunctions. At the time, the prevailing judicial doctrine held that workers who formed organizations to better their working conditions were guilty of unlawful conspiracy charges.

Even as some state courts began to recognize the rights of workers to form organizations in the mid-nineteenth century, the legal environment in which workers were allowed to operate was highly circumscribed. While some courts recognized the right of workers to strike, they also recognized the employer's right to continue operations using striker replacements (referred to by striking or unionized workers as "scabs") along with the right of an employee to remain at work if he or she chose not to honor the strike.

At the same time courts frequently issued labor injunctions prohibiting unions from peaceful picketing on the grounds that such actions interfered with the rights of the employer to continue operations. Under these terms the ''right to strike'' was seriously undermined if not rendered ineffective altogether.

The centerpiece of U.S. federal labor law is the National Labor Relations Act of 1935. The act was declared constitutional by the Supreme Court in 1937 and established employee rights and employer unfair labor practices. The **National Labor Relations Board (NLRB)** was established to administrate the NLRA. Its limited jurisdiction extends only to unfair labor practices and union elections covered in Sections 7-9 of the NLRA. In these matters it adheres to set procedures established by the statute and by regulations established by the board. Besides the NLRB, other government agencies play an important role in the administration of labor law. For instance, the U.S. Department of Labor administers portions of the Labor Management Reporting and Disclosure Act of 1959, the **Fair Labor Standards Act of 1938**, the Occupational Safety and Health Act of 1970, and the **Employee Retirement Income Security Act of 1974 (ERISA)**. The **Equal Employment Opportunity Commission (EEOC)** administrates Title VII (the statute regulating equal employment opportunity) of the Civil Rights Act, as well as the Equal Pay and Age Discrimination in Employment Acts.

The NLRB's Board has five members appointed by the president and confirmed by Senate vote. The president selects one of the five members to serve as chairperson subject to Senate confirmation. Each member serves five years; member appointments are staggered, and do not expire simultaneously. Along with the board, the statute set up a separate, independent general counsel, also appointed by the president subject to Senate approval for a four-year term. The relationship between the five member board and general counsel imitates that of prosecutor and judge in cases of unfair labor practice only (Section 8), were the board acts as judge and the general counsel as prosecutor. Matters related to election procedures (Section 9) are handled solely by the board and have nothing to do with the general counsel.

In 1947, under conservative political pressure, Congress passed the Taft-Hartley Act. In an attempt to redress the imbalance between labor and management, the Taft-Hartley Act significantly altered the pro labor provisions of the NLRA and later renamed it the **Labor Management Relations Act of 1947**. A controversial part of this act are the statutory restrictions contained in Sections 8(b)(4) and 8(b)(7), which comprehensively regulate the right to engage in picketing. The U.S. Constitution permits a limited right to picket as a matter of free speech. But union challenges to overturn the LRMA's picketing statues have been unsuccessful. The courts have maintained that picketing is a form of action, not just speech, thus subject to regulation. The Supreme Court has upheld this argument and ruled that a union's right to picket is determined by the LMRA and not based on constitutional grounds.

Since the 1970s, U.S. union leaders and organizers have routinely voiced concerns about legal obstacles set up to discourage unionization. They are quick to mention that many companies that domestically oppose union organizing drives here have no trouble recognizing unions abroad at their foreign operations. Unfavorable comparisons between U.S. labor laws and those of other industrial democracies do not escape U.S. union advocates.

In mid-to-late 1980s, during the Reagan and Bush administrations, pro-labor forces charged that the NLRB had become stacked with administration appointees intent on obstructing union certification campaigns. At first the Reagan administration practiced a policy of benign neglect. Over an extended period of time, cases piled up as vacant NLRB sets went unfilled. This added prolonged delays to a certification process that already worked to an employer's advantage. Moving from benign neglect to calculated activism, Reagan appointed four corporation lawyers and a chair to the board. Sounding very much like a throwback to the days when public officials were virtually indistinguishable from employers, they openly declared that ''collective bargaining frequently means the destruction of individual freedom,'' that ''unionized labor relations'' figured as one of ''the major contributors to the decline and failure of our healthy industries,'' and characterized strikes as ''a concerted effort employing violence, intimidation and political intervention to prevent people who want to work from working.'' During the board's tenure, complaints against employers that were dismissed increased 300 percent while dismissed complaints filed against unions decreased only 40 percent.

Indeed, by 1994, findings released by The Dunlop Commission, convened during the Clinton administration, confirmed this apparent antiunion bias. In the area of labor law, the commission reported the following: illegal firings occurred in one out of four union election campaigns compared to one in every twenty elections in the 1950s; only two-thirds of union certified elections were recognized by employers agreeing to negotiate contracts, while employers incur no monetary penalty for refusing to engage in good faith bargaining; and, in general, recourse to legal relief through the courts was not an option for a majority of employees, whose low income levels precluded them from paying the high costs and contingency fees required by private lawyers.

PRE-NLRA HISTORY AND DEVELOPMENT

The history and development of U.S. labor law legislation based on independent and legally recognized union organizations divides into two periods—before and after the NLRA. In the pre-NLRA period, roughly 1800-1935, the dominant employer methods used to combat and deny the legal formation of independent unions took two forms: the threat or actual use of private and public armed force and espionage; and employer recourse to a punitive legal system that served as little more than an appendage to employer property interests.

As early as 1806, Pennsylvania courts found cordwainers (shoemakers) guilty of a criminal conspiracy when they combined for the purpose of raising their wages. In 1842, the Massachusetts Supreme Court in *Commonwealth vs. Hunt* repealed criminal conspiracy laws imposed on unions, but left them with little room to function legally. Following the Civil War, especially during the period of a resurgent labor movement in the 1870s and 1880s, labor conspiracy prosecutions soared. These, along with the upsurge in labor injunctions, proved effective weapons by which employers thwarted the formation of a legally constituted labor movement. By the early twentieth century, many state courts were in agreement over the individual laborer's uncontested "right to strike." But then, echoing the 1906 opinion of the Massachusetts Supreme Court, state courts continued to declare many strikes illegal because of the "increase in power which a combination of citizens has over the individual citizen." In short, in most instances a combination of workers was outlawed from doing what one individual worker could do alone.

The use of labor injunctions (a court order prohibiting numerous union actions) rose to prominence during the upsurge in labor activities during the late 1870s and the unrest that was to follow. Just before the Haymarket Square confrontation in 1886, the focal rallying point of one of the first genuine national strikes in U.S. labor history, union strength had reached an all-time high. Leading the way were the Knights of Labor, with more than 700,000 members.

The use of labor injunctions continued well past the 1880s. During the period of 1880-1930, 1,845 labor injunctions were handed down by federal and state courts. And, for approximately the last 10 years of this period, a total of 921 were issued. Among the more notable were the injunctions issued in 1919 during the miners' strike, in 1922 against the national railway shopmen's strike, and in 1922 during the United Mine Workers' campaign to organize West Virginia and Kentucky miners. During the entire period of strife, the U.S. Supreme Court steadfastly upheld injunctions served up by the lower courts.

In 1890, the Sherman Antitrust Act of 1890 outlawed combinations in restraint of interstate trade and commerce including labor. The Sherman Act was invoked 12 times in the first seven years of its passage. It was first used on a national level in breaking the American Railway Strike of 1894. The courts ruled that the union's national strike in solidarity with the Pullman workers violated the Sherman Act. Injunctions were issued, the U.S. Army intervened, and eventually Eugene Debs and other strike leaders were imprisoned.

Between 1908 and 1914, the Sherman Act was used some 20 times. But on the eve of World War I, a respite arrived in the form of the Clayton Antitrust Act. It declared that "the labor of a human being is not a commodity or article of commerce." Not long after the war's end, however, the courts ruled that the Clayton act did not prevent "private parties" from obtaining antitrust injunctions, only the federal government. As a result, antitrust actions against unions reached a new high in the 1920s. Unions and unionists were charged with some 72 violations. Nearly all the injunctions requested under law were obtained, and more than half of the cases resulted in convictions and lengthy prison terms.

The use of criminal prosecutions was heavily used during the 1920s and early 1930s. Felony charges typically included murder, riot, assault, criminal libel, unlawful assembly, malicious mischief, and sedition. Misdemeanor charges included trespassing, loitering, disorderly conduct, assembling without permit, and disturbing the peace. In many instances, hobos riding trains in search of work were charged with any one of these misdemeanors and then required to work for little or no pay as a punishment. In mining states like Idaho, Colorado, Montana, and West Virginia that were policed by national guard units, a person could be arrested without any charge save for "military necessity" and frequently held in prison for long periods of time.

From the 1900s to early 1930s, a common, legally sanctioned tactic was the discharge of an employee for union activities. It was used repeatedly by employers as a means of discouraging unionization. Some states eventually did make the tactic illegal, but courts routinely invalidated these laws. Early in the 1900s, federal legislation was passed that prohibited interstate carriers from discharging employees for union activities, but it was declared unconstitutional by the U.S. Supreme Court in 1908. Existing laws gave an employer the right to coerce or threaten employees who wanted a union. They also empowered an employer with the right to fire an employee that joined a union, to refuse to bargain with a union if it did exist, and the right to form a company union and force employees to join it. During this period arose the term "yellow dog contract," which was a written legally enforceable contract that forbade workers from joining unions. Most courts faithfully enforced these contracts. The penalty for violation was automatic dismissal, and, since the contract was legally binding, unions were outlawed from organizing yellow dog contract workers. With some success, unions agitated for legislation against yellow-dog contracts. But, the U.S. Supreme Court struck down these laws with passage of the Norris-LaGuardia Act of 1932.

Prior to labor's formation of the Congress of Industrial Organizations (CIO) in 1932, it was not unusual for employers to finance their own private ''armies'' or else contract out services intent on crushing new labor organizations. Through mercenaries and spies, employer agencies engaged in subversion, violence, and deliberate lawbreaking. Upon infiltrating a union organization, employer agents identified union activists, gathered information on union organizing drives, fomented factional and ethnic strife among employees, and gained leadership positions with the intent of undermining other elected leaders. By assuming militant postures, these agents incited others to sabotage the union process or provoke violence in order to publicly discredit unions and invite employer retaliatory violence. Employers had no difficultly legally deputizing agents and mercenaries for strikebreaking and union-busting purposes.

Despite the scale and length of this war-like climate, no official casualty figures of those involved in labor disputes were ever kept, despite the fact that this was a time when the recording of statistics for all types of social and scientific phenomena was commonplace. However one report, limited to reviewing newspaper coverage of strikes from 1877 to 1968, tallied 700 dead and thousands of others suffering serious injuries; the overwhelming majority the dead and injured were workers.

In 1912, the Congressional Commission on Industrial Relations investigated the activities of labor espionage agencies. A second investigation was conducted in the mid-1930s by the LaFollette Civil Liberties Committee of the U.S. Senate. Despite being conducted in two different time periods, both investigations uncovered similar patterns of corporate spying practices and private police activities. Their findings proved influential in framing the legal substance of what was soon to emerge as federal labor law.

In the pre-NLRA period employers also turned to public armed force as a means of intervening against labor unions. At times, because of a sanctioning legal system, the difference between private and public armed forces was indistinguishable. Intervention occurred from local and state police, sheriffs, deputies, state militia (later to be national guard units), and all branches of the U.S. armed forces, including air corps mobilization. The advantages gained by employer use of public force were several: in the eyes of the populace, public force struck a chord of legitimacy; they were empowered to arrest, jail, and punish strikers; and usually, but not always, being publicly financed and equipped for violence, less costly to employers. At other times, employers used state militia that proved less than reliable due to lengthy call-up time and lack of loyalty. Most books dealing with labor history amply document the use of public armed forces to intervene in labor disputes. Even after the passage of NLRA, public armed forces were used in labor disputes although for different reasons. For example, President Richard Nixon's used 30,000 federal and national guardsmen to replace postal workers during a 1970 strike and, 11 years later, President Reagan used military personnel to break the air controllers' strike.

Unlike past strikes, when public armed forces were used to break strikes by using their authority and violence, public forces were used in these two cases to maintain services that were deemed essential to the U.S. economy.

American labor began with the legal system clearly stacked against it. One historical study (as noted by Klaus van Beyme, 1980) analyzing comparative labor law legislation throughout Europe and the United States covering the same time period concluded that most often, U.S. employers ''have made and enforced their own laws, acquired the services of public officials and law enforcement agents, resisted labor's claim to legal legitimacy, and assumed an imperial 'We are the law' posture.''

THE NLRA AND ITS LEGISLATIVE AFTERMATH

Enacted during the later years of the Great Depression, the NLRA was prompted by a rising wave of labor union militancy and a sympathetic Roosevelt Administration. It is often referred to as the Wagner Act after the New York Senator who sponsored the legislation. The NLRA established employee rights to organize, join unions, and participate in collective bargaining or mutual aid activities. It also established unfair labor practices, making employer interference with an employee's right to join a union and participate in concerted union activities unlawful. By law, employers were obliged to bargain in good faith with the union and refrain from discharging or otherwise discriminating against workers due to their involvement in union activities. Prior to the NLRA's passage, workers secured bargaining rights in two ways: through a forced strike or recognition based on the voluntary approval of their employer. In matters related to the enforcement of labor law, Congress created the administrative agency of the NLRB in full recognition of the dismal historical performance of the common law courts. At the time this was unheard of, since enforcement of all earlier law had been the sole domain of the courts.

In 1947, Congress passed, over President Truman's veto, the Taft-Hartley Act, named for its cosponsors, Senator Robert Taft and Congressman Hartley. Citing the restoration of ''balance,'' and ''individual rights over collective rights,'' Taft-Hartley significantly revised the NLRA's unfair labor practices Section 8. As a result the NLRA was officially renamed the Labor Management Relations Act. At the time of Taft-Hartley's passage, the United States was caught up in the hysteria of McCarthyism. The House's Dies Committee, later known as the House Un-American Activities Committee (HUAC), took serious charges that the prolabor LaFollette Civil Liberties Committee, communists, the CIO, the NLRB, and the Democratic National Committee had all conspired to engage (in the words of steel tycoon Tom Girdler) in a ''cold-blooded plot'' against business. Among one of its provisions was the requirement that union officers sign noncommunist loyalty oaths as a precondition for using the NLRB. Within the ranks of organized labor, a divisive factionalism resulted over how to best respond to the implementation of Taft-Hartley.

Out of such a political atmosphere did Taft-Hartley emerge. It added broadly interpreted union unfair employee practices. Its provisions prohibited unions from interfering with **employee rights**, from coercing or discriminating against employees through the unions' activities, and required union bargain in good faith. With respect to the employee rights provision, an employee could not be forced to engage in collective bargaining and any or such union activities against their will. Subsequent restrictions on secondary boycotts and free speech and picketing were also an outgrowth of Taft-Hartley.

In 1959, Congress passed the next substantial piece of labor law legislation, the Landrum-Griffin Act. Named after its two Congressional cosponsors, the legislation is formally called the Labor Management Reporting and Disclosure Act of 1959 and primarily governs internal union affairs. It established a ''Labor Bill of Rights'' for union members, such as internal union election procedures and reporting and disclosure stipulations for unions, union officers, and employers. It also added Section 8(e) to the LRMA, prohibiting ''hot cargo'' clauses whereby one employer was forbidden from dealing with other employers who were nonunion or on strike.

Soon to follow was passage of the Civil Rights Act of 1964. Under Title VII of the act, discriminatory wage differentials based on race, color, religion, sex, and national origin were prohibited. The **Occupational Health and Safety Act (OHSA)** was passed in 1970 to the applause of organized labor. Yet disillu-

sionment with OHSA soon set in; both labor and management were critical of it, but for different reasons. For management, it was costly and overly regulatory. Labor complained that with fewer than 3000 inspectors available to visit five million places of work, each establishment would be inspected on an average of every 75 years. At the same time, the average penalty per violation amounted to $25. In 1981, the Reagan administration cut the number of inspectors to 1,100.

Congress enacted the **Employee Retirement Income Security Act of 1974 (ERISA)**. With respect to private pension plans, ERISA was passed to curb practice of administrative misuse and the discharge or permanent layoff of employees just prior to being vested. To further ensure that employees would receive retirement pension benefits, ERISA set up the employer funded Public Benefit Guaranty Corporation government agency. In 1986 it guaranteed pensions up to a maximum of $1,858 per month should the employer go out of business and/or terminate the plan.

In 1993, the Family and Medical Leave Act of 1993, endorsed by organized labor, finally became law. It permitted workers at firms of 50 or more employees to take up to 12 weeks of unpaid, but job protected leave—for the birth or adoption of a child; the critical illness of a child, spouse, parent; or worker illness. In addition, health benefits would continue for the duration of the leave (if the worker had been receiving health benefits prior to the leave). By contrast, most workers in other advanced economies of the world have had this benefit (with pay and for longer periods) from at least World War II.

In 1994, the House of Representatives passed The Workplace Fairness Act bill. The bill never came up for a vote in the Senate. The bill would have banned the use of ''permanent replacements'' during a legally constituted strike. The ban on permanent replacements would not have interfered with the employer's use of replacement workers during a strike, but would have contested their retention as permanent employees in the aftermath of a strike.

[Daniel E. King]

FURTHER READING:

The Encyclopedic Dictionary of Economics. 3rd ed. Duskin Publishing Group, 1986.

Feldacker, Bruce. *Labor Guide to Labor Law*. 3rd ed. Prentice-Hall, 1990.

Gould, William B., IV. *Agenda for Reform: The Future of Employment Relations and the Law*. The MIT Press, 1993.

Sexton, Patricia Cayo. *The War on Labor and the Left*. Westview Press, 1991.

Sloane, Arthur A., and Fred Witney. *Labor Relations*. 6th ed. Prentice-Hall, 1988.

Townley, Barbara. *Labor Law Reform in U.S. Industrial Relations*. Gower Publishing Company Limited, 1986.

van Beyme, Klaus. *Challenge to Power*. Beverly Hills, CA: Sage, 1980.

LABOR-MANAGEMENT RELATIONS

The majority of key turning points in labor-management in the United States relations have been associated with periods of economic hardship. The Great Depression saw the establishment of comprehensive federal legislation designed to protect workers' right to organize. With the slowdown in economic growth and the intensification of global competition after the early 1970s, a number of labor-management cooperation programs were advocated to improve the efficiency of U.S. firms. In 1993, the Clinton administration established the Commission on the Future of Worker-Management Relations to address a broad range of issues, among them labor-management cooperation programs and the reform of U.S. labor law.

The federal government first guaranteed the right to organize and bargain collectively for railroad workers with the passage of the Railway Labor Act of 1926. The National Industrial Recovery Act of 1933 (NIRA) was part of the New Deal policies of the Great Depression era. The NIRA was intended to protect workers' right to unionize. It stated ''That employees shall have the right to organize and bargain collectively through representatives of their own choosing. . . .'' The NIRA had several shortcomings, among them a lack of enforcement provisions, and the act did little to promote workers' rights.

The basic law regulating labor-management relations and collective bargaining in the United States is The National Labor Relations Act of 1935, commonly referred to as the Wagner Act. A key provision of the act guarantees the right of nonmanagerial employees who work for firms engaged in interstate commerce to join unions and bargain on a collective basis. The legally protected right of workers to unionize was first established at the state level. In Massachusetts, for example, the state Supreme Court recognized this right in an 1842 decision.

The Wagner Act was primarily the work of Robert Wagner, a Democratic Senator from New York who wished to address the shortcomings of the NIRA. In 1933, Wagner began meeting with representatives from the American Federation of Labor and the National Labor Board, which was set up to administer the NIRA. These meetings culminated in the writing of the Wagner Act in February of 1934. The act failed to receive congressional support when initially introduced, but passed after the Democrats made substantial gains in the congressional elections of 1934; it was signed into law by President Roosevelt in July of 1935.

The most controversial part of the Wagner Act was Section 8, which prohibited what it called ''unfair labor practices'' on the part of employers. Under Section 8, employers could not legally fire workers for joining unions, could not refuse to bargain with a union that represented a majority of workers, and could not establish company unions. In large part due to the Wagner Act, union membership increased from 4 million in 1935 to 12 million in 1947. The National Labor Relations Board (NLRB) was established to administer the Wagner Act and is still the key agency regulating labor-management relations at the national level.

The constitutionality of the Wagner Act was affirmed in 1937 by the Supreme Court in *National Labor Relations Board vs. Jones and Laughlin Steel Corporation.* Shortly thereafter, probusiness organizations such as the National Association of Manufacturers sought to amend the Wagner Act. The Wagner Act was not amended, however, until the record wave of strike activity that followed World War II, in which President Truman personally intervened to settle disputes in the coal mining, railroad, and steel industries.

The National Labor Relations Act of 1947, also called the **Taft-Hartley Act**, became law over the objections of the **National Labor Relations Board (NLRB)** and Truman's veto. Important amendments were made to Section 8, that clarified what were considered unfair labor practices by unions and employees; the Wagner Act had covered only unfair practices by employers.

Another key amendment was the addition of Section 14(b), which legalized what came to be called right-to-work laws. These laws, enacted at the state level, prohibited what's known as a union shop, in which *all* workers in a unionized factory are forced to join the union and pay dues. Right-to-work laws make union organizing much more difficult and continue to be opposed by organized labor into the 1990s. As of the late 1980s, 21 states in the United States had right-to-work laws, most of them in the Southeast and Southwest.

Attempts to overturn Taft-Hartley began just after its passage and intensified with the merger of the American Federation of Labor and the Congress of Industrial Organizations in 1955, forming the AFL-CIO. These efforts were greatly weakened by investigations into union corruption by the McClellan Committee of the Senate from 1957 to 1959 that culminated in the Labor Management Reporting and Disclosure Act of 1959, also known as the Landrum-Griffin Act. Landrum-Griffin outlined a Bill of Rights for union members. It did not, however, greatly weaken those elements of Taft-Hartley that opposed unions and was devoted in large part to regulating the internal affairs of unions in response to the McClellan Committee's findings of widespread union corruption.

Union membership expanded steadily in the post-World War II years until the recession of the late 1950s, when it declined from just over 17.5 million to 16.5 million members by the early 1960s. The period from the mid 1960s to the late 1970s saw a steady and substantial growth in the number of union members, peaking at about 24 million workers in 1977. From 1978 through the 1990s, however, union membership plummeted, reaching lower levels than in worst years of the early 1960s. Looking at union membership as a percentage of the private sector labor force yields a somewhat less dramatic picture, since this ratio declined in almost all years after 1955, though at an accelerated rate after the mid-1970s. Entering the 1990s, less than 20 percent of the private sector labor force was unionized.

The decline in union membership was associated with a number of other factors that led to a substantial transformation of labor-management relations in the United States. Among these factors were intensified global competition, substantially slower average growth rates for the economy as a whole, declining real wages, the deregulation of key industries, the shift in employment from the industrial to the service sector and from the union strongholds of the Midwest and Northeast to the Sunbelt states, greatly increased anti-union efforts on the part of employers, and reduced resources devoted to organizing on the part of unions.

In the face of their reduced power, unions were compelled to make substantial bargaining concessions beginning in the early 1980s. These included wage and benefit givebacks, the acceptance of two- and three-tiered wage systems, and greater demands by employers for flexibility and cooperation.

Numerous ideas regarding labor-management cooperation came into vogue among managers during the 1980s and continued into the 1990s. Modelled on Japanese labor-management relations and systems of production, these practices were referred to variously as joint programs, team concept, lean production, employee involvement, and labor-management participation, among others. These programs typically advocated non adversarial relations between management and labor, the establishment of work groups or quality control circles, and soliciting workers' input regarding the efficiency of the production process. Many advocated greater flexibility in the production process and workers' schedules.

These programs received mixed responses from organized labor. The Saturn automobile plant in Spring Hill, Tennessee was organized on the principles of flexibility and cooperation, and initially labor-management relations were positive. More recently, 29 percent of the plant's unionized labor force voted for change, believing that union leaders were becoming too closely allied with management. Relations were also strained by 50-hour work weeks with irregular schedules.

General Motors Corp. and Toyota entered into a joint venture in the mid-1980s, resulting in the opening of the New United Motor Manufacturing (NUMMI) plant in Fremont, California. The plant was hailed as a model of lean production and the team concept. Workers voted in 1994 to replace George Nano, head of the bargaining unit since the plant opened, with Richard Aguilar, who advocated a more independent union stance. In August of 1994, NUMMI's workers went on strike, in large part over the company's demands for a so-called alternative work schedule. This would have required three shifts working consecutive ten-hour days, with one shift working through the weekend. No premiums were to be paid for the additional two hours per day or for weekend work. Though it took only two hours for management to back down, this was the first strike in the plant's existence and marked a turning point in labor-management cooperation within the plant.

The rise of **employee stock ownership plans (ESOP)** marked another change in labor-management relations in recent years. One of the largest ESOPs went into effect at United Airlines in 1994. The plan gave United employees ownership of 55 percent of outstanding shares in exchange for wage cuts averaging 14 percent. In addition, the two unions involved were each to get a representative on the 12-member board of directors.

Robert Reich, the Clinton administration's Secretary of Labor, created a Commission on the Future of Worker-Management Relations in mid-1993. This was commonly referred to as the Dunlop Commission after its chairman, John Dunlop, Secretary of Labor under President Ford. The Dunlop Commission studied a broad range of labor-management issues for the purpose of making policy recommendations, in particular with amending federal labor legislation.

The commission's fact-finding report from mid-1994 stated that "stagnation of real earnings and increased inequality of earnings is bifurcating the U.S. labor market, with an upper tier of high-wage skilled workers and an increasing 'underclass' of low-paid labor." The report noted the shift from high-paying production work to low-paying service work, the large number of full-time workers whose income did not provide an adequate standard of living, and the fact that workers in the United States put in longer work weeks than any other advanced industrialized country, except Japan. The report also noted that an increasing number of workers were illegally fired for union organizing activities.

The Dunlop Commission was generally supportive of labor-management cooperation programs but noted that many firms were reluctant to implement them because of Wagner Act restrictions on company unions. In 1993, the AFL-CIO expressed to the Dunlop Commission its willingness to accept weakening of restrictions on company unions in exchange for reforms that would make union organizing easier. In hearings held in August of 1994, the AFL-CIO backed off on this offer.

In June of 1993, the National Labor Relation Board ruled that employee involvement programs at E.I. du Pont de Nemours & Co. violated federal labor laws. A number of employers and business associations argued that the ruling would jeopardize labor-management cooperation programs.

[David Kucera]

FURTHER READING:

Barbash, Jack. *The Elements of Industrial Relations*. University of Wisconsin Press, 1984.

Berberoglu, Berch (ed.). *The Labor Process and Control of Labor: The Changing Nature of Work Relations in the Late Twentieth Century*. Praeger, 1993.

''The Dark Side of Flexible Production,'' *Technology Review*, May 1994.

Kilborn, Peter T. ''Ready to Put Theories into Action, Secretary Finds Ideas Are Not Allies,'' *New York Times*, July 5, 1993.

Kochan, Thomas (ed.). *Challenges and Choices Facing American Labor*. MIT Press, 1985.

Lesnik, Rich and Malik Miah. ''United's Workers Trade Wages for 'Employee Ownership,' '' *Labor Notes*, September 1994.

Lipset, Seymour Martin (ed.). *Unions in Transition: Entering the Second Century*. Institute for Contemporary Studies, 1986.

Lund, Caroline. ''Union Beats 10-Hour Day at NUMMI,'' *Labor Notes*, September 1994.

Noble, Barbara P. ''At Work; Labor-Management Rorschach Test,'' *New York Times*, June 5, 1994.

Noble, Barbara P. ''Worker-Participation Programs Are Found Illegal,'' *New York Times*, June 8, 1993.

Parker, Mike. ''Election of Dissident Reveals Discontent at Model 'Team Concept' Plant,'' *Labor Notes*, July 1994.

Sandver, Marcus Hart. *Labor Relations: Process and Outcomes*. Little, Brown and Company, 1987.

''Saturn: Labor's Love Lost?,'' *Business Week: Industrial Edition*, February 8, 1993.

''Soothing Report on Labor Relations,'' *New York Times*, June 7, 1994.

LABOR UNIONS

A labor union is an organization of wage earners or salary workers established for the purpose of protecting their collective interests when dealing with employers. Though unions are prevalent in most industrialized countries, union representation of workers has generally declined in most countries over the past 30 to 40 years. For example, in the United States, unions represented about one-third of all workers in the 1950s. Today, unions only represent about 16 percent of the labor force. There have also been significant declines in many of the Western European countries and in Japan. Although weakened in many areas, labor unions continue to be an important force in most of these economies.

TYPES OF UNIONS

Unions can be categorized according to ideology and organizational forms. *Ideology* refers to the union's goals and objectives: what its members see as its mission. A distinction is often made between *political unionism* and *bread and butter unionism* (also termed *business unionism*). Although the goals and objectives of politically oriented unions may overlap those of business unions, political unions are primarily related to some larger working-class movement. Most political unions have some formal association with a working-class political party, usually socialist or Marxist.

Political unions range from those dedicated to revolutionary activity (rarely found today) to those seeking change through the electoral process (as in the case of labor unions associated with labor and social democratic parties in Western Europe). In most instances, politically oriented unions see fundamental conflicts between the interests of workers and the capitalist system. The more radical political unions may advocate nationalization of key industries and substantial limitations on free enterprise. In contrast, the mainstream political unions common in Western Europe advocate greater worker voice in business **decision making**. One example policies is the German *codetermination* system. This system requires, by law, the appointment of worker representatives to a company' **board of directors**. Companies in Germany must also establish *works councils*, which are shop-floor level worker committees that provide input into organizational **problem-solving** and decision-making.

In contrast to Western Europe and a number of developing countries, contemporary American labor unions are best viewed as business unions. Business unions generally support the capitalist economic system and focus their attention on protecting and enhancing the economic welfare of the workers they represent, usually through some form of collective bargaining. By law in the United States, unionized employers need only bargain with unions over wages, hours, and working conditions.

This does not mean that business unions are not involved in the political process. Most large national unions, as well as the American Federation of Labor-Congress of Industrial Organizations (AFL-CIO) which is an association of national unions, are involved in lobbying and electoral activities at all levels of government. However, such political efforts serve to supplement their principal economic goals. Political objectives are usually reformist in nature. For example, the many unions campaigned against passage of the **North American Free Trade Agreement** (NAFTA). The labor movement feared that NAFTA would undercut jobs of union workers and weaken the ability of unions to negotiate favorable **contracts** with employers. Although many American unions are active in the Democratic party, they are not formally affiliated with that party. In fact, some unions regularly support Republican candidates, including presidential candidates. Consequently, the political complexion of American labor unions is varied and driven primarily by economic concerns.

There are several different *organizational forms* characteristic of labor unions. The earliest unions in the United States were *craft unions*. Craft unions represent employees in a single occupation or group of closely related occupations. The members of craft unions are generally highly skilled workers. Examples of craft unions include the various skilled trades in the construction industry. Separate unions exist for each major skill (e.g., carpenters, electricians, plumbers). Craft unions are most common in occupations in which employees frequently switch employers. A construction worker is usually hired to complete work at a specific job site and then moves on to work elsewhere (often for another employer). In addition to collective bargaining, craft unions often serve as a placement service for members. Employers contact the union's hiring hall and union members currently out of work are referred to the job.

Closely related to craft unions, though distinct in many respects, are *professional unions*. A professional is generally understood to be an employee with advanced and highly specialized skills, often requiring some credential, such as a college degree and/or a license. Professional unions are much more recent than craft unions and are most common in the public sector. The American Federation of Teachers (AFT) is one of the oldest professional unions. Many professional unions began as professional associations, then became more union-like in character (e.g., the National Education Association).

Most unionized workers in the United States belong to *industrial unions*. An industrial union represents workers across a wide range of occupations within one or more industries. A good example of a typical industrial union is the United Auto Workers (UAW). It represents skilled craft workers, assembly-line workers, and unskilled workers in all of the major American automobile companies. The UAW negotiates separate contracts for workers in each of these companies. Although most industrial unions began by organizing workers in a single industry or group of related industries, most have diversified over the past 30 to 40 years. For example, the UAW represents workers in the tractor and earth-moving equipment industry (e.g., Caterpillar and John Deere) and in the aerospace industry (e.g., Boeing Corporation).

Another organizational form is the *general union*. General unions organize workers across all occupations and industries. Although some highly diversified unions, such as the Teamsters, appear to be general unions, this form of organization does not really exist in the United States. Because they are typically politically oriented, general unions are more common in Europe and developing countries. There were some general unions in the United States in earlier times (such as the Knights of Labor in the late 1800s), but none of these continue to exist.

UNION GROWTH AND DECLINE

Union membership in the United States has varied considerably throughout the country's history. Although American unions have, at times, exerted considerable economic and political power, the level of unionization has generally been considerably lower than in many other advanced industrialized countries (e.g., Britain, Germany, Japan, and Scandinavia). Although there have been unions in the United States for nearly 200 years, prior to the 1930s unions represented, at most, ten to 12 percent of the labor force. Union membership prior to the Depression era rose and fell often, generally corresponding to fluctuations in the business cycle.

The period from about 1935 to the mid-1950s was one of sustained economic growth. The unionization rate went from about 12 percent of the labor force in 1935 to between 32 percent and 35 percent in the mid-1950s. A number of factors were responsible for this unprecedented growth. By the 1930s, the American economy had shifted from an agricultural to an industrial base. Industrial workers were concentrated in urban areas and most were native born and English-speaking. Consequently, there was a common culture among workers absent in earlier generations. The Depression created a backlash against big business, which was largely viewed as the cause of the country's economic difficulties. Another very important factor was the election of Roosevelt in 1932. Active support for organized labor was an integral part of Roosevelt's New Deal. The most important change was the passage of the National Labor Relations Act of 1935 (NLRA) (see below). The NLRA provided a means for official recognition of labor unions. Once recognized, an employer was legally bound to bargain with the union, enforceable by government action. Economic growth during World War II and in the post-war era also facilitated union growth.

By the mid-1950s, the most union-prone sectors of the American economy had largely been organized. Unions maintained their strength at around one-third of the labor force until about 1960. Union membership declined gradually, decreasing to about 25 percent of the labor force in the mid-1970s. The rate of decline was much sharper in the 1980s; unions today represent only about 16 percent of the labor force, although this number has been somewhat stable in recent years. (Mills 1994, 72).

Why has union membership and its corresponding economic and political power declined so much in recent years? There have undoubtedly been many factors. The changing nature of the global economy has been a leading cause. Over the past 20 to 30 years, American companies were increasingly exposed to foreign **competition**. This especially affected many sectors of the economy that were heavily unionized (e.g., automobiles, steel, and textiles). As these industries became more competitive globally, employer resistance to unions often increased. In addition, it became feasible for employers to relocate production facilities to areas of the country which have traditionally been less supportive of unionism (such as the southern and Mountain states) or overseas to less developed countries that have low wages and few unions.

Another important factor has been the shifting nature of the labor force. In the 1930s, "blue collar" workers represented a large proportion of the labor force. Now "white collar" workers (i.e., managers, professionals, and clericals) are a very large component of the labor force. In general, white collar workers have been difficult to organize (except in the public sector). There are also more service employees working in industries that are highly competitive (e.g., fast foods) and thus less easily organized (since employers that recognize unions and make concessions to them are apt to be driven out of business because of higher costs).

The role of the government in relation to unions has changed considerably since the New Deal era. As early as 1947, amendments were added to the NLRA that significantly expanded employer rights and limited the rights of unions. This law, called the **Taft-Hartley Act**, is considered by many scholars to weaken the position of organized labor. Individuals appointed to the National Labor Relations Board (NLRB) (which enforces the NLRA) by the Nixon, Reagan, and Bush administrations often took positions unfavorable to labor unions in Board rulings. This, coupled with a substantial increase in **management** opposition to unions in the 1980s, made it increasingly difficult for unions to organize new members. In addition, many unionized employers, confronting increasing competitive pressures, began to take especially hard bargaining positions in dealing

with unions. Such an approach was not seen as a violation of NLRA standards by the new generation of National Labor Relations Board (NLRB) appointees. Consequently, unions often lost ground in established areas. A number of **consulting** firms specializing in union avoidance activities became highly visible in the late 1970s and throughout the 1980s. Termed ''union busters'' by a scornful labor movement, there is considerable evidence that these **consultants** have played a substantial role in the decline of the contemporary labor movement.

Unions have traditionally been strong in four sectors of the American economy: **manufacturing**, mining, construction, and transportation. They have lost substantial ground in all four of these sectors in the last 20 years. In the transportation sector, an important factor has been deregulation, particularly in the trucking and airline industries. Substantial increases in competition in those industries have made it difficult for unions to negotiate favorable contracts or organize new units. In construction, the growth of nonunion contractors, able to hire qualified workers outside of the union hiring hall system, undercut union contractors. At one time, more than 80 percent of all commercial construction in the United States had been unionized; today, that figure is no more than 25 percent of commercial construction. Foreign competition and technological change have weakened mining unions. In manufacturing, the whole range of factors previously discussed has been responsible for union decline.

The only sector of the economy where unions have gained strength in recent years has been public **employment**. Financial stringency in the public sector has severely impacted public employees. Although public sector unions engage in collective bargaining with employers, they play an even more important role in lobbying legislative bodies regarding the financing of government agencies. Consequently, the relative success of public sector unions is most likely attributable to their role as a lobbying force rather than because of success at the bargaining table. Currently, more than one-third of public employees at all levels of government—local, state, and federal—are unionized.

INTERNAL STRUCTURE AND ADMINISTRATION

Labor unions are complex and vary considerably with respect to internal structure and administrative processes. It is easiest to differentiate among three distinct levels within the labor movement: local unions, national and international unions, and federations.

LOCAL UNIONS. Local unions are the building blocks of the labor movement and represent the interface between the union and its rank-and-file members (Sayles and Strauss 1967). Although there are some free-standing local unions, the vast majority of locals are in some way affiliated with a national or international union. Most craft unions began as local unions, which then joined together to form national (or international) organizations. Some major industrial unions also began as amalgamations of local unions, though it was generally more common for national organizations to be formed first, with locals to be established later. At present, there are around 71,000 local unions in the United States (Mills 1994, 89).

The duties of a local union almost always include the administration of a union contract, which means assuring that the employer is honoring all of the provisions of the contract at the local level. In some instances, local unions might also negotiate contracts, although unions vary considerably in terms of the degree to which the parent national or international union is involved in the negotiation process.

Another important function of the local union is servicing the needs of those represented by the union. If a worker represented by the union believes his or her rights under the union contract have been violated, then the union may intervene on that person's behalf. Examples of such situations include the discharge of an employee, failure to promote an employee according to a contract seniority clause, or failure to pay an employee for overtime. Virtually any provision of a contract can become a source of contention. The local union may try to settle the issue informally. If that effort is not successful, the union may file what is known as a *grievance*. This is a formal statement of the dispute with the employer and most contracts set forth a grievance procedure. In general, grievance procedures involve several different steps, with higher levels of management entering at each step. If the grievance cannot be settled through this mechanism, then the union may, if the contract allows, request a hearing before a neutral arbitrator, whose decision is final and binding.

Most craft unions have **apprenticeship programs** to train new workers in the craft. The local union, usually in cooperation with an employers' association, will be responsible for managing the apprenticeship program. In addition, local unions with hiring halls are responsible for making job referrals.

The jurisdiction of a local union depends to a large extent on the organizational form of the parent organization. Locals of industrial unions most often represent workers within a single plant or facility of a company (and thus are termed *plant locals*). For example, in the case of the UAW, each factory or production facility of each automobile manufacturer has a separate local union. In some instances, a factory

may be so big that it requires more than a single local, but this is not usually the case.

In contrast to plant locals, local craft unions (as well as some industrial unions) are best described as *area locals*. An area local represents all of a union's members in a particular geographical region and may deal with many different employers. Area locals are typically formed for one of two reasons. First, members may in the course of a year work for a number of different employers, as in the case of craft unions. Consequently, it would be difficult, if not impossible, to establish and maintain a separate local in each work location. Second, members may work continuously for a single employer, but each employer or location may be too small to justify a separate local union. The latter case is more typical of some industrial unions. An example is the United Food and Commercial Workers (UFCW), which represents, among others, clerks in retail outlets. Although an industrial union, the UFCW may only have a few members in each store, so a single local is established to serve an entire region. The size of the region served by a local union depends on the number of members available. In large metropolitan areas, an area local might serve only members in a particular city. In less densely populated regions, an area local may have a jurisdiction that covers an entire state (in a few cases, more than one state).

Internal structures and administrative procedures differ between plant and area locals. In almost all local unions, the membership meeting represents the apex of power, as the officers of the union are accountable to the members much as the officers of a corporation are accountable to stockholders. However, in practice, membership participation in union affairs is usually quite limited, so local union officers often enjoy considerable power.

Plant locals have a number of elected officials, usually a president, vice president, secretary, and treasurer. In almost all cases, the officers are full-time employees of the company the union represents, and the contract generally allows some release time for union affairs. In addition to the principal officers of the local, there are also a number of *stewards*. Stewards may be elected or appointed, depending upon the union. The steward serves as the everyday contact between the union and its rank-and-file members. If members have concerns about the affairs of the union, these may be voiced to the steward. The steward's most important responsibility is handling grievances. Should a worker represented by the union have a dispute with the employer over his or her rights under the contract, the steward has the initial responsibility of representing the worker. Usually the steward will discuss the matter with the employee's supervisor to see if the dispute can be resolved. If not, then a formal grievance may be filed and it then proceeds through the grievance system. At higher levels in the grievance system the employee may be represented by a chief steward or union officers.

Area locals typically have more complex internal structures than plant locals. This is usually because of the large geographical region under the local's jurisdiction, along with the greater dispersion of members within the region. As in the case of plant locals, area locals hold periodic meetings in which the officials of the union are accountable to members. There are also elected officers in area locals, as well as stewards for the various work sites in the local's jurisdiction. The principal difference between a plant local and an area local is that the latter typically employs one or more full-time staff members to handle the affairs of the union on a daily basis. These staff members are usually called *business agents*. Given the dispersion of members over a large geographical area and the possibility that the local may be responsible for administering many different contracts, it is the business agent's responsibility to visit work sites regularly and deal with problems that may arise. The business agent may also be responsible for managing any apprenticeship programs and the union's hiring hall. Contracts are often negotiated directly by local unions and the business agents are usually responsible for these negotiations. In some unions, elected officers may serve as business agents, but normally business agents are separate staff members. Depending on the size of the local union, there may be a number of assistant business agents.

NATIONAL AND INTERNATIONAL UNIONS. There are approximately 190 national unions in the United States, along with about 30 professional associations that carry on union activities (Mills, 1994, 73). National unions are composed of the various local unions that they have chartered. Some unions have locals in Canada and therefore call themselves *international* unions. However, the terms *international union* and *national union* are generally used interchangeably.

As with local unions, the administrative structures of national unions vary considerably in complexity. One important factor is the size of the union: larger unions are structurally more complex. Structural complexity also differs between craft and industrial unions. Not only do craft unions tend to be smaller, but decision-making tends to be decentralized. Contracts usually have a limited geographical scope and are negotiated by local unions. The national pools the resources of local unions, thus helping out with things such as strike funds. The national union may also provide research services and be involved politically at the national and state levels. In general, there are few intermediate units between the national office and the local craft unions. National officers, elected periodically, generally work on a full-time basis for the union. Such unions also hold national conventions, most often every couple of years. The officers of the national union are accountable to the convention, much as the officers of a local are accountable to membership meetings.

National industrial unions are typically more complex. They tend to be larger and have a more heterogeneous membership than craft unions (both in terms of skills and demographic traits). Although there are exceptions, contracts in industrial unions tend to be negotiated primarily by staff members from the national office. In many cases, the bargaining unit will include all locals from a particular company (across the entire country). Even if contracts are negotiated by locals, representatives from the national union will often participate in talks to assure that the contract conforms to patterns established by the national organization.

As with craft unions, national unions have periodic conventions and national officers. Depending upon the union, the national officers may be elected directly by rank-and-file members or by some other body (such as convention delegates). National unions generally have a substantial paid staff who provide a variety of different services (e.g., research, legal representation, organizing new members, negotiating contracts, and servicing locals). National unions may also have one or more layers of hierarchy between the local unions and the national offices. For example, in the case of the UAW, there are different divisions responsible for the major industries in which that union represents workers (see above). Within the automobile industry, there are divisions that correspond to each of the major producers. There are other divisions that deal with the needs of special groups within the union (such as minority workers and skilled craft workers). Consequently, the structures of large industrial unions are often as complex as the companies with which they deal.

FEDERATIONS. A federation is an association of unions. It is not a union in the usual sense of the term. Rather, it provides a range of services to affiliated unions, much as an organization such as the National Association of Manufacturers provides services to its member firms. The AFL-CIO is currently the only national federation in the United States. The AFL-CIO formed in the mid-1950s as the result of the merger of what were then two competing federations: the American Federation of Labor (AFL) and the Congress of Industrial Organizations (CIO). The AFL was established in the 1880s and consisted almost exclusively of craft unions. Craft unionists feared that industrial unions might undercut their position, thus they generally opposed formation of industrial unions. The most famous of the AFL's early leaders was Samuel Gompers (1850-1924), who is generally viewed as the "father" of the American labor movement.

Pressures during the Great Depression seemed to favor industrial unionism, so several unions within the AFL broke away to form the rival CIO. Most influential in formation of this federation was John L. Lewis (1880-1969), long-time president of the United Mine Workers (UMW). Initially, the competition between the two federations, which chartered competing unions, probably helped the labor movement to grow in the United States. However, as it became apparent that further competition was only self-defeating, the merger was ultimately negotiated.

There are about 90 national unions, with over 50,000 locals, affiliated with the AFL-CIO; these unions represent about 14 million workers, or about 83 percent of all unionized workers in the United States (Mills 1994, 73). In addition, there are about 60 independent local unions that are also directly affiliated with the federation. A guiding principle of the AFL-CIO is *national union autonomy*. That is, the federation does not control the affiliates nor dictate their internal policies (though it often tries to influence affiliates).

The federation serves a range of functions. It acts as a lobbying body in the political arena and uses its financial resources in election campaigns. It works to resolve conflicts between affiliated unions, such as disputes between construction craft unions over jurisdiction of different areas of work and disputes between affiliated unions that may be competing in efforts to organize new members. It provides research services to affiliated unions and also helps unions organize new members. The diversity of AFL-CIO standing committees reflects the range of federation functions. These include the Legislative Committee, the Organization and Field Services Committee, the Civil Rights Committee, and the Community Services Committee.

The structure of the AFL-CIO is quite complex and also reflects the federation's multiple functions. The federation holds a convention every two years. Each affiliated union sends delegates to the convention. The day-to-day business of the federation is handled by its principal officers (president and secretary-treasurer), who confer regularly with an executive council consisting of more than 30 vice presidents, virtually all of whom are drawn from the ranks of the affiliated unions. In addition to the standing committees, the federation has several staff units. There are also several different departments within the federation that serve the specialized needs of different affiliates. An affiliate can choose to associate with those departments relevant to its particular needs, such as the Building Trades Department, the Industrial Union Department, the Metal Trades Department, and the Public Employees Department.

The national AFL-CIO offices are in Washington. However, there are state-level bodies of the AFL-CIO in all 50 states. These bodies duplicate the federation's national activities at the state level (e.g., lobbying state legislatures and supporting pro-labor candidates in state elections). There are also AFL-CIO central bodies in more than 700 communities (Wallihan 1985, 158). Local unions are affiliated with the city centrals and these organizations provide services at the community level.

The influence of the AFL-CIO has varied over time. George Meany (1894-1980), the first president of the federation, exerted considerable power and influence within the labor movement. However, many feel that Meany worked to maintain an old guard within the labor movement that prevented organized labor from fully appreciating the implications of the many political, economic, and social changes that have taken place over the past 30 years. Lane Kirkland, the current president of the federation, has worked hard, along with many staff members, to introduce innovative policies and programs. However, the federation's influence has declined substantially, within both the labor movement and society at large, since Meany's time. Consequently, these policies have had only limited impact.

[John Lawler]

FURTHER READING:

Elkouri, F., and E. Elkouri. *How Arbitration Works*. Washington, D.C.: Bureau of National Affairs, 1985.

Freeman, R., and J. Medoff. *What Do Unions Do?* New York: Basic Books, 1984.

Kochan, T.A., H.C. Katz, and R.B. McKersie. *The Transformation of American Industrial Relations*. New York: Basic Books, 1986.

Lawler, J.J. *Unionization and Deunionization: Strategy, Tactics, and Outcomes*. Columbia, SC: University of South Carolina Press, 1990.

Lipsky, D.B., and C.B. Donn. *Collective Bargaining in American Industry*. Lexington, MA: Lexington Books, 1987.

Mills, Daniel Quinn. *Labor-Management Relations*. 5th ed., New York: McGraw-Hill, 1994.

Sayles, Leonard, and George Strauss. *The Local Union*. New York: Harcourt, Brace, and World, 1967.

Taylor, B.J., and F. Witney. *Labor Relations Law*. Englewood-Cliffs, NJ: Prentice-Hall, 1987.

Wallihan, J. *Union Government and Organization*. Washington, D.C.: Bureau of National Affairs, 1985.

LAISSEZ-FAIRE

The centuries-old doctrine known as laissez-faire is defined by *The New Encyclopaedia Britannica* as a "policy based on a minimum of governmental interference in the economic affairs of individuals and society." To this meaning *Merriam Webster's Collegiate Dictionary* adds the broader sense of "a philosophy or practice characterized by a usually deliberate abstention from direction or interference, especially with individual freedom of choice and action." Phrases like "rugged individualism," "**free trade**," "market economics," "free enterprise," and "free competition" reflect a posture of laissez-faire, as does Thomas Jefferson's observation that "the least governed are the best governed."

While sources translate the term *laissez-faire* variously—as "allow to do," "leave it alone," "let things alone," and "let go and let pass," among other things—most agree that the expression originated with a 17th century French merchant, François Legendre, who was protesting his government's overregulation of commerce and industry. Subsequently, a group of late 18th century French economists known as the Physiocrats developed and popularized laissez-faire as a principle.

In essence, the Physiocrats believed that the laws of nature, and not of governments, would foster economic and social prosperity. Their efforts and formulations represented a reaction against the widespread practice of mercantilism, a system in which the state exerts significant controls over industry and commerce, particularly foreign trade. Pervading much of Western Europe from the 17th to the 19th centuries, mercantilism manifested itself in the form of a host of navigation laws, tariffs, and other measures constraining merchants' activities.

The concept of laissez-faire was further boosted in the 18th century when the Scottish economist Adam Smith (1723-1790), often called the "father of modern economics," published *The Wealth of Nations* in 1776. In this pathbreaking volume Smith advocated a free enterprise system that was grounded in private ownership, driven by individual initiative, and unencumbered by governmental bureaucracy. In the same work, Smith argued that the "invisible hand" of naturally arising competition would monitor and regulate individual enterprise far more effectively than governmental restrictions would; he, like the Physiocrats, believed in a natural harmony that, if allowed to operate free of institutional restraints, would lead to a beneficent economy and promote the welfare of individuals and communities alike.

As a formal and widely accepted economic and political doctrine, laissez-faire came into full flower during the 19th century, especially in the United Kingdom, where it served to embody the ideas propounded by the English classical school of economists. In his 1828 work *Principles of Political Economy,* the British economist and political philosopher John Stuart Mill (1806-1873) argued vigorously for a society ruled by natural law. Espousing the individual's right to be free of governmental interference in economic pursuits, Mill asserted that "laissez faire . . . should be the general practice: every departure from it, unless required by some great good, is a certain evil."

During the 20th century, especially in the wake of the Industrial Revolution, laissez-faire lost much of its force, giving way to policies and philosophies favoring collective action, as evidenced by the growth of trade associations and trade unions. With the rise of big business, state controls were increasingly seen as a way of breaking up monopolies, advancing international trade, and promoting "the good of all." Resulting from these developments was a multitude of antitrust and other legislation, as well as numerous government policies and regulations addressing such issues as worker safety, the environment, and employment discrimination. While President Ronald Reagan and others initiated a variety of deregulatory actions in the latter part of the 20th century, laissez-faire became just one of several doctrines influencing western economic thought.

In practical terms, it should be noted that although laissez-faire endorses a "hands-off" economic and political posture on the part of government, few economists past or present have embraced the doctrine in a literal sense. Rather, most have supported some form of governmental involvement to promote and safeguard the nation's welfare. Adam Smith, for example, conceded the importance of government's role in protecting certain home industries against encroachment by foreign competitors and in maintaining a system of national defense. Similarly, many of the British classical economists favored government's involvement in such areas as child labor legislation. Other economists have endorsed a primary role for government in spheres ranging from sanitation to education, from public utilities to national transportation networks. Indeed, toward the close of the 20th century, the extent to which government should regulate business activity remained a topic of considerable debate among contemporary economists.

SEE ALSO: Antitrust Acts and Laws

[Roberta H. Winston]

FURTHER READING:

Mill, John Stuart. *Principles of Political Economy.* Viking Penguin.

Smith, Adam. *The Wealth of Nations.* Alfred A. Knopf.

LATIN AMERICAN INTEGRATION ASSOCIATION

The Latin American Integration Association (LAIA) was established August 12, 1980 in Montevideo, Uruguay, when the Montevideo Treaty of 1980 was signed by representatives of 11 Latin American countries. The signatories to the treaty were Argentina, Bolivia, Brazil, Chile, Colombia, Ecuador, Mexico, Paraguay, Peru, Uruguay, and Venezuela. By March 1982 all 11 countries had ratified the treaty. The purpose of LAIA is to increase trade between member countries by reducing barriers to trade. Under the terms of the 1980 treaty LAIA also succeeded the Latin American Free Trade Association (LAFTA) which was established by the Montevideo Treaty of 1960.

LAFTA was formed following discussions that took place throughout 1958 under the direction of the United Nations Economic Commission for Latin America. The original signatories to the 1960 treaty were Argentina, Brazil, Chile, Mexico, Paraguay, Peru, and Uruguay. Membership increased throughout the 1960s with Colombia and Ecuador joining in 1961, Venezuela in 1966, and Bolivia in 1967. Originally LAFTA did not seek a common external tariff. Nor did it immediately seek to form an economic union, although a Latin American Common Market was a long-term goal. Rather the association called for the dismantling of tariffs and other trade barriers between member states. In 1969, however, at a meeting in Caracas, Venezuela, rancor developed over proposals to begin working towards a common market. Although consideration of this subject was postponed until 1980, Colombia and Uruguay continued to disagree with the precepts of the 1969 meeting. Because of internal dissension, by the 1970s LAFTA was little more than a trade and marketing association and by 1980 only 14 percent of trade between LAFTA members was due to the agreement.

In June 1980 representatives of LAFTA meeting in Acapulco, Mexico, and later in Montevideo, voted to dissolve LAFTA and replace it with the Latin American Integration Association (LAIA). It was decided that the new association would have more loosely defined goals, less strictures, and no timetable for goal implementation. Like LAFTA the aim of LAIA is to reduce or remove trade barriers, but unlike LAFTA there are no deadlines and members are free to enter into separate trade and tariff agreements. While LAIA does not call for all-inclusive tariff cuts, there are preferential tariffs for regional products and regional agreements on matters related to agricultural products, technology exchange, and environmental and tourism affairs. LAIA also recognizes an economic hierarchy and trade and tariff agreements take into account the level of economic development of each country. Argentina, Brazil, and Mexico are at the top of the hierarchy; Bolivia, Ecuador, and Paraguay are considered to be the least developed; and Chile, Colombia, Peru, Uruguay, and Venezuela fall in the category of intermediate development.

In 1984 LAIA members ratified the Regional Tariff Preference (RTP) program which was expanded by protocols in 1987 and 1990. The RTP program is a system of tariff cuts based on the level of development of participating countries. During this period LAIA also approved various financial and monetary cooperative programs, as well as assistance programs for less-developed member countries, and ended various nontariff trade barriers. Also in 1984 an important LAIA proposal was the Regional Trade System. This program was aimed at enhancing intraregional trade and controlling bilateral trade agreements. In 1986 LAIA issued the ''Buenos Aires Letter'' and in 1987 the association expanded the RTP program. Both of these plans were aimed at furthering trade between members and lessening trade sanctions and trade barriers. In 1988 LAIA expanded its areas of activity and responsibility to include construction, transportation, information services, tourism, and insurance. By the early 1990s LAIA members had signed 104 bilateral commercial agreements, and 20 agreements with non-LAIA countries, and substantially increased trade between member states.

The principal governing organ of LAIA is the Council of Ministers of Foreign Affairs. This body is composed of the foreign ministers of member countries and meets annually to review activities and set policy. Implementation of policy is the responsibility of the Committee of Representatives.

The Evaluation and Convergence Conference reviews LAIA activities and promotes new programs. Various other administrative units include: the Advisory Commission on Financial and Monetary Affairs, Advisory Council for Export Financing, Advisory Entrepreneurial Council, Advisory Nomenclature Commission, Council for Financial and Monetary Affairs, and the Council on Transport for Trade Facilitation.

[Michael Knes]

LAYOFFS

Layoffs refer to either temporary or permanent **employment** adjustments. Prior to the 1980s, layoffs were typically associated with business cycle downswings, with laid-off workers recalled as business conditions improved. Beginning in the 1980s, a greater proportion of layoffs resulted from plant and office closures and were, therefore, permanent. Many of these layoffs were associated with so-called re-engineering, restructuring, and downsizing—efforts to make U.S. firms more profitable in the face of intensified global competition. As the U.S. economy improved in the early 1990s, large-scale layoffs continued even at highly profitable firms, indicating a break with historical patterns. Layoffs resulting from re-engineering and restructuring were also unique in that a large proportion of managerial positions were affected.

Unlike other advanced capitalist countries, firms in the United States faced with demand variations generally relied on changes in employment rather than changes in working hours. From 1970 to 1983, for example, variations in employment due to fluctuations in production were substantially greater in the United States than in Japan or West Germany. Changes in employment in the United States mostly resulted from temporary layoffs during downswings and recalls of laid-off workers during upswings. The greater reliance on overtime work in Japan and West Germany, rather than layoffs and recalls, may have been due to the fact that overtime is paid only a 25 percent premium in these two countries, compared with 50 percent in the United States.

The U.S. Bureau of National Affairs conducted a survey in 1985 to determine the nature of layoff provisions in labor agreements. Of the agreements studied, 91 percent had some type of layoff provision. In 89 percent of these cases, seniority played a role in determining who would be laid off, and in 49 percent of those cases, seniority played the only role. In addition, 60 percent of labor agreements with layoff provisions allowed a senior employee to bump a junior employee in a different department or job classification should the senior employee's job be subject to layoff.

Senior employees were favored not only in layoffs but in recalls, as the laid-off employees with the greatest seniority were generally called back to work first. In most labor agreements, all laid-off workers had to be recalled before any new employees were hired. Violations of such layoff provisions often resulted in union grievance procedures. Seniority also played an important role in the layoff criteria of non-union firms. A 1982 survey revealed that 42 percent of non-unionized firms followed strict seniority rules in determining layoffs.

Most labor unions favored the use of seniority as the only criteria in determining who would be laid off. In addition, many unions favored ''superseniority,'' in which union officers and stewards were granted highest seniority. Superseniority was favored on the grounds that union officers and stewards must be working in order to protect the rights of fellow workers. In contrast, firms generally preferred to first lay off workers they regarded as least productive. Firms were also generally opposed to bumping, as this often resulted in less-experienced workers taking over an operation.

In their volume *What Do Unions Do?*, Freeman and Medoff addressed the issue of why unionized workers were more affected by temporary layoffs than were non-unionized workers. They wrote as follows:

> ''Why do unionized workers and firms [in the United States] choose temporary layoffs rather than reductions in wages or hours? Perhaps the most important reason is that temporary layoffs mean laying off junior workers, not the senior employees who have a greater influence on union policies than they would on the policies of a nonunion firm.... Except in the cases where mass layoffs are threatened, this will lead him or her to prefer layoffs to other forms of adjustment.''

Freeman and Medoff argue that union members' preference for temporary layoffs, rather than work-sharing, increased in the post World War II years, noting the decreasing number of union contracts with work-sharing provisions. In the face of plant shutdowns, however, unions have accepted not only work-sharing measures but substantial give-backs in terms of wages and benefits.

During the 1990s, many of the largest firms in the country underwent re-engineering or downsizing. This constituted an important shift in the U.S. labor market in which even highly profitable firms laid off employees. At the end of 1993, Xerox Corp. showed consistent profitability; nonetheless, they announced the layoff of over 10,000 workers, nearly one-tenth of its **workforce**. The layoffs disproportionately affected managerial rather than production employees. Also in 1993 Procter and Gamble Co. announced the layoff of 13,000 workers. Procter and Gamble's chairman stated that the layoffs were necessary to improve the firm's position in the face of increasing price **competition**. General Electric, AT&T, and Johnson & Johnson were among other profitable firms to announce layoffs. Other firms announcing large-scale permanent layoffs in 1993 and 1994 included: Amoco Corp., laying off 3,800 workers; Mobil, 2,300 chemical workers; Aetna Life & Casualty, 4,000 workers; Nynex, 19,000 workers; including 13,000 managers; Digital Equipment Corp. (DEC)., 20,000 workers; Bristol-Meyers Squibb, 5,000 workers; Westinghouse, 3,400 workers; US West, 9,000 workers; E.I. du Pont de Nemours & Co., 4,500 workers; Eastman Kodak Co., 10,000 workers; and IBM, 85,000 workers. These layoffs occurred despite an expansion in overall employment in the early 1990s, when openings were increasingly filled by part-time and temporary workers. A disproportionate number of layoffs occurred in the industrial sector while gains occurred in the service sector, accounting for 70 percent of new jobs in 1993.

A study published in *Fortune* magazine (May 30, 1994) reported that 30 percent of all jobs existing in 1989 no longer existed at the end of 1993. Fully two-thirds of the jobs lost resulted from plant or office closings, and, thus, were permanent layoffs. The study noted that layoffs were spread across all regions of the country and occurred in both large and small firms. Of the new jobs created since 1989, 70 percent were created by just three percent of firms. Another study published in the *Washington Post* (February 9, 1994) noted that in January of 1994 alone, U.S. firms announced the permanent layoffs of over 100,000 employees. More than 600,000 workers were permanently laid off in 1993—double the rate for 1989, when the economy was growing at a substantially slower rate.

The American Management Association published survey results based on 870 companies. They found that one-half of these firms had laid off an average of just over ten percent of their employees in 1992. Managerial employees accounted for nearly 60 percent of these layoffs—the first time this share exceeded 50 percent in the seven years the survey was conducted. Significantly, the survey revealed that, of the firms that laid off employees, fewer than one-half showed increased profitability and only one-third showed increased labor productivity.

The National Employment Priorities Act, which proposed that firms be required to give advance notice to workers of impending layoffs or plant closures, was first introduced in Congress in 1974. This legislation, introduced by Congressmen Walter Mondale from Minnesota and William Ford from Michigan, failed to gain sufficient congressional support. Similar laws were passed at the state level, however, with Maine and Wisconsin among the first states requiring firms to give advance notice. Congressman William Ford re-introduced layoff notification legislation at the national level with the proposed Labor-Management Notification and Consultation Act of 1985. Advance notification legislation eventually passed in the form of the Worker Adjustment and Retraining Notification Act. Depending on the size of the firm, the Act required that workers be given prior notice from 60 days to six months of plant closures or large scale layoffs.

[David Kucera]

FURTHER READING:

"A Profitable Xerox Plans to Cut Staff by 10,000," *New York Times*. December 9, 1993.

Addison, John, ed. *Job Displacement: Consequences and Implications for Policy*. Wayne State University Press, 1991.

Cross, Michael. *U.S. Corporate Personnel Reduction Policies: An Edited Collection of Manpower Layoff, Reduction and Termination Policies*. Gower, 1981.

"Despite Big Layoffs, Employment Grows," *Wall Street Journal*. October 8, 1993.

Freeman, Richard B., and James L. Medoff. *What Do Unions Do?* Basic Books, Inc., 1984.

"Job Insecurity," *Fortune*. May 30, 1994.

Sandver, Marcus H. *Labor Relations: Process and Outcomes*. Little, Brown and Company, 1987.

Staudohar, Paul D., and Holly E. Brown. *Deindustrialization and Plant Closure*. Lexington Books, 1987.

"Strong Companies are Joining Trend to Eliminate Jobs." *New York Times*. July 26, 1993.

"Study: Layoffs Haven't Boosted Profits, Productivity," *Washington Post*. September 26, 1993.

Tachibanaki, Toshiaki. "Labour Market Flexibility in Japan in Comparison with Europe and the U.S." *European Economic Review*. April, 1987.

"U.S. Companies Speed Pace of Downsizing," *Washington Post*. February 9, 1994.

LEADERSHIP

Although a number of definitions have been applied to the term "leadership," most interpretations reflect the assumption that leadership is a process of social influence whereby one person motivates another person to accomplish an objective. Differences in definitions, however, relate primarily to which types of influences or motivating forces should qualify as leadership.

Leadership in business generally focuses on action-oriented activities related to interpreting events, determining objectives, building a consensus, and motivating others to accomplish goals. Thus, leadership is different from management, which stresses administrative activities related to planning, organizing, controlling, and sustaining processes. Nevertheless, leadership and management are intertwined, as the success of a leader (manager) is often contingent upon his or her management (leadership) ability.

This text focuses on leadership rather than management. Various approaches to leadership research in organizations are described, four contrasting leadership styles are examined, and leader attributes are provided.

BACKGROUND

Numerous observations and theories regarding leadership have been posited by great thinkers throughout history. The prevailing paradigm prior to the 18th century, and even during much of the 19th century, was that some men are born with the capacity and skills, particularly charisma, to lead other men.

Only during the 1900s, especially after World War II, did the notion that men and women could acquire leadership skills gain broad acceptance. The consensus during that period was that, although some of the characteristics of effective leadership are indeed innate, other attributes can be instilled during early childhood, learned through formal education, and developed through life experiences.

Much of the reason for the shift in paradigms about leadership occurred as a result of detailed studies about leadership in organizations during the 1940s, 1950s, and 1960s. In the 1950s, for instance, research about leading small groups resulted in the identification of two distinct leadership functions: (1) to organize and structure groups to accomplish tasks proficiently; and (2) to facilitate ongoing cooperation within the group until the task is complete. A corollary of this delineation was the identification of noninnate leadership qualities and skills—such as expertise, the ability to plan, and **time management**—as important factors influencing the leadership success.

Subsequent research during the 1970s advanced the view of leadership in organizations as a process that could be learned, particularly within the context of business organizations. The scope of the leadership function was broadened to include activities such as interpreting information important to the decision-making process, negotiating, and securing the support of people outside of an organization that do not have an implicit interest in the objectives of the group. Identification of such traits as important for leadership in modern organizations reinforced the concept of leadership as a learned skill that was complemented by inborn virtues, such as charisma.

Augmenting the concept of learned leadership within organizations was a concurrent increased interest in self-improvement and altering individual behavior to influence other people to engage in a desired behavior. Chief among the examples of this new ideology was Dale Carnegie's famous book, *How to Win Friends and Influence People* (Simon and Schuster, Inc., 1936). That text, which provided guidelines for achieving personal and professional success, essentially laid the foundation for many of the practical leadership training programs and techniques that were developed throughout the mid-1900s. Carnegie's book, as well as the training seminars offered by his foundation, taught such practical leadership skills as arousing enthusiasm among associates, how to spur others on to success, and how to win people to a particular way of thinking.

During the 1980s and 1990s, major trends in organizational leadership theory and practice have been characterized by concepts like participative management, employee **empowerment**, and bottom-up management. In general, those leadership processes emphasize less coercive motivational techniques.

LEADERSHIP RESEARCH

Research conducted during the 20th century helped to identify and define the dynamics of leadership in organizations. It also helped to shape modern perceptions and styles of leadership. Most of the research can be classified into one of four approaches: trait, behavior, power-influence, and situational (*Leadership in Organizations*, Prentice-Hall, 1994). These approaches largely exclude the study of charismatic and transformational leadership, which are discussed below.

The earliest of the four approaches used to study leadership was trait, which focuses on the personal characteristics of leaders. During the 1930s and 1940s, hundreds of studies tried to define leadership qualities and characteristics. Much of the research during that period was still being conducted under the assumption that leadership qualities are innate. Most efforts failed to find traits that would ensure leadership success. It was this failure that lead many researchers to focus on the study of leader attributes in relation to behavior and effectiveness.

The behavior approach to leadership research emerged during the 1950s. Studies were conducted on two fronts: (1) researchers examined how leaders spent their time and how successful they were at their jobs; and (2) they compared, and attempted to measure, the effectiveness of observed leaders. This research helped to shed light on the actions of successful leaders in relation to their personal qualities.

Another category of research that evolved during the mid-1900s was the power-influence approach. It emphasized the study of power within organizations and how leaders use their power to get people to act toward a goal. Leadership effectiveness was explained partially in terms of the amount of influence the leader wielded. The power-influence approach broadened the study of leadership to encompass the role of the follower—followers were viewed as a base from which a leader's power is derived, and as an entity that influences the leader.

The situational approach to research helped to lay the foundation for many of the organizational leadership styles popularized during the 1980s and 1990s, including employee empowerment and bottom-up management (discussed below). This approach focuses on the characteristics of the followers and their work in relation to the leader. Research investigates the way the managers react to the needs and demands of their group as well as to outside constraints, and seeks to correlate leader behavior and effectiveness in different circumstances. The situational approach is distinguished by its assumption of a ''contingency'' theory of leadership, which holds that different behavior patterns will be effective in different situations. In contrast, research approaches based on ''universal'' theories assume that an ideal pattern of behavior exists for all situations.

MODERN LEADERSHIP STYLES

Different leadership styles can be used to accomplish the same objectives. Some styles emphasize charisma or diplomacy to persuade or convince other people to follow, while other leadership strategies rely on motivating followers through fear of retribution, including physical harm. In fact, that difference often leads to discrepancies as to what constitutes leadership. For example, should the act of influencing a person by threatening to physically harm them constitute leadership? Perhaps not, some behaviorists would argue. On a lesser scale, though, should influencing someone to act by implying the loss of a promotion to a better job be considered a form a leadership? After all, other behaviorists would contend, the leader was simply using a tool at his or her disposal to get a coworker to achieve a desired objective—and don't all forms of motivation carry some implied threat, even if it is only the risk of not attaining some internal need, such as a feeling of acceptance or high self-esteem?

Three fundamental leadership styles or philosophies within the context of business are identified below: political, directive, and participative. They differ in the means and methods that people within organizations employ to influence others to accomplish objectives, and in the parties that are served by the objectives. Most individuals and organizations employ a mix of some or all of these strategies. In addition, a fourth style, charismatic leadership, is distinguished. It differs from the other three in that it is more suited to realizing radical visions or handling crises, and less oriented toward influencing behavior toward the attainment of long-term goals or day-to-day management activities.

POLITICAL LEADERSHIP

Business people who adopt a political leadership style recognize that the ability to lead people in organizations requires the acquisition of power that is necessary to manipulate the forces within the entity toward common objectives. This philosophy assumes that the company is a political arena, fraught with deception, in-fighting, and selfish goals, as well as positive attributes like teamwork and self-sacrifice. Political leaders realize that they often must push,

bargain, and manipulate to advance the interests of their departments and themselves.

Although the leader may be well-intentioned, honest, and acting in the best interests of the company, he or she may be willing to deceive others and act selfishly in order to achieve a desired result. In fact, most successful leaders within an organization must employ some political savvy to influence others to achieve a goal. If they have strong, creative ideas about the direction a company or department should be going, they may have to strive to achieve their goals indirectly to reduce destructive, internal resistance. This is achieved by keeping their goals flexible or vague, advancing patiently, and resourcefully coordinating and influencing different political channels.

The theory of political leadership (*Leadership and the Quest for Integrity*, Harvard Business School Press, 1989) is founded on assumptions about human and organizational behavior. Those assumptions can be split into two categories: (1) individual or departmental interests and myopia diffuse leadership efforts—efforts that would otherwise benefit the overall organization; and (2) bureaucracy and inflexibility exist. The second category of assumptions results from people in an organization seeking security and resisting change for personal interests. In other words, a leader may have trouble influencing others to act toward an objective because those people are afraid that change may threaten their unique position in the company. To overcome this problem, leaders often must employ political tactics to assuage people's concerns or negotiate with them to get their support.

The first category of assumptions on which the theory of political leadership is founded includes four major factors that diffuse positive initiatives and create stumbling blocks for leaders. The most powerful of these factors is self-interest, such as a manager sabotaging a colleague's efforts. The second most formidable deterrent is scarcity of resources, which results in groups within a company thwarting the efforts of others in an effort to secure those resources. The third negative force is increased specialization, which in larger companies results in divided authority and dispersed skills and information—it causes groups within a company to see the world from their unique viewpoint, which becomes a detriment of the overall organizational vision. Finally, even when departments within a company do seek to act in the best interests of the company, their efforts are often flawed by a lack of understanding of operations outside of their specialization.

As an example of the political leadership philosophy at work, consider an executive at a meat processing company that has just been named chief executive. In an effort to improve the organization's profitability, he wants to revise the budget, restructure some departments, and implement a new computer **information processing system**. However, in preparing his overall strategy he meets resistance from managers—they withhold information from other departments, insist that changes will not work, or provide enthusiastic lip service despite having no intent of supporting the initiatives with action.

Rather than confronting the dilemma head on, a leader that ascribed to the political leadership philosophy would likely seek gradual change through compromise and diplomacy. His approach would recognize the force of established power structures that could undermine his efforts, and would cautiously seek to win those powers to his way of thinking through manipulation, negotiation, and mitigating irrational fears. He may have to alter his initial goals during the leadership process to gain the support of different power bases or to reduce confrontation and conflict.

DIRECTIVE LEADERSHIP

The directive leadership style emphasizes the use of facts, sound strategy, and assertiveness. Leaders focus on gathering information, developing clear-cut objectives through a careful assessment of data, devising strategies to accomplish goals, and then compelling subordinates and coworkers to achieve those ends. Directive leaders are less concerned about building a consensus for their vision than they are about motivating others to achieve it. Directive leadership differs from political leadership in that the former is proactive and the latter is reactive. Thus, directive leaders must be willing to confront resistance to their goals and assume the risk inherent in conflict.

Three assumptions about human and organizational behavior are inherent to the directive management style: (1) people are motivated more by internal than external forces, such as threats or rewards; (2) companies benefit from strong, decisive leadership; and (3) unity and substance is more important than appearance and style.

The first assumption of directive leadership, that people are motivated primarily by internal forces, holds that the most talented individuals are heavily influenced by base needs, such as security, financial rewards, and status. In companies, people fill these needs largely through achievement, which causes them to want to assume responsibility for making decisions, autonomy, and control over their jobs. They are also driven by the desire to be part of a winning team. A company that rewards these individuals for making good decisions and attributes the company's success to their efforts can influence those workers to perform at a high level. In essence, the workers are motivated by a desire to see the company succeed, which becomes a mark of their own victory. In this

type of environment, workers are more willing to risk failure and are less resistant to change.

The need for strong leadership, the second assumption of the directive leadership theory, arises from the tendency for divisive forces to develop in larger organizations. Like political leaders, adherents to the directive style recognize the propensity of individuals and departments in a company to become myopic and self-centered. However, directive leaders believe that the institution of negative energies is largely the result of a lack of leadership. Indeed, directive leaders posit that in-fighting and self-interest undermines the goals of the overall organization, erodes team spirit, and causes the most talented individuals to flee the company. Therefore, it is part of the role of the leader to confront and overcome these forces, rather than react to them with political maneuverings.

The third assumption of directive leadership, substance over style, implies that it is a mistake for a leader to adapt his or her mode of leadership to accommodate people who comprise the common denominator of society. Instead, a good leader can motivate ordinary people to accomplish extraordinary things through decisive, intelligent, objective leadership.

Consider the chief executive of the meat processing company from the previous example—he has developed a new vision for his company, but is meeting resistance from his subordinates. As a directive leader, he would naturally reject political leadership strategies, fearing that even the appearance of compromise and political pandering will sustain the status quo and foster ill will. Instead, a directive leader would be more likely to gather his managers together and clearly and objectively define the problems that they, as a team, faced. He would then outline his strategy for overcoming and correcting the problems. After explaining the game plan, the leader would directly confront apparent opposition—he may even welcome confrontation as a means of clarifying the company's goals and eliminating ambiguity. He would then work to make sure that his managers felt like they had autonomy to get their jobs done, and that their contributions to the team were recognized and rewarded.

PARTICIPATIVE LEADERSHIP

The participative, or values-driven, style of leadership emphasizes joint decision making, decentralization, the sharing of power, and democratic management. It also recognizes the inevitability of myopia and negativity within larger organizations, and seeks to abolish those forces by keeping workers informed, seeking their input, and giving them a large degree of control over the processes in which they participate.

Participative leadership, then, is behavior-oriented, while political leadership tends to be relationship-oriented and directive leadership is more task-oriented.

The participative philosophy assumes that humans are highly motivated by the need to do good work—work enables them to contribute to worthwhile purposes, allows them to exercise their creativity, and gives them a sense of pride and accomplishment. Specifically, people value work that results in outstanding products or services. They are motivated by work that challenges them, builds skills, and is accomplished with teams of people that they respect.

The participative philosophy views traditional organizational leadership strategies as transactional, meaning that workers exchange time and effort for money, power, and prestige. It implies that transactional systems often result in boredom, dissatisfaction, and alienation. By recognizing individual needs related to doing a good job and making a contribution to a worthwhile cause, companies can maximize the effectiveness of the overall organization. Thus, it is the role of the leader to shape an organization so that its values, norms, and ideals are appealing to its members.

Unlike directive leadership, the participative style focuses on building a consensus during the decision-making process. It also stresses bottom-up management, whereby information and expertise is gleaned from workers in lower levels of the organization that is used to direct decisions and goals. Once decisions have been made and goals have been set, participative leaders are apt to utilize employee empowerment techniques, whereby workers are given the freedom and responsibility to accomplish objectives in the way that they believe is best.

Using a participative leadership style, the CEO of the meat processing company would likely include his fellow managers, and perhaps some of their subordinates, in the initial goal-setting process. He then would propose a tentative plan to revitalize the company, record feedback about his proposal, and then integrate applicable ideas and suggestions into a revised plan. Next, he would give his managers the autonomy and tools necessary to accomplish the goals, all the while striving to facilitate an atmosphere of teamwork and excellence.

CHARISMATIC LEADERSHIP

Charisma is Greek for "divinely inspired gift." Indeed, charisma has been defined as a form of influence based not on formal authority, but on follower's perceptions that the leader embodies extraordinary qualities. Charismatic leadership in business organizations is a style often used by entrepreneurs who are starting new companies. It has also been termed "transformational" leadership to describe leaders that use charisma to revitalize old or large companies. Charismatic leaders often rise to a position of influence by providing a radical vision or solution to a crisis. Because such radical visions are usually difficult to initiate in established organizations, charismatics are often forced to start new enterprises.

The successful application of charismatic leadership is generally assumed to result from both the personal attributes of the leader and the circumstances to which he or she is responding. Charismatic leaders usually possess such character traits as self-confidence, strong convictions, poise, excellent speaking ability, and a flair for drama. They are usually able to motivate followers through emotional appeal and by instilling a sense of team spirit and unity within a group. Although their penchant to take risks sometimes makes them vulnerable, their willingness to assume personal risk is likely to enhance their perceived credibility and to motivate their followers. All of these virtues are useless, however, if the leader lacks the ability to postulate a credible vision—a charismatic individual with an incredible or irrelevant vision would likely be viewed as unstable, rather than charismatic.

Because of their emotional appeal, charismatic leaders can accumulate great power and exercise great influence within organizations. This power and influence can be used to achieve great works, such as defeating enemies or placing a man on the moon. On the other hand, charismatic leaders may also use their influence as a negative force; an extreme example of this is Adolph Hitler, one of the most charismatic leaders of the 20th century. Within a business context, "negative charismatics" may use their power to disrupt an organization or to achieve personal gain at the expense of the company. "Positive charismatics" are generally identified by their devotion to the organization and their followers, rather than to themselves.

The primary downside of positive charismatic leadership, in comparison to the other three management styles, is that it is less useful for the accomplishment of long-term goals. In addition, it typically does not complement management practices necessary to sustain an organization after the start-up or revitalization phase. Furthermore, charismatics often fail to pay attention to the details necessary to accomplish their broad vision. They are also likely to alienate people that don't buy into their goals, may fail to recognize major flaws in their plans because they are over-confident, and often fail to develop long-term plans to sustain the success of their endeavors.

In the meat processing company example, for instance, a charismatic leader might be very successful at convincing his subordinates to embrace a radical (but credible) plan of revitalization, and then to enthusiastically strive to implement the plan. After the plan had been implemented, however, he may lack the leadership and management skills required to keep the company profitable during a noncrisis situation. For this reason, many companies will employ a visionary to lead their organization through a transitional stage with the intent of eventually replacing him with a more management-oriented leader. This facet of the charismatic style also explains the rapid rise and fall of many entrepreneurial concerns.

ATTRIBUTES OF LEADERS

The characteristics of successful leaders in large, complex organizations are vastly different from those associated with the stereotypical charismatic leader that emerges to lead a group through a crisis or to an exigent goal. Instead, leaders in business organizations must have traits and practice styles that are compatible with the day-to-day management of operations and the pursuit of long-range objectives. Furthermore, leaders at both high and low levels within an organization must possess attributes that can only be learned and cultivated over time, as well as inborn skills that complement their objectives and circumstances.

At least six major groups of traits have been identified that encompass the attributes necessary for leaders in large organizations to be effective:

1. motivation

2. personal values

3. abilities

4. reputation and track record.

5. relationships in the firm and industry and

6. industry and organizational knowledge (*The Leadership Factor*, The Free Press, 1988).

Likewise, the origins of those characteristics have been identified as: (1) genetic; (2) early childhood experiences; (3) formal education; and (4) career experiences. Of the six trait groups, only the first (motivation) and the third (abilities and skills) are considered innate. However, motivation can also be learned during early childhood or acquired during career experiences. Likewise, abilities and skills can be acquired through any of those channels, as well as by formal education. Characteristics in the remainder of the trait groups are acquired through combinations of early childhood experiences, education, and career experiences.

In other words, most of the traits necessary for effective leadership in organizations are learned or acquired after birth. For instance, in order to attract the resources and acquire the expertise necessary to accomplish a substantial objective, an effective leader must have credibility with his superiors, peers, and even subordinates. Credibility is acquired through: (1) established, cooperative relationships with critical players in the company and/or industry; (2) a good track record and a solid professional reputation; and (3) the interpersonal ability to develop credible relationships with a broad network of people quickly and easily, and to effectively communicate goals to those people.

Although learned and acquired traits play the most important role in the leadership process, characteristics that are largely inborn also factor into the equation. For instance, the most successful high-level leaders typically possess a keen mind that has the ability to quickly absorb and process large amounts of information for use in the problem-solving process. They are also characteristically multidimensional, have a capacity to see the big picture and think strategically, possess a high energy level, and have a strong desire to lead that is backed by high self-confidence. Furthermore, they usually show initiative in originating personal contacts, persevere, are flexible, have a dominant personality that allows them to assert themselves during confrontation, are good listeners, and exhibit equanimity, or the ability to retain their composure despite outside pressures.

Interestingly, a number of attributes that seemingly have no direct effect on an individual's ability to lead are statistically indicative of the likelihood of a person to be a high-level leader in an organization. For instance, a disproportionately large number of high-level leaders are first-borns (the oldest sibling in their family) and/or relatively slender.

THE MACHIAVELLIAN PERSPECTIVE

Niccolo Machiavelli (1469-1527) was an influential Italian military and political leader during the late 15th and early 16th centuries. In his book *The Prince*, he outlines his approach to leadership and the use of influence within organizations. *The Prince* is perhaps one of the most influential treatises on the subject of power and influence ever written, and has served as a guide for political, military, and business leaders for centuries. Despite advanced leadership research and theory postulated during the 20th century, *The Prince* remains a chief text on the subject of leadership and is required reading in many business school and leadership courses.

Although his views are often considered utilitarian and stoic by today's standards, his basic insights still have application. For instance, Machiavelli suggested that when a leader is forced to make difficult decisions regarding subordinates, he should act decisively and quickly to end the pain and turmoil as soon as possible. This tenant has been applied to the business world to propose, for example, that executives should conduct corporate layoffs and cutbacks all at once, rather than phasing them in over a long period of time. By doing this, the morale of the remaining workers quickly recovers because they know that their jobs are not at risk, and the company can move on with its business.

Machiavelli also recognized that leaders that come to power through the fortune of others, because they have money or are related to somebody important, are often short on leadership knowledge and lack faithful troops and subordinates. Along those lines, he suggested that in many instances a leader who comes to power should harshly quell any hint of opposition, replace most of the leaders below him that were in service during the old regime, and initiate changes despite opposition. These doctrines have been incorporated into successful transfers of power between new corporate chief executives. By assembling a hand-picked team and by firing or striking fear into subordinates that may have allegiance to the old chief executive, a new CEO is able to quickly gain loyalty and respect, thus averting subversion.

More controversial precepts advocated by Machiavelli relate to his appreciation of cruelty and force to achieve positive goals. Leniency and compassion, he argued, can often betray weakness and ineptness, which imperils the state. Instead, a leader's subordinates must fear and respect him before they love him out of choice, because effective leadership is built on what lies in his own powers rather then on the pleasures of other men.

[Dave Mote]

FURTHER READING:

Badaracco, Joseph L., Jr. and Richard R. Ellsworth. *Leadership and the Quest for Integrity*. Boston: Harvard Business School Press, 1989.

Barricelli, Jean-Pierre. *The Prince: Text and Commentary*. Woodbury, NY: Barron's Educational Series, Inc., 1975.

Carnegie, Dale. *How to Win Friends and Influence People*. New York: Simon and Schuster, 1936.

Cohen, William A. *The Art of the Leader*. Englewood Cliffs, NJ: Prentice Hall, Inc., 1990.

Kotter, John P. *The Leadership Factor*. New York: The Free Press, 1988.

Sayles, Leonard R. *Leadership: Managing in Real Organizations*. 2nd ed. New York: McGraw-Hill Book Company, 1989.

Yukl, Gary. *Leadership in Organizations*. 3rd ed. Englewood Cliffs, NJ: Prentice Hall, Inc., 1994.

LEADING ECONOMIC INDICATORS

A leading economic indicator is a statistic, such as housing starts, that is considered to signal the future direction of economic activity. Leading indicators tend to reach cyclical high and low points earlier than corresponding peaks and troughs in the overall economy, which makes them useful for predicting economic downturns or recoveries. In contrast, lagging indicators, such as the average prime interest rate charged by **banks**, generally trail behind changes in **business cycles**. Coincident indicators, like **manufacturing** and trade sales, tend to rise and fall along with overall economic activity.

The most popular forecasting tool of this type is the Composite Index of Leading Economic Indicators (CLI), which is published monthly by the U.S. Department of Commerce. The CLI was created in the late 1950s by a group of economists led by Geoffrey Moore. It appears in numerous magazines and newspapers across the country and is monitored closely by government policy makers, financial analysts, and business leaders who seek to predict and prepare for the future direction of the economy. The CLI is composed of a series of 11 indicators from different segments of the economy selected specifically for their tendency to predict business cycles in the near future. The Commerce Department revises the data, definitions, and procedures used to construct the CLI periodically to ensure its accuracy.

The specific components of the CLI are: the average length of a work week for manufacturing employees; the average number of initial claims for **unemployment** insurance in state programs; the dollar value of new orders placed with manufacturers in the consumer goods and materials industries; the percentage of vendor deliveries that are slower, or require a longer lead time; the dollar value of **contracts** and orders for industrial plants and equipment; the number of new private housing units authorized by local building permits; the dollar change in manufacturers' unfilled orders in the durable goods industries; the percent change in sensitive materials prices; the average prices of 500 **common stocks**; the dollar change in the money supply M2; and the change in consumer expectations.

In order to successfully predict cyclical changes in economic activity, leading indicators must be interpreted using a filtering rule. One popular rule of thumb for interpreting the movement of leading indicators is that three successive periods of decline signal an imminent **recession**, while three successive periods of increase signal the beginning of a recovery. Economists apply much more sophisticated statistical models to interpret the performance of individual leading indicators or the CLI.

In an analysis for the *Journal of Forecasting*, Lahiri and Wang found that the CLI predicted turning points in the economy successfully, with a lead time of about three months using real-time data, but also sent some false signals of impending downturns.

Koenig and Emery, in an article for *Contemporary Economic Policy,* found that the CLI predicted peaks in the business cycle an average of 8.2 months in advance and troughs an average of 4.2 months in advance. However, they still claimed that the CLI "failed to provide reliable advance warning of both recessions and recoveries" for several reasons: there is usually a one-month delay in publication of the CLI; the peaks and troughs are gradual and difficult to recognize in real time; and the **index** is subject to frequent revisions.

Still, the researchers emphasized that their results do not necessarily mean that the CLI is useless. Instead, the index may be relied upon to a great extent by government policy makers. These officials may respond to changes in the CLI by enacting policies to counteract the cyclical trends in the economy. For example, the Federal Reserve might raise **interest rates** in order to slow an economic expansion that is accompanied by **inflation**. Any successful counter-cyclical actions would make the CLI appear less reliable as a predictor.

[*Laurie Collier Hillstrom*]

FURTHER READING:

"Composite Indexes: Leading Index Components," *Survey of Current Business.* March 1995, p. C-9.

Koenig, Evan F., and Kenneth M. Emery. "Why the Composite Index of Leading Indicators Does Not Lead," *Contemporary Economic Policy.* January 1994, pp. 52-66.

Lahiri, K., and J. G. Wang. "Predicting Cyclical Turning Points with Leading Index in a Markov Switching Model," *Journal of Forecasting.* May 1994, pp. 245-63.

Linden, Dana Wechsler. "Sentinel on the Inflation Watch," *Forbes.* September 12, 1994, pp. 126-27.

LEARNING CURVES

SEE: Experience and Learning Curves

LEASING

A lease is a form of financing under which the owner of an asset (the lessor) temporarily transfers the right to use, and sometimes act as owner of, the asset to another party (the lessee). The lessor typically makes the lease for a specified period in return for a lump sum or periodic rental payments from the lessee.

The modern concept of leasing dates back to at least 1800 B.C., when the Babylonian king Hammurabi described the transaction in his Code of Hammurabi. In that code, the king outlines the basic concept behind leasing—use, rather than ownership, of equipment is what produces wealth. Leasing has been used for centuries in different forms and for different applications. By the early 1900s, however, its application was confined primarily to **real estate** rentals, although leasing was also used to finance less expensive assets such as cars and farm equipment.

As a result of several factors, including tax laws and more efficient financial markets, leasing became a common financing tool after 1950 for a variety of goods. By the mid-1990s people and companies were leasing everything from airplanes and oil rigs to televisions and office furniture. In fact, in the United States leasing was the most common way to finance plant and equipment for **manufacturing** companies, and it was being used to finance a growing number of consumer purchases.

As intimated above, the chief advantage of leasing is that it provides an alternative to ownership. The party that leases an asset benefits from not having its resources invested in equipment. Indeed, many companies that lease equipment do so because they believe higher productivity and profits are derived from productive use of equipment, rather than equipment ownership. A trucking company, for example, might benefit from investing its limited resources in **marketing** or inventory tracking operations, rather than in trucks. Similarly, an individual who leases a car may believe that her money would provide a better return invested in stocks. In turn, companies that lease equipment to others believe that they can do a better job of buying, financing, servicing, and selling equipment than their customers.

But there are also numerous logistical motivations behind leasing. A company that leases an office machine, for example, avoids the risk of investing its resources in an asset that may soon become technologically obsolete. The company may also benefit from having access to the machine for only a short time, to complete a big project for example, without having to invest in the equipment and then dispose of it. In addition, companies can reduce their apparent debt burden by leasing. Finally, for individuals who cannot afford to buy or who are unable to obtain loans for consumer goods such as furniture, leasing provides an important financing alternative.

Lessors also benefit in several ways. Compared to their lessees, they are often able to acquire equipment at a low cost, liquidate it efficiently, and obtain acceptable financing terms. Those advantages result from various **economies of scale**, such as increased buying power over sellers of equipment. Lessors are also better positioned to take advantage of some tax laws, such as **depreciation** allowances and investment tax credits. Importantly, lessees also benefit from a number of tax advantages. A firm that leases equipment or real estate, for example, will be able to deduct its lease payments from its taxable income rather than deducting depreciation.

The two primary types of leases are operating and financial (also known as capital leases). Financial leasing companies essentially sell equipment to their customers. The lessee typically rents the item for its entire useful life, or agrees to eventually pay for and own the item through a lease-to-own arrangement. The agreement effectively involves transfer of ownership to the lessee, who cannot cancel the lease without a penalty. The payments typically amortize most of the economic value of the asset. Most financial leases are net leases, meaning that the lessee is responsible for maintaining and insuring the asset and paying all property taxes. Financial leases are often used for heavy capital equipment such as airplanes and earth moving machines, as well as for consumer items such as furniture and electronics.

In contrast, operating leases, or service leases, mimic short-term loans. Lessors usually rent an item more than once during its useful life, and lessees do not commit to purchase the equipment in the lease. Unlike a financial leasing arrangement, however, a lessee can usually cancel an operating lease, assuming prior notice, without a major penalty. Furthermore, the lessor is usually responsible for maintenance, insurance, and taxes related to the asset. Motor vehicles are often leased under operating leases, as are computers, copiers, and other office machines.

Several types of leases, each of which combine different financial and tax advantages, are actually hybrids of financial and operating leases. The dollar-out lease and the bargain lease, for example, both give the user the option of acquiring the equipment for a negligible or undetermined amount at the end of the lease. Among the most popular hybrid leases is the sale-and-leaseback, whereby a company sells its own assets and then leases them back from the buyer. Sale and leasebacks are most commonly used to finance the use of real estate. The company benefits from an infusion of cash, and may also enjoy certain tax advantages.

Real estate and motor vehicles are the most commonly leased assets in the United States—nearly 50 percent of all new motor vehicles were being leased going into the mid-1990s. The next most popular lease items in the United States are airplanes, office machines, and furniture. Airplanes constituted about 16 percent of all equipment leased (under nonfinancial) arrangements in 1991. An estimated 17 percent of all business machines in use in the United States were leased in the early 1990s, and office machines accounted for over 5 percent of all equipment rented in the United States. Approximately 6 percent of all office furniture was leased, and a growing number of individuals were renting their furnishings going into the mid-1990s.

[Dave Mote]

FURTHER READING:

"Equipment Leasing Is a Wise Investment." *Office*. July, 1993.

Shapiro, Alan C. *Modern Corporate Finance*. New York: Macmillan Publishing Company, 1990.

U.S. Department of Commerce. *U.S. Industrial Outlook 1993*. Washington, DC: GPO, June 10, 1993.

LEAST SQUARES

The least squares criterion is a statistical approach used to provide the most accurate estimate of relationships between sets of variables in sample data. It is used to define regression lines and planes that yield estimates of a dependent variable, given values for an independent variable.

Least squares analysis is the most popular approach to the computation of regression lines because it is relatively simple and highly accurate. Particularly in linear relationships, it is the best linear unbiased estimator (BLUE), of sample data. It also gives the maximum likelihood estimator (MLE), in regressions where errors from the **regression** line form a normal bell-shaped distribution.

In order to understand how a least squares analysis is performed, it is important to first understand the properties of a regression analysis. Simply described, regression analysis uses algebraic formulas to estimate the value of a continuous random dependent variable, using other independent variables as indicators. These formulas produce an estimate of the dependent variable that is most correct (or least incorrect), given any value of an independent variable.

The least squares approach is nearly 100 years older than regression analysis. It was independently developed by the French mathematician Andrien-Marie Legendre (1752-1833), the German mathematician and astronomer Carl Friedrich Gauss (1777-1855), and Adrain between 1805-09. These mathematicians were working on ways to estimate the paths of comets.

Astronomical observations had suggested that these comets maintained highly erratic orbits. In fact, the deviations were due to observational errors. This led the discoverers to develop a method, the least squares criterion, that would factor out these errors and produce a correct prediction of a comet's path.

The mathematicians work yielded important insights into estimating relationships between other types of graphical coordinates—specifically, how to rationalize deviations from a theoretical line of best fit. By the definition of such an estimated line, there are as many negative deviations as positive ones. As a result, all deviations must be expressed as absolute values, a condition met through squaring (the square of any number, whether positive or negative, is positive).

The least squares criterion produces a line in which the sum of the squared deviations of every value Y from the line are lowest. The line represents a continuous *estimate* of Y values for every value of X, based on the sample data (see Figure 1).

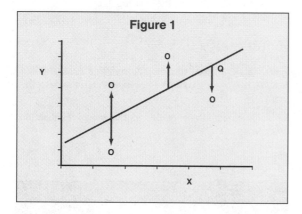

Figure 1

This simple example demonstrates that it is impossible to draw a straight line, or linear regression, that touches all four points on the graph. Instead, we use the least squares criterion to determine the location of a straight line (Q) that comes closest to the points.

Squaring also places the regression line precisely where deviations from the line are lowest. If the sums of deviations were not squared, the line may drift upward or downward until it meets a coordinate. Increased deviation on one side of the line would be made up exactly by decreases on the other side of the line. (See Figure 2)

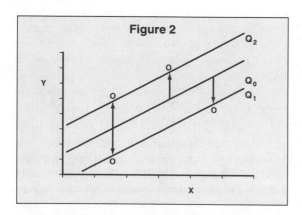

Figure 2

When the deviations are squared, the degree of their deviation is amplified. The difference between 2.5, 3.5, 4.5 and 5.5 is 1, but the difference between their squares—6.25, 12.25, 20.25, 30.25—increases incrementally, 6, 8, and 10.

As a result, the least squares formula indicates a specific slope β, and places that slope at a specific reference point α, the Y intercept.

[John Simley]

FURTHER READING:

Johnson, Robert R. *Elementary Statistics*, 3rd ed. North Scituate, MA: Duxbury Press, 1980.

Kachiga, Sam Kash. *Statistical Analysis*. New York: Radius Press, 1986.

Kazmier, Leonard J. *Basic Statistics for Business and Economics*. New York: McGraw-Hill, 1990.

Monks, Joseph G. *Statistics for Business*, Science Research Associates, 1988.

LETTERS OF CREDIT

A letter of credit is an instrument issued to a buyer of goods by a bank for a mutually agreed upon amount of credit. The letter of credit allows the seller of the goods to draw on the issuing bank for payment. The term letter of credit was legally defined in the case of *American Steel Company v. Irving National Bank* as: "A letter requesting one person to make advances to a third person on the credit of the writer is a letter of credit. These letters are general or special. They are general if directed to the writer's correspondents generally. They are special if addressed to some particular person."

Letters of credit thus involve four parties: the buyer or opener; the buyer's bank, which issues the letter of credit; an associated bank in proximity to the seller; and the seller, also known as the beneficiary. The purpose of a letter of credit is to expedite commercial transactions, usually involving foreign or domestic trade. A letter of credit works by going through the following steps:

1. A buyer and a seller reach a commercial agreement.

2. The party that wishes to buy the goods applies to a bank for a letter of credit.

3. The issuing bank approves a credit line and forwards the necessary information to a corresponding bank used by or in the vicinity of the seller.

4. The corresponding bank confirms the letter of credit (hence the bank is also referred to as the confirming bank) to the seller.

5. The seller transfers the goods to the buyer.

6. The seller notifies the confirming bank that the goods have been transferred to the buyer.

7. The seller is paid by the confirming bank.

8. The confirming bank apprises the issuing bank that the transaction has taken place.

9. The confirming bank is reimbursed by the issuing bank.

10. The issuing bank notifies the buyer that it has reimbursed the confirming bank.

11. The buyer reimburses the issuing bank.

In order to comply with the above steps, letters of credit are generally consistent with proscribed attributes and responsibilities. A letter of credit must refer to itself as such and must clearly state so. A letter of credit must have an expiration date and a set credit line. The issuing bank is not required to reimburse the confirming bank without proper documentation, and the issuing bank is not obligated to referee any legal disputes arising between the buyer and the seller. Finally, the buyer has a total obligation to reimburse the issuing bank.

Letters of credit are advantageous to both the buyer and the seller. Payment to the seller is guaranteed by either the issuing bank or the confirming bank, or sometimes by both. The buyer's funds are not immediately tied up by the transaction and, because payment is guaranteed, a discount price is often negotiated. Since letters of credit have expiration dates, the delivery of the goods is usually guaranteed before that date occurs. The banks receive a fee for their respective services. There is usually no predetermined table of fees, but rather a fee determination based on risk.

An international code of rules pertaining to letters of credit is known as the Uniform Customs and Practices for Documentary Credits (UCP). This code is issued by the International Chamber of Commerce, which is headquartered in Paris. Although there is no formal legislative or judicial enforcement of the code, it is adhered to worldwide by most banks and other commercial enterprises. A similar code in the United States that governs letters of credit practices is the **Uniform Commercial Code**. Like the UCP, there is no formal judicial or legislative enforcement of the UCC. However, most deliberative bodies in the United States write applicable legislation based on the Uniform Commercial Code. In 1994, the International Chamber of Commerce revised UCP-400, which was its protocol for controlling letters of credit. Most of the changes in the new protocol apply to banks issuing and confirming letters of credit rather than the buyers or sellers involved in the transaction.

Generally the above information applies to commercial letters of credit. There is also a traveler's letter of credit. This is a letter of credit issued by a bank to a traveler that serves to introduce the holding party to the correspondent banks in foreign countries. There are actually two variations of traveler's letters of credit, circular and specially advised. Specially advised letters of credit are addressed to a particular foreign bank, while a circular letter of credit is issued for foreign banks in general. The holder of a traveler's letter of credit generally makes payment to an issuing bank in advance and in an amount equal to the credit line. However, the holder may make arrangements to have withdrawals made from a deposit account as drafts are received by the issuing bank.

[Michael Knes]

FURTHER READING:

Aster, Charles E. and Patterson, Katheryn C. *A Practical Guide to Letters of Credit*. Executive Enterprises Publications Co. Inc., 1990.

Rowe, Michael. *Letters of Credit*. Euromoney Publications, 1985.

LEVERAGE

Leverage refers to the use of fixed cost assets and liabilities to boost returns to shareholders. There are two types of leverage, operating and financial. Operating leverage refers to the use of fixed costs in the firm's earnings stream to magnify operating profits—earnings before interest and taxes (EBIT). Financial leverage results from the use of **debt** and preferred stock, to magnify earnings per share. Both types of leverage not only magnify the expected returns, but also increase inherent economic risk.

OPERATING LEVERAGE

Operating leverage is the extent to which a firm uses fixed costs in producing its goods or services. By using fixed production costs, the firm's EBIT is magnified, or leveraged. For example, assume two firms, A and B, produce and sell widgets. Firm A uses a highly automated production process with robotic machines, whereas firm B assembles the widgets using primarily semi-skilled labor. Table 1 shows both firm's operating cost structures.

Highly-automated firm A has fixed costs of $35,000 per year and variable costs of only $1.00 per unit; labor-intensive firm B has fixed costs of only $15,000 per year, but its variable cost per unit is much higher at $3.00 per unit. Both firms produce

Table 1
Illustration of Operating Leverage

	Firm A (High Automation)	Firm B (Low Automation)
Units produced	10,000	10,000
Sales price per unit (P)	$5.00	$5.00
Variable cost per unit (V)	$1.00	$3.00
Fixed costs (F)	$35,000	$15,000

and sell 10,000 widgets per year at a price of $5.00 per widget.

Firm A has a higher amount of operating leverage because of its higher fixed costs. This can be measured by the degree of operating leverage at a specific production level Q (DOL$_Q$).

$$DOL_Q = \frac{Q(P - V)}{Q(P - V) - F} \qquad (1)$$

where Q = the production quantity,
V = the variable cost per unit,
P = the sales price per unit,
F = the total fixed operating costs.

Firm A's degree of operating leverage at a quantity of 10,000 units is given by equation 1 as:

$$DOL_{10,000} = \frac{10,000(5.00 - 1.00)}{10,000(5.00 - 1.00) - 35,000} = 8$$

Firm B, on the other hand, has a lower degree of operating leverage because of its lower fixed costs:

$$DOL_{10,000} = \frac{10,000 (5.00 - 3.00)}{10,000(5.00 - 3.00) - 15,000} = 4.0$$

The degree of operating leverage measures the percentage change in EBIT for a given percentage change in sales.

$$DOL_Q = \frac{\%\Delta EBIT}{\%\Delta SALES} \qquad (2)$$

This definition of the degree of operating leverage shows that if firm A's sales increase by 1 percent, its earnings before interest and taxes (EBIT) will increase by eight percent. However, this magnification is a double-edged sword; if firm A's sales decrease by one percent, its EBIT will decrease by eight percent. The degree of operating leverage shows the responsiveness of EBIT to a given change in sales. Firm A's EBIT will increase (decrease) by a factor of eight for a given increase (decrease) in sales, whereas firm B's EBIT will only increase (decrease) by a factor or four for a given increase (decrease) in sales.

The degree of operating leverage can also be determined using this alternative definition. Table 2 shows partial income statements for firms A and B.

Panel A shows that EBIT are $5,000 for both firms. However, if sales increase by 10 percent to 11,000 units, firm A's EBIT will increase to $9,000, whereas firm B's EBIT increases to only $7,000. Firm A's higher degree of operating leverage results in a greater magnification of EBIT. Equation 2 can be used to calculate the DOL$_Q$ directly from the partial income statements:

$$DOL_Q = \frac{\%\Delta EBIT}{\%\Delta SALES} = \frac{\frac{EBIT_{NEW} - EBIT_{OLD}}{EBIT_{OLD}}}{\frac{SALES_{NEW} - SALES_{OLD}}{SALES_{OLD}}}$$

Table 2
Illustration of Operating Leverage
Panel A: At Current Levels of 10,000 Units

	Firm A	Firm B
Sales (PxQ)	$50,000	$50,000
less variable costs (VxQ)	(10,000)	(30,000)
less fixed costs (F)	(35,000)	(15,000)
EBIT	5,000	5,000

Panel B: At Production Levels of 11,000 Units

	Firm A	Firm B
Sales (PxQ)	$55,000	$55,000
less variable costs (VxQ)	(11,000)	(33,000)
less fixed costs (F)	(35,000)	(15,000)
EBIT	9,000	7,000

For Firm A:

$$DOL_{10,000} = \frac{\dfrac{9,000 - 5,000}{5,000}}{\dfrac{55,000 - 50,000}{50,000}} = \frac{\dfrac{4,000}{5,000}}{\dfrac{5,000}{50,000}} = 8.0$$

For Firm B:

$$DOL_{10,000} = \frac{\dfrac{7,000 - 5,000}{5,000}}{\dfrac{55,000 - 50,000}{50,000}} = \frac{\dfrac{2,000}{5,000}}{\dfrac{5,000}{50,000}} = 4.0$$

Even though a higher degree of operating leverage magnifies the operating earnings of the firm, it increases the inherent risk of the firm as well. Firm A has a higher degree of operating leverage because of its higher fixed costs, and that makes it less financially stable than firm B. One way to see this is by a break-even analysis. In the event of an economic downturn, firm A would be more adversely affected than firm B. Because of its higher amount of fixed costs, firm A must produce and sell more widgets than Firm B to reach its operating break-even point (where EBIT = 0). The operating break-even point, in units is:

$$Q^* = \frac{F}{P - V}$$

Firm A's operating break-even point is:

$$Q^* = \frac{35,000}{5.00 - 1.00} = 8,750 \text{ widgets}$$

whereas firm B's operating break-even point is only:

$$Q^* = \frac{15,000}{5.00 - 3.00} = 7,500 \text{ widgets}$$

In the event of an economic downturn, firm A would have a more difficult time earning an positive operating profit, because of its higher break-even point, than would firm B. An additional measure of the inherent risk with operating leverage is that the variability of the firm's EBIT (as measured by standard deviation) is higher.

In summary, higher fixed costs result in higher degrees of operating leverage. This not only magnifies the firm's EBIT, but increases its operating, or business risk, as well.

FINANCIAL LEVERAGE

Financial leverage results from financing the firm's assets with debt or preferred stock. Similar to operating leverage, financial leverage also magnifies the firm's returns and increases its risk as well. Financial leverage is concerned with the relationship between EBIT and EPS. Using debt or preferred stock

financing magnifies EPS for a given change in EBIT. Recall the two firms, A and B. At production levels of 10,000 widgets, they both had operating earnings (EBIT) of $5,000. Let us assume that both firms have total assets of $40,000. Table 3 shows how the $40,000 of assets are financed for both firms. Firm A is financed with $10,000 of debt which carries an annual interest cost of eight percent, and $30,000 of stockholders' equity (3,000 shares), firm B is financed entirely with $40,000 of stockholders' equity (4,000 shares).

Table 3 Asset Financing		
	Firm A	Firm B
Long-term debt (8%)	$10,000	$ 0
Stockholders' equity	30,000	40,000
Total liabilities & equity	40,000	40,000

Firm A, which uses some debt to finance its assets, is said to have financial leverage, which magnifies the EPS and increases the firm's risk. Table 4 shows the results of financial leverage on the firm's earnings.

Panel A shows that as a result of the $800 interest expense from the debt ($10,000 $\times$ .08 = $800), firm A's earnings per share are lower than firm B's. However, because firm A is financially leveraged, an increase in EBIT will result in a greater increase in EPS. Panel B shows the results of a 10% increase in EBIT for both firms. Firm A's EPS increased from $0.84 to $0.94, an 11.9% increase, while firm B's EPS increased from $0.75 to $0.825, or 10.0%, the same as the increase in EBIT.

This magnification in EPS can be quantified by the degree of financial leverage.

$$DFL = \frac{Q(P - V) - F}{Q(P - V) - F - I} \qquad (3)$$

where Q = the production quantity,
P = the sales price per unit,
V = the variable cost per unit,
F = the total fixed costs,
I = the annual interest expense on the debt.

Firm A's degree of financial leverage is:

$$DFL = \frac{10,000(5.00 - 1.00) - 35,000}{10,000(5.00 - 1.00) - 35,000 - 800}$$
$$= \frac{5,000}{4,200} = 1.1905$$

The interpretation is that a 1 percent change in EBIT will result in a 1.19 percent change in EPS in the

Table 4
Illustration of Financial Leverage

Panel A Operating Income = $5,000

	Firm A	Firm B
Operating Income (EBIT)	$5,000	$5,000
less: interest expense	800	0
Earnings before taxes (EBT)	4,200	5,000
Less: taxes (40%)	1,680	2,000
Net Profits after taxes (NPAT)	2,520	3,000
÷ number of shares	÷ 3,000	÷ 4,000
Earnings per share (EPS)	$0.84	$0.75

Panel B Operating Income = $5,500

	Firm A	Firm B
Operating Income (EBIT)	$5,500	$5,500
less: interest expense	800	0
Earnings before taxes (EBT)	4,700	5,500
Less: taxes (40%)	1,880	2,200
Net Profits after taxes (NPAT)	2,820	3,300
÷ number of shares	÷ 3,000	÷ 4,000
Earnings per share (EPS)	$0.94	$0.825
Increase in EPS	$0.10	$0.075
Percentage increase in EPS	11.90%	10.0%

same direction. Therefore, if firm A's EBIT level were to increase by 5 percent, EPS would increase by 5 × 1.19 = 5.95 percent. Like operating leverage, financial leverage is also a double-edged sword; if EBIT decreases, EPS will decrease by a factor of 1.19 percent.

Firm B's degree of financial leverage is 1.0, meaning that they do not use any debt or preferred stock financing. Any change in firm B's level of EBIT will be reflected by exactly the same change in its EPS.

$$DFL = \frac{10,000(5.00 - 3.00) - 15,000}{10,000(5,000 - 3.00) - 15,000} = \frac{5,000}{5,000} = 1.0$$

Financial leverage occurs for the same reason that operating leverage occurs, namely fixed costs. But in the case of financial leverage, it is fixed financing costs, rather than fixed operating costs, which cause the leverage. Debt is a fixed cost source of funds. Regardless of the firm's performance, debtholders earn the same fixed return. Therefore, in the absence of defaulting on its interest payment, the cost of debt financing to the firm is fixed.

Preferred stock financing has exactly the same effect. Since preferred stock dividends are constant, the cost of this form of financing is also fixed, and therefore increases the firm's financial leverage. Equation 3 can be easily modified to include preferred stock financing:

$$DFL = \frac{Q(P - V) - F}{Q(P - V) - F - I - P} \quad (4)$$

where P = the total annual preferred stock dividends.

Alternatively, equation 5 can be used to calculate a firm's degree of financial leverage directly from the partial income statements.

$$DFL = \frac{\%\Delta EPS}{\%\Delta EBIT} \frac{\dfrac{EPS_{NEW} - EPS_{OLD}}{EPS_{OLD}}}{\dfrac{EBIT_{NEW} - EBIT_{OLD}}{EBIT_{OLD}}} \quad (5)$$

For Firm A:

$$DFL = \frac{\dfrac{0.94 - 0.84}{0.84}}{\dfrac{5,500 - 5,000}{5,000}} = \frac{11.90}{0.10} = 1.190$$

For Firm B:

$$DFL = \frac{\dfrac{0.825 - 0.75}{0.75}}{\dfrac{5,500 - 5,000}{5,000}} = \frac{0.1}{0.1} = 1.0$$

Financial leverage increases the returns to the shareholders (EPS) and also increases the firm's operating risk. Firms that use financial leverage run the risk that their operating income will be insufficient to cover the fixed charges on debt and/or preferred stock financing. Financial leverage can become especially burdensome during an economic downturn. Even if the firm has sufficient earnings to cover its fixed financial costs, its returns could be decreased during economically difficult times due to shareholders' residual claims to dividends.

Generally, if the firm's return on assets (EBIT/Total Assets) is greater than the pre-tax cost of debt (interest percentage), the financial leverage effect will be favorable. The opposite of course is also true; if the firm's return on assets is less than its interest cost of debt, the financial leverage effect will decrease the returns to the common shareholders.

TOTAL LEVERAGE

The two types of leverage explored so far can be combined into an overall measure of leverage called total leverage. Recall that operating leverage was concerned with the relationship between sales and EBIT, and financial leverage was concerned with the relationship between EBIT and EPS. Total leverage is therefore concerned with the relationship between sales and EPS. Specifically, it is concerned with the sensitivity of EPS to a given change in sales.

The degree of total leverage is defined as the percentage change in EPS for a given change in sales, and can be calculated using equation 6:

$$DTL = \frac{Q(P - V)}{Q(P - V) - F - I} \qquad (6)$$

Equation 6 contains the numerator from the degree of operating leverage formula (Equation 1) and the denominator from the degree of financial leverage formula (Equation 2). This results from multiplying the two formulas together. In fact, a simpler method of obtaining the degree of total leverage is to multiply the firm's degree of operating leverage by its degree of financial leverage (DOL × DFL). For Firm A:

$$DTL = DOL \times DFL = 8 \times 1.19 = 9.52$$

which can be interpreted as a 1 percent change in sales that will result in a 9.52 percent change in EPS in the same direction. For Firm B:

$$DTL = DOL \times DFL = 4 \times 1.0 = 4.0$$

A 1 percent change in its sales will result in only a 4.0 percent change in its EPS. This occurs because firm B has a lower degree of operating leverage than firm A, and no financial leverage. As can be seen from the DTL formula, the relationship between operating leverage and financial leverage is multiplicative, not additive. A firm with little operating leverage can attain a high degree of total leverage by using a relatively high amount of debt. These same DTL results can also be obtained directly from the income statements using DTL's definitional formula.

$$DTL = \frac{\%\Delta EPS}{\%\Delta SALES} \qquad (7)$$

Using the results of %Δ Sales and %Δ EPS for Firm A obtained earlier:

$$DTL_{FIRM\ A} = \frac{\dfrac{0.94 - 0.84}{0.84}}{\dfrac{55,000 - 50,000}{50,000}} = \frac{0.119}{0.1} = 1.190$$

For firm B, a 10 percent increase in sales results in EPS increasing from $0.75 to $1.05. Its DTL is:

$$DTL_{FIRM\ B} = \frac{\dfrac{1.05 - 0.75}{0.75}}{\dfrac{55,000 - 50,000}{50,000}} = \frac{0.4}{0.1} = 4.0$$

IMPLICATIONS

Total risk can be divided into two parts: business risk and financial risk. Business risk refers to the stability of the firm's assets if it uses no debt or preferred stock financing. This is the risk inherent in the firm's operations. It includes operating leverage as well as other factors such as the variability in demand, sales price, and input costs. When a firm uses debt or preferred stock financing (financial risk), additional risk is placed on the firm's common shareholders. They demand a higher expected return for assuming this additional risk, which in turn, raises the firm's cost of equity capital. Firms with high degrees of business risk therefore tend to be financed with relatively low amounts of debt capital. The opposite also holds; firms with low amounts of business risk can afford to use more debt financing while keeping total risk at tolerable levels.

[James A. Gerhardinger]

FURTHER READING:

Dugan, Michael T., and Keith A. Shriver. "An Empirical Comparison of Alternative Methods for Estimating the Degree of Operating Leverage," *Financial Review*, May, 1992, pp. 309-321.

Jaedicke, Robert K., and Alexander A. Robichek. "Cost-Volume-Profit Analysis Under Conditions of Uncertainty," *Accounting Review*. October, 1964, pp. 917-926.

Shalit, Sol S. "On the Mathematics of Financial Leverage," *Financial Management*. Spring 1975, pp. 57-66.

LEVERAGED BUYOUTS

During the 1980s, leveraged buyouts (LBOs) became increasingly common and increased substantially in size. In a leveraged buyout, a company or division is purchased by a group of private investors, which frequently includes the **management** of the economic unit. To demonstrate their commitment, the managers will normally be expected to purchase a significant equity stake in the transaction. This will usually, however, buy a disproportionately large amount of the equity. The transaction is financed with large amounts of **debt** and little **equity**, and the firm ceases to be publicly traded. The interest and borrowings can be repaid from the target's cash flow, with tax benefits obtainable for the interest payments. Subsequently, once the debt is paid down, the organizers of the buyout attempt to take the firm public again in three to five years.

A successful buyout candidate has certain characteristics that can increase its chances of surviving and providing returns to lenders, investors, and managers. Factors that can be found in a successful LBO include: (1) proven earnings growth; (2) a strong market position; (3) an asset base indicating unused debt capacity; (4) an established, unconcentrated customer base; and (5) proven management.

The occurrence of LBOs is positively related to the existence of target firms that have large and stable cash flows. The occurrence of LBOs is positively related to expected future tax savings. Finally, LBO incidence increases when there is potential for employment reductions and redeployment, particularly among corporate staff. Therefore, after the LBO, there should be significant improvements in profitability and operating efficiency.

Empirical studies indicate that the acquired firms' shareholders earn large positive abnormal returns from leveraged buyouts. Similarly, the post-buyout investors in these transactions often earn large excess returns over the period from the buyout completion date to the date of an initial public offering or resale.

SOURCES OF VALUE IN LBOS

Studies have identified several potential sources of value in leveraged buyout transactions. These include: (1) wealth transfers from old public shareholders to the buyout group, (2) wealth transfers from public bondholders to the investor group, (3) wealth creation from improved incentives for managerial **decision making**, and (4) wealth transfers from the government via tax advantages. These potential motivations for leveraged buyout transactions are not mutually exclusive; it is possible that a combination of these may occur in a given LBO.

Much controversy regarding LBOs has resulted from the concern that senior executives negotiating the sale of the company to themselves are engaged in self-dealing. On one hand, the managers have a **fiduciary duty** to their shareholders to sell the company at the highest possible price. On the other hand, they have an incentive to minimize what they pay for the shares. Accordingly, it has been suggested that management takes advantage of superior information about a firm's intrinsic value. The evidence, however, indicates that the premiums paid in leveraged buyouts compare favorably with those in inter-firm mergers that are characterized by arm's-length negotiations between the buyer and seller.

Since leveraged buyout transactions are financed largely with debt, the existing debt of the buyout company, if not covenant protected, becomes more risky and less valuable. Accordingly, it has been argued that there is a transfer of wealth from bondholders to pre- and post-buyout equity investors. The empirical evidence, however, indicates that the transfers from bondholders do not appear to be a major source of value. These studies find that many leveraged buyout companies do not have any publicly traded debt in their capital structures. Moreover, the losses experienced by those firms with noncovenant protected, publicly traded debt are much smaller than the positive abnormal returns earned by equity investors.

Another potential source of value in leveraged buyouts is derived from the reduction in agency costs that accompanies management's increased ownership stake in the company. In a publicly traded company, managers typically own only a small percentage of the common shares, and therefore can share only a small fraction of the gains resulting from improved managerial performance. After an LBO, however, executives can realize substantial financial gains from enhanced performance. This improvement in financial incentives for the firm's managers should result in greater effort on the part of management. The empirical evidence is consistent with efficiency gains in leveraged buyout transactions.

The increased levels of debt that the new company supports after the LBO also decrease taxable income leading to lower tax payments. Therefore, the interest tax shield resulting from the higher levels of debt should enhance the value of firm. Studies indicate that tax advantages are a significant source of value in leveraged buyout transactions.

CRITICISM OF LBOS

Critics of leveraged buyouts argue that these transactions harm the long-term competitiveness of the firms involved. First, these firms are unlikely to have replaced operating assets since the firms' cash flow must be devoted to servicing the LBO-related debt. Thus, the property, plant, and equipment of the LBO firms are likely to have aged considerably during the time when the firm is privately held. In addition, expenditures for repair and maintenance may have been curtailed as well. Finally, it is possible that **research and development** expenditures have also been controlled. As a result, the future growth prospects of these firms may be significantly reduced.

Others argue that these transactions have a negative impact on the stakeholders of the firm. In many cases, LBOs lead to downsizing of operations, and many employees lose their jobs. In addition, some of the transactions have negative effects on the communities in which the firms are located.

Towards the end of the 1980s, the prices paid in leveraged buyouts increased, and buyout organizers invested less equity. As a result, a number of high-profile buyouts, such as Revco Drug Stores, filed for bankruptcy protection. Lenders reacted by tightening the supply of LBO credit and demanded changes in deal structures to lower risk.

SEE ALSO: Junk Bonds; Management Buyouts; Restrictive Covenants

[Robert T. Kleiman]

FURTHER READING:

Fox, Isaac, and Alfred Marcus. "The Causes and Consequences of Leveraged Management Buyouts." *Academy of Management Review.* January, 1992, pp. 62-85.

Kaplan, Stephen. "The Effect of Management Buyouts on Operating Performance and Value." *Journal of Financial Economics.* October, 1989, pp. 217-254.

Latif, Yahya. "What Ails the Leveraged Buyouts of the 1980s."
Secured Lender. November/December, 1990, pp. 56-60.

LEVERAGED RECAPITALIZATIONS

During the latter half of the 1980s, leveraged recapitalizations (recaps) emerged as a popular response of U.S. companies to the increasingly competitive operating environment. In a leveraged recapitalization, a firm replaces the majority of its **equity** with a package of debt securities consisting of both senior bank debt and subordinated debentures. Although these transactions could be either defensive or preemptive maneuvers, the vast majority of leveraged recapitalizations were employed as a defensive tactic to ward off hostile **takeovers**. The financial leveraging of the firm discouraged corporate raiders who could no longer borrow against the assets of the target firm to finance the acquisition.

Candidates for a leveraged recapitalization should have a relatively debt-free capital structure, steady and predictable cash flows, and an experienced and capable management team. The majority of firms undertaking these transactions were in mature, slow growth, non-technology-based industries that do not require substantial ongoing capital expenditures to remain competitive.

TYPES OF LEVERAGED RECAPITALIZATIONS

There are two generic categories of leveraged recapitalizations: leveraged cashouts and leveraged share repurchases. A leveraged cashout (LCO) involves a debt-financed special dividend paid by a firm to its shareholders. In addition, existing shareholders also receive a "stub," a stock certificate that represents ownership in the restructured company. Since the "stubs" are publicly traded, shareholders continue to have the opportunity to share in the future gains (or losses) of the firm. Leveraged cashouts also allow **management** to increase their proportional shareholdings instead of receiving the cash payout.

In a leveraged share repurchase (LSR), the company repurchases a significant percentage of its **common stock** through a **tender offer** in a transaction financed with bank and /or high yield **debt**. Like the LCO, an LSR replaces outside equity with debt which has the impact of significantly increasing the financial leverage of the firm. Assuming that the firm is able to earn a return on its operating assets greater than the after-tax cost of debt, leveraged share repurchases should result in higher earnings per share due to the reduction in the number of shares outstanding after the transaction.

The structure of leveraged recapitalization transactions is similar to that employed in **leveraged buyouts** (LBOs). In both cases, the firm significantly increases its financial leverage, and senior managers/employees generally receive additional equity ownership in the corporation. The tax shields associated with the additional debt used to finance the transactions are one source of additional value. Moreover, the additional equity interests of managers and employees should improve incentives to enhance productivity. since the new organizational structure more closely links managerial rewards to employee performance. Both LBOs and recaps are accompanied by a restructuring in which the company sells off assets that are redundant or no longer a strategic fit in order to reduce debt. Like leveraged buyouts, studies of leveraged recapitalization announcements indicate that these transactions are associated with increases in firms' stock prices. Furthermore, the wealth of bondholders declines, but not a significant amount.

Leveraged recapitalizations, however, differ from leveraged buyouts in a number of fundamental ways. First, following a leveraged recapitalization, the firm remains publicly traded. This differs from an LBO in which the firm is taken private. With a recap, the company continues to incur the costs of providing information to shareholders as well as the expenses associated with satisfying reporting requirements of the **Securities and Exchange Commission (SEC)** for publicly held firms. Second, companies that undertake leveraged recapitalizations still maintain access to the public capital markets which may permit these firms to raise capital on more attractive terms than private firms. Third, in comparison to leveraged recapitalizations, leveraged buyouts may impose costs on managers by forcing managers to hold portfolios that are poorly diversified and/or illiquid due to reduced share marketability of the nonpublic shares. Thus, there is less potential for costly disagreements among stockholders in a recap since shareholders can readily sell their holdings if they disagree with corporate policies.

LEVERAGED RECAPITALIZATIONS AND OPERATING PERFORMANCE

Financial theory suggests that leveraged recapitalizations should result in greater operating efficiency. First, corporate managers' percentage of ownership normally increases in LCOs because executives receive new shares of equivalent value in lieu of cash. Consequently, managers have a reduced incentive to take advantage of corporate perquisites (such as large expense accounts or support staffs) in a manner that reduces corporate profitability. The additional equity ownership also provides performance incentives to managers and employees since their economic well-being is now more closely linked to the firm's performance. Second, the debt taken on in leveraged recapitalizations effectively compels management to pay out future free cash flows. Accordingly, these transactions reduce the cash flow available for discretionary spending making it less likely that management will spend money on subpar investment projects. Third, high levels of financial leverage have a powerful disciplining effect since default on the debt could cost managers their managerial independence and even their jobs. Risk-averse managers, fearing the high debt level of the newly recapitalized company, should have a strong motivation to generate additional cash flows.

The principal disadvantage associated with these transactions is the risk incurred from the large amount of debt. In considering a recap, the company must ensure that its debt capacity is sufficient to service the additional debt. In order to meet its debt obligations, a highly leveraged company needs steady and predictable cash flows. A firm that encounters cash flow problems jeopardizes its future operating flexibility, and may be forced to sell assets or declare bankruptcy. Therefore, following a recapitalization, management needs to focus on the fundamentals of the business, selling underperforming or underutilized assets and paying down debt quickly.

Empirical studies indicate that managers significantly improve their management of the firm's **working capital** after undertaking a leveraged recapitalization. Managers substantially decrease days of sales outstanding and improve inventory turnover. In addition, firms are able to generate more sales per dollar of assets. The results for profitability measures that are calculated before interest expense indicate that both the operating return on assets and operating profit margin increase. This suggests that firms increase their gross profit margins and reduce their selling, general, and administrative expense following the recapitalizations.

Improvement in post-recapitalization cash flows, however, appears to be achieved at the expense of long-term viability. Following recaps, firms experience significant decreases in sales and capital expenditures reflecting lower levels of discretionary investment spending and asset sales. This reduction in capital expenditures could have negative implications for the long-term value of these firms.

[Robert T. Kleiman]

FURTHER READING:

Gupta, Atul, and Leonard Rosenthal. "Ownership Structure, Leverage, and Firm Value: The Case of Leveraged Recapitalizations." *Financial Management*. Autumn, 1991, pp. 69-83.

Handa, Puneet, and A. R. Radhakrishnan. "An Empirical Investigation of Leveraged Recapitalizations with Cash Payout as Takeover Defense." *Financial Management*. Autumn, 1991, pp. 58-68.

Kleiman, Robert T. "Shareholder Gains from Leveraged Cash-Outs." *Journal of Applied Corporate Finance*. Spring, 1988, pp. 46-53.

LIABILITIES

A liability is a **debt** assumed by a business entity as a result of its borrowing activities or other fiscal obligations (such as funding pension plans for its employees). Liabilities are paid off under either short-term or long-term arrangements. The amount of time allotted to pay off the liability is typically determined by the size of the debt; large amounts of money usually are borrowed under long-term plans.

Payment of a liability generally involves payment of the total sum of the amount borrowed. In addition, the business entity that provides the money to the borrowing institution typically charges interest, figured as a percentage of the amount that has been lent.

A company's liabilities are critical factors in understanding its status in any industry in which it is involved. As John Brozovsky noted in *Journal of Commercial Lending*, "a basic understanding of **ac-**

counting for liabilities is necessary to assess the viability of any company. Companies are required to follow certain accounting rules; however, the rules allow considerable flexibility in how a company accounts for liabilities.''

CURRENT LIABILITIES

Current liabilities are short-term financial obligations that are paid off within one year or one current operating cycle, whichever is longer. (A normal operating cycle, while it varies from industry to industry, is the time from a company's initial investment in inventory to the time of collection of cash from sales of that inventory or of products created from that inventory.) Typical types of current liabilities include such accrued expenses as wages, **taxes**, and interest payments not yet paid; accounts payable; short-term notes; cash **dividends**; and revenues collected in advance of actual rendering of services or delivery of goods.

Economists, creditors, investors, and other members of the financial community all regard a business entity's current liabilities as an important indicator of its overall fiscal health. One financial indicator associated with liabilities that is often studied is known as **working capital**. Working capital refers to the dollar difference between a business's total current liabilities and its total current assets. Another financial barometer known as the current ratio also examines a company's current liabilities. Creditors and others compute the current ratio by dividing total current assets by total current liabilities, which provides the company's ratio of assets to liabilities. For example, a company with $1 million in current assets and $250,000 in current liabilities would have a four-to-one ratio of assets to liabilities.

LONG-TERM LIABILITIES

Liabilities that are not paid off within a year, or within a business's operating cycle, are known as long-term or noncurrent liabilities. Such liabilities often involve large sums of money necessary to undertake major expansion of a business, replace assets, or make a purchase of significant assets. Such debt typically requires a longer period of time to pay off. Examples of long-term liabilities include notes, mortgages, lease obligations, deferred income taxes payable, and pensions and other postretirement benefits.

When debt that has been classified as long-term is paid off within the next year, the amount of that paid-off liability should be reported by the company as a current liability in order to reflect the expected drain on current assets. An exception to this rule, however, comes into effect if a company decides to pay off the liability through the transfer of noncurrent assets that have been previously accumulated for that very purpose.

CONTINGENT LIABILITIES

A third kind of liability accrued by companies is known as a contingent liability. The term refers to instances in which a company reports that there is a possible liability for an event, transaction, or incident that has already taken place; the company, however, does not yet know whether a financial drain on its resources will result. It also is often uncertain of the size of the financial obligation or the exact time in which the obligation will have to be paid.

Contingent liabilities often come into play when a lawsuit or other legal measure has been taken against the company in question. An as yet unresolved suit initiated against a car manufacturer for an alleged defect in one of its products would be one example of a contingent liability. Environmental cleanup and/or protection responsibility sometimes falls under this classification as well, if the monetary impact on a company is uncertain.

Companies are legally bound to report contingent liabilities. They are typically recorded in notes that are attached to a company's **financial statement** than as an actual part of the financial statement. If a loss due to a contingent liability is seen as probable, however, it should be included as part of the company's financial statement.

[Laurie Collier Hillstrom]

FURTHER READING:

Brozovsky, John. ''A Review of Changes Affecting Accounting for Liabilities.'' *Journal of Commercial Lending*. March, 1994, pp. 48-53.

Smith, Jay M., Jr., and K. Fred Skousen. *Intermediate Accounting*. Cincinnati: South-Western Publishing Co., 1987.

Welsch, Glenn A., Robert N. Anthony, and Daniel G. Short. *Fundamentals of Financial Accounting*. Homewood, IL: Irwin, 1984.

Williams, Georgina, and Thomas J. Phillips, Jr. ''Cleaning Up Our Act: Accounting for Environmental Liabilities.'' *Management Accounting*. February, 1994, pp. 30-3.

Winicur, Barbara. ''Long Term Liabilities.'' *National Public Accountant*. January, 1993, pp. 6, 8.

LICENSING AGREEMENTS

Although licensing agreements were technically in existence in the United States since the first **copyright** and patent were issued in 1790 and the first American trademark was registered in 1870, licensing agreements in the late twentieth century became vital to safeguard intellectual property rights (IPRs) because of virtually uncontrolled access to information. As the **Internet** has expanded and more and more information has become available to more and more people, the problems associated with licensing agreements have increased. Licensing agreements are considered to be divided into five basic categories: copyright licensing, patent licensing, trademark licensing, software licensing, and merchandise licensing.

COPYRIGHT LICENSING

Copyrights apply primarily to original works of artistic merit such as books, plays, magazine and newspaper articles, musical scores, photography, paintings, and sculpture. Contemporary law governing copyright protection has been based on the Statute of Anne, enacted by the British Parliament in 1709. Of the many more recent laws enacted in several countries since then, the most notable changes are contained in the U.S. Copyright Act of 1976 and Canada's Copyright Act of 1985. The Copyright Act of 1976 clearly confirmed that a copyright owner had the following exclusive rights to his or her works:

1. The right to make copies of the work.

2. The right to prepare derivatives (arrangements) of the work.

3. The right to distribute copies of the work to the public.

4. The right to perform the work publicly.

5. The right to display the work publicly.

Church services in particular received two specific exemptions from these exclusive rights:

1. The right to perform a work (songs could be freely sung during a service).

2. The right to display a work (the music director could visually project songs, but the copy of the songs projected had to be legally authorized).

Copyright law is needed to promote the use of copyrights while at the same time protecting the rights of the copyright owner. Basically, a copyright is an exclusive right given to an author of an original work. It is an asset, and a legal interest, protected by law. Included in the exclusive rights given to the copyright owner is the right to copy the work into any form, including in print, on screen, or on tape.

PLAYS. Since copyright laws apply to plays, regardless of who stages the play or where it is performed, playwrights usually rely on play-leasing companies to protect their rights by tracking all productions of their plays and demanding royalties for any play performed before an audience—unless that audience is a school class. Licenses to perform plays do not permit modification of the original script, so that producers and performers who wish to modify scripts can do so only with the permission of the playwright.

MUSIC. In the music field, copying music might have initially been rare. Hymnals, which provide the main access to copyright usage, were purchased by churches and represented a fair way to compensate religious song composers because these composers received a royalty for each hymnal purchased. But the information explosion disrupted this arrangement. With affordable offset printing appearing on the scene, weekly bulletins and liturgies were able to be self-produced by churches, and songs for worship began to be included in bulletins or on songsheet inserts by church song leaders. Helping to expand the convenience of copying music were photocopiers, visual projectors, computers, MIDI (Musical Instrument Digital Interface) instruments, and recorders. Soon, songs could be copied onto overhead transparencies, slides, custom in-house songbooks, and tapes.

Although these copying practices greatly benefited many church activities, enabling a quicker exposure of songs to church congregations, they also deprived songwriters and publishers of revenue. In 1981, a church in Chicago, Illinois, was sued for copyright violations and was ordered by the courts in 1984 to pay $190,400 for making unauthorized music copies for congregational singing. Clearly, the copyright law was not working—it was equitable but not very pragmatic. The copyright law stated that express written permission from the rightful song owner had to be granted before a copy could be made. But obtaining this written permission could often turn out to be an administrative morass.

Christian Copyright Licensing International (CCLI) proved to be a viable solution to this liturgical dilemma. CCLI was founded in 1988 by Howard Rachinski, a songwriter, arranger, record producer, retail sales manager, and music director. It is (a nonprofit organization which acts as a clearinghouse for publishers and copyright owners). A church pays CCLI an annual license fee of from $40 to $795 (assessed according to the size of the congregation) for being able to ''use'' (copy) certain songs. The license fee is then distributed as royalties to all copyright owners involved in the program. The Church Copyright License from CCLI permits the church to:

1. Print songs in bulletins, liturgies, songsheets, and songbooks for the congregation.

2. Make transparencies, slides, or other visual projections of songs for use in the worship service.

3. Make customized instrumental and vocal arrangements if no published version is available.

4. Make worship service tapes for missions, shut-ins, visitors, or friends.

With CCLI, a church can obtain noncommercial permission to use more than 125,000 songs from more than 1,200 Christian publishers, simply by obtaining a CCLI limited license. For individual copyrights, CCLI's per song noncommercial print license was $5.00 per song, per year. For photocopies of the songs printed in CCLI's songsheets or songbooks, the charge was $.50 per copy. So successful were CCLI's efforts as a clearinghouse that, in the early 1990s, it opened branches in England, Australia, and New Zealand.

In 1993, an interesting controversy was resolved concerning music licensing when a U.S. District Court for the Southern District of New York approved an interim decision allowing television stations to pay the American Society of Composers, Authors, and Publishers (ASCAP) for licensed music on a per-program basis instead of paying ASCAP blanket charges. Formerly. television stations had to pay ASCAP a percentage of their net revenue for using licensed music. Under the new decision, stations can determine how much revenue is owed ASCAP by calculating revenues derived from local and syndicated programs that use music unlicensed by ASCAP.

A new music copyright agreement was reached in 1993 when Broadcast Music, Inc. (BMI), and the Higher Education Music Copyright Task Force signed a new five-year BMI Music Performance Agreement for Colleges and Universities. Under this licensing agreement, copyrighted music is subject to the provisions of copyright law and can only be performed in public with the permission of the composer. Music played on college radio stations constitutes a public performance together with background music from compact discs, tapes, and videocassettes. Fees for a one-tier agreement cost 16.5 cents per student, for a two-tier agreement 14.5 cents per student (but with additional quarterly dues).

BMI took a particularly forceful stance toward its commercial-establishment licensees, employing ''music police'' to enforce its agreements. In trying to explain copyright law and to collect royalty fees from commercial establishments for the use of live or recorded music, Meryl Clement, BMI's sole licensing representative in New Jersey in 1994, sometimes met with annoyance or bewilderment from bar and restaurant owners. At issue, according to the majority of restaurateurs, was the ''unjust and capricious'' confusion of fees for the use of live or recorded music. BMI felt the problem arose from association members' extraordinarily lax compliance with copyright law, which required them to pay royalties for the commercial use of music. The association members won a minor victory when the New Jersey General Assem-

bly overwhelmingly approved a bill requiring licensing firms to provide much more information to restaurateurs. As a result, BMI changed its tactics, allowing a reporter to accompany Clement on her rounds and to interview the restaurant and tavern owners.

Restaurateurs complained. Stephen Gross, owner of Stevie G's in Union Beach, New Jersey, balked at having to pay $263 to BMI to cover a 12-month stretch but complied when Clement finally came to visit him. Many of the restaurateurs complained about the purported complexity of the fee structure, maintaining that competitors obtained sweetheart deals from agents or evaded payment entirely. In response, Clement steadfastly denied that she would ever offer such deals, as they might reflect unfavorably on her and on BMI. Furthermore, she pointed to BMI's one-page form, which asked business owners to state their annual use of music. For live music, the fees were based on how much an establishment paid performers; such fees ranged from $175 a year to more than $3,000. For recorded music, the BMI form contained several columns, covering music, music plus visuals, music plus dancing, or all three together. Fees were assessed according to an establishment's legal occupancy, and charges were lower for those that already were paying to use live music. In venues that did not have live performances, BMI's annual charge in 1994 for other music uses ran from $195 to $2,315. Many restaurateurs found the prices too high, but Larry Fidel, vice president of the restaurateurs' association, tacitly acknowledged that some association members protested simply because they were trying to evade royalty payments.

In June 1994 an announcement was made that the U.S. Department of Commerce would replace the compulsory license provision for musical works contained in the U.S. Copyright Law to enhance competition in the music industry. Formerly, the compulsory license had allowed musicians to make cover versions of musical compositions recorded previously. Some industry observers, however, felt that the repeal of this right might be used by recording companies to claim a monopoly over compositions and to use this control to increase mechanical rates. In July 1994 the American Federation of Television and Radio Artists (AFTRA) and the American Federation of Musicians (AFM) called for the revision of existing copyright laws. The groups believed that a digital-performance right in sound recordings should be introduced in order to enable featured artists, musicians, and backup singers to collect compensation whenever their songs were played on the radio. Under then-current law, only the music publishers and songwriters were rewarded for airplay of songs. Although past efforts for the introduction of similar laws had proved futile, many industry observers believed that the 1994 Commerce

Department initiative had a better chance of becoming law because of the outlook of the Clinton administration.

PATENT LICENSING

An interesting aspect of licensing agreements which involved **patents** was the legal tiff regarding states' rights in patent, trademark, and copyright violations. As opportunities to participate in these agreements increased, **intellectual property** rights (IPRs) became more important to states and governmental agencies, since licensing technology could help to raise general revenue, help specific research, or target economic development within a state.

A common example of state involvement with IPRs were licensing agreements between state-affiliated universities and private entities involving technology developed entirely, or in part, through a state university's research program. In this arrangement, the state owned and enforced a portfolio of IPRs through the university. So common was this arrangement that universities employed organizations or formed departments whose sole purpose was to raise revenue through the sale of licensing or intellectual property. Because the enforcement of patents and copyrights was subject to the exclusive jurisdiction of the federal courts, these courts, therefore, effectively determined the market value of state-owned intellectual property through their judgments on validity and infringement. Nevertheless, since states were not subject to federal court jurisdiction to the same extent as private entities due to the state sovereign immunity doctrine incorporated in the Eleventh Amendment to the U.S. Constitution, the market value of state-owned patents and copyrights was different than that of privately-held patents and copyrights.

The Eleventh Amendment prohibited suits against states in limited circumstances, specifically prohibiting federal courts from exercising jurisdiction over consenting states in suits for damages. In 1985, in *Atascadero State Hospital v. Scanlon*, the Supreme Court upheld the applicability of the Eleventh Amendment to patents and copyrights and ruled that states were liable for copyright infringement, thus challenging state sovereignty. In February 1989, the Copyright Remedy Clarification Act (CRCA) was introduced in the U.S. House of Representatives. This bill, which was eventually passed into law, implemented a recommendation from the U.S. Copyright Office that Congress expressly abrogate state sovereignty immunity in copyright infringement cases.

In the CRCA, state liability was defined only for infringement of copyrights. No comparable language existed in the copyright statute subjecting states to federal court invalidity claims. The proposed patent legislation had a similar scenario, whereby the U.S.

Code was amended so that "whoever" infringed would specifically include states and state instrumentalities. Also, the U.S. Code would be amended to maintain that states would be liable for "any other violation" of the patent statutes. Many intellectual property rights (IPR) lawyers felt that neither the copyright legislation existing in 1992 nor the proposed patent legislation illustrated any attempt by Congress to extend the abrogation of the Eleventh Amendment for states as infringers to validity claims against states as property owners. These IPR lawyers felt, therefore, that states defending the validity of their patents would still be able to raise the Eleventh Amendment as a bar to suit.

In *Atascadero State Hospital v. Scanlon*, the Supreme Court's decision changed the status of state-owned patents and copyrights, in that it permitted states to avoid infringement and validity claims in federal courts through the Eleventh Amendment. But this avoidance raised the value of state-owned intellectual property with respect to privately-owned intellectual property. Recognizing the economic harm such state protection could impose on private owners of copyrights, Congress abrogated the Eleventh Amendment for claims of state copyright infringement through the Copyright Remedy Clarification Act (CRCA) in February 1989. This legislation created a problem, however, in that Congress might not have been constitutionally authorized to enact it. And, even if Congress were authorized to enact it, the legislation did not address state Eleventh Amendment protection against copyright invalidity claims.

Likewise, the same authorization problem and validity insufficiency which existed in the CRCA existed with attempts in the early 1990s to abrogate the Eleventh Amendment in patent cases. Concerning both validity and infringement claims, the abrogation of the Eleventh Amendment was necessary to avoid creating a dual enforcement system for patents and copyrights in which the state-owned intellectual property was subject only to state court validity claims. The abrogation of the Eleventh Amendment, with regard to validity, was easily incorporated into the pending patent legislation which also abrogated the Eleventh Amendment for patent infringement claims. Many IPR attorneys felt that such legislation should be incorporated into both the copyright and patent statutes to avoid undermining the federal enforcement system for patents and copyrights.

TRADEMARK LICENSING

Trademark licensing agreements proved to be very profitable for small businesses. Agreements such as these gave a company the right to use a trademark, character, generic mark, descriptive mark, suggestive mark, arbitrary/fanciful mark, or trade dress and to manufacture that image. Characters which have enjoyed great licensing popularity in the twentieth century include Mickey Mouse, Shirley Temple, the Flintstones, Barbie, the Cabbage Patch Kids, the Teenage Mutant Ninja Turtles, and the Lion King.

In 1994, Sleepy Kids PLC was chosen by the Duches of York as the licensing agent for her a children's book character, Budgie, the Little Helicopter. Sleepy Kids PLC was the first private licensing company to enter into a commercial deal with the British royal family. Sleepy Kids, in turn, selected longtime partner Launey Hachmann and Harris, Inc., as its United States licensing and marketing agent for greeting cards, children's clothing, and other items. Indeed, the images of popular characters adorn everything from games to bicycles to sunglasses to jogging shoes; the possibilities in such trademark licensing agreements are endless.

These types of agreements also embrace such items as computer software. In 1993, for instance, Novell, Inc., relinquished its rights to the Unix name by turning over the trademark and branding rights to X/Open Co., Ltd. This transfer resulted in all Unix-named systems being tested and branded by X/Open. Spec 1170, which consisted of 1,170 common application programming interfaces (API) adopted by a consortium of computer manufacturers, was to be used to measure Unix compliance. The X Portability Guide's XPG3 Base would then be used to test products until full test suites for Unix conformity became available late in 1994. Although vendors were unlikely to change the names of their products that were Unix variants, they were predicted to call their products Unix-compliant. As part of this trademark licensing agreement, Novell was made a full shareholder and member of the board of X/Open.

SOFTWARE LICENSING

Licensing agreements for computer **software** entail responsibilities for both users and suppliers. Users need first to select the appropriate package for a specific task and then to abide by the licensing agreement. Software companies need to implement a system for verifying user compliance with the licensing agreement. In addition, software suppliers need to develop reasonable licensing terms that take into consideration the realities of computer usage, such as the nonsimultaneous use of a single license on a variety of systems, whether in the office, on a laptop, or at home. Users, moreover, need to employ procedures and policies for monitoring hard disks to assure compliance with the one-license, one-use principle. Because licensing agreements which prove too complicated and difficult are frequently broken, the language of these agreements needs to be plain and straightforward.

Software licensing agreements are frequently controversial. For instance, in 1992, IBM and Microsoft Corp. battled over the firms' cross-licensing pact—a licensing agreement that allowed each company the rights to the other's operating system code. Because the lack of Microsoft Windows support would have meant the loss of one-third of OS/2's integration, IBM felt it would have been affected more when the agreement was due to end sometime in 1993. Nevertheless, both companies claimed that the expiration of the agreement would not harm them. The controversy began when Microsoft announced in May 1992 that it would not renew the agreement. IBM then accused Microsoft of violating an agreement not to discuss the contract publicly and assured its customers that it would provide whatever compatibility was required.

Over time, licensing agreements have been greatly modified. For instance, in 1994, Digital Software developed a plan called Software Licensing Simplification to increase customers' purchasing flexibility and to decrease the cost. The plan offered four major agreement enhancements: simplified licensing structure, simplified pricing, simplified upgrades and migrations, and simplified licensing policies. A simplified licensing structure offered the consumer a logical way to license his or her software across common computing environments. Under this policy, licenses could be moved across a broad range of products without additional fees or paperwork. With simplified pricing, a single license could be used across a host of systems within a class, thereby giving the user greater flexibility to manage change, reducing upgrade costs, and providing the user with a wide range of computing performance under the same license. Simplified upgrades and migrations protected the customer's investment in Digital Software. Users choosing to upgrade or migrate would receive a credit equal to 75 percent of the price of the license being traded (up to a maximum of 75 percent of the price of the new license). Consumers could then apply this credit toward the purchase of a new license for the same products on a larger system class or a different hardware architecture or operating system. This policy applied to VAX, Alpha AXP, and MIPS platforms. Simplified licensing choices offered two options—license by system and license by user. Licenses based on system classes would replace the previous licenses based on multiple and ClusterWide ratings. In addition, Digital's popular Concurrent Use License (its primary user-based license) was extended to more products, including compilers, resulting in a reduction in incremental license fees and paperwork.

Other software companies were just as innovative in 1994. Novell, Inc., and Microsoft Corp. launched enterprise-level licensing programs for their high-end users late that year. Novell's first comprehensive licensing program integrated the firm's Master Licensing Agreement with WordPerfect's Corporate Advantage Program so that corporate users who subscribed to the revised program would be able to distribute, via CD-ROM, any application or system software program made by either WordPerfect or Novell. The two-CD set would be updated monthly. Moreover, Novell was expected that same month to introduce metering technology that would enable users to measure software usage. Similar to Microsoft's Select program (a multitiered program that enabled users to distribute software from a CD-ROM server), Novell's metering technology would pay an upfront cost based upon the number of desktops at their sites. In Microsoft's program, additional licenses were reported quarterly via a reseller; Novell, on the other hand, required its enterprise program users to report license purchases on a monthly basis. Lotus Development Corporation's Passport Program, which was similar to Microsoft's Select, required users to report software distribution only on an as-you-copy basis. Even though these programs competed with each other and thus saved licensees money, licenses found the compliance and reporting requirements to be quite cumbersome. Additionally, the lack of metering products to track usage left many sites effectively overlicensed. Gartner Group, Inc., estimated that most companies paid for at least 20 percent more software than they actually used.

Pressure from customers eventually forced Novell, Inc., to recast its pricing structure to better reflect the realities of enterprise client/server computing. As a result, all but the biggest of Novell's customers had to purchase NetWare 4.1—which became available in December 1994—through the old server-centric 3.x pricing plan which priced each server license based on how many users concurrently accessed that server. This old pricing policy would severely curtail users' ability freely to access servers enterprisewide; on which servers the users resided did not matter at all. Problematically, while Novell's Network Directory Services (NDS) technically provided that freedom, information systems (IS) staff would have to rein-in usage every time the total number of customers on a given server threatened to exceed the licensing agreement. Erik Dauplaise, a network administrator at Duracell, Inc.'s worldwide technology center in Needham, Massachusetts, believed that what Novell needed was a plan that charged according to the total number of users on the corporate network, as usage patterns dictated, so that if a customer had a 1,000-user license, 900 users could be accessing one server and 100 users the other, or vice versa. Concurrent pricing also forced companies to pay for the number of users accessing a server during peak times but did not compensate them for the valleys that occurred in between. Moreover, these peaks and valleys were

likely to become more numerous and less predictable as companies moved to what Novell called network-centric computing. Instead of being tied to one or two servers for their computing needs, users would hop around the network from, for example, a NetWare for Systems Application gateway on one server to a database on another. Many software consultants believed that one avenue which Novell definitely would not pursue was the per-node or client-based model that Microsoft used for its Windows NT server. In a scenario such as this one, companies paid a set license fee per client, with basic NT file and print services as part of the base price and additional services, such as Remote Access and SNA Server, costing extra. Deemed too burdensome, this scenario would require information systems professionals to keep securing additional licenses each time new users came on board.

IS managers, such as Michael McSorley at the McCarthy Building Company in St. Louis, were open-minded about software licensing agreements. McSorley used Novell's NetWare and Microsoft's Office suite at its sites. While McSorley stated that he would probably move to an enterprisewide agreement to take advantage of the software discounts, he would prefer to pay for the software he actually used. Nevertheless, he conceded that the scenario would not be possible for a multinational company unless tools to meter actual software usage were available.

Thus, the term "software licensing" typically provoked reactions of skepticism from IS managers because licenses many times have been linked to lawsuits, price inflation, and continuous procurement negotiation, resulting in a tendency toward disregard for contractual agreements. Many industry observers feel that software licensing practices are neither safeguarding the intellectual property rights of the vendors nor meeting the needs of the users because these licensing practices have their origins in a mainframe mind-set. Industry analysts feel that basic concepts about software types and potential service measures need to be formulated and models developed from pragmatic syntheses before workable licensing agreements benefiting both vendor and vendee can become a reality. By focusing on fundamental concepts, the software licensing debate can be reduced to important issues only.

MERCHANDISE LICENSING

A good example of this type of licensing lay in the pharmaceutical industry, where, in the early 1990s, the Roberts Pharmaceuticals Corporation marketed drugs researched by other companies. Specifically, Roberts licensed drugs from which significant development risks had already been removed and which were nearing completion of the federal approval process. Instead of using a manufacturing operation, Roberts employed subcontractors for receiving material, storage packaging, labeling, and manufacturing. In addition, the company maintained chemical trial arrangements with approximately 70 research centers. In the mid-1990s every conceivable commodity was capable of being licensed—even shrink wrap.

[Virginia L. Barnstorff]

FURTHER READING:

"AMD Denied Summary Judgment Motion in 287 Action." *Computer Lawyer*. June, 1992, pp. 33-34.

Anderson, Ken. "Preserve the Compulsory License." *Billboard*. June 11, 1994, p. 6.

Best, Jesse. "License to Save." *Computerworld*. July 13, 1992, p. 34.

Bond, Elaine. "Software Licensing: Let's Go Back to Square 1." *Computerworld*. February 15, 1993, p. 27.

Brandel, William. "Vendors to Lighten Up Licensing Woes." *Computerworld*. October 17, 1994, pp. 1, 12.

"The Church Musician and the Copyright Law." Church Music Publishers Association.

Coe, Steve. "Networks Hold Line on License Fees." *Broadcasting*. February 10, 1992, p. 3.

Corcoran, Cate. "Sun to Make Technology Available Sooner for Third Parties." *InfoWorld*. April 20, 1992, p. 30.

"Court Enters Judgment for Nintendo." *Computer Lawyer*. July, 1992, p. 39.

Crain, Rance. "Highly-Placed Friends Have Admen Sky High." *Advertising Age*. February 14, 1994, p. 20.

"Facing the Music Regarding the Copyright Law." Christian Copyright Licensing International.

Foisie, Geoffrey. "ASCAP Music Decision to TV Stations." *Broadcasting & Cable*. March 8, 1993, p. 42.

Foley, Mary Jo. "Novell Hands Off Unix Branding to X/Open." *PC Week*. October 18, 1993, p. 20.

Gilbreth, William J., and William H. Steinmetz. "The Patent Misuse Defense: Its Expansion and Contraction." *Journal of Proprietary Rights*. August, 1992, pp. 7-20.

Goldman, David, Aimee H. Weiss, and Robert A. Magnanini. "Hearings on Federal Software Protection." *Journal of Proprietary Rights*. June 1992, p. 32.

Haring, Bruce. "ASCAP Loses Battle for Cable Licensing Revenues." *Variety*. May 25, 1992, p. 67.

Harper, Blaney. "Intellectual Property and State Sovereignty Immunity: The Eleventh Amendment under Scrutiny." *Computer Lawyer*. July, 1992, pp. 21-27.

Hornaday, Ann. "Cashing in on the Little Green Turtles." *Working Woman*. February, 1992, p. 48.

Horwitt, Elisabeth. "Novell Recasts Enterprise Licensing Paradigm." *Computerworld*. October 17, 1994, p. 12.

Jessell, Harry A. "FCC Favorite Profited in License Deal." *Broadcasting*. January 11, 1993, p. 16.

Joester, Debra. "The Sheer Visibility of Successful, Coordinated Licensing Is a Strong Enticement for Signing Advertisers." *Broadcasting*. May 25, 1992, p. 55.

Kliewer, Warren. "Rights . . . & Wrongs: The Ethics and Etiquette of Performance Rights." *Back Stage*. May 7, 1993, p. 1.

Lindquist, Christopher, and Rosemary Hamilton. "Borland Offers Twist on Licensing Fees." *Computerworld*. July 27, 1992, p. 4.

——. "IBM, Microsoft Battle Rages on: Users Unfazed by the Outcome of Controversy Over Firms' Cross-Licensing Pact." *Computerworld*. June 8, 1992, p. 8.

McCallum, Jack. "Olympic-Sized Squabble." *Sports Illustrated*. March 23, 1992, p. 71.

McLeod, Jonah. "Killing the Competition Legally." *Electronics*. May 24, 1993, p. 15.

Meeks, Fleming. "San Francisco Stand-off." *Forbes*. September 2, 1991, p. 56.

"New Music Copyright Agreement Reached." *School and College*. February, 1993, p. 7.

"Nintendo Sets Jury's Sights on Atari in Antitrust Trial." *Inside Litigation*. June, 1992, pp. 6-8.

Nussbaum, Gerard M. "There Is No Such Thing As a Free Lunch . . . Especially When It Is Software." *InfoWorld*. June 22, 1992, p. 53.

Pike, Helen. "Pharmaceutical Firm Accents the'D' in R&D." *Journal of Commerce and Commercial*. March 10, 1993, p. 7A.

Pride, Dominic. "MTV Europe Sues Majors in Battle over Video Rights." *Billboard*. August 21, 1993, p. 6.

Schlicher, John W. "If Economic Welfare Is the Goal, Will Economic Analysis Redefine Patent Law?" *Journal of Proprietary Rights*. June, 1992, pp. 12-19.

Stern, Christopher. "FCC Incentives Sought in Comparative Hearing Cases: Freeze Creates Uncertainty over Commission Rules: Lift of Settlement Cap Sought." *Broadcasting & Cable*. March 7, 1994, p. 57.

Tyrell, Joe. "Tavern Owners Out of Tune with'Music Police'." *The (Newark, NJ) Sunday Star-Ledger*. November 6, 1994, p. 48.

Weiss, Aimee H., Gregory S. Antollino, Elyse Garmise, and Kenneth P. Held. "Copyright Reform Bill Enacted." *Journal of Proprietary Rights*. August, 1992, p. 32.

York, Bruce. "Copyright Protection Critical for Performers." *Billboard*. July 29, 1994, p. 5.

LICENSING AND CERTIFICATION, OCCUPATIONAL

In the United States occupational licensing and certification is largely a function of state government. There are literally hundreds of occupations and professions that are regulated in one form or another, but not every state regulates every occupation. Licensing requirements for the same occupation or profession often vary from state to state. Individuals licensed for an occupation in one state may not qualify for licensure in another state.

In some cases the federal government has passed legislation that requires states to set up licensure or certification programs for certain occupations. In these instances there is a greater degree of uniformity among the different states regarding their licensing or certification requirements. Real estate appraisers, asbestos contractors and workers, wastewater and water treatment plant operators, and pesticide operators are some of the occupations that are currently licensed or certified at the state level as a result of federal legislation.

Some occupations are licensed at the federal level. These are typically occupations that take individuals into more than one state, such as airline pilots who are licensed by the Federal Aviation Administration (FAA), or that are subject to federal laws, such as air traffic controllers. Many water transportation occupations are licensed by the U.S. Coast Guard. Coastal states and those adjacent to large bodies of water may also regulate water transportation occupations. Generally, state regulations must be at least as restrictive as the applicable federal regulations.

THREE LEVELS OF STATE OCCUPATIONAL REGULATION

There are essentially three levels of state regulation of occupations and professions: licensing, certification, and registration. While these terms are used interchangeably on occasion and definitions are not strictly adhered to, it is useful at least to recognize the three levels of occupational regulation.

Licensing is the most restrictive form of occupational regulation. When states issue licenses under their licensure laws, it is illegal for individuals to engage in the licensed profession or occupation without a license. Physicians, nurses, and attorneys are examples of professions that are licensed and heavily regulated by state governments.

Certification is a somewhat less restrictive form of state regulation. Like licensing, certification requires individuals to meet certain standards that have been established by the state. Uncertified individuals, however, are often allowed to engage in the same profession as long as they do not present themselves to the public as certified practitioners. This type of state regulation affords ''title protection'' to certified individuals. For example, if psychologists were certified but not licensed as defined above in a certain state, then uncertified individuals could not advertise themselves as psychologists or use psychologist as a title. Uncertified individuals, however, could practice under a different title and provide clients with services similar to those of a certified psychologist.

The least restrictive form of state regulation is registration. Registration usually involves providing a state agency with one's name and address and paying a registration fee. Minimal standards—or no standards at all—might have to be met, such as age, citizenship, and moral character. For public protection the state agency would maintain a registry of all practitioners who have registered with it. In some cases the agency may handle complaints and be able to take disciplinary action.

MANDATORY REGULATION AND VOLUNTARY CERTIFICATION

Whatever level of state regulation is in place for a particular occupation, those regulations have the force of law. They are mandatory. Individuals engaging in occupations that are regulated must comply with the state's laws, rules, and regulations governing those occupations. Such regulations not only set standards for individuals entering an occupation, they also typically spell out acts and conduct that are illegal and subject to disciplinary action.

Individuals in many occupations may have the opportunity to become certified on a voluntary basis. Voluntary certification is typically administered by a trade or professional association. In the absence of state regulation voluntary certification enables a profession to set its own standards. While certification standards vary from profession to profession, they usually involve having some experience in the field and demonstrating competency or proficiency by passing a written and/or practical certification examination. Certified individuals are then allowed to use a certain title, designation, or other indication that they are in fact certified by a nationally recognized professional association. Acupuncturists, social workers, automotive mechanics, and athletic trainers are a few of the occupations that have voluntary certification.

REASONS FOR OCCUPATIONAL LICENSING AND CERTIFICATION

If there is one principle behind the maze of state occupational regulations, it is that certain occupations and professions must be regulated in order to protect public health, safety, and welfare. Licensing and certification protect the public from being victimized by individuals who are either incompetent or unethical. As noted above, licensing agencies have disciplinary authority. Their rules and regulations have the force of law. Complaints from the public can be directed to the appropriate licensing agencies. Practitioners who have violated the standards of conduct as set forth in the rules and regulations of the licensing agency may be subject to fines and other penalties including loss of license.

Occupational licensing and certification is not without its costs, however. While the public may be protected from incompetent and unethical practitioners, strict licensing and certification standards may have the unfortunate effect of causing shortages of qualified professionals in certain geographic areas or in certain professions. Often the costs associated with obtaining the necessary education and meeting other licensing and certification requirements are passed along to consumers in the form of higher fees.

IMPLICATIONS FOR BUSINESS

Occupational licensing and certification is in a constant state of flux. It is also a highly decentralized activity that is typically spread out among many different state departments, divisions, agencies, and boards. Determining what regulations apply to a specific business, profession, or occupation can often mean contacting several different state agencies to determine who has jurisdiction. Fortunately, professional and trade associations are often good sources of information about state licensing requirements for specific occupations.

Businesses need to know what occupational licensing and certification regulations apply to them. These licenses are usually separate from those licenses and permits required to conduct business in a particular state. Building contractors, funeral home directors, private investigators, barbers, cosmetologists, engineers, architects, investment advisers, plumbers, and electricians are just some of the many occupations and businesses that are subject to separate occupational licensing and certification requirements in most states.

[David Bianco]

FURTHER READING:

Bianco, David. *Professional and Occupational Licensing Directory*. 2nd ed. Detroit: Gale Research, 1995.

Pare', Michael. *Certification and Accreditation Programs Directory*. Detroit: Gale Research, 1995.

LOANS

As a financial transaction, a loan is the purchase of the present use of money with the promise to repay the amount in the future according to a pre-arranged schedule and at a specified rate of interest. In banking and finance, loan contracts formally spell out the terms and obligations between the lender and borrower. Loans have these distinguishing characteristics:

TIME TO MATURITY. The length of the loan contract is the time to maturity, therefore, loans vary according to maturity. Short-term debt is from one day to one year. Intermediate debt ranges from one-year to seven years. Long-term debt is more than seven years to thirty or forty years.

Overnight funds (Fed funds) are lent among banks to temporarily lift their reserves to mandated levels.

Revolving credit and perpetual debt have no fixed date for retirement. **Banks** provide revolving credit through extensions of a line of credit. Brokerage firms supply margin credit for qualified customers on certain securities.

While the borrower may always be in debt, the borrower constantly turns over the line of credit by paying it down and reborrowing the funds when needed.

A perpetual loan requires only regular interest payments. The borrower, who usually issued such debt through a registered offering, determines the timing of the debt retirement.

REPAYMENT SCHEDULE. Payments may be required at the end of the contract or at set intervals, usually on a monthly basis or semiannual basis. The payment is generally comprised of two parts: a portion of the outstanding principal and the interest costs. With the passage of time, the principal amount of the loan is amortized, repaid little by little until completely retired. As the principal balance diminishes, the interest on the remaining balance also declines.

Interest-only-loans do not pay down the principal. The borrower pays interest on the principal loan amount and is expected to retire the principal at the end of the contract through a balloon payment or through refinancing.

INTEREST. Interest is the cost of borrowing money. The interest rate charged by lending institutions must be sufficient to cover operating costs, administrative costs, and an acceptable rate of return. Interest rates may be fixed for the term of the loan, or adjusted to reflect changing market conditions. A credit contract may adjust rates daily, annually, or at intervals of 3, 5 and 10 years. Floating rates are tied to some market index and are adjusted regularly.

SECURITY. Assets pledged as security against loan loss are collateral. Credit backed by collateral is secured. The asset purchased by the loan often serves as the only collateral. In other cases the borrower puts other assets, including cash, aside as collateral. **Real estate** or land collateralize mortgages.

Unsecured debt relies on the earning power of the borrower.

SHORT-TERM LOANS

A special commitment loan is a single purpose loan with a maturity of less than one year. Its purpose is to cover cash shortages resulting from a one time increase in current assets, such as a special inventory purchase, an unexpected increase in accounts receivable, or a need for interim financing.

Trade credit is extended by a vendor who allows the purchaser up to three months to settle a bill. In the past it was common practice for vendors to discount trade bills by one or two percentage points as an incentive for quick payment.

A seasonal line of credit of less than one year is used to finance inventory purchases or production. The successful sale of inventory repays the line of credit.

A permanent **working capital** loan provides a business with financing from one to five years during times when cash flow from earnings does not coincide with the timing or volume of expenditures. Creditors expect future earnings to be sufficient to retire the loan.

INTERMEDIATE TERM LOANS

Term loans finance the purchase of furniture, fixtures, vehicles, and plant and office equipment. Maturity generally runs more than one year and less than five.

Consumer loans for autos, boats and home repairs and remodeling are of intermediate term.

LONG TERM LOANS

Mortgage loans are used to purchase real estate and are secured by the asset itself. Mortgages generally run ten to forty years.

A bond is a contract held in trust with the obligation of repayment. An indenture is a legal document specifying the terms of a bond issue including the principal, maturity, date, **interest rates**, any qualifications and duties of the trustees, and the rights and obligations of the issuers and holders. Corporations and government entities issue **bonds** in a form attractive to both public and private investors.

A debenture bond is unsecured. Mortgage bonds hold specific property in lien. A bond may contain safety measures to provide for repayment, such as a **sinking fund**.

[Roger J. AbiNader]

FURTHER READING:

Guttman, Robert. *How Credit-Money Shapes the Economy.* M.E. Sharpe, 1994.

McNeil, Jane H, and Edward T. O'Leary. *Introduction to Commercial Lending.* American Institute of Banking, American Bankers Association, 1983.

Rosenthal, James A., and Juan M. Ocampo. *Securitization of Credit.* John Wiley & Sons, Inc., 1988.

Wray, L. Randall. *Money and Credit in Capitalist Economies.* Edward Elgar Publishing Company, 1990.

In the modern office environment, each worker is equipped with a personal computer, containing its own disk drives and processor. Each of these PCs may be set up to communicate with other PCs over a local area network (LAN). In addition, the LAN may also connect the network of PCs with a series of printers, a mainframe computer, or file server, with even greater processing power and memory storage, and other devices that can send messages from the network over telephone lines to another location.

Many aspects of the LAN are overlooked, but its name reveals all of its most important attributes. A LAN is local, meaning that it is a proprietary system limited to a finite number of users. It generally serves an area of less than one mile, and is usually confined to a single building. Finally, it is a network, affording users both functional and communicative diversity through a distribution of resources. A LAN permits workers—isolated in separate offices—to operate off the same system, as if they were all sitting around a single computer.

One of the great attributes of a LAN is that it may be installed simply, upgraded or expanded with little difficulty, and moved or rearranged without disruption. Perhaps most importantly, anyone initiated in the use of a personal computer can be trained to communicate or perform work over a LAN.

But despite their great potential and capabilities, LANs have yet to demonstrate an increase in office productivity. They have certainly eliminated paper and speeded the flow of information, but in many cases they have created additional work. As more people gain experience with these systems, however, it is likely that LANs will prove their worth.

HISTORICAL DEVELOPMENT OF LANS

Local area networks have their genesis in distributed computing systems that were introduced during the 1960s. Initially, they consisted of ''dumb'' terminals connected to a single mainframe processor via a wiring system. Instructions entered on the terminal keyboard were registered at the mainframe, where they were processed, and a visual representation of these instructions was sent back to the terminal for display on a screen.

The first protocols for these distributed computer workstations were proprietary, meaning that they were designed specifically for equipment designed by a certain company. As a result, IBM equipment could not be mixed with DEC, Xerox, Wang, or any other manufacturer's machinery.

By the late 1970s, however, several companies proposed "open" standards under which equipment from one manufacturer could be made to emulate the operating system of another. This allowed manufacturers to compete for business in systems that had previously been closed to all but the system designer.

The first of these standards was Ethernet, a "listen-and-transmit" protocol developed by Digital Equipment Corp. (DEC), Intel Corp and Xerox Corp. Ethernet identified the type of instructions being generated and, if necessary, conditioned them so they could be read by the mainframe on a common terminal, or bus.

In 1980, the Institute of Electrical and Electronic Engineers (IEEE), determined that continued reluctance to open protocols would seriously retard the growth of distributed computer systems. It established a group called the 802 committee to establish networking standards for the entire industry. This would ensure that customers could migrate from one vendor to another without sacrificing their considerable investments in existing systems. The standards also compelled manufacturers to follow the standards, or risk being dealt out of the market.

Ethernet was offered to the 802 committee as a standard. Several manufacturers balked because Ethernet did not work well under heavy traffic. Instead, the Ethernet standard was adapted into three versions, corresponding to network designs. Still, these standards could support 1,024 workstations over an end-to-end distance of two kilometers.

However, processor manufacturing technology had progressed so far that entire computers could be condensed into a single desktop unit. The first of these "personal computers" (PCs) was introduced by IBM in 1981.

IBM's PC featured an open bus architecture, meaning that IBM provided design specifications to other manufacturers in the hope that they would design compatible equipment and software for the system. IBM could impose this architecture on the market because it had very high market penetration and was the leading manufacturer in the industry.

The PC changed the type of information sent over office computer networks. Terminals were no longer "dumb," but contained the power to perform their own instructions and maintain their own memories. This took considerable pressure off the mainframe device, whose energies could now be devoted to more complex tasks.

An analysis of common office tasks revealed that as much as 80 percent of the work performed by the average employee never left the room in which they were produced. This factor established demand characteristics for individual, worker-specific PCs.

The remaining 20 percent of office tasks required transmission of data for access by other workers. LANs enabled this data to be directed to a common printer, serving a dozen or more workers. This eliminated the need for each worker to have a printer and ensured that the one printer provided was not underutilized.

In addition, LANs allowed data to be called up directly on other workers' computers, providing immediate communication and eliminating the need for paper. The most common application was in interoffice communications, or **electronic mail** (e-mail). Messages could be directed to one or several people and copied to several more over the LAN.

As a result, an e-mail system became something of an official record of communications between workers. Addressees became obligated to respond to e-mail messages in a timely manner because their failure to answer could be documented for supervisors.

PCs transformed LANs from mere shared processors to fully integrated communication devices. In fact, developments in processing technology endowed some PCs with even greater capacity than the mainframe computers to which they were attached. For some applications, the need for a mainframe was completely eliminated. With processing power distributed among PCs, the mainframe's main role was eclipsed. While still useful for complex processing, administrative functions and data file storage became the job of a new device, the file server.

PHYSICAL COMPONENTS OF LANS

While software-driven, the physical properties of a LAN include interfaces, called network access units, which connect the PC to the network. These units are actually interface cards installed on PC motherboards. Their job is to provide a connection, monitor availability of access to the LAN, set or buffer the data transmission speed, ensure against transmission errors and collisions, and assemble data from the LAN into usable form for the PC.

The next part of a LAN is the wiring, which provides the physical connection from one PC to another, and to printers and file servers. The properties of the wiring determine transmission speeds.

The first LANs were connected with coaxial cable, the type used to deliver cable television. These facilities are relatively inexpensive and simple to attach. More importantly, they provide great bandwidth (the system's rate of data transfer), enabling transmission speeds initially up to 20 megabits per second.

During the 1980s, however, AT&T introduced a LAN wiring system using ordinary twisted wire pair of the type used for telephones. The primary advantages of twisted wire pair are that it is very cheap, simpler to splice than coaxial and is already installed in many buildings as obsolete or redundant wiring. In fact, many buildings were left with stranded 25-pair wiring once used for key telephone systems.

But the downside of this simplicity is that its bandwidth is more limited. AT&T's first LAN product, StarLAN, had a capacity of only one megabit per second. Subsequent improvements expanded this capacity tenfold and eliminated the need for shielded, or conditioned, wiring.

A more recent development in LAN wiring is optical fiber cable. This type of wiring uses thin strands of glass to transmit pulses of light between terminals. Its advantages are that it provides tremendous bandwidth, allowing very high transmission speeds. And, because it is optical rather than electronic, it is impervious to electromagnetic interference. Its main drawback, however, is that splicing is difficult and requires a high degree of skill.

The primary application of fiber is not between terminals, but between LAN buses (terminals) located on different floors. As a result, fiber distributed data interface (FDDI) is used mainly in building risers. Within individual floors, LAN facilities remain coaxial or twisted wire pair.

Where a physical connection cannot be made, such as across a street or between buildings where easements for wiring cannot be secured, microwave radio may be used. However, it is often difficult to secure frequencies for this medium.

Another alternative in this application is light transceivers, which project a beam of light similar to fiber optic cable, but through the air, rather than over cable. These systems do not have the frequency allocation or radiation problems associated with microwave, but they are susceptible to interference from fog and other obstructions.

LAN TOPOLOGIES

LANs are designed in several different topologies, or physical patterns, connecting terminals. The most common topology is the bus, where several terminals are connected directly to each other over a single transmission path; it is analogous to a street with several driveways. Each terminal on the LAN contends with other terminals for access to the system. When it has secured access to the system, it broadcasts its message to all the terminals at once. The message is picked up by the one or group of terminal stations for which it is intended.

The branching tree topology is an extension of the bus, providing a link between two or more buses. It may be likened to alleyways connecting several streets, each with many driveways. The connections between buses include impedance matching devices.

A third topology, the star network, also works like a bus in terms of contention and broadcast. But in the star, stations are connected to a single, central node that administers access. Several of these nodes may be connected to one another. For example, a bus serving six stations may be connected to another bus serving 10 stations and a third bus connecting 12 stations. The star topology is most often used where the connecting facilities are coaxial or twisted wire pair.

The ring topology connects each station to its own node, and these nodes are connected in a circular fashion. Node 1 is connected to node 2, which is connected to node 3, and so on, and the final node is connected back to node 1. Messages sent over the LAN are regenerated by each node, but retained only by the addressees. Eventually, the message circulates back to the sending node, which removes it from the stream.

TRANSMISSION METHODS USED BY LANS

LANs function because their transmission capacity is greater than any single terminal on the system. As a result, each station terminal can be offered a certain amount of time on the LAN, like a time-sharing arrangement. To economize on this window of opportunity, stations organize their messages into compact packets that can be quickly disseminated.

In contending for access, a station with something to send stores its data packet in a buffer until the LAN is clear. At that point the message is sent out. Sometimes, two stations may detect the opening at the same time and send their messages simultaneously. Unaware that another message has been sent out, the two signals will collide on the LAN. When this happens it is up to the software to clear the wreckage, determine who should go first and ask both machines to try again.

In busy LANs, collisions would occur all the time, slowing the system down considerably. To solve the problem, the LAN software circulates a token. This works like a ticket that is distributed only to one station at a time. Instead of waiting for the LAN to clear, the station waits to receive the token.

When it has the token, the station sends its packet out over the LAN. When it is done, it returns the token to the stream for the next user. Tokens, used in ring and bus topologies, virtually eliminate the problem of collisions by providing orderly, non-contention access.

The transmission methods used on LANs are either baseband or broadband. The baseband medium uses a high-speed digital signal consisting of square wave DC voltage. While it is fast, it can accommodate only one message at a time. As a result it is suitable for smaller networks where contention is low. It also is very simple, requiring no tuning or frequency discretion circuits. As a result, the transmission medium may be connected directly to the network access unit and is suitable for use over twisted wire pair facilities.

By contrast, the broadband medium tunes signals to special frequencies, much like cable television. Stations are instructed by signaling information to tune to a specific channel to receive information. The information within each channel on a broadband medium may also be digital, but they are separated from other messages by frequency. As a result, the medium generally requires higher capacity facilities, such as coaxial cable. Suited for busier LANs, broadband systems require the use of tuning devices in the network access unit that can filter out all but the single channel it needs.

THE FILE SERVER

The heart of the LAN, the administrative software, resides either in a dedicated file server or, in a smaller, less busy LAN, in a PC acting as a file server. In addition to acting as a kind of traffic cop, the file server holds files for shared use in its hard drives, administers applications such as the operating system, and allocates functions.

Where a single PC is used as a workstation and a file server, response times may lag because its processors are forced to perform several instructions at once. In addition, the system will store certain files on different PCs on the LAN. As a result, if one machine is down, the entire system may be crippled. And if the system were to crash due to undercapacity, some data may be lost or corrupted.

The addition of a dedicated file server may be costly, but it provides several advantages over a distributed system. In addition to ensuring access even when some machines are down, it is unencumbered by multiple duties. Its only jobs are to hold files and provide access.

LAN SPEED MEASUREMENTS

The speed of the LAN is measured in terms of throughput, a figure different from transmission speed because it takes into account the capacity of the wiring and the distance between stations. The data rate, which most directly represents response time, is determined by throughput and other factors such as overhead bits and other signals, error and collision recovery, software and hardware efficiency, and the memory capacity of disk drives.

OTHER LAN EQUIPMENT

As mentioned earlier, LANs are generally limited in size because of the physical properties of the network: distance, impedance, and load. Some equipment, such as repeaters, can extend the range of a LAN. Repeaters have no processing ability, but simply regenerate signals that are weakened by impedance.

Other types of LAN equipment with processing ability include gateways, which enable LANs operating dissimilar protocols to pass information by translating them into a simpler code, such as ASCII. A bridge works like a gateway, but instead of using an intermediate code, it translates one protocol directly into another. A router performs essentially the same function as a bridge, except that it administers communications over alternate paths.

Gateways, bridges, and routers can act as repeaters, boosting signals over greater distances. They also enable separate LANs located in different buildings to communicate with each other.

In some cases, separate LANs located in different cities—and even separate countries—may be linked over the public network. Whether these are "nailed up" dedicated links or switched services, the connection of two or more such LANs is referred to as a wide area network (WAN).

WANs require the use of special software programs in the operating system to enable dial-up connections that may be performed by a router. Unless limited to modem speeds, these connections may require special services such as ISDN (integrated services digital network) to ensure efficient transmission, particularly of large data files. Increasingly, companies employing LANs in separate locations also operate WANs.

Another device different from, but related to, the LAN is the data private branch exchange. Private branch exchanges (PBXs) work like an A/B switch, but route messages to specific servers, rather than broadcasting to all stations. Such exchanges are oblivious to operating systems and performs only circuit-switched connections. As a result, PBXs are somewhat slower, and their applications are limited. Nonetheless, they are a suitable adjunct to many LANs because of the PBXs' ability to switch asynchronous terminals to a number of hosts or funnel several terminals into a single terminal port.

LAN DIFFICULTIES

LANs are susceptible to many kinds of transmission errors. Electromagnetic interference from motors, power lines, and sources of static, as well as shorts from corrosion, can corrupt data. Software bugs and hardware failures can also introduce errors, as can irregularities in wiring and connections.

LANs generally compensate for these errors by working off an uninterruptable power source, such as batteries, and using backup software to recall most recent activity and hold unsaved material. Some systems may be designed for redundancy, such as keeping two file servers and alternate wiring to route around failures.

PURCHASING A LAN

When purchasing a LAN, or even investigating the possibility of installing one, several considerations must be kept in mind. The costs involved and the administrative support needed often far exceed reasonable predictions.

A complete accounting of potential costs should include such factors as purchase price of equipment, spare parts and taxes, installation costs, labor and building modifications, and permits. Operating costs include forecasted public network traffic, diagnostics, and routine maintenance. In addition, the buyer should seek a schedule of potential costs associated with upgrades and expansion and engineering studies.

The vendor should agree to a contract expressly detailing the degree of support that will be provided in installing and turning up the system. In addition, the vendor should provide a maintenance contract that binds the company to make immediate, free repairs when performance of the system exceeds prescribed standards.

All of these factors should be addressed in the buyer's request for proposal, or RFP, which is distributed to potential vendors.

SEE ALSO: Computer Networks; Computers and Computer Systems

[John Simley]

FURTHER READING:

Green, Harry James. *The Business One Irwin Handbook of Telecommunications.* 2nd ed. Homewood, IL: Business One Irwin, 1991.

LOGISTICS MANAGEMENT

SEE: Channels of Distribution; Physical Distribution Management (Transportation)

M

MAASTRICHT TREATY

The Maastricht Treaty is more formally known as the Treaty on European Union. It was signed at Maastricht, the Netherlands, on February 7, 1992 by the 12 member states of the European Community. When the treaty went into effect on November 1, 1993, the **European Union** (EU) was established, and the EC became its policy-making body. The EU is an economic union which collectively embraces the European Economic Community, the European Coal and Steel Community (ECSC), and the European Atomic Energy Community. The European Economic Community was established by the Treaty of Rome in 1957 and was originally referred to as the European Common Market. The European Union has such far-reaching goals as a single monetary system, unimpeded movement of European nationals between members states, a transnational right to vote and hold political office, and the eventual dissolution of national frontiers. The 12 members of the EU and signatories of the Maastricht Treaty are: Belgium, Denmark, France, Germany, Great Britain, Greece, Ireland, Italy, Luxembourg, the Netherlands, Portugal, and Spain.

The European Economic Community (EEC) began as an economic union. The purpose of the EEC was to increase the efficiency of member state's economies and subsequently the standard of living of their respective citizens. This was to be achieved by creating a single market via the removal of trade barriers between member countries.

EC members meeting at Maastricht in December 1991 agreed to a number of key provisions to the treaty

A common currency was to be established by the turn of the century for at least some of the countries. Great Britain and Denmark, however, had the option of retaining their own currencies. The concept of a common foreign policy and common defense policy was also established. The treaty called for the definition and implementation of common security and foreign policies and an eventual common defense policy. Security policies are to be implemented under the auspices of the Western European Union which would also serve as a liaison between the EC and **NATO**.

The pan-European social policy provisions of the Maastricht Treaty include the right of the EU to ''support and complement'' the activities of member countries in areas of worker health, safety, and sexual equality. There was much dissension and subsequent compromise over this part of the treaty especially with Great Britain feeling these provisions would compromise existing British law. As with the common currency provision, Great Britain retained the option of unilateral decision making in these regards. The Maastricht agreement also expands EU activities to include: environmental and consumer protection; energy conservation; and education, health, and cultural issues.

Under the treaty greater aid and assistance was granted to Ireland, Spain, Portugal, and Greece, the so-called poorest nations of the EU. The powers of the European Parliament were also expanded under the Maastricht accord to include the formation of ''watchdog'' committees, input in the appointments of European commissioners, and greater control over legislation passed by the Council of Ministers. The treaty also created an advisory Community of the Regions which represents local and regional governing units.

Ratification of the Maastricht Treaty took two years and numerous compromises and national legislative debates before the 12 EC members voted approval amidst an economic downturn in Europe and growing public disenchantment. Great Britain was concerned with loss of sovereignty especially over the issues of common social policies and a single unit of currency. The French National Assembly had to amend the country's constitution because of treaty provisions dealing with transnational voting rights, visa policies, and the common currency. The German parliament also had concerns over the currency issue as well as discomfort with the ambiguous powers of a European union and the relative powers of the European Parliament. Ireland's Maastricht Treaty referendum became tied to a controversy over abortion strictures and EC travel rights. In spite of these roadblocks, in October of 1993 Germany became the 12th and final EC member to ratify the Maastricht accord. The treaty thus became effective November 1, 1993.

[Michael Knes]

FURTHER READING:

Dinan, Desmond. *Ever Closer Union?: An Introduction to the European Community.* Lynne Reiner Publishers, 1994.

Laurent, Pierre-Henri. "The European Community: To Maastricht and Beyond." *Annals of the American Academy of Political and Social Science.* January, 1994.

Sbragia, Alberta M. *Euro-Politics: Institutions and Policymaking in the "New" European Community.* Brookings Institution, 1992.

MACROECONOMICS

Macroeconomics is a social science that studies an economy at the aggregate (or economy-wide) level. For the sake of simplicity, one can consider the discipline of macroeconomics as being composed of three interrelated components: the key attributes that characterize a macroeconomy; the key macroeconomic theories that explain how these attributes behave over time; and the key macroeconomic policy recommendations that emerge from the macroeconomic theories.

THE KEY CHARACTERISTICS OF AN ECONOMY

The characteristics that describe a macroeconomy are usually referred to as the key macroeconomic variables. The following four variables are considered to be the most important in gauging the state or health of an economy: aggregate output or income, the **unemployment rate**, the **inflation rate**, and the interest rate. These will be briefly discussed shortly. It is, however, prudent to point out that numerous additional measures or variables are collected and used to understand the behavior of an economy. In the United States, for example, these additional measures include: the index of leading economic indicators (provides an idea where the economy is headed in the near future); retail sales (indicates the strength of consumer demand in the economy); factory orders, especially for big-ticket items (indicates the future growth in output, as the orders are filled); housing starts (usually a robust increase in housing starts is taken as a sign of good growth in the future); the consumer confidence index (indicates how likely consumers are to make favorable decisions to buy durable and nondurable goods, services, and homes). Sometimes, the variables tracked are more innocuous than the ones included in the preceding list, such as: aluminum production, steel production, paper and paperboard production, industrial production, hourly earnings, weekly earnings, factory shipments, orders for durable goods, new factory orders, new-home sales, existing-home sales, inventories, initial jobless claims, married and jobless, help-wanted advertising, purchasing manager's survey, and the U.S. **trade deficit**.

As is apparent from the preceding list, economists and financial observers use observations on numerous variables to understand the behavior of an economy. Nevertheless, the four key macroeconomic variables summarize the most important characteristics of a macroeconomy.

OUTPUT/INCOME. An economy's overall economic activity is summarized by a measure of aggregate output. As the production or output of goods and services generates income, any aggregate output measure is closely associated with an aggregate income measure. The United States now uses an aggregate output concept known as the **gross domestic product** or GDP. The GDP is a measure of all currently produced goods and services valued at their market prices. One should notice several features of the GDP measure. First, only currently produced goods (produced during the relevant year) are included. This implies that if you buy a 150-year old classic Tudor house, it does not count towards the GDP; but the service rendered by your real estate agent in the process of buying the house does. Secondly, only final goods and services are counted. In order to avoid double counting, intermediate goods—goods used in the production of other goods and services—do not enter the GDP. For example, steel used in the production of automobiles is not valued separately. Finally, all goods and services included in the GDP are evaluated at their market prices. Thus, these prices reflect the prices consumers pay at the retail level, including indirect taxes such as local sales taxes.

A measure similar to GDP is the **gross national product** or GNP. Until recently, the government used to use the GNP as the main measure of the nation's economic activity. The difference between GNP and GDP is rather small. The GDP excludes the incomes earned abroad by U.S. firms and residents and includes earnings of foreign firms and residents in the United States. Several other measures of output and income are derived from the GNP. These include the net national product or NNP (which subtracts from the GNP an allowance for wear and tear on plants and equipment, known as **depreciation**); the national income (which mainly subtracts indirect taxes from the NNP); the personal income (which measures income received by persons from all sources; it is arrived at by subtracting from the national income items such as corporate profit tax payments and social security contributions that individuals do not receive, and adding items such as transfer payments that they do receive but are not part of the national income); and the personal disposable income (which subtracts personal tax payments such as income taxes from the personal income measure). While all these measures move up and down in a generally similar fashion, it is the personal disposable income that is intimately tied to consumer demand for goods and services—the most dominant component of the aggregate demand—and the total demand for goods and services in the economy from all sources.

It should be noted that the aggregate income/output measures discussed above are usually quoted both in current prices (in ''nominal'' terms) and in constant dollars (in ''real'' terms). The latter quotes are adjusted for inflation and are thus most widely used since they are not subject to distortions introduced by changes in prices.

UNEMPLOYMENT. The level of employment is the next crucial macroeconomic variable. The employment level is often quoted in terms of the unemployment rate. The unemployment rate itself is defined as the fraction of labor force not working (but actively seeking employment). Contrary to what one may expect, the labor force does not consist of all able-bodied persons of working age. Instead, it is defined as consisting of those working and those not working but seeking work. Thus, it leaves out people who are not working but also not seeking work—termed by economists as being ''voluntarily'' unemployed. For purposes of government macroeconomic policies, only people who are ''involuntarily'' unemployed really matter.

For different reasons, it is not possible to bring down the unemployment rate to zero in the best of circumstances. Realistically, economists normally expect a fraction of labor force to remain unemployed—this fraction for the U.S. labor market has been estimated to be 6 percent. The 6 percent unemployment rate is often referred to as the benchmark unemployment rate. In effect, if the unemployment level is at

6 percent, the economy is considered to be at full employment.

INFLATION RATE. The inflation rate is defined as the rate of change in the price level. Most economies face positive rates of inflation year after year. The price level, in turn, is measured by a price index, which measures the level of prices of goods and services at given time. The number of items included in a **price index** vary depending on the objective of the index. Usually three kinds of price indexes, having particular advantages and uses are periodically reported by government sources. The first index is called the consumer price index (CPI), which measures the average retail prices paid by consumers for goods and services bought by them. About 400 items, typically bought by an average household, are included in this index.

A second price index used to measure the inflation rate is called the producer price index (PPI). It is a much broader measure than the consumer price index. The producer price index measures the wholesale prices of approximately 3,000 items. The items included in this index are those that are typically used by producers (manufacturers and businesses) and thus it contains many raw materials and semifinished goods. The third and broadest measure of inflation is the called the implicit gross domestic product price deflator. This index measures the prices of all goods and services included in the calculation of the current output of goods and services in the economy, the GDP.

The three measures of the inflation rate are most likely to move in the same direction, even though not to the same extent. Differences can arise due to the differing number of goods and services included for the purpose of compiling the three indexes. In general, if one hears about the inflation rate number in the popular media, it is most likely to be the one based on the CPI.

THE INTEREST RATE. The concept of **interest rates** used by economists is the same as the one widely used by ordinary people. The interest rate is invariably quoted in nominal terms—that is, it is not adjusted for inflation. Thus, the commonly followed interest rate is actually the nominal interest rate. Nevertheless, there are literally hundreds of nominal interest rates. Examples include: savings account rate, six-month certificate of deposit rate, 15-year mortgage rate, variable mortgage rate, 30-year Treasury bond rate, 10-year General Motors bond rate, and commercial bank prime lending rate. One can see from these examples that the nominal interest rate has two key attributes— the duration of lending/borrowing involved and the identity of the borrower.

Fortunately, while the hundreds of interest rates that one encounters may appear baffling, they are closely linked to each other. Two characteristics that account for this linkage are the risk worthiness of the

MACROECONOMICS

ENCYCLOPEDIA OF BUSINESS

borrower and the maturity of the loan involved. So, for example, the interest rate on a 6-month Treasury bill is related to that on a 30-year Treasury bond, as **bonds/loans** of different maturities command different rates. Also, a 30-year General Motors bond will carry a higher interest rate than a 30-year Treasury bond, since a General Motors (GM) bond is riskier than a Treasury bond.

Finally, one should note that the nominal interest rate does not represent the real cost of borrowing or the real return on lending. To understand the real cost or return, one must consider the inflation-adjusted nominal rate, called the real interest rate. Tax and other considerations also influence the real cost or return. Nevertheless, the real interest rate is a very important concept in understanding the main incentives behind borrowing or lending.

MACROECONOMIC THEORIES AND ASSOCIATED POLICY RECOMMENDATIONS

Macroeconomics essentially examines the factors that lead to changes in the main characteristics of the economy—output, employment, inflation, and the interest rate. A set of principles that describes how the key macroeconomic variables are determined is called a macroeconomic theory. Typically, every macroeconomic theory comes up with a set of policy recommendations that the proponents of the theory hope the government will follow. Currently, there are four competing macroeconomic theories: Keynesian economics, **monetarism**, the neoclassical economics, and the supply-side economics. All four theories are based, in varying degrees, on classical economics which preceded the advent of Keynesian economics in the 1930s. Classical economics, as well as the other four theories are briefly described below.

THE CLASSICAL ECONOMICS

The macroeconomic theory that dominated capitalist economies prior to the advent of Keynesian economics in 1936 has been widely known as classical macroeconomics. The classical economists believed in free markets—for example, they held that the economy would always achieve full employment through forces of supply and demand. Classical economists did not see any role for government in economic policy. For example, since market forces led to full employment, there was no need for a government intervention to bring it about. Classical economists recommended the use of neither monetary policy nor fiscal policy by the government. This hands-off policy recommendation is known as the laissez faire policy.

KEYNESIAN ECONOMICS. Keynesian economics was born during the Great Depression of the 1930s and has been, for the most part, followed in most capitalist countries ever since. English economist John Maynard Keynes (1883-1946) argued that self-adjusting market forces would take a long time to restore full employment. He held that the government should intervene to increase aggregate demand through the use of fiscal policy, which involves government spending and taxation. By increasing government spending, for instance, jobs will be created which will increase income levels which will increase the aggregate demand for goods and services and thus create new jobs.

Modern Keynesians (also, known as neo-Keynesians) recommend monetary policy, in addition to fiscal policy, to manage the level of aggregate demand. An increase in the **money supply**, for example, leads to a decrease in the interest rate which increases private investment and consumption, boosting the aggregate demand in the economy.

An increase in aggregate demand under the Keynesian system, however, not only generates higher employment but also leads to higher inflation. This causes a policy dilemma—how to strike a balance between employment and inflation. According to laws that were enacted following the Great Depression, policy makers are expected to use monetary and fiscal policies to achieve high employment consistent with price stability.

MONETARISM. Monetarism was an attempt by conservative economists to reestablish the classical laissez faire recommendation. Proposed by Milton Friedman (1912–), in the 1960s monetarism holds that while it is not possible to have full employment of the labor force all the time, it is better to leave the macroeconomy to market forces. Friedman contended that the government's use of monetary and fiscal policies to stabilize the economy around full employment leads to greater instability in the economy. He argued that while the economy would not achieve a state of bliss in the absence of the government intervention, it will be far more tranquil. Under monetarism, the only policy recommendation is that the money supply should be allowed to grow at a constant rate.

THE NEW CLASSICAL ECONOMICS. The 1970s saw a further push to revive classical orthodoxy. The new classical economists (also known as proponents of rational expectations) provided a theoretical framework and empirical evidence to support the view that neither fiscal nor monetary policy can be effective in altering the output and employment levels in a systematic manner. The concept of rational expectations can simply be considered the use of all available information by economic agents (consumers, businesses, and others). Proponents of the new classical economics argue that if economic agents used rational expectations regarding government policies, they would frustrate any anticipated policy action by the government by altering their own behavior. Thus, there was no point in conducting monetary and fiscal policies—market forces are not amenable to such manipulation.

SUPPLY-SIDE ECONOMICS. While supply-side economics became popular during the Reagan era, it had been a part of U.S. macroeconomic policies for some time. This theory is also rooted in classical economics, even though it accepts some Keynesian demand management policy. Basically, supply siders emphasize enhancing economic growth by augmenting the supply of factors of production (such as labor and capital). This, in turn, is done through increased incentives which mainly takes the form of reducing taxes and regulatory burdens. Reagan used a major tax cut as part of his fiscal policy. The supply siders, in general, want a greater role for market forces and a reduced role for government.

[Anandi P. Sahu]

FURTHER READING:

Froyen, Richard T. *Macroeconomics: Theories and Policies*. 4th ed. Macmillan Publishing, 1993.

Gordon, Robert J. *Macroeconomics*. 6th ed. HarperCollins College Publishers, 1993.

Mayer, Thomas. *The Structure of Monetarism*. W. W. Norton & Company, 1978.

Sommers, Albert T. *The U.S. Economy Demystified*, Lexington Books, 1985.

MAGHREB COMMON MARKET

The Maghreb common market is a proposed economic integration of the five North African countries—Morocco, Algeria, Tunisia, Libya, and Mauritania—which make up the Maghreb, the Arabic term for the western region of the Arab world. The plan for a **common market** by the end of the 1990s was set forth in a treaty of the five nations establishing the Arab Maghreb Union (AMU) in 1989. The Maghreb common market is to be modeled somewhat after the **European Union**'s common market, as the AMU treaty was similar to the European Economic Community Treaty of 1957. Progress towards establishing the Maghreb common market, however, has been slower than anticipated. Despite the cultural unity of the Maghreb, which is predominantly Arabic-speaking and Muslim, with a shared historical sense of identity, there have been economic and political obstacles to swift integration.

The idea of Maghreb integration has existed since Morocco and Tunisia gained independence from France in the 1950s. However, what was foreseen was a political union, and little attention was paid to economics. Political differences and international disputes kept the Maghreb countries from even normalizing their relations until 1988. It was only in that year that the region's two largest nations, Morocco and Algeria, established diplomatic relations after decades of conflict over the former Spanish Sahara (Western Sahara). Relations between Tunisia and Libya also improved in 1988.

The primary impetus for establishing the AMU, which is both a political and economic regional organization, was the threat of being cut off from the Maghreb's major trading partners in Europe with the impending European Union in 1992. At the time almost two-thirds of the Maghreb countries' international trade was with countries of the European Economic Community (EEC), whereas less than three percent was between each other. The leaders of the Maghreb countries realized that the vast inter-Maghreb trade potential was not being realized, especially considering the complementary natural resources and pools of labor of the countries of the Maghreb. Although less economic dependence on Europe was one goal, at the same time it was hoped that the AMU could serve as a negotiating block to achieve better, closer ties with the EEC.

Another reason for seeking economic integration was that the individual Maghreb countries were suffering at the time from economic crises of their own, which could be overcome only through integration. The oil-producing countries Libya and Algeria had become too dependent on revenues from oil exports which had declined due to falling prices. Tunisia and Morocco were undergoing economic restructuring which was having ill short-term effects, and Mauritania was suffering from a stagnant economy and high foreign debt.

The ultimate economic goals of a common market include the adoption of common customs legislation, common financial legislation, and a degree of coordinated economic planning. For the AMU, common customs legislation would involve the removal of internal customs duties and the imposition of a common customs tariff for goods from countries outside the union. Common financial legislation would involve creating a Maghrebi Financial Zone, a Maghreb currency, an independent Maghrebi Fund for Development to coordinate investment and float loans, and a regional budget to fund certain projects, which would be financed through a regional tax. Coordinated economic planning among the members would include public spending, tax legislation, investments, job opportunities, and import-export policies, within a liberal economic framework in which the state would play a lesser role. To these ends, the countries have so far only undertaken feasibility studies. The Arab Maghreb Union had decided at its July 1990 summit session to implement the customs union by 1995, and it determined that Tunis would be the seat of an investment and foreign trade bank.

Initial steps toward a common market have included a freer flow of goods and individuals among the five countries. Visas are no longer required for travel of member nationals and plans have been made for a common identity card. General agreements have been reached on the integration of transportation and improvements on a railway between Tunis, Tunisia, and Marrakesh, Morocco, have begun. Construction has begun on a pipeline from Algeria via Morocco to transport gas to Europe. Other issues that have been discussed include a joint airline, joint agricultural and industrial projects, and intra-Maghreb road improvements. However, greater headway in other spheres, such as standardizing exchange rates and the complete freedom of movement of capital and goods, is still needed.

Slow progress in implementing the common market is largely due to the great deal of economic restructuring required. Since so little of the member countries' trade has been within the region, changing trade patterns will take time. Furthermore, economic integration is hindered by the differing economic structures of the member countries. While Morocco and Tunisia have liberal market-oriented economies, Algeria's and Libya's economics are very much centrally controlled. Mauritania's economy is still largely based on subsistence agriculture, and its gross domestic product in 1991 was only $1.1 billion, compared to a range of $13.6 billion to $24 billion among the other Maghreb countries. Political differences have also resurfaced. The new Algerian military regime, which came to power in 1992, is less compromising than the previous government on the future of the Western Sahara occupied by Morocco. Morocco, meanwhile, has tried to pursue closer relationships with the European Union independent of the AMU, to which it has been giving less attention.

[Heather Behn Hedden]

FURTHER READING:

Chtatou, Mohamed. "The Present and Future of the Maghreb Arab Union." *In North Africa: National, State, and Region*, edited by George Joffe. Routledge, 1993.

Mortimer, Robert. "Regionalism and Geopolitics in the Maghreb." *Middle East Report*. September-October, 1993, pp. 16-19.

"One Club to Beat Another." *The Economist*. May 19, 1990, pp. 48-49.

Owen, Roger. "A New Cold War System? The Middle East in a Regional World." *Middle East Report*. September–October, 1993, pp. 3-6.

"Pragmatism Brings Maghreb Together." *Africa Report*. May–June, 1989, p. 9.

Romdhani, Oussama. "The Arab Maghreb Union: Toward North African Integration." *American-Arab Affairs*. Spring, 1989, no. 28, pp. 42-48.

MAIL-ORDER BUSINESS

A mail-order business is one that receives and fulfills orders for merchandise through the mail. One often hears the terms "mail-order," "**direct mail**," and "**direct marketing**" used as if they were synonymous, when in fact they have different meanings. While a mail-order business may solicit orders using a variety of direct mail packages and catalogs, there are also many businesses, organizations, and agencies that use direct mail that are not mail-order businesses. Direct mail is simply an **advertising** medium that delivers its message through the mail, in much the same way that television, radio, newspapers, and magazines are advertising media.

Direct marketing is a broader term than direct mail and encompasses other media. Mail-order businesses usually use direct marketing techniques to reach potential customers and make sales. Direct marketing may be distinguished from other types of **marketing** by the fact that it always makes an offer and solicits a direct response. While direct marketing makes heavy use of direct mail, it also employs a range of other advertising media to get its message across to target audiences.

Mail-order is simply a way of doing business. While mail-order-businesses originally took orders primarily through the mail, the advent of lower long-distance rates and **toll-free telephone numbers** has made it more convenient for customers to place orders over the telephone. In the early 1990s there were an estimated 200,000 toll-free WATS (wide area telephone service) lines, and the number continues to grow. Mail-order businesses also use the telephone to solicit orders from potential customers.

Mail-order businesses represent a growing segment of the U.S. economy. Estimates of the amount of consumer and business products purchased from mail-order firms vary. The government does not publish statistics on the volume of business done by mail or telephone. Arnold Fishman, as cited in *How to Start and Operate a Mail-Order Business*, estimated that consumers purchased nearly $100 billion of products by mail in 1990, and more than $50 billion of business products were sold through the mail. According to a study of the catalog industry by the Direct Marketing Association, catalog revenue reached $53.4 billion in 1993, an average growth of nearly 7 percent annually since 1987.

THE DEVELOPMENT OF MAIL-ORDER BUSINESSES

How old is mail-order? Garden and seed catalogs were known to be distributed in the American colonies before the Revolutionary War. Mail-order shopping in the area of consumer goods entered a period of growth in the 1880s, when mail-order houses began to fiercely compete with local stores. Their marketing contest centered on three major issues—price, inventory, and assurances—the very factors that made mail-order houses successful.

Aaron Montgomery Ward (1843-1913), regarded as the first of the consumer goods catalogers, started his catalog business in 1872, while Richard Warren Sears (1863-1914) mailed his first flyers in the 1880s. These catalogs had a liberating effect on nineteenth-century consumers. They were no longer captive to their local stores, which had limited inventories and charged higher prices because they were not big enough to receive large volume discounts from their suppliers. With the advent of mail-order, consumers could get attractive goods and prices whether they lived in the middle of Manhattan or a remote rural setting.

The postal system allowed direct-mail companies to operate on a national basis. With **economies of scale** working in their favor, mail-order houses could undercut the pricing of local stores. In 1897, bicycles were selling for $75 to $100 and more, until Sears started offering them for $5 to $20 in its catalog. Sears could offer those low prices because it sold thousands of bicycles every week.

The large volume of business also allowed catalogers to offer a wider variety of goods. Consumers not only wanted low prices, they also wanted variety—twenty kinds of dresses rather than two. Here again, the enormous volume generated by leading mail-order houses made huge inventories not only possible but also practicable.

But price and variety, while important, have only limited value if the goods themselves are shoddy or poorly-made. So the mail-order firms protected consumers with powerful guarantees. Montgomery Ward was one of the first companies to offer a money-back guarantee, and the Sears, Roebuck & Co. pledge of ''satisfaction guaranteed or your money back'' is one of the best-known commitments in American business.

Another successful cataloger, L.L. Bean Inc. of Freeport, Maine, began in 1912 when Leon Leonwood Bean mailed his first single-sheet flyer advertising his Maine hunting boots. Perhaps he got the idea of using direct mail from his brother, Guy Bean, who was the Freeport postmaster. Leon Bean targeted his mailing to individuals who had hunting licenses.

MAIL-ORDER BUSINESSES TODAY

Mail-order businesses today offer consumers a wide array of products and services. Magazine sub-

scription sales represent the largest segment of mail-order sales. Nearly 10 percent of all direct-mail advertising is done on behalf of magazine subscriptions. Books and newspapers also account for a significant portion of mail-order business.

The fastest-growing segment of the mail-order business is that of specialty catalogs. They are fast replacing the large general merchandise catalogs with which consumers are familiar. In fact, several of the major merchandise catalogs have been discontinued and replaced with a series of specialty catalogs. The list of specialty goods sold through the mail is endless and encompasses virtually hundreds of categories. Kitchenware, fancy foods, outdoor clothing, health products, gardening products, sporting goods, records, collectibles, and computer software and equipment are but a few of the more popular categories.

THE GROWTH AND ATTRACTION OF MAIL ORDER

People order through the mail for a variety of reasons. Historically, mail-order businesses became successful because they offered a wider variety of goods than could be found in local retail outlets. Goods purchased through the mail were often cheaper than those available locally. Mail-order shopping offered consumers more convenience than shopping at retail stores. Individuals pursuing a hobby or special interest were more likely to locate those hard-to-find items in a specialty catalog than in a store.

In addition, several recent socioeconomic factors have contributed to the growth of ''at-home shopping.'' These include changing lifestyles, most notably an increase in the number of women working outside the home. Increased consumer acceptance of the telephone as a way to place orders has also helped mail-order businesses. Coupled with telephone-based ordering are faster order fulfillment and the elimination of delays previously associated with the mail. Today, placing an order by phone offers almost the same ''instant gratification'' as picking up a piece of merchandise at the store. This has been made possible largely through the widespread use of credit cards and toll-free telephone numbers.

MARKETING AND ADVERTISING A MAIL-ORDER BUSINESS

Mail-order businesses have a wide range of media to choose from when marketing and advertising their products. Mail-order advertisements are commonly found in direct mail (including catalogs), classified ads, and display ads. Other media that can be used to advertise a mail-order business include television, radio, matchbooks, package stuffers, bill stuffers, transit advertising, comic books, daily newspapers, and free-standing inserts in Sunday newspapers.

Mail-order advertising is usually direct-response advertising. Direct-response advertising is a type of direct marketing. Like all direct marketing, direct-response advertising makes an offer and asks the reader for a response, such as placing an order or requesting more information. The response to any mail-order advertisement can be precisely measured. It is this measurability that allows direct marketers to test a variety of lists, offers, and media before committing valuable resources to a specific campaign.

REGULATIONS THAT AFFECT MAIL-ORDER BUSINESS

Mail-order businesses must comply with the regulations of the **Federal Trade Commission** (FTC) and the U.S. Postal Service. In addition mail-order businesses may be subject to applicable state laws. While recent court decisions have questioned the applicability of state-use tax laws to mail-order businesses, it is still necessary to be aware of state regulations concerning the collection of **sales tax**.

The FTC has issued several directives, guidelines, and advisory opinions concerning mail-order businesses. These and other relevant regulations are published in the Code of Federal Regulations (CFR), Title 16, Chapters 1 and 2, which is available in most large libraries or directly from the FTC. It is worth summarizing a few of the rules that mail-order firms must observe in the conduct of their business.

The Mail-Order Merchandise Rule, also known as the 30-Day Rule, is designed to protect consumers from unexpected delays in receiving merchandise ordered through the mail. It requires a mail-order business to notify customers, when there is a shipping delay, before the promised shipping date or within 30 days after the order was received. The notice of delay must provide the customer with the option of canceling the order for a full refund or consenting to the delay. Among other things, the rule also requires that the option notice be sent by first-class mail.

Another FTC rule requires all mail-order advertising to indicate the country of origin of the product being advertised, but only if the product has a fabric as part of its content. This rule was designed to protect domestic textile and wool producers. Product guarantees and warranties are the subject of additional FTC guidelines that apply to all businesses, not just mail-order businesses.

Mail-order advertising frequently contains endorsements or testimonials. Under FTC guidelines, any endorsement must reflect the views of the endorser, must not be reworded or taken out of context, and the endorser must be a bona fide user of the product. If the endorser has been paid, the ad must disclose that fact, unless they are celebrities or experts. Additional FTC rules apply specifically to endorsements by average consumers and expert endorsements.

The FTC has issued guidelines to help mail-order businesses avoid deceptive pricing. These rules affect two-for-one offers, price comparisons, and other issues. Use of the words "free" and "new" are subject to FTC review. Advertising products that have yet to be manufactured, while legal, is subject to FTC requirements. Also called dry testing, such advertising must clearly state that sale of the product is only planned and that it is possible that consumers who order the product may not receive it. In addition, if the product is not manufactured, consumers who ordered it must be notified within four months of the original ad or mailing, and they must be given the opportunity to cancel their order without obligation.

In addition to FTC regulations, mail-order businesses must also be aware of USPS regulations concerning materials that should not be mailed. Lotteries, for example, are illegal under USPS regulations. A lottery includes the element of chance, consideration, and a prize. Consideration means that consumers must pay something to enter the lottery. Consequently, mail-order businesses often offer consumers the opportunity to enter a sweepstakes that does not require any consideration, payment, or purchase on the part of the consumer. While sweepstakes have proved to be an effective method of advertising mail-order merchandise, many states have laws affecting their use. Particularly deceptive practices in the area of sweepstakes have also drawn the attention of postal officials as a possible violation of laws concerning frauds and swindles.

THE FUTURE OF MAIL-ORDER BUSINESS

The mail-order industry has continued to grow during the early 1990s, and there is every indication it will continue to do so. Catalog revenues, which account for a significant portion of all mail-order sales, grew at an annual rate of approximately 7 percent from 1987 to 1993, according to a 1994 survey by the Direct Marketing Association. The same survey forecast that catalog revenues would grow nearly 6.8 percent annually through 1997, reaching a total of $69.5 billion.

As consumers become more accustomed to at-home shopping, though, they are also showing increasing concern over such issues as privacy and deceptive mail practices. These concerns may lead to increased regulation of mail-order businesses. A variety of federal and state regulations have been proposed to protect consumer privacy. Thus far the mail-order industry has been successful at efforts to regulate itself. Mail-order businesses, however, must remain aware of the constantly changing regulatory environment in which they operate.

SEE ALSO: Catalog Marketing

[David Bianco]

FURTHER READING:

Keup, Erwin J. *Mail-order Legal Guide*. Oasis Press, 1993.

Muldoon, Katie. *Catalog Marketing*. American Management Association, 1988.

Simon, Julian L. *How to Start and Operate a Mail-Order Business*. 5th ed. McGraw-Hill, 1993.

Sroge, Maxwell. *Inside the Leading Mail-Order Houses*. 3rd ed. NTC Business Books, 1989.

MALAYSIA, DOING BUSINESS IN

Malaysia is a rapidly developing nation in Southeast Asia. It is comprised of two distinct regions : Peninsular Malaysia and East Malaysia. The South China Sea separates the two regions by over 540 miles. The nation's total land area is 127,317 square miles, or just over the size of New Mexico. Of the two regions, East Malaysia—consisting of the two states of Sabah and Sarawak on the northern half of the island of Borneo—is disproportionately the larger, covering well over 76,400 square miles. East Malaysia is sparsely populated and relatively undeveloped. By contrast, over 80 percent of Malaysia's 19 million (1994) people live in the rapidly developing Peninsular region. Peninsular Malaysia comprises the southern portion of the Malay Peninsula, bordered on the north by Thailand. Directly off the peninsula's tip is the island nation of Singapore. Just to the west, the Straits of Malacca separates the peninsula from Sumatra in Indonesia.

Since its independence in the wake of World War II, Malaysia has transformed itself from a British colony with an economy almost completely dependent on rubber plantations, tin mining, and agriculture, to emerge as a growing industrial and commercial force in the world economy.

BUSINESS PRACTICES

LANGUAGE. The official language of Malaysia is Bahasa Melayu (literally, ''the Language of Malaysia''). This is a standardized form of the many Malay dialects and is—with mild differences—nearly identical to Bahasa Indonesia spoken in neighboring Indonesia.

While Behasa Melayu is the language required in all governmental communication, and most advertis-

ing, it is not the only language of the country. Approximately 29.7 percent of Malaysia's population are Chinese, speaking various dialects of Chinese. Additionally, just over 8 percent of Malaysians are ethnic Indians, primarily Tamil-speaking but encompassing a wide range of other Indian languages as well.

Additionally, because of long association with Great Britain, most Malaysians of all ethnic groups speak English as their second language. Indeed, government documents generally have an English translation following the Bahasa Melayu version, both for foreigners and for Chinese and Indian Malaysians.

VIEWS OF TECHNOLOGY AND THE ENVIRONMENT. The attitudes of the three main Malaysian ethnic groups—the Bumiputeras, the Chinese, and the Indians—regarding technology significantly differs from that of the United States. The United States is a control culture, while both Bumiputera and Indian Malaysians traditionally are a subjugation culture. This means that U.S. culture views technology as consistently positive and reinforces a belief that people can control their environment to conform to their needs. By contrast, Malaysian groups traditionally view technology with some skepticism and conform their behavior to existing environmental conditions. This traditional view of technology, though still present, is changing toward the control stance in the most-developed urban and industrial areas around the capital city of Kuala Lumpur. These traditional norms, however, remain firmly in place in most of the rest of the country.

Chinese Malaysian culture is more accurately described as a harmonization culture. Here the emphasis is on one's integration into a natural order rather than one's control of that order. This is most evident in the ethnic Chinese following of feng shui (an ancient geomancy dealing with the balance of spiritual forces). The importance of location, lucky or unlucky dates, and numerous other factors determined by feng shui experts guide many of Malaysia's Chinese community. For example, many Chinese would confer with a feng shui expert before deciding on an office location or signing an important agreement. Such practices are important to those who adhere to them, and should be accorded the same respect one would give to a religion, rather than be misinterpreted as the equivalent of minor superstition.

The location of the nation tends to affect certain aspects of Malaysian behavior as well. Work—particularly that conducted outdoors or in areas without air conditioning—is affected by the climate. Malaysia is tropical with high temperatures year-round and unrelentingly high humidity. Additionally, the wet season consists of daily and often torrential rains from roughly September to December.

SOCIAL ORGANIZATION

Social organizational factors in Malaysia affecting business include the importance of religion, the concept of family, and group ties.

RELIGION. Religion plays an important role in Indonesian business. Virtually all Bumiputeras and many of the ethnic Indians are Moslem. Most Malaysian Moslems take Islam very seriously, and follow its precepts as a lifestyle as much as a religion. Because the mosque is regularly visited, it may serve as a place to socialize and nurture business contacts within the Moslem community. Additionally, Moslem sensibilities affect attitudes toward business attire, with most Malaysian women dressing more modestly than their U.S. counterparts.

Five of Malaysia's states (Perlis, Kadah, Kelantan, Terengganu, and Johore) follow the Islamic workweek. In these five states, business offices are open six days a week, Saturday through Thursday, with business closing after a half day on Thursday and the Islamic Sabbath (Friday) off. In the remaining states, the work week follows non-Islamic norms of Monday through Friday, and half days on Saturdays. Still, employers give Moslems time to go to the mosque on Thursday afternoons and part of the day on Friday. As in all Moslem nations, the Islamic holy days are followed. For example, the fasting month of Ramadan is followed, with a resulting effect on work performance.

The ethnic Chinese generally follow a wide range of Buddhist and Taoist practices blended with the precepts of Confucianism. Their observances range from strict adherents to loose practitioners. The Chinese New Year and the importance of feng shui, however, are nearly universally observed.

Most of the non-Moslem Indians are Hindu. The Thomian Indians, however, are among the world's oldest practitioners of Christianity. Additionally, the Sikhs follow their own religion, and some followers of nearly all of India's religions are evident among some Indian Malaysians.

Additionally, because of the influence of Hindu and Chinese spiritual beliefs, Malaysian Moslems (like their Indonesian coreligionists to the south) are more likely than Moslems elsewhere to believe in ghosts and the spirit world. While remaining true to the essential monotheistic beliefs of Islam, Malaysians nonetheless recognize spiritual forces or attributes of the soul in a variety objects. The presence of ghosts, witches, and other spiritual entities remain a real part of life for many Malaysians, and the need to placate these spirits affects all aspects of life, including work. A common mistake of foreigners is to view Malaysia as a traditional Islamic society and therefore to play down the importance of these supernatural forces, to criticize such beliefs, or to mistakenly reduce their importance to that of mere superstition. Fear of ghosts or the believed presence of spiritual forces can prevent employees from coming to work or prevent the conclusion of a business deal.

FAMILY AND GROUP TIES. Most Malaysians hold considerably stronger and more extended kinship bonds than those in the United States. Family connections and obligations influence hiring, deal making and other business issues. Moreover, the definition of immediate relationships reaches far beyond the nuclear family to those who would be considered distant relatives in a North American conception.

For all Malaysian ethnic groups, nepotism extends beyond direct kin relationships to clan ties. This is particularly the case for the various clans of the ethnic Chinese communities.

CONTEXTING

Malaysia is a high context society and the United States is a low context culture. This means that Malaysians are more likely to rely on implicit communication rather than on explicit messages. Malaysians as a result read more into what is said than the words themselves may actually mean. For most Malaysians, what is meant matters more than what is actually said.

In Malaysia, meaning is usually communicated indirectly, especially in the delivery of bad news. As a result, Malaysians are likely to agree to things with which they disagree, allowing the context of the discussion or past relationship to convey their disagreement. This is clear to Malaysians but to those from low context cultures such as the United States, such indirect communication is often misread as dishonesty. Conversely, the direct style of communication practiced by most U.S. businesspeople in Malaysia is perceived as rude and often causes others to lose face.

Malaysians, as a high context culture, place a strong value on face-saving, while most North Americans place little emphasis on face-saving. The Malaysian conception of face-saving takes the form of the avoidance of shame. Most low context U.S. business practice is controlled by the following of the law and adherence to written agreements. In Malaysia, one commonly holds to a contract to maintain appearances rather than from fear of a lawsuit.

The North American businessperson in Malaysia is thus viewed as lacking honor, having no sense of face (and therefore dangerous to deal with) and being foolishly litigious. The Malaysians in turn are viewed by their North American counterparts as dishonoring their contracts and ignoring their own laws. In reality both perceptions are accurate when viewed through the context of the values of the other's culture.

Still, to succeed in business in Malaysia, the foreigner will need to view contracts and other legally binding arrangements as ongoing rather than definitive. Moreover, the foreigner will have to be willing to allow some inconsistencies to stand at times to maintain appearance and avoid shaming the Malaysians who would otherwise terminate the business relationship.

TEMPORAL CONCEPTION

Malaysia is a polychronic culture. Time is more fluid than in monochronic societies such as the United States. The Malaysians value friendship, personal commitments and the completion of tasks at hand at the expense of preset schedules.

Time is seen as malleable. Appointment times are approximate. Work hours are variable. Consequently, the monochronic foreigner needs to adjust his or her concepts of scheduling, deadlines, and other time-linked activities in Malaysia.

SEE ALSO: Cross-Cultural/International Communication

[David A. Victor]

FURTHER READING:

Andaya, Barbara Watson, and Leonard Y. Andaya. *A History of Malaysia*. London: Macmillan, 1982.

Brooks, Guy, and Victoria Brooks. *Malaysia: A Kick Start for Business Travelers*. North Vancouver, BC: Self-Counsel Press, 1995.

Munan, Heidi. *Culture Shock: Malaysia*. Portland, OR: Graphic Arts Center Publishing, 1991.

Schlossstein, Steve. *Asia's New Little Dragons: The Dynamic Emergence of Indonesia, Thailand & Malaysia*. Chicago: Contemporary Books, 1991.

Victor, David A. *International Business Communication*. New York: HarperCollins, 1992.

MANAGEMENT

Business management can be defined as the acquisition, allocation, and utilization of resources through planning, organizing, staffing, leading, and controlling. Discussed below is the evolution of management theory and practice and three modern approaches to management. The popular process approach is emphasized. It explains the basic management functions and how they interrelate and influence organizational effectiveness. In addition, important managerial skills and ancillary roles are identified.

BACKGROUND

The basic elements of modern management practices can be traced to ancient times. The Egyptians, for example, developed advanced management techniques related to labor division, hierarchy of authority, and teams. They developed complex bureaucracies to measure and forecast river levels and crop yields, distribute revenues within the government, manage trade, and complete massive construction projects like the pyramids. The Babylonians, Greeks, Romans, Chinese, and other cultures made similar contributions to management science.

Although management systems existed long before the birth of Christ, it was not until the late eighteenth and nineteenth centuries that advanced business management techniques emerged in response to the Industrial Revolution. The Revolution resulted in the formation of extremely large organizations characterized by job specialization and the administration of large amounts of human resources. A new breed of middle-level managers were needed to plan and direct human efforts and to administer large pools of capital.

Among the most influential American contributors to management practice during the Industrial Revolution was Daniel C. McCallum, the superintendent of the Erie Railroad during the mid-1800s. To more efficiently manage the vast human and capital resources involved with construction of the railroad, he established a set of guiding management principles that emphasized: a specific division of labor and responsibilities; empowering managers to make decisions in the field; compensation based on merit; a clearly delineated managerial hierarchy; and a detailed system of data gathering, analysis, and reporting that would foster individual accountability and improve decision making.

SCHOOL APPROACH

The efforts of McCallum and other managers of his era were reflected in the first of five schools of management that emerged during the early and middle 1900s. The first of these schools was scientific management, which dominated management philosophy between the 1890s and the early 1920s. Scientific management concepts were heavily influenced by the ideas of Frederick W. Taylor. Taylor believed that organizational efficiency could be achieved by using statistics, logic, and detailed analysis to break jobs and responsibilities into specific tasks. The chief contribution of scientific management was that it successfully applied modern techniques of science and engineering to the management of resources and organizational systems.

Scientific management principles were displaced during the 1920s by the classical management school of thought. Classical management theory is largely attributable to Henry Fayol, who is also known as the father of management. Classical management emphasized the identification of universal principles of management which, if adhered to, would lead to organizational success. Universal principles encompassed two broad areas. The first was business functions and the second was structuring organizations and managing workers.

In essence, classical theory holds that management is a process consisting of several related functions, such as planning and organizing. Thus, by identifying specific business functions—including marketing, finance, production, and sub-functions within those and other major categories—companies can efficiently divide an organization into departments that work as a process. Furthermore, by carefully structuring chains of authority and responsibility, an entity can successfully facilitate the performance of individuals within departments to achieve company goals.

Importantly, Fayol is credited with identifying five basic management functions: planning, organizing, commanding, coordinating, and controlling. In addition, his 14 principles of management established a framework for management that continues to influence modern management theory. Those principles included: unity of command, meaning a worker should be responsible to only one superior; unity of direction, which implies that each group of activities having a single goal should be unified in a department or work group, or at least under one manager; centralization, or centralized control and decision making; and stability of tenure of personnel, which suggests that, for efficiency reasons, turnover should be kept to a minimum even it means sacrificing quality for long-term loyalty.

The classical school of management remained dominant from the 1920s until the 1940s. It was gradually supplanted, however, by theories that focused on the importance of individual needs and group interaction in organizations. Human relations management arose in the 1930s, largely as a result of studies and experiments (including the classic Hawthorne experiments) conducted by Harvard University researcher Elton Mayo and his contemporaries. To the surprise of classical theorists, Mayo's research demonstrated that mechanistic, efficiently designed processes did not necessarily create more efficient organizations. Instead, the research demonstrated that success could be attained by showing more concern for workers' psychological needs. The human relations school advocated techniques like employee counseling, feedback, and communication with coworkers, superiors, and subordinates.

Both the classical and human relations management ideologies were eclipsed during the 1950s by the behavioral management school of thought. It also emphasized the importance of the human psyche in management. However, it differed from the human relations approach in that it stressed behavior over

interaction. It sought to rationalize and predict behavior in the workplace through scientific analysis of social interaction, motivation, the use of power and influence, leadership qualities, and other factors. Behaviorists believed that a chief goal of managers should be to increase the effectiveness of workers through motivational techniques like empowerment and participation in decisions, and to redesign jobs to take advantage of individuals' strengths and weaknesses.

Demonstrating the gradual transition from mechanistic management theory to a more humanistic approach is Douglas McGregor's renowned Theory X and Theory Y, which he posited in the 1950s. Theory X depicts the old, repressive, pessimistic view of workers. It assumes that people are lazy and have to be coerced to produce with tangible rewards. It also presumes that workers prefer to be directed, want to avoid responsibility, and treasure financial security above all else. In contrast, Theory Y postulates that: humans can learn to accept and seek responsibility; most people possess a high degree of imagination and problem-solving ability; employees will self-govern, or direct themselves toward goals to which they are committed; and, notably, satisfaction of ego and self-actualization are among the most important needs that organizations should address.

Coinciding with the behavioral management ideology that gained acceptance throughout the 1950s (and remained relevant into the 1990s) was the fifth school of thought, quantitative management. Quantitative management theorists believe that, while the behavioral dimension of organizations merits attention, scientific and analytical techniques related to process and structure can help organizations be much more efficient. Quantitative management entails the application of statistical analyses, linear programming, and information systems to assist in making decisions, allocating resources, scheduling processes, and tracking money. Specifically, it advocates the substitution of verbal and descriptive analysis with models and symbols, particularly those that are computer-generated. In fact, it is because of advanced electronic information systems that quantitative management techniques were broadly applied in the 1980s and early 1990s.

COMPLEMENTARY MANAGEMENT APPROACHES

In addition to the school approaches that dominated much of the twentieth century are three other approaches to management theory and application; process, systems, and contingency. They emerged during the middle 1900s, gained widespread appeal during the latter part of the century, and continued to influence management thought and practice into the mid-1990s. These approaches differ from most of the schools of management thought in that they are not posited as a wrong or right ideology, but rather are complementary—They can exist and be applied simultaneously depending on the particular internal and external environment of individual organizations.

The systems management approach emphasizes the importance of educating managers to understand the overall system so that they will realize how actions in their department affect other units. An organization can be likened to a mobile—If you touch one part, the entire apparatus swings into motion. For example, the hiring of a single individual into a marketing department is bound to have some degree of impact on other divisions of the organization over time. Similarly, incorporating behaviorist theory, if a manager is given more autonomy and responsibility he is likely to perform at a higher level. As a result, subordinates in his department are likely to perform better, which may cause other departments to be more effective, and so on.

The systems approach to management recognizes both open and closed systems. A closed system, like a clock, is self-contained and operates relatively free from outside influences. In contrast, most organizations are open systems and are thus highly dependent on outside resources like suppliers and buyers. Specifically, systems are impacted by four spheres of outside influence: education and skills (of workers); legal and political; economic; and cultural. Management processes must be designed to adapt to those influences. This acknowledgment of outside factors represents a meaningful departure from the earliest school approaches that viewed management within the context of closed systems.

Importantly, the systems approach also recognizes that all large organizations are comprised of multiple subsystems, each of which receives inputs from other subsystems and turns them into outputs for use by other subsystems. At least five types of subsystems, according to systems theory, should be incorporated into management processes in larger organizations. Production subsystems are the components that transform inputs into outputs. In a manufacturing company this subsystem would be represented by activities related to production. In most business organizations all other subsystems are built around the production subsystem.

Supportive subsystems perform acquisition and distribution functions within an organization. Acquisition activities include securing resources, like employees and raw materials, from the external environment. Human resources and purchasing divisions would typically be included in this group. Distribution (or disposal) activities encompass efforts to transfer the product or service outside of the organization.

Supportive subsystems of this type include sales and marketing divisions, public relations departments, and lobbying efforts.

Maintenance subsystems maintain the social involvement of employees in an organization. Activities in this group include providing benefits and compensation that motivates workers, creating favorable work conditions, empowering employees, and other forms of satisfying human needs. Similarly, adaptive subsystems serve to gather information about problems and opportunities in the environment and then respond with innovations that allow the organization to adapt. A firm's research lab or a product development department would both be part of an adaptive subsystem. Finally, managerial subsystems direct the activities of other subsystems in the organization. These managerial functions set goals and policies, allocate resources, settle disputes, and generally work to facilitate the efficiency of the organization.

Like the systems approach, the contingency approach to management views the organization as a set of interdependent units operating in an open system. It differs from all other management approaches, though, in that it is based on the idea that every organization and situation is unique. Its situational perspective implies that there is no single best way to manage. Therefore, specific techniques and managerial concepts must be applied in different ways and in different combinations to achieve organizational or departmental effectiveness. In fact, the contingency theory has been described as a sort of amalgam of all other ideologies. Its chief contribution to modern management theory is its identification of critical internal and external variables that affect management processes.

PROCESS APPROACH

Perhaps the most widely accepted organizational management theory is the process approach. It draws on many of the theories contained in the five schools of management and the systems approach and contingency approach described above. For example, the process approach is centered around Fayol's ideas, particularly his five management functions. And, like the systems approach and the later schools of management thought, it emphasizes the point that management is an ongoing series of interrelated activities rather than a one-time act.

The process approach also recognizes other management theories that have gained acceptance in the late 1900s. Of import is the generally accepted management pyramid model, which is comprised of three hierarchies. At the top of the pyramid is top management, or executives, that handle long-term strategy. At the center is middle management, which translates top management objectives into more specific goals for individual work units. Finally, line managers and supervisors fill the bottom of the pyramid. They handle the day-to-day management of employees and operations.

Adherents to the process approach have altered and elaborated on Fayol's original functions, usually in an attempt to incorporate behaviorist philosophies. Management theorists commonly recognize five management functions: planning, organizing, staffing, leading, and controlling. The five process management functions are linked together by communication and decision-making activities common to all of them.

PLANNING. Planning is the development of specific strategies designed to achieve organizational goals. It occurs at all three management levels: top, middle, and line. As indicated earlier, top managers are charged with making long-term plans that define the mission and policies of the organization. They concentrate on the questions of what and how much in the planning process. In contrast, middle managers implement mission and policy objectives, usually by focusing on the where and when of planning. Finally, line managers effect the specific plans of the middle managers by addressing the pressing questions of who and how.

For example, top executives at a nail factory may decide that the company should become the most productive, highest-quality, largest-volume producer in the world. Middle managers in the production division may decide that accomplishment of that goal requires that over the next 12 months they cut costs by 20 percent, decrease flaws to .01 percent, and increase capacity 40 percent. Likewise, managers in the marketing department may decide that they need to increase sales by 80 percent during the next year. Finally, line managers would have to figure out how to achieve those goals and who would do the actual work. They might increase bonuses for salespeople that boosted volume, for instance, or lower profit margins (and prices) to increase sales. Or, production line managers might implement a new quality management program and increase investments in cost-saving automation.

Another way of viewing the planning process in an organization is by categorizing planning activities as: strategic (top management), tactical (middle), or operational (bottom). The overall process usually entails at least six steps: setting goals; analyzing the external and internal environment to identify problems and opportunities; identifying and evaluating alternatives; choosing a plan; implementing the program; and controlling and judging the results of the implementation. Different stages of the process should ideally overlap management hierarchies, thus fostering organizational unity and informed planning.

In addition to stages of the planning process and hierarchical responsibilities, most planning activities and responsibilities can be categorized into one of four planning roles: 1) resource allocation; 2) environmental adaptation; 3) internal coordination; 4) and organizational strategic awareness. (*Corporate Planning: An Executive Viewpoint*, Englewood Cliffs, 1980). Resource allocation entails decisions related to the apportionment of capital, expertise, labor, and equipment. For instance, a chief executive might decide to not pay shareholder dividends as a way to increase funds for new product development. Or, a production line manager may elect to shift laborers from one product line to another to facilitate shifting output requirements.

Environmental adaptation planning activities are those that serve to improve the company's relationship to its external environment, including such influences as governments, suppliers, customers, and public opinion. These activities address problems and opportunities that arise from those external factors. For example, gas station company managers that choose to attach point-of-sale (credit card) machines to their pumps are reacting to a public demand for convenience. Similarly, a chief executive of a coal mining company might have to plan to reduce toxic emissions in an effort to satisfy government regulators or to appease public sentiment.

Internal coordination planning activities are those that respond to internal influences. They coordinate internal strengths and weaknesses in an effort to maximize profitability (in the case of for-profit companies). Finally, planning activities categorized as organizational strategic awareness strategies create systematic management development systems that allow an organization to evaluate the effects of past plans. This would encompass the sixth stage of the planning process detailed above. It would include activities like making plans to measure the effect of a new commission system on sales volume.

In order to be effective, plans and goals developed and executed at any level will generally exhibit basic characteristics. The plans should be specific and measurable, for example, meaning that they will have definite goals that can be measured against definite results. Plans should also be time-oriented, or should be devised with deadlines for accomplishing parts of the entire goal and a final deadline for completion. Plans should also be attainable. Insufficient resources or impossible goals can thwart motivation and result in underperformance. Finally, plans should be mutually supportive, meaning that plans made in or for one part of an organization should complement other plans and objectives.

ORGANIZING. Organizing is the second major managerial function. It is the process of structuring a company's resources, primarily its personnel, in a way that will allow it to achieve its plans or objectives. Specifically, organizing entails a fundamental three-step process. First of all, managers must determine the exact actions that have to be taken to implement plans and achieve objectives. Secondly, they must divide personnel into teams with areas of responsibility. Thirdly, managers must delegate authority and responsibility to individuals and establish decision-making relationships. Once management accomplishes the first step, it can take number of different routes to organize teams and delegate authority. Most organizations are arranged by either function or division.

A basic understanding of formal authority is integral to an appreciation of different organizational structures. There are three fundamental types of formal authority in businesses. First of all, line authority refers to the relationship between superiors and subordinates. A sales manager with authority over his sales force would exemplify line authority, and the entire sales department would be considered a line department. Secondly, staff authority entails managers' control over subordinates and activities only in their own departments, which serve an advisory or support role in the organization. Examples of staff departments include legal, personnel, and information systems. Thirdly, functional authority gives managers the power to make decisions about projects that involve workers in other departments. For example, a manager of a bowling ball line may have the authority to tell a production manager what color to make a bowling balls, but he has no power to tell him (her) how to reward his workers.

The most common approach to organizing teams and delegating authority in organizations is by function. Under the functional approach, activities are broken down into primary business functions, such as finance, operations, and marketing. Within each major functional group are numerous subfunctions. In the marketing division, for example, might be the sales and promotions departments. The functional approach results in a comparatively efficient division of labor and an authority hierarchy that is easy for workers to understand. However, it may lead to internal rivalries between departments or myopia because different divisions are not aware of the goals and actions of other parts of the company.

In addition to functions, many companies are organized by division. There are several different divisional approaches to structuring teams and delegating power to managers. For example, some companies take a product line approach, whereby the company is broken down into different product or service groups. For instance, an appliance producer may break its organization down into dishwashers, clothes washers and dryers, and vacuum cleaners. Other com-

panies might use a customer approach—industrial products, consumer products, government products, etc. The advantage of both approaches is that they allow managers and the entire company to be focused on the product or customer rather than on support functions, like marketing. However, they may result in an inefficient division of labor (i.e. overlap) because each group is forced to supply their own support functions.

Another common means of organizing a company by divisions is the geographic approach, whereby activities or groups are divided by region. For instance, a multinational bank may have three major divisions: North American, Asia, and European. Those divisions, then, might be divided into sub-regions like northeastern, southern, and western. The geographic approach is often used by companies that specialize in marketing, finance, or some other major business function and operate in a number of different geographic environments. It allows flexibility in relation to different laws, exchange rates, and cultures, and fosters a responsiveness to local markets not attainable under other divisional approaches. The chief drawback of geographic organizations is that they can be relatively expensive to maintain.

A less conventional and increasingly popular approach to structuring organizations is known as the matrix system. In essence, a matrix system creates both functional and divisional groups to form multidisciplinary, integrated teams that combine staff and line authority. The main advantage of the matrix is that it reduces myopia in an organization, fosters cooperation, and promotes a free flow of information. But the matrix approach may also create an ambiguous power structure and may have limitations for many types of companies.

In addition to the basic structure, management authority and responsibility will also be dictated by the level of centralization in a company. In general, companies with more centralized management will be figuratively tall, meaning that power flows down through a chain of command. Decisions are made by a few people and handed down to the masses. In contrast, decentralized, or flat, organizations push management authority down. In flat organizations, many managers (and subordinates) are empowered to independently make decisions about their area of expertise in the company. Because of the trend toward flatter organizations during the 1980s and early 1990s, traditional middle levels of management have become obsolete in many companies. Effectively, all workers become managers to some degree in the flattest organizations.

STAFFING. Staffing, the third major organizational function, encompasses activities related to finding and sustaining a labor force that is adequate to meet the organization's objectives. First, managers have to determine exactly what their labor needs are and then go into the labor force to try and recruit those skills and characteristics. Secondly, managers must train workers. Thirdly, they have to devise a method of compensating and evaluating performance that complements objectives. This includes designing pay and benefits packages, conducting performance reviews, and promoting employees. Finally, managers usually must devise a system of firing ineffective employees or reducing the work force. In addition, management duties related to staffing often entail working with organized labor unions and meeting federal and state regulations.

LEADING. Leading, or motivating, is the fourth basic managerial function identified by the process approach to management. It is defined as the act of influencing other people to achieve goals. In general, the **leadership** role for most managers entails four primary duties: educating, judging, counseling, and representing. Educating includes teaching skills and showing workers how to get along in the company. They do so through both formal and informal means. Examples of informal education are attitudes, work habits, and other behavior that sets an example for subordinates to follow.

Judging activities that are part of a manager's leadership responsibilities include settling disputes, creating and enforcing standards and policies, evaluating output, and dispensing rewards. In fact, much of the respect and esteem that a manager gets from subordinates is contingent upon the ability to judge effectively.

A manager's ability to counsel will also impact his or her effectiveness. Counseling involves giving advice, helping workers solve problems, soliciting feedback from subordinates, and listening to voluntary input or employee problems. Finally, managers lead through representation by voicing the concerns and suggestions of their subordinates to higher authorities. In other words, the manager must show a willingness to back his workers and represent their needs and goals.

Numerous theories have been posited to explain the leadership function and to describe the traits of successful leaders. For example, six traits considered necessary for managers in large organizations to be effective leaders are: 1) motivation; 2) personal values; 3) ability; 4) reputation and track record; 5) relationships in the firm and industry; and 6) industry and organizational knowledge (*The Leadership Factor*, The Free Press, 1988). Contrary to traditional beliefs about leadership, which hold that leadership ability is innate, these trait groups are acquired through combinations of early childhood experiences, education, and career experiences.

In addition to developing leadership traits, effective managers must adopt a style of leadership that complements their position, personality, and environment. In general, managers practice some combination of four recognized leadership styles: directive, political, participative, and charismatic. The directive leadership style emphasizes the use of facts, sound strategy, and assertiveness. The manager focuses on gathering information, establishing objectives through a careful assessment of data, devising strategies to accomplish goals, and then directing subordinates and coworkers to achieve those ends. Managers who subscribe to a directive leadership style are less concerned about building a consensus for their vision than they are about motivating others to achieve it. They are more likely to confront resistance to their goals and to have less patience in pursuing objectives than other types of leaders.

In contrast, managers that embrace a political leadership style believe that their ability to lead requires the power to manipulate forces within the entity toward common objectives. Importantly, they assume that the company is a political arena fraught with deception, in-fighting, and selfish goals. Therefore, they often must push, bargain, and manipulate to advance the interests of their departments and themselves. Although the leader may be well-intentioned, honest, and acting in the best interests of the company, he or she may be willing to deceive others and act selfishly in order to achieve a desired result. Common tactics include keeping goals flexible or vague, advancing their agendas patiently, and manipulating channels of influence and authority.

The participative, or values-driven, style of leadership emphasizes joint decision-making, decentralization, the sharing of power, and democratic management. Managers that are participative leaders assume that their subordinates are highly motivated by work that challenges them, builds skills, and is accomplished with teams of people that they respect. Thus, unlike directive leadership, the participative style focuses on building a consensus during the decision-making process. It also stresses bottom-up management—information and expertise is gleaned from workers in lower levels of the organization that is used to direct decisions and goals—and the empowerment of subordinates to make decisions.

The fourth basic managerial style of leadership, charismatic leadership, differs from the other three styles in that it is more suited to realizing radical visions or handling crises. It is less oriented toward influencing behavior toward the attainment of long-term goals or day-to-day management activities. Charismatic leadership in business organizations is a style often used by entrepreneurs who are starting new companies, or by transformational managers seeking to revitalize established organization.

CONTROLLING. The fifth major managerial function, controlling, is comprised of activities that measure and evaluate efforts at planning, organizing, staffing, and leading. Controlling is typically viewed as an ongoing management process that ensures that the organization is moving toward its goals. The process includes implementing preventive measures, evaluating ongoing activities, and post-performance corrective actions.

Preventive measures usually take the form of preset standards, or specific standards against which performance can be measured. Managers at all levels must determine exactly what they want to accomplish, in quantifiable terms, and then communicate the concrete goals to their subordinates. Examples of standards are budgets, projections, pro forma statements, and production, sales, or quality initiatives.

During the second stage of the control process, evaluation, the manager determines how closely his subordinate's or department's performance matched up with preset standards. Of import is the manager's acceptable range of deviation, or the degree to which actual performance can vary from the standard before corrective action is necessary. In addition, the manager must factor into the performance comparison influences outside of the control of his unit. He must also devise a means of communicating results to subordinates in a constructive manner.

If measured results deviate outside of an acceptable range the manager must take corrective action. Corrective action may mean simply readjusting the preset standards to reflect more realistic goals. Or, the manager may have to analyze the process which lead to the deviation and then act to make changes. For instance, if a production line fails to meet quality goals the manager may choose to rearrange work teams or change the financial incentive system to emphasize quality. He may also determine that the departmental budget needs to be revised to increase spending on quality control.

To be effective, managers must design control systems that are based on meaningful and accepted standards. If standards are too high, subordinates are likely to lose motivation or become frustrated. Standards should also be based on the overall goals of the organization rather than on the narrow objectives of one department or division. The control process should emphasize two-way communication so that controls are understood by subordinates and managers are able to effectively set standards and evaluate performance with the benefit of the workers' perspective. In addition, standards and controls should be flexible to accommodate emerging problems and opportunities. Most importantly, controls should be used only when necessary so that they don't unnecessarily obstruct creativity and drive.

MANAGERIAL SKILLS AND ROLES

In addition to the five basic managerial functions defined by the process approach, a number of ancillary roles can be identified (depending on the position and responsibilities of individual managers) that are necessary to perform the functions. For instance, a manager is generally expected to act as a figurehead for his unit or organization, which entails performing ceremonial duties or entertaining associates. Managers may also serve as liaisons, working with peers in other departments or contacts outside of the organization to gather information and make decisions that impact their subordinates.

Another role is that of monitor, wherein the manager is expected to constantly oversee and observe his unit and to develop a big picture of the department and its place in the organization. Likewise, the manager must be a negotiator to help secure resources for his team or group and to elicit cooperation from other groups or individuals inside and outside the company. Other common roles are entrepreneur, whereby the manager generates ideas about improving his unit's performance, and resource allocator, in which the manager determines how to distribute limited resources within his group to achieve maximum effectiveness.

To succeed in their various roles, managers must possess a combination of skills from three broad groups: conceptual, technical, and relationship. Technical skills refer to knowledge of processes, tools, and techniques particular to a company or industry. For instance, a sales manager that has never worked as a field representative in his company might lack knowledge that would be important in setting sales goals and compensations systems. Conceptual skills allow managers to view each unit as part of the entire organization, and the company as part of a larger industry. Conceptual skills are particularly important for developing long-range goals and solving problems. Finally, relationship skills are those that the manager uses to communicate effectively and work with others.

Effective managers at all levels typically possess an advanced set of relationship skills, particularly in management structures that stress communication and cooperation (e.g. matrix). In general, managers at the top of the management pyramid require a higher degree of conceptual skills. In fact, as managers assume more responsibility and become less involved with day-to-day activities, technical knowledge becomes secondary. Middle managers, on the other hand, usually must possess a roughly equal amount of conceptual and technical knowledge. Finally, line managers near the bottom of the pyramid depend primarily on technical, rather than conceptual, skills.

SEE ALSO: Employee Dismissals; Human Resources Management; Matrix Management and Structure; Organization Development; Organization Theory

[Dave Mote]

FURTHER READING:

Cherrington, David J. *Organizational Behavior: The Management of Individual and Organizational Performance*. Boston: Allyn and Bacon, 1994.

Ivancevich, John M. and Michael T. Matteson. *Organizational Behavior and Management*. Homewood, IL: Richard D. Irwin, Inc., 1990.

Kotter, John P. *The Leadership Factor*. New York: The Free Press, 1988.

Mescon, Michael H. *Management: Individual and Organizational Effectiveness*, 2nd ed. Cambridge, MA: Harper & Row, Publishers, New York.

Plunkett, Warren R. and Raymond F. Attner. *Introduction to Management*, 4th ed. Boston: PWS-Kent Publishing Company, 1992.

Sayles, Leonard R. *Leadership: Managing in Real Organizations*, 2nd ed. New York: McGraw-Hill Book Company, 1989.

Schermerhorn, Jr., John R., James G. Hunt and Richard N. Osborn. *Management of Organizational Behavior*. New York: John Wiley & Sons, 1982.

Wren, Daniel A. and Dan Voich, Jr. *Management: Process, Structure, and Behavior*, 3rd ed. New York: John Wiley & Sons, 1984.

MANAGEMENT AUDIT

Simply defined, the management audit is a comprehensive and thorough examination of an organization or one of its components. The audit is implemented to identify problems or significant weaknesses in the organization or corporation, thus providing management with a tool to address and repair the problem area.

The **audit** is not a new or recent idea. History tells us of the presence of auditors in Pharaoh's Egypt and the classical periods of Greek and Roman history. As businesses developed and grew over the centuries of recorded history, the need for controls became increasingly important. Financial auditing became a standard in American businesses and, following the lead of New York State, certification for accountants was enacted as legislation in many states. The financial audit is now fully integrated in to business practices. The internal audit follows the spirit of financial auditing and surpasses it to examine operational matters as well. Another natural extension is operational auditing. While **internal auditing** is conducted by employees within the organization, an operational audit is generally completed by an internal task force or external analysts.

The management audit is now widely accepted in the business field. For over forty years, corporations and non-profit organizations have utilized the management audit as a comprehensive tool. In 1932, T. G. Rose, a lecturer in management at Cambridge University and former manager for Leyland Motors, embraced the concept of an organizational and management audit annually, and Queens University School of Business professor William P. Leonard followed suit, urging a comprehensive examination of the business entity. Additional credibility stemmed from the **General Accounting Office (GAO)** of the federal government, an office charged with independent audits of government agencies.

The management audit is defined by its scope and objectives. The scope is broad and generally includes all functions of the organization, including objectives and **strategy**, corporate structure, organizational planning, the **budgeting** process, human and financial resources management, **decision making**, **research and development**, **marketing**, equipment and operations, and **management information systems (MIS)**. This breadth extends to recent, present, and future operations and covers external issues as well as internal concerns. Objectives of the management audit includes the development of recommendations and improvements, as well as increased awareness of the credibility and acceptance of the audit's results. The process is more an audit of management, in order to enhance **corporate profits** and financial stability.

The audit follows a logical, step-by-step format, including initial interviews with key managers. A study team uses the interview process to define the scope of the audit, including the areas or functions to be studied. Next, the team requests various forms of documentation, including but not limited to, budgets, planning documents, corporate reports, **financial statements**, policy and procedure manuals, biographical material, and various other documents. Following this stage, the study team then prepares a schedule and detailed plan of study, all aimed at proceeding to the internal fact-finding step. Fact-finding relies once again on interviews, documentation, and personal observation of facilities and organizational work patterns. By the time these steps are completed, the study team develops a thorough understanding of organizational structure and operations.

The team generally turns next to an external review, using interviews to determine opinions and attitudes key people outside the organization have about its operations. Examples of those interviewed are customers, representatives of financial institutions, and employees of federal agencies having contact with the audited organization. These interviews provide the team with more objective evaluations, and lead to an analysis of all the information and data now gathered. Organizational performance is profiled, then efficiency and effectiveness are evaluated and compared against industry norms. While many criteria can be measured quantitatively, team members have to use sound judgement and objectivity when evaluating issues which cannot be measured. In turn, organizational leadership has to be receptive to the audit process and demonstrate clear acceptance of audit findings.

The study team then develops conclusions and recommendations which are communicated to the organization's management. These final two stages—conclusions/recommendations and communication are essential to the management audit process. The audit is expected to identify both corporate strengths and weaknesses, the source of problems, and potential problem areas if not addressed. Recommendations for correction are presented to top management. The final report comes in the form of an overall plan of action, which includes prioritized recommendations, the specific unit and individual to carry out the recommendations, a schedule for action, and expected results. When conducted with thoroughness, objectivity, and timeliness, the management audit becomes a very powerful tool for corporate and organizational executives who seek to improve effectiveness and efficiency.

An important aspect of the management audit is the composition of the study team. Both internal and external analysts are frequently used for an audit team—depending on several factors, including the need for independent appraisal, the lack of human or financial resources to conduct the audit, or the need to provide an external audit to contrast against internal findings. In some instances, associations like the American Institute of Management (AIM) provide audit teams. The AIM has developed ten categories of the management audit, and many audits apply these same categories. They include:

1. economic function
2. corporate structure
3. health of earnings
4. service to stockholders
5. research & development
6. directorate analysis
7. fiscal policies
8. production efficiency
9. sales vigor
10. executive evaluation

Management audits are not limited to business corporations. Non-profit organizations, including educational institutions, hospitals, and churches often utilize the audit in an attempt to improve operations. When conducted effectively, and when recommendations are applied properly, the audit has proved its usefulness as a management technique.

[Boyd Childress]

FURTHER READING:

Craig-Cooper, Michael. *The Management Audit: How to Create an Effective Management Team.* Financial Times Pitman Publishing, 1993.

Leonard, William P. *The Management Audit: An Appraisal of Management Methods and Performance.* Prentice-Hall, 1962.

McNair, Carol Jean. *Benchmarking: A Tool for Continuous Improvement.* HarperBusiness, 1992.

Rose, Thomas G. *The Management Audit.* Gee and Co., 1944.

Talley, Dorsey J. *Management Audits for Excellence: The Manager's Guide to Improving the Quality and Productivity of an Organization.* ASQC Quality Press, 1988.

MANAGEMENT BUYOUTS

A management buyout occurs when incumbent **management** takes ownership of a firm by purchasing a sufficient amount of the firm's **common stock**. These transactions vary due to the conditions under which the firm is offered for sale and the method of financing employed by the managers.

Consider the conditions that may encourage managers to purchase a controlling interest in the firm's stock. The owners of a corporation are its stockholders. These stockholders are concerned with increasing the value of their investment, not only in one specific firm, but for all investments. Therefore, if a majority of the firm's stockholders perceive that the value of their investment will be enhanced by agreeing to be acquired by another firm, they will elect to sell their stock to the acquiring firm at a price they consider fair. Managers of a firm may consider this transfer of ownership a benign event. They may also, however, be concerned that the new owners will not manage the firm most efficiently, that they will have less control over the management of the firm, or that their jobs will be less secure. In this situation, the current managers of the firm may consider purchasing the firm themselves.

Another situation that frequently leads to management buyouts is the case of financial distress. If the firm is having serious difficulties meeting its financial obligations, it may choose to reorganize itself. This can be done by closing failing operations to slow the drain on financial resources and by selling profitable operations to an outside party for the cash needed to restore financial viability to remaining operations. It is not uncommon for firms in this situation to give managers of the divisions being divested the opportunity to buy the assets. This makes sense for two reasons. First, management probably has the greatest expertise in managing the subset of assets offered for sale. Second, it saves the cost of searching for an external party with an interest in the division for sale.

Once incumbent management has decided it is interested in purchasing the firm or a particular portion of a firm they must raise the capital needed to buy it. Managers in many corporations are encouraged to become stockholders in the firm by including stock and the option to buy more stock as part of their compensation package. The nonmanagement stockholders, however, will expect some compensation from this sale and the value of manager-owned stock is not likely to be sufficient to finance the purchase of the firm or one of its divisions. This means that managers must raise cash from other sources such as personal wealth. If managers have sufficient capital in other investments, these can be sold and used to finance the remainder of the purchase price.

While a management buyout is relatively straightforward when managers have sufficient personal capital to meet the purchase price, the more common scenario requires managers to borrow significant amounts. It is not uncommon for managers to mortgage homes and other personal assets to raise needed funds, but in many transactions these amounts are still not sufficient. In these cases, managers will borrow larger amounts using the assets of the firm they are acquiring as collateral. These transactions are called **leveraged buyouts**, or LBOs. The LBO is a common form of financing for large transactions. It provides the management team with the financing needed to control the assets of the firm with only a small amount of **equity**. Nevertheless, the new firm that emerges from this transaction has very high financial risk. The large amounts of debt will require large periodic payments of interest. If the firm cannot meet this obligation during any period, it can be forced into bankruptcy by the debtholders.

It is important to note that managers are no different than other investors. They will assess the risk and rewards associated with a buyout, leveraged or otherwise, and will act in their own best interests. As managers, they have specialized knowledge of the firm that may prove advantageous in charting a future course of action for the acquired firm. By assuming ownership of the acquired firm, they will also assume a riskier position personally. If the potential rewards associated with control are perceived as adequate compensation for this risk, then the management buyout will be consummated.

[Paul Bolster]

MANAGEMENT EDUCATION

SEE: Business Education; Continuing Education; Executive Development

MANAGEMENT INFORMATION SYSTEMS

Management information systems are continuously evolving components of business today. As the business cycle continues to operate at faster rates and competition expands on a global scale, the importance of well-maintained information systems is not to be underrated. The management task continues to grow in complexity as technology changes and the influences of international economies affect business.

A management information system (MIS) typically includes **databases**, **expert systems**, decision support systems, **accounting** and financial information, marketing and sales information, and engineering data. Mainframe computers, while still used effectively by many companies, are a dying trend as new technology embraces the network: **local area networks (LANs)** and **wide area networks (WANs)**. The use of MISs in strategic planning functions is growing, as more reliance is placed on the system. This makes the job of the MIS executive extremely important, as the data enclosed in the system must be accurate, timely, and necessary to provide support to senior managers making encompassing decisions.

Until the mid-1960s, if a company had a computer, its use was limited to accounting functions. There was no specific system for transfer of information aside from papers and memos distributed through the management chain. In 1964, the invention of the silicon chip greatly improved the cost-benefit ratio of owning a computer. More power for less money was available, and computer companies capitalized on the notion of MISs to sell more equipment. Larger companies agreed that an MIS was a good use of the computer because the wealth of information in these companies was difficult to grasp and digest. Nevertheless, by the late 1960s, data processing was the primary function of computers in industry. The use of computers as MISs had failed in many circles due to equipment shortcomings, inadequate literacy of users, and too much ambition without proper planning.

Over the 1970s, the MIS gained acceptance in larger companies as returns on investment were seen. By the 1980s, the equipment evolved exponentially and **software** became more user-friendly, encompassing the entire corporation. The mainframe was introduced and became more pervasive in industry during the 1980s, but leagues of programmers and specialists were necessary to keep the equipment and software up-to-date. Although the mainframe computers were very good for business in this era, they were generally regimented systems, offering little flexibility. The advent of the personal computer (PC) in the 1980s changed the landscape of the MIS again, as software packages became more user-friendly to boost the sales of the PC. A new emphasis on communication was placed on software/hardware development teams, spawning computer networks. Currently LANs and WANs are common system setups. Through the incorporation of data exchange through telephone lines, an MIS can connect with customers around the world to provide more immediate service and instant sales information. Likewise, managers traveling anywhere in the world that has fairly modern telephone systems can connect to the company MIS. Eventually Third World countries will be connected to the electronic web, forever changing the way business is conducted.

Critical issues today include the use of a common operating system, increased bandwidth, plug-and-play capability, and more flexible licensing of software. The biggest challenges are within the corporation. In a 1993 survey, chief financial and operating officers indicated that they wanted to see visible payoffs for MIS investment. Some companies are focusing on justification of expenditures by placing dollar amounts on improved customer service and communication. Approximately 41 percent of executives interviewed said they outsourced some component of or all MIS functions.

A new concept, Commerce at Light Speed (CALS), is changing information standards. CALS is a global information strategy that includes seven networks. Technological information can be shared between industry and government, and information can be easily transferred across the globe. The concept allows a company to develop customized orders and ship these orders quickly. Several companies around the world are using CALS, including Hughes Aircraft, Boeing Corporation, United Airlines, and Tokyo Electric Power Company. Efficiency gains and improvements to manufacturing processes have been observed through the use of CALs.

As companies expand operations to foreign nations, the use of management information systems becomes more critical. Information systems personnel moving away from home-based operations often report to foreign **chief executive officer**s who are not as eager as their American counterparts to adopt new technology. While management and decision-making styles are different across cultures, the information required to make these decisions may also be different. Likewise, cultural differences play a great role in customer relationships and the MIS must adapt to this. Toys 'R' Us uses a Unisys mainframe to house all corporate data within the United States, while in the smaller markets of Europe and Asia simpler interfaces are used.

[Valerie E. Wilson]

FURTHER READING:

Alter, Allan E. "International Affairs." *CIO*. December, 1992, p. 34.

Babcock, Charles. "Unshackling Corporate Data." *Computerworld*. October 3, 1994, p. 6.

Dodge, Marc. "The Mainframe is Dead, But So is the PC." *Computerworld*. March 28, 1994.

LaPlante, Alice. "Life in the Foreign Lane." *Computerworld*. February 20, 1995, p. 117.

Maglitta, Joseph. "Squeeze Play." *Computerworld*. April 19, 1993, p. 86.

Manji, James F. "Aircraft Industry Reaps Benefits from CALS-like Programs." *Industry Week*. October 3, 1994, p. 19A.

Manji, James F. "CALS Concepts Link Multiple Power Plants for Japanese Utility." *Industry Week*. October 3, 1994, p. 17A.

Manji, James F. "CALS Shared Resources Centers: Where Technology Transfer Becomes Reality." *Industry Week*. October 3, 1994, p. 13A.

Manji, James F. "CALS: Sharpen Your Competitive Edge Today and into the 21st Century." *Industry Week*. October 3, 1994, p. 4A.

McLeod, Raymond. *Management Information Systems*. New York: Macmillan Publishing Company, 1990.

Seybold, Patricia. "IS Vision 2000: Dancing to the New Beat." *Computerworld*. December 26, 1994, p. 71.

Smith, Laura B. "Top Issues of '95 Resolved: Not to Let This List Be the Same 20 Years from Now." *PC Week*. December 26, 1994, p. 24.

Williamson, Mickey. "Becoming a World Power." *CIO*. June 1, 1994, p. 40.

MANAGEMENT SCIENCE

Management science is the application of the scientific method to address problems and decisions that arise in the business community and other organizations, such as government and military institutions. This study, which is also commonly known as operations research (OR), operates on the understanding that business managers can make informed decisions only when they have access to scientifically-acquired knowledge.

To gain such knowledge, management science practice requires that its users undertake the major steps of scientific inquiry. It is first necessary to identify the issue or problem. After doing so, one must formulate a hypothesis (theory) about possible solutions to the problem. A practitioner of management science then constructs appropriate models with which the hypothesis can be tested. After the tests have been completed, the results are collected and analyzed. One then determines the best way to resolve the issue or address the problem based on the final results.

J.C. Hsiao and David S. Cleaver commented in *Management Science* that "mathematical models that show interrelationships among decision variables are indispensable to management science. In particular, mathematical models facilitate analysis of the overall structure of the problem and help the decision maker predict the relative effects of alternative courses of action.'' As computers have grown more sophisticated and powerful, they have been used with increasing frequency by those undertaking such complex analysis. By the 1990s, **computers** were well established as integral tools in the execution of management science methods.

Proponents of management science note that the practice and implementation of its information-gathering methods are not intended to replace the valuable insights that people can bring to business decisions based on their own personal experiences. As Shiv K. Gupta and John M. Cozzolino wrote in *Fundamentals of Operations Research for Management*, ''the need for insight and intuition will always be present.'' They point out, however, that a full understanding of all aspects of a business is increasingly difficult to accomplish in a technologically-advanced world of diverse industrial enterprises.

Some scholars admit that management science/operations research is often misunderstood. As R. Nichols Hazelwood observed in *International Science and Technology*, ''OR defies easy definition because it is a way of using some of the tools of scientific research to study things that often are not conventionally the province of scientists. As its techniques become accepted they become part of everyone's way of research. Then there is a tendency to dismiss OR as simply plain 'horse sense.' True. But such fancy horses!'' Indeed, efforts to use management science to find a quantitative basis for making optimal business decisions has become a fundamental cornerstone of corporate and industrial strategy over the past 50 years.

THE EMERGENCE OF MANAGEMENT SCIENCE

Modern management science, declared Hsiao and Cleaver, ''was born during World War II when the British military management called a group of scientists together to study the strategies and tactics of various military operations. The goal was efficient allocation of scarce resources for the war effort. The name operations research came directly from the context in which it was used and developed: research on (military) operations.''

Hsiao and Cleaver noted that the efforts of the British scientific community prompted the United States to initiate similar research activities. Use of the military technology required the knowledge of American scientists. ''After many successes during that war,'' wrote Gupta and Cozzolino, ''operations research began to be transplanted to the industrial environment.'' The post-World War II period was one

wherein the private sector of the United States and other nations experienced explosive growth in technology and economic wealth. Armed with capital and scientific advances, corporations expanded the size of their operations. ''The new business opportunities set the stage for scientific methods to augment the personal experiences of the business managers,'' according to Gupta and Cozzolino.

Management science continued to grow during the 1950s and 1960s as business managers discovered that its use could help reduce problems of huge scale to manageable dimensions. Robert Hayes contended in 1969 in the *Harvard Business Review* that ''quantitative analysis is facilitating communication where it never existed before. When a problem has been stated quantitatively, one can often see that it is structurally similar to other problems . . . And once a common structure has been identified, insights and predictions can be transferred from one situation to another, and the quantitative approach can actually increase communication.''

By the 1990s, management research was well established as a useful tool in all areas of the business community. It was entrenched in government institutions as well, and continues to be used in attacking problems associated with municipal and regional planning, mass transit routes such as highways and airports, and crime prevention and investigation.

[Laurie Collier Hillstrom]

FURTHER READING:

Gupta, Shiv K., and John M. Cozzolino. *Fundamentals of Operations Research for Management*. Holden-Day Inc., 1975.

Hayes, Robert H. ''Qualitative Insights from Quantitative Methods,'' *Harvard Business Review*. August, 1969, pp. 108-117.

Hazelwood, R. Nichols. ''Operations Research,'' *International Science and Technology*. January, 1966, pp. 36-49.

Hsiao, J.C., and David S. Cleaver. *Management Science*. Boston: Houghton Mifflin Company, 1982.

Oran, Daniel, and Jay M. Shafritz. *The MBA's Dictionary*. Reston, VA: Reston Publishing, 1983.

MANAGERIAL ACCOUNTING

Managerial accounting, or management accounting, is a system of providing information to managers. Managers use the information to help them make decisions about production, **marketing**, **finance**, **human resources**, and virtually all other organizational functions. The National Association of Accountants (NAA) has defined management accounting as ''the process of identification, measurement, accumulation, analysis, preparation, interpretation and communication of financial information used by management to plan, evaluate, and control within an organization and to assure appropriate use of and accountability for its resources.''

The chief characteristic of managerial accounting procedures is that they are designed to supply knowledge to decision makers within an entity. Financial accounting, in contrast, is concerned with providing information to stockholders, creditors, and others who are outside an organization. A corollary of that difference is that financial **accounting** procedures generally must conform to standardized principles, while management accounting methods are left to the discretion of individual organizations.

Cost accounting, the third major sphere of accounting, is the process of determining the cost of a specific output or activity. Although it is sometimes confused with the managerial accounting function, cost accounting information is used by decision makers both inside and outside an organization. Cost and managerial accounting differ in that the latter goes beyond the role of cost accounting by combining multiple **management** disciplines with financial information to facilitate internal decision making.

BACKGROUND

The earliest recorded accounting records date back to about 3500 B.C., when ancient Egyptian and Sumerian businessmen recorded agricultural production, **tax collection**, and storehouse inventories. The first evidence of more advanced accounting practices, such as property **depreciation**, has been traced to ancient Greek and Roman record keepers. The earliest accounting records that expressed accounts in terms of common monetary units (currency) are evidenced by records dating back to 1340 from Genoa. In fact, it was during the Middle Ages that an emphasis on arithmetic and writing in commercial trade allowed accounting practices to advance significantly.

The popularization of property ownership and money lending during the Renaissance in Europe necessitated the creation of performance measurement methods to help bankers and investors rate the success or failure of business ventures. Thus, the first advanced accounting procedures evolved that accounted for interest, depreciation, fixed assets, inventory turnover, and other factors that still represent the core of managerial accounting practices. Luca Pacioli, a Venetian, was the first to document the accounting practices in his 1494 book, *Summa de Arithmetica, Geometria, Proportioni et Proportionalita.*

Modern accounting practices emerged during the Industrial Revolution, when the very nature of business activity began to change. Complicated financing techniques and huge capital investment expenditures resulted in the formalized distinction between such factors as income and capital, and fixed assets and inventory. It also prompted the creation of advanced means of allocating **overhead** and accurately determining **liabilities** and net worth within companies.

After the Great Depression, and particularly following World War II, the delineation between financial and managerial accounting became more defined, as government regulations and professional groups began to mandate accuracy and standardization in financial reporting and accounting. The dominant trend in managerial accounting during the latter half of the twentieth century has been the use of increasingly detailed, internally generated accounting data to help steer management decisions and improve profitability. An important reason for the rapid growth in the use of detailed internal accounting information since the 1970s has been the proliferation of computerized information systems that have allowed managers to quickly access and process vast amounts of data.

MANAGERIAL ACCOUNTING THEORY

Professionals within an organization that perform the managerial accounting function generally support two primary functions, which have been described by the American Accounting Association. First of all, they generate routine reports containing information regarding **cost management** and the planning and controlling of operations. Secondly, managerial accountants produce special reports for managers that are used for strategic and tactical decisions on matters such as pricing products or services, choosing which products to emphasize or de-emphasize, investing in equipment, and formulating overall policies and long-range planning.

The specific activities in which managerial accountants theoretically engage while producing reports include: recognizing and evaluating transactions and economic events; quantifying and estimating the value of those events; recording and classifying appropriate transactions and events; and, analyzing the reasons for, and relationships between, the transactions and events. After they have performed those objectives, managerial accountants assemble and document their information and prepare it in a logical format; deliver the information to the interested decision makers in a timely and appropriate fashion; assist the decision makers that use the information; and evaluate the implications of past and future events on proposed plans or decisions. They also work to ensure the integrity of the information that they produce and strive to implement a system of reporting that contributes to the effective measurement of management's performance.

MANAGERIAL ACCOUNTING APPLICATION

The practical role of managerial accounting is to increase knowledge within an organization and therefore reduce the risk associated with making decisions. To accomplish this task, managerial accountants gather, translate, and compile information into various reports, each of which is used by different divisions within the company (or institution). Accountants prepare reports on the cost of producing goods, expenditures related to employee training programs, and the cost of marketing programs, among other activities. The reports are used by managers to measure the difference, or ''variance,'' between what they planned and what they actually accomplished, or to compare performance to other benchmarks.

For example, an assembly line supervisor would likely be interested in finding out how efficient his/her line is in comparison to those of fellow supervisors, or compared to productivity in a previous time period. An accounting report showing inventory waste, average hourly labor costs, and overall per-unit costs, among other statistics, might help the supervisor and superiors to identify and correct inefficiencies. A detailed report might evaluate the assembly line data and estimate trends and the long-term effects of those trends on the overall profitability of the organization.

As another example, a product manager for a line of hair care products at a corporation that manufactured beauty aids would probably want to know how much overhead each of the products is consuming. A report that breaks down the amount of overhead attributable to each product might help the manager better determine the profitability of each item in the line of goods and to find out if the sales and profit goals for each item are being met. For instance, a certain type of shampoo may be selling very well and generating large amounts of cash flow. However, a close accounting of that product's actual costs within the organization may reveal that its contribution to overall profits significantly lags that of other offerings in the hair care line. Armed with that information, the product manager might elect to adjust marketing expenditures to emphasize more profitable items, or to concentrate on reducing expenses related to the shampoo.

Because of the need for detailed information about specific operations within a company, management accounting reports are typically much more in-depth than traditional financial accounting reports, such as balance sheet ratios and net income calculations. Most managerial reports also differ from financial reports in their frequency. Many internal reports, in fact, are generated monthly, weekly, or even daily in the case of information such as cash receipts and disbursements. Despite their emphasis on detail, a critical characteristic of most managerial accounting reports is that they are presented in summary format. Managers can read the summaries, efficiently identify possible problem areas, and then examine the details within those areas to determine a course of action.

PLANNING AND CONTROLLING

In the examples described previously, just as in most managerial accounting applications, information produced for managers is used to make decisions about the future and to judge the effectiveness of past decisions and actions. In managerial accounting, the process of setting goals, determining resource requirements, and devising a means of achieving goals is referred to as ''planning.'' Monitoring financial results and measuring the outcome of planning processes within the enterprise is called ''controlling.'' The person in charge of an entity's accounting department is usually called the ''controller.'' The controller generally plays a key role in both planning and controlling endeavors throughout the organization.

The plans of management are formally communicated as budgets, and the term ''**budgeting**'' typically refers to management planning. The controller oversees the development of budgets by the accounting department, usually on annual basis. Budgets are commonly prepared not only for the overall organization, but also for divisions and departments within a company or institution. Budgets are important to the goal-setting function of an organization because they express the wishes and objectives of management in specific, tangible, quantitative terms.

Once a company's plans, or budgets, have been established, managerial accountants begin gathering information that flows from the organization that indicates whether or not the company is achieving its goals. The accounting department presents its findings in the form of performance reports tailored for individual executives or departments. The detailed performance reports essentially compare budgets with actual results for a given time period, allowing managers to identify problem areas. For instance, a company's store managers may utilize data such as inventory levels and sales volumes to direct advertising and promotional programs.

Besides producing routine reports, management accountants also create special reports for other managers that help them to make decisions about proposed projects or problems that arise. Special reports are often created to analyze the relationship between costs and benefits related to different alternatives in the decision-making process. For instance, if a company's competitor drops its prices, management may ask the accounting department to produce a report comparing possible competitive responses, such as lowering prices, increasing advertising, or even changing its product or service. Such reports often involve forecasting as well as the collection of outside information.

COST INFORMATION

Information gathered by cost accounting methods within an organization make up most of the detailed data used to create managerial accounting reports (and financial accounting reports). Understanding the costs associated with producing goods and services is vital to the decision-making process because that comprehension can help place a measurable value on the results of a company's individual decisions.

Four basic cost accounting activities that support the managerial accounting function are:

1. cost determination, which involves simply determining the actual cost of a product or an activity, such as marketing

2. cost recording, whereby costs are recorded in journals and ledgers

3. cost analyzing, which refers to accountants and managers analyzing the data to help solve problems and make plans and

4. cost reporting, which entails showing the costs in detail, including showing how the costs were measured, what characteristics the costs have, and what the costs actually mean and how they should be interpreted.

PROFESSIONAL GROUPS AND DESIGNATIONS

Numerous professional groups and designations exist for accountants. Chief among the professional designations for management accounts is the Certified Management Accountant designation, which is offered by the NAA. The CMA is the management accounting equivalent of the **Certified Public Accountant** (CPA) designation. Accountants earn the certificate after passing a two-and-one-half-day, five-part examination, and by meeting certain accounting experience requirements. CMAs early in their careers often hold staff and supervisory positions, while more experienced CMAs serve as **controllers**, **chief financial officer**s, or in other executive financial positions.

One of NAA's objectives in establishing the CMA designation was to increase the recognition of management accounting as a professional discipline with an identifiable, underlying body of knowledge, and to outline a course of study by which that knowledge could be attained. Among other goals, the designation helps employers, educators, and students by establishing objective measurements of an individual's knowledge and competence in the management accounting field. The NAA has also promulgated complementary ethical standards related to competence, confidentiality, integrity, and objectivity in the management accounting process.

[Dave Mote]

FURTHER READING:

Garrison, Ray H. *Managerial Accounting*, 6th ed. Boston: Richard D. Irwin, Inc., 1991.

Heely, James A. and Roy L. Nersesian. *Global Management Accounting: A Guide for Executives of International Corporations*. Westport, CT: Quorum Books, 1993.

Heitger, Lester E. and Serge Matulich. *Managerial Accounting*. 2nd ed. New York: McGraw-Hill Book Company, 1986.

Riahi-Belkaoui, Ahmed. *The New Foundations of Management Accounting*. Westport, CT: Quorum Books, 1992.

MANAGERIAL ECONOMICS

Decisions made by managers are crucial to the success or failure of the business. Roles played by business managers are becoming increasingly more challenging as complexity in the business world grows. Business decisions are increasingly dependent on constraints imposed from outside the economy in which a particular business is based—both in terms of production of goods as well as the markets for the goods produced. The impact of rapid technological change on **innovation** in products and processes, as well as in marketing and sales techniques, figures prominently among the factors contributing to the increasing complexity of the business environment. Moreover, because of increased globalization of the marketplace, there is more volatility in both input and product prices. The continuous changes in the economic and business environment make it ever more difficult to accurately evaluate the outcome of a business decision. In such a changing environment, sound economic analysis becomes all the more important as a basis of decision making. Managerial economics is a discipline that is designed to provide a solid foundation of economic understanding in order for business managers to make well-informed and well-analyzed managerial decisions.

THE NATURE OF MANAGERIAL ECONOMICS

There are a number of issues relevant to businesses that are based on economic thinking or analysis. Examples of questions that managerial economics attempts to answer are: What determines whether an aspiring business firm should enter a particular industry or simply start producing a new product or service? Should a firm continue to be in business in an industry in which it is currently engaged or cut its losses and exit the industry? Why do some professions pay handsome salaries, whereas some others pay barely enough to survive? How best to motivate the employees of a firm? The issues relevant to managerial economics can be further focussed by expanding on the first two of the preceding questions. Let us consider the first question in which a firm (or a would-be firm) is considering entering an industry. For example, what led Frederick W. Smith the founder of Fed Ex, to start his overnight mail service—after all, a service of this nature did not exist in any significant form in the United States and people seemed to be doing just fine without overnight mail service provided by a private corporation. One can also consider why there are now so many overnight mail carriers (such as United Parcel Service and Airborne Express. The second example pertains to the exit from an industry, specifically, the airline industry in the United States. Pan Am, a pioneer in public air transportation, is no longer in operation, while airlines such as TWA (Trans World Airlines) are on the verge of exiting the airlines industry. Why, then, have many airlines that operate on international routes fallen on hard times, while small regional airlines seem to be doing just fine? Managerial economics provides answers to these questions.

In order to answer pertinent questions, managerial economics applies economic theories, tools, and techniques to administrative and business **decision making**. The first step in the decision-making process is to collect relevant economic data carefully and to organize the economic information contained in the data collected in such a way as to establish a clear basis for managerial decisions. The goals of the particular business organization must then be clearly spelled out. Based on these stated goals, suitable managerial objectives are formulated. The issue of central concern in the decision-making process is that the desired objectives be reached in the best possible manner. The term best in the decision-making context primarily refers to achieving the goals in the most efficient manner, with the minimum use of available resources—implying there be no waste of resources. Managerial economics helps the manager to make good decisions by providing information on waste associated with a proposed decision.

APPLICATIONS OF MANAGERIAL ECONOMICS

Some examples of managerial decisions have been provided above. The application of managerial economics is, by no means, limited to these examples. Tools of managerial economics can be used to achieve virtually all the goals of a business organization in an efficient manner. Typical managerial decision making may involve one of the following issues:

- Deciding the price of a product and the quantity of the commodity to be produced

- Deciding whether to manufacture a product or to buy from another manufacturer

- Choosing the production technique to be employed by the firm in the production of a given product

- Deciding on the level of inventory to be maintained by the firm of a product or raw material

- Deciding on the advertising media and the intensity of the advertising campaign

- Making employment and training decisions

- Making decisions regarding further business investment and the mode of financing the investment

It should be noted that the application of managerial economics is not limited to profit-seeking business organizations. Tools of managerial economics can be applied equally well to decision problems of nonprofit organizations. Mark Hirschey and James L. Pappas cite the example of a nonprofit hospital. While a nonprofit hospital is not like a typical firm seeking to maximize its profits, a hospital does strive to provide its patients the best medical care possible, given its limited staff (doctors, nurses, and support staff), equipment, space, and other resources. The hospital administrator can use the concepts and tools of managerial economics to determine the optimal allocation of the limited resources available to the hospital. In addition to nonprofit business organizations, government agencies and other nonprofit organizations—such as cooperatives, schools, and museums—can use the techniques of managerial decision making to achieve their goals in the most efficient manner.

While managerial economics is helpful in making optimal decisions, one should be aware that it only describes the predictable economic consequences of a managerial decision. For example, tools of managerial economics can explain the effects of imposing automobile import quotas on the availability of domestic cars, prices charged for automobiles, and the extent of competition in the auto industry. Analysis of managerial economics will reveal that fewer cars will be available, prices of automobiles will increase, and the extent of competition will be reduced. Managerial economics does not address, however, whether imposing automobile import quotas is good government policy. This latter question encompasses broader political considerations involving what economists call value judgments.

ECONOMIC CONCEPTS USED IN MANAGERIAL ECONOMICS

Managerial economics uses a wide variety of economic concepts, tools, and techniques in the decision-making process. These concepts can be placed in three broad categories: (1) the theory of the firm that describes how businesses make a variety of decisions; (2) the theory of consumer behavior that describes decision making by consumers; and (3) the theory of market structure and pricing that describes the structure and characteristics of different market forms under which business firms operate.

THE THEORY OF THE FIRM

Discussing the theory of the firm is an useful way to begin the study of managerial economics, since the theory provides a broad framework within which issues relevant to managerial decisions are analyzed. A firm can be considered a combination of people, physical and financial resources, and a variety of information. Firms exist because they perform useful functions in society by producing and distributing goods and services. In the process of accomplishing this, they use society's scarce resources, provide employment, and pay taxes. If economic activities of society can be simply put into two categories—production and consumption—firms are considered the most basic economic entities on the production side, while consumers form the basic economic entities on the consumption side.

The behavior of firms is usually analyzed in the context of an economic model, an idealized version of a real-world firm. The basic economic model of a business enterprise is called the theory of the firm.

PROFIT MAXIMIZATION AND THE FIRM. Under the simplest version of the theory of the firm it is assumed that profit maximization is its primary goal. In this simplest version of the theory of the firm, the firm's owner is the manager of the firm, and thus, the firm's owner-manager is assumed to maximize the firm's short-term profits (current profits and profits in the near future). Today, even when the profit maximizing assumption is maintained, the notion of profits has been broadened to take into account uncertainty faced by the firm (in realizing profits) and the time value of money (where the value of a dollar further and further in the future is increasingly smaller than a dollar today). In this more complete model, the goal of maximizing short-term profits is replaced by goal of maximizing long-term profits, the present value of expected profits, of the business firm.

Defining present value of expected profits is based on first defining "value" and then defining "present value." Many concepts of value, such as book value, market value, going-concern value,

break-up value, and liquidating value, are encountered in business and economics. The value of the firm is defined as the present value of expected future profits (net cash flows) of the firm. Thus, to obtain an estimate of the present value of expected profits, one must identify the stream of net cash flow in future years. Once this is accomplished, these expected future profit values are converted into present value by discounting these values by an appropriate interest rate. For illustration, assume that a firm expects a profit of $10,000 in one year and $20,000 in the second year—it is assumed that the firm earns no profits after two years. Let us assume that the prevailing interest rate is 10 percent per annum. Thus, $10,000 in a year from now is only equal to about $9,091 at the present ($[\$10,000/(1 + 0.1)] = \$9,091$)—that is, the present value of a $10,000 profit expected in a year from now is about $9,091. Similarly, the present value of an expected profit of $20,000 in two years from now is equal to about $16,529 (since $[\$20,000/(1 + 0.1)^2] = \$16,529$). Therefore, the present value of future expected profits is $25,620 (equal to the sum of $9,091 and $16,529). The present value of expected profits is a key concept in understanding the theory of the firm, and maximizing this profit is considered the primary goal of a firm in most models.

It should be noted that expected profit in any one period can itself be considered as the difference between the total revenue and the total cost in that period. Thus, one can, alternatively, find the present value of expected future profits by subtracting the present value of expected future costs from the present value of expected future revenues.

THE CONSTRAINED PROFIT MAXIMIZATION. Profit maximization is subject to various constraints faced by the firm. These constraints relate to resource scarcity, technology, contractual obligations, and laws and government regulations. In their attempt to maximize the present value of profits, business managers must consider not only the short-term and long-term implications of decisions made within the firm, but also various external constraints that may limit the firm's ability to achieve its organizational goals.

The first external constraint of resource scarcity refers to the limited availability of essential inputs (including skilled labor), key raw materials, energy, specialized machineries and equipments, warehouse space, and other resources. Moreover, managers often face constraints on plant capacity that are exacerbated by limited investment funds available for expansion or modernization. Contractual obligations also constrain managerial decisions. Labor contracts, for example, may constrain a manager's flexibility in worker scheduling and work assignment. Labor contracts may also determine the number of workers employed at any time, thereby establishing a floor for minimum labor costs. Finally, laws and regulations

MANAGERIAL ECONOMICS

have to be observed. The legal restrictions can constrain decisions regarding both production and marketing activities. Examples of laws and regulations that limit managerial flexibility are: the minimum wage, health and safety standards, fuel efficiency requirements, antipollution regulations, and fair pricing and marketing practices.

PROFIT MAXIMIZATION VERSUS OTHER MOTIVATIONS BEHIND MANAGERIAL DECISIONS. The present value maximization criterion as a basis for the study of the firm's behavior has come under severe criticism from some economists. The critics argue that business managers are interested, at least partly, in factors other than the firm's profits. In particular, they may be interested in power, prestige, leisure, employee welfare, community well-being, and the welfare of the larger society. The act of maximization itself has been criticized; there is a feeling that managers often aim merely to "satisfice" (seek solutions that are considered satisfactory), rather than really try to optimize or maximize (seek to find the best possible solution, given the constraints). This question is often rhetorically posed as: does a manager really try to find the sharpest needle in a haystack or does he or she merely stop upon finding a needle sharp enough for sewing needs?

Under the structure of a modern firm, it is hard to determine the true motives of managers. A modern firm is frequently organized as a corporation in which shareholders are the legal owners of the firm, and the manager acts on their behalf. Under such a structure, it is difficult to determine whether a manager merely tries to satisfy the stockholders of the firm while pursuing other goals, rather than truly attempting to maximize the value (the discounted present value) of the firm. It is, for example, difficult to interpret company support for a charitable organization as an integral part of the firm's long-term value maximization. Similarly, if the firm size is increasing, but profits are not, can one attribute the manager's decision to expand as being motivated by the increased prestige associated with larger firms, or as an attempt to make the firm more noticeable in the marketplace? As it is virtually impossible to provide definitive answers to these and similar questions, the attempt to analyze these issues has led to the development of alternative theories of firm behavior. Some of the prominent alternate models assume one of the following: (1) a firm attempts primarily to maximize its size or growth, rather than its present value; (2) the managers of firms aim at maximizing their own personal utility or welfare; and (3) the firm is a collection of individuals with widely divergent goals, rather than a single common, identifiable goal.

While each of the alternative theories of the firm has increased our understanding of how a modern firm behaves, none has been able to completely take the place of the basic profit maximization assumption for several reasons. Numerous academic studies have shown that intense competition in the markets for goods and services of the firm usually forces the manager to make value maximization decisions; if a firm does not decide on the most efficient alternative (implying the need to seek the minimum costs for each output level, given the market price of the commodity the firm is producing), others can outcompete the firm and drive it out of existence. Competition also has its effects through the **capital markets**. As one would expect, stockholders are primarily interested in their returns on **stocks** and stock prices, which in turn, are determined by the firm's value (the discounted present value of expected profits). Thus, managers are forced to maximize profits in order to maximize firm value, an important basis for returns on **common stocks** in the long run. Managers who insist on goals other than maximizing shareholder wealth risk being replaced. An inefficiently managed firm may also be bought out; in almost all such hostile **takeovers**, managers pursuing their own interests will most likely be replaced. Moreover, a number of academic studies indicate that managerial compensation is closely correlated to the profits generated for the firm. Thus, managers themselves have strong financial incentives to seek profit maximization for their firms.

Before arriving at the decision whether to maximize profits or to satisfice, managers (like other economic entities) have to analyze the costs and benefits of their decisions. Sometimes, when all costs are taken into account, decisions that appear merely aimed at a satisfactory level of performance turn out to be consistent with value-maximizing behavior. Similarly, short-term firm-growth maximization strategies have often been found to be consistent with long-term value maximization behavior, since large firms have advantages in production, distribution, and sales promotion. Thus, many other seemingly non-profit-maximizing goals may be intimately linked to value or profit maximization—so much so that the value maximization model even provides an insight into a firm's voluntary participation in charity or other socially responsible behavior.

BUSINESS VERSUS ECONOMIC PROFITS. As discussed above, profits are central to the goals of a firm and managerial decision making. Thus, to understand the theory of firm behavior properly, one must have a clear understanding of profits. While the term profit is very widely used, an economist's definition of profit differs from the one used by accountants (which is also usually used by the general public and the business community). Profit in accounting is defined as the excess of sales revenue over the explicit **accounting** costs of doing business. This surplus is available to the firm for various purposes.

ENCYCLOPEDIA OF BUSINESS

An economist also defines profit as the difference between sales revenue and costs of doing business, but includes more items in figuring costs, rather than considering only explicit accounting costs. For example, inputs supplied by owners (including labor, capital, and space) are accounted for in determining costs in the definition used by an economist. These costs are sometimes referred to as implicit costs—their value is imputed based on a notion of **opportunity costs** widely used by economists. In other words, costs of inputs supplied by an owner are based on the values these inputs would have received in the next best alternative activity. For illustration, assume that the owner of the firm works for ten hours a day at his business. If the owner does not receive any salary, an accountant would not consider the owner's effort as a cost item. An economist would, however, value the owner's service to his firm at what his labor would have earned had he worked elsewhere. Thus, to compute the true profit, an economist will subtract the implicit costs from business profit; the resulting profit is often referred to as economic profit. It is this concept of profit that is used by economists to explain the behavior of a firm. The concept of economic profit essentially recognizes that owner-supplied inputs must also be paid for. Thus, the owner of a firm will not be in business in the long run until he recovers the implicit costs (also known as normal profit), in addition to recovering the explicit costs, of doing business.

As pointed out earlier, a given firm attempts to maximize profits. Other firms do the same. Ultimately, profits decline for all firms. If all firms are operating under a competitive market structure, in equilibrium, economic profits (the excess of accounting profits over implicit costs) would be equal to zero; accounting profits (equal to explicit costs), however would be positive. When a firm makes profits above the normal profits level, it is said to be reaping above-normal profits.

HOW A FIRM ARRIVES AT A PROFIT-MAXIMIZING POINT. Let us assume throughout the discussion that a firm uses an economist's definition of profits. Assume that profit is the excess of sales revenue over cost (now assumed to be composed of both explicit and implicit costs). It can also be assumed, as discussed above, that the profit maximization is the firm's primary goal. Given this objective, important questions remain: How does the firm decide on the output level that maximizes its profits? Should the firm continue to produce at all if it is not profitable?

A manufacturing firm, motivated by profit maximization, calculates the total cost of producing any given output level. The total cost is made up of total fixed cost (due to the expenditure on fixed inputs) and total variable cost (due to the expenditure on variable inputs). Of course, the total fixed cost does not vary over the short run—only the total variable cost does.

It is important for the firm to also calculate the cost per unit of output, called the average cost. In addition to the average cost, the firm calculates the marginal cost. The marginal cost at any level of output is the increase in the total cost due to an increase in production by one unit—essentially, the marginal cost is the additional cost of producing the last unit of output.

The average cost is made up of two components: the average fixed cost (the total fixed cost divided by the number of units of the output produced) and the average variable cost (the total variable cost divided by the number of units of the output produced). As the fixed costs remain fixed over the short run, the average fixed cost declines as the level of production increases. The average variable cost, on the other hand, first decreases and then increases; economists refer to this as the U-shaped nature of the average variable cost. The U-shape of the average variable cost curve is explained as follows. Given the fixed inputs, output of the relevant product increases more than proportionately as the levels of variable inputs used increase. This is caused by increased efficiency due to specialization and other reasons. As more and more variable inputs are used in conjunction with the given fixed inputs, however, efficiency gains reach a maximum—the decline in the average variable cost eventually comes to a halt. After this point, the average variable cost starts increasing as the level of production continues to increase, given the fixed inputs. First decreasing and then increasing average variable cost lead to the U-shape for the average variable cost. The combination of the declining average fixed cost (true for the entire range of production) and the U-shaped average variable cost results into an U-shaped behavior of the average total cost, often simply called the average cost.

The marginal cost also displays a U-shaped pattern—it first decreases and then increases. The logic for the shape of the marginal cost curve is similar to that for the average variable cost—both relate to variable costs. But while the marginal cost refers to the increase in total variable cost due to an increase in the production by one unit, the average variable cost refers to the average variable cost per unit of output produced. It is important to notice, without going into finer details, that the marginal cost curve intersects the average and the average variable cost curves at their minimum cost points (See Figure 1).

The graph in Figure 1 includes a horizontal line, in addition to the three cost curves. It is assumed that the firm can sell as many units as it wants at the given market price indicated by this horizontal line. Essentially, the horizontal line is the demand curve a perfectly competitive firm faces in the market—it can sell as many units of output as it deems profitable at price "p" per unit (p, for example, can be $10 per unit of the product under consideration). In other words, p

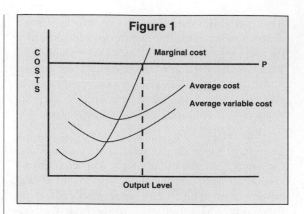

Figure 1

COSTS

Marginal cost

P

Average cost

Average variable cost

Output Level

is the firm's average revenue per unit of output. Since the firm receives p dollars for every successive unit it sells, p is also the marginal revenue for the firm.

A firm maximizes profits, in general, when its marginal revenue equals marginal cost, at point m on the graph in Figure 1. If the firm produces beyond this point of equality between the marginal revenue and marginal cost, the marginal cost will be higher than the marginal revenue. In other words, the addition to total production beyond the point where marginal revenue equals marginal cost, leads to lower, not higher, profits. While every firm's primary motive is to maximize profits, its output decision (consistent with the profit maximizing objective), depends on the structure of the market it is operating under. Before we discuss important market structures, we briefly examine another key economic concept, the theory of consumer behavior.

THE THEORY OF CONSUMER BEHAVIOR

Consumers play an important role in the economy since they spend most of their incomes on goods and services produced by firms. In other words, they consume what firms produce. Thus, studying the theory of consumer behavior is quite important. What is the ultimate objective of a consumer? Economists have an optimization model for consumers, similar to that applied to firms or producers. While firms are assumed to be maximizing profits, consumers are assumed to be maximizing their utility or satisfaction. Of course, more goods and services will, in general, provide greater utility to a consumer. Nevertheless, consumers, like firms, are subject to constraints—their consumption and choices are limited by a number of factors, including the amount of disposable income (the residual income after income taxes are paid for). The decision to consume by consumers is described by economists within a theoretical framework usually termed the theory of demand.

The demand for a particular product by an individual consumer is based on four important factors. First, the price of the product determines how much of

the product the consumer buys, given that all other factors remain unchanged. In general, the lower the product's price the more a consumer buys. Second, the consumer's income also determines how much of the product the consumer is able to buy, given that all other factors remain constant. In general, a consumer buys more of a commodity the greater is his or her income. Third, prices of related products are also important in determining the consumer's demand for the product. Finally, consumer tastes and preferences also affect consumer demand. The total of all consumer demands yields the market demand for a particular commodity; the market demand curve shows quantities of the commodity demanded at different prices, given all other factors. As price increases, quantity demanded falls.

Individual consumer demands thus provide the basis for the market demand for a product. The market demand plays a crucial role in shaping decisions made by firms. Most important of all, it helps in determining the market price of the product under consideration which, in turn, forms the basis for profits for the firm producing that product.

The amount supplied by an individual firm depends on profit and cost considerations. As mentioned earlier, in general, a producer produces the profit maximizing output. Again, the total of individual supplies yields the market supply for a particular commodity; the market supply curve shows quantities of the commodity supplied at different prices, given all other factors. As price increases, the quantity supplied increases.

The interaction between market demand and supply determines the equilibrium or market price (where demand equals supply). Shifts in demand curve and/or supply curve lead to changes in the equilibrium price. The market price and the price mechanism play a crucial role in the capitalist system—they send signals both to producers and consumers.

THEORIES ASSOCIATED WITH DIFFERENT MARKET STRUCTURES

As mentioned earlier, firms' profit maximizing output decisions take into account the market structure under which they are operating. There are four kinds of market organizations: perfect competition, monopolistic competition, **oligopoly**, and monopoly.

PERFECT COMPETITION. Perfect competition is the idealized version of the market structure that provides a foundation for understanding how markets work in a capitalist economy. Three conditions need to be satisfied before a market structure is considered perfectly competitive: homogeneity of the product sold in the industry, existence of many buyers and sellers, and perfect mobility of resources or factors of production.

The first condition, the homogeneity of product, requires that the product sold by any one seller is identical with the product sold by any other supplier—if products of different sellers are identical, buyers do not care from whom they buy so long as the price charged is also the same. The second condition, existence of many buyers and sellers, also leads to an important outcome: each individual buyer or seller is so small relative to the entire market that he or she does not have any power to influence the price of the product under consideration. Each individual simply decides how much to buy or sell at the given market price. The implication of the third condition is that resources move to the most profitable industry.

There is no industry in the world that can be considered perfectly competitive in the strictest sense of the term. However, there are token examples of industries that come quite close to having perfectly competitive markets. Some markets for agricultural **commodities**, while not meeting all three conditions, come reasonably close to being characterized as perfectly competitive markets. The market for wheat, for example, can be considered a reasonable approximation.

As pointed out earlier, in order to maximize profits, a supplier has to look at the cost and revenue sides; a perfectly competitive firm will stop production where marginal revenue equals marginal cost. In the case of a perfectly competitive firm, the market price for the product is also the marginal revenue, as the firm can sell additional units at the going market price. This is not so for a monopolist. A monopolist must reduce price to increase sales. As a result, a monopolist's price is always above the marginal revenue. Thus, even though a monopolist firm also produces the profit maximizing output, where marginal revenue equals marginal cost, it does not produce to the point where price equals marginal cost (as does a perfectly competitive firm).

Regarding entry and exit decisions; one can now state that additional firms would enter an industry—whenever existing firms are making above normal profits (that is, when the horizontal line is above the average cost at the profit maximizing output). A firm would exit the market if at the profit maximizing point the horizontal line is below the average cost curve; it will actually shut down the production right away if the price is less than the average variable cost.

MONOPOLISTIC COMPETITION. Many industries that we often deal with have market structures that are characterized by monopolistic competition or oligopoly. Apparel retail stores (with many stores and differentiated products) provide an example of monopolistic competition. As in the case of perfect competition, monopolistic competition is characterized by the existence of many sellers. Usually if an industry

has 50 or more firms (producing products that are close substitutes of each other), it is said to have a large number of firms. The sellers under monopolistic competition differentiate their product; unlike under perfect competition, the products are not considered identical. This characteristic is often called product differentiation. In addition, relative ease of entry into the industry is considered another important requirement of a monopolistically competitive market organization.

As in the case of perfect competition, a firm under monopolistic competition determines the quantity of the product to produce based on the profit maximization principle—it stops production where marginal revenue equals marginal cost of production. There is, however, one very important difference between perfect competition and monopolistic competition. A firm under monopolistic competition has a bit of control over the price it charges, since the firm differentiates its products from those of others. The price associated with the product (at the equilibrium or profit maximizing output) is higher than marginal cost (which equals marginal revenue). Thus, production under monopolistic competition does not take place to the point where price equals marginal cost of production. The net result of the profit maximizing decisions of monopolistically competitive firms is that price charged under monopolistic competition is higher than under perfect competition, and the quantity produced is simultaneously lower.

OLIGOPOLY. Oligopoly is a fairly common market organization. In the United States, both the steel and automobile industries (with three or so large firms) provide good examples of oligopolistic market structures. Probably the most important characteristic of an oligopolistic market structure is the interdependence of firms in the industry. The interdependence, actual or perceived, arises from the small number of firms in the industry. Unlike under monopolistic competition, however, if an oligopolistic firm changes its price or output, it has perceptible effects on the sales and profits of its competitors in the industry. Thus, an oligopolist always considers the reactions of its rivals in formulating its pricing or output decisions.

There are huge, though not unsurmountable, barriers to entry to an oligopolistic market. These barriers can exist because of large financial requirements, availability of raw materials, access to the relevant technology, or simply existence of patent rights with the firms currently in the industry. Several industries in the United States provide good examples of oligopolistic market structures with obvious barriers to entry, such as the automobile industry where financial barriers to entry exist.

An oligopolistic industry is also typically characterized by **economies of scale**. Economies of scale in production implies that as the level of production rises, the cost per unit of product falls from the use of any plant (generally, up to a point). Thus, economies of scale lead to an obvious advantage for a large producer.

There is no single theoretical framework that provides answers to output and pricing decisions under an oligopolistic market structure. Analyses exist only for special sets of circumstances. One of these circumstances refers to an oligopoly in which there are asymmetric reactions of its rivals when a particular oligopolist formulates policies. If an oligopolistic firm cuts its price, it is met with price reductions by competing firms; if it raises the price of its product, however, rivals do not match the price increase. For this reason, prices may remain stable in an oligopolistic industry for a prolonged period.

MONOPOLY. Monopoly can be considered as the polar opposite of perfect competition. It is a market form in which there is only one seller. While, at first glance, a monopolistic form may appear to be rarely found market structure, several industries in the United States have monopolies. Local electricity companies provide an example of a monopolist.

There are many factors that give rise to a monopoly. Patents can give rise to a monopoly situation, as can ownership of critical raw materials (to produce a good) by a single firm. A monopoly, however, can also be legally created by a government agency when it sells a market franchise to sell a particular product or to provide a particular service. Often a monopoly so established is also regulated by the appropriate government agency. Provision of local telephone services in the United States provides an example of such a monopoly. Finally, a monopoly may arise due to declining cost of production for a particular product. In such a case the average cost of production keeps falling and reaches a minimum at an output level that is sufficient to satisfy the entire market. In such an industry, rival firms will be eliminated until only the strongest firm (now the monopolist) is left in the market. Such an industry is popularly dubbed as the case of a natural monopoly. A good example of a natural monopoly is the electricity industry, which reaps the benefits of economies of scale and yields decreasing average cost. Natural monopolies are usually regulated by the government.

Generally speaking, price and output decisions of a monopolist are similar to a monopolistically competitive firm, with the major distinction that there are a large number of firms under monopolistic competition and only one firm under monopoly. Nevertheless, at any output level, the price charged by a monopolist is higher than the marginal revenue. As a result, a monopolist also does not produce to the point where price

equals marginal cost (a condition met under a perfectly competitive market structure).

MARKET STRUCTURES AND MANAGERIAL DECISIONS. Managerial decisions both in the short run and in the long run are partly shaped by the market structure relevant to the firm. While the preceding discussion of market structures does not cover the full range of managerial decisions, it nevertheless suggests that managerial decisions are necessarily constrained by the market structure under which a firm operates.

TOOLS OF DECISION SCIENCES AND MANAGERIAL ECONOMICS

Managerial decision making uses both economic concepts and tools, and techniques of analysis provided by decision sciences. The major categories of these tools and techniques are: optimization, statistical estimation, **forecasting**, numerical analysis, and **game theory**. While most of these methodologies are fairly technical, the first three are briefly explained below to illustrate how tools of decision sciences are used in managerial decision making.

OPTIMIZATION. Optimization techniques are probably the most crucial to managerial decision making. Given that alternative courses of action are available, the manager attempts to produce the most optimal decision, consistent with stated managerial objectives. Thus, an optimization problem can be stated as maximizing an objective (called the objective function by mathematicians) subject to specified constraints. In determining the output level consistent with the maximum profit, the firm maximizes profits, constrained by cost and capacity considerations. While a manager does not solve the optimization problem, he or she may use the results of mathematical analysis. In the profit maximization example, the profit maximizing condition requires that the firm choose the production level at which marginal revenue equals marginal cost. This condition is obtained from an optimization exercise. Depending on the problem a manager is trying to solve, the conditions for the optimal decision may be different.

STATISTICAL ESTIMATION. A number of statistical techniques are used to estimate economic variables of interest to a manager. In some cases, statistical estimation techniques employed are simple. In other cases, they are much more advanced. Thus, a manager may want to know the average price received by his competitors in the industry, as well as the standard deviation (a measure of variation across units) of the product price under consideration. In this case, the simple statistical concepts of mean (average) and standard deviation are used.

Estimating a relationship among variables requires a more advanced statistical technique. For example, a firm may want to estimate its cost function, the relationship between a cost concept and the level of output. A firm may also want to know the demand function of its product, that is, the relationship between the demand for its product and different factors that influence it. The estimates of costs and demand are usually based on data supplied by the firm. The statistical estimation technique employed is called regression analysis, and is used to develop a mathematical model showing how a set of variables are related. This mathematical relationship can also be used to generate forecasts.

An automobile industry example can be used for the purpose of illustrating the forecasting method that employs simple regression analysis. Suppose a statistician has data on sales of American-made automobiles in the United States for the last 25 years. He or she has also determined that the sale of automobiles is related to the real disposable income of individuals. The statistician also has available the time series (for the last 25 years) on real disposable income. Assume that the relationship between the time series on sales of American-made automobiles and the real disposable income of consumers is actually linear and it can thus be represented by a straight line. A fairly rigorous mathematical technique is used to find the straight line that most accurately represents the relationship between the time series on auto sales and disposable income.

FORECASTING. Forecasting is a method or a technique used to predict many future aspects of a business or any other operation. For example, a retailing firm that has been in business for the last 25 years may be interested in forecasting the likely sales volume for the coming year. There are numerous forecasting techniques that can be used to accomplish this goal. A forecasting technique, for example, can provide such a projection based on the experience of the firm during the last 25 years; that is, this forecasting technique bases the future forecast on the past data.

While the term "forecasting" may appear to be rather technical, planning for the future is a critical aspect of managing any organization—business, nonprofit, or otherwise. In fact, the long-term success of any organization is closely tied to how well the **management** of the organization is able to foresee its future and develop appropriate strategies to deal with the likely future scenarios. Intuition, good judgment, and an awareness of how well the economy is doing may give the manager of a business firm a rough idea (or "feeling") of what is likely to happen in the future. It is not easy, however, to convert a feeling about the future outcome into a precise number that can be used, for instance, as a projection for next year's sales volume. Forecasting methods can help predict many future aspects of a business operation, such as forthcoming years' sales volume projections.

Suppose that a forecast expert has been asked to provide quarterly estimates of the sales volume for a particular product for the next four quarters. How should one go about preparing the quarterly sales volume forecasts? One will certainly want to review the actual sales data for the product in question for past periods. Suppose that the forecaster has access to actual sales data for each quarter during the 25-year period the firm has been in business. Using these historical data, the forecaster can identify the general level of sales. He or she can also determine whether there is a pattern or trend, such as an increase or decrease in sales volume over time. A further review of the data may reveal some type of seasonal pattern, such as, peak sales occurring around the holiday season. Thus by reviewing historical data, the forecaster can often develop a good understanding of the pattern of sales in the past periods. Understanding such a pattern can often lead to better forecasts of future sales of the product. In addition, if the forecaster is able to identify the factors that influence sales, historical data on these factors (variables) can also be used to generate forecasts of future sales.

There are many forecasting techniques available to the person assisting the business in planning its sales. For illustration, consider a forecasting method in which a statistician forecasting future values of a variable of business interest (for example, sales), examines the cause-and-effect relationships of this variable with other relevant variables (for example, the level of consumer confidence, changes in consumers' disposable incomes, the interest rate at which consumers can finance their excess spending through borrowing, and the state of the economy represented by the percentage of the labor force unemployed). Thus, this category of forecasting techniques uses past time series on many relevant variables to forecast the volume of sales in the future. Under this forecasting technique, a regression equation is estimated to generate future forecasts (based on the past relationship among variables).

[Anandi P. Sahu]

FURTHER READING:

Anderson, David P., Dennis J. Sweeney, and Thomas A. Williams, *An Introduction to Management Science: Quantitative Approaches to Decision Making*. 7th ed. West Publishing Company, 1994.

Hirschey, Mark, and James L. Pappas, *Managerial Economics*. 7th ed. Harcourt Brace Jovanovich College Publishers, 1993.

Mansfield, Edwin. ed. *Managerial Economics and Operations Research: Techniques, Applications, Cases*. 5th ed. W. W. Norton & Company, 1987.

Mansfield, Edwin. *Principles of Microeconomics*. 7th ed. W. W. Norton & Company, 1992.

MANAGING MACHISMO

In international business, machismo is not a "woman's" problem. It inhibits the commercial efficiency of both sexes when working abroad. Mainstream Americans perceive gender inequality in negative terms—they rarely realize how favorably machismo is perceived in other global regions. Islamic nations come instantly to mind, but Latins, Africans, Asians, and Southern Europeans also segregate, control, and limit female behavior, particularly in commerce.

Because these limits exist, qualified American businesswomen who seek managerial assignments in any of these regions may wonder if such limits and controls would apply to them. More importantly, female executives have to wonder how the male officers at their own corporation view these limits and controls—will they hesitate to promote a qualified female candidate because they fear she will not be effective in certain regions of the world? How many women find themselves barred from **decision making** posts abroad due to a male **CEO**'s concern about foreign machismo? How many abandon overseas aspirations due to their own anxiety over the reactions of foreign business men? In either case, both sexes suffer, as do their firms.

ARE U.S. CORPORATIONS MACHO?

Current research suggests that senior male executives in most American firms privately believe in gender equality, both here and abroad. One study found that 60 percent of those polled felt a woman could successfully head their subsidiary overseas. They also deplored machismo as practiced abroad. Few American executives, for instance, would applaud a recent decision by Japan's Security Dealers Association to withhold "risky" investment opportunities from female clients, or the Saudi tradition forbidding women to drive, or the Swahili custom restricting bicycles to men.

Nonetheless, the private disapproval of U.S. executives often takes the form of public tolerance. As U.S. companies seek to expand overseas, those that wish to be accepted into foreign business circles face the need to outwardly respect each local culture as host nationals define it. This applies even when the women of that culture are relegated to what Americans perceive as positions of inferiority—a status American women working in those regions cannot easily escape.

As a consequence, many male CEOs oppose sending women to "macho regions" out of concern for foreign reactions. Some feel most nationals would assign insufficient or improper status to an American female decision maker, thereby insulting both her and their firm. Others believe that the corporate hosts in some nations might feel their own commercial status was downgraded by having to deal with female decision makers. Still others fear hosts might resent even the possibility of either consensual or forced sexual interaction between business colleagues. In one study, 72.7 percent of the male managers surveyed saw foreign variations of machismo as posing major barriers to American businesswomen seeking overseas careers. Other researchers draw similar conclusions. Despite their private feelings on gender equality, most American male CEOs feel that sending women abroad in supervisory capacities will cost them foreign business. Such executive ambivalence can quickly form a basis for company policies that hinder female managers seeking overseas posts. Compare the following:

- In a 1975 survey of 171 U.S. firms, all but one of the women who were sent overseas by one of those firms stayed less than 30 days.

- In 1985, less than 3 percent of U.S. overseas managers were female, and only 20 percent of the firms surveyed had sent women abroad.

While the later figures may represent improvement, the potential of most female executives who possess knowledge and skills that would be useful overseas remains vastly under utilized.

FOREIGN MACHISMO: RESPECT IT OR RESEARCH IT

American women who seek foreign posts have two options for coping with bias—both in-house and foreign. One is to accept the judgment of senior male executives who decide that anti-female feelings in specific regions pose too great a barrier to overcome. In such cases, potential overseas candidates may simply decide to "respect" the existing situation, whether by rejecting these assignments, accepting only short-time posts, or restricting overseas tasks to those which limit contact with host nationals.

The other option is to research machismo itself, analyzing local variations the same way any other human factors of a prospective target market would be studied. Women seeking posts in any foreign region should certainly consider which aspects of the host culture may affect their work. In areas known for machismo, this should include male-female relationships.

This type of research should have at least three goals:

1. To investigate host country practices from its citizens' perspective, ascertaining local

expectations regarding female behavior within current business settings.

2. To predict potential conflicts by identifying specific social and commercial situations where male host-national expectations may predictably clash with those of female American business decision makers.

3. To design preemptive strategies, thus "managing" each potential conflict by adapting to local expectations in ways compatible with American self-respect.

STEP ONE: RESEARCH LOCAL PRACTICE

Let us consider a single foreign variation of male/female interaction that most Americans would label as "machismo"—that practiced by Islam. Assume, for instance, that a female American executive is assigned in a decision-making capacity to launch an initial venture within a predominately Moslem region. Many Americans equate Islamic practice with the Arabian Peninsula, but significant Moslem populations are found not only in the Middle East, but in North, West, and Eastern Africa; East, South, and Southeast Asia; and the former USSR.

Clearly, a population of this size will display wide variations in belief. Businessmen in many Moslem areas have had sufficient contact with Western cultures to have adopted Western concepts, including those pertaining to relationship between the sexes. However, there are "modern" Moslems who still embrace traditional beliefs.

Five of these tenets remain so much a part of current Islamic culture that they impinge repeatedly upon contemporary commerce. It therefore seems imprudent for American businesswomen to assume they can be briefly shuttled to one side for business purposes. Rather, the female executive who hopes to create long-range commercial relationships with male Moslem counterparts may find it useful to investigate the following beliefs.

1. 'Ird (female virtue)—Very different from a man's virtue, the 'Ird is the intangible counterpart to her physical virginity, thus subject to similar laws. Both 'Ird and virginity are intrinsic to being female. Preserving both becomes a sacred duty, because what is lost can never be regained—one's 'Ird remains forever. A virtuous woman must diligently guard her own 'Ird and must seek the protection of men to assist her.

2. Sharaf (male honor)—Like 'Ird, its female counterpart, Sharaf is a reflection of male behavior. However unlike 'Ird it can be regained if it is lost. A man can gain or lose sharaf through acts of bravery, cowardice, generosity, inhospitality, etc. Nonetheless, his honor ultimately depends not only on his own behavior but that of every woman in his family—mother, sisters, daughters, cousins etc. Should any one of these commit an act that calls their virtue into question, the sharaf of every male in that family would be lost. Male honor, therefore, requires life time protection of female kin, thus preserving the collective honor of the extended family to which they all belong.

3. Shahua Jenaia (sexual desire/attraction)—The need for the constant protection of women is based on belief in the power of sexual attraction. This power is perceived as being far greater than any man or woman can resist, despite fear of punishment. Thus, traditionalists feel that whenever a man and woman find themselves alone, they will be irresistibly drawn to one another. The man would be unable to restrain himself; the woman, unable to resist.

4. Thaar Aaelie (clan revenge)—Traditional Moslems believe the consequences of sexual attraction are severe. In earlier times, since sexual transgression meant loss of an entire family's honor, men of that family were obligated to restore the loss by killing the woman who had caused it. Meanwhile, the woman's husband was obligated to seek out and kill his wife's seducer. This act, in return, would anger male kinfolk of the slain man, thereby triggering what could become an endless feud. In short, the consequences of sexual transgression could be so great as to damage the fabric of society.

5. Passl (protective segregation)—It is to avoid triggering this violence that Moslem males protect women. It is to shield women from power stronger than themselves that they are segregated, secluded, limited, controlled and thereby removed from sexual temptation. Every woman has the right (and duty) to spend her life in safety and security, under the protection (and thus, jurisdiction) of a man. One who moves outside that jurisdiction invites the possibility of sexual attack, clan revenge, and the subsequent disruption of society. Conversely, men can only provide such permanent protection by restricting female mobility, earning power, and independent action—thereby also ensuring their perpetual dependence. Islamic tradition provides two tools to achieve this level of protection—physical segregation and visual segregation.

Historically, physical segregation has meant creating a dual society of protectors and protected, in which both sexes live largely separate lives. Moslem peoples strive for this ideal, often with considerable innovation. In Oman, for instance, the national university combines Western theories of co-education with centuries of Arab tradition. Classes have separate doors for men and women, as well as segregated seating within. Buildings connect by slender skyways, allowing women to pass between classes unobserved by male students, who walk on the ground. Libraries not only post separate reading hours for each sex, but segregate the bookshelves. The purpose, as Omani see it, is not feminine repression but mutual protection.

Visual segregation means public display of the body is taboo. Clothing must not merely cover the body, but conceal its physical outlines, as well as the face and hair (in some areas). Even eyes must be restricted. Consider, for instance, the way which traditional Moslems cope with public space within the twisting, narrow streets that form the core of many cities. Men walk leisurely down the middle of each path. Women cling to the sides, eyes averted. Both sexes wear cultural blinders: neither side can "see" the other, while every group of chatting women falls silent at the approach of any man.

Americans who walk these streets may also wear cultural blinders. We do see the system: segregation, seclusion, restrictions, controls. We see, for instance, that Saudi women walk behind men, may not drive, and must ride in the back of a bus. However, we do not see the purpose for their restrictions and don't understand why Saudi men and women alike feel the system is needed—not to repress femininity, but to protect it. These feelings extend throughout the Moslem world. A wealthy, educated, and quite Westernized Turkish woman known to the authors expressed widely accepted feelings when she declared:

> ". . . Modern Turks no longer believe we are
> a man's property but we feel safer when we
> obey the laws of Islam and allow ourselves
> to be protected by men."

Most American businesswomen disagree, especially when these allegedly protective restrictions are applied to them. However, the sheer number of foreign markets influenced by Islamic ideals is too great for those seeking overseas posts to avoid. More important, too many similar systems operate in other regions. Consider Japan, South Korea, Greece, Venezuela, Russia, and Somalia; in different ways, each culture limits women within business. Our response should be to research each foreign practice, to the point where we can understand the expectations of practitioners. Only after we can see their side, can we adjust to it effectively.

STEP TWO: PREDICT POTENTIAL CONFLICTS

One reason to research foreign variants of machismo is to identify potential conflicts that may occur once American businesswomen operate within each culture. On one hand, it may be possible to foresee specific problems female managers pose for foreign hosts by adhering to American customs. On the other, it may be equally feasible to predict specific host-national responses that we would label "macho." In such cases, advance knowledge of the values that motivate both sets of behavior may help us to minimize them.

To illustrate, consider three potential conflicts between American businesswomen and Saudi businessmen. Each is predictable, in that the women can reasonably expect to trigger perceived "macho" responses, just by adhering to normal U.S. business practices.

1. DOING BUSINESS ALONE. Consider the problem posed for many Islamic hosts by a woman who conducts business alone. Few American women hesitate to do this. In fact, they pride themselves on their independence, particularly in business settings. Consider the situation created by a female American banking executive sent to Saudi Arabia to negotiate a loan. At the time she was sent, however, no unaccompanied women were allowed into the country. Thus, she displayed a transit visa, implying she was at the airport en route to somewhere else. When no one was looking, she walked out an airport door, and made her way via friends to her foreign contact's firm.

From an American perspective, the decision seemed sound. It facilitated business for both her firm and Saudi contacts. From an Islamic perspective, it was wrong. A woman alone, regardless of nationality, corporate position, or commercial competence, is perceived as a woman in danger. Away from male protection, she may be courted, harassed, or even abused. American women see these responses as proof of machismo and hostility. Islamic males may perceive them as protective and an alternative to social violence.

2. OVERSEAS IMAGE AND PHYSICAL ATTRACTION. American women entering foreign business settings can create images that will predictably enhance their physical attractiveness by unwitting disregard of nuances in local dress codes. Consider, for example, the impact on host nationals that could be created by an American female executive assigned to the Middle East. If aware of Arab sensibilities, she would most likely wear a tailored business suit that covered arms and legs to wrists and ankles. To complete her intended image of precision and efficiency, however, she might carefully style her hair.

In so doing, she creates two predictable problems. Traditional Moslems believe that clothing should not merely cover the female body but conceal its outlines. Female hair—whether styled or unbound—should also be covered, while in more conservative regions, even hairlines are concealed. Key host businessmen might subconsciously prejudge this woman as immodest and perhaps immoral. A tailored business suit is intended to enhance her figure, while the elaborate hairstyle emphasizes femininity. Both detract from the commercial image she intends to present. To ask her hosts to set aside these feelings due to her foreign nationality and corporate status would be as difficult as asking her to set aside her own beliefs and briefly don a veil.

3. CREATING COMMERCIAL CREDIBILITY. The creation of commercial credibility is prerequisite to every foreign venture. Americans and Moslems resolve this need in different ways. We start by sending relevant professional data to future foreign colleagues in advance, then reinforce this first impression at the initial face-to-face meeting by turning instantly to business, using subsequent discussion to establish professional and commercial credentials. For American women, however, this directness poses ''predictable'' problems to her hosts. Moslem businessmen establish credibility by taking private time to forge personal bonds. This can that mean long hours in the business setting will be spent in social conversation. Alternately, it can entail extensive entertainment, either at restaurants or at private homes. But what if male-female behavior codes inhibit/prohibit both aspects of this process? How and where does one build social relationships when forbidden by custom to socialize? No wonder foreign colleagues feel uncertain how to act.

The host businessmen often just do not want to deal with women, while others retreat into excessive formality, providing verbal courtesy to American businesswomen while directing substantive conversation towards their male colleagues.

In the United States, we condemn these reactions as expressions of machismo. The actions of the men in these examples are best described as expressions of frustration, born of uncertainty as to how they should behave. Since habits rarely change when crossing borders, American businesswomen may inadvertently create commercially counterproductive situations for foreign hosts just by behaving like Americans. Luckily, these situations can be avoided by developing preemptive strategies based on prior knowledge of a host culture, thereby easing anxiety on both sides.

HANDLING MACHISMO: PRE-EMPTIVE STRATEGIES

Once potential conflicts are identified, methods can be developed to ''manage'' outbreaks of machismo before they occur. To do this, both the over-seas appointee and her corporate superiors should work in tandem to promote her business image in the foreign setting. In Islamic areas, for instance, four strategies may prove useful:

DEVELOP AREA EXPERTISE BEFORE DEPARTURE. Researching a relevant target culture is critical to success within every foreign target market. Before departure, each new assignee should intensify her level of cultural expertise to the point where she becomes the in-house expert on that region. In Moslem areas, that means learning something of host-nation history, language, and the Koran. Few Moslem males believe that American businesswomen possess knowledge in these areas. Yet, displaying even the most basic interest in all three can undermine a sexist stereotype by creating the feelings of respect and empathy that Moslems find prerequisite for doing business.

Few host nationals expect American expertise. The female author of this article, for instance, proved unable to speak Arabic grammatically during her stay in the United Arab Emirates, despite persistent study. Nonetheless, overjoyed by her efforts, local women taught her formal ''courtesy phrases'' (proverbs, etc.) used traditionally by women in conversation with men to convey respect to the opposite sex. Male business contacts proved delighted when she used them appropriately, thus contradicting their prior stereotype of American women. They subsequently held her in far higher personal—and thus commercial—esteem.

The male author of this article found the same degree of empathy could be created by discussing Islamic history. Knowing too little to converse with authority, he turned what he did know into questions. His lack of knowledge then delighted Moslem business contacts, permitting them to assume the dual roles of tour guide and teacher. Here too, an initial stereotype of U.S. ignorance and arrogance was replaced with common interest in a cherished culture—surely a prerequisite for doing business.

Commercial empathy intensifies when we show interest in the Koran. To Moslems, the Holy Book is more than the Divine Word. It is a practical guide to every facet of human behavior. Many passages carry commercial implications of considerable value to American businesses:

- The well-known ban on pork, for instance, extends to images of pigs, such as stuffed toys and piggy banks.

- The five times daily call to prayer means instant arrest for any American manager who fails to turn off his store's Muzak while the faithful pray—as the manager of Safeway's first market in Riyadh discovered during his first day at work.

- The sadaqat (donation of alms), enjoined on all Moslems, gives U.S. firms opportunities to increase product awareness through selective donations.

To "know Koran" therefore, even through a single reading, allows an American businesswoman to ask perceptive questions that allow her to learn more. To apply Koran to modern business situations, with the guidance of her male hosts, may significantly shift their initial gender stereotype to an opinion more closely related to her professional abilities.

DEVELOP ON-SITE STATUS. Once foreign expertise is acquired, it should be used to create sufficient on-site status to allow the new appointee to do her job. Moslem males feel most uncertain during their initial meetings with American businesswomen. It is during these first encounters that ambiguities of status, authority, level of expertise, etc. prove most disturbing, since they dictate how the males should behave.

One solution is to psychologically prepare host nationals for such meetings by providing "status data" in advance. Here, initial responsibility lies with the corporation. On making overseas appointments, corporate supervisors (and ideally, the CEO) can actively assist each new appointee to create an on-site status by providing a higher job-title to match whatever level of decision making is required.

The second step is to ensure that prior knowledge of both her title and professional expertise arrives on-site before the appointee herself. This will require two separate tasks

- Identifying foreign (host-nation) colleagues working in the United States who might prove commercially useful to the appointee—whether in terms of advice or introductions (setting up an "American net," or network of contacts).

- Asking each contact to be of service to the appointee by providing data, guidance, and further host-nation contacts on-site (setting up a "foreign net").

Thereafter, the CEO should contact each on-site individual he/she feels might be useful, whether to the appointee directly or the proposed commercial project. He/she can ask the on-site contact to be of service to the subordinate employee, both as a personal favor and as a favor to the U.S.-based host-nation contact who provided the initial introduction. Subsequently, the CEO should provide each foreign contact with status data intended to enhance the image of the firm, its projected foreign project, and the new appointee herself. The goal is to create a second net of overseas connections, into which the appointee can move on arrival.

The final step should be taken by the appointee herself. Within 48 hours after each host national has been contacted by her CEO, she should also contact the host national involved and introduce herself, requesting his professional advice and assistance on arrival in his homeland. If accepted she should plan to spend the first few weeks upon arrival conducting field interviews and social visits (to the degree the culture permits) with each contact, using her on-site inexperience as a business tool to learn the local rules and strategies. Only by investing the time to acquire expertise on-site can she reinforce the initial status provided by her firm, to the point where she is truly ready to conduct its business.

LOCALIZE COMMERCIAL IMAGE. The on-site status of a female decision maker may be further enhanced by "localizing" aspects of her business image to conform with foreign feelings regarding feminine behavior and appearance. This does not mean adopting local dress. To do so would undermine the U.S. professional image she intends to represent. Nonetheless, perceptive inquiry into local expectations may lead to changes in both appearance and behavior that may visibly enhance both initial rapport and the potential for commercial progress.

Consider, for example, the American businesswoman's physical image within a traditional Islamic setting. From a Moslem perspective, the standard woman's business suit will require significant modification. While it does meet local sensibilities by covering the arms, legs and shoulders, it emphasizes (rather than conceals) the figure. Moreover, men in various Islamic regions consider the throat, hair, forehead, and even nape of the neck erotic, and a woman who exposes them invites courtship. Clearly American businesswomen could enhance both their professional image and commercial prospects by covering these areas with a scarf. They will do so, however, only if prior research has sensitized them to local custom.

An American businesswoman's vocal image is also out of place within the same Islamic setting. Behaviors that Americans consider feminine may be perceived as masculine abroad. Consider the pitch and volume of the female voice. In American business situations, a woman's voice should grow deeper, louder, and more compelling—the better to be heard and reckoned with. In contrast, non-western cultures restrict female voices to higher pitch and lower volume.

The Japanese, for instance, not only use a special "woman's" language with different grammar, but higher pitch and lower volume to mark the speaker as feminine. Similarly, Moslem women lower their voices in public interaction, to reflect their femininity.

Thus, American women within foreign settings face a double-edged sword. The vocal traits they need at home constrain them when abroad. Host nationals react negatively to what they see as masculinity, while American women label the reaction as machismo. Once again, only prior research can suggest a need to "localize" vocal image.

WORK WITH "SYMBOLIC" MALES. In cultures where men hesitate to work alone with women, it may prove commercially productive to work with male partners. One obvious alternative is to use male-female project teams, in which the man both implements his segment of the venture and facilitates hers. Alternatively, the male might assist his partner in a symbolic capacity, accompanying her when her expertise is in demand but cultural norms (such as evening gatherings) prohibit her to appear alone.

In Oman, for instance, day-long business sessions often end with invitations from one host national for the other professionals to visit either his home or a restaurant. Although unspoken, the invitation is, in fact, a gathering of several males. To ask a single American woman might be awkward; not to do so would be impolite. A foreign pair, however, will always find a local welcome. The simple presence of a male partner makes the woman unavailable for courtship, allowing her to develop business ties in ways no different than an American man.

An American male may also have symbolic value as a fictitious husband. Among Moslems, women gain status through marriage and the birth of sons. Thus, single or divorced U.S. women assigned to these regions may find it useful to imply married status, complete with ring and pictures of a spouse and children. The female author once did this without overtly telling a lie. The ring spoke for itself, while the pictures (in fact, a brother and his sons) were simply displayed with the phrase "my family." The deception illustrates the larger point: in regions where unattached women cause anxiety, a symbolic male presence can reassure host nationals, transforming the status of an American female decision maker so as to conform to local custom.

RECOMMENDATIONS: CAN MACHISMO BE "MANAGED?"

Americans hold strong biases regarding machismo, beliefs we do not leave behind once sent abroad. We disapprove of customs that limit women, even if motivated by desire to protect them. Yet, when dealing commercially with such behavior, it seems best to move past passive disapproval towards active management.

The catalyst that makes such management effective is prior research, examining specific variants of this behavior in ways no different than those used for other aspects of a target clientele. Women seeking

foreign posts can clearly benefit by studying those aspects of host cultures most likely to affect their work. In countries known for machismo, that should include relationships between the sexes. Thus, when working with Islamic businessmen, American businesswomen should consider the following guidelines.

1. Accept the fact that belief systems restricting local women may, in fact, obstruct commercial efforts by American female executives. If so, neither private resentment nor public tolerance may be as effective as actively managing those aspects of the problem that may impede the flow of business. Each system must therefore be researched and analyzed before arrival if it is to be effectively influenced on-site.

2. Research the inner logic of machismo in the specific area to which assigned. This may include initial study of the region's language, history, and holy books. Strive to comprehend each local practice from the perspective of practitioners, learning not only how it works, but why they feel it should. Thereafter, identify specific expectations that key practitioners may hold for U.S. women (however well-regarded by their corporation) who work within the local business setting. Only by viewing foreign behavior through foreign eyes can we develop vision of our own.

3. Identify specific social and commercial situations where expectations of host nationals may clash—predictably—with those of female appointees. Do not assume that corporate status provides exemption from traditions that can go back centuries. These may outwardly be put aside for guests, but still remain within a foreign colleague's mind. This analysis suggests that American businesswomen in contact with Islamic businessmen may encounter problems with physical attractiveness, working alone, and establishing commercial credibility. Further research will certainly suggest others.

4. Develop preemptive strategies to manage each potential conflict so that, ideally, none occurs. Research suggests that the strategies most likely to prevent conflicts between American businesswomen and Moslem businessmen include creating prior in-house expertise, on-site corporate status, a "localized" commercial image, and a supporting network of on-site male partners whose symbolic presence can facilitate the female manager's work.

Americans who work abroad need not be held back by their biases. Many privately condemn machismo. That is their prerogative. Beyond this condemnation, however, whole worlds of foreign thought and feeling call out for further exploration, including those of which we disapprove. To do business in these worlds, we must explore them, transforming private disapproval and passive tolerance into active inquiry and professional concern. Only then will we be able to "manage" machismo so artfully as to prove acceptable to both our foreign colleagues and ourselves.

[Jeffrey A. Fadiman with
Evylyne Meier]

FURTHER READING:

Adler, Nancy. "Expecting International Success: Female Managers Overseas." *Columbia Journal of World Business*. Fall, 1984.

Adler, Nancy. "5 Pacific Basin Managers: A Gaijin, Not a Woman." *Human Resources Management*. Vol. 26 (#2), Summer, 1987.

Adler, Nancy. "Women as Androgynous Managers: A Conceptualization of the Potential for American Women in International Management." *International Journal of Intercultural Relations*. Vol. 3 (#4), 1979.

Alizira, Marianne. "Women of Saudi Arabia." *National Geographic*. October, 1987.

Breen, Katie. "Arabia Behind the Veil." *Marie Clair*. UK, September, 1989.

Gilsenan, Michael. *Recognizing Islam: Religion and Society in the Modern Arab World*. Random House, 1982.

Hashmi, M.S., and K. L. Foutz. "Marketing in the Islamic Context." *Academic Conference Paper*. Presented, Eastern Michigan University, Ypsilanti, Michigan, Spring 1987.

Hooper, John. *The Spaniards: A Portrait of the New Spain*. Penguin Books (UK), 1987.

Kupfer, Andrew. "How to be a Global Manager." *Fortune*. March 14, 1988.

Lamb, David. "1001 Modern Arabian Myths." *Speech to the Commonwealth Club of California*. San Francisco, California, March 14, 1988.

Morgenthaler, Eric. "Women of the World: More US Firms Put Females in Key Posts in Foreign Countries." *Wall Street Journal*. March 16, 1978.

Stasio, Marilyn. "Beyond the Veil." *New Woman*. November, 1987.

Sulivan, Constance. "Machismo and its Cultural Dimension." in *Towards Internationalism*. Luce, L. and E. Smith, eds. Harper and Rowe, 1986.

Taylor, M., M. Odjogov, and E. Morely. "Experienced Women in Overseas Business Assignments." *Academv of Manaaement Proceedinas*. 1975.

Thal, Nancy, and Philip Caetora. "Opportunities for Women in International Business." *Business Horizons*. Vol. 24, December, 1979.

MANUALS

SEE: Handbooks and Manuals

MANUFACTURERS' REPRESENTATIVES

Manufacturers' representatives are independent contractors who work on commission to sell products for more than one manufacturer. They cannot be under the immediate supervision of the manufacturers—typically called principals—that they sell for, therefore the relationship is not like that between a boss and employee, but is a business-to-business relationship.

A manufacturers' rep firm can be run by one person, or it can be a much more extensive organization with numerous sales persons covering specific territories. The typical agency is a corporation employing six people, including those to handle office duties, that sell for an average of 10 different principals, according to the Manufacturers' Agents National Association (MANA). The average rep agency handles annual sales volume of $7 million to nearly $10 million.

The MANA directory lists approximately 6,000 manufacturers' representatives in the United States, located in all 50 states. The firms represent every conceivable product line, from automotive to rubber products, from arts and crafts to jewelry, from electronics to energy, from food and beverage processing equipment to furniture. Virtually any product that is made and sold can be handled by rep firms.

Smaller companies that can't afford to have their own sales staff use agencies, as do billion dollar firms that want to ensure maximum coverage for their products. Some large companies even sell exclusively through manufacturers' representatives.

Representatives generally represent several different companies that offer compatible, but not competing, products to the same industry. This method reduces the cost of sales by spreading the rep's cost over the different products touted to each customer. As a result, manufacturers' agents view themselves not as middlemen, but as a cost-effective alternative to a company hiring a full-time salaried sales force. Tens of thousands of small- and medium-size manufacturers in the United States use agents to sell their products. This is particularly true of new products where a direct salaried force is cost prohibitive. Because reps are paid by commission, the manufacturer incurs no cost until a sale is made.

At different times, however, some large customers—such as Wal-Mart and General Electric—have tried to bypass representatives and buy only directly from manufacturers in an effort to cut costs. This practice, opposed by MANA, was the subject of hearing in 1994 before a U.S. House committee.

HISTORY

Some sales agencies have been around since the turn of the century, but the manufacturers' representative business really began to grow and develop just after World War II. Industry was starting to take off at that time, and many new companies were just getting started and needed ways to get their products to market. These new companies especially liked the economics of the rep business: no cost until a sale was made.

The rep business has grown steadily over the years. While the economics have had a lot to do with the growth, agencies often offer much more than just a salaried sales force. They can bring continuity, as manufacturers and representatives can build relationships that last years and years. While a salaried sales person may move from company to company, many reps and their principals have a business relationship that goes back decades.

ADVANTAGES AND DISADVANTAGES

One of the obvious advantages of utilizing a manufacturers' representative is the economic benefits it offers. A manufacturer has no fixed overhead. Rep firms are paid commissions when they sell products. When they don't sell anything, they aren't paid. When a manufacturer hires salaried sales people, it has to pay salaries, Social Security taxes, and fringe benefits, regardless of what the sales performance is. Hiring a rep firm brings no such upfront costs.

With field sales calls costing an average of $250, a rep trying to sell several products to an individual customer makes the selling process much more efficient. Agents who have created a complete line of products often get more time (and money) from a buyer who is interested in several of the products. The system of agency selling is geared to be highly efficient, because an agency doesn't make money unless it sells products.

Another significant advantage is especially relevant to start-up firms, firms trying to launch a new product, or firms trying to penetrate a new geographic area. By contracting with a manufacturers' rep, a company gains instant access to either industry expertise or knowledge of a particular country or region. This type of knowledge could take a company years to develop on its own, and it could be very expensive. Contracting with a rep bypasses those negatives.

There are other distinct advantages as well. For manufacturers with a narrow product line, agencies offer one of the best ways to access the market. Because they normally sell compatible products to a single market, the rep firms usually are well-connected with the manufacturers' prospects and customers. This offers manufacturers immediate entry to markets that may be hard to reach with a direct sales force.

Start-up companies also can gain an advantage by using reps. Many of the owners of these start-up companies have backgrounds in production, engineering, and finance and have little idea of what goes into sales and marketing. They still see making a superior product as the only thing that matters. Most start-up firms face stiff competition and have to work harder to get noticed. By using manufacturers' reps that handle complementary lines, the reps can see the people these new firm need to influence, usually more easily than a sales person who doesn't have customers in place in the territory.

Rep firms also can give new firms ideas of where to advertise, comment on what the competition is doing, and give estimates of a given territory's potential. Many reps also do service calls for less expense than if it had to be handled from the factory.

There are certain disadvantages to using rep firms, however. Probably the most important drawback is the lack of control. Reps are independent contractors doing business for more than one manufacturer. Because of this, no one manufacturer gets full-time attention from the agent, as he or she must split time among their various principals.

There are also times when it is preferable to have a direct sales person instead of a manufacturers' representative, especially when a product needs highly technical service. When highly skilled technical people are needed for a sale, a direct sales person may have an edge, although some reps have fairly sophisticated backgrounds in the areas in which they specialize.

Some agents also may be reluctant to provide service beyond selling. Such things as start-up assistance and service often are needed and must be supplied by the factory.

AVERAGE AGENCY PROFILE

According to MANA's 1994 survey of manufacturers' agencies, the association's composite profile of the average agency shows the typical agency handled gross sales of about $7 million a year. The average agency had been in operation for more than 18 years, represented 10.4 manufacturers and covered nearly six states in their territories.

Additionally, a typical agency has either one or two offices, employs nearly four sales people, a little more than two office staff employees, and almost two warehouse workers. More than 75 percent of the agencies were owned by the original founder of the firm, owners established the firm, while 20 percent had been acquired, and the rest were formed as the result of a merger.

About 43 percent of the agencies represent foreign manufacturers in the United States, but only 15 percent actually sell product in foreign countries. Among the markets sold to by manufacturers' representatives, by far the top one was original equipment manufacturers, with 55 percent of reps aiming products there. The second most popular area was the wholesaler/distributor market at 44 percent, followed by capital equipment manufacturing at 26 percent. Other main markets included contractors/architects (20 percent), government/municipalities (17 percent), and retail/mass merchandisers (12 percent).

The MANA survey showed a definite correlation between the number of years a rep firm had been in business and the financial results of the company. Fledgling agencies, those in business just 1 to 3 years, handled on average just $2.22 million in total sales and collected gross commissions before costs of about $157,000. For those in business 4 to 10 years, the gross sales rose to $3.53 million, with commissions of nearly $255,000. Agencies in existence 11 to 25 years handled on average $7.51 million in sales, with gross commissions topping $500,000, and rep firms in business more than 25 years had sales of more than $9.2 million and commissions nearing $700,000.

There also was distinct differences pointed out in the survey between agencies established as corporations versus those established as sole proprietorships. The corporate rep firms—the more common of the two—averaged $7.6 million in sales and collected $561,000 in commissions, compared with just $3.13 million in sales and less than $190,000 in commissions for the sole proprietors. Corporations also were more likely to have a greater number of offices, covered more states, had double the number of sales personnel, and had been in business an average of 22 years, compared with about 13 for sole proprietors. A greater percentage of corporate-run businesses also represent foreign manufacturers or sell overseas.

Conversely, 92 percent of sole proprietors established their rep firms, with only 7 percent acquiring the agency, whereas just 71 percent of corporate owners established the firm, with 26 percent acquiring them. It also should be noted that principal owners and partners involved in sole proprietorship take home net income that is a greater percentage of gross sales than their counterparts at corporate rep firms. This likely is because they have less overhead with fewer employees and less office space and warehousing capability.

SELECTING AN AGENCY

Manufacturers have many factors to consider when selecting a manufacturers' representative. They typically will want someone who is knowledgeable about their products and applications. They'll want reps who respond quickly to calls, present the product in terms of how it will meet customer needs, and represent lines fairly, giving enough time to each regardless of how much income each line accounts for.

Manufacturers also need to decide whether to go with a new agency or an established rep firm. Some want agents who are younger while others want the complete coverage they think comes with an established agency that has a large staff. The best rule of thumb for manufacturers is to be patient and do plenty of preliminary research; they should treat the selection process with as much importance as the hiring of a new vice-president. MANA suggest the following guidelines:

1. The manufacturer should define its own needs. If replacing an agency that did well and had a reputation for good service, the replacement better do an equally good job. If appointing a rep for the first time, it's a good idea to make a profile of the customers, their needs, and the way they do business. Ask prospective reps about such things as likely call cycle, problems in the territory, prospective buyers in the area, and how aggressive the people are who sell for competitors.

2. Create a profile of the ideal agency. Make the profile clear, but also be flexible so it never reaches the point that no one ever gets hired because it's impossible to meet all of the perfect standards set down on paper.

3. Create a profile of the manufacturing firm. Many rep firms can be selective and won't take on product lines without knowing quite a bit about their principals. The profile should be honest and touch on growth plans, real advantages of the product, why the territory is open, and what a realistic goal of the territory's potential is.

4. Get referrals from other agencies. Manufacturers' representatives are a close-knit fraternity in the United States, and many can provide the names of several agencies that would be a good fit for the line.

5. Get referrals from other manufacturers. Companies in the same area that sell similar but noncompetitive products can be a good source in finding potential reps. Some may

even recommend their own agencies, while others may be reluctant to have their reps take on additional lines.

6. Manufacturers can create their own agency. Some companies know they have people who won't stay once they've hit the top of the sales department. One way to keep them is by helping them set up their own sales agency. One maker of roofing supplies had seven regional managers who called on distributors and lumber yards. A marketing executive of the roofing firm knew that once they realized the full potential of the territories, they likely would leave. He offered to help them set up as a rep firm by locating other lines to round out their packages. Within five years, all seven were in business for themselves but still selling the roofing lines.

7. Be patient. While manufacturers often don't have the luxury of waiting forever when filling rep openings, doing preliminary research usually is a good idea. Many manufacturers who've admitted making mistakes in hiring agents say it was because they didn't take the time to get to know the prospective rep. In general, it's better to take the needed time to select the right prospect than to rush into a bad situation and have to rectify it later.

8. Be flexible in setting up territories. Reps must have exclusive rights within a territory, but rather than assign arbitrary territories based on geography, it's often preferable to select the agents that best fit your line and let their coverage determine the territories.

DEALING WITH REPS

Manufacturers must remember that their rep firms are independent sales agencies that are not employees of any of its principals, but business partners with each of them. As such, the manufacturers can't have the same type of direct control as they do over their own personnel.

From a legal standpoint, it is important to remember that the manufacturers pay nothing to a rep until a sale is made. They also pay no withholding taxes or Social Security. It also means there is none of the bookkeeping or record keeping done by a direct sales staff. This is an important distinction for the Internal Revenue Service. The IRS typically uses as one of its tests the amount of direct control exercised over sales reps. If regular reports are demanded of independent agents, the IRS can declare the rep an employee and require the various withholding taxes.

Communication remains an integral part of the relationship between reps and their principals. The process of communicating, though, is different than when a salaried sales person is involved. Manufacturers still need field information, but because of the legal ramifications, the question is how will it be supplied. Some agents make regular calls to each of their principals once a month, which is allowable as long as it's not a requirement to keep the line.

The key is that both parties need to know enough about what the other is doing with respect to the program. Reps should let their principals know what they are doing for them in the field, regardless of the level of sales at that particular moment, while agents need updated information on matters such as product specifications and pricing. Manufacturers should expect loyalty, with no conflict in product lines; knowledge of the territory and/or industry; knowledge of product lines after a reasonable amount of exposure; quick response to suggestions; regular follow-up; and a fair share of the agent's time. Reps, on the other hand, should expect a fair contract that recognizes performance and rewards success and longevity; access to customer service, training, and technical backup; a quality product; timely delivery; and a true commitment to build business in their territory.

A GROWING DISPUTE

One legal issue involving the use of manufacturers' representatives has evolved over a number of years. It concerns the growth of superstores—such as Wal-Mart—that represent tremendous buying power. Many of these discount stores have tried to circumvent the normal chain by telling their suppliers they won't deal with independent reps, but only directly with the manufacturer.

The superstores say their economies of scale allow them to undersell small local competitors. They say that ''going direct'' will help them sell at a lower price by eliminating the commission paid to the rep.

MANA said that large retailers have tried this tactic at least six times since 1980. The association filed a complaint against Wal-Mart in 1992 and testified in late 1994 before a U.S. House committee studying the impact of superstores on sales agents.

MANA argued that the practice is ''unethical and illegal,'' causing a domino effect that inhibits the ability of smaller companies that depend on manufacturing reps. The group said that in the American system of marketing, someone makes the sale—be it a direct salaried person or a rep firm—and that this selling function is part of the cost of the product.

EMPLOYEE COMPOSITE

At multiperson sales agencies, 56 percent of firms consider all sales personnel to be employees, according to another MANA survey. About 16 percent of firms use only independent contractors, while 26 percent use a combination of employees and contractors.

A little more than half of the firms, 52 percent, compensate sales people by a combination of salary and commission. A total of 27 percent utilize salary only, while 21 percent pay commission only. Comparing compensation between those paid only by salary and those making a salary plus commission, the study indicates sales people paid with a combination of both generally make more money.

Average compensation for those making just a salary were: sales trainee, $22,647; 1 to 3 years' experience, $29,402; 4 to 6, $36,596; 7 to 10 years, $45,433; and over 10 years, $51,085. For those making a base salary and commission, compensation averaged: sales trainee, $24,600; 1 to 3 years, $32,850; 4 to 6, $44,432; 7 to 10, $53,256; and over 10 years, $62,918.

[Bruce Meyer]

FURTHER READING:

"How to work successfully with manufacturers' agencies." Special Report in *Directory of Manufacturers' Sales Agencies.* Manufacturers' Agents National Association, 1994.

Gibbons, James J. "Recruiting Agents: Do it Right and You'll Never Have to Settle for Second Best." Part of Special Report in *Directory of Manufacturers' Sales Agencies.* Manufacturers' Agents National Association, 1993.

Marshall, Michael, and Frank Siegler. "Selecting the Right Rep Firm." *Sales & Marketing Management.* January 1994, p. 46.

"What Makes for a Long and Rewarding Relationship." *The American Salesman.* November 1992.

"The MANA Manufacturers' Sales Agency Survey." *Agency Sales Magazine.* December 1994, p. 4.

"MANA Testifies Before U.S. House Committee on the Impact of Superstores on Sales Agents." *Agency Sales Magazine.* September 1994, p. 14.

Silliphant, Leigh. *Making $70,000+ a Year as a Self-Employed Manufacturers' Representative.* Berkeley, CA: Ten Speed Press, 1988.

MARKET RESEARCH

Market research is the process where by advertising agencies and advertisers monitor their customers and potential customers to guide future marketing and advertising efforts. Research is needed because consumer and corporate customer behavior is sometimes difficult to predict or explain. People may buy only after carefully studying a product's features and benefits. They may buy after seeing a well-executed advertisement over and over again. Or, they may buy after hearing about a good product from their friends and colleagues. They may even purchase on a whim without knowing anything at all about the product because the packaging caught their eye while walking down the supermarket aisle.

Research tries to find out why a certain television program was watched, why listeners tune in to a certain radio station, why some magazines are read and others lose subscribers. Consumer marketing research tries to find out why a product or service was purchased or ignored. Advertisers believe they can listen better to the customer through market research. They can make changes in existing products and create new products by finding out how consumers view a product. The main objective of market research is to improve the marketing process so marketing budgets are better spent.

Saving marketing money while attracting more customers is at the root of all marketing research. As John Wanamaker, the department store owner who hired the first **advertising** copywriter, said in the 1880s, "I know half the money I spend on advertising is wasted, but I can never find out which half." Market research tries to solve that dilemma.

Market research is critically important but remains imperfect. Although new products are usually researched before introduction, more than 80 percent fail. Campbell's Soup once conducted an exhaustive market research study on sales of their products and on their customers. They discovered that the company wasted more than 60 percent of its marketing dollars targeting people who never buy from a particular product category or those were loyal to other brands. They also found that the small segment that were loyal Campbell's customers delivered three times the profits that occasional Campbell buyers did. This meant that the coupons delivered to regular Campbell's customers took money away from the bottom line since those people would have bought the product anyway.

HISTORY OF MARKET RESEARCH

Advertising was not tested in this country until the 1920s. Until that time copywriters would write what they thought an ad should be, publish it, and hope that readers acted upon the information. During the 1920s, Daniel Starch began expanding his educational surveys into advertising. From those surveys he developed a theory that effective advertising must be seen, read, believed, remembered, and acted upon. By the 1930s he had launched a company that interviewed people in the streets, asking them if they read certain magazines. If they did, his researchers would show them the magazines and ask if they recognized and remembered ads in them. He then compared the number of people he interviewed with the circulation of the magazine to extrapolate how effective those magazine ads were in reaching readers.

Various market research companies started following Starch's example and improved on his techniques. George Gallup (1901-84) developed a rival system of "aided recall" that prompted people to recall the ads they had seen without actually showing the ads. Gallup was able to adapt this system to measure radio and television advertising.

Throughout the last 70 years, market research has grown much more sophisticated and prevalent. One survey of surveying activity found that 73 percent of Americans said they had participated in a survey with 42 percent having been also surveyed in the previous year.

TYPES OF MARKET RESEARCH

AUDIENCE RESEARCH. Research on who is listening, watching, and reading are all important to marketers of television and radio programs and print publications. Television and radio ratings determine popularity of shows and how much stations can charge for advertising spots during show broadcasts. Publication subscription lists are audited by tabulating companies that cross-check magazine subscription records to make sure the people receiving the magazines either subscribe or have requested the publication.

In the early days of television, selected viewer families kept diaries or logs of their viewing habits. Completed logs were mailed to the A.C. Nielsen Company, which then compiled the results. In 1986 the log gave way to a people meter which allows viewers to punch buttons on a remote control-like device that records viewers' choices automatically.

While not yet in place, inventors are experimenting with devices that will no longer depend on viewers, listeners, or readers to actively tell researchers about their habits. The researchers may soon be able to get all the information they need from devices placed in the home. One device under study would be a television capable of looking back at viewers. It would store digitized images of its "television family" in its memory banks then regularly record if they are in the room. The device would even record whether their faces are turned toward the TV to prove they are looking at the show and its accompanying commercials.

Another device under development would not only monitor when people are watching television, but would know when they are reading advertising-filled magazines. The device would record pulses coming from a television or radio and from a transmitter cleverly hidden in the publications' bindings.

The devices sound Orwellian, which is what is slowing their development and implementation. Broadcasters are not sure they want to cooperate with the transmission of the imperceptible pulses, while advertisers are leery about appearing too eager to know everything their customers do in the privacy of their own homes.

PRODUCT RESEARCH. Simple in-person research such as taste tests conducted in malls and in the aisles of grocery stores is market research. So is elaborate, long-term "beta testing" of high-tech products by selected, experienced users. While advertising agencies used to conduct much of the product research, that function has also moved into the marketing department of advertisers.

Product research can be simple: tweaking the taste of an existing product, then measuring consumers' reactions to see if there is room in the market for a variation. Or, it could be more extensive: developing prototypes of proposed new products that may be intended for market introduction months down the road.

Like all research there is a danger to paying too much attention to the wrong things. The introduction of New Coke was based on the outcome of taste tests that showed the public wanted a sweeter product. An angry public, outraged that Coca-Cola was planning to change the familiar formula, forced the company to ignore its taste tests and leave the original Coke on the market. The company had looked closely at taste test studies, but failed to factor in research that showed consumers were happy with the product as is.

BRAND RESEARCH. Brands, the named products that advertising pushes and for which manufacturers can charge consumers the most money, are always being studied. Advertisers want to know if consumers have strong brand loyalty ("I'd never buy another brand, even if they gave me a coupon."); if the brand has any emotional appeal ("My dear mother used only that brand."); and what the consumer thinks could be improved about the brand ("If only it came in a refillable container.").

Brand research has its perils. Campbell's Soup once convened a focus group comprised of its best soup customers. One of the findings was that those customers saw no need for a low-salt alternative soup Campbell's wanted to market. Concerned that the general public seemed to want low-sodium products, Campbell's retested groups other than their best customers. This research found a market interested in a low-sodium soup. The loyal Campbell's customers loved the saltier product as is, while a larger group of potential customers preferred the low-salt alternative.

PSYCHOLOGICAL RESEARCH. Perhaps the most controversial type of market research is psychological research. This research tries to determine why people buy certain products based on a group of researchers' profile of the way consumers live their lives. One company has divided all Americans into more than 60 psychological profiles. This company contends the lifestyles these people have established by past buying habits and their cultural upbringing influences their buying decisions. The researchers assert that individual differences can sometimes be negated.

This research continues to be controversial since it measures attitudes about buying and not the buying itself. Critics point to conflicting information uncovered through other market research studies. In one series of research projects researchers asked people what they were planning to buy before entering a store. After the people surveyed left the store, the same researcher examined what was actually in the shopping cart. In one such study only 30 percent of the people bought what they said they were going to buy just a half hour earlier.

SCANNER RESEARCH. There is no fooling the checkout scanner at the supermarket or the department store. It records is was actually purchased. This is valuable information an advertiser can use to help plan ongoing marketing strategy.

Scanners have changed the way advertisers have typically thought about the sale of consumer products. Before scanners, advertisers received sales information when retailers reordered stock, generally every two weeks. Advertisers had no way to quickly measure the effect of national advertising-supported sales promotions, store sales promotions, or the couponing of similar products by their competitors.

Now, computer technology can send scanner information to advertisers within days or even hours. What scanners have so far confirmed is that consumers are fickle. They may try a product heavily promoted through national television one week. Then the next week they may switch brands based on local promotions from the competition.

DATABASE RESEARCH. Virtually every type of consumer—credit card holders, smokers, drinkers, car buyers, video buyers—shows up on thousands of lists and databases that are regularly cross-referenced to mine nuggets of marketing research. Such database research is growing in popularity among marketers because the raw data has already been contributed by the purchaser. All the marketer has to do is develop a computer program to look for common buying patterns.

Database research can be thought of as the ultimate in market segmentation research. For example, from zip codes lists, marketers may determine where the wealthy people live in a city. That list can be merged with a list of licensed drivers. The resulting list can be merged with another list of owners of cars of a certain make older than a certain year. The resulting list can be merged with another list of car enthusiast magazine subscribers. The final compiled and cross-checked list will deliver a potential market for a new luxury car soon to be introduced and profiled in the car magazines. The people on the potential buyers' list would then be mailed an invitation to come see the new car.

Database research and marketing allow companies to build personal relationships with people who have proven from past purchases that they are potential customers. For example, a motorcycle manufacturer such as Harley-Davidson may discover from database research that a family with a motorcycle has a teenage son. That son is a potential new customer for everything from clothes to a new motorcycle of his own. In another example, movie rental giant, Blockbuster Entertainment, can suggest titles its customers might want to rent based on a check of its database for the types of movies people have rented in the past.

This personal relationship also provides a basis for more detailed and economical market research than might be possible from conducting random calling. From that research, marketing sometimes follows. For example, General Motors Corp., which has collected a database of 12 million GM MasterCard cardholders in just two years, surveys them to determine what they are driving now and when they might buy a new car. Why spend millions of dollars trying to sell to total strangers when you have a list of millions of people you already know?

POST-SALES OR CUSTOMER SATISFACTION RESEARCH. Companies no longer believe that the sale ends their relationship with a customer. Nearly one-third of the research revenues generated by the leading U.S. research companies concern customer satisfaction. Many companies are now waiting a few days or weeks, then contacting customers with survey questionnaires on telephone calls. Companies want reassurance that the customer enjoyed the buying experience and that the product or service lived up to the buyer's expectations.

One research company uses a one dollar check to encourage customer satisfaction responses. It prints a customer survey on the back of the check that is returned when the customer cashes the check. The survey company thus secures a short, but complete, survey of customer satisfaction. Such research can be even more personal. Honda once developed a program in which assembly line workers called new Accord owners to ask them what improvements could be made in the car.

The reason for this sort of research is to ensure current customers are happy and will consider themselves future customers. One study found that 70 percent of customers believe it is important that companies stay in contact with them, but that less than a third of those same customers reported that they had heard from companies whose products they purchased. Nearly 90 percent of those surveyed said they would choose a company's products if it stayed in touch with them and sought their satisfaction.

METHODS OF PERSONAL RESEARCH

CLOSED-END QUESTIONNAIRE. The type of research most people experience is filling out a comment card or questionnaire at a restaurant or hotel asking about the service they received. Another common research method is a telephone survey in which interviewers read from a carefully prepared list of questions designed so answers can be categorized then tabulated by computer.

Both of these are considered closed-ended, meaning that the person being surveyed cannot expound on their answer. Such surveys usually ask for "yes" or "no" answers or several measures of multiple choice opinion (e.g., "extremely interested," "somewhat interested," "not interested at all,"). This type of market research is generally conducted to elicit opinions and beliefs of the public. It is commonly used for political polling and to determine the awareness or popularity of a product or service.

The inherent problem with multiple-choice questionnaires that ask for clear-cut answers is that many people do not think in a clear-cut fashion. If not carefully prepared, closed-ended questions may elicit answers that do not provide a clear view of the person being surveyed. Sometimes, the company conducting the survey may intentionally or inadvertently write questions that elicit the answers it wants to get rather than a true picture of what is happening in the marketplace.

OPEN-ENDED QUESTIONNAIRE. Market researchers have grown more aware through the years that people have their own opinions that may not fit into a multiple-choice questionnaire. To capture these opinions and try to analyze them, researchers are shifting more to open-ended research. They are asking people to say exactly what is on their minds. Manufacturers are giving customers plenty of space on questionnaires to write in their likes and dislikes about products and services. Frequently, telephone researchers will mix closed-end and open-end questions on the same survey to try to delve deeper. A "no" response to why a person does not watch a particular cable television station may trigger an interviewer's follow-up question of "Why not?," the answer to which will be taken down word for word.

There is a problem in both closed- and open-ended questionnaire research, particularly that conducted over the telephone. The person answering the questions could grow increasingly bored or, worse, annoyed at the time it takes to answer the questions. Once they become bored or annoyed, people stop giving true opinions.

One company that has researched the problem of bored interviewees found that falloff in attention can begin as soon as one minute after the person starts answering questions. This also held even when people filled out questionnaires on their own time. The company believes that the longer the person is annoyed, the higher the likelihood that the value of the questionnaire is reduced.

Another study showed that 31 percent of Americans say they refuse to answer marketing research surveys. The survey conductors speculate that the high resistance is a result of consumers lumping telemarketing and survey calls together. Both frequently come at the dinner hour, when many people do not want to participate.

FOCUS GROUPS. In-person, sit-down sessions around a table with groups of consumers, would-be consumers, never-buyers, or any other demographic group a company wishes to bring together are called **focus groups**. This can be the most inexpensive type of research when handled on a local basis by a small business wanting to get a handle on its customers. Or, it can be one of the most expensive if a major corporation wants to test its plans in all sections of the country.

Local, small businesses may invite a focus group to a neighborhood home to sit around the dinner table to discuss how the company can develop new markets. Major corporations conduct their focus groups in a controlled environment, usually with a one-way mirror at one end. This allows executives to unobtrusively watch the proceedings and/or to videotape the session for further study.

The key to gathering good information from a focus group is for the moderator to keep the conversation flowing freely without taking a side. If a company is interested in launching a new product, the moderator usually does not even mention the company that is hosting the focus group, not wanting opinions already formed about the company's other products to influence the discussion. The moderator's job is to involve everyone in the session and prevent any individuals from dominating the conversation. The latter danger is called "The Twelve Angry Men," named after a Henry Fonda movie where a talkative, persuasive Fonda slowly influences 11 other jury members to acquit a man being tried for murder.

Researchers agree that focus group research should be accompanied by other types of research and not be the sole basis for launching new products. The reason is that opinions expressed among strangers may not always reflect the way people would react when alone. For example, a focus group discussing low-fat foods may garner an enthusiastic response from people who want to be publicly perceived as being concerned about their health. The same people, however, might say they never buy low-fat products if questioned during an anonymous phone interview.

SEE ALSO: Scanning Systems

[Clint Johnson]

MARKET SEGMENTATION

Market segmentation is the science of identifying key subgroups of the general market population that have the greatest potential to purchase a product or service, providing indications about how that subgroup might most effectively be motivated to purchase that product or service.

Segmentation is more than merely a method of directing **advertising** and promotion dollars to influence consumer decisions. It performs a very beneficial service to the public, in that it makes the most of often limited advertising and promotion budgets to inform specific members of the population who may have the greatest need for a certain product or brand. It enables people to economically gain information about products that they may otherwise not receive, form opinions about products, and develop motivations about buying decisions.

For example, through segmentation, a marketing manager for a toy intended for use by boys age seven to eleven may seek advertising media that has the greatest exposure to this target market. Marketing analysis indicates that boys in this age group comprise the largest percentage of the audience for a weekly televised professional wrestling show. The marketing manager may direct a substantial amount of the advertising budget for the toy to 30-second advertising spots that run during the wrestling show.

The result of this investment may be measured to provide an indication of the effectiveness of this strategy. In this case, an investment of $200,000 in advertising may produce $1.2 million is sales, or $600,000 in profit. Thus, the advertising yields a 6:1 return on investment for sales and a 3:1 return on investment for profit.

Actual analysis is typically far more complicated, involving multiple subgroups of the target market defined by age, race and gender demographics, geographical location, and a matrix of personality profiles.

If the toy in the above example is a radio-controlled boat, it may be most popular among boys age seven to eleven, but also among single white males age 35 to 44 living in northern states, making $30,000 to $40,000 per year who watch old movies on cable television. In this case, it might make sense to devote a portion of the ad budget to spots on classic movie cable channels.

In any case, segmentation indicates that ad spots during "Murder, She Wrote" (which profiles indicate is most watched by middle-aged women) or "Matlock" (which profiles indicate is watched mostly by older men) would be poor advertising investments. As a result, segmentation is as much about identifying where potential buyers are as where they are not.

SEGMENTATION CRITERIA

One of the most basic concepts in market segmentation deals with ability to purchase by and utility to the buyer. The first consideration is: does the target customer have the *money* to buy the product?

If the toy boat in our example costs $25, it may be assumed that seven- to eleven-year old boys do not have sufficient money for discretionary purchases such as the toy boat. In this case, the target customer lacks the *authority* to purchase the boat. The ad should therefore be aimed at convincing boys to ask their parents to buy the product or convincing parents that the toy would make an excellent gift for such a boy.

Another consideration involves the *desire* of the target customer to use the product—will a seven- to eleven-year-old boy be inclined to use the product. This is a preliminary consideration that is usually resolved in the product design concept stage.

These three considerations are integral parts of the segmentation process and are known by the acronym MAD (money authority, desire).

Recently, a fourth consideration has been added that deals with the *homogeneity* of the target market. In other words, do all members in the subgroup exhibit a predictably or reliably similar propensity to show interest in the product. This adds an "H" (or, sometimes "R," for *response*) to the MAD acronym.

SEGMENTATION STRATEGY

There are three basic segmentation strategies. The first of these, the mass marketing strategy, encompasses products that are identical to every customer in the market.

For example, a national oil company offers automobile gasoline to the entire population of drivers, touting its economy, environmental attributes, and ability to keep an engine in good condition. This message may be delivered to the entire population, regardless of demographic, geographic, or psychographic criteria. Anyone can use the gasoline, and everyone can appreciate its attributes equally. Because the message has universal relevance, it is highly efficient.

The second segmentation strategy involves product differentiation, where a product is unique in its category. For example, based on its characteristics, a single company's line of beers is exclusively popular with blue-collar workers. Advertising portrayals feature workers to reinforce the brand's identity.

While this builds tremendous loyalty to the brand by workers, it limits the scope of advertising to only the subset of the population that can identify with the message. In addition, the brand is solely dependent on this subset of the market for sales. The market for this brand could be destroyed if workers defected to a competing brand line that has greater appeal to this audience.

Third is a target marketing strategy, in which a product is developed specifically for a certain subset of the market. For example, a brand of cigarette is most popular among middle-aged white men. However, extensions to this brand are added, each with different characteristics, reinforced through advertising, to appeal specifically to young women, black women, college-age men, and older people who are trying—but are unwilling—to quit. Each extension is a unique product, a separate franchise, differently promoted and differently profitable.

Target marketing need not involve extension of the same brand identity, but it does involve the creation of versions of the product for specific markets. This strategy avoids the dependence a product may have on a single subgroup (such as with the beer example), and it provides more effective and encompassing appeal to multiple subgroups than mass marketing. However, this subgroup-specific targeting is typically more expensive, because the message must be reiterated for each subgroup.

The key determinant in choosing a strategy is return on investment. If the market for a product is roughly homogeneous with regard to the MADR criteria, it is likely that a mass-marketing or product-differentiated strategy would produce a better return on advertising and promotion than a target market approach.

The key to identifying a market for the targeted strategy lies in three qualification criteria (is the group large enough, is the product available to them, is there demand by the group for the product), and two determining criteria (is the group internally homogeneous, yet heterogeneous with respect to other segments).

The qualifying criteria indicate whether the subgroup comprises a viable (profitable) market. The determining criteria indicate whether subgroups consist of people with highly similar qualities, and whether those qualities are substantially different from other subgroups or the population in general.

SEGMENTATION BASES

Four *segmentation bases* may be used to determine how market subgroups may be divided. Psychographic and behavioristic bases are used to determine preferences and demand for a product and advertising content, while geographic and demographic criteria are used to determine product design and regional focus.

Psychographic bases include personality traits, while behavioristic bases include frequency of use, specific benefits to the subgroup, and readiness to purchase the product. While related, these bases are different. Psychographic bases address predictions of consumer judgements, while behavioristic bases address demonstrations of consumer judgements.

Geographic bases include regional preferences, such as East and West, North and South, urban or rural, and high-income or low-income areas. Demographics include personal criteria such as gender, age, social attributes (such as race, religion, and hobby interests), and income level.

Consider how a snow shovel may be preferred to a snow blower by people in different regions and of different ages and income levels, and how harsh snowy winters may affect the level of demand for these products.

Obviously, a snow shovel manufacturer need not concern itself with southern California, Texas, and Florida, but it would be well advised to concentrate its marketing apparatus on areas with frequent snowfall, such as Colorado, Maine, and Michigan. The same would apply to a maker of snow blowers.

The shovel manufacturer may recognize that its product enjoys a clear cost advantage over the snow blower, and that the shovel may be preferred by younger (more able-bodied) consumers in areas with light snowfalls.

The snow blower manufacturer may recognize that its cost disadvantage may also translate into a luxury advantage, and that older people may be more inclined to spend more for a snow blower, if only to avoid the demanding physical labor associated with shoveling. In addition, older people may be assumed to have more money available to purchase a snow blower.

These segmentation criteria define the bases for marketing strategies for both products. They also indicate specific advantages that comprise a market "niche." Within these niches, each manufacturer enjoys certain attributes that the other cannot overcome.

For example, it would be unwise for a shovel manufacturer to target older, upper-income people living in snowy environs. By the same token, the snow blower manufacturer should not target younger, lower-income people in low snowfall areas.

But in addition, the shovel marketer may identify cracks in the snow blower marketer's niche, specifically by promoting the shovel as a compliment to the snow blower. For example, not every snowfall is substantial enough to justify use of a snow blower. Therefore, owners of snow blowers may opt to also own a shovel for light jobs, and the shovel may be promoted accordingly.

SEGMENTATION PROCESS

Continuums may be developed for different market segments, each showing relative advantages of each type of product. These continuums, consisting of multiple segmentation bases, identify groups that should be specifically targeted for sales efforts.

Within these models, each manufacturer must decide whether (1) the company can deliver a product that will meet customer needs, (2) there are a sufficient number of buyers to justify a sales effort, (3) the product is affordable, (4) the product enjoys special advantages vis-a-vis a competing product, and (5) the product can overcome or neutralize advantages of a competing product.

In addition to helping determine marketing strategies (mass market, differentiated, or target), segmentation bases can indicate how a product should be *positioned*. Where the shovel can compete with the snow blower, it should be positioned as an alternative. Where it cannot compete with the snow blower, it should be positioned as a compliment.

Segmentation strategies are used from the earliest stages of product design, where a company first identifies who is its customer. For example, the toy boat manufacturer may seek opportunities to leverage its favorable acceptance among seven-to eleven-year-old boys to design a product for the twelve- to sixteen-year-old market.

A segmentation analysis reveals that boys in this age group who have experience with the toy boat spend considerable time outdoors (as opposed to watching television or playing video games). This suggests that the new product should be designed for outdoor use.

Boys in the targeted age group also may be determined to be physically active, preferring a product that demands athletic ability, and are employed in odd jobs that give them some discretionary income. Specifically, these boys may have as much as $120 to spend on a product.

A list of products is assembled that meets these criteria, and each is rated for sales potential based on segmentation criteria. The most promising of these products is a skateboard.

A skateboard is designed to be of sufficient size, with the proper balance characteristics and weight-handling capabilities appropriate for a 12- to 16-year-old boy. From focus groups, a variety of color and artistic design schemes are chosen, as is a high-impact product name: "Grungeboard."

Certain demographic, psychographic and behavioristic characteristics have already been accounted for in product design. The skateboard is for boys, age 12 to 16, who enjoy outdoor physical activity and react favorably to the term "grunge." However, further segmentation analysis is necessary to effectively target the promotion strategy.

For instance, skateboarding is necessarily seasonal; the product cannot be used in snow. Therefore, the best geographical markets are warm-weather climates.

Demographic analysis indicates the popularity of skateboarding among boys who are white, black, Asian and Hispanic. At $120, the product is relatively costly with regard to other types of active-lifestyle products, but is competitively priced against competing makes of skateboards. This analysis identifies the market niche for the product.

Promotional media are evaluated with regard to their impact among segments of the target market. These include television and print advertising, point of purchase displays and promotional media in other products (for instance, a catalog enclosed with other products sold by the skateboard manufacturer).

[John Simley]

FURTHER READING:

Sandhusen, Richard L. *Barron's Business Review Series, Marketing.* 2nd Ed. Barron's Educational Series, Inc., 1993.

MARKET VALUE

The standard definition of market value was articulated in the IRS Revenue Ruling 59-60, where it is equated with the price paid for a given property under the construct of a willing buyer and willing seller, both with full knowledge of pertinent facts, and neither being under a compulsion to act. Essentially, market value is the price at which goods trade in an open and competitive market.

For many types of property, the market value is an easily observed quantum. It can be examined by reference to comparable assets that have sold under similar circumstances, such as time, location, condition, terms, and the nature of buyer and seller. In the case of **commodities**, one need only look at the Chicago Board of Options Trading prices to determine at what price crude oil, cotton, pork bellies, etc. are trading on a given day. Similarly, for financial assets, such as shares in publicly traded companies, the New York Stock Exchange, **NASDAQ**, or American Stock Exchange listings can be consulted. The same is true for many debt securities, including corporate, municipal, state, and government **bonds**.

A loaf of bread, a pair of socks, and various consumer products have observable market prices which can be easily determined by sampling prices charged at various retail stores. The same is true, to a lesser extent, about good sold in other venues. Because the information about competitive products and competitive dealers is often less than perfect, different buyers may pay different amounts for the same or similar things. The precision with which market value is defined diminishes as the property becomes more unique and when the relevant information is limited.

Real estate is an example of how apparently similar properties can fetch dramatically different prices. Each parcel of real estate is in some way unique from all others, and the circumstances under which a given buyer approaches the negotiation may be quite varied. Some potential buyers may have a desperate need to buy soon or an emotional attachment to the neighborhood that may encourage them to pay more than could be obtained from another buyer. Thus, a seller may list the property at an unrealistically high price and get ''lucky'' with a particular buyer at the right time and place. Technically, the high trading price establishes a ''market value.'' If the buyer needed to sell shortly thereafter, however, he might find that the property can only be sold for somewhat lower than he recently paid. This price disparity has sparked a philosophical argument over which is the true market value.

The above discussion points out a fact about market value determination: it is easier to quantify and support a market valuation for generic, non-unique property than for unique property. An easily understood example is the case of a new car versus the same car several years later. At the time of a new car sale, identical cars can be found (or ordered) and picked up by buyers with zero miles, no dents or dings and a full manufacturer's warranty. Here the variance of actual transactions should be low; that is, the market values should be within a tight tolerance of some mean price. Four years later, a subset of the same group of cars may be for sale in the used car market. With used cars, many variables that affect value can differ. The cars'

condition and mileage can vary. Availability is more spotty. Therefore, uniqueness is higher, knowledge is less perfect, and comparing competitive options is not as readily done. As a result, the variance of prices paid for the same model used car, at the same point in time, will be much wider about the mean.

In the context of valuing the shares of a company, the observable **stock market** prices, based on minority interests which are less than the controlling interest, represent market value. When applying such empirical data, adjustments may need to be made under certain circumstances. For example, if a valuation is being done of a company in its entirety, the stock market price may need to be appended to capture an element of value known as the control premium. Alternatively, if the shares being valued are in a non-publicly traded company, the stock market price (of a comparable company) may need to be discounted to reflect the lack of marketability, sometimes known as illiquidity.

[Christopher Barry]

FURTHER READING:

Pratt, Shannon. *Valuing a Business: The Analysis & Appraisal of Closely Held Companies.* Burr Ridge, IL: Irwin Professional Publishing, 1988.

MARKETING

Marketing is a very general term that refers to the commercial functions involved in transferring goods and services from a producer to a consumer. It is commonly associated with endeavors such as selling and **advertising**, but it also encompasses activities and processes related to production, product development, distribution, and many other functions. Furthermore, on a less tangible level, marketing facilitates the distribution of goods and services within a society, particularly in free markets. Evidence of the pivotal role that marketing plays in free markets is the vast amount of resources it consumes: about 50 percent of all consumer dollars, in fact, pay for marketing-related activities.

This text recognizes a chief delineation of the subject of marketing, micro- and macromarketing. The latter pertains to the flow of goods and services within and between societies. Micromarketing, in contrast, encompasses specific activities performed by an organization as it attempts to transfer its particular offerings to consumers, primarily through targeted marketing techniques. Case studies and a discussion of multinational marketing nuances complement the very basic review of micro and macro principles.

BACKGROUND

Marketing, as a means of transferring goods and services from suppliers to consumers, predates recorded history. It was born by the transition from a purely subsistent society, in which families and tribes produced their own consumables, to more specialized and cooperative societal forms. The simple act of trading a piece of meat for a tool, for example, entails some degree of marketing. In fact, the term "marketing" is actually derived from the word market, which is a group of sellers and buyers that cooperate to exchange goods and services.

The modern concept of marketing evolved during and after the industrial revolution in the 19th and 20th centuries. During that period, the proliferation of goods and services, increased worker specialization, and technological advances in transportation, refrigeration, and other factors that facilitated the transfer of goods over long distances resulted in the need for more advanced market mechanisms and selling techniques. An example of a major marketing milestone during that time was cataloging, which allowed companies to offer their goods to consumers in remote regions through printed catalogs and order forms. Products could then be delivered by ship or train. Sears, Roebuck & Co. achieved the most notable success with this marketing tool.

Although modern marketing practices were spawned early in the industrial revolution, it was not until the 1930s that companies began to place a greater emphasis on advertising and promoting their products and on striving to tailor their goods to specific consumer needs. Before the 1930s, in contrast, most companies assumed that the market could absorb almost everything they could produce. As manufacturing capacity began to outstrip demand, however, marketing paradigms began to change.

During the 1930s and 1940s, firms innovated new sales techniques to give them an edge over their competitors. By the 1950s, many larger companies were sporting entire marketing departments charged with devising and implementing marketing strategies that would complement, and even direct, the corporation's overall operations. Since the 1970s, and particularly during the 1980s, the chief marketing trend at companies has been a greater focus on providing benefits, rather than products, to customers.

In the United States, General Motors Corp. (GM) is considered one of the pioneers of modern marketing strategy. Although Ford Motor Co. was one of the first organizations to successfully implement mass production techniques, it was the managers at GM that most successfully capitalized on mass production by developing a savvy marketing approach. GM realized that customers wanted a car that reflected a certain economic status, hence the Chevrolet, Buick, and Cad-illac nameplates. GM essentially created a demand for its cars (partially at the expense of its competitors) by differentiating its automobiles within the marketplace in a way that was important to American consumers. Other American companies of import that subsequently helped shape modern marketing strategies during the 20th century include McDonald's, Coca-Cola Co., the Procter and Gamble Co., Wal-Mart, Anheuser-Busch Companies, Apple Computer, Inc., and International Business Machines Corp. (IBM)

MACRO-MARKETING

Macro-marketing refers to the social process that directs the flow of goods and services from producer to consumer—an economic system that determines what and how much is to be produced and distributed by whom, when, and to whom. Economist Richard D. Irwin identifies eight universal macro-marketing functions that make up the economic process:

(1) buying refers to consumers seeking and evaluating goods and services;

(2) selling involves promoting the offering;

(3) transporting refers to the movement of goods from one place to another;

(4) storing involves holding goods until customers need them;

(5) standardization and grading entails sorting products according to size and quality;

(6) financing delivers the cash and credit needed to perform the first five functions;

(7) risk taking involves bearing the uncertainties that are part of the marketing process; and

(8) market information refers to the gathering, analyzing, and distributing of the data necessary to execute the marketing functions listed above.

All of the eight basic macro-marketing functions exist in some form in both command economies and in free markets. In both systems, in fact, consumers have different needs, preferences, and patterns of resource allocation. Similarly, producers have different resources, goals, and capabilities. Although virtually every society has some sort of marketing system that serves to match this heterogenous supply and demand, the success of any macro-marketing system is judged by its ability to accomplish the society's objectives, whether the chief goal is equality of wealth, as in a command economy, or the greatest good for the greatest number regardless of equal distribution, as is the case in a free market system.

In a command economy, government planners perform most of the marketing function for society.

The planners tell producers what and how much to provide and at what price. The goal of the producers is primarily to meet government quotas. Such a system may work well in a small and simple economic system or during a crisis like a war. In a larger economy, however, the process of matching supply and demand tends to become so extraordinarily complex that planners are simply overwhelmed. The complicated dynamics of consumer demands and the capabilities of suppliers elude planners, the result being that many consumer needs are left unfulfilled. Nevertheless, the marketing function may still achieve a primary goal, such as equal distribution of wealth.

In a purely free market economy the marketing function is carried out by individual consumers and producers who essentially act as economic planners by means of numerous day-to-day decisions. In most modern economies, consumers register their purchasing decisions with dollars. Providers of goods and services respond primarily to consumer input in determining what and how much to provide, and at what price. They are motivated by competition rather than incentives to meet government quotas.

The marketing function of free market economies also tends to be characterized by a greater emphasis on middlemen, or parties that specialize in trade rather than production. They bring buyers and sellers together and charge a fee or commission for their services. Likewise, facilitators serve free market economies by providing producers with adjunct services. Examples of facilitators include advertising agencies, transportation firms, banks and other financial institutions, and market research companies.

Although the marketing function in a free economy is generally effective, when judged by its ability to provide the greatest good for the greatest number, it may fail to achieve other goals. For example, some members of society may fail to compete effectively, thus reducing their dollar "vote" in the economy and diminishing their ability to acquire basic necessities. As another example, some producers may profit by providing goods and services, such as addictive drugs, that are detrimental to society as a whole.

Critics of free market systems cite several other flaws. Advertising, for instance, can be used to promote products that are unhealthy, bad for the environment, or cause consumers to make unwise decisions by clouding the facts. Also, the extreme emphasis on promotion consumes vast amounts of resources that are not put to any tangible consumer use. Furthermore, some people believe that the marketing function in a free economy leads to materialism, or an emphasis on things rather than social values.

To overcome some of the negative effects that may result from purely free market economies, most societies without a command economy adopt a market-directed economy that reflects a compromise between the two systems. Market-directed economies use government constraints to temper free markets. In the United States, for example, the federal government sets interest rates, creates import and export rules, regulates advertising medium, mandates safety and quality controls, and even limits wages and prices in some instances.

MICRO-MARKETING

Micro-marketing refers to the activities performed by the providers of goods and services within a macro-marketing system. Those organizations use various marketing techniques to accomplish objectives related to profits, market share, cash flow, and other economic factors that can enhance the organization's well being and position in the marketplace. The micro-marketing function within an entity is commonly referred to as marketing management. Marketing managers strive to get their organizations to anticipate and accurately determine the needs and wants of customer groups. Afterword they seek to effectively respond with a flow of need-satisfying goods and services. They are typically charged with planning, implementing, and then measuring the effectiveness of all marketing activities.

Academic discussions of the marketing management function are often presented within the context of behaviorist Abraham Maslow's famous hierarchy of needs. Maslow (1908-1970) posited that all peopled respond first to vital physical needs, such as food and shelter. Only after those needs have been met, he argued, do people strive to meet social and emotional needs that are important to their psychological well-being. Examples of those needs are security, belonging, and self-esteem. It is these basic biological needs that shape the buying behavior of all consumers.

Because the way that people choose to satisfy their needs can be shaped by past experiences, different groups and individuals may have different "wants" to satisfy the same need. Comprehension of this basic tenet of human behavior reveals an important aspect of the micro-marketing function—that producers are not capable of creating or shaping basic needs, but rather achieve marketing success by influencing wants. In other words, a chief goal of a marketing manager's job is to stimulate customers' "wants" for a product or service by persuading the consumer that the offering can help them better satisfy one or more of their needs.

An implication of Maslow's theory for marketing managers is that customers view products and benefits differently; customers don't buy products (services), they buy the benefits that they believe they will get from them. For instance, when trying to get a consumer to purchase an automobile, marketers must remember that they are selling an image. Car buyers with strong needs for social acceptance might seek a prestigious looking automobile, for example, or be willing to pay more for a particular name brand. This product-versus-benefit element is best evidenced by the strategic marketing of relatively homogenous goods, such as fruit juices, which are differentiated from competing products in the marketplace almost solely on the basis of perceived benefits attached to the product through advertising and promotion.

THE TARGET MARKETING CONCEPT

Micro-marketing encompasses a profusion of related activities and responsibilities. Marketing managers must carefully design their marketing plans to ensure that they complement related production, distribution, and financial constraints. They must also allow for constant adaptation to changing markets and economic conditions. Perhaps the core function of a marketing manager, however, is to identify a specific market, or group of consumers, and then deliver products and promotions that ultimately maximize the profit potential of that targeted market. Often, it is only by carefully selecting and wooing a specific group that an organization can attain profit margins sufficient to allow it to continue to compete in the marketplace.

For instance, a manufacturer of fishing equipment would not randomly market its product to the entire U.S. population. Instead, it would likely conduct research to determine which customers would be most likely to purchase its offerings. It could then more efficiently spend its limited resources in an effort to persuade members of its target group(s). Perhaps it would target males in the midwest between the ages of 18 and 35. The company may even strive to further maximize the profitability of its target market through **market segmentation**, whereby the group is further broken down by age, income, zip code, or other factors indicative of buying patterns. Advertisements and promotions could then be tailored for each segment of the target market.

There are infinite ways to satisfy the wants, and subsequently the needs, of a target market. For example, in the case of a product the packaging can be designed in different sizes and colors, or the product itself can be altered to appeal to different personality types or age groups. Producers can also alter the warranty or durability of the good or provide different levels of follow-up service. Other influences, such as distribution and sales methods, licensing strategies, and advertising media may also play an important role. It is the responsibility of the marketing manager to take all of these factors into account and to devise a cohesive marketing program that will appeal to the customer.

THE FOUR Ps

The different elements of micro-marketing strategy can be divided into four basic decision areas—product, place, promotion, and price—which marketing managers may use to devise an overall marketing strategy for a product or group of goods. These four decision groups represent all of the variables that a company can control. But those decisions must be made within the context of outside variables that are not entirely under the control of the company, such as competition, economic and technological changes, the political and legal environment, and cultural and social factors.

Marketing decisions related to the product (or service) involve creating the right product for the selected target group. This typically encompasses research and data analysis, as well as the use of tools such as focus groups, to determine how well the product meets the wants and needs of the target group. Numerous determinants factor into the final choice of a product and its presentation. A completely new product, for example, will entail much higher promotional costs, whereas a product that is simply an improved version of an existing item likely will make use of its predecessor's image. A pivotal consideration in product planning and development is branding, whereby the good or service is positioned in the market according to its brand name. Other important elements of the complex product planning and management process may include selection of features, warranty, related product lines, and post-sale service levels.

Considerations about place, the second major functional group, relate to actually getting the good or service to the target market at the right time and in the proper quantity. Strategies related to place may utilize middlemen and facilitators with expertise in joining buyers and sellers, and they may also encompass various distribution channels, including retail, wholesale, catalog, and others. Marketing managers must also devise a means of transporting the goods to the selected sales channels. Decisions related to place typically play an important role in determining the degree of vertical integration in a company or how many activities in the distribution chain are owned and operated by the manufacturer. For example, some companies elect to own their trucks, the stores in which their goods are sold, and perhaps even the raw resources used to manufacture their goods.

Decisions about promotion, the third target market functional area, relate to sales, advertising, **public relations** and other activities that communicate information intended to influence consumer behavior. Often promotions are also necessary to influence the behavior of retailers and others who resell or distribute the product. Three major types of promotion typically integrated into a target market strategy are personal selling, mass selling, and sales promotions. Personal selling, which refers to face-to-face or telephone sales, usually provides immediate feedback for the company about the product and instills greater confidence in customers. Mass selling encompasses advertising on traditional mass media, such as television, radio, direct mail, and newspapers, and is beneficial because of its broad scope. It also entails the use of free media, such as feature articles about a company or product in a magazine or related interviews on television talk shows. Finally, sales promotion efforts include free samples, coupons, contests, and other miscellaneous marketing tactics.

Determination of price, the fourth major activity related to target marketing, entails the use of discounts and long-term pricing goals, as well as the consideration of demographic and geographic influences. The price of a product or service generally must at least meet some minimum level that will cover a company's cost of producing and delivering its offering. Also a firm would logically price a product at the level that would maximize profits. The price that a company selects for its products, however, will vary according to its long-term marketing strategy. For example, a company may underprice its product in the hopes of increasing market share and ensuring its competitive presence, or simply to generate a desired level of cash flow. Another producer may price a good extremely high in the hopes of eventually conveying to the consumer that it is a premium product. Another reason a firm might offer a product at a very high price is to discount the good slowly in an effort to maximize the dollars available from consumers willing to pay different prices for the good. In any case, price is used as a tool to achieve comprehensive marketing goals.

COMPETITIVE STRATEGIES

Often times, decisions about product, place, promotion, and price will be dictated by the competitive stance that a firm assumes in its target market. According to Michael Porter's Book *Competitive Strategy*, the three most common competitive strategies are low-cost supplier, differentiation, and niche. Companies that adopt a low-cost supplier strategy are usually characterized by a vigorous pursuit of efficiency and cost controls. A company that manufactures a low-tech or commodity product, such as wood paneling, would likely adopt this approach. Such firms compete by offering a better value than their competitors, accumulating market share, and focusing on high-volume and fast inventory turnover.

Companies that adhere to a differentiation strategy achieve market success by offering a unique product or service. They often rely on brand loyalty, spe-

cialized distribution channels or service offerings, or patent protection to insulate them from competitors. Because of their uniqueness, they are able to achieve higher-than-average profit margins, making them less reliant on high sales volume and extreme efficiency. A company that markets proprietary medical devices would likely assume a differentiation strategy.

Firms that pursue a niche market strategy succeed by focusing all of their efforts on a very narrow segment of an overall target market. They strive to prosper by dominating their selected niche. Such companies are able to overcome competition by aggressively protecting market share and by orienting every action and decision toward the service of its select group. An example of a company that might employ a niche strategy would be a firm that produced floor coverings only for extremely upscale commercial applications.

BUSINESS VERSUS CONSUMER MARKETS

An important micro-marketing delineation is that between industrial and consumer markets. Marketing strategies and activities related to transferring goods and services to industrial and business customers are generally very different from those used to lure other consumers. The industrial, or intermediate, market is made up of buyers who purchase for the purpose of creating other goods and services. Thus, their needs are different from general consumers. Buyers in this group include manufacturers and service firms, wholesalers and retailers, governments, and nonprofit organizations.

In many ways, it is often easier to market to a target group of intermediate customers. They typically have clearly defined needs and are buying the product for a very specific purpose. They are also usually less sensitive to price and are more willing to take the time to absorb information about goods that may help them do their job better. On the other hand, marketing to industrial customers can be complicated. For instance, members of an organization usually must purchase goods through a multi-step process involving several decision makers. Importantly, business buyers will often be extremely cautious about trying a new product or a new company because they don't want to be responsible for supporting what could be construed as a poor decision if the good or service does not live up to the organization's expectations.

A chief difference between marketing to intermediate and consumer markets is that members of the latter are typically considering purchasing goods and services that they might enjoy but don't really need. As a result, they are more difficult to sell to than are business buyers. Consumers are generally less sophisticated than intermediate buyers, are less willing to spend time absorbing individual marketing messages of interest to them, and are often more sensitive to the price of a good or service. Consumers typically make a buying decision on their own, however, (or, for larger purchases, with the help of a friend or family member) and are much more likely to buy on impulse than are industrial customers.

Despite the differences, a dominant similarity between marketing to both intermediate buyers and consumers is that both groups ultimately make purchases based on personal needs, as described earlier. Consumers tend to react strongly to a desire to belong, have security, feel high self-esteem, and enjoy freedom and status. Similarly, business and industrial consumers react more strongly to motivators such as fear of loss, fear of the unknown, the desire to avoid stress or hardship, and security in their organizational role.

MICRO-MARKETING CASE STUDIES

An example of micro-marketing that demonstrates the importance of the marketing function in relation to other business functions, such as production and distribution, is Rubbermaid, Inc.'s strategy. Rubbermaid continued to produce and sell a line of plastic home products for several decades in an industry characterized as undynamic and even stagnant. Nevertheless, Rubbermaid's savvy marketing strategy has allowed it to post continuous gains in sales and market share, particularly during the 1980s when the company's sales rocketed more than six-fold. The company achieved its stellar gains by focusing on new product introductions and by tailoring its existing products to meet new consumer wants and needs. At the same time that it increased its market share, Rubbermaid managed to post strong profit margins by charging high prices. It commanded premium prices because it had positioned its products as unique and high in quality in comparison to competing products. An emphasis on a field sales force and a high level of service to its retailers augmented Rubbermaid's overall stratagem.

The success of Domino's Pizza, Inc. during the 1980s shows how a company that targets a particular market and is sensitive to its customer's needs can achieve success in the marketplace. Tom S. Monaghan opened his first store in 1960 with $500 and grew his tiny enterprise to a chain of four stores by 1965. Strong competition and the lack of a cohesive marketing strategy, however, forced him into bankruptcy. Monaghan researched pizza consumers and entered the pizza business again in 1971. He decided to target residential customers between the ages of 18 and 34 who preferred to have pizzas delivered to their door. He found that consumers were generally dissatisfied with the taste and reliability of delivery available from other pizza shops. As a result, Monaghan developed a pizza that his customers liked and then promised delivery within 30 minutes from the time the order was placed. His restaurants were strictly delivery and carry-out. By the late 1980s, the chain had expanded nation wide with 4,500 outlets and about $2 billion in sales.

One of the most dynamic and telling of all marketing case studies is the U.S. "cola wars." Those battles, which have been waged by major soft-drink manufacturers since World War II, demonstrate the effects of competition on marketing strategies in a free market. Although numerous soft-drink makers competed during the 1950s and 1960s, by the late 1980s the industry had consolidated to just six companies that controlled more than 80 percent of the entire market. The two fiercest competitors, Coca-Cola Co. and PepsiCo, Inc. each spend hundreds of millions of dollars each year to promote their products and to avoid loss of market share. Pepsi bludgeoned Coke during the early 1980s with a taste test promotion. It challenged consumers to taste both colas, which were not labeled, and select the one they believed tasted better. Despite the taste test, both companies have emphasized an emotional appeal to consumers, touting their drinks as fun or "American." Coca-Cola continued to dominate the restaurant and vending markets going into the 1990s and had a near lock on the demand for U.S. colas in Europe. Both companies were battling for market share in emerging Asian and South American markets in the early 1990s, having already garnered more than 70 percent of the U.S. soft-drink market.

Marketing efforts at General Electric (GE) exhibit some of the differences between marketing to industrial and consumer markets. Although GE is generally associated with its production of consumer goods, particularly appliances, only about 25 percent of GE's sales are garnered from consumer markets. Most of its profits come from sales of power generation, heavy industrial, and aerospace equipment. The general public still views GE as a provider of appliances, however, because the company's marketing strategy entails promoting that image in the mass media and through various consumer promotions. In contrast, GE markets its core industrial and technical products primarily through a direct sales force, which consists mostly of highly trained technical sales engineers. GE's marketing program also stresses an extensive lobbying effort at the federal level to secure government contracts and influence policies related to defense spending.

MARKETING FAILURES

Despite a company's best attempts to research and devise effective marketing plans, even the largest and most astute marketing divisions sometimes commit serious marketing mistakes that fail to lure customers and ultimately cost their companies millions of dollars. Such flops illustrate the subjective and complex nature of the micro-marketing process and often show how influences outside of the company's control can play an integral role in the success of any marketing endeavor.

One well-known marketing failure was conducted by the Korvette chain of discount department stores. Started in 1948 by Eugene Ferkauf, Korvette grew during the middle 1900s by undercutting department store prices by ten percent to 40 percent on appliances and other heavy goods. Ferkauf, who grew Korvette to more than $700 million in revenues by 1965, is credited with revolutionizing merchandising and retail marketing techniques and paving the way for mass discount merchandisers like KMart Corp. and Wal-Mart But Ferkauf began to change the market position of his stores in the mid-1960s. He tried to upgrade the image of the chain by bringing in higher-priced merchandise and food and clothing. The new products did not complement Korvette's existing distribution and management infrastructure, however, causing the profitability of the stores to lag. At the same time, moreover, Korvette failed to respond to increased competition in the discount industry. By the late 1960s, Korvette's market presence was quickly fading and Ferkauf was forced out of his management position.

The failure of the Burger Chef hamburger chain to mimic the success achieved by McDonald's exemplifies the importance of a comprehensive and well-executed marketing plan. General Foods purchased the 700-store Burger Chef chain in 1967 with the intent of growing it into a national fast-food powerhouse. By 1969 General Foods had added nearly 600 stores to the chain, primarily through franchising. Unfortunately, the rapid expansion only exacerbated underlying problems that were plaguing the misguided chain.

Burger Chef sported a red and yellow sign and a menu that was a near clone of its leading competitor. Despite Burger Chef's attempt to copy the vastly successful McDonald's, it lacked key marketing elements that had made McDonald's so successful. Its sign, for example, lacked the distinction of McDonald's golden arches, and its chain of restaurants lacked uniformity, thus reflecting an image of inconsistency to consumers. Furthermore, Burger Chef had failed to concentrate enough restaurants in a single area, which would have allowed them to increase the efficiency of local promotions. Most importantly, McDonald's had centered its marketing efforts on a creed of quality, service, and cleanliness, three virtues which Burger Chef failed to adequately imitate. In fewer than four years, General Foods amassed a loss of $83 million from its Burger Chef operations. Many of its stores soon closed.

Perhaps the most notorious marketing flop was Coca-Cola Co.'s introduction of New Coke in the mid-1980s, an effort to diminish gains made by its arch rival, Pepsi, in the youth market. Coke changed its long-revered cola recipe in an attempt to boost interest in its product and to appeal to younger soft-drink consumers who were seeking a sweeter drink. Coca-Cola, long known for its canny marketing prowess, completely misread public reaction to the modification. Outraged at the company's tinkering with what they viewed as an American icon, many consumers rejected the change. Fewer than three months after embarking on its misadventure, Coca-Cola was forced to bring back its old "Classic" Coke, which was soon outselling New Coke by a margin of ten to one. Coca-Cola failed to comprehend both the historical value of, and consumer loyalty to, Coke, both of which it had spent millions of dollars trying to cultivate during much of the 20th century.

MULTINATIONAL MARKETING

As the rapid growth experienced by the U.S. economy during the post World War II boom years faded during and after the 1970s, many companies began to focus on overseas markets for continued growth. While the basic goals of global marketing are the same as marketing a product or service domestically, important differences exist. For example, a product that sells well in the United States may require an entirely different marketing plan to achieve success in another country. General Motors Corp. discovered this when it tried to sell an automobile called the Nova in Mexico (Nova is similar to "no go" in Spanish).

Besides obvious language barriers, cultural subtleties in a country or region can easily thwart a marketing program that has achieved success elsewhere. Other risks associated with global marketing include currency fluctuations, political instability, and unforeseen legal ramifications. Furthermore, the lack of existing market research in many countries and the lack of means to gather information poses a serious roadblock for many would-be competitors. Nevertheless, rampant market growth in emerging countries, as well as relatively untapped markets in established economies, often provide great incentives for U.S. marketers to risk overseas ventures.

Marketers may utilize several different approaches to market their goods to foreign target groups. A common, relatively low-risk strategy is exporting goods through distributors and importers. This technique reduces the company's participation in a foreign country and essentially limits marketing initiatives to various middlemen and their buyers. Retailers and wholesalers in the host country can then select appropriate marketing media, utilize established distribution channels, set prices, and handle other localized marketing endeavors. A second marketing strategy is licensing and franchising, whereby a company sells the right to manufacture or sell its products to a foreign producer. Although this involves a minimal commitment, the company often maintains limited control over the company that purchases the license.

Joint ventures with enterprises in the host country, a third method of overseas marketing, entail a greater commitment on the part of the company trying to sells its goods. Joint ventures reduce political and cultural risks, however, and may help the company compete against local producers. Finally, some manufacturers choose to produce and market their products independently, through a wholly owned subsidiary in another country. Although this last method exposes the organization to greater risk and represents a significant commitment to business in the country or region, it allows more control over operations and provides greater profit opportunities should the venture succeed.

Regardless of the form(s) of participation a company selects to market its products or services abroad, once it makes the decision to go global it typically must establish two separate marketing strategies. First of all, it needs a global strategy that will direct the organization's overall goals abroad—to establish a market presence in Scandinavia, for example, or to control three percent of the East Asian market with five years. Secondly, the company usually devises a separate marketing program tailored to each country or region in which it becomes active—a strategy that is sensitive to the marketing nuances of that particular locale.

Aside from market research, pricing, distribution, advertising, and other marketing activities, the three primary product options available to a company active in overseas markets are: (1) marketing a single "global" product to all countries in which it is active; (2) adapting its product to reflect local markets within a region, such as Asia or Europe; or, (3) changing the product to suit individual countries and locales within each country.

SEE ALSO: International Marketing

[Dave Mote]

FURTHER READING:

Bly, Robert W. *Business to Business Direct Marketing*. NTC Publishing Group, 1992.

Boyd, Harper W., Jr. and Orville C. Walker, Jr. *Marketing Management: A Strategic Approach*. Richard D. Irwin, Inc., 1990.

Buzzell, Robert D. and John A. Quelch. *Multinational Marketing Management: Cases and Readings*. Addison-Wesley Publishing Company, 1988.

Dalrymple, Douglas J. *Sales Management: Concepts and Cases*. John Wiley & Sons, 1982.

Debelak, Don. *Total Marketing*. Richard D. Irwin, Inc., 1989.

Hartley, Robert R. *Marketing Mistakes*. John Wiley & Sons, 1986.

McCarthy, E. Jerome and William D. Perreault, Jr. *Basic Marketing*. Richard D. Irwin, Inc., 1990.

Porter, Michael E. *Competitive Strategy*. The Free Press, 1980.

MARKETING STRATEGY

Marketing strategy is the means by which an organization plans to achieve its desired ends in the marketplace. Subhash Jain defined marketing strategy as "an endeavor by a corporation to differentiate itself positively from its competitors, using its relative corporate strengths to better satisfy customer needs in a given environmental setting."

David Cravens and Charles Lamb stated that "an organization's marketing strategy identifies the buyers to be targeted and the positioning strategy (product, distribution, price, and promotion strategies) to be used for each customer target selected by management." They believe that "the choice of marketing strategies for different competitive situations is affected by the specific business environment of an organization."

Joseph Guiltinan and Gordon Paul asserted that "marketing strategies are plans that specify the impact that a firm hopes to achieve on demand for a product or a product line in a given target market." They indicate that a marketing strategy is a "mechanism for coordinating . . . marketing actions in areas such as advertising, sales promotion, personal selling, customer service, and new-product development."

ORIGIN OF THE MARKETING STRATEGY CONCEPT

A discussion of marketing strategy can be traced back to a discussion of marketing management by Leverett S. Lyon in 1926. Marketing management was perceived as the business function that developed marketing strategy. Lyon stated that "marketing management . . . may be conceived of as the continuous task of re-planning the marketing activities of a business to meet the constantly changing conditions both within and without the enterprise."

MARKETING AND STRATEGY. Marketing strategy has its roots in the basic concepts of **marketing** and **strategy**. Marketing strategy was probably used the first time that two humans engaged in trade, i.e., an "arm's-length" transaction. Certainly, early civilizations, such as the Babylonians, the Chinese, the Egyptians, the Greeks, the Romans, and the Venetians, had developed marketing strategies for their trading activities. They probably discussed appropriate strategies for given situations, and even taught these strategies to friends, family members, and subordinates. The actual function of marketing, i.e., the distribution function, was performed whenever exchange occurred.

Formalized marketing thought was originally developed from economic theory, which in turn, was initially derived from political theory. Robert Bartels cited 1900-10 as the period of discovery of marketing theory.

STRATEGY IS A MEANS TO AN END. It is a conscious approach to accomplishing something. Strategy precedes marketing and marketing strategy. The first time a human planned an approach for achieving a desired end—a goal or objective—he or she was developing strategy. Strategy can be formulated by individual s, groups, and organizations. The organizations can be families, corporations, nations, or groups of nations. In modern times, strategy can be formulated by complicated and sophisticated programmed software operating on computerized systems, personal computers, or personal computer networks.

Original, formalized discussion s of strategy or strategy theory are associated with politics, war, and the military. The term ''strategy'' comes from the Greek word ''strategia'' meaning generalship. It also can mean approach, scheme, design, and system, and is associated with terms such as intrigue, cunning, craft, and artifice.

BUSINESS STRATEGY. Business strategy is usually discussed and developed in the context of competition. It is associated with a struggle for scarce resources. The aim of the ''aggressor'' organization is to improve its position vis-à-vis ''others.'' The competitors, i.e., ''defenders,'' can be other organizations, suppliers, distributors, or customers. The competition is the enemy. Words such as ''campaign,'' ''attack,'' ''battle,'' and ''defeat'' are frequently used. There is an ''I win, you lose''—sometimes called a ''zero-sum game''—mentality. This, of course, is also the operating framework for individuals, families, groups, countries, and alliances when formulating political or military strategy. Hence, business and marketing strategy is frequently associated with political and military strategy.

MARKETING STRATEGY AND MILITARY STRATEGY. A more recent discussion of marketing and military strategy by William Cohen summarized 12 modern military strategies. He also referred to them as the principles of marketing strategy. He identified and described these military strategies as follows:

1. The principle of objective: the strategy should have a clear objective in mind.

2. The principle of initiative: ''act instead of react. . . . Maintain an offensive attitude to control the time and place of action.''

3. The principle of concentration or mass: allocate ''resources to achieve a competitive advantage at a decisive point.''

4. The principle of economy of force: use only the resources you need to achieve the objective, concentrate resources ''against the decisive objective, allocate minimum resources to secondary efforts.''

5. The principle of maneuver or positioning: place your resources in the optimum position for advantage; ''it can be applied to economical or psychological factors as well as geographic, and it incorporates the concept of timing.''

6. The principle of unity of command: ''for every assigned mission there should be one responsible manager, this ensures unity of effort that is necessary to get maximum power from available resources.''

7. The principle of coordination: there should be maximum cooperation and integration among the organizational units in planning and implementing strategy.

8. The principle of security: the enemy ''should never be allowed to acquire an unpredicted advantage; security requires accurate intelligence about the competition [the enemy] as well as in-house security that guards both physical objects and information about your capabilities and intentions.''

9. The principle of surprise: the element of surprise is important; it ''may emanate from deception, secrecy, variation methods, innovation, audacity, or speed of action, and it can compensate for inferior resources. . . . Total ignorance of your intentions is not necessary and probably impossible, but you must be able to accomplish your purpose before your competitors can react effectively.''

10. The principle of simplicity: ''simple direct plans are necessary because operational conditions and pressures make even the most simple strategy difficult to execute.''

11. The principle of flexibility: ''problems and opportunities must be thought about before a strategy is implemented so that alternative [contingency] actions can be planned before they are necessary.''

12. The principle of exploitation—maintain "forward momentum; that is, when winning, don't relax but continue to maintain pressure until maximum success is achieved." As an example, Cohen quoted General George S. Patton as saying "pursue the enemy with the utmost audacity."

THE NATURE OF MARKETING STRATEGY

DECISION MAKING. Marketing strategy is the result of decision making by corporate executives, marketing managers, and other decision makers. In general, the formal organizational titles or jobs of decision makers, or the nature or purpose of the organization, are irrelevant to the formulation of marketing strategy. When the decisions concern products or markets (such as "Should we enter the Mexican Market?"; "Should we subsidize the magnetic-levitation train project?"; "Should we develop a new line of fifth-generation wireless lap-top computers?"; "Should we build a new distribution warehouse in Houston?"; "Should we remodel the store in Miami?"; or "How should we reposition our two-week Grand Canyon Float Trip in the Las Vegas market?"), the results—i.e., the decisions—are all considered marketing strategy.

NARROW PERSPECTIVE. In a narrow sense, marketing strategy is a specified set of ways developed by marketers to achieve desired market ends. E. Jerome McCarthy and William D. Perreault, Jr. state that "a marketing strategy specifies a target market and a related marketing mix. It is a 'big picture' of what a firm will do in some market." In a marketing planning context, where marketing strategy tends to be developed, McCarthy and Perreault indicate that "marketing strategy planning means finding attractive opportunities and developing profitable marketing strategies."

BROAD PERSPECTIVE. In a broad sense, marketing strategy is composed of objectives, strategies, and tactics. Objectives are ends sought. Strategies are means to attain ends, and tactics are specific actions—i.e., implementation acts. Robert A. Lynn and John M. Thies provide military and marketing examples of objectives, strategies, and tactics. A military objective of "destroy enemy's will to fight" is associated with the military strategy to "bomb his homeland" and the military tactic of "regular night bombings." A marketing objective of "raise market share" is linked to the marketing strategy of "revise product line to reach segments not served well now" and to the marketing tactic of "new brand name and package for college market."

STRATEGY LEVELS. Marketing strategy is developed at different levels of an organization (the hierarchical dimension), across core marketing functions (the horizontal dimension), and for marketing execution and control functions (the implementation dimension). Strategy is usually developed in a hierarchical fashion from top to bottom; for example, there could be several layers of objectives where each objective is a function of a superstructure of superior objectives, and a determinant of subordinate objectives (except for the highest and lowest levels of objectives). Higher-level decisions—the superstructure—act as constraints on the one hand, and guides or aids for decision making on the other. The organization levels could include the overall corporate level, strategic business units, product markets, target markets, and marketing units, depending on the complexity of the organization.

MARKETING MIX STRATEGY. Strategy is also developed across the core functional (tactical) areas of marketing, usually referred to as the "marketing mix" or the "4 Ps" of marketing (product, place/distribution, price, and promotion strategies), as well as for marketing implementation (coordination, communication, and motivation strategies) and control functions (such as monitoring systems, variance analyses, and corrective action procedures). Any functional level of marketing, in turn, can have additional levels of marketing strategy decisions where refinement of the strategy might take place. For example, in the advertising component of the promotion function, the organization might develop marketing strategy consisting of advertising objectives, advertising strategies, advertising themes, advertising copy, and media schedules.

MARKETING STRATEGY TYPES

THE BASIC TYPES. There are many different types of marketing strategies. The most basic subdivision of strategy is according to whether the nature of the decision is strategic or tactical. Strategic marketing decisions are broad, long-term decisions covering the next three to five years and beyond. Strategic marketing decisions can involve mission statements, corporate growth goals, strategic alliances, and target markets. These decisions could also be referred to as strategic strategies. Tactical marketing decisions are narrow, short-range decisions covering, for example, next year's operations. Examples of tactical marketing decisions include product-line extensions, dealer contracts for channels of distribution, warehouse and transportation equipment, pricing schedules, advertising copy, and sales force territorial reconfiguration. These decisions could also be referred to as tactical strategies. A given individual might make both strategic and tactical decisions. In other words, the person "wears two hats." In other situations, depending on the size and complexity of the organization, an individual might be involved at only one level, at a parallel position, or at a sublevel. Nevertheless, in practice many of the tactical level decisions are really strategic in nature because of their strategic importance and life span. A good case in point is the decision to change the configuration of a channel of distribution. A decision to eliminate a group of manufacturer's reps and replace them with the organization's own sales force is technically a tactical or marketing mix decision. Yet, its nature is strategic. It is likely a major decision affecting years of operating results.

OTHER TYPES OF MARKETING STRATEGIES. The types of marketing strategies can be organized in many ways. For example, Orville C. Walker, Harper W. Boyd, Jr., and Jean-Claude Larreche, in a strategic (top-level management) approach to developing marketing strategy, discussed marketing strategies for: new markets, growth markets, mature and declining markets, and international markets. Their marketing strategies included pioneer strategy, follower strategy, fortress (position defense) strategy, flanker strategy, confrontation strategy, market expansion (mobile) strategy, contraction (strategic withdrawal) strategy, frontal attack strategy, leapfrog attack strategy, encirclement strategy, guerrilla attack strategy, differentiation strategy, divestment strategy, global strategy, national strategy, exporting strategy, product strategy, pricing strategy, channels strategy, and promotion strategy.

In a third example, Joseph P. Guiltinan and Gordon W. Paul, using a mid-management (e.g., marketing director) perspective, discussed primary demand strategies (market oriented) and selective demand strategies (competitive oriented). They also discuss product-line marketing strategies, including strategies for substitutes (line extension strategies and flanker strategies) and strategies for complements (leader strategies, bundling strategies, and systems strategies). The primary demand strategies include user strategies (increasing the number of users) and rate of use strategies (increasing the purchase quantities). User strategies are, in turn, divided into willingness strategies (emphasis on willingness to buy) and ability strategies (emphasis on ability to buy). The rate of use strategies are divided into usage strategies (increasing the rate of usage—such as brushing your teeth after each meal) and replacement strategies (increasing the rate of use by replacement—such as replacing your toothbrush every month).

The selective demand strategies include retention strategies (retaining the organizations's existing customers) and acquisition strategies (acquiring customers from the competition). Retention strategies are divided into satisfaction strategies (ways to maintain or improve customer satisfaction levels—such as reduction of delivery time from three days to 24 hours); meeting competition strategies (matching or "better-ing" competitive approaches—such as charging the same price or a price stipulated at a percentage lower than the competition); and relationship marketing strategies (establishing enduring relationships with customers—such as developing a computer-based automatic inventory replenishment system). Acquisition strategies are divided into head-to-head strategies (direct, aggressive competition—such as using comparative advertising copy); differentiated strategies (making the organization's offering different from the competition—such as being the only firm to have a wireless feature on a notebook computer); and niching strategies (concentrating on narrow markets—such as a direct marketing mail catalog of premium priced female clothing targeted at large females in the upper-middle and upper classes).

These marketing strategies are not mutually exclusive. They can be used in combination. They also are not exhaustive. In general, additional dimensions and levels can be generated. In other words, other levels and types of strategies at any level can be developed. The actual wording of the final and most refined level of strategy will probably be unique in each situation for each organization for each decision maker. Marketing strategy development is a creative act, requiring an application of science and art.

The decision maker should eventually arrive at a specific stratagem or set of strategies designed to achieve the stated objective. The entire articulated set of decisions (selected strategies) is called the marketing strategy. If the marketing strategy is part of a marketing plan, some or all of the strategy decisions could be formally stated. In some cases, only the lowest level of strategy is indicated. The formal articulation of marketing strategy is a function of the decision-maker's preferences, the organization's policy, user needs, and resources available.

MARKETING STRATEGY PRINCIPLES. The basic principles or theories of marketing appropriate to the successful development of marketing strategy are universal. They can be applied by anyone at any time in any kind of organization to any type of marketing problem in any part of the world. They are relevant to international marketing strategy as-well-as domestic marketing policy. They are useful in both profit-oriented organizations and non-profit institutions, and are appropriate for both services and products.

MARKETING STRATEGY PROCESS

Marketing strategy is produced by the following basic decision process: (1) defining the marketing problem (or opportunity); (2) gathering the facts relevant to the problem (this includes defining the appropriate sources of useful facts or information); (3) analyzing the facts (perhaps with the aid of decision models and computer **software**); (4) determining the alternatives or choices to solve the problem; and (5) selecting an alternative—i.e., making the decision.

MARKETING STRATEGY DETERMINANTS. Marketing strategy is determined by internal and external uncontrollable environmental forces. The internal environment (the environment within the organization) includes previous and higher-level strategies (including objectives), and resources (such as products, processes, patents, trademarks, personnel, and capital). An example of an internal environmental influence on marketing strategy is when a previous strategic decision (such as the choice of a product market for a strategic business unit of an organization) affects current marketing decisions (such as market segmentation and target market selection). Likewise, an organization's financial strength (such as current cash flow) influences its formulation of marketing strategies (such as target market selection, positioning choices, and marketing mix decisions).

The external environment has domestic and global dimensions. The domestic dimension contains home country environments (such as a country's cultural environment). The global dimension consists of international forces (such as the political environment of China) affecting home country environments. The external environment includes the immediate task environment (where there is direct interfacing between the organization and other organizations—such as customers, competitors, suppliers, distributors, and shareholders), and other external environments (such as legal and political environments, economic environments, infrastructures, cultural and social environments, and technological environments). An example of an external environmental influence on marketing strategy is when advertising strategy development is affected by such variables as customer media habits and government al regulations.

TYPES OF MARKETING STRATEGY DEVELOPMENT. Marketing strategy can be formulated with the aid of such tools as marketing concepts, marketing models, and computers. A marketer would use these tools to facilitate decision making. The tool's use would be similar to a carpenter using a saw or hammer to help construct a house. The computer-based method of marketing strategy generation is usually a quantitative approach starting with marketing theory and ending with the processing of data through a specialized computer program that analyzes variables and relationships.

The computer-based method begins with a segment of marketing theory. Marketing theory can be broken down into concepts and subconcepts. A concept is a set of related ideas or variables. For example, the product life cycle (PLC) is a major concept in marketing. It describes market response (in terms of sales or revenues) to a product over the product's commercial life. It depicts four life stages of the product, namely: introduction (or commercialization), growth, maturity, and decline. Each stage of the product life cycle is a function of the nature of competition (such as monopoly or oligopoly) and the maturation of the market. Marketing strategy changes over the life of the product. In general, there is an appropriate (normative) set of marketing strategies or alternatives for each phase of the product life cycle. Market response, stages of the product life cycle, and other ideas constituting the concept are all variables that can assume different values and represent different relationships across the variable set. A marketing model articulate s and quantifies the variables and variable relationships of a marketing concept. It has inputs, processes, and outputs. A model can be constructed intuitively (informally—only in the mind), with pencil and paper (perhaps also using a pocket calculator), or in a computer-based system (e.g., in a computer program or a computerized spreadsheet format).

Nowadays, it is relatively easy to purchase "off-the-shelf" computer operating platforms and generic spreadsheet software, as well as operational marketing models (that operate as files in the generic programs). The marketer then need only change the values of the variables based on the facts that have been gathered in the situation analysis in order to use the output to arrive at a decision. When necessary, the decision maker can add or delete variables and change the functional relationships of the marketing model. Of course, it is also quite easy to assume different situational facts and consider the net impacts on the marketing strategy, or the results of implementing the marketing strategy. Thus, it is relatively easy, using a computerized support system of marketing strategy development, to perform sensitivity (degree of impact of changes) and contingency (alternative scenarios) analyses.

THE FUTURE OF MARKETING STRATEGY DEVELOPMENT

Good marketing strategy is and will continue to be based on relevant knowledge, experience, information, and creativity. To the extent that new technology (such as telecommunications, computers, mathematic al procedures, and marketing concepts) can improve these things (in terms of effectiveness, productivity, and efficiency), marketing management, the decision-making process, and marketing strategy will improve. This is likely to occur based on recent experience s, recent trends, logic, and expert projections.

[Lawrence Dandurand]

FURTHER READING:

Bartels, Robert. "Development of Marketing Thought: A Brief History." In *Science in Marketing*, edited by George Schwartz. John Wiley & Sons, 1965.

Cohen, William A. *The Practice of Marketing Management.* Macmillan Publishing Company, 1991.

Cravens, David W., and Charles W. Lamb, Jr. *Strategic Marketing Management Cases.* Richard D. Irwin, Inc., 1993.

Gardner, David, and Howard Thomas. "*Strategic Marketing: History, Issues, and Emergent Themes.*" In Strategic Marketing and Management, edited by Howard Thomas, and David Gardner. John Wiley & Sons, 1985.

Guiltinan, Joseph P., and Gordon W. Paul. *Marketing Management.* McGraw-Hill, Inc., 1994.

Jain, Subhash C. *Marketing Planning & Strategy.* South-Western Publishing Co., 1993.

Lynn, Robert A., and John M. Thies. "Marketing Strategy and Execution" In *Dartnell Marketing Manager's Handbook,* edited by Stewart Henderson Britt, and Norman F. Guess. Dartnell Corp., 1984.

McCarthy, E. Jerome, and William D. Perreault, Jr. *Basic Marketing.* Richard D. Irwin, Inc., 1993.

Walker, Orville C., Harper W. Boyd, Jr., and Jean-Claude Larreche. *Marketing Strategy.* Richard D. Irwin, Inc., 1992.

MATCHING CONCEPT

In **accounting**, the matching concept is the identification of expenses associated with revenue earned during the same accounting period. Thus, the matching concept states that the expenses of a particular accounting period are the costs of the assets used to earn the revenue that is claimed in that period. It follows, therefore, that when expenses in a period are matched with the revenues generated for the same period, the result is the net income or loss for that period.

ACCOUNTING TERMS

While in everyday vernacular, the terms "cost," "expenditure," and "expense" are used almost interchangeably; in discussing accounting principles, these terms have distinctly different meanings. A cost is the amount of money, or other resources, used for a specific purpose. When a **cost** is incurred, it is associated with an expenditure; expenditures can either result in the decrease of an asset, such as cash, or the increase of a liability, such as accounts payable. Thus, expenditures result in either assets or expenses. If the expenditure will benefit future periods, such as the purchase of office equipment, it is an asset. If it will benefit the current period, such as the purchase of supplies needed to fill immediate manufacturing needs, it is an expense of that period. Logically, then, it follows that an expense is a cost item that is specifically applicable to the current accounting period used during that period to earn revenue.

THE CONSERVATISM CONCEPT

Oftentimes, when deciding which revenues and expenses to match in a given accounting period, ac-

countants have a difficult time recognizing which revenues and expenses are certain for that period. Like many people, accountants and other business professionals tend to be overly optimistic concerning the revenues that their companies generate but tend to be more realistic concerning the associated expenses. Thus, certain accounting principles are used to offset the tendency toward optimism. These principles recognize that increases in retained earnings require stronger proof than do increases in expenses. Therefore, when deciding which expenses and revenues to acknowledge during a given accounting period, accountants are supposed to apply the conservatism concept. This concept has two conditions associated with it: (1) Firms can recognize *expenses* as soon as they are reasonably *possible*. (2) Firms can recognize *revenues* as soon as they are reasonably *certain*.

Usually, a company applies the matching concept by being reasonably certain which items will generate revenue and matching them with any possible expenses for those items. To illustrate, if a company produces an item costing $100 which it later sells for $150, the company must decide the accounting period in which it is reasonably certain to receive the $150. When this is decided, the company must match the $100 cost with the $150 revenue as an expense, resulting in $50 income from sales. Interestingly, not all companies take these steps in the same order; sometimes expenses are first identified and later revenues are matched to them.

REVENUE AND EXPENSE RECOGNITION

The best matching of revenues and expenses occurs under the accrual basis of accounting. Under the accrual basis, revenue (as well as expenses, and other changes in assets, **liabilities**, and **equity** is generally recognized in the period in which the economic event takes place, usually at the point of sale—not when the cash actually changes hands. Revenue recognition occurs at this time because the earnings process is complete and there is evidence supporting the sale price. Earnings, however, can be identified at other times, such as during an item's production, at the end of an item's production but prior to its sale, or when the money is collected, as with payments made on installments. Costs are recognized as expenses in a particular period if (1) there is a direct association between costs and revenues for the period or (2) the costs cannot be assigned to the generation of revenues of any period in the future.

The recognition of revenues and expenses can become more complicated, however, because companies often spend money or assume liabilities for nonmonetary assets affecting more than one accounting period. Examples of transactions affecting more than one period are: (1) supplies purchased in a prior accounting period but used for several periods later; (2) prepaid insurance covering more than one period; (3) buildings and equipment; and (4) expenses—such as salaries—paid after a service has been rendered. Initially, these expenses are recorded at their original costs, which represents the future benefit that the company anticipates receiving from these items. As they are used, the related costs must be matched against the revenues earned for the particular period. For example, for equipment and buildings, accountants gradually expense the costs of these assets over their estimated service life, a concept known as **depreciation**. Broadly, the process of matching costs and revenues for these longer-term assets is referred to as making adjusting entries.

In accounting, adjusting entries are completed at the end of the accounting period to update the accounts for internal business transactions. Thus, the amount of materials used during a particular accounting period would be recorded by an adjusting entry at the end of each period. Expenditures made in the current period for assets not yet used would be recorded as assets and included in the current period's **balance sheet**, not recorded as expenses in the current period. As the assets are used, the related costs would be matched against revenues for that period by making an adjusting entry at the end of the period. If a company fails to make these adjustments at the proper time, the net income and assets of the company could be dramatically overstated.

[Kathryn Snavely]

FURTHER READING:

Anthony, Robert N., and James S. Reece. *Accounting: Text and Cases*. 8th ed. Homewood, IL: Irwin, 1989.

Diamond, Michael A., Eric G. Flamholtz, and Diana Troik Flamholtz. *Financial Accounting*. 2nd ed. Boston, MA: PWS-Kent Publishing Company, 1990.

Eskew, Robert K., and Daniel L. Jensen. *Financial Accounting*. 4th ed. New York: McGraw-Hill, 1992.

Solomon, Lanny M., Larry M. Walther, and Richard J. Vargo. *Financial Accounting*. 3rd ed. New York: West Publishing Company, 1992.

MATRIX MANAGEMENT AND STRUCTURE

Matrix management is a technique of managing an organization's activities that is based on the structure of the entity. In contrast to most other organizational structures, which arrange managers and employees by function or product, matrix management combines functional and product departments in a dual authority system. The term "matrix" is derived from the representative diagram of a matrix manage-

ment system, which resembles a rectangular array of functions and product/project groups.

NEW ORGANIZATIONAL MODELS

In the late 1800s and early 1900s, during the U.S. industrial revolution, a need emerged for more formalized structures in large business organizations. The earliest models emphasized efficiency of process through managerial control. Described as "mechanistic," those systems were characterized by extensive rules and procedures, centralized authority, and an acute division of labor. They sought to create organizations that mimicked machines, and usually departmentalized workers by function, such as finance and production. Important theories during that era included German sociologist Max Weber's (1881-1961) ideal bureaucracy, which was based on absolute authority, logic, and order.

During the 1920s and 1930s, new ideas about the structure and nature of organizations began to surface. Inspired by the work of thinkers and behaviorists such as Harvard researcher Elton Mayo, theories about management structure began to incorporate a more humanistic view. Those theoretical organizational structures were classified as "organic," and recognized the importance of human behavior and cultural influences in organizations. While the mechanistic school of thought stressed efficiency and production through control, organic models emphasized flexibility and adaptability through employee empowerment. From a structural standpoint, mechanistic organizations tended to be vertical or hierarchical with decisions flowing down through several channels. Organic models, on the other hand, were comparatively flat, or horizontal, and had few managerial levels or centralized controls.

Many proponents of organic organizational theory believed it was the solution to the drawbacks of mechanistic organizations. Indeed, mechanistic organizations often stifled human creativity and motivation and were generally insensitive to external influences, such as shifting markets or consumer needs. In contrast, companies that used organic management structures tended to be more responsive and creative. However, many organizations that adopted the organic approach also discovered that, among other drawbacks, it sometimes lacked efficiency and personal accountability and failed to make the most productive use of some workers' expertise.

As an alternative to basic organic structures, many companies during the middle 1900s embraced a model that minimized the faults and maximized the benefits of different organic management structures, as discussed below. Possibly the first application of what would later be referred to as the "matrix" structure was employed in 1947 by General Chemicals in its engineering department. In the early 1960s a more formalized matrix method called ''unit management'' was implemented by a large number of U.S. hospitals. Not until 1965, however, was matrix management formally recognized.

The first organization to design and implement a formal matrix structure was the National Aeronautics and Space Administration (NASA). NASA developed a matrix management system for its space program because it needed to simultaneously emphasize several different functions and projects, none of which could be stressed at the expense of another. It found that traditional management structures were too bureaucratic, hierarchical, slow-moving, and inflexible. Likewise, basic organic structures were too departmentalized (i.e. myopic), thus failing to productively use the unlimited expertise NASA had at its disposal. NASA's matrix solution overcame those problems by synthesizing projects, such as designing a rocket booster, with organizational functions, such as staffing and finance.

Despite doubts about its effectiveness in many applications, matrix management gained broad acceptance in the corporate world during the 1970s, eventually achieving fad status. Its popularity continued during the 1980s as a result of economic changes in the United States, which included slowing domestic market growth and increasing foreign competition. Those changes forced many companies to seek the benefits offered by the matrix model.

MATRIX BASICS

Most organizational structures departmentalize the work force and other resources by one of two methods: by products or by functions. Functional organizations are segmented by key functions. For example, activities related to production, marketing, and finance might be grouped into three respective divisions. Within each division, moreover, activities would be departmentalized into subdepartments. The marketing division, for example, might encompass sales, advertising, and promotion departments.

The chief advantage of functionally structured organizations is that they usually achieve a fairly efficient specialization of labor and are relatively easy for employees to comprehend. In addition, functional structures reduce duplication of work because responsibilities are clearly defined. However, functional division often causes departments to become myopic and divisive, resulting in unhealthy competition between groups within the same company.

Companies that employ a product structure break the organization down into semiautonomous units and profit centers based on activities, or ''projects,'' such as products, customers, or geography. Regardless of

the project used to segment the company, each unit operates as a separate business. For example, a company might be broken down into southern, western, and eastern divisions. Or, it might create separate divisions for consumer, industrial, and institutional products. Again, within each product unit are subdivisions.

One benefit of product or project departmentalization is that it facilitates expansion (because the company can easily add a new division to focus on a new profit opportunity without having to significantly alter existing systems). In addition, accountability is increased because divisional performance can be measured more easily. Furthermore, divisional structures permit decentralized decision making, which allows managers with specific expertise to make key decisions in their area. The potential drawbacks to divisional structures include duplication of efforts in different departments and a lack of horizontal communication. In addition, divisional organizations, like functionally structured companies, may have trouble keeping all departments focused on an overall company goal.

Matrix management structures combine functional and product departmentalization. They simultaneously organize part of a company along product or project lines and part of it around functional lines to get the advantages of both. For example, a diagram of a matrix model might show divisions, such as different product groups, along the top of a table (See Figure 1). Along the left side of the same table, then, would be different functional departments, such as finance, marketing, and production. Within the matrix, each of the product groups would intersect with each of the functional groups, signifying a direct relationship between product teams and administrative divisions. In other words, each team of people assigned to manage a product group might have an individual(s) who also belonged to each of the functional departments, and vice-versa.

Theoretically, managers of project groups and managers of functional groups have roughly equal authority within the company. As indicated by the matrix, many employees report to at least two managers. For instance, a member of the accounting department might be assigned to work with the consumer products division, and would report to managers of both departments. Generally, however, managers of functional areas and divisions report to a single authority, such as a president or vice president.

Although all matrix structures entail some form of dual authority and multidisciplinary grouping, there are several variations. For example, Kenneth Knight identified three basic matrix management models: co-ordination, overlay, and secondment. Each of the models can be implemented in various

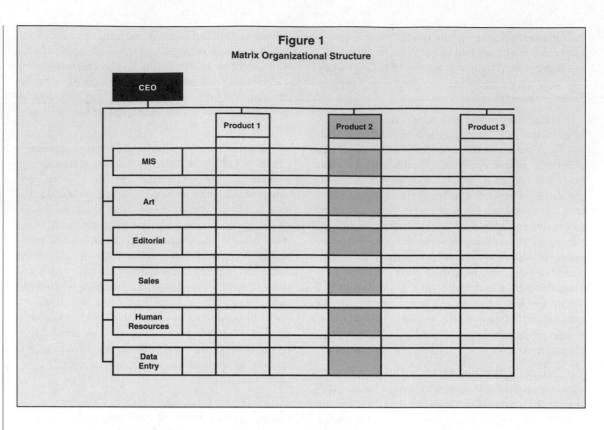

Figure 1

Matrix Organizational Structure

forms that differ in attributes related to decision-making roles, relationships with outside suppliers and buyers, and other factors. Organizations choose different models based on competitive environments, industries, education and maturity level of the workforce, existing corporate culture, and other factors.

In the co-ordination model, the staff remains organizationally and managerially members of their original departments (or the departments to which they would likely belong under a functional or product structure). Procedures are instituted to ensure cross-departmental cooperation and interaction towards the achievement of extra-departmental goals. In the overlay model, staff members officially become members of two groups, each of which has a separate manager. This model represents the undiluted matrix form described above. In the third version, the secondment model, individuals move from functional departments into project groups and back again, but may effectively belong to one or the other at different times.

ADVANTAGES, DISADVANTAGES, AND APPLICATIONS

The cardinal advantage of a matrix structure is that it facilitates rapid response to change in two or more environments. For instance, a telecommunications company might be extremely concerned about both unforeseen geographic opportunities and limited capital. By departmentalizing its company with the

financial function on one axis and the geographic areas on the other, it might benefit from having each of its geographic units intertwined with its finance department. For example, suppose that an opportunity to purchase the cellular telephone rights for a specific area arose. The matrix structure would allow the company to quickly determine if it had the capital necessary to purchase the license and develop the area, or if it should take advantage of an opportunity in another region.

Matrix structures are more fleet and responsive than other types of structures because they permit more efficient exchanges of information. Because people from different departments are cooperating so closely, they are eager to share data that will help them achieve common goals. In effect, the entire organization becomes an information web; data is channeled both vertically and horizontally as people exchange technical knowledge, marketing data, product ideas, financial information, and all other sorts of intelligence that is used to make decisions.

In addition to speed and flexibility, matrix organization may result in a more efficient use of resources than do other organic structures. This occurs because highly specialized employees and equipment are shared by departments. For example, if the expertise of a computer programmer is needed in another department, he or she can move to that department to solve its problems, rather than languishing on tasks of low priority as likely would happen in a nonmatrix setting.

Other benefits of matrix management include improved motivation and more adept managers. Improved motivation results from decisions within groups becoming more democratic and participatory because each member brings specialized knowledge to the table—since employees have a direct impact on day-to-day decisions, they are more likely to experience higher levels of motivation and commitment to the goals of the departments to which they belong. More adept management is the result of top decision makers becoming more involved in, and thus better informed about, the day-to-day operations of the company. This involvement can also lead to improved long-term planning.

Despite its many theoretical advantages, matrix management structures have been criticized as having a number of weaknesses. For instance, matrix structures are typically expensive to maintain, partially because of more complex reporting requirements. In addition, many workers become disturbed by the lack of a chain of command and a seeming inability to perceive who is in charge. Indeed, among the most common criticisms of matrix management is that it results in role ambiguity and conflict. For instance, a functional manager may tell a subordinate one thing, and then his or her product/project boss will tell him or her something different. As a result, companies that change from a comparatively bureaucratic structure to matrix management often experience high turnover and worker dissatisfaction.

Supporting critics' derision of matrix management are several examples of companies that have implemented and later abandoned matrix structures. For example, one study showed that between 1961 and 1978 about one-quarter of all teaching hospitals in the United States moved to unit or matrix management structures. By the late 1970s, though, nearly one-third of those hospitals had rejected the concept, citing reasons such as high costs, excessive turnover, and interpersonal conflict. Although the hospital study suggested that matrix management was better suited to larger organizations, General Motors Corp.' experience indicated otherwise. After a seven-year test of a matrix structure, GM jettisoned matrix management in the 1980s in favor of a more traditional, product-oriented organizational structure. It cited managers' lack of control over incentives as a primary shortcoming of the matrix system.

Although matrix management was often viewed during the 1970s as a cure-all for organizational design, the perceived breadth of its potential for application has gradually diminished. In general, matrix structures are generally assumed to be most appropriate for larger corporations that operate in unique or fast-paced environments; a coal-mining company, for example, might be less likely to benefit from a matrix structure than would a pharmaceutical company. Matrix management also works best for organizations that are managed and staffed mostly by professionals or semi-professionals. Furthermore, matrix management requires a workforce that has a diverse set of skills and employees that have strong interpersonal abilities. Finally, matrix management is usually more effective when a project manager, who is technically working under the authority of a product and a functional boss, is given the authority to make critical decisions.

Because of their limitations, matrix management structures frequently are integrated into an organization as one facet of a larger plan. For example, a research team organized to develop a new product might be placed in a division of the company that is set up as a matrix. After the initial stages of the project are completed, the ongoing management of the product might be moved to a division of the company that reflects a more conventional functional or product/project structure. Indeed, as evidenced by NASA's successes in the 1960s, matrix management is particularly effective in accomplishing "crash" and high-tech projects, such as those related to medical, energy research, aerospace, defense, and competitive threats.

CASE STUDY

Bayer Aktiengesellschaft of West Germany—the company best known in the United States for its Bayer aspirin products—is one of the largest and oldest chemical and healthcare products companies in the world. Because of massive sales gains and increased activity overseas in the early 1980s, Bayer announced a reorganization in 1984. Bayer had been successful with a conventional organizational structure that was departmentalized by function. However, to respond to new conditions the company wanted to create a structure that would allow it to achieve three primary goals: (1) shift management control from the West German parent company to its foreign divisions and subsidiaries; (2) restructure its business divisions to more clearly define their duties; and (3) flatten the organization, or empower lower level managers to assume more responsibility, so that top executives would have more time to plan strategy.

Bayer selected a relatively diverse matrix management format to pursue its goals. It delineated all of its business activities into six groups under an umbrella company called Bayer World. Within each of the six groups were several subgroups made up of product categories such as dyestuffs, fibers, or chemicals. Likewise, each of its administrative and service functions were regrouped under Bayer World into one of several functions, such as human resources, marketing, plant administration, or finance. Furthermore, top managers who had formally headed functional groups were given authority over separate geographic regions, which, like the product groups, were supported by and entwined with the functional groups. The net effect of the reorganization was that the original nine functional departments were broken down into 19 multidisciplinary, interconnected business groups.

After only one year of operation, Bayer management lauded the new matrix structure as a resounding success. Not only did matrix management allow the company to move toward its primary goals, but it had the added benefits of increasing its responsiveness to change and emerging opportunities, and of helping Bayer to streamline plant administration and service division activities.

SEE ALSO: Organization Theory

[Dave Mote]

FURTHER READING:

Cherrington, David J. *Organizational Behavior: The Management of Individual and Organizational Performance.* 2nd ed. Boston: Allyn and Bacon, 1994.

Gray, Jerry L., and Frederick A. Starke. *Organizational Behavior: Concepts and Applications.* 4th ed. Columbus, OH: Merrill Publishing Company, 1988.

Huse, E. F., and T. G. Cummings. *Organizational Development and Change.* St. Paul, MN: West, 1985.

Ivancevich, John M., and Michael T. Matteson. *Organizational Behavior and Management.* Homewood, IL: Richard D. Irwin, Inc., 1990.

Knight, Kenneth, ed. *Matrix Management: A Cross-functional Approach to Organization.* New York: PBI-Petrocelli Books, 1977.

Northcraft, Gregory B., and Margaret A. Neale. *Organizational Behavior: A Management Challenge.* Chicago: The Dryden Press, 1990.

Schermerhorn, John R., Jr., James G. Hunt, and Richard N. Osborn. *Managing Organizational Behavior.* New York: John Wiley & Sons. 1991.

MAXIMARKETING

The common denominators of all types of selling are: it must reach the customers needs, it must make the sale, and it must seek to forge a lasting relationship with the consumer. The manner through which all three of these objectives are reached, however, is dictated, almost completely, by the characteristics of the marketplace. In today's marketplace the old models of marketing to the masses no longer work. Today's marketplace is no longer a ''monolithic'' reality, rather one with millions of market fragments, separated by demographics, lifestyles, and technology. Stan Rapp and Tom Collins created the concept

of MaxiMarketing in an attempt to adapt the promotions and **advertising** industries to this newly-defined market. As Rapp and Collins point out, this new, fast-moving marketplace will require a new marketing vision in order to remain competitive. Their Maxi-Marketing model is built upon the maximization of nine distinct aspects of the marketing mix, including:

1) Maximized targeting

2) Maximized media

3) Maximized accountability

4) Maximized awareness

5) Maximized activation

6) Maximized synergy

7) Maximized linkage

8) Maximized sales

9) Maximized distribution

The common thread running throughout all of these is the ability to achieve measurable responses. These measurements will allow the marketer to determine whether or not the advertising is targeted correctly, compare the relative efficiencies of different media, images and offers, allocate more resources to the advertising budget, and form the foundation for in-house customer databases. The underlying factor of this theory is that advertising can no longer be complacent. It must change and it must strive for active responses. The way to achieve the benefits of this marketing theory is through self-examination of the way marketing has been done in the past, and how it can be better directed towards the needs of the consumer.

MAXIMIZED TARGETING

Maximized targeting, as defined by Rapp and Collins, is the art and science of identifying, describing, locating, and contacting one or more groups of prime prospects for whatever you are selling. Five basic models can be used to achieve maximized targeting.

FISHING. Fishing refers to locating an individual prospect out of the total audience. Fishing can be done in a number of ways. It can be done graphically through pictures and images, through the use of words and phrases, with which the consumer can identify, and by stealing customers from competitors.

In order to determine who these prospects are, the marketer must analyze the Values and Lifestyles (VALS) of the consumer. VALS is a method by which consumers are classified according to values and geographical location. VALS was created by Arnold Mitchell and others at the Stanford Research Institute, in an effort to determine the effect that values and lifestyles had on buying decisions.

MINING. Mining is the process of selection where there is a "rich vein of prospects." Most frequently, this is done through the use of specialized media, such as the established public databases. These public databases list the exact names and addresses of nearly every household using items in your product category.

Once these prospects have been identified and the list narrowed to only the "richest" individuals, you can then concentrate on "no-waste" advertising. No-waste advertisingconsists of mailing to only the prime prospects, the use of persuasive brand advertising, calculating the total sales effect of the advertising, and the collection of the selected individuals into an in-house database for future reference.

PANNING. Panning takes mining a step further. In this process, the prospects are continually whittled down until only the absolute best remain. The primary avenue for panning is list segmentation. List segmentation allows the marketer to begin with a broad category of prospects and refine that list, often through cross-referencing with other lists, to find the individuals that fit the exact description of the ideal consumer. The primary benefit of this method is that the marketer is left with only those individuals that are the most likely to respond to advertising efforts through direct action.

BUILDING YOUR OWN PROSPECT DATABASE. The value of having an in-house database of the best potential consumers cannot be discounted. The advantages of having in-house databases is that they are more cost-effective, time-efficient, and allow the marketer to focus on the long-term value of the consumer.

SPELUNKING. Spelunking is the process of identifying prospects within a niche market. This can be accomplished in two different ways. First, the marketer can find a new niche within which to market an existing product. Second, the marketer can find new products to market to an existing niche. Either way, the marketer is creating opportunities for sales where none previously existed.

MAXIMIZED MEDIA

Maximized media basically means the utilization of various media sources to achieve the highest degrees of cost-effectiveness and accountability. There are a multitude of advertising mediums in our daily lives. The secret to maximizing their utility lies in knowing which mediums are best suited for the product. Some of the greatest challenges facing the advertising world are determining which new and exciting mediums to use and how to achieve the desired responsiveness through their utilization.

It is true that not all mediums are suitable for measuring this responsiveness. However, the point of maximizing media is to apply measuring techniques to those mediums where it is possible, and search for methods of analysis where it appears to be more difficult in an effort to avoid complacency.

MAXIMIZED ACCOUNTABILITY

Maximizing accountability requires the marketing function to accept greater accountability and strive towards more precise measurement of advertising as it occurs. This obviously requires two things from those attempting to achieve maximized accountability. First, it implies that advertising, where possible, must be created such that direct-response capabilities are built into the model. Second, it requires researchers to measure, and perform analysis on, actual responses.

According to the MaxiMarketing concept, this maximized accountability can be achieved by, "incorporating a direct-response element in the advertising; split-testing a variety of approaches, each with the same constant direct-response element, and incorporating the discoveries thus made into the roll-out of the campaign."

MAXIMIZED AWARENESS ADVERTISING

For decades the marketing community has struggled to determine the essence of the advertising function. One side has argued that advertising should target the left-brain, which controls logic and language. The other side has argued that advertising should target the right-brain or the side that controls creativity and intuition. Each method can, and does, have its place. In reality, the conflict centers around targeting the left-brain or the right-brain. MaxiMarketing argues two things. First, it suggests that it is possible to create an advertising scheme that targets both sides of the brain, or the whole-brain, simultaneously. Secondly, it would argue that the type of focus be determined by: what you are selling: to whom you are selling; and how you intend to sell it.

Once again, the marketer should strive for active responses in their advertising. The public response can help you achieve two things. First, it can help you determine the appropriate mix of left/right-brain stimuli. Second, it can help you avoid what the authors call "no-brain" advertising. No-brain advertising refers to messages that are merely clever and bad art direction which obscures good messages. The point of advertising is not to tell the consumer the entire story of a product. Rather, the intent should be to stimulate interest in the product by some clear advantage or benefit.

MAXIMIZED ACTIVATION

Sales promotion, as defined by Rapp and Collins, is the art and science of making something happen. The MaxiMarketing concept employs the idea of activation advertising. This form of advertising, much the same as awareness advertising, should be held accountable by the same types of accountability measures. Once the consumer becomes aware that your product exists, the next step must be to get them to act upon that knowledge.

Coupling sales promotion, or activation advertising, with direct response measures yields a number of benefits to the company. First, it allows for comparative measurement of advertising strategies. Second, it is fairly quick and inexpensive as only the best prospects are targeted as mentioned under maximized targeting. In much the same vein, it is reality-based due to the extensive work that is done in finding potential consumers. Finally, it allows the marketer to further build its prospect database.

MAXIMIZED SYNERGY

Maximizing synergy means that the same advertisement is used to accomplish two tasks, without adding to the total cost. The MaxiMarketing concept offers ten ways this synergy can be achieved:

1. Combine awareness and activation advertising

2. Promote two different channels of distribution simultaneously

3. Do well by doing good—couple your product with a worthy cause

4. Sell an event while selling a product

5. Share advertising, and the associated costs, with another advertiser

6. Support one medium while advertising in another

7. Promote your brand while promoting a separate profit center

8. Build a prospect database while you build your brand

9. Use your **brand names** to sell your premium products and your premium products to sell your brand names

10. Advertise your brand while advertising the distribution channel

MAXIMIZED LINKAGE

Maximized linkage ''links the up-front advertising to the sale with additional arguments and benefits which the up-front advertising didn't have space or time to include.'' This means establishing a process whereby the consumer is ''linked'' to your product through follow-up interaction. Typically, this linkage has been achieved through some form of follow-up letter or correspondence.

However, this follow-up process has historically failed for four simple reasons. First, the follow-up letter is often poorly written or not written altogether. Second, if the follow-up letter is written, it is often written in hard-to-read typography. Third, if the consumer does respond to the follow-up letter, the company's response has been extremely slow, often delaying responses as much as 16 weeks. Finally, the company does not provide clear **purchasing** alternatives, such as location of nearest dealers. The Maxi-Marketing theory strives to increase the attention that is given to this often forgotten stage of the advertising process.

The five structural components to this linkage are: activation, achieved through two-way communication; information; persuasion; propulsion, or action *now*; and consummation of the sale. These components are, by the author's own admission, the same components as those used to complete a profitable **direct-marketing** campaign.

The authors have created the following *Linkage-Assessment Grid* (Figure 1) to help the advertiser determine whether or not linkage is a vital component of what is being sold. The horizontal ''poles'' represent the ends of the high-ticket and low-ticket sales continuum. The vertical ''poles'' represent the ends of the high-involvement and low-involvement continuum.

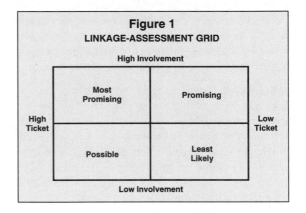

Figure 1
LINKAGE-ASSESSMENT GRID

High Involvement

| High Ticket | Most Promising | Promising | Low Ticket |
| Possible | Least Likely |

Low Involvement

MAXIMIZED SALES

The authors sum up the marketing function by stating that ''all marketing is, or should be, a continuous process. With rare exceptions, it is hoped that making a sale is not the end of a relationship with a customer but rather the beginning or the continuation.'' Maximizing sales means that the value of a consumer is measured by the duration of the relationship, not the margin to be achieved from an individual sale. Through this duration a new kind of synergy emerges. It is a synergy that is achieved through the utilization, and subsequent maximization, of the share of the market and the creation and maintenance of a customer database. Capturing the mind of the consumer and then documenting the characteristics of that consumer, allows the company to forge a lasting, long-term relationship with that customer.

This synergy affords the company a number of luxuries. First, and most obvious, is that it creates the conditions for maximized repeat sales by grabbing and holding on to customer loyalty. Second, it allows for a great deal of cross-promotion through the combination of various databases. Third, it can serve as an effective vehicle through which product lines can be extended. For example, consumers who are known to eat rice-based cereals can be extended to include corn-based cereals in their diets. Finally, it can be used as a "launching pad" for new business ventures as the existing information is readily and easily shared.

MAXIMIZED DISTRIBUTION

As was mentioned in the section on maximizing synergy, the utilization of multiple **channels of distribution** can greatly improve the life and profitability of a product. The secret to maximizing the size of your distribution is to "Think names. Save names. And use names." These names are not restricted to your own databases. They can include both other originators and your own intermediaries. They can be used to fill your product line and "gaps" in the geographic structure of your existing distribution channels. In short, the synergy's created by the simultaneous utilization of existing channels of distribution and newly formed channels can be an incredible source of marketing information and power.

CONCLUSION

The MaxiMarketing concept forces a company to focus on two key issues: accountability and addressability. The true purpose of this concept is to help the marketer eliminate the waste and inefficiencies that have typically been associated with "shotgun" tactics or the approach that "scatters the sales message indiscriminately on prospects and non-prospects alike."

The core goal of accountability is to eliminate the uncertainty of marketing expenditures. It forces the marketer to build in mechanisms which measure the results of an advertising scheme. Accountability requires proactive planning. This enables the company to eliminate front-end waste by narrowing the range of prospects and tailoring the appropriate medium to reach those select individuals. This allows the company to not only build accountability for its efforts, but credibility with the consumer as well.

Once the marketer has successfully narrowed the scope of the prospect market, he/she can address the prospect on an individual basis. No longer are these people merely faces in a crowd. They have been ele-

vated to prospects that the company knows by name and address. This "individual" attention allows the company to establish and maintain an ongoing relationship with the customer.

As was repeated throughout this analysis, the MaxiMarketing concept requires a new way of thinking. This mind-set allows the marketer to evolve into a more efficient and cost-effective player in the marketplace. Once this mind-set has been established, the marketer can then begin to skillfully dissect and exploit the market. However, the MaxiMarketing concept is one that must be adopted throughout the organization. Without the full commitment and dedication of the company, at all levels, MaxiMarketing cannot work. It needs an environment that fosters growth and development on a continual basis. The key to Maxi-Marketing is continual improvement and refining. Once the foundation has been established, the company can begin to reap the benefits.

[John Burnett]

FURTHER READING:

Fox, Stephen. *The Mirror Makers*. New York: William Morrow and Co., 1984.

Levitt, Theodore. *The Marketing Imagination*. New York: Free Press, 1983.

Morgan, Anthony I. "Point of View: Who's Killing the Great Advertising Campaigns of America?" *Journal of Advertising Research*. December, 1984/January, 1985, p. 33.

"Retail Store, Mail Order Catalog: Synergistic Growth," *Direct Marketing*. April, 1983, pp. 44-60.

MERCANTILISM

Mercantilism is considered, at once, a historical period associated with the rise of a particular form of capitalism (in Europe) referred to as merchant capitalism, as well as a doctrine advanced by the writers of this period which tended to advance the power of an alliance of merchants and the declining monarchy. In present times the term is often associated with protectionist trade policies which, through the use of state policies, attempt to subsidize in one way or another, particular industries or firms in order to gain national or regional trading advantages. Whatever the case, mercantilism is associated with nationalistic economic policies as opposed to free trade advocates who argue for minimal state interference in international economic relations.

The term "mercantile system" was coined by Scottish economist Adam Smith (1723-90) to denote the sixteenth and seventeenth century economic doctrine that which advocated nationalist trade policies designed to enhance the wealth of the nation through the import of gold. Smith was highly critical of this concept of wealth and he clearly understood the class bias in the merchant system. In fact, Smith expressed great concern about colonialism and the monopoly of trade routes instituted by the merchant class at the expense of the vast majority.

While generally associated with a historical epoch, the term mercantilism has also been adopted to refer to the general principle of the aggrandizement of state power for the economic gain of a particular country's capitalist class usually through manipulation and control over trading terms. During colonial times, for example, this took the form of military control over trading routes, large tariffs on imported goods (especially manufactured products), and outright plundering of colonies in pursuit of gold and raw materials.

Modern debates surrounding **free trade** invariably invoke the rhetoric of free trade while, often simultaneously, calling for more favorable trading terms for particular industries. For example, the **North American Free Trade Agreement** (NAFTA) encouraged unrestrained capital movements between the United States and Mexico. And yet, U.S. industries have consistently won quotas and subsidies against so-called unfair trade on the part of Japanese corporations (notably autos and steel). The use of state power is in either case a key factor in defining trading terms.

During mercantilist times, aside from the imperatives of empire and colonial conquest, the rationale for such practices was reflected in mercantilist writers' notions of the origins of profit and the nature of exchange. From the perspective of the merchants, the origin of profit was in the unequal exchange of goods, or the mercantilist dictum ''buying cheap and selling dear.'' While this is the goal of any profit-making entity, the mercantilists applied this dictum to the nation as a whole. To them, the gain of the seller is viewed as having occurred only at the expense of the buyer, or in a violation of the sacred market ideology of exchange on the basis of equivalents. Therefore, the nation as a whole could only become richer if it exported more than it imported, thereby amassing gold (the money commodity). The view that profit or surplus originated in the unequal exchange of **commodities** was therefore perfectly consistent with the mercantilist policy of controlling the terms of trade.

While it is debatable whether the merchant system was ever a dominant or stable form of social organization in historical terms, during the transition from feudalism to industrial capitalism, a period certainly existed where large merchant companies (such as the British East India Company) traded goods produced at home over trade routes controlled by mighty empires. The goal was generally to achieve a trade surplus, or more particularly, to maintain a surplus on account of gold, for it was gold that was considered to constitute wealth. The logic of this was that, while all who make a profit sell more value than they buy—since the gain of one business was offset by the loss of another—trade within a nation could not generate a net surplus (or profit) within the nation. Merchants argued that the only way the nation could grow would be to export more than it imports. Armed with this view of the origin of profits, merchants promoted exports as a means of gaining surplus profits. Like all good policy makers, they argued that this would in turn benefit the nation as a whole.

Policies in service of these ends aimed at increasing the nation's wealth and power by encouraging export of goods in return for gold. This involved state subsidy of export industries, the erection of high tariff walls to encourage import-competing industries, the prohibition of the sale of gold to foreigners, subsidization of certain key industries (especially manufacturers), the control over certain types of capital, and the relentless pursuit of raw materials and gold from colonies. Most of these policies involved strict control over trading routes and stable prices fixed by state fiat.

While merchants controlled the trading system, unlike the later system of industrial capitalism, the production of goods and services was not strictly under the control of merchants—production was along the lines of crafts-type production systems or remnants of the old feudal order. As the merchants' power declined, and as the system of industrial capitalism emerged, many merchants would see the benefits of taking over the production process, thereby gaining more direct control over the productivity of labor and potential profitability. While the merchants did not, for the most part, control production (their primary concern was buying and selling), mercantilist policies emphasized the production of high value-added products since these would fetch a higher price relative to raw materials (as opposed to agricultural goods and raw materials) for export. Expansion of gold coffers occurred when trading partners paid off their net balance in precious metals, with these metals being considered wealth.

The period of the rise of mercantile system coincides with the period of early capitalism in sixteenth- and seventeenth-century Europe, mostly in Spain, France, and in the low countries of Belgium and Holland. At that time most of these countries had been transformed into merchant-dominated economies, meaning that a substantial class controlled commerce and to a lesser extent, manufacturing. Meanwhile, modern nation-states were emerging as the political side of the merchant economy. It was this coalition of monarchs and merchants that eventually led to the dissolution of the old feudal order, evolving toward a system regulated instead by a competitive labor market (with an eventual formation of a class of people who were free from feudal ties to the land but were now free only to sell their labor power as their sole source of subsistence). Industrial/manufacturing classes then were "recruited" from the merchant class (i.e., some merchants took over production processes), while some of the direct producers (crafts, guilds, etc.) broke from the merchant companies.

Unable to hold back the emerging forces of industrial capitalism, which lodged the entire system in a generalized structure of commodity production—including a commodified labor market—the merchant class lost control of the new order to the emerging forces of capitalist competition where prices and profits would be regulated by the production and accumulation of capital. While trading was essential to the emerging industrial capitalist system as well, the transactions leading to the final sale of the commodity were seen as merely a sharing out of the total selling price among the buyers and purchasers, including the merchant. Thus, while individual merchants had to achieve a profit, the idea that trade led to profits for the system as a whole was replaced by the classical economists' view that production (and the reinvestment of profit) was the source of the wealth of a nation.

In addition to the shift in focus from trading to production, the new social dynamic of capital accumulation, in turn, led to devastating critiques of mercantilist doctrine by the English classical economists such as Adam Smith, and the French economics tradition known as the Physiocrats. Eventually the doctrine of mercantilist thought gave way to the doctrine of comparative advantage, which enshrined (the ideal at least) that free and open trade (i.e., commodity flows relatively free from state imposed tariffs and other trade barriers) would be the most beneficial system to all who participated, better than any attempts to protect domestic industries from the vagaries of world competition. This could mainly be achieved through the impact of trade on wealth via the reinvestment of profits into any productive activity and hence of accumulation of capital where it, in turn, provides a wider market. The actual historical movement has, of course, been the result of the tension between struggling industries (and in some case dying industries) seeking laws and state assistance to protect themselves and those successful national industries trumpeting the gospel of free trade.

HISTORICAL BACKGROUND

For reasons that have not been entirely determined among historical researchers, the period 1500 to roughly 1750 witnessed a speed up and expansion of market activity in Europe—including international trade—driven essentially by European colonization and the rise of a dominant merchant class. While substantial trading by certain segments of the population was taking place, production and reproduction of European society was still largely under the control of the nobility and production was largely based on the land-based feudal order and craft-based production techniques in the cities. While some of the material production of peasants was sold to merchants by the lord of the manor, most of the direct producers were still peasants tied to the land (who received a portion of the produce to subsist).

By this time, most of England, France, Spain, Belgium, and Holland had been heavily influenced (if not dominated) by merchant capitalists, who controlled commerce but did not have direct control over production. Politically this period was a time of flux, as new coalitions between modern nation-states and the decaying monarchy wrested power from feudal nobility in many areas. The colonial empires of England, Spain, and France each involved an alliance between their respective national merchant classes and the emerging nation-states. Through the large trading companies—for example, the British East India Company—these empires amassed large amounts of wealth from the trading of slaves, products, and extractions of raw materials (especially precious metals) from the colonies, all regulated by national states and national militias who controlled and policed shipping routes.

The resulting emergence of the merchant class and the simultaneous rise of the nation-state led to the spread of gold and the money economy and the declining influence of the old order, namely the church and the old feudal, land-based monarchical institutions. This unstable coalition between merchants worked as follows: merchants paid taxes to support a government military that would protect their industries and trading routes while the crown would extract taxes. Military force maintained exclusive trade routes and command currency to support a military that would deter attacks and contribute to territorial expansion. Meanwhile, on the continent, commerce and industry was growing rapidly, relative to agriculture, and lands were enclosed for the purpose of private capital accumulation, leading to a growing class of landless peasants and craft producers who were increasingly subject to a more intensified division of labor under capitalist relations of production. As the basic preconditions of industrial capitalism took root (namely a commodified labor market, the accumulation of capital funds, and a well-defined market), the merchant view that profit originated in unequal exchange would be replaced by the view, and the reality, that profit originated in production in a context of generalized *equal exchange* of commodities, including labor. While the former ignores the origin of production and profit depends on trade and unequal exchange, the latter is derived from production and wage labor all in the context of apparently equal exchange. While trading is associated with both, the source of gain is different.

MERCANTILIST THEORY AND DOCTRINE

Mercantilist theory was based on the idea that buying cheap and selling dear led to the enhancement of the nation's wealth. While any trader seeks to buy cheap and sell dear—for the system as a whole one's gain must be offset at the expense of another's loss, unless the source of the gain is outside of a nation's trading circuit—thus a merchant could barter $100 worth of goods (for example, to an Indian tribe in the New World) and return and sell them in the imperial country for $200. Here the total material wealth is unchanged yet the colonialist earns a profit (at least in an accounting sense) due to the fact that only one side values the goods in monetary terms. In other words, the tribe might value the use of the goods they acquired in the barter trade while the motive of the merchants is quite different. This simple example illustrates where the merchant view of the origin of profit comes from, yet clearly no additional wealth (for the system as a whole) is generated merely through the exchange.

On the other hand, trade *between* two merchants could only produce gain to one merchant at the loss of another. In this case then, to achieve success (i.e., profit), a merchant had to have some unequal advantage in the exchange of goods. The industrial capitalists would later understand that, under a generalized system of equal exchange, profit for the system as whole could originate only in production—yet the legal conditions of equality in the market place were guaranteed. Soon the economists—Adam Smith, David Ricardo (1772-1823), and Karl Marx (1818-83)—would demonstrate how equal exchange could still embody profit. As one might expect then, merchants did not largely concern themselves with production since to them wealth came from trading. They took advantage of plantations in the colonies to import produce to Europe while exporting high value-added manufacturing and especially luxury goods to America and the Caribbean. Success brought great wealth to some and gave employment to others, especially merchants and artisans connected with shipping.

MAJOR MERCANTILIST WRITERS

While the general perception of mercantilism is one of a long cohesive chapter in the history of economic thought and policy (1500 to 1800), mercantilist authors were typically business and professional people (who existed and wrote long before economics became known as an academic discipline). To paraphrase one writer of the time, the merchants were proselytizing and pamphleteering men of affairs, seeking self-promotion. Thus in contrast to those before them (the Scholastics such as Thomas Aquinas (1224-74), who sought to understand a just or fair price), and in contrast to the systematic theories of Smith, Ricardo, and Marx which were to follow, the mercantilists had no pretension to science.

Mercantilist writing was well scattered within the major colonial empires that emerged at the time. Most representative are the English and French writers of the seventeenth century. Viewed as an economic concept of state building, these eminently practical money-changers sought order and protection that was essential for the expansion of their activities. Meanwhile, in exchange for military protection of trading routes, they often succeeded in gaining monopolistic subsidization from the crown while the state expanded its material means for colonization and wealth accrued to both the crown and the mercantile elite, both in the form of gold and other raw material imports that then fetched an expanded exported value in the form of manufactured goods.

Thus to the mercantilists, production was deemed important only in so far as it led to an export surplus and was thus closely linked not only with the expansion of the flow of specie but especially in the flow of reserves which potentially could expand the wealth through a growing trade balance. With the world volume of wealth taken as given then, how else could a nation expand its wealth except at another nation's expense? To them, prosperity stemmed from spending less than income and so as a nation, promoted a positive trade balance—the profit of one was counterbalanced by the loss of another. In fact, as competition intensified, these practical men further realized the importance of expanded control over the labor process itself in achieving a finer division of labor, greater productivity, and control over the pace and intensity of labor.

While the merchant class was far from cohesive, disagreements about policy within the merchant class were subservient to the aims of the common goal of expanding the trade surplus. They vigorously encouraged exports, except machinery and plant and equipment that might aid foreign competitors and discouraged imports, except raw materials (which fed domestic production) and of course precious metals. The colonies, including the Americas, served as a prime export market and source of tax revenues, military bases, and of course, imports of raw materials, especially gold. The policies required a strong navy and military war machine.

As commodity and money flows became increasingly dominant forms of existence, and as state control over pricing and production began to break down, many writers began grappling with the question of what determines costs, profits, and prices in this emerging system of generalized commodity and money exchange. By the end of the seventeenth century many writers began recognizing some connection between the price and supply and demand for a good, while supply and demand in turn was seen as being regulated by the cost of production of the good (or the portion of the society's labor that must go into producing the good). Only when prices were fully determined by a generalized **commodity exchange** would a theory of prices emerge in the works of the classical economists. Thus, once the society was immersed and regulated by the sale of commodities (i.e., everyone had to buy and sell to exist), economists became more concerned with what determined the prices that must persist to reproduce the society.

Viewing the system of exchange and accumulation and reinvestment of capital, the classical economists looked at the system as a whole, dominated by invisible forces (such as competition, analogous perhaps to the invisible force of gravity) which regulated the movement and stability of the system. They recognized the interconnectedness of the flows of money and commodities (including wages and labor) and sought to determine the prices that must exist in order to allow the production process to repeat itself.

HISTORICAL AND LOGICAL CONTRADICTIONS OF MERCANTILISM

As production became relatively more important, capitalists realized that through control over production, one could cut costs, raise productivity, and undercut competitors through lowering prices. Competition was increasing. This led the later economists (especially Adam Smith) to reject the mercantilist idea that gold (i.e., money) constituted wealth. In a powerful critique of the mercantilists, Smith pointed out that money merely reflected the wealth produced in production and expressed the value of commodities when they circulated in the market. Further, struggles between merchants over the monopoly on trade and prices fostered conflict between merchants. Merchants were compelled to become full-fledged capitalists or fade into the newly emerging working class.

The many criticisms culminated in a devastating critique known as the specie-flow mechanism. Philosopher and political economist David Hume (1711-76) pointed out that (logically speaking) the very success of a nation's mercantilist policies,—i.e., a trade surplus—would set into motion forces which would tend to reverse the trade surplus, all through the normal operation of markets. That is to say, allowing for the free flow of money (at this time, mainly gold), it was argued, would tend to result in balance of trade equilibrium. Of course, this monetarist interpretation of finance and money flows would be sharply criticized later by Marx and others up unto the present day.

While Hume's specie-flow mechanism is the most well-known critique of mercantilist thought, opposition to mercantilist thinking began as early as the late seventeenth century. The main idea here was that the very success of policies set off unintended consequences. If the accumulation of money in a positive balance of trade was a goal, the very success of such a policy might set off forces that would reverse the balance of trade surplus. In the absence of strict controls, it was argued, mercantilist-type policies will fail. This doctrine would later be known as the quantity theory of money. As most forcefully argued by David Hume, a positive trade balance implies a positive net money flow into the surplus country due to the fact that more money is coming in than is being paid out (that is to say, imports greater than imports must be paid for). In so far as money is purely a means of circulation (i.e., it is only spent, not hoarded), and that the economy is assumed to operate at its full capacity to produce (as determined by the profitable capacity in the economy), the only result in this situation is that too much money chases too few goods—the only logical effect is that prices in the "trade surplus country" will tend to rise. While this process is set off in the surplus countries, conversely, for the deficit countries of the world, money is flowing out of the country and prices in these countries are falling. If prices are falling in the deficit countries and rising in the surplus countries that means that the deficit countries are becoming more competitive since their goods are relatively cheaper. Hence trade will shift toward the deficit countries, pushing trade back toward equilibrium. This it was argued was the natural dynamic of markets and thus the laws of the economy override the ethical arguments made by the mercantilists.

In this new scenario, trade—unfettered by government regulation—became the great equalizer, an idea followed through to modern day debates surrounding free trade and protectionism. In modern guise it is still argued that the exchange rate between countries will operate in a similar way as Hume's specie-flow mechanism to bring about equal trade balances. Neither in Hume's time nor in modern times has this mechanism been shown to operate—witness the large and persistent trade imbalances in the world economy.

Despite the dubious and questionable assumptions of Hume's specie-flow mechanism, the idea of unintended consequences would form a cornerstone of the emerging economic thought of Adam Smith's famous "Invisible Hand," Marx's "Laws of Motion," and others. The idea of unintended consequences is a key facet of the operation of capitalist economies. Many, however, have criticized the content of the specie-flow mechanism. For example, a country that is experiencing a trade deficit, and hence a net outflow of money from its borders, need not experience a price increase. If goods are reproducible with the existing capacity (i.e., assuming that the productive capacity is not at its maximum), more goods might be produced at the same cost and prices might stay the same or even fall—decreasing costs and prices. Or the inflow of money might simply lower **interest rates**. Despite these criticisms, however, Hume, along with Sir William Petty (1623-87), Richard Cantillon (1680-1734), Ricardo, and later John Maynard Keynes (1883-1946) clearly anticipated the modern quantity theory of money and free trade arguments.

THE RISE OF INDUSTRIAL CAPITALISM

But the rise of industrial capitalism in Europe required much more than merchants trading goods and services. It would also need an accumulated stock of money to be invested and reinvested, and the propertyless people who now needed to work as wage laborers to survive. It further required a market where goods could be sold. The processes involved in generating these preconditions involved, among others, merchants becoming capitalists, enclosure of land held in common in England, the creation of a large surplus of landless peasants, and the expansion of markets and capital accumulation through the investment and reinvestment of profits in production.

Hence, merchant capitalism provided a transitional form to industrial capitalism. In economic thought it provided a transition from medieval to physiocratic and classical theory by shifting the arena of discussion from ethical and moral/philosophical concerns with justice to one of analyzing a more expansive view of civil society and the economy as a machine or system. Ironically, the idea that profit originated in the realm of exchange would later reappear in the economic thinking of those economists who would follow the classical economists, known as neoclassical economics. Modern **microeconomics** is an elaborate theory of individual behavior based on the idea that the free exchange of goods (including labor) not only provides an understanding of the nature of economic growth and profit, but (logically) leads to a situation where all are better off.

THE INFLUENCE OF MERCANTILISM

In terms of its historical influence, mercantilist policy accelerated the breakup of the feudal economy and the guild crafts system of production. Policy corresponded to the interests of merchant capitalists. The main objective was to foster growth of foreign trade (along with shipping and export industries such as textiles) while encouraging the inflow of metals. This served the role of accelerating the transition from a land-based economy in Europe to a monetary economy.

NEO-MERCANTILISM

Looked at in this light then, the so-called dichotomy between the modern jargon of free trade and protectionism is somewhat of a misnomer. Whatever the trading regime, the various national states (and their collections of workers and capitalists) always struggle to set the rules of international transactions—not only tariffs and taxes but also export quotas, **patent laws**, immigration, nationalization of industries, exchange rates, and property rights all factor into the legal structure upon which the movement of goods, services, financial services, and **direct investment** takes place in the global economy.

In general, then, mercantilist struggles are reflected in the conflict between the degree of state intervention to guide national industries. The strong nations seek to impose **laissez-faire** policy on the relatively weaker ones while calling for help in penetrating the markets of their stronger competitors. This usually takes the form of public subsidy of new industries (or dying industries or companies), tax exemptions and credits for new industries, and perhaps establishment of monopolies over local markets. Trade policies impose tariffs and quotas on imports that compete with local manufacturers; in extreme cases policies may take the form of the prohibition of the export of fixed capital and emigration of skilled labor that may give away a competitive advantage.

[John A. Sarich]

FURTHER READING:

Allen, William R. ''The Position of Mercantilism and the Early Development of International Trade Theory.'' In *Events, Ideology and Economic Theory: The Determinants of Progress in the Development of Economic Analysis,* edited by Robert V., Eagly. Detroit: Wayne State University Press, 1968.

Dowd, Douglas. *U.S. Capitalist Development since 1776: Of, by and for Which People.* M. E. Sharpe, 1993.

Marx, Karl. *Capital.* Vol. III. International Publishers, 1967.

McNally, David. *Against the Market: Political Economy, Socialism and the Marxist Critique.* Verso, 1993.

Mun, Thomas. *England's Treasure by Foreign Trade.* A. M. Kelley, 1986.

Polanyi, Karl. *The Great Transformation.* Beacon Press, 1957.

Ricardo, David. *On the Principles of Political Economy and Taxation,* edited by Maurice Dobb. Cambridge University Press, 1951.

Robinson, Joan. ''The New Mercantilism.'' In *Collected Economic Papers,* edited by Joan Robinson. Vol. Four. MIT Press, 1980, pp. 1-13.

Rubin, Isaac Ilyich. *A History of Economic Thought.* Ink Links, 1979.

Salvatore, Dominick, ed. *The New Protectionist Threat to World Welfare.* North Holland, 1987.

Shaikh, Anwar. ''Foreign Trade and the Law of Value: Part 1.'' *Science and Society.* Fall, 1979, pp. 281-302.

Shaikh, Anwar. ''Foreign Trade and the Law of Value: Part II,'' *Science and Society.* Winter, 1979-80, pp. 27-57.

Shaikh, Anwar. "The Laws of International Exchange." In *Growth, Profits, and Property: Essays in the Revival of Political Economy*, edited by Edward Nell. Cambridge University Press, 1980.

Smith, Adam. *An Inquiry into the Nature and Causes of the Wealth of Nations.* Modern Library, 1937.

Thompson, E. P. *The Making of the English Working Class.* Pantheon, 1963.

MERCHANDISING

Merchandising is a broadly defined **marketing** term that most often refers to the practice of combining the purchase of a product while still promoting the marketing concept that was behind the creation of the product in the first place. While old style marketing sought to create demand that would send consumers looking for products, today's merchandising combines product and demand together. Merchandising becomes the product and the product becomes the merchandising.

Stock retailers such as grocery stores and department stores also use the term "merchandising" to describe how their products are sold, particularly how consumers are steered to the higher **profit margin** items once they enter the store.

Both concepts will be discussed here. First will be the use of merchandising by a myriad of manufacturers all trying to tie their identities to a popular product like a hit movie.

Today's marketing managers developed their understanding of merchandising as children in the 1950s and 60s when they forced their parents to buy metal school lunch boxes with pictures of their favorite cartoon characters on the side. At the time, the cartoon creators were thrilled that millions of kids would advertise their cartoons during lunch. The lunch box manufacturers were simply happy to be selling those character covered lunchboxes. The concept has mushroomed beyond any imagination or control in the 1990's.

Yesterday's lunchbox cartoon merchandising has exploded today into hundreds of products and services that have tangled ties to each other. Sometimes the distinction between what is an original, stand-alone product and what is really a merchandising vehicle has blurred. For example, the *New York Times* criticized the 1994 movie *The Flintstones* as a marketing scheme more designed to sell products than to entertain moviegoers. Dozens of company logos such as "RocDonalds" were embraced by the camera as the action crawled across the screen. Outside the theater, McDonald's and all the other corporations that paid money for product placements were introducing their

"collectible" series of movie paraphernalia. While the 1993 movie blockbuster *Jurassic Park* garnered more fan raves and fewer criticisms for its on-screen merchandising, there were still more than 100 products in the marketplace with ties to the dinosaur movie.

Sometimes a small entertainment concept can be blown up into a full bore merchandising campaign that subsidizes the entertainment. In one case in 1994 an entertainment company created the concept of a syndicated weekly country music TV show that would run on cable. To support and promote it, the company created a two-hour radio show of the same name. It also signed up local country music clubs as affiliates, licensing them to sell merchandise and clothing adorned with the TV show logo. The clothing was designed and produced to promote the show before the show was even on the air. The entertainment company also planned live shows at which the same merchandise would be sold. The live concerts would be promoted as pay-per-view events on the weekly cable show. Producers expected to debut the concept in 120 markets playing to 90 percent of the cable population. Everything was laid out in advance before the first musical note was played on the assumption that country music fans would buy everything they could concerning the show.

If this concept works, other entertainment companies can be expected to experiment with their own versions. Procter and Gamble Co.'s managers have already suggested that TV might return to its roots when programs are produced by one sponsor. Would fans be willing to buy clothing celebrating their favorite soap opera if it also had a little logo selling detergent? Does merchandising work? Did you know a kid who demanded a *Jurassic Park* lunchbox?

The older concept of retail merchandising is to make high profit, high demand products easy to find, and to make shopping seem more like a natural, if not fun process. Grocery stores feature produce at the front of the store because shoppers like to spend time picking out their fruits and vegetables. The frozen foods are near the checkout counters on the left of the store because shoppers want to pick up the ice cream last.

Other items such as expensive cookies, and new **brand names** of coffee and soft drinks are sold differently. Since they are not necessities, the attention of browsing shoppers is caught by signs or displays featuring products. The stores hope shoppers will suddenly decide they need this product and drop it into the cart.

Store merchandising is changing as many consumers are buying less expensive "store brands." One research study for grocery retailers found that store brands accounted for 18 percent of sales in 1993, compared to 12 percent in 1989. If the trend continues, analysts say, store brands could account for 30 percent of sales within a decade. The researchers say the reason behind the trend to cheaper products is that consumers are less influenced by network television **advertising** now that they have more stations to watch on cable television. Since consumers are watching less mass market TV, they are seeing fewer of the mesmerizing TV commercials that sold them on mass market products like **brand name** detergents, cleansers and toilet paper.

Brand name manufacturers are fighting back by slashing the prices of their products and by consolidating their product lines to limit the consumer's choice. Some retailers like KMart have conducted research that indicates such buying behavior might be an irreversible trend with baby boomers purchasers sticking to a low-price, no-impulse-buy, discount-store mentality. The retailing giant has responded by concentrating more on presenting products that its research says boomers are aging into, such as exercise equipment.

What is the future of merchandising? Some manufacturers and retailers fear interactive **computer networks** could change it forever, at least with those potential customers who own computers. Microsoft Corp. CEO Bill Gates is pushing the idea that people could be watching a TV show, see an article of clothing the show's star is wearing, then order the same product by clicking the computer mouse a few times and typing in their measurements. They would not even have to get up from their living room sofa, much less go to the department store to see the merchandising display.

That future is likely a long way off. Homes would have to be rewired to accept such signals. Much more sophisticated interactive technology would have to be developed. And, a phalanx of researchers would have to determine if consumers really mind going to the store.

As one retail vice president says, "Right now, this technology is a solution in search of a problem." As of 1994, the cost of wiring a home to accept the highest level of interactive technology is almost $200,000 per house.

At that cost, there are few consumers who will mind going to the store to pick up the latest movie-theme lunchbox.

[Clint Johnson]

FURTHER READING:

Fleury, Rick. "The Dog That Became a Symbol of the Simple Life," *Brandweek*. July 5, 1993.

Fox, Bruce. "Brand Erosion Potential," *Chain Store Age Executive*. February, 1994.

Harris, Brian and Michael McPartland. "Category Management Defined: What it Is and Why it Works," *Progressive Grocer*. September, 1993.

McLaughlin, Michael and Courtney Kingston. "A Four Point Plant for Serve Merchandising," *Brandweek*. January 3, 1994.

Ray, Susan. "Merchandising Concepts Are Solid as Rock," *Amusement Business*. September 27, 1993.

Schneider, Charles P. "Bridging the Gap: Developing Uniform Criteria for Judging Marketing Efforts," *Progressive Grocer*. December, 1993.

MERCOSUR

Mercosur is a customs union coordinating the economies of Argentina, Brazil, Paraguay and Uruguay. Mercosur eliminates the majority of tariffs among the four member states. Additionally, the four nations share a single external tariff throughout the region. The tariff is intended to spur inter-regional growth and inter-regional investment.

Together, the four member nations represent 59 percent of the land mass of Latin America. Additionally, Mercosur joined together a population of approximately 190 million, or 44 percent of the Latin American total. The combined **gross national product** (GNP) of the four nations was approximately $437 billion at Mercosur's official inception.

Though the customs union formally took effect on January 1, 1995, trade in the entire region had already exploded in anticipation. Trade among the four Mercosur nations grew from $4.7 billion in 1991 to over $10 billion by the end of 1994. For example, Paraguay, a leading producer of cotton, traditionally shipped 90 percent of its product to Brazil, but in the form of raw cotton. In the wake of Mercosur, its textile industry has expanded dramatically as—for the first time—it can ship manufactured cotton products (such as thread, cloth, and clothing) to Brazil duty-free. The resultant demand for cotton goods in the form of value-added garment production has provided in a boost to the Paraguayan economy and created a supporting manufacturing infrastructure.

The common external tariff for the region has successfully encouraged inter-regional investment. In the four year period from Mercosur's signing in 1991 to its enactment at the close of 1994, for example, investment from Brazil into Argentina reached $1 billion. Additionally, the member states have undertaken a proposal to build the world's longest bridge of its kind at the Uruguayan city of Colonia, crossing the Rio de la Plata. The proposed bridge (likely at the time of this writing) will join Uruguay with the Argentine capital of Buenos Aires on the opposite river bank. In addition to allowing for the construction costs previously far in excess of Uruguay's pre-Mercosur ability, the bridge will radically slash the overland trucking time between Argentina's most important economic center and Brazil's major industrial center of Sao Paulo. Additionally, Uruguay will reinforce its position as a trade crossroads, increasing employment at the least and opening its own opportunities to build on the trade traffic between Argentina and Brazil.

Investment in the Mercosur nations from foreign multinational corporations, including the United States, has resulted in an estimated $3.5 billion ranging from factories to franchise operations. While some officials in Mexico, Canada, and the United States see opportunities for expanding the **North American Free Trade Agreement** (NAFTA) to the Mercosur nations, the direction of the Mercosur members at present is leaning away from ties to North America. The Mercosur nations have set the goal of first strengthening their own regional economy and then expanding, if at all, to other South American nations in order to form a South America-wide customs union as a counterbalance to, not in cooperation with, the North American free trade partners.

SEE ALSO: Emerging Markets

[David A. Victor]

MERGERS AND ACQUISITIONS

A merger is the absorption of one firm by another. The acquiring firm retains its identity while the acquired firm ceases to exist. In a consolidation, an entirely new firm is created, and the two previous entities cease to exist. Consolidated **financial statements** are prepared under the assumption that two or more corporate entities are in actuality only one. The consolidated statements are prepared by combining the account balances of the individual firms after certain adjusting and eliminating entries are made. The primary advantage of a merger is its legally simplicity; there is no need to transfer title to each individual asset. A disadvantage is the fact that the shareholders of both firms must vote to approve a merger. Usually a two-thirds majority is required.

Another way to acquire a firm is to buy the voting stock. This can be done by agreement of management or by **tender offer**. In a tender offer, the acquiring firm makes the offer to buy stock directly to the shareholders, thereby bypassing management. In contrast to a merger, a stock acquisition requires no stockholder voting. Shareholders wishing to keep their stock can simply do so. Finally, a minority of shareholders may hold out in a tender offer.

A bidding firm can also buy another simply by purchasing all its assets. This involves a costly legal transfer of title and must be approved by the shareholders of the selling firm.

A takeover is the transfer of control from one group to another. Normally, the acquiring firm (the bidder) makes an offer for the target firm. In a proxy contest, a group of dissident shareholders will seek to obtain enough votes to gain control of the board of directors.

Acquisitions are usually classified as horizontal, vertical, or conglomerate. Horizontal means the firms compete in the same market. Vertical means the firms are at different steps in the production process. Conglomerate means they are in unrelated lines of business.

In principle, the decision to acquire another firm is a capital budgeting decision much like any other. Mergers differ from ordinary investment decisions in at least five ways. First, the value of a merger may depend on such things as strategic fits that are difficult to measure. Second, the accounting, tax, and legal aspects of a merger can be complex. Third, mergers often involve issues of corporate control and are a means of replacing existing management. Fourth, mergers obviously affect the value of the firm, but they also affect the relative value of the **stocks** and **bonds**. Finally, mergers are often ''unfriendly.''

TAXABLE VERSUS TAX-FREE TRANSACTIONS

The tax perspective on mergers and acquisitions is to consider whether a business combination is a tax-free or a taxable event. Certain exchanges of stock are tax-free reorganizations, which permit the owners of one company to exchange their shares for the stock of the acquirer without paying taxes.

The tax status of a transaction may affect the value of the transaction from both the buyer's and the seller's viewpoints. In a taxable acquisition, the assets of the selling firm are revalued or ''written up.'' Therefore, the **depreciation** deduction will rise. Assets are not revalued in a tax-free acquisition. But in a taxable acquisition, the selling shareholders will have to pay **capital gains** taxes and will thus want more for their shares to compensate. (the capital gains effect). The capital gains and write-up effects tend to cancel out each other.

There are three basic types of tax-free reorganizations. In order for a transaction to qualify as a type A tax-free reorganization, it must be structured in certain ways. In contrast to a type B reorganization, the type A transaction allows the buyer to use either voting or nonvoting stock. It also permits the buyer to use more cash in the total consideration since the law does not stipulate a maximum amount of cash that can be used. At least 50 percent of the consideration, however, must be stock in the acquiring corporation. In addition, in a type A reorganization, the acquiring corporation may choose not to purchase all the target's assets.

In instances where at least 50 percent of the bidder's stock is used as the consideration, but other considerations such as cash, debt, or nonequity securities are also used, the transaction may be partially taxable. Capital gains taxes must be paid on those shares that were exchanged for nonequity consideration.

A type B reorganization requires that the acquiring corporation use mainly its own voting **common stock** as the consideration for purchase of the target corporation's common stock. Cash must comprise no more than 20 percent of the total consideration, and at least 80 percent of the target's stock must be paid for by voting stock by the bidder.

Target stockholders who receive the stock of the acquiring corporation in exchange for their common stock are not immediately taxed on the consideration they receive. Taxes will have to be paid only if the stock is eventually sold. If cash is included in the transaction, this cash may be taxed to the extent that it represents a gain on the sale of stock.

In a type C reorganization, the acquiring corporation must purchase 80 percent of the fair market value of the target's assets. In a type C reorganization, a tax liability results when the acquiring corporation purchases the assets of the target using consideration other than stock in the acquiring corporation. The tax liability is measured by comparing the purchase price of the assets with the adjusted basis of these assets.

FINANCIAL ACCOUNTING FOR MERGERS AND ACQUISITIONS

The two principal **accounting** methods used in mergers and acquisitions are the pooling of interests method and the purchase method. The main difference between them is the value that the combined firm's **balance sheet** places on the assets of the acquired firm, as well as the depreciation allowances and charges against income following the merger.

The pooling of interests method assumes that the transaction is simply an exchange of equity securities. Therefore, the capital stock account of the target firm is eliminated, and the acquirer issues new stock to replace it. The two firms' assets and **liabilities** are combined at their historical book values as of the acquisition date. The end result of a pooling of interests transaction is that the total assets of the combined firm are equal to the sum of the assets of the individual firms. No goodwill is generated, and there are no charges against earnings. There is no change in the basis in such a transaction. A tax-free acquisition would normally be reported as a pooling of interests.

Under the purchase method, assets and liabilities are shown on the merged firm's books at their market (not book) values as of the acquisition date. This method is based on the idea that the resulting values, should reflect the market values resulting from the bargaining process. The total liabilities of the combined firm equal the sum of the two firms' individual liabilities. The equity of the acquiring firm is increased by the amount of the purchase price.

Accounting for the excess of cost over the aggregate of the fair market values of the identifiable net assets acquired applies only in purchase accounting. The excess is goodwill that is computed by comparing the cost of an investment with the product of the percentage of the company acquired times the fair market value of the acquired company's identifiable net assets (assets minus liabilities). Goodwill is an asset, which is charged against income and amortized over a period that cannot exceed 40 years. Although the amortization ''expense'' is deducted from reported **income**, it cannot be deducted for tax purposes.

Purchase accounting usually results in increased depreciation charges because the book value of most assets is usually less than fair value because of **inflation**. For tax purposes, however, depreciation does not increase because the tax basis of the assets remains the same. Since depreciation under pooling accounting is based on the old book values of the assets, accounting income is usually higher under the pooling method. The accounting treatment has no cash flow consequences. Thus, value should be unaffected by accounting procedure.

Firms may dislike the purchase method because of the ''goodwill'' created. The reason for this is that goodwill is amortized over a period of years. In the transaction involving company A and company B illustrated in the table on next page, company A has acquired company B. Company B, the target, has assets, net of depreciation, equal to $5 million and total liabilities and total equity each at $2.5 million. Company A, the acquirer, has assets of $20 million, with total liabilities and net worth equal to $10 million each. The transaction is financed by the issuance of $5 million worth of common stock by company A. Under the purchase method, the assets of company B are written up by $1 million. This amount is the premium above book value that is paid for company B.

The assets of company B are revalued at $6 million after the merger instead of $5 million before the merger. The amount that is entered as goodwill, $500,000, is a result of the process of asset balancing.

Example of the pooling versus purchase method				
	Balance Sheet Before Merger		Balance Sheet After Merger	
	Co. A	Co.B	Purchase	Pooling
Assets net of depreciation	$20,000	$5,000	$26,000	$25,000
Goodwill	0	0	500	0
Total assets	$20,000	$5,000	$27,000	$25,000
Total liabilities	$10,000	$2,500	$12,500	$12,500
Equity	$10,000	$2,500	$15,000	$12,500
Total liabilities and equity	$20,000	$5,000	$27,500	$25,000

HOW TO VALUE AN ACQUISITION CANDIDATE

Valuing an acquisition candidate is similar to valuing any investment. The analyst estimates the incremental cash flows, determine an appropriate risk-adjusted discount rate, and the computes the net present value (NPV). If firm A is acquiring firm B, then the acquisition makes economic sense if the value of the combined firm is greater than the value of firm A plus the value of firm B. Synergy is said to exist when the cash flow of the combined firm is greater than the sum of the cash flows for the two firms as separate companies. The gain from the merger is the present value of this difference in cash flows.

The gains from an acquisition may result from one or more of the following five categories: (1) revenue enhancement, (2) cost reductions, (3) lower taxes, (4) changing capital requirements, or (5) lower cost of **capital**. Increased **revenues** may come from marketing gains, strategic benefits, and market power. Marketing gains arise from more effective **advertising**, economies of distribution, and a better mix of products. Strategic benefits represent opportunities to enter new lines of business. Finally, a merger may reduce competition thereby increasing market power. Such mergers, of course, may run afoul of antitrust legislation.

A larger firm may be able to operate more efficiently than two smaller firms, thereby reducing costs. Horizontal mergers may generate **economies of scale**. This means that the average production cost will fall as production volume increases. A vertical merger may allow a firm to decrease costs by more closely coordinating production and distribution. Finally, economies may be achieved when firms have complementary resources, for example, when one firm has excess production capacity and another has insufficient capacity.

Tax gains in mergers may arise because of unused tax losses, unused debt capacity, surplus funds, and the write-up of depreciable assets. The tax losses of target corporations can be used to offset the acquiring corporation's future income. These tax losses can be used to offset income for a maximum of 15 years or until the tax loss is exhausted. Only tax losses for the previous three years can be used to offset future income.

Tax loss carry-forwards can motivate mergers and acquisitions. A company that has earned profits may find value in the tax losses of a target corporation that can be used to offset the income it plans to earn. A merger may not, however, be structured solely for tax purposes. In addition, the acquirer must continue to operate the pre-acquisition business of the company in a net loss position. The tax benefits may be less than their "face value," not only because of the time value of money, but also because the tax loss carry-forwards might expire without being fully utilized.

Tax advantages can also arise in an acquisition when a target firm carries assets on its books with basis, for tax purposes, below their market value. These assets could be more valuable, for tax purposes, if they were owned by another corporation that could increase their tax basis following the acquisition. The acquirer would then depreciate the assets based on the higher market values, in turn, gaining additional depreciation benefits.

Interest payments on debt are a tax-deductible expense, whereas dividend payments from equity ownership are not. The existence of a tax advantage for debt is an incentive to have greater use of debt, as opposed to equity, as the means of financing merger and acquisition transactions. Also, a firm that borrows much less than it could may be an acquisition target because of its unused debt capacity. While the use of financial leverage produces tax benefits, debt also increases the likelihood of financial distress in the event that the acquiring firm cannot meet its interest payments on the acquisition debt.

Finally, a firm with surplus funds may wish to acquire another firm. The reason is that distributing the money as **dividends** or using it to repurchase shares will increase income taxes for shareholders. With an acquisition, no income taxes are paid by shareholders.

Acquiring firms may be able to more efficiently utilize **working capital** and fixed assets in the target firm, thereby reducing capital requirements and enhancing profitability. This is particularly true if the target firm has redundant assets that may be divested.

The cost of debt can often be reduced when two firms merge. The combined firm will generally have reduced variability in its cash flows. Therefore, there may be circumstances under which one or the other of the firms would have defaulted on its debt, but the combined firm will not. This makes the debt safer, and the cost of borrowing may decline as a result. This is termed the coinsurance effect.

Diversification is often cited as a benefit in mergers. Diversification by itself, however does not create any value because stockholders can accomplish the same thing as the merger by buying stock in both firms.

The procedure for valuing an acquisition candidate depends on the source of the estimated gains. Different sources of synergy have different risks. Tax gains can be estimated fairly accurately and should be discounted at the cost of debt. Cost reductions through operating efficiencies can also be determined with some confidence. Such savings should be discounted at a normal weighted average cost of capital. Gains from strategic benefits are difficult to estimate and are often highly uncertain. A discount rate greater than the overall cost of capital would thus be appropriate.

The net present value (NPV) of the acquisition is equal to the gains less the cost of the acquisition. The cost depends on whether cash or stock is used as payment. The cost of an acquisition when cash is used is just the amount paid. The cost of the merger when common stock is used as the consideration (the payment) is equal to the percentage of the new firm that is owned by the previous shareholders in the acquired firm multiplied by the value of the new firm. In a cash merger, the benefits go entirely to the acquiring firm whereas in a stock-for-stock exchange, the benefits are shared by the acquiring and acquired firm.

Whether to use cash or stock depends on three considerations. First, if the acquiring firm's management believes that its stock is overvalued, then a stock acquisition may be cheaper. Second, a cash acquisition is usually taxable which may result in a higher price. Third, the use of stock means that the acquired firm will share in any gains from merger; if the merger has a negative NPV, however, then the acquired firm will share in the loss.

In valuing acquisitions, the following factors should be kept in mind. First, market values must not be ignored. Thus, there is no need to estimate the value of a publicly traded firm as a separate entity. Second, only those cash flows that are incremental are relevant to the analysis. Third, the **discount rate** used should reflect the risk associated with the incremental cash flows. Therefore, the acquiring firm should not use its own cost of capital to value the cash flows of another firm. Finally, acquisition may involve significant investment banking fees and costs.

HOSTILE ACQUISITIONS

The replacement of poor **management** is a potential source of gain from acquisition. Changing technological and competitive factors may lead to a need for corporate restructuring. If incumbent management is unable to adapt, then a hostile acquisition is one method for accomplishing change.

Hostile acquisitions generally involve poorly performing firms in mature industries, and occur when the **board of directors** of the target is opposed to the sale of the company. In this case, the acquiring firm has two options to proceed with the acquisition—a tender offer or a proxy fight. A tender offer represents an offer to buy the stock of the target firm either directly from the firm's shareholders or through the secondary market. In a proxy fight, the acquirer solicits the shareholders of the target firm in an attempt to obtain the right to vote their shares. The acquiring firm hopes to secure enough proxies to gain control of the board of directors and, in turn, replace the incumbent management.

Management in target firms will typically resist takeover attempts either to get a higher price for the firm or to protect their own self-interests. This can be done a number of ways. Target companies can decrease the likelihood of a takeover though charter amendments. With the staggered board technique, the board of directors is classified into three groups, with only one group elected each year. Thus, the suitor cannot obtain control of the board immediately even though it may have acquired a majority ownership of the target via a tender offer. Under a supermajority amendment, a higher percentage than 50 percent, generally two-thirds or 80 percent, is required to approve a merger.

Other defensive tactics include **poison pills** and dual class recapitalizations. With poison pills, existing shareholders are issued rights which, if a bidder acquires a certain percentage of the outstanding shares, can be used to purchase additional shares at a bargain price, usually half the market price. Dual class recapitalizations distribute a new class of equity with superior voting rights. This enables the target firm's managers to obtain majority control even though they do not own a majority of the shares.

Other preventative measures occur after an unsolicited offer is made to the target firm. The target may file suit against the bidder alleging violations of antitrust or securities laws. Alternatively, the target may engage in asset and liability restructuring to make it an unattractive target. With asset restructuring, the target purchases assets that the bidder does not want or that will create antitrust problems or sells off the "crown jewels," the assets that the suitor desires to obtain. Liability restructuring maneuvers include issuing shares to a friendly third party to dilute the bidder's ownership position or leveraging up the firm through a leveraged recapitalization making it difficult for the suitor to finance the transaction. Other postoffer tactics involve targeted share repurchases (often termed "greenmail" in which the target repurchases the shares of an unfriendly suitor at a premium over the current market price) and golden parachutes which are lucrative supplemental compensation packages for the target firm's management. These packages are activated in the case of a takeover and the subsequent resignations of the senior executives. Finally, the target may employ an exclusionary self-tender. With this tactic, the target firm offers to buy back its own stock at a premium from everyone except the bidder.

A privately owned firm is not subject to unfriendly takeovers. A publicly traded firm "goes private" when a group, usually involving existing management, buys up all the publicly held stock. Such transactions are typically structured as leveraged buyouts (LBOs). LBOs are financed primarily with debt secured by the assets of the target firm.

DO ACQUISITIONS BENEFIT SHAREHOLDERS?

There is substantial empirical evidence that the shareholders in acquired firms benefit substantially. Gains for this group typically amount to 20 percent in mergers and 30 percent in tender offer above the market prices prevailing a month prior to the merger announcement.

The gains to acquiring firms are difficult to measure. The best evidence suggests that shareholders in bidding firms gain little. Losses in value subsequent to merger announcements are not unusual. This seems to suggest that overvaluation by bidding firms is common. Managers may also have incentives to increase firm size at the potential expense of shareholder wealth. If so, merger activity may happen for noneconomic reasons, to the detriment of shareholders.

[Robert T. Kleiman]

FURTHER READING:

Auerbach, Alan J., *Corporate Takeovers: Causes and Consequences.* Chicago: University of Chicago Press, 1988.

Coffee, John C., Jr., Louis Lowenstein, and Susan Rose-Ackerman. *Knights, Raiders, and Targets: The Impact of the Hostile Takeover.* New York: Oxford University Press, 1988.

Gaughan, Patrick A. *Mergers and Acquisitions.* New York: HarperCollins, 1991.

METROPOLITAN STATISTICAL AREA

A Metropolitan Statistical Area (MSA) is a designation the U.S. government uses to refer to a region that, broadly speaking, consists of a city and its suburbs, plus any surrounding communities that are closely linked to the city economically and socially. MSAs were known as Standard Metropolitan Statistical Areas (SMSAs) from 1959 to 1983 and, before that, as Standard Metropolitan Areas (SMAs). Having some familiarity with MSAs is useful to businesspeople, for, as Carl Heyel noted in *The Encyclopedia of Management,* data about these regions can be helpful in devising marketing strategies, delineating sales territories, and determining the locations of plant and operating facilities.

The government uses the designation *MSA* for the purpose of applying uniform and consistent standards to the wealth of data collected, analyzed, and published by its myriad departments and agencies. Official definitions for what constitutes an MSA are developed, issued, and periodically revised by the federal Office of Management and Budget (OMB), following public commentary and hearings and in conjunction with the Federal Executive Committee on Metropolitan Areas. And because MSA and similar designations figure prominently in the compilation of statistics for the national census, the U.S. Department of Commerce's Bureau of the Census also plays a part in refining the definitions.

Although the OMB's official standards for defining these regions are highly complex, detailed, and marked by qualifications, in general MSAs can be viewed as part of larger entities known as Metropolitan Areas (MAs). MAs are regions composed of one or more counties and containing either (a) a city whose population is at least 50,000 or (b) a Census Bureau-defined "urbanized area" whose population, together with that of its component county or counties, totals at least 100,000. An important exception to how MAs are defined concerns the New England states, where towns and cities rather than counties are used to designate regions as MAs.

Within the broad category of MAs are three elements, or subcategories: (a) MSAs, generally constituting free-standing MAs whose surrounding counties are nonmetropolitan; (b) Consolidated Metropolitan Statistical Areas (CMSAs), representing the largest metropolitan regions, those with populations of more than one million; and (c) Primary Metropolitan Statistical Areas (PMSAs), consisting of the individual urbanized counties or county clusters within CMSAs.

As an example of how these classifications translate to data that can be useful to businesspeople, the 1992 edition of the *Academic American Encyclopedia* reported that "in 1988 there were 287 officially designated MSAs and CMSAs. Within just 37 of these areas reside 119 million people, nearly half the U.S. population. The New York metropolitan area, with 18 million people, is the largest, followed by Los Angeles, Chicago, San Francisco, and Philadelphia.''

Information on the OMB's standards for defining MSAs and other such designations can be obtained from the Statistical Policy Office of the Office of Information and Regulatory Affairs, Office of Management and Budget in Washington, D.C. Information on the Census Bureau's application of these standards is available from the Secretary of the Federal Executive Committee on Metropolitan Areas, Population Division, U.S. Bureau of the Census, also in Washington, D.C.

[Roberta H. Winston]

FURTHER READING:

Heyel, Carl. *The Encyclopedia of Management.* Van Nostrand.

Office of Management and Budget. ''Revised Standards for Defining Metropolitan Areas in the 1990s; Notice.'' *Federal Register.* April 10, April 30, and May 10, 1990.

U.S. Department of Commerce. Bureau of the Census. *1990 Census of Population and Housing: Summary Population and Housing Characteristics, United States.* Washington, D.C.: Government Printing Office.

MEXICAN LAW

As a result of the **North American Free Trade Agreement** (NAFTA) was implemented on January 1, 1994, United States' business people began trading with Mexico's business people, investing in business opportunities in Mexico, and establishing business facilities in Mexico in unprecedented numbers and ways. U.S. businesses are involved on a daily basis, with Mexico's legal system, which, like most legal systems, is inextricably linked with its economic system and its history. Failure to understand at least the basic elements of Mexico's legal system can pose a significant barrier to U.S. business people trading with or investing in Mexico, because Mexico's legal system is significantly different from that of the United States. Mexico's legal system is a civil law system, which can be traced to sixteenth century law brought by the Spaniards to the land that later was named Mexico. But, it is not the same civil law as exists in other civil law countries, because various aspects of Mexico's legal system can be traced to Pre-Colombian indigenous law as well as to its unique history, social institutions, and economy.

Indeed, the term ''civil law'' is a generalization, because the legal system of each civil law system in the world will vary according to the unique social, economic, political, and historical background of the individual country. A civil law system is a system in which, in general, laws are ''codified,'' i.e., society

relies on a legislative body (or bodies) to pass statutes spelling out their law. Those statutes are then organized, topic by topic, into codes. The codes become the primary resource (research tool) for lawyers and their clients in such a system. In Mexico, the hierarchy of laws is as follows: (1) the Federal Constitution, (2) legislation (found in the ''Codes'' or ''Códigos,'' in Spanish), and (3) regulations interpreting the statutes. Provisions of the Constitution supersede any legislation or regulations, and legislation supersedes any regulations. A final source of law in Mexico, which is least compelling in terms of hierarchy of laws, is ''custom.''

An important consideration for businesses dealing with Mexico is that unlike Mexico's civil law system, the United States legal system is a ''common law'' system. In this system, the roots of which can be traced to England, the Federal Constitution as well as legislation and regulations are recognized as being law just as such documents set down law in a civil law system. However, a crucial difference between the two systems is that a common law system recognizes the decisions of courts as creating ''law.'' Thus, in the United States, our courts create rules of law to fill in the grey areas not clearly covered by legislation or regulations, and they create law where no statutes or regulations exist. For example, entire bodies of law such as tort law (which includes the law of negligence and strict liability for defective products) and contract law (other than contracts for the sale of goods) have been covered in the United States as rules of law established through courts' decisions. Thus, U.S. business people are dealing with a very different way of doing things when dealing with the Mexican legal system.

ATTORNEYS

U.S. business people must recognize that to do business in Mexico, they will nearly always need to hire a Mexican attorney. Reciprocity that would allow U.S. licensed attorneys to practice law in Mexico and vice versa is not a part of NAFTA. This is not surprising in view of the significant differences between the two legal systems and their laws. Further, it is helpful to remember that even in the United States, licensing of attorneys is done by the individual states. Thus, most attorneys in the United States take a bar exam and seek admission to practice law in only one state; only a small percentage of U.S. attorneys go through the extensive efforts necessary to become licensed to practice law in two or more states.

In practical terms, U.S. businesses will usually use their own U.S. attorneys for matters related to U.S. law and will hire Mexican attorneys to work with their U.S. attorneys and to handle legal practice in Mexico. While U.S. attorneys are not allowed to practice law before Mexican courts, they are permitted to register as legal consultants and establish offices in Mexico from which they can advise their clients. Beyond the need for a licensed attorney who is knowledgeable about Mexican law and legal practice, working with Mexican attorneys makes good practical sense. Mexicans place great value on contacts and relationships with people they know and trust as they do business. Thus, working with a Mexican attorney can facilitate business transactions in informal yet important ways, going beyond legal requirements.

In dealing with Mexican attorneys, it should also be recognized that Mexican legal education and licensing are very different from those processes in the United States. In Mexico, there are two levels of attorneys. At the first level, a student of law obtains a five-year degree in law. (This is roughly equivalent to our four-year undergraduate programs in the United States.) After passing courses and oral exams at his or her university, the prospective attorney becomes a *licenciado* and *abogado* (attorney). (The term *licenciado* is applied to graduates of various programs of study at that level in Mexico, not just law. Mexican *abogados* do not take a bar exam such as the exam required of U.S. attorneys in most states.) The abogado can practice law in any part of Mexico. However, the abogado's powers are limited, and many kinds of significant legal transactions, such as transfers of real property, can only be handled by a *notario público*. Although the words *notario público* translate literally to "notary public" in English, the *notario público* is not at all the equivalent of the notary public in the United States. The *notario público* has received advanced education and training beyond that of an *abogado* and has been appointed to serve in a specific geographical area within one of Mexico's states. He or she can move to another part of that state or to another state in Mexico only by applying and competing for another opening in that new location.

THE MEXICAN POLITICAL AND LEGAL SYSTEMS

Mexico has a federal system of government with a national government and 31 states. However, Mexico's national government is far more powerful than those of the United States and Canada.

Mexico's president plays an extremely important role in its legal system. Nearly all federal laws in Mexico are initiated by the president, and his powers (there has been no woman president in Mexico) are such that most laws he proposes are passed with little or no alteration. Further, the president, as the leader of the powerful PRI (the political party of every Mexican president elected since 1928), plays a strong role with respect to policy and enactment of law in the various Mexican states. (PRI stands for the Partido Revolucionario Institucional, or Revolutionary, Institutional Party.)

The structure of Mexico's court system is similar to that in the United States. In each state there are trial and appellate courts. The federal level includes trial courts, circuit courts of appeal, and a Supreme Court. The Supreme Court is divided into four "chambers" with five justices each. Each chamber handles one of four areas of law: criminal, administrative, civil, or labor. It is important to note, however, that the role of the courts in a civil law system such as Mexico's differs from the role of courts in a common law system. In a civil law system, attorneys and judges look to sets of codes in which statutes are set down as their primary source of law, whereas in a common law system, attorneys and judge rely on statutes and rules of law and their interpretation as they are set down in prior-written court opinions.

OVERVIEW OF MEXICAN LAW

The most important legal document in Mexico is its Federal Constitution, which is the basis for all of Mexican law. The current constitution is the 1917 Political Constitution of the United Mexican States (*Constitución Política de los Estados Unidos Mexicanos*). Although the constitution contains many provisions that parallel guarantees found in the United States constitution, such as the right to due process, there are important philosophical differences underlying the two documents. The Mexican constitution is far longer than that of the United States. It includes economic, social, and cultural rights of the Mexican people and calls for a federal government that takes an active role in promoting those rights. Many of the specific provisions of Mexico's constitution are so detailed that in the United States they would be covered through legislation rather than in the Constitution itself.

It is important to note that Mexico's current constitution, which was adopted in 1917, was a product of the Mexican Revolution of 1910-1917. The Mexican Revolution followed a period of history from 1877 to 1911 known as the *Porfiriato* for the ruler of Mexico at that time, Porfirio Díaz. During the *Porfiriato*, Díaz and very few other Mexican people lived in wealth at the expense of the poor, attempting to emulate the lifestyles of the rich in France and the United States. Díaz encouraged and facilitated extensive foreign investment and involvement in Mexico's economy, and he governed the country with an iron hand. There was little or no social or political mobility. Mexican citizens resented foreign ownership of Mexico's railroads and extensive foreign control over Mexico's mining and oil industries.

The revolution ended these social inequities, and led to sweeping changes. Various crucial sections of the Constitution of 1917 were written in reaction to the Díaz era. Among such provisions were Article 27, dealing with agrarian reform and the use and ownership of land and Article 123, dealing with labor and social reform. Both articles have maintained their importance as Mexico moves into a new era and new economy pursuant to NAFTA.

Article 27 gives the Mexican government the power to expropriate private property for public use, and gives all subterranean land, including all minerals, gases, and hydrocarbons, to the Mexican government. It also prohibits foreign ownership of any land within 100 kilometers of Mexico's border and within 50 kilometers of Mexico's shoreline. Further, the Mexican nation itself has control over the transfer of land to private persons. The objective of Article 27 was to break up the monopolies on land, water, and natural resources held by a privileged few.

As a result of Article 27, large parcels of land formerly owned by rich individuals, companies, and religious organizations were taken over by the Mexican government. Many of the lands were converted to use as *ejidos*. *Ejidos* are blocks of land that are operated and farmed by Mexican families that have resided on those lands since the implementation of the 1917 constitution. Prior to the early 1990s, *ejidos* were viewed as a major block to investment in Mexico because, pursuant to Mexican law, such land could not be sold or leased to others. At that time, however, the Mexican government passed an amendment to the 1917 Constitution permitting the sale or lease of *ejido* lands. Use of this new legal option, of course, has not been a simple process. In many cases there simply are no existing titles to the land, which has been used by the families on the land since the 1920s. This has resulted in several scenarios. In some cases, certain parcels are not transferrable because officials are unable to establish ownership. Alternately, certain parcels have been transferred and payments made to those who must leave the land as a result of the transfer. Unfortunately, payments are often minimal and are usually insufficient for peasant farmers and their families to establish themselves elsewhere. Further, it is reported that many peasant farmers are simply being pushed from the land, unable to establish sufficient claim to share in payments being made. Thus, acquisition of land by investors can be a difficult, politically controversial project.

Article 123 of the 1917 Constitution places nearly all labor matters under federal jurisdiction. Article 123 will be discussed below in conjunction with discussion of Mexico's labor laws.

The remainder of this article will review three areas of Mexican law that are of particular importance to businesses: (1) investment law, (2) labor law, (3) and environmental law.

MEXICO'S INVESTMENT LAWS

HISTORICAL DEVELOPMENT. In reaction to the regime of Porfirio Díaz, the Mexican Constitution of 1917 reserved control of land ownership and the exclusive rights to petroleum and other minerals to the Mexican federal government. Thus, throughout the twentieth century, Mexico has been functioning under a constitution that severely restricts foreign investment. Restrictions have been loosened only in some areas, with changes being made recently in preparation for or as a part of the adoption of the North American Free Trade Agreement (NAFTA).

In 1973, the Law to Promote Mexican Investment and Regulate Foreign Investment (also known as the Foreign Investment Law (FIL)) was passed. It mandated that Mexican enterprises could have a maximum of 49 percent foreign ownership. Thus, the rule became known as the "51-49 percent rule." In 1984, the law was changed to allow majority foreign ownership of Mexican corporations in certain industrial and tourism-related industries. Such investment, however, was slow and cumbersome and was permitted only with the approval, on a case-by-case basis, of the Mexican Foreign Investment Commission (FIC). Abolition of this approval process, as well as liberalized foreign investment rules, were included in NAFTA.

THE MAQUILADORA PROGRAM. The Maquiladora program represents a major step by Mexico toward opening its borders to foreign investment. The program was started in 1966, but was not officially authorized by Mexican law until 1983. Under the program, a foreign company can establish a manufacturing facility in northern Mexico and can import equipment, components, and materials to Mexico duty-free, provided that a substantial percentage of the goods produced are exported from Mexico. A plant that operates under the program is called a *maquila*, and the legal structure for the manufacturing program is the *maquiladora*. Most *maquilas* in Mexico are operated in conjunction with a twin plant across the U.S. border. Thus, labor intensive production is done in the Mexican plant, while other aspects of production as well as marketing and distribution are typically handled by the plant in the United States. The 1983 Mexican law required that *maquilas* export at least 80 percent of their production, but new regulations in 1989 allowed up to 50 percent to be sold in Mexico under certain conditions. (It should also be noted that *maquilas* are also required to export their hazardous wastes generated in the production process to the home country of the investor or business.)

For Mexico, the maquiladora program has generated much needed employment. As of 1990, there were approximately 1,500 *maquilas* operating that employed 450,000 workers. U.S. businesses benefit from low labor costs in Mexico and duty-free export of the product from Mexico. Special U.S. tariff schedules place a duty only on the value added by Mexican components and labor.

NEW POLICIES, LAWS, AND REGULATIONS

Under the leadership of Carlos Salinas de Gortari, who served as President of Mexico from 1988 to 1994, Mexico negotiated and approved the North American Free Trade Agreement (NAFTA) with the United States and Canada. During the Salinas administration, several provisions of the Mexican Constitution were amended and new statutes and regulations were passed to facilitate Mexico's move from a protectionist economy to a global one. President Ernesto Zedillo Ponce de León took office in January of 1994 and has continued the economic policies instituted under former President Salinas de Gortari.

Under President Salinas, major changes facilitating foreign investment were made in at least four areas. First, Mexico's new agrarian laws included provisions allowing for foreign ownership of land that was formerly communally-owned. Second, amendments to Mexico's copyright law and a new industrial property law were passed in order to promote investment and prevent unfair competition. The changes also permit joint ventures between landowners and private investors to develop the land for industry or for farming. Third, businesses owned by the Mexican government were sold were sold to private investors. Also, a new 1990 banking law allows foreigners to hold up to a thirty percent ownership interest in a financial institution. (Privatization of those businesses raised funds which were used to help stabilize Mexico's economy.) Fourth, new foreign investment regulations issued in 1989 amended the 51-49 percent rule which limited foreign investment in an enterprise to forty-nine percent.

Upon certain conditions, the new Foreign Investment Regulations of 1989 automatically allow foreign ownership of businesses in Mexico without the prior approval of the Foreign Investment Commission (FIC) or the Ministry of Commerce and Industrial Development (SECOFI). Among those conditions are the following:

1. Foreign investment is limited to $100 million (U.S.);

2. industrial facilities cannot be located in Mexico City, Guadalajara, or Monterrey (areas of "high industrial concentration");

3. the company must train employees and create permanent jobs;

4. the company must abide by Mexico's environmental laws and regulations and use adequate technologies; and

5. the company cannot engage in certain classes of activities listed in the regulations as classified. The list of classified activities for which foreign investment was prohibited or severely limited under the 1989 regulations is extensive.

It should be noted that under the 1989 regulations, a company not meeting the requirements listed above has the option of seeking approval from the FIC. Further, such an application is automatically approved if the FIC does not respond to it within 45 days. However, it is important to note that such approval, either automatic or through FIC action, is not possible for those investments on the list of "classified" activities.

Pursuant to the 1989 regulations, certain activities are restricted in various categories. Among the categories are: (1) activities restricted to the Mexican government; (2) activities restricted to Mexican citizens; (3) Activities in which foreign investment is restricted to a certain percentage, those percentages being 34, 40 or 49 percent; and (5) a final category of activities where 100 percent foreign ownership may be approved by SECOFI and the FIC on a case-by-case basis. The 1989 regulations also exempt all foreign investors from obtaining prior SECOFI approval for any investment (even up to 100 percent) in a *Maquiladora*.

NAFTA'S LIBERALIZING EFFECT. NAFTA eliminates or lessens restrictions on many kinds of investment by U.S. and Canadian citizens and businesses in Mexico. (U.S. or Canadian investors in Mexico are referred to as "NAFTA investors.") Areas where increased opportunities for investment have been created include automotive goods, energy-related services and goods, transportation services, financial institutions, and others.

When NAFTA became effective on January 1, 1994, Mexico immediately removed investment restrictions to allow "NAFTA investors" to invest up to 100 percent in Mexican "national suppliers" of parts. Up to 49 percent of investment in other auto-parts businesses can be by NAFTA investors, with that limit being phased out (allowing up to 100 percent investment) by 1999.

Pursuant to NAFTA, Mexico continues to reserve for the Mexican state exclusive control of investments in oil, gas, refining, basic petrochemicals, electricity, and nuclear energy. However, NAFTA creates opportunities for NAFTA investors in "nonbasis" petrochemical goods and in cogeneration and independent power production.

Opportunities for investment in bus and trucking services have been created under NAFTA, also. By 1997, Mexico will allow NAFTA investors to hold up to a 49 percent investment in bus companies and truck companies that provide international cargo services. That percentage will be increased gradually until 2004, when Mexico will permit 100 percent ownership of such companies by NAFTA investors. Under NAFTA, Mexico is immediately allowing NAFTA investors to own 100 percent of port facilities such as cranes, piers, and terminals for their own cargo. For businesses handling other companies' cargo, 100 percent ownership by NAFTA investors will be allowed contingent upon approval by the Mexican Foreign Investment Commission.

Under NAFTA, Mexico will permit financial institutions organized according to the laws of the United States or Canada to establish such institutions in Mexico. Certain market share limitations will be applied initially, but they will be phased out by the year 2000. Mexico will gradually increase its limits on foreign investment in banking (based on an aggregate market share) from 8 percent to 15 percent by 2004. For securities firms, the limit will increase from 10 percent to 20 percent by 2004. NAFTA investors will be permitted to invest in Mexico in two ways. First they may participate in joint ventures with Mexican insurers, with a phase-in period that will permit 30 percent foreign equity in 1994 rising to 100 percent by the year 2000. Second, insurers from the United States or Mexico may establish subsidiaries, which will be subject to limits on market share that will be phased out gradually. Those limits will be eliminated on January 1, 2000.

MEXICO'S LABOR LAWS

Mexico's labor laws include extensive rights for workers, and, in theory, are designed to provide a mechanism promoting a "just" society. Some of the constitutional provisions do give workers rights and protections that U.S. businesses are not required to provide to their employees in the United States. However, actual application and operation of Mexico's guarantees does not always live up to the words of the Mexican constitution and its statutes. Thus, a description of Mexico's labor laws, such as is given in the paragraphs below, does not provide an accurate picture of actual working conditions for most Mexican workers. Most of Mexico's workers receive insufficient incomes to support their families comfortably, and many work under conditions that threaten their health or safety on a daily or long-term basis. Further, certain guarantees can be circumvented. For example, it is said that Mexican employers avoid hiring women in many cases in order to avoid paying maternity and child care benefits.

The cornerstone of Mexico's labor laws is Article 123 of the Constitution of 1917. Article 123, entitled "Labor and Social Security" was written in response to conditions under the Porfiria regime, during which working conditions were abysmal and unions and strikes by workers were suppressed with violence. Article 123 states that every person "is entitled to suitable work that is socially useful. Toward this end, the creation of jobs and social organizations for labor shall be promoted in conformance with the law." Article 123 provides various protections and guarantees to workers, including an eight-hour work day, a maximum work week of six days, equal pay for equal work, and mandatory childbirth and maternity leave. Mexico's Congress is authorized to enact laws to implement these guarantees and protections and is directed to establish a minimum wage with the authority to consider occupation and geographical areas. According to Article 123, workers are entitled to double pay for overtime work. Also, employers are required to provide employees with a safe workplace and disability pay for work-related injuries. Further, workers are guaranteed the right to form unions and bargain collectively. Workers' rights to organize strikes are recognized, and the rights of employers to impose a lockout, under certain conditions, are recognized. A provision that is unexpected by most U.S. business people is that workers are legally entitled to an 8 percent share of the taxable income of their employers. A second section of Article 123 guarantee the rights of government employees, giving them most of the same rights given to other Mexican workers, although there is no right for them to join unions.

Pursuant to Article 123, all Mexican workers are protected from arbitrary dismissal (unjustifiable discharge). Thus, to some extent, job security is constitutionally guaranteed to the Mexican people. If a business is sold, the new owner must adhere to any existing contract with the workers. These provisions and others in Article 123 illustrate that Mexico's 1917 Constitution is remarkably detailed, and, for its time, set forth remarkably progressive social goals and policies.

Various federal labor "decrees" supplement the provisions of Article 123 of Mexico's Constitution. The most extensive of these is the Mexican Federal Labor Act of 1970, which is a long, detailed statute strengthening the constitutional rights of Mexican workers and placing additional restrictions and duties on employers. Collective bargaining agreements are enforced with the same force as if they were law. A collective bargaining agreement may contain a "closed shop" clause, so long as it is not applied against nonunion workers who were employed prior to the adoption of the agreement.

There are more than 20 million workers in Mexico. Observers say that between 30 and 70 percent of

Mexico's workers are unionized. Unionization is more prevalent in manufacturing than in service-related work. Most Mexican unions are affiliated with regional or national federations, the largest of which is the Mexican Workers Confederation (*Confederacion de Trabajadores Mexicanos*, or CTM). It is estimated that up to 70 percent of all unionized workers in Mexico are affiliated with the CTM.

Although unions are prohibited by statute from ''interfering in political matters,'' in practice that prohibition is ignored. Most trade unions in Mexico, including the CTM, work closely with the dominant PRI political party. The PRI has won all presidential elections since 1928 and has won most Mexican state elections since then also. The CTM rallies labor support for the PRI and is viewed as a significant factor in the PRI's steady record in maintaining political control in Mexico.

Simultaneously, through legal and political mechanisms, Mexico's government maintains a significant degree of control over union operations and affairs. Mexican law requires that labor unions and their leaders be recognized by the government. Thus, independent labor unions can exist, but they are at a disadvantage in dealing with government because often they are not recognized by the Ministry of Labor. On the other hand, a union that is recognized by the PRI and that has leaders who support the PRI has distinct advantages. A labor leader can maintain his (or her) position and power in the union by maintaining close ties with the PRI. Leaders of the CTM who cooperate with the PRI are often offered positions within the federal government as well as in state and local government. Further, there are many reports regarding union leaders who have received substantial bribes from managers, contractors, and others as a result of their public positions.

Collective bargaining agreements generally include provisions on grievance procedures and job security, and they set wages and fringe benefits. Although most agreements set wages that are somewhat higher than the minimums set by Mexican law, even wages agreed upon through collective bargaining are generally only 20 percent (or less) of the amounts typically paid for similar work in the United States. As of 1994, minimum wages set by the Mexican government equalled only about 86 cents (U.S.) per hour, and during the 1980s and early 1990s, wage agreements were consistently negotiated at levels significantly below the rate of inflation in Mexico. (Mexico experienced severe inflation in the late 1980s, which peaked at a rate of about 150 percent around 1986-87.) Therefore, U.S. businesses have been attracted to Mexico to take advantage of lower labor costs than in the United States.

In theory, a U.S. business establishing a manufacturing facility within Mexico can choose its own workers. In practice, however, in at least some cities, political pressures will be such that the U.S. business finds itself compelled to work with the local union and the PRI and to hire workers who have sought jobs through the union.

OVERVIEW OF MEXICO'S ENVIRONMENTAL LAW & ENFORCEMENT

In recent decades, Mexico has been considered a ''pollution haven'' for companies wishing to avoid the more stringent United States' federal and state environmental laws and their enforcement. The worst offenders appear to be the *Maquiladora* factories located along the U.S.-Mexican border. Pursuant to the *Maquiladora* program, raw materials are brought from the United States and assembled in the Mexican plant, with the final product shipped back to the United States. Cancer and birth defect rates are notoriously high in both northern Mexico and in U.S. cities across the border from the plants as a result of air and water pollution.

It must be noted, however, that compared to the United States, Mexico is in its infancy in terms of enactment and enforcement of environmental laws and regulations. Most U.S. environmental laws and their enforcement date from the 1960s and 1970s, while Mexico's General Law on Ecological Equilibrium and Environmental Protection (the *Codigo Ecológico* or General Ecology Law) wasn't passed until 1988.

U.S. companies contemplating doing business in Mexico should be aware, however, that enforcement of Mexican environmental laws and regulations has become more vigorous since 1988, and that trend is expected to continue. From 1988 to 1993, Mexico's environmental enforcement budget increased from $6.6 billion (U.S.) to $77 billion (U.S.), and the number of Mexican environmental inspectors in the border area was increased from 50 to 200. During the six years preceding 1993, environmental compliance inspections resulted in orders closing about 2,000 facilities temporarily for noncompliance. Between June of 1992 and early 1994, Mexican officials conducted over 16,000 inspections of industrial facilities were conducted, 2,400 of them in the area of Mexico's border with the United States. Over 100 facilities have been closed permanently, including a large PEMEX plant near Mexico City. (PEMEX is the Mexican government-owned business that controls the production and sale of petroleum products throughout Mexico.)

In 1992, the U.S. and Mexico agreed to a comprehensive plan to clean up environmental contamination along the 2,000 mile U.S.-Mexican border. They committed a total of about $700 billion to programs to improve pollution control, strengthen environmental enforcement, and increase planning and education. In 1993, Mexico obtained a $1.8 billion loan from the World Bank to strengthen its enforcement of environmental laws in the border area.

In response to concerns about the massive environmental problems in the U.S.-Mexico border area, the United States and Mexico entered into two additional agreements which were approved with in conjunction with NAFTA. The agreements establish a North American Development Bank (NAD Bank) and a Border Environmental Cooperation Commission (BECC). The NAD Bank will provide financing for environmental infrastructure in the border area. The United States and Mexico are each contributing $56 million (U.S.) in paid in capital for each of the first four years of operations. The BECC will work with states, local governments, and nongovernmental organizations to provide technical and financial planning.

PROVISIONS OF MEXICO'S ENVIRONMENTAL LAWS

Mexico's "Código Ecológico," known in English as the "General Ecology Law," was adopted in 1988. It is a comprehensive environmental statute addressing water, air, and ground pollution; resource conservation; and environmental enforcement. The General Ecology Law was modeled on U.S. environmental laws, and its provisions closely parallel those of the Clean Air Act, **Clean Water Act**, and Resource Conservation and Recovery (which regulates handling and storage of wastes). For example, in the area of waste disposal, Mexico's regulations require that generators of waste register with the Registry of Hazardous Waste Generators. They must also store, handle, and label hazardous waste in accordance with government standards. Mexican law requires that polluters pay for clean-up of industrial waste sites, although that requirement, to date, is not actively enforced. However, Mexico does not have community right to know and emergency planning and response provisions such as those included in the 1986 Amendments to the U.S. **Comprehensive Environmental Response, Clean-up and Liability Act (CERCLA) of 1980 (Superfund)**.

During its short history the General Ecology Law has been administered by various agencies. The law and regulations implementing it were placed under the jurisdiction of the Secretary of Urban Development and Ecology (SEDUE) in 1988. In 1992, SEDUE was abolished and the federal Secretariat of Social Development (Secretaria de Desarrollo Social—SEDESOL) took over that responsibility. As of 1994, the Mexican government removed environmental enforcement from the jurisdiction of SEDESOL. At the present, the National Institute for Ecology (Ecology Institute) is responsible for formulating environmental policy and setting regulations implementing the General Ecology Law. It also issues standards, known in English as "NOMS," which stands for "Normas Oficiales Mexicanos." The Procurarduria Federal De Proteccion al Ambiente (PFPA—Federal Attorney General for Environmental Protection) is responsible for enforcement of the law and regulations implementing it.

All industrial facilities, including maquiladoras, must comply with Mexico's environmental registration, licensing, and reporting requirements. The Attorney General's office carries out inspections and works with the National Institute of Ecology to decide how to handle cases in which a company is not in compliance with environmental laws.

It should be noted that Mexico's environmental laws will become more accessible to U.S. business people in the foreseeable future due to the efforts of the Commission for Environmental Cooperation (CEC). That Commission, which was established by the U.S., Mexico, and Canada pursuant to the Environmental Side Agreement to NAFTA, is in the process of compiling the environmental laws of the three countries. That information will be available to business people and their attorneys through the Internet, first in English and later in Spanish and French.

All industrial facilities, including *Maquiladoras*, must comply with Mexico's environmental registration, licensing, and reporting requirements. In order to operate legally, each facility must obtain an Environmental Operating License. The application for such a license must be accompanied by a statement describing the facility's potential impact on the environment. The attorney general has the authority, based on information in that statement, to require that a full environmental impact study be conducted as a precondition to issuing the license.

The General Ecology Law regulates air pollution from both stationary sources (such as industrial facilities) and mobile sources (such as automobiles and buses). For industrial facilities, the General Ecology Law establishes ambient air quality standards called Maximum Permanent Levels (MPL's) that are identical to those in the United States EPA's National Ambient Air Quality Standards (NAAQS). Mexico uses a source permitting system that is administered by the federal SEDESOL. This regulatory structure differs from that used in the United States where, under the **Clean Air Act**, air quality attainment is administered pursuant to State Implementation Plans (SIPs). Mexico's standards for many chemical emissions such as sulphur dioxide are much lower than those set by the

EPA. However, it is in the process of developing higher standards.

The General Ecology Law regulates water pollution resulting from a wide range of activities including: (1) releases from municipalities and industrial, agricultural, and livestock activities; (2) use of pesticides and fertilizers; (3) use of toxic substances at industrial facilities; (4) solid waste dumping; and (5) discharges seeping into aquifers. It should be noted that unlike U.S. federal environmental law, Mexico's law also applies to discharges into groundwater. SEDESOL is in the process of developing regulations covering waste water treatment facilities. (A lack of such facilities is a major problem throughout Mexico at the present.)

Mexico's regulation of hazardous wastes is similar to regulation in the United States pursuant to RCRA. Hazardous wastes and even raw materials must be stored according to the Ecology Institute's regulations. Any plant generating wastes considered to be ''hazardous'' must obtain a generator's license and number from the attorney general. Mexico regulates the handling and transportation of hazardous materials, products or wastes in a manner that is similar to the ''Manifest'' system used in the United States pursuant to RCRA. In Mexico, each shipment of hazardous materials must be accompanied by an ''Ecological Waybill'' which is used to document the shipment's contents, its handling, and its destination. Each industrial facility must keep a permanent record of all hazardous materials on its premises. Companies generating hazardous waste must file a report every two years with Mexican officials.

CONCLUSION

As U.S. businesses increase their trade with Mexico and locate their facilities within Mexico, an understanding of Mexican law and Mexico's legal system will be crucial. Further, as the economies of the two countries become increasingly intertwined thanks to NAFTA, changes in Mexico's laws as well as more stringent enforcement of Mexico's existing laws can be expected.

[Paulette L. Stenzel]

FURTHER READING:

Avalos, Francisco A. *The Mexican Legal System.* New York: Greenwood Press, 1992.

Bartow, Ann M. ''The Rights of Workers in Mexico.'' *Comparative Labor Law Journal.* 11, 1990, pp. 182-202.

Goldin, Amy H. ''Collective Bargaining in Mexico: Stifled by the Lack of Democracy in Trade Unions.'' *Comparative Labor Law Journal.* 11, 1990, pp. 203-225.

Krumholz, Dennis J. ''Under NAFTA, Mexico No Safe Have for Polluters.'' *New Jersey Law Journal.* 133, April 5, 1993, pp. 4, 18-19.

Levy, Charles S., and John J. Kim. ''Outline of NAFTA-Related and International Environmental Issues.'' Paper distributed at the 23rd Annual Conference on Environmental Law of the American Bar Association Section of Natural Resources, Energy, and Environmental Law, Keystone Colorado, March 10-13, 1994.

Newman, Gray. *Business Internationals Guide to Doing Business in Mexico.* New York: McGraw-Hill, 1992.

North American Free Trade Agreement (NAFTA). Washington, DC: U.S. Government Printing Office, 1993.

Silva, Jesus, and Richard K. Dunn. ''A Free Trade Agreement Between the United States and Mexico: The Right Choice?'' *San Diego Law Review.* 27, 1990. pp. 937-992.

Villegas, Daniel Cosio et. al. *A Compact History of Mexico*, 2nd ed. Mexico, D.F.: Colegio de Mexico, 1985.

MEXICO, DOING BUSINESS IN

Mexico is, after Brazil, the second-largest economy in Latin America. At the time the Canadian prime minister and the U.S. president signed the **North American Free Trade Agreement** (NAFTA) with Mexico in 1992, Mexico had a **gross national product** (GNP) of well over $250 billion with pre-NAFTA exports (75 percent of which went to the United States) of just under $40 billion.

Mexico is also, again after Brazil, the second-biggest country in Latin America both geographically and in terms of population. Mexico covers approximately 760,000 square miles, divided into 31 states and the federal district of Mexico City, its capital. Mexico City is the world's largest city with a population of approximately 20 million people, a figure expected to exceed 32 million people by the end of the century. Mexico's two other great industrial cities, Guadalajara and Monterrey, both have exploded from being relatively small cities to having populations of well over 3.5 million and 3 million, respectively. The nation as a whole has a population of approximately 88 million, making it the most populous Spanish-speaking nation in the world.

Mexico has been the focus of considerable attention in the business world with the signing of NAFTA in 1992 and its legislative approval in Canada and the United States in 1994. NAFTA represents an arrangement by which the three nations of North America agreed to reduce tariffs and coordinate limited facets of their trade policy.

NAFTA was of particular importance for Mexico as it represented the first instance in which any developing nation entered into an economic arrangement with two major developed nations. In essence, NAFTA thrust Mexico from a developing nation status to that of the 67 developed nations. For Mexico too, NAFTA cemented for the long term its economic relationship with the United States and Canada while paving the way for increased trade and investment.

CURRENT ECONOMIC EVENTS IN MEXICO

Arguably the strongest economic period in Mexico's history is currently underway. Well before the flurry of attention surrounding NAFTA, Mexico had much to commend itself in the economic sphere. Reaching a postwar low point tied to the collapse of oil prices in the early 1980s, Mexico officially indicated that it had to default on its debt payments and foreign investment fled Mexico while the Mexican peso was devalued by almost 50 percent. By 1987, Mexico was experiencing an annualized **inflation** rate of over 130 percent.

Following the election of President Carlos Salinas de Gortari in 1988, Mexico transformed itself. President Salinas negotiated debt relief from the United States, including a $3.5 billion "debt bridge" loan. Under the Salinas presidency, Mexico privatized more than 100 of its 1,100 state-owned firms in dozens of areas ranging from telecommunications to banking. Mexico's **debt** reduction and **privatization** coupled with an anticorruption campaign and tax restructuring transformed Mexico dramatically cutting its inflation rate, attracting **foreign investment** from around the globe, spurring a rebirth of private enterprise, and supporting a thriving stock exchange. All of this culminated with the full legislative approval of the three NAFTA nations in 1994.

BUSINESS PRACTICES

With the current strength of the Mexican economy and the opening up of Mexico under NAFTA, considerable interest in Mexican business practices has developed.

Mexican business culture differs from any other in the Americas due to its unique history. Moreover, it is profoundly different from the United States whose long northern border it shares.

LANGUAGE. Mexico is the largest Spanish-speaking country in the world. Its form of Spanish is distinctive, drawing heavily on speakers of pre-Columbian native languages and filled with many idioms unique to Mexican Spanish.

Spanish as a language is a useful tool when doing business in Mexico both because it gives access to the large number of Mexicans who speak only Spanish or who speak other languages poorly.

Nevertheless, English is extremely widespread, especially among the educated and the middle class who constitute the majority of the business class in

Mexico. Many government officials and business leaders received degrees from U.S. or Canadian universities, increasing the number of people in leading positions who speak English with great fluency. Indeed, many Mexicans may view the ability to conduct business in English as a sign of their education—suggestions that their use of English is less than fluent or even absent may be a source of loss of face.

While speaking the language of the country in which one conducts business is always advisable for gaining market insight and building relationships, the use of Spanish in Mexico by U.S. businesspeople is of particular value since Mexicans have come to expect that the majority of U.S. businesspeople with whom they come in contact will speak little or no Spanish. For this reason alone, it is an advantage for the U.S. businessperson to learn to speak Spanish as it will likely reflect a presumed interest in and commitment to Mexico that the non-Spanish speaker would have to demonstrate in other ways.

ENVIRONMENT AND TECHNOLOGY. Mexico traditionally has been more ambivalent toward the use of technology than the United States and other control cultures. Mexicans, particularly in nonurban areas, are more likely to see themselves as subject to the forces of nature around them than as controllers of that environment.

Current severe difficulties with pollution and other environmental problems have brought the cost of rapid industrialization further into question in urban areas as well, reviving some traditional skepticism toward the use of technology for its own end. Still, Mexico is rapidly increasing its technological standards. Its infrastructure—**telecommunications**, transportation, and electronics—have all seen dramatic improvement in the last two decades.

SOCIAL ORGANIZATION

FAMILY TIES. Family ties are considerably stronger in Mexico than they are in the United States. "Family," as Eva S. Kras explained, "takes precedence over work and all other aspects of life." Moreover, family ties are not only stronger but broader in Mexico than in the United States. The family in the United States consists of a spouse and children (and occasionally one's parents). In Mexico, family ties are equally strong for kinship relationships such as cousins, in-laws, uncles and aunts, nephews and nieces, as well as *compadrazco* or godparent relationships.

This has far-reaching effects on Mexican-U.S. interactions. The majority of Mexicans define themselves as belonging to a particular family; the majority of people in the United States define themselves by what they do for a living. Thus a Mexican manager is likely to respond first to a query for a self-description with the fact that he or she is a member of the families of his or her father, mother, and spouse. By contrast the average U.S. manager would respond to the same query with the fact that he or she is a manager of some area of specialty. This has direct business application in the way these familial connections are used in the workplace. As John C. Condon explained, ''In Mexico credibility is demonstrated more through position and connections than in the U.S., where one's track record of personal achievements tends to command attention.''

The effect of family on business, however, goes much further than self-definition. Family ties provide access to business joint ventures, to favorable terms on negotiations, and to reaching people in power in Mexico. Family ties provide little of this in the United States. The result is that many U.S. businesspeople in Mexico may not be able to reach people in power in Mexico because they do not know how to employ such connections, while many Mexicans in the United States may place greater faith on such connections than their situation merits.

Finally, **nepotism**—the hiring of relatives—is considered desirable in Mexico and undesirable in the United States. In Mexico, relatives one employs are likely to work harder and be more dedicated than strangers. In the United States, relatives are likely to work less hard and be less dedicated than strangers. In Mexico, nepotism ensures access and loyalty through family ties while fulfilling familial obligations to other family members related to the individual hired (even further strengthening and extending the reach of connections with relatives not hired). Nepotism, by contrast, is disdained in the United States where family ties are assumed to cover up the relative's incompetence; indeed, many organizations in the United States have explicit antinepotism policies.

GENDER ROLES. The genders are more clearly differentiated in Mexico than in the United States. This especially holds true in Mexican social settings where men are more likely than in the United States to rule their households with little open disagreement from wives and where any unchaperoned male-female meetings may be called into question in a way that they would not north of the border.

Machismo does exist in Mexico. Nevertheless, the concept of ''machismo'' is largely misunderstood and exaggerated in the United States. Machismo—essentially the state of acting in a manly manner—is usually misinterpreted in the United States as male boasting of a sexual nature (which is extremely uncommon in the Mexican corporate setting) and a more blatant use of sexually charged stares and innuendos (which do occur at an arguably greater rate but no more so than in, for example, French or Italian culture for which the same concerns are not widely held in the

United States). Machismo, however, also includes a man's sense of earned respect through education (including knowledge of the liberal arts—a distinctly unmacho assumption in the United States), titles, and other distinctions. Finally, machismo includes a sense that men must be decisive and unwilling to show fear—a gender distinction still widely practiced in the United States.

While gender distinctions are more strongly delineated in Mexico than in the United States, Mexico is undergoing a transition as well. Many Mexican women, particularly in the large urban centers, are increasingly active in professional settings ranging from university professors to government leaders and entrepreneurs. Finally, many Mexicans are growing accustomed to the large number of women in the United States and Canada in leading business positions and have become increasingly familiar with working with these foreign businesswomen in positions of authority.

CLASS STRATIFICATION. Advanced education is very widespread in the corporate United States. Indeed, graduate and doctoral degrees are very common in the workplace. Higher education in Mexico is common among business leaders but is nowhere as widespread among the general population as it is in the United States. Among the educated elite, however, the quality and breadth of education is likely to be very high, often including study abroad in the United States, Canada, or Europe, as well as domestically in Mexico.

Educational ties may play a greater role in Mexico than in the United States. Alumni ties as common bonds are strong as they represent a shared experience—a factor that is important in the more personalized nature of business in Mexico described below. The nature of the university is important as well. Foreign education is much more common among upper-level Mexican executives than among their counterparts in the United States, and those educated abroad, of course, are likely to reflect the emphases of the educational institutions of the countries in which they studied. Domestically in Mexico, private universities differ markedly from public universities in their educational emphasis; a distinction almost wholly absent in U.S. public and private colleges. Such private institutions of higher education as the prestigious Instituto Tecnologico y Estudios Superiores de Monterrey (ITESM) and La Salle University in Mexico City emphasize analytical approaches applied to business, legal, and technical education. Public universities, by contrast, reflect a more European-based generalist education with a highly theoretical emphasis by U.S. business or technological education standards.

REGIONALISM. Mexico is divided into numerous regions, each with distinctive histories, accents, and loyalties. Most Mexicans are very proud of their region, and many Mexicans claim ties to the region of their parents even if they were born in a distant urban center such as Mexico City. Mexicans themselves carry many stereotypes and beliefs regarding characteristics of these regions. For example, people from Nuevo Leon are perceived as being very business-oriented and thrifty; people from Oaxaca may be proud of the influence of native Indian cultures, and so forth. Whether true or not, these generalizations are more strongly held than comparable divisions of northerners and southerners in the United States and represent very real points of connection for the business-person aware of their significance.

In recent decades, many Mexicans have been attracted to Mexico's urban centers in the search for jobs and opportunities. While all of Mexico's major cities have seen influxes from the countryside, Mexico City—now the world's largest city—has grown at a pace unmatched anywhere in the industrialized world. Less dramatic but still major migrations of people to Monterrey and Guadalajara have also occurred. These magnet cities represent a major demographic shift for Mexico and break with traditional ties to region and family.

THE CHURCH. Mexico is among the most uniformly Roman Catholic nations. While several hundred-thousand Protestants and several thousand Jews represent significant minorities, Mexico has nowhere near the mix of religion as the United States. Also, while technically Mexico has a separation of church and state (including a period of heavy anticlerical activity early in the twentieth century), the role of religion may seem pervasive by U.S. standards. Conflict of religion in the workplace is negligible since Catholicism is so widely shared; consequently such practices as having a priest bless a new office building or corporate sponsorship of a religious procession are well accepted. Display of religious imagery in the workplace is likewise common and well accepted; by contrast, religion is usually intensely personal in the United States, a fact that makes many Mexicans view their U.S. counterparts as irreligious or at least highly secularized. Widespread belief in God's influence in the workplace (as in all aspects of life) may also provide some Mexicans with more of a sense of acceptance of events that might be fought against in the United States.

CONTEXTING. Mexico is what is called a high context culture As a result, Mexicans place a strong emphasis on how a message is said rather than on the words used alone. The eloquence of the words used are themselves part of the message. Something may be exaggerated in a way known to be an exaggeration but spoken because it is rhetorically satisfying; this is often understood to be lying in the literal understand-

ing of low context cultures such as the United States.

Messages are also understood in terms of the full context of the communicators' relationship with one another. This particularly affects the importance for social etiquette and formality in official situations (including business meetings) and creates an emphasis on face-saving.

As a direct consequence of the high context nature of Mexican communication, it is necessary to build a personal relationship in conducting business with Mexicans. Without the context of that personal relationship, little if any substantive communication can take place, and necessary levels of trust are inadequate to undertake most business arrangements.

As in most high context cultures, Mexican behavior is more likely to be governed by individual interpretation and the need to save face rather than on external rules and regulations. As a result, in Mexico, personal understandings are more binding than contracts. Indeed, contracts in Mexico are often seen as the beginning of a relationship that can be subject to change as the business progresses. This contrasts to the view of low context cultures (such as the United States) in which the contract is viewed as not subject to change.

Finally, in high context societies, understood or unofficial rules are often as important (or even more important) than written rules. This holds true even in relations with government officials. These unwritten rules deal often with issues of respect and family loyalty in Mexico, and remain subject to the context of the situation to which they are applied. As a result, these unwritten rules may be employed in some instances and overlooked in others, depending on the context of the individuals involved and of the situation particular to the incident at hand.

NONVERBAL COMMUNICATION

As with all nations, Mexico has distinctive nonverbal communication unique to itself. It contrasts markedly with the United States in the four areas described below.

PERSONAL SPACE. Mexican concepts of personal distance are considerably closer than in the United States. The average workplace distance while standing face-to-face between two people in the United States is roughly arm's length. While regional differences are notable in Mexico (with interpersonal distance greater as one moves north), the average distance is approximately three to four inches closer than in the United States.

TOUCHING BEHAVIOR. The United States is an ahaptic (or non-touching) culture. Mexico, by contrast, is a much more haptic culture. Most workplace touching in the United States is limited to the handshake. Even the handshake is minimal, limited to one hand and a relatively short duration. Mexican touching behavior is considerably more extensive. Common workplace interactions would likely include back-patting, greeting hugs between men as well as women, and handshakes using both hands often reaching to the upper arm.

MOVEMENT. Movement (kinesics) differs somewhat in Mexico and the United States. Lacking the large waves of immigration that have influenced U.S. body language, Mexicans are more uniform in the sorts of body movement they use when speaking. Generally speaking, Mexicans are more expressive with the hands than many of their U.S. counterparts. Also, most U.S. movement is limited to the arms and head; movement from the torso is not uncommon in Mexican conversation. Finally, most people in the United States, even in formal situations, tend to slouch while sitting; slouching in Mexico is usually a sign of boredom and is thus subject to misinterpretation.

DRESS. Mexicans tend to dress more conservatively in Mexico City than elsewhere in the country. Still, as a whole, business as well as social dress is somewhat more conservative throughout Mexico than it is in the United States. Details—such as shined shoes or well-groomed hair—are often more important in business dress in Mexico than they are in the United States.

TIME CONCEPTION

Mexico and the United States are extremely different in the way each conceives of time. Mexico is what Edward T. Hall termed a polychronic culture; the United States, a monochronic one. Mexico, like all polychronic cultures, ranks personal involvement and completion of existing transactions above the demands of preset schedules. The United States, like other monochronic cultures, adheres to preset schedules which take precedence over personal interaction or the completion of the business at hand.

Because Mexican businesspeople generally complete tasks at the expense of scheduling, people in high authority may become easily overwhelmed with multiple tasks. To prevent overloading, people in positions of high authority rely heavily on subordinates to screen for them. Once a person gets past those screening, the person in authority will generally see the task to completion regardless of its relative importance. By contrast, in the United States, the scheduling of appointments acts as the screen; not the person's subordinates. If a task is not completed within a scheduled time, a new meeting is scheduled.

Because people rather than appointment books act as the screens in Mexico, personal relationships flourish within close circles. In the United States,

personal relationships are discouraged or at least are not allowed to interfere with maintaining the schedule. As a result, in the United States, personal relationships are determined by the terms of the job in a manner that is nearly incomprehensible in Mexico. Conversely, personal relationships are emphasized in the Mexican workplace in a manner that is difficult for most U.S. businesspeople to comprehend. Mexicans make distinctions between insiders and those outside their existing personal relationships. Appointments are secondary. In the United States, one needs only to schedule a meeting with the appropriate people; little or no preference is given to those one knows over complete strangers. In the United States (in direct contrast to Mexico), the outsider is treated in exactly the same fashion as the close associate.

[David A. Victor]

FURTHER READING:

Condon, John C. *Good Neighbors; Communicating with the Mexicans.* Yarmouth, ME: Intercultural Press, 1985.

Hall, Edward T. *The Dance of Life: The Other Dimension of Time.* Garden City, NY: Anchor Press/Doubleday, 1984.

Kras, Eva S. *Management in Two Cultures: Bridging the Gap Between U.S. and Mexican Managers.* Yarmouth, ME: Intercultural Press, 1988.

Paz, Octavio. *The Labyrinth of Solitude: Life and Thought in Mexico.* NY: Grove Press, 1961.

Riding, Alan. *Distant Neighbors: A Portrait of the Mexicans.* NY: Vintage Books, 1984.

Victor, David A. *International Business Communication.* NY: HarperCollins, 1992.

MICROCOMPUTERS IN BUSINESS

Microcomputers form the digital infrastructure of modern business operations. Compared to mainframe and minicomputers, microcomputers offer less computing power and correspondingly smaller physical dimensions. Current powerful microcomputers, however, exceed processing power of yesterday's mainframe and afford generous capabilities for business use. Typically less expensive than mainframe and minicomputers, microcomputers digitize information in the same way and for the same reason. By converting information to coded binary representations, microcomputers capitalize on the extremely reliable and fast operations of a microchip processing unit. Microcomputers rely on a binary coding system to relay basic instructions of an operating system. In binary code, a 0 and a 1 represent a bit of information which is transmitted by the presence or absence of an electric signal. 8 bits of information, or a byte, combine to represent an alphabetic, numeric, or special character. The American Standard Code for Information Interchange (ASCII) forms the standard for text-based information systems.

Well suited in capability and price for business use, microcomputers rely on five key functions to digitally manipulate information: input, processing, output, storage, and control. Physical components—computer hardware—offer the necessary equipment to transfer digitized information. Software programs, or digital manipulation packages, enable the efficient creation and control of machine-readable code. Popular business applications available for microcomputers include spreadsheets, word processors, database management, decision support, graphics, communications, and networking software. Illustrations of business use include transactional, knowledge-based, office automation, management information, decision support, and executive support systems. Spanning the continuum of financial, marketing, managerial, production, and personnel activities, microcomputers pervade almost every aspect of business operations. Ethical questions and concerns for security and privacy accompany the broad use of the microcomputer in business as well as society as a whole. Networked systems of information expand access and leverage information value yet create profound issues of privacy, security, and inquiry. Microcomputers remain the most revolutionary development of the last 50 years and are embraced at all levels of business interest.

HISTORICAL BACKGROUND

In the seventeenth century, the French mathematician Blaise Pascal (1623-62) and the German mathematician Gottfried Leibnitz (1646-1716) almost simultaneously developed the adding machine. Because all mathematical operations in a microcomputer are based on addition and subtraction, the microcomputer owes a great debt to the efforts of these earliest pioneers as well as others. In 1833, British mathematician Charles Babbage (1792-1871) introduced an analytical machine capable of automatically executing a series of mechanized instructions. By the 1940s and 1950s, computer development accelerated to create the first generation of computing: the vacuum tube age. Electric signals transmitted through vacuum tubes created the first mainframe computers, including the ENIAC computer. By virtue of their size, however, vacuum computers remained large and expensive. The vacuum tube soon gave way to smaller and less expensive transistors. A transistor is a small solid-state semiconducting device that relays binary code. Smaller and more cheaply produced, transistor technology fueled the downward spiral of computer cost. By the 1960s, the third generation of computing was well underway with the advent of integrated circuitry. Integrated circuits etch physical pathways onto a semiconducting material, most notably silicon,

to relay binary information. This integrated circuitry accommodated greater complexity of transmission patterns and control. In 1981, International Business Machines (IBM) introduced the first personal microcomputer, the Personal Computer or PC. Combined with increasingly smaller and cheaper components, these personal computers became affordable and easier to use in the 1980s. The current generation of computing, the parallel processing age, employs more than one central processing activity in coordination and synchronization with other processors to further enhance computer capabilities. Though still relatively expensive, microcomputers with parallel processors represent a significant development for complex business activities and operations.

COMPUTER HARDWARE

A computer is a machine capable of receiving, processing, transmitting, storing, and manipulating digital information. Input, process, output, storage, and control functions map directly to the necessary physical hardware components. Together, these functions and components interact as a system and provide information and feedback for continued operation. To receive information, the microcomputer must recognize it in machine-readable format. Input devices transform human touch, sound, and look to digital strings of 0s and 1s. Popular input devices include both keyboard and mouse. A keyboard accepts typed input and converts it to digital format. A mouse maps movement on the desktop plane to a screen display. Other input devices include voice recognition, touch screen, light pen, and graphical capture and conversion machines like fax, scanner, and digital video. Once translated to digital information, a central processing unit (CPU) handles the sorting, selecting and routing of signals. The CPU dictates processing strength and speed. Output through video monitors, printers, and speakers relays computer generated information to the computer user. When information is inactive or not in use, it resides in the primary and secondary storage drives of the system. Hard drives contain large storage areas for digital information. Storage appears internally as well as externally and fixed as well as mobile. External drives plug into the CPU via a socket or pin connection and cable in the back of the computer. Internal drives reside inside the computer CPU casing. Fixed storage resides inside the computer CPU casing while mobile storage include both external hard drive and disk storage. Floppy disks appear as both 3½-inch and 5¼-inch formats according to their physical dimensions. Control activities are performed by a special section of the CPU to coordinate, overall, the instructions to the system. A modem provides another type of control activity. By converting phone signals to computer signals, modems enable computer-based communication with other computers and computer users. A common configuration of a microcomputer system includes a CPU, monitor, keyboard, mouse, modem, and printer. Microcomputer hardware can be classified by size. Handheld, notebook, laptop, portable, desktop, and floor models constitute a wide range of choices ranging from smallest to largest respectively. Smaller and more portable microcomputers increasingly support business activities that require mobility.

COMPUTER SOFTWARE

While the microcomputer components form a system based on electrical connections, another system appears in the arrangement of the computer's instructions. At the core, a computer program is a series of coded instructions to the central processing unit and other hardware devices to perform specified tasks at designated signals. The operating system (OS) comprises the essential computer program. Software platforms, synonymous with operating systems, splits the market in the United States, between DOS (Disk Operating System), Macintosh, and UNIX variant operating systems, with DOS-based machines dominating business use. Popular software programs include word processing, decision support, database management, graphics, communications and spreadsheet, and networking applications.

Word processing programs capture, edit, and store typed input such as letters, memos, reports, and other documents. Templates archive and expedite routine forms. Input can be entered using a keyboard or digitally scanned. Document scanners convert pictures of printed information into machine-readable format. Decision support programs offer expert advice and assistance in decision making and problem solving. Considered to be Knowledge Based Information Systems (KBIS), **decision support systems (DSS)** and **expert systems** combine specialized knowledge and a custom searching program to offer descriptive, interpretive, and predictive information. **Database management** programs provide storage and retrieval functionality. Typically, a database is composed of records, with each record consisting of a series of fields of information. Graphics programs enable the creation and representation of images. Communications programs coordinate the outgoing signals often transmitted using a modem and a phone line. Spreadsheet programs capture, manipulate, and calculate numeric information. Financial documents, reports, and what-if scenarios may be represented using spreadsheet software. Finally, networking software enables individual computers to connect with other computers using a common operating system and shared resources. Novell, Inc.'s NetWare holds the greatest market share among companies providing network software.

REPORTING AND MODELING

The concepts of reporting and modeling underpin all microcomputer applications. In reporting, the superior speed and accuracy of the computer processor increases validity and reliability of data transactions. Applications in this area include warehousing, tracking, sales, purchasing, and inventory. Information reporting of this nature also produces important materials like receipts, invoices, checks, and statements. Transactional reports include various records and communications produced by the business in the course of everyday activity. Microcomputers play an important role in the basic reporting activities of a business by accounting for physical objects and producing reporting and transactional information necessary to the operation of the business. Office automation frequently refers to the concept of automating the reporting function of a business operation.

In modeling, expert systems and decision support systems integrate knowledge with a special searching program to reflect best case and expertly analyzed scenarios, problems, and advice. Companies such as Household Mortgage Corporation employ expert systems such as ASSIST to identify potentially fraudulent information. By providing scarce expert knowledge to assist employees, modeled information systems optimize accuracy, speed, and reliability of employee decision making activities. Expert systems and decision support systems are very similar and overlapping functions and features preclude distinction in many cases. Modeling applications run well on current high powered microcomputers but may require a special math coprocessing circuit to accommodate complex and data-intensive tasks.

BUSINESS USES

Microcomputers emerge as important tools in finance, management, marketing, production, and human resource management across a wide range of companies. Reporting and modeling applications pervade all aspects of business operation.

Financial applications include accounting, budgeting, and forecasting. Accounting functions such as ledger, inventory, payroll, sales, and accounts are easily manipulated on a microcomputer. These reporting activities form the backbone of a financial system. Budgeting, cash management, and investment analysis provide critical decision-making information to a business operation based on modeled information. Assessments of financial condition, forecasting, and projections are a more general yet no less important strategic output for planning and resource allocation. Companies such as Electronic Data Systems Corporation and organizations such as Maricopa Medical Center have both reengineered their financial operations using special software and microcomputers. In the credit union industry, 83 percent of reporting credit unions that use automated processing rely on microcomputers. For numeric manipulation and analysis, microcomputers and financial applications combine to create effective and efficient systems.

In marketing, more than 90 percent of selected marketing research firms employ microcomputers at work. Applications include prospect databases, contracts, and inquiries. These operational uses enable close tracking and monitoring of sales and marketing activities. Companies such as United Artists Cable Systems improve sales by using a microcomputing-based network to track and analyze sales. Tactical and strategic uses include product pricing, sales analysis, and sales forecasting. Computer-automated marketing systems optimize matching between prospect and product by integrating demographics, sales, and advertising activities of a business.

Examples of microcomputer applications in human resource management include succession planning, project management, diversity assistance, and applicant tracking. At AT&T, a microcomputer-based system provides necessary inputs and linkages to manage vacancies in key leadership positions. To more equitably and efficiently allocate project responsibilities, Nordson Corporation uses microcomputer technology to automate scheduling, resource management, and reporting. One particular microcomputer software program, the Culture and Value Analysis Tool (CVAT), collects and analyzes corporate cultural values to facilitate problem-solving and conflict management. Companies that provide applicant tracking software, such as Microtrac Systems, capitalize on the powerful and efficient storage and searching capabilities of the microcomputer to offer automated personnel tracking.

Manufacturing operations enjoy considerable advantages with **computer aided design** (CAD) and **computer aided manufacturing** (CAM) software programs. Both use computer processing and human input to optimize production and inventory operations. Purchasing, receiving, and materials management activities mesh with microcomputers to speed production flow and streamline inventory. Just-in-time (JIT) inventory methods are more easily optimized with the assistance of a microcomputer. At AT&T, enhanced networks of microcomputers reduce inventory, improve productivity, and reduce production time. One important concept for manufacturing operations relies on the idea of programmable or flexible automation. General purpose equipment and software modules result in responsive and effective production when flexible automation concepts are applied. Companies such as the Raymond Corporation use manufacturing resource planning (MRP) to streamline and improve manufacturing operations. The MAP or manufacturing automation protocol pre-sents a standard for industry operations in a digital environment.

Management applications of business software abound. From expert systems such as those used at Cadila Labs to improve pharmaceutical formulation to other applications, these program instructions and microcomputers enhance management activities. Electronic briefcases, JIT, and a host of other management enhancements are based on the power of the microcomputer and its usefulness in business. Expert systems, decision support systems (DSS) and executive support systems provide value-added management information for problem solving, planning, and decision making. Adaptive in nature, the endless loop includes query, model, analyze, and feedback. At Household Mortgage Corporation, an expert system aids in the discovery of fraudulent information. Office automation and reporting applications provide a rich array of facts and transactional history. The smart office of the future relies heavily on microcomputers to optimize management functions. **Electronic data interchange (EDI)** offers an automated and integrated exchange of standard business documents to aid in managerial operations that span financial, human resource, and production tasks.

ETHICAL AND SECURITY ISSUES

Ethical issues involving the microcomputer include privacy, accuracy, property, and accessibility. Privacy issues involve blatant violations, illegal monitoring, caller identification, caller matching, and personal indignities. Blatant violation of electronic privacy might occur with electronic intercept and/or publication of personal information electronically. Illegal monitoring refers to eavesdropping or unauthorized logging of information transactions. Caller identification raises issues of anonymity while caller matching manipulates personal data for other than intended use. Personal indignities might include fraudulent transmission of information. Accuracy of information emerges as an issue when financial and credit decisions are based on inaccurate information. Property issues involve intellectual rights and copyright. Accessibility examines individual use and access to microcomputers and digitized information in the workplace. Legitimate business interests in cost and security frequently conflict with employee freedom and privacy. The Data Processing Manager's Association (DPMA) and the Association for Computing Machinery (ACM) offer codes of conduct for members. Generally these codes recognize the individual right to accuracy, privacy, access, and minimized risk.

Security issues involve both equipment and informational resources. Computer theft, malicious access, and informational alteration present a few examples. Individual motivation for intentional abuse includes self gain and maliciousness. Unintentional security risks are posed by ignorant or untrained users. Security concerns also frequently conflict with individual rights of access. Businesses address these concerns by creating policies to address physical security, user authorization, authentication, encryption, and audit requirements.

NETWORKING

One microcomputer alone represents a powerful digitizing machine. More than one microcomputer sharing resources and processing power comprise a network. Special networking software standardizes the network operating system. **Local area networks (LANs)** feature microcomputers, linked together in a building or office, to maximize the human and system resources. The far-flung operations of a global business realize greater synchronicity and communication using wide area networks (WANs). Medium-sized networks (MAN) cover regional and urban areas. Networks connect using a variety of transmission media and are configured in a variety of ways. Telephone, cable, fiber optic, and radio technologies carry network data from participant to participant. A line or bus network distributes information from one end of a network to the other end. Ring networks are set up with no beginning or end. Tree networks and star networks configure resources in more complex ways to accommodate changing or dynamic networks.

Computer-mediated conferencing (CMS), computer conferencing (CC) and **electronic mail** (e-mail) are all examples of networked information. Many people at remote locations can share information in real-time conversation or in static messaging. Real-time conferencing includes desktop video systems, multiuser (MU) text-based systems, and audio. E-mail, listservers (automated subscription system), and keyboard messaging allow conference members to exchange static messages and comments. All input devices including keyboard, audio, and graphical transmission enable individual participation in specialized discussion and exchange forums. These specialized groups assemble and disband around projects or problems as required. Another form of networked information, groupware, synchronizes the activities of group members in scheduling, project management, and work flow.

[Tona Henderson]

FURTHER READING:

Adams, Lynn E. "Securing Your HRIS in a Microcomputer." *HR Magazine*. February, 1992, pp. 56-61.

Arnold, David O. *Computers and Society: Impact!* McGraw-Hill, 1991.

Brush, Victoria J., and Ron Nardoni. "Integrated Data Supports AT&T's Succession Planning." *Personnel Journal*. September, 1992, pp. 103-109.

Cohen, Eric E. "Manufacturing Inventory Software Review." *CPA Journal*. June, 1992, pp. 83-85.

"Expert Systems for Mortgage Underwriters." *Credit Management*. April, 1993, p. 32.

Forger, Gary. "Real-Time Control Drives JIT Success." *Modern Materials Handling*. October, 1992. p. 68.

Hindin, Eric M. "The Move to Put More Factories on the MAP." *Data Communications*. March, 1992, pp. 51-53.

Levary, Reuven R. "Programmable Automation in Manufacturing Systems." *Industrial Management*. May/June, 1994. pp. 21-26.

"Manufacturing Systems' Software Top 50." *Manufacturing Systems*. July, 1992, pp. 32-76.

Mentzer John T., and Nimish Gandhi. "Microcomputers Versus Mainframes: Use Among Logistics and Marketing Professionals." *International Journal of Physical Distribution and Logistics*. 1993, pp. 3-10.

Merritt, Nancy J., and Cecile Bouchy. "Are Microcomputers Replacing Mainframes in Marketing Research Firms?" *Journal of the Academy of Marketing Science*. Winter, 1992, pp. 81-85.

Meyer, Gary. "Computer Assistance in Managing Diversity and Corporate Culture." *Information Strategy: The Executive's Journal*. Fall, 1992, pp. 42-46.

Names, Judith. "Overhaul Was Only the First Step at Phoenix Facility." *Modern Healthcare*. February 15, 1993, pp. 56-60.

"Nordson Uses Project Management to Balance Workloads." *Industrial Engineering*. April, 1992, pp. 26-28.

O'Brien, James A. *Introduction to Information Systems*. Irwin, 1994.

Pels, Mary Ann. "Invasion of the Mighty Micros." *Credit Union Magazine*. December, 1992, pp. 4a-9a.

Peltz, Michael. "Reengineering the Finance Department." *Institutional Investor*. October, 1993, pp. 151-155.

Ramani, K. V., M. R. Patel, and S. K. Patel. "An Expert System for Drug Formulation in a Pharmaceutical Company." *Interfaces*. March/April, 1992, pp. 101-108.

Schultheis, Robert, and Mary Sumner. *Management Information Systems: The Manager's View*. Irwin, 1992.

Sheldon, Don R. "MRP II Implementations: A Case Study." *Hospital Materials Management Quarterly*. May, 1994, pp. 48-52

Stevens, Tim. "The Smart Office." *Industry Week*. January 17, 1994, pp. 31-34.

Strom, Janine. "Creating an Electronic Briefcase." *I.T. Magazine*. February, 1993, pp. 27-28.

Truelson, Jeff S. "Applicant Tracking Software: Picking the Package Right for Your Company." *Human Resources Professional*. Fall, 1991, pp. 15-19.

MICROECONOMICS

Microeconomics encompasses the study of individual elements in an economy, including the consumer, the producer, and the markets in which they interact. The field is devoted to the examination of choices and motivations of these individuals. By contrast, **macroeconomics** deals with the actions of entire populations, or aggregates, of consumers and producers.

Both sciences seek to resolve many of the same questions, but with different methodology. Unfortunately, these methods are often contradictory. Microeconomics ignores macro phenomena, such as total consumption and production, investment, and employment, choosing instead to deal with resource allocation and distribution of income. Macroeconomics focuses on the whole economy, assuming micro phenomena to be of secondary importance to **inflation** and **unemployment**.

Both sciences are built on models, which are themselves simplified representations of reality. Both must be viewed as mere tools that can be used to gain insight to the behavior of the economic system.

For all their differences, microeconomics and macroeconomics cannot be divorced from each other. Macroeconomic theories must have a strong micro-foundation to be valid; that is, they must make some attempt to resolve microeconomic questions. By the same token, microeconomic theories must provide conclusions that do not contradict macroeconomic circumstances.

HISTORICAL BACKGROUND

The terms microeconomics and macroeconomics have their origin in the early 1930s, when economists strived to gain an understanding of factors that created the Great Depression. Separate mechanisms to describe the actions of individuals and aggregate populations were first described by the Norwegian economist Ragnar Frisch (1895-1973) in 1933.

Frisch called these mechanisms ''micro-dynamic'' and ''macro-dynamic.'' He wrote that micro-dynamic analysis seeks to ''explain in some detail the behavior of a certain section of the huge economic mechanism'' within specific parameters, while macro-dynamics gives ''an account of the whole economic system taken in its entirety.''

John Maynard Keynes (1883-1946), in his seminal 1936 publication *The General Theory of Employment, Interest and Money*, established a popular scientific basis for the separate analysis of micro- and macro-dynamic activity. Economists adopted many of Keynes' assumptions about equilibrium—assumptions required to make the models simple enough to work—and subsequently developed these separate methodologies into often unresolvably dissimilar sciences.

The Dutch economist Peter de Wolff was the first to publish the term ''micro-economics'' in a 1941 article on the income elasticity of demand. Others began using the term in their own works, and by the late 1950s ''microeconomics'' and ''macroeconom-

ics'' made their way into textbooks. Thus, the division of analysis—along two different lines of assumptions about the market—was institutionalized as a central feature of the study of economic systems.

MICROECONOMIC TOOLS

MARGINAL REVENUE AND MARGINAL COST. Microeconomics is sometimes referred to as ''the economics of the firm,'' because it seeks to identify key factors in decisions made by firms. Company managers study the choices made by consumers to establish a basis for their own actions. These are rather simplistically boiled down to two factors: what to produce and how much to produce. Both are determined by consumer demand for a product, relative to supply in the market.

For example, an excess demand for television sets will allow a group of television manufacturers to charge a higher price for their products, yielding them a higher profit. Manufacturers will be induced to produce more televisions to take advantage of the profit the market is willing to provide. In addition, other manufacturers will enter the market, hoping to gain a share of the profits available.

Over time, this will increase the supply of televisions in the market, in effect, helping to satisfy consumer demand for the product. As the excess demand subsides, so does the margin of profit. Eventually, supply will meet demand, theoretically yielding no profit.

This model demonstrates one of the primary tools of microeconomics, the concept of marginal revenue. Marginal revenue is a measure of the extra money a firm can earn by producing one more television set.

Of course, there are costs associated with manufacturing a television set. The firm must also be concerned with the cost it must incur to manufacture one more product. This is another primary tool: marginal cost.

In order to maximize profit, a firm will continue to increase production as long as marginal revenue exceeds marginal cost—that is, as long as it can generate a profit on an additional unit.

But at some point, the costs of production will rise as the optimal capacity of the operation is reached. Increased costs for overtime labor, warehousing, scarcity of resources, and other things will create production inefficiencies that cause the marginal cost to rise. At high production volumes these costs will exceed the revenue generated by the sale of the product. In this case, a firm would lose money on each additional product because its marginal cost exceeds its marginal revenue. To rectify the imbalance, it must reduce production.

In practice, a firm will maintain a level of production that yields a worthwhile profit. If it cannot compete effectively enough to earn an acceptable profit, it may choose to abandon its market and produce something else that will generate a profit, or it will seek to lower its production costs.

In addition to marginal costs and revenues, firms also are interested in average revenue and average cost. Average revenue is computed by dividing the total revenue earned from producing a good by the total number of goods produced. If the firm earns $15,000 from the 1,000 television sets it manufactures, its average revenue is $150. Average revenue increases at every level of production until marginal cost exceeds marginal revenue, and then it declines.

Average cost is derived by dividing the total cost of producing a good by the number of goods produced. For example, if a manufacturer spends $10,000 to produce 1,000 television sets, its average cost is $100.

Average costs typically are high at low production volumes, but as volume increases marginal costs drop. At some point, however, the firm exceeds its production capacity, causing inefficiencies to raise marginal costs. At the point where marginal cost exceeds average cost, average cost begins to rise.

The firm will continue to produce at a volume where marginal cost equals marginal revenue. At that level of production, average cost must exceed the price for that good or, obviously, the firm would do better to go out of business.

ECONOMIES OF SCALE

The factor that causes marginal costs to rise resides in the concept of diminishing returns, or **economies of scale**. For example, a television manufacturer may invest $100,000 to establish a production facility designed to turn out 100 televisions per day. But with a minimal additional investment of, say, $20,000, it will turn out 200 televisions per day. This firm has realized greater economies of scale by making better use of the first $100,000 it invested.

But there are limits to the productive capacity of such an enterprise. An enterprise operating beyond its capacity will incur additional costs.

When it was still a small firm in the mid-1950s, Sony was asked to produce radios for the Bulova Corp. Sony developed a price schedule showing that the more Bulova ordered, the less it would charge per unit. This reflected the declining marginal cost of producing in volume; Sony would merely pass on to its customer its favorable economies of manufacturing on a large scale.

But Sony's plant had a production capacity of only 40,000 radios per year. For every unit ordered in excess of 40,000, Sony's marginal costs would increase. Thus, Sony's price schedule showed the unit price increasing for every radio beyond 40,000. This illustrated Sony's increasing marginal cost and the diseconomies of manufacturing on a very large scale. To build 100,000 radios a year, Sony would have to construct additional facilities. Its price (or marginal revenue) merely reflected the costs of this expansion.

Economies of scale are derived from productive capacity. In Sony's case, an order for 10,000 radios would allow its plant to operate at only a quarter of its capacity. Such diseconomies from underutilization of available resources would yield costly inefficiencies that must be passed on to the customer.

At 40,000 radios, the plant is at full capacity and operating at optimal efficiency. Every available factor of production is employed, yielding a savings that may be passed on to the customer through lower prices. It has achieved full economies of scale.

But at 100,000 radios, the plant is clearly beyond its limits. To meet this production goal, the company would have to build another entire factory specifically designed for the additional capacity demanded. These costly diseconomies are passed on to the customer through higher prices.

Sony determined what to produce but, at least in part, left the decision of how much to produce up to its customer, Bulova. In turn, Bulova's decision would be driven by supply and demand for the product.

SHORT-RUN AND LONG-RUN SCENARIOS. But supply and demand are not static; they will change over time. For that reason, microeconomists use two rather vaguely defined time frames for their considerations, the short run and the long run. Short-run scenarios assume no movement in supply or demand because the time frame involved is too brief to allow manufacturers to alter their output and for consumers to change their demand.

In the long run, however, manufacturers and consumers may exercise changes in supply and demand—manufacturers by producing more or less of a product to maximize profit, and consumers by reacting to these changes in supply.

The common denominator for both manufacturers and consumers is the price mechanism. As in the example of the television market, excess demand in the short run yields high profits, inspiring greater production in the long run. This increases the supply and dries up excess demand, forcing prices down and lowering the margin of profit.

DEMAND ELASTICITIES. Some commodities, however, are so essential that demand is unlikely to change, regardless of changes in price. A good example is provided by the 1973-74 oil crisis, where Organization of Petroleum Exporting Countries (OPEC) producers restricted the supply of oil by raising prices. Consumers had grown highly dependent on oil as a fuel for automobiles; they needed it to go to work and run essential errands. Farmers, freight handlers, and salespeople needed it to do their jobs.

Whether gasoline cost 30 cents a gallon or three times that much, consumers were unwilling or unable to reduce their consumption in proportion to price increases. When the price of gasoline tripled, consumers reduced their consumption by only a few percentage points. As a result, their total expenditures for fuel increased.

Microeconomists measure the sensitivity of demand to changes in price in terms of elasticity: the percentage change in the quantity demanded divided by the percentage change in price. Because one number or the other will be negative, demand elasticity is described as a negative number.

If that number represents a value lower than −1, demand is said to be elastic, because consumers will reduce spending in greater proportion to rises in price. A good example of demand elasticity is provided by airline fares.

American Airlines needs to boost its revenues, so it raises prices by 10 percent. Unfortunately, in doing so it loses half its passengers to competitors. Southwest Airlines, which also needs to boost revenues, drops its prices for tickets by 20 percent. By doing so, it doubles the number of passengers. Both examples indicate an elasticity of −5.

If elasticity is between 0 and −1, consumers will reduce spending in lesser proportion to changes in price. In this case, demand is said to be inelastic. In the case of gasoline, prices tripled, but consumption fell only about 10 percent, indicating an elasticity (or inelasticity) of −0.03.

PRICE ELASTICITY OF SUPPLY. By contrast, price elasticity of supply measures the sensitivity of changes in supply relative to changes in price. It is the ratio of the percentage change in supply divided by the percentage change in price, and is always a positive number.

If supply elasticity is greater than 1, firms will alter production in greater proportion to changes in price. Here, supply is elastic. But if supply elasticity is less than 1, firms will alter production in lesser proportion to changes in price. This is supply inelasticity.

Using the earlier example of television manufacturers, firms in that industry were driven to increase production because excess demand justified an increase in prices. Assume a 10 percent price rise generated a 50 percent increase in production. This

produces a supply elasticity of 5. If, however, prices rose by 20 percent, but production grew only by 10 percent, the measure is 0.5, indicating supply inelasticity.

The factors that would influence the responsiveness of changes in production, or supply, are derived from demand. Companies would be eager to boost production if it meant that increased prices would yield significantly greater marginal revenue. But companies would be less willing to raise production if the price increase raised marginal revenue only modestly.

MICROECONOMIC MARKETS

Firms determine many of the characteristics of the markets in which they operate. A market populated by several companies, each with similar market share, may be said to be competitive. This is because no one firm dominates either the total supply in the market nor the price of the goods it produces.

On the other hand, a firm that is alone in its industry, one with no competitors, is a monopoly. Monopolies may exist because they own proprietary rights to their product (for example, a pharmaceutical company with a patented drug formula) or because competition would raise average costs in the industry (such as with electrical power distribution).

Monopoly markets have no supply curve. Like competitive companies, they merely produce at a level where marginal cost equals marginal revenue. But marginal revenue is derived from the market price which, unlike competitive markets, may be determined by the monopoly.

The monopoly will determine a price based on demand elasticity. In other words, it would lower its price only if that would increase its total revenues. For example, electricity is very nearly a necessity in daily life. The utilities that provide it operate in a natural monopoly (where competition could only raise costs, rather than lower them). If they were allowed to set a high price for electricity, demand might drop only barely. For this reason, governments have created regulatory agencies not only to police monopolies' costs but also to set their prices as well.

Somewhere between competition and monopoly is monopolistic competition, where several firms compete in the same market, but with appreciably unique products. In the example of the pharmaceutical industry, a number of companies may produce different drugs that combat the same affliction. But each may work better for certain types of patients, affording its maker a monopoly in limited areas of the wider market.

Another type of market is the **oligopoly**, where a small number of firms dominate the market, operating with quasi-monopolistic power. The airline industry provides a useful example. United and Delta are the only airlines operating nonstop flights between Chicago and Atlanta. They are likely to charge the same low fare on this route, choosing to compete on the basis of their costs.

But Delta might raise its fare if it is convinced that it might lose only a small number of passengers to United and that it could increase its total revenues. This would provide United with a choice: to raise its total revenue by (1) keeping its low fare and winning passengers over from Delta, or (2) matching Delta's price increase and realizing no gain in ridership. If United opted for the latter choice, its effect on the public would be characteristic of a monopoly. The only difference is that two companies raised the market price rather than one.

The ultimate oligopoly is the **cartel**, and the ultimate cartel is OPEC. In 1973 the countries that comprised OPEC dominated the world supply of oil. That year they all agreed to raise the price of the oil they exported, certain that their customers' demand was inelastic and total revenues would soar.

But there is tremendous pressure for a single member of a cartel not to honor the agreement. By lowering its price to a level below that of its peers, a rogue member can sell all it can produce. As a result, even cartels are endowed with competitive motivations that are capable of ruining them.

In every case but the monopoly, firms are influenced by the actions of competitors. They all strive to maximize their potential to generate profit, based on market characteristics that they form with competitors.

Firms operate in a given market with theoretically identical demand features. Based on their assumptions about costs, they make determinations about production that form industry supply characteristics. These factors dictate a market price and quantity of production that further influence cost and revenue assumptions. Companies may introduce new cost-saving measures or product improvements that influence the demand for their product. These, too, translate into changes in cost and revenue, providing the dynamics of a competitive market.

[John Simley]

FURTHER READING:

Baumol, William. J., and Alan S. Blinder. *Economics, Principles and Policy.* 2nd ed. New York: Harcourt Brace Jovanovich, 1982.

Fischer, Stanley, and Rudiger Hornbusch. *Economics.* New York: McGraw-Hill, 1983.

MINORITY BUSINESSES

Minority-owned businesses have operated in the United States throughout its history. However, it has not always been easy for minorities to establish businesses. For instance, they have experienced difficulties with acquiring financing and purchasing land, as well as attracting complaints and being the targets of unfair competition from other businesses. Many have overcome those problems, however, and today the number of minority-owned businesses is growing.

A BRIEF HISTORY OF EARLY MINORITY-OWNED BUSINESS

Minorities have owned businesses in the United States for hundreds of years. In the early 1700s, for example, several "Negroes," as the historical records called them, owned their own businesses. Historian Carl Bridenbaugh, in his book *Cities in the Wilderness*, wrote that in Charles Town (now Charleston, South Carolina) in the 1730s, "there were many black artisans, like Jack, the ship carpenter, and Prince, 'well known . . . as a Plaisterer (sic) and Bricklayer by trade.' " He also cited Philadelphia and New York as cities that had many black business owners.

Of course, they were not appreciated by their white competitors. As Bridenbaugh wrote, "Philadelphians also objected to blacks who underbid them in servile work. Although harsh legislation in every town restricted his movements, especially at night, the Negro was of too great use and value to be dispensed with as a source of cheap labor."

Similarly, Lorenzo Greene mentioned several black business owners in his book, *The Negro in Colonial New England.* For instance, he cited Jim Riggs, of Framingham, Massachusetts, a jobber and basket maker, who also fought in the American Revolutionary War. One Maine Negro earned his living as a fortune teller. Squire Nep, a Connecticut resident, owned his own barbershop. These men were the exceptions to the rule, though. Minority business owners were not numerous, but they did exist.

Cases abound of Negroes who ran successful businesses in the south after the Civil War. In virtually every large southern city, Negroes were the butchers, barbers, and artisans. They ran successful restaurants and hotels. For example, Jehu Jones ran one of Charleston's most successful hotels. In 1883, Solomon Humphries, a prosperous grocer in Macon, Georgia, was worth about $20,000—and he had more credit than anyone in town. Thomy Lafon, of New Orleans, accumulated real estate estimated to be worth almost half a million dollars.

OTHER MINORITIES JOIN THE BUSINESS WORLD

As the country grew, more minority groups established their own businesses. In 1980, according to the U.S. Bureau of Census, 7.2 percent of all the employed Chinese workers in the country headed their own businesses. Figures for other minorities were also impressive. For example, 11.9 percent of all employed Koreans had their own businesses. Comparable percentages for Vietnamese, Cubans, and Mexicans were 2.2, 5.8, and 3.5 respectively. Enterprising minorities from a variety of ethnic backgrounds seized their chance to open their own businesses.

The theory of middleman minorities attempts to explain the large number of minorities who opened businesses. The theory suggests that entrepreneurial ethnic minorities will cluster in commercial occupations within their societies. Thus, as succeeding waves of Koreans, Vietnamese, Mexicans, and other minorities entered the United States, they tended to live within close proximity. The more financially stable, or more entrepreneurial, members of these communities established the businesses essential to the communities' needs. Eventually, the individual communities became self-supportive, to the point where they established their own banks. The Koreans who established a community in Los Angeles exemplify the benefits of the middleman minority theory.

Many of the Koreans who emigrated to the United States were highly educated and financially well-off. Many of them had business experience in their native country, which they used to their advantage once they reached the United States. Their experience helped them overcome the frustrations and growing pains involved in starting a business. They knew enough to exchange business information among themselves, to mobilize unpaid family members to work, to maintain expected patterns of nepotism and employer paternalism, and to treat their employees with respect. Thus, they benefited tremendously from class resources and old-fashioned ethnic resources to establish a number of successful businesses. It was not just the Koreans who became successful minority business owners, though. Other ethnic groups did and have flourished.

GROWING OPPORTUNITIES

The number of start-up businesses among minorities has been increasing dramatically in the last part of the 20th century. That is due in part to the widespread economic changes that began to occur in the United States in the 1980s. Companies began major restructuring projects that displaced large numbers of workers. Since it is in times of economic slowdown that small business growth occurs, there was a natural tendency among displaced workers to open their own

enterprises. Their timing was good, as many government agencies at the local, state, and federal levels expanded their attempts to encourage the establishment of minority-owned businesses. More and more minorities took advantage of the government's help.

Many of the minority groups established themselves as business owners in urban areas. That was due in large part to historical demographic patterns. For the most part, each succeeding group of immigrants that has entered the United States (e.g., Irish, Chinese, Italian, Polish) settled in large urban areas. They did so simply because that was where the job opportunities existed. So, the entrepreneurial members of their communities opened service businesses of all types to satisfy the consumer demands of the local ethnic groups. Certain categories of business became attractive for minority entrepreneurs. Among the most common business opportunities available to minorities were bowling alleys, contract construction, dry cleaning, furniture stores, real estate brokerages, savings and loan associations, and supermarkets.

Despite opportunities in these and other fields, limitations existed that affected minorities attempting to start their own businesses. One of the most significant problems centered around financing, particularly prior to the 1960s. Up until that time, banks were not anxious to loan minorities money. However, the civil rights movement that began in the in the 1960s theoretically made it easier for minorities to obtain financing. Unfortunately, there was not always enough money to go around. The federal government intervened to alleviate that problem.

GOVERNMENT INTERVENTION

Government agencies became more helpful to minority business owners after the civil rights movement began. President Nixon established the Office of Minority Business Enterprises (OMBE) in 1969 as part of his initiative to spearhead minority capitalism. The agency's purpose was to provide management and technical assistance, information, and advocacy in the private sector for minority business development. OMBE has since been renamed the Minority Business Development Agency, and has become part of the U.S. Department of Commerce. Its six regional offices disperse technical advice and information to a network of over 100 local business development centers around the country.

The **Small Business Administration (SBA)** also stepped up efforts to help minority business owners obtain needed financing. The agency initiated two types of programs—loan assistance and preferential procurement of federal contracts, called ''set-asides.'' Many state and local governments set up similar preferential procurement contracts to assist minority contractors.

Set-asides were created in 1953, when the U.S. government passed a law that set aside five percent of all procurement contracts for small businesses owned by socially and economically disadvantaged people. The SBA has defined and redefined the term "socially and economically disadvantaged" many times since then by adding different groups and deleting others. The core group under the original law included Black Americans, Hispanic Americans, Native Americans, Asian Pacific Americans, and other minorities. In 1982, the SBA added Asian Indians. Six years later, it added Sri Lankans. In 1989, the SBA included Tongans and Indonesians. The agency deleted Hasidic Jews in 1980 and took Iranians off its list when they could not prove long-term bias against them. Decisions such as these led to arguments against the effectiveness and fairness of "set-aside" programs. To exacerbate the arguments, the courts did not always view "set-asides" as legal.

ARGUMENTS OVER "SET-ASIDES"

Large major cities like Atlanta, Baltimore, Detroit, and Philadelphia established "set-aside" programs. Many minority business owners argued that such programs were necessary if they were to survive. Others disagreed. One judge in San Diego, California, ruled that these programs were unconstitutional.

San Diego had an Equal Opportunity Contracting Program that mandated that 20 percent of city-funded construction projects had to be awarded to companies owned by ethnic minorities. Without such mandates, some people argued, the minority-owned companies could not stay in business. In 1993, a U.S. district judge struck down the ordinance. That upset many minority business owners, but others were relieved. They argued that "set-asides" were not helpful to minorities.

John Robinson, who was president and Chief Executive Officer of the New York-based National Minority Business Council, suggested that minority-owned companies that wanted to become successful should ignore "set-asides." They would be better off, he said, entering mainstream business competition. As proof, he cited a black-owned company, TLC Beatrice International, which has annual sales of more than $1.5 billion. Proponents of "set-asides" argued that companies as large as TLC Beatrice did not need such programs. However, they said, smaller businesses such as construction companies and supply distributors did. Forward thinking business experts disagreed.

Anti-"set-aside" experts stated that minority-owned business operators in the late 20th century could no longer rely on "mom-and-pop" operations to sustain themselves. They argued that minority-owned businesses were coming of age and could compete in the mainstream economy. In fact, they

said, "set-asides" impede minority-owned businesses' chances of success, because companies came to depend on them to the detriment of seeking contracts through competition. The success of many minority entrepreneurs supported that argument.

SUCCESS STORIES

In recent years, there have been many examples of minority-owned business success stories on both small and large scales. For example, there is Food from the 'Hood, a black-owned business founded in 1992 in South Central Los Angeles by a group of Crenshaw High School students. Their start-up business took shape after 1992 riots destroyed many business in the area and created economic chaos.

The students planted a quarter-acre lot behind the school's football field with a variety of vegetables. They soon started bottling and selling "Straight Out The Garden," a creamy Italian dressing. Within two years, the young entrepreneurs were selling the low-fat, all-natural dressing in 2,000 supermarkets in 23 states. As important as the sales, though, were the lessons the company's founders learned about the business world.

The founders learned quickly that government restrictions apply equally to all types of businesses, regardless of who owns them. They faced rigid health department standards and steep manufacturing costs. To compensate, they contracted with a manufacturer to produce the dressing and enlisted the aid of a distributor, a supermarket broker, and a law firm. Their funding came through $100,000 in grants and help from an advertising executive and corporate advisers from different companies. The company became successful quickly. By 1994, Von's supermarket chain was selling 360 bottles of the dressing per week and was selling the product in all its 300+ stores. Food From the 'Hood proved that small minority-owned businesses can be competitive in the mainstream business world.

Large minority-owned companies are also finding success, like the aforementioned TLC Beatrice Corporation. Another minority-owned business that has done extremely well is Goya Food, Inc., of Secaucus, New Jersey. This company, founded in 1933, is a wholesale distributor and manufacturer of Hispanic foods. It has manufacturing plants in Puerto Rico, Spain, Santo Domingo, and the Dominican Republic. The company takes in about $330 million in sales revenues annually and is growing rapidly. However, for every major success like TLC Beatrice or Goya, there are thousands of minority-owned businesses struggling. For companies like this, there is help from government and private organizations, although there may not be enough.

HELP IS AVAILABLE

There is no doubt that the federal government's increased involvement in minority business proved valuable. By 1984, the government had provided $9.5 billion in contracts, grants, and loans to minority businesses. That figure may sound impressive, but it does not offer help to as many companies as the government would like. Consider the figures regarding SBA involvement in minority business.

In 1993, the SBA guaranteed 26,812 loans totaling more than $6.4 billion to small- and women-owned businesses. The number reached $7 billion in 1994 and $9 billion in 1995. However, the number of companies that have actually received funds since 1969 (when the SBA established its 8a program to assist minority-owned businesses financially) is only 15,000. (Section 8a is the minority business enterprise section of the Small Business Act.) That pales in comparison to the fact that there existed 1.2 million minority-owned businesses in 1987. The government's help has not been enough. Therefore, private companies and organizations are also helping minority-owned businesses establish themselves and grow.

Cessna Aircraft, based in Wichita, Kansas, spends more than $10 million a year with minority-owned businesses. The company started tracking the amount of business it did with such firms and found that it was not doing enough to help them. The company does not run a "set-aside" program, however. It requires *all* vendors, minority or otherwise, to participate in a bidding process. Sometimes it can take years before minority-owned businesses win contracts, but that is a natural part of the business environment. Cessna provides an example of the type of corporate spirit that is assisting minority-owned businesses in their growing process.

Other organizations upon which minorities can rely for assistance include the NAACP's Community Development Resource Center(s) and the National Black Chamber of Commerce (NBCC). The latter organization was influential in getting the Indianapolis Power and Light Company and PSI Energy, Inc., both of Indianapolis, Indiana, to reexamine their policies regarding minority contractors. At the NBCC's urging, PSI stated that it would like to deliver 4 percent of its business, worth $32 million annually, to minority- and women-owned firms. Help like this is invaluable to minority-owned businesses. More importantly, it bodes well for the future, as more and more minorities establish their own businesses.

MINORITY BUSINESS OWNERS SEIZE OTHER OPPORTUNITIES

More and more minorities are starting to take advantage of government programs, private sector assistance, and established business practices such as networking to assist them in opening their own firms. Networking—interactions among business people for the purpose of discussing mutual problems, solutions, and opportunities—is extremely important to minority business owners. It can take place within a company, an industry, or a group with common characteristics, e.g., race, sex, or religion. One example of a thriving network exists in Cleveland, where the growing Council of Smaller Enterprises of Cleveland comprises over 1,800 members. Organizations such as this are invaluable to minority business owners.

Many companies taking advantage of the assistance available to them have grown quietly into large and respectable firms. One prime example is TRESP Associates Incorporated, a management information systems firm located in Alexandria, Virginia. Owner Lillian Handy started the company from her home. Her only financing was a credit card. She relied on SBA loans through the 8a program to underwrite her business in the early years of the company's business. Only nine years after she started the company, it outgrew the 8A program. The company had 260 employees by 1994 with revenues of $15 million. Ms. Handy projected contracts worth $50 million by 1999. However, the dollar figures do not reflect the true value Ms. Handy has in the area of minority business.

Ms. Handy is also very active in promoting all types of minority-owned businesses. She assumed the chairmanship of the Minority-Owned Business Technology Transfer Consortium in the Washington D.C. area in order to enhance the participation of minority firms in bringing government technology to the private sector. The group also tries to put together joint venture partnerships and to demonstrate to major companies that minority firms are capable of doing quality work. Her own firm serves as a mentor for numerous other minority firms. The help that she and other successful minority business owners provide minority entrepreneurs is extremely important if they are to succeed.

THE FUTURE OF MINORITY BUSINESSES

There is no doubt that the number of minority-owned businesses in the United States will grow considerably in the near future. Many of the barriers that prohibited their growth in the past have disappeared. More and more government agencies are helping with advice and financial aid. There is a growing number of private agencies working with minorities to improve their chances of establishing successful businesses. Private businesses such as Cessna are reexamining their commitments to minority suppliers. Of added importance is the fact that banks are becoming more helpful. For example, a consortium of six South Carolina banks agreed in 1994 to relax some loan requirements to help businesses owned by minorities and women get more financing. The money was needed to help companies acquire the capital to bid on federal contracts. Similar programs in other states have also been helpful in this regard.

The assistance of minority owners like Lillian Handy and the entrepreneurial spirit exhibited by the owners of Food From The'Hood are harbingers of the future. However, the road will still not be easy. Minority business owners will still have to compete seriously for contracts. "Set-aside" programs can only go so far to help them acquire work. Their real success will be in earning contracts and attracting business on their own. There is no doubt they will be successful in doing so based on their past progress.

SEE ALSO: Women in Business

[Arthur G. Sharp]

FURTHER READING:

Bridenbaugh, Carl. *Cities in the Wilderness: Urban Life in America, 1625-1742*. New York: Capricorn Books, 1964.

Green, Shelley and Paul Pryde. *Black Entrepreneurship in America*. New Brunswick: Transaction Publishers, 1990.

Greene, Lorenzo Johnston. *The Negro in Colonial New England*. New York: Atheneum, 1969.

Harmon, J. H., Arnett G. Lindsay, and Carter G. Woodson. *The Negro As Business Man*. College Park MD: McGrath Publishing Company, 1969.

Judd, Richard J., William T. Greenwood, and Fred W. Becker, editors. *Small Business in A Regulated Economy*. New York: Quorum Books, 1988.

Light, Ivan and Edna Bonacich. *Immigrant Entrepreneurs: Koreans in Los Angeles, 1965-1982*. Berkeley CA: University of California Press, 1988.

Urban Business Profiles. Detroit: Gale Research, 1979.

Willie, Charles Vert. *Black and White Families*. Bayside NY: General Hall Inc., 1985.

MISSION

SEE: Strategy Formulation

MIXED ECONOMY

The mixed economy, in economic thinking, is defined by a system in which decisions by the private and public sectors combine to sustain growth and jobs. Government intervention might seem an anomaly for **capitalism**, which in theory puts great stock in the enterprising individual making personal decisions in the marketplace. But, in practice, members of capitalist societies also put great store in economic security. The result is the mixed economy, offering government a voice in sustaining economic growth, while at the same time protecting people from the worst excesses of unfettered competition in the marketplace.

Some examples of intervention by the government include agriculture **subsidies** or price supports for farmers, protective tariffs for steelmakers, deposit insurance for bank depositors and quotas for fishermen. All such measures instituted by government restrain or control competition and the free exchange of goods in an economy—and yet provide security. Therefore, under a mixed economy, neither unfettered capitalism nor centralized government control is possible or preferable. Instead, the public and private sector combine to make economic decisions on what is produced and distributed in an economy, and how. Society as a whole pursues its interests via individual and collective action. Of course, times change and so does the role of government in a capitalist economy. During the 1950s and 1960s, governments used public spending and taxation as fiscal tools to alternately push or restrain demand. This Keynesian prescription held that high investment and growth would come when the uncertainties of economic life were kept to a minimum.

This meant the government spent more public funds when growth flagged and unemployment threatened, or tightened fiscal policy when an economy returned to health. Indeed, government spending among Western economies was highest in the United States during this period due to the effect of high military spending borne of defense needs during the Cold War.

However, by the early 1970s, government spending in Western economies had grown significantly, producing **inflation**, while economic growth stagnated. Suddenly, "stagflation" became the economic buzzword of the day, especially when the 1973 oil embargo inspired fears of concurrent rising inflation and **unemployment**.

In contrast to the Keynesian prescription, monetarist economists argued that high taxes, controls, and regulation imposed by government would suffocate growth. Only when government intervention was minimized, allowing the private sector would significant economic growth resume.

Now individuals were no longer encouraged to shift their economic risks to the government—relying on crop insurance or remaining on welfare—but rather to take more responsibility for their economic destiny in the marketplace.

Put simply, monetarists believed government was more of a problem than a solution when it came to sustaining economic growth. During the 1980s, governments turned to stimulating or restraining an economy on the supply side by adjusting the available

money supply. This they did, once again, through **taxes**. Specifically, Western governments looked to reducing the tax burden as the impetus for releasing private sector energies.

Ironically, despite arguments against government intervention, public spending in Western economies grew, when it was intended to decrease. Politicians insisted that government would no longer assist faltering industrial sectors with public money. And to be certain, a shakeout in smokestack industries did take place during the 1980s recession.

However, bending to political realities, other exceptions were made, and government subsidies grew. The mixed economy was alive and well during the l980s, despite the wishes of supply-side economists. Indeed, their fears were realized, when rising public spending led to higher government borrowing and deficits. This, in turn, led to inflation and higher **interest rates** as the public sector competed with the private sector to borrow on international markets.

In the 1990s, the monetarists went back on the defensive. Control of the money supply, they argued, would reduce the rate of inflation, foster stability, and further economic growth. However, the legacy of this theory has been the steady increase in the federal deficit and the early 1995 recession. Public disillusionment has grown, due to the government's failure to prevent unemployment, and the loss of industrial capacity.

But while monetarism may be dead, the Keynesian prescription is also faltering. Instead, the electorate everywhere insists that governments cannot print money to spur economic growth, and that markets should continue to be allowed to play. Such a balance in attitudes underlines that, however frail economic growth worldwide continues at present, the mixed economy remains a strong and vital component of economies everywhere.

[Etan Vlessing]

MONETARISM

Monetarism states that **monetary policy** is very powerful, but that it should not be used as a macroeconomic policy to manage the economy. There is thus an apparent contradiction—if monetary policy is so powerful, why not use it, for example, to create more employment in the economy?

HISTORY AND BACKGROUND

First of all, it should be noted that monetarism was an attempt by conservative economists to re-establish the wisdom of the classical *laissez faire* rec-

ommendation and was an attack on the *activist* macroeconomic policy recommendations of the Keynesian economists. It is thus helpful to briefly examine the historical background against which monetarism developed as a new school of macroeconomic thought.

THE CLASSICAL ECONOMICS. The macroeconomic thought that dominated capitalist economies prior to the advent of Keynesian economics in 1936 has been widely known as classical **macroeconomics**. Classical economists believed in free markets. They believed that the economy would always achieve full **employment** through forces of supply and demand. So, if there were more people looking for work than the number of jobs available, the wages would fall until all those seeking work were employed. Thus, the full employment of workers was guaranteed by market forces. The full employment level of employment resulted in a fixed aggregate output/income. The price level (and thus the inflation rate) was determined by the supply of money in the economy. Since, the output level was fixed, a 10 percent increase in money supply would lead to a 10 percent increase in the price level—too many dollars chasing too few goods. The real interest rate was also determined by forces of supply and demand in the market for loanable funds. The nominal interest rate was then simply the sum of the real interest rate and the prevailing **inflation** rate. Classical economists thus had an unwavering faith in the self-adjusting market mechanism. However, it was crucial for the working of the market mechanism that there was perfect competition in the market, and that wages and prices were fully flexible.

The classical economists did not see any role for the government. As market forces led to full **employment** equilibrium in the economy, there was no need for government intervention. Monetary policy (increasing or decreasing the **money supply** would only affect prices—it would not affect the important real factors such as output and employment. Fiscal policy (using government spending or taxes), on the other hand, was perceived as harmful. For example, if the government borrowed to finance its spending, it would simply reduce the funds available for private consumption and investment expenditures—a phenomenon popularly termed as crowding out. Similarly, if the government raised taxes to pay for government spending, it would reduce private consumption in order to fund public consumption. Instead, if it financed spending by increasing the money supply, it would have the same effects as an expansionary monetary policy. Thus, classical economists recommended use of neither monetary nor fiscal policy by the government. This hands-off policy recommendation is known as *laissez faire*.

THE KEYNESIAN ECONOMICS. Keynesian economics was born during the Great Depression of the 1930s.

The classical economists had argued that the self-adjusting market mechanism would restore full employment in the economy, if it deviated from full employment for some reason. However, the experience of the Great Depression showed that market forces would not work as well as the classical economists had believed. The unemployment rate in the United States rose to higher than 25 percent of the labor force. Hard working people were out in the street looking for nonexisting jobs. Wages fell quite substantially. However, the lower wages did not re-establish full employment.

Economist John Maynard Keynes argued that the self-adjusting market forces would take a long time to restore full employment. He predicted that the economy would be stuck at the high level of unemployment for a prolonged period, leading to untold miseries. Keynes explained that classical economics suffered from major flaws. Wages and prices were not as flexible as classical economists assumed—in fact, nominal wages were very sticky in the downward direction. Also, Keynes argued that classical economists had ignored a key aspect that determined the level of output and employment in the economy—the *aggregate demand* for goods and services in the economy from all sources (consumers, businesses, government, and foreign sources). Producers create goods (and provided employment in the process) to meet the demand for their products and services. If the level of aggregate demand was low, the economy would not create enough jobs and unemployment could result. In other words, the free working of the macroeconomy did not guarantee full employment of the labor force—the deficient aggregate demand was the cause of unemployment. Thus, if the aggregate private demand (i.e., the aggregate demand excluding government spending) fell short of the demand level needed to generate full employment, the government should step in to make up for the slack.

The central issue underlying Keynesian thought was that those individuals who have incomes demand goods and services and, in turn, help to create jobs. The government should thus find a way to increase aggregate demand. One direct way of doing so was to increase government spending. Increased government spending, would generate jobs and incomes for the persons employed on government projects. This, in turn, would create demand for goods and services of private producers and generate additional employment in the private sector. Keynesian economists thus recommended that the government should use fiscal policy (which includes decisions regarding both government spending and taxes) to make up for the shortfall in the private aggregate demand to reignite the job creating private sector. Keynesian economists even went so far as to recommend that it was even worth-while for the government to employ people to in meaningless jobs, as long as they were employed.

The Roosevelt administration did follow Keynesian recommendations, although reluctantly, and embarked on a variety of government programs aimed at boosting incomes and the aggregate demand. As a result, the Depression economy started moving forward. The really powerful push to the depressed U.S economy, however, came when World War II broke out. It generated such an enormous demand for U.S. military and civilian goods that factories in the United States operated multiple shifts. Serious unemployment disappeared for a long period of time.

Modern Keynesians (also, known as neo-Keynesians) recommend utilizing monetary policy, in addition to fiscal policy, to manage the level of aggregate demand. Monetary policy affects aggregate demand in the Keynesian system by affecting private investment and consumption demand. An increase in the money supply, for example, leads to a decrease in the interest rate. This lowers the cost of borrowing and thus increases private investment and consumption, boosting the aggregate demand in the economy.

An increase in aggregate demand under the Keynesian system, however, not only generates higher employment but also leads to higher inflation. This causes a policy dilemma—how to strike a balance between employment and inflation. According to laws that were enacted following the Great Depression, policy makers are expected to use monetary and fiscal policies to achieve high employment consistent with price stability.

THE MONETARIST COUNTERREVOLUTION

By 1950, Keynesian economics was well established. Keynesian macroeconomic thought became the new standard in place of the old classical standard. The birth of monetarism took place in the 1960s. The original proponent of monetarism was Milton Friedman, now a Nobel Laureate. The monetarists argue that while it is not possible to have full employment of the labor force all the time (as the classical economists had argued), it is better to leave the macroeconomy to market forces. Friedman modified some aspects of the classical theory to provide the rationale for his non-interventionist policy recommendation. In essence, monetarism contends that use of fiscal policy is largely ineffective in altering output and employment levels. Moreover, it only leads to crowding out. Monetary policy, on the other hand, is effective. But, the monetary authorities do not have adequate knowledge to conduct a successful monetary policy—manipulating the money supply to stabilize the economy only leads to a greater instability. Hence, monetarism advocates that neither monetary nor fiscal policy should be used in an attempt to stabilize the economy, and the money supply should be allowed to grow at a constant rate. Friedman contends that the government's use of *active* monetary and fiscal policies to stabilize the economy around full employment leads to greater instability in the economy. He argues that while the economy will not achieve a state of bliss in the absence of the government intervention, it will be far more tranquil. The monetarist policy recommendations are similar to those of the classical economists, even though the reasoning is somewhat different.

A detailed discussion of the key elements of monetarism follows. In particular, an effort is made to explain the theoretical framework that monetarists employ and how they arrive at policy recommendations regarding the use of monetary and fiscal policies.

THE KEY MONETARIST PROPOSITIONS

Based on Richard Froyen in *Macroeconomics: Theories and Policies*, the key propositions advanced by the monetarist economists (in particular, Milton Friedman) can be summarized as follows:

1. The supply of money has the dominant influence on nominal income. Two economic concepts enter this proposition—money supply and nominal income. Money supply can be narrowly defined as the sum of all money (currency, checkable deposits, and travellers checks) with the nonbank public in the economy. The money supply so defined is technically called M1 by monetary authorities and economists. Nominal income can simply be understood as the **gross domestic product** (GDP) at current prices. GDP is thus made up of a price component and a real output component. The current value of the GDP can go up due to an increase in the prices of goods and services included in the GDP or due to an increase in the actual production of goods and services included in the GDP or both.

The above proposition then states that the stock of money in the economy is the primary determinant of the nominal GDP, or the level of economic activity in current dollars. The proposition is vague regarding the breakdown of an increase in nominal gross domestic product into increases in the price level and real output. However, the proposition does assume that, for most part, a change in the money supply is the *cause* of a change in the GDP at current prices or nominal income. Also, the level and the rate of growth of the money supply are assumed to be primarily determined by the actions of the central monetary authority (the **Federal Reserve Bank** in the United States).

2. In the short run, money supply does have the dominant influence on the *real* variables. Here, the

real variables are the real output (the real GDP) and employment. The first proposition only alluded to real output—implied in the break up of the nominal GDP into the real and price components. Where does the employment variable come from? Employment is basically considered a companion of real output. If real output increases, producers must generally employ additional workers to produce the additional output. Of course, sometimes producers may rely on overtime from existing workers. But, generally an increase in employment eventually follows an increase in real output. The second proposition, however, is not confined to real output and employment—prices are influenced as well. Thus, the second proposition effectively states that changes in money supply strongly influence both real output and price level in the short run. Proposition two, therefore, provides a break down of a change in the nominal income, induced by a change in the money supply, into changes in real output and price level components mentioned in the first proposition.

3. In the long run, the influence of a variation in the money supply is primarily on price level and on other *nominal* variables such as nominal wages. Price level is a nominal variable in the sense that a change in price level is in sharp contrast to a change in real output and employment—it does not have the advantages that are associated with the latter two. In the long run, the *real* macroeconomic variables, such as real output and employment, are determined by changes in real factors of production, not simply by altering a nominal variable, such as the money supply. Real output and employment are, in turn, determined by real factors such as labor inputs, capital resources, and the state of technology. As was indicated in the second proposition, in the short run, a change in the stock of money affects both real output and price level. This, in conjunction with proposition three, leads to the implication that the long-run influence of money supply is only on the price level.

4. The private sector of the economy is inherently stable. Further, government policies are primarily responsible for instability in the economy. This proposition summarizes the monetarist economists' belief in the working of the private sector and market forces. The private sector mainly consists of households and businesses that together account for the bulk of private sector demand, consumption, and investment. This monetarist proposition, then, states that these components of the aggregate demand are stable, and are thus not a source of instability in the economy. In fact, the monetarists argue that the private sector is a self-adjusting process that tends to stabilize the economy by absorbing shocks. They contend that it is the government sector that is the source of instability. The government causes instability in the economy primarily through an unstable money supply. Since the

money supply has a dominant effect on real output and price level in the short run, and on price level in the long run, fluctuations in the money supply lead to fluctuations in these macroeconomic variables—i.e., instability of the macroeconomy. Moreover, the government, by introducing a powerful destabilizing influence (changes in the money supply), interferes with the normal workings of the self-adjusting mechanism of the private sector. In effect, the absence of money supply fluctuations would make it easier for the private sector mechanism to work properly.

The above four propositions lead to some key policy conclusions. Based on Froyen, the four monetarist propositions provide the bases for the following two policy recommendations:

1. Stability in the growth of money supply is absolutely crucial for stability in the economy. Monetarists further suggest that stability in the growth of money supply is best achieved by setting the growth rate at a constant rate—this recommendation has been termed as the constant money supply growth rule. The chief proponent of monetarism, Milton Friedman, has long advocated a strict adherence to a money supply rule. Other monetarists favor following a less inflexible money supply growth rate rule. However, monetarists, in general, are in favor of following a rule regarding the money supply growth rate, rather than tolerating fluctuations in the monetary aggregate (caused by discretionary monetary policy aimed at stabilizing the economy around full employment). This policy difference from the activist economists (primarily, the Keynesians) is at the heart of the monetarist debate. This component of the debate is known among professional economists as ''rule versus discretion'' controversy.

One should note that while monetarists are adamant about following a money supply rule, they are not so rigid regarding the rate at which the money supply growth rate should be fixed. A general rule of thumb suggests that the money supply should grow between 4 and 5 percent. How do economists arrive at these numbers? It is assumed that the long-term economic growth potential of the U.S. economy is about 3 percent per annum, i.e., the real GDP can grow at about 3 percent. So, the money supply has to grow at about 3 percent just to keep the price level from falling—economists do not like falling prices because they cause other problems in the economy. An inflation rate of 1 to 2 percent per annum is considered acceptable. To generate 1 to 2 percent inflation, the money supply must grow at 1 to 2 percent above the growth rate of the real GDP. In effect, then, to have a modest 1 to 2 percent inflation, the money supply should grow at about 4 to 5 percent. The issue of the money supply growth rule will be further clarified when theoretical principles underlying monetarism are discussed later.

2. Fiscal policy is ineffective in influencing either real or nominal macroeconomic variables. It has little effect, for example, on either real output/employment or price level. Thus, the government can't use fiscal policy as a stabilization tool. Monetarists contend that while fiscal policy is not an effective stabilization tool, it does lead to some harmful effects on the private sector economy—it crowds out private consumption and investment expenditures.

THEORETICAL UNDERPINNINGS OF MONETARISM

The four monetarist propositions discussed in the preceding section, from which the two policy recommendations follow, are supported by theoretical reasoning and support. In general, the theoretical framework employed by monetarist economists is a modified version of classical macroeconomic theory. The modifications were needed to address the Keynesian criticisms of the classical theory and to establish monetarist policy conclusions. Theoretical support for each of the four propositions will be briefly discussed in this section.

PROPOSITION ONE. This proposition—that money supply has a dominant effect on nominal income—is the most basic part of the theoretical structure of the monetarist counterrevolution. Proposition one is based on a key classical theoretical framework known as the *quantity theory of money*. Classical economists had argued that the quantity (or the supply) of money determines only price level (a *nominal* variable), not *real* variables such as output and employment. The quantity theory of money is used to establish the link between the quantity of money and the price level, and thus its name simply emphasizes the importance of the quantity of money. The quantity theory of money was written in the form of the equation: ''MV = Py''; where M is the quantity or stock of money; P is the aggregate price level; y is a measure of the aggregate real output, say, the gross domestic product; and V stands for the income *velocity* of money that is defined as V = (Py)/M. Apart from the notion of the velocity of money, the other variables that enter the quantity theory of money are relatively straightforward. Noting that ''Py'' is nothing but the nominal aggregate output (the value of the gross domestic product at current prices), the income velocity of money can be thought of as the number of times each dollar in the nation's money supply circulates to finance the current nominal income. The velocity, then, is just the turnover rate of money. Necessarily, the income velocity of money is greater than one. The gross domestic product at current prices in 1993 was about 6,500 billion dollars, and a narrowly defined measure of the money supply (called M1) was about 1,150 billion dollars. These numbers suggested the income velocity of money was approximately 6 in 1993.

How does the classical quantity theory of money provide the linkage between changes in the money supply and changes in the price level? In order to translate the equation "MV = Py" into the quantity theory of money, two main assumptions are made. First, it is argued that velocity is constant. Classical economists, in particular Irving Fisher, argue that the velocity of money is determined largely by payment technology and payment habits of the society. For example, frequent use of charge cards, rather than money (such as cash or checks) increases the velocity of money. Similarly, if workers are paid on a weekly rather than a monthly basis, the velocity will be greater. It is however, argued that the foregoing are examples of institutional characteristics, and institutional factors that determine the equilibrium level of the velocity change very slowly. As a result, the velocity of money can be regarded as fixed or constant in the short run.

The second key classical assumption (in fact, an inference of classical macroeconomic theory) was that real output (measured by real gross domestic product) is constant or fixed. As alluded to in the previous sentence and discussed under a brief overview of classical theory, the constancy of real output is a result of classical macroeconomic reasoning, rather than a simple assumption. The fixed output is a result of the full employment level. The full employment of the labor force, in turn, is assured by a set of assumptions about the labor market. In particular, perfect competition, perfect information, and wage/price flexibility always result in the full employment of workers.

Once the above two assumptions are made (i.e., velocity and real output are fixed), the classical quantity theory of money, given by the expression MV = Py, easily connects the changes in money supply to changes in price level. More specifically, a money supply change leads to a proportionate change in price level. For example, if money supply increases by 10 percent, price also increases by 10 percent. The reasoning behind this linkage between the money supply and the price level is as follows: An increase in the money supply would lead to an increase in spending by individuals. However, given that real output is assumed to be constant, the increased spending can only lead to an increase in the price level. This explanation is often summarized as "too many dollars chasing too few goods."

While monetarists, led by Nobel Prize winner Milton Friedman, initially wanted to use the classical quantity theory of money to explain proposition one (the linkage between the money supply and the nominal GDP/income), in light of the Keynesian theory and the experience of the Great Depression, they could no longer assume that real output level was fixed. Thus, Friedman modified the classical quantity of money to allow for variations in real output. However, if velocity is assumed constant, "MV = Py" still means that an increase in money supply will lead to a proportionate change in "Py." Friedman even argues that the velocity of money does not have to be assumed constant. Instead, he argues that the velocity can be allowed to change. However, the changes in velocity are predictable. This complicates the explanation of the linkage between money supply and nominal income somewhat. It no longer means that an increase in the money supply will lead to a proportionate increase in the nominal GDP, because now the velocity can also undergo a change. However, the modified quantity theory of money still links money supply and nominal income. It should be noted that this linkage between money supply and the nominal income does not separate the effects of money on nominal income into changes in the price level (P) and changes in the real output (y). This issue is further dealt with in propositions two and three.

PROPOSITION TWO. As illustrated above, proposition one does not breakdown a change in nominal output into price and real output components. Friedman argues that, in the short run, both price level and real output increase when the money supply increases. As real output increases, the employment level will change as well, since the increased output has to be produced by a greater number of workers (the level of technology is assumed to remain unchanged in the short run). Monetarists explain the increase in employment and real output as an increase in money supply leads to an increase in price level. However, workers do not ask for increases in nominal wages to offset the price increase, as they are initially unaware of it. However, producers know the increased prices their goods and services are commanding. Thus, from the producers' (employers') point of view, the real wage paid actually falls (i.e., the dollar wage paid remains the same whereas the price level increases). This effectively lowers their cost of hiring workers and they employ increased number of workers, leading to higher employment and higher real output.

An important implication of this proposition is that a change in money supply does more than influence nominal variables such as price level—it affects real variables such as the employment of labor and real output of goods and services. Monetarists further argue that money, of all the sources of demand in the economy, has the most dominant influence on real variables.

PROPOSITION THREE. While proposition two deals with the effects of short-term changes in the money supply, proposition three discusses its long-term effects. Crucial to increases in output and employment in proposition two is the decline in real wages paid to workers. However, the decline in real wage was caused due to workers being unaware of the increase in price levels. It is argued that workers cannot remain uninformed about the price level increase, as they pay higher prices for the goods and services they consume. Once workers understand the true extent of the increase in the price level, they will demand an increase in nominal wages (wages in current dollars) to compensate for the increase in the price level. Strictly speaking, they would want their nominal wages to increase by the same percentage as the increase in the price level to restore the previous level of their real wage. Once the real wage paid to workers rises to the level it was before the increase in the price level, employers no longer enjoy a cost savings due to lower real wages and, as a result, they cut back labor employment to the level that existed before the price increase. Consequently, the real output level also falls back to the previous level.

The foregoing implies that once enough time passes for workers to adjust their price expectations, the effects of money supply on real variables such as employment and real output evaporate. Does this mean that changes in money supply have no effect on the economy? According to monetarists, this is not the case. The effect is only on the nominal variables—in this case the price level and nominal wage rate, both of which rise proportionate to the initial rise in the money supply. As workers recognize the increase in prices and receive nominal wage adjustments, employment and output levels return to their long-term levels, similar to classical fixed output and employment levels. Even as the real variables do not change over the long-term, the increased levels of prices and nominal wages remain.

An important implication of proposition three is that an increase in money supply has no useful effect on the economy, since real variables such as output and employment remain unaffected but prices and wages increase.

PROPOSITION FOUR. The fourth proposition re-emphasizes the monetarists' faith in the private sector and free market. Monetarists rely on a macroeconomic model that illustrates that the private sector of the economy is not prone to massive fluctuations and is inherently stable. On the other hand, the public sector (as reflected by the behavior of the Federal Reserve Bank in manipulating money supply) is unstable. At a more theoretical level, proponents of monetarism argue that investment (a component of private sector demand) is very sensitive to changes in **interest rates**, whereas the demand for money (the amount of money people want to hold in cash and checkable deposits for various purposes) is not very sensitive to changes in interest rates. While the exact theoretical explanation is quite involved, the preced-

ing assumptions regarding the opposite responses of investment and money demand to interest rates lead to a important theoretical outcome—manipulating the money supply leads to instability in the economy in terms of output, employment, and inflation, whereas changes in the levels of consumption and investment lead to minimal fluctuations in the economy.

A corollary of the foregoing argument involves the third component of aggregate demand, government spending. Aggregate demand is considered to mainly comprise consumption, investment, and government spending. Therefore, like consumption and investment, changes in government spending does not trigger large fluctuation in the economy. This also means that fiscal policy in the form of government deficit spending is not very effective in influencing employment and real output in the economy. Monetarists, however, do infer that government deficit spending is not harmless. It leads to increases in interest rates, which reduce private sector spending on consumption and investment—a phenomenon popularly called crowding out.

In sum, the fourth proposition implies that the private sector in itself is stable—instability is introduced by fluctuations in money supply (monetary policy), and fiscal policy, while not causing instability, leads to the crowding out phenomenon.

MONETARIST POLICY RECOMMENDATIONS AND THEIR FOUNDATIONS

Monetarist policy recommendations basically assert that the government should not use monetary and fiscal policies to stabilize the economy. This, not surprisingly, sounds like the *laissez faire* recommendation of classical economists. However, the reasoning behind the policy recommendations advanced by the proponents of monetarism are somewhat different from those used by their classical counterparts.

The monetarist policy recommendations have two key aspects—one relates to the use of monetary policy and the other relates to the use of fiscal policy. The four propositions discussed above form the major foundations for monetarist policy recommendations with respect to the conduct of monetary and fiscal policies. The monetarist reasoning behind their policy recommendations are briefly discussed below.

With respect to monetary policy, monetarists emphatically recommend that monetary authorities (the Federal Reserve System in the United States) should not use discretionary monetary policy. That is, the nations's money supply should not be manipulated to stabilize or fine tune the economy. The notion of stabilization, in turn, implies an effort to create stable economic growth with low or no inflation. Such a stabilization policy, if successful, would smooth out the bumps in the path of economic growth—both recessions and booms would be moderated and the economy would grow at a rate consistent with its long-term potential. Monetarists do not believe that the Federal Reserve can conduct a successful monetary policy aimed at stabilizing the economy. They admit that monetary policy does have a dominant effect on nominal GDP (see proposition one). However, monetary policy affects real variables such as employment and real output, whose growth is considered desirable, only in the short-term (see proposition two). In the long term, real output and employment are determined at the equilibrium level, and thus a money supply increase ultimately only affects the price level and inflation, which is not a desirable outcome (see proposition three). Monetarists, therefore, argue that beneficial effects of monetary policy are short-lived and harmful effects prevail. This is one of the reasons monetarists do not recommend using discretionary monetary policies.

Monetarism supporters further argue that the use of discretionary policy destabilizes the economy even further, rather than stabilizing the economy around full employment with low inflation. Monetarists use propositions one and two to support this contention. However, they argue that the monetary instrument is too powerful to be used successfully in stabilizing the economy. Monetary authorities do not have enough knowledge of the way the economy and monetary policy work to use the policy successfully. In particular, they contend that monetary policy affects the economy with long and variable lags. This implies that we do not know exactly when the effects of a dose of monetary policy will show up in the economy. As a result, use of monetary policy can exacerbate the economic fluctuations in the economy, and the resulting instability would be far greater than that found if no monetary policy were used at all. Consider, for example, that the economy is in recession and that it is going to come out of recession on its own in three months. However, the Federal Reserve, not knowing when the recession will end, conducts an expansionary monetary policy by increasing money supply to eliminate the recession. Now, suppose that the effects of this monetary policy show up in the economy in six months when the economy has already rebounded and is growing rapidly on its own. The powerful push from the monetary policy could have a negative effect—the economy could overheat, leading to unwanted inflation. Thus, monetarists argue that the monetary authorities, even if well-intentioned, do not have the knowledge to successfully conduct stabilization using monetary policy. Of course, monetarists also argue that the Federal Reserve is not to be trusted with the manipulation of money supply. They say that the Federal Reserve has made a number of costly

mistakes in the past in the conduct of monetary policy. The most infamous example is the decrease in money supply during the Great Depression when the economy needed an increase in money supply to cope with the economic crisis. The proponents of monetarism, therefore, advocate that the Federal Reserve should be kept from tampering with monetary policy—instead of manipulating money supply to stabilize the economy, the Federal Reserve should allow money supply to grow at a constant rate. In other words, the Federal Reserve should follow a rule rather than exercising its discretion. This will keep the Fed from being a source of instability. While monetarists agree that following a rule does not imply that the economy would attain *nirvana* (a state of bliss in which there are no fluctuations), the economy would experience smaller fluctuations. Finally, monetarists insist that ultimately, there is no need to stabilize the economy because the private sector is inherently stable (proposition four). It is discretionary monetary policy that introduces instability into the economy. The proponents of monetarism use the inherent stability argument to further strengthen their recommendation of following a constant money supply growth rule,

With respect to fiscal policy, monetarist's policy recommendations are broadly similar to those of the classical economists. The monetarists argue that government fiscal policy (especially deficit spending) is ineffective in affecting employment and real output in any significant manner in either the short or long term (an indirect implication of proposition four). Fiscal policy also does not appreciably influence price level. Thus, on the surface, the conduct of fiscal policy may appear inconsequential. However, monetarists point out that borrowing by the government will lead to an increase in interest rates which, in turn, reduces private expenditures on consumption and investment— government spending crowds out private sector spending. Thus, fiscal policy based on borrowing is not harmless. Increased government spending, financed by printing money, of course, has effects similar to expansionary monetary policy.

Monetarists thus advocate using neither discretionary monetary or discretionary fiscal policy to stabilize the economy—they would like to see money supply grow at a constant rate.

WHO DOES THE GOVERNMENT FOLLOW?

While proponents of monetarism have staged a very vocal and visible attack on the activist policy recommendations of Keynesian economists, they have not been successful in dethroning the Keynesians. One can safely argue that the United States and many other capitalist countries largely follow Keynesian policy recommendations at the current time. In fact, following the Keynesian revolution, the U.S.

Congress has enacted laws that commit the U.S. government to promoting high employment consistent with a stable price level. Officially, both fiscal and monetary policies are considered effective instruments of macroeconomic policies aimed at stabilizing the economy through full employment. However, due to the slow speed at which fiscal policy reacts to developments in the U.S. economy, monetary policy has come to shoulder the major burden of stabilizing the economy.

Does this mean that monetarism has completely failed to influence the conduct of macroeconomic policies? Monetarists did fail in having their key recommendation, the constant money supply growth rule, accepted by monetary authorities. However, they have succeeded in driving home the point that manipulating the money supply has powerful consequences and that it can potentially be harmful to the economy. The monetary policy authorities of today realize the limitations of monetary policy. As a result, they do not take rash steps in either direction. The Federal Reserve watches the economy carefully and collects a great deal of information about the state of the economy before taking a major monetary policy action. Thus, monetarists should not be considered as having failed completely—they have succeeded in, at least, adding a note of caution in the conduct of monetary policy.

[Anandi P. Sahu]

FURTHER READING:

Froyen, Richard T. Macroeconomics: *Theories and Policies,* 4th ed. Macmillan Publishing Company, 1993.

Friedman, Milton, and Anna Schwartz. *Monetary Trends in the United States and United Kingdom.* University of Chicago Press, 1982.

Gordon, Robert J. *Macroeconomics*, 6th edition. Harper Collins College Publishers, 1993.

Gordon, Robert J., ed. *Milton Friedman's Monetary Framework* University of Chicago Press, 1974.

Mayer, Thomas. *The Structure of Monetarism.* W.W. Norton & Company, 1978.

Modigliani, Franco. ''The Monetarist Controversy, or Should We Forsake Stabilization Policies?'' *American Economic Review*, March 1977.

MONEY MARKET INSTRUMENTS

The money market is the arena in which financial, nonfinancial, and banking institutions make available to a broad range of creditors, borrowers and investors, the opportunity to buy and sell, on a wholesale basis, large volumes of bills, notes, and other forms of short-term credit. These instruments have maturities ranging from one day to one year and are extremely liquid. Consequently, they are considered to be near-cash equivalents, hence the name money market instruments.

Retail money market dealers work independently or in syndicated groups to efficiently distribute available supplies of money market instruments to securities dealers, **banks**, and other financial intermediaries who broker them to retail clients. In addition to dealers, institutions and funds repackage money market instruments into money market **mutual funds** to allow participation at almost any level.

The suppliers of funds for money market instruments are institutions and individuals with a preference for the highest liquidity and the lowest risk. Often, money market instruments are a parking place for temporary excess cash of investors and corporations. Interest rates on money market instruments are typically quoted on a bank discount basis.

CERTIFICATES OF DEPOSIT

Certificates of deposit (CDs) are certificates issued by a federally chartered bank against deposited funds that earn a specified return for a definite period of time. Large denomination (jumbo) CDs of $100,000 or more are generally negotiable and pay higher interest than smaller denominations. However, such certificates are insured by the FDIC only up to $100,000. A Yankee CD is a CD issued by domestic branches of foreign banks. Eurodollar CDs are negotiable certificates issued against U.S. dollar obligations in a foreign branch of a domestic bank.

Brokerage firms have a nationwide pool of bank CDs and receive a fee for selling them. Since brokers deal in large sums, brokered CDs generally pay higher interest rates and offer greater liquidity than CDs purchased directly from a bank, since brokers maintain an active secondary market in CDs.

COMMERCIAL PAPER

Commercial paper (CP) refers to unsecured short-term **promissory notes** issued by financial and nonfinancial corporations. CP has maturities of up to 270 days (the maximum allowed without SEC registration requirement). Dollar volume for CP exceeds the amount of any money market instrument other than **Treasury bills**. CP is typically issued by large, credit-worthy corporations with unused lines of bank credit and, therefore, carries low **default** risk.

Standard & Poor's and Moody's provide ratings. The highest ratings are A1 and P(Prime)1, respectively. A2 and P2 paper is considered high quality, but usually indicates that the issuing corporation is smaller or more debt burdened than A1 and P1 companies. Issuers, earning the lowest ratings, find few willing investors.

Commercial paper can be issued directly by the company to creditors, using internal transactors or a bank as an agent. The bank assumes no principal position and is in no way obligated with respect to repayment of the CP.

Companies may also sell CP through dealers who charge a fee and arrange for the transfer of the funds from the lender to the borrower.

BANKERS ACCEPTANCE

Bankers' **acceptances** are generally used to finance foreign trade. A buyer's promise to pay a specific amount of money at a fixed or determinable future time (usually less than 180 days) is issued to a seller. A bank then guarantees or "accepts" this promise in exchange for a claim on the goods as collateral. The seller may obtain immediate cash in lieu of future payment by selling the acceptance at a discount.

[Roger J. AbiNader]

FURTHER READING:

Black, Pam. "CDs That Try a Little Harder." *Business Week*, September 5, 1994.

Dunnan, Nancy. *Dunn and Bradstreet Guide to Your Investments*. 1991.

Munn, Glen G., I. Garcia, and Charles J. Woelfel. *Encyclopedia of Banking and Finance, Library Edition*, 9th ed. Salem Press, 1991.

Nayar, Nandkumar and Michael S. Rozeff. "Commercial Paper and the Cost of Capital, Rating, Commercial Paper, and Equity Returns," *Journal of Finance*. September, 1994, vol. 49, no. 4.

Retkwa, Rosalyn. "New CP-Funded Loans Broaden Market but aren't Always Cheap," *Corporate Cashflow Magazine*, August, 1993, vol. 14, no. 9, p. 45.

MONEY SUPPLY

The supply or stock of money consists of all the money held by the nonbank public at any point of time. Money is defined as the generally accepted medium of exchange, i.e., whatever is generally accepted in paying for goods and services and repaying debt. It must, however, be emphasized that an economist's notion of money differs from the conventional usage of the term.

Commonly, people recognize currency (consisting of notes and coins) as money, since currency in one form or another has been used as a medium of exchange since ancient times. In modern day advanced societies, cash is still "king," but currency is not the dominant part of what economists consider money. The other key component of money is the amount of checkable deposits in the banking system, as people can write checks on their accounts (deposits) to pay for goods and services or to repay debt. The third, and a relatively minor, component of the money supply is the amount of outstanding traveler's checks. The sum of currency held by the nonbank public, checkable deposits, and traveler's checks yield a measure of money supply officially known as the M1 (or money aggregate) measure of money supply in the United States. At the end of 1993, the M1 measure of money supply was estimated at about 1,130 billion dollars, only 28 percent of which was in currency; 71 percent was in checkable deposits and less than 1 percent was in traveler's checks.

It may come as somewhat of a surprise to many people that credit cards are not listed above as being part of the money supply. After all, don't most people use credit cards in numerous ordinary transactions? Some individuals even refer to credit cards as "plastic money." The main reason for excluding credit cards is fairly straight forward—using a credit card is equivalent to buying on **credit**, at least temporarily. In other words, payment by credit cards is inherently different from payment by cash or checks.

MONEY AND ITS KEY FUNCTIONS

To properly understand how the money supply is measured by the federal monetary authorities, one needs to understand the functions of money. While money is defined as anything accepted in payment for goods and services or repayment of debts, it serves several additional functions, such as unit of account and store of value. All three major functions of money are briefly discussed below.

MEDIUM OF EXCHANGE. The definition of money itself refers primarily to the medium of exchange as its key characteristic. Certainly, money in the form of currency or checks serves this function. One can appreciate the contribution of money in facilitating exchanges if one looks into consequences of having to do without money—that is, to depend on a **bartering** system. Imagine a worker working at a farm and being paid in corn that he helped to produce. Further, say this worker does not like to eat corn and has to buy food and nonfood items (such as, clothing, shoes, books, etc.) to satisfy his and his family's needs from his earnings at the farm. He will have to find individuals who will provide him with rice, potatoes, shirts, tennis shoes, children's books, etc. in exchange for his corn. There must always be a double coincidence of wants for a transaction to be consummated. One can easily see that, in the absence of money, the farm worker will have to spend quite a bit of time just converting his earnings in corn into the items he actually wants to consume. When money is introduced into the picture, the farm worker gets paid in dollars.

He then takes his earnings in dollars and buys different items with his income. People who receive the farm worker's dollars also do the same. Thus, the need to find an individual, for example, who wants to exchange shirts for corn is avoided. Use of money as a medium of exchange thus reduces waste and inefficiency by eliminating much of the time spent in exchanging goods and services. As a result, money also promotes specialization, with different individuals specializing in different trades or professions without having to worry about how to trade their services or output to assemble all the items that their incomes can afford. The need for money is so strong that all societies, except those that are extremely primitive, invent some form of money. Money has taken the form of strings of beads (used by American Indians), cigarettes (used in prisoner-of-war camps), gold coins (used by Romans), and traveler's checks used by modern tourists.

UNIT OF ACCOUNT. The second important function of money is to serve as a unit of account—just as we measure weight in pounds or height in inches, the values of goods and services are expressed in terms of money. For example, a shirt costs $45 at a department store, and a crystal ashtray costs $90 at the same store. Thus, the ashtray is twice as expensive as the shirt. The convenience of money, once again, can be seen by contrasting the barter economy scenario. Assume that there are only 10 **commodities** in the economy. With 10 commodities, one must know 45 prices (economic worth of each commodity expressed in terms of the 9 other commodities). However, if money is used to quote values of the 10 commodities, one needs to know only 10 prices to accomplish the same objective that the barter system will do with 45 prices. As the number of commodities increases, the complexity of the barter system multiplies immensely. For example, with 1000 items, nearly half a million prices will be needed in the barter system. Most supermarkets have many more than 1000 items—a total nightmare even for a mathematically inclined shopper. Money thus performs an important function as a unit of account by reducing the transactions costs due to a much smaller number of prices that have to be considered.

STORE OF VALUE. Money also functions as a store of value, although not in all circumstances. Serving as a store of value means that wealth can be held in terms of money for future use—to be spent on items or to be passed on to heirs. Money is not the only asset that functions as a store of value. Many assets, such as **stocks**, **bonds**, **real estate**, and gold, can also be used as a store of value. Money has a minor advantage over competing assets in one respect—it is already in the form that can be spent, while the others first have to be converted into money before being spent. In this sense, money is the most liquid of all assets that can be used to store wealth—stocks and bonds are less liquid than money, but more liquid than real estate. However, money as a store of value has two major disadvantages. First, other assets may yield returns that are far greater than money—say, one individual earns 20 percent a year on stocks and only 3 percent on his checking account. Thus, wealth will multiply faster when held in assets other than money. Secondly, during periods of rapid **inflation**, money may not serve as an useful store of wealth. The decline in the usefulness of money as a store of wealth depends on the rate of inflation. Inflation erodes the purchasing power of money. If price levels double in a year, the stored money will buy only half as much the next year. There are real world examples in history where money became worthless rather quickly. Germany after World War I provides an example of an extreme inflationary environment—the inflation rate sometimes exceeded 1000 percent per month. If a worker did not spend his or her income in the morning, it lost much of its value by the evening.

As the German example illustrates, money is almost useless as a store of value in a highly inflationary environment. Even with a 10 to 15 percent annual inflation rate, money is not considered a good store of value. Because of these difficulties, money is not widely used as a store of value for a prolonged period of time—other assets, despite their relative lack of liquidity, have an edge over money.

DIFFERENT MEASURES OF MONEY SUPPLY

Money as defined above yields the most narrowly defined measure of money supply known as M1. This M1 measure of money supply, most closely corresponds to the ordinary definition of money (i.e., something that is commonly accepted in payment of goods and services).

THE CENTRAL MONETARY AUTHORITY. Every country has a central bank that monitors the money supply and almost always determines the level of money supply in the economy. In the United States, the **Federal Reserve System** serves as the central bank of the country. The Federal Reserve, commonly referred to as the Fed, uses three different measures of money supply—M1, M2, and M3. M2 and M3 measures of money supply build on the narrowly defined M1 measure by successively broadening the money supply measure. Thus, M1 is the narrowest measure of money supply, M2 is broader than M1, and M3 is the broadest measure.

In order to understand why the Federal Reserve System uses successively broader measures of money supply, one has to go back to the ordinary definition of money and then consider what else can be converted into ordinary money with minimum difficulty. The example of savings account deposits can be used to demonstrate why the M1 measure of money supply is broadened. Remember, the narrow M1 definition of money supply includes checkable deposits, but not savings account deposits. The reason for excluding savings account deposits is the inability of a savings account to be directly used in making payments, unlike a checking account. However, with just a phone call to one's bank, one can transfer money from savings into checking and then make the payment by writing checks on the checking account. Alternatively, one can drive to bank and withdraw money in cash from his or her savings account, thus converting resources in the savings account into ordinary money. As this illustrates, there is very little difference between the ''moneyness'' of checkable and savings deposits. Savings account deposits are therefore called near-money. Not considering items that are considered near-money, means that M1 does not properly reflect the extent of true money supply in the economy. The Federal Reserve thus coined broader measures of money supply (M2 and M3) to capture the characteristics of money in items other than those included in the M1 measure of money supply.

THE M1 MEASURE OF MONEY SUPPLY. As pointed out earlier, M1 is the narrowest measure of money supply and closely corresponds to the common definition of money. M1 monetary aggregate can be defined as follows:

M1 = Currency
+ Demand deposits
+ Other checkable deposits
+ Traveler's checks

Currency simply consists of notes (bills of different denominations) and coins. Currency currently accounts for less than one-third of the M1 money supply in the United States. Checkable deposits make up nearly two-thirds of the M1 money supply. The checkable deposits category itself is normally split into demand deposits and other checkable deposits. while both these components of checkable deposits can be used to write checks to make payments for goods and services, there is an important distinction between demand and nondemand checkable deposits. Demand deposits are normally maintained by businesses and they carry no interest payments. They are termed demand deposits because the entire amount in a demand deposit is payable to the deposit holder or a designated person *on demand*. Moreover, some banks charge a service fee from holders of demand deposits, fees that are often waived if the amount in a demand deposit exceeds a certain level. The category ''other checkable deposits'' include different kinds of checkable deposits that pay interest to the deposit holders—NOW (negotiated order of withdrawal) accounts, super-NOW accounts and ATS (automatic transfer from savings) accounts. Therefore, if nondemand checkable deposits can be used both to write checks and to

earn interest, why maintain checkable deposits in the demand deposit form? The answer lies in a restriction associated with nondemand checkable deposits—while balances in demand deposits are payable on demand, checks written on balances in nondemand checkable deposits are negotiated orders of withdrawal. That is, the payment may be delayed for a while, depending on the amount of withdrawal. Even though most people have never experienced this delay in payments from an interest bearing nondemand checking account, it can happen in extreme circumstances. Because businesses deal in larger amounts of money, they cannot entertain this uncertainty and have to maintain demand deposits.

Traveler's checks constitute a very small fraction of the M1 money supply—less than 1 percent of the total M1. Traveler's checks can be used to make payments even outside one's home country, as the issuer of the traveler's checks guarantees payments to the individual or business that receives them (so long as they are properly signed). One can thus consider traveler's checks as checks with added features designed to increase their widespread acceptance.

One can now see how all three components of the M1 measure of money supply—currency, checkable deposits and traveler's checks—are clearly money in the ordinary sense of the term, as they can be directly used in payment of goods and services. One warning about money as it is defined above—it is not universally acceptable (specially, beyond a nation's borders). To make the currency universally acceptable within a country, the government of that country usually provides its currency with legal backing. In the United States, for example, every denomination of paper currency carries the following notice: ''THIS NOTE IS LEGAL TENDER FOR ALL DEBTS, PUBLIC AND PRIVATE.'' Thus, declining to accept a genuine **Federal Reserve** note is literally in violation of the federal law. However, this doesn't mean that U.S. currency would automatically have value in foreign countries, nor does it mean that the currency of other nations is valid in the United States. In fact, stores in U.S. cities bordering Canada often state that Canadian money is not accepted without violating any rules.

THE M2 MEASURE OF MONEY SUPPLY. The M2 measure of money supply is made broader than the M1 monetary aggregate by adding additional items that fall under the near-money category. M2 is formally defined as follows:

M2 = M1
+ Savings deposits
+ Small-denomination time deposits
+ Money market deposit accounts
+ Money market mutual fund shares (noninstitutional)

+ Overnight repurchase agreements
+ Overnight Eurodollars
+ Consolidation adjustment

Basically, six additional assets are added to the narrow measure of money supply known as M1 (the seventh item is merely an adjustment). these items will be briefly discussed below.

SAVINGS DEPOSITS. Savings deposits are maintained by households and individuals. These deposits pay a varying interest based on the balance in an account. Money can be withdrawn from these accounts without penalty. The major inconvenience of a savings account is that checks can't be written on them. Banks have found a way around this inconvenience by permitting automatic transfer of funds from a savings account to pay for checks written on the checking account maintained by the individual. These are called ATS (automatic transfer from savings) accounts. Because of this, ATS accounts are included as part of the M1 money supply. Only the non-ATS portion of savings account deposits are added to the M1 measure when broadening it into the M2 monetary aggregate.

SMALL-DENOMINATION TIME DEPOSITS. Time deposits are commonly known as certificates of deposit. A certificate is issued for a fixed period of time with a specified maturity date and a specified interest rate. Certificates of deposits that are for less than $100,000 are called *small-denomination* time deposits. Unlike the household savings accounts, certificates of deposits (CDs) have a prescheduled maturity date and a financial penalty for early withdrawal of funds, making somewhat illiquid. In order to make certificates of deposits more liquid, banks have begun issuing CDs that are negotiable. Instead of suffering a severe financial penalty, a holder of a negotiable CD can sell it on the secondary market without penalty. Before 1961, bank certificates of deposits were nonnegotiable— they could not be sold to someone else and had to be redeemed, if necessary, from the issuing bank at a substantial penalty. In 1961, Citibank introduced the first negotiable CDs in large denominations ($100,000 or above). Negotiable CDs are now issued by almost all major commercial banks.

MONEY MARKET DEPOSIT ACCOUNTS. Money market deposit accounts are interest bearing accounts where the interest paid on balances in the accounts depends on the interest rate prevailing in the money market. The money market itself consists of short-term financial instruments (those that have maturity periods of one year or less). The key feature of a money market instrument is that its yield reflects the current interest rate and inflation in the economy. A money market deposit thus allows the holder of the account to participate in the money market. Usually, large sums are needed to participate in the money

market directly, which means most individual investors are not able to do so. Banks and other financial institutions, through money market accounts, provide an individual one way to participate in the money market. These often is a minimum investment that an individual must make to use the money market route, although it is less than other investment options.

Most money market deposit accounts also carry limited check-writing privileges and thus resemble interest bearing checking accounts, to a degree. Therefore, many academic scholars in the field believe that money market accounts should be part of the M1 measure of money supply. However, at the current time, listed as a component of M2, not M1.

MONEY MARKET MUTUAL FUND SHARES (NON-INSTITUTIONAL). Money market **mutual funds** are mutual funds that invest in money market instruments. For reasons described above, individuals have difficulty in directly participating in the money market. Opening a money market deposit account at a bank is one way to participate in the money market. Buying shares of a money market mutual fund is another. Money market mutual funds basically pool individual investors' resources and invest them in money market instruments. After subtracting costs, they distribute the gains from the investments to those who contributed to the pool of funds through the purchase of shares. Like money market deposit accounts at banks, most money market mutual funds also provide limited check writing privileges. Checks frequently cannot be written for less than a certain minimum, and a substantial amount of money is initially required to open an account with a money market mutual fund. These restrictions are generally quite similar to those that apply to money market deposit accounts at banks.

OVERNIGHT REPURCHASE AGREEMENTS. Repurchase agreements are essentially short-term loans backed by U.S. **Treasury bills** as collateral. Usually, the maturity period of a repurchase agreement is less than two weeks, although it can be as short as overnight. A repurchase agreement transaction can be illustrated as follows: A large corporation has some idle cash and a bank wants to borrow some funds overnight to make up for the shortfall in the amount of required reserves that it must have at the Federal Reserve. Assume that the corporation uses $10 million to buy Treasury bills from the bank, which agrees to repurchase Treasury bills the next morning at a price slightly higher than the corporation's purchase price. The additional price that the bank pays is a way of paying interest on the overnight use of the $10 million. Should the bank not buy back the Treasury bills that the corporation is holding, the latter can sell those bills to recover its loan. Transferred Treasury bills thus serve as a collateral, which the lender receives if the borrower does not pay back the loan.

Repurchase agreements are a relatively new financial instrument. They have been in existence only since 1969. However, they constitute an important source of funds for banks, where large corporations are considered the most important lenders.

Because of extremely short maturity, overnight repurchase agreements are considered very liquid—the instrument turns back into cash the very next day. However, because it is less liquid than currency or checkable deposits, it is included in the M2 measure.

OVERNIGHT EURODOLLARS. The term Eurodollar originates from the fact that U.S. dollars, at one time, were deposited at banks in Europe by certain individuals and countries. The tradition of Eurodollar deposits was first established when the Soviet Union deposited U.S. dollars in Europe rather than in the United States—it wanted the security that the U.S. dollar provided, along with interest income from its deposits, without exposing the cash to the uncertainty that a deposit in the United States may have entailed. Depositing U.S. dollars outside the United States is no longer confined to Europe—U.S. dollars are now deposited in a variety of locations, including Hong Kong, Singapore, Sydney, and Tokyo. For this reason, Eurodollars are sometimes also referred to as overseas dollars.

Eurodollar deposits are specially attractive to American banks. The advent of Eurodollar deposits was one of the major reasons why so many banks based in the United States have open branches in foreign countries. They can borrow Eurodollar deposits from their own foreign branches or from other banks when they need additional funds. Inclusion of Eurodollar deposits in M2 is a recognition on the part of the Federal Reserve System that the Eurodollar deposits abroad can be converted into dollar holdings in the United States, affecting the U.S. money supply.

CONSOLIDATION ADJUSTMENT. The consolidation adjustment is merely a statistical adjustment applied to the M2 measure to avoid double counting. It is not a fundamental component of the M2 monetary aggregate in the SAME sense that other elements are. The kind of double counting the consolidation adjustment is designed to avoid can be illustrated with the help of an example—the M2 consolidation adjustment subtracts short-term **repurchase agreements** and Eurodollars being held by money market mutual funds, because they are already included in the balances of money market mutual funds.

One can assert that the M2 measure of money supply is a somewhat lower on the liquidity scale, compared to the M1 measure, which is the most liquid. Assets that are added to the M1 aggregate to arrive at the M2 measure are items that are the most easily and most frequently transferred into checking accounts or can otherwise be converted into cash quickly.

THE M3 MEASURE OF MONEY SUPPLY. The M3 measure of money supply further broadens the M2 monetary aggregate by adding additional assets that are less liquid than those included in M1 and M2. Formally, M3 is defined as follows:

$$
\begin{aligned}
\text{M3} = \text{M2} \\
&+ \text{Large-denomination time deposits} \\
&+ \text{Money market mutual fund shares} \\
&\quad \text{(institutional)} \\
&+ \text{Long-term Repurchase agreements} \\
&+ \text{Term Eurodollars} \\
&+ \text{Consolidation adjustment}
\end{aligned}
$$

Many of the items that are added to the M2 measure of money supply to arrive at the M3 monetary aggregate are similar in name to those added to the M1 measure to arrive at the M2 measure, except that the maturity periods associated with the M1 measures are shorter. The five items that are added to the M2 measure to arrive at the M3 measure are briefly discussed below.

LARGE-DENOMINATION TIME DEPOSITS. Certificates of deposits issued in denominations of $100,000 or above are called large-denomination time deposits. These are like small-denomination time deposits (issued in denominations of less than $100,000), with a scheduled maturity date and a specified interest rate. However, large-denomination certificates of deposits are usually negotiable CDs that can be sold in the secondary market before they mature. Thus, large-denomination negotiable CDs serve as an alternative to investing in Treasury bills for corporate treasurers who have idle funds to invest for a short time.

MONEY MARKET MUTUAL FUND SHARES (INSTITUTIONAL). Money market mutual fund shares that are added to M2 to arrive at M3 are the same as those that are added to the M1 measure to arrive at the M2, with a minor difference. Money market mutual fund shares held by institutions also are included when the M3 measure of money supply is calculated, whereas only money market mutual fund shares held by noninstitutions investors were included when the M2 measure of money supply was constructed.

LONG TERM REPURCHASE AGREEMENTS. Repurchase agreements that have maturity periods of more than one night are called long-term repurchase agreements. Thus, long-term repurchase agreements also facilitate borrowing and lending in which Treasury bills are essentially used as collateral. By nature, long-term repurchase agreements are less liquid than overnight repurchase agreements.

TERM EURODOLLARS. Like long-term repurchase agreements, term Eurodollars have a maturity period greater than one night. While the maturity period of a term Eurodollar can vary, a majority of them mature in a few weeks. Obviously, term Eurodollars are less liquid than overnight Eurodollars. That is why term Eurodollars are included only in M3 and not in M2.

CONSOLIDATION ADJUSTMENT. An adjustment, similar to that made to the M2 measure of money supply, is made to the M3 monetary aggregate to avoid double counting.

In sum, one can consider the M3 monetary aggregate to be lower on the liquidity scale than the M2 measure, when all components of M3 are considered together.

WHICH MONETARY AGGREGATE DOES THE FED USE? As was discussed above, the M2 and M3 measures of money supply are, successively, lower on the liquidity scale than M1. While M1 closely corresponds to the ordinary notion of money, M2 and M3 capture the moneyness in assets not included in M1. To monitor the supply of money in the economy, the Federal Reserve looks at all three measures of the money supply but tends to focus on the M2 measure. There is a considerable debate among economists regarding the value of the Fed's emphasis on the M2 monetary aggregate.

While growth rates of all three measures of money supply do have a tendency to move together, there also exist some glaring discrepancies in the movements of these monetary aggregates. For example, according to the M1 measure, the growth rate of money supply did not accelerate between 1968 and 1971. However, if the M2 and M3 measures are used as the guide, a different story emerges—they show a significant acceleration in the growth rate of money supply. Because of this kind of divergent behavior, the battle to find the true measure of money supply continues. Often a weighted average of monetary aggregates—one that captures the moneyness in all assets included in M2 and M3 (remember, M1 is already money in the strict sense of the term)—has been suggested to arrive at the true measure of the money supply.

CONTROLLING THE NATION'S MONEY SUPPLY

As was mentioned earlier, in every free market economy the money supply is controlled by the nation's central bank, the chief monetary authority for the country. A central bank is known by different names in different countries—often, even the adjective "central" may be missing. For example, in the United States, the central bank is known as the Federal Reserve System; in England, it is known as the Bank of England; and in Germany, it is called the Bundesbank.

The Federal Reserve System in the United States uses three different methods to control and manipulate the nation's money supply. However, before discussing these methods, it will be useful to understand the players that participate in increasing or decreasing the levels of monetary aggregates.

MONEY SUPPLY AND THE BANKING SYSTEM. All definitions of money supply underscore the fact that deposits at commercial banks, **savings and loan associations**, **credit unions**, and mutual savings banks (collectively known as depository institutions) are an integral part of the money supply. Why are depository institutions involved in the money supply process? Depository institutions, profit by taking deposits from individuals and businesses and making loans to a variety of borrowers. The difference between what they earn from the loans made and the amount paid to depositors (in additional to the operating costs) constitutes the basis for profits to the depository institutions. This logic will induce banks and other depository institutions to loan out as much of depositors' funds as possible. However, the Federal Reserve has put a restriction on this behavior—the depository institutions are required to keep a fraction of the deposits in reserves at the Federal Reserve. Thus, the depository financial institutions can only lend out the excess reserves—reserves (vault cash and cash deposits at the Federal Reserve) over and above the reserves required, by law, to be kept at the Federal Reserve Bank.

In manipulating the money supply, it is the level of the excess reserves that the Federal Reserve attempts to influence to affect the growth rate of the nation's money supply. To illustrate this, let us assume that through some mechanism the Fed is able to increase the amount of excess reserves in the banking system. Banks, faced with the extra resources, want to lend them prudently to earn interest on loans made. Further, assume that loans are made by simply creating deposits (which are part of the money supply) in borrowers' names. Creating additional deposits results in an increase in the money supply. While the preceding logic may appear like an academic concoction, this is what happens in the real world. The only question that remains to be answered is as to how the Federal Reserve manipulates the level of excess reserves in the banking system.

There are three instruments available to the Federal Reserve Bank that it can use to manipulate the excess reserves in the banking system and thus the level of money supply—the reserve requirement ratio, the discount rate and open market operations.

THE RESERVE REQUIREMENT RATIO. The reserve requirement ratio is the legal ratio determined by the Federal Reserve (within limits established by the Congress) that it requires of the depository institutions in calculating the minimum reserves they must keep to conform to the federal banking law. Thus, if the Fed increases the reserve requirement ratio, it automatically reduces the amount of excess reserves in the banking system. This can be explained as follows. Suppose, a bank has $100 million deposits and the reserve requirement ratio is 10 percent. Further, assume that it has $18 million in reserves. Since the bank is required to keep a minimum of $10 million in required reserves (the 10 percent reserve requirement ratio applied to $100 million in deposits), it has an excess reserve of $8 million. If the Federal Reserve increases the reserve requirement ratio from 10 percent to 15 percent, would then have to keep $15 million in legal reserves. This leads to a decrease in the level of excess reserves from $8 million to $3 million. A decrease in the amount of excess reserves reduces the ability of the bank to make loans, to create additional deposits and to increase the money supply. In this example, the bank started from positive excess reserves and then increased the reserve requirement ratio. If it had started from zero excess reserves and then increased the reserve requirement ratio, the levels of deposits and money supply would be forced to fall—banks caught with deficient minimum legal reserves would have to reduce the level of deposits, consistent with available reserves.

The Federal Reserve can both lower and raise the reserve requirement ratio to affect money supply. However, raising the legal reserve ratio is especially powerful when the banking system has no excess reserves.

Despite the apparent potency of the reserve requirement ratio as an instrument of money supply manipulations, it is seldom utilized by the Federal Reserve in influencing money supply. A change in the reserve requirement ratio is a legal change and it is not advisable to change the rules of the game frequently. Thus, while the reserve requirement ratio may be utilized in a financial emergency, the Federal Reserve does not use the ratio to manipulate the nation's money supply on a regular basis.

THE DISCOUNT RATE. The **discount rate** is the interest rate the Federal Reserve Bank charges banking institutions for the loans it makes to them. The Federal Reserve was initially created as a lender of last resort—its function was to lend to banks in need of funds through discounting banks' holdings of, say, Treasury bills. Essentially, the Fed made loans to banks with Treasury bills serving as collateral.

Of course, if banks can borrow from the Federal Reserve at a low rate of interest and lend to its borrowers at higher interest rates, it will be clearly profitable for them. By lowering the discount rate, the Federal Reserve lowers the cost of borrowing and increases banks' willingness to borrow. This can potentially increase the level of excess reserves in the

banking system and, consequently, the money supply. Raising the discount rate can have the opposite effect on the level of excess reserves and the money supply.

While the discount rate can potentially be used to influence the levels of excess reserves and money supply in the economy, the Federal Reserve does not use this method to induce increased borrowing by banks. The Federal Reserve dislikes profit-based borrowing by the depository institutions—that is, borrowing at a lower interest rate from the Fed and then lending at higher interest rates to banks' customers. The Federal Reserve Bank does not mind need-based borrowing by banks (when banks, due to some unanticipated factors, fall short of funds). Even then, Federal Reserve closely monitors any bank that borrows from the Fed too frequently.

The preceding discussion suggests that the Federal Reserve does not like to use the discount rate as an instrument to manipulate the level of money supply in the economy on a regular basis (by manipulating the level of excess reserves in the banking system). The Fed, however, does utilize this instrument in an indirect way in manipulating money supply—it uses the discount rate as a signalling device. When the Federal Reserve Bank lowers the discount rate, it signals to the banking system and the financial market that it is in favor of increasing money supply. When the Fed increases the discount rate, it sends out the opposite message. In fact, banks often take the Fed's announcement of the discount rate change quite seriously—if the Federal Reserve raises the discount rate, for example, major banks follow up by raising their prime rates (the rate a bank charges its best customers).

THE OPEN MARKET OPERATIONS. Open market operations are the third and the most frequently used instrument by the Federal Reserve in manipulating the money supply. In open market operations, the Federal Reserve Bank uses market forces to manipulate the level of the excess reserves and thus the money supply in the economy.

In open market operations, the Federal Reserve either buys Treasury securities (bills and bonds) from banks or sells Treasury securities to them. When the Federal Reserve sells **Treasury bonds** to banks, the Fed receives cash in exchange for bonds—the excess reserves in the banking system go down and thus the money supply will, potentially, go down also. The opposite is the case when the Federal Reserve sells Treasury securities to the banking system.

The Federal Reserve uses open market operations to manipulate the nation's money supply on a regular basis—the open market operations are considered the main instrument of monetary policy (increasing or decreasing the money supply with a view to influence the state of the economy).

THE MONEY SUPPLY UNCERTAINTY. While the Federal Reserve is fairly successful in manipulating the money supply, there are some uncertainties regarding the magnitude of a monetary aggregate or the exact time when the increase in the money supply materializes after the Fed initiates the process of expanding the money supply. For example, the Federal Reserve increases the level of excess reserves in the banking system to increase the money supply. However, banks are reluctant to loan (and thus to increase the money supply) because of lack of creditworthy borrowers or their desire to wait for better opportunities. Thus, the Federal Reserve's attempt to increase money supply is frustrated. Despite this uncertainty, the Fed is able to determine changes in the money supply since banks have to report periodically to the Federal Reserve.

[Anandi P. Sahu]

FURTHER READING:

Froyen, Richard T. *Macroeconomics: Theories and Policies*, 4th ed. Macmillan Publishing Company, 1993.

Mishkin, Frederic S. *The Economics of Money, Banking and Financial Markets*, 4th ed. HarperCollins Publishers, 1995.

Ritter, Lawrence S. and Silber, William L. *Principles of Money, Banking and Financial Markets*, 6th ed. Basic Books, Inc., 1989.

MONTE CARLO METHOD

The "Monte Carlo" method—the term is derived from the name of the famous gambling casino—is a means of simulating problems by which decision variables and chance processes are used to generate occurrences in the system. In other words, Monte Carlo simulations are used to predict a range of different outcomes from a given set of decisions. The decisions are held constant, but the outcomes are allowed to vary depending on changes in some key influence, such as sales volume. Monte Carlo simulations are distinguished from other types of simulation techniques by their extensive use of random numbers and repeated trials.

Monte Carlo simulations can be used in **decision making** to provide potential solutions to complex problems. As intimated above, the simulations effectively provide an understanding of the possible outcome of a given decision. They are useful when the environment surrounding a problem is too complex for the effects of a decision or set of decisions to be described with a single outcome. Indeed, Monte Carlo simulations can provide a range of potential results based on the same decision(s). As shown in the example below, the simulations typically involve: a decision variable(s) that is chosen and changed by the

person running the simulation; a randomly changing variable; and a key performance indicator that is influenced by the decision variable(s) and the random variable.

As a simple example, assume that the owner of a rolling hot dog stand earns an average of $75 in profit per day. He sells hot dogs for $3 each, and expects daily sales to vary between 100 and 200 hot dogs. All hot dogs that do not sell spoil and are a total loss, and he puts 200 hot dogs in his stand each morning just in case he has a big day. Using Monte Carlo analysis techniques, the owner could study the effects of various business decisions based on the performance of a key indicator, such as daily profit. For example, he could test the profit impact of the decision to start each day with only 175 hot dogs in his cart. He could then generate a series of random numbers to represent daily hot dog sales over a given period to determine his average daily profits. He may find, for instance, that profits rise when he starts out with only 175 hot dogs, despite the fact that he will run out of hot dogs on some days.

The party running a Monte Carlo simulation must adhere to several parameters for the simulation to be useful. For example, the random variable(s)—the number of hot dogs sold in a day in the above example—must reflect the underlying uncertainty of the problem. For this reason, Monte Carlo simulations can be highly complex and require the application of advanced statistical techniques. Because they allow the modeling of complex environments, though, they are often used to simulate difficult scientific and financial problems.

[Dave Mote]

FURTHER READING:

Chase, Richard B. *Production and Operations Management: A Life Cycle Approach.* 5th ed. Homewood, IL: Irwin, 1989.

Kaplan, Robert S., and Anthony A. Atkinson. *Advanced Management Accounting.* Englewood Cliffs, NJ: Prentice-Hall, 1992.

MORTGAGES/MORTGAGE-BACKED SECURITIES

A mortgage-backed security (MBS) is a debt issue secured by groups, or pools, of home mortgages. The mortgages are grouped together by lenders or other institutions and then either sold to investors who purchase ownership shares in the pool or used to back a debt issue. MBSs shift risks related to changes in **interest rates**, prepayment and refinancing of mortgages, and **default** or nonpayment. The investors receive the interest and principal payments in the form of distributions as the loans are paid off by the mortgage holders (or by the federal government in some cases of default), or simple cash disbursements from the institution that owns the mortgages. Besides providing an investment alternative, MBSs serve the important function of bringing additional funding into the mortgage industry that can be used to finance home buyers. By the early 1990s the mortgage-backed securities market was approaching $5 trillion, representing a major segment of the U.S. economy and serving as a primary money supply for the home mortgage industry. Common buyers of MBSs include pension funds, **mutual funds**, and individual investors.

The MBS emerged during the 1970s as the result of U.S. government initiatives related to the secondary mortgage market. The secondary mortgage market was created in 1938, when the federal government created Federal National Mortgage Association (Fannie Mae) to purchase government-backed mortgages, which include Federal Housing Administration (FHA) and Veterans Administration loans. The effort was designed to supply banks and other financial institutions with cash to make new mortgage loans; the banks continued to profit from servicing the mortgages, but Fannie Mae effectively paid the **banks** cash and assumed ownership of the loans.

Fannie Mae was privatized in 1968. In the same year, a similar entity—the Government National Mortgage Association (Ginnie Mae)—was created with the power to purchase and/or provide payment guarantees (timely payment of principal and interest) on securities backed by FHA and VA mortgages. That effectively made it more feasible for loan originators (i.e., banks and other financial institutions) to begin creating securities backed by pools of mortgages. A bank, for example, could package all of its mortgages together into a debt security backed by Ginnie Mae.

Typically, an investment firm underwrites the security for the institution and sells it to investors. The original lender continues to make money servicing the mortgage, and uses the money from the sale of the security to fund new mortgage loans that may also eventually be securitized. Rather than pool the mortgages, lenders can also sell their mortgages to Fannie Mae (and the Federal Home Loan Mortgage Corporation, or Freddie Mac, created in 1970), which use the mortgages to create their own securities.

By the 1980s the MBS industry had expanded to include four major investment vehicles: mortgage pass-through securities (MPTs); mortgage-backed bonds (MBBs); mortgage pay-through bonds (MPTBs); and collateralized mortgage obligations (CMOs). MPTs were initiated by Ginnie Mae in 1968. They most closely represent the MBS structure—the securities are issued by the mortgage originator and backed by the federal government. The minimum size

of a pool in the early 1990s was $100 million and about 1,000 mortgages.

MBBs are used by private mortgage companies such as banks and savings and loans, and may include mortgages not backed by a government entity. They are similar to MPTs, but the cash flows from interest and principal payments do not pass through directly to the security holders. Instead, the entity that creates the security retains ownership of the mortgages in the pool—the mortgages are usually placed in trust with a third party that ensures that the issuer adheres to the bond provisions—and makes predetermined, periodic cash payments to the bondholders. The net effect is that investors are exposed to different kinds of risk; for example, the risk of mortgage prepayment, which reduces income from interest, is borne by the issuer rather than the security holder, as is the case with an MPT. Underwriters are typically used to sell the securities, and the securities are often rated by a bond rating agency. As with other **bonds**, the value of MBBs is influenced by their riskiness and yields in relation to other securities, and by interest rate fluctuations.

MPTBs are a hybrid of MPTs and MBBs. The MPTB is a bond, but the principal and interest payments are passed through to the owners of the securities. Like the MBB, the issuer retains ownership of the mortgages in the pool and the bond is rated by an agency. The MPTB must be overcollateralized to provide protection against default of some of the underlying mortgages. Still, investors are exposed to various risks inherent to both MBBs and MPTs.

CMOs, created in the early 1980s, are complicated versions of MPTBs. The issuer retains ownership of the mortgages, and principal and interest is passed through. The chief difference is that the mortgages in the pool are separated into different groups, or traunches, based on the date the mortgage matures. By separating the mortgages, the issuer can use the pool to create a number of securities with different characteristics. For example, traunches can be designed to simulate low risk, short-term coupon bonds, or higher risk, long-term zero coupon bonds. The different risk classes theoretically maximize the value of the mortgage pool to the overall investment market.

Related to CMOs are real estate mortgage investment conduits (REMICs). A REMIC is essentially a legally recognized entity that creates a CMO. REMICs evolved following Congress' passage of the Tax Reform Act of 1986. The act allowed CMOs, through REMICs, to be issued with a minimum of tax complications.

[Dave Mote]

FURTHER READING:

Brueggeman, William B., Jeffrey D. Fisher, and Leo D. Stone. *Real Estate Finance*. Homewood, IL: Irwin, 1989.

Garner, Robert J., Robert B. Coplan, Barbara J. Raasch, and Charles L. Ratner. *Ernst & Young's Personal Financial Planning Guide*. New York: John Wiley & Sons, 1995.

Shapiro, Alan C. *Modern Corporate Finance*. New York: Macmillan Publishing Company, 1990.

MOST-FAVORED NATION (MFN)

Most-favored nation status (MFN) is granted by countries to one another in formalized reciprocal trade agreements. Under an MFN clause, a country that grants concessions to one party of the agreement must grant the same concessions to all signatories of the agreement. MFN clauses are integral parts of reciprocal trade agreements. The impetus for reciprocal trade agreements is the reduction of tariffs, import taxes, and, in some instances export **taxes**. This reduction of tariffs fosters international trade by opening markets. Reciprocal trade agreements and their all important MFN clauses serve as the basis for the foreign trade policies of most nations.

The idea of granting reciprocal concessions to encourage trade probably began with Islamic and Byzantine commerce. In an effort to attract quasi-permanent settlements of western merchants (mostly from Spanish, French and Italian commercial areas and ports) to more eastern trading centers, the foreign merchants were granted the same rights and guarantees as the citizens of the host countries.

At the outset of the American revolution, John Adams suggested that a commercial treaty with corresponding MFN language, between the colonies and France would keep that country on the side of the Americans and against the British. Adams felt a commercial treaty would be beneficial to both sides and less entangling than a political treaty. In his Farewell Address of 1796, George Washington advised his fellow countrymen to trade impassionately and without regard to political discrimination.

The United States, however, often disregarded Adams's and Washington's counsel. In the late 1700s and through much of the 1800s, the United States drew a distinction between unconditional MFN and conditional MFN status. Unconditional MFN charges a country to grant to a trading partner all concessions granted to third parties of a trade agreement. With conditional MFN status, however, only the opportunity to be the recipient of trade concessions is guaranteed. Concessions are available only if the potential recipient is willing to replicate the reciprocities granted by a third state. If the United States grants a trade concession to France in **reciprocity**, under conditional MFN status the United States will grant the same concessions to Great Britain only if Great Britain matches French reciprocity. Under unconditional MFN language, Great Britain obtains the concessions granted by the United States to France without having to match French reciprocity (Cline, 1982). Although still abiding by treaty arrangements, the United States has routinely and for political reasons revoked its MFN agreements with many socialist countries, including the Soviet Union, Poland, Hungary, Romania and Nicaragua. As late as 1994 the United States was using MFN leverage in an attempt to force the People's Republic of China to cease its human rights violations—especially following the so-called Tiananmen Square massacre of 1989.

The most comprehensive reciprocal trade agreement is the **General Agreement on Tariffs and Trade (GATT)**. GATT was signed in Geneva in 1947 by 23 countries including the United States. By the early 1990s there were 90 signatories to the trade accord. An integral part of GATT is the unconditional most-favored-nation clause.

[Michael Knes]

FURTHER READING:

Cline, William R. *''Reciprocity'': A New Approach to World Trade Policy?* Washington, DC: Institute for International Economics, 1982.

Neff, Stephen C. *Friends But No Allies: Economic Liberalism and the Law of Nations*. Columbia University Press, 1990.

MOTIVATION

SEE: Employee Motivation

MULTICULTURAL WORKFORCE

The multicultural workforce refers to the changing age, sex, ethnicity, physical ability, race, and sexual orientation of employees across all types and places of work in the United States. Other multicultural dimensions span educational, socioeconomic, and individual lifestyle differences. Increasingly, employees with diverse backgrounds enter the workforce and change the face of business with divergent values, customs, and practices. Due to factors such as extended life expectancy, immigration, birth rates, changing social structures, and financial imperatives, the demographic characteristics of the U.S. working population no longer reflect the largely homogenous **workforce** of the past. Demographic shifts in the population refer to statistical characteristics of the population as a whole or in aggregate. Combined with the globalization of corporate activities and changes in mass marketing, a different profile of the American worker emerges than was present 20 years ago. As corporations recognize and adapt to the multicultural workforce, shifts in the labor pool and the consumer base create a competition for talent, a competition for changing markets, and changes in the competitive market. New opportunities and new challenges emerge with a multicultural workforce. Companies are increasingly recognizing the value and significance of a diverse workforce and actively encouraging workforce diversity. Elements of diversity initiatives include training, communications, task forces, and mentoring. Difficulties in implementing a diversity initiative to value multiculturalism arise when companies fail to answer hard questions about conceptual, philosophical, and practical matters. However, there is no prescribed answer or correct combination of answers, however, to minimize challenges or maximize opportunities in the multicultural workforce. In the end, the multicultural workforce mirrors a multicultural market of great significance to future business success.

Both primary and secondary dimensions of diversity combine to define a multicultural workforce. Primary dimensions of diversity include age, ethnicity, gender, physical ability, race, and sexual orientation. Additionally, secondary factors such as education, geographic location, income, marital status, military experience, parental status, religious preference, and work experience also reflect the elements of a multicultural workforce. Both primary and secondary characteristics significantly affect the individual's interaction in the workplace.

HISTORY AND CONCEPT

The American workforce has historically been dominated by the white, male majority in the labor pool. Women entered the workforce in the late 1800s because of financial need and against most of the social norms and mores of the last 200 years. Assimilation, or the practice of suppressing cultural differences to conform to the majority culture, meant that most women and minority workers had to lose a part of their heritage in order to obtain and hold gainful employment. Stereotypes of African Americans, Hispanic Americans, Asian Americans, and women permeated the corporate and industrial culture until well into the 1960s, when federal laws were established to prevent **discrimination**.

DEMOGRAPHIC SHIFTS IN THE LABOR POOL

Workforce 2000, an influential 1987 report, pointed out many changes taking place in the American workforce. In general, the workforce is aging, more women participate now than ever before, ethnic diversity is growing, a gap continues to grow between educated and uneducated employees, persons with disabilities are more frequently employed, and individual values are more varied and divergent.

Older people are participating more frequently in the workforce as advances in healthcare extend average life expectancy. The baby-boom generation (a nickname for the children born immediately after World War II) and the baby-bust generation (a nickname for the children born in the decade following the baby-boom generation) herald changes in the remaining population. While the baby-boom generation comprises about one-third of the U.S. population, the baby-bust generation is considerably smaller and will account for a slow growth rate in the labor pool in the 1990s. Older workers may be less mobile or adaptable to geographic changes. And, an increased emphasis on retirement security, health care, and innovative incentives will reflect an aging perspective in work motivation. Fewer younger workers means that recruiting competition will become fierce for the baby-bust human capital.

By the year 2000 nearly 50 percent of the workforce will be women. Three-quarters of all working women are in their childbearing years while more than half of all mothers work. A decrease in the number of younger workers in the baby-bust generation encourages companies to recruit women, among other diverse groups. In the years between 1975 and 1985, women professionals and managers increased by 77 percent—implications for the workforce are changes in scheduling and benefits to accommodate the primary parental role of many women. Additionally, child-care support remains an important issue for the effective and large-scale employment of women.

U.S.-born people of color and immigrants will represent 43 percent of new entrants to the workforce by the year 2000. In the United States, depending on the geographic locale, ethnic diversity is already a reality. For example, in estimates project that by the year 2005 more than 50 percent of the workforce in California will be people of color. Ethnic groups such as Hispanics and Asians have experienced considerable growth based on such factors as birth rate and continued immigration. Integration instead of assimilation is the key to successfully managing ethnic diversity. Integration refers to the positive melding of many different cultures while assimilation refers to the suppression of ethnic culture in favor of the prevailing majority culture.

As service industries continue to grow and technological changes require increasingly advanced skills, the pool of educated and competent employees declines. As many as one-quarter of all high school graduates cannot read or write above an eighth-grade level. Additionally, somewhere between 10 and 15 percent of all high school students drop out before graduation. On the other hand, the educated work pool is becoming even better educated. These more highly educated workers are better motivated, more participative, and more self-directed. For business, more involvement with community education and remedial training may alleviate problems with uneducated employees, while participative work teams and financial incentives may maximize the **productivity** of educated workers.

Persons with physical disabilities represent a large group of potentially employable applicants with varied competencies and skills. Disabled persons are less likely than other demographic groups to be working. Disabilities may be physical, mental or medical and may be permanent or temporary. Persons with physical disabilities are often more capable and competent than they have traditionally been credited. As such, they represent a significant pool of potential employees within the multicultural workforce.

Finally, individual differences have become increasingly significant for American workers. Differences in sexual orientation, marital status, income level and a host of lifestyle practices represent the current workforce. Business survival and success depends in great part on understanding and valuing these differences in the workplace.

COMPETITIVE CHANGES

The changing demographics of the U.S. population and the resulting shifts in corporate markets create new competitive opportunities for American businesses. In many cases, a multicultural workforce simply makes good business sense. Competition for qualified and skilled employees intensifies as the traditional labor pool of white men shrinks. Recruitment activities change to incorporate new categories of employees or the company risks a shortage of personnel needed to conduct business. For example, companies such as McDonald's and Wal-Mart actively recruit the aging worker and accommodate preferences for part-time work and flexible scheduling. Other companies such as Eastman Kodak Co. pursue younger workers using a scholarship program. In every case, the business of recruitment reflects new benefits and incentives that address the needs and values of a diverse workforce. Shifts in the demographics of the American population and the globalization of business activities herald changes in consumer markets. The competitive market for current business is an international and multicultural market. A multicultural workforce better represents and is better suited to relate to the changing business market. Capitalizing on diversity can increase productivity and competitiveness—yet

comes with a variety of challenges, as well. First and foremost is the challenge of developing an environment that values multicultural employees and their unique contributions.

MULTICULTURAL INITIATIVES

Many different elements may be necessary to create a climate of inclusion and to incorporate genuine value for diversity in the workforce. Four common elements in diversity initiatives that strengthen the multicultural workforce are training, communication, task forces, and mentoring.

Many major companies conduct diversity training for managers and almost half conduct training for all employees. The key to success lies in viewing training as an ongoing process rather than a single event. Core components of the diversity training may include valuing diversity, cultural literacy, corporate inculturation, global perspectives, and individual self-development.

Communications about the value of inclusion and multiculturalism from the top of the organization are critical in the success of a diversity initiative. While this communication is frequently written, companies such as Allstate Insurance employ teleconferencing to communicate multicultural values across the country. Additionally, the creation of a special multicultural manager, as is the case at Hewlett-Packard and AT&T, communicates with actions the real value of diversity from the top.

Task forces engage **management** and employees in the process of dealing with multicultural conflicts, needs, and organizational dynamics. Many task forces operate at high levels within the organization. Yet, increasingly, companies such as Levi Strauss & Co. involve employees at all levels of the company in formulating policies and guidelines.

Mentoring programs directly connect multicultural employees with traditional employees across racial and gender lines. IBM uses a formal mentoring program while Corning employs a more informal "coaching" program.

CHALLENGES IN IMPLEMENTATION

Programs or corporate environments that value multiculturalism must answer hard questions about managing diversity. For example, can multiculturalism be promoted by equal treatment or differential treatment? Antidiscrimination laws prohibit employers from treating applicants differently, yet some argue that this premise seems to ignore the fundamental differences between individuals that form the basis of multiculturalism. On the other hand, treating people differently creates resentment and erodes morale with perceptions of preferential treatment. Some companies such as Pepsi-Cola emphasize the culture-neutral environment of the workplace while others, such as Pacific Bell, deliberately chose to lay off white managers at a higher rate than minorities when downsizing in the early 1980s. Other questions are: will the company emphasis commonalities or differences in facilitating a multicultural environment? Should the successful multicultural workplace recognize differentiated applicants as equals or some as unequals? How does the company achieve candor in breaking down stereotypes and insensitivity towards women and minority groups? These questions pose difficult dilemmas for companies seeking to create an environment conducive to multicultural workers and productivity. To date, there does not seem to be any one correct answer or strategy. Yet, it seems clear that a multicultural workforce represents an increasingly multicultural consumer market that will be critical in positioning for success in the years to come.

[Tona Henderson]

FURTHER READING:

Jackson, Susan E., and associates. *Diversity in the Workplace: Human Resources Initiatives.* New York: Guilford Press, 1992.

Jamieson, David, and Julie O'Mara. *Managing Workforce 2000.* San Francisco: Jossey-Bass Publishers, 1991.

Johnston, William B., and Arnold H. Packer. *Workforce 2000: Work and Workers in the Twenty-First Century.* Indianapolis: Hudson Institute, 1987.

Leach, Joy, and others. *A Practical Guide to Working with Diversity: The Process, the Tools, the Resources.* New York: American Management Association, 1995.

Loden, Marilyn, and Judy B. Rosener. *Workforce America! Managing Employee Diversity as a Vital Resource.* Homewood, IL: Business One Irwin, 1991.

Towers Perrin, and Hudson Institute. *Workforce 2000: Competing in a Seller's Market: Is Corporate America Prepared?* Valhalla, NY: Towers Perrin, 1990.

Winterle, Mary J. *Work Force Diversity: Corporate Challenges, Corporate Responses.* New York: Conference Board, 1992.

MULTILEVEL MARKETING

Multilevel marketing (MLM), or network marketing, is a system of selling that relies on networks of independent distributors to reach customers by word-of-mouth. Multilevel systems provide an alternative to conventional arrangements that involve wholesalers and retailers. Besides eliminating costs associated with middlemen, network marketing reduces advertising and promotion expenses and, in theory, passes savings to the independent distributors and customers.

MLM was conceived by Carl Rehnborg, an American. Rehnborg learned about the value of nutri-

tion while scavenging for food in a Chinese internment camp in the 1920s. After he was freed, he started Nutrilite Products Inc., a manufacturer of vitamin-enriched food supplements. Rehnborg was extremely successful at marketing his products through an innovative distribution process that would become known as multilevel marketing. Nutrilite flourished throughout the 1940s and 1950s and was eventually purchased in 1959 by Amway, a company founded by former Nutrilite distributors. Using similar MLM tactics, Amway Corp. thrived and spawned a string of imitators during the 1960s and 1970s.

During the 1960s and 1970s, fraudulent pyramid schemes exploited the success of MLM companies. Although they closely resembled MLM organizations, pyramids bilked investors and members out of millions of dollars. A mass of legislation passed during the 1970s almost ended MLM altogether, including organizations like Amway. However, laws were eventually modified to accommodate legitimate multilevel marketers and similar organizations.

Tupperware, for example, achieved stellar sales during the 1960s and 1970s with techniques that mimicked MLM systems. In fact, network marketing has traditionally been associated with cosmetics and household items. Still considered in its infancy, MLM was increasingly being used in the 1980s and early 1990s to sell products and services ranging from vacations and books to software and food items.

MLM BASICS

In essence, MLM uses customers to distribute products (or services). A company begins by selling its product to selected customers in specific geographic areas. Those customers then become salespeople by telling friends, associates, and contacts about the product and trying to get them to buy. The salespeople are usually paid a commission for the products that they sell. More importantly, they also receive commissions for the products that their customers, or recruits, sell. In other words, new customers are added to the sales "network," many of whom also become distributors. As the number of levels of customers grows, so does the distribution network. Thus, by trying to sell the products themselves, customers also become recruiters for the company that represents the products.

MLM organizations are based on commissions that accumulate exponentially. For example, assume that Sandy buys a product(s) from a distributor in the MLM company. She then sells the product to five of her friends and receives a commission. Next, three of her friends sell the products to six of their friends. Not only would those three salespeople receive a commission, but Sandy would also receive a (usually smaller) commission for each of the sales. If four of the six new customers each sold to four contacts, the number of people that could potentially be selling products to Sandy's benefit would suddenly lurch past 15. It is easy to see how the sales network originated by Sandy could quickly jump into the hundreds or thousands. In theory, all of the people in the network would benefit from the efforts and purchases of the people below them.

The compensation system is the infrastructure that supports and drives a MLM program. Sellers in the network usually receive relatively large commissions on sales that they make personally. The commission is the difference between what the salesperson sells the products for and what he (she) must pay to buy them from the company. In addition, purchases made by the same customer at a later date will often result in "residual income" to the person that made the first sale to that buyer. As sellers build a network of customers that also become sellers, they also earn group bonuses, or "overrides." An override is the fraction of sales that is paid to the originator of a network. In general, sales made by distributors further down the network, or at lower levels, pay a lower bonus.

Sellers may also get a "leadership bonus," which is effectively a bonus paid to sellers that help distributors in their network to achieve specific levels of sales success. Leadership bonuses provide an incentive for sellers to train and help their customers to become better distributors and recruiters. "Usage" bonuses are provided to sellers based on the total purchases (product usages) by members of their network. Usage bonuses usually take the form of discounts on air travel or long-distance telephone service. They provide an impetus for people in the organization to continue purchasing the goods themselves.

ADVANTAGES AND DRAWBACKS

The obvious enticement for members of a MLM network is the seemingly unlimited profit potential. By purchasing as little as, say, $100 worth of a product, they can become distributors in a network that can pay them thousands or, theoretically, millions of dollars. In addition, MLM sellers get to be their own boss, make their own hours, and choose their own course to success or failure. They also get the advantage of buying the product at nearly the wholesale price.

The company that initiates and supports the network and supplies the products or services may also benefit significantly. It will likely incur costs associated with supporting the organization, including those related to making training videos and audio tapes, warehousing, transportation, and printing brochures. However, even after paying commissions, its advertising and promotion costs may be much lower than those of traditional marketing and distribution channels. Start-up capital requirement are usually much lower because the bulk of the marketing costs are not incurred until the products are actually sold. And the company benefits from strong customer loyalty and a solid base of repeat customers. Furthermore, MLM is more effective for some types of products than is traditional mass media because sales are conducted face-to-face.

Despite its many advantages, network marketing possesses several drawbacks that make it undesirable for many companies. For instance, it usually takes a long time to develop a large, profitable customer base compared to selling techniques like advertising through print and broadcast media. Furthermore, administrative duties and paperwork are usually much greater for MLM operations. Perhaps the greatest disadvantage of network marketing, though, is that the company loses control of its distribution process. It may have no idea of the types of people that are representing (or misrepresenting) its products. A corporate or product image can become quickly tarnished by overly enthusiastic or dishonest salespeople hungry for commissions.

MLM also has several disadvantages for sellers. Long hours are typically required to get a sizable network started, particularly if the product or service is perceived to be of average value by potential consumers. Because of poorly contrived or fraudulent MLM schemes, moreover, many people have attached a stigma to network marketing that sellers must overcome. Indeed, a major drawback of MLM to distributors is risk—they may lose their initial investment or be lured into purchasing additional goods or services that they will never use if the company backing the network is ill-willed or poorly operated.

PYRAMID SCHEMES

Numerous laws exist that regulate MLM organizations to protect consumers against fraud. Most of those laws are designed to discourage pyramid schemes, which closely resemble legitimate MLM systems. The difference between pyramids and legal network marketing is that the latter derives income from the sale of products. In contrast, pyramid organizations get most of their income by bringing new members into the network, or pyramid, and charging them fees.

The classic pyramid scheme is the chain letter. For example, a person might send a letters to ten individuals asking for a $1. He would give each person ten names to which they should send the same letter. Theoretically, as the chain multiplies into a pyramid massive sums of money will flow from the people at the base of the pyramid to those at the top. As the pyramid continues to expand, people that were at the bottom see levels added, effectively moving them away from the bottom and bringing them cash from newcomers. Unfortunately, pyramids inevitably collapse. People at the top profit from the misfortune of those at the base. The problem is obviously more serious than the chain letter example when larger amounts of money and effort are required of pyramid members and promises of wealth go unfulfilled.

Some pyramid organizations disguise their objective by mimicking a MLM company. They integrate into the scheme a product or service that they ''sell'' to newcomers—a strategy known as inventory loading—or they simply charge sellers a fee to join the network. Then they encourage members to recruit, rather than sell the product to, other people.

EXAMPLE

The case of Bios Lite Diet exemplifies a successful, legitimate MLM effort. Bios Lite Diet is a vitamin supplement marketed in the early 1990s by Rexall Showcase, a division of Rexall created explicitly to sell products through MLM. Rexall is headed by Carl DeSantis, who started the company from his bedroom and financed it with a second mortgage on his house. Although DeSantis achieved success with traditional marketing methods during the 1980s, he determined that those techniques were not suited to marketing his newer and more complex Bios Lite Diet.

DeSantis decided to sell his new vitamin using MLM. Because MLM involves face-to-face selling, he reasoned, he would have a better chance of communicating the complicated biochemical benefits of the vitamin to potential customers. Within three years Rexall Showcase was growing twice as fast as Rexall's mail-order and retail divisions and was generating a surprising $36 million of Rexall's $140 million in projected 1994 revenues. DeSantis attributed the success to the seller motivation inherent to MLM.

[Dave Mote]

FURTHER READING:

Boyd, Harper W., Jr. and Orville C. Walker, Jr. *Marketing Management: A Strategic Approach*. Richard D. Irwin, Inc., 1990.

Dalrymple, Douglas J. *Sales Management: Concepts and Cases*. John Wiley & Sons, 1982.

Kishel, Gregory and Patricia Kishel. *Build Your Own Network Sales Business*. John Wiley & Sons, Inc. 1992.

Poe, Richard. ''Wave Three,'' *Success*, June 1994.

MULTIVARIATE ANALYSIS

Multivariate analysis deals with the mathematical application of statistics to a **regression** function to determine the effects of changes in a group of variables on other variables in the function. As a result, **multivariate analysis** can suggest, with a degree of predictive capability, what can be expected to happen when those variables change.

While it involves many kinds of tools, multivariate analysis is primarily a mathematical approach to **decision making**. It has many applications, including problems in engineering, traffic management, biology, economics, **marketing** and even ethics and behavioral psychology. It can quantify how changes in one or more areas of a complex problem will affect an outcome over time, and indicate whether those changes will alleviate or exacerbate a problem.

For example, an airline company may use multivariate analysis to determine how revenue from a certain route might be affected by different fare prices, load factors, advertising budgets, aircraft choices, amenities, scheduling choices, fuel prices and employee salaries. An agricultural engineer would use multivariate analysis to gauge crop yields based on different soil qualities, choices of seed, fertilizer, insecticides and planting schedules, amounts of sunlight and rain and changes in temperature.

In these examples, route revenue and crop yields are dependent variables determined by sets of independent variables, such as fare prices and seed choices. A change in any one of the independent variables will produce a change in the dependent variable. But in some cases, independent variables may affect other independent variables.

For example, lowered airplane fares may affect load factors, and these might affect aircraft choices. Similarly, different fertilizers might affect seed choices, and these might affect planting schedules. Attempts at improving the outcome of the independent variable may have a short-term positive impact but may prove deleterious in the long-term.

Multivariate analysis is not synonymous with classical simultaneous equations methodology, although this form of modeling is an essential component of the analysis. Multivariate analysis includes prescriptions for simplifying parameters and drawing relationships between data over different time periods.

The methods of computation of these functions can be extremely complex and tedious. The application of computer processing power greatly advanced the science of multivariate analysis by freeing analysts from these tasks. As a result, computer programs have become the necessary basic instrument of multivariate analysis.

One of the greatest problems faced by analysts of multivariate data is overparameterization. An overzealous analyst may be inclined to include many types of microphenomena into the analysis which may have little or no bearing on the result.

Part of the art of multivariate analysis is knowing what variables may be excluded. While this simplifies the computations involved, it may also create greater variation in the observed data, making it difficult to identify reliable regression lines. The only way to work past these dilemmas is to repeatedly test the models.

One form of overparameterization has to do specifically with **time series analysis**. This becomes evident in multivariate analysis of biological and sociological phenomena; current conditions may be primarily dependent on the results of previous time series.

For example, the rate of reproduction of trees in a forest depends not only on how many trees there are, but how many there *were*, and how many there were in successive time series before that. Weather conditions 10,000 years ago may be responsible for climatological changes that affect present rates of growth. In some cases, the analyst may be faced with a practically infinite regress. When faced with such chicken-and-egg problems, the analyst must determine where to draw the line, or limit the parameters of the analysis, without corrupting the reliability of the analysis.

These problems also are evident in **econometrics**, where the simultaneous equations methodology cannot reliably predict reduced form structural parameters. Such simplified models can produce series of equations that appear related, but are not. In these cases, econometric analysis can produce invalid estimates of future conditions by suggesting causal relationships between variables that are entirely independent of each other.

An excellent example is provided by weather forecasting. When a hurricane batters Florida, meteorologists look for the cause of the hurricane by following the storm system back through previous time series. Two systems may start out the same way, but one may simply collapse while another erupts into a cataclysmic storm.

This is why hurricane hunters now watch weather patterns in West Africa and measure water temperatures in the Atlantic to estimate what storms might become Caribbean hurricanes 12 days later. Unfortunately, for all their methodology, the forecasters are unable to predict which systems will become hurricanes, and where they might be headed until only hours before they make landfall.

The formulation of monetary policy provides a more complex example. Here, the relationships between variables over time can be frustrated by causality, and priority of causality. In addition to the set of external variables such as **inflation** and **employment**, monetary policy is shaped by results of past time series. But the question arises as to which changes in prior time series caused which outcomes, and in what order of priority.

Such an analysis can indicate trade-offs between factors to determine the lesser of evils that would result from a certain policy decision; whether a drop in unemployment would be worth increased inflation, or vice versa.

Multivariate analysis is suitable for such problems because it can deal with parameterization of variables and time series.

[John Simley]

FURTHER READING:

Eatwell, J., ed. *The New Palgrave Dictionary of Economics*. London: Macmillan, 1987.

Kachiga, Sam Kash. *Statistical Analysis*. New York: Radius Press, 1986.

Kazmier, Leonard J. *Basic Statistics for Business and Economics*. New York: McGraw-Hill, 1990.

Monks, Joseph G. *Statistics for Business*. Science Research Associates, 1988.

MUTUAL FUNDS

A mutual fund is an investment trust in which investors may contribute funds in exchange for a position in the trust. The total of these contributed funds are, in turn, invested in various securities, such as **stocks**, **bonds**, guaranteed investment contracts, Treasury bills, and other vehicles.

Mutual funds are administered by companies employing an investment management board with oversight by a **board of directors**. These companies collect an investment fee—normally about one half percent of invested capital and are provided an administrative expense budget, usually 1 percent of invested capital.

Mutual funds generally feature low minimum investment requirements. Typically, investors may enter a fund with an investment of as little as $1,000 or regular investments of as little as $50 or $100 per month, withdrawn automatically through investor checking accounts.

As a result, mutual funds permit individual investors with less investment capital to build a diversified portfolio of investments. They enable small investors to employ investment managers used by wealthy investors and investment institutions such as pension funds. As a result, individual investors may take advantage of their pooling of assets to retain skilled investment managers capable of making shrewd investment decisions.

	NAV	Price	Volume
Acme Funds			
Amer Gr	4.32	4.55	4350
Intl Telecom	9.88	10.50	255
Global Inv	17.02	18.40	10944
Boston Inv			
Biotech	10.22	12.03	450
Gr & Income A	17.50	19.21	8773
Gr & Income B	22..40	24.63	400
Global Env	4.54	4.90	1221

Table 1

For example, without a mutual fund an individual wishing to invest in a broad number of stocks and bonds would require substantial capital to take maximum advantage of the **economies of scale** associated with purchasing investments. Because the mutual fund assets are invested in dozens of companies, it enables an investor to contribute a much smaller amount, say $1,000, and gain holdings through the fund in all those companies. Consequently, the $1,000 investment may be comprised of $40 worth of shares in one company, $25 in another, $10 in another, and even 40 cents in yet another. The investor could not otherwise gain such small positions in these companies.

Each month, quarter, or year, the fund declares a dividend to its holders. This dividend reflects dividend distributions from each of the companies in its portfolio. In effect, it is the average dividend of all the shares in the portfolio.

The price of each share of a mutual fund is based on the aggregate value of all the shares in the portfolio. In other words, if the value of the shares owned by the fund rises by 5 percent during a quarter, the mutual fund share price may be expected to rise by 5 percent as well.

Mutual funds came into existence as investment clubs during the 1920s, when public interest in the stock market was growing strongly. Due to their popularity, mutual funds came under regulatory authority of the **Securities and Exchange Commission** through the Investment Company Act of 1940. The act established strict fiduciary standards for mutual funds, requiring reporting and disclosure statements similar to those required for publicly traded corporations.

Recent interest in mutual funds has created opportunities for market segmentation of the investment community. Fund managers have tailored investment portfolios to economic and social screens. For example, investors may participate in funds concentrated on power utilities, **telecommunications**, or biotechnology; on companies with good environmental records; on companies that are not involved in tobacco, alcohol, or defense; or on companies whose performance mirrors the performance of the broader market. Many funds are geared specifically toward share price appreciation, while others concentrate on dividend income.

The majority of mutual funds are open-ended, meaning that they may be purchased or sold based on published closing prices. These values are printed in newspaper financial sections, listed first under the management company, and then by fund name. (See Table 1).

Each share is listed first by net asset value (NAV)—calculated as the value of assets in the fund, less management charges, divided by the number of shares outstanding—and second by purchase price, which is higher to reflect marketing and other management charges.

Dividends may be collected by holders either as payments (dividend checks), or reinvested to purchase additional shares. As a result, the number of shares in open-ended funds may be constantly increased.

Other funds are closed-end funds. While also listed in papers, these funds include a finite number of shares. Because no additional shares are issued, dividends are distributed as cash and shares trade based purely on demand.

Loads, or management charges, are figured into share prices through the spread between NAV and purchase price. No-load funds do not feature these spreads, but charge management fees directly out of profits from the portfolio.

[John Simley]

FURTHER READING:

Griffin, Ricky W., and Ronald J. Ebert. *Business*. 2nd ed. NJ: Prentice-Hall, Englewood Cliffs, 1991.

N

NATIONAL ASSOCIATION OF SECURITIES DEALERS AUTOMATED QUOTATIONS

NASDAQ stands for the National Association of Securities Dealers Automated Quotations system. It is a computerized communication system that provides the bid and asked prices of approximately 5,000 over-the-counter (OTC) stocks that have met NASDAQ's registration requirements. Introduced in 1971 by the National Association of Securities Dealers (NASD), NASDAQ is on a path to overtake the New York Stock Exchange (NYSE) in terms of the volume of shares traded. In 1982, NASDAQ accounted for 32 percent of all stock trades, the NYSE 63 percent. By 1992 NASDAQ accounted for 47 percent of all shares traded, the NYSE 50 percent.

In terms of dollar volume, both the NYSE and NASDAQ account for more than $1 trillion of stock trades annually as of 1993. NASDAQ is the second-largest securities market in the United States in terms of share and dollar volume, but it is the largest in terms of the number of companies listed. Internationally NASDAQ was the fifth-largest securities market in terms of dollar volume in 1990, ranking behind the NYSE, Tokyo, London, and the Federal Republic of Germany.

OTC stocks are traded differently than stocks that are listed on the NYSE or the American Stock Exchange (AMEX). Stocks listed on the NYSE or AMEX are traded using the auction method. In the auction method, specialists handle all trades in specific stocks and either passively match orders from buyers and sellers or take a position in the stocks themselves. OTC stocks, on the other hand, are traded using a multiple market maker system. There are approximately 475 firms that make markets in OTC stocks traded on NASDAQ. Some stocks may have 60 market makers, while smaller stocks may only have two.

Under the multiple market maker system dealers make markets in OTC stocks by making bids to buy and offers to sell. A dealer's bid price is the highest price at which someone would buy a stock, and the asked price is the lowest price at which someone would sell the stock. The difference between the market's bid and asked prices is known as the bid-asked spread. Typically, all of the market makers agree on the bid-asked spread, which is usually about half a point ($.50) per share.

Prior to the introduction of NASDAQ in 1971, bid-asked prices were circulated using daily "pink sheets" that were issued by the National Quotation Bureau in three regional editions (East, Midwest, West). During the trading day there was no centralized data on bid and asked prices. Trading in the OTC market was slower, and the bid-asked spreads were higher than under NASDAQ. NASDAQ facilitated OTC trading by providing continuous, up-to-the-minute quotations on bid and asked prices through a centralized computer system.

The approximately 475 member firms that trade on NASDAQ do so using computers and telephone lines. Unlike the NYSE, there is no trading floor where dealers gather to execute their transactions. Rather, it is all done electronically. In some cases trades can be executed without individual dealers calling each other on the telephone. It is estimated that the NASDAQ system handles approximately 1.7 million transactions per day.

NASDAQ offers its dealers three levels of service. Level One service provides bid and asked prices in all securities to all salespersons and dealers through approximately 200,000 terminals. It also provides sales price and volume information on the OTC stocks included in NASDAQ's National Market System. The terminals are usually leased by subscribers from vendor firms such as Quotron. Level Two service utilizes NASDAQ-owned terminals to provide subscribers with a variety of information on the OTC market. Level Three service allows registered market makers to report their trades and daily volume as well as to receive Level Two service.

Other dealer services offered by NASDAQ include the Small Order Execution System (SOES). For trades involving 1,000 shares or less of stocks listed on NASDAQ's National Market System, or 500 shares or less for other NASDAQ issues, trades can be executed electronically under SOES without any telephone calls between dealers. NASDAQ also offers Trade Acceptance and Reconciliation Services, which assists member firms in resolving their uncompared and advisory OTC trades.

Not all securities that trade over-the-counter are listed on NASDAQ. In order to be listed on NASDAQ a **common stock** must be registered under section 12(g) of the **Securities Exchange Act of 1934**, or the equivalent, and must also meet minimum levels for total assets, capital and surplus, public float, number of dealers, and number of shareholders. Those OTC securities that are not listed on NASDAQ trade infrequently and continue to rely on ''pink sheets'' to disseminate information on their bid and asked prices. In addition to listing domestic stocks, NASDAQ also includes foreign securities. During 1990 approximately 184 foreign securities represented $7.1 billion of trading volume on NASDAQ.

[David Bianco]

NATIONAL DEBT

A national debt results when the federal (or central) government spends more than it takes in. To make up for the deficiency in funds, the government must borrow. Therefore the national debt includes not only the money that the government has borrowed, but the interest on the borrowed money. In return, the U.S. government issues IOUs, in the form of Treasury bills, notes, and bonds. If the deficit is not paid up by the end of the fiscal year, it is carried over to the next fiscal year. In this way, the national debt can balloon; for instance, the U.S. national debt stood at more than $4 trillion in 1995. Therefore the U.S. national debt

represents the amount of accumulated deficit since 1969, which was the last year that the federal budget operated in the black. Not only has the national debt gone unpaid from year to year, but each year since then, the federal government has overspent, forcing it to borrow with interest. In fiscal year 1994, for instance, the federal government overspent by nearly $200 billion, with billions more in interest added to this sum. This deficit in turn became part of the overall national debt.

Deficit spending, spending more than what the government takes in taxes, first became acceptable **fiscal policy** at the height of the Great Depression. From the late eighteenth century until that time, the government aimed for a balanced budget, although this ideal was not always possible. Sizable national debts occurred after the War of 1812, the Civil War, and World War I. These debts were eventually paid off, however, and the government operated in the black the majority of the time until the Great Depression. In the 1930s mainstream economists argued that the federal government must spend more than it takes in, in order to stimulate economic growth. President Roosevelt's New Deal implemented deficit spending, which skyrocketed when the country entered World War II. Nevertheless, the federal government once again operated in the black during most of the Truman and Eisenhower administrations.

Because of the unpopularity of imposing higher taxes and massive military spending for the Cold War and the Vietnam War, deficit spending returned in the 1960s. Not until the early 1980s when the Reagan administration simultaneously cut taxes and escalated military spending further, did the federal deficit, and consequently the national debt, grow dramatically. By the end of 1981, the national debt had risen to an all-time high of $1 trillion; five years later, it had doubled. The 1985 Gramm-Rudman Balanced Budget and Emergency Deficit Control Act, which set ceilings on the national debt beyond which the government could not borrow, failed to eliminate deficit spending. Payment of the accumulated national debt and the annual deficit claim an increasingly large portion of federal spending. In 1994, 14 percent of the federal budget went toward payment of interest on the national debt. By the mid-1990s, the size of the U.S. national debt and its persistence had made it into one of the major political issues of the day.

[Sina Dubovoy]

FURTHER READING:

Boettger, Rick. *The Deficit Lie: Exposing the Myth of the National Debt.* 1994.

Turk, James. *Social Security: Lies, Myths, and Reality: The Truth about Social Security, the Trust Funds, and the National Debt.* 1992.

NATIONAL LABOR RELATIONS BOARD (NLRB)

The National Labor Relations Board (NLRB) is an independent federal agency, created by the National Labor Relations Act of 1935 (NLRA). The basic purpose of the NLRB is to enforce the primary labor law in the United States, the NLRA. The NLRB has the power to prevent and remedy unfair labor practices within the scope of private sector employers and unions. The NLRB must also protect employees' rights to organize and decide, through NLRB administered secret ballot elections, whether to have a union represent them for bargaining purposes. In addition, the NLRB also conducts secret ballot elections among employees "who have been covered by a union-security agreement to determine whether or not they wish to revoke their union's authority to make such agreements" (Office of the General Counsel, U.S. NLRB). It is important to understand that although the NLRB is charged with these responsibilities, the processes of the NLRB can begin only when officially requested. These "requests" for NLRB action must be tendered in writing on forms provided by the NLRB and filed with the proper NLRB regional office. Forms used to request an election are called "petitions," and forms used to file unfair labor practices are called "charges." In situations where a jurisdictional dispute arises involving two or more unions, the NLRB determines which competing group of workers (unions) is "entitled to perform the work involved" (U.S. Government Manual). In the event of a national emergency labor dispute, secret ballot elections are conducted among NLRB employees concerning employers' final settlement offers.

CREATION OF THE NLRB

The National Labor Relations Act (NLRA) was developed in Congress in 1935, and is sometimes referred to as the Wagner Act after its chief sponsor in the U.S. Senate. The evolution of the NLRA is traced back to the Railway Labor Act of 1926 (RLA), which essentially was enacted to avoid work stoppages by employees and lockouts by employers through establishing a legal basis for "negotiation, mediation, and arbitration procedure, effectuated by the legislative sanction that previously was lacking" (Labor Law and Legislation). Prior to the RLA of 1926, the fundamental right of workers to engage in labor organization activity without fear of employer retaliation and discrimination was unprotected.

In 1929, the National Industrial Recovery Act of 1933 (NIRA) was enacted by Congress, and under section 7(a) of this Act, employees were guaranteed the right to organize and bargain collectively through representatives of their own choosing, free from the interference of employers. It was this Act, and the RLA of 1926, that Congress drew upon in 1935 when it created the NLRA. The NLRA's power was based on the federal government's power to regulate interstate commerce. Creation of this comprehensive labor code (NLRA) allowed for the removal of obstructions to commerce and restored "equality of bargaining power arising out of employers' general denial to labor of the right to bargain collectively with them from which denial resulted in a number of detrimental consequences, namely, poor working conditions, depression of wage rates, and diminution of purchasing power, all of which had served to cause and aggravate business depressions" (Labor Law and Legislation).

Administration of the NLRA is the responsibility of the NLRB and its General Counsel. There are five members on the Board, all appointed by the President of the United States, with Senate approval, for a term of five years. Board members may be removed, and reappointed at the end of their term. The President also appoints the General Counsel, assigning him or her to a four-year term. All investigation and enforcement functions of the NLRB are executed by the General Counsel. There are offices in Washington, D.C. for the Board and General Counsel, as well as 33 regional and several other field offices of the NLRB. Each regional office is lead by a regional director, and supported by a staff of attorneys, field examiners, and clerical personnel. Typically the division of labor in the NLRB places appellate jurisdiction over election decisions coming out of the regional offices with the Board, while the General Counsel has appellate authority over regional directors' rulings on unfair labor practices.

Provisions of the NLRA allow the NLRB to exercise its powers to enforce the NLRA in all cases involving enterprises whose operations affect commerce, however, the Board does not act in all such cases. The Board itself limits its involvement to cases involving businesses or enterprises whose effect on commerce is considered substantial. For information on which areas of commerce the Board focuses its involvement, please refer to the Office of the General Counsel, NLRB, Washington, D.C. To learn more about the makeup of the NLRB and relevant laws and procedures under the NLRA, contact the Chief Procurement and Facilities Branch, NLRB, Washington, D.C. 20570. Phone, 202-273-4040.

SEE ALSO: Labor Unions

[Art DuRivage]

NATIONAL TECHNICAL INFORMATION SERVICE

The National Technical Information Service (NTIS) is a self-supporting federal agency and is part of the U.S. Department of Commerce. It is charged with collecting, processing, warehousing and disseminating scientific and technical information. The NTIS gathers information from domestic and foreign sources. Although the NTIS is primarily concerned with information the agency also licenses government-owned **patents** to the private sector through its Patent Licensing Program.

The NTIS was preceded by the Publication Board which was created by President Truman's Executive Order 9568 in 1945. The Publication Board reviewed technical and scientific reports and literature generated by the federal government and decided which material could be shared with the public without compromising national security. The Board also reviewed similar material captured from the Axis powers during World War II. It was felt that the release of non-compromising technical information to the American private sector would foster industrial, economic, and technical growth. In 1950 pursuant to Public Law 776, the Department of Commerce became responsible for board activities. In 1970 the board was renamed the National Technical Information Service.

Since its inception the scope of subject matter falling under NTIS operations has continually expanded. In the 1950s NTIS began gathering business and statistical information. By the 1990s medicine, the life and natural sciences, computer science, and many of the social sciences fell under the information gathering purview of the NTIS. In 1980 NTIS began licensing federal inventions and making them available to the private sector on a fee basis. Patents and licenses are handled by the service's Center for the Utilization of Federal Technology.

The NTIS is a self-supporting agency. Its operating budget is derived from the information and services it sells to the private sector. All fees are determined by a cost-recovery formula. All information transferred to the NTIS by other federal agencies was originally submitted on a voluntary basis. In 1992, however, the American Technology Preeminence Act of 1991 became effective. This act mandated the submission of scientific and technical information to NTIS by federal agencies.

Throughout its history there have been attempts to privatize NTIS operations. This was especially true during the later years of the Reagan administration. In 1988, however, Congress passed the Omnibus Trade and Competitiveness Act of 1988 and the National Institute of Standards and Technology Authorization Act. These acts kept NTIS under federal stewardship (subject to Congressional review) and made the NTIS part of the newly created Technology Administration of the Department of Commerce.

All domestic information handled by NTIS is generated directly by the various departments and agencies of the federal government or through federally funded **research and development** grants and projects. By the early 1990s $59 billion was being allocated on an annual basis by the government for R&D.

The NTIS obtains foreign technical information by collecting approximately 25,000 foreign research studies every year. These studies are obtained via numerous NTIS programs such as International Japan which provIdes for NTIS access to the Japanese Information Center of Science and Technology's On-Line Information System. This information system alone covers over 4,000 Japanese scientific and technical journals, articles, reports, and conferences. NTIS also gathers information through agreements with 45 other countries including Canada, China, India, Taiwan and most European nations including the former Soviet bloc.

In addition to its extensive publications program the NTIS has numerous other programs and facilities to handle the massive amounts of both domestic and foreign information. NTIS maintains an archival collection of 2 million scientific and technical titles. 1.6 million of these titles are in electronic databases. This material is permanently available.

As a result of the National Technical Information Act of 1988, the NTIS is authorized to enter into joint or cooperative ventures with the private sector. These ventures have resulted in numerous projects including computerized versions of the **Standard Industrial Classification (SIC)** materials, ''ezBase''—a database management system, and publication of the *R&D Alert Bulletin*. Also available is a CD-ROM version of the NTIS Bibliographic Database which lists NTIS holdings back to 1964.

[Michael Knes]

FURTHER READING:

Caponio, Joseph F., and Dorothy A. MacEvin. *The National Technical Information Service*. Reference Librarian, 1991, no. 32, pp. 217-27.

O'Hara, Frederic J. *Informing the Nation*. Greenwood Press, 1990.

NATIONAL TRANSPORTATION SAFETY BOARD (NTSB)

The National Transportation Safety Board (NTSB) is an independent agency of the federal government that is concerned with the safe conduct of all types of transportation in the United States. Its major activities include investigating a wide range of transportation-related accidents, identifying potential safety problems related to various modes of transportation, and reviewing license and certification matters related to the U.S. Department of Transportation. Its work applies to the transportation industry as well as to other government agencies.

The NTSB was established on April 1, 1975 as an independent agency of the federal government under the Independent Safety Board Act of 1974. It consists of five board members appointed by the President for five-year terms. Two of the members are designated as Chairman and Vice Chairman for two-year terms. Senate confirmation is required for all board members and for the designated Chairman.

The NTSB is responsible for investigating a wide range of transportation accidents. It must conduct an investigation, determine probable cause, make safety recommendations, and report the facts and circumstances of all U.S. civil aviation accidents; all railroad accidents where there is a fatality, substantial property damage, or a passenger train is involved; and all pipeline accidents where there is a fatality or substantial property damage.

The NTSB also investigates selected highway accidents on the basis of recommendations from state government officials. It investigates major marine casualties and marine accidents involving a public vessel and a nonpublic vessel in cooperation with the U.S. Coast Guard. It also has the discretion to investigate other transportation accidents that are catastrophic, involve problems of a recurring nature, or otherwise require investigation in the judgment of the NTSB.

In addition to investigating accidents, the NTSB makes recommendations on issues pertaining to transportation safety. In recent years it has made recommendations for special training for flight attendants in emergency procedures, federal testing of chemical railcars, and studies of weather hazards and conditions affecting airplane safety.

The NTSB's recommendations are often based on the variety of safety studies and investigations it conducts. It also publishes guidelines for accident investigations and recommends specific procedures and techniques. It establishes regulatory requirements for accident reporting.

The NTSB also evaluates the safety policies and procedures of other government agencies with respect to transportation safety and accident prevention. In the area of hazardous materials, the NTSB reviews and investigates the safeguards and procedures in place for their transportation and evaluates the performance of government agencies charged with the safe transportation of hazardous materials.

On appeal the NTSB reviews licenses and certificates issued by the U.S. Department of Transportation that have been suspended, amended, modified, re-

voked, or denied. The NTSB reports annually to Congress on its activities and issues a variety of publications and studies.

The National Transportation Safety Board is located at 490 L'Enfant Plaza SW, Washington, DC 20594. It has ten regional and field offices located throughout the country. The rules and regulations of the NTSB are contained in Title 49, Section VIII, of the Code of Federal Regulations.

[David Bianco]

NEGLIGENCE

Lawsuits based on negligence are the most common kind of civil action in the area of "tort" law. Negligence is usually defined as the failure to exercise the degree of care that a reasonable, prudent person would have exercised under the circumstances. This is sometimes called a lack of "due care" on the part of a defendant. If such lack of care causes injuries (physical, mental, or financial) to the plaintiff, the defendant will usually be ordered to pay compensatory damages. However, if the plaintiff has also been negligent and such negligence contributes to the harm she complains of, her recovery may be reduced or lost entirely. (See "Contributory Negligence" below). This exemplifies the "fault" basis that characterizes this area of tort law.

At the outset, it must be noted that in the United States, tort law in general is largely defined by state rather than federal law. Moreover, the state law of negligence is usually "common law" rather than statutory law, with the effect that what is determined to be a lack of due care will differ from place to place and over time. Similar acts may be found negligent or not negligent, depending on what judges and juries in widely disparate communities may find to be lacking in ordinary care, with outcomes based on the advocacy talents of attorneys for plaintiffs and defendants, the particular judge, the tenor of the times and the personalities of the jury sitting in judgment on a negligence case.

NEGLIGENCE DISTINGUISHED FROM OTHER TYPES OF TORT

Negligence, in short, is unintentional neglect. In strict liability torts, by contrast, fault or neglect is not an issue. Strict liability applies to the seller of a product in a defective condition that is unreasonably dangerous because of that condition and causes harm. The seller may not intend harm or even be negligent, yet where the doctrine of strict liability applies, plaintiffs may obtain a damages award without proving the manufacturer was negligent in the design, production, or marketing of the product.

Negligence actions also differ from intentional torts (such as assault, malicious prosecution, defamation, or intentional interference with contractual relations) since negligence usually involves offending acts that are careless rather than deliberate or malicious. In most states, courts have considered intentional torts to be even more blameworthy than negligent torts. As a result, intentional torts are more likely to bring requests for punitive damages, damages which greatly exceed the actual loss to plaintiff.

A BASIC CASE OF NEGLIGENCE

To succeed in any negligence case in the United States, the plaintiff must prove (1) that the defendant had a legal duty, (2) breached that duty, (3) causing (4) harm with damages to the plaintiff. Proving all four elements of a negligence case requires that the plaintiff introduce some credible evidence for each element. Failing to do so will ordinarily result in the judge granting the defendant's motion to dismiss the plaintiff's case.

THE ESSENCE OF A NEGLIGENCE CASE—DUTY AND BREACH OF DUTY. The first two elements establishing what is sometimes referred to as the defendant's negligence: are the defendant's breach of a legal duty. These elements can be established in one of three ways. Usually, a plaintiff will allege that the defendant had a duty to act as a reasonably prudent person would act. (Corporations are also considered ''persons'' for purposes of civil lawsuits). The ''reasonably prudent'' person standard is a phrase common to most judges when they instruct juries to decide whether the defendant's acts were negligent. Thus, if a defendant fails to warn of a known danger that a reasonably prudent person would have known and warned of, the defendant will likely be found to have breached a legal duty to warn.

In some cases, the burden on the plaintiff to establish the breach of a duty of reasonably prudent care is practically impossible. For a few such cases, the doctrine of *res ipsa loquitur* (''the thing speaks for itself'') may help a plaintiff establish duty and breach of duty. In a seminal case, *Escola v. Coca-Cola Bottling Co. of Fresno* (1944), a waitress had sustained severe injuries to her wrist while transferring freshly delivered bottles of Coke from their cases to the restaurant's refrigerator. One of the bottles exploded. The cause of this explosion could not be explained by the way that the bottles were handled after their delivery. The court found that where the product causing the injury had not been mishandled by the plaintiff and was recently under the exclusive care, custody, and control of the defendant, that the events described by plaintiff would ordinarily not occur without some lack of due care on the part of the defendant. In this way, plaintiff could establish breach of duty without specifying in what way the defendant's conduct had been negligent. Application of the doctrine requires that (1) only the defendant controls the cause of the harm, (2) the event would not ordinarily have occurred without some negligence as its cause, and (3) the event must not have been due to any actions of the plaintiff.

Duty and breach of duty can also sometimes be proven by means of a doctrine known as *negligence per se*. In many cases the defendant's conduct is a violation of a state or federal law. The law establishes the defendant's duty, and the failure to comply with some specific law is the breach of that duty. Taken together, this amounts to *negligence per se*. In such cases, the judge and/or jury need not consider whether the defendant's conduct has been that of a reasonably prudent person. Rather, the law has set standards of conduct and care (reasonable or not) which people are expected to meet, and failing to do so may not only result in sanctions for noncompliance, but may separately be actionable as a tort by those who are harmed by the noncompliance.

ACTUAL AND PROXIMATE CAUSE. Causing harm is critical to the third and fourth elements of a negligence case. The failure to act as a reasonably prudent person, or to comply with some applicable law, may or may not cause harm. A reasonably prudent company would not carelessly produce a product that would cause harm to the ordinary user. But, having negligently produced such a product, the company will not be liable to any consumers unless the product is sold, is used or consumed in the expected manner, and results in actual harm.

Actual harm may often be absent. When a restaurant cooks up supposedly boneless chicken nuggets and one of them has a small bone inside capable of choking a patron, the negligently produced nugget may be discovered by the patron before trying to swallow it. In most courts, the patron's shock at discovering the potential harm will not amount to the kind of harm ordinarily compensated by damages. But if the bone is discovered after it has lodged in the patron's throat, then some damages are likely to be awarded. The amount of such damages will vary greatly, depending on the location of the court, the amount of sympathy that can be generated for the plaintiff, and (often) the apparent ability of the defendant to pay damages.

Where there is actual harm, however, causation is often an issue in negligence cases. The harm to plaintiff must be actually and proximately caused by the defendant's actions. Actual cause means that without (or ''but for'') the defendant's negligence, the harm to plaintiff would not have occurred. Thus, where a delivery van exceeds the posted speed limit by 10 miles per hour and collides with a car that stops suddenly ahead, the jury may reasonably find that the driver's negligence (in this case, *negligence per se*) has actually caused the injuries to occupants inside the vehicle he struck. But if one of the occupants (a young child, say) is killed or seriously injured, and grandparents far from the scene of the accident become consumed with grief, their pain and suffering will not be compensated, even though they would not be so aggrieved ''but for'' the negligence of the driver. In such a case, actual cause is established, but not proximate cause. Proximate cause (sometimes known as ''legal cause'') sets limits on the legal consequences of negligent acts.

Proximate cause limits the legal liability for negligent acts by allowing plaintiffs to recover only in cases where the harm is a reasonably foreseeable result of the negligence. Assume an architect's design for an elevated walkway in a hotel atrium is defective, and the walkway collapses two years after its construction, injuring hotel patrons both on and under the walkway. Assume also that the design defect is the result of the architect's failure to use that degree of care which is usual and customary among members of his profession and is, therefore, a breach of the generalized duty of due care. Finally, assume that three blocks from the hotel, a pedestrian is startled upon hearing the loud crash of the atrium walkway and involuntarily jumps off the curb where he awaits a crossing signal. Struck by a passing car and injured, he later sues the architect in a negligent tort case, and proves duty, breach of duty, and harm. But the third element, cause, is only partly present: although the harm most likely would not have occurred ''but for'' the negligence of the architect, the doctrine of proximate cause would limit the architect's liability to those consequences that were reasonably foreseeable. The pedestrian's injuries from a passing car are consequences too remote and unforeseeable for the law to pin on the architect's original negligence.

THE VARIETIES OF NEGLIGENCE

Businesses may be held liable in a negligence case for providing goods or services. Slightly different standards apply for each kind of case, and liability for negligent goods will be discussed first.

In practice, negligence by a business entity selling goods can mean the failure to properly (1) design the product, (2) select the materials, (3) produce, assemble, inspect, and/or test the product, and (4) place warnings adequate to the average consumer regarding any hazards of which an ordinary person might not be aware. For product design, the usual and customary design practices of an industry will be relevant evidence in establishing the appropriate degree of care. Where a company's product embodies ''state of the art'' design, a finding of negligent product design would be most unlikely.

Manufacturers, distributors, and retailers all have some duties to carefully assemble or inspect merchandise where doing so would be within the realm of reasonably prudent behavior. For example, a car dealership might be held liable for negligently putting customized wheels on a car by failing to properly tighten the lug nuts, so that within twenty miles of operation the car loses a wheel and the driver is seriously injured. But a grocery store will not be liable for failing to inspect all its canned peas for possible metal objects hidden in the cans. (Liability may attach, however, on the basis of strict liability, or on some contractual bases such as the implied warranty of merchantability.)

For services, exposure to claims of negligence will typically arise where the service provider has failed to exercise that degree of care that is usual and customary (a) for members of that profession (b) in the community where such services are delivered. Malpractice is the usual name given to a professional's failure to provide that degree of care, and an aggrieved patient, client, or customer must allege and establish the appropriate level of care for the particular community and also show that the defendant's conduct fell short. Anyone offering a service to the public may be liable, including doctors, lawyers, bankers, insurance agents, hair stylists, architects, or designers.

DEFENSES TO CLAIMS OF NEGLIGENCE

Even where the defendant has breached a duty of due care, it must be remembered that the plaintiff must establish measurable harm *caused* (both actually and proximately) by the defendant's conduct. Plaintiff's failure to do so will typically result in a directed verdict in defendant's favor.

Apart from any defects in plaintiff's part of the case, the defendant can (in appropriate cases) affirmatively plead *contributory negligence* or *assumption of risk* and avoid legal liability even where defendant has been negligent.

CONTRIBUTORY NEGLIGENCE. If a defendant can prove that the plaintiff failed to exercise due care for his or her own protection, and that this failure was a contributing cause to plaintiff's injuries, some jurisdictions will recognize this contributory negligence as a complete defense. Under this defense the plaintiff's conduct is found to fall below a level reasonable for his or her own protection. For example, suppose that a fast food restaurant serves its coffee very hot but does not inform its customers that their coffee is considerably hotter than other restaurants or that customers have often been burned by coffee spills. A drive-through customer who is burned in attempting to open the lid with her teeth while merging into fast-moving traffic may be found to have failed to exercise a reasonable level of care. Moreover, if that failure is found to contribute to plaintiff's injuries, some states' laws would deny any recovery to plaintiff.

Where one party is clearly much more negligent than another, the doctrine of contributory negligence has sometimes led to unjust results. One attempt by states to meet this problem was the doctrine of comparative negligence, which in many states has replaced contributory negligence. In such states, comparative negligence does not bar recovery, but reduces it. The jury is asked to assign a particular percentage for the negligence of both plaintiff and defendant.

Consider a case in which a pizza delivery vehicle speeds through an intersection and collides with another vehicle that has failed to heed a stop sign. The drivers of both vehicles have breached the duty of due care. In the usual collision, there will be damages, and the negligence of each driver can be seen as both an actual and proximate cause of those damages. If the jury determines that the driver who ignored the stop sign accounted for 60 percent of the negligence involved, any damages that a driver can prove in a negligence case against the pizza company or its driver/agent would be reduced by 60 percent. If the nonstopping driver sues the speeding driver (and the pizza company) for $20,000 in provable damages, the court could award him no more than $8,000 in a comparative negligence state. If the speeding delivery driver sues (or counterclaims) against the other driver and has $40,000 in provable damages, this amount will be reduced by 40 percent, leaving a recovery of $24,000. In a state where contributory negligence (rather than comparative negligence) is the rule, neither driver would recover anything.

ASSUMPTION OF RISK. While contributory negligence is characterized by the plaintiff's failure to use proper care for his own safety, the assumption of risk defense arises from the plaintiff's knowing and willing undertaking of an activity generally known to be dangerous. A patron at a baseball game may be injured by a sizzling line drive, and while a cautious ballpark might provide continuous netting to separate players from fans, none do. Knowing this, a patron may elect to sit behind the partial netting in back of home plate, or take the risks inherent in a less protected part of the field. Assumption of the known risk, where found, will negate liability for any finding that the defendant was less than reasonably prudent in its activities. Similar cases involve the well-known risks of colliding with other skiers on a busy slope, watching a stock car race from temporary grandstands near the pit stop area, or attending a hockey game and sitting where pucks are likely to clear the protective glass.

Assumption of risk is different from contributory negligence in that (1) it involves a conscious or presumed decision on the part of the plaintiff to encounter a known risk, and (2) it will never be factored into a comparative negligence calculation; that is, where the plaintiff has assumed a risk, the defendant's negligence (if any) is entirely negated, and no balancing of fault will take place.

Some businesses attempt to protect themselves against claims of negligence by giving customers a statement to the effect that they enter the premises or engage in certain activities entirely at their own risk. Where the risks are of the kind not generally known to the public, however, or where the statement about the risk is hidden in a mass of fine print, the court's acceptance of assumption of risk as a defense is far from automatic. Maximum protection is gained under this doctrine where the risks are well known to the public or clearly articulated to the customer, and where the customer acknowledges receiving and understanding the extent of the risk she is about to assume.

LIMITS ON RECOVERIES BASED ON DEFENDANT'S NEGLIGENCE

As mentioned at the outset, tort law has traditionally been the province of state rather than federal law. Historically, there have been few limits imposed on the courts' abilities to award damages in favor of plaintiffs injured as a result on a defendant's negligence. A large part of the perceived problem has been large awards of punitive damages in cases where the defendant's negligence is perceived by the plaintiff and jury to go well beyond ordinary negligence to negligence that is wilful, wanton, or gross. Large companies believe they are more likely to be tagged with such awards and have urged limits or caps to the multiples by which punitive damages can exceed compensatory damages. Most proposals for tort reform at the federal level have such proposed limitation.

Businesses have also challenged large punitive damage awards as unconstitutional. Where they greatly exceed the amount awarded as compensatory damages, the argument goes, some form of "excessive fine" prohibited by the Eighth and Fourteenth Amendments to the Constitution would apply. But the Supreme Court rejected such arguments in *Browning-Ferris v. Kelco Disposal* (1989) and also rejected an argument in *Haslip v. Pacific Mutual Insurance Co.* (1991) that challenged an Alabama judge's somewhat vague instructions to the jury on punitive damages as a violation of the defendant's due process rights. It remains to be seen whether federal legislation under the commerce clause will address these issues of long-standing concern.

SEE ALSO: Product Liability

[Donald O. Mayer]

NEGOTIABLE INSTRUMENTS

Negotiable instruments are written orders or unconditional promises to pay a fixed sum of money on demand or at a certain time. **Promissory notes**, bills of exchange, checks, drafts, and **certificates of deposit** are all examples of negotiable instruments. Negotiable instruments may be transferred from one person to another, who is known as a holder in due course. Upon transfer, also called negotiation of the instrument, the holder in due course obtains full legal title to the instrument. Negotiable instruments may be transferred by delivery or by endorsement and delivery.

One type of negotiable instrument, called a promissory note, involves only two parties, the maker of the note and the payee, or the party to whom the note is payable. With a promissory note, the maker promises to pay a certain amount to the payee. Another type of negotiable instrument, called a bill of exchange, involves three parties. The party who drafts the bill of exchange is known as the drawer. The party who is called on to make payment is known as the drawee, and the party to whom payment is to be made is known as the payee. A check is an example of a bill of exchange, where the individual or business writing the check is the drawer, the bank is the drawee, and the person or business to whom the check is made out is the payee.

To be valid a negotiable instrument must meet four requirements. First, it *must be in writing and signed* by the maker or drawee. Second, it must contain an unconditional promise (promissory note) or order (bill of exchange) to pay *a certain sum of money* and no other promise except as authorized by the **Uniform Commercial Code**. Third, it must be *payable on demand* or at a definite time. Finally, it must be *payable either to order or to bearer.*

The laws governing negotiable instruments are spelled out in Article 3 of the Uniform Commercial Code. Modeled after the Negotiable Instruments Law, Article 3 has been adopted as law by all 50 states and the District of Columbia. It spells out the basic requirements for valid negotiable instruments and covers such matters as the rights of the holder, types of endorsement, warranties given to subsequent holders, forgeries, dating, and alterations.

A negotiable instrument is said to be dishonored when, upon presentation, payment or acceptance has been refused. To qualify as a holder in due course, an individual or business must have taken the negotiable instrument before it was overdue and without notice that it had been previously dishonored, if such was the case. The negotiable instrument must also be complete and regular upon its face; that is, all of the necessary information must be present. The holder must also take the instrument in good faith and for value. At the time it was negotiated, the holder in due course must have had no notice of an infirmity in the instrument or a defect in the title of the person negotiating it.

If these conditions are met, then the holder in due course generally holds the instrument free from any defect of title of prior parties involved with the instrument. The holder in due course may enforce payment of the instrument for the full amount against all parties liable thereon, free from any defenses available to prior parties among themselves.

Negotiable instruments may be endorsed in various ways, and some negotiable instruments do not require any endorsement. If a negotiable instrument is a bearer instrument, then it may be negotiated by simply delivering it from one person to another with no endorsement required. Such negotiable instruments typically have a blank endorsement consisting of a person's name only. If the negotiable instrument is an order instrument, then the payee must first endorse it and deliver it before negotiation is complete. For example, if the instrument says, ''Pay to the order of Jane Smith,'' then it is an order instrument and Jane Smith must endorse it and then deliver it to the payer or drawee.

Endorsements such as ''Pay to the order of Jane Smith'' are known as special endorsements and have the effect of making the instrument an order instrument rather than a bearer instrument. Restrictive endorsements (''Pay to Jane Smith only'') and qualified endorsements (''Pay without recourse to the order of Jane Smith'') also have the effect of requiring the payee to endorse the negotiable instrument. Qualified endorsements also affect the nature of implied warranties associated with endorsement.

Under the Uniform Commercial Code, an unqualified endorser who receives payment or consideration for a negotiable instrument, provides a series of implied warranties to the transferee and any subsequent holder in due course. An unqualified endorser warranties that he or she has good title to the instrument or represents a person with title, and that the transfer is otherwise rightful. The endorser also warranties that all signatures are genuine or authorized, that the instrument has not been materially altered, that no defense of any prior party is good against the endorser, and that the endorser has no knowledge of any insolvency proceeding involving the payer.

Other issues concerning negotiable instruments are covered in Article 3 of the Uniform Commercial Code. In the case of a forgery, the negotiable instrument becomes inoperative. Antedated or past-dated instruments are not invalid, provided the dating was not done for fraudulent or illegal purposes. Negotiable instruments that have been materially altered without the permission of all parties involved are void. However, a holder in due course who is not party to the material alteration can enforce payment according to the instrument's original terms. Also covered in Article 3 are interpretations of contradictions that may appear from time to time in negotiable instruments.

[David Bianco]

NEGOTIATIONS

SEE: Arbitration and Mediation; Federal Mediation and Conciliation Service; Industrial Relations; International Arbitration; Labor/Management Relations

NEPOTISM

Nepotism in the business world is the showing of favoritism toward one's family members or friends, in both economic and employment practices. The term "nepotism" is applied to the practice of granting favors or jobs to friends and relatives, without regard to merit. Oppositely, "antinepotism" describes the practice of not allowing relatives (by blood or marriage) to work in the same office or firm. On the political scene, "nepotism" is being loosely applied to the phenomenon of "dynasty building"—members of the same political family running for office and trading on their famous name to gain votes.

The word "nepotism" is derived most immediately from the French *népotisme* and the Italian *nepotismo*. These in turn have their origin in the Latin word *nepote*, meaning nephew. The use of the word is passed down from fragmentary information that Roman emperors and generals appointed their nephews to high positions in the empire. In the fourteenth through seventeenth centuries "nepotism" was used to describe the documented practice of French nobility naming their "nephews" (many of whom were their own illegitimate offspring) as prelates and to high office, and of many popes doing the same.

The principle of nepotism migrated to the American colonies along with other political and business concepts. The mainly agrarian economy of the United States was dominated by the family farm. For members of a merchant family to follow in the family business was a given as it was in most of Europe in the eighteenth century. Nepotism on the political scene was not unheard of, but it was not until the election of Andrew Jackson that the practice was seen as rampant on the American political landscape. Jackson extended patronage farther down the scale than just cabinet positions and other high offices. His use of patronage was so widespread that a supporter, Senator William L. Marcy (1786-1857), said in a speech justifying such extensive patronage that there is "nothing wrong in the rule that to the victor belong the spoils of the enemy," thus coining the phrase "spoils system."

The excesses of that era and later administrations led to reforms in the civil service area. The Civil Service Act of 1883 created the basis for the merit hiring system used in the federal service today. Many states followed suit. Nepotism is still a factor on the political scene, in both positive and negative aspects.

While in the **family-owned business** "nepotism" is seen as "succession," many businesses in the modern world try to avoid even the appearance of nepotism, by forbidding relatives from working together, including husbands and wives as well as blood relatives. As women have entered the workforce in greater numbers and have taken on more significant jobs, rules regarding nepotism have begun to change. Both the man and the woman in a marriage often are now too valuable for a company to lose. The general outlook of the 1990s is that these family members can be accommodated within a merit system, especially if there is not a direct or indirect supervisory link between the positions of related employees.

In their book, *The Best Companies for Women*, Baila Zeitz, and Lorraine Dusky list the results of surveys taken in 1980-81 and 1986-87 to verify these changes of policy. The percentage of companies forbidding couples in the same company was 17 percent in 1980-81 and dropped to 2 percent in 1986-87. The companies who forbade couples in the same department or function was 72 percent in 1980-81 and had dropped to 37 percent in 1986-87. Not only have these companies changed their policies, but evidence that their attitude has changed about two-career families is apparent from the development of flexible working practices that allow employees the choice of several child care options, including flexible hours.

Family businesses are the embodiment of nepotism. In the nonfamily business, reasons given for excluding relatives from working together have historically been that the emotional ties of these relationships may negatively affect decision making and growth at the office. The family business, however, encourages participation by all members of the family and the use of emotional ties to bond the relationships more tightly. Recent studies have shown that in the successful family business these bonds are healthy emotionally and good for the business as well. In the family business where there are problems, the type of fears that regular business rightly has concerning nepotism have proven to undermine the family firm. Resources have been developed to help families sort these issues out and to promote the positive aspects of this type of nepotism—the ability to move ahead when all are linked emotionally and mentally and are going in the same direction. The January, 1993, issue of *Nation's Business* offered a very thorough "How-to" on policies and practices that forestall the negative aspects of family business and emphasize the positive. The article concludes that family businesses need to set rules and standards for training and succession by experience, much like the outside world of merit competition, to guide family participation and avoid problems.

SEE ALSO: Career and Family

[Joan Leotta]

FURTHER READING:

Aronoff, Craig E., and John L. Ward, "Rules for Nepotism." *Nation's Business*. January 1993, pp. 64-65.

Baldwin, Deborah, "It's a Small Town After All." *Common Cause Magazine*. Fall 1993, pp. 10-13.

Mehta, Ved. *A Family Affair: India Under Three Prime Ministers*. New York: Oxford Univrsity Press, 1992.

Zeitz, Baila, and Lorraine Dusky. *The Best Companies for Women*. New York: Simon and Schuster, 1988.

NEW PAY

SEE: Strategic Pay/New Pay

NONDURABLE GOODS

Nondurable, or soft, goods are those which are consumed immediately or within a short time. The U.S. Department of Commerce uses three years as the consumption period to distinguish nondurable from durable goods. Nondurable goods consist of food, clothing, and other items that are consumed within three years. Some soft goods, though, are expected to last longer than three years when purchased, such as an expensive suit or coat.

The production of nondurable goods is a component of a country's **gross domestic product** (GDP). As reported in the *Survey of Current Business* by the Bureau of Economic Analysis, nondurable goods that

are sold to consumers appear under personal consumption expenditures. The other two categories of personal consumption expenditures are **durable goods** and services.

Nondurable goods that are produced but not sold are reported as changes in business inventories. Changes in business inventories also include durable goods. If more goods are produced than sold, then business inventories increase. On the other hand, when more goods are sold than are produced during a given period, business inventories decline. The category of changes in business inventories is used as an economic indicator to gauge the direction of a country's economy. Increases in business inventories may signal a weakening of consumer demand or a strengthening of productive activity. Finally, the production of nondurable goods also appears in the GDP as part of a nation's exports and as part of national, state, and local government purchases.

The category of personal consumption expenditures for nondurable goods is not used as an economic indicator. Most nondurable goods are purchased when needed. Changes in the level of consumer expenditures for nondurable goods tend to reflect population growth rather than economic conditions.

The purchase of nondurable goods by consumers represents a significant portion of the United States's GDP, although it is by no means the largest category of expenditures. Personal consumption expenditures in 1993, including durable goods, nondurable goods, and services, amounted to $4.39 trillion in 1993 out of a total GDP of $6.374 trillion, or 69 percent of GDP. Of that total, consumers spent $1.35 trillion on nondurable goods (21.2 percent of GDP), $537.7 billion on durable goods (8.4 percent of GDP), and $2.503 trillion on services (39.3 percent of GDP). In addition, nondurable goods contributed to the GDP in the categories of exports and government purchases. Overall the production of nondurable goods accounted for $1.372 trillion (21.5 percent of GDP) in 1993, of which $1.368 trillion were final sales and $3.8 billion were changes in business inventories.

[David Bianco]

NONPARAMETRIC STATISTICS

NONPARAMETRIC OR DISTRIBUTION-FREE STATISTICS

Many statistical methods apply solely to populations having a specified distribution of values, such as the normal distribution. Naturally, this assumption is not always reasonable in practical applications. The need for techniques that may be applied over a wide range of distributions of the parent population has led to the development of distribution-free or nonparametric statistical methods. In place of parameters such as means and variances and their estimators, these methods use ranks and other measures of relative magnitude—hence the term nonparametric. Distribution-free statistical procedures do not require the normality of underlying populations or that such populations have any particular mathematical form. Although they do require certain assumptions, nonparametric tests are generally valid whatever the population distribution.

Nonparametric counterparts to standard statistical testing procedures are typically used either when an assumption violation that invalidates the standard test is suspected, or in situations where the response variable of interest is not susceptible to numerical measurement, but can be ranked. A common example of this second setting is provided by studies of preference in marketing. For instance, in a taste test, a consumer may be asked to rank a new product in order of preference among several current brands. While the consumer probably has a preference for each product, the strength of that preference is difficult to measure. The best solution may be to have the consumer rank the various products (1 = best, 2 = second best, and so forth). The resulting set of ranks cannot be appropriately tested using standard procedures. Thus, nonparametric methods are often employed when measurements are only available on a nominal (categorical) or ordinal (rank) scale.

NONPARAMETRIC TESTS AND PROCEDURES

Sums of ranks are the primary tools of nonparametric statistics. When comparing samples, the statistician ranks the observations in order, and then considers statistics based on those ranks, rather than on the raw data. Most statistical computer packages will calculate a wide array of nonparametric statistical procedures. The most common rank-based tests are the Wilcoxon rank sum and Wilcoxon signed-rank statistics, used for comparing two populations in, respectively, independent sampling experiments and paired-difference experiments.

For independent samples, another nonparametric analog to the two-sample t test is the Mann-Whitney test, which may be extended, in the case of more than two samples, to the Kruskal-Wallis test. The Kruskal-Wallis test (which tests location) and Friedman two-way ANOVA (which compares variation) are often used as alternatives to the analysis of variance for comparing several populations in a completely randomized experimental design. The Kolmogorov-Smirnov two-sample test is also used for testing differences between sample cumulative distribution functions.

For one-sample tests, a Kolmogorov-Smirnov procedure has been developed to compare the shape and location of a sample distribution to a reference distribution, such as a normal or uniform. The Lilliefors procedure tests standardized values of the sample data (values that have been centered at zero, by subtracting the mean, and also divided by the standard deviation) to see whether they are normally distributed. Also, the Wald-Wolfowitz runs test detects serial patterns in a run of values. In the study of correlation between two variables, methods such as Spearman's rank correlation coefficient (a nonparametric alternative to Pearson's product-moment correlation coefficient), Kendall's tau, and the Goodman-Kruskal gamma statistic may be used to estimate relationships using noninterval data.

NONPARAMETRIC REGRESSION AND SMOOTHING

A regression curve describes a general relationship between one or more predictor variables X and a response variable Y. Parametric regression procedures specify a functional form (such as a straight line with unknown slope and intercept) for the relationship between Y and X. In nonparametric regression, neither the functional form nor the error distribution of the regression curve is prespecified. Instead, a smoothing estimate is developed, often through the use of kernel smoothers, allowing for extremely versatile and flexible methods of presenting and analyzing data. Nonparametric smoothing procedures may be used to model, kinks in nonlinear relationships between, for instance, sales projections for heating oil use and temperature. Additionally, smoothing methods may be used in the diagnosis of outliers, and the analysis of missing data, without reference to a specific parametric model.

THE MISUSE OF NONPARAMETRIC STATISTICS

Some researchers fall back on nonparametric procedures as a substitute for collecting good data. There are, however, explicit assumptions involved in nonparametric analyses, as there are for parametric tests. In most cases, these procedures were designed to apply to data that were categorical or ranked in the first place. Rank-based nonparametric methods may lose much of the information contained in the observed data. Data which violate distributional assumptions for standard probability models may be more effectively transformed using logarithms, roots, or powers than by ranking.

[Thomas E. Love]

FURTHER READING:

Conover, W. J. *Practical Nonparametric Statistics.* 2nd ed. New York: John Wiley & Sons, 1980.

Gibbons, J. D. *Nonparametric Statistical Inference.* 2nd ed. New York: McGraw-Hill, 1985.

Hollander, M., and D. Wolfe. *Nonparametric Statistical Methods.* New York: John Wiley & Sons, 1973.

Lehmann, E. L. *Nonparametrics: Statistical Methods Based on Ranks.* San Francisco: Holden-Day, 1975.

Siegel, S., and N. J. Castellan. *Nonparametric Statistics for the Behavioral Sciences.* 2nd ed. New York: McGraw-Hill, 1988.

NORTH AMERICAN FREE TRADE AGREEMENT (NAFTA)

The North American Free Trade Agreement (NAFTA) is an international agreement among the United States, Canada, and Mexico that became effective on January 1, 1994. NAFTA phases out tariffs among the three countries over a period of 15 years and liberalizes rules related to investment in Mexico. NAFTA's adoption was supported strongly by most businesses and investors in the United States. However, many other citizens opposed its adoption and continue to be wary of its consequences. Labor representatives fear that NAFTA will encourage more U.S. companies to move their operations to Mexico, where wages are lower than in the United States, workers receive fewer protections in terms of occupational safety and health, and enforcement of environmental laws is less stringent.

Many, but not all, environmental groups opposed NAFTA's approval. They fear that its implementation will result in further degradation of the environment in Mexico and the Southwest United States. They also fear that the agreement will lead to challenges to U.S. environmental laws, which are generally more protective of the environment than those of Mexico. As a result of opposition prior to Congress's approval of NAFTA, side agreements on labor, the environment, and import surges were negotiated. Following heated debate and serious concern about whether NAFTA would be approved, NAFTA and the side agreements were approved by the U.S. Congress in November 1993.

NAFTA'S PROVISIONS

NAFTA liberalizes rules for investment by businesses from one NAFTA country in another NAFTA country. It also eliminates tariffs and other barriers to trade among the United States, Canada, and Mexico over a 15-year period beginning January 1, 1994. Thus, it creates what some commentators are calling "the world's largest trading bloc." As of December 31, 1993, there were tariffs on approximately 9,000 products being traded between the U.S. and Mexico. Approximately 4,500 were eliminated on January 1, 1994, and by 1999, tariffs will remain in effect on only about 3,000. The remaining tariffs will be gradually phased out, with the last of them being terminated by the year 2009. NAFTA is a two-volume document covering over 1,200 pages with extremely detailed, complex provisions specifying how tariffs and other barriers for a multitude of different industries will be altered. This description of NAFTA only summarizes some of its salient provisions with respect to certain sectors of the economy.

REMOVAL OF BARRIERS TO INVESTMENT. NAFTA removes certain investment barriers, ensures protections for NAFTA investors, and provides a means for settlement of disputes between investors and a NAFTA country. Coverage includes anticompetitive practices, financial services, intellectual property, temporary entry for business persons, and dispute settlement procedures. One of the most significant aspects of NAFTA for investors is that it minimizes or eliminates many requirements of foreign government approval, which formerly posed significant barriers.

NAFTA includes provisions on anticompetitive practices by monopolies and state enterprises as well as on such practices by privately owned businesses. It also sets out principles to guide regulation of financial services. Under NAFTA, financial service providers of a NAFTA country may establish banking, insurance, securities operations, and other types of financial services in another NAFTA country. With respect to investment in Mexico, there will be a transition period ending by the year 2000 during which certain market share limits will apply. The advantage of this for investors is that they will be able to use the same financial service providers for both domestic and international transactions.

NAFTA provides U.S. and Canadian firms with greater access to Mexico's energy markets and energy-related services. U.S. and Canadian energy firms will be allowed to sell their products to PEMEX, Mexico's state-owned petroleum company, through open, competitive bidding. Under NAFTA, for the first time Mexico will allow foreign ownership and operation of self-generation, cogeneration, and independent power plants in Mexico.

Transportation among the three countries will become more efficient and less costly due to changes in investment restrictions. Pursuant to NAFTA, Mexico is removing its restrictions on foreign investment in its trucking firms. In addition, beginning in 1995, U.S., Mexican, and Canadian trucking companies are able to establish cross-border routes. Such routes were prohibited prior to NAFTA, which made shipping across the U.S.-Mexico border costly and inefficient;

goods had to be unloaded from one truck and put onto another truck as they were moved from Mexico to the United States, or vice versa.

Another market being opened to U.S. investors is Mexico's pharmaceutical market. Under NAFTA, Mexico removed its imports licenses on pharmaceutical products, and it will phase out tariffs on such products by 2004. Mexico is also opening its government procurement contracts for pharmaceuticals to bids from companies from other NAFTA countries.

NAFTA builds on the work of the **General Agreement on Tariffs and Trade (GATT)**, providing substantial protection for intellectual property. Covered are copyrights, including sound recordings; patents and trademarks; plant breeders rights; industrial designs and trade secrets; and integrated circuits (semiconductor chips). NAFTA includes details regarding procedures for enforcement of intellectual property rights and for damages in the event of violations of such rights.

NAFTA does not create a common market for movement of labor. Thus, provisions in NAFTA deal with temporary entry of business people from one NAFTA country into another. On a reciprocal basis, each of the three countries will admit four categories of business persons: (1) business visitors dealing with research and design, growth, marketing and sales, and related activities; (2) traders and investors; (3) intracompany transferees; provided that such transferees are employed in a managerial or executive capacity or possess specialized knowledge; and (4) specified categories of professionals who meet minimum educational requirements or possess specialized knowledge.

ELIMINATION OF TARIFFS. NAFTA's provisions on farm products were of great concern to agriculture business people in the United States. Pursuant to NAFTA, tariffs on all farm products will be phased out, but producers of certain ''sensitive'' products will be allotted extra time to adjust gradually to competition from products OF other NAFTA countries. Tariffs for those sensitive products will be phased out over a period of 15 years. ''Sensitive products'' receiving such treatment include corn and dry beans for Mexico, and sugar, melons, asparagus, and orange juice concentrate for the United States.

Provisions related to the automobile industry were also of special concern in the United States. Pursuant to formulas set out in NAFTA, as of 1995, cars must now contain 50 percent North American content to qualify for duty-free treatment. By 2002, will be required to contain 62.5 percent North American content to receive such treatment. Also, U.S. automobile manufacturers will obtain greater access to Mexican markets. During a transition period, limits on imported vehicles in Mexico will be phased out, and will duties on automobiles, light trucks, and automobile parts.

Mexico's telephone system is of a poor quality and severely underdeveloped. Therefore, it is significant that Mexican investment restrictions on telecommunications services and equipment are being reduced. As of NAFTA's effective date, Mexico abolished tariffs on all telecommunications equipment except telephone sets and central-switching equipment. Tariffs on even those products will be phased out by 1998. U.S. companies will be allowed to compete for contracts for Mexico's telephone system.

DISPUTE RESOLUTION. Administration of NAFTA will be handled by a trade commission composed of ministers (cabinet-level officers) designated by each NAFTA country. A secretariat will serve the commission and assist with the administration of dispute resolution panels.

Whenever a dispute arises with respect to a NAFTA country's rights under the agreement, a consultation can be requested at which all three NAFTA countries can participate. If consultation does not resolve the dispute, the commission will seek to settle the dispute through mediation or similar means of alternative dispute resolution procedures. If those measures are unsuccessful, a complaining country can request that an arbitral panel be established. The panel will be composed of five members selected from a trilaterally agreed upon list of trade, legal, and other experts. After study, the panel will issue a confidential initial report. After receiving comments from the parties, a final report will be prepared and conveyed to the commission. If the panel finds that a NAFTA country violated its NAFTA obligations, the disputing parties have 30 days to reach an agreement. If none is reached, NAFTA benefits may be suspended against the violating country in an amount equivalent to the panel's recommended penalty until the dispute is resolved.

NAFTA'S ENVIRONMENTAL PROVISIONS AND SIDE AGREEMENT

NAFTA has more provisions relating to the environment and, at least on paper, is more protective of the environment than any other international agreement or treaty ever before entered into by the United States. Former U.S. Environmental Protection Agency (EPA) Administrator William K. Reilly observed that it is ''the most environmentally sensitive . . . free trade agreement ever negotiated anywhere.'' Yet consideration and adoption of NAFTA led to a painful division within the environmental community. A coalition of eight major environmental organizations supported it, yet other major environmental groups opposed its approval.

NAFTA's environmental provisions are complex, lengthy, and yet-to-be interpreted as they are implemented. Questions arise in two directions. First, does NAFTA do enough to safeguard *existing* environmental laws and standards? Second, does NAFTA require or at least promote upward harmonization of the environmental laws of the three NAFTA countries?

ENVIRONMENTAL PROVISIONS IN THE PREAMBLE TO NAFTA

The environment and the pursuit of what is called "sustainable development" are mentioned three times in NAFTA's Preamble. However, in NAFTA's Statement of Objectives, which is part of the agreement itself, they are not mentioned at all. Thus, sustainable development is a goal of NAFTA, but there are no substantive provisions in NAFTA to require its pursuit or achievement. "Sustainable development" is a term used often in environmental discussions today. It refers to measures designed to ensure that the needs of the present are met without compromising the ability of future generations to meet their own needs.

ENVIRONMENTAL PROVISIONS WITHIN NAFTA. In terms of our ability to safeguard the "status quo" in environmental regulation in the United States, there are two key articles in NAFTA: Articles 7 & 9. Article 7 covers sanitary and phytosanitary measures. (Phytosanitary refers to measures related to plant and food safety.) This article reserves to each party (those being the United States, Mexico, and Canada) the "right" to set its "appropriate level of protection" for human, animal or plant life or health. It confirms that a party may adopt a measure more stringent than an "international standard, guideline or recommendation." Further, adoption of these "more stringent" measures may be by federal, state, or local governments.

A major concern of U.S. environmental groups is the ability of the United States to maintain its own health and environmental standards. For example, Article 7 says that any trade measure used to achieve a party's level of protection must be "necessary" for the protection of human, animal, or plant life. Some environmentalists are concerned that the term "necessary" might be interpreted very narrowly, as has been the case recently under interpretation of the General Agreement on Tariffs and Trade (GATT).

Article 9 of NAFTA gives each party the right to establish the levels of protection that it considers to be appropriate so long as the choice is made based on a "legitimate" objective. Environmental measures cannot be used to promote unfair discrimination or to serve as a disguised barrier to trade. NAFTA allows only those trade regulations involving "product *characteristics* or their *related* processes and production methods." Thus, a process standard must be related to the characteristics of a product, and a party can't prohibit trade in products grown or manufactured using "unsustainable" methods. Analyzing such provisions of NAFTA, environmentalists fear that specific, individual U.S. environmental laws or regulations might be challenged under NAFTA as being a nontariff barrier to trade without a legitimate objective.

PROVISIONS OF THE ENVIRONMENTAL SIDE AGREEMENT. The North American Agreement on Environmental Cooperation, also known as the "Environmental Side Agreement" was adopted as a part of NAFTA along with two other side agreements, covering labor and import surges.

Part One of the Environmental Side Agreement lists two objectives: (1) to promote environmental concerns without harming the economy, and (2) to open discussion of environmental issues to the public.

Part Two outlines the obligations of the three countries. It confirms that each party has the right to set its own standards and states that the governments of each country are responsible for monitoring and enforcing their environmental laws. It also states that private parties can request government intervention and can seek remedies through the courts of their respective countries.

Part Three establishes a Commission for Environmental Cooperation that will consist of a council, a secretariat, and a Joint Public Advisory Committee. The council consists of cabinet-level representatives who will meet at least once a year. Its function is to implement the environmental side agreement. The secretariat provides a support system for the council.

Nongovernment organizations or private citizens may assert that a country "has shown a persistent pattern of failure to effectively enforce its environmental laws" by filing a complaint with the commission. Thus, private citizens can serve as a watchdog for the commission. This is important to U.S. environmental groups, because such groups have played an active role in overseeing enforcement of U.S. environmental laws and regulations.

The Joint Public Advisory Committee may advise the council on any relevant matter and may provide relevant technical information. The Committee consists of 15 members, 5 appointed by each of the NAFTA countries.

Pursuant to Part Four of the Environmental Side Agreement, each party agrees to cooperate and to provide information to the secretariat upon request.

Part Five allows a party to request consultation with a second party's concerning the party's failure to enforce its environmental laws if such a failure is shown to be part of a persistent pattern. If a mutually satisfactory resolution is not reached within 60 days, a party can request a special session of the council, which must meet within 20 days. If the council is unable to resolve the dispute, it can convene a panel for arbitration of the dispute. The panel will issue an initial report within 180 days, and the parties are allowed to submit comments within 60 days. Next, the panel will submit a final report, which will be made public within 5 days after it is received by the Council. The parties are given an opportunity to reach their own settlement based on the report, and if they cannot reach an ''action plan'' within 60 days, the panel can be reconvened to establish one. If the offending country does not follow the plan, a fine can be imposed. If the fine is not paid, NAFTA benefits can be suspended.

Thus, the Environmental Side Agreement allows citizens and their organizations to serve as ''watchdogs'' by bringing complaints to the attention of the Commission. However, citizens do not have standing to take action on their own. A NAFTA party, however, can file a complaint with the Council in cases in which another party has shown a persistent pattern of failure to enforce its environmental laws and regulations. Ultimate sanctions against an offending party may include suspension of trade benefits, however, the process for reaching such a sanction will take months or years. Commentators predict that suspension of trade benefits will seldom be invoked as a sanction. As of mid-1995, the Environmental Commission had not issued even a draft of its procedures for handling complaints from citizens. It did not receive or process a single complaint during the first nineteen months of NAFTA's implementation.

NAFTA'S SIDE AGREEMENT ON LABOR

The North American Agreement on Labor Cooperation, commonly known as the ''Side Agreement on Labor'' was negotiated in response to concerns that NAFTA itself did little or nothing to protect workers in Mexico, the United States, or Canada. U.S. labor groups have maintained their opposition to NAFTA even with the addition of the Side Agreement on Labor. Representatives of labor groups assert that the Side Agreement on Labor does little to protect workers in the U.S., Canada, or Mexico. The structure and provisions of the Side Agreement on Labor parallel those of the Environmental Side Agreement. Included are a preamble, objectives of the agreement, and obligations of the parties. There are also provisions for a Commission for Labor Cooperation, dispute resolution mechanisms, and sanctions against a NAFTA country found to be in violation of the agreement's provisions.

The Preamble affirms the three parties' desire to create new employment opportunities and to protect, enhance, and enforce basic workers' rights while, at the same time, affirming their respect for each party's constitution and laws.

Part One lists the objectives of the agreement. Its basic goals include the desire to improve labor conditions and encourage compliance with **labor laws**. Another goal is to encourage open sharing of information (transparency) among the three countries regarding their respective labor laws and their enforcement of those laws.

Part Two of the agreement discusses the obligations of the parties. Each party is responsible for enforcement of its own labor laws, but the parties agree that proceedings dealing with enforcement of labor laws will be ''fair'' and tribunals will be ''impartial.'' Labor laws and information about their enforcement are to be made public, and public education will be promoted.

Part Three establishes a Commission for Labor Cooperation. It will consist of a council and a secretariat. The council meets at least once a year or upon the request of one of the parties. Its primary tasks are to oversee implementation of the Side Agreement on Labor and to promote cooperation among the parties on various labor issues.

The secretariat will be headed by an executive director, and that position will be rotated among the three countries. The secretariat's tasks are to assist the council, make public the labor policies of each country, and prepare studies requested by the council.

The U.S., Mexico, and Canada have each established a National Administrative Office (NAO) led by a secretary. NAOs are responsible for gathering information within their respective countries and conveying it to the secretariat and the other two NAFTA parties.

In the event of a dispute related to the Side Agreement on Labor, the leader of one of the NAFTA parties may request a meeting with another leader to attempt to resolve the dispute. The allegation cannot be based on a single failure to enforce its own laws. Instead, any complaint must be based on a ''persistent pattern of failure by the Party complained against to effectively enforce its occupational safety and health, child labor, or minimum wage technical labor standards.'' All three NAFTA parties are allowed to participate in such a meeting. If the matter is not resolved by those leaders, a party-country may request that an Evaluation Committee of Experts (ECE) be established. The ECE will study the matter and submit a report to the council. The purpose of this report is to allow a party to obtain information about the practices and enforcement of labor laws by another NAFTA party.

After the ECE's report is presented, the parties will try to resolve any dispute between themselves. If this fails, the council may attempt to assist the parties in resolving the dispute. Finally, if the matter is not resolved, the council may convene an arbitral panel, chosen from a roster of 45 people chosen pursuant to qualifications outlined in the agreement. The panel convenes, receives input from each of the disputing party-countries, and prepares an initial report. After reviewing comments from each of the parties, a final report is prepared. If it is found that a party ''persistently failed'' to enforce its laws, the disputing parties will prepare an action plan. If the parties do not agree or if the plan is not fully implemented, the panel can be reconvened. If the panel finds that the plan was not implemented, the offending party can be fined. If the fine is not paid, NAFTA trade benefits can be suspended to pay the fine.

Thus, the Side Agreement on Labor provides a mechanism for dealing with a party-country that shows a ''pattern of practice'' of failing to enforce its occupational safety and health, child labor, or minimum wage technical labor standards. However, the enforcement process is slow and cumbersome, and the potential utility of the enforcement mechanism will depend on the council's willingness to vigorously enforce sanctions. Also, it should be noted that the agreement does *not* deal with a country's failure to enforce laws giving workers rights to collectively organize, bargain with, or strike against their employers. This void is a major concern among workers and **labor unions** in the United States.

CONSEQUENCES OF NAFTA

NAFTA is facilitating an unprecedented level of economic integration in North America. It is creating opportunities for investment and growth by private business, and it is promoting more stable relations between and among the United States, Mexico, and Canada. However, NAFTA is not welcomed by all people in the three countries, and some of its effects may be negative.

POLITICAL FACTORS. Investments by U.S. businesses in Mexico have been stemmed by an on-going financial crisis in Mexico. In November of 1994 the Mexican peso was trading for slightly over three pesos per U.S. dollar. However, the exchange rate had dropped to a low of 7.7 pesos per dollar as of March 9, 1995. Further, inflation in Mexico reached an annualized rate of 64% as of February of 1995. In March of 1995, the U.S. extended $20 million in loans and loan guarantees to Mexico. In return, Mexico instituted an economic plan including sweeping budget cuts, increased taxes, and approved provisions allowing the U.S. to oversee Mexico's handling of its economy. The agreement has caused Mexican citizens to lose faith in President Ernesto Zedillo, who has been accused of ''trading his nation's sovereignty'' for American dollars.

In addition, 1994 and 1995 have been tumultuous politically for Mexico. On January 1, 1994, the effective date of NAFTA, there was an uprising in Chiapas, Mexico led by Zaptista rebels. (The rebels take their name from the early twentieth century Mexican Revolutionary leader Emiliano Zapata.) After the initial fighting which resulted in at least 145 deaths, the rebellion has continued to simmer throughout 1994 and 1995. The Zapatistas are protesting political injustices, extreme poverty, and ethnic oppression of the indigenous people of Chiapas. They are also protesting NAFTA and the environmental degradation resulting from increased industrialization of Mexico.

Further, there has been scandal within Mexico's government. On March 23, 1994, Luis Donaldo Colosio, the leading candidate for election to Mexico's Presidency, was assassinated during a political rally. In August of 1994, Ernesto Zedillo was elected to the Presidency. His election was reassuring to investors who were awaiting the results of the election, because he advocates similar economic and political policies to those of former President Carlos Salinas, who led Mexico in approving NAFTA. However, during 1995 there has been scandal within Mexico's government. The brother of former President Salinas was arrested in March of 1995 and accused of planning the murder of Jose Francisco Ruiz, who had been governor of the Mexican state of Guerror from 1987 to 1993. It is said that Francisco Ruiz may have been killed as a result of a battle between political groups. In the aftermath of his brother's arrest, Salinas staged a hunger strike, and, after ending it, he moved to the United States.

Thus, at the present, there are significant economic and political factors to dissuade U.S. businesses from relocating their facilities to Mexico. Those considering investing in Mexico are proceeding cautiously.

ECONOMIC CONSEQUENCES. In the United States, many workers and representatives of organized labor viewed the passage of NAFTA as a major defeat. Individual members of Congress who voted for NAFTA have been denounced by labor groups. Labor representatives feared that substantial numbers of U.S. businesses would relocate to Mexico to take advantage of lower wages and lower costs of compliance with regulations including, but not limited to, environmental regulations.

In his book *Save Your Job, Save Our Country*, former U.S. Presidential candidate and business person Ross Perot warned workers of a ''giant sucking sound'' that would be the flow of American jobs to Mexico. However, that scenario has not materialized during the first two years of NAFTA's implementation. It is reported that NAFTA led to the creation of 100,000 jobs in the U.S. during the first half of 1994, and that as of January 1995 there were at least 700,000 jobs that depended on exports to Mexico. Economists have used economic models to predict NAFTA's effect on jobs in the U.S. During NAFTA's first five years, some economists predict that NAFTA will produce a total gain of 200,000 jobs in the U.S. while others predict a loss of up to 500,000 U.S. jobs. In terms of overall numbers of people employed in the U.S., neither number represents a dramatic shift in numbers of jobs. The jobs that are most vulnerable in the United States will be those that require unskilled labor and those that have been, in the past, protected by high U.S. tariffs. Such industries include the clothing industry, glassware, and manufacture of ceramic tiles. The American Textile Manufacturers Association strongly oppose NAFTA because lower labor costs in Mexico may cause U.S.-manufactured clothing to be unable to compete with low-priced garments made in Mexico.

Economic consequences for Mexico are expected to be more noticeable than those in the United States because Mexico is starting with a much smaller economy. As of 1993, the $6 trillion American economy was 20 times the size of Mexico's. As of 1994, Mexico was both the third largest and the fastest growing trading partner of the United States. However, NAFTA may not represent a blessing for Mexico's unskilled workers and their families. Workers are obtaining employment at low wages in new **manufacturing** facilities. However, their wages are not sufficient to enable them to purchase decent housing, clothing, and good food for their families. Due to a lack of potable water, inadequate sewage facilities, inadequate or unavailable electricity, and other inadequate or unavailable services in the areas around new industrial facilities, life for workers and their families is often a miserable existence. Diseases and illness due to a lack of sanitary facilities and due to industrial pollution are prevalent and are increasing.

CONSEQUENCES FOR ORGANIZED LABOR AND INDIVIDUAL WORKERS. Workers in the United States fear that lure of cheap wages in Mexico (which average one-fifth or less than those in the United States) will cause many U.S. businesses to shift their operations to Mexico, thus losing jobs for this country and shifting much needed capital from this country. With respect to industries requiring unskilled labor, this appears to be true. However, this is a trend that began before the approval of NAFTA. Thus, these consequences of NAFTA appear to represent a continuation of a trend and not a dramatic shift in the way business investors and employers operate.

Representatives of organized labor groups such as the AFL-CIO believe that NAFTA's approval provides businesses with leverage to use against workers and their unions. AFL-CIO representatives believe that businesses will use the threat of moving to Mexico as leverage against unions during negotiation of

labor contracts, and there is some evidence that this is happening.

ENVIRONMENTAL CONSEQUENCES. Environmentalists, business representatives, and the governments of the three NAFTA countries agree that environmental contamination has reached serious proportions in northern Mexico, where U.S. businesses have been operating for over two decades under the "Maquiladora" program. (The *Maquiladora* program was established pursuant to an agreement between the United States and Mexico. The agreement allows U.S. businesses to operate manufacturing facilities in northern Mexico, with restrictions including the condition that all products produced be returned to the United States).

Environmentalists fear that the further industrialization that will occur under NAFTA will continue and exacerbate the degradation of Mexico's environment that has occurred under the Maquiladora program. They also fear that such degradation will extend into the United States. To date, the degradation occurring as a result of the Macquiladora program has not recognized political boundaries. According to the United States EPA, there are nine United States' border communities currently exceeding one or more U.S. National Ambient Air Quality Standards for specified pollutants, including ozone and carbon monoxide.

Mexico does have environmental laws which, on paper, substantially parallel the environmental laws of the United States. Mexico's Codigo Ecologico, adopted in 1988, is known in English as its General Ecology Law. It is a comprehensive environmental statute addressing pollution, resource conservation, and enforcement. Mexico's EPA equivalent is SEDE-SOL (the Secretariat of Social Development). It must be noted, however, that Mexico is in its infancy in terms of environmental enforcement as compared to the United States, with the *Codigo Ecologico* is only six years old. Further, being a poor country, Mexico lacks money for enforcement of those laws; it lacks technology; and it lacks infrastructure such as water treatment plants, sewage systems, and waste disposal facilities. A worst-case scenario under NAFTA is that U.S. industries will locate throughout Mexico, the Mexican government will fail to enforce its environmental regulations, and the problems of the border area will become problems throughout Mexico.

Some steps are being taken to deal with the massive environmental problems of the U.S./Mexican border region. When the signed NAFTA, Mexico and the U.S. also signed agreements establishing a Border Environmental Cooperation Commission (BECC) and the North American Development Bank (NADBank). These two institutions will assist border communities in coordinating and financing environmental infrastructure projects. The NADBank is capitalized in equal shares by the U.S. and Mexican governments. Each is contributing $56 million pr year for each of the first four years of the NADBank's operations to supplement existing funds for environmental infrastruction projects along the U.S./Mexican border. The BECC is working with states, local governments, and nongovernmental organizations to provide technical and financial planning with the objective of developing solutions to environmental problems in the border area.

Some observers are guardedly optimistic that NAFTA may result in better environmental conditions in Mexico and in the U.S./Mexican border area. Such optimism rests on the belief that the success of NAFTA itself will help the environment. If jobs are created in Mexico, and wages increase, and Mexico's economy improves, there should be more money available for what is needed environmentally. Money is needed for personnel to enforce Mexico's environmental laws; money is needed for infrastructure, including waste disposal facilities, water treatment and sewage facilities; and technology and equipment are needed to create safer working conditions inside and outside the walls of industrial facilities.

NAFTA'S FIRST TWO YEARS AND BEYOND

What happened during the first two years of NAFTA? Nothing earthshaking in the economic sense. Business between the United States and Mexico was "business as usual." The effects of NAFTA on trade between Canada and the U.S. were not expected to be great, because the U.S. and Canada already had a separate free trade agreement prior to the negotiation of NAFTA. During 1994, and 1995, investment by U.S. companies in Mexico progressed slowly in view of Mexico's economic and political problems.

In terms of the effect of NAFTA on the environment and labor, the effects of NAFTA will be seen only gradually as its implementation continues and as challenges to actions of NAFTA's party-countries are brought pursuant to the Environmental and Labor Side Agreements.

Meanwhile, NAFTA is being watched closely by observers throughout the word, because it is being used as a model for other agreements. For example, in December of 1994, the United States and thirty-three other Western Hemisphere countries met in Miami, Florida for a "Summit of the Americas." At the Summit, the thirty-four countries agreed to create a Free Trade Area of the Americas (FTAA) by the year 2005. The FTAA will be modeled after NAFTA. And even before the FTAA is negotiated and implemented, NAFTA itself is being expanded. At the close of the 1994 Summit of the Americas, the U.S., Canada, and Mexico announced their plans to admit Chile to NAFTA.

Therefore, NAFTA's provisions and its implementation will continue to be watched closely. NAFTA must be monitored to determine whether its provisions need modification and to determine whether its provisions provide a suitable model for additional trade agreements such as the FTAA.

[Etan Vlessing with Andrea Gacki]

FURTHER READING:

Alexander, Dean C. "The North American Free Trade Agreement: An Overview." *International Tax and Business Lawyer II*, 1993, pp. 48-71.

Carroll, Paul B. and Craig Torres. "Mexico Unveils Program of Harsh Fiscal Medicine." *New York Times*, March 19, 1995, p. A3.

Davis, Bob. "Some Questions and Answers Concerning NAFTA." *Wall Street Journal*, Nov. 19, 1993, p. 14.

Guillermoprieto, Alma. "Zapata's Heirs." *The New Yorker*, May 16, 1994, pp. 52-63.

Hofgard, Kurt C. "Is This Land Really Our Land?: Impacts of Free Trade Agreements on U.S. Environmental Protection." *Environmental Law* 23, pp. 634-81.

North American Free Trade Agreement (NAFTA). Washington, D.C.: U.S. Government Printing Office.

Serrill, Michael S. "Real-Live Soap Opera: As the Economy Slides, the Country Is Transfixed by a Bizarre Political Crime Scandal." *Time*, March 20, 1995, at 56.

Solis, Dianne. "Top Candidate in Mexico Race Is Shot at Rally." *Wall Street Journal*, March 24, 1994, p. A3.

Torres, Craig. "How Mexico's Behind-the-Scenes Tactics and a Secret Pact Averted Market Panic." *Wall Street Journal*, March 28, 1994, p. A10.

NORTH ATLANTIC TREATY ORGANIZATION

The North Atlantic Treaty Organization (NATO) was established April 4, 1949 in Washington D.C. with the signing of the North Atlantic Treaty. The original signatories of the treaty were Belgium, Canada, Denmark, France, Iceland, Italy, Luxembourg, the Netherlands, Norway, Portugal, the United Kingdom, and the United States. The purpose of NATO is to provide its members with a common defense against an aggressor nation. The potential aggressor nation NATO was formed to protect its members against was the now-dissolved Soviet Union and allied members of the Soviet bloc. The eastern counterpart to NATO was the Warsaw Pact.

NATO was formed because of the threat of westward Soviet expansion following World War II. This threat was heightened by numerous Cold War incidents including: the founding of the Communist Information Bureau(Cominform) in 1947, the 1948 communist coup in Czechoslovakia, and the Berlin crisis and the subsequent airlift also in 1948. The invasion of South Korea by North Korea and the subsequent intervention by the People's Republic of China in 1950 also raised fears in the West of Soviet imperialism. Although not in the European theater these events in Asia led many to believe that the Soviet Union was directing events in all communist countries while simultaneously testing the resolve of the West in both political and military arenas. In 1952 Turkey and Greece joined NATO and in 1955 the Federal Republic of Germany (West Germany) was allowed to join after earlier rejection.

Throughout its history the forces of nationalism often played havoc with NATO unity. In 1966 and 1967 France under President Charles de Gaulle (1890-1970) distanced itself from its NATO allies by demanding the withdrawal of NATO forces not under direct French command from home soil. De Gaulle also removed French military units from consolidated commands. In 1976 Iceland nearly withdrew its NATO membership in a fishing rights dispute with Great Britain and throughout much of the 1970s Greece and Turkey were bitterly divided over ethnic problems on the island nation of Cyprus. Greece's problems with NATO were exacerbated in 1981 when a socialist government acceded to power in that country. The Soviet threat and United States' cajoling however overcame the divisive nationalist tendencies of NATO members and the organization remained largely intact.

For an organization with such an overt military function NATO has a unique dual military and civilian administration. The military side of NATO is controlled by the Council and Defense Planning Committee. Directly under this body is the Military Committee which consists of representatives of all member countries except France and Iceland. The Military Committee is responsible for military functions and serves in an advisory capacity to the council. The military responsibilities of NATO are divided geographically into three areas: Allied Command Europe, Allied Command Atlantic (which includes the United States and Canada), and Allied Command Channel.

The North Atlantic Council is responsible for the civilian and political functioning of NATO. The council is responsible for political policy and works closely with the foreign ministries and departments of member nations. Each nation sends a permanent representative with the rank of ambassador to the council. The North Atlantic Council also works closely with the Defense Planning Committee and employs a secretary general to implement policy decisions. Heading NATO's civilian administration is the civilian chief while the president of the United States is the designated Supreme Military Chief of NATO.

By the 1990s NATO had nearly 4.3 million personnel under arms. They were generally considered to be well trained, well equipped and of high morale. The question to be answered however is: Who are they to defend Western Europe against? With the dissolution of the Soviet Union, NATO's greatest adversary has been vanquished. It is ironic that by 1994 Estonia, Latvia, Lithuania, Poland, Bulgaria, Hungary, and the Czech and Slovak Republics (all former Soviet satellites or Soviet Republics) were clamoring for NATO membership. The leaders of these nations felt membership in NATO would ensure against their reincorporation in some future Soviet bloc. Also in 1994 NATO was involved in the ethnic wars in the former Yugoslavia, a military-political-ethnic entanglement of the type that NATO was not designed to fight. Yet many world leaders feel that NATO is the only force in Europe capable of bringing the fighting to a halt. The other question facing NATO at the end of the twentieth century is: With no discernible enemy on the eastern horizon what role if any will NATO play in the Europe of the twenty-first century?

Current (1994) members of NATO are: Belgium, Canada, Denmark, France, Germany, Greece, Iceland, Italy, Luxembourg, the Netherlands, Norway, Portugal, Spain, Turkey, the United Kingdom, and the United States.

[Michael Knes]

FURTHER READING:

Evans, Richard. ''Sidelined by History: NATO's Quest for a Role in the New World Order.'' *Geographical,* vol. 66, March 1994, pp. 32-36.

North Atlantic Treaty Organization: Information Service North Atlantic Treaty Organization: Facts and Figures. Brussels, 1989.

Park, William. *Defending the West: A History of NATO.* Wheatsheaf Books, 1986.

O

OCCUPATIONAL LICENSING AND CERTIFICATION

SEE: Licensing and Certification, Occupational

OCCUPATIONAL MOBILITY AND RETRAINING

The extent of occupational mobility is indicated by the number of workers who change occupations over a given period of time. Occupational mobility can be upward or downward, depending on whether a worker moves to a higher paying, higher status occupation, or vice versa. Since the early 1970s, the growth of higher paying, higher status occupations has slowed in the United States. This includes industrial occupations as well as (more recently) professional occupations and occupations in military-related industries. Combined with a trend towards higher unemployment for all workers, these changes greatly magnify the problem of retraining displaced workers. Worker retraining in the United States is in large part administered under federal government legislation, most recently by the Comprehensive Employment and Training Act of 1973 and the Job Training Partnership Act of 1982.

Occupational mobility is one of the means by which American workers have been able to improve their economic and social circumstances in the post-World War II years. Occupational mobility can be broken down into two types: mobility resulting from overall shifts in the occupational structure, such as from a growing proportion of white-collar occupa-tions; and mobility resulting from workers changing occupations independently of shifts in the occupational structure. The former is referred to as *structural mobility* and the latter as *circulation mobility*.

Until the economic slowdown in the U.S. economy after the early 1970s, there was a tendency towards upward occupational mobility for male workers. In their 1975 article, ''Structural Changes in Occupational Mobility among Men in the United States,'' Hauser et al. wrote, ''despite the many social changes in the United States in the last two decades, it is a more favorable occupational structure, and only that, which has sustained or improved the mobility opportunities of American men.'' With the slowdown in the economy, the rate of structural mobility also slowed, and with it the tendency towards upward mobility.

The U.S. Bureau of Labor Statistics published a detailed study that forecast growth rates of occupations from years 1986 to 2000. The study projected that occupational growth rates would increase at only half the annual average rate from 1986 to 2000 as they had from 1972 to 1986. Higher paid and higher status occupations, such as those in the executive, administrative, and managerial category, were projected to grow particularly slowly. Occupations in this category grew 74 percent between 1972 and 1986 but were projected to grow by only 29 percent from 1986 to 2000. In contrast, lower paid and lower status service occupations grew 46 percent between 1972 and 1986 and were projected to grow 33 percent from 1986 to 2000.

Based on the Bureau of Labor Statistics forecasts, as well as earlier patterns of occupational mobility, a 1992 study traced the probable implications of declining occupational growth on upward mobility for men and women. This study argued that whereas one-half of men were upwardly mobile in 1962, only one-third would be in 2000. This decline was attributed to the slower rate of growth projected for higher status occupations. The projected decline in upward mobility was a continuation of existing patterns through the 1980s. That is, between 1962 and 1989, the rate of upward occupational mobility declined by 7 percent for men. Almost all of this decline occurred after the period of slower economic growth beginning in the early 1970s.

The 1992 study also projected a slower rate of upward mobility for women, although with a smaller magnitude of decrease (9 percent for women compared with 15 percent for men from the early 1970s to 2000). Women's rate of upward mobility remained stable at 55 percent from 1972 to 1985, declining by 3 percent from 1985 to 1989. A 6 percent decline was projected to 2000.

In addition to considering upward mobility, the 1992 study also examined the direction and relative strength of structural and circulation mobility for men and women. The study showed that structural mobility for men decreased from 35 percent in the early 1970s to 23 percent in the late 1980s, a reflection of the less-rapid change in the overall occupational structure of the U.S. economy. For women, structural mobility decreased from 51 percent to 43 percent from the early 1970s to the late 1980s. That is, women's rate of structural mobility was higher than men's and decreased at less than one-half the rate as men's, indicating that women were less affected by the less-rapid changes in the occupational structure than were men. Circulation mobility for men increased from 30 percent to 41 percent over these same years. Circulation mobility for women also increased, although at a more rapid rate, from 21 to 31 percent.

The Bureau of Labor Statistics maintains measures of the occupational mobility rate, defined as the percentage of workers who change occupations over the course of a year. For men and women combined, the occupational mobility rate was stable between the years 1965-66 and 1990-91. This was at odds with the view that the baby boomer generation was more readily inclined to change careers than its parents generation. However, while the occupational mobility rate decreased for men over this span of years, the rate increased for women, as reflected in Figure 1.

The table shows that while men's occupational mobility was higher then women's in the mid-1960s, the pattern was reversed by the early 1990s. The table also shows that the occupational mobility rate declined as workers got older, regardless of sex or time period. This was consistent with the view that older workers had more to lose by changing their occupa-

Figure 1

OCCUPATIONAL MOBILITY RATE

Men	1965-66	1990-91
25 to 34	13.8%	11.6%
35 to 44	7.4%	6.3%
45 to 54	5.2%	4.5%
Women		
25 to 34	8.5%	12.3%
35 to 44	5.3%	8.1%
45 to 54	4.7%	5.5%

tions, especially in seniority, pay, and pensions, among other factors.

RETRAINING

Retraining is generally associated with displaced workers, those who permanently lose their jobs as a result of structural transformations and regional shifts in the economy. The 1,158 community colleges in the United States were the largest providers of workforce retraining in 1993. Many of these received corporate financing for retraining purposes. Community colleges were generally 10 to 20 percent less expensive than firms offering professional training. Community colleges often provide basic retraining of adult workers to accommodate the estimated 40 million American adults who experience some level of illiteracy.

Since 1982, the primary retraining programs in the United States have been administered under the Job Training Partnership Act (JTPA). JTPA programs are part of the overall government system of aiding unemployed workers. Prior to JTPA, retraining programs were largely run by community organizations, but, consistent with the views of the Reagan administration, private industry came to play a greater role under JTPA. JTPA programs are administered by Private Industry Councils; more than one-half of the council representatives are from private industry, while the remainder are divided among state and local government officials, unions, and community groups.

Unlike earlier government sponsored training programs, such as those administered under the Manpower Development and Training Act of 1962 (MDTA) and the Comprehensive Employment and Training Act of 1973 (CETA), JTPA programs are performance based. That is, job trainers are funded not on the basis of how well they train workers, but on whether those workers receive employment. In spite of these changes, the overall effectiveness of JTPA programs has been similar to CETA programs.

A number of JTPA retraining programs are designed to assist displaced industrial workers, a group that has been particularly hard hit as a result of the declining growth of industrial occupations. One of these programs was developed in 1983 to assist displaced miners in the Minnesota Iron Range. Training was provided by community organizations, local government agencies, regional vocational schools, and community colleges. Regional firms also provided short-term training in data processing, truck driving, and welding. The program also provided job search help. For those participating in the program between October of 1983 and June of 1984, 62 percent were able to find new jobs, although one-half of these jobs were outside of the seven county region that the miners lived in. Among the many similar programs administered under JTPA is one developed at the Cummins Engine Company in Columbus, Ohio, and the Metropolitan Pontiac Retraining and Employment Program in Pontiac, Michigan, a project jointly managed by General Motors Corp. and the United Auto Workers.

Facing declining growth after the end of the Cold War, the aerospace industry has posed a significant challenge for worker retraining programs. Starting in 1991, thousands of employees from Martin Marietta's Electronics and Missile Systems and Information Systems divisions in Orlando, Florida lost their jobs as a series of cuts were made in defense spending. With few defense contractors hiring, high regional unemployment, and skepticism towards defense workers on the part of commercial firms, many of these laid-off workers were unable to find new employment. A program was established in 1993 that was administered by the U.S. Department of Labor and partly funded by the U.S. Department of Defense. Additional funds were provided under the Job Training Partnership Act. Managers, engineers, Ph.D.s, and assembly workers were included in the program, which involved evaluating each worker's skills and trying to match them with available openings in the area, particularly in the high-tech medical and entertainment industries. Retraining took place in local community colleges and included education in computer-aided design and computer-integrated manufacturing.

Other programs in which displaced defense engineers were retrained had little success. Two months after an engineer retraining program in Long Island, only one participant out of a total of 44 had been able to find employment as a result of the program. In Los Angeles, a similar program was established to retrain defense engineers to become environmental engineers. Four months after retraining, only six of the 26 participants had found permanent employment as a result of the program and only two of the six had found employment as environmental engineers.

The approach to worker retraining under the Job Training Partnership Act was called into question during the Clinton administration. Under Secretary of Labor Robert Reich, the Department of Labor issued a draft of a bill called the Re-employment Act of 1994. The act would have encouraged states to set up one-stop worker training centers and would have extended unemployment compensation for displaced workers undergoing retraining. The act faced heavy opposition from business groups, who argued that it would increase the federal unemployment tax, and was not passed in 1994.

[David Kucera]

FURTHER READING:

Bellinger, Robert. "Martin-Marietta Retraining Program Flies." Electronic Engineering Times, November 29, 1993.

Bellinger, Robert. "Retrained EEs are Finding Few Jobs: Long Island, L.A. Programs Show Mixed Results." Electronic Engineering Times, March 8, 1993.

"Career Hopping." American Demographics, December 1993.

Cook, Robert (ed.). Worker Dislocation: Case Studies of Causes and Cures. W.E. Upjohn Institute for Employment Research, 1987.

Devroy, Ann, and John Harris. "Clinton Proposes New Job Training." Washington Post, January 11, 1995.

Hauser, Robert M., et al. "Structural Changes in Occupational Mobility Among Men in the United States." American Sociological Review, Volume 40, 1975.

Janoski, Thomas. The Political Economy of Unemployment: Active Labor Market Policy in West Germany and the United States. University of California Press, 1990.

Krymkowski, Daniel H., and Tadeusz K. Krauze. "Occupational Mobility in the Year 2000: Projections for American Men and Women." Social Forces, September 1992.

Rosenbaum, James E. Career Mobility in a Corporate Hierarchy. Academic Press, Inc. 1984.

"Retooling American Workers." Business Week, Industrial Edition, September 27, 1993.

"U.S. Job Training Bill Raises Dander Over Plan's Cost." Crain's, February 28, 1994.

Waddoups, Jeffrey, and Djeto Assane. "Mobility and Gender in a Segmented Labor Market: A Closer Look." American Journal of Economics and Sociology, October 1993.

OCCUPATIONAL SAFETY AND HEALTH ADMINISTRATION (OSHA)

The Occupational Safety and Health Administration (OSHA) was established by the Williams-Steiger Occupational Safety and Health Act (OSH Act) of 1970, which took effect in 1971. OSHA's mission is to "assure, in so far as possible, every working man and woman in the nation safe and healthful working conditions." With the exception of operators of mines, the OSH Act covers every nonpublic United States employer whose business affects interstate commerce. Thus, nearly every private employer in the United States is covered. Operators of mines are exempt from the OSH Act because they are regulated separately pursuant to the Mine Safety and Health Act of 1977. Because OSHA is an administrative agency within the United States Department of Labor, it is administered by an assistant secretary of labor. Under President Clinton, that person is Joseph Dear, who headed the state of Washington's labor department prior to joining OSHA in April of 1993.

OSHA'S OBJECTIVES AND STANDARDS-SETTING

OSHA seeks to make workplaces safer and healthier by making and enforcing regulations, which the OSH Act calls "standards." The OSH Act itself establishes only one workplace standard, which is called the "general duty standard." The general duty standard states: "Each employer shall furnish to each of his employees employment and a place of employment which are free from recognized hazards that are causing or are likely to cause death or serious physical harm to his [or her] employees." In the OSH Act, Congress delegated authority to OSHA to make rules further implementing the general duty standard.

Standards made by OSHA are published in the *Code of Federal Regulations* (*CFR*). The three types of regulations are called interim, temporary emergency, and permanent. Interim standards were applicable for two years after OSH Act was passed. For this purpose, OSHA was authorized to use the standards of any nationally recognized "standards setting" organization such as those of professional engineering groups. Such privately developed standards are called "national consensus standards." Temporary emergency standards last only six months and are designed to protect workers while OSHA goes through the processes required by law to develop a permanent standard. Permanent standards are made through the same processes as the regulations made by other federal administrative agencies. As OSHA drafts a proposal for a permanent standard, it consults with representatives of industry and labor and collects scientific, medical, and engineering data as appropriate. A proposed standard is then published in the *Federal Register*. A comment period is held, during which input is received from interested parties including, but not limited to, representatives of industry and labor. At the close of the comment period, the proposal may be withdrawn and set aside, withdrawn and reproposed with modifications, or promulgated as a final standard. (Promulgated means that it has been made into a permanent standard and has the force and effect of law.) All promulgated standards are first published in the *Federal Register* and are then compiled and published in the *Code of Federal Regulations*. It is important to note that many of OSHA's permanent standards originated as national consensus standards developed by private professional organizations such as the National Fire Protection Association and the

American National Standards Institute. Examples of permanent OSHA standards include limits for exposure of employees to hazardous substances such as asbestos, benzene, vinyl chloride, and cotton dust.

In the OSH Act of 1970, in addition to creating OSHA, Congress established a research institute called the National Institute of Occupational Safety and Health (NIOSH). Since 1973, NIOSH has been a division of the Centers for Disease Control (CDC). The purpose of NIOSH is to gather data documenting incidences of occupational exposure, injury, illness and death in the United States. After gathering and evaluating data, NIOSH develops "criteria documents" for specific standards giving doctors' and scientists' conclusions about specific hazards. For example, they evaluate how much noise is likely to cause deafness or how much exposure to benzene is likely to cause leukemia. Some OSHA standards specifying permissible amounts and levels of exposure to toxic substances are based on criteria documents. However, the administration also considers data gathered by representatives of industry, labor, and other groups.

OSHA'S RECORD-KEEPING REQUIREMENTS

As a means of identifying workplace hazards and as a means of identifying violations of OSHA's standards, all employers covered by the OSH Act are required to keep four kinds of records. These records include: (1) records regarding enforcement of OSHA standards; (2) research records; (3) job-related injury, illness, and death records; and (4) records regarding job hazards.

OSHA'S ENFORCEMENT OF STANDARDS

OSHA inspectors conduct planned or surprise inspections of work sites covered by the OSH Act to verify compliance with the OSH Act and standards promulgated by OSHA. The OSH Act allows the employer *and* an employee representative to accompany OSHA's representative during the inspection. It should also be noted that in 1978, in *Marshall v. Barlow*, the United States Supreme Court declared that in most industries, employers have a right to bar an OSHA inspector from his/her premises if the inspector has not first obtained a search warrant.

If violations are found during an inspection, an OSHA citation may be issued in which alleged violations are listed, notices of penalties for each violation are given, and an abatement period is established. The abatement period is the amount of time the employer has to correct any violation(s). Penalties for a violation can be civil or criminal and vary depending on whether the violation is nonserious or serious, willful or nonwillful, or repeated. For serious, repeated, willful violations, possible civil penalties range up to $70,000. Ironically, however, monetary criminal penalties range up to only $10,000. A six-month jail sentence can be imposed if an employee death results from a violation. Because OSHA must refer cases to the United States Justice Department for criminal enforcement, it has not made extensive use of criminal prosecution as an enforcement mechanism.

An employer has 15 days to contest an OSHA citation, and any challenge is heard by an Administrative Law Judge (ALJ) within OSHA. The ALJ receives oral and written evidence, decides issues of fact and law, and enters an order. If the employer is dissatisfied with that order, it can be appealed to the Occupational Safety and Health Review Commission, which will, in turn, enter an order. Finally, within 30 days of the issuance of that order, the employer or the Secretary of Labor can take the case to the United States federal court system by filing an appeal with a United States court of appeals.

OSHA AND ITS STATE COUNTERPARTS

Pursuant to the OSH Act, an individual state can pass its own worker health and safety laws and standards. If the state can show that its counterpart to OSHA will regulate as stringently as or more stringently than the federal agency, the state counterpart will be certified to assume OSH Act administration and enforcement in that state. As of 1993, counterparts to OSHA were authorized in at least 23 states. Therefore, businesses in those states deal on a day-to-day basis with the state agency instead of the federal administration.

Businesses should be aware that in recent years state attorneys general and prosecutors have brought increasing numbers of criminal prosecutions against employers for crimes ranging from battery to murder. Thus, although the OSH Act provides for maximum penalties of six months of jail for willful violation of a standard, state prosecutors can and do seek much more serious penalties using state criminal statutes.

HISTORY OF THE RELATIONSHIP BETWEEN OSHA AND BUSINESS

OSHA has traditionally used "command and control" kinds of regulation to protect workers. "Command and control" regulations are those which set requirements for job safety (such as requirements for guard rails on stairs) or limits on exposure to a hazardous substance (such as a given number of fibers of asbestos per cubic milliliter of air breathed per hour). They are enforced through citations issued to violators.

In 1984, OSHA promulgated the Hazard Communication Standard (HCS), which is viewed as a new kind of regulation differing from "command and control." The HCS gives workers access to information about long-term health risks resulting from workplace exposure to toxic or hazardous substances. The HCS requires manufacturers, importers, and distributors to provide employers with evaluations of all toxic or hazardous materials sold or distributed to those employers. For each chemical, this information is compiled in a Material Safety Data Sheet (MSDS). The MSDS describes the chemical's physical hazards such as ignitability and reactivity, gives associated health hazards, and states the exposure limits established by OSHA. In turn, the employer must make the MSDSs available to its employees. In addition, the employer must establish a hazard communication program which educates employees about the HCS, explains the potential hazards of materials in their workplace to employees, and trains employees in methods of using those materials safely. The employer must also label all containers with the identities of hazardous substances and appropriate warnings. Worker Right-to-Know, as implemented on the federal level through the HCS, is designed to give workers access to information which, in turn, may enable workers to make choices about their exposure to toxic chemicals.

OSHA has been criticized by businesses throughout its history. In the 1970s, it was criticized for making job-safety regulations that businesses considered to be vague or unnecessarily costly in time or money to enforce. For example, a 1977 OSHA regulation contained detailed specifications regarding irregularities in western hemlock trees used to construct ladders. In the Appropriations Act of 1977, Congress directed OSHA to get rid of certain standards that it described as "trivial." As a result, in 1978 OSHA revoked 928 job-safety standards and increased its efforts to deal with health hazards.

On the other hand, OSHA has been criticized throughout its history for doing too little to protect workers. It has been and continues to be criticized for issuing too few new standards, for failing to protect workers who report violations of OSHA standards, for failing to adequately protect workers involved in the clean up of toxic-waste sites, and for failing to enforce existing standards. For example, in September of 1993, 25 men and women perished in a fire in a chicken processing plant in North Carolina. The workers died because they were trapped inside the burning building behind emergency exits that had been bolted by managers of the plant in violation of OSHA standards. During 11 years of operation in North Carolina, the plant had never been inspected by OSHA inspectors.

The alleged reasons for such failures to protect workers range from inadequate funding for research and enforcement to lack of will to enforce. During the 1980s, Presidents Reagan and Bush publicly supported efforts to keep agencies such as OSHA "off the backs" of business. Therefore, workers' advocates place at least partial blame for lax enforcement on those administrations.

OSHA REFORM LEGISLATION

Although OSHA's HCS and similar state Worker Right-to-Know laws give today's workers access to far more information about their exposure to toxic chemicals than they received a decade ago, knowledge alone does not prevent illness, injury, or death. However, as a result of workers' and other citizens' increased awareness of hazards, there are calls for OSHA to do more to protect workers, and there are proposals for new mechanisms to allow workers themselves to take action to protect themselves.

OSH Act Reform legislation that was pending before the United States Congress in 1995 included a number of proposals for significant changes in the OSH Act. If passed, the law would mandate that every employer implement a health and safety program that identifies and addresses workplace hazards. Also, it would require that each employer with 11 or more employees establish a joint health and safety committee, with equal numbers of employer and employee representatives. Among its duties, the committee would conduct periodic inspections of the worksite, and it would conduct additional inspections in response to employee complaints. The reform bill would expand OSH Act coverage to include federal, state, and local employees, and it would mandate time frames to compel OSHA to act more quickly if NIOSH recommends that a standard be promulgated. Potential fines and prison sentences for criminal violations would be increased significantly. Also, employees who exercise their rights to report violations of OSHA standards would receive greater protection against retaliatory discrimination by their employers.

The OSH Act is more than two decades old, and criticisms of the OSH Act and OSHA abound. Therefore, public debate regarding OSH Act Reform legislation promises to be vigorous, and its outcome will be significant for our society.

[Paulette L. Stenzel]

FURTHER READING:

Amy Bodwin, "Work-Safety System Clogged: State Audit," *Crains Business Detroit,* April 12-18, 1993, p. 1.

Occupational Safety and Health Act of 1970, 29 U.S.C. §§651-678 (1988).

Stenzel, Paulette L., "Right to Act: Advancing the Common Interests of Labor and Environmentalists," 57 *Albany Law Review* 1, 1993.

Boggs, Richard F., "OSHA Can't Do It All," *Safety & Health,* 5 April 1992, p. 25.

Tyson, Patrick R., "OSHA Reform: The Sequel," *Safety & Health,* Dec. 1991, p. 17.

Tyson, Patrick R., "OSHA Reform Under Way," *Safety & Health,* Nov. 1991, p. 23

OCCUPATIONAL SAFETY AND HEALTH REVIEW COMMISSION

The Occupational Safety and Health Review Commission (OSHRC) rules on cases arising from contested enforcement actions of the **Occupational Safety and Health Administration (OSHA)**. Its purpose is to provide a timely and fair resolution of those cases, which involve the alleged exposure of workers to unsafe or unhealthy working conditions.

The OSHRC was established by the Occupational Safety and Health Act of 1970. It is an independent, quasi-judicial agency headquartered in Washington, DC, with regional offices in Atlanta, GA, Boston, MA, Dallas, TX, and Denver, CO. The agency consists of three commissioners, one of which is designated as chairperson, a legal staff, national and regional judges, and assorted other staff.

The Occupational Safety and Health Act affects virtually every employer in the United States. The act is enforced by the Secretary of Labor primarily through OSHA. It requires employers to provide workers with a safe and healthy environment. In recent years specific areas of concern have included, among others, exposure to hazardous materials and process safety management in the oil and gas industries.

OSHA conducts safety and health inspections to insure compliance with the act. Cases are forwarded to the OSHRC by the Department of Labor when OSHA's rulings and enforcement actions are contested either by an employer, an employee, or an employee representative. An employer may contest any alleged job safety or health violation found during an OSHA inspection as well as the penalties assessed and the time allowed to correct such violations. Employees or their representatives may also challenge the appropriateness of the time allowed to correct a hazardous situation. All such challenges must be made within 15 working days after a citation has been issued by OSHA against an employer.

Within the OSHRC there are two levels of adjudication. If the case requires a hearing, it is assigned to an administrative law judge, usually in the community where the alleged violation has occurred. In such a hearing the Secretary of Labor usually has the burden of proving a violation has occurred. Upon completion of the hearing the judge issues a decision based on the facts presented.

In many cases the decisions of the administrative law judges are final. However, each decision may be reviewed at the discretion of one of the three OSHRC commissioners within 30 days. In cases where such a review takes place the OSHRC issues its own decision, which supersedes that of the administrative law judge. Once a case has been decided, either by a judge or by the commission, it may be appealed to the United States Courts of Appeals.

The main office of the Occupational Safety and Health Review Commission is located at 1120 Twentieth Street NW, Washington, DC 20036-3419. The rules and regulations of the OSHRC are contained in Title 29, Section XX, of the Code of Federal Regulations.

SEE ALSO: Occupational Safety and Health Administration (OSHA)

[David Bianco]

OFFICE AUTOMATION

Office automation refers to the varied computer machinery and software used to digitally create, collect, store, manipulate, and relay office information needed for accomplishing basic tasks and goals. Raw data storage, electronic transfer, and the management of electronic business information comprise the basic activities of an office automation system. In its basic form, information exists as letters, memos, graphs, records, messages, etc. When that information is electronically transferred, raw data is exchanged between two or more office employees, either at the same or different locations.

The history of modern **office automation** began with the typewriter and the copy machine, which mechanized previously manual tasks. However, increasingly office automation refers not just to the mechanization of tasks but to the conversion of information to electronic form as well. The advent of the personal computer in the early 80's revolutionized office automation. Popular operating systems like DOS (Disk Operating System) and user interfaces like Microsoft Corp.'s Windows dominate office computer systems. Today, most offices use at least one commercial computer business application in the course of daily activity. Some large companies like AT&T maintain extensive and complex office automation systems, while smaller companies may employ only a word processor.

Office automation involves the receipt and processing of pertinent office information to accomplish office tasks and goals. In order to process information, office automation systems must allow input of new information and the retrieval of stored information. Input of new information refers to the physical transfer of text, video, graphics, and sound into a computer. Input can be typed into the computer or scanned (digitally reproduced) from another document or source. New advances in input devices frequently allow direct handwritten input or voice dictation. Input of pre-existing information means retrieving the electronic materials from an existing storage area. These storage areas can be finite and local, such as the hard drive on the office PC, or as seemingly infinite and global as the Internet, the worldwide collection of computer networks that is growing every year.

THE BASICS OF OFFICE AUTOMATION

Generally, there are three basic activities of an office automation system data storage of raw data, data exchange, and data management. Within each broad application area, hardware and software combine to fulfill basic functions.

DATA STORAGE AND MANIPULATION. Data storage usually includes office records and other primary office forms and documents. Data applications involve the capture and editing of a file, image, or spreadsheet. Word processing and desktop presentation packages accommodate raw textual and graphical data, while spreadsheet applications enable the easy manipulation and output of numbers. Image applications allow the capture and editing of visual images.

Text handling software and systems cover the whole field of word processing and desktop publishing. Word processing is the inputting (usually via keyboard) and manipulation of text on a computer. Word processing is frequently the most basic and common office automation activity. Popular commercial word processing applications include WordPerfect (Novell) and Word (Microsoft). Each provides the office user with a sophisticated set of commands to format, edit, and print text documents. One of the most popular features of word processing packages are their preformatted document templates. Templates automatically set up such things as font size, paragraph styles, headers and footers, and page numbers so that the user does not have to reset document characteristics every time they create a new record.

Desktop publishing adds another dimension to text manipulation. By packaging the features of a word processor with advanced page design and layout features, desktop publishing packages easily create documents with text and images, such as newsletters or brochures.

Image handling software and systems are another facet of office automation. Images, or digital pictures, are representations of visual information. Visual information is an important complement to textual information. Examples of visual information include pictures of documents, photographs, and graphics such as tables and charts. These images are converted into digital files, which cannot be edited the same way that text files can. In a word processor or desktop publishing application, each word or character is treated individually. In an imaging system, the entire picture or document is treated as one whole object. One of the most popular uses of computerized images is in corporate presentations or speeches. Presentation software packages simplify the creation of multimedia presentations that use computer video, images, sound and text in an integrated information package.

Spreadsheet programs allow the manipulation of numeric data. Early popular spreadsheets like VisiCalc and Lotus 123 greatly simplified common business financial record keeping. Particularly useful among the many spreadsheet options is the ability to use variables in pro forma statements. The pro forma option allows the user to change a variable and have a complex formula automatically recalculated based on the new numbers. Many businesses use spreadsheets for financial management, financial projection, and accounting.

DATA EXCHANGE. While data storage and manipulation is one component of an office automation system, the exchange of that information is another equally important component. Electronic transfer is a general application area that highlights the exchange of information between more than one user or participant. Electronic mail, voice mail, and facsimile are examples of electronic transfer applications. Systems that allow instantaneous or ''real time'' transfer of information (i.e. online conversations via computer or audio exchange with video capture) are considered electronic sharing systems. Electronic sharing software illustrates the collaborative nature of many office automation systems. The distinction between electronic transfer and electronic sharing is subtle but recognizable.

Electronic transfer software and systems allow for electronic, voice, and facsimile transmission of office information. Electronic mail uses computer-based storage and a common set of network communication standards to forward electronic messages from one user to another. It is usually possible to relay electronic mail to more than one recipient. Additionally, many electronic mail systems provide security features, automatic messaging, and mail management systems like electronic folders or notebooks. Voice mail offers essentially the same applications, but for telephones, not computers. Facsimile transmissions are limited to image relay and have suffered in popularity with the increase in the use of the personal computer. There are, however, facsimile converters for the personal computer that allow remote printing of ''faxed'' information via the computer rather than a dedicated facsimile machine. These facsimile circuit boards for the microcomputer are slowly replacing stand-alone facsimile machines.

Electronic sharing systems offset the limitations of a store-and-forward electronic mail system. Office automation systems that include the ability to electronically share information between more than one user simultaneously are often called groupware. One type of groupware is an electronic meeting system. Electronic meeting systems allow geographically dispersed participants to exchange information in real time. Participants may be within the same office or building, or thousands of miles apart. Long-distance electronic sharing systems usually use a telephone line connection to transfer data, while sharing in the same often involves just a local area network of computers (no outside phone line is needed). An interesting byproduct of the electronic sharing functions of an office automation system is telecommuting. A telecommuter works for a business from another location (often home) using a computer and a connection to the office automation system. Telecommuting is an increasingly popular style of work for many office workers and companies.

DATA MANAGEMENT. The last major component of an office automation system offers planning and strategic advantages by simplifying the management of the stored information. Task management, tickler systems or reminder systems, and scheduling programs monitor and control various projects and activities within the office. Electronic management systems monitor and control office activities and tasks through timelines, resource equations, and electronic scheduling. As in data exchange, groupware is gaining in popularity for data management. Each member of the work group or larger group may share access to necessary information via the automated office system and groupware.

OFFICE AUTOMATION: PEOPLE, TOOLS, AND THE WORKPLACE

When considering office automation three main areas need further discussion: people, and how automation affects them; the constantly changing tools used in automation; and the ways automation has changed the workplace.

People involved with office automation basically include all users of the automation and all providers of the automation systems and tools. A wide range of people—including software and hardware engineers, management information scientists, and secretaries—are just a few people involved with using office automation. All are also involved with providing information. This dual role of both provider and user gives rise to two critical issues. First, training of personnel to effectively use an office automation system is essential. The office automation system is only as good as the people who make it and use it. Second, overcoming workplace resistance is a must if the full benefits of automation are to be realized. Change is difficult for some workers, yet change must occur.

Practical tools for office automation include computer hardware and software currently available in a number of models, applications, and configurations. Two basic microcomputer platforms are DOS (Disk Operating System)-compatible computers and Apple MacIntosh systems. Applications such as word processing, database management, and spreadsheets are common and constantly changing. Standards are increasing but still not yet completely integrated into all aspects of office automation. Office automation tools may stand alone (without access to information at other computers) or be networked (with access to information at other computers). Configuring complex office systems to share information is difficult and involves a considerable staff commitment. Popular local area network software includes Novell Netware and Lantastic.

Practical workplace issues of office automation often involve the budget and physical considerations involved with creating, exchanging, and managing information. Equipment, rewiring, training, security, and data entry all cost money and require space. New medical problems such as repetitive motion syndrome are a significant issue for some people using office automation systems. Repetitive motion syndrome is a medical disorder associated with lengthy keyboard inputting and seating arrangements. Likewise, environmental safety concerns might also include vision and overall health considerations related to electromagnetic computer emissions. Telecommuting advances enable an increasing number of the workforce to make their home their office and, at the same time, provoke considerable debate on the future of the central office. Businesses must comply with software licenses or face lawsuits. Office automation systems can be complex to acquire and costly to administrate for large organizations. The availability of vital office information in such an easily obtained digital format requires considerable thought and preparation for data security.

By integrating raw information with exchange mechanisms and management structuring and guidance, office automation creates advantages as well as disadvantages. Benefits in using electronic management systems include savings in production and service costs as information is quickly routed for the optimal office performance. Office automation can also be cost effective, as powerful microcomputers continue to drop in price. While office automation often mirrors actual paper transaction and activity, an office automation system may also complement the paper system and provide output only available in digital format. Thus, office automation extends the information workplace and activities of the office to surpass physical or geographic limitation.

[Tona Henderson]

FURTHER READING:

Carter, Leon. ''Office Machines Meet LAN's In The Digital Office of the Future.'' *Purchasing*. November 25, 1993, pp. 71-80.

Dykeman, John. B. ''The State of Office Applications Software.'' *Managing Office Technology*. June 1993, pp. 40-44.

Kimmel, Peter S. ''The Vicious Cycle And New Ways To Manage.'' *Facilities Design and Management*. February, 1994, p. 29.

Laudon, Kenneth C., and Jane P. Laudon. *Management Information Systems: Organization and Technology*. Macmillan, 1994.

Martin, E. Wainright, et al. *Managing Information Technology: What Managers Need To Know*. Macmillan, 1991.

O'Brien, James A. *Introduction to Information Systems*. Irwin, 1994.

Stevens, Tim. ''The Smart Office.'' *Industry Management*. January 17, 1994, pp. 31-34.

Taylor, James R., and Elizabeth J. Van Every. *The Vulnerable Fortress: Bureaucratic Organization and Management in the Information Age*. University of Toronto Press, 1993.

OFFICE MANAGEMENT

According to CEOs responding to a survey from *Inc.* magazine, good office **management** and office managers are the grease that keep the wheels of business rolling smoothly. **Office management** can be virtually anything the company owner wants it to be. Generally, the job is described as organizing and administering the auxiliary chores of the front office. Possible duties of an office manager include ordering and purchase approval of office supplies and services, hiring of front office workers, handling customer service, managing **accounting** functions, and analyzing sales.

There is no traceable history of office management. The job of ''office manager'' is generally found in smaller companies where the owner depends on a single person who performs a variety of tasks to keep the office functioning. As a company grows into a corporation, office managers seem to disappear, while other departments such as purchasing and human resources expand. The office manager is usually not considered to be a member of the management team. She or he probably would not participate in management strategy sessions on how to increase sales, but would participate in sessions on how to cut operating expenses.

In the area of supplies and services, an office manager is usually responsible for buying short-term supplies such as photocopy paper, envelopes, and letterhead, longer-term purchases such as telephone systems, and other ongoing necessities such as making sure the postal meter has enough postage. This person usually handles the company's service purchases, such as long distance telephone service and photocopier service agreements. Ideally, office managers will be given the authority to accept bids and negotiate contracts so that they may tell salespeople that they make the decisions. Office managers must also be savvy enough to recognize fraudulent business practices.

One of the most common scams perpetuated on small companies today involves selling office products over the phone. A scam artist will call the company and try to bamboozle whoever answers the phone into approving an order for photocopier supplies. Many company owners instruct all office personnel to turn such calls over to the office manager who should be trained to recognize such scams. Another popular scam office managers need to recognize is official-looking, but phony, bills that are sent to the company. Such bills look like an invoice for telephone book advertising or a directory listing, but are fraudulent.

Another responsibility of an office manager is staffing. He will recruit, interview, and hire employees for the office. The office manager needs to know how to select the right people and train them. For example, the telephone receptionist will need to be skilled in telephone etiquette and customer service.

Office managers sometimes take on the role of monitoring customer service. They may listen to calls, or answer the phone themselves. They may also ask the customers directly how the company is doing in this area. They then report their findings to the company owner on a regular basis. They also know enough to turn over particularly thorny problems to the company owner immediately so faithful customers do not become angry if they think the company owner is ignoring them and passing them off to an office manager. The key to being successful as a customer service manager is to convince customers that all collected information good and bad, will go directly to the president for review.

Accounting functions are often handled by office managers, provided they have some background in handling money, or can be trained to do so. They may keep track of accounts payable and accounts receivable, assign vendor bills to be paid during specific weeks, prepare outgoing bills as customer orders or jobs are finished, and control the company's petty cash. Many office managers are reluctant to actually sign checks, however, as that could make them appear to be a link in the chain of financial liability if the company were to run into financial problems.

Office managers also frequently take on the job of time accounting, particularly for small service companies such as advertising agencies or law firms that depend on the billing of time as a source of revenue. The officer manager collects the time sheets from billable employees in order to assign the hours to specific jobs. This task is slowly being replaced by software that automatically tracks and assigns time.

A final possible area of responsibility for office managers is to compile and analyze sales information. This might involve calculating the profitability of the company and specific projects or tracking various expenditures. This knowledge is critical to the performance of a company, but too detailed for the company owner to know off the top of his or her head. An office manager performing these duties must be able to retrieve all the necessary documents and be able to analyze the information.

An office manager position can sometimes lead a person up the corporate ladder without a formal business degree. The experience gained from organizing and running the front office successfully can provide a person with a variety of transferable skills.

[Clint Johnson]

FURTHER READING:

Greco, Susan. "What Office Managers Really Do." *Inc.* January, 1992, p. 114.

"Hiring an Office Manager." *American Medical News.* January 27, 1992, p. 9.

Patrick, Alan. "How to Make the Office Work." *Management Today.* January, 1993, p. 54.

OLIGOPOLY

An oligopoly is a market condition in which the production of identical or similar products is concentrated in a few large firms. Examples of oligopolies in the United States include the steel, aluminum, automobile, gypsum, petroleum, tire, and beer industries. The introduction of new products and processes can create new oligopolies, as in the computer or synthetic fiber industries. Oligopolies also exist in service industries, such as the airlines industry.

An oligopoly may be categorized as either a homogeneous oligopoly or a differentiated oligopoly. In a homogeneous oligopoly the major firms produce identical products, such as steel bars or aluminum ingots. Prices tend to be uniform in homogeneous oligopolies. In a differentiated oligopoly, similar but not identical products are produced. Examples include the automobile industry, the cigarette industry, or the soft drink industry. In differentiated oligopolies companies attempt to differentiate their products from those of their competitors. To the extent that they are able to establish differentiated products, companies may be able to maintain price differences.

Being part of an oligopoly affects a company's competitive behavior. In a competitive market situation which is not an oligopoly, firms compete by acting for themselves to maximize profits without regard to the reactions of their competitors. In an oligopoly, a firm must consider the effects of its actions on others in the industry. While smaller firms may operate at the fringes of an oligopoly without affecting the other firms in the industry, the actions of a major firm in the oligopoly typically cause reactions in the other firms in the industry. For example, if one company in the oligopoly attempts to undersell the others, then the other firms will respond by also lowering prices. As a result, price cuts in oligopolies tend to result in lower profits for all of the firms involved.

Prices in oligopolistic industries tend to be unstable to the extent that companies will shade, or lower, their prices slightly to gain a competitive advantage. It must be remembered that collusion between firms to fix prices is illegal under the United States' antitrust laws, so oligopolies must reach industry agreements on pricing indirectly. Companies can signal their pricing intentions indirectly in a variety of ways, such as through press releases, speeches by industry leaders, or comments given in interviews. In some cases there is a recognized price leader in the oligopoly, and other firms in the oligopoly set their prices according to that of the industry's price leader.

Industrial concentration is a matter of degree. This means that there is no absolute definition of an oligopoly in terms of the number of firms accounting for a certain percentage of an industry's output. In the United States the *Census of Manufacturers* reports on each industry's four-firm concentration ratio. This figure indicates what percentage of an industry's output is accounted for by its four largest companies. It is not uncommon for the four largest firms to account for 30 percent or more of an industry's output, and in some cases they account for more than 70 percent of production.

Oligopolies tend to develop in industries that require large capital investments. Studies have shown that industries with high four-firm concentration ratios tend to have higher margins than other industries. In order to maintain an oligopoly, potential investors must be discouraged from establishing competing companies. Oligopolies are able to perpetuate themselves and discourage new investments in several ways. In some cases the oligopoly is the result of access to key resources, which may be either natural resources or some patented process or special knowledge. New firms cannot enter the industry without access to those resources.

The established, experienced firms in an oligopoly also enjoy significant cost advantages that make it difficult for new firms to enter the industry. These cost advantages may be the result of the large scale of production required as well as of experience in keeping manufacturing or operating costs down. Another factor that tends to perpetuate oligopolies is the difficulty of introducing new products into an oligopoly characterized by a high degree of product differentiation. Prohibitively large expenditures would be required of a new firm to overcome consumer reluctance to try a new product over an established one. Finally, oligopolies perpetuate themselves through predatory practices such as obtaining lower prices from suppliers, establishing exclusive dealerships, and predatory pricing aimed at driving smaller competitors out of business.

[David Bianco]

ON-THE-JOB TRAINING

There are two basic types of job training—classroom and on-the-job. In his article, "Public Policy to Retrain Displaced Workers," Duane Leigh distinguished between the two types of training as follows: "The premise of classroom training is that the specific skills of displaced workers have been made largely obsolete, but that marketable skills can be developed through intensive, formal training in a classroom setting. On-the-job training, on the other hand, is appropriate in the acquisition of specific skills that can most efficiently be learned on the job."

On-the-job training is the predominant form of job training in the United States, particularly for nonmanagerial employees. Numerous studies indicate that it is the most effective form of job training. The largest share of on-the-job training is provided by the private sector, though the most widely studied training programs are those sponsored by federal legislation.

On-the-job training programs range from formal training with company supervisors to learning by watching. In this sense, the most formal types of on-the-job training are distinct from classroom training largely in that they take place within the firm. In the face of increased international competition and the more widespread use of computers in production processes, the implementation of more sophisticated forms of on-the-job training has become a critical issue for firms in the United States.

Federal legislation has played a large role in the provision of on-the-job training. Title I of the Comprehensive Employment and Training Act of 1973 (CETA) provides for on-the-job training and "work experience'' for disadvantaged workers. This includes the establishment of subsidized government jobs in an effort to encourage regular work habits and develop job skills for those with little or no previous experience in the labor market.

Several studies of CETA programs have sought to determine the relative effectiveness of classroom versus on-the-job training in improving participants' earnings. These studies have concluded that on-the-job training is generally more effective, especially for minority participants. This results in part from the fact that participants receiving on-the-job training are often able to continue working at the place of training.

CETA expired in 1982, during one of the deepest U.S. recessions since the 1930s. CETA was replaced by the Job Training Partnership Act (JTPA) of 1982. JTPA has three main titles. Title II provides job training for disadvantaged adults and youths as well as summer jobs for these youths. Title III provides job training for displaced workers whose jobs are eliminated by transformations in the economy. Title IV provides training for Native Americans, veterans, and migrant workers.

Unlike CETA, programs under JTPA are intended to train and place workers in the private sector. This is in response to the political unpopularity of subsidized government jobs developed under CETA. JTPA programs also contrast with CETA programs in that they are largely regulated at the state level, give private sector representatives a large administrative role, and focus more on job training than income maintenance.

The **General Accounting Office (GAO)** conducted a nation-wide survey of Title III JTPA programs between 1982 and 1985. The survey indicated that 80 percent of program participants received job search assistance, compared with only 26 percent who received classroom training and 16 percent who received on-the-job training. The low proportion of participants actually receiving training resulted from the fact that trainers were largely funded on the basis of job placement, not long-term labor market preparedness or earnings improvement. Based on the General Accounting Office survey and an additional year of study, the U.S. Department of Labor recommended greater emphasis on job training to meet the needs of specific employers and particularly on on-the-job rather than classroom training.

The Department of Labor's recommendations were realized with the passage of the Economic Dislocation and Worker Adjustment Assistance Act of 1988. The act greatly increased funding for job training programs under JTPA, even though the level of spending was only one-tenth of that under CETA in its peak year. The effectiveness of on-the-job training was examined for four JTPA programs in the late 1980s. Contrary to the emphasis of the new legislation (and in contrast with more comprehensive studies of CETA programs), on-the-job training was not found to significantly improve employment rates or earnings of trainees.

On-the-job training has long been the key form of training for workers in the United States. In their article, ''Joint Union-Management Training Programs,'' Ferman et al. describe this as follows: ''Historically, the provision of worker training in the United States has been highly segmented. Employers generally supported training for executives, managers, and professional and technical employees. The government generally supported training for the disadvantaged and the hard to employ. Unions supported apprenticeship programs for employees in the skilled trades. And, for the majority of U.S. workers, the dominant mode was on-the-job training.''

In 1993, U.S. Labor Secretary Robert Reich cited on-the-job training as one of the five key factors of employee-oriented management, which he advocated as beneficial to a firm's economic performance. The other factors cited by Reich were worker participation, profit sharing, flexible work rules, and a safe work environment.

The U.S. Bureau of the Census conducted a survey in 1984 of 14.8 million training programs delivered or paid for by employers. The survey was broken down by sector and by the percent of training done within firms. The results are shown in Table 1.

Table 1

EMPLOYER-PROVIDED TRAINING COURSE BY SECTOR: 1984 (BUREAU OF THE CENSUS)

Sector	Percent of training done within firm
Transportation, communications, & utilities	75
Agriculture	62
Mining	77
Construction	59
Manufacturing	59
Trade	74
Finance, insurance, real estate	63
Services	69
Public administration	78
TOTAL	69

The table reflects the large extent to which firms relied on on-site locations for the training they provided, ranging from 59 percent in construction to 78 percent in public administration, with an average of 69 percent.

The 1984 Bureau of the Census survey also provided a breakdown of the percent share of employer-provided training within occupations, as well as percent share of employment within occupations, shown in Table 2.

Table 2

EMPLOYER-PROVIDED TRAINING COURSE BY OCCUPATION: 1984 (BUREAU OF THE CENSUS)

Occupation	Percent share of training	Percent share of employment
Executive, managerial	22.0	11.0
Professional specialty	29.8	12.7
Technical & related support	6.4	3.0
Sales	7.3	12.0
Clerical & administrative support	14.1	15.9
Private household service	0.1	0.9
Protective service	2.9	1.6
Other service	5.1	10.9
Farming, forestry, fishing	0.8	3.4
Precision products, craft, repair	7.6	12.4
Machine operators, assemblers	2.0	7.6
Transportation, materials moving	1.1	4.3
Handlers, helpers, laborers	0.8	4.2

Table 2 indicates that executive, managerial, professional specialty, technical, and protective service occupations received shares of training proportionately greater than their shares of employment, while other occupations received proportionately less. This imbalance indicated that while the United States appeared to do fairly well in educating white-collar and technical employees, it did less well in educating production-related employees. This was argued to be problematic, given the increasing skill requirements of industrial production.

Little effort has been made to evaluate the effectiveness of company-provided management training programs in the United States One study of managerial training programs at 100 large firms indicated that while 75 percent of these firms sought to determine the reaction of participants to training, only 20 percent sought to determine whether training changed the behavior of managers. It has been argued that this resulted in part from the prohibitive costs of evaluating management training programs, particularly as regards establishing control groups. In their 1990 essay, "Assessing the Returns to Training," Mangum et al. wrote as follows: "That rate-of-return studies are almost entirely limited to the $5 billion per year spent on publicly supported vocational education and training programs for the economically disadvantaged, while little is done to measure the results of private industry training (variously estimated to cost from $30 billion per year to $210 billion per year), is a phenomenon worthy of note. Involved is a tendency to take training on faith." Rate-of-return studies conducted for company-provided managerial training have provided evidence of effectiveness.

A number of studies have addressed the relative effectiveness of company-provided on-the-job training and other forms of job training, such as classroom training. Among the types of company-provided on-the-job training considered were formal on-the-job training, informal on-the-job training with supervisors, informal on-the-job training with coworkers, and learning by watching. These studies have indicated that company-provided on-the-job training has a larger positive impact on employee earnings than other forms of training. Many of these studies have also indicated that company-provided on-the-job training is associated with increased occupational prestige and a lesser likelihood of becoming unemployed.

The **U.S. Small Business Administration** conducted a survey in the late 1980s to determine the importance of on-the-job training by firm size. The survey revealed that in firms with fewer than 100 employees, 75 percent of employees received their primary training off-the-job, compared to 58 percent of employees in larger firms.

Japanese production and management techniques had a large influence in the American workplace in the 1980s and 1990s. One element of this was the increased use of statistical control techniques and **quality circles**, which required more sophisticated on-the-job training for production workers. Firms such as the Victor Products Division of the Dana Corporation, the First Chicago Corporation, Nestle Foods Corp., and Motorola, Inc. provided basic training to low-skilled and unskilled workers in computers and statistical process controls. In addition, these firms provided on-the-job training in basic skills, including reading and math. An increasing number of firms came to provide such training in basic skills in response to dramatic changes in production techniques, for which such skills were essential.

At the same time, management training also shifted directions. U.S. firms placed increased emphasis on interaction with stockholders, customers, and suppliers. This required greater management knowledge of the details of their firm's products and production processes, knowledge gained through intensified on-the-job training.

On-the-job training programs can be distinguished by the level of centralization at which they occur. Most on-the-job training in the United States is decentralized, occurring at or near the job itself. Centralized training departments generally play a more important role in larger firms, but even in these cases it is estimated that more than half of on-the-job training takes place at a decentralized level. The extent of decentralization depends also on the generality of knowledge that the firm desires in an employee, and this depends on whether the employee is among the managerial, technical, marketing, or production occupations. The Japanese-influenced emphasis on quality control after the 1970s brought with it a greater emphasis on decentralized on-the-job training. This resulted from the implementation of quality circles, in which production workers assume a much larger role in quality control. Previously in the United States, quality control had been largely the domain of management.

In spite of the Japanese influence, however, U.S. firms continue to rely less on on-the-job training and more on formal education for management training than do Japanese firms. Masters in Business Administration (MBA) degrees provide an important credential for managers in the U.S., whereas only one Japanese university offers a degree similar to an MBA Japanese managers often begin their careers by doing production work and are trained by being rotated through a broad range of a firm's operations until they become top-level managers.

The German system of job training is also an influential model in job-training policy debates in the United States The German system relies heavily on on-the-job training, but in a more formal manner than in the U.S. or Japan. About 80 percent of Germans have completed vocational education programs, which prepares them for one of 400 occupations. The system supports approximately 1.5 million apprentices at a time, with an estimated $8,400 (U.S. dollars) spent per year for each apprentice. Though vocational education is overseen by a federal government agency, training takes place largely within firms. These firms take responsibility for the daily supervision of trainees and for the administration of certification exams.

Unlike the Japanese system, trainees in Germany generally do not become employees at the firms in which they received their training. That is, trainees are prepared for the job market at large, not the so-called internal labor market within the firm as in the Japanese system. This difference is a reflection of the life-time employment system in Japan, in which firms benefit directly from investments made in entry-level on-the-job training. Germany and Japan both have lower employee turnover rates than in the United States, however. In this sense, U.S. firms run a higher risk in investing in ongoing on-the-job training for their workers, in that they are less able to secure returns from that training.

During the 1980s, there was a rapid expansion in the number of joint union-management training programs in the United States These programs were most extensive in the automotive, communications, steel, and construction industries, as well as in the public sector. Joint programs offer general worker education as well as on-the-job training, including apprenticeships, certifications, and licensing. The growth of joint training programs is a reflection of the greater emphasis that firms placed on training after the 1970s. This was based on the rapid pace of technical change that often required new forms of work organization, such as flexible and just-in-time production. In these forms of production, workers generally are required to perform a greater number of tasks than with traditional mass production techniques.

Joint on-the-job training programs have also been established between labor unions and institutions of higher education in the form of joint apprenticeship training. The pioneering programs were established under a grant by the U.S. Department of Labor to the International Union of Operating Engineers in 1972. These programs typically give college credits to apprentices engaged in on-the-job training, and these apprentices enroll in college courses for related education. Courses are taken mainly in two-year colleges but also in university labor education centers. An increasing number of these programs emphasize background education in labor studies in addition to the more technical aspects of the apprenticeship.

[David Kucera]

FURTHER READING:

Carnevale, A.P. "Management Training: Today and Tomorrow," *Training and Development Journal*, Vol. 42, 1988.

Collins, Scott. "New Development Tactic: In-House Study," *Crain's Chicago Business*, September 6, 1993.

Cook, James and Carol Panza. "ROI, What Should Training Take Credit For?," *Training*, January 1987.

Cook, Robert (ed.). *Worker Dislocation: Case Studies of Causes and Cures*. W.E. Upjohn Institute for Employment Research, 1987.

Ferman, Louis et al. "Joint Union-Management Training Programs: A Synthesis in the Evolution of Jointism and Training," in Louis Ferman et al. (eds.), *New Developments in Worker Training: A Legacy for the 1990s*. Industrial Relations Research Association Series, 1990.

Ferman, Louis et al. (eds.). *New Developments in Worker Training: A Legacy for the 1990s*. Industrial Relations Research Association Series, 1990.

"Germans' Apprentice System is Seen as Key to Long Boom," *New York Times*, February 6, 1993.

Janoski, Thomas. *The Political Economy of Unemployment: Active Labor Market Policy in West Germany and the United States*. University of California Press, 1990.

Leigh, Duane. "Public Policy to Retrain Workers: What Does the Record Show?," in John Addison (ed.), *Job Displacement: Consequences and Implications for Policy*. Wayne State University Press, 1991.

Mangum, Stephen et al. "Assessing the Returns to Training," in Louis Ferman et al. (eds.), *New Developments in Worker Training: A Legacy for the 1990s*. Industrial Relations Research Association Series, 1990.

"On Being an Employee-Oriented Company," *Industry Week*, November 1, 1993.

OPEN ECONOMY

An open economy is the opposite of a managed economy. It is one that is characteristically market-oriented, with free market policies rather than government imposed price controls. In an open economy industries tend to be privately owned rather than owned by the government. In the area of international trade an open economy is one whose policies promote **free trade** over protectionism.

On the other hand, a managed or **closed economy** is characterized by protective tariffs, state-run or nationalized industries, extensive government regulations and price controls, and similar policies indicative of a government-controlled economy. In a managed economy the government typically intervenes to influence the production of goods and services. In an open economy, market forces are allowed to determine production levels.

A completely open economy exists only in theory. For example, no country in the world allows unlimited free access to its markets. Most nations have fiscal and monetary policies that attempt to improve their economies. Many economies that are open in some respects may still have government-owned, monopolistic industries. A country is considered to have an open economy, however, if its policies allow market forces to determine such matters as production and pricing.

Chile and Argentina are examples of two countries that have moved or are moving from a managed economy to an open economy. Chile has led the way for South America and Central American countries in adopting open economy and free market policies that have led to greater prosperity. As a result of its open economy, Chile became the fastest growing economy in Latin America from 1983 to 1993.

Among the steps Chile took to make its economy more open was a reduction of its protective tariffs to a uniform 11 percent, which is one of the lowest rates in the world. Such a reduction in tariffs forced its domestic producers to become more competitive in the international market. As a result Chile improved its balance of payments to the point of enjoying a surplus of $90 million in 1991, compared to a deficit of $820 million in 1990. The country became less dependent on its copper exports as the economy diversified under new policies. Chile also improved its international trade by negotiating a series of bilateral trade agreements.

Similar measures that have been taken in Argentina to promote an open economy include more favorable treatment of foreign investors. An open economy provides the same treatment to foreign investors as it gives to its own investors. Price controls have been eliminated for most products, and several government owned industries have been privatized.

Economists recognize an open economy as being more efficient than a managed economy. In the 18th century, economist Adam Smith (1723-1790) wrote *Inquiry into the Nature and Causes of the Wealth of Nations* to explain the benefits of an open economy and free trade. He wrote that interventions in international trade, such as tariffs and **duties**, only serve to reduce the overall wealth of all nations. Similarly, interventions in the domestic economy are also regarded as inefficient. Smith developed the concept of "the invisible hand," which in effect stated that when individual enterprises work to maximize their own profits and well-being, then the economy as a whole also operates more efficiently. He argued that the economy does not require government intervention, because the operations of domestic producers are guided, as if by an invisible hand, to benefit the economy as a whole.

SEE ALSO: Central America, Doing Business in; Latin American Integration Association; South America, Doing Business in

[David Bianco]

OPERATIONS MANAGEMENT

Do you drive a car, write checks, have a savings account, or get medical treatment? If so, you are directly affected by operations and **operations management**. Operations are the processes within organizations that transform inputs (labor, capital, materials, and energy) into outputs (services and goods) consumed by the public. Services are intangible products, and goods are physical products. According to the classification scheme used by the U.S. Department of Commerce and Labor, services include: **transportation**, utilities, lodging, entertainment, health care, legal services, education, communications, wholesale and **retail trade**, **banking** and **finance**, public administration, insurance, **real estate**, and other miscellaneous services. Goods are described as articles of trade, merchandise, or wares. Manufacturing is a specific term referring to the production of goods. In this article, in term ''product'' is used to refer to both goods and services.

Operations employ people, build facilities, and purchase equipment in order to provide services or change materials into finished goods. Hospitals, banks, and fire departments, as well as steelmakers and oil refiners, have operations that engage in this transformation process.

People working in operations are capable of much greater output than the same people working alone because these organizations have developed sophisticated facilities and equipment that greatly increase worker productivity. These organizations also apply the principle of division of labor which allows the worker to quickly master a reduced set of job skills. These concepts are essential to achieve economies of scale. As a result of productivity increases, the standard of living for everyone is higher.

Operations management is a multi-discipline field that focuses on managing an organization's operations. The scope of operations management includes **decision making** about the design, planning, and **management** of the many factors that affect operations. Decisions include: what products to produce, how large a facility to build, where to locate the facility with respect to customers and suppliers, what techniques and equipment to use to make the goods or to provide the services, how many units to produce next month, how employees should be trained, and what methods to use to enhance product quality. Operations managers apply ideas and technologies to increase productivity and reduce costs, improve flexibility to meet rapidly changing customer needs, enhance product quality, and improve customer service.

KEY ISSUES IN OPERATIONS

As an organization develops plans and strategies to deal with threats and opportunities in its environment, it should consider issues related to: designing a system that is capable of producing the services and goods in demanded quantities; planning how to use the system effectively; and managing key elements of the operations. Each of these topics is described briefly in the following sections.

DESIGNING THE SYSTEM. Designing the system begins with product development. Product development involves determining the characteristics and features of the product. For example, should a bank offer fund transfers via a touch-tone phone; should a car be equipped with dual air bags? Product development should begin with an assessment of customer needs and include a detailed product design. The facilities and equipment that will produce the service or good, as well as the information systems needed to monitor and control performance, should also be designed. Product development is a cross-functional decision-making process that requires teamwork to install the **marketing**, financial, and operating plans needed to successfully launch a product.

Product design is a critical task because it determines the characteristics and features of the product, as well as how the product functions. Product design determines a product's cost and quality, as well as its features and performance. These are important factors on which customers make purchasing decisions. Techniques such as Design for Manufacturing and Assembly (DFMA) are being implemented to improve product quality and lower costs. DFMA focuses on operating issues during product design. This can be critical even though design costs are a small part of the total cost of a product. Design is important because it may fix up to 90 percent of the total production costs. For example, when a police department designs a procedure for booking a suspect, the procedure dictates the amount of time spent by police officers, clerical staff, and management each time a booking takes place. A procedure which wastes time and duplicates effort will substantially impact the department's **costs**.

Quality Function Deployment (QFD) is also being used to improve product design by focusing design efforts on customer needs. QFD is a set of planning and communication routines that focuses attention on customer wants and coordinates actions.

Process design describes how the product will be made. The process design decision has two major components: a technical or engineering component and a scale economy, or business component. The technical component includes selecting equipment and sequences for production. For example, a fast food restaurant should decide whether its hamburgers will be flame-broiled or fried. A decision to flame broil would limit the equipment design and selection decision. Decisions must also be made about the sequence of operations. For example, should a car rental agency inspect a car that has been returned by the customer first or send it to be cleaned and washed by maintenance? Most likely, the car should be inspected first so the damage that might occur in the cleaning process would not be counted against the customer.

The scale economy or business component involves applying the proper amount of mechanization (tools and equipment) to make the organization's work force more productive. This includes determining: (1) if the demand for a product is large enough to justify mass production, such as a fast food restaurant that purchases specialized equipment to make a large volume quickly (2) if there is sufficient variety in customer demand so that flexible production systems are required, such as a full-service restaurant that purchases general purpose equipment to produce its diverse menu (3) if demand for a product is so small that it cannot support a dedicated production facility, such as demand for the handmade luges for the Olympics.

Facility design involves determining the capacity, location, and layout for the facility. Capacity is a measure of an organization's ability to provide the demanded services or goods in the quantity requested by the customer and in a timely manner. Capacity planning involves estimating demand, determining the capacity of facilities, and deciding how to change the organization's capacity to respond to demand.

Facility Location is the placement of a facility with respect to its customers and suppliers. Facility location is a strategic decision because it is a long-term commitment of resources that cannot easily or inexpensively be changed. When evaluating a location, management should consider: customer convenience, initial investment for land and facilities, government incentives, and operating transportation costs. In addition, qualitative factors may be important, such as recreational activities for employees, an adequate transportation infrastructure, and a favorable labor environment.

Facility layout is the arrangement of the work space within a facility. It considers which departments or work areas should be adjacent to one another so that the flow of product, information, and people can move quickly and efficiently through the production system.

Job design specifies the tasks, responsibilities, and methods used in performing a job. For example, the job design for a word processing specialist at a publishing company would describe needed equipment and would explain the standard operating procedures.

PLANNING THE SYSTEM. Planning the system describes how management expects to utilize the existing resource base created during the original design of production system. One of the outcomes of this planning process may be to change the system design to cope with environmental changes. For example, management may decide to increase or decrease capacity to cope with changing demand, or rearrange layout to enhance efficiency.

Decisions made by production planners depend on the time horizon. Long-range decisions could include the number of facilities required to meet customer needs, or how technological change might affect the methods used to produce services and goods. The time horizon for long-term planning varies with the industry and depends on how long it would take an organization to build new facilities or make major technological changes. For example, in the aircraft industry it may take five to ten years to design a new aircraft and build a facility to produce it. A car rental agency may need a much shorter time horizon for production planning because changes can be made more quickly.

In medium-range production planning, which is normally about one year, organizations find it difficult to make major changes in facilities. At most, modest expansion may be achieved or limited new equipment installed. Here, production planning may involve determining **workforce** size, developing training programs, working with suppliers to improve product quality and improve delivery systems, and determining the amount of material to order on an aggregate basis.

Scheduling has the shortest planning horizon. As production planning proceeds from long-range to short-range, the decisions become more detailed. In scheduling, management decides what products will be made, who will do the work, what equipment will be used, which materials will be consumed, when the work will begin, and what will happen to the product when it is complete. All aspects of production come together to make the product a reality.

MANAGING THE SYSTEM. Managing the system involves working with people to encourage participation and improve organizational performance. Participative management and teamwork are becoming an essential part of successful operations. Motivation, **leadership**, and training are receiving new impetus. In addition, material management and quality are two key areas of concern.

Material management includes decisions regarding the procurement, control, handling, storage, and distribution of materials. Material management is becoming more important because, in many organizations, the costs of purchased materials are over 50 percent of the total product cost. How much material should be ordered, when should it be ordered, and which supplier should it be ordered from are some of the important questions.

Quality management programs and high product quality are essential to compete in today's business environment. Quality is increasingly becoming customer-driven with emphasis put on obtaining a product design that builds quality into the product. Then, the process is designed to transform the product design into a quality product and the employees are trained to execute it.

BUILDING SUCCESS WITH OPERATIONS

To understand operations and how they contribute to the success of an organization, it is important to understand the strategic nature of operations, the value-added nature of operations, the impact technology can have on performance, and the globally competitive marketplace.

Organizations can use operations as an important way to gain an advantage over **competition**. What factors influence buying decisions for most consumers? For most services and goods, price, quality, product performance and features, product variety, and availability of the product are critical. All these factors are substantially influenced by actions taken in operations. When productivity increases, product costs decline and product price can be reduced. As better production methods are developed, quality and variety may increase.

By linking operations and operating strategies with the overall strategy of the organization (including engineering, financial, marketing, and information system strategy) synergy can result. Operations become a positive factor when facilities, equipment, and employee training are viewed as a means to achieve organizational objectives, rather than suboptimal departmental objectives. The criteria for judging operations is changing from cost control, which is a narrowly defined operating objective, to more global performance measures such as product performance and variety, product quality, delivery time, and customer service. When flexibility is designed into operations, an organization is able to rapidly and inexpensively respond to changing customer needs.

Operations should always be a value-added activity. That means that customers should be willing to pay more for the finished product than the total input costs. In the private sector, the difference between the price consumers pay and the cost of production is profit. Profit can be reinvested to build new and better products, thus creating **wealth** for society. In the public sector benefits added by creating products should always be greater than costs. This added value, once again, represents an increase in wealth for society. For example, effective fire protection should reduce fire insurance premiums, decrease the number of fires, and cut the losses from fires because of rapid response and better fire-fighting techniques and equipment. Value-added fire protection would have more benefits to society than the sum of the costs of providing it. All operating decisions, indeed all the decisions made by the organization, should consider how customers or potential customers will value the outcome of the decision. Decisions should not be made simply on how costs will be affected.

Technology is the application of knowledge, usually in the form of recently developed tools, processes, or procedures, to solve problems. Advances in technology make it possible to build better products using fewer resources. As technology fundamentally changes a product, its performance and quality often increases dramatically. For example, an electronic watch is cheaper, more reliable, and takes less care than a traditional mechanical watch. Customer's value the product more and will pay more for it, but as with most electronic products today, the costs of production have declined substantial. When competition is added, prices drop and the market expands substantially because new buyers emerge and existing customers buy more watches.

It is impossible to ignore the impact that the emerging global marketplace and **free trade** are having on organizations and their operations. The **North American Free Trade Agreement** (NAFTA) and the **General Agreement on Tariffs and Trade (GATT)** are increasing the opportunities for countries to focus on areas of trade and commerce where they have a relative advantage. It will be increasingly common for finished products to have components part from many different countries. Global sourcing and production of goods and services will become more common.

Over time, operations management has grown in scope and increased in importance. Today, it has elements that are strategic, it relies on behavioral and engineering concepts, and it utilizes management science/operations research tools and techniques for systematic decision-making and problem-solving. As operations management continues to develop, it will increasingly interact with other functional areas within the organization to develop integrated answers to complex interdisciplinary problems.

[Mark A. Vonderembse]

FURTHER READING:

Blackstone, J.H. *Capacity Management.* Cincinnati, OH: South-Western Publishing Co., 1989.

Chase, R.B., and D.A. Garvin. ''The Service Factory.'' *Harvard Business Review.* 67, 4, 1989, pp. 61-69.

Clark, K.B., and T. Fujimoto. *Product Development Performance.* Boston, MA: Harvard Business School Press, 1991.

Doll, W.J., and M.A. Vonderembse. ''The Evolution of Manufacturing Systems: Towards the Post-Industrial Enterprise.'' *OMEGA Int. J. of Mgmt. Sci.* 19, 5, 1991, pp. 401-411.

Garvin, David A. *Managing Quality.* NY: The Free Press, 1988.

Krajewski, L. J., and L. P. Ritzman. *Operations Management: Strategy and Analysis.* Reading, MA: Addison-Wesley Publishing Company, 1993.

Skinner, W. ''Manufacturing-Missing Link in Corporate Strategy.'' *Harvard Business Review.* 52, 3, 1969, pp. 136-145.

Sule, D. R. *Manufacturing Facilities: Location, Planning, and Design.* Boston, MA: PWS-KENT Publishing Company, 1988.

Suzaki, K. *The New Manufacturing Challenge: Techniques for Continuous Improvement.* NY: The Free Press, 1987.

Tersine, R. J. *Principles of Inventory and Materials Management.* NY: Elsevier Science Publishing Co., Inc., 1982.

Umble, M. M., and M. L. Srikanth. *Synchronous Manufacturing*. Cincinnati, OH: South-Western Publishing Co., 1990.

Vonderembse, M. A., and G. P. White. *Operations Management: Concepts, Methods, Strategies*. St. Paul, MN: West Publishing Company, 1991.

OPPORTUNITY COST

Opportunity cost may be applied to many different situations and considered in several types of circumstances in which scarcity necessitates the election of one option over another. In economic practice, it can be used to calculate the difference between the return on an **investment** and the return on a superior investment. Opportunity **cost** is usually defined in terms of money, but also may be considered in terms of time, person-hours, mechanical output or any other finite, limited resource.

The concept of opportunity cost is ancient, due to the simplicity of the idea. The term itself came into common use with the development of modern economic terminology during the early twentieth century.

One way to demonstrate opportunity cost lies in the employment of investment **capital**. For example, a private investor purchases $10,000 in a certain security, such as shares in a corporation, and after one year the investment has appreciated in value to $10,500. The investor's return is 5 percent.

The investor considers other ways the $10,000 could have been invested, and discovers a bank certificate with an annual yield of 6 percent and a government bond that carries an annual yield of 7.5 percent. After a year, the bank certificate would have appreciated in value to $10,600, and the government bond would have appreciated to $10,750.

The opportunity cost of purchasing shares is $100 relative to the bank certificate, and $250 relative to the government bond. The decision to purchase shares with a 5 percent return comes at the cost of a lost opportunity to earn 6 or 7.5 percent.

Expressed in terms of time, consider a commuter who chooses to drive to work, rather than use public transportation. Because of heavy traffic and a lack of parking, it takes the commuter 90 minutes to get to work. If the same commute on public transportation would have taken only 40 minutes, the opportunity cost of driving would be 50 minutes.

Calculation of opportunity cost is normally subjective and immediate. Opportunity cost is calculated at the time a choice is made between two investment opportunities and becomes irrelevant immediately after the choice is made.

As a result, opportunity costs are necessarily forward-looking. In the example of the commute, the commuter might have naturally have chosen driving over public transportation because he could not have anticipated traffic delays in driving. Once the choice has been made to drive, it is not possible to change one's mind, thus the choice itself becomes irrelevant.

Experience can create a basis for future decisions; the commuter may be less inclined to drive next time, now knowing the consequences of traffic congestion. This knowledge can influence future choices.

Economists frequently misunderstand the concept of opportunity cost. It is the value of the most attractive rejected alternatives. In making a choice, the economist asks, ''What am I giving up in order to do what I have chosen?''

[John Simley]

FURTHER READING:

Baumol, William J., and Alan S. Blinder. *Economics, Principles and Policy*. 2nd ed. New York: Harcourt Brace Jovanovich, 1982.

Fischer, Stanley, and Rudiger Hornbusch. *Economics*. New York: McGraw-Hill, 1983.

OPTICAL CHARACTER RECOGNITION DEVICES (OCR)

OCR or optical character recognition is a term that emerged in the mid-1980s when computer hardware manufacturers and software developers recognized a market for converting paper documents to computer images that could be stored on a computer disk for later retrieval. OCR refers to the computer's learned ability through software programs to recognize that a printed letter (optical character) of the alphabet is the same letter that it already recognizes as the character created when the computer's keyboard key is pushed. The OCR process is simple in theory. A printed page of text is placed on a digital scanner, a device that usually looks similar to the familiar photocopier. The scanner copies the text while OCR software stored in the attached computer looks at each letter of each word in order to covert it to an image that can be read by the computer then stored just like a document originally created by the computer.

OCR developers believed such a process would allow them to create a true paperless office. The idea was that documents and any accompanying illustrations and photos would be scanned into the computer, then stored until they were needed. Books, lengthy documents, even legal contracts taking up file drawer and bookshelf space would be put on disks. People who collect clips from magazines and newspapers would convert them to documents that could be indexed by keywords for later use as reference materials. Important faxes originally printed on paper would be stored on disk with the paper tossed into the recycling bin.

Once-paper documents would be called up on the computer screen instantly rather than with a time-wasting search through scores of file folders for the same document. Once every important piece of existing paper was in the computer (without the necessity of rekeying), all future written communication would be computer-to-computer. There would be no need for paper. File cabinets would go the same way as the ink well.

That was the theory anyway. The paperless office predicted in the 1980s has yet to emerge in the 1990s and likely never will, unless OCR **software** becomes absolutely foolproof and every office in the world converts to it.

ORIGINAL PROBLEMS WITH OCR

One of the problems with OCR when it was first developed was that the computer was frequently baffled by what the human eye and mind readily accepts. The letter ''e'' in the word ''the'' might be interpreted as the letter ''o'' so that it would scan in ''tho'' without a millisecond hesitation. Early OCR software programs boasted accuracy rates of more than 90 percent, which sounds good, but actually results in a computer-stored document riddled with more typographical errors than would probably have been created by a typist. The document would have to be carefully proofread and corrected by a typist anyway, who would have to use the original paper document as a guide.

What usually confused the OCR software was that original documents had to be almost perfect before they could be scanned. The letters had to be crisply printed (not typed on typewriters with dirty keys). Unusual fonts that some type designer thought were avant garde were impossible for the OCR to understand and duplicate. Strikeovers also confused OCR programs. Even slightly blurry, shiny type as might be expected from fax paper feeding off a roll could throw the software into fits.

OCR PROBLEMS IN THE 1990S

The OCR programs available in the mid-1990s have improved—some claim up to a 99 percent efficiency. That is not perfect, but closing in on it. Still, there are problems that usually originate with the documents OCR programs and scanners are asked to copy.

OCR software developers try to find a happy medium between making recognition of characters too strict, or too flexible. Too strict an interpretation of OCR means mistakes when a letter collects a little bit of dirt or suffers a slightly broken letter form. Too flexible, and it will make the same mistakes as it tries to interpret anything it sees as a letter. As one OCR magazine reviewer has written, OCR software that recognizes 2,100 different typefaces is perfect until it encounters typeface number 2,101, invented by a type designer looking for something different to put on the page.

The biggest problem remains ''degraded'' text, such as a slight bit of dirt on the paper that causes the OCR software to interpret a lower case ''h'' as a ''b.'' Faxes remain a problem because even plain paper facsimile machines can leave text just blurry enough to confuse OCR.

Attempts to attract the reader's eye—such as stretching letters as an artistic device or putting in more than normal white space between letters—can also create problems. In the mid-1990s advertising agencies started a practice of throwing all manner of typefaces onto the printed page in attempts to look ''hip.'' Some magazines copied the trend in the layout of articles.

This created problems because today's OCR programs learn the look of a typeface it is asked to scan. Too many variations of the typefaces on one page confuses the software as it looks through its programming for something that it recognizes.

Another problem that OCR has yet to resolve is accurately interpreting handwriting, as any early buyer of Apple's Newton personal digital assistant can testify. OCR programs cannot account for hand-editing, such as a crossed-out or underlined word on a memo. Preserving such memos in a computer always requires editing the memo to show such emphasis. A boss who likes to see his or her own marks on a final memo still has to settle for a hard, paper copy in a file cabinet.

On the plus side, OCR developers are working ever harder to train their software to call attention to the mistakes that it copies. Some OCR programs are preprogrammed to recognize correct grammar and common spellings so it automatically highlights words that it has copied, but that it also finds questionable. The software, in effect, tells its user that it has made a mistake, but it does not know what to do about it. In the end the machine turns control of the scanning back over to the human to make the final decision how to handle what it considers a problem.

OCR DEVICE CHOICES

There are several types of scanners. The most common is flatbed. Flatbed scanners look and act much like a photocopy machine with pages being scanned placed flat on the scanner's glass. They generally copy single pages at a time. Scanning thick, bound books can be a problem as the printing at the binding may curve away into distortion. The handheld scanner looks like and is about the size of a tapered handheld tape recorder. Instead of bringing the page to the scanner, a handheld allows the scanner to go to the page. Software allows wide images to be ''stitched'' together from two passes of a handheld over a large image. While improvements are being made all the time, there is some question how steady a person can scan with a handheld without distorting the image. Some magazines have run tests where they find OCR software does not do as well with a handheld as it does with a flatbed. Another scanner feeds single pages much like a page might pass through a fax machine. Finally, the newest type of scanner looks like a pen. It allows the user to select certain lines of type in a book for scanning. This type of scanner connects to a computer printer port without the addition of any other computer boards, which is necessary in a handheld scanner.

THE FUTURE OF OCR

The paperless office is not here yet and likely never will be. Paper is convenient to handle. It sells for a few dollars per ream. Everyone in the company has easy access to it while not everyone knows how to find something in a computer file.

Still, optical character recognition software and devices will reduce the burden of storing paper. Companies that deal with large numbers of documents such as insurance companies and law firms will no doubt follow the technological development of OCR closely and will purchase each upgrade as it is released. Writers and reporters who spend their time digging for information in mounds of documents will closely follow the further development of the pen-based scanner.

SEE ALSO: Scanning Systems

[Clint Johnson]

OPTIONS CLEARING CORPORATION

The Options Clearing Corporation (OCC) is owned by the four securities exchanges that make markets in listed stock options. These exchanges are the Chicago Board of Options Exchange (CBOE), the American Stock Exchange (AMEX), the Philadelphia Stock Exchange (PHLX), and the Pacific Stock Exchange (PSE). All four exchanges clear all of their option transactions through the OCC. The OCC is regulated by the **Securities and Exchange Commission** (SEC), and is vital to the operations of the exchanges.

The main role of the OCC is to act as a performance guarantor for all stock options. An option buyer and seller who agree on a price for a standardized stock option will negotiate a deal. The OCC then interposes itself between the buyer and seller, becoming the party to whom delivery is made, and from whom delivery is taken. By becoming the opposite party to every contract, the OCC is substituting its own ability to deliver on the contract for the option writer's ability to deliver, thus guaranteeing performance and eliminating counterparty risk.

For example, the seller, or writer, of an IBM call option with a three month expiration date is obligated to deliver 100 shares of IBM stock to the buyer at the striking price, if the buyer decides to exercise his or her option. Buyers of call options will exercise their options when it is economically advantageous to do so. Normally, this occurs at the expiration date, if the current stock price exceeds the strike, or exercise price. Such an option is said to be ''in the money,'' meaning that the buyer will immediately profit from exercising the option. Since an option is an agreement or contract between two parties, the buyers profit will equal the writer's loss. However, there is an incentive for the writer of a call that is in the money at the expiration date to simply ignore his or her obligation to deliver the 100 shares of stock. This could occur because of bankruptcy by the writer, or simply their unwillingness to incur the financial loss. (Recall that the potential loss from writing call options is virtually unlimited because the stock value has no price ceiling.)

Because the OCC becomes the counterparty to all option trades, the buyer of a call option need not worry about the integrity or financial means of the writer. If the writer of the option defaults on his or her obligation, the buyer is unaffected because the OCC will make the delivery. This, in effect, increases the secondary marketability of stock options, plus reduces transaction costs, since buyers will not need to investigate the writer's credit.

The same is true for buyers and sellers of put options. The writer of a put option agrees to purchase the 100 shares of stock from the put buyer at the exercise price on or before the expiration date, if the buyer so decides to exercise. Put buyers will exercise their options when the current stock price is below the exercise price. Although the put writer's loss is limited, because the stock value can only drop to zero, there is still a financial incentive for the writer to **default**. But since the OCC is, in effect the counterparty to both sides, the buyer need not worry about the writer's integrity. If the writer defaults, the OCC will purchase the shares from the buyer, and take legal action against the writer.

In addition to guaranteeing the performance on all option contracts, another way the OCC increases option marketability and liquidity is by enabling option buyers and writers to terminate their positions in the market at any time, by making an offsetting transaction. A buyer of a call option can in effect, close out his or her position by simply writing a call option with the same exercise price and expiration date. The same holds true for puts; buyers and writers of put options can terminate their positions by taking the opposite position with the same exercise price and expiration date. Because of this possibility, more participants are likely to enter the market, thereby improving marketability and liquidity of options. (The other factor that aides marketability and liquidity is the standardized contract).

The OCC also maintains the financial integrity of the option exchanges and markets through margin requirements that are imposed on option writers. The actual margin requirements are established by the SEC and Federal Reserve Board, however, the OCC acts as the clearing house. Put or call buyers pay a premium to the writer at the time the contract is entered into. The buyers do not need to post any margin because they will only exercise the option if it is profitable. In other words, after purchasing the put or call option, no further money is at risk. However, put and call writers have a future financial obligation if the option expires in-the-money. Therefore, option writers are required to post margin equal to the market value of the their obligation, as a performance guarantee.

[James A. Gerhardinger]

FURTHER READING:

Cox, J. and W. Rubenstein. *Option Markets*. Englewood Cliffs, N.J.: Prentice Hall, 1985.

Gastineau, Gary. *Stock Options Manual*. 2nd ed. New York: McGraw-Hill, 1979.

Option Writing Strategies. Chicago: Chicago Board Options Exchange, 1982.

Understanding Options. Chicago: Chicago Board Options Exchange, 1987.

OPTIONS/OPTIONS CONTRACTS

An option is the right to choose a particular action among alternatives. The term is most often associated with "options contracts" to buy or sell stock, but options are available on other **assets**. There are also a number of other financial instruments, such as warrants and convertibles, which include option features. Options and instruments with option features are sometimes called "derivatives" or "contingent claims," since the value of the instrument is derived from or contingent on the value of some underlying asset. More recently, **financial engineering** has produced an array of innovative financial instruments and strategies that employ options or exhibit option characteristics.

An option contract may be a "put" or "call." A call is the right to buy (call in) a fixed amount of the underlying asset at a fixed price, for a set period of time. A put is the right to sell (put onto someone else) a fixed amount of the underlying asset at a fixed price for a set period of time. The seller, or "writer," of the option contract assumes the obligation to buy or sell if the buyer decides to "exercise" the option. The buyer gains the right, but not the obligation, to exercise to option. The fixed price at which the purchase or sale can be executed is called the "strike price" or the "exercise price"; the price of obtaining the option is referred to as the "premium." European options may be exercised only at expiration, while the much more prevalent American option may be exercised at any time on or before expiration.

Conventional option contracts are available over-the-counter from put and call dealers who provide individualized option contracts. In 1973, however, the Chicago Board of Options Exchange (CBOE) began trading standardized options contracts. These standardized listed options are easier and cheaper to trade, provide greater trading depth and have an active secondary market. Additionally, there is no performance risk—performance is guaranteed by the Options Clearing Corporation (OCC). The OCC in effect enters each transaction, becoming a buyer to the seller and a seller to the buyer, maintaining a net zero position. Standardized options are now traded on several exchanges and account for the bulk of options trading. Listed options are available on more than 700 **common stocks**, various foreign currencies, and several stock indexes. Listed options are also available on **futures contracts** for agricultural commodities, precious metals, foreign currencies, and **interest rates**.

TYPES OF OPTIONS

The exact terms of standardized option contracts vary with the nature of the underlying asset. For options on common stock, the contract size is 100 shares. Strike prices are set by the exchange, most often at multiples of $5.00. Not all strike prices are traded. The exchange will begin trading options of a given expiration at a strike price or prices that are close to the market price. If the price of the stock changes, however, the exchange will initiate trading in contracts at other strike prices. Eventually, there may be many contracts traded with the same expiration but different strike prices. Strike price and contract size is adjusted for stock splits, and for stock dividends of more than 10 percent, using the split factor, e.g., a three-for-two stock split would result in an option on 150 shares at two-thirds of the original strike price. Cash dividends have no effect on the option. Listing requirements limit the number of **stocks** on which options can be traded.

The maturity of stock options is usually identified by the month of expiration, with all options expiring on the Saturday following the third Friday of the month. Options with maturities up to two years, called "long-term equity anticipation securities" (LEAPS) are available on some blue-chip stocks. Most stock options have maturities of eight months or less, however, and fall into one of three expiration cycles: (1) January, April, July, and October; (2) February, May, August, and November; or (3) March, June, September, and December. Generally, options with expiration in the next two calendar months, plus the next two closest months in the expiration cycle, are available. When an option is exercised before expiration, the OCC will deliver on the option. In order to maintain the zero balance, the OCC will at the same time exercise the option contract with a seller. In this case the exercise is randomly "assigned" to a broker or dealer, who will then assign the exercise to a client who has written the contract. The broker or dealer must provide an explanation of the exercise assignment procedure to clients at the time the contract is written.

Options on indexes include broad stock market indexes and industry-specific indexes. Expiration dates are similar to those of stock options. An importance difference here is the nature of delivery. The contract is written on 100 units of the underlying index. Since it would be impractical or even impossible for writers to deliver the exact assets and proportions specified in the index, cash settlement is used. At exercise, the writer delivers cash equal to 100 times the (positive) difference between the index value and the strike price. Another important difference is that an order to exercise is executed after the close of trading at the ending price, rather than at the time and the price when the order is given. Although the cash settlement is a desirable feature, it may increase the price volatility of the underlying stock. This occurs because institutional investors with large portfolios use index options to hedge against losses, or to take advantage of small price imbalances. As the options approach expiration, attempts to restructure these positions cause large transactions with attendant price swings.

Foreign currency options are written on a set amount of the foreign currency. Expiration is on the Saturday before the third Wednesday of the month. Maturities available include the next two months, and March, June, September, and December. Interest rate options are written on a specific amount (usually $100,000) of a specific **Treasury notes** or bond. They are available with original maturities of three and six months, but normally options on a given instrument are traded for only one expiration cycle. Rather than introducing new options on the same securities, they are replaced with options on recent issues. Trading volume in these options remains low.

The options discussed so far are based on the spot price, the price for immediate delivery of the asset. A futures contract, however, calls for delivery of the underlying asset at a fixed price at some time in the future. An important difference between an option and a futures contract is that the buyer of a futures contract assumes the obligation to perform. An option on a futures contract, or "futures option," provides the option feature based on the trading price at some time in the future. Futures options are available on agricultural commodities, precious metals, fixed-income securities (called "interest rate options,") and stock indexes. Trading volume in futures options sometime exceeds trading volume in the spot contract. The exact maturities and expiration dates vary among the underlying assets traded.

OPTION PAYOFFS

The key to the analysis of gains and losses on option positions is that the buyer of the option has the right, but not the obligation, to exercise. The buyer would not exercise the option if exercise would result in a loss. For this reason, many options are never exercised and simply expire. This also implies that the maximum possible loss for the buyer, and the maximum gain for the writer, is the premium. Consider a listed call option on XYZ stock with a strike price of $30, purchased for a premium of $200, which is about to expire. The net payoffs at expiration for both the writer and the buyer are given in Table 1 for a range of market values of the underlying stock. At any price below $30, the buyer will not exercise the call option because to do so would be to buy the stock above market—the option is said to be "out of the money." Expiration is preferable to exercise because by not exercising the buyer limits the loss to the premium paid to obtain the option, in this case $200. At $30, the option is "at the money," and the buyer is indifferent. Above $30, the buyer could exercise the option and buy the stock at a price below market—the option is "in the money." Note that this may still result in a net loss, since the premium must be deducted. The loss would be higher, however, if the option was not exercised. At $32, the buyer breaks even, and any further increases in the value of the stock result in proportional ($\times$ $100) net gains limited only by the maximum stock price. The payoffs of the buyer and the writer are always a mirror image, as depicted in Table 1. The writer thus has a maximum gain of $200, and an indefinite maximum loss.

Table 1

STRIKE PRICE = $30.00, PREMIUM = $200

Call Option:

Stock Price	Writer exercise	+	premium	=	net	Buyer exercise	+	premium	=	net
$0.00	NEX*		+$200		+$200	NEX*		-$200		-$200
29.00	NEX*		+$200		+$200	NEX*		-$200		-$200
30.00	-0-		+$200		+$200	-0-		-$200		-$200
31.00	-$1 x100		+$200		+$100	+$1 x100		-$200		-$100
32.00	-$2 x100		+$200		-0-	+$2 x100		-$200		-0-
33.00	-$3 x100		+$200		-$100	+$3 x100		-$200		-$100
34.00	-$4 x100		+$200		-$200	+$4 x100		-$200		+$200
35.00	-$5 x100		+$200		-$300	+$5 x100		-$200		+$300

* not exercised

Put Option:

Stock Price	Writer exercise	+	premium	=	net	Buyer exercise	+	premium	=	net
$0.00	-$30 x100		+$200		-$2800	+$30 x100		-$200		+$2800
26.00	-$4 x100		+$200		-$200	+$4 x100		-$200		+$200
27.00	-$3 x100		+$200		-$100	+$3 x100		-$200		+$100
28.00	-$2 x100		+$200		-0-	+$2 x100		-$200		-0-
29.00	-$1 x100		+$200		+$100	+$1 x100		-$200		-$100
30.00	-0-		+$200		+$200	-0-		-$200		-$200
31.00	NEX*		+$200		+$200	NEX*		-$200		-$200

* not exercised

This same type of analysis can be applied to the payoffs from a put, as is also shown in Table 1 for a put with a strike price of $30 and a premium of $200. Again, the payoffs to writer and buyer are mirror images, and again the buyer's maximum loss and the writer's maximum gain are equal to the premium. The buyer's maximum gain and the writer's maximum loss are limited to $2,800 ($30 × 100 less the $200 premium), which will occur if the stock price goes to zero.

OPTION STRATEGIES

The payoffs shown in Table 1 can be changed by writing or buying combinations of puts and calls. A "straddle" is the combination of a put and a call on the same stock with the same strike price and expiration. For a buyer, a straddle will produce a loss of the two premiums if the price of the stock is at the strike price. If the price moves away from the strike price in either direction, one of the options becomes in the money. The buyer will realize a gain if the price of the stock moves far enough away from the strike price, either up or down, so that the gain on exercise of the in-the-money option will more than equal the premiums. Variations on a straddle include strips (two puts and one call) and straps (two calls and one put). Spreads involve a combination of calls or puts on the same underlying stock, but with differing strike prices or expirations.

A position involving only the option itself is called a naked option, while an option position combined with a long position in the underlying stock is called a covered option. Sales of covered calls, the sale of a call on a stock being held by the investor, has been a popular strategy. The seller of the covered call will lose the possibility of **capital gains**, but will receive additional income from the premium. This strategy would be appropriate if the seller does not expect a price increase, or planned to eventually sell the stock at the call price. The purchase of a put on a stock held by the investor, or "protective put," allows the investor to hedge, or ensure against losses in the stock at the cost of the premium.

Use of options is not limited to individual investors. Index options are used in portfolio insurance. Analogous to protective puts on an individual stock, the portfolio manager will buy puts on a stock index. Although the stock index will likely not move exactly with the portfolio value, for a large portfolio the correlation of portfolio and index will likely be high, and even this imperfect hedge will remove much of the risk of price decreases. Similarly, institutions with low trading costs attempt to **arbitrage**, or take advantage of small differences in value between the index options and the underlying stocks, through program trading.

RISK IN OPTION TRADING

There is no definitive answer to the question of the riskiness of option trading. As shown in Figure 1, the possible outcomes vary widely, and the strategy being followed must also be considered. Sale of a naked put or call exposes the writer to extreme losses, whereas purchase of the call or put has sharply limited loss possibilities. Covered options present limited risk, and protective puts are meant to reduce risk. There is no doubt, however, that some options trades can present significant risk. One reason for the popularity of options as investment vehicles is that they provide leverage. For the amount of the premium, the buyer controls 100 shares of stock, so that a $1 change in the value of the stock underlying the money option results in a much larger change in the premium. Because of the inherent risk, the OCC requires the option writer to post and maintain margin.

OPTION PRICING

Option pricing refers to the size of the premium. There are financial models of option premiums, such as the Black-Scholes Option Pricing Model, that attempt to specify the price on a quantitative basis. The largest influence on the premium is the relationship between the strike price and the market price of the underlying **assets**. The value of a call will be positively related, and the value of a put negatively related, to the market price of the underlying stock. For a given market price, the value of a call will be negatively related, and the value of a put positively related, to the strike price. Even if the strike price is above the market value of a call, or below the value of a put, the option will have value. This value is based on the possibility that the stock price will change enough to

put the option in the money. Because the possibility that the option will become in the money is greater, the greater the volatility of the stock price, the premium for both a put and a call will be positively associated with the volatility of the underlying stock price. Interest rates are positively related to the premium because the leverage effect is more attractive in times of high interest rates.

The option itself has a positive value, and this value is greater the longer the time to expiration. Because of the value of time to expiration, few investors exercise options before expiration. Instead, the buyer or writer of the option will retain this value by engaging in an offsetting trade, which results in the canceling of the investors' position on the books of the OCC. Since there is no adjustment for dividends, which have a tendency to decrease stock price, the value of a call is negatively related, and the value of a put is positively related, to the dividend yield of the stock. Additionally, if a dividend is to be recorded before expiration, investors may wish to exercise calls to capture the dividend.

There is a definite relationship between the price of a put and the price of a call, referred to as the "**put-call parity**" relationship. At maturity, a protective put will have a value equal to the greater of the strike price or the stock price. An investor could, however, purchase a call on the same stock at the same strike price and expiration, and investing enough in **Treasury bills** (T-bills) to equal the strike price at expiration. At expiration, this portfolio also has a value equal to the greater of the strike price or the stock price. Since both of these positions have the same outcome, they should have the same price or arbitrage if possible. Therefore,

$$C + \frac{X}{(1 + r_f)^T} = S + P$$

where C is the call premium, X is the strike price, $(1 + r_f)^{-T}$ is the present value factor for an amount invested at time T in T-bills at rate r_f, S is the stock price, and P is the put premium.

INSTRUMENTS WITH OPTION FEATURES

Analysis of financial instruments with implicit or explicit option features can proceed by decomposing the instrument into a nonoption instrument plus an option or options. This separation provides a different perspective that may allow new insights into value.

Rights arise in stock offerings and are sometimes associated with the preemptive right of common stockholders to maintain their proportional ownership of the firm. The existing shareholders of the firm are given one right for every share that they own. Purchase of one share of the new stock then requires R rights plus $\$S_e$. $\$S_e$ is set at a value below the expected post-offering stock price $\$S_p$. The R rights required for subscription then have a value $\$S_p - \$S_e$, so that the value of one right will be:

$$\frac{\$S_p - \$S_e}{R}$$

There is a market for rights, and investors who do not wish to subscribe or who have odd numbers of rights may capture their value. The lifetime of rights is typically short, and they may be considered as options on the to-be-issued shares.

Warrants are options to buy a fixed number of newly-issued shares at a fixed price, written by the firm. They often are included in bond offerings as "sweeteners" in order to make an issue more attractive, or in executive compensation. They typically have an extended lifetime, some even being perpetual, and originally are "deep" out of the money, carrying an exercise price well above market. The value of a warrant would be affected by the same factors affecting other call options.

Most bonds are callable, meaning that they can be repurchased by the issuer for the price of the bond plus a call premium. The call feature is simply a call option held by the issuer. A callable bond can be analyzed as a purchase of a noncallable bond, plus the sale of a call on the bond—a covered call position in the bond. The call feature would be affected by the same factors affecting other call options.

Convertible bonds may be converted into common stock at some fixed ratio or face value per share. The conversion feature is in essence an option on the common stock, and callable bonds are sometimes analyzed as the combination of a bond and an option. A convertible will be valued at the higher of its value as a straight (i.e., nonconvertible) bond, or its conversion value as the underlying stock, plus an added premium for the value of the option feature.

Financial engineering is the term applied to the creation of innovative financial instruments, and the options feature has been widely used in this activity. Analysis of the instruments often requires sophisticated mathematical treatment. Some of these instruments are individualized, while others are traded to varying degrees. These traded instruments include putable bonds, certificates of deposit (CD's) with payoffs based on various indexes, and LYONS (zero-coupon, convertible, callable, putable bonds).

SEE ALSO: Call and Put Options; Derivative Securities; Hedging

[David Upton]

FURTHER READING:

Bodie, Zvi, Alex Kane, and Alan J. Marcus. *Investments*. 2nd ed. Irwin, 1993.

Chance, D. M. *An Introduction to Options and Futures*. 2nd ed. Dryden Press.

Fischer, Donald E., and Ronald J. Jordan. *Security Analysis and Portfolio Management*. 5th ed. Prentice-Hall.

Hull, John C. *Options, Futures, and Other Derivative Securities*. Prentice-Hall.

Kolb, Robert W. *Financial Derivatives*. Kolb Publishing.

Reilly, Frank K. *Investment Analysis and Portfolio Management*. 3rd ed. Dryden Press.

ORGANIZATION OF AFRICAN UNITY

The Organization of African Unity (OAU) was established May 25, 1963 as the result of a conference attended by 20 African nations at Addis Ababa, Ethiopia. The conference was held at the invitation of Emperor Haile Selassie I of Ethiopia. The aim of the OAU is to promote unity and solidarity amongst the African nations, foster an environment for economic cooperation, and a provide a forum to discuss and deal with respective problems. The OAU is also overtly political in denouncing vestiges of colonialism and in protecting and perpetuating the territorial integrity and the sovereignty of its member states. The OAU has adopted the precepts of the Charter of the United Nations and the Universal Declaration of Human Rights as its guiding principles.

The establishment of the OAU evolved from previously unsuccessful and often acrimonious attempts to form an inter-African association. In 1958 a Conference of Independent States was held in Ghana resulting in a charter that would eventually serve as a defining document for the OAU. In 1961 a conference was held at Casablanca, Morocco. Another charter was drawn up at this conference along with much discussion of an African Common Market and an African Military Command. Nations attending this conference became known as the "Casablanca Group." The early 1960s saw three more conferences at Abidjan (Ivory Coast), Brazzaville (Congo), and Yaounde (Cameroon). These conferences were attended by French-speaking nations and resulted in the establishment of the Organisation Commune Africaine et Mauricienne. Also in 1961 another conference was held at Monrovia, Liberia, which resulted in the formation of the Organization of Inter-African and Malagasy States. Nations attending this conference became known as the "Monrovia Group."

The ideologies of these two groups were quite different. The Casablanca contingent was regarded as radical with their endorsement of socialistic planned economies, strong anticolonialist policies, and pan-Africanism. The Monrovia group was more moderate, placing less emphasis on political unity and favoring a regional approach to problems, increased economic cooperation, and a hands-off approach in regard to the internal affairs of other countries. Despite these differences, the two groups were brought together in Ethiopia in 1963 with the resultant formation of the OAU. The new inter-African organization, however, more closely resembled the ideologies of the conservative Monrovian group. Nevertheless, compromises were made, to the Casablanca group, including limited support of liberation movements and resolutions condemning apartheid and remnants of colonialism on the continent.

By 1984 all independent African nations except South Africa belonged to the OAU, for a total membership of 50. The political agenda of the OAU has presented a united front against colonialism, racial discrimination, and the then-prevailing government in South Africa. The OAU succeeded in excluding South Africa from the Economic Commission for Africa and UNESCO, and nearly succeeded in having South Africa expelled from the **United Nations** while showing strong support for the African National Congress. Among the OAU's economic activities has been the African Economic Summit in 1980 and the Lagos Plan of Action which calls for economic independence by the year 2000. It is hoped that this will be achieved by the creation of regional economic communities that will then be joined together in a continent-wide African Economic Community. In 1989 there was another economic summit with discussions of external debt problems and negotiations concerning reforms mandated by the **International Monetary Fund** and the **World Bank**. In 1991 the OAU Assembly met at Abuja, Nigeria, and drafted the African Economic Community treaty. This treaty deals with the deteriorating economic condition of the continent as a whole and calls for the implementation of six economic steps through 2025. Through gradual steps the OAU will implement the removal of trade barriers and the economic integration of member countries, and establish an inter-African economic union, currency, and parliament. The treaty also calls for an OAU Court of Justice.

There have also been divisions and disunity in the OAU since its inception. These divisions have largely been over political rather than economic or procedural issues. These include a controversial pan-African peacekeeping contingent of soldiers being sent to Chad in 1981. The effort was unsuccessful and soon withdrawn through lack of funding. In 1982 a delegation representing the Sahrawi Arab Democratic Republic (guerrillas from the western Sahara) were seated by the OAU. Intense opposition by the Moroccan representatives and their allies to the seating led to the cancellation of the 19th Assembly of Heads of State meeting. Libya has also boycotted the OAU over the seating of delegates from Chad.

The chief policy-making body of the OAU is the Assembly of Heads of State and Government. The Assembly meets annually and each member nation is allotted one vote. The Council of Ministers meets biannually and is made up of the foreign ministers of each member country. The Council of Ministers advises the Assembly on budgetary matters, policy implementation, inter-African affairs, and relations with nonmember countries and cooperative unions. There is also a Commission of Mediation, Conciliation, and Arbitration that settles intermember disputes, a Liberation Committee that aids continent-wide liberation movements, and various specialized agencies dealing with a wide variety of matters such as sports, aviation, communications, transportation, and scientific research.

[Michael Knes]

FURTHER READING:

El-Ayouty, Yassin. *The Organization of African Unity after Thirty Years*. Praeger, 1994.

Wallerstein, Immanuel. *Africa: The Politics of Unity*. Random House, 1967.

ORGANIZATION OF AMERICAN STATES

The Organization of American States (OAS) traces its ideological beginnings to Venezuelan revolutionary Simón Bolívar (1783-1830) and the Congress of Panama in 1826. The resultant Treaty of Perpetual Union, League, and Confederation was signed by delegates from numerous Central and South American countries. The congress failed, however, as only one country ratified the agreement.

In 1889 the First International Conference of American States was held in Washington D.C. and established the International Union of American Republics and, as its secretariat, the Commercial Bureau of the American Republics. Eighteen nations from North and South America, including the United States, were involved in this commercially oriented organization. In 1910 the Commercial Bureau was succeeded by the Pan American Union. In 1947 a collective security agreement, the Inter-American Treaty of Reciprocal Assistance was signed in Rio De Janeiro. In 1948, in Bogota, the OAS Charter was formally accepted by the Ninth International Conference on American States. The purpose of the OAS is to encourage peace, representative democracy, security, and economic, social and cultural development in the Western Hemisphere. The OAS also acts as a forum for discussing and resolving inter-American disputes and provides for a common defense against outside aggression.

The major function of the OAS has been its role as the peacekeeper of the Western Hemisphere. The organization has played important roles in resolving conflicts between Peru and Ecuador (1981 border dispute), Colombia and Venezuela (1988 naval incident), and Trinidad and Venezuela (1989 incident involving a Trinidad fishing trawler and a Venezuelan naval vessel). The OAS has also imposed political sanctions against Cuba for fomenting revolution in Venezuela (1964), created an inter-American peacekeeping force in the Dominican Republic (1965), helped resolve various border disputes between Honduras and El Salvador (1969, 1970, and 1976), and monitored the border between Costa Rica and Nicaragua (1978). The OAS provided a forum for denouncing Manuel Noriega's drug trafficking in Panama (1989), monitored elections in Nicaragua (1990), and has monitored political developments and subsequent human rights violations in Haiti (1993).

Since its inception the OAS has received strong political and financial support from the United States. American foreign policy, however, has often run afoul of OAS stands on hemispheric issues. This was especially true when the United States supported Great Britain in retaking the Falkland Islands from Argentina (1982), and when the United States invaded Grenada (1983).

The chief administrative body of the OAS is the General Secretariat. The Secretariat is responsible for implementing policy set by the General Assembly and the three councils. The Permanent Council is responsible for relations with other international organizations and promoting harmony between inter-American states. The Inter-American Economic and Social Council promotes economic and social development between member countries, and the Inter-American Council for Education, Science, and Culture administers multinational projects dealing with culture, heritage, education, and infrastructure improvements. The General Assembly is also responsible for the OAS budget and member assessments.

The OAS is associated in diverse ways with a variety of organizations. Some of these organizations are autonomous from the OAS while others are funded in part or in full by the OAS. These organizations include the Inter-American Children's Institute, the Inter-American Commission on Women, the Inter-American Defense Board, the Inter-American Defense College, the Inter-American Development Bank, the Inter-American Institute for Cooperation in Agriculture, the Pan-American Health Organization, the Pan-American Institute for Geography and History, the Inter-American Indian Institute and the Pan-

American Development Foundation. The OAS also works closely with the Inter-American Commission on Human Rights and is involved with drug enforcement through the Inter-American Drug Abuse Control Commission.

In 1993 the operations budget of the OAS was $64 million. Funds came from member assessments with 66 percent coming from the United States. The United States assessment dropped to 54 percent in 1994. The OAS also received $23 million in voluntary funds for technical cooperation and assistance. The United States contributed $11 million to this fund. The OAS has 35 members: Antigua and Barbuda, Argentina, Commonwealth of the Bahamas, Barbados, Belize, Bolivia, Brazil, Canada, Chile, Colombia, Costa Rica, Dominica, Dominican Republic, Ecuador, El Salvador, Grenada, Guatemala, Guyana, Haiti, Honduras, Jamaica, Mexico, Nicaragua, Panama, Paraguay, Peru, Federation of Saint Kitts and Nevis, Saint Lucia, Saint Vincent and the Grenadines, Suriname, Trinidad and Tobago, United States, Uruguay, and Venezuela. Cuba is technically a member, but since 1962 has not been allowed to participate because of its antidemocratic government.

[Michael Knes]

FURTHER READING:

Einuadi, Luigi R. *The United States and the OAS*. U.S. Dept. of State, Bureau of Public Affairs, Office of Public Communications, 1990.

Pan American Union. *Chronicle of the OAS*. Washington D.C.

ORGANIZATION FOR ECONOMIC COOPERATION AND DEVELOPMENT

The Organization for Economic Cooperation and Development (OECD) originated in 1948 as the Organization for European Economic Cooperation (OEEC). It was established to help implement the Marshall Plan following World War II. The Marshall Plan was a massive economic aid package aimed at revitalizing the war-ravaged economies of Western Europe. By the 1960s the economies of Western Europe had achieved dynamic growth highlighted by currency convertibility, the easing of trade restrictions and a greater currency equality with the dollar. In accordance with the Convention of the OECD, the OECD was established on September 30, 1961, superseding the Organization for European Economic Cooperation. In the new organization, the United States and Canada became full members (in the old organization both countries were associate members). The OECD soon attracted other industrial democracies with free market economies including Japan (1964),

Finland (1969), Australia (1971), and New Zealand (1973).

The purpose of the OECD is to promote economic growth, high employment, and financial stability amongst its member nations. The organization is also charged with fostering the economic growth of developing nations and promoting world trade. To achieve these aims the OECD provides a forum in which its members can jointly plan and implement multilateral economic policies. Policy calls for each member state to submit to the OECD secretariat its country's economic plans and forecasts for review and criticism. The secretariat strives to keep critiques and economic advice free from political considerations.

Originally the OECD was concerned with the economic and financial policies of its members. The Organization has since expanded its sphere of responsibility to include agriculture, energy, the environment, science and technology, social matters, and trade. To implement policy in these areas the OECD has created advisory committees and agencies including: the Committee for Agriculture; the International Energy Agency; the Environmental Policy Committee; the Committee for Scientific and Technology Policy; the Employment; Labor and Social Affairs Committee; and the Trade Committee. Two important committees dealing with finance are the Committee on Capital Movements and Invisible Transactions and the Committee on International and Multinational Enterprises.

The OECD is recognized worldwide for its extensive publications program highlighted by the biannual *OECD Economic Outlook*. This publication forecasts global economic trends with information on each member country. *OECD Economic Surveys* are also published by the organization. These surveys are published annually and provide a detailed overview of the economy of each member country. The OECD also publishes *Main Economic Indicators* (monthly), *Employment Outlook* (annually), *Foreign Trade Statistics* (monthly), *Oil and Gas Statistics* (quarterly), *Energy Balances* (quarterly) and *Energy Prices and Taxes* (quarterly). Through its publications program the OECD provided the General Agreement on Tariffs and Trade (GATT) negotiations with much needed technical information. Especially timely were analyses of industrial subsidies, intellectual property rights, and general services.

The council is the governing organ of the OECD. It meets at least once a year and each member nation is represented on the council. The council functions at two levels, the level of government ministers and the official level. At the official level the position of chairman is filled by the OECD secretary general. At the ministerial level the chairman comes from whichever

country is elected to the chairmanship for that respective year. There is also a 14-member executive committee made up of selected council members. The executive committee implements council policy and performs specific assignments. There is also an autonomous international secretariat headed by the secretary general. The secretariat assists the council in that body's duties. The OECD is closely associated with the Centre for Cooperation with European Economies in Transition, the Centre for Educational Research and Innovation, the Development Center, the Nuclear Agency, and the International Energy Agency.

There are 24 OECD members: Australia, Austria, Belgium, Canada, Denmark, Finland, France, Germany, Great Britain, Greece, Iceland, Ireland, Italy, Japan, Luxembourg, the Netherlands, New Zealand, Norway, Portugal, Spain, Sweden, Switzerland, Turkey, and the United States.

[Michael Knes]

ORGANIZATION OF PETROLEUM EXPORTING COUNTRIES

The Organization of Petroleum Exporting Countries (OPEC) was established September 14, 1960 at a conference in Baghdad, Iraq. The purpose of OPEC is to stabilize and control for its members' advantage the production, supply, and price of crude oil. With the forming of OPEC, a cartel was created to coordinate the petroleum policies of OPEC's various members. The founding members of OPEC were Iran, Iraq, Kuwait, Saudi Arabia, and Venezuela. Other countries have since joined including: Algeria (1969), Gabon (1973), Indonesia (1962), Libya (1962), Nigeria (1971), Qatar (1961), and the United Arab Emirates (1967). Ecuador joined OPEC in 1973 but terminated its membership in 1992.

After 13 years of agitation by Dr. Juan Pablo Perez Alfonso of Venezuela, the first Arab Petroleum Conference was held in 1959. Alfonso argued that pro-rationing the production of crude oil would allow oil producers to control prices. Pro-rationing would assign production quotas and schedules to members of the cartel. Opponents argued that attempting to control oil prices through pro-rationing ignores market forces of supply and demand (it must be remembered that not all oil producers wished to join the proposed cartel) and will ultimately fail. Alfonso's view prevailed, however, and OPEC was founded the following year. The immediate impetus for the oil cartel was a soft buyer's market in the early 1960s. The supply of crude oil was greater than the demand, prices were depressed, and prospects for price increases were not realistic. The immediate aim of the new cartel was to restore the price of a barrel of crude oil to its pre-1960s level and unite against multinational oil companies. Prices remained depressed until the 1970s when the growing strength and unity of OPEC coupled with increased demand for oil by western industrialized nations brought about a seller's market.

When OPEC was established, a barrel of oil (42 gallons) was selling for under $5. By the 1980s the price of the same barrel of crude had risen to around $40. Much of this increase was due to global demand for oil, as well as OPEC's initial controls over production and price. By the mid-1980s, however, the price of oil began dropping due to overproduction and a worldwide recession. There was also a concerted effort among non-OPEC oil-producing countries and other industrialized nations to increase oil exploration, develop new and more efficient oil drilling technology, and implement long-term energy conservation projects. By 1985 crude oil was selling for around $25 a barrel. Many OPEC members continued to exceed their production quotas because of growing populations at home, falling oil reserves, foreign debt, and foreign exchange shortages. In 1987, for instance, the OPEC quota for all members was set at 16.5 million barrels of oil a day, but in fact OPEC members were producing more than 20 million barrels. Problems over production quotas continued to plague OPEC well into the 1990s. At a meeting in Geneva in early 1994 OPEC members again failed to agree on an equitable schedule to cut production levels. At that time OPEC was producing nearly 24.5 million barrels of oil per day. Saudi Arabia, which produces nearly a third of OPEC's oil, refused to participate in production cutbacks. This disagreement precipitated a $1 drop in the price of oil bringing it down to $13.75 per barrel, a five-year low. The failure of OPEC to control the price of oil by arbitrarily raising prices while cutting production reenforces the belief of many economists that in order for commodity prices to remain stable over the long-term, the prices must be reasonably tied to the cost of production. In 1994 OPEC nations produced 37 percent of the world's oil.

The supreme authority of OPEC is the Conference which usually meets biannually to formulate policy. Each member country is represented on the Conference which also reviews recommendations from the Board of Governors. The Governors also oversee the administration of OPEC and, like the Conference, each member country is represented on the board. There is a Ministerial Monitoring Committee which formulates long-term strategy, sets production quotas, and Monitors the global petroleum market. The Office of the Secretary-General and the Secretariat are served by the Personnel and Administration Department, the Department of OPECNA (OPEC News Agency) and Information and the Legal Office. There is also a Research Division which is comprised of three departments: Economics and Finance, Energy Studies, and Data Services. The Office of the Secretary-General is responsible for the daily operations of OPEC, implementing policy, and maintaining relations with other governments and international organizations.

OPEC also administers the OPEC Fund for International Development. Headquartered in Vienna, the Fund makes loans and grants to developing countries. This financial aid is usually provided for balance-of-payment support, development projects, technical assistance, and research grants.

OPEC should not be confused with OAPEC, the Organization of Arab Petroleum Exporting Countries. Although they are autonomous, many Arab oil-producing nations belong to both organizations and they share many common goals. OAPEC was responsible for the infamous oil embargo which lasted from October 1973 to March of 1974.

[Michael Knes]

FURTHER READING:

Ahrari, Mohammed E. *OPEC: The Failing Giant*. University of Kentucky Press, 1986.

Kohl, Wilfrid L. *After the Oil Price Collapse: OPEC, the United States, and the World Oil Market*. Johns Hopkins University Press, 1991.

Mabro, Robert. *OPEC and the World Oil Market: The Genesis of the 1986 Price Crisis*. Oxford University Press, 1986.

ORGANIZATION THEORY

An organization, by its most basic definition, is an assembly of people working together to achieve common objectives through a division of labor. People form organizations because individuals have limited abilities. An organization provides a means of using individual strengths within a group to achieve more than can be accomplished by the aggregate efforts of group members working individually. Business organizations (in market economies) are formed to profit by delivering a good or service to consumers.

Researchers have proposed several theories attempting to explain the dynamics of business organizations. Organization theory is examined here primarily from a historical perspective that briefly summarizes its evolution. The open-systems theory—the dominant school of thought throughout most of the twentieth century—is examined in greatest detail, and organizational characteristics, and structures are also reviewed.

BACKGROUND

Modern organization theory is rooted in concepts developed during the beginnings of the Industrial Revolution in the late 1800s and early 1900s. Of import during that period was the research of Max Weber (1864-1920), a German sociologist. Weber believed that bureaucracies, staffed by bureaucrats, represented the ideal organizational form. Weber based his model bureaucracy on legal and absolute authority, logic, and order. In it, responsibilities for workers are clearly defined and behavior is tightly controlled by rules, policies, and procedures. In effect, Weber's bureaucracy was designed to function like a machine; the organization was arranged into specific functions, or parts, each of which worked in concert with the other parts to form a streamlined process.

Weber's theories of organizations, like others of the period, reflected an indifferent toic and impersonal attitude toward the people in the organization. Indeed, personal aspects of human behavior were considered unreliable and were viewed as a potential detriment to the efficiency of any system. Humans were likened to a bundle of skills that could be inserted into the system like a cog in a machine. Although his theories are now considered mechanistic and outdated, Weber's views on bureaucracy provided important insight into process efficiency, division of labor, and hierarchy of authority.

Another important contributor to organization theory in the early 1900s was Henri Fayol. He is credited with identifying four basic managerial functions that characterize successful organizations:

1. planning: thinking before acting

2. organizing: setting up policies and procedures that regulate employee behavior

3. staffing: recruiting a suitable work force

4. controlling: motivating workers to pursue the goals of the organization.

Weber's and Fayol's theories found broad application in the early and mid-1900s, largely as a result of the work of Frederick W. Taylor (1856-1915). In a 1911 book entitled *Principles of Scientific Management*, Taylor outlined his theories and eventually implemented them on American factory floors. Taylor's theory of scientific management mimicked the four basic managerial functions identified by Fayol, and adopted the same basic attitudes about process efficiency championed by Weber. Although elements of Taylor's research and findings have been criticized as being false, he is credited with helping to define the role of training, wage incentives, employee selection, and work standards in organizational performance.

Researchers began to adopt a less mechanical view of organizations and to pay more attention to human influences in the 1930s. This development was motivated by several studies, particularly the Hawthorne experiments, that shed light on the function of human fulfillment in organizations. Primarily under the direction of Harvard University researcher Elton Mayo, the **Hawthorne** studies were conducted in the mid-1920s and 1930s at a Western Electric Company plant known as the Hawthorne Works. The company wanted to determine the degree to which working conditions affected output.

Surprisingly, the studies failed to show any significant positive correlations between workplace conditions and productivity. In one study, for example, worker productivity escalated when lighting was increased, but it also increased when illumination was decreased. The results of the studies demonstrated that innate forces of human behavior may have a greater influence on organizations than do mechanistic incentive systems. The legacy of the Hawthorne studies and other organizational research efforts of that period was an emphasis on the importance of individual and group interaction, humanistic management skills, and social relationships in the workplace.

The focus on human influences in organizations was reflected most noticeably by the integration of Abraham Maslow's "hierarchy of human needs" into organization theory. Maslow's theories had two important implications for organization theory: (1) people have different needs and are therefore motivated by different incentives to achieve organizational objectives; and (2) people's needs change predictably over time, meaning that as the needs of people lower in the hierarchy are met, new needs arise. These assumptions led to the recognition, for example, that assembly-line workers could be more productive if more of their personal needs were met, whereas past theories suggested that monetary rewards were the sole, or primary, motivators.

Douglas McGregor contrasted the organization theory that emerged during the mid-1900s to previous views. In the 1950s, McGregor offered his renowned Theory X and Theory Y to explain the differences. In a nutshell, Theory X depicts the old, repressive, pessimistic view of workers. It assumes that people are lazy and have to be coerced to produce with tangible rewards. In fact, McGregor argued that the old view, assumed that workers preferred to be directed, wanted to avoid responsibility, and cherished financial security (i.e., jobs) above all else.

McGregor believed that organizations that embraced Theory Y were generally more productive. Theory Y adopted a more optimistic view of human nature. Among other things, it theorized that: humans can learn to accept and seek responsibility; most people possess a high degree of imaginative and problem-solving ability; employees will self-govern, or direct themselves toward goals to which they are committed; and, importantly, satisfaction of ego and self-actualization are among the most important needs that have to be met by (profit-maximizing) organizations.

OPEN-SYSTEMS THEORY

Traditional theories regarded organizations as closed systems—autonomous and isolated from the outside world. In the 1960s, these mechanistic organization theories, such as scientific management, were spurned in favor of more holistic and humanistic ideologies. Recognizing that traditional theory had failed to take into account many environmental influences that affected the efficiency of organizations, most theorists and researchers embraced an open-systems view of organizations.

The term "open systems" reflected the newfound belief that all organizations are unique and should therefore be structured to accommodate unique problems and opportunities. For example, research during the 1960s showed that traditional bureaucratic organizations generally failed to succeed in environments where technologies or markets were rapidly changing. They also failed to realize the importance of regional cultural influences in motivating workers.

Environmental influences that affect open systems can be described as either specific or general. The specific environment is a network of suppliers, distributors, government agencies, and competitors. An organization is simply one element of that network. To succeed, or profit, the organization must interact with these influences. They use suppliers, for example, when they purchase materials from other producers, hire workers from the labor force, or secure credit from banks or other companies.

The general environment encompasses four influences that emanate from the geographic area in which the organization operates. The first is cultural values, which determine views about what is right or wrong, good or bad, and important or trivial. Companies in the United States will likely be influenced by the values of individualism, democracy, individual rights and freedoms, and a puritan work ethic, among many others. In addition, regional and local values will affect organizations. For instance, workers and consumers in southern and northwestern states are more likely to be ideologically conservative.

Economic conditions make up the second cluster of general environmental influences on open systems. These influences include economic upswings, recessions, regional unemployment, and many other factors that affect a company's ability to grow and prosper. Economic influences may also partially dictate an organization's role in the economy. For example, as the economy grows the organization will likely become not only larger but more specialized.

A third influence on organizations is the legal/political environment, which effectively helps to allocate power within a society and to enforce laws. The legal and political system in which an open system operates determines, most importantly, the long-term stability and security of the organization's future. For instance, a national government can add stability by maintaining a strong defense force. But legal and political mechanisms can also hamper a company's success by burdening it with regulations, taxes, employee rights laws, and other rules. In general, the larger and more powerful the local, regional, or national government, the less attractive will be the general environment to nongovernment organizations.

The fourth general environmental influence on open systems is educational conditions. For example, businesses that operate in countries or regions with a high education level will have a better chance of staffing a complex organization that requires specialized skills and a precise division of labor.

KATZ AND KAHN

Daniel Katz and Robert L. Kahn developed a framework for open-systems theory that encompasses: (1) energic inputs into the organizations; (2) the transformation of those inputs within the system; (3) the energic outputs; and (4) recycling. Energic inputs, or external influences, include familiar resources like employees, raw materials, and capital. However, they also include intangible external influences, such as status, recognition, satisfaction, or other personal rewards.

The transformation process involves using energies, or inputs, to (in the business context) create products or services. Energic outputs are simply the products or services that are distributed to consumers. Finally, recycling refers to the fact that outputs are indirectly recycled back into the organization. For instance, when a company sells a toaster the revenue becomes an input into the organization that is used, for example, to pay workers or buy materials.

In addition to identifying the four phases of an open system, Katz and Kahn cataloged several other organizational characteristics that support the open-systems theory and have implications for the design of successful organizations. For example, they recognized the universal law of entropy, which holds that all organizations move toward disorganization or death. However, an open system can continue to thrive by importing more energy from the environment than it expends, thus achieving negative entropy. For example, a failing company might be able to revitalize itself by bringing in a new chief executive who improves the way the company transforms energic inputs.

Another characteristic of organizations is dynamic homeostasis, which infers that all successful organizations must be able to achieve balance between subsystems. For example, a sales department might grow very quickly if it is very successful or demand for its products jumps. But if the manufacturing arm of the company is unable to keep pace with sales activity, the entire organization could break down. Thus, subgroups must maintain a rough state of balance as they adapt to external influences.

Katz and Kahn also characterize open systems by equifiniality. This concept suggests that organizations can reach the same final state by a number of different paths. In fact, the course is not fixed and may develop organically as both internal and external influences intervene.

SUBSYSTEMS

Open-systems theory assumes that all large organizations are comprised of multiple subsystems, each of which receives inputs from other subsystems and turns them into outputs for use by other subsystems. The subsystems are not necessarily represented by departments in an organization, but might instead resemble patterns of activity.

An important distinction between open-systems theory and traditional organization theory is that the former assumes a subsystem hierarchy, meaning that not all of the subsystems are equally essential. Furthermore, a failure in one subsystem will not necessarily thwart the entire system. By contrast, traditional mechanistic theories implied that a malfunction in any part of a system would have an equally quashing effect. This could be likened to pulling one cotter pin from the wheel of a go-cart; doing so would make the entire vehicle inoperable.

At least five subsystems identified by Katz and Kahn are important to the success of any business organization. Each of these subsystems may also be comprised of subsystems. For example, production subsystems are the components that transform inputs into outputs. In a manufacturing company this subsystem would be represented by activities related to production. In most business organizations, all other subsystems are built around the production subsystem.

Maintenance subsystems maintain the social involvement of employees in an organization. Activities in this group include providing benefits and compensations that motivate workers, creating favorable work conditions, empowering employees, and fulfilling other employee needs.

Adaptive subsystems serve to gather information about problems and opportunities in the environment and then respond with innovations that allow the organization to adapt. A firm's research lab or a product development department would both be part of an adaptive subsystem.

Supportive subsystems perform acquisition and distribution functions within an organization. Acquisition activities include securing resources, such as employees and raw materials, from the external environment. Human resources and purchasing divisions are typically included in this group. Distribution, or disposal, activities encompass efforts to transfer the product or service outside of the organization. Supportive subsystems of this type include sales and marketing divisions, public relations departments, and lobbying efforts.

Managerial subsystems direct the activities of other subsystems in the organization. These managerial functions set goals and policies, allocate resources, settle disputes, and generally work to facilitate the efficiency of the organization.

BASIC ORGANIZATIONAL CHARACTERISTICS

Organizations differ greatly in size, function, and makeup. Nevertheless, three characteristics of nearly all organizations with more than a few members are: (1) a division of labor; (2) a decision-making structure; and (3) formal rules and policies.

Organizations practice division of labor both vertically and horizontally. Vertical division includes three basic levels—top, middle, and bottom. The chief function of top managers, or executives, typically is to plan long-term strategy and oversee middle managers. Middle managers generally guide the day-to-day activities of the organization and administer top-level strategy. Low-level managers and laborers put strategy into action and perform the specific tasks necessary to keep the organization operating.

Organizations also divide labor horizontally by defining task groups, or departments, and assigning workers with applicable skills to those groups. Line units perform the basic functions of the business, while staff units support line units with expertise and services. For instance, the marketing department (line unit) might be supported by the accounting department (staff unit). In general, line units focus on supply, production, and distribution, while staff units deal mostly with internal operations and controls or public relations efforts.

Decision-making structures, the second basic organizational characteristic, are used to organize authority. They vary in their degree of centralization and decentralization. Centralized decision structures are referred to as ''tall'' organizations because important decisions usually emanate from a high level and are passed down through several channels until they reach the lower end of the hierarchy. Bosses at all levels have relatively few employees reporting directly to them.

In contrast, flat organizations, which have decentralized decision-making structures, employ only a few hierarchical levels. The few bosses or authority figures have many employees reporting directly to them. Such organizations, however, usually practice some form of employee empowerment whereby individuals make decisions autonomously. Decentralized structures are more representative of humanistic organization theories, while traditional tall organizational structures are more mechanistic. Besides meeting human needs, flat structures yield faster response times to internal and external influences.

Formalized rules and policies is the third standard organizational characteristic. Rules, policies, and procedures serve as substitutes for managerial guidance. For example, they may indicate the most efficient means of accomplishing a task or provide standards for rewarding workers. The benefit of formalized rules is that managers have more time to spend on other problems and opportunities. The disadvantage of rules is that they sometimes stifle workers' creativity and autonomy, thereby reducing their satisfaction and effectiveness.

Thus, organizations can be categorized as informal or formal, depending on the degree of formalization of rules. In general, formal organizations are goal-oriented and rational, and the relationship between individuals and the organization is comparatively impersonal. Subordinates have less influence over the process in which they participate, with their duties more clearly defined. The extreme case of a formal organization would resemble Weber's ideal bureaucracy.

Informal organizations are those that have relatively few written rules or policies. Instead, individuals are more likely to adopt patterns of behavior that are influenced by a number of social and personal factors. Changes in the organization are less often the result of authoritative dictate and more often an outcome of collective agreement by members. Informal organizations tend to be more flexible and more reactive to outside influences. But they may also diminish the ability of top managers to effect rapid change.

BASIC ORGANIZATIONAL STRUCTURES

In addition to the three root characteristics of business organizations are two basic types of structure: functional and divisional. Most companies represent an amalgam of both. Functional organizational structures are more traditional. They departmentalize the company based on key functions. For example,

activities related to production, marketing, and finance might be grouped into three respective divisions. Within each division, moreover, activities would be departmentalized into subdepartments. Within the marketing division, for example, might be the sales, advertising, and promotions departments.

The advantage of functionally structured organizations is that they typically achieve an efficient specialization of labor because people with specific skills can follow a career path within their department. In addition, this type of structure is relatively easy for employees to comprehend. Therefore, they are more likely to identify with their group and enjoy a sense of accomplishment through the gains of the department. Finally, functional structures reduce duplication of work because responsibilities are clearly defined.

On the other hand, functional structures are often divisive, causing departments to become adversarial and employees to engage in behavior that benefits their department at the expense of the overall organization. Furthermore, employees in departments often become myopic, thus losing sight of the goals of the entire organization. In addition, functional structures typically fail to make full use of the talents of workers and they are often less reactive to environmental influences.

Companies that employ a more divisional structure break the organization down into semiautonomous units and profit centers based on activities related to products, customers, or geography. Regardless of the activity group used to segment the company, each unit operates as a separate business. For example, a company might be broken down into southern, western, and eastern divisions. Or, it might create separate divisions for consumer, industrial, and institutional products. Again, within each division are subdivisions.

One benefit of a divisional structure is that it facilitates expansion because the company can easily add a new division to focus on a new profit opportunity without having to significantly alter exiting systems. In addition, accountability is increased because divisional performance can be measured more easily. Furthermore, divisional structures permit decentralized decision making, which allows managers with specific expertise to make key decisions in their area.

The potential drawbacks to divisional structures include duplication of efforts and a lack of communication. For example, separate consumer and industrial divisions of the same air-conditioner company may both be trying to develop a better compressor. In addition, divisional organizations, like functionally structured companies, may have trouble keeping all departments focused on an overall company goal. A corollary is that top management sometimes loses touch with the goals and inner-workings of each division.

SEE ALSO: Organizational Behavior; Organizational Growth; Organizational Life Cycle

[Dave Mote]

FURTHER READING:

Cherrington, David J. *Organizational Behavior: The Management of Individual and Organizational Performance*. Boston: Allyn and Bacon, 1994.

Gray, Jerry L., and Frederick A. Starke. *Organizational Behavior: Concepts and Applications*. 4th ed. Columbus, OH: Merrill Publishing Company, 1988.

Huse, E. F., and T. G. Cummings. *Organizational Development and Change*. St. Paul, MN: West, 1985.

Ivancevich, John M., and Michael T. Matteson. *Organizational Behavior and Management*. Homewood, IL: Richard D. Irwin, Inc., 1990.

Katz, Daniel, and Robert L. Kahn. *The Social Psychology of Organizations*. 2nd ed. New York: Wiley, 1978.

Northcraft, Gregory B., and Margaret A. Neale. *Organizational Behavior: A Management Challenge*. Chicago: The Dryden Press, 1990.

Osborn, Richard N., James G. Hunt, and Lawrence R. Jauch. *Organization Theory: An Integrated Approach*. New York: John Wiley & Sons, 1980.

Schermerhorn, John R., Jr., James G. Hunt, and Richard N. Osborn. *Management Organizational Behavior*. New York: John Wiley & Sons. 1982.

ORGANIZATIONAL BEHAVIOR

Organizational behavior is an academic discipline concerned with describing, understanding, predicting, and controlling human behavior in an organizational environment. It is a fairly new discipline, dating back to the early 1900's, although some experts suggest that it came into existence right after the American Civil War. Organizational behavior has evolved from early classical management theories into a complex school of thought—and it continues to change in response to the dynamic workforce in which today's businesses operate.

THE CLASSICAL MANAGEMENT SCHOOL

In 1911, Frederick W. Taylor's book, *Principles of Scientific Management*, was published. This book marked the first serious attempt to publish the results of scientific management studies aimed at motivating workers to produce more. Taylor was the best known of a group of people, primarily mechanical engineers, who applied time-and-motion study concepts in the workplace. These engineers focused on the task concept to show that workers could be motivated to pro-duce more, especially if they were offered an incentive to do so.

The task concept centered around the idea that if managers planned workers' tasks at least one day in advance, production would increase. Taylor devised a differential piece-rate system based on two different rates of pay. His system was simple: workers who did less than the expected output received a low rate of pay. Those who exceeded the standard earned more money. That was a radical idea for the time. It separated the worker from the machine and indicated that employees could control how much they produced. Taylor also suggested in his approach that money motivated workers. This, too, was a unique idea. What Taylor did not do, however, was take into account group behavior. He, like most classical managers, had no concept of the importance of workers as members of groups. The next wave of theorists, the human relations experts, addressed the issue of group behavior.

THE HAWTHORNE EXPERIMENTS

Human relationists tried to add a human dimension to classical theory in their studies. They did not try to refute the classical management proponents. Rather, they introduced the idea that workers would be willing to accept as part of their reward humane treatment, personal attention, and a chance to feel wanted. To prove their point, human relationists embarked on a series of experiments.

Perhaps the most significant experiments were the **Hawthorne experiments**. The studies began in 1924 at the Hawthorne Works, part of the Western Electric Company, located in Cicero, Illinois. The researchers' original goal was to measure the effect of illumination on output. In simplified terms, what they actually learned was that an individual's work performance, position, and status in an organization are determined not only by the individual, but by group members, too. They also learned that workers formed cliques that affected their production and that there were certain codes of conduct members of individual cliques were expected to follow. The Hawthorne studies opened the door to more experiments by other human relationists.

HUMAN RESOURCES THEORY

The next group to take center stage in the organizational behavior arena postulated that a manager's role was not to control workers, but to facilitate employee performance. According to human resources experts, people work to make a living, but their efforts go far beyond just laboring. They also work to fulfill certain needs, e.g., contributing to organizational objectives, attaining a feeling of accomplishment, and using their creativity in the work environment. Managers were well advised to keep all these needs in mind when dealing with workers. According to the human resources theorists, managers should apply mutual goal-setting and problem-solving approaches to their workforce members.

Managers were encouraged to make use of whatever training was necessary to ensure maximum performance. The training could take a variety of forms, i.e., technical, human, or conceptual. They were also advised to open communication lines in all directions to promote organizational effectiveness. After all, the theorists emphasized, workers welcome self-direction and self-control and will perform well when managers take an interest in their lives. In short, the human resources advocates said, managers should place their primary emphasis on using workers as if they are important human assets.

THE SYSTEM APPROACH TO ORGANIZATIONAL BEHAVIOR

Modern theorists apply a five-part system approach to organizational behavior: the individual; the formal organization; the informal organization; the fusion process, in which the first three modify and shape one another; and the physical environment. Each part is essential. None can exist alone in the system. This system approach is the basis for modern organizational theory, which is founded on behavioral science studies.

THE BEHAVIORAL SCIENCES

There are three behavioral sciences: psychology (the study of individual behavior), sociology (the study of social behavior within societies, institutions, and groups), and anthropology (the study of the origin, cultural development, and behavior of man). Each has made important contributions to the study of organizational behavior.

From an organizational standpoint, psychologists are concerned with the processes of learning, perception, and motivation. Sociologists study the various organizations that compose society, e.g., political, legal, business, governmental, and religious bodies. Finally, anthropologists are interested in the impact of culture on behavior. The three disciplines have had a major impact on the study of organizational behavior.

Organizational behavior scientists study four areas: individual behavior, group behavior, organizational structure, and organizational processes. They investigate facets of these areas like personality and perception, attitudes and job satisfaction, group dynamics, politics and the role of leadership in the organization, job design, the impact of stress on work,

decision-making processes, the communications chain, and company cultures and climates. They use a variety of techniques and approaches to evaluate each facet and its impact on individuals, groups, and organizational efficiency and effectiveness.

In regard to individuals and groups, researchers try to ascertain why people behave the way they do. They have developed a variety of models designed to explain individuals' behavior. They investigate the factors that influence personality development, including genetic, situational, environmental, cultural, and social factors. Researchers also look at personality types such as authoritarian (people who adhere closely to conventional values) and dogmatic (people who are extremely rigid in their beliefs). They want to find out what causes a person to form either type of personality and learn whether one or the other—or neither—is a positive trait for people in the business world.

Researchers have also studied a number of concepts, including:

1. Stereotyping—the process of categorizing people based on limited information

2. Halo effect—the use of known personal traits as the basis for an overall evaluation

3. Perceptual defense—the process of screening out or distorting information that is disturbing or that people do not care to acknowledge

4. Projection—people attribute their own undesirable traits or characteristics to others.

They evaluate perception versus reality, individuals' locus of control, (whether they believe they or outside forces are in control of their lives), and common problems resulting from these personality traits and characteristics. Finally, they look at an individual's attitudes and correlate them to job satisfaction and job performance.

THE IMPORTANCE OF JOB SATISFACTION STUDIES

The study of job satisfaction is central to organizational behavioral scientists. Companies want to know why their employees are or are not satisfied. If they are not happy, executives look to the behavioral scientists for ways to improve individuals' attitudes and to suggest ways of improving the work environment. This implies that the theorists have to look well beyond the tangible factors influencing job satisfaction, such as pay, benefits, promotional opportunities, and working conditions. They have to study how groups influence the workplace and individuals' expectations.

THE DYNAMICS OF GROUP BEHAVIOR

The first factor that researchers addressed in the area of group behavior was the definition of ''group.'' They agreed that there is no one definition. Therefore, they looked more at why people join groups, types of groups, and group activities and goals. Studies focused on group norms, individuals' behavior within groups and how it changed, their roles within groups, and what groups could accomplish that individuals could not. The researchers discovered that a group is more than the sum of the individual members, even though its goals, interactions, and performance are determined primarily by the individuals comprising it. This led them to a study of leadership within the group setting.

Organizational behavior scientists drew a distinction between leadership and management. They defined management as the process of accomplishing tasks, whereas leadership was the process of getting things done by influencing other people. Their next question was whether leaders are born or made. In order to answer that question, researchers sought common characteristics shared by leaders. They found a few—intelligence, dependability, responsibility, social activity, and high originality—but there were not enough to form any definitive conclusions of common leadership characteristics.

POWER, POLITICS, AND CONFLICT

Organizational behavior scientists have identified five basic types of power managers and leaders use to influence their subordinates: reward, coercive, legitimate, referent, and expert.

Reward power, which is based on an individual's expectation of receiving desired outcomes, was found to be a positive force. However, if the members of a group do not believe they will be rewarded for their efforts, the person in a position to offer rewards will not be able to influence the individuals. Similarly, managers who rely on coercive power, which is based on fear, will probably be unable to influence workers, especially group members, for a long period of time.

The other three types of power also have advantages and disadvantages. For instance, legitimate power, which exists as part of a manager's position in the hierarchy, is often ignored by workers who do not respect the individual filling the role. Referent power, which is based on the manager's charisma, influences only those individuals or group members who are swayed by the charismatic leader. Finally, expert power, which is power acquired from experience and learning, is a positive force, but only in so far as managers can convince individuals and group members that their leadership skills go beyond expertise alone.

People attempting to exercise power in the organization often resort to political tactics to do so. They blame others for mistakes, form power coalitions, praise co-workers and subordinates when they think it will help them achieve goals and reinforce their images. In short, they use every stratagem possible to win friends and influence people. In the process, however, they often create conflict. This prompted researchers to study conflict and its possible solutions.

Organizational behavior scientists recognize that conflict exists at both the individual and group levels. They have devised a number of ways to deal with it. Among them are mutual problem solving, compromise, and avoidance. Significantly, they discovered that conflict resolutions are most often temporary, and they have looked for ways to make them more permanent. In order to find permanent solutions, they have performed more in-depth studies of organizational structure and processes and how both affect individuals and groups.

ORGANIZATIONAL DESIGN AND PROCESSES

Organizational behavior scientists have conducted entensive studies on job definitions and the tasks a job comprises. They have looked at how each job fit into different groups within the organization, a process called departmentalization. The researchers have studied managerial spans of control, i.e., the number of people an individual manager can manage most effectively. The process required that researchers reduce to its most basic level each task performed and then find ways to perform jobs more efficiently and effectively.

Many researchers have suggested viable ways that organizations could restructure jobs and relationships to stimulate job satisfaction and productivity simultaneously. They have devised better communications programs, identified the elements that create stress, and explained how it could be better managed.

Organizational behavior scientists performed extensive studies on company cultures and climates with an eye to upgrading employees' quality of life in the workplace. They have sought ways to include more people in the managerial and decision-making processes. Their suggestions have included such techniques as **quality circles** and participative management programs.

Quality circles, which are team approaches to identifying and resolving work-related problems, became popular in some businesses. So, too, did participative management efforts, which gave a wider variety of people opportunities to comment on—and implement—new ideas in the workplace. One prominent organizational behavior scientist, William Ouchi, recommended that American companies integrate more Japanese management, such as these concepts into their management practices. His approach became known as Theory Z.

The ideas promulgated by organizational behavior scientists have caught on in managerial circles. Not surprisingly, not all of the programs can used by all companies. If there is one thing that researchers have recognized, it is that no two companies are alike. To compensate for the dissimilarities, behavioral scientists reformed detailed cultural profiles to determine which programs fit individual companies' needs. These profiles have the illustrated importance of culture in the field of organizational behavior. Researchers have examiined how company cultures control individual and group behavior, promote innovation, foster personnal commitment, etc.

THE FUTURE OF ORGANIZATIONAL BEHAVIOR

The international economy has taken on added importance in organizational behavior circles in recent years. Researchers currently are studying such things as communications between and among foreign business operations, cultural differences and their impact on individuals, language difficulties, motivation techniques in different cultures, as well as the differences in leadership and decision-making practices from country to country.

Today, organizational behavior scientists are dealing with a wide range of problems confronting the business world. For instance, they are studying downsizing, career development in the global economy and in the face of a shrinking workforce, social problems such as substance abuse and the breakdown of the family unit, and the global economy. They are trying to determine just what effects such factors are having on the workplace and what can be done to alleviate problems.

[Arthur G. Sharp]

FURTHER READING:

Hodgetts, Richard M. *Organizational Behavior: Theory and Practice.* New York: Macmillan Publishing Company, 1991.

Ouchi, William. *Theory Z: How American Business Can Meet the Japanese Challenge.* Reading, MA: Addison-Wesley Publishing Co., 1981.

Taylor, Frederick. *Principles of Scientific Management.* New York: Harper & Brothers Publishers, 1911.

ORGANIZATIONAL DEVELOPMENT

Organizational development (OD) is an application of behavioral science to organizational change. It encompasses a wide array of theories, processes, and activities, all of which are oriented toward the goal of improving individual organizations. One of numerous definitions interprets OD as ''a system-wide application of behavioral science knowledge to the planned development and reinforcement of organizational strategies, structures, and processes for improving an organization's effectiveness'' (*Organizational Development and Change*, West, 1985).

OD differs from traditional organizational change techniques in that it typically embraces a more holistic approach that is aimed at transforming thought and behavior throughout an entity. Like many other organizational change techniques, the basic OD process consists of gathering data, planning changes, and then implementing and managing the changes. However, OD initiatives are usually distinguished by the use of ''action research,'' change agents, and ''interventions.''

BACKGROUND

Organization development is rooted in behavioral research that proliferated in the United States after World War II. That research led to the development in the late 1940s and 1950s of behavioral development strategies like sensitivity training, survey feedback, sociotechnical systems, and quality management.

Chief among the early endeavors in the field of behavioral science were Kurt Lewin's contributions to sensitivity training, or T-groups, during the mid-1940s (Lewin was the director of the Research Center for Group Dynamics at the Massachusetts Institute of Technology). Lewin's research showed that informal discussions about individual and group behavior, when combined with feedback, were more educational for group members than were lectures and seminars. T-groups (''T'' stands for training) became popular with several major corporations as a means of improving group performance. In fact, during the 1950s and 1960s, organizational change and development was often considered synonymous with sensitivity training.

Also emerging in the mid-1940s were the behavioral techniques of survey research and feedback, many of which were originally developed by Rensis Likert and fellow researchers at the University of Michigan Survey Research Center. Likert and his associates used questionnaires, statistical samples, and feedback to managers to improve organizations. They found that when managers shared the information with subordinates and discussed potential routes to improvement, overall group performance was enhanced.

Also of import to the evolution of OD were sociotechnical system models developed during the

1950s and originating from England's Tavistock Institute. These models were developed to help sustain meaningful social interaction and fulfill workers' social needs in the face of technological change. Such methods of responding to change were later adapted to help manage organizational turbulence caused by other factors, such as restructuring or layoffs, and to create more efficient management structures. In the context of modern OD, a sociotechnical system approach usually involves work teams.

Although they were not integrated into OD in the United States until the 1980s, quality management philosophies and processes were also formulated during the 1940s and 1950s. W. Edwards Deming and J.M. Juran are generally credited with developing continuous quality improvement techniques that they successfully implemented in many corporations. Both Deming and Juran achieved great success with their programs in Japan following World War II before returning to the United States to help American firms. Their contributions to OD have included statistical analysis techniques and methods for creating conditions of perpetual improvement in organizations.

During the 1950s and 1960s, researchers and managers began to pull together different elements of the behavioral development strategies described above to create more comprehensive processes for planning and executing change in organizations. For example, Lewin (1958) devised a renowned three-step change process that entailed ''unfreezing,'' changing, and then ''refreezing'' the behavior of individuals and groups within organizations. In fact, it was during the 1960s and 1970s that the term ''organizational development'' was popularized to describe a multidisciplinary approach to achieving organizational change and improvement. OD evolved during the 1970s and 1980s to encompass a variety of change techniques and processes.

Interest in OD was bolstered in the United States during the 1980s by global and domestic economic influences. As domestic market growth slowed and foreign competition increased, many U.S. companies were forced to implement extensive changes in their organizations. For example, in their pursuit of quality and productivity, many corporations slashed payrolls, introduced new technology, adopted new management structures, and altered worker incentive systems. In an effort to effect change, many companies utilized OD techniques.

ORGANIZATIONAL DEVELOPMENT BASICS

Although the field of OD is broad, it can be differentiated from other systems of organizational change by its emphasis on process rather than problems. Indeed, traditional group change systems have focused on identifying problems in an organization and then trying to alter the behavior that creates the problem. OD initiatives, in contrast, focus on identifying the behavioral interactions and patterns that cause and sustain problems. Then, rather than simply changing isolated behaviors, OD efforts are aimed at creating a behaviorally healthy organization that will naturally anticipate and prevent (or quickly solve) problems (*Organizational Behavior: A Management Challenge*, Dryden Press, 1990).

OD programs usually share several basic characteristics. For instance, they are considered long-term efforts of at least one to three years in most cases. In addition, OD stresses collaborative management, whereby managers and workers at different levels of the hierarchy cooperate to solve problems. OD also recognizes that every organization is unique and that the same solutions cannot necessarily be applied at different companies—this assumption is reflected in an OD focus on research and feedback. Another common trait of OD programs is an emphasis on the value of teamwork and small groups. In fact, most OD systems implement broad organizational changes and overcome resistance largely through the efforts of small teams and/or individuals.

An integral feature of most OD programs is the change agent, which is the group or individual that facilitates the OD process. Change agents are usually outside consultants with experience managing OD programs, although companies sometimes utilize inside managers. The advantage of bringing in outside OD consultants is that they often provide a different perspective and have a less biased view of the organization's problems and needs.

The drawback of outside change agents is that they typically lack an in-depth understanding of key issues particular to the company (or institution). In addition, outside consultants may have trouble securing the trust and cooperation of key players in the organization. For these reasons, some companies employ a external-internal team approach, which combines the advantages of internal and external change agents.

IMPLEMENTING OD PROGRAMS

OD efforts basically entail two groups of activities; ''action research'' and ''interventions.'' Action research was originated in the 1940s by Lewin and another U.S. researcher, John Collier. It is a process of systematically collecting data on a specific organization, feeding it back for action planning, and evaluating results by collecting and reflecting on more data (*Managing Organizational Behavior*, John Wiley & Sons, 1982). Data gathering techniques include everything from surveys and questionnaires to interviews, collages, drawings, and tests. The data is often evalu-

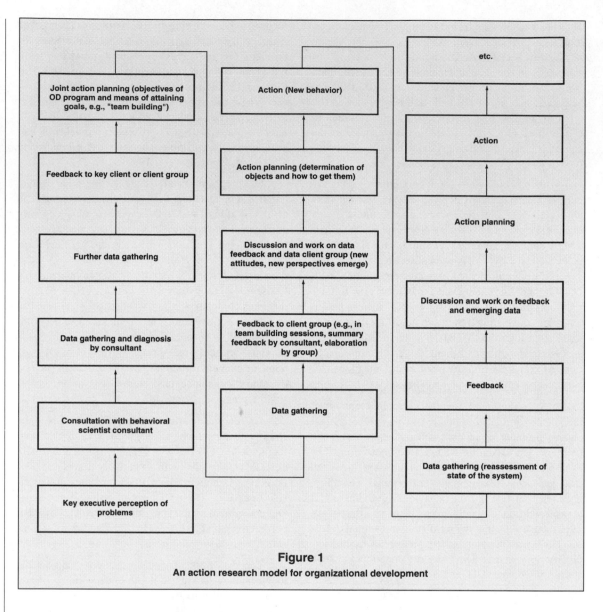

Figure 1
An action research model for organizational development

ated and interpreted using advanced statistical analysis techniques.

Action research can be thought of as the diagnostic component of the OD process. But it also encompasses the intervention component, whereby the change agent uses actions plans to intervene in the organization and make changes, as discussed below. In a continuous process, the results of actions are measured and evaluated and new action plans are devised to effect new changes. Thus, the intervention process can be considered a facet of action research.

A standard action research model was posited by W.L. French in his essay ''Organization Development: Objectives, Assumptions, and Strategies'' in *Sloan Management Review*, (1969, Vol. XII, No. 2.). As shown in the chart, the first step in the OD process is recognition of a problem by key executives. Those

managers then consult with a change agent (a group or individual), which gathers data, provides feedback to the executives, and then helps them determine change objectives. Next, the agent does new research within the context of the stated OD goals, gives more feedback, devises a plan of action, and then intervenes in the company to effect change. After (or during) the intervention(s), data is gathered, feedback is supplied, actions are planned and implemented, and the process is repeated.

INTERVENTIONS

OD interventions are plans or programs comprised of specific activities designed to effect change in some facet of an organization. Numerous interventions have been developed over the years to address different problems or create various results. However, they all are geared toward the goal of improving the entire organization through change.

In general, organizations that wish to achieve a high degree of organizational change will employ a full range of interventions, including those designed to transform individual and group behavior and attitudes. Entities attempting smaller changes will stop short of those goals, applying interventions targeted primarily toward operating policies, management structures, worker skills, and personnel policies.

OD interventions can be categorized in a number of ways, including function, the type of group for which they are intended, or the industry to which they apply. In fact, W.L. French identified 13 major ''families'' of interventions based on the type of activities that they included—activity groups included team-building, survey feedback, structural change, and career-planning (*Behavioral Science Interventions for Organization Improvement*, 3rd ed., Prentice-Hall, 1983).

One convenient method of classifying OD interventions is by group size and interrelationship, including: interpersonal relationships, group processes, intergroup systems, and the entire organization (*Organizational Behavior: The Management of Individual and Organizational Performance*, 2nd ed., Allyn and Bacon, 1994). Typically, an OD program will simultaneously integrate more than one of these interventions. A few of the more popular interventions are briefly described below.

INTERPERSONAL. Interpersonal interventions in an OD program are designed to enhance individual skills, knowledge, and effectiveness. One of the most popular interventions in this class are T-groups, which help workers become more aware of their own and their coworker's behavior patterns. A typical T-group consists of 10 to 20 volunteers. They usually meet at a specific time for one or two weeks. The meetings are unstructured, leaving the group to determine subject matter within the context of basic goals stipulated by a facilitator. As group members try to exert structure on fellow members, anxiety ensues and the group becomes more aware of their own and other's feelings and behaviors.

For example, a group of managers in a marketing department might participate in a T-group together. The members would then describe their perception of each member's behavior and the group might suggest improvements. Finally, each member would identify areas of personal improvement and then act to make changes. The end result would be that the team would become more proficient because of greater understanding and subsequent efforts to improve.

A second example of an interpersonal intervention is process consultation, which helps a company understand and alter processes by resolving interpersonal dilemmas. Although they are similar to T-groups, process consultations are more task-oriented and involve greater input by the change agent. For example, a change agent may observe an individual manager in meetings and conversations during a workday, and then make specific suggestions as to how the manager could alter his or her behavior to improve performance.

Other types of interpersonal interventions include those designed to improve the performance review process, create better training programs, help workers identify their true wants and set complementary career goals, and resolve conflict.

GROUP. OD group interventions are designed to help teams and groups within organizations become more effective. Such interventions usually assume that the most effective groups communicate well, facilitate a healthy balance between both personal and group needs, and function by consensus as opposed to autocracy or majority rule.

Group diagnostic interventions are simply meetings wherein members of a team analyze their performance, ask questions about what they need to improve, and discuss potential solutions to problems. The benefit of such interventions is that members often communicate problems that their coworkers didn't know existed (or were perceived to exist). As a result, many problems are resolved and group dynamics are improved simply as a result of the meeting(s).

Team-building meetings are similar to diagnostic interventions, but they usually involve getting the group away from the workplace for a few days. In addition, the group members go a step further than diagnosing problems by proposing, discussing, and evaluating solutions. The purpose of the meetings is to formulate specific procedures for addressing problems. The chief advantage of such interventions is that they help the team reach a consensus on solving problems (away from the pressures of the workplace), thus eliminating incongruent actions and goals that diminish the group's efficiency.

Role analysis technique (RAT) is used to help employees get a better grasp on their role in an organization. In the first step of a RAT intervention, people define their perception of their role and contribution to the overall company effort in front of a group of coworkers. Group members then provide feedback to more clearly define the role. In the second phase, the individual and the group examine ways in which the employee relies on others in the company, and how they define his or her expectations. RAT interventions help people to reduce role confusion, which can result in either conflict or the perception that some people are not doing their job. A popular intervention similar to RAT is responsibility charting, which utilizes a matrix system to assign decision and task responsibilities.

INTERGROUP. Intergroup interventions are integrated into OD programs to facilitate cooperation and efficiency between different groups within an organization. For instance, departmental interaction often deteriorates in larger organizations as different divisions battle for limited resources or become detached from the needs of other departments.

Conflict resolution meetings are one common intergroup intervention. First, different group leaders are brought together to get their commitment to the intervention. Next, the teams meet separately to make a list of their feelings about the other group(s). Then the groups meet and share their lists. Finally, the teams meet to discuss the problems and to try to develop solutions that will help both parties. This type of intervention helps to gradually diffuse tension between groups caused by lack of communication and misunderstanding.

Rotating membership interventions are used by OD change agents to minimize the negative effects of intergroup rivalry that result from employee allegiances to groups or divisions. The intervention basically entails temporarily putting group members into their rival groups. As more people interact in the different groups, greater understanding results.

OD joint activity interventions serve the same basic function as the rotating membership approach, but it involves getting members of different groups to work together toward a common goal. Similarly, common enemy interventions achieve the same results by finding an adversary common to two or more groups and then getting members of the groups to work together to overcome the threat. Examples of common enemies include competitors, government regulation, and economic conditions.

COMPREHENSIVE. OD comprehensive interventions are used to directly create change throughout an entire organization, rather than focusing on organizational change through subgroup interventions. One of the most popular comprehensive interventions is survey feedback. This technique basically entails surveying employee attitudes at all levels of the hierarchy and then reporting the findings back to them.The employees then use the data in feedback sessions to create solutions to perceived problems. A number of questionnaires developed specifically for such interventions have been developed.

Structural change interventions are used by OD change agents to effect organizational alterations related to departmentalization, management hierarchy, work policies, compensation and benefit incentives programs, and other elements. Often, the implemented changes emanate from feedback from other interven-

tions. One benefit of change interventions is that companies can often realize an immediate and very significant impact as a result of relatively minor modifications.

Sociotechnical system design interventions are similar to structural change techniques, but they typically emphasize the reorganization of work teams. The basic goal is to create independent groups throughout the company that supervise themselves, including administering pay and benefits, disciplining team members, and monitoring quality, among other responsibilities. The theoretic benefit of sociotechnical system design interventions is that worker and group productivity and quality is increased because workers have more control over (and subsequent satisfaction from) the process in which they participate.

A fourth OD intervention that became extremely popular during the 1980s and early 1990s is **total quality management** (TQM), which is largely a corollary of Deming's work. TQM interventions utilize established quality techniques and programs that emphasize quality processes, rather than achieving quality by inspecting products and services after processes have been completed. The important concept of continuous improvement embodied by TQM has carried over into other OD interventions.

OD SUCCESS STORY

An exemplary illustration of how OD can change an organization for the better is the initiative undertaken by General Motors Corp. at its Tarrytown, New York auto assembly plant in the 1970s. By the late 1960s, Tarrytown had earned a reputation as one the least productive plants in the company. Labor relations and quality were at an all-time low, and absenteeism was rampant, when GM finally decided to take action.

Realizing the seriousness of the situation, plant managers tried something new—they sought direct input from laborers about all aspects of the plant operations. Then they began to implement the ideas with success, sparking interest in a more comprehensive OD effort. Thus, in the early 1970s, GM initiated a quality-of-work-life (QWL) program, an OD program that integrates several types of interventions. The goal of QWLs is to improve organizational efficiency through employee well-being and participative decision-making.

In 1973, the union leaders signed a "letter of agreement" with management in which both groups agreed to commit themselves to exploring specific OD initiatives that could improve the plant. The plant hired an outside consultant to oversee the change process. The initial research stage included a series of problem-solving training sessions, during which 34 workers from two shifts would meet for eight hours on Saturdays. Those meetings succeeded in helping plant managers to improve productivity. Therefore, in 1977 management increased the scope of the OD program by launching a plantwide effort that included 3,800 managers and laborers.

Although the OD program eventually cost GM more than $1.5 million, it paid off in the long run through greater productivity, higher quality, and improved labor relations. For example, the number of pending grievances plummeted from 2,000 in 1972 to only 32 by 1978. Absenteeism dropped as well, from more than seven percent to less than three percent. In fact, by the late 1970s the Tarrytown plant was recognized as one of the most productive and best run in the entire GM organization.

[Dave Mote]

FURTHER READING:

Burke, W. Warner. *Organization Development: A Normative View.* Reading, MA: Addison-Wesley Publishing Company, 1987.

Cherrington, David J. *Organizational Behavior: The Management of Individual and Organizational Performance.* Boston: Allyn and Bacon, 1994.

Connor, Patricke E. and Linda K. Lake. *Managing Organizational Change.* New York: Praeger Publishers, 1988.

French, W.L. "Organization Development: Objectives, Assumptions, and Strategies." *Sloan Management Review* 12 No. 2.

French, W.L. *Behavioral Science Interventions for Organization Improvement*, 3rd ed., New York: Prentice-Hall, 1983.

Gray, Jerry L., and Frederick A. Starke. *Organizational Behavior: Concepts and Applications*, 4th ed. Columbus, OH: Merrill Publishing Company, 1988.

Huse, E.F., and T.G. Cummings. *Organizational Development and Change.* St. Paul, MN: West, 1985.

Ivancevich, John M., and Michael T. Matteson. *Organizational Behavior and Management.* Homewood, IL: Richard D. Irwin, Inc., 1990.

Northcraft, Gregory B., and Margaret A. Neale. *Organizational Behavior: A Management Challenge.* Chicago: The Dryden Press, 1990.

Schermerhorn, Jr., John R., James G. Hunt, and Richard N. Osborn. *Managing Organizational Behavior.* New York: John Wiley & Sons. 1982.

ORGANIZATIONAL GROWTH

Growth is something for which most companies, large or small, strive. Small firms want to get big, big firms want to get bigger. Organizational growth, however, means different things to different organizations. How, then, is growth defined? How is it achieved? How does a company survive it?

MEASURING GROWTH

There are many parameters a company can select to measure its growth. The most meaningful yardstick is one that shows progress with respect to an organization's stated goals as in the following examples.

NUMBER OF EMPLOYEES. Some businesspeople boast of the number of employees in their companies or departments. Employees in and of themselves, however, cost money. A better employee-based measure of growth is change in company or departmental revenue generated per employee. This, then, becomes a valuable measure of increasing (or decreasing) productivity, rather than a measure of labor and salary expense.

DOLLAR REVENUES. Every business magazine or newspaper describes a company by its revenues as an "X million dollar company." Although used frequently, the pitfall of relying on gross revenue or gross margin as a measure of growth for an organization is that it completely ignores the expenses associated with generating those revenues. Greater revenues do not necessarily mean greater profitability. In periods of very quick "growth," expenses can spiral upward and out of control leaving a company strapped for cash and facing an uncertain future, at best.

More useful, revenue-based measures of growth are increases (or decreases) in net profit or net margins. These methods account for the expenses incurred in generating revenues for the firm and identify the portion that is truly added to the bottom line. This amount is the cash flow that can be invested to fuel the real growth of a company.

ACHIEVING GROWTH

While there are many academic models depicting the growth stages of a company, management guru Tom Peters strongly suggests several real-world ways for companies large and small to achieve organizational growth. The business press routinely reports on the activities of companies employing these suggestions.

JOINT VENTURE/ALLIANCE. This strategy is particularly effective for smaller firms with limited resources; however, in a business environment where changing demand, supply, and manufacturing or service conditions are an everyday occurrence, "partnering" makes sense for the large organization as well. Forming joint ventures or alliances gives all companies involved the flexibility to move on to different projects upon completion of the first, or restructure agreements to continue working together. Subcontracting, for example, allows firms to concentrate on those portions of their businesses which they do best.

Joint ventures and alliances inject partners with new ideas, access to new technologies, new approaches, and new markets, all of which can have positive implications for the growth of all firms involved. Creating ventures with upstart or overseas firms may present the best opportunities for accomplishing this.

LICENSING. "License your most advanced technology," advised Tom Peters. The idea behind this is that no technologies can be truly proprietary today. A rival or an outsider will soon copy whatever a company has developed. Save competitors the hassle of and profit from copying by selling current technology. This creates cash flow for the company to fund future **research and development** and creates switching costs by making others dependent upon a firm's applications.

SELL OFF OLD WINNERS. Getting rid of the **cash cow** operations to focus on growing newer enterprises can make sense for organizations trying to grow. Even though it sounds contradictory at first, top dollar is commanded in the market for this kind of business and the necessary capital to fuel growth of other operations is generated. The decline of a sold cash cow is left up to the new owner. Meanwhile, ventures that were new at the time of that sale may now be cash cows ripe for picking. An addendum to this line of thinking is the divesting of older technology or products. Emerging markets such as Latin America and Eastern Europe have been favorite places for companies to get rid of outdated products or technology. These markets may not yet be able to afford state-of-the-art goods, but can still benefit from older models.

NEW MARKETS. Entering new markets is an obvious way to expand a company. Creating additional demand for a firm's product or service, especially in a market where competition has yet to fully develop, is a much sought after experience for growing enterprises. As more and more companies move parts of their operations off-shore, more opportunity and awareness is created for other companies to serve the markets in those foreign locations.

NEW/COMPLEMENTARY PRODUCT DEVELOPMENT. Some of the strategies suggested here benefit the firm in generating cash. Product or service development is a smart place to use that cash in order to create future growth for the firm. Put that money to work by investing in new products, either outright new products or those that complement existing products. These products will be the basis for future revenues and cash flows.

VENTURE CAPITAL/IPO. For companies small or large, growth must be funded, but where can one get the money? Where large public firms issue stock or **debt**, smaller private firms search for capital from **banks**, private investors, or **venture capital** firms. A venture capital firm will provide cash to firms it expects will have extremely fast growth. The venture capital firms will expect to be rewarded for its capital infusion with large payoffs at an initial **public offering** (IPO), the point at which the small private firm issues public stock.

ACQUISITION. Both small and large firms get bigger by buying other companies. Merger-mania cyclically sweeps the business world as a preferred method to increase a company's size, revenues, product or service offering, etc. The takeover frenzy of the 1980s has returned to Western markets. Successful **mergers and acquisitions** will blend resources to create a synergy while improving existing core competencies.

For any company that has achieved growth, the work has just begun. Managing and sustaining that growth is imperative if the initial progress is to have any lasting positive effects for the company.

[Richard C. Cuthie]

FURTHER READING:

Bildner, James L. "Hitting the Wall." *Inc.* July, 1995, pp. 21-22.

Churchill, Neil C., and Virginia A. Lewis. "The Five Stages of Small Business Growth." *Harvard Business Review.* May-June, 1983, pp. 30-42.

Grousbeck, H. Irving, Michael J. Roberts, and Howard H. Stevenson. *New Business Ventures and the Entrepreneur.* 4th ed. Boston: Richard D. Irwin, 1994.

Jemison, David B., and Sim B. Sitkin. "Acquisitions: The Process Can Be a Problem." *Harvard Business Review.* March-April, 1986.

Kotter, John P., Vijay Sathe, and Leonard A. Schlesinger. *Organization: Text, Cases, and Readings on the Management of Organizational Design and Change.* Homewood, IL: Richard D. Irwin, 1986.

Peters, Tom. "Get Innovative or Get Dead, Part I." *California Business Review.* Fall, 1990, pp. 9-26.

ORGANIZATIONAL LIFE CYCLE

Organizational life cycle (OLC) is a model which proposes that over time business firms move through a fairly predictable sequence of developmental stages. This model is linked to the study of **organizational growth** and development. It is based on a biological metaphor, that is, business firms resemble living organisms because they demonstrate a regular pattern of developmental process: birth, growth, maturity, decline, and death. In a summary of OLC models, Quinn and Cameron (1983, p. 33) state that the models typically propose that "... changes that occur in organizations follow a predictable pattern that can be characterized by developmental stages. These stages are sequential in nature; occur as a hierarchical progression that is not easily reversed; and involve a broad range of organizational activities and structures."

Hanks *et al.* (1993) propose five OLC stages: start-up, expansion, maturity, diversification, and decline.

While a number of business and **management** theorists alluded to developmental stages in the early to mid 1900s, Mason Haire (1959) is generally recognized as one of the first theorists to use a biological model for organizational growth and to argue that organizational growth and development follows a regular sequence. Chandler (1962) influenced later OLC research with his argument, based on a study of four large U.S. firms, that as a firm's **strategy** changed over time, there must be associated changes in the firm's structure. In the period 1972-1993, a very conservative estimate of the number of scholarly articles and books which focused specifically on OLC is about 65. The number of life cycle stages proposed in these works ranges from three to ten; the most frequently occurring number of stages is five, with a four-stage model a close second. Organizational life cycle is an important model because of its premise and its prescription. The model's premise is that requirements, opportunities, and threats both inside and outside the business firm will vary depending on the stage of development in which the firm finds itself. For example, threats in the start-up stage differ from those in the maturity stage. As the firm moves through the developmental stages, changes in the nature and number of requirements, opportunities, and threats exert pressure for change on the business firm. Baird and Meshoulam (1988) state that organizations move from one stage to another because the fit between the organization and its environment is so inadequate that either the organization's efficiency and/or effectiveness is seriously impaired or the organization's survival is threatened. The OLC model's prescription is that the firm's managers must change the business' goals, strategies and strategy implementation devices to fit the new set of issues. Thus, different stages of the company's life cycle require alterations in the firm's objectives, strategies, managerial processes (planning, organizing, staffing, directing, controlling), technology, culture, and **decision making**. For example, in a longitudinal study of 36 corporations, Miller and Friesen (1984) proposed five growth stages: birth, growth, maturity, decline, and revival. They traced changes in the organizational structure and managerial processes as the business firms proceeded through the stages. At birth, the firms exhibited a very simple organizational structure with authority centralized at the top of the hierarchy. As the firms grew, they adapted more sophisticated structures and decentralized authority to middle- and lower-level managers. At maturity, the firms demonstrated significantly more concern for internal efficiency and installed more control mechanisms and processes.

What else must change as an organization moves through the stages of the life cycle? Quinn and Came-ron (1983) propose that the criteria for an organization's effectiveness change. Smith, Mitchell, and Summer (1985) note changes in the organization's reward system, type of organization structure, communication and decision-making processes, and the composition of top-level management staff. Types of employees and **human resource management** practices may also require alteration.

Hanks *et al.* (1993) asked two salient questions in comparing ten life cycle models: what constitutes a life cycle stage and what are the characteristics of each stage? In answer to the first question, they conclude that a given life-cycle stage is a multidimensional phenomenon and is distinguished from other stages "... by differences in the pattern and magnitude of these dimensions" (p. 7). These stage-distinguishing dimensions are categorized as either contextual or structural. Contextual dimensions were "... organization age, size, growth rate, and focal tasks or challenges faced by the firm." Stage-distinguishing structural dimensions were "... structural form, formalization, centralization, and vertical differentiation, the number of organization levels." Table 1 provides Hanks *et al.* (1993) "... synthesis of the ten models by dimension and stage."

While about 65 scholarly works focusing on organizational life cycles have appeared in the period 1972-1993, the majority are conceptual and hypothetical. Only a small minority attempt to test empirically the organizational life cycle model. A widely-cited conceptual work is that by Greiner (1972). Greiner used five growth phases: growth through creativity; growth through direction; growth through delegation; growth through coordination; and growth through collaboration. Each growth stage encompasses an evolutionary phase, "... prolonged periods of growth where no major upheaval occurs in organization practices," and a revolutionary phase—"... periods of substantial turmoil in organization life." The evolutionary phases are hypothesized to be about four to eight years. The revolutionary phases are characterized as the crisis phases. At the end of each one of the five growth stages listed above, Greiner hypothesized that a crisis will occur. Phase (1), growth through creativity eventually leads to a crisis of **leadership**. More sophisticated and more formalized management practices must be adopted. If the founders can't or won't take on this responsibility, they must hire someone who can, and give this person significant authority. Phase (2), growth through direction, eventually leads to a crisis of autonomy. Lower-level managers must be given more authority if the organization is to continue to grow. The crisis involves top-level managers' reluctance to delegate authority. Phase (3), growth through delegation, eventually leads to a crisis of control. As "... autonomous field managers prefer to run their own shows" without interference from the

Table 1
Life-Cycle Stage Characteristics: Common Patterns

Dimension	Start-Up Stage	Expansion Stage	Consolidation Stage	Diversification Stage	Decline Stage
Age	Young	....	....	Older	Any Age
Size	Small	....	Large	Largest	Declining
Growth Rate	Inconsist	Rapid positive	Slow growth	Rapid positive	Declining
Structural Form	Undifferentiated, Simple	Departmentalized, Functional	Departmentalized, Functional	Divisional	Mostly Functional
Formalization	Very informal, personal flexible; Few policies	Formal system begin to emerge, but enforcement is lax	Formal bureaucratic: Planning & control systems are enforced	Formal, bureaucratic	Excessive bureaucratization
Centralization	Highly centralized in founder	Centralized; Limited delegation	Moderately centralized	Decentralized	Moderately centralized
Business Tasks	Identify niche; Obtain resources; Build prototype; Set up task structure	Volume production & distribution; Capacity Expansion; Set up operating systems	Make business profitable; Expense control; Establish management systems	Diversification; Expansion of product market scope	Revitalization; Redefinition of mission and strategy

rest of the organization, top management perceives that they are losing control of a diversified company. Phase (4), growth through coordination, eventually leads to crisis of red tape. Coordination techniques like product groups, formal planning processes, and corporate staff become, over time, a bureaucratic system that causes delays in decision making and a reduction in **innovation**. As Greiner notes: "... the organization has become too large and complex to be managed through formal programs and rigid systems." Phase (5), growth through collaboration, is characterized by the use of teams, a reduction in corporate staff, matrix-type structures, the simplification of formal systems, an increase in conferences and educational programs, and more sophisticated information systems. While Greiner does not formally delineate a crisis for phase (5), he guesses that it may revolve around "the psychological saturation of employees who grow emotionally and physically exhausted by the intensity of team work and the heavy pressure for innovative solutions." Greiner summarizes his model in Table 2. Greiner reminds the reader that managers must realize that solutions to a given crisis will cause a future crisis to emerge and that not all companies survive each crisis point. He also cautions against skipping phases because "each phase results in certain strengths and learning experiences in the organization that will be essential for success in subsequent phases." Crises "... provide the pressure, ideas and awareness that afford a platform for change and the introduction of new practices."

[John G. Maurer]

FURTHER READING:

Baird, L., and I. Meshoulam. "Managing Two Fits of Strategic Human Resource Management," *Academy of Management Review* 13(1), January, 1988, pp. 116-128.

Chandler, A. *Strategy and Structure: Chapters in the History of the Industrial Enterprise.* Cambridge, MA: MIT Press, 1962.

Churchill, N., and V. Lewis, "The Five Stages of Small Business Growth," *Harvard Business Review*, 61 (3) May-June 1983, pp. 30-50.

Dodge, H., and J. Robbins, "An Empirical Investigation of the Organizational Life Cycle Model for Small Business Development and Survival," *Journal of Small Business Management*, 30 (1) January, 1992, pp. 27-37.

Greiner, L. "Evolution and Revolution as Organizations Grow," *Harvard Business Review*, 50 (4), July-August, 1972, pp. 37-46.

Haire, M. "Biological Models and Empirical Histories of the Growth of Organizations," M. Haire (Ed.) *Modern Organization Theory.* New York: John Wiley & Sons, 1959, pp. 272-306.

Hanks, S., C. Watson, E. Jansen, and G. Chandler, "Tightening the Life-Cycle Construct: A Taxonomic Study of Growth Stage Configurations in High-Technology Organizations," *Entrepreneurship Theory and Practice*, 18 (2) Winter, 1993, pp. 5-29.

Kazanjian, R. "Relation of Dominant Problems to Stages of Growth in Technology-Based New Ventures," *Academy of Management Journal,* 31 (2) June 1988, pp. 257-279.

Miller, D., and P. Friesen, "A Longitudinal Study of the Corporate Life Cycle," *Management Science,* 30 (10) October, 1984, pp. 1161-1183.

Quinn, R., and K. Cameron, "Organizational Life Cycles and Shifting Criteria of Effectiveness: Some Preliminary Evidence," *Management Science,* 29 (1) January, 1983, pp. 33-51.

Smith, K., T. Mitchell, and C. Summer, "Top Level Management Priorities in Different Stages of the Organizational Life

Table 2

Organization Practices During Evolution in the Five Phases of Growth

Category	Phase 1	Phase 2	Phase 3	Phase 4	Phase 5
Management Focus	Make & sell	Efficiency of operations	Expansion of market	Consolidation of organization	Problem solving & innovation
Organization Structure	Informal	Centralized & functional	Decentralized & geographical	Line-staff & product groups	Matrix of teams
Top Management Style	Individualistic & entrepreneurial	Directive	Delegative	Watchdog	Participative
Control System	Market results	Standards & cost centers	Reports & profit centers	Plans & investment centers	Mutual goal setting
Management Reward Emphasis	Ownership	Salary & merit increases	Individual bonus	Profit sharing & stock options	Team bonus

Cycle," *Academy of Management Journal,* 28 (4) December, 1985, pp. 799-820.

Tyebjee, T., A. Bruno, and S. McIntyre, "Growing Ventures Can Anticipate Marketing Stages," *Harvard Business Review,* 61 (1) January-February, 1983, pp. 62-66.

ORIGINAL ISSUE DISCOUNT (OID)

Original issue discount (OID) refers to a **debt** instrument initially issued at a price substantially below its face amount (i.e., at a deep discount). OIDs can also be **bonds** issued as zero-coupon bonds. A zero-coupon bond (also referred to simply as a zero) has no stated or coupon interest rate and therefore pays no periodic interest. Non-zero deep discounted bonds are priced well below par at issuance but have regular semi-annual or annual interest payments based on their stated interest rate.

BACKGROUND

In the late 1970s and early 80s, **interest rates** were at historic highs. In an attempt to reduce their periodic cash outflows for interest, borrowers, both corporate and governmental, began issuing bonds carrying very low stated or coupon interest rates relative to those prevailing in the marketplace. During the 1980s many **leveraged buyouts** were financed with deep discount bonds of questionable **credit** worthiness and earned the name "**junk bonds.**"

The U.S. Treasury has been selling zero coupon bonds for many years in the form of Series E and EE U.S. savings bonds. For example, a $37.50 investment in a U.S. savings bond can return $50.00 at its matu-rity with no periodic interest payments. The interest return to the investor is implied in the difference between the deep discounted price ($37.50) and the maturity value of the bond ($50.00). The U.S. Treasury adjusts their yield by changing the time to maturity.

By 1982 the popularity of zeros encouraged the U.S. Treasury to allow U.S. government securities dealers to strip the semi-annual interest coupons from a group of bonds, and to sell blocks of same-maturity coupons and principal to investors as a zero-coupon bond derivative (ZCBD). Broker/dealers developed portfolios of ZCBDs bearing the name of aggressive, coy animals:

- LIONs - Lehman Brothers' Lehman Investment Opportunity Notes;

- TIGRs - Merrill Lynch's Treasury Investment Growth Receipts;

- CATS - Salomon Brothers' Certificate of Accrual on Treasury Securities.

In 1985 the U.S. Treasury began issuing notes and bonds tailored as zeros known as Separate Trading of Registered Interest and Principal Securities (STRIPS).

Municipalities also worked zeros into their debt structures. The high interest rates during the 1980s made it almost impossible to issue municipal bonds. The Tax Reform Act of 1986 lowered the maximum tax bracket to 33 percent, making the tax-free aspects of munis less attractive. In the face of high debt costs, declining demand, and decreasing bond ratings, municipalities began issuing zeros with U.S. Treasury-backed zeros as collateral.

PROS AND CONS OF OIDS

There are advantages of OIDs and zeros for both issuers and investors and a distinct tax disadvantage for the investors. The tax effects are discussed below.

ISSUERS. The major advantage to an issuer is that because of the lower coupon or stated interest rates, the issuing firm's periodic interest payments are considerably smaller than would otherwise be the case. Another advantage to the issuer is that OIDs tend to carry original yields to maturity which are less than those of similar quality non-OID bonds.

INVESTORS. OIDs, whether purchased at issue or in the secondary market, are convenient and affordable in that they require a low initial investment and provide an implied automatic reinvestment of interest. However, there are some special tax rules. Investors are also attracted to deep discount or zero coupon bonds because they have very little reinvestment rate risk. One of the problems facing an investor in securities which pay periodic returns to their holders (either **dividends** or interest) is how to reinvest those payments in instruments yielding at least as much as the anticipated yield to maturity of the original security. When interest rates are declining, this becomes an increasingly difficult task. By purchasing a zero coupon bond, an investor eliminates this problem because there are no periodic interest payments. Therefore, there is no reinvestment rate risk.

Aside from the adverse tax ramifications discussed below, the major disadvantage of an OID is that because of its very low interest rate relative to the prevailing market rate, the price volatility of these instruments is much greater than traditional debt instruments (see illustration).

PRICING AND YIELDS

The pricing of a zero coupon bond is a straight forward present value computation. It is simply the present value of the face amount of the bond discounted for the time remaining to maturity at the prevailing market rate of interest for bonds of similar risk. For example, assume a 20 year, $10,000 face value zero is issued in a market demanding a seven percent yield to maturity, compounded semi-annually. Its price would be 0.2526 of par, or $2,526, plus commissions. Investors purchasing at that price are able to lock in a compounded rate of interest of seven percent regardless of what subsequently happens to market rates until the bond matures. Recognize this is a two-edged sword: an upward change in interest rates, of course, will decrease the market value of zeros and OIDs just as a decrease in interest rates will increase market value.

Assuming market interest rates remain at seven percent, our seven point zero percent. 20-year zero,

compounded semi-annually, per $10,000 face value, if held by the original purchaser, would have the following values:

End of Year	Theoretical Value
Table 1	
Value of Zero Coupon Bond	
1.	$2,706
2.	2,898
5.	3,563
10.	5,026
20.	10,000

Recalling the statement made earlier about the price volatility of OIDS, note that if interest rates should rise to eight percent at the end of the first year, this bond would decline in value to $2,253 or − 16.7 percent. Had the bond been originally issued with a seven percent coupon its price would fall from $10,000 to only $9,032 or nine point seven percent.

The yield to maturity of an OID is calculated the same as for any other bond. The yield to maturity is that interest rate which equates the present value of the remaining interest payments and the face amount of the bond to the bond's current market price. The yield to maturity can be derived from present value tables, bond yield tables, or by using internal rate of return programs in financial calculators or in computer spreadsheets.

TAX CONSIDERATIONS

OIDS WITH A COUPON. Investors in OID debt with a coupon or stated interest rate will pay income taxes on both the periodic interest payments received and the annual **amortization** of the OID. The amortization is calculated using the compound, or effective, interest rate implied in the bond. Both components are taxed at ordinary (i.e., non-capital gain) income tax rates. Investors purchasing previously issued OID bonds at less than face are also subject to this provision.

Brokers who sell OIDs are responsible for keeping a list of OIDs, their issue dates, and issue price to facilitate taxpayers' filing requirements, and are required to file a form 1099-OID to accounts holding OIDs. This form may be insufficient if OIDs are purchased after the issue date in the secondary market, and also because the reporting requirements have periodically changed, as explained in IRS Publication 1212. Pub. 1212 also contains a list of OIDs as does *Moody's Municipal Bond Guide.*

The simplest reporting of OID involves an investor who holds an original issue. The 1099-OID will indicate the taxable portion of the OID for the period. Pub. 1212 provides the per-diem rate to use if the bond was sold during the year.

There are special rules for: (1) the reporting of OID for bonds which were originally issued with OID and are then purchased in the secondary market, and (2) the determination of the gain or loss on the sale of a bond with OID. Holders of either taxable or tax-exempt OIDs are referred to **Internal Revenue Service** Publication 550, ''Investment Income and Expense.'' OID rules do not apply to U.S. Savings Bonds or to OID bonds or obligations with a maturity date of one year or less from the date of issue.

ZEROS. The taxation of both the related implied interest income and interest expense on zeros is covered by special provisions within the Internal Revenue Code.

Since zeros have no stated or coupon interest rate, no interest is either paid or received annually. However, the taxpayer must report and pay taxes on the amount accrued each year as though received, and the issuer expenses the accrued amount as though paid. Using the above example, in the first year of the bond, an investor would report interest income and the issue would report interest expense of $180 ($2706-$2526). Because of the need to pay tax on income never received in cash and the increase in marginal tax rates between 1987 and 1995, the demand for taxable zeros has dried up in recent years. However, even taxables may be appropriate investments if they are going to be used to fund IRAs (**Individual Retirement Accounts**) or Keogh plans since no tax is paid on the earnings in these accounts.

Some of the more generous zeros and OIDs have call provisions which issuers would exercise if the refunding would reduce their overall liabilities in the long run. If an OID bond is issued with the intention of calling the debt before maturity, any gain on the retirement or refunding is treated an ordinary income to the investor.

Corporate borrowers find zeros very attractive for the opposite reason: they are able to take tax deductions for the implied interest they never paid, thus effectively lowering their after-tax cost of borrowing.

MUNICIPAL ZEROS. The market discount and the OID income of munis are tax free. As a result, except for their use in tax-exempt retirement plans, investors now find taxable zeros much less attractive than non-taxables.

SEE ALSO: Refinancing

[Ronald M. Horwitz]

FURTHER READING:

Bierman, Harold, Jr. and Seymour Smidt. *Financial Management for Decision Making.* Macmillan Publishing Company, 1986.

Sharpe, William, F., and Gordon J. Alexander. *Investments.* 4th ed. Prentice Hall, 1990.

Shillinglaw, Gordon, and Philip E. Meyer. *Accounting, A Management Approach.* 7th ed. Richard D. Irwin, Inc., 1983.

OUTPLACEMENT

SEE: Employee Outplacement

OUTSOURCING

Outsourcing is when a company purchases products or services from an outside supplier, rather than performing the same work within its own facilities, in order to cut **costs**. The decision to outsource is a major strategic one for most companies, since it involves weighing the potential cost savings against the consequences of a loss in control over the product or service. Some common examples of outsourcing include **manufacturing** of components, computer programming services, **tax** compliance and other **accounting** functions, and payroll and other human resource functions. According to research conducted by *CFO: The Magazine for Senior Financial Executives,* there were 146,000 outsourcers providing products or services to other companies in the United States as of December 1994, an increase of 65 percent from the 88,000 that existed in 1989.

The growth in outsourcing in recent years is partly the result of a general shift in business philosophy. Prior to the mid-1980s, many companies sought to acquire other companies and diversify their business interests in order to reduce risk. As more companies discovered that there were limited advantages to running a large group of unrelated businesses, however, many began to divest **subsidiaries** and refocus their efforts on one or a few closely related areas of business. Companies tried to identify or develop a ''core competence,'' a unique combination of experience and expertise that would provide a source of competitive advantage in a given industry. All aspects of the company's operations were aligned around the core competence, and any activities or functions that were not considered necessary to preserve it were then outsourced.

Successful outsourcing thus requires a strong understanding of the organization's capabilities and future direction. As William R. King explained in *Information Systems Management,* "Decisions regarding outsourcing significant functions are among the most strategic that can be made by an organization, because they address the basic organizational choice of the functions for which internal expertise is developed and nurtured and those for which such expertise is purchased. These are basic decisions regarding organizational design." Outsourcing based only upon a comparison of costs can lead companies to miss opportunities to gain knowledge that might lead to the development of new products or technologies. *Business Week* called companies that had outsourced too many of their core functions "hollow corporations," and claimed that they had relinquished their reason for existence.

Outsourcing can be undertaken to varying degrees, ranging from total outsourcing to selective outsourcing. Total outsourcing may involve dismantling entire departments or divisions and transferring the employees, facilities, equipment, and complete responsibility for a product or function to an outside vendor. In contrast, selective outsourcing may target a single, time-consuming task within a department, such as preparing the payroll or manufacturing a minor component, that can be handled more efficiently by an outside specialist. The opposite of outsourcing is insourcing, when a staff function within a company markets its product or service to external as well as internal customers.

STRATEGIES FOR OUTSOURCING

Companies that decide to outsource do so for a number of reasons. The primary reason is to achieve cost savings or better cost control over the outsourced function. Companies usually outsource to a vendor that specializes in a given function and performs that function more efficiently than the company could. Anticipated cost savings sometimes fail to materialize, however, because the vendor must make a profit and because the company incurs additional **transaction costs** when interacting with the vendor. Another common reason for outsourcing is to achieve headcount reductions or minimize the fluctuations in staffing that may occur due to changes in demand for a product or service. Companies also outsource in order to reduce the workload on their employees, or to provide more development opportunities for their employees by freeing them from tedious tasks.

Some companies outsource in order to eliminate distractions and force themselves to concentrate on their core competencies. Still others outsource to achieve greater financial flexibility, since the sale of assets that formerly supported an outsourced function can improve a company's cash flow. A possible pitfall

in this reasoning is that many vendors demand long-term **contracts**, which may reduce flexibility. A common reason for outsourcing computer programming and other **information technology** functions is to gain access to new technology and outside expertise. Some experts claim, however, that companies are exposed to new technology by vendors anyway, and that they could simply hire people with the expertise they seek. Company politics is another common reason for outsourcing. For example, some companies might begin outsourcing initiatives after observing the successful efforts of a competitor. Others might be pushed toward outsourcing by managers seeking personal gain or by a desire to eliminate troublesome departments. Finally, outsourcing provides an attractive option for start-up firms as they grow.

Some of the major potential disadvantages to outsourcing include poor **quality control**, decreased company loyalty, a lengthy bid process, and a loss of strategic alignment. There may also be inherent advantages of maintaining certain functions internally. For example, company employees may have a better understanding of the industry, and their vested interests may mean they are more likely to make decisions in accordance with the company's goals. A general rule of thumb is that companies should never outsource any function that directly affects quality or service.

Once a company has made the decision to outsource, there are still a number of factors it must consider in making a successful transition and forming a partner relationship with the vendor. Ethel Scully recommended a series of steps for companies to follow in *National Underwriter.* First, the company needs to obtain the support of key personnel for the decision to outsource. Many companies encounter resistance from employees who feel that their jobs are threatened by outsourcing. Scully suggested forming a team consisting of an outsourcing expert, representatives from senior **management** and human resources, and the managers of all affected areas of the company to help address employee concerns about the decision. Then the company can begin contacting potential vendors, either formally or informally, and asking specific questions about the services provided and the terms of the contract. It is also important for the company to develop tangible measures of job performance before entering into an agreement. Finally, the company should select a vendor it trusts in order to develop a mutually beneficial partner relationship.

[Laurie Collier Hillstrom]

FURTHER READING:

Elliot, Vince. "Outsourcing without Risk," *Journal of Property Management.* January/February 1995, pp. 40-41.

Foxman, Noah. "Succeeding in Outsourcing," *Information Systems Management.* Winter 1994, pp. 77-80.

Hammond, Keith H. "The New World of Work," *Business Week*. October 17, 1994, pp. 76-87.

King, William R. "Strategic Outsourcing Decisions," *Information Systems Management*. Fall 1994, pp. 58-61.

Lacity, Mary, Rudy Hirschheim, and Leslie Willcocks. "Realizing Outsourcing Expectations: Incredible Expectations, Credible Outcomes," *Information Systems Management*. Fall 1994, pp. 7-18.

Mello, John P. "Outsource Taxes? Why Not?," *CFO: The Magazine for Senior Financial Executives*. January 1995, pp. 75-76.

Meyer, N. Dean. "A Sensible Approach to Outsourcing: The Economic Fundamentals," *Information Systems Management*. Fall 1994, pp. 23-27.

Scott, Miriam Basch. "Outsourcing Affords Employers Improved Administration, Benefits," *Employee Benefit Plan Review*. November 1994, pp. 44-45.

Scully, Ethel. "Many Factors to Weigh in Decision to Outsource," *National Underwriter*. January 16, 1995, pp. 10-11.

Springsteel, Ian. "Outsourcing Is Everywhere," *CFO: The Magazine for Senior Financial Executives*. December 1994, p. 23.

OVER-THE-COUNTER SECURITIES MARKETS

An over-the-counter (OTC) securities market is a secondary market through which buyers and sellers of securities (or their agents or brokers) consummate transactions. Secondary markets (securities markets where previously issued securities are re-traded) are mainly organized in two ways. One is to form an organized exchange, where buyers and sellers of securities (mostly represented by their agents or brokers) meet at a central place to conduct their transactions. The New York Stock Exchange (NYSE), the American Stock Exchange (located in New York) and the Chicago Board of Trade for Commodities are examples of major organized exchanges in the United States. An over-the-counter securities market provides an alternative way of organizing a secondary market—in this, dealers with inventories of securities at different geographical locations are in contact with each other through a computer network. In other words, these dealers of securities are ready to buy or sell securities over the counter to anyone who contacts them and accepts their quoted price. One may thus describe an over-the-counter securities market as an electronic market. The **National Association of Securities Dealers Automated Quotations System (NASDAQ)** is an example of an over-the-counter securities market in the United States.

THE EVOLUTION OF THE OVER-THE-COUNTER MARKETS

The NASDAQ over-the-counter market was established in 1971. Before the NASDAQ was insti-
tuted, trading in OTC securities used to be a rather haphazard operation—individual broker/dealer firms bought and sold securities for their own accounts. In doing so, they acted as dealers, not brokers. For larger OTC **stocks**, a dozen or so firms quoted bid and asked prices for securities—account executives relied on these quoted prices in buying and selling securities for their customers. However, for many small over-the-counter securities, only a couple of firms made a market—that is, quoted bid and asked prices. Thus, one could never be sure if one got the best price. Moreover, record keeping was done on "pink sheets" that recorded bids and offers, not actual trades. The computer system replaced the telephone communications mechanism in 1971 and has provided a far better method of uncovering the best price.

EFFICIENCY OF THE OTC MARKETS

Since over-the-counter securities dealers are in computer contact with each other, they know the prices set by one another. As a result, an OTC market is very competitive and is not significantly different from a securities market that utilizes an organized exchange. Nevertheless, it is fair to say that the stocks of the largest and the best known corporations are traded on the NYSE, often called the Big Board. This provides the NYSE with high visibility—it is considered the real marketplace. The trading in shares of approximately 2,000 corporations takes place on the floor of the exchange; transactions are recorded on an electronic ticker tape flashed on the floor itself as well as in brokerage offices throughout the country. As a consequence of the emphasis on Big Board stocks, the common stocks listed on over-the-counter markets are often called secondary issues.

OVER-THE-COUNTER MARKETS FOR DIFFERENT SECURITIES

There are over-the-counter securities markets for a variety of financial securities or instruments. The most widely followed is the over-the-counter market in common stocks. While the largest corporations have their stocks traded at the New York Stock Exchange, not all common stocks traded in the NASDAQ market are small. For example, IBM Corp., AT&T, or General Motors Corp. stocks (that are also part of the 30 common stocks included in the widely followed Dow Jones Industrial Average index) are traded on the Big Board. However, many widely known common stocks, such as Intel Corp. or MCI Communications Corp. are traded in the over-the-counter stock market. Both the NYSE and the NASDAQ market have a large number of small common stocks.

The financial market in U.S. government **bonds** is also set up as an over-the-counter market. It is important to note that the U.S. government bond market has a larger trading volume than the NYSE. The OTC market in government bonds was established by approximately forty dealers in Treasury bonds who were ready to buy and sell Treasury securities.

Over-the-counter securities markets exist in other financial instruments, in addition to common stocks and government bonds. Markets for several money-market financial instruments are also established as over-the-counter markets. For example, negotiable certificates of deposit, banker's acceptances and federal funds are all traded in over-the-counter securities markets. There are OTC markets in non-money market instruments as well. These include trading in a **foreign exchange**.

DERIVATIVES AND THE OTC MARKETS. The newly issued financial instrument known as a derivative is also traded in the OTC securities markets. Peter Abken (in *Economic Review*) discusses the implications of **derivative securities** trading in the over-the-counter markets. He points out that, aside from their complexity, the largely unregulated character of the OTC derivatives markets sets them apart from the financial markets for other securities, due to their extremely rapid growth and fast pace of innovation. In recent years, over-the-counter derivatives have become a mainstay of financial risk management and are expected to continue growing in importance, according to Abken. The current structure of the OTC markets is being closely examined, and a set of recommendations have been made. The central policy question in derivatives regulation debated by Abken is whether further federal regulation is appropriate, or whether the existing structure can oversee these markets.

BID-ASK PRICES AND THE DEALER'S SPREAD

The bid price is the amount that a securities dealer must pay to obtain a security, while the ask price is the amount that a securities dealer receives after selling it. Frederic S. Mishkin commented in *The Economics of Money, Banking, and Financial Markets* that ''you might want to think of the bid price as the 'wholesale price' and the asked price as the 'retail' price.''

The ask price for securities is higher than the bid price. The difference between the two prices provides the dealer with his profit margin, compensating the dealer for his work. This compensation amount is known as the dealer's spread. Since securities can rise or fall in price during the period that the dealer owns them, thus impacting a dealer's ability to secure an acceptable asking price, this business can be a tricky one.

[Anandi P. Sahu]

FURTHER READING:

Abken, Peter A. ''Over-the-counter Financial Derivatives: Risky Business?'' *Economic Review* [Federal Reserve Bank of Atlanta], March/April 1994, pp. 1-22

Mishkin, Frederic S. *The Economics of Money, Banking, and Financial Markets*, 4th ed. HarperCollins Publishers, 1995.

Ritter, Lawrence S. and William L. Silber. *Principles of Money, Banking, and Financial Markets*, 6th ed. Basic Books, Inc., 1989.

OVERHEAD EXPENSE

Overhead expenses are those production and nonproduction costs not readily traceable to specific jobs or processes. Overhead expense encompasses three general areas: indirect materials, indirect labor, and all other miscellaneous production expenses such as **taxes**, insurance, **depreciation**, supplies, utilities, and repairs. Therefore, overhead expense is part of the total costs of maintaining and staffing a facility.

Production overhead includes such items as factory supplies and materials that are used in the production process, supervisors' salaries, maintenance and repairs of machinery, and utilities. Nonproduction overhead includes salaries of building maintenance, medical, and security personnel, rent or depreciation on plant and equipment, insurance on plant and equipment, the costs of meeting government regulations, and administration salaries and expenses.

DETERMINING OVERHEAD RATES

The accurate **accounting** and allocation of overhead expenses are very important in calculating the cost of goods sold and in setting a profitable selling price. The accounting of overhead is part of the control established during the budget process. The accounting department, along with line supervisors and decision-point managers, develops projections of the volume of sales, the volume of production, and the cost of production for the coming year. If the company produces only one product, accounting merely divides the total overhead by the expected volume of output to derive the standard overhead rate, burden rate, or indirect cost rate (an overhead rate per unit).

During the fiscal year, accounting counts the number of finished goods going into inventory and allocates overhead for these units by multiplying the units by the standard overhead rate. The finished goods are said to have absorbed a portion of the total overhead costs.

In a company with more than one product, the procedure is much more complex. The accounting department's allocation of overhead is complicated by the variations in the different production processes. One item may require a labor-intensive finishing process, while another relies more on machinery. The relationships apparent between the finished product and these production processes provide accounting an activity base upon which to calculate the allocation of overhead according to a formula similar to the following:

$$\frac{\$S_p - \$S_e}{R}$$

$$\text{Overhead Rate Per Unit Activity Base} = \frac{\text{Overhead to be Allocated (dollars of overhead)}}{\text{Volume of Activity Base (direct labor-hours)}}$$

For a process mostly reliant on machinery, the divisor, in the above formula, would be machine-hours instead of labor-hours. A company provides for overhead absorption by combining a number of these activity-based overhead rate allocation methods.

ABSORPTION AND OVERHEAD VARIANCES

The monthly job cost ledger may indicate that, in applying the predetermined rate, the allocation either exceeded or fell short of actual costs. This variance, termed the "burden variance," means that overhead was either: (1) overabsorbed (overapplied): the application of the predetermined rate exceeded the actual overhead used, or (2) underabsorbed (underapplied): the application of the predetermined rate fell short of the actual overhead used.

Burden variance can result from the following spending variations, or budget variance:

1. The total amount actually spent for production overhead varied from the budget.

2. The price paid for units of overhead factors varied from the budgeted prices.

3. The quantity of overhead factors per unit of finished product varied from the quantity per budgeted unit.

4. The mix of overhead factors used changed so that the average cost of overhead per unit of product varied from the amount budgeted.

Burden variance also results from the following volume variances:

1. Actual volume varied from the volume used to set the predetermined overhead rates.

2. Seasonal fluctuations distorted the averages.

Underabsorbed overhead exists as a debit balance in the production overhead clearing account at the end of the year. Overabsorbed overhead is a credit balance. To report these balances in the **financial state-ments**, the accountant examines the cause of the variance and chooses a method to satisfy the reporting objective. In reporting the variances the accountant considers at least three alternatives:

1. Divide the under- or overabsorption in any period between the **income statement** and the **balance sheet** in direct proportion to the distribution of the overhead absorbed during the period. The objective of this method is to have inventory cost and the cost of goods sold approximate the average costs of production in the period.

2. Report the variance in full as a loss or a gain on the income statement for the period in which it arises. The purpose of this method is to measure the inventory at its normal cost, with the income statement accounting for all variances from the budget. Inefficiencies due to overspending or underproduction are costs of the period rather than costs of the products manufactured during the period. When plant utilization falls short of budget, there is a loss (or an expense for idle capacity) to be reported in the income statement for the period.

3. Carry all burden variances to the balance sheet for the end of the period to be added to or offset against similar amounts arising in preceding or succeeding periods. Management exercises this option when it expects that a portion of the burden variance may be offset. **Management** does not extend this practice to the annual reporting, however, where it splits the burden variance between inventory and the cost of goods sold if the variance is (1) large enough to have a material effect on the financial statement and if it represents overabsorption, or (2) likely to be recoverable from the sale of the inventory in later periods.

COST CLASSIFICATION PROBLEMS

In some instances the cost of classifying production costs to specific units may be prohibitive. Therefore, management recognizes them as part of the production overhead to be absorbed on a per-unit basis and may devise some arbitrary method of allocation. Some examples of these costs are:

- Glue, staples, nuts, bolts, nails, plastic wrap, tape, etc.–elements common to a variety of products without specific measurements.

- Shared time and travel expenses resulting from performing services at a number of customer sites.

- Overtime premiums, resulting from over-scheduling, are averaged over the entire production for the period.

SUMMARY

Production overhead costs are of many different types and can be associated only indirectly with product units. The allocation of overhead is one of the most challenging problems of accounting. It provides management with an accurate accounting of costs and with the ability to set profitable market prices.

Differences in production processes call for the use of activity bases in setting standard overhead rates. Production overhead variances, resulting from over- or underapplied overhead, often occur when using standard rates. Accounting makes the necessary adjustments in internal and external reporting.

SEE ALSO: Budgeting; Cost Control; Costing Methods (Manufacturing)

[Roger J. AbiNader]

FURTHER READING:

Black, Homer A., John E. Champion, and Gibbs U. Miller. *Accounting in Business Decisions: Theory, Method, and Use.* Prentice Hall, 1973.

Meigs, Robert F., and Walter B. Meigs. *Accounting: The Basis for Business Decisions.* 8th ed. McGraw-Hill, 1990.

Shillinglaw, Gordon, and Philip E. Meyer. *Accounting: A Management Approach.* 7th ed. Irwin, 1983.

Welsch, Glenn A. *Budgeting: Profit Planning and Control.* Prentice Hall, 1976.

P

PACKAGING

Packaging is the container or wrapper that holds a product or group of products. Types of commercial packaging include shipping cartons, containers for industrial goods, and holders for consumer products. Discussed below are consumer packaging and shipping cartons designed for promotional use. Such packaging serves two basic functions: to contain the product and to communicate to the consumer.

BACKGROUND

Before World War II, packaging was used primarily to surround and protect products during storage, transportation, and distribution. Some packages were designed with aesthetic appeal and even for ease-of-use by the end consumer, but package design was typically left to technicians. Since the beginning of the Industrial Revolution in the mid-1800s, in fact, the "build it and they will come" maxim had prevailed. After World War II companies became more interested in marketing and promotion as a means of enticing customers to purchase their products. As a result, more manufacturers began to view packaging as a way to lure buyers.

During the mid-1900s, several influences contributed to turn packaging into an integral part of most companies' marketing mix. Consumers became better educated, and wealth and expectations generally increased. Consequently, consumers began to rely much more heavily on manufactured goods and processed food items. New technologies related to production, distribution, and preservatives led to a massive prolif-

eration in the number and type of products and brands available in industrialized nations. Thus, packaging became a vital means of differentiating items and informing inundated consumers.

The importance of consumer packaging was elevated in the United States during the late 1970s and 1980s. Rapid post-war economic expansion and market growth waned during that period, forcing companies to focus increasingly on luring consumers to their product or brand at the expense of the competition. Package design became a marketing science. And, as a new corporate cost-consciousness developed in response to increased competition, companies began to alter packaging techniques as way to cut production, storage, and distribution expenses. Furthermore, marketers began to view packaging as a tool to exploit existing product lines by adding new items and to pump new life into maturing products.

PACKAGE DESIGN

Consumer packaging serves to contain and communicate. A product's "packaging mix" is the result of several requirements that determine how a package accomplishes those two basic functions. Robert D. Hisrich identified eight major package requirements that dictate the mix. A package must: protect the product, be adaptable to production-line speeds, promote or sell the item, increase the product's density, help the consumer use the product, provide reusable value to the user, satisfy legal requirements, and keep packaging-related expenses low. Two classes of package design criteria are: functional requirements and sales requirements.

FUNCTIONAL REQUIREMENTS

Package design must meet five groups of functional criteria in-home, in-store (or warehouse), production, distribution and safety, and legal. In-home requirements usually dictate that packaging be easy to use and store, remind users when and what to repurchase, reinforce consumers' expectations of the product, and tell them how to safely and effectively use the product. In addition, increasing numbers of consumers expect packaging to be recyclable and environmentally sensitive.

In-store criteria require that packaging attracts attention on the shelf, instills confidence in the buyer, identifies the product or brand and differentiates it from the competition, communicates benefits and uses, and entices customers to actually purchase the item. The product must also be easy for retailers to store and stock on the shelves or the floor, and simple to process at a check-out counter or other final point of distribution. For instance, packaging that is oddly shaped and takes up a large amount of space may draw attention, but it may also be shunned by mail-order sellers concerned about shipping costs or by space-conscious store retailers.

Production demands, the third group of functional criteria influencing packaging, are primarily based on cost. A designer may create a fantastic package that would perform excellently in the marketplace, but if the company can't find a way to produce the package cost-effectively, the design is useless. Among the most important considerations is production line speed. If a container is too long, wide, or short, it could significantly slow the speed of the production machines. Or, if the top or spout of a container is too small or is oddly shaped, the product may not flow easily into the package.

Packaging considerations related to distribution and safety are important and numerous. If an unacceptable portion of the goods are damaged during storage, transportation, or distribution, the package has failed. Likewise, if the package injures the user future sales could be lost or the company could be liable for damages. As a result, numerous technical considerations face engineers that have a residual impact on the final look and feel of the package. For instance, packages must be able to withstand the pressure of several other crates stored on top of them. They must also be able to resist moisture, adapt to temperature changes, and withstand rough handling. From a cost standpoint, packages must also be designed to suit standardized transportation requirements related to weight, size, and durability.

Furthermore, packages should ideally be designed to handle normal use by consumers. For example, a vegetable oil container must be able to fall from

a counter without breaking and to have very warm oil poured back into it without melting. Examples of packages that may result in harm to consumers include: those with sharp edges, such as some pull-top canisters; glass containers that hold products made for use in the shower, which could cause serious injury if dropped; and heavy item boxes which might break when the customer is carrying them or cause strain or injury to the consumer when picked up or set down.

The fifth basic group of packaging requirements is laws and legislation. Various federal laws have been passed to protect consumers from misrepresentation and unsafe products. For instance, some laws require that containers for potentially dangerous goods, such as gasoline or drugs, be stored in specially constructed containers. Other laws forbid producers from misrepresenting the product quality or quantity through misleading packaging. Perhaps the most influential class of laws that affect packaging, however, is that related to **labeling**.

PRODUCT LABELING. The label is the text printed on a product package or, in the case of items like clothing, attached to the product itself. Legally, labels are all written, printed, or graphic material on the container of products that are involved in interstate commerce or held for sale. The main body of legislation governing packaging and labeling is the Fair Packaging and Labeling Act of 1966. It mandates that every product package or label specify on its "principal display label" (the part of the label most likely to be seen by consumers): (1) the product type; (2) the producer or processor's name and location; (3) quantity (if applicable); and (4) number and size of servings (if applicable). Furthermore, several restrictions apply to the way that the label is displayed. For example, mandatory copy required by the act must be in boldface type. Also, if the company is not listed in the telephone book, the manufacturer's or importer's street address must be displayed.

Other information required by the act relates to specific foods, toys, drugs, cosmetics, furs, and textiles. For instance, under the act labels for edible products must provide sodium content if other nutritional information is shown. They must also show ingredients, beginning with the one of highest quantity and descending in order. Certain food items, such as beef, may also be required to display qualitative "grade labels" or inspection labels. Likewise, "informative labeling" may be required for products such as home appliances. Informative label requirements mandate information about use, care, performance capability, life expectancy, safety precautions, gas mileage, or other factors. Certain major home appliances, for example, must provide the estimated cost of running each make and model for one year at average utility rates.

Congress passed significant new labeling legislation in 1990 (the Nutrition Labeling and Education Act of 1990) that became effective in the mid-1990s. This act is intended primarily to discourage misleading labeling related to health benefits of food items. Specifically, many package labels subjectively claimed that their contents were "low-fat," "high-fiber," or possessed some other health virtue when the facts indicated otherwise. Basically, the new laws require most food labels to specify values such as calorie and cholesterol content, fat and saturated fat percentages, and sodium levels.

SALES REQUIREMENTS

In additional to functional requirements, product packaging must be designed in a way that will appeal to buyers. The four principal merchandising requirement areas are: apparent size, attention drawing power, impression of quality, and brand-name readability.

Apparent size entails designing packaging to look as large as possible without misrepresenting the actual contents. This objective can be achieved by ensuring that the panels or dimensions of the package most likely to be viewed by the consumer are the largest, and that the product or brand name is shown on the most visible areas in large letters. In addition, the package can be made to look larger by using solid colors and simple, bold designs free of borders, superfluous art work, and unnecessary print. The pretense of largeness is particularly important for packages containing commodity items, such as rice, driveway salt, and canned fruit or vegetables.

Attention drawing power refers to the aesthetics and obtrusiveness of the package design. Depending on the product and the goals of the marketers, the package may be made to appear attractive, exciting, pure, soft, sexy, scary, intriguing, or to evoke some other emotion. In most cases, though, the product is displayed on the front of the package in the form of a picture, art, or see-through window. In addition, bright colors, glossy stock, obtrusive carton displays, and other elements can garner positive attention if used prudently.

A quality impression is an important sales requirement for packaging because items that are perceived to be of low quality are usually assumed to be a poor value, regardless of price. Examples of packaging mistakes that convey low quality or poor value include: faded lettering or colors, tacky designs or strange typeface, outdated pictures and designs, and cheap construction.

Readability, the fourth basic sales requirement for successful package design, means that the package must be extremely simple and easy to read. This is of paramount importance for products like breakfast cereal that are shelved next to several competing brands and products. If the package attempts to convey too many messages, it will likely fail to connect with the consumer. Because of the mass of buying choices, buyers typically do not take time to absorb messages on packaging, with the possible exception of high-priced specialty items. Among other guidelines, letters or logos should be large and printed in the same type style as that used in complementary print and television advertising. The requirement of readability contributes to the difficulty in packaging completely new products.

PACKAGING STRATEGY

One of the most critical roles for packaging is promoting products. Indeed, just as ease-of-use and readability are elements of the strategic packaging mix, packaging is an important part of a company's strategic marketing mix. Most packages for consumer products are designed for one of three purposes: (1) to improve the packaging of an existing product, (2) to add a new product to an existing product line, or (3) to contain an entirely new product.

Redesign of packaging for existing products may be prompted by several factors. Many times, a company may simply want to breathe new life into a maturing product by updating its image or adding a new gimmick to the package, such as an easy-pour spout. Or, a company may redesign the package to respond to a competitive threat, such as a new product that is more visible on the shelf. Other strategic reasons for package redesign are: changes in the product; economics, which may require less or more expensive packaging; product line restructuring; alterations in market strategy, such as aiming the product at a different age group; trying to promote new uses for a product; or legal or environmental factors that lead to new materials or technology.

Even small packaging changes for established brands and products typically require careful consideration, since millions of dollars are often at risk if a company alienates or confuses customers. In 1988, for example, the Adolph Coors Co. changed the words "Banquet Beer" on its beer container labels to "Original Draft." Although the label change was generally successful, sales dropped in southern California and west Texas, the two regions where Coors beer had been sold since the 1940s. Many customers there were confused by the change and assumed that Coors had altered the product. Coors changed the label back to "Banquet Beer" in those two areas and sales recovered.

A second reason for package design is to extend a product or brand line. An example of a product line extension is Anheuser-Busch Companies' Busch

Light beer, which is an extension of the Busch beer product line. Another example is the Tide detergent brand line, which was extended to include Tide Free, a detergent without dyes or perfumes. In the case of product extensions, the packaging strategy is usually to closely mimic the established brand or product, but to integrate the benefits of the new feature into the existing package in such a way that customers will be able to easily differentiate it from other products in the line.

Chief risks inherent in packaging for extensions are the that new package will confuse customers or frustrate retailers. Ralston Purina Company had to overcome the latter when it designed packaging for an extension to its Tender Vittles cat food line. It wanted to add an additional flavor, but was concerned that retailers would be hesitant to use more linear space to stock the large line. Therefore, Ralston changed the package dimensions of all six existing Tender Vittles' lines. It made the boxes slightly taller and narrower, thus allowing the seven packages to fit conveniently within the same amount of horizontal shelf space.

The third impetus for package design is the need to generate housing for an entirely new product. This is the most difficult type of packaging to create because it often requires the designer to instill consumer confidence in an unknown product or brand, and to inform the buyer about the product's uses and benefits. Packaging for products and brands that are entirely new to the marketplace require the most education, and are therefore the most challenging to develop. In contrast, packaging for goods that are entering established product categories require less education, they must, however, overcome established competition. In general, packaging strategies for such products entail mimicking the packaging of leading products, which helps to assure the buyer that the product is "normal." Consider, for instance, how similar packaging is for every brand of salad dressing, soda, eggs, toothpaste, and milk.

An example of a new product launch that demonstrates the importance of packaging in the marketing mix is Ore-Ida Foods, Inc.'s introduction of Deep Fries in the early 1970s. Deep Fries were frozen, oil-coated french fries that were cooked in the oven. Although they were comparatively expensive, Deep Fries were more convenient to prepare and better tasting than other frozen fries. The package was designed to convey to consumers that the product was premium and it offered "Deep Fried flavor and crispness without deep frying."

The initial launch was successful and Deep Fries soon cultivated a small group of loyal customers. Nevertheless, sales growth failed to meet projections. Consumer research showed that the Deep Fries package succeeded in conveying a premium image but had failed to inform customers of the benefits of Deep Fries. In fact, many customers had purchased the product simply because of the quality of the packaging. Other would-be customers never tried the product because they were unable to justify its high price. Those that did buy the product realized its benefits, were satisfied, and continued to buy.

Ore-Ida developed two new packages and eventually selected one that proved, through market tests, to achieve the desired sales growth. Its new package changed the quote "Deep Fried flavor and crispness without deep frying" to "The Self Sizzlers, they make your oven work like a deep fryer." In addition, the Ore-Ida name was replaced with Ore-Ida's parent company name, H.J. Heinz Co., which served to soften the expensive, premium image. The phrase "Heinz, Self Sizzling Deep Fries" was also added to the package. The product eventually captured a loyal groups of customers characterized as working women who habitually purchased the best, most convenient products.

[Dave Mote]

FURTHER READING:

Boyd, Harper W., Jr., and Orville C. Walker, Jr. *Marketing Management: A Strategic Approach*. Boston: Richard D. Irwin, Inc., 1990.

Hisrich, Robert D. *Marketing*. New York: Barron's Business Library, 1990.

Lusch, Robert F., and Virginia N. Lusch. *Principles of Marketing*. Boston: Kent Publishing Company, 1987.

McCarthy, E. Jerome, and William D. Perreault, Jr. *Basic Marketing*. Boston: Richard D. Irwin, Inc., 1990.

Schoell, William F., and Joseph P. Guiltinan. *Marketing: Contemporary Concepts and Practices*. 5th ed. Boston: Allyn and Bacon, 1992.

Stern, Walter. *Handbook of Package Design Research*. New York: John Wiley & Sons, 1981.

PASSIVE MANAGEMENT (FIXED INCOME)

Passive bond portfolio management takes advantage of the implications of bond market efficiency. Because bond markets are efficient, investors are not able to use past price and volume data or publicly available information to achieve superior rates of return. The limitations on portfolio management imposed by market efficiency preclude achieving superior rates of return by either superior bond selection or superior market timing. Investors achieve market rates of return by buying a randomly diversified **bond** index fund or investors immunize the bond portfolio by taking advantage of the concept of duration.

The simplest approach to creating a bond index fund is to buy a market-weighted random selection of bonds in each of the major bond categories in the domestic bond market: Treasury bonds, federal agency bonds, corporate bonds, state and municipal bonds, and mortgage-backed bonds. This portfolio, with proper rebalancing, will provide the investor with the bond market rate of return. If the objective of the investor is more narrow, a bond portfolio could be constructed that meets a specific need. For example, a bond portfolio of only corporate bonds could be constructed. The rate of return for this portfolio would mirror the rate of return for corporate bonds in general. A smaller sector of the bond market, such as AAA rated bonds, could be used to construct an index that would mirror only the highest quality bonds.

Portfolio immunization is more complex than indexation and takes advantage of bond duration to eliminate interest rate risk from the bond portfolio. When the interest reinvestment rate rises (falls), the value of the principal repayment falls (rises) and the value of the interest on interest rises (falls). A bond portfolio is immunized when the duration of the bond portfolio is equal to the duration of the liabilities hedged by the bond portfolio Thus, total interest rate change effects are offset.

An investor with multiperiod obligations can take advantage of duration on a period-by-period basis. This technique is known as dedication.

The duration of the bond portfolio will vary over time. Changes in the bond portfolio duration can be rebalanced by reinvesting coupon payments or replacing longer duration bonds with shorter duration bonds.

[Carl B. McGowan, Jr.]

FURTHER READING:

Reilly, Frank K. *Investment Analysis and Portfolio Management*. 3rd ed. Chicago: The Dryden Press, 1989.

PATENT LAW/PATENTS

A patent is a legal document issued by the federal government that gives an inventor the exclusive right to manufacture and sell his or her invention for a period of 17 years. Any infringement of this right is punishable by law. Hence a patent is a monopoly that the government protects for the purpose of encouraging inventors and inventorship. Sole rights to an invention allow the inventor (or joint inventors, as the case may be) to profit from it. He or she can then commercialize the invention, often selling the monopoly in the form of a license to other manufacturers, who in turn must abide by the inventor's stipulations.

At the conclusion of the 17 year period, other manufacturers have a right to make the product and sell it to their advantage, without permission. Ideally, the inventor by then has enjoyed the commercial benefits of his or her invention, and has a market edge over any new competitor. This was not the case, however, with the giant Xerox Corp., which fostered the invention of xerography. When the Xerox patent expired in 1979, the Japanese company Canon Inc. quickly seized and overtook Xerox' market share, and nearly destroyed the company in the process. Hence a patent is meant to encourage invention; what the inventor does with the patent depends on his or her business acumen.

The patent document itself is written by the inventor and describes the invention in great detail, underscoring its uniqueness and setting forth its advantages. The Patent and Trademark Office (PTO) then publishes the document, and nowadays, all U.S. patents are accessible on-line as well as in print. Each year the PTO issues over 100,000 patents to U.S. citizens as well as to foreigners seeking American patents.

Besides patents, the PTO also registers trademarks, which is a quite different matter. For a business that uses trademarks (brand names and corresponding logos) to identify its products or services, trademark registration does not secure monopoly rights. There is also confusion between patents and copyrights. A copyright, issued by the Library of Congress, is similar to a patent in that it grants to the author of a book, the composer of music, or a sculptor, choreographer, sound recorder or motion picture producer, an exclusive right not to have their work copied without their permission. This right lasts for the lifetime of the creator of the work plus 50 years thereafter.

Hence patents do not cover written works, music, or art, but do include computer software products, because of their technical applications. In all, there are three categories of inventions that are patentable: technical objects, instruments, applications, and formulas (as in chemical compounds in medicine) that are of use to the general public—the largest category; designs, as on eyeglass frames or jewelry; and, lastly, plants that are asexually propagated (i.e., without seeds). In short, patentable items are always practical; copyrighted material often is not. Both fall under the rubric of **intellectual property**. Almost all countries have patent laws. If the world were without patents, there would be little incentive for an individual to create an original product or design or a unique plant, unless perhaps if the person were independently wealthy. Moreover, there might be endless lawsuits in the United States if there were no specific patent laws. In this country, patents historically have always been awarded to the original inventor, and not to the ''first filer,'' as in all other countries. Hence if an inventor files for a patent in the United States, he must prove that he is the first to invent rather than the first to file the invention.

The U.S. Constitution in 1789 explicitly granted Congress the right to authorize patents to inventors. Patents in those days were quite familiar to the general public, and were characteristic of the most advanced countries. Patents in these formative years of the republic were modeled on those of Great Britain; even the colonies, most notably Massachusetts and South Carolina, had granted patents to inventors as early as the 1640s. Britain, however, had not been the originator of patents: the Italian merchant republics, specifically Venice and Florence, awarded the earliest known ones in the mid-fifteenth century. The first patents in the British Isles were awarded a century later, in Elizabethan England.

As a result of Article 1, Section 8 of the Constitution that specified "the Congress shall have power . . . to promote the progress of science and useful arts, by securing for limited times to authors and inventors the exclusive right to their writings and discoveries," the first patent law was passed in 1790. This spelled out the criteria for granting patents: that they were to go to the original inventor; that the invention was not to have been "known before or used," hence, be original; and that the invention or discovery be useful. The first inventor to be awarded an American patent under the new law was Samuel Hopkins, for his formula for making "Pot and Pearl Ashes."

The patent law of 1790 was ahead of any country's and would be widely imitated. The law, however, did not establish a separate office or administrator to award patents. Instead, examining and awarding patents was considered a part-time job that the secretaries of war and state and the attorney general could perform in their spare time. It was up to them to give patents, deciding either collectively or individually. Secretary of State Thomas Jefferson, himself an inventor, had perhaps the keenest interest in this sideline. However, soon he, too, was inundated, bringing many public complaints about the slowness and cumbersomeness of the patenting process. Nonetheless, in three years, 57 patents were issued for such inventons as type punches, a machine for manufacturing nails, and various steam-power innovations.

To streamline the patenting process and cut down on the time it took to award patents, Congress passed a new law in 1793 that effectively nullified the previous one. This law was decidedly inferior to the one it replaced, since all it did was require a person to register an invention without the stipulation that it be examined and determined to be original or useful. While this certainly simplified the patenting process, it opened the door for all kinds of chicanery, which gave rise to a large number of lawsuits. For the next

few decades, however, this law remained in force, until a backlash produced a reformed and stronger patent law in 1836.

The new law reinstated the requirement that an invention's originality had to be proven, which in essence was a restatement of the 1790 patent statute. The difference between the two major patent laws was the 1836 provision for a separate patent bureau, with its own staff that worked full-time on patent processing. While Congress in 1802 had created a discrete patent office within the State Department, this one-person office was mandated to do little more than register patents. Hence the 1836 reformed patent statute set up what amounted to a modern patent office, headed by a commissioner of patents; and for the first time, an inventor had the right to appeal if his patent application was rejected.

This new law reinstated the 1790 patent statute's liberal stance toward foreign inventors, who were once again eligible for patents. As in the 1790 and 1793 laws, the inventor, and not the first to file an invention, had the sole right to apply for a patent. That meant that an inventor could freely sound out her ideas or attempt the commercialization of her invention as long as this occurred within 12 months of the first filing date of her patent application.

Even by twentieth century standards, the 1836 patent statute ushered in a modern system of patent processing that was liberal in application, protecting the inventions of foreigners as well as citizens of the United States for a period of 14 years and granting them the right of appeal. While the law would be superseded by another law in 1870 and by the codification of 1952, these later laws would incorporate the features of the 1836 statute. Other changes in patent law occurred in 1842, when design patents were granted for the first time; and 1861, when the 14-year limitation on a patent was extended to the current seventeen years. In 1930, plant patents went into effect, while in 1952, all patent laws were codified; for the first time in patent history, the principle of "non-obviousness"—a refinement of the criterion of originality—became a permanent part of patent law. In essence this meant that an invention not only had to be original, but its originality could not be "obvious" even to a specialist in the field.

The United States was so far ahead in its patent application procedure in the nineteenth century that in 1869 the Patent Office issued seven times more patents (13,997) than Great Britain, which at that time was considered the world's "workshop." The kinds of inventions no doubt presaged this country's industrial supremacy in the twentieth century. Some of the most notable patents were the steam-powered engine (1811), the mechanized reaper (1834), the telegraph (1840), the sewing machine (1846), the typewriter (1868), the telephone (1876), the phonograph (1878), the electric light bulb (1880), and the motion picture projector (1893). Eli Whitney's cotton gin went into use in the first half of the nineteenth century, but was patented in 1794. In addition, Charles Goodyear's vulcanization of rubber—an example of a process, rather than an instrument or object—received a patent in 1844 and later made the modern bicycle and car tire possible.

Meanwhile, one industrializing country after another was adopting patenting statutes. In 1900 Japan sent an observer to the United States to learn about patenting, and adopted many of the features of the American patent system, including the first to invent criterion rather than first to file. In 1883, those countries which had patent laws in place agreed to the Paris Convention, which meant that an inventor who filed for a patent in one member country could use that same filing date in the other member countries. An American who applied for a patent outside of the United States or its territories, however, would have to file before he or she could disclose the invention publicly. The Paris Convention was followed 87 years later with the Patent Cooperation Treaty of 1970. In this treaty, only a single application had to be filed for a patent, which could be made in English, and was automatically applicable in other member nations.

The U.S. Patent Office, established in its own building as a result of the 1836 patent law, burned to the ground that year, and with it, all of its records, numbering in the thousands. It was quickly rebuilt, becoming part of the Interior Department in 1849. No doubt because of this catastrophe, all patent applications since then, along with their drawings, had to be submitted in duplicate. The Patent Office remained a division of the Interior Department until 1925; since then, it has remained part of the Commerce Department.

Basically the U.S. patent law and supplements, amalgamated into one single patent law in 1870, remained unchanged until 1952. On July 19, 1952, the new patent statute, which is still in force, became law and went into effect on January 1, 1953. It codified all previous patent laws, modifications and amendments, specified what was patentable, and spelled out the application procedure and the duration of patents. For the first time, it established the principle of ''nonobviousness,'' which meant that an invention not only had to be original, but ingenious, and not obvious to a practitioner or expert on the subject. Excluded from patents was any invention contrary to the public welfare, and any patent that utilized nuclear material for weapons' purposes. The Patent Office was renamed the Patent and Trademark Office (PTO), its most important activity being the time consuming, exhaustive study of each patent application.

Of the three types of inventions that are patentable, the majority are applications or instruments (in-

cluding chemical compounds), followed by designs, and new plants. Even within these categories, not all inventions are patentable. They must be in accord with the legal criteria for patentability: an invention must be useful, original and beyond that, not obvious even to a practitioner or expert in the field, and cannot have been publicized more than one year prior to filing. The application process for a patent is not difficult. Almost always an inventor hires a patent attorney to assist in writing up the application and in researching the possibility that the invention, or some form of it, might have existed prior to the application (known as the ''prior art''), which would disqualify it. An application is not judged ready until there is a workable model, in the form of a drawing or actual model, of the invention. The written application must contain the date of the invention's conception, and must be signed by a witness.

Once the application is submitted to the PTO, the application undergoes detailed examination. To facilitate this, the PTO began an extensive, billion-dollar computerization program in 1984 that will be in place by the turn-of-the-century. It rigorously scrutinizes the prior art of the invention in order to establish its originality, even though the inventor has already done so. This entails researching all previous U.S. patents ever filed, as well as foreign patents, and relevant literature on the topic.

Often an invention is original, but not so ingenious that an expert in the field could not have deduced it. In such cases, it is rejected, and the inventor has the right to appeal the decision. The PTO has its own board of appeals, and from there, an inventor can go even higher, to the Court of Appeals of the Federal Circuit of the District of Columbia (CAFC). Theoretically, it is possible to bring a rejected patent application all the way up to the Supreme Court; surprisingly, this has not yet happened.

A person can apply for more than one patent, or two individuals can file a joint patent. In the case of the latter, there is joint ownership of the patent, with neither owner obligated toward the other. This can create problems if one of the owners only contributed marginally to the invention, and sells his or her share, which the joint patentee has the legal right to do. To avoid possible future conflict, joint filers usually have a written agreement between them. Patents are legally considered property and hence inheritable by law, should the patentee (or one of them) die before the expiration date of the patent.

A patented invention is no guarantee of future commercial success. Statistically, the number of successful inventions is minuscule. One avenue of commercialization open to a patentee is licensing his or her patent to a company, or a number of companies, provided a firm is willing to risk investing in a wholly untried product or process. The patent holder, however, cannot demand that royalties from the product continue beyond the stipulated 17-year patent period, nor can the patentee set the product's price or determine its use.

Often an American inventor will seek a foreign patent. The Paris Convention, adhered to by over 90 countries, gives foreign patentees the same rights as their own citizens. Nonetheless, most foreign countries require that a product be manufactured in the country for a stipulated period. Many countries, especially in Asia, Eastern Europe, and Russia, have patent laws that are either not strictly enforced or not very advanced. This has troubled many manufacturers of commercial software products, who cannot profit from their products in these countries because of lax patent laws or patent laws that do not cover software and computer applications.

There is great international pressure on the United States to harmonize its patent criteria with the rest of the world's—i.e., the stipulation that the first to file for a patent is the one who is eligible for a patent, whether or not this person is the original inventor. The PTO also has recommended this change, which would save taxpayer dollars because it would simplify the patent scrutinization process. If implemented, the first to file principle would be a radical change from the tradition of recognizing only the inventor's right to file, first established over 200 years ago in the patent law of 1790. Moreover, it would eliminate the one-year grace period prior to filing, which allows the inventor to publicize or even commercialize his or her invention. Critics of "harmonization," mainly from the academic world, charge that it would benefit only big business, which has ample resources to file first. Filing a patent application costs little—under one hundred dollars. Engaging a patent attorney, however, is expensive. While do-it-yourself patent books abound, few inventors take the risk of filing without assistance. With Congress taking a hard look at patent harmonization and cost cutting, adoption of the first to file principle is gaining favor.

Despite the fact that the PTO is considered to be one of the most cost effective agencies of the government and one of the most efficient, it is subjected to criticism on all sides. This has usually preceded major changes in patent law. The criteria for patentability are becoming outmoded, as so much of the world is moving toward technological inventions that defy the traditional concepts of what is useful and tangible, especially in the fast-growing realm of biotechnology and software. No one, however, suggests that we do away with the expensive, time-consuming patenting process or with patents themselves.

[Sina Dubovoy]

FURTHER READING:

Feinberg, Rick. *Peculiar Patents: A Collection of Unusual and Interesting Inventions from the Files of the U.S. Patent Office.* Secaucus, NJ: Citadel Press, 1994.

Foster, Frank H., and Robert L. Shook. *Patents, Copyrights, and Trademarks.* 2nd Ed. New York: Wiley, 1993.

Kingston, William. *Innovation, Creativity & Law.* Dordrecht and Boston: Kluwer Academic Publishers, 1990.

U.S. Patent and Trademark Office. "The Story of the U.S. Patent and Trademark Office (Washington, D.C.)." U.S. Government Printing Office, 1988.

Warshofsky, Fred. *The Patent Wars: The Battle to Own the World's Technology.* New York: Wiley, 1994.

PAY-PER-CALL TELEPHONE SERVICE (900 NUMBERS)

Calls to 900 telephone numbers, or pay-per-call services, are paid for by the caller. The charge is greater than, or added to, the carrier's charge for the transmission of the call. As of November 1, 1993, the 900 prefix became the only one through which interstate pay-per-call services could be offered. Pay-per-call services for local or intrastate calls often use other prefixes, such as 976 or 560. A 1992 survey found that between one-third and one-half of all adult Americans did not realize that they had to pay for calls to 900 telephone numbers.

Pay-per-call services offer a variety of audio information, audio entertainment, simultaneous voice conversation, and other services ranging from product offerings to personal dating services. The operator of a pay-per-call service is known as an information provider (IP). IPs determine the information or service to be provided, the amount of the charge, and whether it will be assessed on a per-call or time-interval basis, and how the service will be advertised. IPs typically use service bureaus to handle incoming calls.

900 telephone numbers have a variety of applications. Since the caller pays a charge for making 900 calls, many IPs have established 900 services as money-making ventures. In the political arena, one of the first applications of the 900 number was to poll voters. Following the Reagan-Carter debates in 1980, viewers were given the opportunity to call one of two 900 numbers to cast a vote for the presidential candidate of their choice. Similarly, television networks have established 900 numbers to allow viewers to cast votes for programs that were scheduled to be cancelled. Television programs airing rock videos have allowed viewers to call 900 numbers to cast their votes for their favorite videos. When an incentive was added to the call, one NBC program received more than 450,000 responses during a 90-minute show.

Since 900 telephone numbers are an effective means of establishing a caller's involvement, they have been used in marketing and sales promotion campaigns. These applications are not designed to make money from the 900 number. Rather, they are used to create an affinity between the consumer and a particular company or product. In one example, a record company offered a special CD and other merchandise to consumers who called a 900 number. In addition to the 900 charge, callers also paid for the merchandise, some of which could only be obtained by calling the 900 number.

The use of a 900 telephone number in a marketing or sales promotion campaign provides a variety of benefits. In terms of lead generation, 900 numbers provide better qualified leads than do 800 numbers. If the marketer wants to create a mailing list or database of callers, it is easy to obtain the necessary information using the audiotext, or prerecorded message, feature of the 900 call. When 900 numbers are used in television advertising, they usually provide an indication of the response rate within minutes or hours. Finally, the charges associated with a 900 number can help the company recoup its promotion costs.

As a result of widespread abuses of 900 telephone numbers by IPs, their use is now subject to regulation by the **Federal Trade Commission (FTC)** and the **Federal Communications Commission (FCC)**. Under the authority of the Telephone Disclosure and Dispute Resolution Act of 1992 (TDDRA), the FTC and FCC adopted their final rules governing 900 numbers and pay-per-call services effective November 1, 1993. These rules apply to IPs, service bureaus, and carriers. They are limited to interstate services, but individual states may adopt and enforce more stringent regulations.

The FTC regulations cover the preamble, advertising disclosures and prohibitions, and billing rights and responsibilities. The preamble is an introductory message that a caller hears at the beginning of the call. It must include the name of the IP, a description of the service, the cost of the call, and a statement that gives the caller the opportunity to hang up within three seconds to avoid any charge. A preamble is not required when the call costs two dollars or less, or when it is made between data devices and no human is involved.

The FTC requires that all advertisements for pay-per-call services include the cost adjacent to the 900 number. In television advertising, both video and audio disclosures of the cost must be made, unless the ad is 15 seconds or less or contains no audio information about the 900 service. Either the total cost of the call must be given, or the cost per minute and any minimum charges. In the case of infomercials, the cost and other disclosures must be made at least three times during the infomercial—at the beginning, middle, and end.

Other advertising disclosures that must be made include the odds of winning and alternate methods of entry for sweepstakes advertising that employs a 900 number. Advertising a 900 service to children under 12 years of age is prohibited unless it is a bona fide educational service. Advertising aimed at individuals between 12 and 18 years of age must disclose that parental consent is required.

The FTC also created rules affecting billing rights and responsibilities, including the right of consumers to have 60 days from the date of billing to communicate errors to carriers. The FCC rules apply mainly to carriers. Consumers must be able to request their carriers block interstate 900 services. Carriers must also provide consumers with local or toll-free numbers from which to obtain information about 900 services. Carriers may not terminate telephone service for failure to pay for 900 calls. Both the FTC and the FCC will enforce a rule prohibiting callers from being charged for calls to an 800 number in any manner without a presubscription agreement.

The rules and regulations covering 900 telephone numbers are designed to protect consumers from fraudulent and deceptive practices. Such practices in the past have tarnished the image of 900 numbers, to some degree slowing their acceptance in the marketplace as legitimate marketing and sales promotion tools. There are many legitimate for-profit IPs providing 900 services. The future of 900 services is dependent on a number of factors that include consumer acceptance, the ability of the industry to police itself, and the effect of federal and state regulations on legitimate providers.

[David Bianco]

PER CAPITA INCOME

Per capita income is the average amount of money each person in a nation makes during the course of a year. It is calculated by dividing national income, which is the sum of all the individual and corporate income arising from a nation's production of goods and services, by the total population of the nation. Per capita real **income** is the same figure, but adjusted to eliminate changes in prices or **purchasing** power over time. Many economic terms are commonly divided by population and expressed as per capita, or per person, amounts. Examples might include per capita **gross national product** (GNP) and per capita savings.

It is important to remember that per capita income figures represent a national average; in reality, income is not distributed evenly among all members of the population. Income varies by geographical region, for example, because the primary source of income in one area might be industry while in another it might be agriculture. Another geographical difference is based on the fact that wages tend to be higher in large cities than in small towns or rural areas. Income also tends to differ between individuals with different educational backgrounds.

Due to the difficulties of interpreting per capita income figures within a nation, per capita income is most often used to compare the standard of living in different countries. Per capita income varies greatly around the world, and the gap between relatively poor and relatively rich countries is becoming larger all the time. According to Susan Dentzer in *U.S. News and World Report,* the top 20 percent of countries worldwide (based on annual national income) reported per capita income figures an average of 65 times greater than the bottom 20 percent of countries in 1988.

In the United States, per capita income nearly doubled from 1959 to 1993 to reach $20,864 in current dollars, as Ben Stein noted in *New York.* In fact, the annual growth rate of per capita income over the 20-year period from 1973 to 1993 was 1.38 percent. In addition, there were many indications that Americans had more money and were living better than before. Three times as many newly constructed homes contained more than two bathrooms in 1992 than in 1970, for example, while the average square footage of new houses increased by one-third over the same period. Stein argued that such statistics are misleading, however. After adjusting for **inflation**, Stein found that per-hour private-sector earnings, excluding agricultural work, rose only .3 percent per year, or 10.6 percent over the past 34 years. In addition, he reported that inflation-adjusted weekly earnings had actually declined by 2 percent since 1959.

Stein attributed the decline in real income in part to the fact that the overall American labor force has increased by 12 percent from 1954 to 1993. An increase in the number of people working means that national and per capita income tends to rise, even though the average income per worker remains the same or declines because it is divided among more people. In addition, Stein noted that the government figures for per capita income growth include nonmonetary benefits received by workers, such as health care and **retirement** coverage. These payments, which have increased markedly in recent years, tend to inflate per capita income figures and hide underlying trends affecting wages. Other factors Stein found to reduce per capita income growth include fewer people pursuing higher education and companies keeping wages low in order to compete with foreign firms.

[Laurie Collier Hillstrom]

FURTHER READING:

Bureau of Economic Analysis. *Survey of Current Business.* March 1995.

Dentzer, Susan. "The Wealth of Nations: A Growing Slice of the World Economy Is Now in the Hands of the Affluent," *U.S. News and World Report.* May 4, 1992, p. 54.

Pomice, Eva, and Robert F. Black. "Is Your Job Safe?," *U.S. News and World Report.* January 13, 1992, pp. 42-48.

Stein, Ben. "Whining and Dining: Why We're Richer and Poorer," *New York.* April 11, 1994, p. 14.

PERESTROIKA

Perestroika is a Russian word, meaning "restructuring" or "reconstruction." It refers to the series of political and economic reforms and foreign policy changes undertaken by the Soviet Communist Party in the years 1985 to 1991. In that time, the Soviet Union was transformed from a tightly controlled communist state to a fledgling parliamentary democracy based on a free market economy. In the process, the Soviet Union was dissolved and the fifteen former communist republics achieved independence. The largest of these is the Russian Federation, which is 8.5 million square miles in size. While this includes the vast expanse of Siberia, for the first time in Russian history it excludes the Ukraine. The architect of perestroika as an official policy was Mikhail Gorbachev, who became party secretary in 1985, and thus head of state.

Unlike the preceding five communist party heads, all of whom had died of old age or illness, Gorbachev was a relatively young and vigorous man of 53. He had come to the helm of the Soviet Union when, to all the world, the country appeared to be militarily invincible, stable, and changeless. The sizable cracks in the facade of the U.S.S.R. were visible to only a very few outsiders.

Nearly seven decades of control by the communist party of the Soviet Union (CPSU) had isolated the country from the world economy and generated an aggressive Cold War with the United States that was a serious financial drain on the Soviet Union. The state controlled system of "collective" farming had produced a perpetual agrarian crisis, leading to dependency on American and Canadian grain imports to avoid a shortage of bread. In 1979, the U.S.S.R. imported a record 25 million tons of grain from the United States alone. By 1985, the free world had long entered the "microchip era," with economies and business life anchored to computers and sophisticated telecommunications systems. In the Soviet Union, state controlled businesses still widely employed the ancient abacus and the banking system was decrepit.

Widespread serious environmental damage caused by antiquated manufacturing industries was carefully hidden from the outside world, until the Chernobyl nuclear plant disaster in 1986.

Real progress in these years occurred in education, with a nearly 100 percent adult literacy rate and 99 percent of high school age children in school. Urbanization also had made rapid strides, with a majority of Soviet citizens living in cities. The restlessness of this educated population, denied the right to travel abroad or the right to freedom of expression, was evident in the growing dissident movement, whose spiritual leader was former communist physicist Andrei Sakharov (1921-1989), who had been sentenced without trial to exile and isolation in the Russian city of Gorky.

Outwardly a loyal communist who had risen through the ranks, Mikhail Gorbachev was determined to reverse the downhill spiral of the Soviet Union when he became Secretary General. Against party opposition he launched the policies that would be known as *perestroika* and *glasnost*. The horrendous nuclear power disaster at Chernobyl in the Ukraine the following year convinced doubters of the serious need for reform in the Soviet Union.

Glasnost (or "openness") took the form of greater freedom of expression (i.e., relaxed censorship), culminating in Gorbachev's personal invitation to dissident Andrei Sakharov to return from his exile in 1989 to help in the reconstruction of his homeland. *Perestroika* involved a series of political and economic reforms that, modest at the outset, unleashed a torrent of change that led to the collapse of the Soviet Union.

Among the reforms initiated by Gorbachev was the introduction, for the first time since 1917, of a limited free market economy, which involved the gradual elimination of communist party control and ownership of the economy; for this he turned to western capitalist countries for financial assistance. On the political front, *perestroika* involved the introduction of multicandidate elections, eventually ending the monopoly of political control by one party. In foreign policy, the changes brought about by *perestroika* were very radical, with consequences that are still being felt today. Renouncing the Brezhnev Doctrine that gave the Soviet Union the right to intervene militarily in Warsaw Pact countries, communist governments in eastern Europe were overthrown; the Berlin Wall collapsed; and the breakup of the Soviet Union itself ensued, with the former Soviet states proclaiming their right to self-determination. The world watched in amazement as the U.S.S.R. and the United States became allies in many areas.

The beginning of liberal reforms in the Soviet Union revealed the weaknesses of the totalitarian system that had been in power for seven decades by means. Unfortunately, the changes instigated by *perestroika* took on an uncontrollable momentum, leaving chaos and disruption in their wake and lowering the already low standard of living in the former Soviet Union. A new nostalgia for the stability and even the prosperity of the Soviet Union appeared even among the well-educated, leading to political polarization. Diehard communist sympathizers staged a surprise coup in August, 1991, while Gorbachev vacationed with his family. This was foiled by the timely support of Boris Yeltsin's (1931–) followers, who called for reforms more radical than *perestroika*. Gorbachev, who had received the Nobel Peace Prize in 1990, resigned as president of the near defunct Soviet Union in December, 1991, officially bringing *perestroika* to an end. Under his successor Yeltsin, the communist party was outlawed, and the loosely organized "Commonwealth of Independent States," whose political capital was not even in Russia, replaced the former monolithic Soviet Union.

[Sina Dubovoy]

FURTHER READING:

Boznak, Rudolph. "Moscow Diary: Momentum Unleashed by *Perestroika* Can't be Reversed," *Industrial Engineering*. November, 1990, p. 31.

Castro, Janice. "Perestroika to Pizza (U.S.-Soviet Business Ventures Beginning Again," *Time*. May 2, 1988, p. 52.

Davidow, Mike. *Perestroika: Its Rise and Fall*. New York: International Publishers, 1993.

Dowlah, A.F. *Perestroika: An Inquiry Into Its Historical, Ideological and Intellectual Roots*. Stockholm: Bethany Books, 1990.

Gorbachev, Mikhail. *Perestroika: New Thinking for Our Country and the World*. New York: Perennial Press, 1988.

Shlapentokh, Vladimir. "Privatization Debates in Russia: 1989-1992," *Comparative Economic Studies*. Summer, 1993, p. 19.

"The Sixth Wave (Russia Survey—Economic Reform)," *The Economist*. Dec.5, 1992, p. S3.

Steele, Jonathan. *Eternal Russia: Yeltsin, Gorbachev, and the Mirage of Democracy*. Cambridge: Harvard University Press, 1994.

Taranovski, Theodore, ed. *Reform in Modern Russian History: Progress or Cycle?*. Washington, D.C.: Woodrow Wilson Center Press, 1995.

PERFORMANCE APPRAISAL AND STANDARDS

Performance appraisal is a process by which organizations evaluate **employee performance** based on preset standards. The main purpose of appraisals is to help organizations achieve objectives. When conducted properly, appraisals serve that purpose by: 1) showing employees how to improve their performance; and 2) helping managers to assess subordinates' effectiveness and take actions related to hiring, promotions, training, compensation, job design, and other responsibilities.

Following, the role of performance appraisal systems are described, the structure of effective programs are reviewed, different evaluation techniques are examined, and legal influences are discussed.

In the early part of this century performance appraisals were used in larger organizations mostly for administrative purposes, such as making promotions and determining salaries and bonuses. Since the 1960s, however, companies and researchers have increasingly stressed the use of employee evaluations for motivational and organizational planning purposes. Indeed, for many companies performance appraisal has become an important tool for maximizing the effectiveness of all aspects of the organization, from staffing and development to production and customer service.

That shift of focus was accompanied during the 1970s, 1980s, and early 1990s by a number of changes in the design and use of appraisals. Those changes reflected new research and attitudes about **organizational behavior** and theory. In general, employee evaluation systems have recognized the importance of individual needs and cultural influences in achieving organizational objectives. For example, traditional appraisal systems were often closed, meaning that individuals were not allowed to see their own reports. Since the mid-1900s, most companies have rejected closed evaluations in favor of open appraisals that allow workers to benefit from criticism and praise.

Another change in appraisal techniques since the mid-1900s has been a move toward greater employee participation. This includes self-analysis, employee input into evaluations, feedback, and **goal setting** by workers. Appraisal systems have also become more results-oriented, which means that appraisals are more focused on a process of establishing benchmarks, setting individual objectives, measuring performance, and then judging success based on the goals, standards, and accomplishments. Likewise, appraisals have become more multi-faceted, incorporating a wide range of different criteria and approaches to ensure an effective assessment process and to help determine the reasons behind employees' performance.

Performance appraisals and standards have also reflected a move toward decentralization. In other words, the responsibility for managing the entire appraisal process has moved closer to the employees that are being evaluated; whereas past performance reviews were often metered out by centralized **human resources** departments or upper-level managers, appraisals in the 1990s are much more likely to be conducted by line managers directly above the appraisee. Furthermore, the appraisal process has become increasingly integrated into complementary organizational initiatives, such as training and mentoring.

In addition to reflecting new ideas about personal needs and cultural influences, performance appraisal systems have evolved during the late 1900s to meet strict new federal regulations and to conform to labor union demands. A flurry of legislation during the 1970s and 1980s, for example, prohibited the use of performance appraisals to discriminate against members of selected minority groups. Other laws established restrictions related to privacy and freedom of information. The end result of new laws and labor demands was that companies were forced to painstakingly design and document their appraisal programs to avoid costly disputes and litigation.

THE ROLE OF PERFORMANCE APPRAISAL

Competent appraisal of individual performance in an organization or company serves to improve the overall effectiveness of the entity. The three main functional areas of performance appraisal systems are: administrative, informative, and motivational. (*The Human Side of Enterprise*, McGraw-Hill, 1960). Appraisals serve an administrative role by facilitating an orderly means of determining salary raises and other rewards, and by delegating authority and responsibility to the most capable individuals. The informative function is fulfilled when the appraisal system supplies data to managers and appraisees about individual strengths and weaknesses. Finally, the motivational role entails creating a learning experience that motivates workers to improve their performance.

Benefits of effective performance appraisal accrue to: 1) appraisees; 2) appraisers (managers); and 3) the organization. Appraisees benefit in a number of ways. For example, they discover what is expected of them and are able to set goals. They also gain a better understanding of their faults and strengths and can adjust behavior accordingly. In addition, appraisals create a constructive forum for providing feedback to workers about individual behavior, and for allowing workers to provide input to their managers. Finally, appraisees are (ideally) given assistance in creating plans to improve behavior, and are able to get a better grasp on the goals and priorities of their superiors.

Appraisers gain from evaluations as well. They are able to effectively identify and measure trends in the performance of their employees, and to more accurately compare subordinates. They also get a better understanding of their workers' needs and expectations. Managers are able to use the information to assist their subordinates in planning long-term and short-term goals and career objectives, and to tailor their job responsibilities to make fuller use of their skills. Importantly, the appraisal process helps managers to make informed decisions about promotions and assignments based on applicable facts.

Chief benefits that can accrue to the entire organization from the appraisal process include: improved communication, which results in more cooperation and better **decision making**; greater staff motivation; and a more informed **workforce**, which leads to a greater organizational focus on comprehensive goals. Specifically, the performance appraisal process allows the organization to achieve a more productive division of labor, develop training and education programs, eliminate bias and irrelevant data from evaluations and decisions, and design effective compensation and reward systems.

PERFORMANCE APPRAISAL SYSTEMS

Most effective systems of appraising performance are: 1) pragmatic; 2) germane; and 3) uniform. Pragmatism is important because it helps to ensure that the system will be easily understood by employees and effectively put into action by managers. Appraisal structures that are complex or impractical tend to result in confusion, frustration, and nonuse. Likewise, systems that are not germane, or not specifically related to the job, may result in wasted time and resources. Indeed, most successful appraisal programs identify and evaluate only the critical behaviors that contribute to job success. Systems that miss those behaviors are often invalid, inaccurate, and result in **discrimination** based on non-related factors. Finally, uniformity of the appraisal structure is vital because it ensures that all employees will be evaluated on a standardized scale. Appraisals that are not uniform are less effective because the criteria for success or failure becomes arbitrary and meaningless.

Keeping in mind the three key traits of effective performance appraisal programs, companies must address four decisions when structuring their appraisal systems: 1) What should be assessed?; 2) Who should make the appraisal?; 3) Which procedure(s) should be utilized?; and 4) How will the results be communicated? In determining what to evaluate, designers of an appraisal system usually consider not only results, but also the behaviors that lead to the results. The actions and results that are measured will depend on a variety of factors specific to the company and industry. Most importantly, criteria should be selected that will encourage the achievement of comprehensive corporate objectives. This is accomplished by determining the exact role of each job in accomplishing company goals, and which behaviors and results are critical for success in each position. Furthermore, different criteria for success should be weighted to reflect their importance.

In determining who should address performance, managers of the performance appraisal system usually select an employee's immediate supervisor to provide the assessment, which is then reviewed by a higher-level manager or the personnel department. In addition, other appraisers may be selected depending on: their knowledge of, and opportunity to observe, the appraisee's behavior; their ability to translate observations into useful ratings; and their motivation to provide constructive input about the employee's performance. (*Personnel/Human Resource Management*, Business Publications, 1988). Other evaluators may include coworkers, subordinates, or even the employees themselves.

After selecting performance appraisal criteria and evaluators, the designers of the system must determine which assessment techniques to use. Numerous methods may be applied depending on the nature of the industry, company, or job. As noted earlier, many organizations utilize a combination of several techniques throughout the organization. In general, the most popular rating techniques fall into one of four categories: 1) rating, in which evaluators judge workers based on different characteristics; 2) ranking, whereby supervisors compare employees to one another; 3) critical incidents, in which evaluators create descriptions of good and bad behavior and then assign those descriptions to employees; and 4) techniques that use multiple or miscellaneous criteria, such as employee-directed standards. Popular appraisal techniques are detailed below.

In addition to selecting evaluation techniques, managers of appraisal systems must devise a means of effectively communicating the results of assessments to employees. Often, the communication process is built-in to the appraisal technique, but sometimes it isn't. Feedback about performance is important for improving worker behavior. For instance, a worker who receives a very positive appraisal will likely become motivated to perform. On the other hand, a poor appraisal could have the opposite effect. For that reason, assessors have a number of feedback techniques at their disposal to help ensure that the end result of any assessment is constructive. Examples of feedback methods are written follow-ups, goal-setting to overcome deficiencies, and allowing workers to have input into their appraisal to explain reasons for success or failure. Importantly, most feedback techniques stress a delineation between an employee and his negative behavior (i.e. the employee still has value, despite his/her deficient behavior).

After addressing the four questions of what, who, which and how, an organization must evaluate the system itself to determine if it is helping to achieve designated organizational objectives (and conforming with legal guidelines, as discussed below). Managers of the appraisal system need to determine whether or not the system is being implemented properly: Are managers being rewarded for conducting appraisals?;

Are they being trained to perform the evaluations properly?; Are evaluations based on specific job-related criteria? Furthermore, they need to take action to determine whether or not the system is producing measurable results: Are the results of individual appraisals valid?; Is the system producing consistent and reliable information for use in making decisions?; Are employees developing and achieving goals as a result of appraisal and feedback?

BIAS AND ERRORS

Even when a performance evaluation program is structured appropriately, its effectiveness can be diluted by the improper use of subjective, as opposed to objective, measures. Objective measures are easily incorporated into an appraisal because they are quantifiable and verifiable. For example, a fast-food worker may be rated on the number of cars he (she) can serve at a drive-through window during an eight-hour period. Other objective measures commonly include error rates, number of complaints, frequency of failure, or other tangible gauges. In contrast, subjective measures are those that cannot be quantified and are largely dependent on the opinion of an observer. For example, an appraisal of the fast-food worker's courteousness and attitude would be subjective.

Subjective measures have the potential to dilute the quality of worker evaluations because they may be influenced by bias, or distortion as a result of emotion. To overcome the effects of prejudice, many organizations train appraisers to avoid six common forms of bias: **cross-cultural**, error of central tendency, halo effect, leniency and strictness, personal prejudice, and recency effect. The recency effect is a corollary of the natural tendency for raters to judge an employee's performance based largely on his most recent actions rather than taking into account long-term patterns.

Cross-cultural bias is a consequence of an evaluator's expectations about human behavior. Those expectations often clash with the behavior of appraisees that have different beliefs or cultural values. For instance, an evaluator with an Asian heritage may be more likely to rate an older employee higher because he has been taught to revere older people. Likewise, personal prejudice results from a rater's dislike for a group or class of people. When that dislike carries over into the appraisal of an individual, an inaccurate review of performance is the outcome. For example, studies have shown that black raters and white raters are much more likely to give high rankings to members of their own race. (Kraiger and Ford, *Journal of Applied Psychology*, 1985).

Like cross-cultural and personal prejudice biases, the halo effect is caused by a rater's personal opinions about a specific employee that are not job-related. The term "halo" stems from the distortion that the ap-

praisee, like an angel with a halo over its head, can do no wrong. However, this type of bias also applies to foes of the rater. The effect is particularly pronounced when the appraisee is an enemy or very good friend of the evaluator.

Leniency and strictness bias results when the appraiser tends to view the performance of all of his employees as either good and favorable or bad and unfavorable. Although these distortions are often the result of vague performance standards, they may also be the consequence of the evaluator's attitudes. For example, some evaluators want their subordinates to like them (leniency bias) or want to feel like they are being a "tough judge" (strictness). Similarly, the error of central tendency occurs when appraisers are hesitant to grade employees as effective or ineffective. They pacify their indecisiveness by rating all workers near the center of the performance scale, thus avoiding extremes that could cause conflict or require an explanation.

In addition to bias, flaws in the execution of an appraisal program can be destructive. For instance, managers may be downgrading their employees because high performance reviews would outstrip the department's budget for bonuses. Or, some managers may be using performance appraisals to achieve personal or departmental political goals, thus distorting assessments. Problems are usually indicated, for example, by extremely high numbers of poor or positive appraisals, or by a general lack of individual improvement over the long term. In any case, appraisal managers must identify and overcome the causes of these flaws to ensure the usefulness of the system. This is typically accomplished through a formal process of evaluating the effectiveness of the appraisal program itself, as discussed above.

PERFORMANCE APPRAISAL TECHNIQUES

In addition to separating them into the four general categories discussed above, different performance appraisal techniques can be classified as either past-oriented or future-oriented. (*Human Resources and Personnel Management*, 3rd ed., McGraw-Hill, 1989). Past-oriented techniques assess behavior that has already occurred. They focus on providing feedback to employees about their actions, feedback that is used to achieve greater success in the future. In contrast, future-oriented appraisal techniques emphasize future performance by assessing employees' potential for achievement and by setting targets for both short- and long-term performance. A few of the more popular techniques from each category are explained below.

PAST-ORIENTED. Rating scales are among the most popular and traditional form of performance appraisal. They entail an assessor providing a subjective assessment of an individuals' performance based on a scale effectively ranging from good to bad. Typically, basic criteria like dependability, attitude, and attendance are listed, and the evaluator simply checks a box beside each factor to indicate, for example, excellent, good, fair, or poor. A value may be assigned to each level of success—a rating of fair, for instance, might be worth two points—and the appraisee's score totaled to determine his (her) **ranking**. The obvious advantage of rating scales is that they are inexpensive and easy to administer. Primary disadvantages include the fact that these scales are: highly susceptible to all forms of bias; often neglect key job-related information and include unnecessary data; provide limited opportunities for effective feedback; and fail to set standards for future success. Furthermore, subjective techniques like rating scales are vulnerable to legal attack.

Checklist and adjective checklist appraisals are similar to rating scales, except the assessor puts checks next to pre-written statements (or adjectives) that he believes describe the individual. Examples of statements would be "works well with others" or "never works overtime when asked." To each statement is ascribed a value that is subjectively determined by the creator of the checklist and is not disclosed to the rater. The values are totaled to determine the worker's performance—a high rating is usually positive. Like rating scales, checklists are easy and inexpensive to administer. But they also suffer from the same disadvantages as rating scales. An additional drawback of checklists is that they don't allow relative rankings; a worker who is excellent at cooperating with others would receive the same ranking as a coworker who is simply good at working with other people.

Behaviorally anchored rating scales (BARSs) are designed to identify job-related activities and responsibilities and to describe the more effective and less effective behaviors that lead to success in specific jobs. The rater observes a worker and then records his behavior on a BARS. The system is similar to checklist methods in that statements are essentially checked off as true or false. However, BARSs differs in that they use combinations of job-related statements that allow the assessor to differentiate between behavior, performance, and results. Therefore, BARSs can be more effectively utilized in the goal-setting process. The advantage of BARSs is that they are extremely job specific, easy to administer, and eliminate most biases. However, they can be difficult and expensive to develop and maintain.

Forced-choice appraisals consist of a list of paired (or larger groups of) statements. The statements in each pair may both be negative or positive, or one could be positive and the other negative. The evaluator is forced to choose one statement from each

pair that most closely describes the individual. An example of a pair of statements might be "Always on Time" and "Never on Time." By incorporating several question groups that test different levels or degrees of the same behaviors, evaluators are able to generate an accurate representation of the individual's learning ability, interpersonal competence, drive, and other characteristics. Forced-choice appraisals are typically easy to understand and inexpensive to administer. However, they lack job-relatedness and provide little opportunity for constructive feedback.

Critical incident evaluation techniques require the assessor to record statements that describe good and bad job-related behavior (critical incidents) exhibited by the employee. The statements are grouped by categories like cooperation, timeliness, attitude, etc. An advantage of this system is that it can be used very successfully to give feedback to employees. Furthermore, it is less susceptible to some forms of bias. On the other hand, critical incident assessments are difficult for managers to maintain (or record incidents as they occur), and they do not lend themselves to **standardization**.

Field review appraisal techniques entail the use of human resource professionals to assist managers in conducting appraisals. The specialist asks the manager questions about an employee's performance, records the answers, prepares an evaluation, and sends it to the manager to review and discuss with the employee. This type of system improves reliability and standardization because a personnel professional is doing the assessment. For the same reason, it is less susceptible to bias or to legal problems. But field reviews are generally expensive and impractical for most firms, and are typically utilized only in special instances—to counteract charges of bias, for example.

A separate category of past-oriented appraisals are comparative evaluations, which encompass several techniques used to compare employees to one another. In general, employees in a group or department are ranked from best to worst by a single supervisor. The results are often not shown outside of the department, and sometimes are kept from employees. Comparative appraisals are useful for creating pay scales, splitting bonuses between departments, and making promotions. Comparative evaluations are, by nature, subjective, and therefore open to bias. They also offer few feedback opportunities and may even create bitter conflict if the ratings are made available to the group. However, they offer the ultimate form of appraisal standardization within a department (assuming bias is not involved), and are easy and inexpensive to administer.

There are at least four general categories of comparative evaluations. Paired comparisons force raters to contrast the performance of each individual with that of each member of the group. The employee that receives the greatest number of favorable comparisons is the best of the group. A second form of comparison is the point allocation method, in which the assessor allocates a fixed number of points to the employees. Forced distributions are similar, but the evaluator must sort employees into different categories (such as top 20 percent, middle 40 percent, and bottom 20 percent). In simpler ranking comparisons, the fourth category of comparative evaluations, workers are simply rated in order from best to worst.

FUTURE-ORIENTED. One of the most popular future-oriented performance appraisal techniques utilizes the management by objectives (MBO) approach. In MBO, managers and employees work together to set goals. In fact, MBO is usually goal-oriented, with the intent of helping employees to achieve continuous improvement through an ongoing process of goal-setting, feedback, and correction. As a result of their input, employees are much more likely to be motivated to accomplish the goals and to be responsive to criticism that arises from subsequent objective measurements of performance. Although it achieved fad status in the late 1970s and into the 1980s, critics of MBO cite its propensity to focus on objectively measured behaviors, such as quantity of output, at the expense of subjective criteria, like quality of output. The result can be employee frustration or lackluster performance.

Assessment center evaluation is a more complex assessment method that is usually applied to managerial or executive prospects. It is a system of determining future potential based on multiple evaluations and raters. Typically, a group meets at a training facility or evaluation site. They are evaluated individually through a battery of interviews, tests, and exercises. In addition, they are evaluated within a group setting during decision-making exercises, team projects, and group discussions. Psychologists and managers work together to evaluate the employees' future management potential and to identify strengths and weaknesses. Assessment centers are susceptible to bias, have been criticized as not being specifically job-related, and are extremely costly. However, they have also proven effective and have achieved broad appeal in the corporate world.

Psychological tests are a much less intricate method of determining future potential. They normally consist of interviews with the employee and his supervisors and coworkers, as well as different types of tests and evaluations of intellectual, emotional, and work-related characteristics. The psychologist puts his findings and conclusions in a report that may or may not be shared with the employee. Psychological testing is slow and costly, and must be administered extremely carefully because of the long-term implica-

tions of the evaluation on the employee's future. Success is largely dependent on the skill of the psychologist.

Another appraisal technique included in the future-oriented category is self-appraisal, which entails employees making evaluations of their own performance. Although self-assessment techniques may also be coordinated with past-oriented evaluations, they are particularly useful in helping employees to set personal goals and identify areas of behaviors that need improvement. The advantage of such appraisals, which may be relatively informal, is that they provide an excellent forum for input and feedback by superiors. In addition, they allow supervisors to find out what employees expect from themselves and from the organization or department. Furthermore, because the employee is much less defensive about the criticism, self-improvement is much more likely.

LEGAL INFLUENCES

Federal laws related to performance appraisals, most of which are enforced by the **Equal Employment Opportunity Commission (EEOC)**, as well as a plethora of court decisions have turned the evaluation process into a legal mine field for many companies. Because appraisals are used to make promotions, give raises, establish salaries, and terminate workers, they must conform to strict EEOC Uniform Guidelines on Employee Selection Procedures. Specifically, the law requires that performance appraisals: 1) are job related and utilize behavior-oriented, rather than trait-oriented, criteria; 2) use tests, measurements, scales, feedback and other evaluation tools derived from an analysis of each individual job; 3) not reflect a bias based on race, color, sex, religion, age, or nationality; and 4) be conducted by persons that have distinct knowledge of the position.

In addition to explicit federal guidelines, court cases have also had an impact on appraisal processes. For example, court decisions have demonstrated that, even if it designs its appraisal system according to legal guidelines, a company may be at fault if the numeric results of its appraisal system reflect bias against a protected minority group. Suppose, for example, that statistics showed that a company's appraisal system resulted in a disproportionate number of employees of Mexican descent receiving promotions and raises, while a disproportionate number of African-American workers did not receive the same rewards. Unless the organization could prove that its decisions were based only on specific job-related factors, its appraisal system could be judged as biased in the courts. Therefore, managers of appraisal systems must be careful to monitor results as well as structure.

In addition to legal ramifications related to bias, numerous other laws affect appraisal systems. Evaluations must conform to a battery of privacy laws, for example. Companies are not allowed to divulge personal information to outside sources, for instance, and are required to make most information gathered during the evaluation process available to employees at their request. Likewise, evaluators must be careful to steer clear of protected personal information that does not relate specifically to the ability of the worker to perform his or her job. Such questions include inquiries about pregnancy, age, sexual practices, family, and health. For instance, a company would be leaving itself open to legal attack if it asked an employee whether or not she planned to have children in the near future and then made a decision not to promote her based on that answer.

An organization could opt out of conducting any type of appraisal program as a way of avoiding litigation risks. But even that option becomes risky if the company's promotion/salary practices can be shown to be statistically discriminatory (because the company is left with no documentation to prove the legal validity of its decisions). A safer approach is to structure the performance appraisal system in accordance with EEOC guidelines, and to: carefully record all decisions related to staffing, promotions, bonuses, and other actions impacted by appraisals; create specific job requirements; share appraisals only with staff members and people that have an interest in the assessment that is specifically related to the job; document and follow procedures that eliminate bias and errors from the process; and conduct periodic evaluations of the program to ensure that the appraisal process is producing unbiased results.

[Dave Mote]

FURTHER READING:

Anderson, Gordon C. *Managing Performance Appraisal Systems.* Cambridge, MA: Blackwell Publishers, 1993.

Brown, Robert D. *Performance Appraisal as a Tool for Staff Development.* San Francisco, CA: Jossey-Bass, 1988.

Kraiger, Kurt, and J. Kevin Ford. "A Meta-Analysis of Ratee Race Effects in Performance Ratings." *Journal of Applied Psychology.* 1985.

McGregor, D. *The Human Side of Enterprise.* New York: McGraw-Hill, 1960.

Milkovich, George T., and John W. Boudreau. *Personnel/Human Resource Management: A Diagnostic Approach.* Plano, TX: Business Publications, 1988.

Werther, William B., Jr., and Keith Davis. *Human Resources and Personnel Management.* 3rd ed. New York: McGraw-Hill, 1989.

Schuster, Frederick E. *Human Resource Management: Concepts, Cases and Readings.* 2nd ed. Reston, VA: Reston Publishing Company, 1985.

PERSONAL INCOME TAX

Tax on one's personal income, or income tax, had a haphazard evolution prior to the passage of the Sixteenth, or "income tax," Amendment in 1912. Prior to the Civil War, property tax was the main form of personal tax, although strictly defined, this was not an income tax. The federal government, with a budget operating in the black for most of the nineteenth century, obtained the bulk of its revenues from the imposition of high tariffs on imports, including food products.

The colony of Massachusetts was the first in the New World to impose a personal income tax in 1634, even though the property tax still remained the most important source of revenue. By then the idea had gained acceptance that wealth was more than just visible property. That is, a person had certain skills and knowledge that could produce income, even if he owned no property. Hence the colony imposed a tax on the incomes of artisans and doctors, for example. The difficulty that the colony faced with income tax is an old one: taxpayers concealed their taxable income and paid as little as possible.

The U.S. Constitution, which was ratified in 1788, contained an explicit guarantee of the central government's power to tax in Article I, Section 8, but did not say anything about a tax on personal income, nor was one adopted on a national scale.

This changed with the outbreak of the Civil War, when the federal government desperately needed more revenue. The Revenue Act signed by President Lincoln in July 1862 restored the office of Commissioner of Internal Revenue (which Thomas Jefferson had abolished). The commissioner was empowered to establish a system to collect a progressive income tax based on mandatory income withholding (a tax return form was duly created), as well as to collect numerous other internal taxes. For the first time, an individual's failure to comply with the tax laws could result in punishment, and confiscation of **assets** in the most extreme cases. Taxpayers had to sign their tax returns under oath.

By the end of fiscal year 1863, the new revenue bureau took in, through its assessors and collectors, the sum of $40 million. By war's end, the Bureau of Internal Revenue had mushroomed from one employee to over 4,000.

The income tax was discontinued after the Civil War, since Congress had intended it originally as a wartime expedient only. In 1894, however, with import tariffs under increasing criticism, Congress once again passed an income tax law, only to have the Supreme Court annul it a year later. The problem lay in the vagueness of the Constitution which gave the federal government the right to tax, but did not give it the explicit right to tax personal incomes.

In February 1913, the states approved the Sixteenth Amendment. It quite simply invested Congress with authority to ''lay and collect taxes on incomes, from whatever source derived.'' On October 13, 1913, Congress once again passed an income tax law, the first since the abortive 1894 bill. It stipulated that all incomes above $3,000 would be taxed. An annual salary of over $3,000 in those days was a generous middle class income; below that, no one paid income tax. Hence, fewer than 1 percent of working people would file tax returns. Reform-minded Americans hailed the graduated income tax as a sound blow to ''special interests.'' The Bureau of Internal Revenue, a division of the U.S. Department of the Treasury, would administer and collect the new income tax, as it had during the Civil War. Nine years later, it established an intelligence division for the surveillance of income tax evaders.

As late as 1940 only 11 percent of working people were required to file, despite the huge cost of the preceding New Deal social legislation. World War II increased the need for more and better collection of revenue; in 1943, Congress mandated personal payroll deductions, which increased revenue to $45 billion in 1945, up from a mere $7.4 billion in 1941.

Unlike the Civil War period when payroll deductions were introduced for the first time only to be discontinued (with the dismantling of income tax) after the Civil War, mandatory payroll deductions remained in force after 1945. Moreover, by war's end, all working people were required to file income tax returns.

With the increase in taxpayers, the number of penalties that the **Internal Revenue Service** (IRS) had the power to enforce on errant taxpayers escalated from a mere 13 in 1954 to 150 in 1990, the year in which the IRS made nearly three million seizures of taxpayers' assets.

Under President Ronald Reagan, tax reform became a high priority. Taxes seemed too high and tax forms too complicated. In 1986, his tax reform package inaugurated the most sweeping changes in American income tax since 1913.

In essence, Reagan's tax measure slashed individual income taxes and drastically cut government spending, all in the hope of putting more money into the consumer's pocket. Individual tax brackets were reduced to two in number: all incomes up to $17,600 were taxed 15 percent; over that amount, 27 percent. Six million low-income working people were exempt from paying any federal income tax at all. For the middle class on up, dozens of deductions were eliminated, including the traditional deductions for pay-

ment of state income tax and **individual retirement account (IRA)** deposits. The business and corporate world would carry the tax burden, according to the 1986 tax reform bill, and not the individual. Despite the Reagan tax reform measure, personal income tax has continued to be a controversial issue. On the eve of the twenty-first century, proponents of a flat tax and the elimination of income tax have gained increasing popularity.

Since 1911, when Wisconsin introduced the first state income tax in the nation, 42 states have followed suit. Most taxpaying individuals must thus file two separate income tax returns each year.

SEE ALSO: Taxes and Taxation

[Sina Dubovoy]

FURTHER READING:

Bartlett, Donald L., and James B. Steele. *America: Who Really Pays the Taxes?* New York: Simon & Schuster, 1994.

Cnossen, Sijbren, and Richard M. Bird, eds. *The Personal Income Tax: Phoenix from the Ashes?* Amsterdam and New York: Elsevier Science Publication Co., 1990.

PERSONAL SELLING

Personal selling is communicating with a potential buyer (or buyers) face-to-face with the purpose of selling a product or service. The main thing that sets personal selling apart from other methods of selling is that the salesperson conducts his or her business with the customer *in person.*

Personal selling dates back to the beginning of history. According to Philip Kotler, renowned marketing expert and author of *Marketing: An Introduction*, selling goes back as far as the Bronze Age. Traveling sales kits made up of bones and stones have actually been found from this era. In the United States, the first salesmen were Yankee peddlers who carried their goods from the east on their backs. They traded clothing, spices, pots and pans, and other household goods to settlers in the western frontier. The father of modern selling techniques is considered to be John Henry Patterson the head of National Cash Register company. As far back as the late 1800s he was implementing sales training programs, quotas, and sales territories for his sales staff. He also introduced the notion of canned sales talks.

Personal selling is one part of the promotion mix, the various ways businesses choose with reach or communicate to their customers. The main elements in a promotion mix are advertising, sales promotion, public relations, and personal selling. **Advertising** is any form of paid presentation or promotion that is not done face-to-face. Television commercials are a well-known form of advertising. Sales promotion is the use of incentives to entice a customer to buy a product or service, such as **coupons**. Public relations is the act of building up the image of a company in the eyes of the community in the hopes of translating the feelings of goodwill into sales. An example of public relations is a company sponsoring a charity event. The final component of the promotion mix is personal selling. Personal selling is giving a demonstration or presentation to a potential customer in person.

Deciding on the promotion mix involves many factors. Businesses may choose to use any or all of the promotion mix tools and must decide how to allocate resources for each component. Some of the things organizations should consider when deciding on a promotion mix are the type of product or service sold, the unit value of the product or service, and the budget allotted for the promotion mix. Of all the industries involved in the promotion mix, the personal selling industry involves the most people. As a comparison, there are about 500,000 people involved in the advertising industry but more than 13 million people in personal selling.

In general, if a product has a high unit value and requires a demonstration, it is well suited for personal sales. For example, an encyclopedia is a high-priced item and most people do not feel they need one. After a demonstration, however, most people agree it would be a useful item to have. Therefore, encyclopedias are well suited to a promotion mix that emphasizes personal selling. Highly technical products are also primarily sold through personal sales methods. Computers and copiers are good examples of technical products that are best sold through personal sales. Products that involve a trade-in are also best sold through personal selling to help facilitate the trade-in process. Automobile sales often involve a trade-in and almost always involve a personal sales transaction. And finally, an organization that cannot afford an advertising campaign (which is a very expensive endeavor) might consider personal selling as an alternative to advertising. A personal **sales force** is a relatively inexpensive alternative to advertising as the primary cost is the sales force compensation. Since sales force compensation is largely based on actual sales, a sales force is an investment that requires much less money up front than do other forms of the promotion mix that need time to pay off.

Personal selling as a career is unique and offers many benefits. It is, however, not for everyone. In general it involves long, irregular work hours and extensive travel. A personal salesperson should also be able to handle rejection face-to-face, which is a large component of the job. On the other hand, personal sales offers great rewards for those who are successful. Because most compensation involves commissions-based on sales made, the potential for income is great. With personal sales, there is no ceiling on what a person can earn, as there is with other salaried jobs. Also, many people enjoy the freedom of flexible hours, and the fact that a personal salesperson has little contact with a supervisor. A career in personal sales offers a person the chance to develop interpersonal, communication, organizational, and time-management skills.

Sales force compensation varies from one organization and industry to another. All compensation plans, however, contain one or more of the following components: commission, bonuses, **expense accounts**, incentives, benefits, and a salary or draw. Commission is the most common type of sales force compensation—when a salesperson is paid a percentage of the sale he or she makes and so directly ties compensation to performance. Bonuses based on performance are often employed as well. With expense accounts or allowances, some companies will reimburse salespeople for business expenses incurred. Another form of compensation, and one that can be extremely motivating for some people, is incentive prizes earned through sales contests. Cars, trips, cash, and any other number of prizes are offered in exchange for meeting certain sales goals. Many companies offer benefits such as life and health insurance, although these benefits too can be tied to sales performance. And finally, some companies pay a base salary or draw, usually in conjunction with one or some of the other compensation elements. A draw is a fixed amount that is held against future sales earnings of a salesperson. This is usually offered to a new salesperson to offer earnings stability while he or she is learning the business. Usually if the salesperson does not make future sales, he or she is not held responsible for the amount.

In general, the tighter the control a company has over a salesperson, the larger the role salary plays in compensation. For example, an IBM salesperson, based in a branch office and receiving extensive training and supervision, may have a large part of his beginning compensation plan made up of a base salary or draw. At the other end of the spectrum you may find a *World Book* salesperson, based in her home, with little training and supervision. She may never even see a branch office and will be compensated entirely in commissions and bonuses.

Just as you will find many different types of sales force compensation, you will also find many different types of personal sales jobs. A noted industrial psychologist, Robert McMurry identified the main types of personal sales jobs:

- Driver-sales person: this person merely delivers the product and has few selling responsibilities.

- Inside order taker: In this position a person takes orders from within a selling environment. Examples include a sales clerk in a retail store, or a phone representative working for a catalog sales company. Some selling skills are required.

- Outside order taker: These salespeople go to the customer's place of business and take orders. Most of these sales are repeat business. Some selling is required, especially to establish new accounts.

- Missionary sales person: This type of sales involves selling goodwill but not any actual product or service. This salesperson's goal is to make a customer feel good about the company and products or services he or she represents. Some businesses that employ missionary salespeople are in the pharmaceutical and liquor industries.

- Sales engineer: These positions are found in technical industries such as computers and copiers. Sales engineers provide technical support, explain the products, and adapt the product to the customer's needs.

- Creative sales person: These sales people must be the most creative of all sales people as they attempt to sell goods (vacuum cleaners or encyclopedias) but more often ideas, such as services (insurance) or causes (charities). These salespeople are usually dealing with customers who are unaware of their need for the service or product, and so, the salespeople must possess the most selling skills of all the types of salespeople.

Although there are many different types of salespeople, they all go through the same basic steps when making a sale. Prospecting and qualifying, preapproach, approach, presentation and demonstration, handling objectives, closing, and follow-up are frequently identified as the steps to a sale, and are employed by all personal salespeople to one extent or another. Although training for personal sales forces may vary from one organization to another, the majority of the training will include some version of these steps.

Prospecting and qualifying are the acts of finding potential customers and finding out if they are in a buying position. Prospecting, or lead-generation, can be as simple as asking current customers for names of acquaintances, or as sophisticated as using a database or mailing list. Often the salesperson's company provides leads, but a truly successful salesperson will also be able to generate his or her own leads. Generally, prospecting involves an element of cold-calling—that is calling an unknown potential customer and introducing yourself and your product. Often this

is the least favorite part of a salesperson's job but ultimately one of the most important. In addition to prospecting for clients, a salesperson needs to qualify the customer. Is the potential customer in a buying decision-making position? Does this customer need the product or service? Can the customer afford the product? In all sales positions, the salesperson needs to contact many, many prospects before making a sale.

The preapproach is the step salespeople take when they are researching their prospective customer—often another company. They may read up on the company, talk to other vendors, or find out more about the industry. The salesperson will also take time to set sales call objectives and try to determine the best time to make the sales call.

The next step is the approach. This step is crucial for a salesperson to start out on the right foot. The salesperson should introduce himself or herself, the company represented, and the product or service being offered. It is also important that the salesperson listen carefully to the prospect and respond appropriately. All of this will make sure the sales call starts out right.

Once the approach has been made the salesperson should be ready to launch into the demonstration or presentation. Depending on the company and the product or service, there are generally three types of presentations. The canned approach is a tightly scripted talk that is either memorized or read. The formula approach is less rigid and, depending on the buyer's response to some carefully asked questions, the seller will go to a formula presentation that he or she hopes will meet the customer's needs. The third presentation style is the need-satisfaction approach where the seller tries to find out the customer's needs mostly by listening.

Presentations and demonstrations may involve any number of visual aids, such as flip-charts, or demonstrations of the products themselves. One of the keys to a successful presentation is product knowledge. The more the salesperson knows about the product or service, the more relaxed he or she will be, and the more able to answer questions, fill the customer's need, and handle objections.

Handling objections is the next phase of selling. Almost every customer will present objections to making a purchase, whether real or not. A good salesperson is not flustered by these objections and handles them in a positive, confident manner. One approach to objections, used frequently with canned presentations, is to simply acknowledge the objection then continue to make the presentation. In the more tailored presentations the salesperson can handle the objection by turning them into reasons to buy.

The next step of a sale is often identified by novice salespeople as the toughest step. That step is closing, or asking the buyer to purchase. Some new salespeople are so reluctant to be perceived as being aggressive that they never try to close and the customer may become annoyed and decide not to purchase just for that reason. Customers must be given the chance to purchase. Salespeople need to learn to look for signals that a closing is appropriate. Common signals that customers give include asking questions, making comments, leaning forward or nodding, or asking about price or terms.

The last step of a sale is often neglected but is important for many reasons. The final step is the follow-up which can be done in person or by telephone. This gives the customer the chance to ask questions and reinforce his or her buying decision. The salesperson can review how to use the product, go over instructions and payment arrangements, and make sure the product has arrived in proper working order. This step ensures repeat business, is a good opportunity to get referrals, and increases the chances that subsequent payments will be made.

Personal selling involves specific steps, requires training and experience, and employs some of the finest salespeople around. Unfortunately, however, personal selling is often perceived as being a less than reputable field of work. Unethical salespeople, aggressive or hard sell tactics, and misleading sales pitches have made many buyers wary of personal sellers. Fortunately, much has been done to address this issue. Selling associations such as the Direct Selling Association have adopted codes of ethics that dictate standards of behavior that all members are to follow. Most organizations with large personal sales forces have also adopted their own codes of ethics that provide guidelines regarding the type of sales pitch that can be made, the hours a sales call may be made, and the prohibition of using misleading information or pressure tactics to make a sale. Much progress has been made in making personal selling a more reputable field, and efforts toward that goal will continue.

[Judith A. Zimmerman]

FURTHER READING:

Armstrong, Gary, and Philip Kotler. *Principles of Marketing*, 4th ed. Prentice-Hall, Inc., 1989.

Kimball, Bob. *AMA Handbook for Successful Selling*. NTC Business Books, 1994.

Kotler, Philip. *Marketing Management*, 8th ed. Prentice-Hall, Inc., 1994.

Kotler, Philip, and Gary Armstrong. *Marketing: an introduction*, 3rd ed. Prentice-Hall, Inc., 1993.

Stair, Lila B. *Careers in Marketing*. VGM Career Horizons, 1991.

Stanton, William J., Michael J. Etzel, and Bruce J. Walker. *Fundamentals in Marketing*, 10th ed. McGraw-Hill, Inc., 1994.

THE PETER PRINCIPLE

Co-written in 1969 by Dr. Laurence J. Peter and Raymond Hull, *The Peter Principle—Why Things Always Go Wrong* was a slim, 167-page management self-help book that became a best seller. It also added a catch phrase to business management that has been regularly quoted for the past 25 years.

The book stated and restated in a number of ways the observation Peter had made in his contact with store clerks, actors, business managers and other people he met outside the academic world he occupied. The Peter Principle: "In a hierarchy every employee tends to rise to his own level of incompetence."

The Peter Principle states that a good employee who is fulfilled doing a particular job may become a poor employee if promoted to a new position without evidence that he or she has the desire, ability and training to handle the job. Peter's observations and theories apply equally to the lowest level, undertalented employees to top corporate officers who may spend their time on trivial matters because their well-promoted underlings are doing all the interesting work.

His book was hailed as an explanation of why top producing salesmen sometimes make mediocre sales managers. It also explains today why founders of hot entrepreneurial companies frequently sell out to larger corporations because their skills at managing growing concerns have been overmatched by the task's requirements. The frustrated entrepreneurs sell out, then happily start building new companies, which was the strength they exhibited in the first place.

The book, co-written by a Canadian and a British-born writer living in Canada, suffers somewhat in reading today from a heavy emphasis on academic examples and nonexistent companies making nonsense products. Many examples in the book are of teachers and principals, reflecting Peter's history as a former teacher and a college professor. The book is also filled with theories given fancy, if sometimes made-up names, such as "hierarchal exfoliation" (the firing of both super-competent and super-incompetent employees) and "Peter's Circumbendibus" (a "veiled" detour up the corporate ladder around a "super incumbent" who is entrenched in a comfortable staff position and who has no intention of moving up the ladder by promotion so an eager underling can fill his slot in the hierarchy).

Peter and Hull filled the book with 19 other theories, including "Peter's Corollary" which says "In time, every post in a hierarchy tends to be occupied by an employee who is incompetent to carry out its duties." So, if that is true, how do corporations or any organizations accomplish anything? Peter's explanation is that all of the work is completed by people who have not yet reached their level of incompetence.

Peter also handles seeming exceptions to his principle such as the person who is ''kicked upstairs,'' promoted from a job where he is incompetent to a job where he will be even more incompetent. In Peter's view this promotion was made so to keep other employees thinking that the person really does know what he is doing (despite perceptions) and that if he can be promoted, they can too. Such promotions are supposedly given to keep incompetents who know how the business operates from joining the competition.

One of the unexpected theories in the book is that people in charge of hierarchies dislike super-competents as much as they dislike incompetents. According to Peter, simple incompetence is not always a reason for dismissal from a company because the employee can probably find a job he can do. However, super-competents, the men and women who seem to know everything and do everything well at all levels in anticipation of always moving up, are more likely to be fired because they disrupt the hierarchy. In Peter's view, these people attract too much attention to themselves, worrying others in the organization so much that they derail the super-competent's climb to the top.

Peter's book unabashedly champions finding a patron within the organization who will provide the ''pull'' necessary to create job opportunities for the competent person wishing to advance. On the other hand, he thinks ''push,'' self-initiative and self-promotion, have been given too much emphasis. He claims that no amount of push can overcome an employee who is on the rung of the ladder above (super incumbent), and push might be interpreted by superiors as not having focus in the current job.

In yet another emphasis on the inertia of hierarchies, Peter asserts that higher ranks frequently dislike ''leaders'' coming from the lower ranks because they are usually disruptive to the hierarchy. Disruption translates to insubordination, which translates to incompetence. He says what most take as leaders are really followers moving to the head of the following crowd. They are obeying precedents set before them by still higher leaders, who do not want or need anyone changing the rules of how to run the organization.

Peter touches on organizational politics in the book, pointing out that most companies organize around favoritism of some class over another. He points to the '60s definition of a ''Harvard'' man as at the top of his profession while graduates of ''Outer Sheepskin College'' are never admiringly called ''A Sheepskin Man.''

What happens when a person rises to the top of an organization without reaching a level of incompetence Peter says is inevitable? He sometimes changes jobs to find other ''challenges.'' Peter sites as examples military men who join industry, or retired politicians who go into higher education. He believes these successful people did not spend enough time in their previous careers to find their own level of incompetence.

The other possibility for the top level person is that they reach the top and then become almost instantly incompetent. Peter cites corporate board members who tell jokes rather than deal with company problems, or who spend their time rearranging reporting responsibilities instead of planning future successes.

Essentially, the Peter Principle asserts that everyone has skills that can fit somewhere, but in due time a person's skills will outstrip the requirements for the job. A person will eventually land in a job for which he or she is incompetent.

[Clint Johnson]

FURTHER READING:

Peter, Dr. Laurence J., and Raymond Hill. *The Peter Principle*. William Morrow & Company, 1969.

PHILANTHROPY

SEE: Corporate Image; Corporate Philanthropy

PHYSICAL DISTRIBUTION MANAGEMENT (TRANSPORTATION)

Physical distribution (or logistics management) is concerned with the transporting of merchandise, raw materials, or by-products (such as hazardous waste) from the source to the customer. A manager of physical distribution must also assess and control the cost of transporting these goods and materials, as well as determine the most efficient way to store them, which usually involves some form of warehousing. Hence, physical distribution (PD) is concerned with **inventory control**, as well as with **packaging** and handling. **Customer relations**, order processing, and **marketing** are also related activities of PD.

In essence, physical distribution management (PDM) involves controlling the movement of materials and goods from their source to their destination. It is a highly complex process, and one of the most important aspects of any business. PDM is the ''other'' side of marketing. While marketing creates demand, PDM's goal is to satisfy demand as quickly, capably, and cheaply as possible.

One could maintain that PD is as old as civilization. Even merchants in ancient times had to move goods and raw materials to their destination, and to engage in storage and inventory control. Until the Industrial Revolution, however, these activities were carried out inefficiently: goods usually were replenished slowly, and there were far fewer goods than in the era of mass production. If marketing was conducted at all, it was usually done at the point of purchase.

The Industrial Revolution ushered in mass production and, by the late nineteenth century, the beginnings of mass marketing. Goods and raw materials also were conveyed over greater distances. Nonetheless, until World War II, PD was far less important than production and marketing. Physical distribution of goods and materials also remained basically unchanged, carried out as separate, unrelated activities—transportation and handling, storage, and inventory control.

The postwar years witnessed an unprecedented explosion of consumer goods and brands, thanks to modern mass marketing, the population explosion, and the increasing sophistication of the average consumer. The sheer volume and variety of goods enormously complicated their distribution and storage. A wholesaler of breakfast cereals, for instance, no longer handled a few cereal brands, but dozens of them, and with the proliferation of supermarkets, was confronted with the problem of greater demand and continuous product turnover. The cost of distribution escalated as well, further adding to the complexity of distribution. A seminal article on physical distribution (''New Strategies to Move Goods''), appearing in a September 1966 issue of *Business Week*, for the first time fostered an awareness of PD as a separate category of business. This eventually generated textbooks on physical distribution management, as well as courses in business schools. For the first time, PD, as well as **cost control**, became central concerns of upper management.

By this time, computers had slowly entered the realm of PD, at least in the United States. It was not until the 1970s, however, that computers were fully utilized. Their effect over time was to integrate the hitherto disparate categories of PD—transportation, storage, inventory, and distribution—into closely related activities. Most recently, computerization is performing the major functions of physical distribution management, from long-range strategic planning to day-to-day logistics, inventory, and market forecasting. The next stage of computerization in PDM already has arrived, namely, one computer system communicating with and interpreting another system.

Up to now, PDM has been concerned with the movement of physical objects. In the future, however, it will have to accommodate the increasing shift of the economy away from goods manufacturing and into service industries. In this new realm, environmental cleanup and the disposal of waste undoubtedly will be increasingly important to PDM. The shift from domestic to global markets also will affect the future of PDM, requiring enormous technical and operational refinement.

[Sina Dubovoy]

FURTHER READING:

Ballou, Ronald H. *Basic Business Logistics*. 2nd ed. Englewood Cliffs, NJ: Prentice-Hall, 1987.

DeRoulet, David G. ''ECR: Better Information Cuts Costs.'' *Transportation & Distribution*. October, 1993, p. 63.

Doherty, Katherine. ''Distribution's '93 Newsmakers (A Look at 1993's Distribution Trends & Innovations).'' *U.S. Distribution Journal*. December 15, 1993, p. 23.

Muller, E. J. ''Conquering the Global Market.'' *Chilton's Distribution*. October, 1993, p. 32.

PLANNING

SEE: Business Planning; Financial Planning

POISON PILLS

A poison pill is a type of financial or structural maneuver that a company may make to frustrate an attempted takeover by a hostile bidder. The poison pill affords directors of a company sufficient latitude to restructure or acquire **debt** or sometimes sell **assets**, specifically to make the takeover target a much less attractive prospect. If the poison pill is effective, the acquiring company will abandon its takeover and allow the target company to remain independent.

For all the criticism directed at **takeovers**, it has been suggested that they perform a highly useful task: they motivate the directors of potential target companies to consistently maximize shareholder value and to restructure underperforming companies into profitable, competitive and usually smaller enterprises.

HISTORY AND BACKGROUND

Poison pills have existed in various forms for many decades, but were viewed merely as anomalies in corporate finance. Over an approximately ten-year period beginning in the late 1950s, several large conglomerates formed out of the philosophy that any company involved in only one industry would be ravaged by periodic downturns in that industry. Diversification would enable companies to maintain consistent profitability by offsetting losses in struggling operations with profits from other unrelated and more successful operations.

Conglomerates such as LTV, Textron, General Dynamics, TRW, General Electric, Teledyne, and Tenneco built enormous corporate empires that had interests in several major industries, specifically to achieve diversification. In the process, many companies lost their independence to these conglomerates because few among them were able to mount successful defenses against unwelcome bids.

The rash of conglomerate activity and the pace of **mergers and acquisitions** caused concern that takeovers were causing excessive concentration in certain industries and were allowed to proceed without sufficient notification or care. This led to congressional lobbying efforts by business federations, unions, and institutional investors that culminated in passage of the Williams Act in 1968.

The Williams Act obliged parties to a takeover to fully disclose the terms of an impending acquisition and to allow a period in which competing offers for a target company could be made. The act became the basis for other federal laws regarding corporate mergers and acquisitions, and established a basis for legal challenges that could hamstring takeovers in several ways, including bad faith, misrepresentation, and antitrust arguments.

During the period that followed, many state legislatures passed more specific and restrictive legislation on takeovers, based on the Williams Act. This, for the first time, involved legislators in corporate mergers and acquisitions and required companies to maintain strong government relations groups.

The Williams Act and the various state laws that were modeled after it caused many companies to alter their articles of incorporation by changing their legal domiciles to states with the most favorable environments. By far, the most attractive was Delaware (and this explains why most companies today are incorporated in that state). State laws—particularly those in Delaware—provided grounds for statutory and legal defenses that could frustrate all but the least unwelcome takeovers. By the late 1970s, the pace of acquisitions nearly ground to a halt.

But in 1982 the U.S. Supreme Court passed a landmark ruling in the case of *Edgar v. MITE Corp*, which invalidated the basis for antitakeover laws in 37 states. Helped to some degree by a noninterventionist U.S. Department of Justice under the Reagan administration, restrictive takeover laws were severely weakened. No longer able to take shelter in statutory and legal defenses, many firms were once again vulnerable to takeover offers.

TYPES OF POISON PILLS

The most common type of poison pill—used by more than nine out of ten companies—is the shareholder rights, or "flip-over," plan.

A shareholder rights plan commonly allows a company facing an unwelcome bid to declare a special stock dividend consisting of rights to purchase additional, newly created shares. The exercise price to these rights is purposely set far above market value, so that a suitor company would have to spend substantially more to acquire control. The company may redeem the rights after the bid has been abandoned, but usually at only five cents per share.

If the takeover bid is successful, the shareholder rights may be transferred, or "flipped over," to the successor firm. The rights would entitle shareholders to purchase shares in the surviving firm at a discount of as much as 50 percent, causing tremendous dilution of the surviving firm, and possibly even placing control of that firm in jeopardy.

A variation of the flip over is the "flip-in" plan. This plan is designed to hasten the exit of a suitor with a substantial minority of shares who cannot, or will not, affect a merger—and who may be playing the shareholders for a gain through **greenmail**. The flip-in offers shareholders in the target company—but not the suitor—rights to buy additional discounted shares.

As these rights are exercised, the suitor's position is diluted and share value drops. The suitor is faced with mounting losses the longer he or she hesitates, and is motivated to liquidate his or her holdings as quickly as possible.

Both poison pill plans enable a company to thwart all but the most determined and deep-pocketed suitors, while allowing shareholders to benefit greatly if the suitor succeeds. Nevertheless, no poison pill or any other type of defense is ever meant to be used. Their greatest utility is in their deterrent influence; a company is unlikely to launch a takeover of a firm whose defenses are sufficiently formidable.

THE EFFECTS OF POISON PILLS ON COMPANIES

Few companies have been able to maintain their independence indefinitely after employing a poison pill. While effective at fending off unwelcome bids, poison pills have tended to indicate to the financial community that the companies using them suffer from some financial or structural weakness and are ripe for some form of merger.

Many shareholder activists, concerned with the potential abuses that might result, have sponsored proposals that would require shareholder approval prior to including a poison pill in the corporate charter or activating an existing poison pill.

Their argument is that by preserving the independence of firms, poison pills have the effect of perpetuating inefficiencies and poor **management** that result in declining **productivity** and competitiveness that is reflected in lower share value.

Boards of directors frequently argue that poison pills have exactly the opposite effect on share value. They maintain that poison pills are brutally effective bargaining tools that may be used to extract only the most favorable terms from potential suitors. Negotiating positions can only be strengthened by poison pills, and this will lead to the most favorable bids.

While there is merit to both arguments, it is most often the case that these effects cancel each other out and have little or no effect on share value. Shareholder activists, however, remain increasingly vigilant about possible abuses that may arise from poison pill plans, and takeover defenses in general. Meanwhile, state legislatures have spent the years since the Supreme Court ruling on *Edgar v. MITE Corp* gradually reconstructing restrictive antitakeover laws.

[John Simley]

FURTHER READING:

Griffin, Ricky W., and Ronald J. Ebert. *Business*. 2nd ed. Englewood Cliffs, NJ: Prentice-Hall, 1991.

POLICIES AND POLICY MAKING

Policy making at one time was the term used to describe top-level decision making in organizations. In recent years, however, this managerial process has been elaborated on both the academic and practitioner literature and taken on more descriptive designations, such as strategy formulation or strategic planning. Policy making now, more aptly, simply describes the development of organizational policies. Some policies appear in the highest level of organizations and are essential components of the strategic process. But, the vast majority of policies apply at lower levels and are operational in nature.

THE NATURE OF POLICIES

Very simply, policies are standing plans that provide guidelines for decision making. They are guides to thinking that establish the boundaries or limits within which decisions are to be made. Within these boundaries, judgment must be exercised. The degree of discretion permitted will very from policy to policy. Some policies are quite broad and allow much latitude, whereas others are narrowly constructed and leave little room for judgment. To illustrate, a policy of selecting the best qualified candidate for a managerial position permits more discretion than a policy of promoting the best qualified candidate from within the organization. The latter is a narrower policy because it limits the choices to current employees. A policy of promoting from within the organization based on standardized test scores and seniority would, of course, be an even more restrictive policy.

To better comprehend the nature of policies, it is useful to differentiate them from other standing plans—i.e., plans designed to deal with recurring issues—such as rules, standard operating procedures, and standard methods. Rules are specific statements of what must or must not be done in a given situation. Unlike policies, they provide no room for managerial discretion. ''No smoking in the work area'' and ''Wash your hands before leaving the restroom'' are examples of company rules. Rules by their very nature are designed to suppress thinking whereas policies require varying degrees of judgment.

Standard operating procedures, or SOPs, are detailed instructions for the execution of a particular operation. They specify an exact chronological sequence of steps to be followed and permit little room for discretion. Most procedures cut across departmental lines and involve several employees. SOPs are frequently used to support the implementation of major policies. For example, a policy of purchasing from the qualified bidder with lowest price might be routinely implemented through a prescribed SOP.

Standard work methods are established ways of performing specific tasks. Like SOPs, they designate an exact sequence of actions but, unlike SOPs, they are only concerned with the task of a single worker. The prescribed set of steps in ironing and folding shirts at a commercial laundry is an example of a standard work method.

FUNCTIONS OF POLICIES

Policies perform several important functions in organizations. First and foremost, they simplify decision making. They delimit the area of search for possible alternatives and preclude the need for repeated, in-depth analysis of recurring, similar problems. Consequently, they promote efficiency in the utilization of managerial time.

Policies also permit managers to delegate to subordinates more decisions and more important decisions than they would otherwise. Thus, if a manager establishes a policy governing a specific class of decisions, he or she will feel more comfortable delegating these decisions to subordinates because they will have set guidelines within which to make choices. The delegation of decision-making authority is important because it frees up managerial time for activities such as opportunity finding and planning that typically are put off.

Finally, policies help secure consistency and equity in organizational decisions. Thus, if several managers make decisions in a particular policy area, their decisions will be consistent within the limits established by the governing policy. Equity is also promoted through the policy mechanism, especially with regard to personnel and vendors. For example, an announced policy of permitting the company employees with the greatest seniority to have first choice of vacation times would tend to be viewed as more equitable than allowing managers to make these decisions without guidelines. By the same token, a policy stating that supply contracts will be awarded to the lowest qualified bidder would normally be viewed as fair by vendors.

FORMULATION OF POLICIES

Policies can emerge in four very different ways. First, and most commonly, they may be originated by management. Managers originate policies to assure that decisions within the organization will be in line with its objectives. Generally, they are written and embodied in the company's policy manual, if it has one.

The second way policies come about is through appeal. The appeal process typically works something like this. A situation develops where an executive is uncertain whether he has the authority to make a decision. Consequently, he appeals to higher-level management for the decision. Once the decision is made, it becomes precedent for similar decisions in the future. The process is analogous to the way common law develops in the Anglo-American judicial system. There is a danger, however, of allowing too many policies to be made through appeal. A set of unwritten, incomplete, and uncoordinated policies may emerge because the various appealed decisions will, in all likelihood, be made on the basis of the individual merits of the particular situations without regard for their broader implications.

Third, policies may be implied from the decisions and actions of the company's executives. In fact, it is not uncommon to find that some of the "real" policies of a company differ from its stated policies. For example, a company may have a stated policy of promoting strictly on the basis of merit whereas in reality, relatives and personal friends of top management are given priority.

Finally, policies can be externally imposed. Not infrequently, outside institutions, such as various departments of government, trade unions, and trade associations, impose requirements on organizations.

Labor contracts and federal regulations are familiar examples. Consider how the equal opportunity employment laws have led to major modifications in the personnel policies of many firms.

HIERARCHAL STRUCTURE OF POLICIES

Policies are found at all levels of organizations. At the very top, key policies may be important elements of the company's overall strategy and help define how it differentiates itself from its rivals and competes in the marketplace. Such policies are commonly called functional strategies because they guide strategic decision making at the functional level. Consider Polaroid's principal functional strategies under its founder, Edwin Land. In the financial area, there were two atypical policies: no long-term debt and growth strictly through internal development (i.e., no acquisitions). The company's product policy was to bring only unique, high-tech products to the market. A key marketing policy called for very heavy initial advertising of new products. Other strategic marketing policies emphasized the introduction of successively less expensive camera models and the pricing of instant film as a high-margin cash cow. Production policy dictated subcontracting of high-volume, repetitive manufacturing work and keeping technically critical, high value-added work in-house. Taken together, these policies defined, to a large extent, Polaroid's competitive posture during its "glory years."

High-level policies typically must be interpreted and narrowed at lower organizational levels. This reality results in a hierarchial structure of policies within organizations. To explicate, a company might have a functional strategy of aggressive price competition. At the sales manager level, this policy might be refined to state that the company will meet competitors' prices on all of the firm's nonproprietary products. And, at the district level, the policy might be narrowed again to read that district sales managers can make price concessions up to 10 percent on their own authority but, beyond that, they must get approval from above. As the example illustrates, policies tend to be broad at higher organizational levels and become successively more restrictive as they move down the hierarchy.

POLICY AUDITS

Organizational policies have a tendency to become obsolete. Stated policies commonly change much more slowly than do the conditions that led to them. One approach to dealing with this problem is to conduct periodic reviews or audits of the organization's policies. These audits can help identify and eliminate outmoded policies. This regimen, however, tends to result in a time lag between the actual need for policy changes and the recognition of that need. It is therefore prudent for managers also to review policies on a more or less ongoing basis by asking questions such as, "What is the purpose of this policy?" and "Does it still make sense?" If the answers are negative or ambiguous, the policy may be a candidate for modification or elimination before the next scheduled audit. The astute manager will also be on the lookout for appealed and implied policies that may not be contributing to the achievement of the firm's goals.

SUMMARY

Policy making is concerned with the formulation of general statements or understandings that guide or channel managerial decisions. Policies, whether written or implied, are essential components of a company's planning framework because they simplify the making of recurring decisions and facilitate the delegation of these decisions. Successive delegations tend to result in a hierarchy of policies within large organizations.

It is not overly far-fetched to suggest that without policies, because of excessive analyses and the concentration of decisions at the top, corporate decision making would be slowed to the point of bringing operations to a virtual standstill. Yet, in today's fast-moving business world there is also a great danger of policies becoming rapidly outmoded. For this reason, audits and on-going reviews are a must, if a company's policies are to remain effective decision guides.

[Edmund R. Gray]

FURTHER READING:

Gray, Edmund R. and Larry R. Smeltzer, *Management: The Competitive Edge*, 2nd ed. Kendall/Hunt Publishing Company, 1993

Koontz, Harold and Heintz Weihrich, *Management*, 9th ed. McGraw-Hill Book Company, 1988

Newman, William H., *Administrative Action: The Technique of Organization and Management*, 2nd ed. Prentice-Hall, Inc., 1963

POLLUTION

SEE: Clean Air Act; Clean Water Act; Comprehensive Environmental Response, Compensation and Liability Act of 1980 (Superfund); Corporate Image; Environmental Law and Business; Environmental Protection Agency (EPA); Recycling

PONZI SCHEMES

A Ponzi scheme is an investment swindle whereby some early investors are paid returns from the money acquired from new investors; eventually the scheme collapses when there is not enough new investment to continue the payouts.

The original Ponzi scheme began in Boston in 1919. Charles Ponzi, a dapper 37-year-old Italian immigrant, conceived a unique arbitrage system. Member nations of the Universal Postal Union had agreed to a permanent exchange rate not affected by currency fluctuations. Ponzi saw he could buy depressed liras and francs, turn them into International Reply coupons, and then convert the coupons into U.S. dollars for a profit of up to 250 percent. He began paying investors 50 percent interest in 45 days.

This bonanza started a frenzy that went beyond the Italian North End and spread throughout New England. When Ponzi was exposed by the Boston *Post*, he had taken in $10,000,000 and purchased less than $30 worth of International Reply coupons. He had been redeeming his promissory notes with new funds from would-be greedy investors standing in block-long lines to reach his 16 clerks.

In 1920 Ponzi went to federal prison for using the mails to defraud and later to Massachusetts state prison for grand larceny. Receivers for his bankrupt Securities Exchange Company paid back about 35 cents on the dollar after puzzling over his bookkeeping for years. Ponzi died a pauper in Brazil in 1949.

Modern Ponzi scheme victims are less likely to be ignorant immigrants but are still vulnerable because they are preoccupied with other concerns. Doctors and entertainers, for example, are frequent targets of Ponzi-scheme promoters.

Use of the term "Ponzi scheme" has broadened considerably since the 1920s. For example, the Drexel/Milken junk-bond craze of the 1980s, which fueled an unprecedented wave of corporate **takeovers** and caused the collapse of the savings and loan industry, has been described, with some justification, as a Ponzi scheme.

The term is often applied to the practices of certain Third World governments that borrow billions from the **International Monetary Fund** and then more billions to pay back the billions previously borrowed. The word "Ponzi" implies that these governments have no intention of repaying in full.

Social Security has frequently been called a Ponzi scheme by conservatives who claim that young workers will be cheated because the fund must inevitably go bankrupt. The word "Ponzi" in this context suggests that irresponsible politicians are looting the fund to disguise budget deficits and pyramiding benefits in the form of COLA entitlements to win votes from elderly recipients at the expense of future generations.

What distinguishes a true Ponzi scheme is motive. If the promoters intend to bilk investors by paying for borrowed money with more borrowed money, fully realizing that the pyramid must collapse, then it can correctly be characterized as a Ponzi scheme. Otherwise the term must be understood as an ambiguous derogatory epithet.

[Bill Delaney]

FURTHER READING:

Bogdanich, Walt. "Ponzi Schemes Allegedly Increasing, Fooling Even the Savviest Investors." *Wall Street Journal.* May 8, 1985, p. 33(E).

Bulgatz, Joseph. *Ponzi Schemes, Invaders from Mars, and More Extraordinary Popular Delusions and the Madness of Crowds.* NY: Crown Publishing Group, 1992.

Dunn, Donald H. *Ponzi! The Boston Swindler.* NY: McGraw-Hill, 1975.

J.B.C. "Where Are They Now? The Rise of Mr. Ponzi." *The New Yorker.* May 8, 1937, pp. 18-22.

Nash, Jay Robert. *Hustlers and Con Men: An Anecdotal History of the Confidence Man and His Games.* NY: M. Evans & Co., 1976.

PORTFOLIO MANAGEMENT THEORY

The theory of portfolio management describes the process of combining assets in an efficient manner. Here, efficiency means the highest expected rate of return on an investment for a specific level of risk. The primary starting point for portfolio theory requires an assumption that investors are risk averse. This simply means that they will not consider a portfolio with more **risk** unless it is accompanied by a higher expected rate of return.

Modern portfolio theory was largely defined by the work of Harry M. Markowitz in a series of articles published in the late 1950s. This theory was extended and refined by William Sharpe, John Lintner, James Tobin, and others in the subsequent decades. Portfolio theory integrates the process of efficient portfolio formation to the pricing of individual assets. It explains that some sources of risk associated with individual assets can be eliminated, or diversified away, by holding a proper combination of assets (see Figure 1).

To begin the development of a theory of effective portfolio management, consider the set of four individual securities as shown in Figure 1. If investors are restricted to holding a single security, and since they prefer higher returns to lower returns, they will prefer B to D. Likewise, investors prefer less risk to more risk, so they will prefer B to C and A to D. Thus no rational, risk-averse investor will hold C or D. But

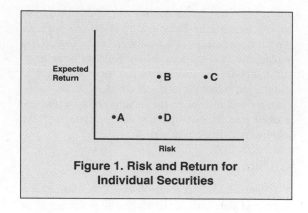

Figure 1. Risk and Return for Individual Securities

what about the remaining portfolios A and B? The decision here is less clear. Neither portfolio is dominated by the other. Thus, investors must decide whether the additional expected return of B is adequate compensation for the additional risk it also exhibits. If these are the only four alternatives, then A and B are efficient portfolios since they exhibit the highest return for a given risk level. Rational investors, however, may now disagree on which of the two portfolios to select.

Now, suppose that investors can apportion their investment into A, B, or some of each. The expected return of this new set of two security portfolios will be a simple weighted average of the expected returns of the individual elements. For example, if the expected return on A was 12 percent and the expected return on B was 20 percent, then a portfolio with an equal proportion of each would be expected to return 16 percent. If the proportion of B was increased, the expected return would rise. Conversely, it would decline if the proportion of A was enhanced. Determining the risk inherent in these two security portfolios is somewhat more complex. There is a risk component contributed from A, another from B, and a third that results from the comovement of A and B. Statistically, this third component is referred to as covariance, or correlation. This comovement term can be strong or weak. It can also be positive, indicating that the returns from A and B tend to move in the same direction, or negative, indicating that A and B tend to move in opposite directions.

Although the comovement component makes risk analysis of portfolios more complicated, it also represents the source of risk diversification and provides superior investment alternatives for many investors than can be attained by holding A or B in isolation. This is the insight that Markowitz was able to formalize. For example, if the returns generated by A and B exhibit moderate and positive comovement (or correlation), then portfolios of A and B would have expected return and risk characteristics as illustrated in Figure 2.

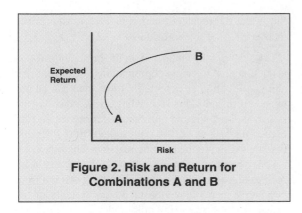

Figure 2. Risk and Return for Combinations A and B

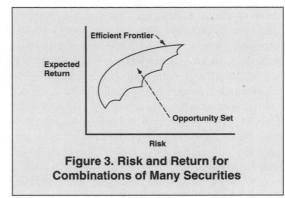

Figure 3. Risk and Return for Combinations of Many Securities

The set of combinations of A and B illustrated in Figure 2 are referred to as the opportunity set. Note that some portfolios that are attainable would not be desirable to a risk-averse investor. For example, no investor will hold a 100 percent A portfolio since there is a combination containing some B that has the same level of risk and greater expected return. In fact, this is true for all portfolios represented on the lower half of the curve. The efficient frontier is the name given to the subset of the opportunity set containing the highest expected return portfolio for every possible level of risk. The shape of the graph and the resulting efficient frontier are both a function of the strength and direction of the correlation between the two securities. If the correlation was stronger and more positive, the curve would flatten and eventually become a straight line connecting the two points if the correlation became perfect. On the other hand, the curve would become more pronounced and approach the vertical axis of the graph if the correlation became weaker and possibly negative.

Next, consider this same problem with more than two securities to consider. The expected return of any combination of any number of securities remains a weighted average of the expected returns of the individual components, but the risk calculation must now contain a comovement, or correlation term for each unique pair of securities under consideration. Even though this requires a large amount of calculation, it can be accomplished. The resulting opportunity set is now represented by the area behind the curve in Figure 3. The efficient frontier of combinations of these risky individual securities, however, are the portfolios represented along the upper edge of the curve itself.

Which of these efficient portfolios is best for an individual investor? It depends upon that investor's personal level of risk aversion. Investors with high risk tolerance will choose portfolios to the right and those with low levels of risk tolerance will choose portfolios toward the left. Regardless, all investors should consider only those portfolios that are members of the efficient frontier. A further refinement in this analysis

can be obtained if there are risk-free assets to consider as well. A truly riskless security will have a certain return and will therefore have no correlation with the uncertain returns from other individual securities or portfolios. Combinations of the risk-free security and a risky portfolio, Y, are illustrated in Figure 4.

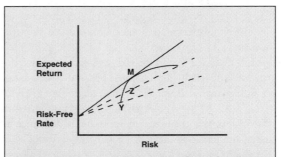

Figure 4. Risk and Return for Combinations of Risky Portfolios and a Risk Free Security

Note that investors can now achieve lower risk positions than are possible by holding only combinations of risky securities. Investors choosing to place a portion of their wealth in Y and the rest in the risk-free security will attain a portfolio that appears on the straight line segment connecting those two components. If it were possible to borrow at the risk-free rate, investors could actually attain higher returns (for higher risk). These portfolios are represented by points on the dotted line to the right of Y. These combinations, however, would not be efficient since there are pure combinations of risky securities that offer higher returns at similar risk levels.

Since portfolio Y is not unique, consider a different combination of risky assets, Z. Combinations of Z and the risk-free security lie upon a line connecting these two points. Clearly, any investors, regardless of their attitude toward risk, would prefer to select among combinations of Z and the risk-free security than combinations of Y and the risk-free security since there are higher expected returns at all risk levels. Portfolio Z, however, is not unique either and there are other risky portfolios that would provide superior returns when combined with the risk-free security. This process can be repeated until a particular portfolio M is identified. The line defining the expected returns and risk of combinations of M and the risk-free security is tangent to the former efficient frontier. Risky portfolios with higher expected return than M would not offer superior alternatives in conjunction with the risk-free security. Therefore, M is a unique combination. Investors who prefer a level of risk below that of M will hold a combination of M and the risk-free security. Their portfolios would plot between these two points on the graph. Investors who desire a risk level in excess of M can borrow at the risk-free rate and invest more than 100 percent of their original wealth in M. This will allow them to position themselves at points on the line above and to the right of M.

While M is unique in geometric terms, it is also unique in economic terms. Once this portfolio is identified, every investor, regardless of risk preferences, should choose combinations of M and the risk-free security. All investors should be allocating their wealth between M and the risk-free security. This has several important implications. First, all risky assets must be included in M. If not, then the price of excluded assets will quickly fall to a point where its rate of return will suggest membership in M. Since all assets are included in M, it is commonly referred to as the market portfolio.

The line passing through M is called the capital market line (CML). The slope of this line represents the price of additional units of expected return per unit of additional risk. Once the CML is defined, the next step is to determine the implications of portfolio M in deriving proper required returns for the individual securities it contains. One model that does this is the **capital asset pricing model**. The CAPM indicates that the proper expected return for an individual security is related to its risk relative to the overall risk level of M. This relationship can be defined in the following equation.

$$\text{Expected Return for an Individual Security} = \text{Risk-free rate} + \beta \, (\text{Expected Return on M} - \text{Risk-free rate})$$

The return a security (or portfolio) is expected to generate in excess of the risk-free rate is called a risk premium. The expected return for a security must include a risk premium that is some multiple of the risk premium for the entire market. In this equation, β (or Beta) is the risk of the individual security relative to the overall risk level of the market. A security with above-average risk would have a β in excess of 1 and a below-average risk security would have a β below 1.

Since the aggregate of individual securities is the market itself, β for portfolio M is exactly 1.

Recall that the main benefit of forming portfolios is the potential to create combinations with lower risk and possibly higher expected returns than can be obtained from individual securities. Now consider the risk associated with an individual security as the sum of two parts. One part is represented by risk factors that are unique to the specific security. The other part is represented by risk factors that are essentially common to all securities. For example, the potential for a key employee to leave the firm unexpectedly or the possibility of discovering gold under corporate headquarters are unique risk factors that are not shared with other firms. On the other hand, risk factors concerning the potential for unexpected and rapid growth in the national (or international) economy or the enactment of new legislation that affects the operating costs for all firms represent examples of common risk factors. While portfolio formation reduces the influence of unique risks associated with individual securities, it cannot eliminate exposure to common risk factors. Stated differently, properly constructed portfolios allow for diversification of unsystematic (unique) risk, but not for systematic (market) risk.

Using this latest interpretation, β represents the level of systematic risk of an individual security. Since investors have the potential to eliminate unsystematic risk from their portfolios, the return they expect should only include compensation for the systematic risk component. This is the underlying message of the CAPM.

There are other theories that attempt to explain how individual securities are priced. A prominent one is arbitrage pricing theory (APT). While CAPM essentially uses the market's risk premium as the sole determinant of a security's return, APT allows for multiple systematic risk factors. A simple representation of the APT model is provided below.

$$\text{Expected Return on an Individual Security} = \text{Risk-free rate} + \beta 1 \, (\text{Risk premium on M}) + \beta 2 \, (\text{Change in Inflation rate}) + \beta 3 \, (\text{Change in GNP growth})$$

Systematic risk is now measured with respect to a variety of factors, not just market returns. While three factors are listed here, there may be more or fewer. Furthermore, the factors themselves are not specified by the theory. This means that any application of the theory requires the user to commit to a specific set of factors that can be justified both economically and statistically.

This is a good place to review the implications of portfolio theory. First, investors are risk averse and will accept more risk only if there is the expectation of higher return as well. This suggests that they will seek and hold only efficient combinations of securities. These efficient combinations have exploited the role of comovement among the individual securities to eliminate all diversifiable, or unsystematic, risk. The returns expected from individual securities will therefore include no premium for diversifiable risk since it can be eliminated. The only source of risk requiring compensation is systematic, or market, risk.

It is also worth noting that if a risk-free asset is also available, there is a single risky portfolio (referred to as M, or the market portfolio) that is optimal for all investors. Investors will seek their desired level of risk exposure by selecting the proper proportions of the risky portfolio, M, and the risk-free asset.

As a practical matter, it is difficult to identify the true market portfolio since it, by definition, must contain proportions of all assets that have value. This means that investors and portfolio managers must create proxies for the market portfolio from some subset of all possible investments. Even if this proxy can be identified and created, the efficient frontier moves around as expected return and risk of the individual securities, and correlation among these elements, change over time.

Two alternative approaches to portfolio management arise from these considerations. Many investors default to a passive portfolio strategy. A passive strategy requires the investor to buy and hold some replica of the market portfolio and accept an expected return equal to the market. For example, an investor may choose to hold a portfolio of stocks that is identical to the Standard & Poor's Index (S&P 500) or some other broad market index. This becomes the risky component of the portfolio and is combined with a proportion of a risk-free security (e.g., **Treasury bills**) to achieve the desired risk level. Underlying this strategy is the assumption that markets are reasonably efficient and that any attempt to improve the rate of return from risky securities is not likely to succeed.

Active portfolio management strategies attempt to ''beat the market'' by identifying ''mispriced'' securities and forming efficient portfolios from those securities. This strategy clearly requires more effort from the investor. If such securities can be identified and the market eventually prices them properly, the active portfolio will generate returns in excess of those provided by the market on a risk-adjusted basis.

SEE ALSO: Diversification in Investments

[Paul Bolster]

FURTHER READING:

Bodie, Zvi, Alex Kane, and Alan J. Marcus. *Investments*. 2nd ed. Irwin, 1993.

Markowitz, Harry. *Portfolio Selection: Efficient Diversification of Investments*. John Wiley & Sons.

PRESENT VALUE

The present value (PV) of an amount to be received in the future is the discounted face value considering the length of time the receipt is deferred and the required rate of return (or appropriate **discount rate** under the circumstances). It is the result of the time value of money concept that recognizes that today's dollar is worth more than the same dollar received at a future point in time. This notion can be demonstrated by examining several common financial transactions:

- Money invested in bank **certificates of deposit** may earn interest at 5 percent. At that rate, $1,000 deposited on January 1 will accumulate $50 of interest by December 31, making the total available to the investor $1,050. Since this investor is willing to lend his money to the bank for 5 percent annual interest, that rate may be viewed as the required rate of return, or the discount rate. The $1,050 to be received on December 31 had a PV to that investor at January 1 of exactly $1,000 $(1,050/(1 + .05)^1)$.

- Annuity contracts can be bought from insurance companies whereby a single payment is made to the insurance company in exchange for a defined series of annual (or monthly) payments made back to the buyer. In these cases the simple sum of the periodic repayments from the insurance company to the buyer exceed the original annuity purchase price, in absolute terms. However, when considering the deferred repayment and the implied rate of return on the money loaned, the amounts exactly equate, on a present value basis.

- Mortgage loans are basically the reverse of the above described annuity contract. Here, the individual borrows the money, promising to make scheduled repayments to the mortgage holder or lender. Again, due to the differential timing of cash flows, and the fact that the bank requires interest to be paid on the borrowed funds, the PVs equate. That is, the PV of the sum of the future mortgage payments is exactly equal to the amount borrowed (which by definition is at the PV on the date of the loan).

The formula for calculating the present value of a series of future receipts is:

$$PV = CF1/(1+i)^1 + CF2/(1+i)^2 + \cdots + CFn/(1+i)^n$$

Where CF1 to CFn = future receipts
i = the interest, or discount rate appropriate for the stated period
n = the number of periods over which future receipts occur

The interest, or discount, rate used in PV calculations is a key element in determining the PV. This importance is emphasized when the future amounts occur over an extended period of time, due to the power of compounding. For example, the final payment on a 30-year loan at 7 percent interest would be worth approximately 13.1 percent of its face amount on a present value basis at the date of loan origin $[1/(1 + .07)^{30}]$. By contrast, the 30th payment on a loan with a 9 percent interest rate would be worth only 7.5% $[1/(1 + .09)^{30}]$ of its face amount in present value terms at the origin. This simple example shows the power of compounding when time periods are long.

The discount rate used in a given circumstance must provide for compensation to the lender of funds for three elements of return:

1. Inflation: just to keep even in terms of buying power, the return of money at a future date must be appended by the CPI rate. In other words, if a person lends an amount of money adequate to buy a loaf of bread at t = 0, he will require repayment at t = 1 of the original amount *plus* the fraction of that amount representing the CPI increase over the period. That way he will be able to buy the same loaf of bread at t = 1.

2. Time value of money (TVM): beyond simply keeping even with inflation, the investor or lender has a basic preference for consumption sooner rather than later. The cost of compensating for this aspect of human nature has been found to be about 1 to 2 percent per year. That is, the real rates of return on riskless assets has averaged about 1.5 percent.

3. **Risk**: in addition to postponing the preferred immediate consumption and having to reimburse for inflation's erosion of buying power, many types of investment involve a risk of default. That is, the investor may never again see his funds, for example if the company goes bankrupt. Compensating for this element of required return can be considerably more expensive than the first two combined. For example, junk bonds may be paying interest at 12 percent, while anticipated inflation is only 4 percent and TVM is about 1.5 percent. This would mean that the risk premium component of the overall in-

terest rate is 6.5 percent (12 percent − 4 percent − 1.5 percent).

SEE ALSO: Discounted Cash Flow

[Christopher C. Barry]

PRICE/EARNINGS (P/E) RATIO

The price/earnings ratio (P/E ratio) provides a comparison of the current market price of a share of stock and that stock's earnings per share, or EPS, (which is figured by dividing a company's net income by its number of shares of **common stock** outstanding). For example, if a company's stock sold for $30 per share and it posted earnings per share of $1.50, that company would have a P/E ratio of 15. A company's P/E ratio typically rises as a result of increases in its stock price, an indicator of the stock's popularity.

''The price-earnings ratio is part of the everyday vocabulary of investors in the stock market,'' noted Richard Brealey and Stewart Myers in *Principles of Corporate Finance*, because a company's P/E ratio is often viewed as an indicator of future stock performance. ''The high P/E shows that investors think that the firm has good growth opportunities, that its earnings are relatively safe and deserve a low **capitalization rate**, or both.''

John B. Thomas observed in the *Indianapolis Business Journal*, however, that ''while accepting that a high P/E ratio is usually a sign of high expectations, analysts and brokers nonetheless are quick to caution that the ratios are only part of the puzzle.'' A company may post an artificially high P/E ratio as a result of factors that can either boost stock prices or diminish earnings per share. Restructuring charges, merger and acquisition rumors (whether true or false), and high dividend yields all have the capacity to push a company's P/E ratio upward. In other instances, legitimately high P/E ratios can be adversely impacted down the road by such factors as market conditions, technology, and increased **competition** from new rivals (who may, in fact, be drawn to the industry by the company's previously posted P/E ratios).

Conversely, while a low P/E ratio is often a good indication that a company is struggling, appearances can again be deceiving. In addition, different industry sectors often have diverse P/E ratio averages. A company may have a fairly low P/E ratio when compared with all other corporations; when compared with the other companies within its industry, however, it may be a leader.

Finally, a company that posts a loss has no earnings to compare with its stock price. As a result, no P/E ratio can be determined for the company. Still, these companies may remain viable choices for investment if an investor decides that the company under examination is headed toward future profitability.

Since so many factors can influence a company's P/E ratio, industry analysts caution against relying on it too heavily in making investment decisions. As one analyst remarked to the *Indianapolis Business Journal*, while a company's P/E ratio is a valuable and often accurate investment tool, "if you're going to buy and sell **stocks** based on a P/E ratio, you're not going to make money. You'd better look at why it is high or low."

EARNINGS PER SHARE (EPS)

Earnings per share is one of the two factors that determine a company's P/E ratio; the other is the price of the company's stock. EPS is derived by dividing a corporation's net income by the number of shares of common stock that are outstanding. A company with 30,000 outstanding shares of common stock and a net income of $270,000 would thus have an earnings per share of $9.

An essential part of determining the P/E ratio, earnings per share has also come to be regarded as an important piece of information for the investment community in and of itself. "A primary concern of investors is how profitable a company is relative to their investment in the company," wrote Jay M. Smith, Jr., and K. Fred Skousen in *Intermediate Accounting*. "The investor is concerned with how net income relates to shares held and to the market price of the stock. . . . Only by converting the total amounts to per share data can a meaningful evaluation be made," because EPS figures can illustrate the degree to which a company's net income is keeping pace with its **capital structure**. In recognition of the importance of this information, corporations are required to report EPS amounts on their **income statement** (the requirement was suspended for nonpublic entities in 1978).

[Laurie Collier Hillstrom]

FURTHER READING:

Bierman, Harold, Jr., and Seymour Smidt. *Financial Management for Decision Making*. New York: Macmillan Publishing Company, 1986.

Brealey, Richard, and Stewart Myers. *Principles of Corporate Finance*. 2d ed. New York: McGraw-Hill Book Company, 1984.

"Don't Get Burned by Hot Stocks," *Money*. October 1994, p. 72.

Smith, Jay M., Jr., and K. Fred Skousen. *Intermediate Accounting*. Cincinnati: South-Western Publishing Co., 1987.

Thomas, John B. "P/E Ratios Driven by Variety of Factors, Carry Variety of Meanings," *Indianapolis Business Journal*. May 23, 1994, p. B10.

Welsch, Glenn A., Robert N. Anthony, and Daniel G. Short. *Fundamentals of Financial Accounting*. Homewood, IL: Richard D. Irwin, Inc., 1984.

PRICE INDEXES

Price indexes are used to measure the rate of inflation in the economy. There are three key price indexes that are routinely calculated and reported to the public by government agencies in the United States. These three measures differ with respect to the number of items they take into account. Before discussing these measures, it is worthwhile to explain why an index is needed to calculate the rate of inflation.

THE NEED FOR AN INDEX

Most economic variables are measured in measured in absolute terms. For example, it was reported that 12 million cars were produced in 1994 in the United States and that the gross output of goods and services in the United States was estimated at $6.5 trillion during 1993. It is not possible, however, to measure the price associated with a group of **commodities** in absolute terms; only the price for one commodity can be measured in absolute terms. For example, we can thus say that the average price of a loaf of bread in the United States, was $1.05 in 1994. The difficulty arises when we have to deal with a number of commodities together. So, once we start asking what happened to Joe Smith's cost of living in 1994 compared to 1993, it is no longer logical to compute the average price of all the goods and services bought by him in 1993 and compare it with the average price of all the goods and services bought by him in 1994. After all, what meaning can we attach to the average of prices paid for, for instance, a fancy stereo system and a pound of hamburger? An index helps us out of this quandary. In the most basic terms, an index attaches weights to the prices of items whose collective price movement we are interested in. Below is a detailed discussion of the three main price indexes used widely in the United States and how they are constructed.

THE THREE MAIN PRICE INDEXES AND THE INFLATION RATE

The inflation rate is derived by calculating the rate of change in a price index. A price index, in turn, measures the level of prices of goods and services at a particular time. The number of items included in a price index varies depending on the objective of the index. Government agencies periodically report three types of price indexes, each having their particular advantages and uses. The first index is called the **consumer price index** (CPI), it measures the average retail prices paid by consumers for goods and services bought by them. A couple thousand products, grouped into 224 sets of items, are included in this index. These items are selected on the basis of their inclusion in the household budget of a consumer. Each of the product prices is assigned a weight based on the importance of the item in the household budget. As a result, the CPI reflects changes in the cost of living of a typical urban household. The CPI is considered the most relevant **inflation** measure from the point of view of consumers, as it measures the prices of goods and services that are part of their budgets. Nevertheless, the CPI will not precisely measure changes in the cost of living of every consumer due to differences in consumption patterns.

A second price index used to measure the inflation rate is called the producer price index (PPI). It is a much broader measure than the consumer price index. The PPI measures the wholesale prices of approximately 3,000 items. The items included in this index are those that are typically used by producers (manufacturers and businesses) and thus include many raw materials and semifinished goods. A change in the PPI reflects a change in the cost of production, as encountered by producers. Since producers may pass a part or all of the increase in the cost of production to consumers, movements in the PPI indicate future movements in the CPI. The producer price index can thus forewarn consumers of coming increases in the cost of living.

The **implicit price deflator** is the third measure of inflation. This index measures the prices of all goods and services included in the calculation of the current output of goods and services in the economy, known as **gross domestic product** (GDP). It is the broadest measure of price level. This index includes prices of fighter bombers purchased by the Defense Department as well as paper clips used in any office. Thus, the implicit price deflator is a measure of the overall or aggregate price level for the economy. Movements in the implicit GDP price deflator capture the inflationary tendency of the overall economy.

The three measures of the inflation rate are most likely to move in the same direction, even though not to the same extent. Differences can arise due to the differing number of goods and services included in compiling the three indexes. The preceding three price indexes are discussed in further detail below.

CALCULATIONS OF THE CONSUMER PRICE INDEX AND THE INFLATION RATE

The construction of the consumer price index employs an index number technique, in which a fixed basket of commodities (a collection of goods and services considered relevant to the index) is valued using prices at different points of time. This type of index is technically known as a Laspeyres index, named after the statistician who invented the method.

First, a point of reference is selected, commonly known as the base year. Normally, a particular year is selected as the base year—prices prevailing in the selected base year are used in comparing changes in the price level. Currently, however, the 1982-84 period (rather than a single year) is used as the base in the construction of the consumer price index in the United States. In this case, the average price of a commodity over the three-year period is used as the base price for the commodity. This implies that the average of 1982, 1983, and 1984 prices for any given item included in the CPI is used in comparing the prices of that commodity in successive months and years. The price of each item in the basket of commodities selected is attached a weight in accordance with its importance in the budget of a typical urban family. In other words, the government first identifies the goods and services that are used by a typical urban consumer. Then, it assigns a weight to each of the items in the fixed basket—the basket thus contains a collection of goods and services in quantities that, presumably, a representative consumer consumes. Next, the government evaluates the fixed basket of commodities using prices at successive points and compares its costs (or values) with the cost to buy the same basket in the base period. This results in a series of price ratios that are usually multiplied by 100 for convenience. Thus, the price index is 100 in the base period and its value at other points reflect movements in the price level, which can be used to calculate the inflation rate between any two points of time.

For example, the CPI in the United States for 1982 was 96.5, for 1983 it was 99.6, and for 1984 it was 103.9. The average of the CPI numbers for these three years is equal to 100, since the 1982-84 period is used as the base period or point of reference. The consumer price index stood at 141.9 at the end of 1992, and at 145.8 at the end of 1993. The latter two values of the CPI imply that the cost of the fixed basket of commodities, compared to the 1982-84 period, had gone up by 41.9 percent by the end of 1992, and by 45.8 percent by the end of 1993. They also imply that the inflation rate during 1993 was roughly 2.7 percent on an annual basis (inflation rate = {(145.8 − 141.9)/141.9}*100).

ITEMS INCLUDED IN THE CONSUMER PRICE INDEX. The consumer price index is calculated by the U.S.

Bureau of Labor Statistics (BLS) and is published on a monthly basis. The broad categories of items that are included in construction of the CPI, in a highly simplified form, are: food and beverages, housing, apparel and upkeep, transportation, medical care, entertainment, and other goods and services. In reality, however, the CPI is based on a couple thousand products that are grouped into 224 sets of items. BLS employees visit thousands of stores in 85 geographical areas every month and collect more than 100,000 prices. Then the average prices of related items, such as poultry and honey are combined to yield group indexes—in this particular case, food and beverages. Next, the group indexes are combined to yield the overall price index called the "all-items CPI."

THE MEASUREMENT ERROR IN THE CONSUMER PRICE INDEX. Until 1983, the consumer price index data inflated the extent of true inflation, due to a measurement error. This error arose from the treatment of mortgage interest rates. The BLS attached excessive weights to this item, which rose quite rapidly during the 1970s. The government agency, in calculating price statistics, assumed that increased mortgage rates led to higher housing costs for homeowners—this is incorrect, since homeowners do not take out new **mortgages** every month. The mention of this measurement error is important, since the CPI series, unlike many other economic statistics, is not revised to correct for errors. Thus, the measurement error is still present in the CPI series and it can lead to misleading impressions. For example, the consumer price index data suggest that real earnings (earnings adjusted for inflation) fell between 1972 and 1982, but according to another price index—also published by the federal government—real earnings grew slightly from 1972 to 1982.

THE USEFULNESS OF THE CONSUMER PRICE INDEX. The consumer price index is widely used, both in the private and public sectors. The CPI is most commonly used in calculating the inflation rate for general purposes. The movement in the CPI reflects changes in the cost of living for urban consumers. **Labor unions** often use the CPI in bargaining for wage increases. Also, most government pensions, including the level of Social Security benefits, are indexed to the consumer price index.

CALCULATIONS OF THE PRODUCER PRICE INDEX AND THE INFLATION RATE

The producer price index (PPI) is also published by the U.S. Bureau of Labor Statistics (BLS) on a monthly basis. For the PPI, the BLS collects prices on more than 3,000 commodities that are not bought by consumers directly but instead are purchased by businesses. In a simplified form, the producer price index can be thought of as having the following broad categories: finished goods; intermediate materials, supplies, and components; and crude materials for further processing. Each of these broad categories is further subdivided in smaller groups. For example, the finished goods category consists of foods, energy, and finished goods excluding food and energy (the last subcategory includes capital equipment).

The PPI uses an index number construction methodology similar to at used for the CPI. While price data are directly collected by the BLS workers, the actual prices for the PPI index are obtained from questionnaires that are mailed to thousands of firms that sell products included in the PPI.

Currently, 1982 is used as the base year for the producer price index series. The interpretation of the PPI series is similar to the CPI series—the PPI can also be used to calculate the inflation rate.

USEFULNESS OF THE PRODUCER PRICE INDEX. One should recognize that the producer price index serves as an index relevant to the producers' cost. In other words, the PPI tells what is happening to the cost of production. If the cost of production is rising, however, producers may also increase the prices at which they sell. This, in turn, is likely to increase the retail prices that consumers pay in stores across the nation. The importance of the producer price index, then, is that it forewarns of changes in the consumer price index and, therefore, the cost of living of ordinary households.

CALCULATIONS OF THE IMPLICIT PRICE DEFLATOR AND THE INFLATION RATE

The implicit price deflator is arrived at in an indirect manner, thus the adjective implicit. Calculation of the consumer price index (CPI) and the producer price index (PPI) are explicit or direct—indexes calculated from price data on the items included. The implicit price deflator, on the other hand, is inferred indirectly from the estimates of gross domestic product (GDP) in nominal terms (in current dollars) and in real terms (the nominal value of GDP adjusted for inflation by reevaluating the GDP in prices that prevailed during a chosen base year).

Currently, 1987 is be used as the base year for calculating the real value of GDP in the United States. For example, the 1993 U.S. output of goods and services is first evaluated at prices prevailing in 1993. Then, the 1993 output of goods and services is also evaluated at prices that prevailed in 1987 (thus the terms "GDP in 1987 dollars" or "GDP in constant dollars." One can easily see how the ratio of GDP in 1993 prices and GDP in 1987 prices would yield a measure of the extent of the rise in price level between 1987 and 1993. According to federal government statistics, this ratio is estimated at 1.242 or 124.2 when multiplied by 100 (as is customarily done to be able to see the extent of price increases more conveniently). The value of the implicit price deflator of 124.2 in 1993 implies that the price level increased by 24.2 percent from 1987 to 1993 (note that the value of the implicit price deflator in the 1987 base year, is equal to 100).

The above method of expressing gross domestic product into its value in 1987 prices is routinely done every year (of course, sometimes the base year itself may be changed to a later year to keep the data series closer to the current period). Thus, we have 1992, 1991, 1990 (and so on) GDPs expressed in 1987 prices. This helps to calculate the inflation rate between subsequent years. For example, the implicit price deflator stood at 121.1 at the end of 1992. Given that the deflator was at 124.2 at the end of 1993, we arrive at the annual inflation rate of roughly 2.6 percent during 1993 (1993 inflation rate = [(124.2 − 121.1) / 121.1] * 100).

One should also notice that the term "deflator" is not used in the CPI or PPI. This is because, if you know the implicit price deflator, say, for 1993 and the 1993 GDP in current prices, you can arrive at the GDP in 1987 prices by deflating the 1993 GDP in current prices by the deflator for 1993 (expressed in plain ratio form, rather than the one multiplied by 100). Despite the use of term "deflator," one should not lose sight of the fact the implicit price deflator is essentially a price index.

USEFULNESS OF THE IMPLICIT PRICE DEFLATOR. As was pointed out earlier, the implicit price index is the broadest measure of price level. Although this index is all-inclusive and changes in it reflect inflation pressure underlying the whole economy, it may not be directly useful to ordinary households and even businesses—the CPI and PPI are more relevant to these units.

USEFULNESS OF THE THREE PRICE INDEXES

As mentioned earlier, all three price indexes can be used to calculate the inflation rate. There are, however, two important differences among these indexes. First, the consumer and producer price indexes are published every month, whereas the implicit price deflator figures are reported on a quarterly basis. Thus, more frequent users of inflation data would be inclined to use the CPI or the PPI. Second, the coverage of the three indexes are dramatically different. Thus, one of these price index series can be more suitable than the other two a particular in case. To measure the cost of living for an urban consumer, for example, the CPI will be overwhelmingly preferred to the PPI and the implicit price deflator. Nevertheless, one must be aware that even the CPI is an average price measure

that is based on certain weights. While the CPI may reflect the cost of living changes for the average consumers, it cannot precisely reflect changes in the actual cost of living for a particular consumer—his or her consumption pattern may be quite different from that assumed in assigning weights to the fixed basket of commodities. One thus needs to interpret the price index numbers carefully.

Despite the slight caution one must exercise in interpreting the price indexes, a good understanding of the inflation rate is important for every individual and household. Most economies face positive rates of inflation year after year. If the inflation rate is positive and an individual's income remains constant, his or her real standard of living will fall since the individual's income will be worth less and less in successive periods. For example, a household earns $50,000 per year and its income remains fixed at this level in the future. If the inflation rate persists at 10 percent per year, the purchasing power of the household income will also keep declining at the rate of 10 percent per year. At the end of a five-year period, prices will be one and a half times greater. This will lead to the household being able to buy only two-thirds of the goods and services it was able to buy at the beginning of the period.

An understanding of inflation is also crucial in making plans to save for retirement, children's education, or a boat. One must use an appropriate price index in calculating the funds required for a given purpose. The CPI is a good guide for retirement purposes. But if one is saving to buy a boat, even the CPI may not produce a good result—the individual may want to specifically know the way boat prices are increasing. Nevertheless, an understanding of price indexes prepares an individual adequately to explore such questions further.

SEE ALSO: Index/Indexes

[Anandi P. Sahu]

FURTHER READING:

Froyen, Richard T. *Macroeconomics: Theories and Policies*. 4th ed. New York: Macmillan Publishing Company, 1993.

Gordon, Robert J. *Macroeconomics*, 6th ed. New York: Harper-Collins College Publishers, 1993.

Sommers, Albert T. *The U.S. Economy Demystified*. Lexington, MA: Lexington Books, 1985.

PRIME RATE

The prime rate has different meanings in different contexts. It most commonly refers to a commercial bank's prime lending rate, or the interest rate charged by **banks** for short-term commercial loans to their most credit-worthy customers. Different banks may have different prime rates, and specific loans may vary from the prime rate due to a number of factors. Banks use the prime rate as a benchmark in setting the rates for a wide range of loans, including small business loans, home equity loans, and credit card balances. Banks also refer to their prime rate as their base lending rate.

In the context of **interest rates** in general, the prime rate refers to the rate of interest that would be charged on a riskless loan. In a sense it represents the ''pure'' cost of money in the absence of financial risk. Comparing yields on a riskless investment, such as U.S. government **securities**, with those of other investments, such as corporate **bonds**, provides a measure of the interest rate premium that must be paid for assuming some financial risk.

In the case of Federal Reserve banks, their prime rate is the discount rate they charge to member banks for advances that are secured by U.S. government securities. The Federal Reserve Board may raise or lower its discount rate as a matter of monetary policy. The prime lending rate of commercial banks is sensitive to the Fed's monetary policies; increases in the discount rate are usually followed by major banks raising their prime rates. However, it should be noted that when the Federal Reserve Board raises its discount rate, it is not actually raising what is commonly called the prime rate. Rather, it is individual banks that raise or lower their prime rates in response to changes in the Federal Reserve's discount rate.

Changes in the prime rate are usually made first by the nation's largest banks, after which other banks follow suit. In some cases a few smaller banks may raise or lower their prime rates on their own, but normally other banks do not follow along. Most of the large banks tend to have the same prime rate, and changes in the prime rate affect the interest rates charged by banks on other types of loans and credit as well as the interest paid on investments such as **certificates of deposit**. While rates on loans tend to rise quickly in response to increases in the prime rate, they are generally much slower to respond to decreases in the prime rate.

The Federal Reserve Board can influence the prime rate through its **monetary policy**. In general the Fed increases its discount rate in times of economic growth in order to slow the economy's growth and reduce inflationary pressures. In slow economic times, the discount rate is likely to go down. As was noted, bank's tend to raise or lower their prime rates in response to the announced monetary policies of the Federal Reserve Board.

Since 1965 the prime rate has reached a low of approximately 5 percent in 1965 and a high of more than 22 percent in 1980. Depending on economic conditions the prime rate may be relatively stable, or it may change frequently. In 1965, for example, the prime rate changed once, while in 1980 it changed 37 times as it fluctuated from just under 12 percent to just over 22 percent. Between March of 1989 and March of 1994, the prime rate declined steadily to a low of 6 percent before it began to rise again.

[David Bianco]

PRISONER'S DILEMMA

The prisoner's dilemma is only one of many illustrative examples of the logical criteria and complex decisions involved in **game theory**. It establishes a crisis situation where a person must make a decision that will have consequences not only for himself, but also for others. Likewise, the decisions of others will have a profound effect on this person and his decision choices. When it is first described, the prisoner's dilemma seems absolutely rudimentary; the decisions a person makes about his own welfare and those of others depends on his relationship with those other people. But this is where it gets hard. What if the person has doubts about the loyalty of others? Can the person afford to risk the betrayal of his or her partners? What retribution might he or she face for abrogating his or her cooperation with the others? What is the optimal strategy?

If these aspects can be understood properly, they may be translated to hundreds of other more complex dilemmas. The mechanisms that drive the prisoner's dilemma are the same as those that are faced by marketers, military strategists, poker players, and many other types of competitors. The simple models used in the prisoner's dilemma afford insights on how competitors will react to different styles of play, and these will reveal suggestions on how those competitors can be expected to act in the future.

The prisoner's dilemma was first described in the 1950s by Al Tucker, who used it to illustrate the failure of lowest-risk strategies and the potential for conflict between individual and collective rationality. Tucker suggested a model in which two players must choose an individually rational strategy, given that this **strategy** may affect the other player and that the other player's strategy may affect his own.

In the example, two suspects are apprehended by police for robbing a store. Prosecutors cannot prove either actually committed the robbery, but have enough evidence to convict both on a lesser charge of possession of stolen property.

Both suspects are isolated and offered an opportunity to plea bargain. Each is asked to confess and testify against the other. If both prisoners refuse to confess, they will be convicted of the lesser charge and must serve a year in jail. If both confess and implicate each other, they will be convicted of robbery and sentenced to two years in jail.

However, if prisoner A refuses to confess while prisoner B confesses and agrees to testify against A, prisoner B will be set free. Meanwhile, prisoner A may be convicted on the basis of prisoner B's testimony and be sentenced to six years in jail. The reverse applies if prisoner A confesses and prisoner B remains silent.

The choices available to the prisoners, and the consequences for those choices, may be represented in the matrix shown in Figure 1 (numbers are years sentenced to jail):

		Prisoner A	
		Confess	Stay Silent
Prisoner B			
Confess		A:2 B:2	A:6 B:0
Stay Silent		A:0 B:6	A:1 B:1

Figure 1

If the prisoners hope to avoid spending six years in jail, and are willing to risk serving two years to guarantee this, they will be motivated to confess. A confession for either will ensure that he or she will serve no more than two years, regardless of what the other does.

This strategy of confession is called a dominating strategy because it yields a better outcome for the prisoner—in this case, avoiding a six-year jail term—regardless of what his or her partner does. It is also known as the "sure-thing" principle, because the confessing prisoner can be assured that he or she will not serve more than two years.

But where the dominating strategy of confession is individually rational, an even more optimal outcome may be gained from a strategy that is collectively rational. For example, if prisoners A and B can be assured that neither will confess, and both are willing to serve a year to ensure this, they will be motivated not to confess.

This strategy, which yields the prisoners the lowest total number of years in jail, two, is called a cooperative strategy. The matrix in Figure 2 illustrates collectively optimal choices. It repeats the choices presented earlier, but shows the total number of years that will be served by both in each instance.

		Prisoner A	
		Confess	Stay Silent
Prisoner B			
Confess		4	6
Stay Silent		6	2

Figure 2

Obviously, if the two prisoners are very loyal and refuse to implicate the other, they will both opt to remain silent and minimize the number of years they must serve together. This assumes that the two have an agreement that is reasonably enforceable and effective.

If the agreement is not effective, either prisoner may be motivated to adopt the dominating strategy because he or she can improve upon his or her situation; one prisoner may be allowed to go free, while the crestfallen partner spends the next six years behind bars.

Indeed, one of the prisoners may be motivated to construct an agreement not to confess, specifically to cheat his or her partner and ensure his or her own freedom. This demonstrates how noncooperative play can subvert cooperative strategies, and why knowledge is absolutely essential to making an individually optimal decision.

The prisoner's dilemma provides few insights when it is done only one time. For example, assume that in a test prisoner A stays silent and prisoner B confesses. Prisoner A goes free while prisoner B marks the next six years in jail. Clearly, unless he is a martyr, prisoner B has misjudged his or her partner.

Meanwhile, prisoner A returns to a life of crime and is picked up under identical circumstances with another partner, prisoner C. Prisoner C is aware of what A did to B last time, and has no pretensions about confessing and testifying against prisoner A because he knows prisoner A cannot be trusted, and because he does not want to join prisoner B for six years.

Prisoner C possesses something B did not: superior knowledge about how prisoner A might act. Prisoner A knows this, and like C will be motivated to confess. Both are sentenced to two years.

The fact that the game is repeated, or iterated, affords the players indications of each other's style of play based on past performance. By allowing opportunities for retribution, iterated play provides indications of how players will interact and how they will react to the consequences of noncooperative strategies.

For example, prisoner A would be well-advised to retire from crime because his or her past actions are likely to doom his chances that another partner who knows prisoner A's history will ever cooperate with prisoner A.

Iterated play against a programmed player—one whose decisions are predictable—will indicate how a player will react to opportunities to exploit the other. Assume that a player named Bob merely repeats the moves of another named Ray. Ray knows that whatever he does, Bob will do on the next move. Therefore, if Ray takes advantage of Bob on one move, Bob will reciprocate on the next move. This destructive cycle will continue until both can be convinced that they would benefit more from a cooperative style of play.

For example, if Bob and Ray are prisoners A and B, they might realize that repeatedly confessing against each other in a series of crimes is causing more damage than if they were to cooperate. This is illustrated in the tables, where both get two years if they confess, but only one if they cooperate and stay silent.

Examples of iterated play show that, as long as the benefits of cooperation outweigh the benefits of noncooperation, players will eventually adopt a cooperative style of play. That is because, over a series of repeated games, collective rationality becomes analogous to individual rationality.

The prisoner's dilemma may be extended to competitive market situations. Assume for instance that there are only two grocers in a given market, grocer Bill and grocer Mary. Bill decides to attack Mary by undercutting her prices. George reciprocates by matching the price cuts. Both foresake profits, and even incur losses, hoping to force the other into submission.

Finally, Bill gives up and raises his prices. Mary who can no longer afford underpricing Bill, raises her prices as well. Now neither are at a disadvantage. They have reached a cooperative agreement after learning that the consequences of noncooperation are mutually deleterious.

The prisoner's dilemma forces each individual to weigh the collective consequences of his individual action. This quality translates to many situations where individual action may damage collective welfare.

Assume, for example, that ten farmers share a single pasture where their 20 cows may graze. Each farmer decides to purchase an extra cow because each can benefit individually from the increased milk production. But if the pasture can support only 24 cows, the farmers' herd of 30 will overgraze it, ruining its ability to regenerate grass and depriving the entire herd of food.

A real-world example of the extended prisoner's dilemma exists in the fishing industry, where the rate of catches by fishers has increased faster than the ability of the fish to reproduce. The result is a depleted supply which has caused every fisher greater hardship.

The individually optimal strategy for each fisher is to cooperate with other fishers by restraining the volume of his or her catches. Fishers forgo higher profits in the near term, but are assured of protecting their livelihood in the long term.

These examples directly contradict the accepted principle in economics that the individual pursuit of self-interest in a freely competitive market yields an optimal aggregated equilibrium. They demonstrate the application of diminishing returns to a finite resource.

The claim that cooperative strategies will prevail over noncooperative ones in iterated games gained support from a most unusual source: theoretical biology. Scientists concerned with evolutionary dynamics postulated that species which fight to the death work their way toward extinction.

It seems elementary, that an animal determined to kill others of its kind would eventually cease to exist. But contests within species are common, particularly in the selection of a mate. However, these contests are often not lethal. They reward the winner with a mate and reward the loser with survival for accepting defeat and walking away.

Assuming that the male and female of a species are produced randomly in equal numbers, repeated situations in which two males fight to the death for a single mate will yield a population in which females will outnumber males. If this limits the number of females that may reproduce, population growth of this species will be retarded or turned negative.

If two males under the same conditions fight only for supremacy, rather than to the death, the loser may prevail in another contest with another yet weaker opponent, and still be allowed to reproduce. Thus, nonlethal combat may be viewed as cooperative in the collective sense.

The prisoner's dilemma becomes relevant in evolutionary biology when one constructs a matrix to analyze the outcomes of contests between animals that are killers and those that are nonkillers (see Figure 3.)

A single killer will prevail in three of the four contests, while two non-killers will survive in one of the four. In iterated play, the killers will eventually destroy all the non-killers. In a population left only

	Killer A	Non-Killer A
Killer B	A or B	B
Non-Killer B	A	A and B

Figure 3

	Prisoner A	
Prisoner B	Confess	Stay Silent
Confess	A: 2 B: 2	A: 3 B: 2
Stay Silent	A: 2 B: 3	A: 2 B: 2

Figure 5

with killers, successive contests between killers will yield fewer and fewer killers until the species cannot sustain itself.

Meanwhile, populations in which there are no killers will suffer no decrease in the male population due to lethal contests. A roughly equal distribution of males and females will remain, and the animals will pair off and reproduce the species. This example once again proves that cooperative strategies are dominant in iterated play.

One instance where noncooperative play may benefit a player is in the case where the highest penalty is removal from the game. For example, if the two prisoners are implicated in a murder, but prosecutors can't determine who was the hit man, they may offer to plea bargain (see Figure 4).

	Prisoner A	
Prisoner B	Confess	Stay Silent
Confess	A: 25 B: 25	A: Executed B:12
Stay Silent	A: 12 B: Executed	A: 8 B:8

Figure 4

If both confess, each gets 25 years. If they refuse to cooperate, they each get eight years. But, if prisoner A testifies that B actually did the murder, and B remains silent, prisoner B will be executed. While extreme, such a model by its nature precludes iteration because prisoner B will be dead.

Another case where noncooperative strategies may prove dominant is where the penalties to each player are insufficient to provide cooperative motivations. Consider the following example in Figure 5.

Here, prisoners A and B are indifferent about confessing or staying silent because in either case they would get two years. But each is aware that if he remains silent while the other agrees to implicate him, he might face a third year in jail. Thus, in order to avoid the heavier penalty, both will adopt a noncooperative defensive strategy and confess.

The prisoner's dilemma may be extended to contests between more than two players. Assume for example that three prisoners, rather than two, are apprehended for robbery. Each prisoner must now weigh the possible outcomes of cooperation and noncooperation with two counterparts. This may be represented in a three-dimensional matrix with eight, rather than four possible outcomes.

If there was a fourth partner, the matrix would require a fourth dimension, or array, with 16 possible outcomes. The number of outcomes in a multiple-player dilemma may be expressed as a formula: $(C)^n$, where C is the number of choices available to each player and n represents the number of players.

Tests with multiple-prisoner dilemmas support the position that cooperative strategies remain individually optimal, particularly in iterated play.

[John Simley]

FURTHER READING:

Eatwell, J. ed. *The New Palgrave Dictionary of Economics.* London: Macmillan, 1987.

Johnson, Robert R. *Elementary Statistics*, 3rd ed. North Scituate, MA: Duxbury Press, 1980.

Maynard Smith, John. *Evolution and the Theory of Games.* Cambridge: Cambridge University Press, 1982.

PRIVACY

SEE: Employee Rights; Right of Privacy

PRIVATELY HELD COMPANY

A corporation may be publicly owned or privately owned. In the case of a privately owned, or closely held, corporation, all of the stock is concentrated in the hands of a few individuals. When the privately held corporation first issues its stock, it is not offered for sale to the general public. On the other hand, the stock of a **publicly held corporation** is offered to the general public for sale. A privately held company may decide to ''go public.'' That is, it may make a stock offering to the general public in order to raise capital. The first public stock offering of a company is known as its initial **public offering** (IPO).

In order for a company to be privately held, it must be organized as a corporation. A corporation is a legal form of business that is established by a corporate charter granted by a particular state. The corporate charter establishes the corporation as a separate legal entity from its owners. The corporation is said to be a ''legal person'' and may enter into agreements, make contracts, and sue or be sued.

The owners of a corporation, whether public or private, are its **common stock**holders. There are two types of stock, common and preferred. **Preferred stock**holders generally receive a stated dividend of a specific amount. Common stockholders receive a dividend based on corporate profits, although in some cases common stock pays no dividend. The corporation's charter specifies how many shares and what types of stock it is allowed to issue. While both preferred stockholders and common stockholders are investors in the corporation and provide it with capital, it is the common stockholders who actually own the firm.

In a privately held corporation, the owners and managers may be the same individuals. In the case of a small grocery store organized as a corporation, for example, it would not be uncommon for the owners of the store to also run it. The president of a small manufacturing firm that is privately held may be the sole stockholder or hold a majority of the stock.

The corporate form of business organization allows a distinction to be made between a corporation's owners and its managers. In a large, privately held corporation, the shareholders who own the firm are likely to be different from the managers, executives, and directors who run the firm. In that case, the company's board of directors would be responsible for running the corporation to maximize profits for the shareholders. The directors may themselves be the sole shareholders. In practice the corporate directors establish corporate policy, make major decisions, and hire managers and others to oversee the daily operations of the corporation. Shareholders can express their satisfaction or displeasure with the board of directors of a corporation by voting them in or out of office.

Whether publicly held or privately held, corporations provide their owners with a degree of limited liability. The shareholders of a publicly held corporation may lose their investment in a company, but they have no personal liability beyond that. The same is also true for privately held corporations. However, if an owner of a privately held corporation is also actively engaged in managing and directing the operations of the company, then he or she may be held personally liable in a lawsuit against the firm. The concept of limited liability still applies to some extent in that situation, so that in the case of multiple owners or shareholders, one shareholder is not personally liable for the wrongdoings of another shareholder. A parallel situation exists for publicly held companies, where a company's directors may be held personally liable for specific cases of wrongdoing.

Unlike publicly held companies, privately held companies are not required to make public their profits and other financial results. Of course, they are also not able to raise capital by selling shares of stock to the general public. Successful and relatively young privately held companies often attempt to facilitate their growth by becoming publicly held companies and making an IPO. It must be remembered, however, that not all privately held corporations are small; there are some very large corporations that remain privately held, such as Levi Strauss & Co. and Hallmark Cards, Inc.

[David Bianco]

PRIVATELY PLACED SECURITIES

Privately placed securities are those that are sold directly to institutional investors instead of being offered for sale to the general public. Privately placed securities are usually bond issues, including corporate bonds; they also include other debt instruments as well as equity securities. Privately placed securities are issued primarily by smaller companies, although even Fortune 500 companies occasionally make use of the private placement market. The major purchasers of privately placed securities are life insurance companies, with other institutional investors such as **mutual funds**, pension funds, **banks**, **savings and loan** institutions, and limited partnerships also participating in buying private placements.

Certain securities offerings, including privately placed securities, are exempt from the **Securities and Exchange Commission**'s registration requirements.

These include securities that are purchased for investment rather than for distribution. Exempt securities must be offered through direct communication with the purchaser without general advertising. Such investors are assumed to have access to significant financial information concerning the issuer and the issue and thus do not require the guarantee of full disclosure afforded by Securities and Exchange Commission (SEC) registration. Accordingly, exemption from SEC registration applies to the sale of securities involving a limited number of financially sophisticated purchasers.

Privately placed securities are generally considered less liquid than comparable public issues. That is, it is easier for a purchaser to resell publicly issued securities than privately placed securities. This is due to the conditions under which private placements are issued as well as the restrictions that exist on resales. As a result of this liquidity risk, privately placed securities generally pay higher rates of interest than comparable public issues.

In 1990, bonds represented 87 percent of all privately placed securities, with equity securities accounting for the remaining 13 percent. Approximately $87 billion of privately placed bonds were issued in 1990, representing 29 percent of the $299 billion of new bonds issued in the United States that year. The $87 billion in privately placed bonds represented a decline from the high of $128 billion issued in 1988. One factor accounting for the decline was the desire of life insurance companies, the primary purchaser of private placements, to find more liquid investments to better cope with changing financial conditions.

Private placement offers several advantages to both borrowers (issuers) and lenders (purchasers). Since private placement is based on direct negotiations, it is possible to tailor the loan terms to fit the needs of both parties. Direct negotiation also makes it easier to structure complex offerings that would not be easily understood by the public. For lesser-known firms and smaller companies, private placements may represent their only source of long-term **capital**. For larger firms, private placements offer less expensive borrowing than with registered public offerings. Private placement also provides the issuer with some confidentiality regarding its financial records. In the case of public offerings and SEC registration, sensitive financial data must be disclosed.

Restrictive covenants are commonly used in private placements to protect the lender and ensure that the borrower conducts its business in a manner that will protect the value of the privately placed securities. While covenants are also written into loan agreements affecting public issues, they are generally more detailed in private placements. Among the areas covered by covenants are provisions for collateral to the security, delivery of financial data to the lender, and restrictions regarding the amount of additional long-term debt the borrower may take on. In addition the loan agreement may contain provisions limiting the issuer's ability to call in the security during times of falling **interest rates** and other restrictions designed to protect the purchaser's investment.

[David Bianco]

PRIVATIZATION

Privatization is an alternative to government production of goods and services that relies increasingly on the private sector to satisfy residents' needs and less on government. The term refers to a shift from public to private provision of services. Typically, these services are those for which absolutely private markets are considered deficient. The purpose of privatization is to take advantage of the perceived cost efficiencies of private firms. Even after privatization, however, government intervention is necessary in order to ensure that satisfactory services are provided to residents. Privatization of public services has been largely a "bottom up" experience in the United States, with local governments in the forefront and state and federal levels of government trailing behind.

WHAT IS PRIVATIZATION?

The term privatization has been applied to three different methods of increasing the activity of the private sector in providing public services: (1) private-sector choice, financing, and production of a service; (2) public-sector choice and financing with private-sector production of the service selected; (3) deregulation of private firms providing services. In the first case, the entire responsibility for a service is transferred from the public sector to the private sector, and individual consumers select and purchase the amount of services they desire from private providers. As an example, solid-waste collection is provided and produced by private firms in some communities. The third form of privatization means that government reduces or eliminates the regulatory restrictions imposed on private firms providing specific services.

The second version of privatization refers to joint activity of the public and private sectors in providing services. In this case, consumers select and pay for the quantity and type of service desired through government, which then contracts with private firms to produce the desired amount and category of service. Although the government provides for the service, a private firm produces it. The government determines the service level and pays the amount specified in the contract, but leaves decisions about production decisions to the private firm.

Although privatization alters who provides public services, it does not change who pays for the service. Suppose that prior to privatization, a service was produced by government employees and funded by the government. Upon privatization, the service would be provided by private sector employees, but the government could continue its financing role.

Services differ in the extent to which they are privatized. Local governments are more likely to contract out for services that typically are offered by the private sector or other levels of government. Furthermore, most privatization efforts at the local level have been applied to either routine housekeeping services in which government itself is the customer or public services with well-defined tangible outputs. Conversely, governmental units tend not to contract out for services that are commonly the responsibility of local government. For example, fire protection, sewerage systems, and water distribution and treatment are among the least-likely services to be contracted out. Townships are more likely to contract out than municipalities or counties. Privatization differs across geographic regions, with the Midwest and West South Central regions having the greatest and the South Atlantic the least tendency for private production.

ADVANTAGES AND DISADVANTAGES OF PRIVATIZATION

REDUCED COSTS AND OTHER POTENTIAL ADVANTAGES. Proponents of privatization argue that government producers have no incentive to hold down production costs, whereas private producers who contract with the government to provide service do. The lower the cost incurred by the firm in satisfying the contract, the greater profit it makes. Competition among potential private suppliers to obtain this contract is expected to provide the government with the lowest cost for the specified level of service. On the other hand, the absence of competition and profit incentives in the public sector is not likely to result in cost minimization.

Although private firms may pay lower wages and fringe benefits than local governments, the major cause of the cost differences between the private and governmental sectors is employee **productivity**. Lower labor costs may arise either from lower wages (which means that the government was paying wages higher than necessary for a given skill) or from less labor input (which means that the government was hiring unnecessary workers). Government agencies are normally less productive per paid labor hour than private firms. Private firms have more flexibility than governmental units to use part-timers to meet peak loads, to fire unsatisfactory workers, and to allocate workers across a variety of tasks. Moreover, governments tend not to reward individual initiatives or punish aberrant behavior, in relation to its private sector counterparts, contributing to the lower productivity.

Private firms may also more readily experiment with different approaches to service provision, whereas government tends to stick with the current approach since changes often create political difficulties for elected officials. In addition, private firms may use retained earnings to finance research or to purchase new capital equipment that lowers unit production costs. On the other hand, government may not be able or willing to allocate tax revenues to these purposes as easily, given the many competing demands on the government's budget.

Another fundamental reason for the cost disparity is attributable to the greater efficiency associated with a private sector firm operating in a competitive environment. Private owners have a strong incentive to operate efficiently, while this incentive is lacking under public ownership. If private firms spend more money and employ more people to do the same amount of work, competition will lead to lower margins, lost customers, and decreased profits. The disciplining effect of competition, however, does not occur in the public sector. Government agencies tend to operate in noncompetitive environments and therefore can charge more for services and provide unwanted services.

Public employees have a vested interest in having the government grow. Elected officials who promotes higher spending levels gain the support of the beneficiaries of the government's largess. Higher government expenditures also lead to increased staffing levels, larger salaries for department heads, higher status, and more perquisites.

Private ownership produces the public benefits of lower costs and high quality only in the presence of a competitive environment. Privatization cannot be expected to produce these same benefits if competition is absent. In addition, the idea that government has no incentive to hold production costs down may be too strong because local officials face competition from potential candidates and communities face competition from other communities both for residents and businesses. If the government's costs for a service in one community are higher than they need be, then taxes in that community are also higher. Accordingly, households and businesses might move to communities with lower costs for a given level of services.

BURDENS FOR PUBLIC EMPLOYEES AND OTHER POTENTIAL DISADVANTAGES. Potential problems with the private provision of government services might arise from the bidding process, the precise specification of the contract, and the monitoring and enforcement of the contract. First, competitive bidding may not provide the service at lowest cost to the contracting government if there are only a few potential suppliers and the government has only a limited idea about the level of total costs.

Furthermore, there is concern that potential suppliers may initially offer a price to the government that is less than actual production costs to induce the government to transfer the service to the private sector or to win the contract. Subsequently, the contractor would then demand a higher price after the government has dismantled its own production system. Such ''low-balling'' in the bidding process may be reduced if the local government requires relatively long-term contracts, or if it is easy to switch contractors.

The second potential difficulty with privatization concerns the specification of the service to be provided in the contract. It is particularly difficult to characterize output for some services. If society is not certain what ''good'' education is and how to measure it, for instance, how can government contract for it?

The third potential problem concerns monitoring the service quality provided by the private firm and enforcing the contract when problems arise. Monitoring the performance of the private supplier creates costs, which may be substantial, for the government. In addition, there must be a remedy if the supplier does not provide or stops the service. For example, suppose that the private contractor underestimates its costs so that the price charged the government is not sufficient to cover all production costs, resulting in losses for the firm. This could result in serious implications in the case of critical services such as police and fire protection if the firm shuts down. Although there are scattered examples of contractors who failed to live up to expectations, the average experience does not appear to be negative.

The burdens of contracting are concentrated on the public sector **workforce**. In some cases, privatization results in layoffs of public sector employees, although governments often reassign them to other government jobs, place them with private contractors, or offer them early retirement programs. Because their jobs and incomes are at risk, public employee unions have an incentive to block privatization. Surveys have indicated that this opposition lowers the likelihood that public services will be contracted out.

PRIVATIZATION'S EFFECTIVENESS: EVIDENCE BASED ON THE U.S. EXPERIENCE

Contracting out services is the most popular form of privatization for state and local governments. The available evidence shows that the number of state and local governments contracting with private firms to provide final services to consumers and intermediate services to the government has increased substantially in the past decade. Recent surveys indicate that over one-half of state and local governments have to some degree privatized services.

In a wide variety of cases, contracting has resulted in the same level of service being provided at substantially lower cost, although utilities seen to be an exception. A number of surveys have indicated that municipal executives cite cost reductions as the primary benefit of contracting out, and that most indicated that they were satisfied with the quality of the work performed by the private contractor. There is also substantial and increasing evidence that the use of private firms to produce services has resulted in lower costs, especially for the more typical types of privatization. In general, the studies found that private firms provided at least the same level and quality of service at cost savings in the range of 10 to 30 percent.

Smaller municipalities may incur relatively high unit costs if they operate their own services as a result of not being able to achieve **economies of scale**. These localities may benefit from turning to a contractor that serves multiple communities. Privatization is also more acceptable in fast-growing communities. If services are being expanded to cover new residents, private contractors are less likely to displace existing public sector employees. Finally, contracting out varies with the number of services provided to residents. As the number of services increases, differences in the cost and effectiveness with which they are provided become more apparent. Therefore, municipalities providing diverse services may be more open to exploring private sector options than those localities where services are more limited.

INTERNATIONAL PRIVATIZATION

In some countries, governments have privatized state-owned enterprises involved in the production of goods and services that elsewhere are commonly produced by the private sector. Western European countries, especially Great Britain and France, have sold off state-owned enterprises in industries such as automobiles, glassmaking, **telecommunications**, airlines, finance, and insurance. The countries of the former Soviet bloc are now engaged in similar privatization efforts, on a more massive scale. According to some estimates, privatization can be expected to raise $800 billion for governments by the year 2000. Once enterprises have been sold, they function like any other private business.

There are four main approaches to international privatization: (1) traditional privatization, which stresses receipts to government from the sale of state-owned **assets**, or improvements in the balance of payments from **foreign investment** inflows; (2) an approach that minimizes social upheaval associated with privatization, while pursuing rapid divestiture; (3) mass ownership transformation, which attempts rapid transfer of ownership in hundreds of medium and large state-owned enterprises to private owners through vouchers; and (4) internal privatization, which relinquishes control of state-owned enterprises to internal groups such as **management** and workers.

Among the objectives cited in connection with privatization are: reducing the government's operating deficit and its external and internal debt, increasing domestic and international business confidence in the country's economy, and reducing the role of the state in the economy. Therefore, privatization is more likely to be pursued by countries with high budget deficits, high foreign debt, and high dependence on international agencies such as the **World Bank**. In Latin America and Asia, the trend is also more likely in countries that have overused state enterprises in the past and those in which the private sector has grown faster than average and is more ready to assume responsibilities once assigned to state enterprises. In Africa, privatization has often been imposed by external agencies on countries that are not necessarily ready for privatization.

Those countries that have implemented extensive privatization programs have achieved substantial benefits. Empirical studies have compared the pre- and post-privatization financial and operating performance of companies that experienced full or partial privatization through public share offerings during the period 1961-90. The studies have documented strong performance improvements. After being privatized, firms increase real sales, become more profitable, increase their capital investment spending, improve their operating efficiency, and increase their workforce. Furthermore, these companies significantly lower their debt levels and increase dividend payouts. The improved efficiency of state-owned enterprises can lead to gains for investors as well, as the stock of newly privatized firms are frequently good buys. From 1988 to 1993, newly privatized companies appreciated an average of 14 percent a year.

Other major issues of privatization concern political aspects and institutional support. Some industries, such as defense, are considered too sensitive to put out to bid. Other firms are too union-dominated. In many nations, **labor unions** do not support the idea of turning government-owned assets over to private enterprise. Restrictions on the participation of foreign investors are common in most countries for some privatizations. In some cases, such as France, the state will retain 10 percent to 20 percent or more of the enterprise after privatization, which is suggestive of government regulation after privatization.

[Robert T. Kleiman]

FURTHER READING:

Henkoff, Ronald. "Some Hope for Troubled Cities." *Fortune*. September 9, 1991, pp. 121-128.

Kodrzycki, Yolanda. "Privatization of Local Government Services: Lessons for New England." *New England Economic Review*. May/June, 1994, pp. 31-46.

Lieberman, Ira W. "Privatization: The Theme of the 1990s—An Overview." *Columbia Journal of World Business*. Spring, 1993, pp. 8-17.

Megginson, William L., Robert C. Nash, and Matthias Van Randenborgh. "The Financial and Operating Performance of Newly Privatized Firms: An International Empirical Analysis." *Journal of Finance*. June, 1994, pp. 403-452.

Poole, Robert, and Philip Fixler "Privatization of Public-Sector Services in Practice: Experience and Potential" *Journal of Policy Analysis and Management*. 6:4, 1987, pp. 612-625.

PRO FORMA STATEMENT

Pro forma is a Latin term applied to the process of presenting projections or a series of projections for a specific time period in a standardized format. For the purpose of comparison and analysis, pro forma statements provide the **management** of a business, investment analysts, and **due diligence** or **credit** officers the opportunity to get a feel for the particular nature of a business's financial structure for the past, in the present, and for the projected time period.

The dictionary definition of *pro forma* only intimates the structure and purpose of pro forma statements. Literally translated "for (the sake of) form" or "as a matter of form," the "form" of pro forma statements has been the subject of recommendations and regulations by both the American Institute of Certified Public Accountants (AICPA) since 1923 and of the **Securities and Exchange Commission** since 1933. Both organizations require standard formats when constructing and presenting pro forma statements.

Businesses use pro forma statements for **decision-making** in planning and control, and for external reporting to owners, investors, and creditors.

PRO FORMA STATEMENTS IN BUSINESS PLANNING

A company uses pro forma statements in the process of **business planning** and control. Because pro forma statements are presented in a standardized, columnar format, management employs them to compare and contrast alternative business plans. By arranging the data for the operating and **financial statements** side-by-side, management analyzes the projected results of competing plans in order to decide which best serves the interests of the business.

In constructing pro forma statements, a company recognizes the uniqueness and distinct financial characteristics of each proposed plan or project. Pro forma statements allow management to:

1. Identify the assumptions about the financial and operating characteristics that generate the scenarios.

2. Develop the various sales and budget (expenses and revenues) projections.

3. Assemble the results in profit and loss projections.

4. Translate this data into cash flow projections.

5. Compare the resulting balance sheets.

6. Perform ratio analysis to compare projections against each other and to those of similar companies.

7. Review proposed decisions in **marketing**, production, **research and development**, etc., and to asses their impact on profitability and liquidity.

Competing plans constitute simulation models that are quite useful in evaluating the financial effects of the different alternatives under consideration. Based on different sets of assumptions, these plans propose various scenarios of sales, production costs, profitability, and viability. Pro forma statements for each plan provide important information about future expectations such as:

- Sales and earnings forecasts
- Cash flows
- Balance sheets
- Proposed capitalization
- Income statements

Management also uses this procedure in choosing among budget alternatives. Planners present sales revenues, production expenses, **balance sheet**, and cash flow statements for competing plans with underlying assumptions explained. Based on an analysis of these figures, management selects an annual budget. After choosing a course of action, it is common for management to examine variations within the plan.

If management considers a flexible budget most appropriate for its company, it would establish a range of possible outcomes generally categorized as *normal* (expected results), *above normal* (best case), and *below normal* (worst case). Management examines contingency plans for the possible outcomes at input/output levels specified within the operating range. Since these three budgets are projections appearing in a standardized, columnar format and for a specified time period, they are pro forma.

During the course of the fiscal period, management evaluates its performance by comparing actual results to the expectations of the accepted plan using a similar pro forma format. Management's appraisal tests and re-tests the assumptions upon which it based its plans. In this way pro forma statements are indispensable to the control process.

FINANCIAL MODELING

Pro forma statements provide financial statements and data for calculating financial ratios and for mathematical calculations. Financial models built on pro forma projections contribute to the achievement of corporate goals if they (1) test the goals of the plans, (2) furnish findings that are readily understandable, (3) and provide time, quality, and cost advantages over other methods.

Financial modeling tests the assumptions and relationships of proposed plans by asking the ''What If'' questions:

- What would be the impact on cost of goods sold if the prices of labor, materials, and overhead increased? Decreased? Changed in mix?

- What would be the impact on the income statement if the cost of goods sold increased 20 percent? Decreased 5 percent?

- What would be the impact on cash flow if the cost of borrowing increased? Decreased?

- What would the impact be on revenues if the volume of sales increased 10 percent? Decreased 15 percent?

- What would be the impact on the financial statement if inventory valuation increased 10 percent? Decreased 5 percent?

Computer-assisted modeling has made assumption testing more efficient. The use of powerful processors permits on-line, real-time decision making through immediate calculations of alternative cash-flow statements, balance sheets, and the income statements.

PRO FORMA FINANCIAL STATEMENTS

A company prepares pro forma financial statements when it expects to experience or has just experienced significant financial changes. The pro forma financial statements present the impact of these changes on the financial position as depicted in the income statement, balance sheet, and the cash-flow statement.

When management contemplates a merger or **joint venture** involving two or more companies, it will prepare pro forma financial statements to facilitate the analysis of the financial position and earnings of the combined enterprise. If a business combination is to occur during the course of a fiscal year, a company structures the pro forma financial statement for the full year to determine what the operating results would have been if the combination had taken place at the beginning of the current year.

In its decision to refinance debt through issuance of preferred stock, **common stock**, or other **debt**, a company constructs a series of pro forma financial statements depicting the impact of each choice on cash flow and income.

EXTERNAL REPORTING

Businesses also use pro forma statements in external reports prepared for owners (stockholders), creditors, and potential investors. For companies listed on the stock exchanges, the SEC requires pro forma statements for any filing, with registration statements, and for proxy statements. The **SEC** and organizations governing **accounting** practices require pro forma statements when essential changes in the historical character of a business's financial statements have occurred or will occur. Financial statements change because of:

1. Changes in accounting principles due to adoption of a generally accepted accounting principle different from one used previously for financial accounting. Management's decision to change accounting principles may be based (a) on the issuance of a new accounting principle by the **Financial Accounting Standards Board (FASB)**, (b) on internal considerations taking advantage of revised **valuations** or tax codes, or (c) on the accounting needs of a new business combination.

2. A change in accounting estimates dealing with the estimated economic life and net residual value of assets.

3. A change in the business entity resulting from the acquisition or disposition of an asset or investment, and/or the pooling of interests of two or more existing businesses.

4. A correction of an error made in report or filing of a previous period.

CHANGES IN ACCOUNTING PRINCIPLES

By changing its accounting practices, a business might significantly affect the presentation of its financial position and the results of its operations. The change also might distort the earnings trend reported in the income statements for earlier years.

Accountants must find appropriate methods of reporting these accounting changes to users of financial statements to clarify the effects of the changes and to facilitate a meaningful comparison

TYPES OF ACCOUNTING CHANGES. Changes in accounting principle involve the methods used to measure **assets** and **liabilities**. For example, changing the method of computing **depreciation** from straight-line to an accelerated method. Another example is changing the method of valuating inventory from last in, first out (LIFO) to first in, first out (FIFO).

When a company changes an accounting method, it uses pro forma financial statements to report the cumulative effect of the change for the period during which the change occurred. To enable comparison of the pro forma financial statements with previous financial statements, the company would employ the following four principles in reporting the changes.

1. Present the financial statements for prior periods as originally reported.

2. Include in the net income of the period of the change the cumulative effect of the change on the amount of retained earnings (if applicable) at the beginning of the period. The cumulative effect of the change is the difference between the actual amount of retained earnings at the beginning of the period of the change, and the amount of retained earnings that would have been reported on that date if the company had applied the new accounting principle retroactively for all periods in the comparison.

3. Disclose the effect of adopting the new principle on income before extraordinary items and on net income. Express the results on a per share basis, if applicable.

4. Show income before extraordinary items and net income are computed on a pro forma basis in the income statement, for all prior accounting periods presented, and as if the newly adopted accounting principle had been used in prior periods.

Pro forma statements, based on these principles, indicate that a different accounting principle was used to prepare the financial statements. The accountants would also include (1) an income statement for the current period, (2) the actual and pro forma amounts (including earnings per share) for the immediately preceding period, (3) the total and per-share amounts of the cumulative effect in the income statement below any extraordinary items, and (4) appropriate consideration for income **taxes**.

A change in accounting estimate may be required as new events occur and as better information becomes available about the probable outcome of future events. For example, an increase in the percentage used to estimate doubtful accounts, a major write-down of inventories, a change in the economic lives of plant assets, and a revision in the estimated liability for outstanding product **warranties** would require pro forma statements.

A change in the reporting entity occurs when the basic business entity changes through the pooling of interests, because of a major acquisition, or due to the disposition of a part of the entity. The company would restate the historical statements on a pro forma basis to provide sufficient disclosure of the impact on the financial statements.

A correction of an error is required when a company discovers errors in previously issued financial statements. The complexities of tax codes, changing markets, and business practices may cause a company to improperly record material amounts of depreciation, especially in light of changes made in accounting principles and estimates.

THE SEC FORMAT

In Rule 10-11 of Regulation S-X, the SEC prescribes the form and content of pro forma statements for companies subject to its jurisdiction in circumstances such as the above. Some of the requirements are:

1. An introductory paragraph describing the proposed transaction, the entities involved, the periods covered by the pro forma information, and what the pro forma information shows.

2. A pro forma condensed balance sheet and a pro forma condensed income statement, in columnar form, showing the condensed historical amounts, the pro forma adjustments, and the pro forma amounts. Footnotes provide justification for the pro forma adjustments and explain other details pertinent to the changes.

3. The pro forma adjustments, directly attributable to the proposed transaction, which are expected to have a continuing impact on the financial statements. Explanatory notes provide the factual basis for adjustments.

PRO FORMA FINANCIAL STATEMENTS FOR CHANGES IN ENTITY AND FOR BUSINESS COMBINATIONS

The FASB, the AICPA, and the SEC have provided significant directives to the form, content, and necessity of pro forma financial statements in situations where there has been a change in the form of a business entity due to changes in financial structure

resulting from the disposition of a long-term liability or asset, or to a combination of two or more businesses.

The purpose of pro forma financial statements is to facilitate comparisons of historic data and projections of future performance. In these circumstances users of financial statements need to evaluate a new or proposed business entity on a basis comparable to the predecessor business in order to understand the impact of the change on cash flow, income, and financial position. *Pro forma adjustments* to accounting principles and accounting estimates reformat the statements of the new entity and the acquired business to conform with those of the predecessor.

The following discussion provides an overview of the kind of adjustments and pro forma financial statements required by the SEC for companies under its jurisdiction.

MERGER AND ACQUISITIONS. Pro forma statements report the impact of the acquisition upon the acquiring company resulting from (a) a new capital structure, and (b) the new valuation placed upon the fixed assets to be required. The pro forma assists in assessing the new entity's coverages of liquidating values, any possible dividend requirements, and the change in earnings per share.

The pro forma consolidating balance sheet gives effect to the recapitalization and acquisition.

The pro forma income statement calculates the income, changes in tax liabilities, and depreciation changes resulting from the increased valuation of acquired fixed assets.

EXCHANGE OFFERS. A company, trying to reduce its debt-to-equity ratio, may issue common or preferred stock in exchange for outstanding debt. To help in the understanding of the impact of the exchange, the company would provide (1) historical financial statements, (2) a pro forma statement of income, and (3) the necessary pro forma adjustments made, especially in interest expense and the gain or loss on the exchange.

ACQUISITION OF A PARTNERSHIP OR SOLE PROPRIETORSHIP. Occasionally, a partnership or sole proprietorship will sell all or part of the business interest. Sometimes it is necessary, especially if the business is "going public," to reorganize into a corporation. The financial statements on a corporation with a very short history are not helpful in a thoughtful analysis of future potential. Similarly, because of the differences in federal income tax liabilities, a restatement of the predecessor business in historical terms only confuses the picture. Since the financial statements of the predecessor business do not contain some of the expense items applicable to a corporation, the pro forma financial statements make adjustments to restate certain expenses on a corporate basis. In particular these would include:

1. Stating the owners' salaries in terms of officers' salaries.

2. Calculating the applicable federal taxes on the predecessor business as though it were a corporation.

3. Including corporate state franchise taxes.

4. For partnerships acquired through the pooling of interests, adding the balance of the partners' capital to contributed capital in the combined company rather than to retained earnings.

Sub-Chapter S corporations exercise the tax-option of the shareholders individually assuming the tax liability rather than the corporation as a whole. If the shareholders choose to go public or change their qualifications, the corporation looses the tax-option. Therefore, in addition to the pro forma statement showing historical earnings, the new company will make pro forma provision for the taxes that it would have paid had it been a regular corporation in the past.

When acquisition of the Sub-Chapter S corporation is accomplished through the pooling of interests, the pro forma financial statement may not include any of the retained earnings of the Sub-Chapter S corporation in the pooled retained earnings.

In preparing a pro forma income statement for the acquisition of a partnership, the accountant would add adjustments such as:

Net income, as stated, minus:

1. Increase/(decrease) of officers' salaries over partners' salaries

2. Directors' fees, estimated

3. Federal capital stock tax, state franchise tax, and social security tax applicable to officers' salaries

4. Provision for federal income taxes

Equals, adjusted net income

In regard to the officers'/partners' salaries, the acquiring company, on a certain date, established officers' salaries different from partners' salaries. If officers' salaries increased, the excess is subtracted from income. If the officers' salaries decreased, the difference is added to net income.

When presenting the historical operations of a business previously operated as a partnership, the accountant would make adjustments to bring the statement in line with the acquiring corporation. Historical data listed would include net sales; cost of sales; gross profit on sales; selling, general, and administrative expenses; other income; other deductions; and income before taxes on income. Pro forma adjustments would include pro forma adjustments to restate partnership operations on a corporate basis, including estimated partnership salaries as officers and estimated federal and state taxes on income; as well as pro forma net income and pro forma net income per share.

Accountants make similar adjustments to pro forma statements for businesses previously operated as sole proprietorships and Sub-Chapter S corporations.

THE ACQUIRED BUSINESS OPERATED AS A DIVISION. A company may derive many benefits from the inclusion of its various divisions in tax filings. There may not have been arms-length apportionment and allocations of costs and expenses, nor an allocation of federal income taxes to each division. Therefore, the restatement of earnings in pro forma financial statements should include:

1. A projection of the impact of new **depreciation** and **amortization** schedules for the properties acquired.

2. The impact of long-term financing carried over from the predecessor's parent.

3. The restatement of earnings and expenses, including state and federal tax liabilities, as though the division operated as an independent company.

4. Additional operating costs or increased efficiencies resulting from the combination.

ACQUISITION OR DISPOSAL OF PART OF A BUSINESS. A meaningful pro forma statement would include pro forma adjustments to the historical figures to demonstrate how the acquired part would have fared had it been a corporation. Pro forma statements would also set forth conventional financial statements of the acquiring company, and pro forma financial statements of the business to be acquired. Notes to the pro forma statements explain the adjustments reflected in the statements.

A pro forma income statement would combine the historical income statement of the acquiring company and a pro forma income statement of the business to be acquired for the previous five years, if possible. Pro forma adjustments would exclude overhead costs not applicable in the new business entity such as division and head office expenses.

THE ACQUISITION OF REAL PROPERTY BY A REAL ESTATE COMPANY. Real estate investment trusts and other issuers whose business is primarily that of acquiring and holding real estate for investment include pro forma statements in SEC filings to indicate how it will apply the proceeds of an offering. If the acquisition is clearly a significant part of the real estate company, the registration statement will include an operating statement of the property.

The operating statement, covering a minimum of five years, is essentially historical in character, with pro forma adjustments eliminating items not comparable to the proposed future operation of the property, such as mortgage interest, depreciation, leasehold rental, corporate expense, and income **taxes**. If the acquiring company plans to manage the new property, it would include statements showing the estimated taxable operating results of the combined business based on the most recent 12-month period.

PRO FORMA STATEMENTS UNDER THE POOLING METHOD. When a company is considering a business combination under the pooling method of accounting, the pro forma statement for the proposed pooling would present a balance sheet at a current date giving effect to the combination as if it had occurred at that date. For a historical perspective, pro forma statements of earnings for the preceding five fiscal years, and for any interim periods deemed appropriate, would give effect to the combination as if it had occurred at the beginning of the earliest period included in the statements.

The Accounting Principles Board (APB) requires certain disclosures in the notes to the financial statements in the period in which a combination occurs. It also calls for similar information on a pro forma basis in data to be given shareholders in connection with a proposed business combination. These disclosures include the following:

1. A detailed comparison of the results of the operations of the previously separated company prior to an actual combination. These details should include such items as revenue, extraordinary items, net income, other changes in stockholders' equity, and the amount and manner of accounting for intercompany transactions.

2. A description of the nature of any adjustments of the net assets of the combining companies necessitated by changes in accounting principles and accounting estimates.

3. A description of the impact of accounting changes on the net income previously reported by the separate companies.

4. Details of the increases or decreases in retained earnings for the fiscal year of a combining company.

5. Explanatory notes containing a reconciliation of the revenue and earnings previously reported by the acquiring company with the pooled amounts currently shown in the financial statement.

In situations where the pooling of interests occurs or is completed after the date of the balance sheet, the APB requires certain disclosures in the notes to the

financial statements with respect to the details of the effect of the pooling. The details would include revenue, net income, **earnings per share**, and the effects of the anticipated changes in accounting methods as if the combination had been consummated at the date of the financial statements. In addition, a company should furnish a pro forma balance sheet as of the same date in order to comply with SEC practice.

PRO FORMA STATEMENTS UNDER THE PURCHASE METHOD. The APB requires certain supplemental information when a company accounts for a business combination under the purchase method. This supplemental information applies only to the combination of regular corporations.

1. Pro forma financial statements showing the results of operation for the current period as though the companies had combined at the beginning of the period.

2. Pro forma statements showing the results of operations for the immediately preceding priod as though the companies had combined at the beginning of that period.

3. Supplemental information showing revenue, income before extraordinary items, net income, and earnings per share.

4. Pro forma adjustments to interest and preferred stock **dividends**, income taxes, depreciation and amortization of assets in conformity with the accounting basis recognized in recording the combination.

5. A pro forma presentation of the results of operations for only the immediately preceding period.

The SEC requires that the acquiring company state the contribution to sales and earnings of the acquired company, not only for the year in which the purchase occurs, but also in the succeeding years. The SEC may require additional disclosures if the line of business of the acquired company is different from that of the acquiring company.

The purchase of a sole proprietorship, partnership, Sub-Chapter S corporation, or business segment requires pro forma statements for a series of years in order to reflect pro forma adjustments for such items as owners' or partners' salaries and income taxes. In this way, each year reflects the results of operations of a business organization comparable with that of the acquiring corporation. However, the pro forma statements giving effect to the business combination should be limited to the current and immediately preceding periods.

SUMMARY

Pro forma statements are an integral part of business planning and control. Management uses them in the decision-making process when constructing the annual budget, developing long-range plans, and choosing among **capital** expenditures. Public accounting and external reporting find pro forma statements indispensable in assisting users of financial statements in understanding the impact on the financial structure of a business due to changes in the business entity, or in accounting principles or accounting estimates.

[Roger J. AbiNader]

FURTHER READING:

Merrill, Ronald E., and Henry D. Sedgwick. *The New Venture Handbook: Everything You Need to Know to Start and Run Your Own Business.* AMACOM, 1987.

Mosich, A. N., and E. John. Larsen. *Intermediate Accounting.* McGraw-Hill Book Company, 1986.

Rappaport, Louis H. *SEC Accounting Practice and Procedure.* The Ronald Press Company, 1966.

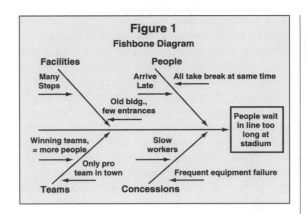

Figure 1
Fishbone Diagram

PROBLEM-SOLVING STYLES

A number of different problem-solving styles have evolved to deal with the problems that people and organizations face. These problem-solving styles deal with some or all of the stages of the problem-solving process. These stages can be divided into:

1. Problem Identification

2. Identification of Potential Solutions

3. Evaluation of Potential Solutions

4. Anticipation of Negative Consequences

5. Overcoming Obstacles to Carrying Out a Solution

6. Detailed Plan for Carrying Out a Solution

PROBLEM IDENTIFICATION

An approach that is meant to aid in problem identification is the Ishikawa "fishbone diagram" form of root cause analysis. In this method, all of the possible major causes and sub-causes of the end effect are enumerated along the "bones" of the diagram. Then all of the possible sub-causes are evaluated to see if they might cause the problem under consideration. A potential difficulty is that it may be difficult to identify the actual cause of a specific problem with this approach. Figure 1 shows an example of a fishbone diagram.

An approach that can help with the stage of problem identification and identification of potential solutions is the Crawford Slip Method, in which group participants submit ideas in writing on slips of paper.

The nominal group technique has some similarities in its approach, and is meant to deal with the same stages as the Crawford slip method. Another approach that deals with these stages is Alex Osborn's brainstorming technique, which has some limitations due to personal interaction that the Crawford slip method and the nominal group technique are designed to avoid.

IDENTIFICATION OF POTENTIAL SOLUTIONS

The simplest problem-solving style is informal enough that it does not appear to have a name. It involves using a list of potential solutions to a problem and identifying the positive and negative aspects of each solution, choosing the best solution. This assumes that both the problem and the potential solutions are already well identified. While this approach is simple and requires little expertise, its disadvantage is that the more complex the problem, the less satisfactory it is.

The use of a **decision tree** is a more complex problem-solving style that also requires the prior identification of the problem and potential solutions. Decision trees show, in detail, the sequence of actions and events that will follow from an initial decision point, where one of a number of alternative actions can be taken. This sequence of actions and events can then be evaluated using expected monetary values based on probability judgments. These two approaches concentrate on the stages of evaluation of potential solutions and anticipation of negative consequences.

Another approach to potential solution identification, is Fritz Zwicky's morphological approach, in which a two- or three-dimensional matrix is used to force the consideration of possible solutions that might otherwise be overlooked. Also employed identify solutions is Edward de Bono's use of "lateral thinking" to generate unconventional new ideas. This has some similarity to Roger Von Oech's "whack on the side of the head" approach to thinking of the problem and its effects in unconventional terms.

Probably the best explanation for the success of Zwicky's, de Bono's, Von Oech's, and others, approaches to thinking about problems "outside the box" is Arthur C. Koestler's 1964 masterwork, *The Act of Creation*. Koestler explained in great detail the concept of "bisociation," in which the intersection of two incompatible but internally consistent frames of reference can lead to a solution that would otherwise not be discovered. He showed how all of humor, most of literature and art, and nearly all breakthrough scientific discoveries can be traced to the occurrence of bisociation on the part of the creator. He cited the example of Archimedes, counselor to Hiero II, king of Syracuse in ancient Greece. The king had been given a golden crown and had assigned Archimedes the task of determining how much gold the crown contained, since he suspected that it had been alloyed with less expensive silver. What Archimedes needed was to use the weight and volume of the crown to determine its density, since it could then be compared with pure gold. While Archimedes could weigh the crown, he did not know how to determine its volume without melting it down into a bar, which would of course destroy the crown and its value as a work of art. While this was on his mind, Archimedes happened to notice, for the first time, that as he climbed into his bathtub, the water level rose. He immediately realized that his body displaced a volume of water that had to be equivalent to the volume of his own body. Since the volume of displaced water could be easily measured, he had in effect found a way to melt himself down and measure the volume of his own body. Applying this principle to the crown gave him the answer to his problem. He could now determine the volume of the crown in the same way.

What Archimedes had done was to take a common, usually neglected observance that the water in his bathtub rose, and connect it with the other frame of reference regarding his problem with the crown. This bisociation between the two frames of reference allowed Archimedes to think of the problem in a completely different way, and to reach a creative solution. Zwicky's morphological approach, de Bono's lateral thinking, and Von Oech's "whack on the side of the head" approach all make use of this kind of creative look at a problem from a different point of view.

Synectics, developed by William J. J. Gordon and George M. Prince, is an approach that deals with the stages of identifying solutions and overcoming obstacles to carrying out a solution. In the synectics approach, a team working on possible solutions to a problem takes an "excursion" into a fantasy environment somehow related to the problem. The ideas developed in the fantasy environment, using an open form of team participation, are then translated back into the real-world environment of the problem to become potential solutions. This consideration of the problem in a fantasy context allows the team to develop solutions that would otherwise not be discovered.

EXPLANATION OF SELECTED PROBLEM SOLVING APPROACHES

While it is not possible to explain each of the problem-solving approaches mentioned in this article, the decision tree, Kepner-Tregoe, and **theory of constraints** "thinking process" approaches deserve a further (although necessarily limited) explanation.

DECISION TREES. Decision trees are used to evaluate situations where a decision must be made between alternative actions in a probability context. In this case, a tree structure is used to specify the time ordering of actions and events that are part of the decision situation. A simple example would be the sequence of actions and events involved in deciding whether or not to buy an instant scratch-off lottery ticket.

The basic structure of a decision tree can be seen in Figure 2, which depicts the decision situation of a person with the opportunity of buying an instant scratch-off lottery ticket. The action forks and event forks which make up the decision tree are shown in a time-sequenced order, according to the following rules:

1. An action fork is placed on the tree at the time when the decision becomes irrevocable.

2. An event fork is placed on the tree at the time when the outcome of the event will become known.

An action or event fork is conditional on the sequence of specific action choices and event outcomes that will have happened beforehand. In other words, in order to learn whether an instant lottery ticket is a winner or not, you must first buy the ticket. With regard to the time ordering, even though the winning or losing nature of the specific lottery ticket is determined at the time it is printed, the buyer does not learn of the outcome until after the purchase.

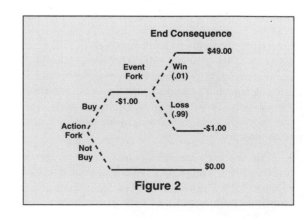

Figure 2

The starting point at the left of Figure 2 is the decision to buy or not buy the lottery ticket. This is an action fork, at which the mutually exclusive decision alternatives are shown. If the alternative to buy is chosen, the ticket cost of $1.00 is subtracted from the starting cash position. If the alternative to not buy is chosen, there is no net change in the cash position due to that choice.

Following the choice to buy is the event fork that depicts the outcomes shown as win or lose. These outcomes are mutually exclusive, and the probabilities of their occurrence must add to 100 percent. The probability of a win is judged to be $1/100$ or .01, while the probability of lose is $99/100$ or .99. The end consequences shown at the right of Figure 2 are the net changes in cash position at the end of each branch of the tree, as a result of the revenues and costs incurred for that branch. Since a winning lottery ticket pays $50, the $1 cost of the ticket is subtracted from that, resulting in an end consequence of $49 for the combination of buy and win. The combination of buy and lose has an end consequence of minus $1. The end consequence of not buy is no net change, or $0.

Once a decision tree is completed, with all of the probability judgments and end consequences correctly stated, it can be "folded back" from the end to the starting point, to indicate the best choice for the initial decision, based on the expected results of choosing each path. Assuming that the end consequences reflect risk neutrality on the part of the decision maker, the tree can be folded back by taking the expected value at each event fork, choosing the best valued alternative at each action fork, and carrying them forward from the end consequences toward the starting point. The expected value of the buy and win branch is the end consequence value of $49 times the win probability of .01, or $.49. The expected value of buy and lose is $-$1 times .99, or $-$.99. Adding these expected values for the branches gives the expected value for the win or lose event fork of $-$.50, as shown in Figure 3.

The $-$.50 expected value of the event fork is brought forward to represent the end consequence of the buy branch of the buy or not buy action fork. The $0 value is brought forward to represent the end consequence of the not buy branch. Because the $0 value is preferred to $-$.50, the not buy alternative is chosen, and all other branches are removed from consideration. (If the tree were to be folded back further, the $0 value would be brought forward, and considered as the end consequence of the next previous branch). In this case, the conclusion is that buying the lottery ticket is not worth it from an expected value point of view.

This decision tree example is trivially simple, but it should serve to illustrate some of the construction and evaluation procedures involved in using decision analysis. This discussion only scratches the surface with regard to the use of decision analysis, and does not include the possibility of obtaining additional information from such sources as **market research** or **forecasting** that could be used to improve the decision maker's ability to choose wisely.

THE KEPNER-TREGOE APPROACH TO PROBLEM-SOLVING

In 1965, Charles H. Kepner and Benjamin B. Tregoe wrote a book, *The Rational Manager: A Systematic Approach to Problem-solving and Decision Making*, that documented the problem-solving approach they had developed. They updated this work in 1981 with the publication of *The New Rational Manager*, to reflect the latest developments in their approach. The Kepner-Tregoe approach was in use at more than 3,000 corporations worldwide as of 1981, and had been accepted as a proven approach to problem-solving in industry, government, and other applications. In fact, the authors detailed the use of their problem-solving approach by the National Aeronautics and Space Administration (NASA) to successfully diagnose the problems encountered by the Apollo 13 astronauts and bring about their return. NASA personnel credited the Kepner-Tregoe approach with enabling them to discover the cause of the problem and find a solution under extraordinary time pressure with no tolerance for mistakes and no second chances available.

The Kepner-Tregoe approach covers stages 1 through 5 of the problem-solving process. The components of the Kepner-Tregoe approach are: situation appraisal, problem analysis, decision analysis, and potential problem analysis.

While situation appraisal is meant to be the first technique employed in a Kepner-Tregoe analysis, in order to sort out the relevant from the irrelevant in a problem situation, it is the last technique explained in teaching this problem-solving approach. The reasoning for this is that the techniques of situation

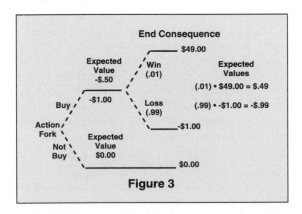

Figure 3

appraisal are used to guide the user toward the use of problem analysis, decision analysis, or potential problem analysis, whichever is relevant to the situation. Until those techniques are understood, however, it is difficult to show how situation appraisal should be used to choose among them.

Problem analysis is used to "identify, describe, analyze, and resolve a situation in which something has gone wrong without explanation." The process uses cause and effect thinking to isolate the problem from the confusing mass of detail that usually surrounds problem situations. The concepts of identity, location, timing, and magnitude are used to home in on the cause of the problem's effects.

Decision analysis is used to examine the purpose behind making a decision, the possible options to achieve that purpose, and the risks for each of those alternatives. Once these factors are outlined, the alternative with the best balance between positive and negative factors can be chosen.

Potential problem analysis is used to analyze what could happen in a specific situation. If a situation could result in problems or might lead to trouble, this analysis can be used to foresee what could possibly go wrong and to develop measures which could either head off the problems altogether, or could deal with the problems once they actually arise.

THE THEORY OF CONSTRAINTS "THINKING PROCESS" APPROACH. The most complete and most advanced problem-solving style yet developed to deal with complex and difficult problems is the logic-based theory of constraints "thinking process." It encompasses all six of the stages of the problem-solving process. Although most of it is based on commonly-known methods from the field of informal logic that began in the 1970s, this approach has much to offer as an integrated set of techniques that can deal with even the most complex and difficult-to-grasp problems. It offers a means of creatively breaking through the seemingly unsolvable problem and then evaluating the solution to make sure that positive results occur and any negative results are avoided.

The "thinking process" was developed by Eliyahu M. Goldratt as an outgrowth of the theory of constraints that he originated. The theory of constraints originally was intended to deal with problems encountered in manufacturing. This approach concentrates on the constraint that limits the ability of a system to get things done. The main idea is that the system should be managed to get the most from the constraint, which means that other parts of the system should be subordinated to the way the constraint is managed. For physical systems, the theory of constraints suggests a five-step process of continuous improvement:

1. Identify the system's constraint(s). (This could be machines, market demand, policies, procedures, or corporate thinking.)

2. Decide how to exploit the system's constraint(s). (Squeeze the most possible from the limits of the current constraint.)

3. Subordinate everything else to the decisions made in step 2. (Avoid keeping non-constraint resources busy doing unneeded work.)

4. Elevate the system's constraint(s). (If possible, reduce the effects of the constraint. Offload some of its demand, or expand its capability. Make sure everyone in the firm knows what the constraint is and what its effects are. Marketing, engineering, sales, and other functions should know about it and make decisions based on its effects.)

5. If the constraint is broken in step 4, go back to step 1.

For any system, the constraint is defined as anything that limits the system from achieving a higher level of performance relative to its goal. Obviously, this means that the system's goal must be defined before the constraint can be identified. Constraints can be either physical or nonphysical. A physical constraint could be the speed of a machine or the capacity of a vehicle, while a nonphysical constraint could be a policy or procedure based on someone's way of thinking.

The five-step improvement process described above is oriented toward solving problems in a system with physical constraints. If the constraint in a system is nonphysical, however, such as a policy that has outlived its usefulness, the five-step process above should be replaced by the five-component "thinking process." The five components are: the current reality tree, evaporating cloud, future reality tree, prerequisite tree, and transition tree. The current reality tree is used to diagnose the core problem from its symptoms by using a form of cause-effect logic flowcharting. The evaporating cloud approach is used to creatively develop potential solutions to problems that seem intractable. The future reality tree is used to identify the results of the potential solution, both the positive results hoped for, and the negative consequences that otherwise would not be anticipated and headed off. The prerequisite tree is used to overcome obstacles that stand in the way of accomplishing the solution. The transition tree is a logical form of implementation plan for carrying out the solution.

In developing a current reality tree, a list of symptoms is developed that apply to a specific problem situation. From this list of symptoms, called undesirable effects (UDEs), one of the symptoms is chosen as a starting point. For this effect, its immediate cause is hypothesized, and the relationship is shown with an arrow connecting the statement of the cause to the statement of the effect. It is read in the following fashion: "If the cause, then the effect." This cause-effect relationship can be confirmed, if need be, by looking for another effect from the same cause. If this effect is observed, this tends to confirm that the cause-effect analysis is aimed in the right direction. If the effect does not occur, this is sufficient to disconfirm the original cause-effect hypothesis, and indicate that the analysis should aim in a different direction.

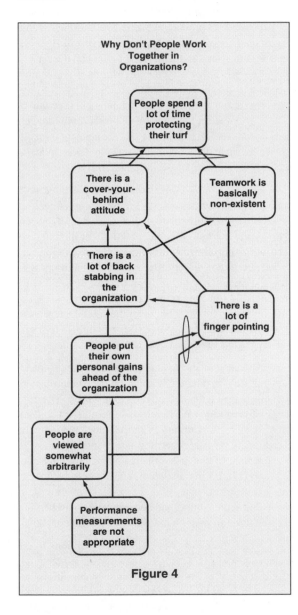

Figure 4

Once the original cause and effect relationship is deemed satisfactory, the cause can be considered as an effect, and its immediate cause can be hypothesized in turn. This process is repeated until the core problem is identified. The core problem is considered to be the cause that results in a sufficient number of the original symptoms of the problem. The current reality tree in Figure 4 shows an example of the use of this approach. An ellipse joining arrows from cause to effect is an indicator that all of the causes joined are required to produce the effect. Otherwise, a cause is considered sufficient to result in the effect by itself. In Figure 4, note the effect of inappropriate performance measurements on the behavior of people in organizations.

While space limitations preclude a discussion of the other components of the theory of constraints "thinking process," it should be noted that this approach has proven to be a powerful means of problem-solving across a wide variety of environments, as well as a very effective means of communication.

[James T. Low]

FURTHER READING:

Adams, James L. *Conceptual Blockbusting: a Guide to Better Ideas.* 3rd ed. Reading, MA: Addison-Wesley, 1986.

Barker, Wayne. *Brain Storms: A Study of Human Spontaneity.* New York: Grove Press, 1968.

Brassard, Michael, and Diane Ritter. *The Memory Jogger II: A Pocket Guide of Tools for Continuous Improvement & Effective Planning.* Methuen, MA: GOAL/QPC, 1994.

Brown, Rex V., Andrew S. Kahr, and Cameron Peterson. *Decision Analysis for the Manager.* New York: Holt, Rinehart and Winston, 1974.

Crawford, C. C., and John W. Demidovich. *Crawford Slip Method: How to Mobilize Brainpower by Think Tank Technology.* Los Angeles: School of Public Administration, University of Southern California, 1983.

de Bono, Edward. *New Think: The Use of Lateral Thinking in the Generation of New Ideas.* New York: Avon Books, 1971.

Delbecq, Andre L., Andrew H. Ven de Ven, and David H. Gustafson. *Group Techniques for Program Planning: A Guide to Nominal Group and Delphi Processes.* Glenview, IL: Scott, Foresman and Company, 1975.

Dettmer, William H. *The Theory of Constraints: A Systems Approach to Continuous Improvement.* Los Angeles: University of Southern California, 1995.

Fiero, Janet. "The Crawford Slip Method." *Quality Progress.* May, 1992, pp. 40-43.

Goldratt, Eliyahu M. *It's Not Luck.* Great Barrington, MA: North River Press, 1994.

Goldratt, Eliyahu M., and Jeff Cox. *The Goal.* 2nd ed. Great Barrington, MA: North River Press, 1992.

Gordon, William J. J. *Synectics: The Development of Creative Capacity.* New York: Harper, 1961.

Ishikawa, Kaoru. *What Is Total Quality Control? The Japanese Way.* translated by David J. Lu. Englewood Cliffs, NJ: Prentice-Hall, 1985.

Kepner, Charles Higgins, and Benjamin B. Tregoe. *The New Rational Manager.* Princeton, NJ: Princeton Research Press, 1981.

Kepner, Charles Higgins, and Benjamin B. Tregoe. *The Rational Manager: A Systematic Approach to Problem-solving and Decision Making.* New York: McGraw-Hill, 1965.

Koestler, Arthur C. *The Act of Creation*. London: Hutchinson, 1964.

Noreen, Eric, Debra Smith, and James T. Mackey. *The Theory of Constraints and Its Implications for Management Accounting*. Great Barrington, MA: North River Press, 1995.

Osborn, Alexander Faickney. *Applied Imagination: Principles and Procedures of Creative Thinking*. Rev. ed. New York: Scribner, 1957.

Prince, George M. *The Practice of Creativity: A Manual for Dynamic Group Problem-Solving*. New York: Collier Books, 1972.

Von Oech, Roger. *A Whack on the Side of the Head: How to Unlock Your Mind for Innovation*. Menlo Park, CA: Creative Think, 1983.

Watzlawick, Paul. *Change: Principles of Problem Formation and Problem Resolution*. New York: Norton, 1974.

Zwicky, Fritz. *Discovery, Invention, Research through the Morphological Approach*. New York: Macmillan, 1969.

Zwicky, Fritz. *Morphology of Propulsive Power*. Pasadena, CA: Society for Morphological Research, 1962.

PRODUCT LIABILITY

Product liability issues have become increasingly important to manufacturers and marketing managers. In the last twenty years the liability of a manufacturer has been greatly expanded as a result of the spread of the doctrine of strict liability and the adoption of new theories that permit recovery in so-called "delayed manifestation" cases. According to Section 102(2) of the Uniform Product Liability Act, product liability includes "all claims or action brought for personal inquiry, death, or property damage caused by the manufacture, design, formula, preparation, assembly, installation, testing, warnings, instructions, marketing, packaging, or labeling of any product."

In the early history of law affecting issues of product liability, responsibility was based in the law of contract: *Winterbottom v. Wright* (10 Mees & W 109, 11 L.J. Ex. 4.5 [18427]). In 1840, a coachman for the royal mail was injured when the coach overturned due to insecurely bolted axles. The coachman sued the man who had contracted with the postmaster general to keep the coaches in good working condition. The court found that the coachman was not a party to the contract and, therefore, ruled against him.

In time, social policy changed with respect to this strict interpretation of contract law. The courts began to argue that there was a "duty" owed to users by sellers to provide reasonable care in the manufacture of goods. After the mid-1800s, sellers were held liable to third parties for manufacturing or sales negligence of goods inherently dangerous to human safety. Product examples included food, beverages, drugs, firearms, and explosives.

By 1962, the changes in social policy resulted in the application of tort principles to product liability. The landmark case of *MacPherson v. Buick Motor Co.* (1961) concerned liability of the auto manufacturer to the buyer of a car sold through a dealer. Although the concept of "inherently dangerous" goods was still held to be significant, there was a shift from the analysis to negligence (tort) principles in this case—that is, the producer was required to apply "due care" in the marketing of goods to users. (According to *Black's Law Dictionary*, 1990 edition, a product is "inherently dangerous" where danger of an injury arises from the product itself, and not from defect in the product.) *MacPherson v. Buick Motor Co.* first applied the theory of negligence to product liability. The opinion, written by Judge Cardozo of the New York Court of Appeals, had an immediate and widespread effect on the state of law. The principles laid down in *MacPherson* are now accepted throughout the country, followed by all American courts and adopted by the Restatement (Second) of Torts. Eventually, the concept of "inherently dangerous" products fell into disuse and the concept of negligence expanded beyond product ion to include labeling, installation, inspection, and design.

The *MacPherson* decision took legal thinking a step beyond previous rulings on inherently dangerous goods. It established that because manufacturers knowingly market products which affect the interests of consumers, they owe a legal duty of caution and prudence to consumers. Because manufacturers may foresee potentially harmful product effects, they are responsible for attempting to minimize harm. Establishing this legal duty between the manufacturer and the consumer made it possible for plaintiffs to argue the negligent breach of that duty.

A weakness in the negligence approach to product liability results in burdening the plaintiff with having to prove the defendant's negligence. The concept of warranty was developed in an effort to limit this problem. A warranty is an assurance made by the producer to the user regarding safety and soundness of the product. In this case, only the original purchaser of an item could bring an action, and it could be against only the person who sold the product to him. This provided more limitations because most merchandise passes through many hands en route to the consumer.

Again the courts began to find exceptions to the rule. For example, during the early twentieth century, the discovery of substandard sanitary conditions resulted in a public hysteria about adulteration and mislabeling of foods. Food marketers had long been held to special responsibilities, but in order to protect the public welfare, food businesses were held to an absolute responsibility to provide unadulterated food products. Soon after, the position was expanded to include drugs, beverages, and cosmetics.

The four elements of a negligent tort as applied to product liability cases are as follows:

1. A duty owed by the particular defendant to the particular plaintiff to act as a reasonably prudent person under the same or similar circumstance.

2. A breach of such a duty by the defendant that is, a failure to act reasonably.

3. Injury, including personal injury or property damage.

4. A causal link between defendant's breach of duty and injuries sustained by plaintiff.

The concept of negligence is applicable to every activity preceding a product's availability in the market. So everything from product design, the inspection and testing of materials, the manufacture and assembly of the product, the packaging, the accompanying instructions and warnings, through the inspection and testing of the final product are all susceptible to negligence. Negligence can result from omission as well as commission—failure to discover a flaw is as negligent as creating one. Similarly, failing to provide adequate warnings about potential dangers in the use of a product is a violation of duty.

Still it may be difficult to prove negligence in product liability cases. Defendants only must meet the general standards of reasonable behavior as judged against the behavior of a reasonably careful competitor who demonstrates the standard skills and expertise of the industry. In reality, a manufacturer must only show that "ordinary care under the circumstances" was applied to avoid liability for negligence. This is easy compared to the task of consumers showing evidence to the contrary.

Many products, even the most ordinary, pose some level of risk and the law recognizes that it is often not possible to design a totally safe product. However, manufacturers are legally obligated to warn consumers about known dangers. Manufacturers may be found negligent if:

(1) they fail to warn users about recognized risk,

(2) the warning is too vague to be adequate, or

(3) the warning is not brought to the user's attention.

There is no duty to warn against misuse that is so rare or unusual that it cannot be foreseen. This poses a unique difficulty for manufacturers who must not only provide warnings, but must communicate them such that a reasonable person will find and understand them. In some cases a warning buried in an instruction ID may be judged inadequate; in other situations, a warning sticker on the product may be considered sufficient.

STRICT PRODUCT LIABILITY

The most recent evolution in tort law, strict liability, has transformed the very nature of inquiry because it eliminates the entire question of negligence, i.e., fault. Strict liability requires only demonstrating that a product caused an injury because it was defective; the reason for the defect is irrelevant. The product itself, not the defendant's use, is under investigation.

Under strict liability, the manufacturer is held liable for allowing a defective product to enter the marketplace. The issue is a matter of public policy, not the manufacturer's unreasonable or negligent conduct. The introduction of a defective product into the marketplace brings each member of the product's distribution channel into liability for negligence. The theory of strict liability holds that manufacturers:

1. have the greatest control over the quality of their products;

2. can distribute their costs by raising prices;

3. have special responsibilities in their role as sellers.

The tort of negligence at least provided the responsible person a standard by which to measure negligence although it imposed the added burden of proving that the defendant was negligent. (According to Section 282 of the *Restatement (Second) of Torts*, negligence includes any "conduct which falls below the standard established by law for the protection of others against unreasonable risk of harm.") Although strict liability eases those burdens for the plaintiff and improves chances of recovery, it does not provide a universally accepted standard for measuring failure.

Section 402A of the *Restatement (Second) of Torts* relies on what has become known as the "consumer-expectation" test:

One who sells any product in a defective condition unreasonably dangerous to the user or consumer or to his property is subject to liability for physical harm thereby caused to the ultimate user or to consumer, or to his property if

(1) the seller is engaged in the business of selling such a product, and

(2) the product is expected to and does reach the user or consumer without substantial change in the condition in which it is used.

In *Legal Environment of Business*, George Spiro defines "unreasonably dangerous" as "dangerous to an extent beyond that which would be contemplated by the ordinary consumer who purchases it, with the ordinary knowledge common to the community as to its characteristics." Despite its great influence, this definition has not been universally accepted. In California, for example, the court has rejected the necessity to prove unreasonable danger, arguing that such an expectation defeats the purpose of strict liability by imposing a negligence-like burden of proof on the plaintiff.

The *Restatement (Second) of Torts* recognizes that some products beneficial to society cannot be made entirely safe. Prescription drugs and vaccines are notorious examples. Such a product is not held defective simply because of its inevitable hazards; something else must be wrong with it also. Therefore, the *Restatement* does not hold drug companies strictly liable for a properly manufactured product accompanied by appropriate directions and warnings. In sum, design defects are not the same as manufacturing defects.

One defense manufacturers have employed with controversy is called "state of the art." This means that manufacturers should be held accountable only for information available to them at the time of manufacture. Flaws or defects which arose due to unavailable knowledge are not considered in questions of liability. The problem interpreting this defense concerns the variation of knowledge and its applications across the country.

The **Uniform Commercial Code** has provided alternatives for persons injured by products. This code contains warranty provisions. Recall that a warranty is an assurance made to the buyer of a product. Three types are most common: express warranties, implied warranties of merchantability, and implied warranties of fitness for a particular purpose.

Express warranties affirm facts about a product and become a t of the sales bargain. They may be written with or without the words "guarantee" or "warranty" or may be implied by samples that demonstrate certain characteristics, such as a genuine leather binding. The implication is that all pieces in the lot purchased will have the same type of leather binding. Express warranties are defined and governed by Section 2-313 of the UCC.

Implied warranties pertain to the applicability of the goods purchased. The implied warranty of merchantability suggests that professional sellers have special skill or knowledge of their goods and sell goods which are "fit for the ordinary purpose for which such goods are used." When the buyer is dependent on the seller's expertise, has indicated specific needs and the need to rely on the seller's advice, the seller is then liable to provide the right product. These warranties were created to serve public policy and did not result from agreement between parties to a sale. The courts construe implied warranties to protect buyers. The warranty of merchantability is governed by Section 2-314 of the UCC and is only applicable to merchants. The warranty of fitness for a particular purpose is governed by Section 2-315.

PRIVITY

Historically, a plaintiff had to have a relationship or connection, called privity, with a defendant in order to legally challenge that defendant. This factor became a defense used by manufacturers to avoid product liability cases of all kinds. The erosion of this defense has been important to the development of product liability, especially implied warranties.

Three types of privity exist. Horizontal privity refers to all persons making use of a product. Vertical privity concerns a product's channel of distribution. Market share privity stems from the notion of collective liability whereby an entire industry is liable for product injury. In this case, the specific manufacturer causing the product defect leading to injury cannot be determined.

[John Burnett]

FURTHER READING:

Clement, David E. "Human Factors, Instructions and Warnings, and Product Liability," *IEEE Transactions on Professional Communication.*PC-30, No. 3, September, 1987, pp. 149-56.

Downs, Philip E. and Douglas N. Behrman, "The Product Liability Coordinator: A Partial Solution," *Journal of the Academy of Marketing Science* 14, No. 3, Fall 1986, pp. 58-65.

Morgan, Fred W. "Tampered Goods: Legal Development and Marketing Guidelines," *Journal of Marketing* 52, April, 1988, pp. 86-96.

Spiro, George W. *Legal Environment of Business.* Prentice Hall, 1993.

PRODUCT SAFETY

Consumer protection refers to a number of activities that are designed to protect consumers from a wide range of practices that can infringe on the rights of consumers in the marketplace. These activities stem from a broad and aggressive movement, usually called consumerism, that is supported by consumers themselves, by many business organizations, and by the government. Consumerism ensures that the rights of consumers are respected.

Although specific legislation protecting the consumer from potentially harmful products is a rather recent event, consumer protection per se is not a current phenomenon. Consumers obviously have been concerned about the products they buy ever since the marketplace has existed. But in terms of the development of consumer protection in this country, there are three distinct periods that ultimately led to the current status of product safety.

The first period, between 1879 and 1905, is referred to as the Muckraking Era. It was during this period that a number of bills were introduced into Congress to regulate the sale of food and drugs and protect consumers from a growing power of large business enterprises. However, these bills were apparently the work of a small group of consumer advocates because both Congress and the public at large were rather apathetic about any public policy measures directed to protect consumers. This apathy, coupled with strong business opposition to the bills, meant that no action was taken on the consumer front during these years. However, all this changed in 1905 when Upton Sinclair published *The Jungle*, a sordid tale of conditions in the Chicago meatpacking industry. The book gave gruesome examples of the way meat was processed, portraying meatpacking plants where rats and parts of the human body were often processed along with sausage meat. This book, more than any other single event, jolted the public out of its apathy and made the need for consumer protection apparent to many people. Congress responded by passing the following public policy measures: Pure Food and Drug Act (1905); Federal Meat Inspection Act (1907); Federal Trade Commission Act (1914); Water Power Act (1920).

The next era, known as the Information Era, began in the 1930s and was sparked by a book called *Your Money's Worth* written by Stuart Chase and F. J. Schlink. This book pictured the consumer as an "Alice" in a "Wonderland" of conflicting product claims and bright promises. It focused on advertising and packaging that inundated the consumer with information designed to sell a product rather than help the consumer make an intelligent decision. The book made a plea for impartial product testing agencies that had no vested interest in the product and thus could supply the consumer with objective and trustworthy information about the performance of the product. The 1930's, then, saw the development of independent product testing agencies, such as Consumers Union, that would test products and publish the results. In addition, the following important public policy measures were also passed in the 1930's: Food, Drug, and Cosmetic Act (1938); Wool Products Labeling Act of 1939.

The modern consumer movement began in 1965 with the publication of another book, Ralph Nader's *Unsafe at Any Speed*. The book criticized about the safety of the Corvair automobile and indicted its producer, General Motors Corp., for a lack of concern about automobile safety. The issue received national attention when it became public knowledge that General Motors had hired private investigators to follow Nader and investigate him while he was a witness for a Senate subcommittee. The time was ripe for a new consumer movement concerned with a range of issues that affected an increasingly affluent population, a technologically sophisticated marketplace, and a society that had high expectations and aspirations for the fulfillment of higher needs. The complexity of many modern products made it difficult for the average consumer to rationally choose them, and the products were impossible to repair if they broke. During the latter half of the 1960s and early 1970s, Congress passed dozens of pro-consumer laws, the most significant being the Consumer Product Safety Act.

The Consumer Product Safety Act was signed into law by President Richard M. Nixon on October 27, 1972. It went into effect on December 26, 1972, creating an independent, full-member **Consumer Product Safety Commission**. The intent of the CPSC was to protect the public against unreasonable risks of injury associated with the wide range of consumer products. The background of this act was a national commission study on product safety, which found that 20 million Americans were injured severely enough each year in product-related accidents to require medical treatment. Some 110,000 of these people were permanently disabled and 30,000 were killed, at a cost to the economy of more than $5.5 billion annually. A crisis situation was believed to exist that demanded government attention, and the solution to the crisis was direct regulation.

The CPSC is headquartered in Washington, D.C., with 14 field offices and testing laboratories around the country. At the present time, more than 10,000 products are subject to the legal powers of the Consumer Product Safety Commission, including ladders, swings, blenders, televisions, stoves, stairs, ramps, window sills, doors, and electrical wiring. The only consumer products not covered by the act are foods, drugs, cosmetics, automobiles, firearms, tobacco, boats, pesticides, and aircraft, all of which are regulated by other agencies. The agency also has responsibility for enforcing specific consumer legislation, including the Flammable Fabrics Act, the Refrigerator Safety Act of 1956, the Hazardous Substances Act of 1960, and the Poison Prevention Packaging Act of 1970.

The CPSC has the authority and responsibility to (1) develop and enforce uniform safety standards governing the design, construction, contents, performance, and labeling of all consumer products under its jurisdiction; (2) ban consumer products deemed to be hazardous; (3) initiate and monitor recall of hazardous products; (4) help industry develop voluntary safety standards; (5) help consumers evaluate the comparative safety of products; (6) conduct applied research and develop test methods for unsafe products; (7) collect, analyze, and publish inquiry and hazard data; and (8) help to harmonize federal, state, and local product safety laws and enforcement.

The five-member commission has a great deal of responsibility and power to resolve substantial hazards, as defined under section 15 of the act. Some people feel that the authority of the commission is too extensive because it can determine the fate of many new or existing products. The commission tries to use discretion when reviewing products because not all risk can be eliminated, however, it does try to eliminate what it considers to be unreasonable risks.

Despite its desire to operate in the background, the commission's first regulatory action made resulted in controversy. It ruled that mattresses had to be made of material that would not catch fire from cigarettes, and during a six month transition before the new requirements took effect, the mattresses had to be labeled flammable. Both consumer groups and the mattress industry took the commission to court. The consumer groups wanted the commission to require that all mattresses meet federal safety requirements immediately. The industry claimed the ruling to be unfair because of the high cost of switching materials and because it felt that it had been given the total burden of resolving a problem caused by negligent cigarette smokers. (The reaction of the mattress industry is a common one from the standpoint of industries forced to bear the responsibility for careless consumers).

Regarding its enforcement powers, success depends significantly on cooperation from business. The commission can order a manufacturer, wholesaler, distributor, or retailer to recall, repair, or replace any product that it determines to be unreasonably risky. When a product is deemed to be particularly hazardous, the commission can simply ban the product from the market. It can also fines ranging from $50,000 to $500,000 and impose jail terms of up to one year for violations. In addition, the commision requires manufacturers, wholesalers, distributors, or retailers to report within 24 hours the existence of any substantial product hazard that is known. Failure to report a defect or furnish required information during this time period can result in civil and criminal penalties. This initial notification must include the following information:

1. Identification of the product.

2. Name and address of the manufacturer, if known.

3. Nature and extent of the defect.

4. Name and address of the person informing the commission.

The agency can then demand corrective action, including refunds, recalls, dissemination of public earnings, and reimbursement of buyers for expenses that incur in the process. In 1984, the Toy Safety Act was passed, which gave the Commission the power to recall dangerous toys from the marketplace much more quickly than before. Previous to that act, the CPSC had to order recalls of children's products under the Federal Hazardous Substances Act, which required a lengthy banning process.

The commission's section-15 group is responsible for determining whether or not a product defect may pose a substantial risk of injury. It contacts the party making the notification to gather details about the product and the associated injuries. The risk of injury, if found to be substantial, results in a ''pre-15(b) letter'' to the manufacturer, distributor, or retailer indicating the commission's knowledge of the situation. This letter requests that the firm provide an estimate of the number of products involved and explain any corrective action that may have been taken. If the commission and the firm concur that no substantial hazard exists, no future action is taken.

Consumer Product Safety Standards are the means by which the objectives of the act are attained. These standards ''consist of (1) requirements as to performance, composition, contents, design, construction, finish, or packaging, or (2) requirements that a consumer product be marked with or accompanied by clear and adequate warnings—or (3) any combination of (1) or (2).'' According to the specifications of the Consumer Protection Act, the development of standards begins with a majority agreement by the five commissioners that a product poses ''an unreasonable risk of injury'' thus necessitating some criteria for safety. The commission then publishes a notice in the Federal Register and the press inviting any person or group to submit an existing standard or an offer to develop a mandatory standard. This offer is extended by the commission to ensure representative public participation in the development of these standards. The act allows any trade association; consumer organization; professional society; testing laboratory; university or college department; wholesaler; retailer; federal, state, or local government agency; ad hoc association; or any company or person to submit an offer to develop a proposed consumer product safety standard.

Once the commission evaluates any responses, it can then proceed in one of three ways: (a) publish an existing standard as a proposed mandatory standard, (b) accept one or more offers to develop a standard, or (c) proceed independently to develop a standard. These standards fulfill the main objective of the Consumer Product Safety Act: reducing unreasonable risks of injury associated with the use of consumer products.

During the first year of operation, the Consumer Product Safety Commission received about 130 defect notifications involving some 14 million product units. These complaints included such products as baby cribs, soft drink bottles, bicycles, swimming pools, minibikes, snowmobiles, power lawn mowers, sliding doors, and artificial turf. Over the course of its existence, the CPSC has adopted only six mandatory standards but has forced business to adopt several voluntary standards. It has also imposed two labeling requirements and six product bans under the Product Safety Act and forced recalls of many others. Since 1973, the commission has initiated more than 1,300 recalls or other corrective actions that involved over 200 million products. The agency has also issued five rules under the Federal Hazardous Substances Act and requirements for child-resistant caps for numerous products under the Poison Prevention Packaging Act.

The Consumer Product Safety Amendments of 1981 changed the rule-making procedure of the commission by placing more emphasis on voluntary standards. An advance notice of proposed rule-making has to invite the development of a voluntary standard. The commission must then assist industry in developing a voluntary standard, and if it appears likely that this standard will eliminate or adequately reduce the risk of injury and it is likely that there will be substantial compliance with the standard, the CPSC must terminate its mandatory rule-making effort and defer to the voluntary standard. This provision along with other provisions in the amendments, severely restricts the agency's rule-making authority.

Although the commission has established itself as an important element in product safety, its members feel that the agency needs better tools to accomplish its responsibilities. Some of the areas needing improvements are:

1. The power to independently file civil and criminal cases against violators rather than working through the Justice Department, which in many instances, has declined to pursue referred cases.

2. Authority to seize products judged to pose substantial hazards.

3. Elimination of the present system of public participation in setting standards so that the commission may avoid delay and confusion, especially because it usually rewrites the standards anyway.

[John Burnett]

FURTHER READING:

Chew, W. Bruce, and Timothy B. Blodgett. ''The Case of the High-Risk Saftey Product.'' *Harvard Business Review*. May-June, 1992, pp. 14-27.

FIC. *Guides for the Use of Environmental Marketing Claims: The Application of Section 5 of the Federal Trade Commission Act to Environmental Advertising and Marketing Pratices*. Washington, D.C., 1992.

Geyelin, Milo. ''Product-Liability Groups Take Up Arms.'' *The Wall Street Journal*. January 29, 1993, pp. B1, B2.

Mayer, Robert N., Debra L. Scammon, and Jason W. Gray-Lee. ''Update On National Audit of Environmental Claims.'' 1994, working paper.

Mergenhagen, Paula. ''Product Liability: Who Sues?'' *American Demographics*. June, 1995, pp. 48-54.

Sterling, Anthony. ''Warning: Marketers Must Do Better With Product Warnings.'' *The Marketing News*. June 19, 1995, p. 4.

PROFESSIONAL AND TRADE ASSOCIATIONS

Professional and trade associations are non-profit membership organizations which serve the interests of members who share a common field of activity. Professional organizations—also called professional societies—consist of individuals of a common profession, whereas trade associations consist of companies in a particular industry. The activities of both trade and professional associations are similar and the ultimate goal is to promote, through cooperation, the economic activities of the members while maintaining ethical practices. Professional associations have the additional objectives of expanding the knowledge or skills of its members and providing professional standards.

The definition of a profession is an occupation that requires considerable education and specialized training, such as medicine, law, **accounting**, and engineering. However, the definition has been broadened by an increasing number of occupational groups that desire the prestige of a professional status. There is a fine line between professional associations and scientific or academic societies, especially in certain fields, such as the applied sciences or education. Academic societies aim exclusively at advancement of the discipline, rather than being concerned with the methods of practice and economic well-being of the members. At the other end of the spectrum, the differentiation between professional associations and trade unions can be blurred, as some unions claim the added distinction of being professional associations.

The definition of an industry, as far as trade associations are concerned, is very flexible. Some associations deal with a specific activity, such as paper manufacturing, whereas others consist of company members involved in all aspects of a given product, such as the publishers, printers and marketers of calendars. Associations exist for both specialized sectors of an industry and the broader industry categories.

The best known professional associations include the American Bar Association and its affiliated state bars, the American Institute of Certified Public Accountants (AICPA) with 280,000 members, and the American Medical Association, with 250,000 members. Some of the larger and more influential trade associations include the American Iron and Steel Institute (AISI) with 1,200 members, the National Association of Manufacturers, with 12,500 members, the American Bankers Association (ABA)with 10,000 members, and the Pharmaceutical Manufacturers Association, with 93 members. The membership figures of trade associations, unlike professional associations, are not a good indicator of size, for the companies belonging to a trade association may be very large, and the associations may have budgets of millions of dollars. Some trade associations have less than ten members.

The activities of both professional and trade associations may include providing public relations for the field, collecting and publishing statistics on the industry or profession, advising members on technological or management issues, promoting research, sponsoring conferences, keeping members informed of developments or regulations in the field, and lobbying government. Associations typically publish a newsletter or magazine distributed to members and many produce additional publications for the public. Activities particular to trade associations include sponsoring trade shows and awards, providing market statistics for their members, promoting research on new products or manufacturing methods, offering scholarships or fellowships, and encouraging ethical business practices. Professional associations are uniquely involved in sponsoring or certifying training programs or examinations for individuals in the field. Almost all professional associations hold conferences or seminars to discuss techniques of practice. Professional associations also provide opportunities for personal networking and job information for members.

Both professional and trade associations set their own membership requirements and charge membership dues. Full members may vote in association affairs and run for office. Professional associations may require specialized training or certification as a requirement for membership. Some professional associations also accept certain corporate members. National organizations with large memberships—which is typically the case for professional associations—often have local chapters to which their members also belong. The proliferation of organizations in both narrow and broad fields makes it common for a company or an individual to belong to more than one association.

[Heather Behn Hedden]

FURTHER READING:

Daniels, Peggy Kneffel and Carol A. Schwartz, eds. *Encyclopedia of Associations*, 28th ed. Detroit, MI: Gale Research Inc., 1994.

Pemberton, J. Michael. "The Professional Association: Some Basics," *Records Management Quarterly*. January 1994, pp. 50-55.

Russell, John J., et al. *National Trade and Professional Associations of the United States,* 29th ed. Columbia Books, Inc., 1994, pp. 5-15.

PROFIT MARGIN

The profit margin is an **accounting** measure designed to gauge the financial health of a business firm or industry. In general, it is defined as the ratio of profit earned to total sales receipts (or costs), over some defined period. The margin is a measure of the amount of profit accruing to a firm from the sale of a product and is a measure of efficiency because it captures the amount of surplus generated per unit of the product sold. For example, if firm A, in July 1994, made a profit of $10 on the $100 sale of television sets, then that firm's profit margin would be 0.10 or 10 percent, meaning that each dollar of sales generated on average ten cents of profit. Thus, as a measure of the competitive success of a business, the profit margin is very important because it captures the firm's unit costs. A low-cost producer in an industry would generally have a higher profit margin. This is because firms tend to sell the same product at roughly the same price (adjusted for quality differences); therefore, lower costs would be reflected in a higher profit margin. Lower cost firms also have a potentially deadly strategic advantage in a competitive price war because they have the leverage to undercut their competitors by cutting prices in order to gain market share and potentially drive higher cost (and therefore lower profit margin) firms out of business.

Firms clearly exist to expand their profit and, while a growing absolute amount of dollar profit is desirable, by itself it has minimal significance unless it is related to its source. This is why firms use measures such as the profit margin and the profit rate. Profit is a flow concept and the profit margin measures the flow of profits over some period compared with the costs, or sales incurred over the same period. Thus, one could compute the profit margin on costs (profits divided by costs), or the profit margin on sales (profit margin divided by sales).

Other specific profit margin measures often calculated by businesses are: (1) gross profit margin—(gross profit divided by net sales), where gross profit is the total money left over after sales and net sales is total revenues; (2) net profit margin—(net profit divided by net sales), where net profit (or net income) is profit after deducting costs such as advertising, **marketing**, interest payments, and rental payments.

The profit margin is related to other measures such as the rate of profit (sometimes called the rate of return), which comprise various measures of the amount of profit earned relative to the total amount of capital invested (or the stock of capital) required to generate that profit. Thus, while the profit margin measures the amount of profit per unit of sales, the rate of profit on total assets indicates the efficiency of the total investment. Or, put another way, while the profit margin measures the amount of profit per unit of capital (labor, **working capital**, and **depreciation** of plant and equipment) consumed over a particular period, the profit rate measures the amount of profit per unit of capital advanced (the entire stock of capital required for the production of the good). Using our previous example, if a $1,000 investment in plant and equipment were required to produce the television set, then a profit margin of 10 percent would translate into a profit rate on total investment of only 1 percent. Thus, in this scenario, Firm A's unit costs are low enough to generate 10 percent profit (profit margin) on the capital consumed (assuming some market price) to produce the TV, set but in order to achieve that margin, a total capital expenditure of $1,000 must be made.

The difference between the profit margin measure and the profit rate concept then lies in the rate at which the capital stock depreciates; and the rate at which the production process repeats itself, or turnover time. In the first case, if, say, the entire capital stock for a particular firm or industry is completely used up during one production cycle, then the profit margin would be exactly the same as the profit rate. In the case of turnover, if a firm succeeds in, for example, doubling the amount of times the production process repeats itself in the same period, then twice as much profit would be made on the same capital invested even though the profit margin might not change. More formally, the rate of return equals the profit margin times the ratio of sales to average assets: rate of return = (profit margin) × (sales/average assets), where average assets is the total capital stock divided by the number of times the production process turns over. Thus, the rate of return can be increased by increasing the profit margin or shortening the production cycle. Of course, this will largely depend on the conditions of production in particular industries or firms. To give a broad view of the spectrum of profit margins for U.S. manufacturing industries, shown in Table 1 are profit margins (taxable income) on sales as reported to the U.S. Bureau of the Census for the third quarter of 1992.

For U.S. manufacturing firms as a whole, although absolute levels of profits are continually reaching new peaks (firms would hardly be induced to invest if their investment gained them the same profit—or less profit—each year), the profit margin is highly cyclical and, according to data on taxable income reported to the U.S. Bureau of the Census, on a downward trend since the late 1970s, as illustrated in Figure 1 on the next page.

Table 1
Profits Per Dollar of Sales by Industry

Taxable Income Before Taxes (cents per dollar of sales), third quarter, 1992

All manufacturing corporations	**5.3**
Nondurable manufacturing corporations	6.9
Food and kindred products	7.4
Textiles	5.7
Paper and paper products	4.3
Printing and publishing	7.3
Chemicals	10.3
Industrial chemicals	6.7
Drugs	19.4
Petroleum and coal products	3.0
Rubber and miscellaneous plastics	4.6
Durable manufacturing corporations	3.6
Stone, clay, and glass products	4.7
Primary metal industries	4.6
Iron and steel	4.9
Nonferrous metals	4.4
Fabricated metal products	6.0
Machinery (except electrical)	-3.2
Electrical and electronics equipment	6.9
Transportation	0.8
Motor vehicles and equipment	-2.2
Aircraft, guided missiles, parts	5.2
Instruments and related products	13.5

If costs rise and prices do not rise to keep up, then the profit margin will fall. In times of business cycle upturns, prices tend to rise; in business cycle downturns, prices tend to fall. Of course, many factors, and not only costs, will affect the profit margin, namely, industry-specific factors that relate to investment requirements, pricing, type of market, and conditions of production (including production turnover time).

SEE ALSO: Income Statement

[John Sarich]

FURTHER READING:

Raiborn, Cecily A., Jesse T. Barfield, and Michael R. Kinney. *Managerial Accounting*. West Publishing Company, 1993.

U.S. Department of Commerce. Bureau of the Census. *Quarterly Financial Report for Manufacturing, Mining, and Trade Corporations*. Third Quarter, 1992. Series QFR-92-3. Washington, D.C.: GPO, 1992.

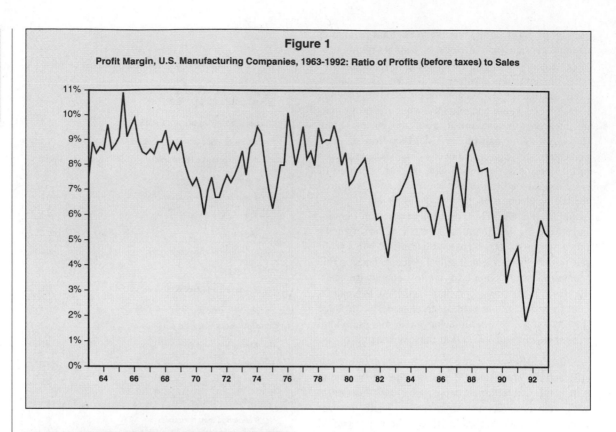

Figure 1

Profit Margin, U.S. Manufacturing Companies, 1963-1992: Ratio of Profits (before taxes) to Sales

PROFIT SHARING

Profit sharing refers to the process whereby companies distribute a portion of their profits to their employees. Profit sharing plans are well established in American business. The annual U.S. **Chamber of Commerce** Employee Benefits Survey indicates that somewhere between 19 and 23 percent of U.S. companies have offered some form of profit sharing since 1963. Other estimates place the number of companies offering profit sharing plans in the 1990s somewhere between one-fourth and one-third of all U.S. firms.

Historically, profit sharing plans have their roots in the nineteenth century, when companies such as General Foods and Pillsbury distributed a percentage of their profits to their employees as a bonus. The first deferred profit-sharing plan was developed in 1916 by Harris Trust and Savings Bank of Chicago. There was a sharp increase in profit-sharing plans during World War II, when wages were frozen. Deferred profit-sharing plans enabled wartime employers to provide additional compensation to their employees without actually raising their wages.

The **Employee Retirement Income Security Act of 1974 (ERISA)** provided a further boost in the use of profit-sharing plans. ERISA regulates and sets the standards for pension plans and other employee benefit plans. Many employers found that a simple profit-sharing plan avoided many of ERISA's rules and regulations that affected pension plans.

Many companies have turned to profit-sharing plans during hard economic times, when they are unable to provide guaranteed wage increases. Chrysler Corp., for example, introduced profit-sharing for its union and nonunion employees in 1988 during an economic recession. Its profit-sharing plan was offered as part of its union contract in exchange for wage concessions made by its **workforce**. Corporate earnings at the time were weak, so profit-sharing payouts were small. By 1994, however, Chrysler had recovered and was paying an average profit-sharing bonus of $4,300 per person to 81,000 workers, a total outlay of approximately $348 million.

TYPES OF PROFIT-SHARING PLANS

Companies may use any number of different formulas to calculate the distribution of profits to their employees and establish a variety of rules and regulations regarding eligibility, but there are essentially two basic types of profit-sharing plans. One type is a cash or bonus plan, under which employees receive their profit-sharing distribution in cash at the end of the year. The main drawback to cash distribution plans is that employee profit-sharing bonuses are then taxed as ordinary income. Even if distributions are made in the form of company stock or some other type of payment, they become taxable as soon as employees receive them.

To avoid immediate taxation, companies are allowed by the **Internal Revenue Service** (IRS) to set up qualified deferred profit-sharing plans. Under a deferred plan, profit-sharing distributions are held in individual accounts for each employee. Employees are not allowed to withdraw from their profit-sharing accounts except under certain, well-defined conditions. As long as employees do not have easy access to the funds, money in the accounts is not taxed and may earn tax-deferred interest.

Under qualified deferred profit-sharing plans, employees may be given a range of investment choices for their accounts. Such choices are common when the accounts are managed by outside investment firms. It is becoming less common for companies to manage their own profit-sharing plans due to the fiduciary duties and liabilities associated with them.

OTHER ISSUES CONCERNING PROFIT-SHARING PLANS

Deferred profit-sharing plans are a type of defined contribution plan. Such employee benefit plans provide for an individual account for each employee. Individual accounts grow as contributions are made to them. Funds in the accounts are invested and may earn interest or show capital appreciation. Depending on each employee's investment choices, their account balances may be subject to increases or decreases reflecting the current value of their investments.

The amount of future benefits that employees will receive from their profit-sharing accounts depends entirely on their account balance. The amount of their account balance will include the employer's contributions from profits, any interest earned, any **capital gains** or losses, and possibly forfeitures from other plan participants. Forfeitures result when employees leave the company before they are vested, and the funds in their accounts are distributed to the remaining plan participants.

Employees are said to be vested when they become eligible to receive the funds in their accounts. Immediate vesting means that they have the right to funds in their account as soon as their employer makes a profit-sharing distribution. Companies may establish different time requirements before employees become fully vested. Under some deferred profit-sharing plans employees may start out partially vested, perhaps being entitled to only 25 percent of their account, then gradually become fully vested over a period of years. A company's vesting policy is written into the plan document and is designed to motivate employees and reduce employee turnover.

In order for a deferred profit-sharing plan to gain qualified status from the IRS, it is important that funds in employee accounts not be readily accessible to employees. Establishing a vesting period is one way to limit access; employees have rights to the funds in their accounts only when they become partially or fully vested. Another way is to establish strict rules for making payments from employees accounts, such as at retirement, death, permanent disability, or termination of employment. Less strict rules may allow for withdrawals under certain conditions, such as financial hardship or medical emergencies. Nevertheless, whatever rules a company may adopt for its profit-sharing plan, such rules are subject to IRS approval and must meet IRS guidelines.

The IRS also limits the amount that employers may contribute to their profit-sharing plans. The precise amount is subject to change by the IRS, but recent tax rules allowed companies to contribute a maximum of 15 percent of an employee's salary to his or her profit-sharing accounts. If a company contributed less than 15 percent in one year, it may exceed 15 percent by the difference in a subsequent year to a maximum of 25 percent of an employee's salary.

Companies may determine the amount of their profit-sharing contributions in one of two ways. One is by a set formula that is written into the plan document. Such formulas are typically based on the company's pretax net profits, earnings growth, or some other measure of profitability. Companies then plug the appropriate numbers into the formula and arrive at the amount of their contribution to the profit-sharing pool.

Rather than using a set formula, companies may decide to contribute a discretionary amount each year. That is, the company's **board of directors**—at its discretion—decides what an appropriate amount would be.

Once the amount of the company's contribution has been determined, different plans provide for different ways of allocating it among the company's employees. The employer's contribution may be translated into a percentage of the company's total payroll, with each employee receiving the same percentage of his or her annual pay. Other companies may use a sliding scale based on length of service or other factors. Profit-sharing plans also spell out precisely which employees are eligible to receive profit-sharing distributions. Some plans may require a certain length of employment, for example.

[David Bianco]

PROGRAM EVALUATION AND REVIEW TECHNIQUE (PERT)

Program Evaluation and Review Technique (PERT) is a scheduling method originally designed to plan a **manufacturing** project by employing a network of interrelated activities, coordinating optimum cost and time criteria. PERT emphasizes the relationship between the time each activity takes, the costs associated with each phase, and the resulting time and cost for the anticipated completion of the entire project.

PERT is an integrated **project management** system. These systems were designed to manage the complexities of major manufacturing projects, the extensive data necessary for such industrial efforts, and the time deadlines created by defense industry projects. Most of these management systems developed following World War II, and each has its advantages.

PERT was first developed in 1958 by the U.S. Navy Special Projects Office on the Polaris missile system. Existing integrated planning on such a large scale was deemed inadequate, so the Navy pulled in the Lockheed Aircraft Corporation and the management consulting firm of Booz, Allen, and Hamilton. Traditional techniques such as line of balance, Gantt charts, and other systems were eliminated, and PERT evolved as a means to deal with the varied time periods it takes to finish the critical activities of an overall project.

The line of balance (LOB) management control technique collected, measured, and analyzed data to show the progress, status, and timing of production projects. It was introduced at Goodyear Tire and Rubber Company in 1941 and fully utilized during World War II in the defense industry. Even older is the Gantt chart, developed during World War I by H e n r y Gantt, a pioneer in the field of scientific management. It is a visual management system, on which future time is plotted horizontally and work to be completed is indicated in a vertical line. The critical path method (CPM) evolved parallel to PERT. CPM is a mathematically ordered network of planning and scheduling project management; it was first used in 1957 by E.I. du Pont de Nemours & Co.. PERT borrows some CPM applications. PERT proved to be an ideal technique for one-of-a-kind projects, using a time network analysis to manage personnel, material resources, and financial requirements. The growth of PERT paralleled rapid expansion in the defense industry and meteoric developments in the space race. After 1960, all defense contractors adopted PERT to manage the massive one-time projects associated with the industry. Smaller businesses, awarded defense related government contracts, found it necessary to use PERT. At the same time, DuPont developed the critical path method (CPM), applied particularly in the construction industry. In the last 30 years, PERT has spread, as has CPM, as a major technique of integrated project management.

PERT centers on the concept of time and allows flexible scheduling due to variations in the amount of time it takes to complete one specific part of the project. A typical PERT network consists of activities and events. An event is the completion of one program component at a particular time. An activity is defined as the time and resources required to move from one event to another. Therefore, when events and activities are clearly defined, progress of a program is easily monitored, and the path of the project proceeds toward termination. PERT mandates that each preceding event be completed before succeeding events, and thus the final project, can be considered complete.

One key element to PERT's application is that three estimates are required due to the element of uncertainty and to provide time frames for the PERT network. These three estimates are classed as optimistic, most likely, and pessimistic, and are made for each activity of the overall project. Generally, the optimistic time estimate is the minimum time the activity will take—considering that all goes right the first time and luck holds for the project. The reverse is the pessimistic estimate, or maximum time estimate for completing the activity. This estimate takes into account Murphy's law—whatever can go wrong will, and all possible negative factors are considered when computing the estimate. The third is the most likely estimate, or the normal or realistic time an activity requires. Two other elements comprise the PERT network, the path, or critical path, and slack time. The critical path is a combination of events and activities which will necessitate the greatest expected completion time. Slack time is defined as the difference between the total expected activity time for the project and the actual time for the entire project. Slack time is the spare time experienced in the PERT network.

A vital aspect of PERT is the formula used for the calculation of expected project time. The project reads:

$$T = \frac{A + 4M + B}{6}$$

where T = expected completion time; A = optimistic estimate; M = most likely estimate; and B = pessimistic estimate.

Applying real numbers to the PERT formula, the result is as follows, where A (optimistic time) = 7 weeks; M (most likely time) = 11 weeks; B (pessimistic time) = 15 weeks:

$$\frac{7 + (4 \times 11) + 15}{6} = 11 \text{ weeks}$$
(or T, expected completion time)

Once the expected time is computed, the critical path is established. The PERT network considers all potential variables, thus quantifying the scheduling and planning of the project. In a comprehensive view of PERT, it becomes clear that despite the fact that some steps of the process are independent, the next step will depend on the successful completion of prior steps. This principle is shown in this rather simple PERT network.

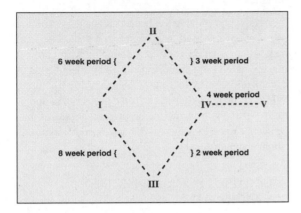

Here, steps II and III are the independent phases of project planning, but step IV depends directly on the successful completion of II and III, as does step V. The critical path in this PERT example is the longest period of time possible for project duration, or fifteen weeks.

Another key to PERT is to analyze and revise the data owing to a constant state of flux. Factors influencing project management take many forms, including personnel, materials, equipment and facilities, utilities, and environmental conditions. For example, **absenteeism**, sickness, vacations, and even strikes can affect personnel supply, or sudden changes in climatic conditions (snow, flooding from rains, etc.) may have an environmental impact. Various methods have been established to adjust the PERT network in order to allow for unpredictable situations. In recent years, computers have provided one major means of network analysis and revision, especially on larger projects. Computers are significantly useful for computations of the critical path and slack time. Smaller networks can generally be managed with manual computations and are usually developed, evaluated, and revised without great difficulty.

PERT has advantages as well as disadvantages, but time has seemingly not diminished its applicability. Planning a major network reveals potential problem areas and interdependent events which are not so obvious in conventional project development methods. One advantage is the three time estimate process, again useful in identifying difficulties as well as more effective interrelated processes. When utilizing the latest computer applications to PERT networks, managers have additional benefits with which to plan. A final advantage is the use of what is termed the management-by-exception principle, whereby data accumulated and analyzed by various means can be applied to the planning and execution of a major project. When managers have used PERT in integrated project management, experience gained is reapplied to future projects, especially in developing bids for project estimates. When appropriate costing techniques are implemented with PERT networking, the project sponsors realize significant financial benefits.

The PERT/cost system was developed to gain tighter control over actual costs of any project. PERT/cost relates actual costs to project costs. Job cost estimates are established from an activity or a group of activities on the basis of a time network. Labor and nonlabor estimates are developed for the network targeting the control of time and costs and identifying potential areas where time and cost can be traded off—all aimed at more effective, efficient project management.

Clearly PERT is a manufacturing-based project planning and scheduling network. In many instances, managers have attempted to apply PERT principles to other types of projects, including hospital planning for such issues as costs and social security, educational planning and development, various accounting functions, and even **real estate** development.

[Boyd Childress]

FURTHER READING:

Evarts, Harry F. *Introduction to PERT*. Allyn and Bacon, 1964.

Moder, Joseph J. *Project Management with CPM, PERT, and Precedence Diagramming*. Van Nostrand Reinhold, 1983.

Soroush, H.M. "The Most Critical Path in a PERT Network." *Journal of the Operational Research Society*. May, 1994, pp. 89-99.

Spinner, M. Pete. *Elements of Project Management*. Prentice-Hall, 1992.

Wiest, Jerome D. *A Management Guide to PERT/CPM*. Prentice-Hall, 1969.

PROJECT MANAGEMENT

Many times a business must make a systematic change, such as constructing a building, installing a computer system, merging with another company, developing a new product, entering a new market, etc. These changes are the result of projects.

A project is an organized undertaking intended to produce a specific outcome (goal) subject to the limitations of people, time, and money. Projects usually require coordinated work from multiple groups of people, exist only for a limited time, and have goals that become more detailed over time.

Project management consists of processes to plan, direct, monitor, redirect, and complete the project. During these processes, tradeoffs must be made between the amount of work (scope), acceptability of the work (quality), cost, and schedule so the project results are useful, timely, and affordable.

HISTORY OF PROJECT MANAGEMENT

Projects, sometimes of massive size, have occurred through human history. Early construction projects included the building of pyramids, cities, and medieval cathedrals. Other early projects include waging wars and empire building. While the results of these projects are incredible, the human cost and time required to complete them were sometimes staggering. Many thousands of workers and decades of time were often required.

In the twentieth century, project managers have had to learn to manage costs, schedules, and results. In the 1950s and 1960s, many techniques for planning and controlling project schedules and costs were developed, primarily on huge aerospace and construction projects. Much of this development was based on the concept of determining precedence relationships—that is, identifying which work activities must be done before other activities. In the 1980s and 1990s, many software companies have begun offering ever more powerful and easy ways to plan and control project costs and schedules. The result is that formal project management is now used in a wide variety of industries.

The project management usage trend is likely to continue. Business is faced with the challenges of downsizing, more complex products and services, the need to produce higher quality, cost-conscious customers, faster development cycles, international **competition**, and increased regulation. These challenges force businesses to quickly and inexpensively develop complex solutions. Project management is designed to help business leaders do just that.

RELATED CONCEPTS AND TERMS

There are many terms that can be confused with project management. The differences are usually one of size or organization. For example, enormous projects are often called programs. A program can usually be divided into multiple projects. The multibillion dollar development of a new jet can be described as a program composed of many projects that involve subsystems such as engines or avionics. Alternatively, the new jet program could have separate projects for various phases, such as design or testing.

Projects, in turn, can be broken down into smaller sets of activities. These smaller sets of work are sometimes called tasks, subprojects, hammock activities or work breakdown structure (WBS) summary activities. Responsibility for these smaller sets of work is often assigned to one person or department, while the project itself requires multiple people, departments, or companies to complete. Project management techniques can apply to both these larger and smaller undertakings.

As stated previously, project management is the set of processes used to accomplish a goal. The term task force is often used interchagably with project management. Functional, matrix, and project forms of organization refer to how a business is structured. While companies that have many projects are sometimes structured as matrix or project organizations, projects can be managed under any form of organizational structure.

A DETAILED LOOK AT PROJECT MANAGEMENT

All projects are performed to achieve a specific desire output. This output can be described both by its amount, size, or performance characteristics (scope), and by how well it serves its intended purpose (quality). Scope and quality collectively are the project goals.

All projects have finite amounts of time, money, and other resources. They are also limited by technology and legal requirements. All of these limitations must be taken into account when managing project activities.

There are many tools for planning, scheduling, monitoring, and reporting project activities. These tools, collectively referred to as project management tools, are used by business managers to accomplish project goals subject to the limitations faced.

All of the project activities occur in a predictable pattern called the project life cycle. A project has several overlapping stages in its life cycle. Different industries and professional groups have defined project life cycles with four or more stages and minor differences in specific activities. A simplified generic description of the project life cycle with typical names for the various phases follows.

The first project phase is often titled initiate or conceive. This starts with establishing a need for the project output. Then a project manager and possibly other key staff members are assigned. The scope (desired output) is defined and approximate time and resource estimates are made to determine if it is feasible to achieve the desired output. Different strategies or alternative approaches are explored and one is selected. Finally, approval to proceed to the next phase is obtained.

The second project phase is called the planning, design, or development phase. Additional project members may be assigned. Scope, quality standards, work activities, resource needs, and responsibilities are defined or further refined. Once this detailed planning is complete, approval to proceed to the next phase is obtained.

The third phase, often called the implementation, construction, or production stage, is when most of the actual project work is completed. Goods and services needed to complete the project are procured. (This is sometimes defined as a separate phase.) The project organization, procedures, and reporting mechanisms are established. Project work activities are directed, monitored, and redirected, always, keeping the project goals and limitations in mind.

The final phase is the completion, turn-over, or start-up phase. Activities include ensuring that project work is complete and acceptable, transferring responsibility for the project outcome to the user, reassigning workers and other resources, and evaluating the project with an eye toward improving future projects.

Project management is a process that includes planning, directing, monitoring, redirecting, and completing work so that the project goals can be completed while taking into consideration limitations such as time and money. Many work endeavors are already managed as projects. Competitive pressures and better software are likely to encourage more work endeavors to be managed as projects in the future.

[Timothy J. Kloppenborg]

FURTHER READING:

Duncan, William R. ''The Process of Project Management.'' *Project Management Journal.* September, 1993, pp. 5-10.

Kloppenborg, Timothy J., and Samuel J. Mantel, Jr. ''Tradeoffs on Projects: They May Not be What You Think.'' *Project Management Journal.* March, 1990, pp. 13-20.

Meredith, Jack R., and Samuel J. Mantel, Jr. *Project Management: A Managerial Approach.* 2nd ed. John Wiley & Sons, Inc.

PMI Standards Committee. *Project Management Body of Knowledge.* Project Management Institute.

Shtub, Avraham, Jonathon F. Bard, and Shlomo Globerson. *Project Management: Engineering, Technology, and Implementation.* Prentice Hall.

PROMISSORY NOTE

A promissory note is a written agreement from one party to another that promises the payment of a specific amount of money on a specified date. A promissory note is an alternative means of obtaining **credit** that is not widely used; it is more common to obtain business credit through an open account with a line of credit. A promissory note may be negotiable, so that the holder can sell or transfer the note to another party by endorsing it. In such cases the transferred note would usually be discounted somewhat from its face value.

Promissory notes of large corporations are also known as commercial paper. Commercial paper offers large corporations an alternative means of obtaining short-term financing. Most commercial paper is due in two to six months. It is usually sold to other business firms, insurance companies, pension funds, and banks. There is also an open market of commercial paper dealers. These kinds of promissory notes are usually issued in denominations of at least $1 million. The interest paid on prime commercial paper is usually slightly lower than that charged for prime business loans, so large firms with good credit ratings often choose to issue commercial paper rather than obtain a bank loan or use their line of credit.

The use of commercial paper on the open market is generally limited to large firms that are good credit risks. Purchasers often require that the issuer have enough open credit to back the note. Otherwise, payment of the promissory note may be dependent on the issuer having excess funds on hand. It is possible for a company's promissory notes to go into default if the company declares bankruptcy.

[David Bianco]

PROPERTY MANAGEMENT

Property management, also called real estate management, is the business of overseeing income-producing properties for third parties in exchange for a fee. A property manager typically has responsibility either directly or indirectly for the following aspects of a building's operations: **marketing**; financial administration and **budgeting**; **leasing**; tenant or resident relations; maintenance; property analysis; and **risk management**. The building's property managers oversee are commonly categorized as residential, office, shopping center, or industrial.

Property management began to be a recognized profession after 1890 as the construction of urban **real estate** shifted from single-family homes and two- or three-unit dwellings to larger, multi-family buildings. Construction of early urban multi-family residences was at its height in the mid-1920s. Another trend that gave rise to the need for third-party fee managers of real estate was the advent of the skyscraper in cities such as Chicago, IL where soon after the Great Fire of 1871, the cityscape transformed itself—from horizontal to vertical. High-rise, multi-tenant office space required specialized skills, particularly in the area of leasing.

From 1920 to 1922, investors in real estate found themselves awash in profits. Faced with the quandary of how to spend so much extra income and at the same time manage their assets, many investors turned to real estate agents, asking them to collect rents, pay for building maintenance and utilities, maintain heating systems, and send in net profits at the end of the month. Building managers did not usually make extraordinary expenses without express instructions to do so, and owners were usually present during the leasing season. Real estate agencies often provided management services in order to obtain sales clients. Management business volume, however, started to become important in areas with high rents and large numbers of multi-family properties.

During the 1920s, split **mortgages** became popular. These finance instruments broke large **loans** into smaller **bonds** available to the investing public. Overlending on real estate, about which investors were often not knowledgeable, was an ominous prelude to the decade that followed. With the Great Depression of the 1930s came mass foreclosures and for all intents and purposes, the liquidation of individual ownership of investment properties.

What most in the industry today describe as the field of property management ironically has its roots in this disastrous failure of real estate as an investment vehicle for the common citizen in the years preceding the depression. With defaults on the mortgages of the vast majority of the income-producing properties in the nation, banks, insurance companies, **savings and loan associations**, trust companies, and investment protective committees were suddenly saddled with large numbers of multi-family and commercial properties. They formed management departments to oversee the operations of their real estate assets.

By the time the United States entered World War I in 1941, demand for urban property was high enough to diminish the need for specialists who could rent buildings under difficult conditions and create profit scenarios. In addition, during the war, federal rent controls applied to residential properties, so there was no longer a need for someone who could apply successful rental increases. With what was basically a captive market, building owners often neglected building upkeep. These market conditions generally lasted until the end of 1957.

The scenario changed after a construction boom from 1946 to 1956 created a housing surplus. Suburbs began springing up where there was once farmland or woods, and by the end of 1963, rental space was more readily available, rental rates were more stable, and occupancy rates were falling. Property managers experienced greater demand for their services.

A voracious demand for office space also colored the post-war period. Greater employment levels in the areas of government, retailing, and services were partly responsible. Another contributing factor was increased prosperity, which led many businesses to seek more space. Specialized space needs, e.g., for computing functions, also created a need for office space with plus value.

During the 1960s and 70s, the onslaught of condominiums created another source of demand for property management services. Many condominiums were second homes in buildings under multiple ownership in resort areas, and their owners needed full-time managers. Also, an increase in the mortgage money supply allowed for the development of large income-producing properties. The popularization of **Real Estate Investment Trusts (REITS)**, which offered investments in real estate in the form of securities, and the subsequent collapse of many of these trusts from 1974 to 1975, created another period of high demand for property management services.

Since the real estate development boom years of the 1980s, the office market has been glutted with space in most regions. During the late-1980s and early-1990s, an important market for many property managers consisted of banks with real estate owned properties (REOs) on their books. As in the early years of the Depression, financial institutions in the early 1990s needed outside specialists to manage real estate assets while they sought to sell them.

Also during the early 1990s, some property management firms targeted their services at large corporations that had downsized their organizations and were outsourcing services such as facilities management, previously provided in-house. Facilities managers offer property management services for a corporation's headquarters or other owner-occupied space. Other property management firms have branched into asset management services, through which they manage and maximize the value of the real property held by a client.

Another topic that is increasingly important in property management for all building types is risk management, through which managers analyze the real or potential risks at a piece of property and control them by reducing or transferring them to third parties through insurance or indemnification clauses in legal contracts. Risks property managers often assess and manage relate to emergencies, negligence, premises security, general liability, negligent hiring or other employment issues, and environmental liability.

RESIDENTIAL MANAGEMENT

Property managers of residential buildings often administer the financial, budgeting, and reporting functions for a portfolio of properties, and manage site managers at individual buildings who perform other tasks. A site manager frequently lives in an apartment on the premises of the property managed and usually supervises leasing, maintenance, and other employees who work on the grounds of the building. A property manager usually reports directly to the owner or owners of properties in the portfolio; a site manager usually reports directly to a property manager.

A typical job description for a site manager includes responsibilities for the following: budget preparation assistance; purchase order and **inventory control**; oversight of building maintenance and physical operations; supervision of on-site employees; management of resident relations and retention; assistance in the design and implementation of marketing programs; administration of resident selection and application process; rental payment collection; record keeping.

OFFICE BUILDING MANAGEMENT

Office building managers frequently have the following responsibilities for the buildings they manage: budgeting and financial administration; reporting and owner relations; publicity and tenant relations; leasing and lease administration; emergency procedures planning; supervision of contractors or in-house employees for maintenance, security, cleaning, elevators, landscaping, and other services. For leasing functions, property managers use either in-house leasing staffs or outside brokers.

SHOPPING CENTER MANAGEMENT

Shopping centers fall into the following categories: community, regional, specialty, mall, and convenience. Managers of shopping centers generally have the same responsibilities as managers of office buildings: budgeting, reporting, and financial administration; publicity and tenant relations; leasing and lease administration; emergency procedures planning; supervision of contractors for maintenance, security, and other services.

Leasing of shopping centers differs from that of office buildings in that leases are often at least partially percentage-based. This usually means that after a tenant begins to generate a certain amount of money per square foot, a percentage of this income is paid as rent. In part because of percentage-based leases, shopping center managers must pay close attention to the profitability of tenants. Managers usually seek to provide tenant synergies by bringing tenants to the center who draw business for each other rather than compete with each other. Tenants are sometimes concerned with obtaining lease clauses that give them the exclusive right to provide a particular service or product at the center. The stable presence of an anchor tenant such as a large department store or supermarket is usually crucial to the profitability of a shopping center.

Finally, a trend in real estate development of the 1980s and early-1990s was to construct mixed-use developments, meaning properties that may have office, shopping, residential or other space all under the same roof. An important role of a property manager of a mixed-use development is to capitalize on marketing and functional synergies among the building uses present in the complex.

[Dorothy Walton]

FURTHER READING:

Bachner, John Philip. *The Guide to Practical Property Management*. McGraw-Hill, 1991.

Leasing Retail Space. Institute of Real Estate Management, 1990.

Managing the Office Building. Institute of Real Estate Management, 1985.

Managing the Shopping Center. Institute of Real Estate Management.

Pappas, Stephen G. *The Property Manager's Handbook*. Dearborn Financial Publishing, 1991.

Principles of Real Estate Management. Institute of Real Estate Management, 1991.

Roberts, Duane F. *Marketing and Leasing of Office Space*. Institute of Real Estate Management, 1986.

Shear, Mel A. *Handbook of Building Maintenance Management*. Prentice-Hall, 1983.

Walters, William. *The Practice of Real Estate Management for the Experienced Property Manager*. Institute of Real Estate Management, 1979.

Zankel, Martin I. *Negotiating Commercial Real Estate Leases*. Dearborn Financial Publishing, 1990.

PROPRIETARY INFORMATION

Proprietary information, also known as a trade secret, is information that a company wishes to keep confidential or secret from those outside the company. Proprietary information can include secret formulas, processes, and methods used in production. It can also include a company's business and marketing plans, salary structure, customer lists, contracts, and computer system. In some cases the special knowledge and skills that an employee has learned on the job are considered to be a company's proprietary information.

There is no single standard by which to determine if information is proprietary or not. Some 39 U.S. states have laws that define a trade secret and the conditions under which it is considered to have been stolen. In general, for information to be considered proprietary, companies must treat it as such. Information that is readily available in public sources will not be treated by the courts as proprietary. The body of case law covering proprietary information and trade secrets recognizes a company's right to have proprietary information and provides it with remedies when its trade secrets have been misused or appropriated illegally.

There are several ways for a company to protect its proprietary information. Key employees with access to proprietary information may be required to sign restrictive covenants, also called non-compete agreements, that prohibit them from competing with their employer for a certain period of time after leaving the company. These restrictive covenants are usually enforced by the courts if they are reasonable with respect to time and place and do not unreasonably restrict the former employee's right to employment. In some cases the covenants are enforced only if the employee has gained proprietary information during the course of his or her employment.

Companies may also develop security systems to protect their proprietary information from being stolen by foreign or domestic competitors. Business and industrial espionage is an ongoing activity that clandestinely seeks to obtain trade secrets by illegal methods. A corporate system for protecting proprietary information would include a comprehensive plan ranging from employee education to data protection to securing phone lines and meeting rooms. In some cases a **chief information officer** (CIO) would be responsible for implementing such a plan.

An employee who divulges a trade secret is committing a tort by violating a duty of loyalty that includes nondisclosure of proprietary information. Once the employee leaves the company, however, that duty no longer exists. For this reason companies often require employees to sign a restrictive covenant, or non-compete agreement.

In addition, the courts generally consider it unfair competition for one company to induce employees of another company who have acquired unique technical skills and secret knowledge during their employment, to terminate their employment and use their skills and knowledge for the benefit of the competing firm. In such a case the plaintiff company could seek an injunction to prevent its former employees and the competing company from using the proprietary information.

[David Bianco]

PUBLIC DEBT

Any federal budget gap between revenues (from taxes and tariffs) and expenditures (on agencies and programs) creates a fiscal-year deficit. The U.S. government meets this deficit by borrowing in international credit markets and floating **bonds** through the U.S. Department of the Treasury and the **Federal Reserve System**. Federal borrowing to cover annual deficits accumulates as the public debt, which is administered by the Department of the Treasury.

HISTORY AND BACKGROUND

The politics of public debt in the United States date back to the birth of the nation. In 1790, Alexander Hamilton (1755-1804) called the repayment of the **national debt** (then at $75 million) stemming from the Revolutionary War a "sacred obligation." War, in fact, traditionally has been the cause of surges in public debt. The public debt jumped from $65 million in 1860 to $3 billion in 1865 because of the Civil War, and to $24 billion after World War I. During the World War II years of 1940-45, the public debt increased sixfold from $43 billion to $259 billion.

THE POLITICS OF PUBLIC DEBT

The public debt is one component of a far larger political question: the role, scope, and prerogatives of the federal government. The problem of the public debt becomes intertwined with questions about global and domestic priorities, the administration of the income tax system, and the function of the Federal Reserve. Federal spending can promote global prosperity, stimulate the domestic economy, develop the national **infrastructure**, provide access to education, and protect disadvantaged populations, among other purposes that benefit all Americans. Escalating interest payments on deficit spending, however, ultimately crowd out vital expenditure and investment, sap energy from the business sector, and stifle economic productivity and growth. In addition, as Alexander Hamilton recognized, there are moral objections to passing on debt to future generations.

THE CONTEMPORARY PUBLIC DEBT

Public debt shot up to unprecedented heights during the 1980s, although the decade was one of relative peace. Deficits resulted from lowered taxes and increased defense spending during the Reagan administration, along with the growing burden of older entitlement programs such as Social Security and Medicare. The public debt more than tripled from $907.7 billion in 1980 to $3.2 trillion in 1990, and quadrupled to $4 trillion by 1992. Annual interest payments on the public debt correspondingly rose from $75 billion in 1980 to $200 billion in 1992. In that year, the budget deficit peaked at approximately $350 million. Voter pressure on President Clinton and the Congress led to a trimming of the deficit over the next few years.

Three strategies for curbing the public debt—raising taxes, cutting programs, and balancing the federal budget—often pit Congress against the presidency, the legislative branch of government against the executive. The congressional elections of 1994 provided a notable example: riding on Newt Gingrich's ''Contract with America''—which called for the passage of a balanced-budget amendment ''to force the government to live within its means''—the Republican Party gained the majority in the House of Representatives for the first time in 40 years.

[David Sprinkle]

FURTHER READING:

''Deficit Lessons: Hamilton the Hero.'' *New York Times*. May 2, 1993, 3:13.

Heilbroner, Robert L., and Peter Bernstein. *The Debt and the Deficit: False Alarms, Real Possibilities*. NY: Norton, 1989.

Stabile, R. Donald, and Jeffrey A. Cantor. *The Public Debt of the United States: An Historical Perspective, 1775-1990*. Westport, CT: Praeger, 1991.

Thompson, Roger. ''Restoring the American Dream.'' *Nation's Business*. May, 1995, pp. 18-24.

U.S. Department of the Treasury. *Monthly Statement of the Public Debt of the United States*. Washington, DC: GPO.

PUBLIC OFFERING

In order to raise **capital** corporations offer their securities for sale to the general public. An initial public offering (IPO) is the first instance in which a corporation offers a specific, registered security for sale. A corporation whose securities are already trading publicly may also offer a new block of stock from its treasury stock or from a large investor in a secondary offering.

An IPO of **common stock** converts a business owned by one person or several persons into a business owned by many. Taking a company public serves two main purposes:

1. It provides an immediate injection of cash that can be used to enhance the possibilities of successful growth, to buy out and/or to retire the owners, and to establish a base value for estate purposes.

2. It expands the equity base increasing the possibility of stock value appreciation.

There are disadvantages, however. The registration process is expensive and cumbersome, and requires not only the extensive disclosure of the inner workings of the business but also a scrutinizing of the principal(s). Sharing ownership also means dilution of earnings and loss of control.

Secondary public offerings and IPOs involve the transfer of wealth from suppliers of capital to demanders of capital in exchange for (1) direct ownership of the business through stock ownership, and/or (2) a claim on future earnings through debt securities.

THE CAPITAL MARKETS

The **capital markets** are comprised of a diverse set of firms that perform the function of bringing together the suppliers and demanders of capital. Their primary marketplaces are the New York Stock Exchange, the American Stock Exchange, and the **over-the-counter securities markets**.

The **Securities Act of 1933** prohibited market players from unscrupulous dealings by requiring disclosure statements, and imposing criminal and civil penalties for inadequate and inaccurate disclosure of ''material fact,'' i.e., information that would likely cause potential investors to reconsider the feasibility of the investment. In 1934 the **Securities and Exchange Commission** was conferred with the authority for implementing and enforcing the 1933 act.

The SEC is a quasi-judicial administrative agency authorized to regulate securities industry personnel and the trading of public companies. The SEC is responsible for a formal system of underwriting securities, offering them to the public, raising funds in the public markets, and supervising the continuing trading of securities.

The SEC requires the education, testing, and licensing of individuals engaged in the sale of securities. To keep the investing public properly informed, the SEC has established a series of periodic reports to be filed by publicly listed companies. To oversee public offerings, the SEC has a long and involved registration, disclosure, and review process.

BLUE-SKY LAWS. In order to prevent securities fraud, each state passed legislation to prevent the sale of dubious investments such as the blue sky. These laws are more or less similar to SEC rules and regulations. Issuers of securities must comply with the blue-sky laws in each state in which they expect to offer the securities.

THE SECURITIES PLACEMENT PROCESS

INITIAL PUBLIC OFFERING. The process of going public, i.e., making an initial public offering, is complex and involved. It begins with the process of incorporation (if it is not already), for only corporations are publicly listed.

The corporation secures a financial adviser to consult on the feasibility of going public and in what manner to do so. After the decision has been made to go forward, the corporation seeks the services of a person who has access to funds. An investment banker serves as the liaison between investors and the company.

The company assembles an experienced team of accountants, auditors, and attorneys along with the investment banker. Together they complete and submit the registration forms and the initial offering prospectus required by the SEC. The prospectus provides a detailed discussion of the company, its performance and profitability, the **management**, and the intended uses for the funds raised.

Meanwhile, the company works with the underwriters to determine the appropriate offering price for the new securities, the underwriter's compensation, the size and timing of the offering, and the method of distributing the securities to the public.

The company and all of its team members are to honor a "quiet period" of 90 days from the date of commencing the work on the financial planning to the effective date of the registration statement. The SEC prohibits any publicity during the registration period other than the distribution of the preliminary prospectus.

The SEC review, termed **due diligence**, determines the consistency and completeness of the statements to insure full disclosure of material facts. If incomplete, the company performs a "cleanup" to resolve SEC concerns.

In order to determine the public's interest in the IPO, the underwriter circulates an attention getter called a "red herring," whose cover page is printed in red as a warning that it is merely a preliminary prospectus. The red herring usually does not give an offering date, price, or number of shares but inside the red herring is a wealth of company information, **financial statements**, and notes.

Upon approval of the registration statements and the prospectus, the SEC notifies the company, and the security may then be listed on an exchange and sold to the public. SEC approval does not constitute a statement of investment merit or fairness of the offering price, but only that full disclosure of relevant facts has been made.

If there are changes to the initial prospectus, the company will revise, reprint, and redistribute it. Sales are permitted only after the potential investor has a prospectus in hand long enough for adequate review. In the instance where only the price and share information is needed, the company merely sticks a completed label on the cover sheet.

The led investment banker supervises the public sale of the security. For a larger offering, the lead investment banker will form a syndicate of other investment bankers to underwrite the issue as well as a selling group to assist with the distribution. During the offering period, investment bankers are permitted to "stabilize" the price of the security in the secondary market by purchasing shares in the secondary market. This process is called pegging, and it is permitted to continue for up to ten days after the official offering date.

After a successful offering, the underwriter meets with all parties to distribute the funds and settle all expenses. At that time the transfer agent is given authorization to forward the securities to the new owners.

An IPO closes with the transfer of the stock, but the terms of the offering are not completed. The SEC requires the filing of a number of reports (Form SR) ascertaining to the appropriate use of the funds as described in the prospectus. If the offering is terminated for any reason, the underwriter returns the funds to the investors.

IMPORTANT SEC FORMS

- S-K: Standard Instructions for Filing Forms under Securities Act of 1933, **Securities Exchange Act of 1934**, and Energy Policy and Conservation Act of 1975 specifies the requirements for the nonfinancial portion of the registration.

- S-X: Form and Content of and Requirements for Financial Statements, Securities Exchange Act of 1933, Securities Act of 1934, Public Utility Holding Company Act of 1935, and Energy Policy and Conservation Act of 1975 specifies the financial statements required and denotes the form, content, and time periods for submission of the information.

- Reg C: describes the proper procedure for filing a registration statement: the mechanics and paper size, the number of copies, the size of the type, and the definition of terms.

SEE ALSO: Privately Placed Securities; Underwriting

[Roger J. AbiNader]

FURTHER READING:

Arkebauer, James B., with Ron Schultz. *The Entrepreneur's Guide to Going Public*. Upstart Publishing Company, 1994.

Malone, Michael S. *Going Public: MIPS Computer and the Entrepreneurial Dream*. Edward Burlingame Books, 1991.

Shillinglaw, Gordon, and Philip E. Meyer. *Accounting: A Management Approach*. 7th ed. Irwin, 1983.

Welsch, Glenn A., Robert N. Anthony, and Daniel G. Short. *Fundamentals of Financial Accounting*. 4th ed. Irwin, 1984.

PUBLIC RELATIONS

The term ''public relations'' is practically self-explanatory, yet over the years it has meant different things to different people. To some the term conjures up negative images of publicity ''hacks,'' press agents, and propagandists. To others public relations means making corporations and other types of organizations more responsive to the demands of public opinion. In its simplest form, public relations means relating to the public. As practiced in the first years of the twentieth century before the term ''public relations'' was coined, it meant one-way communications from an organization to its audience, or simple publicity. As public relations evolved during the 20th century, it recognized the importance of public opinion and its impact on the organization, and thus the necessity for two-way communication between an organization and its publics.

Edward L. Bernays, an important founding father of modern public relations, began practicing public relations in 1920. He coined the term ''public relations counsel'' and taught the first university course on public relations in 1923 at New York University. That same year his book, *Crystallizing Public Opinion*, was published and became the first book on public relations. In an interview that was published in the Winter 1956 issue of *Public Relations Quarterly*, Bernays described public relations as ''a field of activity which has to do with the interaction between an individual, a group, an idea, or other unit with the public on which it depends. A counsel on public relations is an expert who advises on relations with these publics. He attempts to define the socially sound objectives of his client or project. He attempts to find out by research what the adjustments or maladjustments are between his client and the publics on which he depends.''

Philip Lesly, a leading authority on public relations and author of *Lesly's Handbook of Public Relations and Communications*, succinctly defined public relations as ''helping an organization and its public adapt mutually to each other.'' Other definitions of public relations point to its role in protecting and developing goodwill or characterize it as how one organization or group tells other organizations or groups about itself. Yet public relations involves more than words; it also requires an organization to act. The effect of good public relations is to lessen the gap between how an organization sees itself and how others outside the organization perceive it.

Bernays, Lesly, and other experts agree that public relations involves two-way communication between an organization and its public. It requires listening to the publics on which an organization is dependent as well as analyzing and understanding the attitudes and behaviors of those audiences. Only then can an organization undertake an effective public relations campaign consisting of actions as well as words.

Public relations involves many different types of audiences and organizations. Public relations is practiced not only by companies and business firms, but also by trade associations on behalf of specific industries, **professional and trade associations** on behalf of their members, and other nonprofit organizations as well as cities, states, countries, and a variety of government agencies.

The publics with which these organizations are concerned are also quite varied. Depending on the type of organization, they include its stockholders and investors, employees or members, customers and consumers, government regulators, the media, the community in which it is located, and others.

PUBLIC RELATIONS: A MULTIFACETED ACTIVITY

If we examine some of the goals and objectives of public relations, it becomes clear that it is a multifaceted activity involving many different functions. Topping the list of objectives, public relations seeks to create, maintain, and protect the organization's reputation, enhance its prestige, and present a favorable image. Studies have shown that consumers often base their purchase decision on a company's reputation, so public relations can have a definite impact on a company's sales and revenue. Public relations can be an effective part of a company's overall marketing strategy. In the case of a for-profit company, public relations and marketing may be coordinated to be sure they are working to achieve the same objectives.

Another major public relations goal is to create goodwill for the organization. This involves such functions as employee relations, stockholder and investor relations, media relations, community relations, and relations with the many other publics with whom the organization interacts, affects, or is affected by.

Public relations also has an educational component that can help it achieve such goals as outlined above. Public relations may function to educate certain publics about many things relevant to the organization, including educating them about business in general, new legislation, and how to use a particular product as well as to overcome misconceptions and prejudices. A nonprofit organization may attempt to educate the public regarding a certain point of view. Trade associations may undertake educational programs regarding particular industries and their products and practices.

PUBLIC RELATIONS AND TWO-WAY COMMUNICATION

Effective public relations requires a knowledge, based on analysis and understanding, of all the factors that influence perception of and attitudes toward the organization. The development of a specific public relations campaign follows these basic steps, which can be visualized as a loop that begins within the organization, extends to the target audience(s), and returns back to the organization.

While a specific public relations project or campaign may be undertaken proactively or reactively, the first basic step in either case involves analysis and research to identify all the relevant factors of the situation. In this first step the organization gains an understanding of the key factors that are influencing the perceptions of the organization and the nature of the publics involved.

The second step, policy formation, builds on the first. Here the organization establishes an overall policy with respect to the campaign, including defining goals and the desired outcome as well as the constraints under which the campaign will operate. It is necessary to establish such policy guidelines in order to evaluate proposed strategies and tactics as well as the overall success of the campaign.

In step three strategies and tactics are outlined. Here the organization brings into play its knowledge of its target audiences and develops specific programs consistent with established policies to achieve the desired objectives. Then the organization is ready for step four, actual communication with the targeted publics. Specific public relations techniques, such as press conferences or special events, are employed to reach the intended audience.

Up to this point the public relations loop has gone in one direction from the organization to its target audiences. In step five the loop turns back toward the organization as it receives feedback from its publics. How have they reacted to the public relations campaign? Are there some unexpected developments? Here the organization listens to its publics and, in the final step, assesses the program and makes any necessary adjustments.

PUBLIC RELATIONS PRACTICES AND TECHNIQUES

Public relations is a multifaceted activity involving different publics and audiences as well as different types of organizations, all with different goals and objectives. Specific areas of public relations will be reviewed next, with examples of practices and techniques and their use in effective campaigns covering a variety of situations. Many of the examples cited first appeared as case studies in the weekly *PR News* and were later collected in the *PR News Casebook*.

PRODUCT PUBLIC RELATIONS. Public relations and marketing work together closely when it comes to promoting a new or existing product or service. Public relations plays an important role in new product introductions by creating awareness, differentiating the product from other similar products, and even changing consumer behavior. For example, when the Prince Matchabelli division of Chesebrough-Pond's USA introduced a new men's cologne, there were twenty-one other men's fragrances being introduced that year. To differentiate its new offering, called Hero, Prince Matchabelli created a National Hero Awards Program honoring authentic male heroes and enlisted the participation of Big Brothers/Big Sisters of America to lend credibility to the program. When Coleco introduced its Cabbage Patch Kids, public relations helped increase awareness through licensed tie-in products, trade show exhibits, press parties, and even window displays in Cartier jewelry stores. When one bank began using **automated teller machines** (ATMs), it created a friendly new image of the new customer-operated machines by introducing them first to children. Public relations can also help introduce new products through staging a variety of special events and in the handling of sensitive situations.

Public relations is often called on to give existing products and services a boost by creating and renewing visibility. The California Raisins Advisory Board organized a national tour featuring live performances by the California Dancing Raisins to maintain interest in raisins during a summer-long advertising hiatus. The tour generated national and local publicity through media events, advance publicity, trade promotions, and media interviews with performer Ray Charles. Before denim became fashionable, the Denim Council helped gain public acceptance of the fabric with a multifaceted campaign that included a range of special events, book tie-ins, promotional giveaways, and specially designated ''Denim Weeks,'' resulting in high-profile magazine and newspaper feature stories.

Other public relations programs for existing products involve stimulating secondary demand, as when Campbell Soup Co. increased overall demand for soup by publishing a recipe booklet, or identifying new uses for the product, as when Rit Household Dyes took advantage of the tie-dying craze of the 1960s and 1970s to increase demand for its products. Public relations can interest the media in familiar products and services in a number of ways, including holding seminars for journalists, staging a special media day, and supplying the media with printed materials ranging from ''backgrounders'' (in-depth news releases) to booklets and brochures. Changes in existing products offer additional public relations opportunities to focus consumers' attention. An effective public relations campaign can help to properly position a product and overcome negative perceptions on the part of the general public.

EMPLOYEE RELATIONS. Employees are one of the most important publics a company has, and an ongoing public relation program is necessary to maintain employee goodwill as well as to uphold the company's image and reputation among its employees. The essence of a good employee relations program is keeping employees informed and providing them with channels of communication to upper levels of management. Bechtel Group, a privately held complex of operating companies, published an annual report for its employees to keep them informed about the company's operations. The company used employee surveys to determine what information employees considered useful. A range of other communication devices were used, including a monthly tabloid and magazine, a quarterly video magazine, local newsletters, bulletin boards, a call-in telephone service, and ''brown bag'' lunches where live presentations were made about the company. Suggestion systems, which originated in World War II, are another effective way to improve employee-management communications.

Other public relations programs for employees include training them as company public relations representatives, explaining benefits programs to them, offering them educational, volunteer, and citizenship opportunities, and staging special events such as picnics or open houses for them. Other programs can improve performance and increase employee pride and motivation. Public relations also plays a role in recruiting new employees; handling reorganizations, relocations, and mergers; and resolving labor disputes.

FINANCIAL RELATIONS. Financial relations involves communicating not only with a company's stockholders, but also with the wider community of financial analysts and potential investors. An effective investor relations plan can increase the value of a company's stock and make it easier for it to raise additional capital. One successful plan involved financial presentations in ten major cities, mailings to the financial community, and financially oriented advertisements, resulting in the stock price increasing 50 percent and

the price-earnings ratio doubling. In some cases special meetings with financial analysts are necessary to overcome adverse publicity, negative perceptions about a company, or investor indifference. Such meetings may take the form of full-day briefings, formal presentations, or luncheon meetings. A tour of a company's facilities may help generate interest among the financial community. Mailings and ongoing communications can help a company achieve visibility among potential investors and financial analysts.

Annual reports and stockholder meetings are the two most important public relations tools for maintaining good stockholder relations. Some companies hold regional or quarterly meetings in addition to the usual annual meeting. Other companies reach more stockholders by moving the location of their annual meeting from city to city. Annual reports can be complemented by quarterly reports and dividend check inserts. Companies that wish to provide additional communications with stockholders may send them a newsletter or company magazine. Personal letters to new stockholders and a quick response to inquiries insure an additional measure of goodwill.

COMMUNITY RELATIONS. Comprehensive, ongoing community relations programs can help virtually any organization achieve visibility as a good community citizen and the goodwill of the community in which it is located. Banks, utilities, radio and television stations, and major retailers and corporations are some of the types of organizations most likely to have ongoing programs that might include supporting urban renewal, performing arts programs, social and educational programs, children's programs, community organizations, and construction projects. Support may be financial or take the form of employee participation.

Organizations have the opportunity to improve goodwill and demonstrate a commitment to their communities when they open new offices, expand facilities, and open new factories. One company increased community awareness of its presence by converting a vacant building into a permanent meeting place. Another company built its new headquarters in an abandoned high school that it renovated. Mutual of Omaha scheduled an anniversary celebration and awards dinner to coincide with the dedication of its new underground office building to generate additional media coverage.

One of the more sensitive areas of community relations involves plant closings. A well-planned public relations campaign, combined with appropriate actions, can alleviate the tensions that such closings cause. Some elements of such a campaign might include offering special programs to laid-off workers, informing employees directly about proposed closings, and controlling rumors through candid and direct communications to the community and employees.

Organizations conduct a variety of special programs to improve community relations, including providing employee volunteers to work on community projects, sponsoring educational and literacy programs, staging open houses and conducting plant tours, celebrating anniversaries, and mounting special exhibits. Organizations are recognized as good community citizens when they support programs that improve the quality of life in their community, including crime prevention, employment, environmental programs, clean-up and beautification, recycling, and restoration.

Sometimes it is necessary for an organization to gain community support for a particular action, such as a new development or factory. One real estate developer elicited favorable media coverage and brought praise from local government by preserving a historic estate that was on a site that had been proposed for development. A utility company mobilized its employees to win community support for a proposed nuclear power plant. They participated in a telephone campaign, attended council meetings in area communities, and volunteered as guides for plant open houses.

CRISIS COMMUNICATIONS. Public relations practitioners become heavily involved in crisis communications whenever there is a major accident or natural disaster affecting an organization and its community. Other types of crises involve bankruptcy, product failures, and management wrongdoing. After the San Francisco earthquake of 1989, the Bank of America utilized its public relations department to quickly establish communications with customers, the financial community, the media, and offices in forty-five countries to assure them the bank was still operating. When faced with bankruptcy, Chrysler Corp. embarked on an extensive public relations campaign under the direction of its public affairs department to convince Congress to approve a $1.2 billion government loan guarantee. In some cases, crises call for an organization to become involved in helping potential victims; in other cases, the crisis may require rebuilding an organization's image.

GOVERNMENT AND POLITICAL PUBLIC RELATIONS. Public relations in the political arena covers a wide range, including staging presidential debates, as the League of Women Voters has done, holding seminars for government leaders, influencing proposed legislation, and testifying before a congressional committee. Political candidates engage in public relations, as do government agencies at the federal, state, and local levels.

Trade associations and other types of organizations attempt to block unfavorable legislation and support favorable legislation in a number of ways. The liquor industry in California helped defeat a proposed tax increase by taking charge of the debate early, winning endorsements, recruiting spokespersons, and cultivating grassroots support. A speakers bureau trained some 240 industry volunteers, and key messages were communicated to the public through printed materials and radio and television commercials.

In another example, many cities considered adopting legislation that banned the sale of spray paint to retail customers because of a rash of graffiti. The National Paint and Coatings Association launched a campaign that focused on the crime of vandalism. The collective research that went into the campaign resulted in an ongoing legislative monitoring operation through which the industry is alerted to new developments.

PUBLIC RELATIONS IN THE PUBLIC INTEREST. Organizations attempt to generate goodwill and position themselves as responsible citizens through a variety of programs conducted in the public interest. Some examples are environmental programs that include water and energy conservation, antipollution programs, and generally publicizing an organization's environmental efforts. Health and medical programs are sponsored by a wide range of nonprofit organizations, healthcare providers, and other businesses and industries. These range from encouraging other companies to develop **AIDS in the workplace** policies to the American Cancer Society's Great American Smokeout.

A variety of programs for young people may be conducted in the public interest. These range from providing educational materials to schools to sponsoring a radio program for students and teachers. International Paper developed a program to help older students and recent graduates improve their reading and writing skills by having celebrities write ''how-to'' articles which were printed as advertisements in popular magazines and major newspapers. Other programs offer political education, leadership and self-improvement, recreational activities, contests, and safety instruction.

CONSUMER EDUCATION. Organizations have undertaken a variety of programs to educate consumers, building goodwill and helping avoid misunderstandings in the process. Some examples of trade association activity in this area include the Soap and Detergent Association preparing a guide on housecleaning to be used in educational programs for new public housing residents. The National Association of Manufacturers held local open houses to educate the public about local businesses. The general public was allowed to make toll-free calls to a pesticide symposium conducted by two agricultural associations. The automotive industry established the Automobile Information Council as a source of industry news and information. An association of accountants undertook to educate the public concerning new tax laws.

Other opportunities for educating consumers include sponsoring television and radio programs, producing manuals and other printed materials, producing materials for classroom use, and releasing the results of surveys. In addition to focusing on specific issues or industries, educational programs may seek to inform consumers about economic matters and business in general.

OTHER PUBLIC RELATIONS PROGRAMS. Other types of programs that fall under the umbrella of public relations include corporate identity programs ranging from name changes and new trademarks to changing a company's image and identity. Milestones and anniversaries are observed in a variety of ways to improve an organization's public relations.

Special events may be held to call attention to an organization and focus the public's goodwill. These include anniversary celebrations, events related to trade shows, special exhibits, fairs and festivals, and other types of events.

Speakers bureaus and celebrity spokespersons are effective public relations tools for communicating an organization's point of view. Speakers bureaus may be organized by a trade association or an individual company as well as by virtually any other type of organization. The face-to-face communication that speakers can deliver is often more effective than messages carried by printed materials, especially when the target audience is small and clearly defined.

The examples of public relations practices given here indicate the range of activities and functions that fall within public relations. It is clear that while communication is the essence of public relations, an effective public relations campaign is based on action as well as words. Whether it is practiced formally or informally, public relations is an essential function for the survival of any organization.

[David P. Bianco]

FURTHER READING:

Bernays, Edward L. *The Later Years: Public Relations Insights, 1956-1986.* H&M Publishers, 1986.

Bianco, David, ed. *PR News Casebook: 1000 Public Relations Case Studies.* Gale Research Inc., 1993.

Lesly, Philip, ed. *Lesly's Handbook of Public Relations and Communications.* AMACOM, 1991.

Weiner, Richard. *Professional's Guide to Public Relations Services.* AMACOM, 1988.

PUBLICLY HELD COMPANY

A publicly held company exists when that company's stock is owned by members of the general public. The stock of a publicly held company is openly traded. In order for a company to be publicly held, it must be organized as a corporation. A corporation is a legal form of business that is established by a corporate charter granted by a particular state. The corporate charter establishes the corporation as a separate legal entity from its owners. The corporation is said to be a "legal person" and may enter into agreements, make contracts, and sue or be sued.

A corporation may be publicly or privately owned. In the case of a privately owned, or closely held, corporation, all of the stock is concentrated in the hands of a few individuals. When the privately held corporation first issues its stock, it is not offered for sale to the general public. On the other hand, the stock of a publicly held corporation is offered to the general public for sale. A privately held company may decide "to go public." That is, it makes a stock offering to the general public in order to raise capital. The first public stock offering of a company is known as its initial public offering (IPO).

The owners of a corporation, whether public or private, are its common stockholders. There are two types of stock, common and preferred. Preferred stockholders generally receive a stated dividend of a specific amount. Common stockholders receive a dividend based on corporate profits, although in some cases common stock pays no dividend. The corporation's charter specifies how many shares and what types of stock it is allowed to issue. While both preferred stockholders and common stockholders are investors in the corporation and provide it with capital, it is the common stockholders who actually own the firm.

In a privately held corporation, the owners and managers may be the same individuals. That is not the case with a publicly held company. A distinction is made between a publicly held corporation's owners and its managers. While the shareholders own the firm, the company's managers, executives, and directors run the firm. The **board of directors** is responsible for running the corporation to maximize profits for the shareholders. In practice the corporate directors establish corporate policy, make major decisions, and hire managers and others to oversee the daily operations of the corporation. Shareholders can express their satisfaction or displeasure with the board of directors of a publicly owned firm by voting them in or out of office.

While the shareholders of a publicly owned company are its owners, they are not liable for the actions of the company. Through the concept of limited liability, the shareholders may lose their investments in a company, but they have no personal liability beyond that. For example, they are not personally responsible for the debts of the corporation. Although they are owners of the corporation, the shareholders have in effect agreed to give up immediate control of the corporation. As a result, they are not held personally liable for the actions of the corporation.

Publicly held companies must follow the financial reporting and disclosure requirements of the **Securities and Exchange Commission**. The SEC regulations are designed to keep stockholders informed of the financial condition of the corporation. In addition, the SEC regulates all stock offerings and requires that new stock offerings be registered and fully described in a document called a prospectus. Privately held corporations, on the other hand, are not required to make public their profits and other financial results.

Publicly held companies are responsible for much of the business activity of the United States. Corporations that have the ability to raise capital by selling shares of stock to the general public can accumulate large amounts of capital for use in their business. Successful and relatively young privately held companies often attempt to become publicly held companies when their management believes there is enough public confidence in their ability to turn a profit. However, it must be remembered that not all corporations are publicly held, and there are some very large corporations that remain privately held.

[David Bianco]

PURCHASING POWER

Purchasing power refers to the amount of goods and services a fixed amount of money can purchase. The purchasing power of the dollar is related to changes in prices for different goods and services. Published price indices periodically measure the prices of commodities, retail prices, and prices for the economy as a whole. When prices for commodities increase, the purchasing power of the commodity dollar decreases. When retail prices increase, the purchasing power of the retail dollar decreases. And when prices for the economy as a whole, as reported in the consumer price index (CPI), increase, then the purchasing power of the consumer dollar decreases.

Individuals living on fixed incomes are those who are most affected by price increases and corresponding decreases in purchasing power. Payments to such individuals, including government Social Security payments and a variety of pension payments from private industry, are often tied to changes in the consumer price index. When the consumer price index rises and the purchasing power of the dollar decreases, pension and Social Security payments typically add what is known as a cost of living factor. These addi-

tional payments are made to individuals living on fixed incomes in an attempt to maintain the level of their purchasing power when prices have gone up.

In order to more accurately reflect the purchasing power of the dollar, economic statistics are usually reported in current dollars and in constant dollars. Constant dollars are measured against a base year in which a current dollar equals a constant dollar. Then for years before and after the base year, a current dollar is multiplied by a figure known as an implicit deflator to obtain the equivalent value in constant dollars. The deflator takes into account price increases and, depending on the behavior of prices, may change from year to year.

Reporting economic statistics in terms of constant dollars enables economists to compare economic performance from one year to another. Increases of such economic measures as the **gross national product** (GNP) or disposable personal income that are reported in current dollars would not accurately measure increases in productivity or in real income. Rather, much of the increase in GNP and disposable personal income would simply be due to inflationary factors, such as price increases. However, when such statistics are reported in constant dollars, then the effect of price increases is eliminated and a truer picture of actual production or purchasing power is given.

Economists refer to income reported in current dollars as money income, and income reported in constant dollars as real income. Real income provides a measure of purchasing power, since it takes into account the effect of price changes. When people speak of a dollar not being what it used to be, they mean that it no longer has the purchasing power it once had.

[David Bianco]

PUT-CALL PARITY

Put-call parity is a relationship that must exist in order to prevent **arbitrage** profits in a situation where puts and calls on the same underlying stock with identical exercise prices and expiration dates are trading simultaneously.

Let

C_o = call price at t = $\varnothing$
P_o = put price at t = $\varnothing$
E_1 = exercise price at t = 1
S_o = current market price of underlying stock
i = current market rate of interest

S_1 = market price of underlying stock at expiration

In order to avoid arbitrage, identical assets (i.e., investment portfolios that provide the same payoff) must sell for the same payoff. For example, each of the following investment portfolios provide the same payoff at option expiration:

Portfolio 1:

Buy Put and Share of Stock
Cost of Portfolio: $P_o + S_o$
Payoff at Expiration:
    If $S_1 > E_1$, put is worthless,
    portfolio value = S_1
    If $S_1 < E_1$, exercise put,
    portfolio value = E_1

Portfolio 2:

Buy Call and make bank deposit equal to present value of exercise price

$$\left[\frac{E_1}{(1 + i)^1} \right]$$

Cost of Portfolio:

$$C_o + \frac{E_1}{(1 + i)}$$

Payoff at expiration:
    If $S_1 > E_1$, use bank balance of E_1 to exercise call, portfolio value = S_1
    If $S_1 < E_1$, call is worthless, portfolio value = E_1

Since Portfolio 1 and Portfolio 2 have the same payoff, they are identical assets and must sell for the same price. Therefore,

$$P_o + S_o = C_o + \frac{E_1}{(1 + i)^1}.$$

The above equation is called the put-call parity theorem, and it must hold in order to avoid the existence of an arbitrage opportunity.

[Glen Wolfe]

QUALITY CIRCLES

The interest of U.S. manufacturers in quality circles (or quality control circles) was sparked by the dramatic improvements in the quality and economic competitiveness of Japanese goods in the post-World War II years. In their volume *Japanese Quality Circles and Productivity*, Ross and Ross defined a quality circle as follows: ''A quality circle is a small group of employees doing similar or related work who meet regularly to identify, analyze, and solve product-quality and production problems and to improve general operations. The circle is a relatively autonomous unit (ideally about ten workers), usually led by a supervisor or a senior worker and organized as a work unit.''

Quality circles were generally associated with **Japanese management and manufacturing techniques**. The introduction of quality circles in Japan in the post-War years was inspired by the lectures of W. Edwards Deming (1900-1993), a statistician for the U.S. government. The newly-formed Union of Japanese Scientists and Engineers was familiar with Deming's work and heard that he would be coming to Japan in 1950 to advise the Allied occupation government. Accepting JUSE's invitation, Deming addressed Japanese industry's top fifty executives.

Deming based his proposals on the experience of U.S. firms operating under wartime industrial standards during World War II. Noting that American management had typically given line managers and engineers about 85 percent of responsibility for quality control and only about 15 percent to production workers, Deming argued that these shares should be reversed. Production processes should be re-designed to more fully account for quality control, and all employees in a firm from top down should understand statistical control technologies and undergo continuous education on quality control. Quality circles were the means by which this continuous education was to take place for production workers.

Were Japanese firms to adopt the system of quality controls he advocated, Deming predicted that nations around the world would be imposing import quotas on Japanese products within five years. His prediction was vindicated. Deming's ideas became very influential in Japan, and in 1951, JUSE established the annual corporate and individual Deming awards for achievements in quality improvement. Deming was also awarded the Second Order Medal of the Sacred Treasure from Emperor Hirohito for his contributions to the Japanese economy. A 1954 lecture series in Japan by American quality control expert Dr. J.M. Juran gave further impetus to the development of quality control circles.

The principles of quality circles emphasized the importance of preventing defects from occurring rather than relying on product inspection following a production process. Quality circles also attempted to minimize the scrap and downtime that resulted from part and product defects. Deming's idea that improving quality could increase productivity led to the development in Japan of the **Total Quality** Control (TQC) concept, in which quality and productivity are viewed as two sides of a coin. TQC also required that a manufacturer's suppliers make use of quality circles.

Quality circles often rely on visual representations such as scatter diagrams, flow charts and cause-and-effect diagrams. In one common format, various aspects of the production process were categorized by materials, manpower, methods, and machines. The reliance on statistical representations of the production process and statistical production controls was another of Deming's legacies in Japan.

Quality circles in Japan were part of a system of relatively cooperative **labor-management relations**, involving company unions and lifetime employment guarantees for many full-time permanent employees. Consistent with this decentralized, enterprise-oriented system, quality circles provided a means by which production workers were encouraged to participate in company matters and by which management could benefit from production workers intimate knowledge of the production process.

Recommendations from employees played an important role in Japan, and two associations, the Japanese Association of Suggestion Systems and the Japan Human Relations Association, were developed to improve the process. These associations reported that in 1980 alone, changes resulting from employee suggestions resulted in savings of $10 billion for Japanese firms and bonuses of $4 billion for Japanese employees.

Active American interest in Japanese quality control began in the early-1970s, when U.S. aerospace manufacturer Lockheed organized a tour of Japanese industrial plants. This trip marked a turning point in the previously established pattern, in which Japanese managers had made educational tours of industrial plants in the United States. Lockheed's visit resulted in the gradual establishment of quality circles in its factories beginning in 1974. Within two years, Lockheed estimated that its fifteen quality circles had saved nearly $3 million, with a ratio of savings to cost of six to one.

As Lockheed's successes became known, other firms in the aerospace industry began adopting quality circles, including Hughes Aircraft, Northrop, Sperry Vickers, Martin Marietta, and Westinghouse. Thereafter quality circles spread rapidly throughout the U.S. economy; by 1980, over one-half of firms in the *Fortune* 500 had implemented or were planning on implementing quality circles. By the early-1980s, General Motors Corp. had established about 100 quality circles among its Buick, Oldsmobile, Cadillac, Chevrolet, and Fisher Body divisions.

In the early-1990s, the U.S. **National Labor Relations Board (NLRB)** made important rulings regarding the legality of certain forms of quality circles. These rulings were based on the 1935 Wagner Act's prohibition of company unions and management-dominated labor organizations.

In December of 1992, the NLRB ruled that Electromation Inc. of Elkhart, Indiana was operating unlawful quality circles and employee-involvement programs, referred to as 'action committees' by the firm. These programs were found unlawful in that they were established by the firm, that their agendas were dominated by the firm, and that they addressed the conditions of employment within the firm. The NLRB stated that its ruling was not a general indictment against quality circles and labor-management cooperation programs, but was aimed specifically at the practices of Electromation. Electromation had been a non-union firm, but was unionized by the Teamsters shortly after the 'action committees' were eliminated.

The NLRB made a similar ruling against E.I. du Pont de Nemours & Co., a unionized firm, in June of 1993. The NLRB ruled that Du Pont's seven labor-management committees in its Deepwater, New Jersey plant were in effect labor organizations that were used to bypass negotiations with the plant's union, the Chemical Workers Association. The NLRB stated once again that its ruling was limited to the facts in the case at hand. Nonetheless, a number of employer representatives expressed their concern that the ruling would hinder the development of labor-management cooperation programs of all kinds.

[David Kucera]

FURTHER READING:

Gryna, Frank M., Jr. *Quality Circles: A Team Approach to Problem Solving.* AMACON, 1981.

"New Rules on Employee Involvement," *Industry Week*, February 1, 1993.

McMillan, Charles J. *The Japanese Industrial System.* Walter de Gruyter, 1984.

Noble, Barbara Presley. "Worker-Participation Programs are Found Illegal," *New York Times*, June 8, 1993.

"Recent NLRB Decisions Shed Light on Employees Rights," *US Glass, Metal and Glazing*, February 15, 1993.

Ross, Joel E. and William C. Ross. *Japanese Quality Circles and Productivity.* Reston Publishing Company, 1982.

Sasaki, Naoto and David Hutchins. *The Japanese Approach to Product Quality.* Pergamon Press, 1984.

Uchitelle, Louis. "Workers Seek Executive Role, Study Says," *New York Times*, December 5, 1994.

QUALITY CONTROL

The American Society for Quality Control's (ASQC) *Glossary and Tables for Statistical Quality Control* defines quality control as:

"the operational techniques and the activities which sustain a quality of product or service that will satisfy given needs; also the use of such techniques and activities . . . the aim of quality is to provide quality that is satisfactory, e.g., safe, adequate, dependable, and economical, . . . [This requires] integrating several related steps including proper specification...; design of the product ... to meet the requirements; production [processes which] ... meet the specification; inspection to determine [the degree of conformance] ... to specification; and review of usage to provide for revision of specification [if necessary]."

These steps are required for a firm to design, produce, market, and profit from a quality product. "Control charts" are one technique used in sustaining quality control. Statistical process studies are also an important tool in improving quality by reducing process variation. "Total Quality Control" (TQC) or "**Total Quality Management**" (TQM) refers to quality control beyond the "sustaining" of quality.

Dr. Kaoru Ishikawa, recipient of many awards, including the Deming Prize, defines total quality control as a system of introducing and implementing quality technologies into various departments of a company, such as engineering, production, sales, and service, for the purpose of satisfying customers. He states that viewed chronologically, TQC is only the first stage of company-wide quality control (CWQC). CWQC incorporates quality function deployment (QFD), whereas TQC does not. QFD is a design procedure which introduces quality control in product development. It is a formal mechanism which guarantees that "the voice of the customer" is heard throughout all the phases of manufacturing a product or providing a service.

As Besterfield states in his book *Quality Control*, the deliverance of a quality product or service requires the responsible integration of all the firm's departments: marketing, product engineering, purchasing, manufacturing engineering, manufacturing, inspection and testing, packaging and shipping, and product service. Total quality control or total quality management is far more than sustaining quality, as it may include control systems, employee relations and organizational behavior, statistical process control, and Japanese management techniques.

Beginning in the Middle Ages, the maintenance of quality was generally guaranteed by the guilds. They required long periods of training, which instilled in craftsmen a strong pride in the quality of their work.

The Industrial Revolution initiated the specialization of labor. Consequently, workers no longer produced the whole product, only a part. This transformation lead to a decline in workmanship. At first, quality was not greatly diminished since manufacturing processes were fairly simple in the early days of the Industrial Revolution. However, as manufacturing processes became more complicated and work more specialized, the trend toward post-manufactured product inspection began.

During the 19th century, modern industrial systems arose. At this time in the United States, Frederick W. Taylor's "scientific management" dominated. His philosophy placed work and production planning exclusively in the hands of management and industrial engineers. (The ultimate expression of Taylorism was Henry Ford's moving assembly line). Before scientific management, quality was manufacturing's responsibility. Since meeting production deadlines became the production manager's main priority, the responsibility for quality was placed increasingly in the hands of the "chief inspector" and the quality control department.

In 1924, at Bell Telephone Laboratories, Walter A. Shewhart developed statistical control charts. These charts pinpointed the sources of variation within processes and were used to control the quality of, and to improve the processes that delivered, the output. It is a total quality management principal that, generally, quality is maintained and improved through the reduction of process variation.

The introduction and implementation of Shewhart's control charts inaugurated statistical quality control. The value of statistical quality control became obvious during World War II. Unfortunately, American management failed to understand this value, and its brief and limited application was abandoned after the War as many companies viewed quality control as a wartime effort only. It seemed unnecessary in the booming postwar years when quantity seemed to be all that mattered.

In 1946, the American Society for Quality Control was founded. Under its auspices, quality professionals developed failure analysis methods to problem-solve, quality engineers became engaged in early product design, and a number of companies began to test the environmental performance of products.

In 1950, W. Edwards Deming (1900-1993), a statistician who had worked with Shewhart at Bell Labs, was invited by the Union of Japanese Scientists and Engineers (JUSE) to speak to Japan's leading industrialists. He presented a series of lectures on statistical quality techniques and on the responsibilities of top management for delivering quality products and services. The Japanese industrialists and engineers embraced Deming's teaching, and Japanese quality, productivity, and competitive position significantly increased. Under Deming, Joseph M. Juran, and Armand V. Feigenbaum, the concept of quality control, no longer viewed as principally a corrective activity, was extended to all areas, from design to sales.

During the 1960s, 1970s, and 1980s, Japanese management and engineering professionals such as Ishikawa, Imai, and Taguchi—the latter having developed the statistical design of experiments for quality—have built on Deming's and Juran's ideas.

SUSTAINING QUALITY: IMAI AND KAIZEN TECHNOLOGY

A crucial aspect of TQC is maintaining the quality of existing processes, of processes pertaining to new products or services, and of processes resulting from innovative technologies (discoveries based on new scientific principles). Of course, design of experiments can assure that the new product has quality built into it and then the problem becomes one of maintaining and improving the quality. An example of an innovative technology is **computer aided design** and **computer aided manufacturing** (CAD-CAM) as such a project revolutionizes existing systems.

Improving and sustaining the quality of processes is designated Kaizen technology. The activity of improving is included because Kaizen technology assumes that any process, based on innovative technology or otherwise, is subject to steady deterioration (entropy) unless constant efforts are made to maintain and improve the process's standards. Kaizen technology is the accumulation of small technological improvements continually made upon the production or service process.

Dr. Donald J. Wheeler, co-author of *Understanding Statistical Process Control*, further describes entropy: "Entropy is relentless. Every process will naturally and inevitably migrate toward the state of chaos. The only way this migration can be overcome is by continually repairing the effects of entropy." Having the ability to repair a process assumes that its effects are known. This knowledge can be achieved through control charts and process capability studies. Unlike today's common U.S. management practices, which are based on the Taylor model, Kaizen technology requires virtually every employee's personal contribution and effort to quality. This requires a substantial management commitment of time and effort; infusions of capital are no substitute for this investment in time, effort, and people. Unlike the Taylor model, Kaizen technology assumes that all employees can contribute to the improvement of the production processes both in terms of quality and productivity.

Taylor argued that all important knowledge and information was known by management, and it was the exclusive responsibility of management to use "science" to establish an optimal production system. This optimal system was to be based on the close supervision of all work procedures. Workers were to follow, without deviation, the procedures proscribed by management. Their performances were to be judged on the basis of the standards of these procedures.

Cooperation within such a system meant that the workers would adhere to the directives of management. Taylor argued if any deviations occurred, they were caused by the worker's failure to adhere to his job specifications. Many in management believe this is not "science" because science recognizes that variation generally exists within any process whether or not specifications are meet.

It is the opinion of a number of managers and scientist that management based on the Taylor model is incompatible with achieving as Kaizen technology does, long-run and long-lasting (but undramatic) quality improvements because such improvements only come about when workers are actively involved in the production processes. The Kaizen approach asserts that those closest to the work have a great deal of skill, energy, and knowledge that must be tapped. Many believe the Taylor model ignores this work force potential; it does not support the empowerment of employees. The Kaizen approach stresses gradual and consistent changes and improvements as a result of both labor and management slowly learning more and more about the processes and systems in which they are involved.

Consequently, Japanese firms are committed to the notion that the customer comes first. However, for most U.S. firms, there is considerable doubt that this is so. Delavigne and Robertson state that, "despite lip service to the importance of the customer, observations still show that most companies concentrate on what they can get from customers (money, profits) than on what they are going to provide to the customer (the quality of the product, and extensions to the product such as spare parts, courteous support, a product line that grows with the customer's needs, and so on)."

Delavigne and Robertson use the term "Neo-Taylorism" in describing current U.S. management practices and conclude that "the state of management was even worse at the end of the 1980s than when the decade began."

SUSTAINING AND IMPROVING QUALITY: TWO ILLUSTRATIVE CASES OF KAIZEN TECHNOLOGY

The first case is the Calsonic Corporation. Calsonic manufactures a "uniquely-designed flat motor" for automobiles. Instead of wire-wound magnetic cores, Calsonic uses laminated copper sheets which are perforated by high speed stamping machines to form the electromagnetic circuitry. This technology used by Calsonic was conceived over twenty-five years ago by a French engineer. He sold the rights to an American firm which was not able to commercialize it. Calsonic then purchased the rights and through a joint venture with the Yaskawa Electric Company found a way to manufacture the motor.

Calsonic feels that this manufacturing success was only possible due to Kaizen technology. Many Calsonic employees made technological improvements on the original idea, especially in the areas of production engineering, precision stamping technology, product quality, assembly design, and machine maintenance.

The Calsonic Corporation's application of Kaizen technology underlines Masaaki Imai's observation that Kaizen technology "includes those actions which make the best use of the resources at hand (such as people, machines, facilities, technology and so forth) . . . to improve little by little—the point is not to use money (unnecessarily)." Sustaining and improving the quality of output means quality control. For a firm to have the ability to do so requires TQM, and the application of such techniques as control charts and process capability studies. This is different from the common American managerial approach of attempting to find a quick fix, e.g., the attempt to find a new optimal situation by some new capital expenditure.

In the Calsonic example, employee involvement is critical. However, Kaizen technology does not assume that workers and management have identical roles. Certainly both labor and management spend time on quality improvement activities, with first-line supervisors and middle management spending the most time. But the Kaizen approach asserts that workers spend the most time on maintenance activities that sustain quality. As one moves up the management ladder, that time decreases. Middle and top management spend far more time on innovative technology and new product development.

This is in contrast to the Taylor model, which asserts that workers must spend their time exclusively on maintenance and none on improvement. As a result, management based on the Taylor model, according to many administrators, fails to tap the tremendous pool of information, knowledge, skill, and energy of the workers.

The second example of sustaining and improving quality is dynamic random-access memory chips, DRAMs. Most of the technology for this high-tech product was developed in the West, but today Japanese companies hold seventy-five percent of the world market.

The most important break-even factor for the manufacture of this product is the defective percentage. To control this factor, Kaizen technology is necessary since any minor change in the manufacturing environment must be checked with great care to guarantee uniform production. At one Japanese plant, a small increase in the defective rate was noticed for a few hours one day. But, at first, no abnormal manufac-turing conditions were discovered. Further investigation revealed the problem. A truck had parked by a ventilation tunnel for the DRAM plant's air conditioning system. The defective chips were caused by particles from the truck's exhaust. A new standard was introduced at the plant which prevented the problem from recurring. This new standard, obviously, resulted in sustaining and improving the quality of the output.

For quality control to occur, the top management of any company must have totally committed itself to TQC or TQM. Sustaining and improving the quality of manufacturing or service processes requires such tools as control charts, process capability studies, business ethics, organizational change and development, and excellent employee relations.

SEE ALSO: Taguchi Methods

[Dr. Peter B. Webb]

FURTHER READING:

American Society for Quality Control: Statistics Division. *Glossary & Tables for Statistical Quality Control*. American Society for Quality Control, 1983.

Besterfield, Dale H. *Quality Control*. Prentice Hall, 1990.

Bhote, Keki R. *World Class Quality*. Amacom, 1991.

Bossert, James L. *Quality Function Deployment: A Practitioner's Approach*. ASQC Quality Press, 1991.

Box, G. E. P., William G. Hunter, and J. Stuart Hunter. *Statistics for Experimenters: An Introduction to Design, Data Analysis, and Model Building*. John Wiley & Sons, 1978.

Delavigne, Kenneth T., and J. Daniel Robertson. *Deming's Profound Changes: When Will the Sleeping Giant Awaken?* PTR Prentice Hall, 1994.

Deming, W. Edwards. *Out of the Crisis*. MIT Center for Advanced Engineering Studies, 1986.

DeVor, Richard E., et. al. *Statistical Quality Design and Control*. Macmillan Publishing Company, 1992.

Feigenbaum, Armand V. *Total Quality Control*. American Society for Quality Control, 1991.

Gitlow, Howard, et. al. *Tools and Methods for the Improvement of Quality*. Richard D Irwin, Inc., 1989.

Imai, Masaaki. *Kaizen: The Key to Japan's Economic Success*. Random House Business Division, 1986.

Ishikawa, Kaoru. *Guide to Quality Control*. Asian Productivity Organization, 1987.

——. "Quality and Standardization Programs for Economic Success," *Quality Progress*. January, 1984, pp. 16-20.

Lochner, Robert H., and Joseph E. Matar. *Designing for Quality: An Introduction to the Best of Taguchi and Western Methods of Statistical Experimental Design*. ASQC Quality Press, 1990.

Taylor, Frederick W. *The Principles of Scientific Management*. Harper & Row, 1911.

Thurow, Lester C. "A Weakness in Process Technology," *Science*. December 18, 1987, pp.1659-1663.

Wheeler, Donald J., and David S. Chambers. *Understanding Statistical Process Control*. Statistical Process Controls, Inc., 1986.

Yoshida, Shuichi. "Two Technological Developments," *Kaizen Communique*. January, 1990, p. 3.

QUEUING THEORY

In its broadest sense, queuing theory is the study of contention for the use of a shared, but limited, resource. It is comprised of models and formulas that describe the relationships between service requests, congestion, and delay.

Queuing theory may be extended to cover a wide variety of contention situations, such as how customer check-out lines form (and how they can be minimized), how many calls a telephone switch can handle, how many computer users can share a mainframe, and how many doors an office building should have. These are diverse applications, but their solutions all involve the same dynamics.

The nature of the queue is one of cost shifting and burden averaging. A provider of some service whose resources are limited may serve only a small number of people at a time. Any number of people beyond that are obliged to wait their turn.

Assuming everyone's time is worth something, those who must wait for service are expending a valuable possession—their time. By waiting in line, the service provider is ensured that none of his resources will stand idle. In effect, the waiting customer is forced to pay in time for the privilege of being served, shifting costs from the service provider to the customer.

In a post office, where there is usually one line but several clerks, the next person to be served is the one who has stood longest in line. The burden of the wait is shared by all those in line—the larger the line, the longer the average wait.

The burden is less equally shared in a grocery store, where each clerk has a line. If one line happens to have five simple orders, and another has five patrons with large orders, coupons, and fruit to weigh, the simple line will probably move much faster. Those lucky enough to be in that line will be served before those in the complex line. Thus, grocery shoppers will not share the burden of the wait as equally as in the post office.

The question for the service provider is simple: how to provide good service. Indeed, the highest level of service would be achieved by providing resources equal to the number of patrons; a cashier for every shopper. However, this would be extremely costly and logistically impractical; dozens of cashiers would stand idle between orders.

To minimize **costs**, the manager may provide only one cashier, forcing everyone into a long, slow-moving line. Customers tiring of the wait would be likely to abandon their groceries and begin shopping at a new store. The question arises: what is an acceptable level of service at an acceptable cost to the provider?

These examples seem simple, but the questions they raise extend far beyond the average grocery store. Queuing theory is the basis for traffic management—the maintenence of smooth traffic flow, keeping congestion and bottlenecks to a minimum. Once the nature of the traffic flow is understood, solutions may be offered to ease the demands on a system, thereby increasing its efficiency and lowering the costs of operating it.

HISTORICAL DEVELOPMENT OF QUEUING THEORY

The first to develop a viable queuing theory was the French mathematician S.D. Poisson (1781-1840). Poisson created a distribution function to describe the probability of a prescribed outcome after repeated iterations of independent trials. Because Poisson used a statistical approach, the distributions he used could be applied to any situation where excessive demands are made on a limited resource.

The most important application of queuing theory occurred during the late 1800s, when telephone companies were faced with the problem of how many operators to place on duty at a given time. At the time, all calls were switched manually by an operator who physically connected a wire to a switchboard. Each customer required the operator only for the few seconds it took to relay directions and have the plug inserted and the time recorded. After the call was set up, the operator was free to accept another call. The problem for an early telephone traffic engineer was how many switchboards should be set up in an area.

Beyond that, supervisors were faced with the problem of how many operators to keep on the boards. Too many, and most operators would remain idle for minutes at a time. Too few, and operators would be overwhelmed by service requests, perhaps never catching up until additional help was added.

Often, callers who were unable to gain an operator's attention simply hung up in frustration and, suspecting it was a busy time for the operators, would wait several minutes before trying again. Others stayed on the line, waiting their turn to talk to the operator. Yet others would call repeatedly, hoping the operator would be sufficiently annoyed by repeated calls to serve them next.

These behavioral discrepancies caused problems for traffic engineers because they affected the level of demand for service from an operator. A call turned away was lost, not to come back until much later, and was effectively out of the system. Callers who held were more predictable, while repeat callers only increased demands on the system by appearing as several requests. Poisson's formula was meant only for the latter situation.

Because few callers acted as aggressively as the Poisson formula assumed, systems were often overengineered, resulting in a substantial waste of resources. Operator offices were equipped with 24 switchboards when they never used more than 20.

A Danish mathematician named A.K. Erlang developed a different approach to traffic engineering based on Poisson's work. He established formulas for calls that are abandoned (called Erlang-B) and for those that are held until service is granted (Erlang-C).

The Poisson and two Erlang formulas made some basic assumptions about the system. Because user behavior is unpredictable, the types of calls that are received are assumed to be randomly distributed. That is, unusual calling characteristics in one period are likely to be normalized over time yielding a more normal distribution.

EXAMPLES OF QUEUING THEORY APPLICATIONS

The most unusual recurring period is the ''busy hour,'' which provides a pattern upon which the system should be engineered. For example, if a system receives its highest number of calls between 9 and 10 a.m., the office should be equipped with enough switchboards to handle that level of requests. The issue of how many operators to assign depends on calling patterns from one hour to the next.

What is interesting about the Poisson and Erlang formulas is that the relationship between operators and congestion is not parallel. For example, assume that 10 operators are inundated by 30 percent more calls than they usually handle. A supervisor calls in an 11th operator and, even though the rate of incoming service requests remains constant, the backlog will gradually fall. After the backlog is eliminated, the 11th operator may actually force others to go idle for extended periods.

We might assume that 10 operators handling 130 percent of their normal volume would require 13 operators. In fact, the addition of only one is more than enough to resolve the problem. This is because repeated calls are disposed of, and the aggregate wait of everyone holding (which grows multiplicatively) is reduced one factor at a time. The backlog simply cannot regenerate itself fast enough.

Put differently, 11 operators may be able to dispose of service requests at a faster rate than they are coming in. It may take a few minutes to eliminate the backlog, but the backlog will decline eventually.

Consider the situation in a grocery store where there are five lines open and 12 people in each line. The addition of only one extra cashier will quickly reduce the lines to one or two people, even though the same number of people are entering checkout lines. When the backlog is eliminated, the sixth cashier may be taken off and put on some other job.

As well as a system may be engineered, unusual nonrandom disturbances can cause the system to collapse in spectacular fashion. This was demonstrated by a problem with the New York water system during the 1950s. Engineers discovered that water pressure dropped significantly—and for firemen, perilously—during a period of hours every Sunday evening. A study revealed an unusual culprit: Milton Berle.

The comedian hosted an immensely popular weekly television show every Sunday which was watched by nearly everyone with a set. When the show went to a commercial break, tens of thousands of people, having finished dinner, retreated to their bathrooms at the same time.

With thousands of toilets being flushed within minutes of each other, sewers were inundated. More importantly, toilet tanks were refilling, each consuming two or three gallons of fresh water. The coordinated demand for water in a brief period of time virtually eliminated water pressure. In fact, some toilets took a half hour to refill, and water pressure took hours to recover.

Serious consideration was given to cancelling the show. The solution, however, was relatively simple. The addition of only a few more water towers was sufficient to maintain adequate water pressure. In essence, the system was reengineered to handle more demanding peaks.

This situation may be repeated in a telephone system when everyone is motivated to place a call at the same time. During the 1989 San Francisco earthquake, vast numbers of people in the metropolitan area attempted to make a call at the same time—immediately after the quake subsided—hoping to learn whether friends and relatives were safe. Although the switching systems were automated, they were completely unable to handle the volume of requests for dial tone.

Only a small percentage of calls (enough to meet the capacity of the system) were allowed to go through. Indeed, radio and television reporters urged people to stay off the lines so that emergency calls could be handled.

There was no need to reengineer the system because the occurrence of earthquakes, while random, are not consistently repeated. It would be uneconomic to engineer the telephone network for peak usages that occur only once every decade or so. As a result, every earthquake yields a temporary breakdown in the telephone network.

Other slightly less offensive instances occur every time a radio host offers a prize to "caller number x." Telephone companies and public officials have convinced many radio stations to discontinue the practice.

FUTURE APPLICATIONS OF QUEUING THEORY

The most relevant and promising future applications of queuing theory are likely to occur in the areas of computer science and manufacturing systems. In computer science, queuing is a necessary consideration in contention for processing resources. Given that the highest-cost component in advanced computation is processing power, systems are moving increasingly toward network solutions in which processing power is distributed. The result of this trend toward greater distribution is that systems will contend for access to a network and to diverse processors and files.

In manufacturing, queuing is a necessary element of flexible systems in which factors of production may be continually adjusted to handle periodic increases in demand for manufacturing capacity. Excess capacity in periods of low demand may be converted into other forms of working capital, rather than be forced to spent those periods as idle, nonproductive assets.

The concept of **flexible manufacturing systems** is very interesting. Consider that today a company such as Boeing endures long periods of low demand for its commercial aircraft (a result of cycles in the air transportation industry), but must quickly tool up for expanded production when demand rises. The company must alternately open and mothball millions of dollars worth of manufacturing capacity (and hire and lay off thousands of workers) through every demand cycle.

During periods of low demand, floor space, machinery and inventories remain tied up. If, on the other hand, demand flows could be better managed, Boeing could convert these assets to more productive applications. The primary focus of queuing theory on flexible manufacturing remains centered on machine reliability and depreciation and processing and cycle times.

[John Simley]

FURTHER READING:

Eatwell, J., ed. *The New Palgrave Dictionary of Economics*. London: Macmillan, 1987.

Green, Harry James. *The Business One Irwin Handbook of Telecommunications*, 2nd ed. Homewood, IL: Business One Irwin, 1991.

R

RANDOM WALK THEORY

The random walk theory concerns the random behavior of stock prices and holds that the prices of stocks change independent of one another. Although randomness had previously been studied in a business context to little notice (for instance, the Frenchman Louis Bachelier's 1980 doctoral thesis on random processes and food economist Holbrook Working's 1934 paper on the random behavior of commodity prices), it was Maurice Kendall's paper in 1953 that caused a flood of controversy. Looking for regular price cycles, the statistician found that the prices wandered, coining the term "random walk." The reason Kendall's paper survived ongoing scrutiny was due to the development of **computers**: the theory was supported by numerous calculations and random number generators.

In a study of various model evaluation statistics, in the short term fundamental exchange-rate models perform no better than random walk models. Over the long term, however, error-correction terms perform significantly better. This coincides with a 1992 study that showed risk is a two-component quantity in determining the behavior of stock prices. The asset class (stock, bond, cash) is one component; the length of time is the other. Therefore, while stock prices in the short term exhibit a totally independent, relationship (or random walk), the long term tends toward growth.

Interestingly, Swedish stock prices have not exhibited the random walk pattern of U.S. stock prices during a 72-year period. The implications of such a finding are far-reaching when considering the establishment of a long-term stock portfolio.

The random walk can be most easily thought of as a coin toss. Richard A. Brealey and Stewart C. Myers use the following example: "You are given $100 to play a game. At the end of each week a coin is tossed. If it comes up heads, you win 3 percent of your investment. If it is tails, you lose 2.5 percent. Therefore your capital at the end of the first week is either $103.00 or $97.50. At the end of the second week the coin is tossed again." The possible outcomes are shown below.

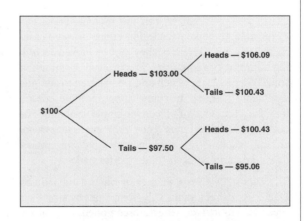

"This process is a random walk with a positive drift of .25 percent per week. (The drift is equal to the expected outcome: $0.5(3) + 0.5(-2.5) = .25\%$)."

[Valerie E. Wilson]

FURTHER READING:

Brealey, Richard A., and Stewart C. Myers. *Principles of Corporate Finance*. 4th ed. New York: McGraw-Hill, 1991.

Chinn, Menzie D., and Richard A. Meese. "Banking on Currency Forecasts: How Predictable Is Change in Money?" *Journal of International Economics*. February, 1995, p. 161.

Frennberg, Per, and Bjorn Hansson. "Testing the Random Walk Hypothesis on Swedish Stock Prices: 1919-1990," *Journal of Banking & Finance*. February, 1993, p. 175.

Holton, Glyn A. "Time: The Second Dimension of Risk." *Financial Analysts Journal*. November-December, 1992, p. 38.

Kendall, M. G. "The Analysis of Economic Time-Series, Part I. Prices." *Journal of the Royal Statistical Society*. 1953, pp. 11-25.

Working, Holbrook. "A Random Difference Series for Use in the Analysis of Time Series." *Journal of the American Statistical Association*. March, 1934, pp. 11-24.

RANKING

A business ranking is one in which different companies or products are listed, or ranked, in order based on specific criteria. Within a particular industry, companies are typically ranked by criteria appropriate to that industry. Banks would be ranked in terms of their dollar volume. Advertising agencies are ranked according to their annual billings. Insurance companies may be ranked according to premiums earned. General businesses could be ranked by sales volume, profits, number of employees, and other criteria.

A ranking tells at a glance who the top performers are in a given category. *Business Rankings Annual*, published by Gale Research, contains approximately 10,000 different rankings that have been published during the year. Examples include the top ten advertisers, top ten retailers, top ten mutual funds, etc. Firms may be ranked according to one or more criteria. In the case of retailers, they may be ranked according to profits per employee, sales, return on equity, or some other measure. Each criterion is used to compile a separate ranking. In some cases, multiple criteria may be combined to create a single ranking. The ranking of mutual funds tends to be based on several criteria, resulting in a more complex indexing procedure to determine each fund's performance.

Dun's Business Rankings, published annually by Dun & Bradstreet, ranks U.S. companies by size. Two separate national rankings are compiled, one on the basis of sales volume, the other on the number of employees. In addition to the national rankings, the book ranks firms within each state and within industry category.

Perhaps the most well-known business ranking is the *Fortune* 500. Published annually in an April issue of *Fortune* magazine, the *Fortune* 500 ranks the top 500 U.S. companies by sales for the previous year. Through 1994, the *Fortune* 500 included only industrial companies. However, in 1995, the list included service and retail firms for the first time. *Fortune* editors said the change was made to reflect the growing importance of those sectors of the economy. *Fortune* also publishes the Service 500 (May), the Global Industries 500 (July), and the Global Services 500 (August).

Product rankings are generally more complex, being based on multiple measures of performance. A ranking of personal computers, for example, might be based on such performance measures as the speed of its central processing unit (CPU), the speed at which it writes to and reads a file from a disk, and the time required to copy a file from one disk to another. Then, using a mathematical process called multidimensional scaling, it would be possible to obtain a single ranking of different computer models on the basis of all the relevant performance criteria.

Rankings are also used in the physical and social sciences. Rankings help interpret the results of survey research and are used in manufacturing quality control, for example. In whatever field they are used, rankings allow for the comparision of similar entities on the basis of fair and consistent criteria.

[David Bianco]

RATIOS

SEE: Financial Ratios; Price Earnings (PE) Ratios

REAL ESTATE

Real estate is land and all that is permanently a part of it, either on, or under, including water, trees, buildings, minerals, oil. "Real estate," also called "real property," is a term that developed in medieval times. When contests were held over the title of a piece of land, the person judged as rightful owner received the real (actual) property as the settlement of the dispute.

The term "real estate" today, is used to refer to land and the property on it, and to the real estate industry—including both domestic and commercial land, appurtenant property, the leasing of same, and financing of and investment in same.

In the selling and renting of both domestic and commercial real estate, brokers buy and sell and appraisers fix value. Property managers and a host of others work rentals. Another whole set of persons is involved with the financing of the purchase or rental and mortgage issues for purchase.

Because of the many facets of the industry, determining who are the largest firms requires asking further questions. What part of the industry? By what measure? Volume of sales? Number of brokers? Number of offices? The industry itself is at odds on ranking issues. A March 22, 1993 *Advertising Age* article documented the squabble over ranking issues between Century 21 and Re Max, two undisputably large players in domestic real estate.

Century 21 is one of the largest franchise real estate brokers in the United States, with Weichart Realtors operating nationally as one of the largest independent realtors. Trends in twentieth-century realty brokerage include the development of mortgage financing companies that handle financing and refinancing for domestic real estate sales, the increased training and professionalism of real estate broker and the use of the term "realtor," developed by the National Association of Realtors.

As a force in the economy, the real estate industry holds power in its own right. Real estate brokers and managers form the seventh-largest industry by receipts (nearly $75 billion in 1992) in the nation among nonmanufacturing and service industries. Investment in real estate development by individuals and businesses, for one's own or the firm's use and as speculation, grew to be a significant force in the 1990s. Real estate investment trusts (REITs) are, according to the Standard & Poor's *Industry Survey* of November, 3, 1994, a "formidable economic force." Standard and Poor's stated that "as of September 30, 1994, the REIT industry total market capitalization had ballooned to some $42.7 billion up from $8.7 billion as of year end 1990." Some of the major players in the REIT market are Development Diversified, Rouse Company, and Kimo Realty.

The two largest foreign investors in U.S. real estate are Canada and Japan; the strength of the yen has made U.S. real estate even more attractive to Japanese investors. The outlook for the future of real estate, both commercial and domestic, is tied to the fate of **interest rates**, to changes in the tax laws to make investment trusts easier to set up, and to the activities of REITs both in the stability of their investments and their activity in the stock market.

[Joan Leotta]

FURTHER READING:

"Banking." *Industry Surveys.* December 3, 1994, pp. B59-60.

Bergsman, Steve. "Choosing the REIT Stuff." *Black Enterprise.* February, 1995, pp. 57-58.

Hylton, Richard D. "Why Real Estate Stays Grounded." *Fortune.* December 13, 1993, pp. 141-143.

Kimelman, John. "What Recovery?" *Financial Planner.* February 21, 1995, pp. 68-69.

Levin, Gary. "Realty Firms Wage War over Ads." *Advertising Age.* March 22, 1993, p. 8.

"Two Real Estate Investment Trusts Agree to Merge." *New York Times.* February 28, 1995, p. D4.

REAL ESTATE INVESTMENT TRUSTS (REIT)

A real estate investment trust, (REIT), pronounced reet, is a corporation or trust that combines the capital of many investors to acquire or provide financing for all forms of **real estate**. A corporation or trust that qualifies as a REIT generally does not pay corporate income tax to the **Internal Revenue Service**. Most states honor this federal treatment and do not require REITs to pay state income tax either. This means that nearly all of a REIT's income is distributed to shareholders, without double taxation on the income. Unlike a partnership, a REIT cannot pass its tax losses onto its investors.

President Dwight D. Eisenhower signed the Real Estate Investment Trust Act of 1960, creating an industry that grew over the next 34 years to more than 270 REITs with combined real estate assets in excess of $60 billion. The basic provisions of the law have not changed since it was enacted, although several improvements have been made. REITs were created to provide investors with the opportunity to participate in the benefits of ownership of larger-scale commercial real estate or mortgage lending and receive an enhanced return because the income is not taxed at the REIT level.

In order for a corporation or trust to qualify as a REIT, it must comply with certain provisions within the Internal Revenue Code. As required by the tax code, a REIT must: be a corporation, business trust, or similar association; be managed by a **board of directors** or board of trustees; have shares that are fully-transferable; have a minimum of 100 shareholders; have no more than 50 percent of the shares held by five or fewer individuals during the last half of each taxable year; invest at least 75 percent of the total assets in real estate assets; derive at least 75 percent of gross income from rents from real property, or interest on mortgages on real property; derive no more than 30 percent of gross income from the sale of real property held for less than four years, securities held for less than one year, or certain prohibited transactions; and pay dividends of at least 95 percent of REIT taxable income.

The REIT industry started off slowly, following its 1960 inception. By 1968, industry assets totaled only $1 billion. By 1974, however, total assets exceeded $20 billion. But rising **interest rates**, a national **recession**, and an overbuilt real estate market affected the performance of the early REITs, and the industry experienced its first general shakeout.

A restructuring and stabilization period followed. 1984 tax law changes made competitive, tax-motivated real estate syndications less attractive, causing renewed growth in REITs.

According to Richard Saltzman, managing director and head of Merrill Lynch's Real Estate Investment Banking Division, the real watershed event for the industry was the tax law change of the late 1980s that permitted the management of properties directly by the REIT.

REIT industry analysts classify REITS in one of three investment approaches: equity REITs, mortgage REITs, and hybrid REITs. Equity REITs own real estate, and their revenue principally comes from rent. Mortgage REITs lend money to real estate owners, and their revenue principally is derived from interest earned on mortgage loans. Some mortgage REITs also invest in residuals of mortgage-backed securities. Hybrid REITs combine the investment strategies of both equity REITs and mortgage REITs.

Pension funds, endowment funds, insurance companies, bank trust departments, **mutual funds**, and investors—both U.S.-based as well as non-U.S.-based—own shares of REITs. An individual who chooses to invest in a REIT seeks to achieve current income distributions and long-term stock appreciation potential. REIT shares typically can be purchased for $2 to $40 each, with no minimum purchase required.

Over 80 percent of the REITs operating in the United States today are traded on the national stock exchanges, including the New York Stock Exchange, the American Stock Exchange, and the NASDAQ National Market System. Dozens of REITs, however, are not traded on a stock exchange.

Analyzing the performance and value of current REITs values is not an easy task. Asset values may be derived using different rent multipliers and capitalization rates; but these values are derived from appraisal reports, which do not always reflect the same standards.

Rather than using asset values to analyze performance, the following criteria are recommended: 1) **management** (prospective investors in a particular REIT should carefully examine the experience level of the management team); and 2) future growth (which is contingent on the future income from the REIT's holdings). **Income**, in turn, depends on rent, which is influenced by vacancy levels, regional economic growth, and units available in an area. It is also affected to some degree by the sales level of the REIT's properties.

SEE ALSO: Banks and Banking; Dividends; Mortgages/Mortgage-Backed Securities; Stocks; Taxes and Taxation; Trusts and Trustees.

[Susan Bard Hall]

FURTHER READING:

Haight, G. Timothy, and Deborah Ann Ford. *REITs: New Opportunities in Real Estate Investment Trust Securities*. Chicago: Probus Publishing Company, 1987, pp. 49.

Real Estate Investment Trusts: Frequently Asked Questions about REITs. Washington, D.C.: National Association of Real Estate Investment Trusts, 1994.

The REIT Industry Today. Washington, D.C.: National Association of Real Estate Investment Trusts.

REBATES

Rebates, widely known as refunds, are a popular tool used by businesses to promote their products and services. The term "rebate" derives from the Middle English *rebaten*, meaning "to deduct." Rebates are distinct from coupons and other forms of discounting in that they reimburse a customer for part of the purchase price following rather than at the time of sale. A relatively new method of promotion, rebating evolved from the marketing technique of offering coupons when couponing proved broadly successful, in the latter half of the twentieth century. Rebates were initially offered by producers of grocery-store goods and subsequently by manufacturers of nonfood items. Currently, businesses making use of rebates are diverse and include the manufacturers of health and beauty aids, household supplies, and small and large appliances, as well as automakers, wine and liquor manufacturers, and segments of the computer industry. The cash amounts these companies offer their customers is similarly wide-ranging and can be less then a dollar or as much as fifty dollars or more, depending on the retail price and nature of the product being promoted.

The first step in rebating, as outlined by Susan J. Samtur in *Cashing in at the Checkout,* is for the manufacturer to issue an offer of a rebate to all who purchase its product; typically the offer carries an expiration date of six to eight months. The purchaser then completes a form provided by the manufacturer and mails it—along with any other items the manufacturer may require, such as a cash-register receipt or the Universal Product Code (UPC) snipped from the packaging—to the address specified on the form.

Most commonly, the purchaser sends the rebate form and related ("proof of purchase") items not to the manufacturer but to one of several large clearinghouses hired by the manufacturer to handle these transactions—for instance, the Young America Corporation in Minnesota or the Nielson Clearing House in Texas. The clearinghouse then processes the form and sends the purchaser a check in the manufacturer's name, usually within four to eight weeks from the time the purchaser mails in the required information.

Companies use a number of means to get their rebate forms into the hands of customers. Many companies supply a pad of tear-off rebate forms to the stores selling their products; others print the form directly on the packaging or on a tag hanging from the merchandise; a few instruct the purchaser to write in for the form. To announce the rebate offer and distribute the forms, companies may also place advertisements in newspapers and magazines, utilize home mailers, and/or place ads in the myriad refunders' newsletters developed by consumers to avail themselves of these offers. In addition, companies frequently use television and radio advertisements to publicize their rebate promotions.

For consumers, rebating is highly attractive, offering a partial cash reimbursement for their purchases that is tax-free, inasmuch as the **Internal Revenue Service** views rebates as a reduction in the price paid for a product, rather than as income. And for manufacturers, rebating provides numerous advantages: it induces prospective customers to try their products; it boosts company sales and visibility; and it attracts interest from retailers, who often help promote the offer and expand the shelf space allotted to the manufacturer's goods accordingly. Rebate promotions can thus help a company increase its leverage with retailers and develop brand loyalty and repeat business among consumers over the long run—not just a one-time incentive to buy.

Indeed, a study conducted by United Marketing Services (UMS) found that participating in a rebate promotion makes customers better able to remember a product than is the case with other promotional vehicles. UMS also found the rate of consumer participation in rebate promotions to be on the rise—about 60 percent in 1987, compared with 45 percent the preceding year. Other sources cite consumer participation in rebating to range from 25 to 40 percent and find that most participants request only two or three refunds per year. Hence, because the number of purchasers who actually request the refunds is relatively small, the dollar outlay in cash refunds for the manufacturer may be minimal in comparison with the sales and other benefits generated by the promotion.

In the 1990s several innovative offshoots of rebating began to emerge. Among these were the linking of customer purchases to rebates in the form of contributions to retirement plans, tuition costs, and air-mileage credits. Other variations on rebate promotions include offering to refund a fixed percentage of the purchase price, rather than a set dollar amount; providing a "bounceback coupon" that can be redeemed on a later purchase; and making contributions to charitable causes based on customer participation in the promotion.

[Roberta H. Winston]

FURTHER READING:

A-S-M Communications, Inc. "How Rebates Affect Purchases Behavior." *Adweek's Marketing Week.* January 16, 1989, p. SP11.

Joyce, Marion. *The Frugal Shopper.* New York: Perigree Books/Berkeley Publishing Group, 1986.

Samtur, Susan J., with Tad Tuleja. *Cashing in at the Checkout.* Stonesong Press/Grosset & Dunlap, Inc.

Smith, Anne Kates. "Buying Shopper Loyalty." *U.S. News & World Report.* April 27, 1992, p. 77.

RECESSION

A recession is a downturn in the business cycle that occurs when the real **gross national product (GNP)**—the total output of goods and services produced by the U.S. population—declines for two consecutive quarters, or six months. Recessions are usually characterized by a general decrease in output, **income**, **employment**, and trade lasting from six months to a year. A more severe and long-lasting economic crisis is known as a depression.

Virtually all advanced world economies that are not controlled centrally have experienced recurring cycles of slump and recovery in business activity since the Industrial Revolution. The United States suffered through four severe depressions in the 1800s, as well as the Great Depression in the 1930s. These crises cost a great deal in terms of national **wealth** and personal hardship. Since then, however, sophisticated analysis of economic trends has combined with increased government intervention to prevent such extreme fluctuations in economic activity. In fact, no depressions have occurred in industrialized nations since World War II, although many recessions have occurred. Governments monitor the business cycle closely and take various steps to stabilize the economy before it reaches extreme peaks and troughs. Formerly, the typical stages in the business cycle were depression, recovery, prosperity, and recession. Today, the phases are usually defined using the more moderate terms upswing, peak, recession, and trough.

THE BUSINESS CYCLE

Prior to entering the recession phase of the business cycle, the economy reaches the peak of its expansion. When it nears the full-employment level of output, its rate of growth begins to slow. Prices are generally rising, so consumers demand fewer products and services. As a result, companies begin to hire fewer new workers, and demand falls even further with the reduction in incomes. **Productivity** and output begin to decline as **costs** increase, and companies respond by decreasing investment. Gradually, the overall economy **contracts**, as the decrease in investment reduces production and employment. Eventually, government intervention and the natural progression of **business cycles** cause the recession to end, or reach a trough or turning point, and the upswing stage begins.

Though the general pattern of the business cycle is understood, in reality the situation is not usually so clearly defined. The economy progresses through the stages very gradually, and not all regions, sectors, or businesses are affected in the same way at the same time. In addition, there are many other patterns of economic activity that interact with and complicate the business cycle. For example, economists often observe seasonal variations in output and sales in some sectors of the economy. Retail sales tend to pick up around Christmas, while construction tends to increase during the summer months. Economists also describe independent cycles of investment in certain industries, such as shipbuilding or agriculture. Finally, the overall level of economic activity tends to expand every year. These factors combine to make recessions difficult to predict or define.

A number of changes have taken place or been instituted by the government to stabilize fluctuations in economic activity, and thus reduce the incidence and severity of recessions, over the years. For example, the growth of the service sector, with its relatively stable demand and its tendency to employ salaried personnel, has been a stabilizing influence. The corporate trend toward stable dividend policies has also helped, as has increased federal regulation of the **stock market** and the **banking** industry. Some experts claim that instituting a progressive income **tax** and an **unemployment** insurance program have also worked to moderate fluctuations in the business cycle. Finally, the government often intervenes directly with monetary or fiscal controls to prevent **inflation**, and with job training programs and public welfare to reduce the negative effects of unemployment.

THE U.S. RECESSION OF 1990-1991

Despite such measures, however, recessions still occur in the United States and worldwide. During the U.S. recession that lasted from July 1990 through March 1991, the economy showed the lowest growth rate since the Great Depression. *U.S. News and World Report* called the recession "unlike any the country has experienced in the post-World War II era, the

result of years of profligacy and irresponsible government policies," and claimed it was responsible for the loss of 1.9 million jobs through early 1992. In fact, some analysts stated that this recession could have been as bad as the Great Depression if not for increased government spending—which represented 25 percent of GNP in 1991 as opposed to 3 percent in 1930—and **federal deposit insurance** for **banks**.

Still, economists disagreed on what caused the recession and the slow recovery, how long the recession officially lasted, and how a similar situation could best be prevented in the future. Some experts attributed the prolonged recession to industrial overcapacity, which led to falling value of the assets of many businesses. Others claimed that an overall decrease in consumption was responsible, whether in response to an increase in oil prices following the Persian Gulf War or due to a slowdown in the rate of population growth. Some analysts blamed technology, stating that the proliferation of electronically controlled credit cards led consumers to build up personal **debt**. Whatever the reasons for the recession, however, it seemed clear that the best course of action for individuals, businesses, and the government was to include the likelihood of another recession in their future plans.

[Laurie Collier Hillstrom]

FURTHER READING:

"America's Sluggish Recovery," *Economist*. June 5, 1993, p. 18.

Blanchard, Oliver. "Consumption and the Recession of 1990-1991," *American Economic Review*. May 1993, p. 270.

"Brightening Up: The Economy," *Economist*. December 11, 1993, p. 29.

Caballero, Ricardo J., and Mohamad L. Hammour. "The Cleansing Effect of Recessions," *American Economic Review*. December 1994, p. 1350.

Hall, Robert E. "Macro Theory and the Recession of 1990-1991," *American Economic Review*. May 1993, p. 275.

Hansen, Gary D., and Edward C. Prescott. "Did Technology Shocks Cause the 1990-1991 Recession?," *American Economic Review*. May 1993, p. 280.

"On Understanding the History of Capitalism," *Monthly Review*. October 1992, p. 1.

Pomice, Eva, and Robert F. Black. "Is Your Job Safe?," *U.S. News and World Report*. January 13, 1992, pp. 42-48.

Ulan, Michael. "Is the Current Business Cycle Different? Does How We Measure Matter?," *Business Economics*. April 1994, p. 41.

RECIPROCITY (COMMERCIAL POLICY)

In the area of international trade, reciprocity refers to an agreement between two or more countries to mutually reduce tariffs and duties on goods traded between them. Reciprocity has played an important role in the trade policy of the United States since 1934, when the Reciprocal Trade Agreements Program was initiated to lower tariffs and other trade barriers. Under that program the United States negotiated bilateral trade agreements with other countries. In the years following World War II, the **General Agreement on Tariffs and Trade (GATT)** took effect. It provided for multilateral trade agreements to be negotiated in a series of "rounds," the most recent of which was the Uruguay Round that concluded in 1993. GATT represents overall reciprocity, where the consenting nations agree to mutual and equivalent reductions of trade barriers.

In the United States, tariffs had reached a peak in the early 1930s as a result of the country's protectionist policy. In 1934 the Reciprocal Trade Agreements Program went into effect. Under that program the United States sought to increase its exports and pull the country out of the depression. The President was empowered to negotiate bilateral treaties with other nations to reduce tariffs by as much as 50 percent of their 1934 levels. For such a treaty to be concluded with another country, it was necessary for the other country to reciprocate, or agree to an equivalent tariff concession.

Countries with whom the United States had negotiated reciprocal tariff reductions were given **most-favored nation status** (MFN). All countries with MFN status were then eligible to receive the same tariff reductions that were negotiated in the bilateral agreements. In the case of commodities, the United States often granted the MFN tariff reduction only to the chief supplier of the commodity to the United States.

Two amendments introduced in the late 1940s modified the original Reciprocal Trade Agreements Program and gave the United States more flexibility in granting and withdrawing tariff reductions. An escape clause introduced in 1947 allowed the United States to reimpose tariffs on any imports that caused unforeseen damage to domestic producers. In 1948 the peril-point clause was added that gave the U.S. International Trade Commission the power to recommend maximum permissible tariff reductions that would not damage domestic producers.

Reciprocal trade agreements may encompass more than the lowering of tariffs. Equivalent market access is a type of reciprocity in which trading partners agree to allow each other's firms to operate in each other's countries. Reciprocity may involve the extension of restricted nationalistic treatment by one nation to another country's firms operating in its country, but only to the extent that its firms are allowed to operate in the other country. National treat-

ment, another type of reciprocity also known as equivalent treatment, is the treatment of goods produced in another country as if they were domestic goods.

Reciprocity is generally considered a politically safe policy as well as an economically safe one. Economically, reciprocity eliminates the risks associated with unilaterally reducing tariffs, such as a balance-of-payments deficit. Politically, reciprocity makes all tariff reductions appear as exchanges rather than concessions.

[David Bianco]

RECRUITING

SEE: Employee Recruiting

RECYCLING PROGRAMS

Recycling programs are comprised of three elements in a continuum represented by the "chasing arrows" symbol: collection of recyclable materials from the waste stream, processing the **commodities** into new products, and purchasing products containing recycled materials. It has been estimated that each office worker in America produces from one-half to one and one-half pounds of solid waste each day, of which 70 to 90 percent is paper. Whereas paper comprises at least 40 percent of the American waste stream and businesses contribute one-third of the nation's solid waste, recycling programs in the business world commonly address wastepaper. However, corporate recycling programs have come to include all types of waste.

Although the word "recycle" was not coined until the late 1960s, recycling has been a trash disposal option for centuries. Native Americans and early settlers routinely reused resources and avoided waste. Materials recovery was also a significant contributor to the United States' World War II effort, when businesses and citizens alike salvaged metal, paper, rubber, and other scarce commodities. But the emergence of the "throwaway society" of the 1950s helped extinguish any residual recycling impetus. With seemingly unlimited landfill space, disposable and single-use products and packages became the norm in the ensuing decades. Recycling did not regain popularity until the late 1960s and early 1970s, when environmental concerns rose to the fore in a "green revolution." The first national Earth Day celebration in 1970 heralded anti-litter campaigns, the creation of the federal **Environmental Protection Agency (EPA)**, and some municipal and corporate recycling programs.

Legislation during that period provided an additional impetus for recycling programs, especially in the federal government. The Solid Waste Disposal Act had established resource recovery goals as a priority for U.S. environmental and energy conservation programs. The Resource Recovery Act of 1970 amended the previous legislation, mandating paper recycling and procurement of recycled products in federal agencies wherever economically feasible. The well-known Resource Conservation and Recovery Act of 1976 completely revised both acts, imposing requirements regarding hazardous waste disposal and mandating the recycling of non hazardous waste in federal facilities. The legislation included the requirement that federal agencies "purchase items that contain the highest percentage of recovered materials practicable given their availability, price and quality." Deposit laws enacted around the country encouraged recycling of glass beverage bottles.

The Environmental Protection Agency and the **General Services Administration (GSA)**, which were jointly charged with administration of the program, launched "Use It Again, Sam," an earnest and widespread federal office paper recycling program, in 1976. Within two years, 90 federal agencies and their 115,000 employees were recycling, enjoying the support of President Jimmy Carter and guided by a comprehensive, EPA-issued manual. The recycling program declined in the 1980s, however, due to a lack of enforcement and oversight, budget cuts, apathy, and the EPA's concentration on administration of the **Superfund** hazardous waste cleanup program. Many state and local governments around the country stepped in to fill this void in the ensuing decade. Overall, however, low disposal costs relegated recycling to little more than an afterthought of solid waste management in the 1970s and early 1980s.

In the late 1980s, however, several factors converged to revive interest in recycling as an attractive alternative to traditional disposal. Evidence of toxic leaks from, and dangerous buildups of methane gas in, landfills around the country brought closures, increased regulation, and public opposition to location and expansion of landfills. Incineration was briefly tested as an expedient solution to the mounting solid waste crisis, but problems with stack emissions and the disposal of toxic ash undermined that option. Public recognition of the crisis crested in 1987, when a garbage barge originating from New York City traveled to six states and three countries before dumping its load back in its home state. The number of operating landfills in the United States decreased from 18,500 in 1979 to 6,500 in 1988, and it was projected that by the year 2000 only 3,250 landfills would be open for business. The dearth of disposal options in the latter years of the 1980s caused disposal expenses to rise dramatically: landfill costs in some regions (especially the Northeast and Northwest) doubled and tripled within a few years. At the same time, some states (e.g., Rhode Island, New Jersey and Connecticut) adopted mandatory recycling legislation. These factors combined with increasing consumer demand for environmental responsibility to prompt a second green revolution that swept the country—including the business world—in the 1990s.

Recycling programs emerged as "good business for business" in the last decade of the twentieth century for a variety of reasons. Perhaps most importantly, recycling holds out the "bottom line" benefit of reducing waste disposal expenses. It also offered substantial, positive benefits for the local and global environment: recycling one ton of office paper saves seventeen trees, conserves enough energy to meet the requirements of at least 4,000 people, and saves three cubic yards of landfill space.

Fort Howard Corporation, of Green Bay, Wisconsin, is a sterling example of the practicability of recycling programs. Established in 1919, the company made its first official commitment to the environment in 1930. Recycling became an economic imperative during the 1940s, when a shortage of pulp pushed Fort Howard to reprocess waste paper. By the late 1970s, the paper manufacturer had reduced its use of virgin pulp to "an almost negligible percentage," according to a 1993 article in Managing Office Technology. Fort Howard worked with municipal governments near plants to collect household and office waste paper, winning the EPA's first Administrator's Award for Recycling Leadership in 1990 and keeping more than one million tons of waste paper out of landfills each year in the 1990s.

Adopting a recycling program can also enhance a company's reputation with its customers, employees, and surrounding community. As environmentalism gained ascendancy in the 1990s, a corporate recycling program can also offer a substantial basis for "green marketing." IBM Corporation focuses its recycling programs on environmental and public relations benefits. Like so many other American concerns, IBM got its first shot at recycling by salvaging metals during World War II. The oil crisis of the 1970s provided the impetus for the corporation's energy conservation programs. The company undertook its office paper recycling program around that time, but still found room for improvement in the early 1990s. By that time, almost two-thirds of IBM's more than 9,000 employees worked in an office environment. Internal investigations estimated that high-quality white bond and computer paper constituted 70 percent (or 512 tons annually) of its office waste. With participation rates of about 80 percent, IBM expected to recover

480 tons of wastepaper annually, and set a goal of 50 percent waste reduction. In the 1990s, the corporation expanded its program to include: wooden pallets, lawn clippings, and corrugated cardboard.

If for no other reason, many firms were compelled to reduce their solid waste to comply with legislation. AT&T undertook paper recycling in New Jersey in 1984, three years before mandatory recycling legislation took effect in that state. The model program's waste paper sales earned $372,000 in 1987 alone, in addition to saving disposal costs. The program was expanded nationwide in the 1990s, and set a 60 percent recycling goal. In 1992, the company recycled 12,565 tons of waste.

Some firms report the best success rates with a comprehensive recycling program encompassing their entire waste stream. Veryfine Products, Inc. of Littleton, Massachusetts, started its recycling program in 1982 with copy and computer paper. The company took a proactive stance to environmental legislation in 1989, when impending EPA waste water treatment and source reduction standards demanded attention. The company designed a "state-of-the-art," $8.5 million water purification plant, as well as water-conserving cooling towers. By the early 1990s, the company was recycling 90 to 95 percent of all solid waste generated in the juice-making process, including glass, aluminum, paper, plastic, pulp, cardboard, wood and steel. The program included an environmental newsletter, recycling committee, and suggestion system. Veryfine's president, Samuel Rowse, plays a vital leadership role in these programs. In 1993, he noted that the corporation's programs had not only avoided nearly $400,000 in landfill costs in recent years, but also gained $158,000 through the recovery and sale of aluminum and glass. Rowse asserted that "Fragmented attempts at recycling, source reduction and environmentally friendly packaging are not enough to make a significant difference in the years ahead. Rather, comprehensive environmental efforts should be integrated into every facet of the business—from the front office to the shipping-and-receiving dock."

The federal government's 1993 "Office Recycling Program Guide" notes five basic, interconnected components of a comprehensive recycling program: education, collection, marketing, procurement, and monitoring and evaluation.

Education encompasses training of both leaders and participants in a recycling program. Studies have shown that the most successful recycling programs involve top-level management and require employee participation. Experts advise the appointment of a recycling coordinator or committee responsible for setting up, implementing, and monitoring the program. Some organizations employ environmental consultants to perform this function. Any recycling coordinator's first order of business is self education. There are a wide variety of resources available to personnel charged with organizing recycling programs. Regional Environmental Protection Agency (EPA) offices and state-affiliated natural resource departments throughout the country offer information packets and recycling kits.

While recycling technically encompasses collecting, processing and **marketing**, experts urge source reduction as an integral aspect of successful corporate recycling programs. Source reduction precludes waste management and its costs. Experts suggest several simple ways to reduce waste and reuse resources. Copy and write on both sides of a sheet of paper. Use coffee mugs instead of disposable cups. Reuse packing material and/or make it from shredded waste paper. Ensure that office equipment has a long life by negotiating strong service contracts. Route documents, or use electronic mail, instead of disseminating multiple copies. Have laser printer and copier toner cartridges refilled. Sears, Roebuck and Company packaging reduction program, implemented in the early 1990s, saved the retailer an estimated $5 million annually. McDonald's well-publicized partnership with the Environmental Defense Fund greatly reduced its packaging. "Pollution Prevention Pays," a source reduction program started in 1975 by 3M Company, generated enough employee suggestions to save over $500 million in operational costs by 1989.

After learning about recycling in general, recycling coordinators should acclimate themselves to the particulars of their company's waste management program through a waste audit. A waste audit should note the sources, amounts and types of trash generated; the current methods and cost of disposal; and the volume of potentially recyclable trash. Based on these findings, leaders of recycling programs can determine which materials to target. Some experts advise beginning recyclers to limit their programs to one type of waste, usually high-quality bond and computer paper. Once participants have grown accustomed to recycling, the program can be expanded to include aluminum, newspaper, plastics, glass, and cardboard, for example. Some companies eventually recycle virtually all their waste. The types and volumes of materials to be recycled will govern the methods of collection employed.

Collection comprises the nuts-and-bolts logistics of separating, gathering and storing recyclables from trash at their source. The most common methods are the desktop container, a series of designated containers, or a central collection area, but some businesses employ vendor sorting, where mixed recyclables are stored together and sorted off-site by the waste hauler. These containers are usually brought by janitorial or mailroom staff to a storage area, where they are kept until pickup by the waste paper dealer. Some companies dealing with sensitive, proprietary, or confidential information may also need to consider destruction (by shredding, for example) as part of this step. Maintenance of quality standards is paramount to this facet of a successful recycling program. Similar materials, like white and colored paper, may have a market separately, but are nearly worthless when mixed. Processors of most types of paper discourage commingling of ''stickies'' (labels, stickers and tape), food and other contaminants. Although source separation has proven to be the best collection method, a new technology from James River Corp. of Virginia marketed under the trade name Office Pack will allow businesses to collect virtually all grades of paper in one container. Such technological advances characterize the field of recycling, and are sure to continue as recycling enters the mainstream.

Marketing the recyclable materials to a processor involves research and contracting. Waste paper dealers can be found in local phone directories or through contact with the Paper Stock Institute of America. The EI Environmental Services Directory, ''the nation's largest, most in-depth directory of environmental service providers,'' lists and describes over 2,000 vendors. This component of the program obviously incorporates outside forces, including the solvency of the contractor and vagaries of the waste paper market. It holds out the prospect, however, of converting disposal expenses into profits from scrap marketing.

Procurement helps ''close the recycling loop'' by arranging to purchase and use supplies made from recycled materials. These can include newsprint, tissue products, paperboard, and printing and writing papers. Some recycling experts suggest that companies only purchase materials that they can recycle, for example, only white paper or envelopes without plastic windows. The Environmental Products Guide, published by the federal government's General Services Administration, lists nearly 3,000 products that meet or exceed the Environmental Protection Agency's guidelines for recycled content products. First published in 1989, The Official Recycled Products Guide, includes nearly 4,000 entries on recycled products, with indexes, classifications, and cross-references. Although sometimes overlooked, procurement is a vital component of recycling programs. Some purchasing officers, in fact, report returns of ten percent to 25 percent of materials' original purchase price. More importantly, however, without sufficient demand for recycled products, there will be no incentive for recyclers to reprocess waste. This aspect of office recycling in America appears to be lacking. A 1991 Purchasing World survey noted that while 87 percent of respondents collected used or excess materials for recycling, only half of the respondents' companies purchased recycling materials for use in their own operations. This shortfall has been called ''recycling's greatest problem'' in the 1990s.

Each aspect of the recycling program must be monitored and evaluated for efficiency and progress. A cost-benefit analysis of the program can strengthen management support and encourage expansion to other areas of the company and/or other products in the waste stream. Periodic bulletins noting the number of trees, kilowatts of energy and gallons of water saved by the program can keep enthusiasm high.

In light of the economic, political and social influences that came to bear on the solid waste issue in the late twentieth century, hundreds of major American businesses have launched recycling and waste reduction programs. Although the concept has received widespread media attention, the Environmental Protection Agency reported in 1993 that less than five percent of offices in the United States participated in office paper recycling programs.

[April Dougal Gasbarre]

FURTHER READING:

American Recycling Market Annual Buyers' Guide. Ogdensburg NY: American Recycling Market, Inc., 1991.

Beverly, Dawn. Business Recycling Manual. New York: INFORM, Inc. and Recourse Systems, Inc., 1991.

Cichonski, Thomas J., and Karen Hill. Recycling Sourcebook. Detroit: Gale Research, Inc., 1993.

Curry, Gloria. ''Increasingly Cost-Effective, Recycling Programs Continue to Grow,'' Office, v. 118, August, 1993, 30-31, 51, 55.

Kimball, Debi. Recycling in America: A Reference Handbook. Santa Barbara CA: ABC-CLIO, 1992.

Kornegay, Jennifer. ''Security Goes Green,'' Security Management, v. 35, August, 1991, 95-96.

MacEachern, Diane. Save Our Planet. New York: Dell Publishing, 1990.

Office Paper Recycling Guide. St. Louis: Federal Executive Board, 1992.

Ortbal, John. ''How to Cultivate an Office Recycling Program,'' Modern Office Technology, v. 36, April, 1991, 32-36.

The Recyclers' Directory. Portland OR: Resource Recycling, Inc., 1993.

Rowse, Samuel. ''A Veryfine Approach to Environmental Awareness,'' Beverage World, v. 112, October, 1993, 76-78.

Steuteville, Robert. ''Corporate Recycling Reaps Savings,'' BioCycle, v. 34, August, 1993, 34-36.

——, ''More Mixing, Better Paper Diversion,'' BioCycle, v. 34, August, 1993, 60-61.

Stundza, Tom. ''Treat Scrap as Trash and You Throw Money Away,'' Purchasing, vi 11, July 18, 1991, 66-69.

United States, Federal Supply Service. Environmental Products Guide. Washington, D.C.: U.S. General Services Administration, 1994.

United States, General Accounting Office. Wastepaper Recycling: Programs of Civil Agencies Waned During the 1980s. Washington, D.C.: The Office, 1989.

United States, *Office of Administrative and Management Services. Office Recycling Program Guide.* Washington, D.C., 1993.

Webb, Nan. "Recycling Tasks Are Part of the Job," *Purchasing World,* v. 35 March, 1991, 42-3.

REFINANCING

Refinancing is the refunding or restructuring of **debt** with new debt, equity, or a combination of both. The refinancing of debt is most often undertaken during a period of declining interest rates in order to lower the average cost of a firm's debt. Sometimes refinancing involves the issuance of equity in order to decrease the proportion of debt in the borrower's **capital structure**. As a result of refinancing, the maturity of the debt may be extended or reduced, or the new debt may carry a lower interest rate, or a combination of both.

Refinancing may be done by any issuer of debt such as corporations and governmental bodies and holders of **real estate**, including home owners. When a borrower retires a debt issue, the payment is in cash and no new security takes the place of the one being paid-off. The term "refunding" is used when a borrower issues new debt to refinance an existing one.

CORPORATE OR GOVERNMENT DEBT REFINANCING

The most common incentive for corporations or governmental bodies to refinance their outstanding debt is to take advantage of a decline in interest rates from the time the original debt was issued. Another trigger for corporate debt refinancing is when the price of their **common stock** reaches a level which makes it attractive for a firm to replace its outstanding debt with equity. Aside from reducing interest costs, this latter move gives a firm additional flexibility for future financing because by retiring debt, they will have some unused debt capacity. Regardless of the reason for the refinancing, the issuer has to deal with two decisions: (1) is the time right to refinance, and (2) what type of security should be issued to replace the one being refinanced?

If a corporation or governmental body wishes to refinance before the maturity date of the outstanding issue, they will need to exercise the call provision of the debt. The call provision gives the borrower the right to retire outstanding **bonds** at a stipulated price, usually at a premium over face amount, but never less than face. The specific price which an issuer will need to pay for a call appears in the bond's indenture. The existence of a call premium is designed to compensate the bond holder for the firm's right to pay-off the debt earlier than the holder expected. Many bond issues have a deferred call, which means the firm cannot call in the bond until the expiration of the deferment period, usually five to ten years.

The cash outlay required by exercising the call provision includes payment to the holder of the bond for any interest which has accrued to the date of the call and the call price, including premium, if any. In addition, the firm will need to pay a variety of administrative costs, including a fee to the bond's trustee. Of course, there will be flotation costs for any new debt or equity that is issued as part of the refinancing.

Sometimes an issuer may be prohibited from calling in the bonds (e.g., during the deferred call period). In these instances, the issuer always has the opportunity to purchase its bonds in the open market. This strategy may also be advantageous if the outstanding bond is selling in the market at a price lower than the call price. Open market purchases involve few administrative costs and the corporation will recognize a gain (loss) on the repurchase if the **market value** is below (above) the amount at which the corporation is carrying the bonds on its books (face value plus or minus unamortized premium or discount).

The major difficulty with open market purchases to effect a refinancing is that typically the market for bonds is "thin." This means that a relatively small percentage of an entire issue may be available on the market over any period of time. As a result, if a firm is intent on refinancing a bond issue, it almost always needs to resort to a call. This is why virtually every new bond that is issued contains a call provision.

If an outstanding issue does not permit a call, another option available to the issuer is to seek tenders (offers to sell at a predetermined price) from current bond holders.

The new debt instrument issued in refinancing can be simple or complex. A corporation could replace an existing bond with traditional bonds, serial bonds (which have various maturity dates), zero-coupon bonds (which have no periodic interest payments), or corporate shares (which have no maturity date, but which may have associated dividend payments). One factor that a firm needs to consider is that the administrative and flotation costs of issuing either common or preferred shares are higher than for new debt. Furthermore, dividend payments, if any, are not **tax** deductible.

The decision to refinance is a very practical matter involving time and money. Over time the opportunity to refinance varies with changing interest rates and economic conditions. When a corporation anticipates an advantageous interest rate climate, it then analyzes the cash flows associated with the refinancing. Calculating the present value of all the cash

Exhibit 1

Example of Analysis Required for Refinancing

Original Issue:

Outstanding principal	$300,000
Call premium (5%)	15,000
Annual interest	30,000
Years remaining to maturity	30

Refinancing Alternatives:	Cash	New 8% Debt 30 Year	Preferred Stock-9%
New amount	$ 0	$300,000	$300,000
Flotation costs	0	27,000	45,000
Annual interest		24,000	
Annual dividend			27,000
Initial cost of refinancing:			
Face amount of old issue	300,000	300,000	300,000
Call premium, net of taxes	9,000	9,000	9,000
New issue proceeds, net of costs		275,000	255,000
Initial cost	$309,000	$34,000	$54,000
Annual savings, net of taxes	18,000	3,960	-9,000
Net present cost (savings) of refinancing	$106,356	$-26,288	$146,466

outflows and the interest savings assists in comparing refinancing alternatives that have different maturity dates and capitalization schemes.

Exhibit 1 demonstrates the type of computation that needs to be made to determine the financial feasibility of refinancing alternatives. We are assuming a call premium (tax deductible) of five percent and a tax rate of 40 percent. The discount rate used in the **present value** computations is the after-tax interest/dividend cost of the respective alternative. For simplicity, we are assuming annual interest payments.

As can be seen, the most favorable alternative is to refinance with the 30 year debt. This results in a net present value savings of $26,288. The other alternatives each have a net present value *cost*.

MORTGAGE REFINANCING

The above method of analyzing the refinancing decision is also applicable to mortgage refinancing for residential or commercial real estate. In residential real estate the conventional wisdom applied the "2-2-2 rule": if interest rates had fallen two points below the existing mortgage, if the owner has already paid two years of the mortgage, and if the owner plans to live in the house another two years, then refinancing is feasible. However, this approach ignores the present value of the related cash flows and the effects of the tax deductibility of interest expense and any related points.

Therefore, the analysis of a mortgage refinancing decision should be similar to the corporate decision illustrated. For a mortgage you would:

1. Calculate the present value of the after-tax cash flows of the existing mortgage

2. Calculate the present value of the after-tax cash flows of the proposed mortgage

3. Compare the outcomes and select the alternative with the lower present value. The interest rate to be used in steps one and two is the after-tax interest cost of the proposed mortgage.

[Ronald M. Horwitz]

FURTHER READING:

REGRESSION ANALYSIS

Regression analysis employs algebraic formulas to estimate the value of a continuous random variable, called a *dependent* variable, using the value of another, *independent*, variable. Statistical methods are used to determine the most correct estimate of that dependent variable, and whether the estimate is valid at all.

Regressions may be used for a wide variety of purposes where estimation is important. For example, a marketer may employ a regression to determine how sales of his product might be affected by investments in advertising. An employer may perform a similar analysis to estimate an employee's job evaluation scores based on his performance on an aptitude test. A biologist can even use a regression to see how temperature changes might affect the rate of reproduction in frogs.

While closely related, regression differs from *correlation analysis* in an important way. Where regression is used to estimate the value of independent variables, correlation measures the degree of relationship between variables. In other words, correlation analysis can indicate the strength of a linear relationship between variables, but it is left to regression analysis to provide predictions of the dependent variable based on values of an independent variable.

Both regression and correlation deal with *statistical relationships*, where there is an approximate relationship between variables. Regression analysis takes sampling error into account and can therefore only provide an estimate, rather than a prediction, of independent variables.

Unfortunately for many regression analysts, many people reading the information provided from such an analysis cannot make—or need to be reminded of—the distinction between prediction and estimation. As a result, the analyst can be unfairly blamed for bad analysis when his estimate is "wrong."

A *simple regression analysis* is one in which a single dependent variable is used to determine an independent variable. The relationship between the variables is assumed to be consistent, or *linear*. Figure 1 shows examples of linear, non-linear and curvelinear scatter diagrams, as well as one where there is no consistent relationship between X and Y variables.

The equation that represents the simple linear regression is

$$Y_i = \alpha + \beta X_i + e_i$$

where

Y_i represents the value of the dependent variable in a certain observation, i (sometimes denoted X_0);

α indicates the value of Y when X is equal to zero, and may be thought of as the intercept (sometimes denoted β_0);

β indicates the slope of the regression line;

e_i is the random error in the observation i.

The values of both the independent variable X and the dependent variable Y are provided by a survey, or set of observed numerical samples. These sets of numbers are maintained as ordered pairs—a range of values of Y is indicated for each value of X. The value e_i represents the sampling error associated with the dependent random variable Y.

Some assumptions must be satisfied to perform the regression analysis. Firstly, if we plot the values of X on a scatter diagram, the sampling error e_i, or variance from a mean, must be reasonably consistent for all values of X. In other words, for each value of X, the variation in values of Y must be reasonably consistent. This quality is called *homoscedasticity*.

Secondly, observed values of the random variable and amounts of random error must be uncorrelated, a condition usually satisfied by random sampling of the dependent value.

A simple regression analysis uses only one independent variable. However, there are many situations where a dependent variable is determined by two, three, five, or even a hundred independent variables. As a result, it becomes difficult to represent the relationships between the variables in a visual model.

For example, a simple regression with two variables can be represented on a graph, with one variable measured on the X axis and the other on the Y axis. But add a third variable, and the graph requires a third dimension, X_2. As a result, the regression line becomes a regression *plane*.

Add a fourth variable, and the regression can no longer be represented visually. Conceptually, it has four dimensions, also called *hyperplanes* or *arrays*. The same applies for regressions with even more variables; eight variables requires eight dimensions.

These relationships can only be expressed only in complex mathematical formulas. They are no longer simple regressions, but *multiple* regressions.

[John Simley]

FURTHER READING:

Johnson, Robert R. *Elementary Statistics*. 3rd ed. North Scituate, MA: Duxbury Press, 1980.

Kachiga, Sam Kash. *Statistical Analysis*. New York: Radius Press, 1986.

Kazmier, Leonard J. *Basic Statistics for Business and Economics*. New York: McGraw-Hill, 1990.

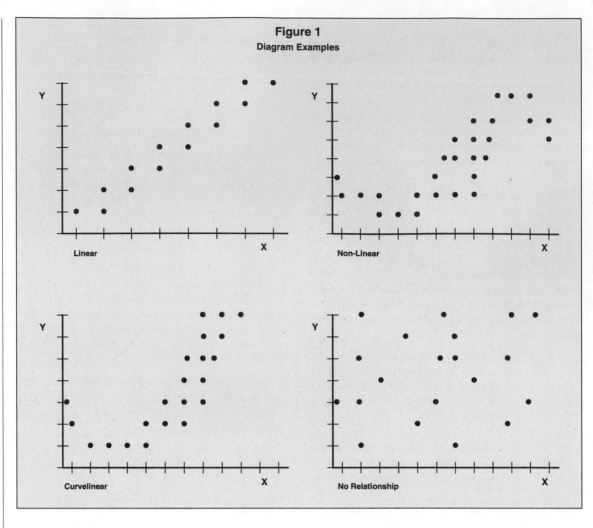

Figure 1
Diagram Examples

Linear

Non-Linear

Curvelinear

No Relationship

Monks, Joseph G. *Statistics for Business*. Worthington, OH: Science Research Associates, 1988.

RELIABILITY

The concept of reliability or dependability is used in a variety of business and industrial settings. In general, the concept of reliability is applied where it is important to achieve the same results again and again. A **manufacturing** process is said to be reliable when it achieves the same results, within defined limits, each time it occurs. An automobile, or other type of product, is reliable if it performs consistently and up to expectations. The reliability of financial and other types of data may depend on how they have been compiled and prepared. Personnel are considered reliable when they perform consistently and are able to achieve defined objectives.

Reliability is measured by results. It is the yardstick against which performance is measured and

evaluated. Reliability is applied to the performance of individuals, products, processes, and data, among other things. Reliable performance in all of these areas is critical to successful **business planning** and results. In order for a business to be successful, all of its components must be reliable.

In the area of finance and accounting, data is reliable when an independent audit has confirmed that financial records have been prepared according to generally accepted **accounting** principles. Annual reports and other financial disclosures from **publicly held companies** generally contain a statement from the **auditing** firm as to the reliability of the data contained therein. The statement of reliability affirms that the information contained in the financial report is free from error and bias and reasonably reflects the facts of the business operation.

Accounting data can be reliable without necessarily being verifiable. In order for such data to be verifiable, it must be possible to reconstruct the financial data and achieve the same results. In addition, two or more accountants working independently must be able to achieve the same results for financial data to be verifiable.

Reliability is also an important concept in manufacturing and engineering. Plants, processes, materials, and a host of other aspects of the manufacturing process are continually tested for reliability. Since reliability does not necessarily mean perfection, constant attention is paid to improving the reliability of a wide range of manufacturing functions. The reliability of such processes directly affects the profitability of a manufacturing firm as well as the reliability of its products.

Product reliability is important not only to the manufacturer, but also to the consumer. When consumers purchase products, they have certain expectations as to how well those products will perform and for how long. When manufacturers offer product warranties, they are standing behind the reliability of their products. A computer that has a three-year warranty can be expected to be more reliable than one with only a two-year warranty. During the warranty period, the manufacturer generally assumes the cost of any repairs or defects and, in some cases, may even replace the product at no additional charge.

A variety of legislation exists at the state and federal levels to protect consumers from faulty, defective, and unreliable products. Perhaps the most well known is California's so-called "lemon law," which provides consumers with remedies when they purchase consistently unreliable automobiles. That law also prevents automobile dealers from knowingly reselling "lemons" without notifying consumers of the car's repair history. The reliability of some services, such as **telecommunications**, is also regulated by the government.

In the area of human resources and personnel, the reliability of individuals seeking employment is of concern to businesses. So-called dependability and integrity tests have been developed to screen potential employees. Businesses can give these tests to applicants to determine the probability of their having disciplinary problems, **absenteeism**, tardiness, and other counterproductive traits. Dependability tests complement mental and physical ability tests to provide employers with a better evaluation of potential new hires.

[David Bianco]

REPLACEMENT COST

Under generally accepted **accounting** principles, the value of a company's assets is based on its historical costs. The present book value of an asset is determined by its acquisition, or historical, cost, less any depreciation. A company's **financial statements** will reflect this, usually valuing its assets at their present book value.

Replacement costs provide an alternative way of valuing a company's assets. The replacement, or current, cost of an asset is the amount of money required to replace the asset by purchasing a similar asset with identical future service capabilities. In replacement cost accounting, assets and **liabilities** are valued at their cost to replace.

If replacement costs are used to establish the value of assets, then the replacement method of depreciation is also used to adjust the value of an asset as it is used over time. Under the replacement method of depreciation, an anticipated replacement cost for the asset is estimated. The depreciation expense is then calculated as the sum of the depreciation based on the historical cost, plus a percentage of the difference between the historial cost and the replacement cost. Using the replacement method, the depreciation expense associated with an asset is based on a combination of its historical cost and its replacement cost.

When an acquiring company seeks to obtain an estimate of a target company's value before making a pruchase offer, the replacement costs of the company's assets often provide a more accurate value than does the present book value of the assets. The value of an asset is intended to reflect its earnings potential. Present book value, calculated on the basis of historical costs and depreciation, does not take into account such factors as inflation, for example. Replacement costs, on the other hand, are more likely to accurately reflect economic conditions that can affect the value of a company's assets.

[David Bianco]

REPURCHASE AGREEMENTS

Repurchase agreements are considered to be money market financial instruments. Money market financial instruments, in turn, consist of short-maturity or short-term financial instruments. A financial instrument is considered "short-term" if it matures within one year. The definition of "short-term" as used for money market purposes is different from that used by the **Internal Revenue Service**; the latter uses six months as the cut-off between short and long terms. Among the many market instruments, repurchase agreements are among those that have the shortest maturity periods. Based on maturity period, repurchase agreements are usually classified under two sub-groups—overnight repurchase agreements and long-term repurchase agreements.

OVERNIGHT REPURCHASE AGREEMENTS

Repurchase agreements, or RPs, are essentially short-term loans backed by Treasury bills as collateral. Usually, the maturity period of a repurchase agreement is less than two weeks, overnight RPs being the shortest maturity repurchase agreement instrument. A repurchase agreement transaction can be illustrated as follows: corporation ''A'' has some idle cash and corporation ''B'' wants to borrow funds overnight to make up for the shortfall in the amount of required reserves that it must have at the Federal Reserve. Assume that corporation A uses $10 million to buy Treasury bills from corporation B, which agrees to buy back (repurchase) Treasury bills the next morning at a price slightly higher than corporation A's purchase price. The higher price that corporation B pays is a form of interest on the overnight use of corporation A's $10 million. Thus, in effect, corporation B borrows $10 million from corporation B for overnight use at a specified interest (implied in the purchase and repurchase prices of Treasury bills). Should corporation B not buy back the Treasury bills that IBM is holding, the latter can sell those bills to recover its loan. Transferred Treasury bills thus serve as collateral, which the lender receives if the borrower does not pay back the loan.

Repurchase agreements are a relatively new financial instrument. They have been in existence only since 1969. However, they constitute an important source of funds for banks, where large corporations are considered the most important lenders.

Because of extremely short maturity, overnight repurchase agreements are considered very liquid—the instrument turns back into cash the very next day. Since RPs are liquid, but less liquid than currency or checkable deposits, they are included, by the **Federal Reserve**, in broader definitions of money supply.

LONG-TERM REPURCHASE AGREEMENTS

Repurchase agreements that have maturity periods of more than one night are called long term-repurchase agreements, or term RPs. Thus, long term repurchase agreements also facilitate borrowing and lending in which Treasury bills are essentially used as collateral. By nature, long-term repurchase agreements are less liquid than overnight repurchase agreements.

[Anandi P. Sahu]

FURTHER READING:

Mishkin, Frederic S. *The Economics of Money, Banking, and Financial Markets*, 4th ed. HarperCollins Publishers, 1995.

Ritter, Lawrence S. and William L. Silber. *Principles of Money, Banking, and Financial Markets*, 6th ed. Basic Books, Inc., 1989.

Request for Proposal or RFP is the process by which a corporate department or government agency prepares bid documents to acquire equipment or services. The RFP is frequently published in the legal documents section of pertinent newspapers or in trade journals covering the industry in which the department operates. The RFP can also be distributed to a list of qualified potential bidders that have already been contacted and prequalified as eligible by the agency or department.

''Qualified'' is a key word in answering or preparing any RFP. Qualification frequently depends on follow-up investigation on the part of the hopeful bidder, and careful wording of the original RFP. A company that deals only in Macintosh computers and **software** written for Apple Computer, Inc. could not hope to win the RFP bid and fulfill the needs of a government agency that is totally equipped with IBM personal computers. On the other hand, Dell Computer, which sells IBM clones, may indeed fill the needs of the department if it can prove that its computers can mesh with the existing IBM machines and MS-DOS software.

Private corporations sometimes employ the practice of issuing RFPs, usually when purchasing **commodities** or services that do not bear directly on the company's own products or services. Government agencies are closely associated with preparing and evaluating RFPs since their responsibility to get equipment and **consulting** talent at the lowest possible price is closely monitored by the press and *tax watchdogs.* This attention to low cost as monitored by the RFP process led long ago to the old joke asking how astronauts feel about sitting on top of a rocket designed and built by a long string of low bidders.

PREPARING GOOD RFPS

There are some elements that an issuing agency should make sure to include in a good RFP. Be specific when describing what is needed to fulfill the agency needs. A request for ''five 486 PC computers'' is not specific. ''Five 486 PC computers, each powered by DX/66 microprocessors with 8 megabytes of Random Access Memory and expandable to 32 MB of RAM with 430 MB hard drives with both 5.25 inch (1.2 MB) and 3.5 inch (1.44 MB) floppy disk drives'' goes a long way towards being specific. Much more description is needed to make sure that every potential vendor is bidding on the same equipment. Some companies may even want to specify the manufactures of components that will be inside the computers. This would eliminate the potential problem of a vendor substituting a poor quality component that meets the specifications on paper, but is known for problems.

Make sure the potential vendors understand the nature of the RFP agency, what it does, how the equipment will be used, the problem that is being addressed by the RFP, and any future goals that the agency plans that might relate to the equipment.

Look as far into the future as possible. If the equipment will eventually be networked to a building that is not yet built, but is in the company's long range plans, alert the bidders to that possible future need. It may make a difference sometime in the future and does not hurt to see how the bidders respond to the possibility.

Alert the bidders to any environmental situations that the equipment might face. If the equipment is being purchased to go to Europe or South America, tell them. Foreign standards might be entirely different from what is acceptable in the United States. If the equipment is planned to go into an old building on the second floor, check with the bidders that the equipment is not too heavy. Bidders might assume that the RFP agency knows that the item weighs a ton, while the RFP agency might not even have thought about where it will be used.

Give vendors plenty of time to study the RFP before the deadline. Some companies give vendors as much as one month from the time the RFP is published before the bids are due. This allows bidders time to tinker with their bids, possibly allowing them to seek out new vendors of their own to help meet the needs of the RFP.

Enforce standards on replying bidders. If a company returns a bid for "five 486 DX/33 computers," return it to the company, or throw it out without comment, since the vendor did not follow the RFP's specifications for DX/66 computers running at 66 mghtz.

Enforce deadlines on vendors. When buying off-the-shelf equipment, an agency should be suspicious of any vendor claiming to need more time than the contract requires in order to meet the needs of the agency. Why does the vendor need more time to deliver 486 DX/66 computers when that type of computer is a commodity? If the RFP is for equipment that is "cutting edge," the RFP agency should require the winning vendor to sign a peformance bond that guarantees it will deliver by a certain date. Such **bonds** carry a monetary penalty that the vendor agrees to pay if it misses the delivery date.

Try to limit the number of vendors since every bid requires staff scrutiny. Who makes the list? Who doesn't? That is up to the agency staff to determine. Many government agencies and some corporate departments are reluctant to cut vendors off bid lists out of fear of favoritism charges. One way to keep the list manageable is to require potential vendors to refile every few years and to meet certain criteria, such as listing past sales and experience or number of employees available to service the account. Shaky companies that would not be good vendors are unlikely to keep up with such refiling requirements.

Make sure replying companies specifically address the problem that was the original purpose of issuing the RFP. Bids that address both the company's current problem and future needs carry more weight than those that just cover the minimum the company asked.

A lawyer may be needed to make sure the RFP and the equipment or services it seeks are legal under local, state, and federal laws. For example, a company advertising for bids for fuel oil storage tanks should make absolutely sure that the tanks offered by companies responding to the RFP fit all federal environmental standards as set down by the **Environmental Protection Agency (EPA)**.

ANSWERING RFPS

Companies wishing to bid on RFPs should monitor the legal notices in local newspapers and trade magazines, and contact the purchasing departments of corporations and government agencies likely to request services and equipment. Investigate the requirements to be added to the "bid list."

There may be more to answering the RFP than just providing the lowest cost or the highest level of customer service. Some corporations and government agencies give special consideration on their bid lists to minority- and women-owned companies with "set-asides," a certain percentage of a job predetermined to go to companies that are usually smaller and newer to business.

Read the RFP carefully, paying particular attention to deadlines and performance clauses. Some RFPs may require that the winning bidder provide the service by a certain date. If that date is missed, the bidder might be forced to return cash to the organization that issued the RFP.

Determine if the RFP is for both equipment and service. Companies that sell equipment might not be able to adequately service it, yet that service performance may be written into the RFP in a separate section from the equipment specifications. Responders must know they can fulfill the entire contract before answering it.

[Clint Johnson]

FURTHER READING:

Stein, Murry. "Don't Bomb Out When Preparing RFPs." *Computerworld*. February 15, 1993, p. 102.

RESEARCH AND DEVELOPMENT

Research and development (R & D) represents a large and rapidly growing effort in both industrialized and semi-industrialized nations. In 1992, the United States spent $99 billion on industrial R & D and $58 billion on military R & D, for a total of $157 billion, equal to 2.5 percent of the **gross national product**. Similar ratios exist for economically advanced countries, like Germany, France, the United Kingdom, and Japan. In order to compete in the international marketplace, rapidly industrializing countries such as South Korea, Indonesia, and Brazil have national policies in place for developing indigenous R & D. The goal is substitution of strategic imports and development of exports.

The reason for this increased emphasis on R & D is that it creates new or improved technology that in turn can be converted through **technology management** a competitive advantage at the business, corporate, and national level. While the process of technological innovation (of which R & D is the first phase) is complex and risky, the rewards can be very high, as witnessed, for example by the GE Engineering Plastics business. Started in 1957 and based on R & D, the company grew to $5 billion in sales in 1993.

The relationship between R & D and economic growth is complex, but several economic studies have come to the conclusion that it is very significant. The social rate of return of industrial and agricultural R & D is of the order of 50-70 percent, while the *private* rate of return is of the order of 25 to 50 percent. The reason that the private rate is approximately half the social rate is that the originator of R & D cannot appropriate all the benefits of its innovations and must share them with customers, the public, and even competitors. At the business level, the Strategic Management Institute determined that the return of R & D for 42 major U.S. corporations was 33 percent in 1978. Therefore, R & D is a good investment for business, but a risky one—the majority of R & D projects fail to provide the expected financial results, and the successful projects (25 to 50 percent) must also pay for the projects that are unsuccessful or terminated early by management.

OBJECTIVES AND TYPES OF R & D

The objective of academic and institutional R & D is to obtain new knowledge, which may or may not be applied to practical uses. In contrast, the objective of industrial R & D is to obtain new knowledge *applicable to the company's business needs*, that eventually will result in new or improved products, processes, systems, or services that can increase the company's sales and profits.

The National Science Foundation (NSF) defines three types of R & D: basic research, applied research, and development.

1. *Basic research* has as its objectives a fuller knowledge or understanding of the subject under study, rather than a practical application thereof. As applied to the industrial sector, basic research is defined as research that advances scientific knowledge but does not have specific commercial objectives, although such investigation may be in the fields of present or potential interest to the company.

2. *Applied research* is directed towards gaining knowledge or understanding necessary for determining the means by which a recognized and specific need may be met. In industry, applied research includes investigations directed to the discovery of new specific knowledge having specific commercial objectives with respect to products, processes, or services.

3. *Development* is the systematic utilization of the knowledge or understanding gained from research toward the production of useful materials, devices, systems, or methods, including design and development of prototypes and processes.

At this point, it is important to differentiate development from engineering, which can be defined as utilization of state-of-the-art knowledge for the design and production of marketable goods and services. In other words, research creates knowledge, development develops and builds prototypes and proves their feasibility. Engineering then converts these prototypes into products or services that can be offered to the marketplace or in to processes that can be used to produce commercial products and services.

In modern industrial practice, the distinction between R (research) and D (development) is not always clear. At General Electric's (GE) R & D Center, a relatively small percentage (5 to 10 percent) of the total effort is devoted to "exploratory research," with results expected within a time span of 10 to 15 years and no specific commercial applications. All the remaining efforts are lumped together and accounted for as R & D. Also, the relative importance of R & D varies according to a company's strategy and culture. Some companies, such as E.I. du Pont de Nemours & Co. and Sony, still rely heavily on research to eventually develop new products such as Kevlar or the VCR. Other companies prefer to conduct little or no research and instead develop new products from the results of research generated by others that may be generally available in the public domain or acquired legally. In the United States, Apple Computer Inc. and Microsoft Corp. conduct relatively little research but are exceptionally creative at development. Of course, the Japanese consumer electronics industry initially utilized the results of American and European research creatively and effectively to enter the international marketplace through new low-cost, high-quality products, developed, designed, and manufactured in a relatively short time. As technology became harder to acquire, many Japanese companies switched from development to research. For instance, in the 1950s, Toshiba was heavily dependent on GE's technology, but it now has a major independent R & D laboratory.

R & D AND TECHNOLOGY ACQUISITION

In many cases, technology required for industrial purposes is available in the marketplace, usually for a price. Before embarking on the lengthy and risky process of performing its own R & D, a company should perform a "make or buy" analysis and decide whether or not the new R & D project is strategically and economically justified.

The following influencing factors should be considered: proprietariness, timing, risk and cost.

PROPRIETARINESS. If a technology can be safeguarded as proprietary, and protected by patents, trade secrets, nondisclosure agreements, etc., the technology becomes exclusive property of the company and its value is much higher. In fact, a valid patent grants a company a temporary monopoly for 17 years to use the technology as it sees fit, usually to maximize sales and profits. In this case, a high-level of R & D effort is justified for a relatively long period (up to 10 years) with an acceptable risk of failure.

On the contrary, if the technology cannot be protected, as is the case with certain software programs, expensive in-house R & D is not justified since the software may be copied by a competitor or "stolen" by a disloyal employee. In this case, the secret of commercial success is staying ahead of competition by developing continuously improved software packages, supported by a strong marketing effort.

TIMING. If the market growth rate is slow or moderate, in-house or contracted R & D may be the best means to obtain the technology. On the other hand, if the market is growing very fast and competitors are rushing in, the "window of opportunity" may close before the technology has been developed by the new entrant. In this case, it is better to acquire the technology and related know-how, in order to enter the market before it is too late.

RISK. Inherently, technology development is always riskier than technology acquisition because the technical success of R & D cannot be guaranteed. There is always the risk that the planned performance specifications will not be met, that the time to project completion will be stretched out, and that the R & D and manufacturing costs will be higher than forecasted. On the other hand, acquiring technology entails a much lower risk, since the product, process, or service, can be seen and tested before the contract is signed.

Regardless of whether the technology is acquired or developed, there is always the risk that it will soon become obsolete and be displaced by a superior technology. This risk cannot be entirely removed, but it can be considerably reduced by careful technology forecasting and planning. If market growth is slow, and no winner has emerged among the various competing technologies, it may be wiser to monitor these technologies through "technology gatekeepers" and be ready to jump in as the winner emerges. For instance, in the development of nonimpact magnetic printers, several technologies were researched and developed: lasers, laser xerography, electrostatic, magnetic, and ink jet. In the 1970s, GE jumped on the magnetic technology band wagon on without considering alternative technologies; after spending nearly $10 million and ten years to develop its product, the company found no takers for its poor performing printer. In the meantime IBM, Xerox Corp., Honeywell and Japanese companies had developed successful printers using the other technologies listed above. In retrospect, GE could have reduced its risk by monitoring the various competing technologies by gatekeepers in the R & D Center and by starting a crash program (as it did with CAT, Computerized Axial Tomography, a medical diagnostic imaging system) as soon as the market was ready and the winning technology had emerged.

COST. For a successful product line with relatively long life, acquisition of technology is more costly, but less risky, than technology development. Normally, royalties are paid in the form of a relatively low initial payment as "earnest money," and as periodic payments tied to sales. These payments continue throughout the period of validity of the license agreement. Since these royalties may amount to 2 to 5 percent of sales, this creates an undue burden of continuing higher cost to the licensee, everything else being equal. On the other hand, R & D requires a high front-end investment and therefore a longer period of negative cash flow. There are also intangible costs involved in acquiring technology: the license agreements may have restrictive geographic or application clauses, other businesses may have access to the same technology and compete with lower prices or stronger marketing. Finally, the licensee is dependent upon the licensor for technological advances, or even for keeping up to date, and this may be dangerous. As a typical example, General Electric gave a general license for heavy electrical equipment (hydraulic turbines, transformers, circuit breakers) to its subsidiaries in Italy, CGE (Compagnia Generale di Elettricitá) and in Spain, GEE (General Eléctrica Española), with only $1\frac{1}{2}$ per cent of sales. The problem arose when GE Power Systems decided to abandon the three businesses and drastically cut back R & D on steam turbines. The GE subsidiaries were stuck with obsolescent technologies and had to scramble to find other sources, since they lacked the resources and the time to perform in house R & D.

MOVING AHEAD WITH R & D

Once the decision has been made to perform R & D, the company should decide where and how such R & D should be carried out. There are various possibilities: in-house R & D in the company laboratories, externally contracted R & D, and joint R & D. In-house R & D commands a strategic advantage, since the company is the sole owner of the technology and can protect it from unauthorized uses. In addition, since R & D is basically a learning process, the company can develop a group of experienced scientists and engineers that can be employed in developing more advanced products and processes and in transfering the results of their R & D to operations and to customers. However, since R & D personnel do not like to work alone and are stimulated by peers, the laboratory should have a critical mass in the core technologies and support services; this critical mass may exceed the company resources.

External R & D is usually contracted out to specialized nonprofit research institutions, such as Battelle Memorial Institute or SRI International in the United States, or to universities. The advantages are that these institutions may already have experienced personnel in the disciplines to be researched, as well as the necessary laboratory and test equipment. This will save money and especially time with respect to in-house R & D. The disadvantages are that the company will not benefit from the learning experience, and may become overly dependent on the contractor. Also, the technology transfer may be difficult and there is always the possibility of leaks to competitors. In the case of universities, costs are usually lower and there is the additional benefit of identifying graduate students who may be hired later and researchers who may be employed as consultants when needed.

Joint R & D has been carried out systematically in Europe and Japan and has now become popular in the United States after **antitrust** laws were relaxed and tax incentives offered to **R & D consortia**. In a consortium, several companies with congruent interests join together to perform R & D, either in a separate organization (such as SEMATECH, the Semiconductor Manufacturing Technology Consor-

tium), or in a university. The advantages are lower costs, since each company does not have to invest in similar equipment, a critical mass of researchers, and interchange of information among the sponsors. The disadvantages are that all the sponsors have access to the same R & D results. However, because of antitrust considerations, the R & D performed must be precompetitive, and each participant in the joint R & D must apply separately the information obtained to its products, processes, and services. In some countries (for example Japan), this joint research is sponsored, if not imposed, by the government and the companies have no choice but to comply with the "directives" of MITI, the Ministry of Technology and Industry.

R & D LABORATORY ORGANIZATION AND FUNDING

R & D is usually performed within R & D laboratories, also called R & D centers, for reasons of efficiency and control and to facilitate communications and synergy among researchers. The organizational positioning and the funding of these laboratories is often a controversial matter and is still evolving. There have been three phases in the evolution of R & D in large and medium companies since the 1950's.

PHASE I. After World War II, it was believed that R & D was the key to the success of a technology-based company. All that was needed was to have the "best" (in terms of creativity and training) scientists available, give them well-equipped research laboratories, plenty of money, maximum freedom to do their own research, and wait for the inevitable scientific discoveries. According to the Director of Research of Eastman Kodak Co. "the best person to decide what research shall be done is the man who is doing the research." The laboratory, in order to insure full independence, was part of the corporate staff and was entirely funded by the corporation, which "assessed" its cost to operations. Little attention was given to how to transfer the research results to operations, and how to couple R & D activities with the company business strategies. In effect, technology management was not practiced.

Unfortunately, this *"laissez faire"* management approach produced few useful results. In some cases, the scientists met insurmountable technical barriers (for instance high-efficiency low-cost solar cells) or made important discoveries unrelated to the firm's strategic and business thrust (for instance, Nobel prizes in astrophysics and cosmology awarded to a telephone company). Some laboratories were unable to transfer their new technologies to the company operations and, in frustration, turned to more receptive audiences, including competitors. A well-publicized example is the development of the STAR PC by the Xerox PARC (Palo Alto Research Center). The computer section of Xerox was interested only in main-frame computers and disdained the STAR as a toy. Steve Jobs, the founder of Apple Computer, Inc., visited PARC, realized the potential of the new technology, hired the PARC researchers, developed the Lisa and Macintosh personal computers, and made a fortune.

PHASE II. As a reaction to these problems, operations were encouraged to set up their own laboratories, mostly to do development for a specific business. GE, for instance, had two central laboratories: the Research Laboratory and the Consulting and Engineering Laboratory, both located in Schenectady, NY. These were later joined to form the present GE R & D Center. In addition, GE set up an Electronics Lab in Syracuse, NY, a Space Sciences Lab in Valley Forge, PA, an Appliance Lab in Louisville, KY, and a Plastics Application Lab in Pittsfield, MA. The R & D Center's mission was to perform research and longer-term development of benefit to several operating units. The mission of the other laboratories was to perform shorter-term research and mostly development for the businesses to which they were organizationally responsible and from which they received funding. To insure closer coupling between the R & D Center and operations, only about two-thirds of the required funds came from the corporation through assessments. The remaining one-third was obtained through contracts that had to be negotiated with the interested operations. Naturally, operations would only fund contracts for short- or medium-term results, usually less than three years, and would not renew the contract annually unless they were satisfied. A separate ''liaison office'' was set up in the R & D Center to ensure close coupling with operations, to listen to their requirements (market pull) and to persuade them to adopt the new technologies (technology push), and to help sell the R & D contracts.

PHASE III. This system worked relatively well until the economic crises of the 1980s and the intensification of international competition. Many large and medium corporations, faced with staggering losses and major reductions in employment, questioned the need for, and the role of, the corporate laboratory, especially its funding. Some central labs were simply eliminated, or drastically reduced in size, with their mission restricted to R & D for developing new businesses at the corporate level. Most researchers were transferred to operations, where the climate was less benign, others resigned, moving to universities or starting their own businesses. In the case of GE, there was a major cutback in the support functions of the R & D Center, and the liaison function was eliminated. The laboratory and section managers are now responsible for coupling with operations. At the same time, the funding sources of the laboratory were re-versed. Before 1982, the corporation was contributing 67 percent of the budget in assessed funds, and contracts with operations amounted to the remaining 33 percent. Under the new president, Jack Welch, contract funds now amount to 75 percent and assessed funds to 25 percent. In theory, assessed funds are for exploratory research and for new business development. In practice, some may be shared with operations, for projects of longer-range impact or higher risk, which operations are unwilling to fund alone. This new funding approach does ensure close coupling with operations, but targets the R & D Center activities towards the larger, and richer, GE businesses, while neglecting the poorer, less glamorous core businesses, such as GE Power Systems.

An R & D laboratory can be organized internally according to three patterns: by functions, by projects, and matrix. In the *functional* organization, all researchers working in a specific discipline, for instance laser optics or polymers, are grouped in a unit and report to a manager, who is a recognized expert in the field. This organization is similar to the various academic departments of a university. The advantages are close interaction with peers and competent evaluations of the scientific value of the researchers' work. The main disadvantage is that most industrial R & D projects require the contributions of different disciplines, and there is often nobody responsible for managing the project and integrating the work of the researchers.

In the *project* organization, all researchers working on a given project report to a project manager, who is usually not an expert in their specific disciplines. The project manager evaluates the researchers on the basis of practical results, time, and money, rather than on the value of their scientific and technical contributions. The advantages are that the project can be professionally managed and corrective actions taken if the results expected are not forthcoming or budgets are not met. The main disadvantage is that projects have, by definition, a limited life. A project team, as an organization, is disbanded as soon as the work has been completed. The researchers now have no ''home'' and must look for work on new projects, which may or may not be forthcoming.

The *matrix* organization attempts to combine the best features of the functional and project organizations, by assigning every researcher to two superiors: a functional manager and a project manager. The functional manager is responsible for evaluating the scientific value of the researcher's work, planning his/her career development, and providing a ''home'' between projects. The project manager is responsible for evaluating the researcher's contributions to the project and giving him/her the resources needed to get the job done. Obviously, the two managers must work closely together in assigning the duties of the researchers, integrating their evaluations, and reporting them to higher management.

In practice, small and shorter-term projects are run according to a functional organization, with one researcher taking on the project administration (*not* management) duties. Larger, longer-range projects, such as the GE CAT (Computerized Axial Tomography) and MRI (Magnetic Resonance Imaging) medical diagnostic imaging systems are organized as independent projects with strong professional project management. When project responsibility is transferred to operations, some of the researchers move too, thereby ensuring an effective transfer of technology.

R & D PROJECT SELECTION, MANAGEMENT, AND TERMINATION

Industrial R & D is generally performed according to projects (i.e., separate work activities) with specific technical and business goals, assigned personnel, and time and money budgets. These projects can either originate "top down" (for instance, from a management decision to develop a new product) or "bottom up" from an idea originated by an individual researcher. The size of a project may vary from a part-time effort of one researcher for a few months with a budget of tens of thousands of dollars, to major five or ten year projects with large multidisciplinary teams of tens of researchers and budgets exceeding millions of dollars. Therefore, project selection and evaluation is one of the more critical and difficult subjects of R & D management. Of equal importance, although less emphasized in practice, is the subject of project termination, particularly in the case of unsuccessful or marginal projects.

Normally, a company or a laboratory will have requests for a higher number of projects than can be effectively implemented. Therefore, R & D managers are faced with the problem of allocating scarce resources of personnel, equipment, laboratory space, and funds to a broad spectrum of competing projects. Since the decision to start on an R & D project is both a technical and a business decision, R & D managers should select projects on the basis of the following objectives, in order of importance:

1. maximize the long-term return on investment

2. make optimum use of the available human and physical resources

3. maintain a balanced R & D portfolio and control risk

4. foster a favorable climate for creativity and innovation.

Project selection is usually done once a year, by listing all ongoing projects and the proposals for new projects, evaluating and comparing all these projects according to quantitative and qualitative criteria, and prioritizing the projects in "totem pole" order. The funds requested by all the projects are compared with the laboratory budget for the following year and the project list is cut off at the budgeted amount. Projects above the line are funded, those below the line delayed to the following year or tabled indefinitely. Some experienced R & D managers do not allocate all the budgeted funds, but keep a small percentage on reserve to take care of new projects that may be proposed during the year, after the laboratory official budget has been approved.

Since R & D projects are subject to the risk of failure, the *expected value* of a project can be evaluated *ex ante* according to the following statistical formula:

$$\text{E.V.} = P \times p_t \times p_c \times p_f$$

where P is the payoff if the project is successful, that is, the stream of net income accruing to the company over the life of the new product (or process, or service) resulting from the project. The payoff P is then multiplied by the probability of success, which is the product of three separate probabilities:

1. p_t is the probability of technical success, i.e., that the new product or process will meet the technical and functional specifications

2. p_c is the probability of commercial success, i.e., that the new product will be accepted by the marketplace and will achieve the forecasted market share

3. p_f is the probability of financial success, i.e., that the new product will achieve the forecasted financial goals, in terms of profits, return on investment, and cash flow.

Consequently, project evaluation must be performed along two separate orthogonal real dimensions: technical evaluation, to establish the probability of technical success, and business evaluation, to establish the payoff and the probabilities of commercial and financial success. Once the expected value of a project has been determined, it should be divided by the forecasted cost C of the project, in order to obtain a benefit/cost ratio R of the form R-E.V./C. Obviously the higher this ratio, the more desirable the project.

For more advanced and longer term projects, leading to major (rather than incremental) innovation, it may be difficult to establish reliable values of P, C, p_t, p_c, and p_f. In this case, a *relative* comparison of projects is made based on their respective *technical quality* and *potential business value*.

Technical quality is evaluated by analyzing and rating the clarity of the project goals; the extent of the technical, institutional, and market penetration obstacles that must be overcome; the adequacy of the skills and facilities available in the laboratory for carrying out the work; and, finally, how easily can the project results be transferred to an operation.

Potential business value of a project is defined in terms of the market share of an existing market that can be captured by the new product, or by the size of a new market that can be developed by the new product, or by the value of new technology that can be sold by the company or transferred to its customers.

After the first tentative list of projects has been established in order of priority, it is "matched" with the existing laboratory human and physical resources to make sure that these resources are well utilized. In fact, creative human resources are the laboratory's most valuable asset, and these should not be wasted by asking researchers to do work outside their disciplines and interests. Also, it is difficult to change in a short time the "mix" of available disciplines and equipment, and to hire and fire researchers as is done for labor. Thus, a shift towards new disciplines should be done gradually, avoiding the underutilization or overloading of the existing resources.

Once the tentative list of prospects has been modified according to the above, the entire *project portfolio* of the R & D laboratory should be balanced, in order to control risk, according to three types of probabilities listed above.

Technical risk is controlled in two ways: (a) by having a spectrum of projects ranging from low to medium-high technical risk; (b) by avoiding "bunching" too many projects in the same technology, particularly if the technology could be replaced by a superior technology during the expected lifetime of the new product.

Commercial risk can be controlled by not having "too many eggs in one basket," that is, by targeting different market segments (government, capital equipment, consumer, industrial, international, etc.) and attacking different competitors, since directly targeting a major competitor may trigger a dangerous counter offensive and a price war.

Financial risk is controlled by having a majority of small- and medium-size projects (in terms of R & D expense), a few large projects, and no projects that, in case of failure, could bankrupt the company. Financial risk, in terms of cash flow, is also controlled by having a spectrum (in time-to-payoff) of more short- and medium-term projects than long-term projects. This type of spectrum is also psychologically important to maintain the credibility of the R & D laboratory in the face of upper-level executives who keep asking "What have you done for me lately?"

By definition, R & D is a risky activity, and there are no "zero risk" R & D projects, since these would then be engineering projects. While the majority of the projects in an R & D portfolio should be categorized as low-risk, some medium-risk projects are justified, and even a few high-risk projects, provided their expected value is high.

Finally, project evaluation and selection should be made objectively, in order to develop and maintain a favorable climate for creativity and innovation. Researchers will be naturally disappointed when their projects are not approved. Some may even suspect that other projects were preferred for subjective reasons, such as the "halo" effect (the past track record and prestige of other, more senior, researchers), the reluctance of management to terminate less deserving projects, and especially political influences to select "pet" projects of executives. If there is a feeling that project selection is not done objectively, many researchers, particularly the junior ones, will lose their enthusiasm and renounce proposing new projects of a high potential value for the company. Eventually, if this situation persists, the laboratory will lose its creativity and concentrate on routine low-risk (but also low-payoff!) or "political" projects, and it will have difficulty in keeping and attracting the best researchers. Therefore, it is desirable that the project evaluation and selection criteria be properly explained and that all researchers be asked to participate in the evaluation process. Also, the finalized project portfolio should be presented to, and discussed with, all the researchers.

The management of R & D projects follows basically the principles and methods of project management. There is, however, one significant caveat in relation to normal engineering projects: R & D projects are risky, and it is difficult to develop an accurate budget, in terms of technical milestones, costs, and time to completion of the various tasks. Therefore, R & D budgets should be considered initially as tentative, and should be gradually refined as more information becomes available as a result of preliminary work and the learning process. Historically, many R & D projects have exceeded, sometimes with disastrous consequences, the forecasted and budgeted times to completion and funds to be expended. In the case of R & D, measuring technical progress and completion of milestones is generally more important than measuring expenditures over time.

Finally, termination of projects is a difficult subject because of the political repercussions on the laboratory. Theoretically, a project should be discontinued for one of the following three reasons:

1. there is a change in the environment, for instance new government regulations, new competitive offerings, or price declines, that

make the new product less attractive to the company

2. unforseen technical obstacles are encountered and the laboratory does not have the resources to overcome them

3. the project falls hopelessly behind schedule and corrective actions are not forthcoming

Due to organizational inertia, and the fear of antagonizing senior ''prima donna'' researchers or executives with pet projects, there is often the tendency to let a project continue, hoping for a miraculous breakthrough that seldom happens.

In theory, an optimal number of projects should be initiated and this number should be gradually reduced over time to make room for more deserving projects. Also, the monthly cost of a project is much lower in the early stages than in the later stages, when more personnel and equipment have been committed. Thus, from a financial risk management viewpoint, it is better to waste money on several promising young projects than on a few maturing ''dogs'' with low payoff and high expense. In practice, in many laboratories it is difficult to start a new project because all the resources have already been committed and just as difficult to terminate a project, for the reasons given above. Thus, an able and astute R&D manager should continuously evaluate his/her project portfolio in relation to changes in company strategy, should continuously and objectively monitor the progress of each R&D project, and should not hesitate to terminate projects that have lost their value to the company in terms of payoff and probability of success.

In conclusion, by assuring a close coupling with the company's strategic goals and by maintaining close contacts with operations, the laboratory and the R & D function will maintain credibility and strengthen its strategic value for the corporation.

[Pier A. Abetti]

FURTHER READING:

Hampton, John J., ed. *AMA Management Handbook.* ANACOM, 1994.

Martin, Michael J.C. *Managing Technological Innovation and Entrepreneurship.* Reston, 1984.

Roussel, Philip. A., Kamal N. Saad, and Tamara J. Erikson. *Third Generation R & D.* Harvard Business School Press, 1991.

Twiss, Brian. *Managing Technological Innovation.* 3rd ed. Pitman, 1985.

RESEARCH AND DEVELOPMENT CONSORTIA

Research and development consortia are formed by manufacturing companies, often with the support of government, for the purpose of conducting shared research on new technologies for the benefit of the consortium's member companies. Government-supported R & D consortia *(kumaia)* have been common in Japan since the 1960s, and now number more than 200. In the United States, however, the formation of industry-specific R & D consortia was hindered by **antitrust laws** that penalized cooperation among competitors until Congress passed the National Cooperative Research Act of 1984 (NCRA).

Under the NCRA, firms within an industry may form consortia to conduct ''precompetitive'' research. Precompetitive research is research that is considered generic to the development of multiple products of basic value to all participants. By forming R & D consortia, manufacturing firms can avoid duplicating basic research tasks and share the results more cost effectively. As a result they are able to compete more effectively in the global marketplace.

Research and development consortia are required by the NCRA to register with the U.S. Department of Justice, which recorded more than 300 new consortia between 1984 and 1994. In 1993, the NCRA was expanded to cover joint manufacturing agreements. While the NCRA does not provide exemption from antitrust laws, it limits the damages that may be assessed if an antitrust violation occurs. Where as antitrust laws provide for triple damages to be assessed, the NCRA limits liability to single damages. However, in the decade since NCRA was passed, no antitrust proceedings have been brought against registered consortia.

Research and development consortia can provide member companies with many benefits. They are formed to share expenses and resources and to pool talent and expertise. Consortia that are formed in the United States to compete globally are eligible for government funding. The most common type of consortia are horizontal, consisting of competing firms within an industry. Vertical consortia include firms ranging from materials suppliers to finished product manufacturers.

Research and development consortia have been successful in spurring innovation. SEMATECH, a Texas-based consortia of major semiconductor manufacturers founded in 1987, has had dramatic success in helping its member companies regain dominant market shares in the international semiconductor equipment and silicon-chip markets. Another consortia, the U.S. Council for Automotive Research, was formed to accelerate technological innovation among the major automobile manufacturers.

After manufacturing companies have agreed to form a consortium and have registered with the Department of Justice, they then assign personnel and budget funds to it. Joint research is usually conducted at a single specified site. Under the NCRA, the research must be precompetitive, concerning areas generic to the products of each member company. As the consortium develops new technologies and improves on existing ones, individual companies may begin to apply those technologies to their own products. At a certain point in time, the companies may agree to dissolve the consortium to focus on their own applications.

Research and development consortia may consist exclusively of companies from a single nation, or they may be international in scope. Japan's Ministry of International Trade and Industry (MITI), which supports and directs R & D consortia in Japan, began opening some of its R & D consortia to foreign companies in 1990. In the European Community, U.S. companies are allowed to participate in publicly supported R & D consortia. In the United States, consortia that receive government funds are limited to domestic companies.

In the United States, joint ventures between private industry and federal laboratories offer similar research sharing and development opportunities as R & D consortia. Called Cooperative Research and Development Agreements (CRADAs), they are becoming more commonplace as federal laboratories refocus their efforts away from Cold War defense projects to help domestic industries develop new technologies.

[David Bianco]

RESOLUTION TRUST CORPORATION (RTC)

The Resolution Trust Corporation (RTC) becomes either a conservator or a receiver for an insolvent savings and loan institution (S&L) when the Office of Thrift Supervision (OTS) determines the S&L is being operated in an unsafe or unsound manner. If the RTC becomes conservator, the S&L's financial condition is further evaluated and is prepared for sale with designated assets. The S&L's deposits and franchises are marketed to pre-qualified bidders. Once the question of the failed S&L's ownership has been resolved, any remaining assets are held in receivership for disposition and are sold in accordance with RTC asset disposition sales policies.

The RTC has established Sales Centers to respond to investor needs and to facilitate the sale of real estate and loans in cooperation with local real estate brokers and contracted asset management firms. These RTC Sales Centers have been organized into two areas: real estate; and financial instruments, to coordinate the sale of all other assets, including mortgage and consumer loans.

The Resolution Trust Corporation (RTC) was established on August 9, 1989 when the Financial Institutions Reform, Recovery and Enforcement Act (FIRREA) was signed into law. The law provided for a major restructuring of the nation's thrift industry and a reorganization of the federal agencies that oversee this industry. The mission of the RTC is to sell all assets in such a manner that maximizes the net present value return from the sale or other disposition of thrifts and their assets, to minimize the impact of such transactions on local real estate and financial markets, and to maximize the availability and affordability of residential real estate for low- and moderate-income individuals.

The RTC created the Small Investor Program (SIP) in June 1993 to meet the needs of investors with moderate levels of investment capital. Under the SIP, the RTC will offer real estate assets on an individual basis for at least 120 days, either through a broker, auction, or sealed bid sale. Assets marketed under SIP are offered with an emphasis on geographic focus to attract small investors who want to invest in their local market.

The RTC acquires its assets when the Office of Thrift Supervision (OTS) appoints the RTC as conservator or receiver for an insolvent savings and loan, which the RTC has determined is being operated in an unsafe or unsound manner.

The RTC sells its real estate owned (REO), loans, and other assets (including subsidiaries, mortgage servicing rights, and furniture, fixtures and equipment) depending upon product type, geographic location, complexity, market demand and marketing, and holding costs. Individual sale, sealed bid sale, open outcry auctions, and securitization are strategies the RTC uses.

Some select assets, including short-term loans, may be held to maturity. Loans are packaged and sold primarily through open outcry auctions, sealed bid sales, or securitization.

Individual sale is the strategy the RTC uses to make real estate assets that are immediately deliverable upon closing available to the public.

The sealed bid sale method is often selected when two or more parties are interested in the same asset or when a sealed bid sale can effectively establish a high level of competition that may command a higher sale price.

Open outcry auctions are used to sell REO, loans, and furniture, fixtures, and equipment (ff&e). Auctions provide the opportunity to expose a large volume of assets to the marketplace and dispose of them quickly. Minimum bids or reserve prices are usually established, although the RTC may conduct absolute auctions or auctions with no minimum reserve on some of its smaller assets and ff&e.

Securitization is the process of restructuring cash flows from pools of whole loans into securities which are liquid assets.

Among the assets in the RTC's inventory are:

- COMMERCIAL: Office complexes; retail shopping centers; bank branches; mobile home parks; storage facilities/mini-warehouses; industrial park/warehouses; restaurants; parking garages/lots; medical facilities/private hospitals; nursing/retirement homes; hotels/motels; resorts/golf courses; apartments; office condominiums; and mixed-use zoned land.

- RESIDENTIAL: Single-family detached (1 to 4); townhouse; condominium; co-op; and timeshare.

- LAND: Unimproved, commercial and residential; developed, commercial and residential; agricultural; and ranch/pastures.

- FINANCIAL INSTRUMENTS: Residential/commercial mortgages; consumer loans (secured and unsecured); judgments/deficiencies; business loans; leasing portfolios; and securities.

- SUBSIDIARIES: Mortgage banking/servicing; title; insurance; and real estate development.

- FURNITURE, FIXTURES & EQUIPMENT (FF&E): Art; banking equipment; computers; gallery/restaurant equipment; office equipment; heavy equipment; and vehicles.

SEE ALSO: Banks and Banking; Savings and Loan Associations.

[Susan Bard Hall]

FURTHER READING:

"Complete Guide to the Resolution Trust Corporation," Resolution Trust Corporation, January 1994, pp. 1, 5, 6, 8, 9, 11, and 26.

RESOURCE CONSERVATION AND RECOVERY ACT

In 1976 the Resource Conservation and Recovery Act (RCRA) was enacted as an amendment to the Solid Waste Disposal Act. RCRA regulates both household and hazardous solid wastes, with regulations covering hazardous waste that are particularly detailed and are described as being "cradle to grave." ("Cradle to grave" refers to regulation from the point of generation of the waste through and including its ultimate point of "disposal" or storage.) The act was amended by Congress in 1978, 1980, 1984, 1986, and 1988, with the 1984 amendments making the most substantial additions to the program. The 1984 amendments, called the Hazardous and Solid Waste Amendments (HSWA), expanded RCRA's coverage and requirements significantly to deal with hazardous industrial wastes.

Most of RCRA's programs are designed to be proactive; that is, they are designed to provide for safe handling and containment of both hazardous and nonhazardous wastes as they are generated. RCRA does not address the problems associated with inactive or abandoned dump sites or those associated with chemical spills or releases requiring immediate, emergency response. Those problems are dealt with under the **Comprehensive Environmental Response, Compensation, and Liability Act (CERCLA) of 1980**, commonly known as Superfund. Both RCRA and CERCLA are administered by the federal **Environmental Protection Agency (EPA)**. RCRA's programs regulating businesses are administered by regional offices of the EPA except in states that have been authorized to administer their own RCRA programs. In such states, businesses deal directly with a state counterpart to the EPA.

HISTORY—THE NEED FOR RCRA

Prior to 1965, regulation of solid wastes was considered to be the responsibility of state and local governments. When the Solid Waste Disposal Act was enacted in 1965, a great deal of our waste (garbage) disposal was through open dumping or in local "landfills." The Solid Waste Disposal Act was the first federal statute dealing with the effects of such dumping on our environment. The act's goal was to promote better solid waste disposal methods. It did so primarily by providing grants to states and local governments for research on waste disposal.

The Solid Waste Disposal Act was amended in 1970 by the Resource Recovery Act and in 1976 by RCRA. RCRA was designed to eliminate "the last remaining loophole in environmental law, that of unregulated land disposal of discarded materials and hazardous wastes" according to a report issued by the U.S. House of Representatives. In its enactment of RCRA in 1976 and in the 1984 and 1986 amendments to RCRA, Congress addressed three sets of needs and concerns. First, it focused on the need for a *system* for management of solid wastes. Second, it recognized the need for special provisions for dealing with hazardous wastes. Third, it included provisions to encourage resource conservation and recovery (recycling and reuse of resources).

Prior to enactment of RCRA, a great deal of the hazardous waste in the United States was "disposed of" or dumped at or near the site at which it was generated. In other cases, generators of hazardous waste hired transporters to take the wastes to off-site disposal areas. A lack of record-keeping and lack of efforts to contain wastes at disposal sites created serious problems for today and for future generations. When on-site disposal was used, records were not kept and property was often sold to parties who had no information about the presence of hazardous materials on the premises or buried on the property. When off-site disposal was used, generators often knew nothing about the location of or operations of the site to which transporters took hazardous wastes. Typically, a disposal site went through several changes of ownership during its period of operation, which averaged about 20 years. A site usually received hazardous wastes from numerous transporters and generators, and site operators had few or no records documenting the kinds of wastes located there. Further, after a site was closed, it was often sold (or occasionally donated) to purchasers who had no idea of its prior use. An example of this is the Love Canal site near Niagara Falls, New York, where in the late 1970s about 200 families experiencing unusually high rates of cancer, birth defects, and other health-related problems discovered that their homes and their children's elementary school had been built on top of a former waste dump for hazardous chemicals. Land for the school had been donated to the local school district.

RCRA'S PROVISIONS AND PROGRAMS

RCRA includes four distinct programs designed to implement its goals. First, it encourages states to develop plans to manage nonhazardous waste (household waste). Second, it establishes a "cradle to grave" system for monitoring and controlling the disposal of hazardous waste. The system of paperwork for monitoring such disposal is called a manifest system. Third, it regulates underground storage tanks through a program called the Underground Storage Tank (UST) program. Fourth, the EPA has conducted a new demonstration program to track medical wastes from generation through disposal.

In Subtitle D of RCRA, states are encouraged to implement their own solid waste management plans. This has become increasingly difficult for states due to at least two factors. First, with population growth and the increased use of "disposable" products, the amount of waste being generated each year is increasing dramatically. Second, there is a phenomenon which has been labeled the "NIMBY Syndrome."

("NIMBY" stands for "Not In My Back Yard.") Our present solid waste disposal sites are being filled quickly; most are filled to capacity within 20 (or fewer) years after their opening. Yet, because of opposition of local residents, it has become extremely difficult for private waste disposal companies or local municipalities to find locations for and open new facilities for disposal of such wastes. No one wants to live next to or near such a site. As a result, in the 1984 Hazardous and Solid Waste Amendments, Congress authorized the EPA to take a more active role in assisting the states in handling nonhazardous waste landfills. The EPA has been working on strategies to deal with disposal of household wastes.

In Subtitle C of RCRA, Congress established a "cradle to grave" system for management of hazardous wastes. Pursuant to Subtitle C, the EPA has issued criteria for identifying hazardous wastes, and, in turn, it has used those criteria to issue a list of those wastes which are considered to be "hazardous" for purposes of administration of RCRA. That list is published in the Federal Register and is updated periodically. As a part of this "cradle to grave" system, the EPA was directed to issue three sets of standards regulating three sets of parties: (1) generators who produce hazardous waste, (2) transporters of the waste, and (3) those who own or operate disposal sites. The EPA has issued standards regulating how generators handle, label, and store hazardous wastes. Similar standards cover transporters of hazardous wastes. A transporter must obtain a license (permit) for hauling of wastes and that license will cover only specified types of waste, depending on whether the transporter has met the EPA's requirements for each type. Similarly, any facility accepting hazardous wastes for disposal must obtain a license (permit) from the EPA in which the EPA specifies which kinds of hazardous waste can be accepted by the facility. Such facilities are subject to extensive regulation by the EPA covering location and construction of the site as well as its ongoing operation. As a precondition to issuance of licenses (permits) to transporters or owners or operators of sites, the EPA applies extensive standards (regulations) to those parties.

Tying together the EPA's regulation of generators, transporters, and owners or operators of sites is the "manifest system." A manifest is a set of paperwork that accompanies any "batch" of hazardous waste from the generator, through any and all transporters, and to the site of ultimate disposal. The disposal site might be better conceptualized as the site of "permanent storage," because such wastes never "go away." (In some cases, however, wastes may be treated to reduce hazards or to recover materials for reuse.) The RCRA and the EPA refer to disposal sites as "treatment, storage and disposal facilities" (TSDFs).

The manifest is a form that is obtained from the EPA or its state counterpart in states that have been authorized to administer RCRA. The manifest form includes five or six copies of a form with copying materials in-between. The generator fills out his or her portion of the form, identifying the wastes to be hauled; keeps a copy; and conveys the remaining copies to the transporter. It should be noted that this manifest system affects most businesses in this country. Any company generating one-half of a 50-gallon barrel of hazardous wastes or more per month must comply with the manifest system.

Next, the transporter completes the remaining forms, giving the transporter's EPA-assigned identification number. The transporter keeps one copy. If there is a second transporter, he or she does the same. Finally, the disposal site owner or operator completes the remaining forms with his or her EPA-assigned identification number. The owner or operator keeps one copy, sends one to the EPA or its state counterpart, and sends one to the generator. The result is a complete "paper record" of a batch of hazardous wastes from the point of generation to its ultimate "disposal" site. Generators of waste can be held liable for civil or criminal penalties for failure to complete a manifest, for failure to hire an EPA-licensed transporter, or if the wastes are not placed in an EPA-licensed facility. There are also civil or criminal penalties for transporters or facilities which are either unlicensed or which handle or accept wastes not allowed under their licenses.

Subtitle I of RCRA, regulating underground storage tanks, was added to RCRA through 1984 amendments. Pursuant to the program, states are required to inventory all underground storage tanks containing hazardous substances or petroleum products. Testing of all such tanks is required and use of tanks which are subject to leaking must be discontinued by 1997. If an owner or operator of the tank can be identified, he or she is required to undertake and pay for cleanup of the tank and contamination caused by the tank. When an owner or operator cannot be identified or is insolvent, funding may be available from a $500 million Leaking Underground Storage Tank Trust Fund which was established through the 1986 amendments to RCRA. The program is funded by federal taxes on motor fuels. The program has become controversial, however, because various states have run out of funds without having finished testing and cleanup of the numerous leaking tanks within their borders.

Subtitle J was added to RCRA in 1988 when U.S. citizens became alarmed in response to reports about medical wastes being washed up on beaches in the United States and in other parts of the world. Pursuant to Subtitle J, the EPA conducted a two-year demonstration project designed to track medical waste from generation to disposal, following the model of Subtitle C, which regulates disposal of hazardous wastes. To this date, Congress has not enacted a nation-wide program for medical waste regulation. Some states, however, are regulating such wastes.

Sanctions for violations of the various requirements of RCRA include civil and criminal penalties. Civil penalties range up to $25,000 per day per violation. Criminal penalties can include up to one year in prison, fines of up to $25,000 per day per violation, or both.

CRITICISMS OF RCRA AND ITS FUTURE

Corporate managers have been frustrated by the amount of paperwork required under RCRA, the minute details of operation covered by RCRA regulations, and by the EPA's slow action in reviewing applications for permits. RCRA limits the duration of permits to ten years, yet it may take up to four years to obtain a permit from the EPA. Thus, operators of a facility may feel as though they are continuously involved in the process of applying for permits. Some critics allege that as a consequence of this process the most reputable companies which make good-faith efforts and devote substantial resources to waste minimization and waste handling are unduly burdened by the EPA's regulation of their activities pursuant to RCRA. Those critics allege that at the same time RCRA's burdensome requirements encourage other less reputable companies to avoid the regulatory process altogether. Such companies dispose of their wastes in illegal ways creating hazards to which the public will be exposed.

Further, as the United States is becoming more involved in a global economy, its handling of hazardous waste has taken on global consequences. As a result of a scarcity of sites for disposal of both nonhazardous and hazardous wastes, new companies have been established in the United States that make a business of shipping our wastes abroad. Such waste is reportedly being hauled to sites in the Caribbean, the South American country of Guyana, various countries in Africa, and to other sites throughout the world. The attention of the world was captivated when from 1988 to 1990 a shipment of ash from Philadelphia spend two years traveling from country to country including the Bahamas, Bermuda, Honduras, the Dominican Republic, Guinea-Bissau, and Haiti trying to find a place to dump its cargo of waste. Environmentalists fear that impoverished Third World countries are becoming dumping grounds for the hazardous wastes of more prosperous, industrialized countries. As a consequence, traffic in international wastes has become the subject of international agreements, including, for example, the 1989 Basel Convention.

A sound environmental policy for the United States must include provisions for management of hazardous wastes. Environmentalists agree that businesses must be encouraged to develop innovative programs for management of hazardous waste. The current RCRA program may be discouraging such innovation by placing substantial costs and inconvenience on responsible businesses. Yet, our businesses must behave in a responsible manner in the international area and avoid taking advantage of citizens of Third World countries which may be coerced to accept hazardous wastes due to financial need. Thus, it is likely that Congress will give serious consideration to proposals for amendments to RCRA as it considers its reauthorization in the near future. In addition, issues related to management of wastes will extend beyond RCRA into negotiation of international agreements and treaties as our interconnections with other countries expand.

[Paulette L. Stenzel]

FURTHER READING:

Findley, Roger W., and Daniel A. Farber. *Environmental Law in a Nutshell*. 2nd. ed. 1988, pp. 162-168.

Feder, Miriam. "Failures of the Current Waste Management Policy." *Environmental Law*. 18, 1988, pp. 671-681.

Sheppard, Nathaniel, Jr. "West Shipping Waste Woes to Third World." *Chicago Tribune*. July 11, 1988, Sec. 1, pp. 1, 8.

Dufour, Jean-Paul, and Corinne Denis. "The North's Garbage Goes South." *World Press Review*. November, 1988, pp. 30-31.

Kummer, Katharina. "The International Regulation of Transboundary Traffic in Hazardous Wastes: The 1989 Basel Convention." *International and Comparative Law Quarterly*. 41, 1992, pp. 530-562.

RESTRAINT OF TRADE

"Restraint of trade" is a phrase that is part of the Sherman Antitrust Act of 1890. This historic piece of federal legislation was designed to halt the excessive monopolistic and anti-competitive activities of burgeoning industrial combinations and trusts. The words appear in the first section of the act: "Every contract, combination in the form of trust or otherwise, or conspiracy in restraint of trade or commerce among the several states, or with foreign nations, is declared to be illegal." Named after Senator John Sherman of Ohio, the act was written by Senators George Edmunds of Vermont and George Hoar of Massachusetts.

Prior to the Sherman Antitrust Act there was no legislation dealing specifically with anticompetitive business behavior. While contracts that allegedly restrained trade were unenforceable under certain circumstances there were no laws allowing for punitive action or sanctions against offending parties. Monopolies and **trusts** were also quite legal. The Sherman

Act was meant to curtail two types of anticompetitive behavior: the growth of giant monopolies through mergers and various price-fixing agreements.

The years between the Panic of 1873 and the passage of the Sherman Antitrust Act saw a steady growth of monopolistic combinations or trusts. This monopolistic trend was particularly evident in heavy industry and railroads. There was a worrisome feeling in many segments of society that trusts were harming the economy by reducing or eliminating **competition** which subsequently caused a slowdown or reduction in economic output. A strident antimonopolistic fervor soon developed that called for legal reform to curtail trust activity. There is contradictory historical evidence, however, as to which segments of nineteenth-century American society opposed the trusts. Many economists felt that although a lack of competition tended to drive prices up, the inherent efficiency and cost effectiveness of trusts tended to drive prices down. Much of the antitrust fervor came from the so called "muckrakers" and "yellow journalists" of the late nineteenth-century and was based on emotional appeals rather than empirical evidence. By the late 1880s the outcry for reform was growing unabated and by 1890 15 states had enacted antimonopolistic legislation. Pressure continued to mount for more effective and comprehensive federal legislation and the Sherman Act was enacted by a large bipartisan congressional majority on July 2, 1890.

The Sherman Antitrust Act does not define "restraint of trade." That was left for the courts, which they did in a number of different and sometimes controversial ways. In early decisions (*Trans-Missouri Freight Association*, 1897; *Joint Traffic Association*, 1898; and *Addyston Pipe*, 1899) the courts found that any agreement to limit competition was illegal under the Sherman Act. In 1911, however, the courts found that only unreasonable restraints of trade were illegal. These decisions (*Standard Oil Co. of NJ v. United States* and *United States v. American Tobacco Co.*) employed the so-called "rule of reason." This concept led to the Clayton Antitrust Act of 1914, which specifically addressed price discrimination, mergers, and tying the purchase of a set of goods with the required purchase of another. Under the Clayton Act these acts were illegal but only when they weakened competition or contributed to other monopolistic behaviors.

In the 1940 *Socony-Vacuum Oil Company* case the "per se" concept was established following 20 years of mixed decisions (*Chicago Board of Trade*, 1918; *Trenton Potteries*, 1927; *Appalachian Coals*, 1933). In the Socony case the court found that even though there were previous specific exceptions, tampering with price structure is nonetheless unlawful and ". . . raising, depressing, fixing, pegging or stabilizing the price of a commodity in interstate and foreign commerce is illegal per se.'' Alleged anticompetitive activities could now be judged as ''illegal per se'' when they have no justification or redeeming value, or they could be judged as falling under the ''rule of reason,'' which is a much more situational way of viewing anticompetitive behavior.

There are two general categories of restraint of trade practices: vertical restraints and horizontal restraints. Vertical restraints occur when a company purchases or otherwise acquires control over another company that is either its supplier or customer. The controlling company is then in position to impose various anticompetitive restrictions on its former customer or supplier. These restrictions can include:

- Resale price maintenance where the supplier dictates a minimum price at which its products can be resold. This practice is generally regarded as being illegal per se.

- Maximum resale price maintenance is similar to resale price maintenance except the supplier sets a maximum price at which its products can be resold. This practice is also illegal per se.

- Mandating territorial or other customer restrictions is also a vertical restraint. This occurs when a manufacturer dictates to whom its products may be resold. Originally courts ruled such activity was illegal per se but recently such activity is judged under the rule of reason.

- Tying arrangements occur when a seller demands that a certain lot of its goods can only be purchased by a customer if that customer also purchases a different lot of goods. The purchase of one lot is tied to or dependent upon the purchase of the second lot. Under certain circumstances tying arrangements may be illegal per se.

Vertical restraints occur in the relationship between suppliers and customers and almost always at a wholesale level. There is still controversy among economists over the anticompetitive impact of vertical restraints.

Horizontal restraints deal with price-fixing agreements and are highly illegal. Similar to price-fixing agreements and just as illegal are other practices such as ''bid rigging,'' **boycotts**, territorial impositions, and imposed minimum fee schedules. The *Socony-Vacuum Oil Company* case determined that horizontal restraints represent the type of anticompetitive practices the Sherman Antitrust Act was written to curtail and that decision remains the rule of law today.

[Michael Knes]

FURTHER READING:

Areeda, Phillip. *Antitrust Analysis*. Boston: Little, Brown, 1988.

Bork, Robert. *The Antitrust Paradox*. New York: Basic Books, 1978.

RESTRICTIVE COVENANTS

Creditors use protective covenants in bond indentures to protect their interests by restricting certain activities of the issuer that could endanger the creditor's position. Similarly, **banks** employ loan covenants to ensure that the borrower uses the funds for the stated purpose. Auditors (or trustees in the case of bond issues) must certify that the borrowing firm has not violated the covenants. If a covenant is violated, then the debtor is in technical default, and the creditor can require immediate repayment of the bond issue or the loan.

COVENANTS IN BOND AGREEMENTS

The American Bar Association's *Commentaries on Debentures* provides a summary of the typical covenants found in bond agreements. These covenants can be divided into four basic categories: (1) those restricting the issuance of new debt; (2) those restricting dividend payments; (3) those restricting merger activities; and (4) those restricting the disposition of the firm's assets. Bond covenants that restrict subsequent debt financing are by far the most common type. The provisions are typically stated in terms of **accounting** measures in order to make them easier to monitor. The issuance of **debt** may require the new bond issue to be subordinate to existing debt. This restriction is designed to prevent the firm from increasing the riskiness of existing debt by issuing new bonds with a superior claim on the firm's assets. Other covenants may prohibit the issuance of additional debt unless the firm maintains certain prescribed financial ratios between tangible net worth and long-term debt, tangible assets and long-term debt, and income and interest charges.

Creditors also attempt to limit stockholders' ability to transfer assets to themselves through dividend restrictions. Bond covenants that restrict **dividends** are necessary to protect bondholders against the payout of assets that serve as collateral. In the extreme case, shareholders could vote to pay themselves a liquidating dividend leaving only an empty corporate shell. Most dividend restrictions refer not only to cash dividends, but also share repurchases. Payout restrictions generally require that dividends can be increased only if the firm's earnings are positive, if the firm issues new equity capital, or if dividend distributions since the bonds were issued are maintained below some predetermined maximum level.

Bond covenants allow merger activity only if certain conditions are met. Mergers can have a negative effect on existing bondholders if the acquiring firm has more debt in its capital structure than the target firm, or if the debt of the acquiring firm matures sooner than the debt of the target firm. Thus, bond covenants allow mergers only if the net tangible assets of the combined firms meet a certain minimum dollar amount or are greater than a certain fraction of long-term debt. The mergers-related covenants could also make the merger contingent on the absence of default after the transaction is completed.

Debt covenants that restrict asset disposition decisions take the following forms: (1) restrictions on common stock investments, **loans**, and extensions of credit; (2) restrictions on the disposition of assets; and (3) covenants requiring the maintenance of minimum levels of assets. Assets that provide collateral cannot be disposed of under the provisions of the indenture agreement.

In addition to restrictions on the activities of the firm, covenants may also be expressed in the maintenance of certain levels of accounting based measures, such as retained earnings, **working capital**, net assets, and debt-to-equity ratios. These affirmative covenants are generally related to the restrictions above by limiting a certain activity if the accounting variable drops below a certain level.

LOAN COVENANTS

To protect the surety of their loans, banks also require covenants in loan agreements. Loan covenants are similar to those found in bond issues, and are of two primary types. Affirmative covenants describe actions which a firm agrees to take during the term of the loan. These include such activities as providing **financial statements** and cash budgets, carrying insurance on assets and against insurable business risks, and maintaining minimum levels of net working capital. Negative covenants describe actions which a firm agrees not to take during the term of the loan. These may include agreements not to merge with other firms, not to pledge assets as security to other lenders, or not to make or guarantee loans to other firms. The covenants in private lending agreements often modify generally accepted accounting principles (GAAP). For example, off-the-balance-sheet debt may be included in calculating the debt-to-equity ratio.

[Robert T. Kleiman]

FURTHER READING:

Copeland, Thomas E., and J. Fred Weston. *Financial Theory and Corporate Policy*. 3rd ed. Reading, MA: Addison-Wesley Publishing Company, 1987.

RÉSUMÉS

A résumé is a document presented by a job applicant to a prospective employer outlining and summarizing that person's qualifications for **employment**. A résumé generally includes data on education, previous work experience, and personal information. The résumé is formatted in such a way as to make the applicant attractive as a potential employee. A résumé is generally accompanied by a cover letter which introduces the applicant and the résumé to the employer. The purpose of a résumé is to obtain an interview, not to land a job. This is an important distinction. Whether or not a person is hired is largely determined by what transpires during the job interview, not by the résumé. A résumé is extremely important because it provides the employer with a first impression of the job applicant. From this first impression a decision will be made as to whether or not an interview will be granted.

Résumés are read from two perspectives: the physical document itself and the content of the résumé. In the first regard the employer will become aware of any typographical errors, poor grammar usage, or sloppy sentence structure. Many résumés also employ various gimmicks to attract attention. These can include odd-sized sheets of paper, garish colors, and unconventional type. Many prospective employers feel that applicants utilizing such tactics are attempting to cover a weakness in their background. There is also disagreement among employers concerning professionally prepared résumés. Many such résumés are done in a style that makes it evident that the résumés were professionally written. Employers often prefer résumés to be in the applicants' own words and style so as to better judge their communication skills.

The content of most résumés falls into four broad categories: education, previous work experience, personal data, and social data. The first two are self-explanatory. Personal data includes such things as address and telephone number. Social data includes military status, club memberships, references, etc. Handbooks that provide detailed advice on compiling résumés are available in most bookstores and libraries. These guides generally agree on the types of information to include on a résumé but sometimes differ on the format and hierarchical arrangement of the résumé. Some authors feel that educational information should be presented first while others feel previous work experience should be foremost. Other authors of such handbooks offer advice on tailoring a résumé to fit one's particular employment situation be it first job, re-entering the job market, or changing fields or vocations. Most of these handbooks, however, have one thing in common: they generally lack empirical data on what a prospective employer is looking for in a résumé. References in these handbooks to this aspect of the applicant, résumé, and employer scenario is largely anecdotal.

In 1984 Professor Kevin Hutchinson surveyed 500 large corporations and organizations throughout the United States. A summary of Hutchinson's study showed the percentage of personnel administrators' preferences regarding résumé content: educational qualifications and previous work experience were highest (92 percent) followed by professional objectives (90 percent), special aptitudes—computer skills, foreign language skills, etc. (78 percent), special interests related to one's vocational field (75 percent), personal information (72 percent), and finally, social data (57 percent). Hutchinson's research also supported the importance of résumé content over format, showing no support for the inclusion of references to personality traits, little support for the inclusion of information on hobbies and outside activities, and a strong feeling that race, religion, and gender should not appear on the résumé. There was mixed and sometimes contradictory support for information relating to age, marital status, and dependents.

When reading résumés, employers generally are looking for hard data and information. Functional résumés (résumés with no dates) are often viewed as indicators of excessive job movement or attempts to hide large gaps in one's career. Nebulous phraseology such as "exposure to" or "assisted in" indicate a lack of depth of work experience as does excess space devoted to education, personal, and social data. Employers are also on the lookout for deliberately falsified information and often hire outside firms to verify data and information appearing on résumés.

There are also a number of automated résumé banks in the United States. Upon request these banks will, for a fee, mail out copies of résumés to prospective employers. Using technical terminology and job related phrases a computer will match the résumés it stores in its data bank with job descriptions supplied by its clients. Résumé banks, however, are not professional recruiters who are compensated for their services, in terms of a percentage of a recruit's salary. Résumé banks charge a sliding fee for their services generally in the range of a few hundred dollars.

[Michael Knes]

FURTHER READING:

Half, Robert. "Managing Your Career: How Do You Read a Résumé?" *Management Accounting*. May, 1988.

Hutchinson, Kevin L. "Personnel Administrators' Preferences for Résumé Content: A Survey and Review of Empirically Based Conclusions." *Journal of Business Communication*. Fall, 1984, pp. 5-13.

RETAIL TRADE

Retail trade is the section of the economy that offers goods and services for sale directly to the ultimate consumers. Wholesale trade is the purchase of goods or services in bulk by businesses or persons who may add something to those goods or services, or use them in production, and then sell them to others, rather than to ultimate consumers.

The retail industry accounted for 21 percent of all nonfarm jobs in the United States in 1993. The U.S. Industrial Outlook for 1994 predicted that retail sales would reach an estimated $2.1 trillion in 1994. According to the National Retail Federation (NRF), almost 90 percent of 21 million retail workers were employed in businesses with fewer than 20 workers.

There are more than one million retail companies in the United States. Retailers offer a wide variety of durable and nondurable merchandise. The Census Bureau classifies these establishments according to their principal merchandise line—the line that accounts for at least 50 percent of the total sales of the store. Thus a store such as Kmart which carries furniture, but sells far more clothing, would have its furniture sales reported under the principal line, "clothing." According to the U.S. Industrial Outlook for 1994, retail establishments selling both durable and nondurable goods experienced an increase in sales in 1993 over 1992, 5.7 percent for nondurables and 7 percent for durables. The U.S. Industrial Outlook covers most, but not all of the retail trade through the gathering of census data. Census data is not collected for discount stores, warehouse stores, convenience stores, catalog sales, and video sales firms, although these are a significant part of the retail trade market. Other sources, such as the NRF, do capture this data.

HISTORY

In the late 1700s in Europe and slightly later in the United States, the societal mix of ample goods with enough people with disposable income to purchase those goods reached the critical mass needed to fuel the rise of a merchant class and a multitude of shops. Colonial American towns were lined with shops where the purchase of goods and the exchange of social niceties was a way of life. Frontier settlers were treated to "portable" stores in the form of peddler wagons until enough people lived in one area to support a store. This pattern continued well into the twentieth century with a cluster of stores downtown that sold many goods, and a few food and general merchandise stores in the neighborhoods.

In the sixties, retailing began to take on a new face. Retailers followed their customers to the suburbs with an array of strip malls, then in the seventies and eighties giant indoor shopping malls, and in the nineties the return to the strip mall and the beginning of the electronic shopping place.

Retail trade has always been an important factor in the nation's economy and in the nation's **credit** outlook. Retailers purchase items for sale with no guarantee of selling them, often borrowing large sums to make the goods available to customers. Customers, in turn, often purchase items on credit using store or national credit cards.

The NRF's booklet, ''Retailing: On Every Main Street'' noted that retailing is highly competitive and that large discount chains and specialty retailers were competing aggressively for consumer dollars at the end of the twentieth century. Food retailing entered the discount/warehouse wars as well with customers seeking to buy in bulk at a discount. Retailers began to look at tailoring their methods to reach consumers who were increasingly short of time, looking to get the best buy for their dollar, and demanding superior customer service. At the same time, the very act of shopping was undergoing a change. Standard & Poor's, in its 1993 quarterly report on retailing noted ''Going shopping has lost its charm.'' Standard & Poor's concluded that shopping is no longer the all-day, white-glove, out-to-lunch affair it used to be. Shopping at the end of the twentieth century is viewed as a utilitarian task. In women's retailing, where the traditional store concept is most alive, inroads have been made by electronic shopping, shopping in catalogs, and shopping by television and phone; all time-saving efforts.

Even at the gas pump there were innovations in retailing to gain a larger share of the consumer dollar. A new type of store, called a ''G'' store, sells snacks and sundries at the gasoline station and began to encroach on the market share of the more traditional convenience store. Table A provides a better picture of market share.

In addition to experiments with new store formats, the retail industry seeks to maintain and even increase its share of profit by looking for efficiency in management, using technology, and redirecting its **advertising**. The Occupational Outlook for 1994 quoted David Glass, the Wal-Mart CEO in 1993 and preisdent in 1994: ''All concepts of doing business are changing.'' Part of the reason for these changes in retailing is that the demographics of the U.S. market have changed significantly in the last quarter of the twentieth century.

The percentage of married couples reported in the United States in 1991 was 55.3 percent, down from 60.8 percent in 1981. And women who were married in 1991 were more likely than their eighties counterparts to have remained in the job market, even when their children were under six years of age.

Table A

Item	% Market Share
Supermarkets	35.0
Discount stores	21.0
Department stores	13.0
General merchandise	8.0
Specialty apparel	7.0
Warehouse clubs	6.0
Drug stores	5.0
Convenience stores	3.0
Variety stores	2.0

Two-parent two-child homes are no longer the standard. There are large sectors of single people—elderly, teens, and single parents. Each of these sectors has its own buying power and market needs. Recognizing a diversified market, many retailers are tailoring their ad campaigns to segments of the market once ignored. There are new campaigns for larger-sized women's clothing, ads targeted specifically toward Hispanics or African Americans, and the plethora of media efforts to gain the dollars of the fickle but lucrative teen market.

Targeting customers for advertising became easier with electronic **inventory control** which allows merchants on a more timely basis not only to keep track of items bought and sold, but also to maintain information on the buyer. Vendor merchant relationships changed in the 1990s as well. Reducing their own risk and need to borrow, retailers used electronic control to buy smarter and on a shorter time frame. Seeking quality control and a direct line as a better guarantee of service for their customers and themselves, many retailers now also often work directly with the vendor in the apparel industry. Garr Consulting Group noted in 1994 that 59 percent of apparel store managers surveyed noted that they have entered into some degree of ''strategic alliance'' with their vendors to implement a quick response system that will keep their racks full of the latest fashions at the best prices, while ensuring top quality.

In the volatile retailing field of women's apparel, *Women's Wear Daily* magazine noted at the end of 1993 that those chains which were battling tight sales should adopt such strategies as:

- tightening inventories
- working with vendors to lower initial prices on items

- shifting away from high fashion to more basic items and current trends

- restructuring their management

- trimming their number of suppliers.

Dan Walker, CEO of the GAP stores, in the introduction to *Opportunities in Retailing Careers*, added, "Giant retailing institutions of the eighties have two critical factors in common, a well-defined and focused business concept and an abundance of talent."

Employment prospects in the retail sector have always been most abundant in sales and the majority of that workforce has been, traditionally, female. Retail employment expanded by three percent annually between 1985 and 1990 and declined between 1990 and 1992 according to the 1993 U.S. Industrial Outlook. The 1990-92 decline reflected the recession and the need for fewer sales force employees due to the inroads made by QVC Home Shopping and catalog sales. Significant also is the fact that the 1993 Industrial Outlook stated that two of every five retail sales employees were part-time workers. This is significant in that many part-time workers do not earn pension or health benefits. In addition, the use of many part-time workers means that merchants do not have to pay overtime to stay open seven days a week. Salaries in the retail industry have historically been low and the hours difficult.

The move toward more electronic equipment in the retail field means that fewer and fewer of the sales staff will be able to get by with a high school education. More and more will need at least some additional training on computers.

The retail staff includes buyers (usually college educated), workers to stock the shelves and keep tabs on inventory, and sales people. Management includes financial managers, human resource specialists, finance and accounting specialists, advertising specialists, photographers and display specialists, and a security staff that guards against shoplifting and employee theft. The larger the business the more specialized these jobs become; the smaller the establishment, the more of these functions one person handles.

The retail job market should remain a large segment of the economy for some time to come. The basic jobs may require more education, but the necessity for workers who will meet customer service needs will remain.

The Occupational Outlook for 1994 forecasts small, but continued improvements in retailing overall. The optimistic forecast is based on an assumption that low interest rates and diminished inflationary pressures will continue and that retailers will continue to be quick to adapt to innovations in technology and in their own marketing strategies that will keep them in line with consumer needs and interests and thus continue to stoke their own engines of profitability.

[Joan Leotta]

FURTHER READING:

Dolber, Roslyn. *Opportunities in Retailing Careers*. Lincolnwood, IL: VGM Career Horizons, 1989.

US Department of Labor, Bureau of Labor Statistics Staff. *Occupational Outlook: 1994-95 Edition*. Scottsdale, AZ: Associated Book Publishers, Inc., *1994*.

RETIREMENT PLANNING

Retirement planning is a fairly complicated issue that continues to capture the attention of the public. The debate over whether Social Security will be available for the youngest members of the current workforce only adds legitimacy to the necessity of early retirement planning. Mortality studies show that most people will need retirement income for at least 15 years. This, combined with the uncertainty of investment returns and inflation, makes retirement planning a critical topic in today's business and political spectrums.

Retirement benefits have been available to some employees of some companies for a number of years. Private pension plans in the United States are a result of the Industrial Revolution in the late 1800s, as the industrial base shifted from agriculture to manufacturing. The Social Security Administration was created in the 1930s as a part of Franklin Roosevelt's New Deal. Shortly after the creation of Social Security, private pension plans grew—offering coverage to millions of employees. In 1962 the Self-Employed Individuals Retirement Act (also known as Keogh plans) was enacted through the efforts of New York Congressman Eugene J. Keogh. This act established tax-deferred retirement plans with withdrawals starting between ages 59 ½ and 70 ½. The plan is for the self-employed and those who have income from self-employment on the side (freelancers, moonlighters, etc.). Embezzlement from these plans by trustees led to the passage of and the **Employee Retirement Income Security Act of 1974 (ERISA)**. That same year another entity was formed by the government, the Pension Benefit Guaranty Corporation, which serves as the insurer of many pension plans.

Deferred compensation, defined benefits, and defined contribution plans are common forms of retirement plans. All plans having to do with retirement are considered pension plans. In the 1980s, defined-benefit (DB) plans have lost popularity in favor of defined contribution plans. DB plans are standard retirement accounts which currently require a five-year vesting period. In 1979, 17 percent of pension plans were DC. By 1988 this percentage had grown to 34 percent. **Labor unions** tend to use DB plans extensively, and this may account for some of the decline. A primary reason for the growth of DC, however, is the emergence of **401(k) plans**, in which employers match a percentage of employee contributions; these are generally invested in **mutual funds** or stock plans. Also, as the workforce becomes more mobile DC plans are preferable because the amount invested can be rolled into another account at another employer. DC plans, however, face scrutiny by many financial advisers for two reasons: (1) the investment decisions made by the company may be too restrictive for the employee to meet individual goals; and (2) many times employees are not educated about the risk and returns available through the given investment vehicles.

In 1990 DC and DB plans distributed $126 billion in lump-sum payments, an amount that was equal to half of all Social Security checks posted that same year. Rollover activity into similar tax-deferred plans continues to increase as tax laws require a 20 percent withholding tax to be paid on the lump-sum if it is not rolled over. Merrill Lynch leads the market in attracting this rollover business. In 1993 65,000 new retirement accounts were opened at Merrill Lynch, averaging $100,000 each.

Perhaps the most significant difference between DB and DC plans is the voluntary nature of the DC plan. DB plans are generally automatic, reserved for union and salaried employees. DC plans are fully voluntary, deferred-compensation plans in which an hourly or salaried employee elects to have a certain percentage of money deducted—before taxes—from the paycheck. Adding to the financial pressure of DB plans on employers, nondiscrimination rules have been enacted for 1996. These rules state that public sponsors must offer the same benefits to all employees regardless of their compensation. Many state and local municipalities have moved to DC plans to avoid this new mandate. Similarly, the voluntary nature of DC plans makes detractors wonder if ill-informed employees will have less in their DC accounts at retirement than if the DB plans had been available.

Two possible changes in the laws that govern retirement accounts have recently been the center of debate. Senator Howard Metzenbaum of Maryland introduced a pension reform bill in 1994 that would allow all employees to participate in a company's retirement plan (if the company has one), reduce the term of full vesting to 750 hours, and ease rollover requirements should an employee change employers. The proposed bill also provides for immediate vestment of employer contributions to DC plans. The other change is encompassed in the proposed Retirement Protection Act of 1993. The idea behind the act is that age and service-weighting factors are not in line

with nondiscrimination rules. These factors supposedly tend to favor highly-paid employees who can use the DC plans as a tax shield.

[Valerie E. Wilson]

FURTHER READING:

Connor, John B., Jr. ''Pay Me Later.'' *Small Business Reports*. July, 1994, p. 44.

Elgin, Peggie R. ''Uncle Sam Prepares to Block Fat Cats' Age-Weighted Plans.'' *Corporate Cashflow Magazine*. January, 1994, p. 5.

Ippolito, Richard. ''Toward Explaining the Growth of Defined Contribution Plans.'' *Industrial Relations*. January, 1995, pp. 1-20.

''IRS Has Safe Harbor Model for Rabbi Trusts.'' *Employee Benefit Plan Review*. October, 1992, p. 50.

Philip, Christine. ''Value of Defined Contribution Plans Debated.'' *Pensions & Investments*. February 20, 1995, p. 39.

Reilly, Meegan M. ''Metzenbaum Pension Bill Would Expand Coverage Requirements.'' *Tax Notes*. October 31, 1994, pp. 589-590.

Ritter, Mark S. ''Rabbi Trust Administration: An Overview.'' *Benefits Quarterly*. Summer, 1994, p. 43.

Rohrer, Julie. ''Darwinian Economics.'' *Institutional Investor*. January, 1994, p. 137

Rohrer, Julie. ''The Great Nest Egg Hunt.'' *Institutional Investor*. March, 1994, p. 97.

Silverstein, Ken. ''DC Plans.'' *Pension Management*. November, 1994, p. 9.

Sloane, Leonard. *The New York Times Book of Personal Finance*. NY: Times Books, 1992.

Smith, Rodger F. ''DC Plans Accepted, Assets Growing . . . What's the Problem?'' *Pension World*. February, 1993, p. 28.

Sollinger, Andrew. ''Defined-Contribution Plans: In the Public Interest?'' *Institutional Investor*. June, 1993, p. 159.

''Work Force Mobility Lends Itself to Defined Contribution Approach.'' *Employee Benefit Plan Review*. June, 1994, p. 55.

RETRAINING

SEE: Occupational Mobility and Retraining; Vocational Rehabilitation

REVENUE

SEE: Income and Revenue

RIGHT OF PRIVACY

At no time in American history has the ''right of privacy'' generated such heated controversy and been the focus of so much attention as at present. The Watergate scandal in the 1970s brought to the public's attention, for the first time, the damaging effects of sophisticated electronic technology on privacy, and the public's need to control it. Watergate provided the impetus for the landmark Privacy Act of 1974, passed by Congress in 1974; the law limits the federal government's ability to disclose information about a citizen. In 1978, Congress strengthened the law on illegal government wiretapping. States have followed the federal government's lead in passing laws protecting the privacy of their residents. Nonetheless, the computerization of business and government since the 1970s has made relentless onslaughts on the individual's privacy, most often without his or her knowledge or consent.

In American history, "privacy" traditionally has meant the right to be left alone. The Bill of Rights guarantees freedom of speech, press, and religion; prohibits the government from conducting "unreasonable searches and seizures"; and protects the individual from self-incrimination and "cruel and unusual punishment." These constitutional guarantees, while not defining privacy outright, implicitly uphold the sanctity and autonomy of the individual, which is the essence of privacy.

Hence for the first hundred years of this country's history, constitutional guarantees respecting privacy adequately protected it. Information files were few, while the frontier made surveillance virtually impossible. However, late nineteenth-century technology, in the form of telegraphs and telephones, was beginning to make inroads into privacy, drawing the attention of Louis D. Brandeis (1856-1941) future justice of the Supreme Court and his law firm colleague Samuel D. Warren (1852-1910). In 1890 their article, "The Right to Privacy," appeared in the *Harvard Law Review*, and largely focused on the invasion of the individual's "right to be left alone" by the popular press. The ensuing legal debate over privacy contributed to the evolution of the concept of privacy in American law. In 1923 the Supreme Court struck down a Nebraska law—that prohibited the teaching of any language other than English—on the grounds that it violated personal autonomy, which was recognized for the first time as a legal principle. In 1965 the Supreme Court, in the case of *Griswold v. Connecticut*, held that the Constitution implicitly guaranteed the right of sexual privacy. The Griswold case as well as the 1973 *Roe v. Wade* decision, recognizing a woman's right to an abortion, personified for many the individual's right to personal privacy. The *Roe v. Wade* case, however, dramatized as no other issue could, the ever present tension between the right of society to intervene versus the right of the individual to personal autonomy.

The clash between society—usually government and business interests—and the individual's right to personal autonomy has heightened since *Roe v. Wade*, thanks in large part to the "information revolution." The sophistication of surveillance technology and the invasion of **computers** into all realms of life, including churches and schools, have heightened the assault on individual autonomy to a degree undreamed of when the Constitution was written. The government's abuse of electronic surveillance to spy on its citizens during the Nixon administration drew national attention to the misuse of technology and the need for legal curbs. The result was the Privacy Act of 1974. This law was meant to empower the individual by giving him or her access on demand to any personal records held by a federal agency; the law also limited the power of any federal agency to "swap" records with another agency, as well as to disclose information on an individual.

Critics of the law since its passage cite its lax enforcement, loopholes, and exceptions, as well as the near absence of committed oversight and enforcement. Following on the heels of this law was the 1976 Supreme Court case, *United States v. Miller*, in which the court ruled that an individual's bank records belong to the bank, and not to the individual, who "surrenders" his or her right to privacy upon becoming a bank customer. This opened the door to the individual's "surrendering" the right of privacy to insurance and credit card companies, and many other businesses and government agencies that provide services. Computerization of business and government has also invaded the workplace, in which millions of Americans may be monitored by computers, telephone tapping, and closed circuit cameras.

The "right to privacy," guaranteed by the Constitution and buttressed by state and federal law, has required constant vigilance as it is increasingly being identified with the essence of democracy itself. Hence the issue of privacy will not diminish, but will loom larger in the future.

[Sina Dubovoy]

FURTHER READING:

American Civil Liberties Union. *Your Right to Privacy; A Basic Guide to Legal Rights in an Information Society*. Carbondale, IL: Southern Illinois University Press, 1990.

Hershey, Robert D., Jr. "I.R.S. Staff is Cited in Snoopings;" *The New York Times*. July 19, 1994, pp. C1(N), D1(L).

"I Spy (Congress Is Considering Bill to Limit Electronic Workplace Surveillance)." *Inc.* April, 1994, p. 110.

Linowes, David F. *Privacy in America, Is Your Private Life in the Public Eye?* Champaign-Urbana, IL: University of Illinois Press, 1989.

Nelson, Corey L. "Is E-mail Private or Public? Employers Have No Right to Snoop through Mail." *Computerworld*. June 27, 1994, p. 135.

RIGHTS (SECURITIES)

The preemptive right allows stockholders to purchase a pro rata share of any new stock issues. The rights offering allows current shareholders to maintain their relative control and to prevent the dilution of the value of their shares. The number of new shares that need to be issued is calculated as the total amount of new funds to be raised divided by the subscription price per new share. The subscription price is the amount that current shareholders must pay to purchase one new share. The number of rights needed to purchase one new share is equal to the ratio of the number of old shares outstanding divided by the number of new shares to be issued.

If a firm currently has 1,000 shares outstanding at a market price of $10 per share, the market value of the firm is $10,000. If the firm decides to sell $4,000 of new equity with a rights offering and if the subscription price is set at $8, the firm needs to issue 500 new shares. One new share may be purchased for each two old shares. Two rights are needed to buy one new share. The value of each share after the rights issue is equal to the new total market value, 10,000 plus 4,000 divided by the new number of shares outstanding, 1,000 plus 500. The new price per share, ex rights, is $9.33 = (10,000 + 4,000)/(1,000 + 500).

Prior to the rights issue, the rights and the share sell as one unit. The share is said to be selling rights on. After the holder of record date, the rights and the shares sell separately. The share is said to be selling ex rights.

The value of each right is equal to the difference between the current market price of the stock, rights on, and the subscription price of the rights issue divided by the number of rights needed to purchase one new share plus one. In this example, that is equal to $0.67 = (10 − 8)/(2 + 1). The value of the rights can be determined from the ex rights price. The value is equal to the ex rights market price minus the subscription price divided by the number of rights required to buy one new share, $0.67 = (9.33 − 8.00)/2. The value of the right is equal to the difference between the rights on share price and the ex rights price per share, $0.67 = ($10.00 − 9.33).

Prior to the rights offering ten shares represented a market value of $100 = ($10 * 10 shares). Assuming that a shareholder exercises all rights, this shareholder will have ten old shares and five new shares worth $140 = ($9.33 * 15 shares). The shareholder will have purchased the five new shares for $40. The value of the shareholder's ten shares holding from prior to the rights issue is $100.

If a shareholder chose not to exercise the ten rights but sold them, the shareholder would still have $100. Ten shares would be worth $93.33 = ($9.33 * 10 shares). Ten rights would be worth $6.67 = ($0.67 * 10 shares). The total is $100.

The ten shares prior to the rights offering represented 1 percent of the old total outstanding shares. The 15 shares after the rights offering represents 1 percent of the new total outstanding shares. Thus, both relative control and value are maintained.

[Carl B. McGowan, Jr.]

FURTHER READING:

Reilly, Frank K. *Investment Analysis and Portfolio Management*. 3rd ed. Chicago: The Dryden Press, 1989.

RISK MANAGEMENT AND INSURANCE

Risk management is the identification, measurement, and treatment of exposures to accidental loss to an organization or individual. The practice of risk management utilizes many tools and techniques, including insurance, to manage a wide variety of risks facing any entity, from the largest corporation to the individual. The term "risk management" has usually pertained to property and casualty exposures to loss but recently has come to include financial risk management, i.e., **interest rates**, **foreign exchange** rates, derivatives, etc.

The term risk management is a relatively recent (the last 20 years) evolution of the term "insurance management." The reason for this evolution is that the concept of risk management encompasses a much broader scope of activities and responsibilities than does insurance management. Risk management is now a widely accepted description of a discipline within most large organizations. The myriad risks faced by most organizations today necessitate a department solely devoted to managing these risks. Basic risks such as fire, windstorm, flood, employee injuries, and automobile accidents as well as more sophisticated exposures such as **product liability**, environmental impairment, and employment practices are the province of the risk management department in a typical corporation.

According to *Risk Management and Insurance* by Williams and Heins, the risk management process includes six steps. These steps are (1) determining the objective of the organization, (2) identifying exposures to loss, (3) measuring those same exposures, (4) selecting alternatives, (5) implementing a solution, and (6) monitoring the results. The objective of an organization—i.e., growth, for example—will determine the strategy for managing various risks. Identification and measurement are relatively straightforward. Earthquake may be identified as a potential exposure to loss but if the exposed facility is in New York the probability of earthquake is very low and will have a low priority as a risk to be managed.

There are many alternatives available for the management of risk. Loss prevention involves preventing a loss from occurring, via such methods employee safety training. Loss reduction is concerned with reducing the severity of a loss, through—for example—the installation of fire sprinklers. While sprinklers will not prevent fire from occurring, they will reduce the damage it may cause. Other techniques include risk transfer, which refers to the practice of contractually transferring risk to another party. Examples would include the indemnity provision of a purchase order or a lease. Risk avoidance is another available tool for managing risk. An example of this might include a drug company deciding not to market a drug because of potential liability claims.

Self retention of certain risks—sometimes referred to as "self-insurance"—is also a valid risk management tool. Insurance is the last resort for managing risk. If there is no other way to manage a particular risk, it may be insured, subject to the terms of the insurance policy. Awareness of, and familiarity with, various types of insurance policies is necessary for the risk management process. In the implementation step, combinations of the above tools may be used. The final step, called monitoring, is necessary to determine if the solution employed actually obtained the desired result or if that solution requires modification.

The management of risk is important to everyone, from the most massive corporation to the corner store, and from large charitable organizations and churches to individuals. All face risks that need to be managed.

[Louis J. Drapeau]

FURTHER READING:

Williams, C. Arthur, Jr. and Richard M. Heins. *Risk Management and Insurance.* McGraw-Hill Book Company, 1989.

Head, Dr. George L. and Stephen Horn, II. *Essentials of Risk Management, Vols. I-II.* Insurance Institute of America, 1991.

RISK AND RETURN

The term "risk and return" refers to the potential financial loss or gain experienced through investments in **securities**. An investor who has registered a profit is said to have seen a "return" on his or her investment. The "risk" of the investment, meanwhile, denotes the possibility or likelihood that the investor could lose money. If an investor decides to invest in a security that has a relatively low risk, the potential return on that investment is typically fairly small. Conversely, an investment in a security that has a high risk factor also has the potential to garner higher returns. Return on investment can be measured by nominal rate or real rate (money earned after the impact of inflation on the value of the investment has been figured in).

Different securities—including common **stocks**, corporate **bonds**, government bonds, and **Treasury bills**—offer varying rates of risk and return. As Richard Brealey and Stewart Myers noted in *Principles of Corporate Finance*, "Treasury bills are about as safe an investment as you can get. There is no risk of default and their short maturity means that the prices of Treasury bills are relatively stable." Long-term government bonds, on the other hand, experience price fluctuations in accordance with changes in the nation's interest rates. Bond prices fall when interest rates rise, but they rise when interest rates drop. Government bonds typically offer a slightly higher rate of return than Treasury bills.

Another type of security is corporate bonds. Those who invest in corporate bonds have the potential to enjoy a higher return on their investment than those who stay with government bonds. The greater potential benefits, however, are available because the risk is greater. "Investors know that there is a risk of default when they buy a corporate bond," commented Brealey and Myers. Those corporations that have this default option, though, "sell at lower prices and therefore higher yields than government bonds." In the meantime, investors "still want to make sure that the company plays fair. They don't want it to gamble with their money or to take any other unreasonable risks. Therefore, the bond agreement includes a number of restrictive covenants to prevent the company from purposely increasing the value of its default option."

Investors can also put their money into common stock. Common stockholders are the owners of a corporation in a sense, for they have ultimate control of the company. Their votes—either in person or by proxy—on appointments to the corporation's board of directors and other business matters often determine the company's direction. Common stock carries greater risks than other types of securities, but can also prove extremely profitable. Earnings or loss of money from common stock is determined by the rise or fall in the stock price of the company.

There are other types of company stock offerings as well. Companies sometimes issue preferred stock to investors. While owners of preferred stock do not typically have full voting rights in the company, "no dividends may be paid on the common [stock] until after the preferred dividend has been paid."

RISK AND RISK AVERSION

Many types of risk loom for investors hoping to see a return on their money, noted Jae K. Shim and Joel G. Siegel in *Handbook of Financial Analysis, Forecasting, & Modeling*. Business risk refers to the financial impact of basic operations of the company. Earnings variable in this area include product demand, selling price, and cost. Liquidity risk is the possibility that an asset may not be sold for its market value on short notice, while default risk is the risk that a borrower company will be unable to pay all obligations associated with a debt. Market risk alludes to the impact that market-wide trends can have on individual stock prices, while interest rate risk concerns the fluctuation in the value of the asset as a result of changes in interest rate, capital market, and money market conditions.

Individual risk aversion is thus a significant factor in the dynamics of risk and return. Cautious investors naturally turn to low-risk options such as Treasury bills or government bonds, while bolder investors often investigate securities that have the potential to generate significant returns on their investment. Certain types of common stock that fit this description include speculative stocks and penny stocks.

Many factors can determine the degree to which an investor is risk-averse. William Riley and K. Victor Chow contended in *Financial Analysts Journal* that "relative risk aversion decreases as one rises above the poverty level and decreases significantly for the very wealthy. It also decreases with age—but only up to a point. After age 65 (retirement), risk aversion increases with age." Riley and Chow note that decreases in risk aversion often parallel higher degrees of education as well, but speculate that "education, income and wealth are all highly correlated, so the relationship may be a function of wealth rather than education."

Economically disadvantaged families are, on the surface, often seen as risk-averse; in actuality, however, decisions by these households to avoid investment risk can be traced to a lack of discretionary income or wealth, rather than any true aversion. As Riley and Chow noted, "risk aversion can ... be expected to decrease as an individual's wealth increases, independent of income. Someone whose stock of wealth is growing can be expected to become less risk-averse, as her tolerance of downside risk increases."

[Laurie Collier Hillstrom]

FURTHER READING:

Bierman, Harold, Jr., and Seymour Smidt. *Financial Management for Decision Making*. New York: Macmillan, 1986.

Brealey, Richard, and Stewart Myers. *Principles of Corporate Finance*. 2d ed. New York: McGraw-Hill, 1984.

Brigham, Eugene F. *Financial Management: Theory and Practice*. Fort Worth: Dryden Press, 1991.

Riley, William B., Jr., and K. Victor Chow. "Asset Allocation and Individual Risk Aversion," *Financial Analysts Journal*. December, 1992, pp. 32-7.

Shim, Jae K., and Joel G. Siegel. *Handbook of Financial Analysis*, Forecasting, & Modeling. Englewood Cliffs, NJ: Prentice Hall, 1988.

ROBOTICS

The Robotic Industries Association defines robot as follows: "A robot is a reprogrammable, multifunctional manipulator designed to move material, parts, tools or specialized devices through variable programmed motions for the performance of a variety of tasks." This definition has become generally accepted in the United States and other Western countries. The most common form of industrial robot is made up of a single automated arm that resembles a construction crane.

The word "robot" was coined by Czech playwright Karel Capek (1890-1938) in his 1921 play *R.U.R* (Rossum's Universal Robots). Robot is spelled *robota* in Czech and means forced labor. The word found its way into English-language dictionaries by the mid-1920s. The word "robotics" was first used by science fiction writer Isaac Asimov (1920-92) in his 1942 story "Runaround," in which he wrote what became known as Asimov's Three Laws of Robotics: "1. A robot may not injure a human being, or, through inaction, allow a human being to come to harm. 2. A robot must obey the orders given it by human beings except where such orders would conflict with the First Law. 3. A robot must protect its own existence as long as such protection does not conflict with the First or Second Law." Though fictional, these laws and Asimov's robot stories were influential to Joseph Engelberger, who is arguably the most important figure in the development of industrial robots. Though the word "robot" is relatively new, the concept is centuries old, and prior to the 1920s robot-like mechanisms were called automatons. In one of Noah Webster's earliest dictionaries, an automaton is defined as "A self-moving machine or one which moves by invisible springs."

In a number of respects, robots are like numerically-controlled automated machine tools, such as an automated lathe, in that they are both reprogrammable

ROBOTICS

to adapt to producing a number of different objects. What distinguishes robots is their flexibility, regarding both range of tasks and motion. In one typical **manufacturing** application, robots move parts in their various stages of completion from one automated machine tool to the next, the system of robots and machine tools making up a **flexible manufacturing** workcell. Robots are classified as soft automata whereas automated machine tools are classified as hard automata. The Japanese Industrial Robot Association also classifies manually-operated manipulators and nonreprogrammable, single-function manipulators as robots, and one must bear this in mind when comparing data on robot use between Japan and the West.

Since robots are defined by their capacity to move objects or tools through space, key issues in robotic control are location and movement, referred to in the industry as kinematics and dynamics. The position of an object in a three-dimensional space can be defined relative to a fixed point with three parameters via the Cartesian coordinate system, indicating placement along x, y, and z axes. The orientation of an object requires three additional parameters, indicating rotation on these axes. These parameters are referred to as degrees of freedom. Together these six parameters and the movement among them make up the data of kinematic control equations. Robots carrying out simpler tasks may operate with fewer than six degrees of freedom, but robots may also operate with more than six, which is referred to as redundancy. Redundancy gives a robot greater mobility, enabling it to more readily work around obstructions and to choose among a set of joint positions to reach a given target in less time.

Two types of joints are commonly used in robots, the prismatic or sliding joint, resembling a slide rule, and the revolute joint, a hinge. The simplest type of robot to control is one made up of three sliding joints, each determining placement along a Cartesian axis. Robots made solely of revolute joints are more complex to control, in that the relation of joint position to control parameters is less direct. Other robots use both types of joints. Among these, a common type uses a large sliding joint for vertical placement of an arm made of revolute joints. The vertical rigidity and horizontal flexibility of such robots make them ideal for heavy assembly work (this configuration is referred to as SCARA for Selectively Compliant Arm for Robot Assembly). Robots may also be made of a system of arms each with restricted movement (i.e., with relatively few degrees of freedom) but which together can perform complex tasks. These are referred to as distributed robots. Such robots have the advantage of high speed and precision, but the disadvantage of restricted range of movement.

Robots are actuated by hydraulic, pneumatic, and electrical power. Electric motors have become in-

creasingly small with high power-to-weight ratios, enabling them to become the dominant means by which robots are powered. The hand of a robot is referred to in the industry as an end effector. End effectors may be specialized tools, such as spot welders or spray guns, or more general-purpose grippers. Common grippers include fingered and vacuum types.

One of the central elements of robotics control technology involves sensors. It is through sensors that a robotic system receives knowledge of its environment, to which subsequent actions of the robot can be adjusted. Sensors are used to enable a robot to adjust to variations in the position of objects to be picked up, to inspect objects, and to monitor proper operation. Among the most important types are visual, force and torque, speed and acceleration, tactile, and distance sensors. The majority of industrial robots use simple binary sensing, analogous to an on/off switch. This does not permit sophisticated feedback to the robot as to how successfully an operation was performed. Lack of adequate feedback also often requires the use of guides and fixtures to constrain the motions of a robot through an operation, which implies substantial inflexibility in changing operations.

Robots may also be able to adjust to variations in object placement without the use of sensors. This is enabled by arm or end effector flexibility and is referred to as compliance. Robots with sensors may also make use of compliance.

Robots are programmed either by guiding or by off-line programming. Most industrial robots are programmed by the former method. This involves manually guiding a robot from point to point through the phases of an operation, with each point stored in the robotic control system. With off-line programming, the points of an operation are defined through computer commands. This is referred to as manipulator level off-line programming. An important area of research is the development of off-line programming that makes use of higher-level languages, in which robotic actions are defined by tasks or objectives.

Robots may be programmed to move through a specified continuous path instead of from point to point. Continuous path control is necessary for operations such as spray painting or arc welding a curved joint. Programming also requires that a robot be synchronized with the automated machine tools or other robots with which it is working. Thus robot control systems are generally interfaced with a more centralized control system.

Industrial robots perform both spot and electric arc welding. Welding guns are heavy and the speed of assembly lines requires precise movement, thus creating an ideal niche for robotics. Parts can be welded either through the movement of the robot or by keeping the robot relatively stationary and moving the part. The latter method has come into widespread use as it requires less expensive conveyors. The control system of the robot must synchronize the robot with the speed of the assembly line and with other robots working on the line. Control systems may also count the number of welds completed and derive productivity data. The Ford Motor Co. uses German-made robots for welding operations in its European plants.

Industrial robots also perform what are referred to as pick and place operations. Among the most common of these operations is loading and unloading pallets, used across a broad range of industries. This requires relatively complex programming, as the robot must sense how full a pallet is and adjust its placements or removals accordingly. Robots have been vital in pick and place operations in the casting of metals and plastics. In the die casting of metals, for instance, productivity using the same die-casting machinery has increased up to three times, the result of robots' greater speed, strength, and ability to withstand heat in parts removal operations. In 1992, CBW Automation Inc. of Colorado announced the development of the world's fastest parts-removal robot for plastics molding. Their robot moves through a four-foot stroke in under one-fifth of a second.

Assembly is one of the most demanding operations for industrial robots. A number of conditions must be met for robotic assembly to be viable, among them that the overall production system be highly coordinated and that the product be designed with robotic assembly in mind. The sophistication of the control system required implies a large initial capital outlay, which generally requires production of 100,000 to 1,000,000 units per year in order to be profitable. Robotic assembly has come to be used for production of printed circuit boards, electronic components and equipment, household appliances, and automotive subassemblies. As of 1985, assembly made up just over ten percent of all robotic applications.

Industrial robots are widely used in spray finishing operations, particularly in the automobile industry. One of the reasons these operations are cost-effective is that they minimize the need for environmental control to protect workers from fumes. Most robots are not precise enough to supplant machine tools in operations such as cutting and grinding. Robots are used, however, in machining operations such as the removal of metal burrs or template-guided drilling. Robots are also used for **quality control** inspection, to determine tightness of fit between two parts, for example. The use of robots in nonindustrial applications such as the cleaning of contaminated sites and the handling and analysis of hazardous materials represent important growth markets for robotics producers.

The first industrial robot was developed in the mid-1950s by Joseph Engelberger (1925–), who has been referred to as the father of industrial robots. Engelberger also founded Unimation, Inc., which became the largest producer of industrial robots in the U.S. His early research involved touring Ford, Chrysler Corp., General Motors and 20 other production plants. Engelberger observed that men performed the higher-paying jobs in which they lifted heavy objects with two hands simultaneously, while women performed tasks in which they used their hands asynchronously. Economic and technical considerations thus led Engelberger to focus on the development of a one-armed robot. Engelberger developed his first prototype in 1956, the design of which is very similar to Unimation robots produced decades later. General Motors purchased a test model in 1959, though by 1964, Unimation had sold only 30 robots. It was not until the late-1960s that sales increased strongly and not until 1975 that the firm turned a profit. Together with number two producer Cincinnati Milacron, Unimation accounted for 75 percent of the U.S. robotics market in 1980. Unimation Inc. became a wholly-owned subsidiary of Westinghouse in 1982. By 1983, the firm had sales of $43 million.

The U.S. robotics industry suffered a severe setback in the mid-1980s, largely the result of declining orders from the automobile industry. This resulted in a number of firms leaving the industry and the consolidation of many remaining firms. Conditions improved considerably for the industry as it entered the 1990s, as Table 1 indicates (from the *U.S. Industrial Outlook*). Orders increased by 21 percent from 1991 to 1992, and at a similar rate into the first half of 1993. Orders were especially strong for welding, assembly, painting, and material handling operations. As of 1993, fewer than 1,000 robots were manufactured each year in the United States, as most U.S. producers manufactured their robots abroad. U.S. firms remained leaders in the areas of **software**, control systems, and sensors.

The *U.S. Industrial Outlook* for 1994 summarized prospects for the robotics industry as follows: "The long-term outlook for the U.S. robotics industry remains promising. The North American market remains largely untapped with less than 50,000 robots now installed in the United States out of a world population of more than 500,000. . . . Non-industrial applications for robots in security, commercial cleaning, and health care are also on the rise. These so-called 'service robots' present a great opportunity for U.S. robotics manufacturers because the U.S. producers hold the lead in service robot technology." A 1994 study by Frost & Sullivan Market Intelligence forecasted that the U.S. robot market would double from 1992 to 1999. A particularly promising new robot was unveiled by Reis Machine in 1993. Their

Table 1

U.S. FACTORY SHIPMENTS OF ROBOTS, ACCESSORIES & COMPONENTS BY SELECTED CATEGORIES AND TOTAL SHIPMENTS ($ MILLIONS, CURRENT) : 1984-1991

	1984	1985	1986	1987	1988	1989	1990	1991
POINT-TO-POINT TYPE								
Welding, soldering, brazing and cutting	57	75	86	65	32	29	28	30
Assembly	21	18	19	20	8	8	9	10
Material handling and parts transfer	35	45	45	48	27	26	25	27
CONTINUOUS-PATH TYPE								
Welding, soldering, brazing and cutting	17	22	14	9	4	2	2	2
Spraying, painting, gluing and sealing	46	41	37	41	30	35	38	41
Other machining	24	49	48	17	33	26	27	29
ACCESSORIES								
End-of-arm tooling	1	4	8	6	3	4	4	4
Vision, sonic, force tactile and proximity sensors	15	18	15	16	18	21	22	24
Misc. accessories	28	43	44	38	45	73	85	91
TOTAL	281	345	346	284	229	256	275	294

robot was developed with **computer-aided design** and used only one-half the parts of conventional models. The robot featured a large range of operation, low price, and low operating and service costs.

Entering the 1990s, Japan produced and used more robots than any other country. Its production of industrial robots quadrupled from the mid-1980s to 1990, when it possessed over 40 percent of all industrial robots in use worldwide. Prior to 1978, the largest user of industrial robots in Japan was the automobile industry, after which the electric and electronics industries became most important. Unlike the United States, Japan makes extensive use of SCARA configuration robots, which offer substantial advantages in assembly work.

Recent **research and development** has addressed a number of aspects of robotics. Robotic hands have been developed which offer greater dexterity and flexibility. Most visual sensors in use were designed for television and home video, and do not process information quickly for optimal performance in many robotics applications. Consequently, solid-state vision sensors came into increased use, and developments were also made with fiber optics. The use of superconducting materials offered the possibility of substantial improvements in the electric motors that drive robotic arms. Attempts were made to develop lighter robotic arms and also to increase their rigidity. Standardization of software and hardware to facilitate the centralization of control systems was also an important area of development.

[David Kucera]

FURTHER READING:

Asimov, Isaac, and Karen Frenkel. *Robots: Machines in Man's Image*. Harmony Books, 1985.

Breger, Bill, and Angela Charles. "Strong Sales Favor U.S. Robot Production." *Plastic News*. November 29, 1993, p. 5.

Dorf, Richard, ed. *Concise International Encyclopedia of Robotics: Applications and Automation*. John Wiley & Sons, 1990.

"The Droid Void Is Ending." *Ward's Auto World*. January, 1994, p. 56.

Durrant-Whyte, H.F. *Integration, Coordination and Control of Multi-Sensor Robot Systems*. Kluwer Academic Press, 1988.

Electronic Market Data Book. Electronic Industries Association, 1993.

"New Articulated Arm Robot Is Simpler, at Half the Price." *Material Handling Engineering*. September, 1993, p. 38.

Ranky, P.G., and C.Y. Ho. *Robot Modelling—Control and Applications with Software*. IFS Publications, 1985.

"Robots with Tender Touch Move into Medicine." *Nikkei Weekly*. November 29, 1993, p. 9.

Taylor, P. M. *Understanding Robotics*. CRC Press, 1990.

U.S. Industrial Outlook. U.S. Department of Commerce, 1994.

S

S CORPORATIONS

An S corporation, (formerly Subchapter S corporation), is a variation of traditional C corporations. A corporation is a legally recognized entity defined in federal and state tax codes that furnishes certain benefits to the owners of a company. Advantages enjoyed by owners of organizations that incorporate include: marketability of ownership shares; ease of estate planning; and continuity of the company's life. Among the most important benefits of incorporation is limited liability—if a company is sued in court or is unable to pay its debts, the owners, officers, and directors are usually not held personally liable.

The traditional C corporate form of ownership is usually best suited to large companies, for several reasons. For example, the cost of incorporating can be prohibitive for small companies. More importantly, smaller companies may suffer from double taxation. Indeed, C corporations pay income tax on all income, and corporate shareholders (owners) pay personal income tax on any dividends that they receive from the company. Although incorporation is financially burdensome, many small business owners still want the benefits of incorporation related to limited liability. To accommodate small business owners, the federal government has established the S corporation. The federal government allows certain companies to adopt the S corporation format if they qualify as a small business corporation under the provisions of the Internal Revenue Code. Many states also allow a special tax status for S corporations.

S corporations offer the best of both worlds for owners of small companies. They convey the benefits of limited liability offered by C corporate status, but are taxed similarly to sole proprietorships or partnerships. In other words, profits from an S corporation are taxed only once as they pass directly to the shareholders. Furthermore, the owners' taxable income in the case of losses is reduced. Unlike a C corporation, moreover, owners are able to write off losses from the S corporation against other income. S corporations, however, generally enjoy less protection from liability than do larger corporations. And S corporations are more complex, more expensive to set up, and more difficult to account for than either a limited partnership or sole proprietorship. Also, some states do not recognize certain tax benefits identified in the Internal Revenue Code. Finally, S corporations allow less flexibility in allocating **income** and **capital gains** to different owners than do partnerships.

The S corporation can be useful in a number of different circumstances. For example, it continued to be especially useful in the mid-1990s for start-up companies that expected to bear high costs for equipment and to post losses early. As an example, assume that three investors are starting an ice cream store and they incorporate under Subchapter S. If they invest $100,000 in equipment and furnishings they would be eligible for a 10 percent investment tax credit. Also assume that the store loses money during its first year. Under S corporation laws, the credit would pass directly to the investors to be used immediately against other income. In contrast, in an ordinary C corporation there would be no income against which the credit could be taken during that first year—it would have to be carried over until the company showed a profit.

As intimated above, the S corporation format is useful for owners who expect to accumulate earnings, because there is no tax on earnings distributions at the corporate level. In a C corporation, of course, the earnings would be paid out as **dividends** to individuals and taxed for a second time as personal income. Another circumstance in which S corporations can be useful is for speculative ventures. That is because S corporation laws provide for immediate tax write-offs of operating losses up to the amount paid into the company as **equity** or as **loans**. S corporate status can also be utilized to reduce taxes related to transferring a business between family members. For example, the owner of a company could incorporate under Subchapter S and then give the stock to her children. Assuming the children are in a lower tax bracket than their mother, the S corporation would effectively act as a tax shelter for future profits from the business.

Companies that incorporate under Subchapter S often elect to convert to a C corporation at a later date to avoid some of the disadvantages of S corporations. For example, when a firm begins generating cash that it reinvests for growth, the C corporation may be superior. That is because income tax rates at the corporate level are lower than rates for high-income individuals—the cash reinvested in a C corporation is being taxed only once, so the overall tax burden may be lower than it would for an S corporation owned by individuals in high income tax brackets. Once a company elects to convert to C status it cannot change back to an S corporation for a specified period; the specified period was five years in the early 1990s.

[Dave Mote]

FURTHER READING:

Bodie, Zvi, with Alex Kane, and Alan J. Marcus. *Investments*. Homewood, IL: Irwin, 1989.

Brueggeman, William B., with Jeffrey D. Fisher, and Leo D. Stone. *Real Estate Finance*. Homewood, IL: Irwin. 1989.

Garner, Robert J., Robert B. Coplan, Barbara J. Raasch, and Charles L. Ratner. *Ernst & Young's Personal Financial Planning Guide*. New York: John Wiley & Sons, 1994.

Shapiro, Alan C. *Modern Corporate Finance*. New York: Macmillan Publishing Company, 1990.

SALES CONTRACTS

A sales contract is an agreement between a buyer and seller covering the sale and delivery of goods, securities, and personal property other than goods or securities. In the United States domestic sales contracts are governed by the **Uniform Commercial Code**. International sales contracts fall under the **United Nations** Convention on Contracts for the International Sale of Goods (CISG), also known as the Vienna Sale Convention.

Under Article 2 of the UCC, which has been adopted by every state (except Louisiana), the District of Columbia, and the Virgin Islands, a contract for the sale of goods for more than $500 must be in writing in order to be enforceable (UCC 2-201). The sale of securities is a special case covered in Article 8 (UCC 8-319); to be enforceable a contract for the sale of securities must be in writing regardless of the amount involved. For the sale of other kinds of personal property, a minimum of $5,000 must be involved before an enforceable contract must be in writing. Otherwise, an oral agreement is enforceable as a binding contract.

Contracts that must be in writing to be enforceable are said to be within the Statute of Frauds. The Statute of Frauds dates back to 1677, when the English Parliament decreed that certain types of contracts must be in writing. The applicable parts of the UCC effectively define the types of sales contracts that must be in writing. In addition, every state has its own version of the Statute of Frauds.

Under the UCC a written sales contract should specify the parties involved, the subject matter to be sold, and any material or special terms or conditions. Some states also require that the consideration—the amount and type of payment for what is purchased—be specified. The UCC does not require a formal sales contract, though. In many cases a memorandum or collection of papers is sufficient compliance. The courts have held that a written check can be considered a written memorandum of a sales agreement. The UCC allows a written sales contract to be enforced even if it leaves out material terms and is not signed by both parties. However, one party may not create a sales contract on its own that is binding against another party, and an enforceable contract must be signed by the defendant, or the one against whom the contract is sought to be enforced.

In many cases a purchase order, pro forma invoice, or order acknowledgment may serve in place of a formal sales contract. A purchase order is issued by the buyer and sent to the seller, stating the type and amount of goods to be purchased, the price, and any other material terms such as a time limit on filling the order. A pro forma invoice is issued by the seller and sent to the buyer, often in response to a purchase order or oral agreement. In international transactions, the pro forma invoice may enable the buyer to open a line of credit with which to pay for the goods ordered. The pro forma invoice typically includes relevant terms and conditions that apply to the sale.

A formal order acknowledgment is useful for establishing the seller's position in case a dispute should arise. The order acknowledgment is drawn up by the seller in response to a received purchase order. It does not necessarily repeat the details of the purchase order, but it may clarify details such as delivery schedules. When a formal order acknowledgment is countersigned by the buyer, it becomes a type of sales contract.

For international transactions, the Vienna Sale Convention is binding on signatory countries, of which the United States is one. Each of the nations that has signed the convention may state up to five reservations. For example, the United States has stipulated that it shall apply to U.S. companies only when the transaction involves another signatory country. Much of the convention parallels the UCC, with these notable exceptions: (1) Acceptance of an offer that includes a request for additions or modifications constitutes a counteroffer; (2) There is no provision requiring a contract be written in order to be enforceable; and (3) The period for discovering defective merchandise may be as long as two years.

Sales contracts are useful in providing for a common understanding between buyer and seller, minimizing disputes. When a dispute does occur, the sales contract can help provide for a fair settlement.

[David Bianco]

SALES FORCE

A company's sales force consists of its staff of salespeople. The role of the sales force depends to a large extent on whether a company is selling directly to consumers or to other businesses. In consumer sales, the sales force is typically concerned simply with taking and closing orders. Salespeople don't call on customers; the days of the door-to-door salesperson are long past. Salespeople don't create demand for the product, since demand for the product has already been created by **advertising** and promotion. They may provide the consumer with some product information, but individuals involved in consumer sales are often not concerned with maintaining long-term customer relationships. Examples of consumer sales forces include automobile salespersons and the sales staffs found in a variety of retail stores.

The sales force takes on a completely different role in business-to-business sales. Industrial sales forces, for example, may be required to perform a variety of functions. These may include prospecting for new customers and qualifying leads, explaining who the company is and what its products can do, closing orders, negotiating prices, servicing accounts, gathering competitive and market information, and allocating products during times of shortages.

Within the business-to-business market, a distinction can be made between selling to retailers, industrial sales, and other types of business-to-business sales and marketing. The concerns and activities of the sales force tend to vary in each type of business market. What they have in common, however, is the desire of the sales force to establish a long-term relationship with each of its customers and to provide service in a variety of ways.

In selling to retailers, for example, the sales force is not concerned with creating demand. Since consumer demand is more a function of advertising and promotion, the sales force is more concerned with obtaining shelf space in the retailer's store. The sales force may also attempt to obtain more promotion support from the retailer. The sales force relies on sophisticated marketing data to make a convincing presentation to the retailer in order to achieve its sales and marketing objectives.

The largest sales forces are involved in industrial selling. An average industrial field sales force ranges in size from 20 to 60 people and is responsible for selling throughout the United States. The sales force may be organized around traditional geographic territories or around specific customers, markets, and products. An effective sales force consists of individuals who can relate well to decision makers and help them solve their problems. A sales manager or supervisor typically provides the sales-force with guidance and discipline. Within the company the sales force may receive support in the form of specialized training, technical backup, inside sales staff, and product literature. **Direct mail** and other types of marketing efforts can be employed to provide the sales force with qualified leads.

Since the early 1970s, the cost of a single business-to-business industrial sales call has risen from less than $60 in 1971 to more than $250 by the end of the 1980s. Consequently, companies are very concerned about the efficiency of their sales force. Sales managers and supervisors can measure the efficiency of their sales force using several criteria. These include the average number of sales calls per salesperson per day, the average sales-call time per contact, the average revenue and cost per sales call, the entertainment cost per sales call, and the percentage of orders per 100 sales calls. The sales force can also be evaluated in terms of how many new customers were acquired and how many customers were lost during a specific period. The expense of a sales-force can be measured by monitoring the sales-force-to-sales ratio, or sales-force cost as a percentage of total sales.

Using such criteria to evaluate the effectiveness of the sales force allows companies to make adjustments to improve its efficiency. If the sales force is calling on customers too often, for example, it may be possible to reduce the size of the sales force. If the sales force is servicing customers as well as selling to them, it may be possible to shift the service function to lower-paid personnel.

In industrial and other business-to-business sales, the sales force represents a key link between the manufacturer and the buyer. The sales force is often involved in selling technical applications and must work with several different contacts within a customer's organization. Industrial salespeople tend, on average, to be better educated than their consumer counterparts, and to be better paid. However, their cost as a percentage of sales is lower than in consumer sales, because industrial and business-to-business sales generally involve higher-ticket items or a larger volume of goods and services.

The sales force may be compensated in one of three ways: straight salary, straight commission, or a combination of salary plus commission. From 1950 through 1990 more companies began using a combination of salary plus commission to compensate their sales forces, and fewer companies based their sales force compensation on straight commission. It appears that, as a percentage of all sales forces, the use of straight salaries remains constant. Whatever type of compensation system is used for the sales force, the important consideration is that the compensation adequately motivates the sales force to perform its best.

SEE ALSO: Sales Letter

[David Bianco]

SALES FORECASTING

Sales bring in the revenues that provide the funds that support a business. No matter the product, the good, or the service, sales are the primary means for obtaining unencumbered cash, free reserves, and **working capital**. Revenues from sales are the key indicators of management's ability to successfully implement the **business plan**. Sales forecasting is management's primary tool for predicting the volume of attainable sales. Therefore, the whole budget process hinges on an accurate, timely sales forecast.

A sales forecast is a technical projection of the potential customer demand for specific products, goods, or services, for a specific company, within a specific time horizon, and with specified underlying assumptions. While a sales forecast is a prediction of company sales, market potential is a projection of total potential sales for all companies. Market potential relates to the total capacity of the market to absorb the entire output of a specific industry. On the other hand, sales potential is the ability of the market to absorb or purchase the output from a single firm.

MARKET POTENTIAL

The methodology of assessing market potential consists of developing relationships among the dynamic factors of the market served. Analysts on the industry level look for causal factors that, when linked together, demonstrate which economic, demographic, social, and political variables connect to support a market for various products. Analysts for a company must derive their own market potential for specific products based on which variables they believe are most important.

THE INDEX METHOD. Many agencies and organizations publish indexes of market potential. They base their findings on extensive research and analysis of certain relationships that exist among basic economic data—for example, the location of potential consumers by age, education, and income for products that demonstrate a high correlation between those variables and the purchase of foreign cars. This information allows analysts to calculate the market potential for consumer or industrial goods.

Sales and Marketing Magazine publishes buying power indexes. Its commercial indexes combine estimates of population, income, and retail sales to derive composite indicators of consumer demand according to U.S. Census Bureau regions, by state, or by the bureau's organized system of metro areas. The BPI, buying power index, provides only a relative value which analysts adjust to determine the market potential for local areas.

SALES POTENTIAL AND FORECASTING

Forecasting methods and levels of sophistication vary greatly. Each portends to assess future events or situations which will impact either positively or negatively on a business's efforts. Managers prepare forecasts to determine the type and level of demand for products currently produced or that it can produce. They consider a broad spectrum of data for indications of growing and profitable markets. Technically trained economists, analysts, and statisticians use numerous sophisticated methods to estimate the potential size of the market available to the company. Forecasting involves not only the collecting and analyzing of hard data but also the applying of management's proven business judgment in their interpretation and application.

Individual departments, such as sales, and divisions, such as manufacturing, also engage in forecasting. Sales forecasting is essential to setting production volume. Production forecasting determines the materials, labor and machines needed.

Computer-aided sales forecasting has revolutionized this process. Advances in computer technology, information highways, and statistical and mathematical models provide almost every business with the ability to execute complex data analyses, thus reducing the risks and pitfalls prevalent in the past. These advances have made the process and costs of forecasting practical and affordable.

FACTORS IN SALES FORECASTING

Sales forecasts are conditional in that a company prepares the forecast prior to developing strategic and tactical plans. The forecast of sales potential may cause management to adjust some of its assumptions about production and marketing if the forecast indicates that (1) current production capacity is inadequate or excessive and (2) sales and marketing efforts need revisions. Management, therefore, has the opportunity to examine a series of alternate plans that propose changes in resource commitments (such as plant capacity, promotional programs, and market activities), changes in prices and/or changes in production scheduling.

Through forecasting the company determines markets for products, plans corporate strategy, develops sales quotas, determines the need and number of salespeople, decides on distribution channels, prices products or services, analyzes products and product potential in different markets, decides on product features, determines profit and sales potential for different products, constructs **advertising** budgets, determines the potential benefits of sales promotion programs, decides on the use of various elements of the marketing mix, sets production volume and standards, chooses suppliers, defines financing needs, and determines inventory standards. For the forecasting to be accurate, managers need to consider these factors.

THE HISTORICAL PERSPECTIVE. As a starting point, management analyzes previous sales experience by product lines, territories, classes of customers, and other relevant details. Management needs to consider a time line long enough to detect trends and patterns in the growth and the decline of dollar sales volume. This period is generally five to ten years. If the company's experience with a particular product class is shorter, management will include discernible experience of like companies.

The longer the view, the better management is able to detect patterns which follow cycles. Patterns which repeat themselves, no matter how erratically, are considered to be ''normal,'' while variations from these patterns are ''deviant.'' Some of these deviations may have resulted from situations in society that dampened sales temporarily. Management would compensate for these abnormalities by adjusting

the figures to reflect normal trends under normal conditions.

THE BUSINESS ENTITY. The ability of a company to respond to the results of a sales forecast depends on its production capacity, marketing methods, financing, and leadership, and its ability to change each of these to maximize its profit potential.

MARKET POSITION. Forecasting also considers the competitive position of the company with respect to its market share; **research and development**; quality of servicing, pricing and financing policies; and public persona. In addition, forecasters also evaluate the quality and quantity of the customer base to determine brand loyalty, response to beneficial promotions, economic viability, and credit worthiness.

GENERAL ECONOMIC CONDITIONS. Although consumer markets are becoming more segmented, the condition of the overall economy primarily determines the general level of sales and those of many niche markets. Forecasters incorporate relevant data that correlate well or demonstrate a causal relationship with sales volume.

PRICE INDEX. If the prices for products have changed over the years, changes in dollar volume of sales may not correlate well with volume of units. At one point in time when demand is strong, a company raises its prices. At another time, a company may engage in discounting to draw down inventories. Therefore, accountants devise a price index for each year which compensates for price increases. By dividing the dollar volume by the price indexes, a company can trend its volume growth. This process is similar to an inflation index which provides prices in constant dollars. As a result, management is able to compare the price-adjusted dollar sales volumes.

SECULAR TRENDS. The secular trend depicts (1) general economic performance or (2) the performance of the specific product for all companies. If a company's trend line rises more rapidly than the secular trend line, a company would be experiencing a more rapid growth in the rate of sales. If a company's trend line is below the secular trend line, its performance is below the market's average. Management also uses this type of comparison to evaluate and control annual performance.

TREND VARIATIONS. Although the secular trend represents the average for the industry, it may not be ''normal'' for a particular company. The comparison of company trends to secular trends may indicate that the company is serving a specialized market, or that the company is not faring well. Forecasters study the underlying assumptions of trend variations to understand the important relationships in determining the volume of sales. Although markets may be strong, the sales force might need to be adjusted.

INTRA COMPANY TRENDS. By analyzing month-to-month trends and seasonal variations over both the long and short terms, management can adjust the sales forecast to anticipate variations that prove to repeat themselves during budget periods. Management may then construct a budget reflecting these variations, perhaps increasing volume discounts during traditionally slow periods, exploring new territories, or having sales representatives solicit product and service ideas from current customers.

PRODUCT TRENDS. Forecasters also trend individual products, using indexes to adjust for seasonal fluctuations and price changes. Product trends are important for understanding the life cycle of a product.

FORECASTING TECHNIQUES. There are a variety of forecasting techniques and methods. Not all of them are applicable in every situation. To allow for adequate forecasting, a company must (1) choose those methods which best serve their purposes, (2) provide forecasters accurate and relevant data, and (3) formulate honest assumptions appropriate to the market and product.

SOURCES AND MAGNITUDE OF PRODUCT DEMAND. In the past the introduction of new and improved products drove much of the demand. Currently, consumer attitudes and lifestyles anticipate product introductions and technological changes. Individual consumers are pushing technology to anticipate the needs of an increasingly segmented market. Demand based on anticipation is becoming the dominant feature of the technological age. The rapid pace of technological development and new product introduction have shortened product life-cycles. The combination of demographic considerations and technological change dominate consumer trends to a greater degree than in the past. Forecasters need to know how and why markets are segmented.

DEVELOPING A SALES FORECAST

Forecasting sales is inherently more difficult than the construction of the subsequent sales budget. Although management exerts some degree of control over expenditures, it has little ability to direct the buying habits of individuals. The level of sales depends of the vagaries of the marketplace. Yet, a sales forecast must attain a reasonable degree of reliability to be useful.

Fundamentally, sales forecasting is the job of the sales organization which follows steps similar to these in developing a forecast of sales potential:

1. Determine the purposes for using the forecasts.

2. Divide the company's products into homogeneous groups.

3. Determine those factors affecting the sales of each product group and their relative importance.

4. Choose a forecasting method or methods best suited for the job.

5. Gather all necessary and available data.

6. Analyze the data.

7. Check and cross-check deductions resulting from the analyses.

8. Make assumptions regarding effects of the various factors that cannot be measured or forecast.

9. Convert deductions and assumptions into specific product and territorial forecasts and quotas.

10. Apply forecasts to company operations.

11. Periodically review performance and revise forecasts.

HISTORY OF FORECASTING

Since the 1920s, with the introduction of scientific methods of planning business activities and measuring potential sales, the collection of data and analytical techniques have improved greatly. Improved forecasting techniques primarily resulted from three developments. First, the pioneering work at the National Bureau of Economic Research and parallel improvements in data collection by a vast number of agencies, university research groups and private firms, led to a better understanding of the causes of business fluctuations and vastly improved data for the analysis of general business conditions. Second, the development of statistical sampling techniques, motivational research and operation research, gave businesses the tools to conduct better market research and to develop more successful marketing programs. Finally, technical advances in computers and database programs assisted in the development and general application of statistical techniques.

The gap between the ideal goal and the actual performance is steadily improving. Although sales forecasting is more reliable, it will never be totally accurate because it deals with future events. A company can improve the odds, however, by:

- using more than one forecasting technique.

- remembering that forecasts are conditional and subject to change.

- carefully monitoring market developments for changes which test the assumptions.

- conducting periodic reviews and making changes when necessary.

FORECASTING TECHNIQUES AND APPROACHES

Sales forecasts may be general if they calculate aggregate sales attainable in an industry. Conversely, forecasts may be very specific, detailing data by individual products, sales territories, types of customers, and so forth. In recent decades market analysts have increased their use of **focus groups**, individual surveys, interviews, and sophisticated analytical techniques aimed at identifying specific markets.

In the causal approach forecasters identify the underlying variables that have a causal influence on future sales. The company has no influence over those causal variables in the general society such as population, gross national product, and general economic conditions. A company does, however, maintain control over its production lines, prices, advertising and marketing, and the size of its sales force. After studying the underlying causes and variables in depth, the analysts use a variety of mathematical techniques to project future trends. On the basis of these projections, management derives its sales forecast.

The non-causal approach involves an in-depth analysis of historical sales patterns. Analysts plot these patterns in graphs in order to project future sales. Because no attempt is made to identify and evaluate the underlying causal variables, the analysts assume that the underlying causes will continue to influence the future sales in the same manner as in the past. Although analysts may apply certain statistical techniques to extrapolate past sales into the future, this approach is frequently referred to as "naive."

Analysts employ the indirect method by first projecting industry sales. From this data they project the company's share of the industry total. The direct approach skips the industry projection with a straightforward estimate of sales for the company. Either of these methods are applicable to the causal and noncausal approaches.

FORECASTING METHODOLOGIES

BOTTOM-UP FORECASTING. The analysts divide the market into segments, and then separately calculate the demand in each segment. Typically, analysts use sales force composites, industry surveys, and intention-to-buy surveys to collect data. They aggregate the segments to arrive at a total sales forecast. Bottom-up forecasting may not be simple because of complications with the accuracy of the data submitted. The usefulness of the data is contingent upon honest and complete answers from customers, and on the importance and priority given to a survey by the sales staff.

TOP-DOWN FORECASTING. This is the method most widely used for industrial applications. Management first estimates the sales potential, then develops sales quotas, and finally constructs a sales forecast. Problems arise when the underlying assumptions of the past are no longer applicable. The correlation between economic variables and quantity demanded may change or weaken over time.

These two forecasting methods encompass a number of methodologies which can be divided into three general categories: qualitative, times-series analysis and regression, and causal

QUALITATIVE METHODS. Qualitative methods rely on non statistical methods of deriving a sales forecast. A company solicits the opinion or judgment of sales executives, a panel of experts, the sales force, the sales division supervisors, and/or outside expert consultants. Qualitative methods are judgmental composites of expected sales. These methods are often preferred when (1) the variables which influence consumer buying habits have changed, (2) current data is not available, (3) none of the qualitative methods work well in a specific situation, (4) the planning horizon is too far for the standard quantitative methods, and (5) the data has not yet factored in technological breakthroughs taking place or forthcoming.

The probability assessment method (PAM) forecasts sales volume by utilizing in-house expert opinion that provides probabilities between one and 99 percent, plus and minus, on certain target volumes. Analysts translate these estimates into a cumulative probability curve by plotting the volumes by the probability assigned to them. They use this curve to aid in forecasting.

The **program evaluation and review technique (PERT)** requires estimates of "optimistic," "pessimistic," and "most likely" future circumstances. Analysts weigh these three estimates to form an expected value from which they compute a standard deviation. In this way analysts convert the expert's estimates of the most likely and the extreme values into measures of central tendency and dispersion. The standard deviation enables the forecaster to estimate a confidence interval around the expected value. While PERT is only an approximation, it is quick and easy to use. The forecaster can take into account the expert's opinion as a check on estimates produced by other methods.

The **Delphi technique** relies on the assumption that several experts can arrive at a better forecast than one. The Delphi solicits a panel consensus and reprocesses the results through the panel until a very narrow, firm median is agreed upon. By keeping the panel participants isolated, the Delphi excludes many aspects of group behavior, such as social pressure, argumentation, and domination by a few members, from causing undue influence.

A visionary forecast relies on the personal insights and judgment of a respected individual. Although often supplemented by data and facts about different scenarios of the future, the visionary forecast is characterized by subjective guesswork and imagination and is highly nonscientific.

Historical analogy attempts to determine future sales through an in-depth analysis of the introduction and sales growth of a similar product. Historical analogy seeks patterns applicable to the product considered for current introduction. This method requires several years' history for one or more products, and is generally applicable to new product introductions.

The sales force composite gathers forecasts from each individual salesperson for a particular territory. The sales forecast is the aggregate of the individual forecasts. The usefulness of this method is dependent on the accuracy of the data submitted in the composites.

An intention-to-buy survey measures a target market's intention to buy within a specified future time period. Market analysts conduct such surveys prior to the introduction of a product or service. Analysts provide consumers with an adequate description or explanation of the product or services with the hope that respondents will provide honest answers. If respondents tell analysts ''what they want to hear,'' the survey will not be accurate. In addition, certain environmental factors, such as a competing technological breakthrough or a recession, may influence respondent buying habits between the time of the survey and the product introduction.

TIME SERIES ANALYSIS AND PROJECTION. Trend projection techniques may be most appropriate in situations where the forecaster is able to infer, from the past behavior of a variable, something about its future impact on sales. Forecasters look for trends that form identifiable patterns which recur with predictive frequency. Seasonal variations and cyclical patterns form more obvious trends, while random variables make projection more complex.

While time series methods do not explicitly account for causal relationships between a variable and other factors, analysts find the emergent historical patterns useful in making forecasts. Analysts typically use time series for new product forecasts particularly in the intermediate and long-term. The data required varies with each technique. A good rule of thumb is a minimum of five years' annual data. A complete history is very helpful.

Market research involves a systematic, formal, and conscious procedure for evoking and testing hypotheses about real markets. Analysts need at least two market research reports based on time series analyses of market variables, and a considerable collection of market data from questionnaires and surveys.

In its simplest form, trend projection analysis involves the examination of what has happened in the past. Analysts develop a specific linear percentage trend with the expectation that the trend will continue. The problem with the simple trend projection is the fact of randomness—that is, the random event or element that has a major impact on the forecast.

Moving averages is a more sophisticated type of trend projection. It assumes the future will be an average of the past performance rather than following a specific linear percentage trend. The moving average minimizes the impact of randomness on individual forecasts since it is an average of several values rather than a simple linear projection. The moving average equation basically sums up the sales in a number of past periods and divides by the number of periods.

Industry surveys involve surveying the various companies that make up the industry for a particular item. They may include users or manufacturers. The industry survey method that uses a top-down approach of forecasting has some of the same advantages and disadvantages as the executive opinion and sales force composites.

A **regression analysis** may be linear or multiple. With linear regression analysts develop a relationship between sales and a single independent variable and use this relationship to forecast sales. With multiple regression, analysts examine relationships between sales and a number of independent variables. Usually the latter is accomplished with the help of a computer which helps analysts to estimate the values of the independent variables and to incorporate them into a multi-regression equation. If analysts find a relationship among various independent variables, they can develop a multiple regression equation for predicting sales for the coming year.

Exponential smoothing is a time series approach similar to the moving average. Instead of using a constant set of weights for the observation made, analysts employ an exponentially increasing set of weights so that more recent values receive more weight than do older values. More sophisticated models incorporate various adjustments for such factors as trends and seasonal patterns.

Analysts look at the leading indicators because the National Bureau of Economic Research has clearly demonstrated their value in forecasting. These indicators include prices of 500 **common stocks**, new orders for durable goods, an index of net business formation, corporate profits after taxes, industrial materials prices, and the change in consumer installment debt. Despite their widespread use, the leading economic indicators do not relate well with specific products. Nevertheless, when such relationships can be established, analysts construct multiple regression models with which to forecast sales.

CAUSAL METHODS. When analysts find a cause-effect relationship between a variable and sales, a causal model may provide better forecasts than those generated by other techniques. Life-cycle analysis forecasts new product growth rates based on analysts' projections of the phases of product acceptance by various groups—innovators, early adapters, early majority, late majority, and laggards. Typically, this method is used to forecast new product sales. Analysts' minimum data requirements are the annual sales of the product being considered or of a similar product. It is often necessary to do market surveys to establish the cause-effect relationships.

THE SALES BUDGET

The sales forecast provides the framework for the detailed planning presented in the master budget. Based on planned strategies and its best business judgment, management converts a sales forecast into a sales plan through the commitment of resources and the establishment of control mechanisms. The sales budget provides an evaluative tool by presenting monthly indexes of volume of units and of dollars as hard targets for the sales team. Deviations from these indexes indicate to managers where they need to adjust their efforts to take advantage of hot products or to remedy difficult situations.

Management determines its sales policies and strategies within its ability to respond to customer needs, technological changes, and the financial prerequisites of marketing. The sales budget projects that portion of potential sales the sales team believes it can achieve. The forecast, then, sets the parameters on the top side while the production capacity and sales acumen of the team sets the floor.

CAPABILITIES OF THE COMPANY. Although sales forecasts may accurately project significant changes in market conditions, a company needs to thoroughly examine its own resources to determine its ability to respond to these changes. A huge drop in demand may decrease the strain on the production process to where a company regains cost efficiencies or a large increase in demand might be required by a company that needs cash for other projects. The sales budget, therefore, is predicated on a company's ability to meet expected demand at or near its maximum profit potential.

THE PRODUCTION BUDGET. A company constructs the production budget within its own limitations of production, warehousing, delivery, and service. Subsequently, a company attempts to schedule production at maximum efficiency. By anticipating the variations in monthly sales, management can keep production at

levels sufficient to provide adequate supply. Labor costs generally comprise the greatest single production costs. Therefore, management may adjust labor hours to production schedules.

Production levels remain rather constant if current inventory is sufficient to meet increases in sales. If management expects an increase, it may build inventories during the first quarter of the budget, and sell them down to planned levels during the remaining three quarters. From the production budget, a company estimates the mix of materials, labor and production overhead needed to meet planned production levels.

SEE ALSO: Budgeting; Business Conditions; Business Planning; Discriminant Analysis; Histograms; Program Evaluation and Review Technique (PERT); Time Series Analysis

[Roger J. AbiNader]

FURTHER READING:

Cohen, William A. *The Practice of Marketing Management.* Macmillan Publishing Company, 1988.

Gruenwald, George. *New Product Development.* NTC Business Books, 1985.

Welsch, Glenn A. *Budgeting: Profit Planning and Control.* 4th ed. Prentice-Hall, Inc., 1976.

SALES LETTERS

The sales letter is the most important element of the standard direct-mail package. It takes the place of a salesperson and provides sellers with the opportunity for personal, one-on-one communication with their prospects. In addition to their use in **direct mail**, sales letters are also used by salespeople in a variety of situations—from customer communications to internal letters written for others on the **sales force**.

A standard direct-mail package usually includes an outer enevelope, a reply envelope, a brochure, and a response device in addition to the sales letter. The direct-mail letter is a sales letter and provides the opportunity to directly address the interests and concerns of the recipient. In a sense the letter replaces the salesperson in face-to-face selling. The letter typically spells out the benefits of the offer in detail. The more personal the sales letter, the more effective it generally is. To be successful the letter writer must be intimately familiar with not only the product or service and its benefits, he or she must know and understand the person to whom the letter is addressed.

A sales letter can be analyzed and discussed in terms of its components, including the letterhead and size of the letter, the salutation, the lead or opening, the body of the letter and its close, the signing of the letter, and the postscript. The look of a direct-mail sales letter is also important. Typeface selection, use of a second color, frequent indents and bullets, and other ways to highlight or emphasize certain parts of the letter play an important role in a sales letter's success.

Successful sales letters usually begin by spelling out some of the benefits of the product or service being sold. This is done in a way that captures the reader's attention. It may involve placing a lead sentence over the salutation or inside what is known as a Johnson Box, so named after 20th-century copywriter Fred Johnson who effectively used boxed messages to sell magazine subscriptions. Once the letter's lead has grabbed the reader's attention, the body of the letter follows to generate interest and motivate the reader to action. This is often accomplished by addressing the reader in a direct, personal manner and spelling out additional benefits that match the reader's known interests and needs. A successful sales letter may be as long as four pages or as short as one. There is no rule covering the length of a sales letter, only that it be long enough to tell an effective sales story.

The postscript, or P.S., is one of the most effective parts of a sales letter. Studies have shown that people who don't spend time reading the entire letter usually glance at the end of the letter and read the postcript—if there is one. Good letter writers know that the postscript is likely to be read, so they manage to include an especially attractive restatement of the offer, a key benefit, or other inducement to action in the postscript.

A "lift letter" is a variant of the direct-mail sales letter that is often added to a direct-mail package to "lift" the response rate. The lift letter often carries the message, "Read this only if you've decided not to accept our offer," or something similar to grab the recipient's attention one more time.

Another variant of the direct-mail sales letter is the testimonial, or endorsement, letter. While some sales letters may incorporate testimonials into the body of the letter, in other cases it becomes desirable to include an entire letter that serves as a testimonial for the product or service being sold. Product endorsements from real people are used to provide credibility and overcome the reader's reluctance to accept advertising or sales copy at face value.

Outside the realm of direct-mail, sales letters are used by salespeople to deal with a variety of situations. They may send sales letters to customers and prospects as a lead-in or follow-up to a telephone call or appointment, to confirm an appointment, as a letter of introduction, as a "reminder" to buy, and to cover a variety of other selling situations. Sales letters help salespeople build relationships with their customers.

They are used to sell and service accounts. Customers often perceive letters as being more thoughtful than telephone calls.

Sales letters can also be used effectively to build a marketing team or sales force. Letters from the sales manager can be used to provide encouragement and inform the sales staff in a variety of ways. Sales letters are used to announce changes in territories or commissions, incentive award offers, recognition of achievement, and other business matters affecting the sales force.

[David Bianco]

SALES MANAGEMENT

Sales **management** refers to the administration of the personal selling component of an organization's **marketing** program. It includes the planning, implementation, and control of sales programs, as well as recruiting, training, motivating, and evaluating members of the sales force. The fundamental role of the sales manager is to develop and administer a selling program that effectively contributes to the achievement of the goals of the overall organization. The term "sales manager" may be properly applied to several members of an organization, including: marketing executives, managers of field sales forces, district and division managers, and product line sales administrators. This text emphasizes the role of managers that oversee a field sales force.

BACKGROUND

The discipline of marketing management emerged during the Industrial Revolution, when mass production resulted in the creation of large organizations, and technological advances related to transportation and communication enhanced access to geographic markets. The two developments contributed to a growing need for the management of groups of sales people in large companies.

Since the start of the industrial revolution, sales management has progressed through four evolutionary stages. The first stage, which lasted until the beginning of the Great Depression, was characterized by an emphasis on engineering and production. Managers in those functional areas generally determined the company's goals and plans. They developed products and set prices with the assumption that the customers would naturally buy whatever they could get to the market. The job of the sales departments, then, was simply to facilitate the smooth flow of goods from the company to the consumer.

The maxim "build a better mousetrap and the people will come," was effectively dashed by the Depression, when producers found that selling products could be much more difficult than churning them out. Sales people and managers were elevated to a new status, and their input into product planning and organizational goal setting increased. It was also during this period that "hard sell" tactics, which still embody the stereotype often ascribed to automobile and aluminum siding salesmen, were developed. The hard sell philosophy reflected the propensity of most organizations to focus on getting the customer to want the product that was being offered rather than delivering what the customer desired. This second evolutionary stage extended from the 1930s into the 1950s.

During the 1960s and 1970s, companies in the United States began to embrace the concept of marketing, which initiated a shift of the organizational focus from selling to customer satisfaction and more efficient advertising and promotional practices. The adoption of marketing techniques essentially involved the integration of the selling side of business into related functions, such as budgeting, inventory control, warehousing, and product development. Despite the emergence of the marketing philosophy, however, most manufacturing companies continued to emphasize the production side of their business.

Sales management at U.S. companies entered a fourth evolutionary stage during the 1980s, characterized by a marked shift from production-orientation to customer orientation. Several factors prompted this change. Increased foreign competition, particularly from Japan, posed a serious threat to American companies, which were comparatively inefficient and unaware of customer wants. In addition, a slowdown in U.S. market growth resulted in greater competition between domestic rivals. Finally, a change in social orientation demanded that companies focus on creating and selling products that would provide a better quality of life, rather than a higher material standard of living. This change was evidenced by the proliferation of laws protecting the environment and mandating product safety.

The result of changes during the 1980s and early 1990s was that sales managers were forced to concentrate their efforts on determining precisely what customers wanted, and efficiently providing it. This change necessitated greater involvement by sales managers in the goal-setting and planning activities of the overall organization. This broadened scope meant that sales managers were expected to develop a more rounded body of knowledge that encompassed finance, operations, and purchasing.

At the same time, sales managers were forced to deal with other pivotal economic and social changes. Chief among socioeconomic trends of the 1980s and early 1990s was the evolution of marketing media. As the cost of the average industrial sales call rocketed from less than $100 in 1977 to more than $250 by the late 1980s, marketing and sales managers began to stress other sales tools. **Direct mail** and telephone sales became efficient **direct marketing** alternatives to face-to-face selling. They also surfaced as important media that sales managers could use to augment the efforts of their sales people in the field.

THE ROLE OF SALES MANAGEMENT

Although the role of sales management professionals is multidisciplinary, their primary responsibilities are: (1) setting goals for a sales-force; (2) planning, **budgeting**, and organizing a program to achieve those goals; (3) implementing the program; and (4) controlling and evaluating the results. Even when a sales force is already in place, the sales manager will likely view these responsibilities as an ongoing process necessary to adapt to both internal and external changes.

GOAL SETTING

To understand the role of sales managers in formulating goals, one must first comprehend their position within the organization. In fact, sales management is just one facet of a company's overall marketing strategy. A company's marketing program is represented by its marketing mix, which encompasses strategies related to products, prices, promotion, and distribution. Objectives related to promotion are achieved through three supporting functions: (1) **advertising**, which includes direct mail, radio, television, and print advertisements, among other media; (2) **sales promotion**, such as contests and coupons; and (3) personal selling, which encompasses the **sales force** manager.

The overall goals of the sales force manager are essentially mandated by the marketing mix. The mix coordinates objectives between the major components of the mix within the context of internal constraints, such as available capital and production capacity. For example, the overall corporate marketing strategy may dictate that the sales force needs to increase its share of the market by five percent over two years. It is the job of the sales force manager, then, to figure out how to achieve that directive. The sales force manager, however, may also play an important role in developing the overall marketing mix strategies that determine his objectives. For example, he may be in the best position to determine the specific needs of customers and to discern the potential of new and existing markets.

According to Irwin in the book *Management of the Sales Force*, one of the most critical duties of the sales manager is to accurately estimate the potential of the company's offerings. An important distinction exists between market potential and sales potential. The former is the total expected sales of a given product or service for the entire industry in a specific market over a stated period of time. Sales potential refers to the share of a market potential that an individual company can reasonably expect to achieve. According to Irwin, a sales forecast is an estimate of sales (in dollars or product units) that an individual firm expects to make during a specified time period, in a stated market, and under a proposed marketing plan.

Estimations of sales and market potential are often used to set major organizational objectives related to production, marketing, distribution, and other corporate functions, as well as to assist the sales manager in planning and implementing his overall sales strategy. Numerous **sales forecasting** tools and techniques, many of which are quite advanced, are available to help the sales manager determine potential and make forecasts. Major external factors influencing sales and market potential include: industry conditions, such as stage of maturity; market conditions and expectations; general business and economic conditions; and the regulatory environment.

PLANNING, BUDGETING, AND ORGANIZING

After determining goals, the sales manager must develop a strategy to attain them. A very basic decision is whether to hire a sales force or to simply contract with representatives outside of the organization. The latter strategy eliminates costs associated with hiring, training, and supervising workers, and it takes advantage of sales channels that have already been established by the independent representatives. On the other hand, maintaining an internal sales force allows the manager to exert more control over the salespeople and to ensure that they are trained properly. Furthermore, establishing an internal sale force provides the opportunity to hire inexperienced representatives at a very low cost.

The type of sales force developed depends on the financial priorities and constraints of the organization. If a manager decides to hire salespeople, he needs to determine the size of the force. This determination typically entails a compromise between the number of people needed to adequately service all potential customers and the resources made available by the company. One technique sometimes used to determine size is the "work load" strategy, whereby the sum of existing and potential customers is multiplied by the ideal number of calls per customer. That sum is then multiplied by the preferred length of a sales call (in hours). Next, that figure is divided by the selling time available from one sales person. The final sum is

theoretically the ideal sales force size. A second technique is the "incremental" strategy, which recognizes that the incremental increase in sales that results from each additional hire continually decreases. In other words sales people are gradually added until the cost of a new hire exceeds the benefit.

Other decisions facing a sales manager about hiring an internal sales force are what degree of experience to seek and how to balance quality and quantity. Basically, the manager can either "make" or "buy" his force. Young hires, or those whom the company "makes," cost less over a long term and do not bring any bad sales habits with them that were learned in other companies. On the other hand, the initial cost associated with experienced sales people is usually lower, and experienced employees can start producing results much more quickly. Furthermore, if the manager elects to hire only the most qualified people, budgetary constraints may force him to leave some territories only partially covered, resulting in customer dissatisfaction and lost sales.

After determining the composition of the sales force, the sales manager creates a budget, or a record of planned expenses that is (usually) prepared annually. The budget helps the manager decide how much money will be spent on personal selling and how that money will be allocated within the sales force. Major budgetary items include: sales force salaries, commissions, and bonuses; travel expenses; sales materials; training; clerical services; and office rent and utilities. Many budgets are prepared by simply reviewing the previous year's budget and then making adjustments. A more advanced technique, however, is the percentage of sales method, which allocates funds based on a percentage of expected revenues. Typical percentages range from about two percent for heavy industries to as much as eight percent or more for consumer goods and computers.

After a sales force strategy has been devised and a budget has been adopted, the sales manager should ideally have the opportunity to organize, or structure, the sales force. In general, the hierarchy at larger organizations includes a national or international sales manager, regional managers, district managers, and finally the sales force. Smaller companies may omit the regional, and even the district, management levels. Still, a number of organizational considerations must be addressed. For example:

- Should the force emphasize product, geographic, or customer specialization?

- How centralized will the management be?

- How many layers of management are necessary?

The trend during the 1980s and early 1990s was toward flatter organizations, which possess fewer levels of management, and decentralized decision-making, which empowers workers to make decisions within their area of expertise.

IMPLEMENTING

After goal setting, planning, budgeting, and organizing, the sales force plan, budget, and structure must be implemented. Implementation entails activities related to staffing, designing territories, and allocating sales efforts. Staffing, the most significant of those three responsibilities, includes recruiting, training, compensating, and motivating sales people.

Before sales managers can recruit workers to fill the jobs, they must analyze each of the positions to be filled. This is often accomplished by sending an observer into the field. The observer records time spent talking to customers, traveling, attending meetings, and doing paperwork. The observer then reports the findings to the sales manager, who uses the information to draft a detailed job description. Also influencing the job description will be several factors, chiefly the characteristics of the people on which the person will be calling. It is usually important that salespeople possess characteristics similar to those of the buyer, such as age and education.

The manager may seek candidates through advertising, college recruiting, company sources, and employment agencies. Candidates are typically evaluated through personality tests, interviews, written applications, and background checks. Research has shown that the two most important personality traits that sales people can possess are empathy, which helps them relate to customers, and drive, which motivates them to satisfy personal needs for accomplishment. Other factors of import include maturity, appearance, communication skills, and technical knowledge related to the product or industry. Negative traits include fear of rejection, distaste for travel, self-consciousness, and interest in artistic or creative originality.

After recruiting a suitable sales force, the manager must determine how much and what type of training to provide. Most sales training emphasizes product, company, and industry knowledge. Only about 25 percent of the average company training program, in fact, addresses personal selling techniques. Because of the high cost, many firms try to reduce the amount of training. The average cost of training a person to sell industrial products, for example, commonly exceeds $30,000. Sales managers can achieve many benefits with competent training programs, however. For instance, research indicates that training reduces **employee turnover**, thereby lowering the effective cost of hiring new workers. Good training can also improve customer relations, increase employee morale, and boost sales. Common training methods include lectures, cases studies, role playing, demonstrations, on-the-job training, and self-study courses.

After the sales force is in place, the manager must devise a means of compensating individuals. The main conflict that must be addressed is that between personal and company goals. The manager wants to provide sufficient incentives for salespeople but also must meet the division's or department's goals, such as controlling costs, boosting market share, or increasing cash flow. The ideal system motivates sales people to achieve both personal and company goals. Good salespeople want to make money for themselves, however, a trait which often detracts from the firm's objectives. Most approaches to compensation utilize a combination of salary and commission or salary and bonus.

Although financial rewards are the primary means of motivating workers, most sales organizations employ other motivational techniques. Good sales managers recognize that sales people, by nature, have needs other than the basic physiological needs filled by money: they want to feel like they are part of winning team, that their jobs are secure, and that their efforts and contributions to the organization are recognized. Methods of meeting those needs include contests, vacations, and other performance based prizes in addition to self-improvement benefits such as tuition for graduate school. Another tool managers commonly use to stimulate their workers is quotas. Quotas, which can be set for factors such as the number of calls made per day, expenses consumed per month, or the number of new customers added annually, give salespeople a standard against which they can measure success.

In addition to recruiting, training, and motivating a sales force to achieve the sales manager's goals, managers at most organizations must decide how to designate sales territories and allocate the efforts of the sales team. Many organizations, such as real estate and insurance companies, do not use territories, however. Territories are geographic areas such as cities, counties, or countries assigned to individual salespeople. The advantage of establishing territories is that it improves coverage of the market, reduces wasteful overlap of sales efforts, and allows each salesperson to define personal responsibility and judge individual success.

Allocating people to different territories is an important sales management task. Typically, the top few territories produce a disproportionately high sales volume. This occurs because managers usually create smaller areas for trainees, medium-sized territories for more experienced team members, and larger areas for senior sellers. A drawback of that strategy, however, is that it becomes difficult to compare performance across territories. An alternate approach is to divide regions by existing and potential base. A number of computer programs exist to help sales managers effectively create territories according to their goals.

CONTROLLING AND EVALUATING

After setting goals, creating a plan, and setting the program into motion, the sales manager's responsibility becomes controlling and evaluating the program. During this stage, the sales manager compares the original goals and objectives with the actual accomplishments of the sales force. The performance of each individual is compared with goals or quotas, looking at elements such as expenses, sales volume, customer satisfaction, and cash flow. A common model used to evaluate individual sales people considers four key measures: the number of sales calls, the number of days worked, total sales in dollars, and the number of orders collected. The equation below can help to identify a deficiency in any of these areas:

$$\text{\$ Sales} = \text{Days worked} \times \frac{\text{Calls}}{\text{Days worked}} \times \frac{\text{Orders}}{\text{Calls}} \times \frac{\text{Sales \$}}{\text{Orders}}$$

An important consideration for the sales manager is profitability. Indeed, simple sales figures may not reflect an accurate image of the performance of the overall sales force. The manager must dig deeper by analyzing expenses, price-cutting initiatives, and long-term contracts with customers that will impact future income. An in-depth analysis of these and related influences will help the manager to determine true performance based on profits. For use in future goal-setting and planning efforts, the manager may also evaluate sales trends by different factors, such as product line, volume, territory, and market.

After the manager analyzes and evaluates the achievements of the sales force, that information is used to make corrections to the current strategy and sales program. In other words, the sales manmager returns to the initial goal-setting stage.

ENVIRONMENTS AND STRATEGIES

The goals and plans adopted by the sales manager will be greatly influenced by the industry orientation, competitive position, and market strategy of the overall organization. It is the job of sales managers, or people employed in sales-management-related jobs, to ensure that their efforts coincide with those of upper-level management.

The basic industry orientations are industrial goods, consumer durables, consumer nondurables, and services. Companies or divisions that manufacture industrial goods or sell highly technical services tend to be heavily dependent on personal selling as a marketing tool. Sales managers in those organizations characteristically focus on customer service and education, and employ and train a relatively high-level sales force. Sales managers that sell consumer durables will likely integrate the efforts of their sales force into related advertising and promotional initiatives. Sales management efforts related to consumer nondurables and consumer services will generally emphasize volume sales, a comparatively low-caliber sales force, and an emphasis on high-volume customers.

Michael Porter's book, *Competitive Strategy,* lists three common market approaches that determine sales management strategies: low-cost supplier; differentiation; and niche. Companies that adopt a low-cost supplier strategy are usually characterized by a vigorous pursuit of efficiency and cost controls. A company that manufactures nails and screws would likely take this approach. They profit by offering a better value than their competitors, accumulating market share, and focusing on high-volume and fast inventory turn-over. Sales management efforts in this type of organization should generally stress the minimizing of expenses—by having sales people stay at budget hotels, for example—and appealing to customers on the basis of price. Sales people should be given an incentive to chase large, high-volume customers, and the sales force infrastructure should be designed to efficiently accommodate large order-taking activities.

Companies that adhere to a differentiation strategy achieve market success by offering a unique product or service. They often rely on brand loyalty or a patent protection to insulate them from competitors and, thus, are able to achieve higher-than-average profit margins. A firm that sells proprietary pharmaceuticals would likely use this method. Management initiatives in this type of environment would necessitate selling techniques that stressed benefits, rather than price. They might also entail a focus on high customer service, extensive prospecting for new buyers, and chasing customers that were minimally sensitive to price. In addition, sales managers would be more apt to seek high-caliber sellers and to spend more money on training.

Firms that pursue a niche market strategy succeed by targeting a very narrow segment of a market and then dominating that segment. The company is able to overcome competitors by aggressively protecting its niche and orienting every action and decision toward the service of its select group. A company that produced floor coverings only for extremely upscale commercial applications might select this approach. Sales managers in this type of organization would tend to emphasize extensive employee training or the hiring of industry experts. The overall sales program would be centered around customer service and benefits other than price.

In addition to the three primary market strategies, Raymond Miles and Charles Snow claim that most companies can be grouped into one of three classifications based on their product strategy: prospector, defender, and analyzer. Each of these product strategies influences the sales management role. For example, prospector companies seek to bring new products to the market. Sales management techniques, therefore, tend to emphasize sales volume growth and market penetration through aggressive prospecting. In addition, sales people may have to devote more time to educating their customers about new products.

Defender companies usually compete in more mature industries and offer established products. This type of firm is likely to practice a low-cost producer market strategy. The sales manager's primary objective is to maintain the existing customer base, primarily through customer service and by aggressively responding to efforts by competitors to steal market share.

Finally, analyzer companies represent a mix of prospector and defender strategies. They strive to enter high-growth markets while still retaining their position in mature segments. Thus, sales management strategies must encompass elements used by both prospector and defender firms.

REGULATION

Besides markets and industries, another chief environmental influence on the sales management process is government regulation. Indeed, selling activities at companies are regulated by a multitude of state and federal laws designed to protect consumers, foster competitive markets, and discourage unfair business practices.

Chief among anti-trust provisions affecting sales managers is the Robinson-Patman Act, which prohibits companies from engaging in price or service discrimination. In other words, a firm cannot offer special incentives to large customers based solely on volume, because such practices tend to hurt smaller suppliers. Companies can give discounts to buyers, but only if those incentives are based on savings gleaned from manufacturing and distribution processes.

Similarly, the Sherman Act makes it illegal for a seller to force a buyer to purchase one product (or service) in order to get the opportunity to purchase another product, a practice referred to as a "tying agreement." A long-distance telephone company, for instance, cannot necessarily require its customers to purchase its telephone equipment as a prerequisite to buying its long-distance service. The Sherman Act also regulates reciprocal dealing arrangements, whereby companies agree to buy products from each other. Reciprocal dealing is considered anticompetitive because large buyers and sellers tend to have an unfair advantage over their smaller competitors.

Also, several consumer protection regulations impact sales managers. The Fair Packaging and Labeling Act of 1966, for example, restricts deceptive labeling, and the Truth in Lending Act requires sellers to fully disclose all finance charges incorporated into consumer credit agreements. Cooling-off laws, which commonly exist at the state level, allow buyers to cancel contracts made with door-to-door sellers within a certain time frame. Additionally, the Federal Trade Commission (FTC) requires door-to-door sellers who work for companies engaged in interstate trade to clearly announce their purpose when calling on prospects.

SALES MANAGEMENT CAREERS

In many ways, sales managers are similar to other marketing managers in the organization in that they are assigned a profit center for which they are ultimately responsible and for which they are expected to oversee all activities. Naturally sales manager's jobs also differ from other marketing-related management positions. Foremost among the differences is the geographical positioning of subordinates. In order to cut sales costs, companies attempt to disperse their sales forces evenly throughout the entire selling zone. This division reduces the sales manager's ability to directly oversee their work. As a result, sales managers must spend much more of their time traveling than other managers.

Another distinguishing characteristic of sales management positions is their high exposure. Sales managers are usually on the "front lines" of their company's war in the competitive market. And, because of detailed weekly, or even daily, reports showing sales and profit data, their performance can be easily judged by superiors and coworkers. A corollary of the ease in measuring their performance is that their compensation plans typically differ from managers in areas such as finance or operations. Often, much of their compensation comes in the form of bonuses linked to statistics indicative of the success of the overall sales force. In the late 1980s, sales managers at medium-sized to large companies generally earned between $60,000 and $200,000, depending primarily on industry, product type, and experience/education level, whereas district managers' salaries fell into the $50,000 to $70,000 range with pay increasing at the regional and national levels.

Despite their administrative orientation, many sales managers continue to spend much of their time selling. In fact, at least one study made during the 1970s indicated that sales managers spend about 35 percent of their time engaged in sales activities, including making important sales calls with their sales people and dealing with problem accounts. The study also revealed that about 20 percent of the managers' time, on average, was used to train people, establish performance standards, and handle other personnel matters. The remainder of the time was dedicated mostly to marketing, administrative, and financial tasks. The trend going into the mid-1990s was toward increased awareness, and time allotted to, activities such as finance and (particularly) purchasing.

POSITIONS

Sales managers commonly begin their careers as salespeople. In some instances, particularly in companies that sell products and services directly to customers, sales people may assume a management role in as little as six months. Typically, however, at least a few years of field sales experience is required to become eligible for a management position. In the case of firms that market highly technical industrial products, a competent sales person may have to work in the field for five or ten years before being promoted.

A common progression for a manager of a field sales force is district, regional, and then national sales manager. Some companies also have unit managers, who are typically placed in charge of four or five sales people. All of these territorial management positions are usually in direct authority over the sales force and generally entail the responsibilities outlined in this text. Most companies have a chief sales executive, or the equivalent thereof. Regardless of his or her title, that person is ultimately in charge of overseeing the successful operation of the entire field sales force program.

Some companies organize their sales forces by markets, products, or customer types, rather then territories. In those instances, sales force managers are commonly referred to as market sales managers or product sales managers. Furthermore, high-level field sales force managers, particularly in large organizations, may employ one or several assistant sales managers to handle budgeting, forecasting, research, and other duties. Finally, in addition to field sales force management positions, there are a number of sales management professionals who do not oversee sales people in the field. Such jobs include managers of sales training, customer service, and research departments.

SEE ALSO: Management Science; Marketing Strategy; Training and Development

[Dave Mote]

FURTHER READING:

Churchill, Gilbert A., Jr., Neil M. Ford and Orville C. Walker, Jr. *Sales Force Management: Planning, Implementation, and Control*, 3rd ed. Irwin, 1990.

Dalrymple, Douglas J. *Sales Management: Concepts and Cases*. John Wiley & Sons, 1982.

Miles, Raymond and Charles C. Snow. *Organizational Strategy, Structure, and Process*. McGraw-Hill Book Company, 1978.

Newton, Derek A. *Sales Force Management: Text and Cases*, 2nd ed. Irwin, 1990.

Porter, Michael E. *Competitive Strategy*. The Free Press, 1980.

Stafford, John and Colin Grant. *Effective Sales Management*. Nichols Publishing Company, 1986.

Stanton, William J. and Richard H. Buskirk. *Management of the Sales Force*, 7th ed. Irwin, 1987.

SALES PROMOTION

Sales promotion is an important component of a company's **marketing** communication strategy along with **advertising**, **public relations**, and **personal selling**. The American Marketing Association (AMA) defines sales promotion as, ''media and nonmedia marketing pressure applied for a predetermined, limited period of time in order to stimulate trial, increase consumer demand, or improve product quality.'' Unfortunately, this definition does not capture all the elements of modern sales promotion. An alternative definition follows: sales promotion is a marketing activity that adds to the basic value of the product for a limited time and directly stimulates consumer purchasing, selling effectiveness, or the effort of the sales force.

Three issues clarify sales promotion. First, sales promotion ranks in importance with advertising and requires similar care in planning and strategy development. Second, three audiences are targeted by sales promotion: consumers, resellers, and the sales force. Lastly, sales promotion as a competitive weapon provides an extra incentive for the target audience to purchase or support one brand over another. This last factor distinguishes sales promotion from other promotional mix tactics. For example, unplanned purchases may be directly related to one or more sales promotion offers. Sales promotion stems from the premise that any brand or service has an established perceived price or value. Sales promotion is believed to change this accepted price-value relationship by increasing the value and/or lowering the price.

In order to understand the basic role and function of sales promotion, one must differentiate between sales promotion and other components of the marketing mix. Sales promotion usually operates on a short time line, uses a more rational appeal, returns a tangible or real value, fosters an immediate sale, and contributes highly to profitability. The idea of contribution to profitability may be confusing. It is simply the ratio between what is spent on a promotional mix compared to the direct profitability generated by that expenditure. A few exceptions to the above traits do exist. For example, a sweepstake might use a very emotional appeal, while a business-to-business ad may be very rational.

GROWTH OF SALES PROMOTION

Sales promotion has grown substantially in recent years. Donnelley Marketing estimates that expenditure on sales promotion hit $150 billion in 1993. More promotion dollars are being spent on sales promotion than on advertising (roughly 65 percent versus 35 percent). There are several reasons for this dramatic growth in sales promotion.

First, the consumer has accepted sales promotion as part of buying decision criteria. There are inherent reasons why consumers have become amenable to sales promotion. Primarily, sales promotion offers consumers the opportunity to get more than they thought possible. Product sampling, for example, allows consumers to try the product without buying it. Furthermore, many people are reluctant decision makers who need some incentive to make choices. Sales promotion gives them the extra nudge they need in order to become active customers. Finally, sales promotion offers have become an integral part of the buying process, and consumers have learned to expect them.

The progression of sales promotion has been spurred by business, especially big business. Top managers and product managers have played direct roles in encouraging the recent growth of sales promotion. The product manager's goals and desires have provided the initial impetus. Product managers are challenged to differentiate their product in a meaningful way from competitors' products because buyers have many choices among brands and types of products offering similar satisfactions. Sales promotion techniques provide solutions to this dilemma. Heads of companies today focus increasingly on short-term results. They want sales tomorrow, not next quarter or next year. Sales promotions can provide immediate hikes in sales.

New technology, especially the computer, has also created greater acceptance of sales promotion by managers wanting to measure results. For example, scanning equipment in retail stores enables manufacturers to get rapid feedback on the results of promotions. Redemption rates for coupons or figures on sales volume can be obtained within days.

The growth in power of retailers has also boosted the use of sales promotion. Historically, the manufacturer had the power in the channel of distribution. Mass marketers utilized national advertising to get directly to consumers, creating a demand for the heav-

ily advertised brands which stores couldn't ignore. With consolidation, retailers have gained access to sophisticated information. For example, use of computers and bar codes on packages is shifting the balance of power in their favor. Custom designed programs will help retailers to complete and increase sales in their market area. Sales promotion is an effective and satisfying response to the demand for account-specific marketing programs. Increased sales volume provided through sales promotion enhances small profit margins. Retailers also benefit from the immediate feedback of sales promotion that readily reveals unsuccessful programs.

LIMITATIONS

Although sales promotion is a competent strategy for producing quick, short-term, positive results, it is not a cure for a bad product, poor advertising, or an inferior sales team. After a consumer uses a coupon for the initial purchase of a product, the product must then take over.

Sales promotion activities may bring several negative consequences, primarily clutter from increased competitive promotions. New approaches are promptly cloned by competitors, with efforts to be more creative, more attention getting, or more effective in attracting the attention of consumers and the trade.

Also, consumers and resellers have learned how to milk the sales promotion game. Notably, consumers may wait to buy certain items knowing that eventually prices will be reduced. Resellers, having learned this strategy long ago, are experts at negotiating deals and manipulating competitors against one another.

TECHNIQUES OF CONSUMER PROMOTIONS

Consumer sales promotions are steered toward the ultimate product users—typically individuals—especially shoppers in the local supermarket. The same techniques promote products sold by one business to another such as computer systems, communication networks, automobile fleets, cleaning supplies, and machinery. In contrast, trade sales promotions target resellers—wholesalers and retailers—who carry the marketer's product. Following are some of the key techniques in the storehouse of varied consumer-oriented sales promotions.

PRICE DEALS

A consumer price deal saves the buyer money when a product is purchased. The price deal hopes to encourage trial use of a new product or line extension, to recruit new buyers for a mature product, or to reinforce existing customers' continuing their purchasing, increasing their purchases, accelerating their use, or purchasing of multiple units of an existing brand. Price deals work most effectively when price is the consumer's foremost criterion or when brand loyalty is low. Four main types of consumer price deals are used: price discounts, price pack deals, refunds (**rebates**), and **coupons**.

Buyers learn about price discounts and cents-off deals either at the point of sale or through advertising. At the point of sale, price reductions may be posted on the package or signs near the product or in storefront windows. Ads that notify consumers of upcoming discounts includes fliers, newspaper and television ads, and other media. Price discounts are especially common in the food industry, where local supermarkets run weekly specials.

Price discounts may be initiated by the manufacturer, the retailer, or the distributor. For instance, a manufacturer may "pre-price" a product and then convince the retailer to participate in this short-term discount through extra incentives. Effectiveness of national price reduction strategies requires the support of all distributors. The frequency of these programs is seen in the supermarket where the manufacturer's price is covered by the retailer's price serves as witness to the power of retailers.

Existing customers perceive discounts as rewards and often then buy in larger quantities. Price discounts alone, however, usually don't induce first time buyers. Other appeals must be available, such as mass media ads or product sampling.

A price pack deal may be either a bonus pack or a banded pack. When a bonus pack is offered, an extra amount of the product is free when a standard size of the product is bought at the regular price. This technique is routinely used in cleaning products, food, and health and beauty aids to introduce a new or larger size. A bonus pack rewards present users but may have little appeal to users of competitive brands. It is also a way to "load" customers up with the product.

When two or more units of a product are sold at a reduction of the regular single-unit price, a banded pack offer is being made. Sometimes the products are physically banded together, such as in toothbrush and toothpaste offers. More often, the products are simply offered in a two-for, three-for, or ten-for format. The smaller size of the product may be attached to the regular size.

A refund or rebate promotion is an offer by a marketer to return a certain amount of money when the product is purchased alone or in combination with other products. Refunds aim to increase the quantity or frequency of purchase, to encourage customers to load up. This dampens competition by temporarily taking consumers out of the market, stimulates purchase of postponable goods such as major appliances,

and creates on-shelf excitement or encourages special displays. Consumers seem to view refunds and rebates as a reward for purchase. They appear to build brand loyalty rather than diminish it.

Coupons are legal certificates offered by manufacturers and retailers. They grant specified savings on selected products when presented for redemption at the point of purchase. Manufacturers sustain the cost of advertising and distributing their coupons, redeeming their face values, and paying retailers a handling fee. Retailers who offer double or triple the amount of the coupon shoulder the extra cost. Retailers who offer their own coupons incur the total cost, including paying the face value. Retail coupons are equivalent to a cents-off deal. In 1859, Grape-Nuts cereal created this promotional technique by offering a 1-cent coupon.

Manufacturers disseminate coupons in many ways. They may direct deliver by mailing, dropping door to door, or delivering to a central location such as a shopping mall. They may distribute them through the media—magazines, newspapers, Sunday supplements, or freestanding inserts (FSI) in newspapers. They may insert a coupon into a package, attach it to, or print it on a package. Coupons may also be distributed by a retailer who uses them to generate store traffic or to tie in with a manufacturer's promotional tactic. Retailer-sponsored coupons are typically distributed through print advertising or at the point of sale. Sometimes, specialty retailers such as ice cream or electronics stores or newly opened retailers will distribute coupons door to door or through **direct mail**.

CONTESTS/SWEEPSTAKES

Historically, a great deal of confusion about the terms contests and sweepstakes has existed. Simply, a contest requires the entrant, in order to be deemed a winner, to perform a task (for example, draw a picture, write a poem) that is then judged. This is termed a contest of skill. On the other hand, a sweepstake is a random drawing or chance contest which may or may not have a requirement such as buying a ticket or purchasing a product. A contest requires a judging process; a sweepstake does not.

The use of sweepstakes has grown dramatically in recent decades, thanks largely to changes in the legal distinctions that determine what is and is not a lottery. A lottery is a promotion that involves the awarding of a prize on the basis of chance with a consideration required for entry. Before these changes, being associated with a lottery carried negative stereotypes of gamblers or organized crime. In a sales promotion, the consideration is the box top or other token asked for by the advertiser. For many years, advertisers employed contests, thus eliminating the element of chance and removing the lottery stigma. The familiar "twenty-five words or less" contest and many other similar devices were common. The liberalization of legal interpretations, including the ability to ask for a sales receipt as proof of purchase, made sweepstakes feasible.

Besides legal changes, concern for costs favored a switch to sweepstakes. Judging and processing contests are expensive procedures. Administering a contest once cost about $350 per thousand entries, while the cost of processing a sweepstake has recently ranged from just $2.75 to $3.75 per thousand. In addition, participation in contests is very low compared to that of sweepstakes. Contests require participants to compete for a prize or prizes based on some sort of skill or ability. Sweepstakes, on the other hand, require only that participants submit their names for a drawing or another type of chance selection. Although the figures are rough, an estimated $87 million was spent on contests and sweepstakes in 1977, and $175 million in 1989. Surprisingly, fewer than 20 percent of all households have ever entered a contest or sweepstake.

SPECIAL EVENTS

According to International Events Group (IEG), an events consulting firm, businesses spend over $2 billion annually to link their products with everything from jazz festivals to golf tournaments to stock car races. In fact, companies like RJR Nabisco and Anheuser-Busch Companies have special divisions or departments that handle nothing but special events. One of the world's largest agencies, Saatchi & Saatchi DFS Compton, has a group called HMG Sports that manages sports events, including the Olympics, a ski tour for Sanka and Post Cereals, a bass-fishing contest for Hardee's, and a worldwide yacht-racing event for Beefeater's Gin.

Several good reasons explain why so many marketers have jumped on the special events bandwagon. First, events tend to attract a homogeneous audience very appreciative of the sponsors. Therefore, if a product fits with the event in terms of the expected stereotypic homogeneity of the audience, the impact of the sales promotion dollars will be quite high. To illustrate, Lalique Crystal should not sponsor a tractor pull, but Marlboro should. Second, events sponsorship may build support from trade and from employees. Those employees who manage the event may receive acknowledgment and even awards. Little is more appealing to the president of Kemper Insurance than presenting a $300,000 check to the winner of the Kemper Open on national television. Finally, compared to producing a series of ads, event management is simple. Many elements of events are prepackaged. For example, MCI Communications Corp. can use the same group of people to manage many events. It can use booths, displays, premiums, and ads repeatedly by simply changing names, places, and dates.

PREMIUMS

A premium is tangible compensation, an incentive, given for rendering a particular deed, usually buying a product. The premium may be free, or, if not, the cost is well below the usual price. Getting a bonus amount of the product is a premium, as is receiving the prize in a cereal box, a free glass with a purchase of detergent, or a free atlas with a purchase of insurance.

Incentives given free at the time of a purchase are called direct premiums. With such bonuses there is no confusion about cost, returning coupons or box tops, clipping weight circles or bar codes, risk or gamble, or saving proofs. And, there is instant gratification.

Four variants of direct premium programs may be identified. First, the simple direct premium provides an incentive given separately as a product is purchased. For instance, when a shopper pays for a new coat, she learns it has a direct premium—a hanging travel bag. Second, in-packs may be enclosed with a package at the factory. A snack food company, for example, may include a serving tin inside its holiday package. On-packs are another type of factory-added packaging that lies outside the package, well attached by a plastic strip, wrapper, or other apparatus. Free dental floss attached to toothpaste is an example. Fourth, container premiums reverse the presentation of the in-pack by placing the product inside the premium such as fancy liquor decanters which often hold the goods at Christmas.

Other types of direct premium are traffic builders, door-openers, and referral premiums. The traffic-builder premium is an incentive—such as a gift of a small garden tool—to lure a prospective buyer to a store. A door-opener premium is directed to customers at home or business people in their offices. Door-opening favors are a staple device in the direct-sales field. The use of this premium type may create a subtle entry during house-to-house canvassing or a clincher when telephoning for an appointment. Door-openers serve similar functions in many other industries. For example, an electronics manufacturer offers free software to an office manager who agrees to an on-site demonstration. The final category of premiums is the referral provided by the purchaser. Sales leads from satisfied customers are awarded to sellers along with rewards for their assistance.

Mail premiums, unlike direct premiums, require the customer to perform some act in order to obtain a premium through return mail. The self-liquidator is the basic type of mail premium. It was created during the 1930s Depression, a time of enforced economy. Savings counted to the penny were vital to the ordinary consumer. Since promotion budgets were usually tight, the premium which cost the advertiser nothing was most appealing. The self-liquidator fit the bill. Self-liquidating meant the price the customer paid for the premium was the same as the cost paid by the advertiser. That is, the costs canceled themselves. A self-liquidating premium may be available in exchange for one or more proofs-of-purchase and a payment or charge covering the cost of the item plus handling, mailing, packaging, and taxes, if any. The premium represents a bargain because the customer cannot readily buy the item for the same amount.

CONTINUITY PROGRAMS

Continuity programs retain brand users over a long time period by offering ongoing motivations. Self-liquidating premiums are one-time opportunities, whereas continuity programs demand that consumers keep saving something in order to get the premium in the future. Trading stamps, popularized in the 1950s and 1960s, such as S&H and Gold Bond, are prime examples. The bonus was usually one stamp for every dime spent at a participating store. The stamp company provided redemption centers where the stamps were traded for merchandise. A catalog listing the quantity of stamps required for each item was available at the participating store.

Today, airlines' frequent-flyer clubs, hotels' frequent-traveler plans, as well as bonus-paying credit card programs have replaced trading stamps continuity programs. Looking back, it seems that when competing brands have reached parity, continuity programs have provided the discrimination factor among those competitors. Continuity programs have also opposed a new threatening competitor by rewarding long-standing customers for their continuing loyalty. A continuity program is all about sustaining brand loyalty through continuous reward. Retail-driven frequent-shopper plans focus on core customers to solidify store loyalty; manufacturer-sponsored programs usually encourage product loading and repeat purchase from stores.

SAMPLING

A sign of a successful marketer is getting the product into the hands of the consumer. Sometimes, particularly when a product is new or is not a market leader, an effective strategy is giving a sample product to the consumer either free or for a small fee. The first rule is to use sampling only when a product can virtually sell itself. Thus, the product must have benefits or features obvious to the consumer. Also, the consumer must be given enough of the product to enable an accurate judging of its value. Trial sizes of a product dictate how much will be received.

There are several means of disseminating samples to consumers. The most popular has been through the mail. Increases in postage costs and packaging and bundling requirements, however, have made this method increasingly less attractive. An alternative is door-to-door distribution, particularly when the items are bulky and/or when reputable distribution organizations exist. The product may simply be hung on the doorknob or delivered face to face. This method permits selective sampling of neighborhoods, dwellings, or even people.

Another method is distributing samples in conjunction with advertising. An ad may include a coupon that the consumer can mail in for the product, or an address or phone number for ordering may be mentioned in the body of an ad. Direct sampling is achieved through prime media using scratch-'n'-sniff cards and slim foil pouches.

Products can also be sampled directly through the retailer who sets up a display unit near the product or hires a person to give the product to consumers as they pass by. This technique may build goodwill for the retailer and be effective in reaching the right consumers. Some retailers resent the inconvenience and require high payments for their cooperation.

The last form of distribution deals with specialty types of sampling. For instance, some companies specialize in packing samples together for delivery to a homogeneous consumer group such as newlyweds, new parents, students, or tourists. Such packages may be delivered at hospitals, hotels, or dormitories.

TRADE PROMOTIONS

A trade sales promotion is pointed to resellers who distribute products to ultimate consumers. The term "trade" traditionally refers to wholesalers and retailers who handle or distribute marketers' products. It is synonymous with resellers, the term used here for wholesalers and retailers. Making matters more confusing, the term "dealers" is also used to represent these two groups. For clarity, "trade" will be used throughout this section.

Commonly, a senior marketing officer or product manager is responsible for planning a trade promotion. Decisions about the nature of the deal and its timing are made jointly by the marketing officer, sales manager, and campaign manager. Because such deals have direct bearing on the pricing strategy and resulting profitability, they may require clearance by top management as well.

The objectives of sales promotions aimed at the trade are different from those directed to consumers.

Trade sales promotions hope to accomplish four overall goals:

1. Develop in-store merchandising support or other trade support. Strong retail support at the store level is the key to closing the loop between the customer and the sale.

2. Control inventory. Sales promotions are used to increase or deplete inventory levels and to eliminate seasonal peaks and valleys.

3. Expand or improve distribution. Sales promotions can open up new areas or classes. Sales promotions are also used to distribute a new size of the product.

4. Motivate channel members. Sales promotions can generate excitement about the product among those responsible for selling it.

TYPES OF TRADE SALES PROMOTIONS

Manufacturers provide point-of-purchase (POP) display units free to retailers in order to promote a particular brand or group of products. The forms of POP displays include special racks, display cartons, banners, signs, price cards, and mechanical product dispensers. Probably the most effective way to ensure that a reseller will use a POP display is to design it to generate sales for the retailer.

High product visibility is the basic goal of POP displays. In industries such as the grocery field where a shopper spends about three-tenths of a second viewing a product, anything increasing product visibility is valuable. Beyond getting attention for a product, POP displays also provide or remind about important decision information such as the product name, appearance of the product, and sizes. Consumers may have seen or heard some of the information in ads before entering the store. The theme of the POP should be coordinated with the theme used in ads and by salespeople.

For resellers and salespeople, sales contests can be an effective motivation. Typically, a prize is awarded to the organization or person who exceeds a quota by the largest percentage. For example, Cepacol Mouthwash offered supermarket managers cash prizes matched to the percentages by which they exceeded the sales quota, plus a vacation to Bermuda for the manager who achieved the highest percentage. Often such programs must be customized for particular reseller groups.

Thousands of manufacturers display their wares and take orders at trade shows. Companies spend over $9 billion yearly on these shows. For many companies, maximum planning effort and much of the marketing budget are directed at the trade show. Success for an entire year may hinge on how well a company performs there.

Trade shows provide unique opportunities. First, trade shows provide a major opportunity to write orders for products. Secondly, they are a chance to demonstrate products, provide information, answer questions, and be compared directly to competitors. All the companies are attempting to provide a clear picture of their products to potential customers, consequently, quality, features, prices, and technology can be easily compared.

Related to trade meetings but less elaborate are sales meetings sponsored by manufacturers or wholesalers. Whereas trade shows are open to potential customers, sales meetings are targeted to the company sales force and/or independent sales agents. These meetings are usually conducted regionally and directed by sales managers and their field force. Sometimes a major marketing officer from corporate headquarters directs the proceedings. The purposes of sales meetings vary. The meetings may occur just prior to the buying season and are used to motivate sales agents, to explain the product or the promotional campaign, or simply to answer questions.

An extra payment given to salespeople for meeting a specified sales goal is called push money; it is also known as spiffs or PM. For example, a manufacturer of refrigerators might pay a $30 bonus for sales of model A, a $25 bonus for model B, and a $20 bonus for model C between March 1 and September 1. At the end of that period, the salesperson would send evidence of these sales to the manufacturer and receive a check in return. Although push money has a negative image since it hints of bribery, many manufacturers offer it.

A deal loader is a premium given by a manufacturer to a retailer for ordering a certain quantity of product. Two types of deal loaders are most typical. The first is a buying loader which typically is a gift given for making a specified order size. The second is a display loader which means the display is given to the retailer after the campaign. For instance, General Electric may have a display containing appliances as part of a special program. When the program is over, the retailer receives all the appliances on the display if a specified order size was achieved. Trade deals are often special price concessions superseding, for a limited time, the normal purchasing discounts given to the trade. Trade deals include a group of tactics having a common theme—to encourage sellers to specially promote a product. The attention may be special displays, purchase of larger-than-usual amounts, superior in-store locations, or greater advertising effort. In exchange, retailers may receive special allowances, discounts, goods, or money.

Money spent on trade deals is considerable. In many industries, trade deals are the primary expectation for retail support. There are two main types of trade deals: buying allowances and advertising/display allowances.

A buying allowance is a bonus paid by a manufacturer to a reseller when a certain amount of product is purchased during a specific time. All the reseller has to do is meet the criteria of the deal. The payment may be a check or a reduction on the face value of an invoice. For example, a reseller who purchases ten to 15 cases receives a buying allowance of $6.00 off per case; a purchase of 16 to 20 cases would result in $6.75 off per case, and so forth.

In order to enjoy a buying allowance, some retailers engage in forward buying, a practice very common in grocery retailing. In essence, more merchandise than needed during the deal period is ordered. The extra merchandise is stored to be sold later at regular prices. The savings gained through the buying allowance must be greater than the cost of warehousing and transporting the extra merchandise.

The count and recount technique is an approach used in the buying allowance strategy. It involves a certain amount of money for each unit moved out of the wholesaler's or retailer's warehouse during a specified period.

A buy-back allowance is another type of buying allowance. It immediately follows a previous trade deal and offers a specified bonus for new purchases of the product related to the quantity of purchases from the first deal. The purpose is motivating repurchase immediately after the first trade deal on the product has depleted warehouse stock.

The slotting allowance is the most controversial form of buying allowance. Slotting allowances are fees retailers charge manufacturers for each space or slot on the shelf or warehouse that new products will occupy. The controversy stems from the fact that in many instances this allowance amounts to little more than paying a bribe to the retailer.

The final type of buying allowance is a free goods allowance. The manufacturer offers a certain amount of product to wholesalers or retailers at no cost if they purchase a stated amount of the same or a different product. The bonus is free merchandise instead of money. For example, a manufacturer might offer a retailer one free case of merchandise for every 20 purchased.

An advertising allowance is a common method exercised primarily for consumer products. The manufacturer pays the wholesaler or retailer a dividend for advertising the manufacturer's product. The money can only be used to purchase advertising. Controlling this scheme may be difficult. Some resellers may view the advertising allowance as a type of personal bonus and engage in devious behavior such as billing the manufacturer at the much higher national rate rather than at a lower local rate. Therefore, many manufacturers require some verification.

A display allowance is the final form of promotional allowance. Some manufacturers pay retailers to select their display from the many available every week. The payment can be in the form of cash or goods. Retailers must furnish written certification of compliance with the terms of the contract before they are paid. Retailers tend to select displays that yield high volume and profits and are easy to assemble.

SEE ALSO: Brands and Brand Names

[John Burnett]

FURTHER READING:

Blattberg, Robert C. and Scott A. Neslin. *Sales Promotion: Concepts, Methods, and Strategies*. Prentice Hall, 1990.

Lodish, Leonard M. *The Advertising & Promotion Challenge*. Oxford University Press, 1986.

Ovid, Riso, ed. *Sales Promotion Handbook*. 7th ed., Dartnell Corporation 1979.

Quelch, John A. *Sales Promotion Management*. Prentice Hall, 1989.

SALES REPRESENTATIVES

SEE: Manufacturer's Representatives; Sales Force

SALES TAX

A sales tax is a tax that is levied on the sales of goods and, in some cases, services. Sales taxes apply to transactions and are based on expenditures. Depending on what types of exemptions are allowed, businesses as well as individuals pay sales taxes. The retail sales tax and the **value-added tax** are the two most common types of sales tax that are applied to a broad range of goods. The **excise tax** is a type of sales tax that is applied to a specific commodity or type of goods, such as cigarettes, gasoline, and alcoholic beverages.

Since World War II sales and excise taxes have become a major source of revenue for state and local governments. In the United States 45 states and the District of Columbia have a general sales tax. Mississippi became the first state to apply a general sales tax in 1930. During the 1930s 24 states adopted a sales tax, followed by six states in the 1940s, five states in the 1950s, and eleven states in the 1960s. Currently Alaska, Delaware, Montana, New Hampshire, and Oregon do not have a state sales tax. In addition, 31 states permit local governments to levy their own sales tax.

In the United States the general sales tax is strictly the function of state and local governments. The United States is the only developed nation that does not levy some type of federal general sales tax. A national sales tax usually takes the form of a value-added tax (VAT). VATs are common in Western Europe, Canada, and other developed countries. A VAT is assessed on the value added at every stage of production and distribution. At each stage the seller pays a tax on the value added, or the difference between the seller's cost and the selling price. Then, the purchaser applies for a credit on that portion of the VAT that has already been paid by the seller. At the retail level, the different VATs that have been paid along the way are incorporated into the selling price to the consumer. The net result is that all of the businesses involved in production and distribution receive credits for the VAT they have paid, and the cost of the VAT is passed along to the consumer.

While the VAT is a multistage tax, the general sales tax that is collected at the retail level is a single-stage tax. The sales tax is usually an *ad valorem*, or flat-rate, tax that is based on the price of the goods or services being taxed. A VAT is also usually an *ad valorem* tax. On the other hand, excise taxes are usually assessed on a per unit basis (e.g., per gallon of gasoline or per package of cigarettes).

The tax base for sales tax was originally confined to merchandise or tangible goods. More recently, sales tax has been applied to services as well. One reason for adding services to the sales tax base is that services are accounting for a greater portion of the U.S. economy each year. The size of a state's sales tax base is further affected by any exemptions that have been granted. Sales of goods that will be resold are usually exempt from sales tax. States that have adopted a component-part rule exempt ingredients and component parts of products that are manufactured for sale. A direct-use rule extends the sales tax exemption to the sales of machinery, equipment, fuels, lubricants, and similar items used directly in industrial or agricultural production.

Another area that may be exempt from sales tax in some jurisdictions is that of necessities. More than half of all states with a sales tax exempt prescription drugs, for example. Many states do not charge sales tax on food unless it is purchased in a restaurant or has already been prepared as a meal for carry-out. For every exemption granted, a state or local government loses a certain amount of revenue. In addition, a long list of exemptions may make it difficult for the state to administer the tax and for retailers to properly collect it.

Exemptions of specific categories of goods and services from the sales tax are often made in an attempt to make the sales tax more equitable. It is generally recognized that a sales tax is regressive. That is, individuals and families with lower incomes pay a greater proportion of their income for sales taxes than people with higher incomes. By exempting food and other necessities from the sales tax, it is argued, lower-income families are relieved from part of their tax burden.

Businesses as well as individuals pay sales taxes. To date there has been no attempt to exclude interbusiness transactions from sales taxes. To attempt to do so would greatly complicate the administration of the tax. While businesses in states that have adopted a component-part rule or direct-use rule may enjoy exemptions, and goods purchased for resale are also usually exempt, nevertheless businesses and individuals alike must pay the same sales tax on the goods and services they purchase.

[David Bianco]

SALVAGE VALUE

All assets have a salvage value, which is the estimated value each asset will have after it is no longer going to be used in the operation of a business. Also known as the residual value or scrap value, the salvage value may be zero or a positive amount. An asset's salvage value is arrived at based on estimates of what it could be sold for or, more likely, a standard figure.

The salvage value of an asset is used in **accounting** to determine its net cost, which is its acquisition, or historical, cost minus its salvage value, if any. An asset's net cost is used as the basis for most **depreciation** methods, except the double declining balance method. For each accounting period, a percentage of the net cost of the company's assets is used to calculate depreciation expense. For example, if an asset has a useful life of five years, the annual depreciation expense using the straight-line method would be 20 percent of its net cost. Some accelerated methods of calculating depreciation are also based on the net cost of assets.

On the other hand, the double-declining balance method is based on the historical cost of an asset. For each accounting period, a rate double that of the straight-line method is applied to the historical cost of the asset minus any accumulated depreciation. Thus, the salvage value of the asset has no effect on depreciation when the double declining balance method is used.

The salvage value is necessarily an estimate of an asset's value after it has been used over a period of time. A common method of estimating an asset's salvage value is to estimate how much the asset could be sold for. Its salvage value in this case would be based on its estimated market value after it had been in use for a certain length of time. Since different owners might estimate different market values for an asset, standard values that have achieved industry acceptance are often used for salvage values. The use of standard values in certain situations eliminates discrepancies that may arise from individual estimates.

It is clear that the amount of wear and tear on an asset can significantly affect its salvage value. In other words, it is not simply the length of time an asset is in use that affects its potential resale value. The way an asset has been operated, used, and otherwise maintained during its useful life can have a real effect on its future market value. Such considerations may affect a company or individual's decision whether to lease or buy an asset. In the case of a decision whether to lease or purchase a new car, for example, the dealer's estimate of the market value of the car at the end of the lease period affects the amount of the monthly lease payments. An individual may decide it is better financially to purchase a car than lease it if he or she believes it will have a higher resale value than is assigned by the dealer. The individual may calculate that at the end of the lease period, the car would be worth more than the resale value assigned by the car dealer, especially if he or she plans to take good care of it and generally does not drive a lot of miles. In that case a higher resale value should result in lower lease payments, and if the dealer will not lower the lease payments the individual would be better off financially to purchase the car and then resell it in the future for more than the dealer's resale value.

[David Bianco]

SANCTIONS

Sanctions involve the deliberate withdrawal, or threat of withdrawal, of customary trade or financial assistance by one or more countries against another country. Also known as embargos, economic sanctions refer to measures taken by one or more nations against another country to halt trade with the target country. Sanctions may be imposed on exports or imports of specific products, financial assistance, and specific methods of transportation. When a government imposes a sanction, businesses that violate the sanction are subject to legal penalties.

There are a variety of political and economic reasons for imposing sanctions, or embargos, against other countries. Under international law, the **United Nations** may impose economic sanctions on a nation that is deemed to be a threat to international peace and security. When the United Nations imposes an embargo or sanction, as it has done against such countries as Southern Rhodesia, South Africa, and the former Yugoslavia, member nations are requested to stop trading with the specified country. The embargo or sanction may cover all trade, or it may be limited to specific goods, such as the arms embargo that was in effect against South Africa.

Outside of the United Nations, sanctions may be imposed unilaterally by a single country, as the United States did against Nicaragua in the 1980s, or multilaterally by a group of countries, as the Arab States have done against Israel. Imposing economic sanctions puts economic pressure on a country to change its political or economic policies. However, unilateral and multilateral sanctions may be broken by rival countries that do not agree with them. For example, the United States has had an embargo on trade with Cuba since the early 1960s, but its effect was diminished by the massive aid Cuba received from the former Soviet Union during the Cold War.

Unilateral sanctions are typically imposed by one country on another for the purpose of applying pressure or in retaliation for certain economic or political policies. For example, in an effort to open the Japanese market for cellular telephones, the United States resorted to trade sanctions against selected Japanese products in 1994. In 1994 the United States also imposed economic sanctions on Taiwan to protest that nation's illegal trade in tigers and rhinoceroses. Thus, the objective of a particular sanction may be very limited, or it may be very ambitious, as in the case of sanctions imposed during wartime between hostile nations.

More than 100 sanctions were applied between the end of World War II and the United Nations embargo against Iraq during the Gulf War. The United States took a leading role in approximately two-thirds of them. For the United States, economic sanctions were a major foreign policy tool during that period. Since 1990, however, the United States has imposed unilateral sanctions much less frequently. Examples include those mentioned as well as sanctions against Russia and India for selling missile technology and expanded sanctions against Cuba.

Under the **General Agreement on Tariffs and Trade (GATT)**, economic sanctions could be imposed by a newly created World Trade Organization (WTO). GATT members could request that sanctions be imposed on countries they felt were obstructing trade. It remains to be determined how such powers would be used to affect a country's nontariff barriers. For example, the United States is concerned that such powers to impose sanctions could affect its food labeling and pollution standards laws, for example, if they were regarded by other nations as obstructing international trade.

[David Bianco]

SAVINGS & LOAN ASSOCIATIONS

The nature of savings and loan associations (S&Ls) has changed over time, and as the S&L industry faces an uncertain future in the 1990s and beyond, it is essential that they evolve to become competitive. S&Ls, along with savings banks and credit unions, are known as thrift institutions. Thrifts and commercial banks are also known as depository institutions and are distinguished from nondepository institutions such as investment banks, insurance companies, and pension funds. S&Ls traditionally have taken savings, time, and demand deposits as their primary liability, and made most of their income from loaning deposits out as mortgages.

The first savings and loan association was organized in 1831 as the Oxford Provident Building Association of Philadelphia. Like the building societies of England and the credit cooperatives of Europe, it was a membership organization that took savings deposits from its members and in turn made home loans to them. S&Ls soon accepted deposits from the general public and became public depository institutions. They also became the primary source of credit for working individuals to purchase their own homes at a time when commercial banks did not offer mortgages. By the end of the 19th century there were nearly 6,000 S&Ls in existence.

S&Ls may be member owned, or they may be owned by stockholders. Member-owned S&Ls are known as mutual associations. Individual states may allow S&Ls to incorporate under general corporation laws and issue stock. An S&L may have a federal charter or a state charter. Federal charters became available to S&Ls in 1933 with the passage of the Home Owners' Loan Act. Federal charters are issued by the Home Loan Bank Board (HLBB) and may be obtained by new institutions or by converting from a state charter. Since the start of 1934, savings deposits at S&Ls have been insured by the Federal Savings and Loan Insurance Corporation (FSLIC). The establishment of both the HLBB and the FSLIC came in the aftermath of the Great Depression.

The S&L industry thrived in the post-war era of the 1950s and 1960s until the interest rate volatility of the 1970s and early 1980s exposed it to losses on its holdings of long-term, low-interest-rate mortgages. As interest rates rose, investors were able to obtain a better return on their investments by purchasing money market certificates that were tied to the higher rates. The assets of money market funds increased from $12 billion in 1979 to $230 billion by the end of 1982. A lot of that money came from deposit accounts at S&Ls as well as from low-paying accounts at commercial banks.

It wasn't only rising interest rates, however, that brought on the S&L crises of the 1980s. By their very nature, S&Ls were always in a position of borrowing short and lending long. That is, the deposits they took in could be withdrawn on short notice, but their assets were tied up in long-term mortages for the most part. In an era of stable interest rates, that formula worked fine, allowing S&Ls to increase their assets from just $17 billion in 1950 to $614 billion in 1980. During that period S&Ls were not allowed by law to pay an interest rate higher than 5.5 percent on demand deposits.

With 85 percent of all S&Ls losing money in 1981, the S&L industry was entering its first crisis of the decade. The federal government responded by lowering the capital standards for S&Ls while at the same time increasing the deposit insurance ceiling per account from $40,000 to $100,000. It was an era of federal deregulation in many industries, and in effect many S&Ls were not subject to rigorous examinations for years at a time.

In an attempt to keep S&Ls competitive with other financial institutions, many of the regulations were changed during the 1980s. S&Ls were allowed to engage in a variety of banking activities that had previously been prohibited. They could offer a wider range of financial services and were given new operating powers. Two key pieces of legislation were the Garn-St. Germain Depository Institutions Act of 1982 and the Depository Institutions Deregulation and Monetary Control Act of 1980.

While the government's policies were intended to encourage growth in the S&L industry, the effect was entirely different. The increase in deposit insurance meant that it was the FSLIC and not the S&L managers who were at risk when bad loans were made. As a result of the lowering of capital standards, many insolvent and weakly capitalized S&Ls made risky loans that eventually led to the second S&L crisis in the late 1980s.

The full extent of the S&L crisis and its effect on the viability of the S&L industry has not yet been determined. In 1988 over 200 S&L failures were resolved by the HLBB selling them to individuals and firms. In 1989 Congress passed the Financial Institutions Reform, Recovery and Enforcement Act (FIRREA), which among other things established the **Resolution Trust Corporation (RTC)** to seize control of an estimated 500 insolvent S&Ls. Within a few years that number had risen to approximately 800 insolvent institutions.

In addition to selling insolvent S&Ls and otherwise trying to resolve them, the RTC also has the power to prosecute S&L officials for criminal wrongdoing. Congress recently increased the statute of limitations on S&L-related crimes from three years to five years.

[David Bianco]

SCANNING SYSTEMS

Digital scanning refers to optical and electronic processes that capture and convert printed materials to digital format. Scanning is one component of a larger document imaging system which includes image capture, storage, display, and retrieval. Document imaging systems typically differentiate between page imaging and text imaging although, increasingly, systems integrate both capabilities. Page scanners rely on bitmap images while text images rely on **optical character recognition** (OCR).

Bitmap images are arrays of horizontal and vertical dots or pixels that carry information about light and dark components of the image. A pixel in a simple black and white scanner carries one bit of information—whether the pixel is black-or-white. The number of available pixels or dots per inch determines the resolution of the image. The more dots per inch, the greater the resolution or level of visual sharpness of the image. These two critical concepts in digital scanning are called gray scale and resolution. Gray scale refers to the differentiated intensity of light and dark, while resolution refers to the level of detail available for display.

Scanning technology relies on photoelectric measures of light and dark to create bitmapped displays. The number of total photoelectric sensors and the amount of information contained about each pixel combine to create gray scale and resolution. The conversion of sensor data to digital format is obtained through the use of an analog-to-digital converter. The resulting digital information may be manipulated, stored, retrieved, or display on request as a digital mirror image of the original.

Scanner components typically include document input or reading devices, scan engines, and scanning software. Desktop digital scanners rely on either flat-bed or sheet-fed operations to input hard-copy printed materials into digital form. Scanning engines incorporate cylinders and drums to record digital information and frequently use charge-coupled devices (CCDs). Scanning software enables manipulation of both text and images. Using special scanning software, text

recognition or optical character recognition (OCR) translates printed alphabetical symbols to digital words. These digital words may be edited or manipulated with a word processing software package.

Trends in scanning include availability of color and higher resolutions. Color scanners, while still expensive, provide image representations that include color. Several considerations affect business use of scanners including evaluation of needs, potential hazards, and maintenance activities. Advantages of scanning include potential reductions in both direct and indirect costs, while disadvantages include hardware investment and lack of industry standards. Purchasing a scanner involves assessing speed, resolution, gray scale, color, type, and special features required.

HISTORY OF DIGITAL SCANNING

In 1925, AT&T produced the wirephoto scanning service and with it, the first commercial image scanning system. Used by the news media, this service allowed photos taken around the world to be transmitted and printed in other newspapers. Additional experimentation and development resulted in the first color scanner patented by Alexander Murray and Richard Morse in 1937. Lacking digital processing and storage capabilities, however, scanning remained unchanged within the news media and undeveloped commercially. In the late 1960s, the National Aeronautics and Space Administration (NASA) spurred the use of image scanning in lunar explorations. Original lunar images were created and transmitted to Earth in analog (continuous) signals for later digitization. The Jet Propulsion Laboratory, under contract with NASA, developed a system to convert these images to digital form for computer processing. During the same period, analog facsimile scanners were developed for use in the business sector and within ten years, converted to digital facsimile scanners (fax). Medical uses of scanning increased and heralded the development of computerized tomography (CT scan) and magnetic resonance imaging (MRI) during the late 1960s. With the advent of personal computers in the early 1980s, scanner devices dropped in price and were actively marketed for use with home and business applications. USAA, and other companies, have incorporated scanning to improve insurance records and customer service, while others, such as Northwest Airlines, effectively use scanners in accounting and auditing. In 1993 almost 876,000 scanners were installed in the United States.

DOCUMENT IMAGING SYSTEMS

Document imaging systems facilitate the initial input, storage, retrieval, and display of digital images. Specialized image processing systems additionally provide for image enhancement, image restoration, image analysis, image compression, and image synthesis. Image enhancement activities include, for example, sharpening edges and adjusting contrast. Restoration activities, like photometric correction, adjust images to compensate for conversion errors. Image analysis may extract features or classify objects within an image, while image compression concerns itself with decreasing the overall size of a digital image file. Finally, image synthesis may incorporate activities like visualization and image mergers. Scanning software may incorporate features of an image processing system for user convenience and effectiveness.

Document imaging systems capture information based on full or partial pages of data or based on text or optical character recognition. Full or partial pages of information are converted to bitmap images using a digital process that creates software addresses for each small component of the image. OCR scanners map bitmaps to character symbols to convert text to digital format. In both cases, the beginning point of all document imaging systems is typically the initial input using a scanner.

GRAY SCALE AND RESOLUTION

Two of the most important concepts in digital scanning are resolution and gray scale. Resolution refers to the level of detail available in a printed image or the relative degree of visual sharpness. The number of pixels per inch or dots per inch (dpi) determines the quality of the image resolution. Gray scale information for any pixel is a relative value of light intensity and is determined by the number of bits allowed for each pixel (a bit is a binary digit or the smallest element of the binary language). Frequent configurations include 4 bits per pixel (16 levels of gray scale) and 8 bits per pixel (256 levels of gray scale). Although higher gray scale levels create better resolution, trade-offs to resolution include increased scan time and increased storage requirements.

Gray scale is necessary to provide automatic scaling without loss or distortion. Scaling is the process of adding or removing pixels from an image. Because image resolution and image size are reciprocal functions, they are related by a scaling factor—scanner resolution multiplied by scanned size. Imaging continuous tone art and photographs requires gray scaling to accommodate shades. While print media represent shades with different sizes of dots, pixels are all the same size and must be manipulated by controlling the size or configuration of groups of pixels. Two methods (dithering and true gray-scaling) simulate shades. Black-and white images may be converted to gray scale using a process called dithering. Dithering creates a simulated number of gray tones using geometric groupings of pixels that form patterns. These patterns represent shades of gray. Dithered images are often grainy and poor. True gray scaling, on the other hand, uses pixels that contain gray scale information. These pixels are grouped into symmetric patterns.

SCANNING TECHNOLOGY

Scanners reflect light onto a printed page to illuminate light and dark areas of the page. These light and dark areas are recorded to a logical grid within the computer. Using a charge-coupled device (CCD), scanners record information by accumulating a charge proportional to the light intensity in a solid-state array of wells. Scanning and recording cylinders preserve photoelectric charges. The resolution at which an image can be scanned depends on the number of light sensors or CCD's in the scanner. Functionally, a CCD breaks up the scanned image into thousands of pixels. Each CCD photoreceptor cell converts light or dark into electrical voltage proportional to the light intensity. Exporting these voltages creates a bitmapped image. Raster scanning, line by line from top to bottom and left to right, yields a bitmap image.

A bitmap treats an image or document as a rectangular array of pixels by using a binary digital technique to represent the black-and-white pixels. Black pixels, represented by ones and a white pixel represented by zeros are mapped to a grid to represent the light and dark areas of an image or document. When pixels hold information about a scale of light or dark (as opposed to simply black or white), they are consider to have gray scale definitions.

Digital scanners capture images (pictures and text) and convert them to computer files. These computer files represent the zeros and ones of the binary language that the computer understands. Image scanners identify a picture as thousands and thousands of individual elements. These individual elements are known as pixels or pels and vary in density and pattern to accurately reproduce a graphic image. A picture element, or pel, is used when each element contains only black or white elements, while a pixel is used when the element contains intermediate shades of gray. Pixels are the smallest element of a display surface that hold information about color or light intensity. Bitmaps are the mapped pixel location and intensity necessary to recreate the original document or image.

SCANNER COMPONENTS

There are three main subsystems to a digital scanner: the document feed, the scan engine, and the scanning software. First, the document feed system provides a means by which the printed material is entered into the computer. The scan engine consists of a light source, such as mirrors and lenses, and a light intensity sensor and recording medium. Finally, the scan control system is typically a software program that manages and directs the scanning process including resolution and gray scale detection.

DOCUMENT FEED. Document feed systems ensure that paper documents or images enter the scanning device for digitization. Four scanner designs are available with different document feed formats. The flatbed scanner (or full-page scanner) resembles a photocopier with a flat glass area on which to lay documents. Almost any document type including books, heavy card stock, paste-ups, or other materials may be scanned on a flatbed scanner. By comparison, the document feed scanner can only handle single sheets and operates like a fax machine. While document feed scanners cannot scan a book, they can handle multiple sheets of paper automatically. Contemporary scanners frequently offer both flatbed and document feed in the same design. A third type of document feed system, the overhead scanner is more specialized and used for three-dimensional objects. The scanning cylinder is usually encased above the scan bed and the light source points downward and is reflected upwards. The fourth, and increasingly popular, document feed system is the handheld scanner. Handheld scanners provide inexpensive scanning capabilities for small digitization activities. Most cover a four-inch swath of the document.

SCAN ENGINE

Scanning engines are the nuts and bolts of the digital scanner. Consisting of a light source (a moveable or fixed path of mirrors and lenses) and a light intensity sensor (a charge-coupled device), a document is scanned line by line. The light source, often fluorescent lamps, illuminates the document and the reflected light is focused on a CCD by a mirror or prism. The resolution at which an image can be scanned depends on the number of CCDs in the scanner. For example, a 300-sensor-per-inch scanner can provide an image at 300 dots per inch. When the scan is in progress, either the sensors themselves or the document move at a fixed rate. As these sensors or CCDs are exposed to light, they generate a charge related to each pixel's level of light intensity or gray scale. One line at time, an image is produced that consists of an array of horizontal and vertical dots with varying intensity of light. An analog-to-digital converter generates digital information from the CCDs continuous analog signal. This information contains data about individual pixel elements and gray scale. The scan engine relays this information to the scanning software for processing, displaying, filing, or printing.

SCANNING SOFTWARE. Scanning software frequently incorporates interactivity with the user. In addition to determining how the image is scanned, scanning software manipulates files, scales images, edits, rotates, and performs a wide variety of other functions including image enhancement and alteration. Scanning parameters such as page contrast, gray scale, thresholds, area dimensions, scaling, and resolution are all setup using scanning software. In addition to the scanning set up parameters, scanning software may also include programs to manipulate, edit, and save images. Specialized software is available to convert file formats for import or export. One special type of scanning software, optical character recognition (OCR), is specifically designed for use with textual materials.

OPTICAL CHARACTER RECOGNITION (OCR). OCR breaks down a bitmapped image into smaller bitmaps of individual character cells. Assuming that each character is unbroken and surrounded by space, OCR scanning software identifies text characters using pattern and feature recognition, and saves them as individual letters and words. In pattern recognition, a preexisting library of symbols is compared to the bitmapped character. The closest match determines the character code. In feature recognition, curves and lines and their relationships are derived from a sample character. Again, the closest match determines the character code. Errors occur when incomplete or unknown matches are encountered. Error rates in OCR range from 1 to 5 percent. OCR sales doubled between 1988 and 1990 as converting text became increasingly popular with businesses.

The simplest and most popular application of OCR is as a replacement for keyboard entry. In high-volume fields, such as law and business, OCR scanners speed document entry appreciably. Forms may also be used with OCR to capture questions and responses more accurately. OCR is a processor-intensive function best suited to high-end work stations. With the advent of inexpensive, powerful microcomputers, OCR applications are increasingly effective and available.

COLOR SCANNERS

Color scanners require detecting and processing and storing three pixels to accommodate red, blue, and, green colors within each range of gray scale. A four-bit color scanner provides only 16 colors. Typical color scan engines use an illumination system of fluorescent red, blue, and green lamps and filters. Balance and adjustment tables are provided by the computer and may updated and altered using scanning software. Color scanners are processor-intensive and, while decreasing in price, remain somewhat specialized and expensive.

MANAGERIAL CONSIDERATIONS

Evaluating the potential and practical use of a scanner includes evaluation of needs, consideration of environmental hazards, and discussion of maintenance activities. Needs evaluation includes performance goals, user access, and identification of materials to be scanned. Environmental hazards such as temperature, humidity, dust, static electricity, and power supply present critical issues in the location and use of digital scanners. Cleaning and maintaining the scanning and recording cylinders, lenses, and mechanical components are additional factors in evaluating the potential use of scanners in the workplace.

Considerations in the purchase of a scanner include speed, resolution, gray scale, color, type, and special features. Speed refers to the scan speed of both black-and-white and gray scale images. Resolution refers to the optical resolution range given in dots per inch or dpi. The number of detectable gray levels and color capabilities impact both cost and capability. Many scanners now incorporate both flatbed and sheet feed types. Special features include paper size, supported printers, documentation and support, and image editing options. The two initial steps in selecting a scanner are: (1) determining the type of scanning to be done (OCR versus image) and (2) determining the best scanner system. Price range and compatibility with current computer resources are additional factors to consider when selecting a scanner.

Image processing offers many advantages, although not all business will benefit all the time. Direct cost savings are available when scanning systems free storage space and permit reductions in workforce. These savings may be offset, however, by higher skill levels required for existing personnel. Fast retrieval, concurrent access, processing and distribution control, and reductions in lost documents can all contribute to improved productivity and competitive advantage. Nevertheless, initial costs for large-scale scanning operations can be expensive. Additionally, because image processing and scanning applications are relatively new applications, few experts or reputable vendors may exist. Incompatibility with current computerized resources and a lack of industry-wide standards may also create problems in installation, exchange, and use of digitized images. Companies in the credit industry such as American Express have capitalized on the advantages of scanning and minimized the disadvantages. By effectively using scanning technology, American Express Co. improved the aesthetic quality of the billing statement, reduced mailing time, reduced funding costs, and reduced document entry errors. Likewise, British Airways has improved cabin crew services by using scanning to facilitate the creation and entry of the voyage report. For these companies and others, image scanning and processing is a powerful tool in the management of critical information.

[Tona Henderson]

FURTHER READING:

Amedon, Don. *Introduction to Electronic Imaging.* Silver Spring, MD: Association for Information and Image Management, 1992.

Baxes, Gregory A. *Digital Image Processing: Principles and Applications.* New York: John Wiley & Sons, 1994.

Bennet, Garner R., and George Church. "Scanning Market Update." *IMC Journal.* January/February, 1992, pp. 9-11.

Clark, John M. "Using Image Scanners to Create and Access Electronically Stored Documents." *ARMA Records Management Quarterly.* July, 1991, pp. 9-13, 16.

D'Alleyrand, Marc R. *Image Storage and Retrieval Systems.* New York: McGraw-Hill, 1989.

Field, Gary G. *Color Scanning and Imaging Systems.* Pittsburgh: Graphics Arts Technical Foundation, 1990.

Francis, Bob. "OCR Comes Down to the Desktop." *Datamation.* September 15, 1991, pp. 46, 44.

Gillooly, Brian. "Scanners Gain In Popularity." *Computer Reseller News.* February 14, 1994, p. 114.

Green, William B. *Digital Image Processing: A Systems Approach.* New York: Van Nostrand Reinhold, 1989.

Hu, Darwin. "Scanner Vendors Offer Many Choices." *Computer Technology Review.* May, 1993, p. 15.

Keen, Peter G. W. *Every Manager's Guide to Information Technology: A Glossary of Key Terms and Concepts for Today's Business Leader.* Boston: Harvard Business School Press, 1995.

Khoshafian, Setrag. *Intelligent Offices: Object-Oriented Multi-Media Information Management in Client Server Architectures.* New York: John Wiley & Sons, 1992.

Martin, James A. "All About Scanners." *Macworld.* October, 1992, pp. 150-155.

Parker, John. "Desktop Scanning Moves into the Office." *Electronic Business.* April 22, 1991, pp. 66-68.

Weinberg, Neil. "Bypassing the Keyboard." *Forbes.* July 18, 1994, pp. 300-302.

Wetzler, Fred U. *Desktop Image Scanners and Scanning.* Silver Spring, MD: Association for Information and Image Management, 1989.

SECURITIES ACT OF 1933

The Securities Act of 1933, sometimes referred to as the truth-in-securities act, is primarily concerned with the initial issuance of securities from enterprises to the investing public in the United States. The intention of the 1933 act is to ensure that all relevant information about the security be disclosed to potential investors. This information must be filed with the **Securities and Exchange Commission** (SEC) prior to issuance of the securities. In fact, it is unlawful to offer securities unless a registration statement is filed and in effect with the SEC. Some securities are exempt from this registration, such as government securities, nonpublic offerings, intrastate offerings, and certain offerings not exceeding $1.5 million. In the event that a securities registration statement contains erroneous information, the statement's effectiveness may be refused or suspended, based on a public hearing.

The key to the registration statement is that it provides the investor with information necessary to make an "informed and realistic evaluation of the worth of the securities." Registration of the securities, however, does not imply approval of the issue by the SEC, or that the SEC has found the registration disclosures to be accurate. Those individuals found guilty of intentionally filing false securities with the SEC are at risk for fines, prison terms, or both. Along with that, those who are found to be connected with the securities, such as directors, accountants, and any other experts, may also be held liable and subject to discipline as well.

PURPOSE OF SECURITIES REGISTRATION

Securities registration requires, but does not guarantee, accuracy in the registration statement and prospectus. Investors who ultimately suffer economic losses after the purchase of securities do have important recovery rights under the law, if they can prove either incomplete or inaccurate disclosure of material facts in the registration statement or prospectus. In the event that investors wish to exercise these rights, they must be handled through the appropriate federal or state court, as the SEC has no power to award damages. The only standard that must be met when registering securities is adequate and accurate disclosure of required material facts concerning the company and the securities it is proposing to offer. The issue of fairness of terms, the issuing company's potential success, and other factors that affect the merits of investing in the securities (regardless of price, potential profits, etc.) has no bearing on the question of whether or not securities may be registered.

JUSTIFICATION PROCESS

Registration forms, to be filed with the SEC, require specific information such as: (1) description of the registrant's properties and business, (2) description of the significant provisions of the security to be offered for sale and its relationship to the registrant's other capital securities, (3) information about the management of the registration, and (4) **financial statements** certified by independent public accountants.

Registration statements and prospectuses on securities become public immediately upon filing with the SEC. Following the filing of the registration statement, securities may be offered orally or by certain summaries of the information in the registration statements as permitted by SEC rules. It is unlawful, however, to sell the securities until the effective date.

Most registration statements shall become effective on the twentieth day after the filing. The SEC, however, may pull ahead the securities effective date if it is deemed appropriate given the "interests of investors and the public, the adequacy of publicly available information, and the ease with which the facts about the new offering can be disseminated and understood."

EXEMPTIONS FROM REGISTRATION

As a general rule, registration requirements apply to securities of both foreign and domestic issuers, and to securities of foreign governments sold in domestic securities markets. The following represent exemptions: (1) private offerings to a limited number of persons or institutions who have access to the kind of information that registrations would disclose and who do not propose to redistribute the securities; (2) offerings restricted to residents of the state in which the issuing company is organized and doing business; (3) securities of municipal, state, federal, and other governmental instrumentalities as well as charitable institutions, banks, and carriers subject to the Interstate Commerce Act; and (4) offerings of small business investment companies made in accordance with rules and regulation of the commission.

Regardless of whether the securities are exempt from registration, antifraud provisions apply to all sales of securities involving interstate commerce or the U.S. postal system.

Exemptions are available when certain specified conditions are met. These conditions include the prior filing of a notification with the appropriate SEC regional office and the use of an offering circular containing certain basic information in the sale of the securities.

SEE ALSO: Securities Exchange Act of 1934; Stocks

[Arthur DuRivage]

SECURITIES EXCHANGE ACT OF 1934

The Securities Exchange Act of 1934 (SEA 1934) was enacted June 6, 1934 and was meant to oversee and regulate trading on the various securities markets. The **Securities and Exchange Commission** (SEC) was also created as part of the 1934 legislation and was charged with enforcing the provisions of the 1934 act and the prior **Securities Act of 1933**.

The SEA 1934 legislation came about as a result of the Great Depression and was part of President Franklin D. Roosevelt's New Deal program that was meant to contribute to the reform and revitalization of the American economy. It was believed by the president and many congressmen that the stock market crash of 1929 was precipitated by underregulation of securities markets which in turn encouraged unsafe and fraudulent trading practices. In 1933 Congress passed the Securities Act that required companies and firms offering securities to provide detailed financial data on all new issues. This legislation applied to securities being traded in interstate commerce or offered through the mails. Provisions of the 1933 act were enforced by the **Federal Trade Commission**. SEA 1934 transferred regulatory enforcement to the newly created SEC, which was given increased federal control over securities markets—more than the FTC could provide. The SEC was first headed by Joseph P. Kennedy (father of President John F. Kennedy) and later by future Supreme Court Justice William O. Douglas.

SEA 1934 assigns the SEC broad regulatory and oversight powers. The commission's responsibilities include: securities markets, self-regulatory organizations, and the conduct of personnel involved in security trading (such as brokers, dealers, and investment advisers). The SEC investigates cases of suspected fraudulent behavior and oversees **takeovers** and proxy fights for violations. Regulation of **mutual fund** activities also falls under the purview of the SEC as of the Investment Company Act of 1940. Other legislation that expanded SEC regulatory powers includes: the Public Utility Holding Company Act of 1935; the Maloney Act of 1938 (which deals with the establishment of organizations responsible for self-regulation in the various securities markets, such as the National Association of Securities Dealers); the **Investment Advisers Act of 1940**; and the Bankruptcy Code (which involves the SEC with failing companies). The SEC is a quasi-judicial agency and its decisions may be appealed to the federal courts for review.

SEA 1934 also regulates trading procedures and practices, especially short sales, wash sales, matched orders, and insider trading. Short sales involve the "borrowing" of a security lot from a broker. Anticipating a drop in the price of the security, the borrower covers the sale by agreeing to buy a future lot of the same security at a hoped-for lower price. The anticipated drop in value represents a profit for the borrower. An increase in the value of the security, however, will mean a loss for the borrower. Selling short, while perfectly legal, is nonetheless carefully regulated by the SEC. By contrast, matched orders, wash sales, and insider trading are all illegal. Matched orders involve a person buying a security lot from one broker while simultaneously selling an identical security lot through another broker. When done on a large scale, matched orders give the appearance of the stock being active and are executed with the intention of

driving up the value of the security. Wash sales are similar to matched orders except the collusion in the buying and selling of the security is between two or more brokers. Inherent in a wash sale is the agreement that neither party will be responsible for actually paying for or delivering the security being manipulated. Corporate officers, members of a company's **board of directors**, and those holding more than 10 percent of the stock of a company are considered by the SEC to be "insiders." Insiders are allowed to trade but must register their stock portfolios with the SEC and report all changes on a monthly basis. Insider rules are meant to minimize the unfair advantage that insiders have because of their privileged access to strategic information.

SEE ALSO: Stocks

[Michael Knes]

FURTHER READING:

Shields, Robert E. *Securities Practice Handbook*. American Law Institute-American Bar Association, 1987.

Skousen, K. Fred. *An Introduction to the SEC*. South-Western Publishing Co., 1991.

SECURITIES AND EXCHANGE COMMISSION, UNITED STATES

The U.S. Securities and Exchange Commission (SEC) is responsible for administering federal securities laws written to provide protection for investors. The SEC also ensures that securities markets are fair and honest, and if necessary, the SEC may provide for the means to enforce securities laws through the appropriate sanctions. The SEC may also serve as adviser to the federal courts in Chapter 11 cases (corporate reorganization proceedings under Chapter 11 of the Bankruptcy Reform Act of 1978).

The SEC was created by Congress in 1934, under the **Securities Exchange Act**, as an independent, nonpartisan, quasi-judicial regulatory agency. The commission is made up of five members: one chairman and four commissioners. Each member receives a five-year term appointment from the President. The five-year terms are staggered such that each June 5th an appointed member's term expires. It is a policy that no more than three of the commissioners may be of the same political party.

The chairman and commissioners are responsible for ensuring that publicly held entities, broker-dealers in securities, investment companies and advisers, and other participants in the securities markets comply with federal securities law. These securities laws were designed to provide for informed investment analysis and decision making by the public investors—

principally by ensuring adequate disclosure of material information (as directed in the **Securities Act of 1933**).

The commission's staff is made up of lawyers, accountants, financial analysts, engineers, investigators, economists, and other professionals. The SEC staff is divided into divisions and offices, which includes 12 regional and branch offices, each directed by officials appointed by the SEC chairman.

LAWS ADMINISTERED BY THE SEC

There are six major laws that the SEC is responsible for administering:

- **Securities Act of 1933**
- Securities Exchange Act of 1934
- Public Utility Holding Company Act of 1935
- Trust Indenture Act of 1939
- Investment Company Act of 1940
- **Investment Advisers Act of 1940**

The Securities Act of 1933, also known as the "truth in securities" law has two primary objectives, both of which the SEC must ensure occurs: (1) to require that investors be provided with material information concerning securities offered for public sale; and (2) to prevent misrepresentation, deceit, and other fraud in the sale of securities.

In 1934, the U.S. Congress enacted the Securities Exchange Act of 1934 in which the "disclosure" doctrine (from the Securities Act of 1933) was extended to securities listed and registered for public trading on the U.S. securities exchanges. In 1964, the Securities Act Amendments extended disclosure and reporting provisions to equity securities in the over-the-counter market. The act seeks to ensure (through the SEC) fair and orderly securities markets by prohibiting certain types of activities and by setting forth rules regarding the operation of the markets and participants.

The SEC also administers the Public Utility Holding Company Act of 1935. Subject to regulation under this act are interstate holding companies engaged in the electric utility business or in the retail distribution of natural or manufactured gas. Reports to be filed with the SEC by these **holding companies** include detailed information concerning the organization, financial structure, and operations of the holding company and its subsidiaries. Holding companies are subject to SEC regulation in areas such as structure of the system, acquisitions, combinations, and issue and sales of securities.

The Trust Indenture Act of 1939, under the watchful eye of the SEC, applies to bonds, debentures, notes, and similar debt securities offered for public sale and issued under trust indentures with more than $7.5 million of securities outstanding at any one time. Other provisions of the act include prohibiting the indenture trustee from conflicting interest; requiring the trustee to be a corporation with minimal combined capital and surplus; and imposing high standards of conduct and responsibility on the trustee.

The SEC must ensure that the intentions of the Investment Company Act of 1940 are followed. The Investment Company Act seeks to regulate the activities of companies engaged primarily in investing, reinvesting, and trading in securities, and whose own securities are publicly offered. It is important for potential investors to understand that although the SEC serves as a regulatory agency in these cases, the SEC does not supervise the company's investment activities, and the mere presence of the SEC as a regulatory agency does not guarantee a safe investment.

The Investment Advisers Act of 1940 establishes a style, or a system, of regulating investment advisers (for the SEC). The main thrust of this act is simply that it requires all persons, or firms, that are compensated for advising anyone about securities investment opportunities to be registered with the SEC and conform to the established standards of investor protection. The SEC has the power and ability to strip an investment adviser of his or her registration if a statutory violation has occurred.

Finally, the SEC is given some responsibility connected with corporate reorganizations, commonly referred to as Chapter 11 proceedings. Chapter 11 of the Bankruptcy Code in the U.S. grants the SEC permission to become involved in any proceedings, but the SEC is primarily concerned with proceedings directly involving a large portion of public investor interest.

[Arthur DuRivage]

SECURITIES AND INVESTMENTS

"Investments" refers to the process of applying resources so as to increase wealth. Investment may take the form of directly holding and using assets. For some assets such **direct investment** is cumbersome, limited in size and liquidity, and requires close involvement by the investor. These problems make directly holding such assets risky. Consequently, investors using this direct form of investment demand higher return and are hesitant to undertake new ventures. If this were the only form of investment, economic growth would be slow. Many of these problems can be reduced or avoided by indirect investment through "securities." Securities are instruments that represent an interest in, or claim on, other assets. Use of securities separates ownership from possession and use of assets. This separation allows widespread ownership and easy transfer, facilitates reduction of risk by diversification, and encourages professional management. This in turn helps create **capital markets** with efficient application of resources, encouraging economic growth. The advantages of the security form of investment are not limited to physical assets. The appeal of securities over direct acquisition is evidenced by the recent "securitization" of financial assets. In this process normally illiquid assets are pooled, and shares in this diversified pool are then issued.

Securities simplify the investment process, but do not remove all problems. Analysis of securities, and their combination into portfolios, requires a high level of expertise. Additionally, the investor must be concerned with risk, or uncertainty about the anticipated returns. Much of investment theory treats anticipated returns as a random variable described by a probability distribution. Assets exhibit a "risk return trade-off"—i.e., assets with higher risk (more uncertainty about the actual outcome) must on average provide a higher anticipated return to induce investors to accept the risk. This trade-off was demonstrated in a study of returns to **bonds** and **stocks** over the period 1926 to 1990. The safest asset class (**Treasury bills**, or T-bills) returned an average annual return of 3.7 percent, while the riskiest asset class (stocks of smaller firms) returned an average return of 17.1 percent. Analysis of securities is aided by the concept of "risk return space." Return is measured on the vertical axis, while risk is plotted on the horizontal axis. The risk return trade-off is then represented as a line of positive slope (see Figure 1).

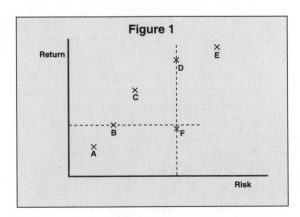

Figure 1

SECURITIES

An amazing diversity of securities has developed over time. People have been very creative in developing securities, and there are many variations on the general types described here. The pace of innovation has increased in recent years with the development of quantitative analysis and investment models. New types of securities are being created, and old types modified, at an unprecedented pace. **Financial engineering**, which is the design of new and often very complex instruments and strategies, has emerged as a separate new discipline. The standard forms of securities predominate, however, and are typically classified according to various common characteristics into equity, fixed income, derivatives, and money market securities. There are also some investment instruments that have security characteristics, but are less readily traded. While investors need not live in constant fear, it is not advisable to invest without complete understanding of the nature of the security involved.

EQUITY SECURITIES

Equity securities are simply evidence of a partial share in the ownership of an enterprise. Thus, individual **common stock**s are referred to as "shares." Sale of shares is more attractive to the firm than direct investment. Since many shares can be issued for the same enterprise, the firm has access to a much wider pool of capital. This enables the firm to raise larger amounts and so consider larger projects.

Sale of shares is also attractive to **management**, at least in part, because it has more control over the firm due to the diffusion of ownership. The holder of a share does not have a direct voice in the management of the enterprise, but has an indirect control through the election of the members of the **board of directors**, who in turn choose the management of the firm. Voting for directors may be through simple majority voting or through cumulative voting. In the majority system, each investor may cast one vote per position for each share held, and the director receiving more than 50 percent of the votes wins. Under majority voting, a group holding more than 50 percent of the voting stock could lock out minority groups. In the cumulative system, each investor receives one vote per position for each share held, but may "cumulate" the votes received by casting them all for one candidate. Under cumulative voting fewer shares are required to guarantee election of a director, so that excluding minority stockholder groups is more difficult. Managements of firms that are takeover targets or are facing challenges from stockholders prefer to be under majority voting. Even under cumulative voting mounting a successful dissident drive faces formidable hurdles, however, since management may dominate the board of directors and controls the assets of the firm. If there is a disagreement with management, the conventional wisdom of Wall Street has been to sell the stock rather than mount a challenge. This conventional wisdom has changed somewhat in recent times because of a willingness of stockholders to take on the role of activists. Also, large positions held by institutions such as mutual funds or pension funds make challenges to management easier to pursue.

The cash flows to an equity investor are not specified in advance. They depend on the success of the enterprise, are uncertain or risky, and are properly described in terms of probability distributions. As part owner of the firm, the owner shares in the success or failure of the firm in two ways. The first way is through returns from **capital gains** and **capital losses**, increases or decreases in the value of the stock. The second way is through cash flows arising from the distribution of earnings in the form of **dividends**. The distribution of earnings through dividends is not automatic. Dividends are not obligation, but instead are ''declared'' at the discretion of the board of directors. In practice, dividends are usually not just a function of earnings. Dividends are thought to be a signal to investors as to firm performance. Management prefers to present positive signals, ''smoothing'' dividends by avoiding decreases and increasing dividends only if it is likely that the higher level can be maintained. In some cases, firms have raised funds in the capital markets so as to maintain the dividend. An exception is the extraordinary dividend, so labeled by management as a sign that the increase is not permanent.

In case of bankruptcy, common stock has limited liability. Legally, the firm is considered to be an individual, able to assume its own **liabilities** separately from the shareholders. As a result, liability is separated from ownership. The investor is not liable for the debts of the firm, and should the firm fail the investor's loss will be limited to no more than the amount invested. In bankruptcy the various claims on the firm follow a well-defined priority, with common stockholders assigned the lowest priority. It is for this reason that the common stockholders are sometimes called the residual owners of the firm. Limited liability is very important to investors, and is considered a major factor in the development of the corporate form of business.

There are other characteristics of equity that are less universal, and there are other exceptions to these general properties of equity securities. Some firms have multiple classes of stock with different voting power and/or share of dividends. Other stock may be restricted as to trading. **Common stock**s are traded in several exchanges and over the counter. The size of the underlying firm, and the trading volume of the stock, vary widely. Consequently, the liquidity and the amount of information available on a stock also vary widely.

FIXED-INCOME SECURITIES—BONDS

Unlike equity securities, the cash flows to fixed-income securities are fixed or specified in advance and are a contractual obligation. The cash flows are the interest payments, generally paid semiannually, and the repayment of principal at maturity. Thus, a $1,000, 20-year, 12 percent bond will make 40 semiannual payments of $60, plus one payment of $1,000 at the end of 20 years. Purchase of a bond is considered a form of lending. The investor must still bear credit risk, which is the risk that the issuer will default by failing to meet some or all of the obligations. Bonds are often separated by issuer into governments, municipals, and corporates.

GOVERNMENT BONDS. Government bonds are securities issued by the U.S. Treasury and by U.S. government agencies. Treasury securities are backed by the full faith and credit of the United States government, and are considered to have no credit risk. **Treasury notes** have original maturities ranging up to 10 years, while Treasury bonds have original maturities from 10 to 30 years; both notes and bonds have specified interest payments and maturity values. Treasury bonds are typically callable in the last five years before maturity. Treasury securities enjoy one of the most active markets, and are highly liquid. The market is an over-the-counter market where government securities dealers stand ready to buy or sell, providing continuous quotes.

Notes and bonds are issued on regular cycles for various maturities. Competitive bids specify the yield and the amount of securities desired. Noncompetitive bids specify only the amount of securities desired. The total amount of noncompetitive bids is first subtracted from the size of the offering, and the remaining amount is then allocated among the competitive bids by ascending yield. All noncompetitive bids are then accepted at the average price paid by the competitive bidders. Competitive bidders run the risk of winners curse (overpaying) or of not having the bid accepted in hopes of getting a low price. Noncompetitive bidders avoid the winner's curse of overbidding and know that the order will be filled, but do not know the price and miss the chance of buying at a low price.

Agencies are bonds issued by government agencies, with fixed interest payments and maturity value. These securities are technically are not directly obligations of the U. S. government. Nonetheless, it is widely assumed that the U.S. government would support the obligation, and the bonds are considered to have very low credit risk.

MUNICIPAL BONDS. Municipal bonds are issued by state and local governments, with fixed interest payments and maturity values. Interest payments on municipal bonds are exempt from federal taxes, and from state and local taxes within the state of issue (but not in other states). Because of this tax exempt feature, these bonds tend to have a lower yield than taxable bonds, so that the after tax yield is similar to that of similar taxable bonds. Capital gains on municipal bonds are fully taxable. It is important to recognize, however, that not all bonds issued by state and local governments qualify for this tax treatment, and the investor is advised to use caution.

General obligation bonds are supported by the full faith and credit of the issuer. In reality, this means that the bonds ultimately rely on the taxing power of the municipality. The credit risk of a given issue is thus a function of the prosperity and existing tax load of the municipality. Revenue bonds, on the other hand, are bonds issued to finance a particular project, such as a bridge or sewer line. Revenue bonds are meant to be paid by the proceeds from the project, such as bridge tolls or fees, and are not backed by the municipality itself. The credit risk of a particular issue depends on the viability of the project being financed. Various maturities are available, usually up to 30 years. Municipals are sometimes issued as serial bonds. A serial bond issue is one that has staggered maturities, so that a certain number of the bonds will mature in any given year. The investor can then choose from a variety of maturities.

CORPORATE BONDS. Corporates are simply bonds issued by corporations, typically with fixed interest payments and maturity. The credit risk of a corporate bond is a reflection of the viability of the issuer, and variations are wide. Beyond the credit risk there are a number of characteristics and arrangements which affect the risk of the bond. These characteristics and arrangements are spelled out in the indenture, or legal agreement under which the bond is issued.

One important characteristic of a bond is the collateral. Mortgage bonds are secured by a claim on a specific asset, usually real property. They may be open end, limited open end, or closed end, depending on the extent to which the collateral can be used as security for other issues. Equipment trust certificates are a variation of mortgage bond using equipment as security, while collateral trust certificates use securities of other entities as security. In bankruptcy, the asset would be sold and the proceeds used to pay the claims of the mortgage bondholders. Any excess proceeds would go the claimants of next highest priority. If the proceeds were insufficient, the mortgage bondholders claims for the balance would simply be joined to the holders of debentures. Debentures are secured by a general, nonspecific claim on the firm's assets. In some cases the security of mortgage bonds or debentures may be augmented by the existence of subordinated debentures. In case of bankruptcy the holders of subordinated debentures must subordinate their claims to another specific class of bonds, and will receive payments only after the claims of the other class have been met in full.

Callable bonds are bonds that can be repurchased by the firm at its option. The call price at which the forced repurchase is carried out includes a call premium, which is often equal to one year's interest. The call premium may vary over the life of the bond, typically becoming smaller as maturity nears. The premium may also vary in size depending on the reason underlying the call. This feature is to the benefit of the firm, primarily if the firm desires to refund the issue by replacing it with an issue with lower interest cost. Despite the attraction of receiving the call premium, the investor faces the prospect of being forced to replace the investment with a security of lower yield. This will be the case since the firm will only recall the issue when recall is to its advantage—i.e., when yields are low. Further, the call price becomes in effect an upper limit to the price of the bond. Since this feature is disagreeable to investors, callable bonds typically have a higher yield than similar noncallable bonds. Bonds are often call protected for a certain period to make the feature more acceptable to investors and allow issue at a lower yield. At the other extreme is the putable bond, which may be sold back to the issuer at the option of the investor. This feature is attractive to investors.

The maturity date of a bond issue is a time of some concern. While the firm may be able to make the periodic interest payment, the repayment of principal at maturity may be beyond the ability of the firm. Normally, an issue will simply be replaced by a new issue, but this may prove difficult or impossible. A **sinking fund** is a way of avoiding this end of life crisis. Originally, a sinking fund requirement actually created a fund to which the firm made payments, so that all or at least a portion of the maturity payments were available. At present, however, the sinking fund usually requires that a certain number of bonds be retired each year. If the bonds are selling below the call price, the requirement will be met through purchase on the open market. If the bonds are above the call price, they will be called. Often the call premium for purchases to meet sinking fund requirements are less than call premiums for refunding. This feature is thus a mixed blessing for investors. On the one hand the possibility of end of life crisis is lessened, the average life of the issue is shortened, and it is also thought that sinking fund repurchases will support the value of the bonds. On the other hand, the investor faces the possibility of call at a reduced premium. The effect is similar to that of municipal serial bonds.

Convertible bonds are bonds that can be converted into the **common stock** of the issuing firm. Zero coupon bonds are bonds that have no interest payment, but instead provide a return by being sold at a discount. In fact, there are a large variety of other characteristics that have been written into the bond indenture, the agreement under which the bond is issued, and the instrument is very flexible.

MORTGAGE-BACKED SECURITIES. Mortgage-backed securities, or pass throughs, are securities that represent a claim to proceeds from a pool of mortgages. Ownership of an individual mortgage would be quite risky and would have high default risk, but ownership of a pool spreads default risk (allows diversification) over all investors holding securities based on the pool. The cash flows from the instrument are the principal and interest payments of the mortgages, which are passed through to the bondholders. Another source of cash flows is prepayment of the mortgages. Because of the right of the mortgagees to repay, which is strongly affected by interest rates, the cash flows are hard to predict.

FIXED-INCOME SECURITIES—PREFERRED STOCK

In the case of preferred stock, the specified cash flows take the form of a fixed dividend to be paid at set intervals. While some preferred stock has a maturity with a final payout, more often there is no fixed maturity. The stock is called preferred for two reasons. The first is that no dividends may be paid on common stock unless the dividend on preferred stock has been paid. Second, in bankruptcy the preferred stockholders have a higher priority for payment than the common stockholders. Balancing these preferences is the characteristic that preferred stock usually has no voting power.

The specification of dividends is a promise, rather than a contractual obligation. Dividends are declared at the discretion of the directors. The directors have no legal obligation to declare dividends at the indicated time and preferred stockholders cannot legally force payment. There are several reasons, however, why it is advisable for the directors to declare the dividend. First, the dividend is usually cumulative, and any skipped dividend is not forgotten but is due and payable. Second, no dividends may be declared to common stockholders while preferred dividends are in arrears. Finally, the preferred stockholders are often granted voting power if preferred dividends are in arrears. Thus, theoretically, the directors will declare the dividends, if possible, to avoid the wrath of the now-voting and annoyed preferred stockholders. In reality, given the difficulties of mounting a challenge to an entrenched management, this may not be all that powerful a motivation. It may be that investor antipathy to a firm in arrears on preferred dividends, and the resulting isolation from capital markets, is more important.

It has been suggested that preferred stock may not be a desirable investment for individual investors. This suggestion arises from the tax treatment because dividends on preferred stock are not tax deductible, and hence the earnings supposedly behind the dividend have already been taxed once. When the dividend is paid to an individual, it is taxed again, for double taxation. If the dividend is passed through another firm that then pays the dividend earnings as a dividend, the earnings would have been subject to triple taxation. In order to reduce this multiple taxation effect, 70 percent of the dividends on preferred stock held by other firms are excluded from taxes (this exclusion does not extend to common stock). At a given price, the return on preferred stock is higher for firms than for individuals. Demand from firms thus results in overpricing from the individual viewpoint.

MONEY MARKET SECURITIES

Money market securities are instruments that are highly marketable, have low credit risk, and are of short maturity, usually one year or less. These securities generally trade on a discount basis, where the cash flow is the final repayment of principal. The instruments provide a return by selling at a discount from maturity value. They are usually used by large institutions and **mutual funds**, and are seldom held by individual investors. Negotiable CDs are large certificates of deposit that can be traded among investors. Banker's acceptances are simply drafts on a bank, to be paid at some future date, which the bank has promised to honor or "accepted." These banker's acceptances are traded on a discount basis. Commercial paper is simply an unsecured loan to the issuing firm—they are sometimes called corporate IOUs. Only a small number of firms are able to use this instrument. T-bills, short-term government securities having original maturities of 91 days or 182 days, are issued weekly, while 52-week maturities are issued monthly. Eurodollars are dollar-denominated deposits at foreign banks or at the foreign branches of American banks. The term "Euro" is historic in origin, and the deposits may be in banks worldwide. Both these and the similar Eurodollar CDs escape regulation by the U.S. Federal Reserve Board. Repos are the purchase of government securities, with an agreement by the seller to repurchase the securities back at a set higher price—in effect, a very short-term collateralized loan.

DERIVATIVE SECURITIES

Derivative securities or contingent claims are securities that provide payoffs according to the values of other assets such as **commodities**, stock prices, or values of a market index. In short their value is contingent on or derived from the value of other assets.

OPTIONS. Call and put options grant the holder the right to decide whether or not a particular action will be taken. A call option grants the right to buy a fixed amount of assets, at a fixed price, for a fixed period, a put option grants the right to sell a fixed amount of an asset, at a fixed price, for a fixed period. The buyer of the option literally buys the right to decide whether or not the trade will be executed (the option exercised): the seller or writer must comply with the decision of the buyer. Most trading is in standardized options traded on an exchange, although individualized contracts are available. Options contracts are available on common stock, commodities, foreign currency, and bonds. Some options are actually written on futures rather than directly on the asset in question, although there is no practical difference. Since delivery of a market index is infeasible, the delivery on index options is made in cash. Options provide tremendous flexibility in creating financial strategies, and are often used to create hybrid securities. Options permit high leverage and may be very speculative, but can also be used to reduce exposure to some types of risk.

FUTURES AND FORWARD CONTRACTS. A forward contract is a commitment to trade a fixed amount at a fixed price at some future date. **Futures contracts** are simply a standardized form of forward contract that are traded on an exchange. The futures contract has the added feature of a clearinghouse that guarantees performance, and the daily marking to market or payment of gains or losses. Futures may be used by both producers and users of an asset to hedge against price changes, or they can be used as speculative investments.

OTHER INSTRUMENTS

There are other instruments that separate ownership from possession and use, and provide limited liability. For various reasons, however, these instruments lack liquidity or other characteristics of securities. In limited partnerships, for example, only the managing partner exercises management control and assumes full risk. The rest of the partners are called limited partners. The limited partner's have no say in the management of the partnership, but in exchange have limited liability. This arrangement has been widely used in real estate investing. The major drawbacks to limited partnerships is the almost total reliance on the ability of the managing partner and the lack of liquidity.

INVESTMENTS

The process of investing in securities can be visualized in terms of three problems. The first problem is choice—which of the individual assets will be acquired. The second problem is allocation—how the assets will be combined into a portfolio. The final problem is one of timing—how to respond to changing market conditions. This description is helpful in understanding the process, but in practice all three problems are interrelated and must be solved together.

CHOICE

The problem of choosing among the many securities is called security analysis. The traditional advice of "Buy low, sell high" does not answer the question of what is high and what is low—security analysis attempts to answer this question. While three general philosophies can be identified, few investors adhere solely to one philosophy. All three are relevant in some way, and there are in reality as many approaches to security analysis as there are investors.

FUNDAMENTAL ANALYSIS. The origin of fundamental analysis is often identified with J. B. Williams' suggestion that securities could be valued as the present value of the anticipated cash flows. This suggestion prompted the application of quantitative economic analysis to securities. Fundamental analysis is based on the belief that it is possible to identify incorrectly priced securities on the basis of the underlying conditions in the economy, industry, and company—the fundamentals. Analysts using this approach gather and evaluate information about all facets of a firm and its industry. This includes sources such as **accounting** data, items published in the financial press, information from trade publications, and almost any other source that can be accessed. Professional security analysts usually specialize in one industry or sector of the economy, often maintaining a relationship with the management of the firms under analysis. Using this information and forecasts of economic conditions, fundamental analysts attempt to evaluate the intrinsic value, or the economically rational, correct value for the firm. This intrinsic value is often indirectly expressed on the basis of expected return, rather than on price. The approach is optimal as a technique for comparison across similar firms, where the intent is to identify incorrectly priced assets. Statistical concepts can be applied to provide probabilistic estimates of value or return.

Outside this common philosophy, there is often little in common among the techniques or strategies applied. One common approach is to analyze "P/Es," or **price-earnings ratios**. The difficulty of this approach is that it requires specification of the suitable P/E ratio, which is in turn a function of the fundamentals. Somewhat more specific are the **discounted cash flow** (or DCF techniques). Essentially, these techniques estimate the future cash flows from the asset, and take the intrinsic value of the asset as the present value of the cash flows. The present value is the amount that, if invested today at the required rate of return on the investment, would just recreate the estimated cash flows. This in turn raises the question of the required rate of return, which is defined as the rate of return on other, similar securities. There are numerous variations of these approaches. Another classification of fundamental analysis is based on management style, which is based on the strategy followed. Value managers, for instance, attempt to identify undervalued firms, while growth managers attempt to identify firms that will grow more rapidly than average.

INDEXING. This approach is identified with the efficient markets hypothesis arising from **portfolio management theory**. Indexing is based on the belief that analysts not only can correctly identify mispriced assets but also are so efficient at this endeavor that very few stocks will be mispriced, and then only fleetingly. This implies that at any given time the best estimate of the value of an asset is the market price, and the expensive search for incorrectly priced stocks will be unlikely to produce unusually high returns. Under this belief, the optimal course is to purchase a well-diversified portfolio of assets. The approach is called indexing because the portfolio is usually created in such a way as to mimic some market index, such as the Standard & Poor's 500. This approach is most often used for those common stocks that are widely traded.

TECHNICAL ANALYSIS. Technical analysis has its origins in the Dow theory. It agrees with the belief that stock values depend on the fundamentals. Due to the complexity of the relationships, the constantly changing conditions, and uncertain investor psychology, however, technicians believe that fundamental analysis is futile. Instead, this approach assumes that prices and investor sentiment adjust slowly, producing trends in security prices over time. The emphasis of technical analysis is thus on the detection of trends based on observance of price and trading data. The original theory has over time come to encompass a wide array of possible detection devices.

ALLOCATION

This is the problem of portfolio management. The idea of diversification—holding multiple assets—has always been stressed as correct investment procedure. Historically, however, this was based on an intuitive reasoning such as ''Don't put all of your eggs into one basket,'' and diversification was primarily a matter of the number of different assets to be held. A more exact, quantitative analysis of the nature of was first provided by Harry M. Markowitz in the early 1950s. Markowitz noted that a combination of assets that are not perfectly correlated produces risk and return combinations that are superior to those available from the individual assets. The lower the correlation between the assets, the larger the effect. For example, all other things being equal, the owner of a ski resort would be better off investing in a beach resort than in another ski resort. The reason is the

relationship of the pattern of earnings of the investment as compared to the earnings of the ski resort. If the owner acquires another ski resort, in cold years with good snow both would do well; in warm years with poor snow both would do poorly. The result would be a highly variable, risky total-earnings stream. If the beach resort is purchased, however, it will do well in warm years and poorly in cold years. This pattern of earnings would balance out the fluctuations of the ski resort earnings, and produce a predictable, less risky total earnings flow.

This analysis led to the development of what is called modern portfolio management, (or portfolio management theory) and the understanding that asset correlations strongly affect the diversification process. The implication is that the decision to include an asset in a portfolio depends not only on the asset but also on its relationship with the other assets in the proposed portfolio. Finally, for a given set of assets there are many combinations, and the risk and return of the combinations can vary greatly. The task of the portfolio manager is thus to choose both assets and proportions that will result in a portfolio with a suitable risk and return profile.

For an example of this, return to the example of ''risk return space'' shown in Figure 1. The portfolio manager will avoid a portfolio such as F because portfolio F is ''dominated'' by portfolios B, C, and D. Portfolio F is said to be dominated because there are alternatives that are unarguably better. In this case, Portfolio B has less risk but provides the same return, portfolio C provides more return for less risk, and portfolio D has more return for the same risk. An economically rational investor would always prefer B, C, or D to F. None of the other portfolios can be said to dominate one another. Portfolio E has higher return than portfolio A, but it also has higher risk. While a young doctor might prefer portfolio E because of its high return, and a widow with several children might prefer portfolio A because of its low risk—this is a matter of personal choice, not of dominance. Portfolios A, B, C, D, and E are said to be efficient, where an efficient portfolio is simply a portfolio which is not dominated. The role of the portfolio manager, then, is to choose asset proportions that produce an efficient portfolio with appropriate risk and return.

Study of the effect of diversification led to a new way of thinking about risk itself. It became apparent that the risk of an asset had two components. Part of the risk, called diversifiable risk, could be reduced or eliminated through diversification. The reduction of risk through diversification has a natural limit. Although risks that affect individual assets or limited groups of assets can be reduced or eliminated by diversification, risks that affect all assets cannot be diversified. These nondiversifiable risks are those that cause entire capital markets to go through bull and bear phases—i.e., they affect the entire economic system. Another name for the nondiversifiable risk is thus systematic risk, while another name for diversifiable risk is nonsystematic risk. If an investor holds a well-diversified portfolio, it is only the nondiversifiable, systematic risk that is of concern. This systematic risk is measured by the beta of the asset. Portfolio management theory suggests that the beta of a security is the determinant of the required return on an asset. This analysis, and the use of beta as a risk measure, is most often applied to common stock analysis. The underlying analysis of the nature of diversification, however, is applicable to all investment problems. Finally, this analysis points out a major reason for the growth of international investing. Foreign economies do not move directly with the domestic economy, and provide the opportunity to diversify beyond the domestic systematic risk.

TIMING

Given that the market exhibits bull and bear stages, timers focus on buying and selling according to the market stages. Thus, a timer who anticipates a bull market would increase the proportion of stocks in the portfolio and decrease the amount of cash, and vice versa for a bear market. Cash in this usage is taken to mean money market securities rather than cash itself, since these securities provide return with nearly the liquidity and safety of cash itself. The timer might use either fundamental analysis of economic variables or technical analysis to form expectations. A pure timer would buy or sell an index portfolio, but the strategy is more often combined with fundamental or technical analysis. Timing may also take other forms. A bond portfolio manager might lengthen the maturity of the portfolio if **interest rates** are expected to decrease, or shorten the maturity if interest rates are expected to increase. Another version of timing is to attempt to buy stocks ahead of the business cycle, or sector rotation.

PROFESSIONAL DESIGNATIONS

There are a number of professional designations in the field of securities analysis. These include:

1. Registered representative stockbroker. Brokers are essentially the salespeople of the securities industry. Brokers must successfully complete the Series Seven examination given by the National Association of Security Dealers (NASD). The examination covers the basics of securities and markets, and is roughly equivalent in content to a college-level investments course.

2. Certified financial planner. This designation is relevant to professionals who provide financial guidance to individuals. This in-

cludes brokers, insurance representatives, and others dealing in investment products. The designation is granted by the College of Financial Planners, and requires successful completion of a ten-part examination covering an array of topics relevant to financial planning for individuals. The content would be equivalent to several college-level courses.

3. Chartered financial analyst. This designation has become widely accepted as a requirement in the **investment management** industry. The designation is granted by the Institute of Chartered Financial Analysts after successful completion of three six-hour examinations covering various aspects of securities analysis and portfolio management, plus three years of experience in investment decision making. The content is equivalent to a master's degree.

SEE ALSO: Capital Assets Pricing Model; Diversification in Investments

[David Upton]

FURTHER READING:

Bodie, Zvi, Alex Kane, and Alan J. Marcus. *Investments*. 2nd ed. Irwin, 1993.

Chance, Don M. *An Introduction to Options and Futures*. 2nd ed. Dryden Press, 1992.

Cottle, Sidney, Roger F. Murray, and Frank E. Block. *Security Analysis*. 5th ed. McGraw-Hill, 1988.

Ellis, Charles D., and James R. Vertin, eds. *Classics: A Treasury of Investment Literature*. Irwin Professional Publishing, 1988.

Ellis, Charles D. and James R. Vertin, eds. *Classics No. II: The Most Interesting Ideas & Concepts from the Literature of Investing*. Irwin Professional Publishing, 1991.

Ellis, Charles D. *Investment Policy: How to Win the Loser's Game*. 2nd ed. Business One Irwin, 1992.

Fabozzi, Frank J. *Bond Markets: Analysis, and Strategies*. 2nd ed. Prentice Hall, 1992.

Fischer, Donald E., and Ronald J. Jordan. *Security Analysis and Portfolio Management*. 5th ed. Prentice Hall, 1995.

Malkiel, Burton G. *A Random Walk Down Wall Street*. 4th ed. W. W. Norton & Company, 1989.

Reilly, Frank K. *Investment Analysis and Portfolio Management*. 3rd ed. Dryden Press.

SELF-EMPLOYMENT

Classification of someone as an employee or a self-employee is ambiguous and depends on several factors, including degree of independence, the freedom to hire others to do the work taken on, the freedom to work for others, and the assumption of risks. Courts have held that the individual does not necessarily have to provide the equipment to do the job, as in the case of independent television and film mixers working on equipment owned by client production companies. Employees have more statutory rights, benefits, and protections than subcontractors, who must generally provide these for themselves.

Variations of the term include "independent contractors," "**free-lancers**," "consultants," "sole proprietors," and, creatively, "soloists," "virtual employees," "corporate refugees," "corporate mutineers," "lone wolves," "lone rangers," and "lone eagles."

The America of Thomas Jefferson's imagination was made up of independent farmers and merchants, and at the beginning of the twentieth century most Americans were self-employed. After decades of corporate life, the concept of self-employment received increased attention in the 1980s and 1990s as many large firms responded to the growth of competition and a lingering recession by "downsizing," or reducing the size of their "permanent" staffs and hiring temporary employees and independent contractors to reduce overhead. Some such groups of businesses have been called "virtual corporations," as they perform functions formerly grouped under a single corporation, but legally do not exist under one ownership. While in the past a large company using freelancers seemed to imply a crisis, it became a commonplace way to control costs and try out new talent in the 1990s.

In most industrialized countries, nonagricultural self-employment increased in the 1980s after decades of decline. In the first three quarters of 1993, one-fifth of all new jobs in the United States were created by self-employment and 400,000 new businesses started; job growth in this category increased almost twice as fast as overall job growth. The highest growth came in the finance, insurance, property, and business services industries—areas where professionals could expect to earn more by becoming independent. A survey in Great Britain in the spring of 1993 put the number of self-employed British at 3,103,000, up 57,000 from the winter. In Great Britain in 1990, the self-employed made up 11.6 percent of the workforce, in Japan it was 11.5 percent. In the United States, where 50 percent of the newly self-employed left an existing job and 20 percent had been unemployed, the self-employed made up 7.6 percent of the workforce. The self-employed comprised 11 percent of the workforce of Organization for Economic Cooperation and Development (OECD) countries in 1990, from 28 percent in Turkey, and 27 percent in Greece, to six percent in Austria and Norway.

The increase in self-employment can be attributed partially to **workers' compensation**, social security, and job protection laws, which have made employers cautious about hiring full-time employees. In addition, smaller companies can afford to temporarily hire professionals who have had experience at larger, more sophisticated companies. The self-employed also benefit from more personal treatment than when dealing with a large corporation.

There are many different types of independent contractors: professionals leaving corporate life, youngsters delivering papers, single parents stuffing envelopes at home. Generally, professionals have built up their skills and their reputations working for others. The overall number of self-employed in the United States in the 1990s has been estimated at 20 million. While this rate has been increasing, the number of self-employed men actually declined. One study estimated the number of self-employed women in the United States at ten million. According to 1992 Census Bureau statistics self-employed men earned slightly more (a median of $31,812 per year gross) than their organizationally-employed counterparts in private industry ($30,087), while self-employed women earned much less ($15,032 versus $20,644). Many self-employed women held very low-paying positions, such as **child care**.

Some individuals begin their own enterprises to work fewer hours, as eighty-hour weeks are not unheard of in corporate life. For women, being able to take time off to raise their children can be priceless perquisite, as can the freedom to bring the children into the workplace. Another factor leading workers to consider self-employment is the downsizing trend itself, which has done much to erode the belief that salaried jobs are more secure. It is also very difficult for older workers to secure permanent jobs after they have been dismissed. Freedom from the necessity of commuting is one factor in the increase in number of home-based businesses in the United States from 3.6 million to more than 5.6 million between 1985 and 1991.

The burden of managing others is often cited among professionals as a motivator for starting a business. The responsibility of personnel management even causes some small business owners to dismiss their staffs in order to spend more time practicing their trades.

Self-employed individuals as a whole tend to work longer (an additional 17.5 hours per week, according to one study) and harder than their colleagues who are organizationally-employed, and they do it for irregular pay and, frequently, fewer benefits. In addition, their salaries and assets are dependent on their work contributions in a more direct way than are those of their colleagues. Not surprisingly, a study of certified public accountants in 1986 found the self-employed ones to have higher levels of organizational commitment. However, greater freedom, autonomy, and job satisfaction do not necessarily arise from being self-employed.

In a survey of college graduates, self-employed respondents tended to be older and reported higher earnings than their cohorts. Studies concerning the length of education of self-employed individuals have had mixed results, however it has been supported that self-employment and success are influenced by a longer formal education and a general education.

The self-employed have been found to report lower absences, which has been attributed not to superior health but the feeling of being indispensable. In fact, their jobs tend to be more physically and psychologically stressful due to the investments in energy the jobs demand. Certain stress factors are generally absent from self-employment—such as corporate meetings and employee discipline problems. However, dealing with clients presents its own stress, such as rush orders and negotiations.

Governments in many developed countries have instituted self-employment assistance—including small loans, grants, and advice—as part of their aid for the unemployed. In Great Britain 500,000 people were assisted with such programs between 1983 and 1990; over half of the participants were still self-employed after three years. Massachusetts tested similar programs, offering business development advice, loans, and a stipend equivalent to their unemployment compensation. Program participants used fewer unemployment benefits overall.

Self-employment is a necessary way of life for many in developing nations. It became legal in Cuba in July of 1993, part of liberalizations designed to relieve economic hardships. By the end of the year, 40,000 Cubans had established enterprises in order to earn hard currency. Self-employment was considered crucial for the development of Eastern Europe after the demise of Soviet control, although **entrepreneurship** there stimulated social differences in cultures unused to free enterprise. The spread of smaller enterprises from the West to the East was cited as one way to provide models for development.

Various personal characteristics seem to steer people into self-employment, such as being the oldest child or having parents who were self-employed. In addition, individuals are more likely to become self-employed if they have been fired from more than one job, have been previously employed in small businesses, are college graduates, are realistic risk takers, and are well-organized and good at organizing others. Many are immigrants or children of immigrants. Some personality requirements for success as an independent contractor are confidence, a positive outlook, friendliness, and the determination to succeed. Inde-

pendent contractors should also be prepared to accept tedious tasks if they expect to gain repeat business.

Professionals can often expect to earn more after establishing themselves as independent contractors, but the pay differential has been shrinking. Generally, these "lone eagles" do not bring large staffs with them, nor do they expect to build a great deal of equity in their ventures. At the end of their careers, there is usually very little besides office equipment to sell from the one-person office.

The small business owner must make many management decisions, such as keeping precise accounting and tax records, projecting cash flow, and making purchasing decisions. More successful individuals can—and frequently must—hire another professional to take on some of these tasks, particularly accounting, but also sometimes filing, manufacturing, billing, maintaining databases, mailing brochures, or selling.

Intermittent income is one of the most important difficulties the newly independent businessperson must face. Downtime can be avoided by overscheduling or moonlighting or by also working a salaried job. New business owners are advised not to rely on their enterprises for income for at least the first six months; comfortable returns may not follow for months afterward.

The self-employed often undercharge for their services or products at the beginning of their enterprises, at times even doing work for free with the hope of impressing new clients. This is partly due to a lack of confidence and partly because of their justified concerns about competing in the marketplace. This can pose a serious dilemma, as underpricing may not necessarily lead to more contracts; in fact, it can connote a lack of quality. However, freelancers starting out are advised to take all the work they need in order to survive—frequently, all they work they can find, including low-paying projects. Market values for their work can be determined through colleagues or contacts in the business.

Two things which cannot be escaped when going into business are marketing and sales (including collecting from clients). These can be daunting concepts, even to those trained in these areas, given the added challenge of selling one's own self, without a corporate image. Rejections can be psychologically very damaging.

Different tactics are called for in marketing one's self. While time-consuming and expensive cold calls and mailing lists may help sell corporate products; when the entity is unknown, introductions and referrals are essential. Speaking and writing on topics of professional expertise are more cost-effective ways of reaching people, from an audience of a dozen in the case of public speaking to several hundred or several thousand in trade periodicals. In both cases, the prospective client has a chance to evaluate the professional's expertise and personality. Keeping informed of markets is also crucial.

An additional psychological strain for the consultant is isolation. The environment of the typical self-employed individual is quite different from the corporate environment where many professionals gain their experience. This is one reason contact with supportive colleagues becomes crucial. In addition, these mentors can provide advice regarding business aspects of the consultant's operation. **Professional and trade associations** can be an excellent way to establish contacts with peers. Tenacity in networking has been cited as a key to survival for some business owners, some of whom maintain databases of thousands of contacts. These contacts are also vital in referring clients and providing market information. The role of the contact is made more important as the self-employed individual typically has no staff for marketing support.

It is difficult to exaggerate the importance of referrals to the typical independent professional. Since relationships are so vital, one must exercise the utmost delicacy in terminating employment with one's former employer or turning down a job. One's former employer can even become a good client, besides providing valuable referrals. When turning down clients, the self-employed person can protect those relationships by making referrals or even subcontracting to other colleagues in their network. Provided the work done is of quality, this can strengthen one's reputation as a purveyor of talent—whether one's own or an associate's. When the client calls back with a more appropriate assignment, the contractor has the choice of the business.

As they begin their enterprises, self-employed individuals feel compelled to accept a variety of assignments due to sheer scarcity of work. However, specialization can help ensure their long-term survival. For one thing, corporate clients can often find a generalist's abilities in-house. Also, specialization may allow professionals to broaden their client base geographically—freeing their fortunes from fluctuations in the local economy. These factors can enable the specialist to earn higher fees and work more consistently. Paradoxically, one's work as a specialist can garner referrals outside one's specialty, so specialization might not be as limiting as a strict definition would imply. The self-employed should be cautioned against changing their specialties too often, as this can confuse clients and make their own operations inefficient.

The personal computer and communications technology made working at home more feasible throughout the 1980s and 1990s. Mastering these technologies has become essential for those without staffs. Through cellular telephones and pagers, the self-employed professional can stay in touch with clients throughout the day. Fax machines and modems make business over a large geographic area feasible and help the one-person office get work out quickly. Computerized spreadsheet and database programs are necessary to deal with administrative tasks quickly and efficiently. In addition, on-line services and electronic bulletin boards made instantaneous local, cross-country, and international networking and research feasible. Consultants can also use their **computers** to "manufacture" or "distribute" their work product. In most cases, they make their work process more efficient, as well.

By 1992 the one-person office accounted for $7.5 billion in sales of computer and office products. The relatively low price of the personal computer, peripherals, and communications equipment have enabled many to conduct business independently; frequently, it is their only capital equipment.

Self-employment has long been a focus of the **Internal Revenue Service** (IRS). In 1992 the **IRS** estimated the self-employed underpaid $20 billion a year in taxes. To reduce taxes paid, forming a subchapter **S corporation** is an option, particularly when income before expenses and taxes exceeds $150,000. In an S corporation, income is not subject to self-employment taxes. There are other tax disadvantages for unincorporated businesses. For example, owners of such businesses are not able to fully deduct employee contributions to health insurance.

Not surprisingly, this discourages the self-employed from getting health insurance for themselves and their employees. Health insurance may be available through one's prior employer. The Consolidated Omnibus Budget Reconciliation Act (COBRA) requires companies with more than 50 employees to offer health care coverage up to 18 months after an employee leaves; this may be the only option for people with preexisting conditions that preclude new insurance coverage. Under this plan, however, employees must pay 102 percent of their insurance premiums (including a two percent administrative fee). Under COBRA, the departing employee is also credited with deductibles already paid, while temporary plans reset deductibles. Other options include a spouse's company plan, a trade organization plan, or individual coverage.

Independent life insurance plans tend to give better coverage than company plans that are converted within 30 days of leaving a job. Disability coverage typically can't be converted, but it can be necessary to cover business overhead during an out-of-work period. A single-premium insurance policy, where only one premium payment is required, is one solution to the problem of pensions that irregular earnings creates.

There are tax advantages to self-employment, found in retirement plans and home-office and transportation deductions. In the simplified employee pension plan (SEP-IRA), a maximum of 13.1435 percent of net income can be contributed to these accounts annually, up to $30,000. A portion of the home dedicated exclusively to business use may be depreciated over 31½ years. A standard deduction, 30 cents per mile in 1995, may be used for business-related transportation costs, or actual fuel and maintenance costs. Also, up to 25 percent of medical insurance premiums may be deducted for sole proprietors, partners, and more-than-2 percent S corporation shareholders; also, the self-employed pay Federal Insurance Contributions Act (FICA) tax on net, not gross, earnings. For these reasons, it is essential to keep an accurate record of expenses.

The legal definition of self-employment is ambiguous. One's status as an independent contractor can be reinforced by having multiple clients, being paid by work done rather than by the hour, or obtaining an employer identification number from the IRS by filing form SS-4. Working under a business name also helps reinforce this status. For some independent contractors, it's simply their own name, plus an ''Inc.'' if they've incorporated. Stipulating in written contracts that either party can be dismissed on 30 days' notice helps differentiate oneself from employees, who often cannot be fired at will. Printing invoices, business cards, and stationery help identify oneself as independent. Independent contractors typically accept no fringe benefits and pay Social Security, Medicare, and income tax installments directly. The freedom to work without supervision, at one's own speed and with one's own methods, are the hallmarks of self-employment.

SEE ALSO: Small Business

[Frederick C. Ingram]

FURTHER READING:

Arzeni, Sergio. ''Encouraging the Entrepreneur.'' *OECD Observer*. February/March, 1992, pp. 19-22.

Banerjee, Abhijit V., and Andrew F. Newman. ''Occupational Choice and the Process of Development.'' *Journal of Political Economy*. April, 1993, pp. 274-298.

Bianchi, Alessandra. ''New Businesses.'' *Inc.* May, 1993, p. 58.

Dermota, Ken. ''If Che Could See Me Now.'' *Business Week*. December 20, 1993, pp. 30a-30d.

Edwards, Colin C. ''A Career in Contracting . . . Is It a Viable Alternative?'' *Management Services*. March, 1992, pp. 30-32.

Eliason, Carol. *The Business Plan for Homebased Business*. Denver: U.S. Small Business Administration, Office of Business Development, 1991.

Ellis, Barbara. ''Tips for the Self-Employed Professional.'' *Accountancy*. January, 1994, p. 48.

Fairchild, Tony. ''Don't Go to Work: Let the Work Come to You.'' *Australian Business Monthly*. November, 1993, pp. 118-119.

Greene, Jeffrey J. ''When Is a Rental Not a Rental?'' *Tax Adviser*. August, 1993, pp. 498-499.

Hise, Phaedra. ''The Last Hurdle.'' *Inc.* January, 1994, p. 50.

Lear, Jeffrey. ''The IRS and Personal Property Rental Income.'' *National Public Accountant*. August, 1993, pp. 10-12.

''LFS Help-Line.'' *Great Britain-Department of Employment-Employment Gazette*. October, 1993, pp. LFS1-LFS7.

Lohse, Deborah. ''The Greenest Tax Breaks of All Go to the Self-Employed.'' *Money*. August, 1992, pp. 153-156.

Mahar, Maggie. ''White-Collar Wash: For Women, More Jobs, Less $.'' *Working Woman*. March, 1994, p. 16.

McRae, Hamish. ''Work: Where Will It Be Found?'' *Director*. January, 1994, pp. 24-30.

Monheit, Alan C., and P. Holly Harvey. ''Sources of Health Insurance for the Self-Employed: Does Differential Taxation Make a Difference?'' *Inquiry*. Fall, 1993, pp. 293-305.

Murphy, Anne. ''Do-It-Yourself Job Creation.'' *Inc.* January, 1994, pp. 36-50

Nelton, Sharon. ''Putting Women into Business.'' *Nation's Business*. October, 1992, p. 56.

Novack, Janet. ''The Tax Cheater Handbook.'' *Forbes*. November 8, 1993, p. 202.

Oliver, Suzanne. ''Moonlighter's Delight.'' *Forbes*. June 21, 1993, p. 198.

Phalon, Richard. ''How the Bar Girls Beat the IRS.'' *Forbes*. February 15, 1993, p. 136.

Pridna, John P., and Charles J. DeLanoy. ''Maximizing Deductions for Self-Employed Persons' Medical Expenses.'' *Tax Adviser*. May, 1993, pp. 293-294.

Robinson, Peter B., and Edwin A. Sexton. ''The Effect of Education and Experience on Self-Employment Success.'' *Journal of Business Venturing*. March, 1994, pp. 141-156.

Staber, Udo, and Dieter Bogenhold. ''Self-Employment: A Study of Seventeen OECD Countries.'' *Industrial Relations Journal*. June, 1993, pp. 126-137.

Thompson, Cynthia A., Richard E. Kopelman, and Chester A. Schriesheim. ''Putting All One's Eggs in the Same Basket: A Comparison of Commitment and Satisfaction among Self- and Organizationally Employed Men.'' *Journal of Applied Psychology*. 1992, pp. 738-743.

Torroll, Sam. ''Clinton's Tax Package: A Trader's P&L.'' *Futures: The Magazine of Commodities & Options*. November, 1993, pp. 58-60.

Vijverberg, Wim P. M. ''Educational Investments and Returns for Women and Men in Cote d'Ivoire.'' *Journal of Human Resources*. Fall, 1993, pp. 933-974.

Watson, Mark, and Ian Hunter. ''Employment Law.'' *Director*. March, 1994, p. 70.

Wells, Melanie. ''Big Shops Put Faith in Free-Lancers.'' *Advertising Age*. May 31, 1993, p. 13.

''Working for Yourself.'' *The Economist*. August 29, 1992, p. 61.

SERVICE INDUSTRIES

The ''service'' economy is becoming one of the buzzwords of the late 20th century. It characterizes an economy and a market that are quite distinct from what they were as recently as 25 years ago, when they were based on industrial manufacturing. In the 1960s, General Motors Corp. was the largest producer in the world, bigger than the 10 most important manufacturers in western Europe combined; the United States was still the world's most important manufacturing nation.

This has changed dramatically because of the growth of the service sector of the economy, which has far outstripped that of **manufacturing**, **agriculture**, and mining. The most important, fastest growing areas of the service sector are telecommunications, health care, financial services, and the most rapidly growing of all, computer services. To point out how sweeping the takeover of the service industries has been, one can point to the city of Des Moines, Iowa. While firmly in the heart of the nation's farm belt, Des Moines' economy has little to do with agriculture, but is almost entirely grounded in services.

Des Moines mirrors the economic trend of the country as a whole, where only one in six workers is employed in manufacturing and 60 percent of the **gross national product** (GNP) is derived from the service industries, translating into approximately $900 billion. In other words, McDonald's is a bigger industry in this country than the U.S. Steel Corporation, in terms of the number of employees. In Great Britain, only one worker in five is employed in manufacturing, and in Germany and Japan, one in three. Even "undeveloped" industrializing countries as India and China are making the transition to service industries.

What is a service industry? Definitions and descriptions abound. Both service industries and manufacturing industries produce, and manufacturing has always included service. However, in a service based industry, the "product" is intangible and simultaneous, in that a consumer uses the service as soon as it is produced, hence it is always perishable and cannot be warehoused or inventoried. While manufacturing in this country has included service to the customer (as seen in the use of advertising), profits are tied to the tangible commodities produced rather than to servicing the consumer. Moreover, human interaction is an important component of services and cannot be easily separated from the product as in manufacturing. Lastly, information is at the heart of a service business. Not surprisingly, online information services are experiencing the most explosive growth (worth $750 million in 1993) in the service sector, an indication that information is the key to a service's quality and to its timely delivery. By the year 2000, only 8 percent of the nation's GNP is projected to derive from manufacturing, and 85 percent from service industries.

THE SWITCH TO A SERVICE ECONOMY

How and why the changeover to a service based economy occurred is not hard to divine. The new service economy of the late 20th century reflects an evolutionary development that began when this nation became independent. At that time, the nation's wealth was derived from agriculture; mechanized industry began in the early part of the 19th century with the development of new sources of energy, especially steam, followed by electricity. These developments culminated in the Industrial Revolution of the latter part of the century, which supplanted agriculture as the major employer and the major source of wealth in this country.

Manufacturing, which led workers to congregate in cities and thus hastened the urbanization of America, spawned the need for services. These services, however, were largely byproducts of manufacturing such as transportation, **banking**, **advertising**, and legal services. By the 1920s, however, the United States already was beginning to move away from manufacturing. By the 1940's, the number of employees in services roughly equalled the number in manufacturing for the first time. In 1956, when the United States was considered the greatest manufacturing powerhouse in the world, the majority of Americans were actually employed in service enterprises.

However, it would take more than another decade for the new economy to assert itself and attract notice. The recession of the late 1970s led to the collapse of the steel and automobile industries and ruined the economies of the cities that depended on those industries. The steel town of Pittsburgh recovered slowly from the recession by attracting service based businesses to the city, which now has as little to do with steel as Des Moines has with agriculture.

Hence the new service economy evolved out of manufacturing and began to experience rapid growth with the advent of advanced automation, computerization, and the globalization of business. By the mid-1980s, manufacturing industries were shifting to robots and, consequently, were becoming much less labor intensive. As workers were losing manufacturing jobs, eight out of every ten new jobs being created were service industry jobs. (Even service industries are affected by automation, however—automated teller machines (ATM) have made banks less dependent on human tellers, and telephone operating is also automated).

Even traditional manufacturing industries have realized the importance of service. In the era of massive computerization and rapid automation of mundane tasks, products are roughly equal in quality no matter who produces them. The result is that the difference between two of the same commodities is virtually nil. In the face of eroding market share, manufacturing industries nationwide have come to emphasize service to the customer as the only difference between them and a competitor.

For example, with cloned computers selling at a fraction of the price of premium brand models, computer manufacturers were pressured to shift their focus and provide computer repair and other services. The shift from production to service is also strikingly evident at major companies such as Motorola and General Electric. They no longer produce the appliances and electronic products that made them world famous, but rather have converted their businesses wholly to telecommunications and an array of consulting services. The giant Philip Morris Companies, Inc. also has transformed itself into a service oriented firm, offering market research and management services to offset the declining market shares of its products.

THE INCREASING DIVERSITY OF SERVICES

The explosion of services and their increasing diversity is amazing when compared to the extremely limited range of services available in 1900. At that time, unskilled personal services predominated, chiefly street vending, shoe shining, and housekeeping. Of the skilled and semi-skilled services available, financial services were primitive by today's standards, while telephones, accounting, and advertising were still in their infancy.

By the late 20th century, all this had changed. Services had becom so widespread that several major groups of services have become apparent. First are traditional personal services, such as drycleaning, hair styling, and housekeeping, which still thrive. A fairly new group is entertainment and leisure, which includes tourism, travel, and the booming physical fitness field. The social services group includes the fastest growing and most profitable service industry— health and medical related services. Other social services include education, government services, and virtually all nonprofit organizations. Distribution services, a fourth grouping, includes transportation of all kinds, storage services, the wholesale and retail industries, and the fast-growing telecommunications industry. The last group is producer and consumer services such as legal services, accounting and financial services, architectural and engineering services, and insurance and real estate.

DEREGULATION AND FOREIGN MARKETS

While the inauguration of the ''information age'' and the de-industrialization of the economy largely paved the way for the explosive growth in service businesses, their proliferation has much to do with the wholesale deregulation of service businesses that occured in the 1970s and 1980s. This was set in motion with the Justice Department's antitrust suit against AT&T in 1974 that ended the phone giant's monopoly hold over long distance service. Soon afterward, the air freight and banking industries were deregulated, as were trucking, busing, trains, and airlines. This deregulation created a far greater number of choices for consumers, and usually, lower prices as well. Competition among service businesses has since increased dramatically, forcing marketing to become more targeted and ''niche'' oriented.

Another interesting outcome of deregulation has been its ripple effect—in the wake of deregulation in this country, western Europe, Australia, and even some Asian countries have followed suit. The fall of communism in eastern Europe and Russia further opened the world market. With the United States approving the **Global Agreement on Tarrifs and Trade (GATT)**, the global market is becoming one huge free market. This will accelerate the trend towards service businesses (as seen after the signing of the **North American Free Trade Agreement (NAFTA)**, and the United States is the global leader in service business and the leading exporter of services. Major American companies, especially banks and telecommunications and accounting firms derive more than half of their incomes from foreign business. World trade in services is growing at a faster rate than for commodities.

WHAT DOES THE FUTURE HOLD?

The factors favoring the explosive growth of the service economy are obvious; less so are the reasons for the decline of manufacturing, since commodity consumption is at an all-time high in the United States and worldwide. In the face of this product saturation, the decline of manufacturing appears paradoxical.

The answer to the puzzel is automation. Just as automation has meant fewer workers producing the same amount of food in agriculture, so has automation in manufacturing drastically reduced the demand for workers without a corresponding decrease in output. Moreover, manufactured goods in this country are now largely imported or produced abroad. However, nations that are currently manufacturing goods cheaply for the highly industrialized countries will eventually cease doing so as their economies transform into service economies. In that eventuality, either goods will become more expensive in the 21st century or manufacturing will be wholly automated.

If the service economy is but another stage in the nation's, and the world's, economic growth, where does it evolve from here? It appears that the service economy already has developed from a ''low technology'' economy to a ''high technology'' one, and presumably technology will keep advancing, unless technology, too, is finite.

While it is difficult to discern exactly how the service economy will develop, some trends and implications of the service economy can be ascertained. While eight out of ten jobs by the year 2000 will be found in the service industries, growth will continue only as long as the service sector expands. Service businesses, especially in the telecommunications industry, have not been immune to downsizing and automation.

Another trend in the new service economy is the increasing number of women employed and the decreasing number of white males. By the year 2000, only 39 percent of the workforce is expected to be composed of white males, a decrease from the 46 percent in 1993. Greater numbers of women than ever will be working, constituting at least 60 percent of the employed by 2000. The workforce also will be getting older, and few service industries seem to be responding to the implications of an aging population in the workforce.

In the new service economy developing globally, bigger is not always better. By switching from an emphasis on products to services, it is theoretically possible for a single individual to hone his or her own talents and skills and establish a service business. The service economy may in fact become a boon to immigrants, who are generally young and entrepreneurial. Already the number of small, home-based businesses is exploding, and it will continue to increase. The decline, to minuscule numbers, of the blue-collar workforce bodes negatively for labor unions, unless they, too, respond imaginatively to the revolutionary changes in the economy.

Many continue to identify the service economy with low wages and McDonald-type jobs. However, the service industries are and will continue to be extremely diverse, requiring highly skilled labor and specialization. Therefore, fast food chains represent the ''low end'' of the service sector and it is not inconceivable that the routine jobs performed in these restaurant chains will become automated and disappear. Many service businesses, moreover, have proven to be recession resistant, in contrast to the manufacturing sector of the economy.

[Sina Dubovoy]

FURTHER READING:

Chant, Ben. *How to Start A Service Business.* Avon Books, 1994.

Daniels, P.W. *Service Industries in the World Economy.* Blackwell, 1993.

Giarini, Orio, Stahel, Walter R. *Limits to Certainty: Facing Risks in the New Service Economy.* 2nd ed. Boston: Kluwer Academic Publishers, 1993.

Glasmeier, Amy. *The Role of Service Industries in Rural Economic Development.* Council of Planning Librarians, 1990.

Grigoli, Valorie. *Service Industries.* F. Watts, 1984.

National Research Council, Commission on Physical Science, Mathematics and Applications. *Information Technology in the Service Society: A Twenty-First Century Lever.* Washington, D.C.: National Academy Press, 1994.

Palmer, Adrian. *Services Marketing: Principles and Practice.* Prentice Hall, 1995.

SERVICE MARKS

Service marks are a special type of trademark, one designating a company's services rather than its products. The U.S. Patent and Trademark Office (PTO) of the U.S. Department of Commerce provides the following definition: ''A trademark is either a word, phrase, symbol or design, or combination [thereof], which identifies and distinguishes the source of the goods or services of one party from those of others. A service mark is the same as a trademark except that it identifies and distinguishes the source of a service rather than a product. . . . Normally, a mark for goods appears on the product or on its packaging, while a service mark appears in advertising for the services.'' Elaborating on this idea in *Intellectual Property: Patents, Trademarks, and Copyrights,* Richard Stim remarks, ''When any party performs services or labor for the benefit of others, then the mark that identifies those services is a service mark. The federal courts have interpreted a service to be an activity that is (1) real; (2) for the benefit of someone other than the applicant; and (3) qualitatively different from what is necessarily done in connection with the sale of goods.''

In practice, the terms *service mark* and *trademark* are often used interchangeably. Examples of service marks include American Express Co., Prudential Insurance Company of America, Hilton Hotels Corp., and American Airlines.

Service marks offer several advantages to their users. By providing a name or symbol that consumers can readily identify, they aid in word-of-mouth **advertising** and help build customer loyalty. By constituting a distinctive mark customers associate with a company's services, service marks foster goodwill—the tendency for customers to repurchase services from that company. Service marks attract attention from consumers and help them distinguish among competitors and find the services sold under a particular mark. As Thomas G. Field, Jr., notes in *Trademarks and Business Goodwill,* these marks ''are often the most important asset of an established business. . . . People who are starting out cannot afford not to make the most of trademarks.''

Under the federal Trademark Act of 1946, service marks are afforded protection from illegal use by others—a form of unfair competition known as trademark infringement. While any company can gain some protection by merely using a mark in the course of selling or advertising its services, most authorities advise registering the mark, preferably with the PTO at the federal level, to gain the fullest possible protection against piracy. Among the many benefits to the owners of federally registered service marks are the right to exclusive, nationwide use of their marks; the right to sue in federal court for trademark infringement; and a basis for applying to use the mark in foreign countries, as well as to prevent foreign competitors from using the mark in the United States. Moreover, federal registration can last indefinitely, so long as the registrant—the owner of the mark—meets certain requirements, such as continuing to use the mark and periodically renewing registration with the PTO.

States too offer trademark protection, generally simpler, quicker, and cheaper to obtain than federal registration. Not all states offer registration for service marks, however, and legal protection is limited to the particular state, rather than to the entire United States and its territories and possessions. Furthermore, federal registration usually takes precedence over state registration when legal disputes arise. On the other hand, state registration can be useful for businesses that don't meet the requirements for federal registration.

Obtaining federal registration for a service mark is a lengthy—often lasting a year or more—and complex process that begins with the company filing a written application with the PTO. To be eligible for filing such an application, a company must either have established prior use of the service mark or have a bona fide intention of using it on services rendered in "commerce," defined by the PTO as "all commerce which may lawfully be regulated by the U.S. Congress, for example, interstate commerce or commerce between the U.S. and another country." This stipulation is important and has resulted in numerous legal claims and lawsuits, such as a case in which Bookbinder's Restaurant in Philadelphia was found ineligible to register its name as a service mark, whereas a pit-barbecue restaurant located on an interstate highway was found eligible.

Companies meeting these criteria submit a written application form (obtainable from the PTO), along with a filing fee and a drawing of the service mark; those businesses basing their application on prior use must also submit samples—brochures, advertisements, business cards—of the mark's use in commerce. The PTO then reviews the application, gives it a serial number, and assigns an examining attorney to determine whether the mark can be registered; if it

can, the PTO publishes the mark in the weekly *Official Gazette,* giving other parties a chance to oppose the registration. In time, successful applicants are issued a certificate of registration.

The PTO maintains two registers, principal and supplemental, the former conferring more rights than the latter. The PTO also specifies eight categories of services for which applicants can apply for registration of a service mark. Applicants should contact the PTO for current information regarding filing fees, which are subject to change.

The PTO's examining attorneys can refuse registration for various reasons—among them that a mark is merely ornamental or descriptive, that it's disparaging or deceptive, or that it too closely resembles a mark already registered. Thus, a key part of the examining attorney's job is to search the PTO's library of existing and pending service marks to ascertain whether an applicant's mark conflicts with marks already in use.

Companies in the process of choosing a service mark are advised to conduct a preliminary search to verify that the mark hasn't already obtained national, state, or other rights. To aid in such efforts, the PTO maintains a trademark search library in Arlington, Virginia. Alternatively, companies can conduct a search through a patent and trademark depository library, available in most states, or hire an attorney or search firm to conduct the search, in which case companies can contact local bar associations for a list of attorneys who specialize in trademark law or consult the Yellow Pages under Trademark Search Services to locate search firms.

In selecting a service mark, Field recommends choosing a strong name, an original mark, an "arbitrary or fanciful" mark, or one conveying a positive image; he cautions against marks that are descriptive or misdescriptive or that are surnames or geographic names. Companies should also avoid marks bearing similarity to others' marks; McDonald's restaurants, for instance, won an infringement suit against a chain of motels using the name McSleep.

It should be noted that while any business can use the service mark symbol (SM) without obtaining federal registration of a service mark, only federally certified registrants are entitled to use the registration symbol (®) or, as alternatives, the phrases "Registered in U.S. Patent and Trademark Office" or "Reg. U.S. Pat. & Tm. Off."

[Roberta H. Winston]

FURTHER READING:

Borchard, William. *Trademark Basics*. New York: International Trademark Association, 1995.
Everyone's Guide to Copyrights, Trademarks, and Patents: Philadelphia: Running Press, 1990.

Field, Thomas G., Jr. *Trademarks and Business Goodwill.* Washington, D.C.: Office of Business Development, U.S. Small Business Administration, 1990.

Rolfe, Robin. "Making Your Mark." *Association of Management.* August, 1992, pp. 101-102.

"Single-Location Business Can Get Service Mark Protection for Its Name." *Profit-Building Strategies for Business Owners.* June, 1991, p. 12.

Stim, Richard. *Intellectual Property: Patents, Trademarks, and Copyrights.* Albany, NY: Lawyers Cooperative Publishing/Delmar Publishers.

U.S. Department of Commerce/Patent and Trademark Office. *Basic Facts about Registering a Trademark.* Washington, D.C., 1994.

SEX DISCRIMINATION

Sex or gender discrimination in the United States has a long tradition, partaking of a much wider phenomenon of discrimination against women that is both ancient and global. Only recently have social movements and laws in some countries recognized the right of women to own property, vote, marry whom they choose, limit the number of children they will bear, or have equal opportunities in the workplace. Such equal opportunity laws are gender-neutral, and tend to allow for claims of discrimination by men on the basis of gender, but the vast majority of cases involve discrimination against women. Historically, the common law of most states allowed employers to hire and fire "at will" unless their right to do so was limited by contract or statute. Under this system, white men dominated the labor market.

It was also common for states to legislatively limit the kinds of work that women could do. The usual justification for such laws was the protection of women, yet the prohibited jobs typically paid considerably more. But during World War II, the contribution of women in industry to the war effort became obvious, and it was more and more difficult to maintain arguments based on "protection." In 1964, during debate on Title VII of the Civil Rights Act, a southern legislator and civil rights opponent, Judge Howard Smith, offered to amend Title VII by including "sex" as a prohibited basis of discrimination in hiring, firing, or working conditions. His hope was to weaken the bill, which was primarily directed at problems of racial inequality, but the bill passed anyway.

Title VII's prohibitions on sex discrimination have given significant help to women seeking equality in the workplace. Yet 30 years after passage of Title VII, nearly 80 percent of female workers were in "women's work," as secretaries, administrative support workers, and salesclerks. In 1993, only 19 of the 4,000 Fortune 500 officers and directors were women, and more than half the Fortune 500 boards had no women as members. A 1989 *New York Times* poll of women found that job discrimination was "the most important problem facing women today." Despite significant gains among women in U.S. business and political life by 1990, 80 to 90 percent of women said they suffered from job discrimination and unequal pay, and gender discrimination charges filed with the **Equal Employment Opportunity Commission (EEOC)** rose nearly 25 percent in the 1980s. When Congress revisited civil rights legislation in 1991, its amendments to the 1964 Civil Rights Act included the establishment of a Glass Ceiling Commission to investigate barriers to female and minority advancement in the workplace.

Worldwide, a comprehensive 1989 survey of women concluded that in most countries women were "poor, pregnant, and powerless." In many countries, women are still regarded as the property of men, are denied access to birth control information, are not allowed to vote, and are prohibited from working with men. In patriarchal societies, being born female can be fatal, as male children are greatly preferred. In many countries, young girls (and some boys) are sold by their families into the prostitution trade.

Many of these countries have subscribed to the Convention on the Elimination of All Forms of Discrimination against Women, adopted by the **United Nations** General Assembly in 1979. Article 2 of the Convention provides that states agree to pursue a policy of eliminating discrimination against women and take appropriate measures, including legislation, to modify or abolish existing laws, regulations, customs, and practices that constitute discrimination against women. Yet in subscribing to the Convention, many countries note that they will not adhere to Article 2's direction. In Europe, specific laws have been enacted with the aim of ameliorating the effects of gender discrimination. What follows is a discussion of the specific rights created by U.S. law relating to sex discrimination in the workplace.

U.S. FEDERAL LAWS MANDATING GENDER EQUALITY IN THE WORKPLACE

Title VII of the Civil Rights Act of 1964 is the primary federal law establishing gender equality in the workplace. The other laws are the Equal Pay Act of 1963 and Executive Order 11246. Title VII and the Equal Pay Act were established in accordance with Congress's powers under the Commerce Clause of the U.S. Constitution; employment discrimination was deemed by Congress to sufficiently affect interstate commerce, and the exercise of federal power in this area has been upheld by the courts as constitutional.

EQUAL PAY ACT. The Equal Pay Act of 1963 forbids only sex discrimination regarding pay, directing that men and women doing equal work are to receive equal pay. While the terms of the legislation are gender-neutral, and men could conceivably be plaintiffs, the typical plaintiff is a woman, and she must show the court that she has received lower pay than a male employee who performed substantially the same work for the same employer. "Substantial equivalence" can be shown where the two jobs involve (1) equal effort, (2) equal skill, (3) equal responsibility, and (4) similar working conditions. Once these elements are established by the plaintiff, the defendant may show that the pay disparity is justified by (1) seniority, (2) merit, (3) quality or quantity of production, and (4) any factor other than sex. For any of the first three defenses, employers cannot rely on subjective estimates but must offer fairly precise criteria that are equally applied and communicated to all employees. The fourth defense is a catch-all category, which may include practices such as paying more for certain less-desirable shifts.

Remedies for successful claimants under the Equal Pay Act include recovery of back pay. Plaintiffs may also receive an equal amount as liquidated damages. Unlike Title VII actions, claimants need not pursue administrative remedies through the EEOC, even though the EEOC enforces the Equal Pay Act.

EXECUTIVE ORDER 11246. Under Executive Order 11246, first signed into law by President Lyndon B. Johnson in 1965, employers who contract to furnish the federal government with goods and services of $10,000 or more must agree not to discriminate against employees on the basis of race, color, religion, gender, or national origin. For the smallest contracts, employers must agree that they will not discriminate in soliciting, hiring, training, and retaining employees, and will post notices that it is an equal opportunity employer. These notices must be posted in conspicuous places. Small contractors must also agree to certain record-keeping and inspection requirements.

If a contractor has 50 or more employees and a nonconstruction contract of $50,000 or more, the contractor must develop an **affirmative action** plan within 120 days of the beginning of the contract. Many of the "voluntary" affirmative action programs (those plans not mandated by a court order after pervasive patterns of discriminatory conduct are found) arise from the mandate of Executive Order 11246, which has remained in force through the successive presidencies of Presidents Nixon, Ford, Carter, Reagan, Bush, and Clinton. The listed strategies for complying with Executive Order 11246 include a workplace assessment in which the employer lists how many women are in each of seven categories, from unskilled workers to managers. Employers must compare the percentage of women in these positions with the percentage of such qualified employees available in the appropriate geographic area.

The executive order is enforced by the Office of Federal Contract Compliance Programs (OFCCP) in the U.S. Department of Labor. The OFCCP issues numerous regulations to implement the order. Penalties for noncompliance include publishing the names of nonconforming contractors, recommending to the EEOC or U.S. Department of Justice that proceedings be instituted under Title VII, canceling or suspending the contract (either absolutely or conditionally, depending on future compliance with affirmative action plans), or (only rarely) barring the contractor from entering into further government contracts until the secretary of labor is satisfied that equal opportunity/affirmative action will be realized at the contractor's place of business.

TITLE VII. The Civil Rights Act of 1964 was intended to discourage discrimination on various "suspect" bases in a variety of settings. The suspect bases are race, color, religion, sex, or national origin. Title II, for example, prohibits discrimination on all five suspect basis in public accommodations (such as hotels, motels, restaurants), while Title IX prohibits discrimination on the same bases in public education. The essence of Title VII is to discourage employment discrimination on any of the suspect bases.

Section 703 of Title VII makes it an unlawful employment practice: "to fail or refuse to hire or to discharge any individual, or otherwise to discriminate against any individual with respect to his compensation, terms, conditions, or privileges of employment, because of such individual's race, color, religion, sex, or national origin." Thus, the law covers employer discrimination in hiring, promotion, or firing, or working conditions such as training, pay, discipline, layoffs, and benefits. Similar provisions apply to labor organizations (unions), and employment agencies must not classify, refer, or fail to refer people to others on any of the suspect bases. Employers are also forbidden to retaliate against any employee who makes a charge, testifies, or otherwise participates in an investigation or hearing under the act or opposes any unlawful practice.

Several exceptions were made. If an employee is a member of the Communist Party of the United States or of any other organization considered a "Communist-action or Communist-front organization," discrimination is not unlawful. Nor is discrimination on any of the suspect bases unlawful where the job "is subject to any requirement imposed in the interest of national security of the United States."

Other exceptions are more likely to apply. Title VII allows for unintentional discrimination that arises from a bona fide seniority or merit system. It also provides an exception where religion, sex, or national origin is a bona fide occupational qualification (BFOQ) ''reasonably necessary to the normal operation of that particular business or enterprise.'' Thus, a Jewish synagogue need not seriously consider a Baptist minister for possible employment, and may impose a religious affiliation requirement for its hiring process. But the exception is very limited. The courts have allowed use of the BFOQ exception when an acting part is cast as male or female. But airlines were not successful in claiming that males would not be suitable as flight attendants. If persons of one sex can perform the essential functions of the job as well as persons of the other sex, the BFOQ exception will ordinarily not justify gender discrimination.

Title VII applies to private employers with 15 or more employees, **labor unions** with 15 or more members, employment agencies, state and local governments, public and private educational institutions, and the federal government (including, most recently, Congress itself). Title VII has been amended several times with the Equal Employment Opportunity Act of 1972 and the Pregnancy Discrimination Act of 1978. The 1978 amendment added pregnancy discrimination as a type of gender discrimination. The 1972 amendment widened Title VII's coverage to include government employees and strengthened the powers of the Equal Employment Opportunity Commission (EEOC), the agency charged with enforcement of Title VII. Amendments in 1991, among other things, (1) allowed recovery of compensatory and punitive damages, rather than just back pay; (2) allowed jury trials where compensatory or punitive damages are sought; and (3) extended Title VII's application beyond U.S. boundaries to include U.S. citizens working for U.S. companies abroad.

THE EQUAL EMPLOYMENT OPPORTUNITY COMMISSION. The Civil Rights Act of 1964 not only set substantive limits on workplace discrimination but also created an administrative agency to enforce the act. The EEOC is composed of five members, not more than three of whom may be members of the same political party. The members are appointed by the president with the advice and consent of the Senate; each serves a five-year term. The EEOC has authority to set guidelines for adherence to the Civil Rights Act of 1964, as well as other legislation such as the Age Discrimination in Employment Act of 1967 and the **Americans with Disabilities Act**. It has authority to hold hearings, obtain evidence, and subpoena and examine witnesses under oath.

An aggrieved employee or the EEOC may file a civil lawsuit to complain of discriminatory acts by an employer, labor union, or employment agency. First, however, each must exhaust administrative efforts to settle the claim. An employee must file a complaint to the EEOC within 540 days of the alleged unlawful practice; the EEOC then serves notice of the charge to the employer within ten days. The EEOC will investigate the complaint by talking with both the employer and employee (or ex-employee). (A claimant who remains an employee has some protection from the anti-retaliatory provisions of Title VII, which makes it a separate offense for an employer to retaliate against any employees pursuing their rights under Title VII.) After investigating the complaint, the EEOC may find that there is no cause, and will issue a right to sue letter. The claimant, having exhausted administrative remedies, must then file a lawsuit within 90 days in federal or state court or lose the right to pursue a Title VII action. Claimants also have a right to sue if the EEOC does not act on the complaint within a certain time.

The EEOC may, however, find reasonable cause to charge the employer with discrimination, and will attempt to conciliate the matter in an informal way. Conciliated resolution of Title VII disputes may include the employer's agreement to write a favorable letter of recommendation, to reinstate, or promote or to adjust the pay or working conditions. If no conciliation is made, the EEOC may file a civil action.

Whether the EEOC brings an action or whether the claimant brings an action, the usual remedies sought include back pay awarded for time an employee was not working because of illegal discrimination, and front pay for time an employee would have been in a job were it not for the illegal discrimination. Both such remedies are aimed at making the claimant ''whole''; that is, putting the claimant in approximately the same economic position that she or he would have been in had the illegal discrimination not occurred.

To such damages the **Civil Rights Act of 1991** added compensatory damages and punitive damages as possible remedies. Compensatory damages could include emotional pain, suffering, inconvenience, mental anguish, and other nonpecuniary losses. Punitive damages are allowed when the employer's acts are malicious or done with reckless indifference to the employee's Title VII rights. Both compensatory and punitive damages are capped at various levels. For employer with:

- 15 to 100 employees, there is a cap of $50,000.

- 101 to 200 employees, there is a cap of $100,000.

- 201 to 500 employees, there is a cap of $200,000.

- More than 500 employees, there is a cap of $300,000.

TITLE VII LAWSUITS. To win a Title VII sex discrimination lawsuit, a plaintiff must show that actions taken by the employer were based on gender. Generally, two types of cases are distinguished: the disparate treatment allegation (in which the plaintiff must convince the court that the employer intentionally discriminated against the plaintiff) and the disparate impact allegation (in which the plaintiff must show that the employer's seemingly neutral or nondiscriminatory acts, policies, or practices had a disproportionately negative impact on women in that particular workplace). Sexual harassment cases are a variety of disparate treatment cases; the essential allegation is that the plaintiff has been treated differently by the employer because of her gender.

A MODEL DISPARATE TREATMENT CASE

If an employer intentionally treats minority applicants or employees differently from the majority group, based on their sex, that would be disparate treatment under guidelines established by the EEOC, the U.S. Civil Service Commission, the U.S. Department of Labor, and the U.S. Department of Justice. These four agencies have a common set of rules for interpreting and enforcing the Civil Rights Act—the Uniform Guidelines on Employee Selection Procedures. Sexual harassment is a type of disparate treatment case because the victim would not have suffered the harassing conduct except for her (or his) sex. In *McDonnell Douglas Corp. v. Green* in 1973, the Supreme Court established a four-step decision rule for inferring intentional discrimination in disparate treatment cases involving hiring decisions:

1. plaintiff belongs to a protected classification;

2. plaintiff applied for and was qualified for a job for which employer was seeking applicants;

3. despite their qualifications, they were rejected; and

4. after their rejection, the position remained open and the employer continued to seek applicants from persons of complainant's qualifications.

Similar yet somewhat different proofs must be offered by plaintiffs who are aggrieved by promotion or layoff decisions or working conditions, where the gender of the plaintiff is alleged to be the primary cause of the nonpromotion, layoff, or adverse working condition. Adverse working conditions may include conditions of sexual harassment.

SEXUAL HARASSMENT CASES. Sexual harassment cases are, in essence, claims of disparate treatment under Title VII. The employee's complaint is typically based on a perceived difference in treatment based on gender. Sexual harassment claims are either *quid pro quo* or hostile working environment claims. A *quid pro quo* claim alleges that the employer re-

quired favors of a sexual nature in exchange for continued employment or in exchange for certain working conditions. If, for example, an employer asks an employee to kiss him or her or have sex with him or her, and makes such behavior a requirement of continued employment, a *quid pro quo* claim of sexual harassment is evident. But if there is no physical contact between employer and employee, there may still be sexual harassment under the hostile working environment type of claim. If an employer repeatedly makes comments of a sexual nature or leers at employees, he or she may be liable for creating a hostile working environment.

The "employer" in either *quid pro quo* or hostile working environment claims can include any managerial or supervisory employee who engages in sexual harassment, and can also include co-workers who sexually harass. The Supreme Court determined in *Meritor Savings v. Vinson* (1986) that, in general, agency principles would apply, and that a company would generally be responsible for the acts of its employees as agents; still, the court was willing to consider that a company might not actually have knowledge of sexually harassing behavior on the part of its employees, and that this might operate as a defense to liability. The Court cautioned, however, that businesses cannot simply insulate themselves from liability by making it difficult for upper management to know about sexual harassment allegations; businesses should have some means for aggrieved employees to make complaints of sexual harassment, should have a clearly stated policy covering sexual harassment, and must enable employees to bypass a harassing supervisor in order to make a complaint.

Prior the Supreme Court's decision in *Harris v. Forklift Systems, Inc.* (1993), many federal circuit courts of appeal had used a "reasonable woman" standard in sexual harassment cases. The use of such a standard, in contrast to a "reasonable person" standard, requires that the alleged sexual harassment of a woman be judged on a gender-specific basis. That is, the particular sensibilities of women would be acknowledged by the courts in evaluating whether the alleged harassment was actionable under Title VII as a form of sex discrimination in the workplace. Legal scholars and social critics had either hailed or condemned the use of the "reasonable woman" standard. Supporters of the standard believed it was the only feasible way to reverse the reality that many men have been brought up to believe that gender abuse and harassment is their birthright; critics believed that a gender-specific standard was needlessly divisive and would tend to elevate relatively trivial forms of workplace harassment into a federal cases and "chill" the exercise of free speech and normal social intercourse.

But in *Harris v. Forklift Systems, Inc.*, the Supreme Court laid the "reasonable woman" standard to rest. On appeal, the plaintiff sought to undo the lower court's requirement that she prove "psychological harm" from the harassment. The Court, speaking through Justice Sandra Day O'Connor, firmly rejected any such requirement in Title VII sexual harassment cases. Without addressing the "reasonable woman" standard directly, O'Connor's opinion clearly embraced the "reasonable person" standard in saying that "Conduct that is not severe or pervasive enough to create an objectively hostile or abusive work environment—an environment that a reasonable person would find hostile or abusive—is beyond Title VII's purview."

In *Harris v. Forklift Systems*, the owner/manager allegedly made numerous sexual innuendoes about Harris's and other women's clothing, suggested that he and Harris "go to the Holiday Inn" to negotiate her raise, and occasionally asked female employees (including Harris) to get coins from his front pants pocket. At least once, Harris was called a "dumb ass woman." The owner/manager also threw objects on the ground in front of female employees and asked them to pick up the objects.

In finding that no proof of psychological injury was required, the Supreme Court tried to steer a "middle path between making actionable any conduct that is merely offensive and requiring the conduct to cause tangible psychological injury." But the Court disavowed any set criteria, other than the "test" that "so long as the environment would reasonably be perceived, and is perceived, as hostile or abusive" there may be sexual harassment without a finding of psychological injury. O'Connor continued:

> But we can say that whether an environment is "hostile" or "abusive" can be determined only by looking at all the circumstances. These may include the frequency of the discriminatory conduct; its severity, whether it is physically threatening or humiliating, or a mere offensive utterance; and whether it unreasonably interferes with an employee's work performance.... while psychological harm, like any other relevant factor, may be taken into account, no single factor is required.

True to the dictates of judicial conservatism, the Court has avoided deciding cases not before it; the tradition of case-by-case analysis by "looking at all the circumstances" is invoked, leaving managers and organizations with scant guidance. Given that under the Civil Rights Act of 1991, Title VII cases can now take place before juries empowered to award punitive damages, a certain confused caution may be the order of the day for business organizations. Lacking more specific guidance, businesses are likely to err on the side of protecting all sensibilities, however fragile or idiosyncratic. A prudent set of policies would include a systematic yet unintrusive survey of employee attitudes about what kinds of speech and behaviors are perceived and harassing and which are not. Such surveys, fortunately, are available.

A MODEL DISPARATE IMPACT CASE

Disparate impact cases are somewhat different from disparate treatment: showing an intent to discriminate is not a necessary part of plaintiff's burden of proof. In effect, an employer may have a policy or practice that, on its face, is seemingly neutral as to gender. In practice, however, the policy may systematically disadvantage applicants or employees of a particular sex.

In the leading case on disparate treatment, *Duke Power Co. v. Griggs*, the Supreme Court found that the company's policy of requiring a high school diploma or passing an high school achievement test was seemingly neutral, yet disproportionately affected African-American employees and applicants. Plaintiffs prevailed even though there was no showing of an intent to discriminate. In sex discrimination cases, certain policies that, for example, require employees to be able to lift 80 pounds deadweight from a standing position would be facially neutral, yet may disproportionately affect the chances women might have to gain employment. Yet the facially neutral requirement may be reasonable, in which case the courts will allow a defense of business necessity. Business necessity as a defense in disparate impact cases requires that the employer show (1) that qualities measured by the test or requirement are, in good faith, reasonably necessary to an adequate performance at the job in question, and that (2) any test actually examines what it purports to examine, is valid, and measures accurately what it purports to measure. The EEOC specifies three forms of test validation under its 1978 Uniform Guidelines on Employee Selection Procedures.

Yet there are many policies and practices that may have a disparate impact that are not as clearly defined as a test or requirement. Candidates for mid-level and upper-level management are usually not evaluated by tests or specific requirements; they are typically chosen by rather more subjective methods. Such methods are difficult for disadvantaged employees to pin down, yet the courts require that a specific practice or policy that is the cause of the disproportionate impact must be identified. Statistical evidence alone—even where the workforce is nowhere near representing the racial and gender mix of eligible and available employees—will generally not suffice to establish disparate impact. More is required: the identification of a specific policy, practice, or procedure which disadvantages the complainant(s). Moreover, that practice or policy must be causally related to the impact shown.

AFFIRMATIVE ACTION AND REVERSE DISCRIMINATION

In disparate treatment cases, the issues of affirmative action and reverse discrimination may arise. A company which has intentionally and systematically excluded people of one sex from its workplace may find itself sued under Title VII and ordered to institute an affirmative action plan under court supervision. A company which is fearful of litigation over its personnel practices may decide to have a voluntary affirmative action program designed to increase the representation of previously excluded minorities, including women (or men). Voluntary affirmative action plans have been challenged in court as a kind of reverse discrimination: a male who is passed over for promotion in favor of a female may claim disparate treatment, and the court must determine whether the voluntary affirmative action plan is valid. The Supreme Court will generally allow an affirmative action plan in any case where the plan (1) is temporary, designed to attain rather than permanently maintain some balance in the workforce; (2) does not impose rigid quotas setting aside a certain number of positions for women; (3) does not bar affected males, in the long-term, from further advancement; and (4) has the purpose of correctting manifest, long-standing imbalances in the employer's workforce.

Affirmative action has been controversial in contexts of both race and gender. Any forced changes in the status quo are likely to produce some backlash; moreover, many people object to using some form of discrimination to end discrimination, and many others are not convinced of the long-term utility of affirmative action for women or people of color. Title VII specifically allows affirmative action, but there are likely to be some new limits placed on its use by Congress.

STATE LAWS ON SEX DISCRIMINATION

The majority of states also have laws prohibiting discrimination by employers on the basis of race, sex, or religion, as well as discrimination on a variety of other grounds. Michigan's Elliott-Larsen Act, for example, prohibits discrimination on the grounds of obesity if the employee is otherwise capable of performing his or her assigned tasks. Such state laws are not preempted by federal law in Title VII, since Congress neither stated nor implied that states could not also regulate on the subject of job discrimination. Thus, some state laws on equal opportunity could provide different or even more generous remedies to affected employees, and could protect classes of employees not otherwise protected by Title VII.

A potential claimant may thus pursue both federal and state remedies. Typically, states have their own agencies to administer and enforce nondiscrimination laws. Under Section 706 of the Civil Rights Act of 1964, state agencies may contract with the EEOC to be a "706" agency and process claims of discrimination for the EEOC in addition to state-based claims. If a claimant comes to the EEOC when there is a 706 agency in the jurisdiction, EEOC must defer to that agency for 60 days before beginning its investigation.

In filing suit, Title VII claimants with right-to-sue letters typically resort to federal district courts within the applicable time limits. If a plaintiff has a state claim as well, the state claim will be heard as part of the federal courts' pendant jurisdiction. But a state court may hear a Title VII claim unaccompanied by a state claim, since state courts have concurrent jurisdiction of all types of claims unless exclusive jurisdiction resides with the federal courts. In passing Title VII, Congress empowered federal courts to hear complaints of job discrimination based on race, color, sex, religion, and national origin, but did not limit the available post-EEOC dispute resolution forums to the federal courts. Thus, state courts and arbitral forums are also available for the resolution of Title VII claims.

ARBITRATION OF EMPLOYMENT DISCRIMINATION CLAIMS

In Section 118 of the Civil Rights Act of 1991, Congress encouraged the use of alternative dispute resolution mechanisms to settle claims of job discrimination. Earlier that year, the Supreme Court had interpreted the Federal Arbitration Act to require an employee to arbitrate an age discrimination claim even though he preferred to litigate in federal court (*Gilmer v. Interstate/Johnson-Lane*). In one of many documents signed as part of his application for employment, Gilmer had unknowingly agreed to arbitration of any disputes arising between him and his employer. After the alleged discrimination, resulting in his discharge, Gilmer sued but was compelled to arbitrate his age discrimination claim instead of having it heard by the federal court. Since the Gilmer case was decided, federal courts have overwhelmingly enforced predispute arbitration agreements where sex discrimination or other Title VII causes of action are alleged.

Only a few courts have made exceptions. In *Prudential Ins. Co. of America v. Lai and Viernes et. al.* (1994), the Ninth Circuit Court of Appeals determined not to enforce a predispute arbitration clause where the plaintiffs had no opportunity to read the forms they signed, where they were told they were applying to take a test, and where arbitration was never mentioned. Until the Supreme Court speaks to these issues, prudent employers desiring arbitration of sex discrimination claims are well-advised to make full disclosure of any predispute arbitration agreements.

Courts are also grappling with the extent to which arbitrators may award punitive damages. Predispute arbitration agreements, particularly in the securities industry, choose New York state law as the basis for interpreting the agreement. Under New York law, however, public policy prevents arbitrators from awarding punitive damages. In 1995, the Supreme Court decided *Mastrobuonno v. Shearson Lehman* and directed courts to allow arbitrators to award punitive damages unless the parties had clearly agreed that the arbitrator had no power to do so.

EXTRATERRITORIAL APPLICATION OF TITLE VII

In the 1991 amendments to Title VII, Congress also made clear that the law applies outside U.S. boundaries, but only where the claimant is a U.S. citizen and the employer is a U.S. company. Earlier that year, the Supreme Court had held that the Title VII claim of a U.S. citizen should be dismissed where the discriminatory actions by a company incorporated in the United States had taken place in Saudi Arabia. (*EEOC v. Boureslan*). Under international law, nations have the power to prescribe and enforce laws beyond their borders with respect to acts by their citizens (nationals). Where a U.S. company is subject to laws in a host country that would prevent the hiring of women for certain jobs, the bona fide occupational qualification (BFOQ) exception would resolve the conflict between Title VII and the host country's law. In one case, a U.S. citizen tried to use Title VII to recover damages because he had not been employed to fly planes to Mecca. But the plaintiff was a Baptist, and Saudi Arabian law required that anyone in Mecca must be Islamic. The defendant U.S. company had imposed the same requirement, and the Court held that its requirement was a BFOQ (*Kern v. Dynalectron*). The more difficult cases will arise when the U.S.-based company encounters cultural norms hostile to gender equality.

SEE ALSO: Civil Rights Act of 1991; Handbooks and Manuals

[Donald O. Mayer]

FURTHER READING:

Aaron, Titus E. *Sexual Harassment in the Workplace: A Guide to the Law and a Research Overview for Employers and Employees.* Jefferson, NC: McFarland, 1993.

Bennett-Alexander, Dawn D., and Laura B. Pincus. *Employment Law for Business.* Irwin, 1995.

Bureau of National Affairs. *Sex Discrimination Handbook.* Washington, DC: BNA Books, 1992.

Clark, Belinda. "The Vienna Convention Reservations Regime and the Convention on Discrimination against Women" *American Journal of International Law.* Vol. 85, p. 81.

Docksey, Christopher A. "Sex Discrimination in Britain, the United States, and the European Community" *Denver Journal of International Law and Policy.* Vol. 13, 1984, p. 181.

Mayer, Donald, and Kenneth York. *In Search of the Reasonable Person Standard after Harris v. Forklift Systems: Use of Surveys to Determine Contemporary Community Standards.* Academy of Management National Proceedings, 1994.

Otten, Laura A. *Women's Rights and the Law.* Westport, CT: Praeger, 1993.

Rhoodie, Eschel. *Discrimination against Women: A Gobal Survey of the Economic, Educational, Social, and Political Status of Women.* Jefferson, N.C.: McFarland, 1989.

Thomas, Claire Sherman. *Sex Discrimination in a Nutshell.* St. Paul, MN: West Publishing, 1991.

Velasquez, Manuel. *Business Ethics: Concepts and Cases.* Englewood Cliffs: Prentice Hall, 1993, pp. 319-36.

York, K. M. "Defining Sexual Harassment in Workplace: A Policy-Capturing Approach." *Academy of Management Journal.* 1989, pp. 830-850.

U.S. Supreme Court, 1993: *Harris v. Forklift Systems, Inc.* United States Law Week (Bureau of National Affairs), p. 4004.

U.S. Supreme Court, 1986: *Meritor Savings Bank v. Vinson*, Vol. 477 United States Reports, p. 57.

SEXUAL HARASSMENT

Sexual harassment is the term given to two particular types of illegal discrimination in the workplace. Both of these involve behavior which subjects people of one gender to job conditions which those of the other gender do not face. This creates a situation which takes away the worker's right to equal employment opportunity, a violation of employment discrimination laws.

The federal law which covers sexual harassment is Title VII of the Civil Rights Act of 1964. Title VII makes it illegal for employers or their agents to discriminate in the compensation, terms, conditions, or privileges of employment on the basis of the employee's race, color, national origin, religion, or sex. Labor organizations and employment agencies are also covered by Title VII with regard to their dealings with members and prospective employees. Many states also have laws which prohibit sex discrimination in workplaces within that state. Sexual harassment has been determined by the courts to be discrimination on the basis of sex and, thus, is deemed to be illegal in the employment setting.

At the federal level, the **Equal Employment Opportunity Commission (EEOC)** handles sexual harassment complaints, and employees are required to file a charge with the EEOC before taking a case to court under Title VII. Sometimes the EEOC will mediate the complaint and in other situations it will grant the party the right to file a lawsuit, giving them a ''right to sue'' letter. Generally, a complaint must be filed with the EEOC within 180 days after the last alleged incident of harassment occurred, with some differing requirements when state law proceedings are also being undertaken. State laws vary with regard to filing requirements, with some states allowing an employee to institute a lawsuit without filing a formal charge with a state agency.

One of the two types of sexual harassment being alleged in lawsuits today is called *quid pro quo* harassment. *Quid pro quo* is a contract term which means ''something for something.'' Usually in this type of discrimination, a person with authority in the workplace offers a subordinate some sort of employment benefit in return for sexual favors. If the employee refuses, he or she stands to suffer some detrimental consequences and, thus, is subjected to employment conditions because of his or her sex which other employees do not face. The employment benefits offered in return for the sexual favors vary in the many cases in which *quid pro quo* has been alleged, ranging from the granting of a job promotion to a promise not to give an unsatisfactory job evaluation which had otherwise been contemplated. Often, employees also allege that they were fired because they did not give in to a supervisor's demands.

In order to prove a *quid pro quo* case, an employee must generally give credible evidence which shows: that someone with authority made such a demand; that the employee was denied some workplace benefit—such as an available promotion—or was subjected to some other detrimental economic consequences—such as a bad evaluation or demotion—by the person making the demand; and that the employee was entitled to the benefit or did not otherwise deserve the adverse treatment. The employer must then show evidence of a legitimate or non-discriminatory reason for the denial of the benefit or for the detrimental economic consequences. For example, an employer might show that the employee was discharged for unsatisfactory job performance, rather than for refusing to agree to the illegal terms of employment. If the court is satisfied that there is adequate proof of a legitimate reason, then the employee is given the opportunity to show that the employer's reasons are a pretext or a cover-up for what was really an illegal practice. Often, this means showing that others in the workplace with identical work records were not denied this benefit or that the evidence given by the employer is offset by conflicting evidence or by extenuating circumstances. Recently, the Supreme Court opinion in *Hopkins v. Price Waterhouse* has also been used as a precedent for courts to allow an employee to win a case, even if there is a mixed reason for the

decision: one legitimate and one discriminatory. In such a situation, once an employee has proven that the illegal condition of employment at least played a part in the consequences he or she suffered, then the employer must prove that the same decision would have been made if the employee's refusal had not been taken into consideration.

The situation is somewhat different when an employee goes along with the *quid pro quo* offer and then files a case. Courts often view these cases as ''hostile environment'' situations, a second type of sexual harassment which will be discussed later in this article.

If the employee is able to prove that, in fact, they were subjected to this illegal term of employment, the employer will find itself strictly liable for the supervisor's actions. This means that even if the employer did not know of the situation or had a policy which prohibits this, if it happens and the employee suffers a detriment, the employer must pay the damages. Under the amendments to Title VII passed in 1991, these damages, in a federal lawsuit, can now include money for the pain and suffering of the employee, as well as backpay or front pay, which is designed to help the employee with expenses while he or she finds another job. In addition, an employee who is successful in a lawsuit is entitled to reinstatement, lost seniority, a court order to stop the discrimination, his or her attorney fees, and court costs. Most states which provide protection against discrimination, also allow for these types of damages.

Quid pro quo cases were the first type of cases to be filed with regard to sexual harassment. Most sexual harassment lawsuits filed by men are of the *quid pro quo* type, although women continue to be the victims in most cases. Another type of case, however, has been almost exclusively filed by women because of its unique nature. It was not until about 1981 that this new type of lawsuit began to appear. These cases did not allege that there was a tangible economic workplace benefit offered or a threat of detrimental action made but, rather, that the atmosphere in the workplace was adverse to the success of people of one gender. These cases are known as the ''hostile or intimidating work environment'' cases and for some years, the courts were unsure if they were, in fact, allowable under the laws against discrimination. In 1986, the United States Supreme Court settled the matter in the federal courts by deciding, in the case of *Vinson v. Meritor Savings Bank*, that such lawsuits could be filed under Title VII.

The *Vinson* case was representative of the types of cases in which hostile environment was originally alleged. The woman making the claim of discrimination worked in a bank and was subjected by her supervisor to continual sexual advances, up to and including what amounted to several instances of rape. Because there was no direct economic benefit offered to the woman, nor were any overt threats made of economic consequences if she did not go along with the situation, the lower court had decided that she could not prove a *quid pro quo* discrimination case. The woman claimed, however, that the actions of her supervisor created an environment for her which was discriminatory because the men at the bank did not have to put up with this type of behavior. As she put it, her workplace was hostile and intimidating and she was being subjected to conditions of employment which differed from those of males. In other words, the supervisor's conduct created an environment which made it harder for her to carry on her daily work or to succeed than for the men. This, she contended, meant that her employer was violating Title VII.

The Supreme Court agreed with the woman and set a precedent which continues to expand. The Court stated that certain workplace conduct could be viewed as affecting a term, condition, or privilege of employment when it reached the level of being severe or pervasive. In other words, conduct becomes sexual harassment under the legal definition when it alters the conditions of employment for one gender and creates an abusive work environment. Many people contend that this type of harassment is used as a power play and has little to do with sexuality. By using certain behaviors to intimidate, humiliate, or place someone in an uncomfortable position, the harasser can get the ''upper'' hand and make the victim feel that they do not belong at the work site or that they are inferior or subordinate to the person or people involved in the harassing behavior.

Since the *Vinson* case, the courts have continued to expand the definition of hostile environment harassment. At first, as in the *Vinson* case, only conduct which could be viewed as criminal sexual abuse was seen as serious enough to alter the conditions of employment. Recently, however, many judges have accepted the argument of some victims that such conduct as hanging ''girlie'' calendars, pestering someone with requests for dates, making unwanted comments about a person's appearance, or touching someone where they do not wish to be touched can also create an environment which is not conducive to one gender or the other. Usually, as stated earlier, this means that it creates an environment which makes it more difficult for women to succeed than for men.

A common misconception about hostile environment sexual harassment is that it involves conduct which is only sexual in nature. This is not true, although certainly sexual behavior can create a discriminatory work environment. In addition, any demeaning behavior, such as comments or actions which portray a belief that one gender is inferior in the workplace or conduct designed to belittle or humiliate is also sexual harassment. This is because, in fact, what is prohibited is harassment based on gender and that can take many forms.

In order to prove a hostile environment sexual harassment case against an employer, a party bringing a claim must, generally speaking, prove three elements: that the conduct was pervasive, that it was unwelcome, and that the employer is liable for the conduct. All three must be proven for a claim to be successful.

Pervasive simply means that the conduct was not merely annoying or trivial but that it was severe enough to create an environment where one gender is denied an equal opportunity to succeed. The courts will look at the severity of the conduct, its frequency, and its intensity in making this determination but, as time passes, less and less is being required before a court concludes that conditions of employment have been altered.

One of the problems with this area of the law is that it is not precise and is not subject to hard and fast rules. This is especially true with regard to the ''pervasive'' element. What conduct does create this type of environment? What is appropriate behavior and what behavior denies someone equal opportunity? How much harassing behavior must occur before the environment becomes hostile? The Supreme Court has not given much direction in this regard, stating only that every case must be judged on its own facts and on the totality of the circumstances. This has, of course, resulted in some widely varying decisions, although all courts do seem to be moving more and more toward finding hostile environments exist when the behavior might have once been termed ''trivial.''

Before 1993, some courts had been requiring that the conduct be severe enough to seriously affect the psychological well-being of the reasonable employee, but in that year, the Supreme Court made it clear that this was too strict a standard. The key, according to the high court in the case of *Harris v. Forklift Systems, Inc.*, is whether the conduct is adequately severe to detract from an employee's job performance, discourage them from remaining on the job, or keep them from advancing in their careers. This meant that it need not be so serious that it would cause a psychological injury of the type which some courts had required.

It is interesting that there are various views as to what conduct does have the kind of effect that the Supreme Court required in *Harris*. This is because of the argument that the effect of certain behavior can be viewed as quite different for men and for women. Several courts have accepted this argument and have specifically stated that, in order to adequately decide these cases, they must use the perspective of the person claiming hostile environment, which usually is a woman. There has been much debate about this difference, as courts begin to consider the possibility of using what has been termed the "reasonable woman" standard for judging potentially harassing behavior.

Many hostile environment cases now involve a great deal of psychological testimony specifically presented to show that certain behaviors, both sexual and demeaning, have a different effect on women than they do on men because of the unique socialization of each gender. Sexuality in the workplace may not be a problem for men but many psychologists and sociologists claim that, for women, it has a debilitating effect. Sexuality, attractiveness, and a focus on their appearance puts women in a less authoritative or competent light, according to many researchers, an effect which does not occur with men. Thus, it is argued, to be judged in a sexual manner or to be in a place where women are viewed in a sexual light creates an environment where women do not feel as competent as they should and where they may be judged on stereotypical criteria. In one highly publicized case, for example, the court agreed with expert psychological testimony that women in a sexually charged environment may be evaluated more on their attractiveness or sexuality than on their ability to do the job. This case, *Robinson v. Jacksonville Shipyards*, involved a complaint filed by female shipyard workers who were required to work in an environment in which sexual innuendoes, "girlie" displays, and sexual "horseplay" were a normal part of the daily routine. Such environments are commonplace, according to studies, in workplaces which have been traditionally male. Women in these non-traditional jobs are now beginning to demand changes, claiming that such behavior inhibits their job performance, even though it does not create problems for the men.

Thus, many commentators and lawyers argue, it can make a great deal of difference as to which perspective the court uses to decide whether this conduct creates a hostile environment: the "reasonable woman" or the "reasonable man." Courts have traditionally used a "reasonable person" perspective but many in the law contend this is not possible in these cases because the behavior must be viewed either from the eyes of a man or a woman in order to determine its effect. This is one of the many issues in the hostile environment arena which are currently unresolved.

Another issue in these cases involves what some have termed the "status quo" defense. Some employers have claimed women should not be allowed to claim that they have been subjected to a hostile environment when the behavior which created it was the "normal banter" which has always gone on in the workplace. Those defendants who try to use this defense have argued that the law requires equal treatment of men and women and that is what is happening. Men and women are being treated equally and are being subjected to the same environment. The argument which is usually used against this is that Title VII and the state's anti-discrimination laws require equal opportunity and a work environment which has been set up to be comfortable for men is not necessarily conducive to women's success. Thus, the argument goes, equal treatment is not necessarily equal opportunity and just because men were there first and set up the "norms" does not mean that women need to adapt to those norms if they work against women's best job performance. A few courts have allowed this "status quo" defense but most refuse to accept that any environment is legal just because it has existed for many years. As most judges note, Title VII was designed to change such "norms."

Closely related to the "status quo" defense is another argument which is not looked on with favor in most courts. This is the "society" defense. The case which is most cited for the court's acceptance of this defense is *Rabidue v. Osceola Refining* which was decided by the Sixth Circuit Court of Appeals, a federal court which is inferior to the Supreme Court and which sets precedent only for the federal district courts in three states: Michigan, Ohio, and Tennessee. In *Rabidue*, the company had argued that the victim could not claim to be affected by the demeaning comments or sexual displays in the workplace because she was faced with them throughout society. The court accepted this argument and said that women who see pornography on street corners and on newsstands and all around, could not possibly claim that it caused them problems in the workplace. Few courts have agreed with this view, however, most finding that Title VII was supposed to change the workplace not all of society. In addition, the courts note, sexuality outside of the work environment was quite different than in the workplace where women need to be viewed in a professional manner.

After proving that the harassment was "pervasive," the person bringing the claim of hostile environment must prove that the conduct was "unwelcomed" by the victim. The U.S. Supreme Court has drawn a sharp distinction between the terms "involuntary" and "unwelcomed." The Court noted in the *Vinson* case that despite the fact that the woman may have been found to have voluntarily gone along with the supervisor's sexual behavior because she did not complain or appear to resist, she could still prove that the conduct was not welcomed by her and that it created a hostile environment. Because a subordinate might be seen to have little choice but to go along with the situation, the Court concluded that the true way to judge this element was not by asking whether she resisted, complained or voluntarily went along, but, rather, whether, given a choice she would have wanted this situation to occur; thus, did she welcome the behavior?

This element, although it may appear more clear cut than the ''pervasive'' requirement, in fact, has also resulted in much debate. While it is probably clear that demeaning, belittling, or humiliating behavior would easily be seen as ''unwelcomed'' by anyone, a real problem occurs with regard to sexuality in the workplace. When are sexual overtures, sexual comments, sexual pictures, etc. welcomed in the workplace by—as is the usual party complaining or filing a lawsuit—women who are subjected to them? This, of course, becomes very complex, tied up with the sexual interplay between the sexes. Also, it is sometimes difficult to know how to judge whether a certain person welcomes the behavior because, for some, silence may manifest approval, for others, it might mean that they are humiliated and unable to respond. Thus, courts are grappling with what type of evidence should be presented to show that the person claiming a hostile environment actually welcomed the behavior.

The Supreme Court in *Vinson* stated that evidence of a complaining person's dress, speech, or participation in harassing behavior was not irrelevant to a determination of unwelcomeness. While few people would contend that a person might dress in such a way that she or he should be viewed as wanting demeaning or belittling comments, situations involving sexual behavior are more problematic for judges. In those kinds of cases, defendants often want to present evidence of certain actions by the person making a claim of hostile environment to prove that the complaining party wanted or invited sexual overtures, jokes, or comments. The evidence which an employer might wish to present could include testimony about the victim having worn clothes which were deemed sexually attractive, using words which were deemed sexually offensive, telling off-color jokes, or laughing at others' jokes or comments. The Supreme Court's statement that such evidence was not irrelevant still left the decision as to whether specific evidence should be allowed in the hands of the judges trying the cases.

The trial judges, then, are the final deciders of whether facts to be presented are relevant to that particular case. Most judges who do allow evidence of a person's participation, dress, or speech to be presented by the defendant in hostile environment cases, draw a sharp line, however, between the victim's behavior in and outside the workplace. The fact that one dresses in a sexual manner in one's private life, for example, is usually not deemed relevant to a charge that she or he was subjected to a hostile environment at work. This is true even though the victim may socialize and work with the same group of people.

An interesting twist to the workplace/private life issue was presented in a case where a woman claimed that she was subjected to a hostile environment in her workplace, partly because nude pictures of the woman were displayed by other co-workers. The woman had posed for the pictures some years before. The employer claimed that the displays could not be seen as unwelcomed by the alleged victim because she had done the posing herself. The court in that case stated that what a person does outside of the workplace has no bearing on whether potentially harassing behavior is welcomed in the work environment.

In addition, the courts usually will find that a person may welcome behavior from some people in the workplace but not from others. Thus, an alleged victim's welcoming of sexual comments coming from someone in whom she or he has a personal interest does not necessarily mean that the same behavior would be deemed welcomed from another person.

Often, employers will try to use the fact that the person filing the lawsuit never complained about the problem as evidence that the behavior was not unwelcome. This is also a difficult issue, and judges view this type of situation in differing ways. First, if the person doing the harassment is a supervisor, most courts have said that the situation is quite different than when a co-worker is causing the problem. People often find it difficult to complain about a supervisor and in many workplaces an employee may suffer consequences for such a report. Thus, lack of a complaint when a supervisor is the harasser is rarely seen as important evidence that the conduct was welcomed, unless, as will be seen shortly, the employer has in place a policy and procedures which invite such complaints and provides a safe way to register them.

When the behavior originates from co-workers, the situation is somewhat different. Courts allow non-reporting to be used more often in those situations but are still careful because psychologists and sociologists often testify that women, especially, are hesitant to complain, feeling that they will not be believed and that even more problems will result from a report of harassing behavior. Once again, however, if there are policies and procedures in place to assure the workers that complaints will be taken seriously and no retaliation will result, silence about the problem is more often allowed as evidence that the behavior was welcomed.

In order to successfully bring a hostile environment harassment lawsuit against a company, the person bringing the claim must, finally, prove that her or his employer is liable for the situation. Unlike the *quid pro quo* situation, the employer is not strictly liable for every hostile environment situation. While businesses have been found liable in cases where supervisors, co-workers, or customers or clients have been involved in creating the problem, specific standards for employer liability vary according to the person involved in the harassment.

When the harassment is carried out by a supervisor, the Supreme Court has stated that agency principles apply with regard to the employer's liability. Briefly, this means that if the supervisor was acting as the employer's agent while harassing the employee, then the employer will be responsible for the behavior. Normally supervisors are seen by the law as having authority to supervise subordinate employees, so the potential for liability when a supervisor is involved in creating a hostile environment is extensive. The only way to avoid liability is to take away even the apparent authority to conduct the workplace in this manner by instituting a policy and rigid procedures which are communicated to the workers and which give them the real opportunity to complain if this occurs.

When co-workers are involved in creating the hostile environment, the standard for liability is not so extensive. Courts and the EEOC state that an employer will be liable in those situations when it knew or should have known of the problem and failed to take appropriate corrective measures. A company is deemed to know about a situation when a report or complaint is filed or when a supervisor is told of the harassment. Courts believe that an employer should have known of the harassment, even if no complaint is filed, when it is so extensive that the agents of the company should have noticed, had they been supervising the workplace in a reasonable manner. In either case, the law does recognize that, without an adequate policy or procedures which encourage people to report, the company may not be able to claim that it did not know of the situation. Courts state that the employer would have known had it had such a program and, thus, it "should" have known. The standard for liability when a customer or client is involved is somewhat less clear, but it appears that most courts are using the same standard as when a co-worker is involved.

It has become clear, with regard to hostile environment sexual harassment claims, that the best course for a company to take to try to avoid liability is to adopt a strong policy against sexual harassment and procedures designed to successfully carry out that policy. Interestingly, while many companies currently have a policy against discrimination, studies indicate that most do not meet the requirements set by the EEOC and the courts for an adequate anti-harassment policy and procedures. There are many components to a successful program against harassment, including: a policy which deals exclusively with sexual harassment and not other types of discrimination; "failsafe" systems which allow reporting to several alternative people; specific and increasing penalties for violations; a commitment that there be no retaliation for registering a complaint; a program of training and education; and follow-up procedures after remedial measures are carried out. It is also clear that investigations must be carefully undertaken so that the process itself does not increase the hostile environment and create more liability for the company.

Sexual harassment continues to be an expanding area of liability for businesses. The law is constantly shifting and changing as new fact situations occur. While the victim in the *Vinson* case was subjected to a horrendous situation, the law today does not require that level of abuse before finding an environment exists which is hostile or abusive to people of one gender.

[Anne Levy]

FURTHER READING:

Abrams, Kathryn. "Gender Discrimination and the Transformation of Workplace Norms." 42 *Vanderbilt Law Review* 1183 (1989).

Astrachan, Anthony. *How Men Feel: Their Response to Women's Demands for Equality and Power.* Anchor Press/Doubleday: 1986.

Burns v. McGregor Electronic Industries, 989 F.2d 959 (8th Cir. 1993).

EEOC Guidelines on Discrimination Because of Sex, 29 Code of Federal Regulations, Part 1604 (1980).

Ellison v. Brady, 924 F.2d 872 (9th Cir. 1991).

Gutek, B.; Stromberg, A; Larwood, L., eds., *Women and Work: An Annual Review*, Vol. 3. Sage Publications: 1988.

Harris v. Forklift Systems, 62 U.S.L.W. 4004 (1993).

Hearn, J.; Sheppard, D.; Tancred-Sheriff, P.; Burrell, G., eds. *The Sexuality of Organization.* Sage Publications: 1989.

Levy, Anne C. "Sexual Harassment Cases in the 1990s: 'Backlashing' the 'Backlash' Through Title VII." 56 *Albany Law Review* 1 (1992).

MacKinnon, Catherine A. *Sexual Harassment of Working Women.* Yale University Press, 1979.

Meritor Savings Bank v. Vinson, 477 U.S. 57 (1986).

Milwid, Beth. *Working With Men: Professional Women Talk About Power, Sexuality, and Ethics.* Beyond Words Publishing: 1990.

Paludi, M. & Barickman, R. *Academic and Workplace Sexual Harassment: A Resource Manual.* SUNY Press: 1991.

Price Waterhouse v. Hopkins, 490 U.S. 228 (1989).

Proposed EEOC Guidelines on Harassment Based on Race, Color, Religion, Gender, National Origin, Age, or Disability, 29 Code of Federal Regulations, Part 1609 (1993).

Rabidue v. Osceola Refining, 805 F.2d 611 (6th Cir. 1986).

Robinson v. Jacksonville Shipyards, 760 F. Supp. 1486 (M.D. Fla. 1991).

SIMPLE INTEREST

Interest can be an expense or a revenue. Interest expense is the cost of borrowed money. Interest income is the earnings on money that has been loaned or invested. The sum against which interest is calculated is known as the principal. Interest on the principal may be calculated as simple interest or compound interest.

The primary difference between simple interest and compound interest is the treatment of the length of time for which interest is paid or earned. In simple interest calculations, the number of time periods is disregarded. For example, $100 earning ten percent simple interest results in interest income of $10 per year regardless of how many years are involved. That is, the amount of interest equals the interest rate times the principal. The accumulated interest and the number of time periods do not enter into the calculation.

On the other hand, in compound interest calculations, each time period affects the amount of interest earned or paid. That is because the accumulated interest itself earns interest, or is said to be compounded. For example, $100 earning ten percent compound interest results in interest income of $10 in the first year. In the second year, interest income increases to ten percent of $110, or $11, because the first year's interest is added to the principal. In the third year the interest payment increases to $12.10, or ten percent of $121.

Thus, it can be seen that using simple interest, a $100 investment would earn $30 over three years at ten percent. Using compound interest, the same investment would result in interest income of $33.10. Compound interest is widely used in financial planning, because it is assumed that interest on the principal would earn the same interest rate as the principal does. Simple interest is useful in situations where the interest payments are not being reinvested.

[David Bianco]

SIMPLIFIED EMPLOYEE PENSIONS

Simplified employee pensions (SEP), also known as SEP-IRAs (**individual retirement accounts**), can be defined as pension plans for successful small business people and the self-employed. Created by Congress and monitored carefully by the **Internal Revenue Service**, SEPs are designed to give small business owners and employees the same ability to set aside money for later retirement as traditional large corporate pension funds.

SEPs, however, can be much more flexible and attractive than corporate pensions. They can even be used to supplement the pension, and the corporate **401(k) plans**. Many full-time employed people use SEPs as a way to save and invest more money for retirement than they might normally be expected to put away under IRS rules. *Forbes* magazine described SEPs as a "moonlighter's delight" in a 1993 article.

The reason for the magazine's enthusiasm is that SEPs, while created for the self-employed and small business people, also allow full-time employees to contribute a portion of self-employment income from consulting or freelancing.

The rules governing SEPs are fairly simple, but are subject to change with any Congressional action so yearly checks of IRS publications 560 (retirement plans for the self-employed) and 590 (IRAs) are necessary. Through 1994, SEPs could be set up with a simple form and did not require any separate trustee, which is required of larger, more complicated pension plans. The maximum allowable tax-deductible SEP contribution per employee is 15 percent of salary or income (up to a maximum income of $150,000) or $22,500, whichever is less. The maximum amount an employer can contribute to his or her own plan is 13.0435 percent of income. Still, compared to the $2,000 allowable standard IRA contribution, which has not been fully tax deductible for all contributors since 1986, the advantages of SEPs are obvious. Again on the plus side, people can contribute to their existing IRAs and 401(k)s, and still hold a SEP.

One word of caution for small business people: SEP plans must be set up for everyone in the company, not just the owners. That even includes part-time employees—everyone in the company must be covered. That does not mean that the SEP must be funded each year. If the company is experiencing a lean year funding of the SEP may be skipped. All of the SEP's funding is deductible as a business expense in the year it is made.

A similar program is the salary reduction simplified employee pension (SARSEP). SARSEPs are similar to 401(k) plans, where employees defer part of their annual compensation into an IRA. Any employer contributions to the program are deductible as business expenses. The employer can still establish a separate SEP to handle employer contributions. SARSEPs are available to businesses with 25 or fewer employees, but at least 50 percent of the employees must elect to participate in the program to launch it.

[Clint Johnson]

FURTHER READING:

Rowland, Mary. "Pension Options for Small Firms.," *Nation's Business*. March, 1994, pp. 25-27.

SINKING FUND

A bond indenture may contain a sinking fund provision which provides for the orderly retirement of the **debt**. Under a sinking fund provision, the issuer may annually transmit funds to the trustee who is responsible for (1) purchasing similar investments which will mature in time to retire the debt, (2) calling a portion of the bonds (typically at a premium) for early retirement, or (3) purchasing the issuer's bonds in the open market. Alternatively, the issuer may perform one of the aforementioned tasks itself and subsequently transfer the resulting instruments to the trustee.

Operationally, a sinking fund provision may require either uniform annual payments, uniform increments over time, or contributions determined by the level of earnings. Since a bond issue with a sinking fund provision is generally considered to be safer than a similar bond issue without one, a sinking fund provision has the effect of lowering the interest rate on a bond issue.

BENEFITS OF A SINKING FUND

An issuer accepts sinking fund provisions for the following reasons:

1. If the **credit** worthiness of the issuer is in question, lenders may not grant credit without a sinking fund since it provides a measure of protection for the creditor. The **opportunity costs** of the sinking fund requirement may be the inability to secure long-term debt needed to purchase highly profitable equipment.

2. The accumulation of funds in a special account also provides the issuer with security against future business conditions which may be detrimental to its ability to retire the debt.

3. The insurance provided by a sinking fund decreases the **interest rates**, therefore, the interest expenses. This results in increased cash flow.

4. When the purchase of productive assets requires a sinking fund, the sinking fund mirrors the **depreciation** schedule of those asset. The issuer benefits in two ways. Depreciation allows the issuer to recover the costs while simultaneously retiring the debt of equipment going out of service.

5. The issuer can book **capital gains** on debt retirement if it purchases bonds in the open market below book value.

6. A sinking fund enhances the tax benefits of financial **leverage**. First, interest expense and depreciation are tax-deductible. The issuer can use the tax-savings to fund part of the annual sinking fund payment. Second, the sinking fund could earn compounded interest, helping to reduce the cost of borrowing. Finally, the interest expense decreases proportionately to the amount of **bonds** outstanding. If the sinking fund accumulates and compounds, the earnings grow geometrically. At some point the issuer will benefit from a positive after-tax cash flow.

SEE ALSO: Depreciation

[Roger J. AbiNader]

FURTHER READING:

Bierman, Harold. *Financial Management for Decision Making.* Macmillan Publishing Co., 1986.

Vichas, Robert P. *Handbook of Financial Mathematics, Formulas, and Tables.* Prentice Hall, 1979.

SMALL BUSINESS ADMINISTRATION

The Small Business Administration, created by Congress in 1953, is the only federal agency whose sole charge is to provide service to owners of small businesses. The SBA's mission is to counsel, assist, and protect the interests of small business; to assist small business start-ups; and to ensure that small business concerns receive a fair portion of government purchases and contracts. The SBA also licenses and regulates Small Business Investment Companies (SBICs), and assures that small business owners have a chance to buy a fair share of government property for sale. There are various criteria used to determine if a business is small. Small retail businesses are generally deemed to be those whose receipts do not exceed between $3.5 and $13.5 million. Depending on the industry, companies may employ up to 1500. Small manufacturing companies must have 500 or fewer employees.

The SBA also makes loans under limited circumstances. Loans are of two basic types: guaranty and direct. Guaranty loans are made by private lenders, usually banks, and guaranteed up to 90 percent by the SBA. Well over 90 percent of loans are of the guaranty type; traditionally very little money is available for direct loans.

Applicants for loans must be of good character, show sufficient management expertise and commitment to run a successful operation, and have enough capital to operate on a sound financial basis. For new businesses, this amount—including both loan proceeds and personal capital—must be enough to meet start-up expenses and to sustain the business for the initial operating phase during which losses are likely to occur.

The SBA also provides guidance in preparing a business plan, widely considered the most important step in starting a new business. It is a blueprint that focuses the goals of, and helps gauge the progress of the new endeavor. It defines the planned business and its major products or services, outlines the management team, and defines targets for sales, growth, new product development, etc.

Many SBA district offices hold pre-business workshops for aspiring entrepreneurs. These sessions offer advice to those who want to start small retail and service businesses. Information about these aspects of the SBA can be obtained from any Small Business Administration office.

Counseling for owners of existing small businesses is one of the SBA's most important programs. Help is available in the areas of marketing, buying, producing, selling, financial management, record keeping, and administration through SCORE (Service Corps of Retired Executives). SCORE is a free service consisting of thousands of retired volunteers who span the full range of business management—office managers, accountants, advertising and public relations experts, and sales managers.

The Small Business Institute is another SBA management counseling systems. Started in 1972, SBI is a three-way cooperative among more than 500 collegiate schools of business administration, members of the small business community and the Small Business Administration. Under the supervision of university faculty and SBA staff, business degree candidates work directly with the owners of small firms, providing on-site counseling at no charge in the areas of market research, accounting systems, inventory control, and cost-benefit analysis. Applicants for this service are carefully screened to assure that both students and business owners will benefit from the program.

The SBA also funds Small Business Development Centers (SBDC), which bring together the resources of universities, colleges, private companies, and governmental agencies at all levels to provide assistance to small businesses. The Small Business Administration is the principal agency of the U.S. government that furnishes disaster assistance to small businesses. Once an area has been officially declared a disaster due to fire, flood, earthquake or riot, the SBA is authorized to make or guarantee loans to small businesses located in the region, repair property, and replace inventory. Homeowners and renters are sometimes eligible for disaster relief assistance as well. The SBA also extends physical-disaster loans to nonprofit companies, schools, religious organizations and charitable institutions.

The SBA also provides expertise in the areas of procurement and small business development and advocacy for women and minorities. Small business owners seeking to do business with the federal government are helped by procurement specialists at district offices. These specialists identify for business owners which government agencies are prospective customers, how small businesses can have their names included on bidders' lists, and how owner's can obtain specifications and drawings for specific contracts.

The Office of Advocacy attempts to evaluate the effect of proposed legislation and other policy issues on small businesses. The chief counsel for advocacy acts as the primary spokesperson for small business and represents their views before Congress, local governments, and other agencies.

A comprehensive range of business development booklets is published by and made available from the SBA for modest prices. Topics covered include cost accounting, record keeping, planning for growth, training sales people, and exporting. SBA local offices are located in more than 100 cities across the United States.

[Ruth Pittman]

FURTHER READING:

Emerich, Amy., ed. *Small Business Sourcebook*. Gale Research, Inc., 1996.

Handbook for Small Business: A Survey of Small Business Programs of the Federal Government, 5th ed., Washington, D.C.: U.S. Government Printing Office, 1984.

Pittman, Ruth. *Small Store Success*. Holbrook, MA: Bob Adams, Inc., 1992.

SMALL BUSINESSES

Small businesses and entrepreneurs form the backbone of the American economy. Without one, there would not be the other. Certainly, not all small businesses are owned by entrepreneurs, but it is entrepreneurs who generate the ideas that lead to opportunities for people to begin their own companies. That has been the case since the early days of American history, and will no doubt continue to be for the foreseeable future.

SMALL BUSINESSES ARE THE MAINSTAY OF THE AMERICAN ECONOMY

By some definitions, anywhere from 70 to 99 percent of American businesses fall into the "small" category. The actual percentage is difficult to estimate, since there is no clear-cut definition of what constitutes a small business. For example, the U.S. Chamber of Commerce defines a small business as a company that employs fewer than 500 people. Another definition suggests that a small business is one that employs fewer than 100 people. Yet a third definition eschews numbers and states simply that a small business is one that is independently owned, i.e., not a subsidiary of a large company. Whatever definition applies, one thing is certain: small businesses account for the bulk of businesses in the United States. That has been the case since the first settlers set foot on American soil in the early 1600s.

THE HISTORY OF SMALL BUSINESS

Small businesses were the lifeblood of the American economy between the time the first settlers arrived in the early 1600s and the Industrial Revolution. In almost every early American community, small business owners abounded. For example, a profile of Northampton, Massachusetts in 1773 shows that workers other than farmers were not day laborers who toiled for wages. Rather, they were skilled artisans who worked for themselves. They comprised blacksmiths, goldsmiths, tanners, weavers, tailors, traders, barbers ... in short, any specialist whose services were needed by others. This situation continued until the Industrial Revolution.

The British industrial revolution occurred between 1760-1830. By contrast, the American Industrial Revolution did not begin until the 1830s. The proliferation of machines and assembly line processing altered the way Americans did business, but, contrary to what many people predicted at the time, it did not eliminate the need for small business owners. That has never changed. Even today, when corporations are undergoing massive changes in their work structures, the need for small business owners has remained steady or even increased.

In the late 1980s, corporations began divesting themselves of large numbers of employees, particularly those in middle management. Many of these displaced workers opted to start their own businesses rather than take a chance on working for corporations and being downsized again. So, in the early 1990s, there began a trend toward more small business ownership. Many of the people who started these new businesses were merely exercising entrepreneurial skills that had either been dormant or simply never used. These were the new breed of entrepreneurs, whose presence is necessary if any economy is to flourish.

Entrepreneurs are generally innovative people who turn new ideas into thriving businesses. Often, the businesses they start based on a simple idea turn into major corporations. Their endeavors pave the way for less innovative people with shrewd business minds to run small businesses of their own. Thus, entrepreneurs and business operators feed off one another—and feed the American economy.

As is the case with the term "small business," entrepreneur is hard to define. To some people, an entrepreneur is simply an individual who starts a new enterprise. To others, the word connotes an individual who organizes and manages natural resources, labor, and capital in order to produce goods and services with the intention of making a profit—but who also runs the risk of failure. However the word is defined, entrepreneurs are the linchpin of the American economy. They make it possible for small business owners to survive, in whatever form of operation they choose.

OWNING A SMALL BUSINESS DOES NOT GUARANTEE SUCCESS

Running a successful small business requires a tremendous amount of dedication and a variety of skills. A successful small business owner must have a wide range of entrepreneurial skills, e.g., a knowledge of financing, selling, accounting, bookkeeping, regulatory procedures—in short, just about every facet of business. But, knowledge of the various business activities alone does not guarantee an owner success. There are other factors involved, such as location and luck. The bottom line is that small business operators must be dedicated to succeed—and not all of them do. Many small business owners fall victim to the pitfalls of the economy and fail due to no fault of their own. At other times, they end up in bankruptcy because they do not adhere to the basic rules of business.

TYPES OF SMALL BUSINESS

There exist several forms of small business—**S corporation**, sole proprietorships, general partnerships, **franchises**, and others. Regardless of what type of business owners choose, their goals are the same: to make a profit and to avoid bankruptcy.

The most common form of small business is the sole proprietorship, a business owned and usually operated by one person who is personally responsible for the firm's debts. According to the U.S. Department of Commerce, approximately 11.9 million of the nation's 16.9 million businesses are sole proprietorships. They account for less than six percent of total business revenues in the country. Individual sole proprietorships may be small, but from them grow some major corporations. Many of today's large companies (for example, Sears, Roebuck & Co. and Ford), began as sole proprietorships.

One of the reasons sole proprietorship is so popular is because it offers many advantages to the small business owner. The biggest advantage of a sole proprietorship is the freedom it allows the owner. Sole proprietors answer only to themselves. They alone enjoy the profits. On the other hand, they are solely responsible for debts. Another advantage is the privacy involved in running a sole proprietorship. The owner does not have to reveal information regarding the business to anyone.

Sole proprietorships are also relatively simple to start up. People interested in starting their own businesses often need do no more than hang out a sign. The lack of complex regulations governing the opening of a small business is extremely appealing to entrepreneurs, many of whom thrive on starting businesses and then divesting them. Perhaps the biggest advantage, though, is that owners of sole proprietorships can dissolve them as easily as they start them. That is why many sole proprietorships are designed to be short-lived.

There are people who form sole proprietorships to run a single athletic event or rock concert. As soon as the event is over, the business is terminated. Because of the ease of starting such a business, promoters can—and often do—"open" and "close" such businesses frequently. This is possible for several reasons, not the least of which is the low cost of starting such a business.

Low start-up costs encourage many people to open their own businesses. In many cases, there are no legal fees involved. Often, a person starting a sole proprietorship need only register it with a state agency as protection against another person using the business' name. There are some sole proprietorships that require the owners to have licenses, for example, hair salons or saloons.

Consider a writer who wishes to start a business. There are no licenses involved, thus no fees to pay. The need for legal assistance is rare—possibly only for cases where copyright infringement is involved. Generally, writers can work out of office space in their homes without worrying about zoning regulations. And, comparatively speaking, there is very little equipment for a writer to purchase—writers need little more than a computer, a fax machine, a printer, a telephone, and a modem. They also need sundry items like paper and reference books. Thus, to start a writing business, all that is needed is a pronouncement that "I am a small business owner" and a desire to succeed. Most importantly, writers enjoy the ultimate benefits of a sole proprietorship: they keep the profits and get tax breaks.

There are cases in which sole proprietors (and other business owners) suffer losses in the early stages of their operations. Tax laws allow sole proprietors to treat the sales revenues and operating expenses of the business as part of their personal finances. As a result, sole proprietors can reduce their taxes by deducting allowable operating losses from income earned from sources other than the business. This is an extremely important benefit, since most businesses lose money in the beginning.

The possibility of losing money is but one of the disadvantages of a sole proprietorship. One major disadvantage is the fact that sole proprietors are responsible for all debts incurred by their businesses. This unlimited liability is a deterrent to some people seeking to start their own businesses. If a business does not generate the projected income in its existence, owners must pay any debts incurred out of their own pockets. If they do not—or cannot—creditors can claim the owners' personal property such as cars and houses. (Laws vary from state to state. Some states do allow business owners to protect some of their personal property.)

Another disadvantage associated with sole proprietorships is the lack of continuity. If an owner dies, the business is not passed down automatically to heirs, family members, etc. A sole proprietorship is dissolved legally when the owner dies. Of course, there is nothing to stop other people from reorganizing the business if there is a successor available who is trained and willing to take over the business. If there is not, the deceased owner's executors or heirs must liquidate the assets of the business. The effects of an owner's death point up another major disadvantage to a sole proprietorship: it is frequently dependent on the resources of one person.

Often, sole proprietors are responsible for all of the operations involved in running a business. They alone are responsible for the firm's cash flow and finances. Often, they find it difficult to borrow money from legitimate sources such as banks when they need it. This applies to money for starting and expanding businesses. Banks, for example, are sometimes reluctant to lend money to sole proprietors for fear they will not recover it if the owners die or become disabled. Therefore, proprietors must rely on the cash generated by the business, personal savings, or family loans to finance their operations. Disadvantages aside, many sole proprietors succeed in business—as do their counterparts in general partnerships, the next type of small business.

General partnerships are fairly common in the world of small business even though they are legally one of the least popular form of business organization. There are roughly 1.7 million partnerships in existence, which generate only 4 percent of total U.S. sales revenues. A general partnership is a business with two or more owners who share in the operation of a firm and in financial responsibility for its debts. There is no legal limit to the number of partners allowed. The number can run from two to hundreds. Partners do not have to invest equal amounts of money. They may earn profits that bear no relationship to the amount they have invested in the business. It is up to the partners to arrange the financial dealings and other management aspects of the organization.

Sometimes partnerships are created when sole proprietors can no longer run their businesses as one-person operations. Or, sole proprietors may simply want to expand, and taking on a partner or partners is the best way to accomplish it. A general partnership can be a start-up operation, too.

One example of a successful general partnership is ValueNet International, Inc., based in Hartford, Connecticut. In 1993, Rick Wise and Bob Fenn, both of whom had worked previously for a major financial institution, opened ValueNet with a very simple premise: ValueNet would teach small businesses how to cut costs in non personnel areas, e.g., on office equipment, supplies, technology, training and development, and employee benefits. Their company's goal is to save businesses money on everyday purchases. ValueNet analysts scour clients' accounts payable for the past year in areas where they may have been overpaying. They identify areas where their customers can find meaningful savings. Once they have done so, the analysts make specific recommendations for saving money without sacrificing quality or service. ValueNet does not suggest cuts in staff or salaries. Ultimately, the analysts make their clients' employees more cost conscious without being perceived as a threat.

The company's service does not stop there. ValueNet representatives will negotiate for clients with present or prospective vendors. They may recommend new suppliers. They leave all final decisions to the clients. In payment, they receive fifty cents of every dollar of first-year savings. After that, the savings belong totally to the clients. The idea has caught on. ValueNet moved out of the incubator in which it started and is a thriving business. (An **incubator** is an organization that nurtures new businesses in their very early stages by providing shared space, usually at a site housing other new businesses as well, stimulation, support, and a variety of other basic services, often at reduced fees.)

Like any other type of business, general partnerships have their advantages and disadvantages. One of the advantages is that partnerships can add talent and money as they go along. They also have an easier time borrowing money. Normally, banks and other lending institutions prefer to loan money to businesses that do not depend on one person. Another advantage is that partners in a business have access to one another's funds. This is especially important in a business which comprises a large number of partners.

Another advantage is that partnerships are easy to organize. There are few legal requirements involved in forming a general partnerships. Wise partners, however, will draft some type of agreement among themselves. The agreement may be written, oral, or unspoken. The important thing is that one must exist. Some of the questions that might be asked include general ones such as who invests what sums of money in the partnership, who receives what share of the partnership's profits, who does what and who reports

to whom, and how the partnership may be dissolved if the need arises. What is included in the agreement is up to the individuals involved. The document is not a legal requirement; it is strictly a private document that no government agency needs to see.

A partnership is not a legal entity in the eyes of the law. It is simply an agreement between two or more people working together. From an **Internal Revenue Service** standpoint, partners are taxed as individuals. That, too, is an advantage for partnerships. But, there are the inevitable disadvantages, too.

Unlimited liability is a major drawback for partnerships, just as it is for sole proprietors. By law, each partner may be held personally liable for all debts incurred in the partnership's name. If any partner incurs a debt, even if the other partners do not know about it, they are all liable for it if the responsible partner cannot pay it. This legal stipulation remains even if the partnership agreement states that all notes and bills are to be endorsed by the other partners.

Again, as is the case with the sole proprietorships, lack of continuity can be a disadvantage in partnerships. If one partner dies or withdraws from the business, the partnership may dissolve legally. This can happen even if the other partners agree to stay. They can, however, form a new partnership immediately if they wish, and retain the old firm's business. This arrangement prevents the loss of revenues that might otherwise affect the partners. The lack of continuity problem is closely associated with the difficulty of transferring ownership.

In a general partnership, no individual may sell out without the permission of the other partners. In addition, partners who want to retire or transfer their interests in the firm to family members cannot do so without the express permission of all the remaining partners. As a result, the continuation of a partnership may depend on the ability of retiring partners to find someone acceptable to the other partners to buy their shares. If retiring partners cannot find such a person, the partnership may have to be liquidated. As an alternative, the remaining partners may buy out a retiring partner.

Another major problem involved frequently with partnerships is the lack of conflict resolution. When sole proprietors have problems with the way their businesses are being run, they resolve the problems themselves. That is not the case with partners. If one partner or group of partners wants to expand a business, and another partner or group does not, there is a conflict. That conflict may be difficult to resolve, especially if the partners are evenly divided. Conflicts may involve virtually anything, ranging from partners' personal habits to personnel matters. The lack of resolution can lead to dissolution.

Another type of small business is the corporation, which is normally associated with large businesses. Indeed, even though only 20 percent of the nation's businesses (about 3.3 million firms) are corporations, they generate 90 percent of the revenues. Nevertheless, a corporation does not have to be a large business.

Any business owner can incorporate. In legal terms, a corporation is a legal entity separate from its owners with many of the legal rights and privileges a person has. It is a form of business organization in which the liability of the owners is limited to their investment in the firm. Corporations may sue and be sued; buy, hold, and sell property; make and sell products to consumers; and commit crimes and be punished for them. As far as small businesses go, many of the attributes associated with corporations may be inappropriate. For example, a writer or a newsstand owner may not want to sell stock in their businesses, form boards of directors, or deal in proxy votes. Nevertheless, small business owners can incorporate to take advantage of benefits endemic to corporations.

The biggest advantages corporations experience include limited liability, continuity, greater likelihood of professional management, and easier access to money. On the other hand, there are disadvantages. For example, corporations may undergo stockholder revolts, experience high start-up costs, be subjected to excessive regulation, and pay high taxes.

ALTERNATIVE SMALL BUSINESSSES

Small business owners' choices are not limited to sole proprietorships, general partnerships, and corporations. The alternative forms most likely to be considered by small business owners include limited partnerships, master limited partnerships, and S corporations. Like other forms, they each offer advantages and disadvantages.

Limited partnerships are businesses that have both active and inactive partners. They exist mainly so owners can avoid the problem of unlimited liability. The active partners run the company. The limited partners have no active role in the company's operations. (For this reason, they are sometimes called silent partners.) Should the business fail, they are liable only to the extent of their investment. They can invest their money without being held liable for the active partners' debts. There are legal stipulations that affect how a limited partnership is run. For example, each limited partnership must have at least one active partner designated as the general partner. This is primarily for liability purposes. In most cases, the general partner oversees the day-to-day operations of the company and holds the responsibility for its survival and growth.

In a master limited partnership, the business is organized much like a corporation. However, all the profits are paid out to investors. The company is run by a single "master" partner, who holds a majority of the stock. The major advantage to a master limited partnership is that it helps owners avoid double taxation. In this arrangement, the company sells shares to investors, just as a corporation does. However, all of the profits go to the investors, unlike what happens in a corporation.

Corporations retain some portion of any profits for growth and expansion. They pay income taxes on these profits, and the stockholders must pay income taxes on the dividends they receive from the company. Under the master limited partnership arrangement, this double taxation is avoided. There are disadvantages, though. For instance, since more of the earnings are paid to investors than is normally the case in a corporation structure, per-share prices for **stocks** are higher. This dissuades potential investors from buying into the company. Nevertheless, the master limited partnership form of ownership is growing in popularity.

Another form of business receiving a lot of attention from small business owners is the S corporation, so named because it is part of the Subchapter S of the U.S. Internal Revenue Code. Congress created the S corporation in 1958 to help small businesses compete better and to provide them with some relief from excessive taxation and regulation, both of which have increased since World War II.

The S corporation allows businesses to avoid double taxation. It is based on the premise that owners enjoy the limited liability benefits of corporate ownership but the taxation advantages of a partnership. Stockholders of an S corporation are taxed simply as if they were partners. As with other forms of small business, the corporations do not pay income taxes on earnings and the stockholders do not pay income taxes or tax on their dividends. Of course, there are limitations on the S corporation.

First, in order to qualify as an S corporation, a business must meet some stiff legal requirements. For example, it must be a domestic corporation that is independently owned and managed and not part of any other corporation. It cannot have any more than 35 stockholders. The stockholders that do exist may only be estates or individuals. They cannot be nonresident aliens. Lastly, no more than 25 percent of the firm's sales revenues may come from dividends, rent, interest, royalties, annuities, or stock sales, and no more than 80 percent of sales revenues may come from foreign markets. Despite these restrictions, S corporations do offer small business owners significant advantages.

FRANCHISES

Generally, small business owners are on the look-out for any advantages that will help them survive in the increasingly competitive business environment. One of the most sought after advantages is security. That is why many business owners invest in franchises, which offer a reasonable amount of security. However, franchisees (the individuals who purchase franchises) give up a lot for that security. In fact, many experts do not consider franchise owners to be small business operators at all.

A franchise is a continuing arrangement between a franchiser (a manufacturer or sole distributor of a trademarked product or service who typically has considerable experience in the line of business being franchised) and a franchisee. The franchisee purchases a franchise. In the process, the franchisee receives the opportunity to enter a new business, hopefully with an enhanced chance of success. That is not always the case, although failure rates among franchises run at less than five percent. By contrast, the **U.S. Small Business Administration** has reported that 65 percent of business start-ups fail within five years.

Franchises best demonstrate the difference between an entrepreneur and a small business owner. For example, Dave Thomas founded the Wendy's chain of hamburger restaurants in the early 1970s. By the end of the 1980s, the chain included 2,615 franchised outlets and 1,208 company-owned stores. Franchises existed in Canada, Ireland, Italy, Japan, Spain, Taiwan, New Zealand, and several other geographically diverse countries. Thomas's dream had grown considerably. He had developed an entrepreneurial idea into a flourishing chain of restaurants. His idea made it possible for people wanting to own their own businesses to do so.

It was Thomas who had taken the risks in opening his first Wendy's outlet. He secured the financing. He prepared the **business plan**. He oversaw the chain's growing pains. By the time he was ready to sell franchises, the company was profitable and stable. Thus, the entrepreneur made it possible for others to capitalize on his success. That is the story of **franchising**. An entrepreneur develops an idea and lays the groundwork for small business owners who buy relatively safe franchise outlets. Often, they must pay a stiff price for doing so.

Buying a franchise is not cheap. For instance, the total cash investment to open a Wendy's outlet in 1990 was between $593,000 and $1,346,000. This is relatively expensive in light of some franchise costs. None of the top ten franchises for the 1990s is that high. The total start-up cost for a McDonald's franchise averages $610,000. For a Merry Maids franchise, which provides residential cleaning services,

the start-up cost ranges from $28,500 to $33,500. This type of business is ideal for two-career families seeking to supplement their incomes. And Precision Tune, which specializes in automotive services, sells franchises for between $146,620 and $163,620.

Wendy's, like most franchisers, does not sell to just anybody. The company requires that prospective franchisees have successful business track records and a sense of commitment as an owner/operator. In return for their investments, franchisees receive access to Wendy's proven business records and established reputation. They also receive training and assistance from the franchiser. The assistance lowers the chances that the franchise will fail. This is certainly a plus for franchisees, but there are trade-offs.

People who operate franchises forego independence in running their business. They cannot make major modifications to their facilities without corporate approval and they are subject to monitoring from the franchiser's office. Another disadvantage is that they may be locked into long-term contracts with suppliers that are dictated by the corporation. Whether or not franchisers can live with such restrictions is for them to decide. Restrictions, aside, however, purchasing a franchise is a good way for people to start their own small businesses.

STARTING A SMALL BUSINESS

Franchising is one of the three basic ways people can start their own small businesses. The other two are starting a new firm from the ground floor and buying an existing business.

A start-up firm is one that a business owner builds from scratch. The process takes a lot of work. Owners have to obtain financing, choose an appropriate location, hire trustworthy personnel, plan for continuity, etc. They must make major decisions regarding all aspects of the operation. For example, should they finance continuing operations through debt capital (financing that involves a loan to be repaid, usually with interest) or equity capital (financing which usually requires that the investor be given some form of ownership in the venture)? Who will manage the company if the owner dies or is disabled? These are critical questions for small business operators.

The loss of key employees hurts small business owners much more than it does large corporations. It is problems like these that differentiate between small business owners and their large corporation counterparts. That is why these problems must be addressed in the early stages of a business' existence. The solutions can mean the difference in whether a small business survives or fails. It is problems like these that often prompt small business owners to buy existing businesses, rather than starting their own.

People generally buy existing businesses with an eye toward keeping them in basically the same form and avoiding growing pains. Some owners, basically those who fall into the entrepreneurial category, may buy an existing business with the intention of changing it dramatically so they can take it in new directions. Some entrepreneurs will purchase existing businesses they know are in financial trouble just for the challenge of reviving them. This is another approach that differentiates entrepreneurs from small business owners. For whatever reason a person buys an existing business, there are several key questions that must be considered before the purchase is made.

One of the key issues is whether the product or service the business provides falls into the prospective owner's areas of expertise and interests. Another is whether the purchase price is reasonable. A third addresses the business' turnaround prospects. Then there is the question of the target firm's financial condition: is it favorable or poor? Naturally, the most salient question deals with how to finance the purchase and continuing operations.

FUNDING SMALL BUSINESSES

There exist several sources through which small business owners can finance their operations. These include, but are not limited to, Small Business Administration (SBA) loan programs, commercial banks, venture capitalists, business development corporations, and stock shares.

The SBA offers a variety of loan programs for small businesses that cannot borrow from other sources on reasonable terms. The SBA normally places limits on the amount of money available, but interest rates are usually slightly lower than those on commercial loans.

Commercial banks are good sources of loans for existing small businesses, but they are often reluctant to fund start-up firms that have no track record or cannot demonstrate adequate assets. Banks generally require security and guarantees before they will make start-up loans. They sometimes impose other stringent restrictions on borrowers. Hence, commercial banks are not a major source of loans for start-up businesses.

Venture capitalists are institutional risk takers who tend to specialize in certain types of businesses. (There are also state-funded venture capital programs. For instance, Connecticut and South Carolina operate programs that provide financing for new and existing businesses.) They usually have formulas for evaluating a business and prefer strong minority ownership positions. Venture capitalists often structure deals with both equity and debt characteristics. They can be lucrative sources of funds—and they are not hard to locate.

CPAs, attorneys, and bankers can generally locate venture capitalists for small business owners. On occasion, they can be found at conferences designed to match small business owners with investors. For example, in December 1994, owners and investors met at the 7th Annual Southeast Capital Connection in Charleston, South Carolina. The purpose of the conference was to attract venture capitalists and investment bankers to the area to fill a vacuum for small- and medium-sized start-up companies. Companies like Alternative Control Systems Corporation, based in West Charleston, South Carolina, and Concepts Development, of Charleston, were represented.

Alternative Control Systems Corporation has developed a patented process to steer fire ants, snails, slugs, and other bugs away from pet food bowls. Concepts Development has designed a hospital bed with a built-in commode. It is these types of companies with innovative ideas that attract venture capitalists, in large part because banks are often reluctant to loan money to business with unproven products. In fact, 20 companies had representatives at the meeting, some from as far away as New Jersey. This highlights the importance of venture capitalists in the world of small business, where owners are always seeking funding.

Business development corporations are privately owned companies chartered by states to make small business loans. They can develop creative financing packages. The most attractive facet of these corporations is that their loans are generally guaranteed by the SBA.

Another way of funding a small business is through the issuance of shares. In order to attract outside investors, business owners can sell shares in the business at private or public offerings. However, such offerings are highly technical and usually require expert legal help to conform to state and federal securities laws. The share process also removes a large part of business owner's independence, however, since stockholders are given a say in how the business is run and receive a portion of the profits.

There are other sources of funding besides those mentioned above. For example, there are family members and wealthy individuals who might be willing to provide financial backing for partial ownership in a company or interest payments. The source of funding a business owner chooses is based on the type and size of the business and other factors dictating the direction in which it is going.

DETAILS, DETAILS, DETAILS

Small business owners must concern themselves with advertising, public relations, the legal aspects of operating a business, and other details. There are expenditures like insurance and personnel costs to be considered. There are business policies and procedures to establish. Inattention to these details can lead a small business to failure and possible bankruptcy.

THE PITFALLS OF SMALL BUSINESS

It is an unfortunate fact of small business that many companies do not survive. There are several reasons. The most prominent are economic recessions, inefficient management, insufficient capital, bad-debt losses, competition, decline in the value of assets, and poor business location. Some of these are not within a small business owner's control. Most, however, are. It is essential, then, that small business owners pay strict attention to every aspect of their operations. Attention to details is the key to success in any type of business—small businesses in particular.

THE FUTURE OF SMALL BUSINESS

There is no doubt that small businesses will continue to be the cornerstone of the American economy. They will provide the wide array of products and services that large corporations either cannot or will not provide. Consequently, there will be opportunities galore for entrepreneurs and owners alike who wish to exercise their independence by operating their own businesses. More importantly, small business owners will create the jobs so badly needed by people looking for employment opportunities. Simply put, the country cannot survive without a strong small business base. That has always been the case in the United States—and it will continue to be so for the foreseeable future.

[Arthur G. Sharp]

FURTHER READING:

Dorland, Gilbert N. and John Van Der Wal. *The Business Idea from Birth to Profitable Company.* Van Nostrand Reinhold Company, 1978.

Hawken, Paul. *Growing A Business.* Simon and Schuster, 1987.

How to Set Up Your Own Small Business. American Institute of Small Business, 1990.

Kuriloff, Arthur H., John M. Hemphill, Jr., and Douglas Cloud. *How to Start Your Own Business . . . and Succeed.* McGraw-Hill, Inc., 1993.

Mancuso, Joseph R. *How to Start, Finance, and Manage Your Own Small Business.* Prentice Hall, 1987.

SOCIALISM AND COMMUNISM

The word ''socialism'' was coined in 1832 by Pierre Leroux, editor of the Parisian journal, *Le Globe.* From then on, ''socialism'' took on many different meanings as the varieties of socialism grew and expanded, from western Europe to Russia, America, Asia, and Australia. It is mistakenly believed that Russians invented both socialism and communism and exported them, when in fact they borrowed these creeds from western Europe, developing their own versions of them.

Socialism, as distinct from ''socialistic'' ideas and practices that are evident as far back as biblical times, is a set of ideas, or theories, at the heart of which is a strong belief in social justice. All socialist theories are critical of wealth and the concentration of wealth in private hands; all of them advocate the elimination of poverty by equalizing the distribution of wealth, most often by some degree of collective (i.e., public) ownership. Only the most extreme socialist creeds have advocated the total elimination of private property. Because socialism also advocates some form of collective action, it can be defined not only as a theory but also as a movement.

The many varieties of socialism evolved in part from the disagreement on the means by which a more equitable distribution of wealth in society is to be achieved, a point on which no two socialist philosophies seemed to agree. Marxist socialism proposed the forceful establishment of a workers' dictatorship; conservative social democrats advocated parliamentary reform and trade unions; syndicalists favored a general strike of the workers; Christian socialists advocated a stringent application of the principles of the Bible (and also trade unions, or ''associations,'' as they called them). Furthermore, no two socialist creeds could agree on why poverty existed or how it had come about in the first place.

In short, the goal of a more just society based on an elimination of poverty was shared by virtually all socialist theories, including communism; how to achieve that goal led to the evolution of many different varieties of socialism. Finally, to make matters more difficult, socialism in theory often differed significantly from socialism in practice. Marxist socialism (that is, communism) in theory espoused workers' control of the means of production; Marxism in practice, however, be it in Russia, Cuba, or Cambodia, involved a communist-led government taking control of the means of production. Ironically, this produced permanent poverty for the mass of working people.

While socialistic ideas and practices have existed for thousands of years (the biblical Jesus was highly critical of wealth, defended the poor, and practiced a communal lifestyle), modern socialism was not born until the Industrial Revolution arrived in western Europe in the late eighteenth and early nineteenth centuries. The degrading poverty of the factory workers was nothing new—poverty has always been around—but their crowding into cities and their wretched living conditions made their particular kind of poverty so much more glaring and difficult to avoid. In addition to this new kind of poverty were two other important elements that would give rise to modern socialism: widespread literacy and the critical spirit that was the legacy of the Enlightenment. The difference therefore between a modern socialist and pre-modern socialist thinking was in the attitude towards poverty: Jesus, for example, took for granted that there always would be poverty; a modern socialist questioned the necessity of poverty, was convinced it could be abolished, and had a program to achieve this goal.

Bitter critiques of private wealth and intellectual theories about poverty became especially frequent preceding and during the French Revolution of 1789-99. Jean Jacques Rousseau (1712-78) was one of the earliest-known proponents of the state's responsibility for the equal distribution of wealth, but did not go so far as to advocate the dispossession of the rich. During the French Revolution, the supporters of the radical Jacobins in power demanded greater social justice and the equalization of wealth, but were not opposed to private property.

One of these French agitators, Gracchus Babeuf (1760-97), has frequently been cited as the "father" of modern communism for evolving a socialist creed (embodied in the *Manifesto of the Equals* written by a follower of Babeuf's) based on the belief that poverty was caused by class differences. The solution to poverty, according to Babeuf, was for the lower classes to overthrow the propertied class by force, establish themselves in power (i.e. create a "commonwealth" of equals), and proceed to distribute all property equally and hold it collectively. When Babeuf's secret organization, "The Conspiracy of the Equals," staged an abortive uprising in Paris in 1796, it was mercilessly crushed, his movement was outlawed, and Babeuf himself was guillotined.

Babeuf had been a poor, but highly literate, rural laborer, whose legacy was carried on by a number of disciples who were forced to live in permanent exile throughout western Europe. His followers came to be known as anarchists. The most famous names associated with anarchist socialism were August Blanqui (1805-81), who coined the term "dictatorship of the proletariat," and Pierre-Joseph Proudhon (1809-65), whose famous dictum, "property is theft," identified what many anarchist socialists by then believed was the primary cause of poverty.

Anarchism was the most extreme socialism before Karl Marx's *Capital*, the bible of Marxist socialism, was first published in London in 1867. Long before then, anarchism would move away from its roots in rural poverty to embrace the cause of the exploited factory worker during the Industrial Revolution. Blanqui believed in a violent insurrection of the

proletariat (factory workers), who afterwards would establish a dictatorship during which time the workers would dispossess the rich and distribute their wealth equally among all. Blanqui referred to socialism as "communism," and his anarchist followers were popularly referred to as "communists," although this communism had nothing to do with Marxism, which was a later development. Because anarchists rejected centralized government and some advocated violence, they were considered by the public to be dangerous radicals. They were in fact among a small minority of socialists.

There were at the same time, in the first half of the nineteenth century, far "milder" versions of socialism. These creeds had their roots in the Enlightenment as well, but were spawned largely by the misery and poverty engendered by the early stages of the Industrial Revolution. They disdained violence and did not believe in dispossessing the propertied.

A milder variant of socialism was embodied in the almost quaint ideas of Charles Fourier (1772-1837). This dreamy French intellectual disdained crowded cities and technology, advocating instead rural, self-sufficient agricultural communes, or phalansteries, where all property would be held in common, all inhabitants would do useful work but according to their own capacity and enjoyment (children, he reasoned, who loved playing in dirt, should be assigned garbage collecting), and adult love would be "free" and not chained by marriage. Women were to be absolutely equal and free (and could seek their own partners). Too poor to establish such a commune himself, many of his devoted followers brought his ideas to the United States, where they set up utopian communities in the midwest. Similar ideas were espoused by the Welsh owner of Scottish factories, Robert Owen (1771-1858), whose followers also set up a utopian community in New Harmony, Indiana.

Christian socialism, most often associated with Anglican author and activist Charles Kingsley (1819-75), developed in the 1850s and advocated a practical Christianity with the church involved in the improvement of workers lives. This version of socialism had the greatest impact in England, but also had a significant influence in Germany by the late nineteenth century.

The German Karl Marx (1818-83) would scoff at all of these socialisms as "utopian," although he would not admit how heavily they influenced him, especially anarchism. Marx's own variant of socialism was known as dialectical materialism, based on a dialectical model borrowed from the German historian Georg Hegel (1770-1831), who had taught at the University of Berlin shortly before Marx became a student there. The dialectic, acted out in a pattern of thesis, antithesis, and synthesis, gave form and logic to history, and explained how history evolved from one stage to the next.

Unlike Hegel, however, Marx was first and foremost a materialist. "Materialism" is any system of belief in which matter (which can be any impersonal force or influence over which a person exercises no control) is the only reality. In a materialistic philosophy, where impersonal forces are the agent, the individual is of little consequence. For Marx, only economic forces and the class struggle mattered. Therefore, an individual was important only in so far as he or she was part of an economic class. Marx's materialism (and atheism) owed much to the writing of the German intellectual, Ludwig Feuerbach (1804-72). In fact, Marx's dialectical materialism, fully expressed in his popular 1848 treatise, *The Communist Manifesto*, was thoroughly German.

By borrowing the dialectical model (and logic) of Hegel, Marx set out to prove that the driving force throughout history has been the class struggle between the owners of the means of production (the thesis), and those who labored for them (the antithesis). In ancient times, the laborers were slaves; in Marx's own time, they were the proletariat. The tension, the class struggle, between laborers and private property owners, would be resolved only in the final stage of the dialectic. This would occur when the class-conscious proletariat united to overthrow the "bourgeois" or capitalist state by means of revolution. The workers would then proceed to establish a temporary dictatorship in order to forcibly dispossess the capitalist bourgeoisie of their property, and hence, of the means of production. With the means of production in the hands of the actual producers for the first time in history, a classless society would result. Consequently, the class struggle would end, and the final stage of the dialectic (and of history) would be achieved.

With occasional financial support from his friend and mentor Friedrich Engels (1820-95), Karl Marx was able to spend years doing research in the British Museum (he was forced into exile in 1848, spending the next 35 years in London, where he died). He buttressed his dialectical theory with statistics of industrial growth in Great Britain, the most advanced capitalist country, and with current British economic theories. One of these was promulgated by David Ricardo (1772-1823), who argued that labor was the source of all value. Marx interpreted this to mean that capitalist profits were really wages stolen from the workers. Marx predicted that capitalism in Great Britain would lead to greater impoverishment of the workers, with wages continuously falling; in time, capitalism would collapse. The result of his intensive study was his turgid two volume work in German, *Das Kapital*, which was quickly translated into English (*Capital*) and eventually into Russian (it escaped

Russian censorship because of its highly theoretical content).

Marxism (that is, dialectical materialism) is only an economic theory. Instead of being regarded in this light, it became in a few years a secular religion. A generation of educated Europeans were won over by the "scientific" logic of dialectical materialism, next to which all other existing socialist creeds seemed infantile and utopian. Until well into the twentieth century, true believers of Marxism referred to it as "scientific socialism."

Since dialectical materialism is not a political theory, there is nothing about it that suggests the kind of totalitarianism with which the world has come to identify communism (a word Marx and Engels used loosely). Moreover, dialectical materialism or Marxism was put into practice for the first time in the least likely country, Russia. Marx and Engels would not have dreamed that a communist state would arise in an agrarian country, and they had only contempt for peasants and farmers who owned property, or desired to own it.

Nonetheless, this economic theory of Karl Marx, together with other writings of Marx and Engels besides *Capital*, bear out the totalitarian characteristics of Marxism: the proletariat and it alone would own all property (which is to say, the state); peasants, businessmen, professional people, would be dispossessed forcibly, since they were considered bourgeois, or petty bourgeois (as the peasants). Moreover, Marx and Engels had contempt for civil and political rights, which they also considered "bourgeois" and a means by which the bourgeoisie asserted its control. Finally, Marx adopted Blanqui's idea of the "dictatorship of the proletariat" as a necessary final (but temporary) stage of the dialectic, when the bourgeoisie would be compelled to give up their property, and capitalism would come to an end. Hence the necessity of compulsion and of a dictatorship, however temporary, are ominous indications that dialectical materialism, even in theory, was antidemocratic. Marx would have scoffed at this, insisting that a worker's state, where all were equal, could only be democratic. Of the rights of minorities he had not a clue, while due process of law was "bourgeois."

Even before Marx's *Capital* was published and disseminated, factory workers in many countries in Europe were being organized into unions and demanding better working conditions and wages. Many labor leaders had been influenced by the socialist creeds popular before Marx, and had even organized a "Worker's International" (the First International) in which Marx himself had become briefly involved. It is not surprising that Marxism, wholly concerned with the factory worker and predicting the ultimate triumph of labor, would make a deep impact on labor leaders as well as dissatisfied intellectuals.

It was in Marx's native Germany that Marxist socialism made its greatest impact before World War I; German Marxism in turn would have enormous impact on the socialist movements in Scandinavia and Russia, as well as on the Polish, Bulgarian, and Serbian labor movements. The first Marxist party in the world was the German Social Democratic Workers' Party, founded by August Bebel (1840-1913) in 1868, at a time when Germany was politically divided and still largely agrarian (that would change after 1871). "Social Democratic" and "Socialist" meant the same thing to most Germans, and the name stuck. In the 1870s and 1880s, Marxist labor parties, or "social democratic labor parties," sprang up throughout Europe. Unlike the American trade unions which arose independently of political parties, European trade unions were established by labor parties; hence, **labor unions** as a rule were closely tied to a political party. More often than not, the party was Social Democratic (meaning Marxist).

By 1889, Marxism as a movement had made such headway that Social Democratic party leaders throughout western Europe gathered in Paris and established the Second Socialist International (the First International had expired in London in the 1860s). The Second International had a permanent headquarters in Brussels called the ISB (International Socialist Bureau), and held periodic congresses every two years. During its brief history, from 1889 to 1914, the Second International was extremely successful in its role as promoter of Social Democracy throughout the world. Its leaders, such as Karl Kautsky (1854-1938) of the German Social Democratic Labor Party, Rosa Luxembourg (1870-1919; who was Polish, but most active in the German labor movement), Jean Jaures (1859-1914) in France, and Belgian Camille Huysmans (1871-1968; head of the ISB), gave the world the impression that the "socialist" (that is, Marxist) movement was invincible.

In fact, it was far from that. With the spread of universal male suffrage throughout western Europe, heretical voices within the Social Democratic parties and trade unions were questioning whether the lot of the worker was really getting worse, as Karl Marx had predicted, and whether the ballot box would not be a better means of serving the worker than the violent overthrow of the bourgeois state. Furthermore, most workers in the Social Democratic trade unions were not very interested in class struggle or the theoretical issues of dialectical materialism. Finally, by 1901, a respected leader of the German Social Democratic Labor Party, Eduard Bernstein (1850-1932), had broken with Marxism altogether. Having lived for years in England, he was impressed by what parliamentary democracy could do for workers who had the vote,

and he observed that the quality of their lives and their wages had improved steadily over the years. Nevertheless, his break with Marxism was not a break with socialism. Rather, he was siding with a less dogmatic, more liberal socialism of the kind that had taken root in England, and that was best represented by the Fabian socialists (not a political party, but an eclectic group of men and women—George Bernard Shaw was one of their most famous members).

While Bernstein was condemned within the International and by his own party, his dramatic break with Marxism heralded a schism in Social Democracy between the right wing (or "revisionists"), increasingly drawn to parliamentary democracy and to working within the system, and the left wing. Leftists were the hard-core Marxists, usually from eastern Europe and the Russian Empire, where democracy was weakest. This split between the left and right wings of the Social Democratic movement affected all the members of the International, including the American Social Democrats (led by Eugene Debs and Daniel De Leon). With the outbreak of World War I in 1914, it became permanent.

The self-appointed leader of the left-wing Social Democrats was Vladimir Lenin (1870-1924). He headed the Russian Social Democratic Labor Party's bolshevik wing (which had split off from the majority party in 1903), which he already was calling the "Bolshevik" party. In 1920, Lenin demanded that any Marxist party which joined the Third Communist International (or Comintern, headquartered in Moscow) shed the name "social democratic" and adopt the name "communist" to distinguish it from those parties that retained the name "social democratic" after World War I, but had shed Marxism.

It is ironic that the first communist government to be established in the world was in Russia, at the height of World War I. In the Russian Empire more so than in the other belligerent states, the unbearable strain of total war had undermined the shaky political regime. When popular pressure forced the tsar to abdicate in March 1917, the provisional government which replaced him doomed the country to chaos because of its efforts to promote democracy and civil liberties in the midst of total war. The newly amnestied Bolshevik leaders took advantage of the liberal atmosphere to undermine the democratic regime. With the help of the paramilitary Red Guards, they succeeded in toppling the new liberal government by force on November 7, 1917.

Even before he became head of state, Lenin had shifted the Marxist position on the peasantry (which Marx and Engels had lumped with the property-owning bourgeoisie) in order to win the support of Russia's vast mass of peasants. He declared that the peasantry were future proletariat; backed by plentiful statistics, Lenin proved in his writings that urbanization and industrialization in Russia were inevitable, and that the peasants were proletariat in the making. Nevertheless, only the Communist Party, and not the peasantry-turned-factory workers, could lead Russia along the path to a workers' state.

This emphasis on the primary and exclusive role of the party distinguishes ''Leninism'' from traditional Marxism. Traditional Social Democratic parties before World War I had not considered the party to be the ''vanguard'' of the revolution, nor did this concept of the party's leadership role fit into the scheme of the dialectic. Lenin's variant of Marxism, however, caught on especially in economically backward areas, where there were few factories and, hence, almost no proletariat.

Under Lenin, all enterprises, large and small, including the banking system, were nationalized. While small farmers could keep their land, this exception was meant to be only temporary. The Communist Party under Lenin felt too weak to directly challenge the majority of Russia's population.

Lenin also believed in rule by terror, which meant the secret police. This, too, would have horrified Social Democratic parties before World War I. To Lenin (who was a lawyer by profession), terror was justified since Russia was the only ''worker's state'' in the world, surrounded by capitalist enemies.

The Soviet Union (Russia and its satellite republics in the Caucasus and Central Asia) officially came into being in the 1920s. Lenin's successor, Joseph Stalin (1879-1953), became General Secretary of the Communist Party of the Soviet Union in 1928, and assumed complete control in 1929, turning the Soviet Union into one of the world's most totalitarian countries.

Democracy had no tradition or roots in Russia, and Soviet-style (Marxist-Leninist) communism took root subsequently in areas of the world where democratic traditions were weak or nonexistent. While communism has virtually disappeared 120 years after Karl Marx declared the imminent collapse of capitalism, totalitarianism (of which Marxist socialism is one variant) continues to attract its true believers.

[Sina Dubovoy]

FURTHER READING:

Kernig, C. D., ed. *Marxism, Communism and Western Society: A Comparative Encyclopedia*. 8 vols. New York: Herder & Herder, 1972-73.

Lichtheim, George. *The Origins of Socialism*. London: Weidenfeld & Nicolson, 1969.

Lichtheim, George. *Marxism, An Historical and Critical Study*. New York: Columbia University Press, 1982.

Lichtheim, George. *A Short History of Socialism*. London: Weidenfeld & Nicolson, 1970.

Meyerson, Adam. ''The Ash Heap of History. Why Communism Failed.'' *Policy Review*. Fall, 1991, p. 4.

Mosse, George L. *The Culture of Western Europe, The Nineteenth and Twentieth Centuries*. New York: Rand McNally, 1969.

SOFTWARE

Software is the collective term for computer programs, which are instructions in code telling a computer what to do in response to specific user inputs. Software is part of a functioning computer system, which also consists of hardware, the actual computer machinery and equipment.

Although computers were commercially introduced in the early 1950s, the term software did not appear until the early 1960s. Originally, commercial software was either developed and sold exclusively by computer hardware manufacturers and their value-added resellers as part of a computer system, or it was custom-written by computer programmers for individual clients. It was only in the 1970s, once the mainframe and minicomputer market had sufficiently grown and microcomputers had appeared, that independent software companies emerged.

There are two different types of software—operating system software and applications software—both of which are needed to perform most common functions on a computer.

Operating systems software is the basic set of instructions of how a computer operates, and most types perform similar functions. Operating systems may be either proprietary—that is designed and sold only with a specific computer hardware brand—or they may be sold independently of a computer brand, as long as the operating systems and the computers meet certain industry standards. During the course of the 1980s operating systems became increasingly independent of hardware. Widely used proprietary system software include MVS for IBM mainframe computers and VMS for Digital VAX minicomputers. MacOS was the proprietary operating system of Apple Macintosh computers until late 1994 when the company began licensing it to other computer manufacturers. The most common nonproprietary operating systems include DOS, OS/2, and the various versions of UNIX. All applications software must be designed to run on a given operating system, although some operating systems, such as OS/2, can execute software designed for other operating systems. Many common commercial applications software packages are made available in different versions for various operating systems.

There is also a type of software known as a **graphical user interface (GUI)**, which, until the mid-1990s, complemented, but did not replace the operating system. The most widely used GUI software is Windows; version 3.1 ran on DOS, but its replacement that was released in 1995 was both an operating system and a GUI. Windows also requires that applications software be tailored for its use.

A special category of systems software is network operating systems. This software, in conjunction with network adapter hardware, allows multiple computers to be connected together and share data and the use of peripheral equipment. A common network operating system for **local area networks (LANs)** (within an office) is Novell, Inc.'s NetWare.

Applications software may be custom-designed by or for an individual corporate user, developed and sold as part of a computer hardware system with its own proprietary operating system, or developed and marketed independently for use on one or more of the standard operating systems, also referred to as off-the-shelf software. The trend has been towards more off-the-shelf-software packages.

Software applications used in business may be of a generic type, sometimes called horizontal software, or be tailored to the very specific needs of an industry segment, which is referred to as vertical software. Common horizontal software types are word processing, **spreadsheet**, **database management**, and communications software. Commonly used word processing programs are Microsoft Word and WordPerfect; common spreadsheet programs are Lotus 1-2-3 and Microsoft Excel; and common database management programs are dBASE and Paradox. Communications software includes programs for internal communications over a local area network (LAN), such as cc:Mail, and software for transmitting data remotely over telephone lines, such as CrossTalk or Microphone II. These same software applications that serve various administrative needs are used by enterprises of all sizes in all industries, nonprofit and governmental entities, and consumers at home.

Certain software applications, while not industry-specific, are designed mostly for business applications because of their capabilities to handle large volumes of data. This is particularly the case with database management software, especially transaction processing software. This includes payroll and billing processing software and software used in retail and wholesale trade. Such software is typically developed for larger, more powerful computers, such as mainframes and minicomputers.

Software for a specific industry, or vertical software, is often at its core a combination of generic software types, such as database management plus communications software, often with the addition of certain data and features. Examples of vertical software include transaction processing software used by banks, computer reservations software used by travel agents to book airline flights and hotel rooms, appointment scheduling software used in medical offices, software that keeps track of customer orders in mail-order houses, and software to keep track of parts and labor for appliance repair contractors. Vertical software is more often proprietary than horizontal software, but it, too, is becoming increasingly available in off-the-shelf packages as its respective markets expand.

Other kinds of industry-specific software that are not so directly business related are those that facilitate engineering, manufacturing, and other production needs. Computer-aided design (CAD) software facilitates the design of engineering or architectural projects. Automated industrial machinery, such as in manufacturing or materials handling, uses software to control the machinery and processes. Desktop publishing software is used in publications design and typesetting and has become widely used not only by publishing and printing companies but also by many organizations and individuals wishing to create attractive documents.

The ability to integrate different software applications is a growing trend in business software. Different activities of a company have historically used independent software programs, such as one for accounts receivable, another for inventory management, another for manufacturing process control, and yet another for product design. Newer software tends to offer expanded features or the ability to "interface" with, or be connected to, other software programs. Similarly, various "add-in" software has been developed to add features to specific existing software packages. For example, in the retail/wholesale industries, the same software is now being used to record retail sales, keep track of inventories, and place orders with suppliers. In engineering, a CAD program can be linked to a database of information on component prices and labor costs to provide instant cost estimates for a specific design, which aids in budget planning. In some kinds of manufacturing, process control software not only automatically adjusts the flow of additives into product for desired quality, but also keeps track of the amount and rate of additive use; this data can be analyzed on a connected spreadsheet program to keep track of costs. General-purpose horizontal software is similarly being integrated, whereby the user can search and retrieve texts from a database, edit the texts, and then electronically transmit them to the computer of another user, all without exiting a software program.

[Heather Behn Hedden]

Figure 1

Takei Bussan	Ownership	Takei Oil, K.K.	Ownership
Takei Heavy Industries	6.2%	Takei Bussan	9.1%
Takei Bank	6.0	Oita Electric	8.0
Takei Steel	5.5	Takei Heavy Industries	7.8
Marubishi Glass	4.9	Takei Steel	7.6
Oita Electric	4.0	Takei Bank	7.2
Takei Oil	3.9	Dai Ichi Chemical	7.0
Dai Ichi Chemical	2.8	Marubishi Glass	6.5
Total	33.3%	Total	53.2%

FURTHER READING:

Dayton, Doug. *Computer Solutions for Business.* Microsoft Press.

Seymour, Jim. "The Real Add-In Story: Making 1-2-3 More Vertical." *PC Magazine.* April 16, 1991, p. 103.

Vizard, Michael. "Vertical Applications Will Build on Suites." *Computerworld.* December 27, 1993, p. 68.

"Why Study Vertical Markets?" *Computer Industry Report.* March 27, 1992, p. 4.

SOGO SHOSHA

The sogo shosha is a form of industrial organization unique to Japan in which a number of independently incorporated companies maintain substantial equity interests in each other, forming loose conglomerates that are vertically integrated. At the center of these organizations is a trading company which arranges financing, coordinates activities, and handles **marketing** functions for the companies in its group. These subordinate companies may be considered operating companies, because they specialize in certain types of business.

While the term *sogo shosha*, which is Japanese for "general trading company," is derived from the central organization, the name generally refers to the entire group of operating companies that comprise the conglomerate.

Typically, as the head of the several companies that comprise a group, the trading company is the primary shareholder of operating companies in its group. The trading company commonly places several of its own officials on the boards of these companies, while senior officials of the largest companies in the group maintain seats on the trading company's **board of directors**. This arrangement comprises a loose system of interlocking directorships.

The sogo shosha differs from classical conglomerates, such as those in the United States and Europe, in that no single entity in the group owns more than a small percentage of any other company in the group. But taken together, the trading company and several of the other companies in its group may own a majority of shares in one of these companies, in effect, comprising a controlling interest.

All the companies in a typical sogo shosha own aggregate majority shares in each other, forming a complex system of cross-ownership. As a result, companies in a sogo shosha cannot technically be considered **subsidiaries** in the classical sense. Subordinate companies are merely "associated" with the sogo shosha because they are independently listed and substantial minority interests are held by investors outside the sogo shosha.

Some sogo shosha comprise as few as a half dozen companies, while other larger organizations might contain as many as 150 or more subordinate companies.

The matrix of cross ownership is illustrated in Figure 1. The Takei Group, consists of eight companies, headed by the Takei Bussan trading company.

What is striking about this example is that the operating companies in the group control a third of the trading company's shares, while a majority of the operating companies' shares are owned by the trading company and its associated operating companies. The remaining shares—those not owned by entities within the Takei Group—may be owned by other institutions, pension funds, brokerages, and individual shareholders. This allows shares in these companies to be independently listed on stock exchanges to raise additional investor capital.

Commensurate with the majority position group companies have in each other is representation on boards of directors. Officials of numerous Takei Group companies may hold a majority of seats on the boards of subordinate companies in which the Group has a majority interest. The remaining seats are held by nominally independent directors who have no official employment relationship with a Takei Group company.

This form of cross-ownership and board representation is not permitted in the United States, where strict **antitrust laws** preclude this type of control. For example, General Motors Corp. may hold shares in its EDS subsidiary, but EDS may not simultaneously hold shares in General Motors. Similarly, neither company's board may include more than one or two directors from the other company. In Japan, however, these are common features of a sogo shosha. This form of organization is allowed for several reasons.

First, the sogo shosha system has been in existence for more than a hundred years and has become a traditional, if not essential, feature of industrial organization in Japan. Secondly, the Japanese government recognizes that sogo shosha are highly efficient and synergistic: each company has a stake in the financial success of every other company and concentrates its resources to realize that success.

Third, sogo shosha generally are not anticompetitive. There are about a dozen such conglomerates in Japan, each of which is highly diversified and competes in specific industrial sectors against other sogo shosha and independent companies. For the most part, no sogo shosha dominates any of the industries in which it is involved—and it is likely that none would even if it could.

If, through expansion and acquisition, a sogo shosha was to build a large market share in a certain industry, the resulting concentration would enable that company to frustrate **competition** within that industry. Government regulators would require the company to reduce its presence in that market, specifically to preserve competition and protect the investments of other companies in that industry.

Such brash moves to dominate certain industries could seriously disrupt the business of competitors. While concern for the welfare of competitors is not particularly important in the United States, it would be treated gravely in Japan, where social mores demand a high level of respect for competitors, because many are capable of retribution which might prove destructive to the business of other enterprises in the group.

The government maintains a powerful agency— the Japanese Ministry of International Trade and Industry—to regulate and coordinate the actions of the conglomerates. In addition, the conglomerates have established an executive council called the Keidanren specifically to prevent such actions and maintain industrial harmony. This ''coordination'' among major producers would clearly constitute collusion in the United States.

The sogo shosha are basically marketing organizations. They maintain large international networks to collect information on numerous markets and facilitate the sale of products in those markets. A typical sogo shosha serves as an agent for products manufactured by companies in its group and, under a contract arrangement, by smaller independent manufacturers.

As a result, the sogo shosha may supply tens of thousands of products, from can openers, calculators and bicycles to automobiles, locomotives and ships. This is why consumers might see **brand names** like

Mitsubishi on a wide variety of products, including televisions, automobiles and vacuum cleaners.

In addition to their ability to make the greatest use of the marketing intelligence network, the sogo shosha work on extremely thin margins, commonly little more than 1.5 percent. It is therefore necessary for these companies to maintain very high sales volumes and remain focused on long-term business development.

The sogo shosha are populated with largely homogeneous personalities. They are male-dominated organizations whose staff are culled from the finest universities and placed on extensive socialization programs that include years of cultural preparation. By this process, a profound team mentality is established among the work force. Employees of one company may deal with counterparts elsewhere in the organization free from cultural barriers and acclimated to a common code of conduct.

The sogo shosha system has its origin with a political rebellion in 1868, in which the Tokugawa government was replaced by a restoration of the Meiji emperor. The new government initiated an ambitious industrial modernization program in which large state enterprises were established, using the British East India Company, Jardine Matheson, and other firms as models.

But because government officials lacked the managerial expertise to run these companies, the government was forced to turn the enterprises over to existing companies that, while small, had nonetheless demonstrated strong management skills.

These family-run businesses—which included Sumitomo, Mitsui, Mitsubishi, Ono and Shimada— were primarily involved in import and export trading. Most were not manufacturers; their primary function was marketing products made by other companies, and so were sogo shosha from the very beginning.

During the 1870s, many of these companies grew tremendously. Mitsui became Japan's leading trading firm, while Mitsubishi grew to dominate the shipping industry, and Sumitomo the mining industry. Ono and Shimada eventually dissolved, but were replaced by Yasuda, which became Japan's largest bank.

These enterprises continued to grow in scope and scale, helped by strong relationships with local and national political figures and their involvement in Japan's military conquests of Korea, Manchuria, Taiwan and China. So dominant were these companies in Japanese trade and industry, that they became known as *zaibatsu*, or ''money cliques.''

The zaibatsu commonly consisted of a primary enterprise—usually a sogo shosha—surrounded by subsidiaries engaged in banking, insurance, shipping, mining, real estate, food processing and manufacturing. By virtue of their assets in human and fixed capital, as well as their considerable political power and technological expertise, the zaibatsu became essential components of Japan's economic modernization, and remained so through the 1920s, when they reached the peak of their power.

Japanese colonial interests in Korea, Manchuria, and China were developed mainly by zaibatsu companies. They provided their homeland with a wealth of natural resources from these areas, including lumber, coal, and agricultural and animal products. Several of these areas became highly developed industrial centers.

During this period, the majority of Japan's import and export trade was conducted through the zaibatsu companies. This placed them in positions to identify promising new industries and either capitalize them for an equity interest or purchase them outright. In either case, growth companies were quickly made captive to a zaibatsu very early in their development stages.

The zaibatsu gradually lost their independence from political forces during the 1930s, after a nationalist military faction gained power over government and political organs. The zaibatsu were made targets of this faction, which denounced the companies as monopolist (in fact, Mitsui's chairman was assassinated by military fanatics).

For the most part, this was a valid criticism. The zaibatsu benefitted greatly from recessions and other public crises, and exercised extensive control over government and public resources.

In 1937, the militarists launched a war of conquest against China. Despite their disdain for the zaibatsu, the military leaders recognized that these enterprises were essential to a successful prosecution of the war. By 1941, the zaibatsu had become synonymous with the Japanese military-industrial complex.

That year, the war expanded to include Britain, the United States and the Netherlands. Far from reducing the companies' influence, the military leaders placed the zaibatsu in charge of large areas of the economy, resulting in tremendous concentration of the industrial sector.

When the war ended in 1945, government authority was assumed by the American military occupation authority, known by its acronym SCAP. The first priority of SCAP was to prosecute war criminals, including senior officials of the zaibatsu who had been sympathetic to military.

SCAP saw the zaibatsu companies not only as the core of Japan's ability to wage war, but also as an impediment to democratization. Furthermore, the high concentration of manufacturing capacity in the zaibatsu was incompatible with the American tradition of antitrust law.

As a result, SCAP decreed the establishment of antimonopoly laws that necessitated the dissolution of the zaibatsu into thousands of independent companies, none of which was allowed to retain its association through the old zaibatsu or even use the zaibatsu name.

Despite this, the captains of the defunct zaibatsu established in 1946 a loose federation called the keidanren to coordinate reconstruction projects with the government. After the Occupation ended in 1950, the keidanren lobbied for the relaxation of antimonopoly laws that limited contact between former zaibatsu affiliates. This was largely achieved by 1952, and over the ensuing years, Mitsui, Mitsubishi, Sumitomo and others gradually re-established their groups around the banks that had been members of their groups.

At this stage, the relationships were merely commercial. As the former zaibatsu companies expanded the scope and volume of their business, they became known as keiretsu, "banking conglomerates," and zaikai, "financial circles."

The banks provided a legitimate medium for association between former affiliates, but the cross-ownership and interlocking directorships which had been features of the prewar zaibatsu were still prohibited. Several of the old groups reconstituted themselves through acquisitions, but also used the opportunity to expand into completely new lines of business.

The government recognized that the old zaibatsu groups could be very effective at rebuilding the shattered Japanese economy. They were best positioned to provide capital to small start-up enterprises and, given Japan's lack of natural resources, to develop a neomercantilist economy that would generate growth through exports.

They established foreign offices to sell goods in new markets, generating capital to develop primary industries, such as steel making, ship building, oil refining, automobile manufacturing, power generation and road building.

The new sogo shosha conglomerates—again led by Mitsui, Mitsubishi, Sumitomo and others—participated in the construction of a modern industrial infrastructure that facilitated the growth of thousands of smaller enterprises, fueling economic expansion through exports as they had 60 years earlier.

Through the keidanren, the new sogo shosha worked closely with the government's Ministry of International Trade and Industry (MITI) to develop industries in which Japan had a distinct international competitive advantage. They brought products such as textiles, handicrafts and simple electronics to markets in the United States, Europe, and Asia.

The cycle of investment enabled many of the sogo shosha to capitalize new ventures in heavy industry. By the 1960s, Japan was positioned to enter international markets for automobiles, electronics, steel, and maritime products.

The sheer size of the sogo shosha made them essential partners in carrying through government policies. They employed most of the available managerial talent, and their banks had more capital than any other source.

The sogo shosha helped to create an environment in which independent companies were able to grow. Companies such as Honda, Hitachi, Kubota, Toyota, Sony, Ricoh, Canon Inc., Matsushita, Minebea and Hino—none of which were officially associated with sogo shosha—built their own marketing networks independent of the sogo shosha. This forced many of the sogo shosha into increasingly risky ventures.

Despite their size, the sogo shosha operated on such narrow margins that the failure of even a small venture was catastrophic. Indeed, a medium-size sogo shosha called Ataki was forced into insolvency when its Canadian oil venture failed.

By 1978, Japan had nine major sogo shosha, led by Mitsubishi and Mitsui, and followed by C. Itoh, Marubeni, Sumitomo, Nissho-Iwai, Kanematsu-Gosho, Tomen, and Nichimen. Smaller groups included Chori, Itoman, Okura and Toshoki.

Strictly speaking, the trading company is a middleman whose only functions are marketing the products it handles and occasionally capitalizing promising infant firms. As a result, its only real assets are managerial expertise and financial capital.

Modern sogo shosha remain loosely organized. There is no powerful central parent company as there was before World War II. Contact between the principals of operating companies usually takes place in informal weekly or monthly gatherings, called clubs.

Despite the re-emergence of limited cross-ownership and interlocking directorships and the collusory nature of the keidanren and the club system, the concentration of industrial capacity in Japan is little different from that in the United States. In fact, in many cases there are fewer competitors in certain American markets than in Japanese ones.

The government maintains a strong degree of control over the sogo shosha through MITI, although its relationship with the companies is almost exclusively cooperative. MITI and the Keidanren frequently hold panels to study the companies' investment plans as part of an effort to coordinate production.

However, there are patterns of price leadership in certain markets. This feature of cartel organization is allowed, and sometimes even condoned, by the government as a measure of demand control.

While the sogo shosha frequently cooperate in certain areas, they avoid oligopolistic patterns by mounting rivalries that produce high rates of investment in new industries, often yielding low-cost products in brief cycles.

But as more independent Japanese companies have grown in sales and volume, they have outgrown the need for representation and capitalization by the sogo shosha and established their own international marketing networks. This has forced the sogo shosha ''down market'' into lower-technology goods in declining industries.

This stems from the fact that most of the sogo shosha are historically concentrated in basic industries, handling low-margin primary—rather than higher-margin finished—products.

In addition, the sogo shosha tend to lack experience in marketing products—automobiles, electronics, and cosmetics—which require extensive consumer research and sales support. Firms in these industries are less likely to do business through a sogo shosha because the trading companies lack the necessary expertise—a deficit in experience that is self-perpetuating.

The sogo shosha form of organization is by no means monolithic; groups vary in scale, scope and degrees of cross-ownership. While some sogo shosha are very tightly knit (to the extent of sharing strategies, names, and even chairmen), others are little more than associations of convenience whose companies may not even hold shares in each other.

The only modern equivalent to sogo shosha occur in South Korea, where conglomerates such as Lucky-Goldstar, Samsung, Hyundai, Ssangyong and others—called chaebol—have been encouraged to follow the example of Japanese companies. While there are obvious differences between sogo shosha and chaebol, they have produced strikingly similar forms of industrial organization and economic growth; South Korea is today approximately where Japan was 20 years ago.

Despite the difficulties encountered by many sogo shosha during the late 1980s and early 1990s, it is unlikely that any will imminently meet their demise. The sogo shosha remain the largest companies in Japan and are sufficiently diversified to withstand periodic downturns in certain sectors of the economy.

Due to their size, the sogo shosha have had problems adjusting to new dynamics in the Japanese economy. It is by no means necessary for the sogo shosha to emulate the activities of specialized high-growth companies to survive. They continue to dominate essential sectors of the economy, such as petroleum, chemicals and metals processing, machinery manufacturing, engineering, transportation, and banking.

In addition, the sogo shosha are powerful instruments of government policy and industrial planning. It is unlikely that the government would allow the decline of such an effective system of industrial organization and capitalization.

[John Simley]

FURTHER READING:

Allen, George Cyril. *A Short Economic History of Modern Japan*. New York: St. Martin's Press, 1981.

Oppenheim, Phillip. *Japan Without Blinders*. Tokyo: Kodansha International, 1992.

Richardson, Bradley, and Taizo Ueda. *Business and Society in Japan*. New York: Praeger Publishers, 1981.

Tsurumi, Yoshi. *Sogoshosha: Engines of Export-based Growth*. Montreal: Institute for Research on Public Policy, 1980.

SOUTH AMERICA, DOING BUSINESS IN

South America is a huge continent of dramatic contrasts, with a population of only 285 million people, fewer than in tiny western Europe, and only 50 million more than in the United States. The biggest country in South America, Brazil, is approximately the size of the United States, but has only half of the number of inhabitants. The official language of most of South America is Spanish (English and Dutch are spoken in Surinam and Guyana, French in French Guiana, and Portuguese in Brazil), with Indian dialects spoken widely in the countryside.

South America is an incredibly rich continent; for instance, only the Middle East has more oil than Venezuela. Besides oil, the continent is very rich in minerals, metals, and other raw materials. Yet most ordinary people living in the 12 nation states (and one colony) of South America are poverty stricken; in extremely oil rich Venezuela, the gross domestic product (GDP) per person averages only a little over $2,000. Despite the fact that the entire continent experienced European colonialism (via Spain and Portugal) and Roman Catholicism, discord and disunity have prevailed throughout most of South America's modern history. Neither Spain nor Portugal had parliamentary governments, consequently, the political legacy in South America has been a highly authoritarian one. Slave-based agriculture prevailed as late as 1888 (in Brazil), but mining also played an important economic role in the Andean countries of Chile, Bolivia, and Peru. Until well into the 20th century, South American economies have focused on only one or two products, be it tin or bananas or coffee. Political instability and authoritarian regimes by and large stymied economic growth and diversification in every South American nation, as well as the building of sound infrastructures. Strongly protectionist trade policies until recent times did their part to discourage significant foreign trade.

POLITICAL AND ECONOMIC CLIMATE

The United States government has not always had a positive impact on this continent, Cold War tensions between the United States and Soviet Union brought outright interference and intervention in domestic politics, such as in the forcible overthrow of the Marxist government of Salvador Allende in Chile in 1973. Anti-communist South American dictators, many of questionable ethics, usually found support from the U.S. government, fueling anti-American hostility on the part of the native populations.

Accordingly, most American businesses have been skeptical about doing business in this unstable region. However, the fall of communism in the U.S.S.R. and the end of the Cold War have triggered a dramatic transformation throughout Latin America, beginning with the volatile, politically polarized Central American region (a barometer for the rest of Latin America). Free market reforms and economic liberalization have been evident in every Latin American and Caribbean island nation. In addition, everywhere in Latin America military dictatorships and other forms of authoritarianism have given way to democratic parliamentary rule. Foreign firms doing business in many South American countries now encounter a sophisticated business climate where business managers are the equal of those in the United States or Europe.

The 1990s has seen an unusual trend—a movement away from military rivalry towards aggressive economic competition. To win in the economic sphere, nations that were once rivals have down played their differences in favor of regional economic cooperation. (A similar situation has occurred in Europe and Asia.)

The trend towards economic regionalism in this hemisphere first became serious in 1988, when the Cold War was on the wane. The free trade pact between the United States and Canada that year later developed into the **North American Free Trade Agreement** (NAFTA). Approved by the U.S. Congress in the fall of 1993, NAFTA created the largest free trade zone in the world. NAFTA's ratification was impelled in part by the creation of the **European Union**.

Even before the ink was dry on the NAFTA accord, the United States, in a reversal of decades of indifference to Latin America's economic future, decided to encourage the growth and development of the economies there. The reason for this change was the hope that, in time, all of Central and South America would be joined with North America in an economic accord known as the Western Hemispheric Free Trade Area (WHFTA).

Hence the U.S. government has given unequivocal support to the unprecedented efforts of several South American governments to unify their economic policies for the sake of greater economic power. As with North America, no single South American country could hope to match the economic clout of the European Community, especially since virtually all South American governments have labored under huge deficits. Ecuador alone has spent as much as 40 percent of its national budget annually just to service its $12 billion debt. As a member of the Andean Pact, however, Ecuador has already increased its foreign capital reserves from $200 million in 1990 to more than $1 billion dollars.

REGIONAL ECONOMIC PACTS

In the summer of 1990, Washington unveiled the Enterprise for the Americas (EAI) initiative. With the promise of U.S. assistance in debt reduction, increased trade, and bilateral or multilateral preferential trade treaties with the U.S. (on the condition that major economic reforms occurred), the stage was set for the launching of regional economic pacts in Latin America and the Caribbean. Three years later, four major alliances had developed: the Caribbean Common Market, the Central American Common Market (CACM), Mercosur, the Southern Cone Common Market (consisting of Argentina, Paraguay, Uruguay, and Brazil, with Chile promising to join in 1995), and the Andean Pact (Ecuador, Peru, Bolivia, Venezuela, and Colombia). Guyana and Surinam belong to the Caribbean economic union. French Guyana is a department of France, which makes it a member of the European Common Market.

Of these four regional economic alliances, the biggest and most important has been MERCOSUR, which was established in 1991. Members of this common market pledged to from an economic union (which means that economic policies among the member states must be merged) in December 31, 1994. This was the first time in South American history that any two major economies would be joined together, let alone five nations. The members of MERCOSUR are among the most economically sophisticated in Latin America, and any American firm doing business with a member of this common market would not be dealing with a developing, dependent region. MERCOSUR already has opened an information center (Mercosur Consulting Group, Ltd.) in New York City as a way of marketing the business opportunities within member states.

The Andean Pact includes countries as potentially wealthy as Venezuela and as extremely poor as Ecuador. By and large, the less well to do and most troubled nations of South America—Peru, Bolivia, and Colombia—are members of the Andean Pact. (Peru faces ongoing terrorism difficulties, while Bolivia and Columbia continue to battle the cocaine trade.) Hence in March 1992, two months after the five Andean Pact members officially inaugurated **free trade** within their region, the White House unveiled the Andean Trade Initiative. This policy extends to the Andean Pact members the same benefits that the Caribbean Basin Initiative grants Caribbean Basin countries: duty-free entrance into the United States of 94 product categories manufactured in the Andean Pact countries; the establishment in the AP member states of development banks, chambers of commerce, and free trade zones; the funding of job training and self-help programs; and most importantly, financial assistance to U.S. companies doing business in this region with attractive terms. The Andean Trade Initiative expires in 2002.

AMERICAN BUSINESS IN SOUTH AMERICA

Because of the many positive changes in the political and economic fortunes of South America, American businesses have begun to take a fresh look at opportunities there. Currently, economic blocs are still in flux. Competition from Asian and European companies is still relatively low in some South American countries, especially within the Andean bloc. In fact, it may well be in an American company's interest to take trade and investment in South America seriously before this century runs out. The economic blocs still in the process of forming can negotiate favorable terms with foreign businesses; these favorable terms will be more difficult to obtain in the future, when European and Asian companies have established a presence in South America. In addition, so long as the Andean Trade Initiative is in force, there are many financial benefits to starting a business before 2002.

Other advantages to doing business in South America are more obvious: in virtually every South American country, labor is cheap and raw materials are abundant. Most American businesses concentrate on producing goods for shipment back to the United States, but within the economic blocs themselves, there is a sizable market for U.S. products, which are very popular among consumers. Tourism is also becoming a vital industry. South America is the one region of the world in which the United States has enjoyed a trade surplus, exporting considerably more than it has imported.

However, doing business in South America is not easy. Unlike establishing a business in the developing island nations of the Caribbean or in Central America, it is not possible for a company to do business in South America without seasoned business professionals with a great deal of international marketing experience. Knowledge of the native language is essential. Having a partner in the host country is also imperative. While markets are becoming more open and tariffs are declining, the legacy of political instability and corruption (especially severe in the Andean Pact nations) will take years to overcome.

Clearly the difficulties and the requirements of doing business in a South American country can be formidable, but there are always difficulties and roadblocks in doing business with any foreign region. A number of South American countries, such as Colombia, Venezuela, and Ecuador, have a trade relationship with the United States that dates back decades. And unlike Europe and Asia, South America needs **foreign exchange** to reduce soaring debts, so every government there is willing to bend over backwards to attract it. **Privatization** of government services is one result of this in all South American countries, even in the formerly semi-communist country of Ecuador. Low tariffs are already common, and repatriation of profits back to the United States is universal.

Argentina is an example of a South American country that for decades had one of the most isolated and overregulated economies in the world. By 1990, superinflation had reached 20,000 percent. Since then, however, the economic and political scenarios have changed rapidly under the democratic rule of President Carlos Menem and, for the first time in 60 years, foreign capital and investment are welcome. Large scale privatization is underway, and all export taxes and government caps on prices have been abolished. A 1991 treaty between the United States and Argentina guarantees American businesses in Argentina equal government treatment with native-based companies.

Such incentives are necessary to lure foreign business to a country that still suffers from corruption and favoritism, factors that have to be taken into account when doing business in Argentina. In Brazil, another **MERCOSUR** member, there are still so many obstacles to doing business that only the most seasoned U.S. companies should consider it. However, to ignore the largest country in South America (when Asians and Europeans do not) is to risk being left out when economic reforms have finally taken hold. Perhaps the most lucrative markets in Brazil are those for environmental products and computers, for which there appears to be a perpetual demand.

Of the five members of the Andean Pact, oil rich Venezuela is perhaps the best place to invest. Ecuador is just beginning to open up to foreign investment. While overwhelming red tape and corruption still plague the business person wishing to establish trade links with Venezuela, it has made the largest strides within the Andean Pact towards opening up to foreign trade and instituting economic reforms. Unlike Argentina and Chile, however, Venezuela is still very much a developing country, despite its huge oil sales. While a quarter of Venezuela's GDP comes from its petroleum sales, there is no thought of privatizing the giant petroleum industry, which is in serious need of modernization. The population is poverty stricken, with low rates of education and literacy and low health standards. However, the country's labor is cheap, abundant, and much of it is skilled. The country's location astride the Caribbean makes it very accessible to trade, and there is continuous and strong demand for computer and telecommunications products and systems, medical equipment, and even foodstuffs.

Finally, perhaps the most progressive and developed country in Latin America is Chile. Privatization is nearly complete, having been begun in 1973 with the ouster of Marxist leader Salvador Allende Gossens (1908-1973). Adult literacy is at the same level than in the United States and **unemployment** is low. Chile is an aggressive member of MERCOSUR and a tough business partner, comparable to any in Europe or Asia. Its relative remoteness means shipping and transportation to and from the United States is very costly. However, Chile's vast Pacific coastline and proximity to Asian and Australian markets makes it a strategically located country. Best of all, the domestic market is very open to foreign products, especially American (one of the few countries in which this still holds true). Unlike all other South American countries, there is no red tape or corrupt bureaucracy. Citibank has had a branch in Santiago for years that specializes in trade finance and lends money on easy terms.

Because of the great diversity of opportunities and obstacles in doing business in South America, a company must be sure that its product line will have a niche before doing business there. Market studies are necessary and can be conducted easily by a native marketing agency. Finding a business partner is essential, as is developing exhaustive knowledge about doing business in any South America country. If the chosen country is a member of MERCOSUR, information is available from the MERCOSUR office in New York City. The Latin American/Caribbean Business Development Center in Washington, D.C., an office of the U.S. Commerce Department, also has up to date information on doing business in South America and offers one-on-one assistance. It is perhaps the best source of information on doing business in South America, and the best place to start. If the chosen country belongs to one of the other two common markets in South America, the consulate office of that country or the trade section of the embassy can supply additional information.

With tariffs at all-time lows, a cheap supply of labor, abundant natural resources, and governments eager for **foreign trade**, South America is poised for business growth.

[Sina Dubovoy]

FURTHER READING:

Crow, Patrick. "Ecuador Seeks Foreign Investors," *Oil & Gas Journal*. December 27, 1993, p. 33.

Edwards, Sebastian. "Latin American Economic Integration: A New Perspective on an Old Dream," *World Economy*. May, 1993, p. 317.

Foster, Kent, and Dean Alexander. "Investment Spurts in Uruguay," *Global Trade & Transportation*. January, 1994, p. 6.

Gitli, Eduardo, and Gunilla Ryd. "Latin American Integration and the Enterprise for the Americas Initiative," *Journal of World Trade*. August, 1992, p. 25.

Holman, Richard L. "Peru To Re-Enter Trade Bloc (Andean Pact)," *The Wall Street Journal*. April 7, 1994, p. A10(W), A11(E).

Jennings, Horace. "Brazil: A'Hot' U.S. Market, Despite Lagging Reforms," *Business America*. April 19, 1993, p. 9.

Kissenger, Henry A. "A Hemisphere of Free Trade (Enterprise for the Americas Initiative)," *Washington Post*. May 17, 1992, p. C7.

Long, William R. "Trade Winds Are Blowing Across Americas," *Los Angeles Times*, January 1, 1994.

MacNamara, Laurie. "Andean Region Makes Integration Effort," *Business America*. March 23, 1992, p. 5.

McCrary, Ernest S. "It's Testing Time for Latin America's Free Market Will," *Global Finance*. May, 1993, p. 69.

Murphy, Tom. "MERCOSUR to Maintain Schedule for Toppling Trade Barriers," *Journal of Commerce and Commercial*. December 13, 1993, p. 3A(1).

"NAFTA Draws Attention to Other Key Trade Pacts," *Journal of Commerce and Commercial*. February 28, 1994, p. 3C(1).

Robinson, Danielle. "Chile Sets Sights Further Afield," *Euromoney*, March, 1993, p. 157.

"Texas's Southern Neighbors Hold Promise for Future Trade," *San Antonio Business Journal*. September 3, 1993, p. 48.

Tuller, Lawrence W. *Doing Business in Latin America and the Caribbean*. New York: Amacom, 1993.

SPECTRAL ANALYSIS

Spectral analysis as used in business, is applied to statistical economic trend calculations. Cyclic economic factors, or variables of business interest, are like the oscillating patterns on a heart monitor in that they represent, both visually and mathematically, the pulse of the economy. To more clearly understand the business applications of spectral analysis, one needs to understand the principle in a broader sense.

Spectral analysis is a mathematical technique for studying physical phenomena that occur in cycles. Although it has wide-reaching applications in the sciences, its beginnings lie in the observance of nature.

Ancient humans became aware of cycles with the changing of the seasons, the rising of tides, and the movement of the stars. Early astronomers and those persons living in agriculture-based civilizations first learned the values of recognizing patterns and of being able to make predictions and forecasts based on empirical observations of cyclic trends.

The foundations of spectral analysis lie in the broader area of times series analysis. The Fourier theorem, named for Baron J. B. J. Fourier (1768-1830), a French geometrician and physicist, states that periodic functions can be defined by the mathematical components of cyclical series decomposed, or broken down, into multiples of the functions sine and cosine. These are the components which create the spectrum which is analyzed. Astronomers, physicists, mathematicians, and other scientists grasped this concept and have used it extensively ever since, but it did not readily lend itself to economic studies.

Another major step in the development of time series analysis came with the work of Sir Arthur Shuster from 1898 to 1906. Shuster popularized the use of the periodogram method. In the 1920s, further advances were made by grappling mathematically with the ideas of the ebbs and flows of business economics. E. Slutsky and G. U. Yule made advances on previous methods with the idea of an auto regressive moving average.

FUNDAMENTALS OF SPECTRAL ANALYSIS

Waves on a pond have the physical shape characteristic of cycle, or wave, phenomena. By using this pond wave model, one can observe that while the waves are constant, they vary in their pitch, or distances apart, and their heights. These variations are termed wave frequency and amplitude, respectively. Frequency is measured in cycles per time unit, also referred to as the time period of a cycle. Amplitude is measured in the indexes relative to the variable of interest, such as unemployment expressed as a percentage, interest rates also expressed as a percentage, capital expenditures expressed in currency, and so on. By plotting historical data, it can be seen that variables change relative to the constant measure of time. A point can be found on the wave by a given value of one variable when the equation is used that describes the function of the sine wave. In this equation, we express the effect of change on one variable relative to the other, or codependency with, the functions of sine and cosine. Nevertheless, business or economic conditions do not behave in a smooth, regular, cyclic pattern. They are irregular and, like our pond wave model, are stochastic, or random.

Economics statisticians plot variables of business interest against time and through the use of mathematical refinement techniques—such as smoothing and filtering—that produce the sine wave cycles. Some of the items or occurrences the statistician would be likely to filter out are cycles with wildly exaggerated amplitude, or noise, such as the price of steel during World War II. Noise can be compared to someone throwing a stone into the pond wave model. It cannot be predicted or taken into account in plotting general trends.

Analysis can be undertaken considering the entire time plot limits or at specific times or time intervals. These are termed the continuous spectrum and the discrete spectrum, respectively. Once a clarified sine wave cyclic pattern emerges from the plot of all the data, the statistician would then perform a regression analysis of the plot to determine the pattern of a trend. A projection can then be made by extending the variable of interest out along the trend line to a given time in the future.

The primary application of spectral analysis in business is in **forecasting** economic conditions. By no means is it suggested that this is an exact prediction, but rather more an indication of a trend.

[Karen L. Boyd]

FURTHER READING:

Griliches, Zvi, and Michael D. Intriligator. *Handbook of Econometrics*. Vol. 2. North-Holland, 1984.

Horn, Robert V. *Statistical Indicators for the Economic and Social Sciences*. Cambridge University Press, 1993.

Hu, Teh-wei. *Econometrics: An Introductory Analysis*. University Park Press, 1973.

Judge, George G., R. Carter Hill, William Griffiths, Helmut Lutkepohl, and Tsoung-Chao Lee. *Introduction to the Theory and Practice of Econometrics*. John Wiley & Sons, 1982.

Kennedy, Peter. *A Guide to Econometrics*. MIT Press, 1979.

Klein, Lawrence R. *A Textbook of Econometrics*. 2nd ed. Prentice-Hall, 1974.

SPIN-OFFS

Spin-offs occur when a parent corporation distributes its entire holdings of stock in a subsidiary on a pro-rata basis to the parent's shareholders. These transactions have the effect of completing the separation of the assets and **liabilities** of the parent and subsidiary. Prior to the spin-off, shareholders only own the parent company's stock, whereas after the spin-off they own shares in both the parent and the subsidiary. In these transactions, no funds change hands, and the assets of the subsidiary are not revalued. The transaction is considered to be a stock dividend and a tax-free exchange under Internal Revenue Code Section 355. The spin-off of AT&T's regional operating **subsidiaries** exemplifies this type of corporate reorganization.

It is important to distinguish corporate spin-offs from three types of related transactions—equity carve-outs, split-offs, and split-ups. Under an equity carve-out, a portion of the subsidiary's shares are offered for sale to the general public. This has the effect of injecting cash into the parent firm without the loss of control. Under a split-off, shareholders exchange their parent stock for the shares of the subsidiary. These transactions provide the company an opportunity to dispose of a subsidiary in a tax-free manner, and even to relieve itself of an unwanted shareholder. A split-up occurs when the parent distributes shares in each of its subsidiaries, and the parent firm liquidates and ceases to exist.

Parent corporations are not likely to spin-off their more attractive businesses. Instead, corporations which are spun-off are typically slower-growth businesses, whereas faster-growing subsidiaries are typically offered to the public via equity carve-outs.

ADVANTAGES OF SPIN-OFFS

Many portfolio managers prefer "pure play" companies. Investment professionals may be interested in one or the other of a company's basic businesses, but not both. To the extent that financial markets are incomplete, spin-offs provide investors with a wider range of investment opportunities appealing to different investor clienteles. In addition, the issuance of separate financial reports on the operations of the subsidiary facilitate the evaluation of the firm's performance. Thus, this technique enables managers to uncover the hidden value of the subsidiary.

Another rationale advanced for spin-offs is a major shift in the economic environment affecting the corporate entity. While a combined organizational structure may have been optimal in the past, the separation of operations may now be appropriate. In particular, management synergy may be nonexistent for firms in unrelated businesses. Spin-offs enable managers to focus on the specific operating and financial characteristics of the subsidiary rather than being overly concerned with the impact of subsidiary decisions on the performance of the parent company.

Incentive contracts tied to the performance of the **common stock** of the parent company may not be meaningful for managers in the subsidiary. On the other hand, a spun-off subsidiary has the advantage of an independent stock price which should reflect the capital market's assessment of management's performance. Thus, compensation can be more directly related to performance with the existence of the spun-off unit.

Another important motive for corporate spin-offs is tax and/or regulatory advantages. Tax advantages can be achieved by the creation and spin-off into natural resource royalty trusts or real estate investment trusts. As long as these entities pay out 90 percent of their earnings to shareholders, they are tax exempt, permitting the parent company to shield income from taxes. In addition, regulated subsidiaries are sometimes penalized by their association with profitable parents if regulators consider the parent's earnings when considering a rate increase. The spun-off subsidiary may have a greater chance of being granted a rate increase, and the nonregulated operations of the parent would be freed from regulatory scrutiny.

IMPACT OF CORPORATE SPIN-OFFS

Studies which have investigated the effects of voluntary spin-off announcements on the shareholder wealth of parent firms indicate that these firms experience significantly positive abnormal returns at the time of the spin-off announcement. In addition, larger spin-offs are associated with larger positive shareholder returns. These studies also found that decreases in value of corporate bonds was not a significant source of shareholders' gains.

Newly spun-off companies usually incur negative stock market returns in comparison to the overall market once they start to trade separately. Initially, there is a tendency for institutional investors to reduce their holdings of spun-off shares after the restructuring. Institutions may be constrained from owning stock in these firms because they do not meet various criteria. For example, index funds may dispose of the shares because they are not included in the Standard & Poor's 500 Index. Similarly, other institutions may sell the shares because they do not pay **dividends**. Therefore, institutional investors typically liquidate the newly created post-spin-off shares they receive leading to a significant, seller-induced price pressure effect that is temporary in nature.

Because these issues are new to the market, only a few analysts generally evaluate the merits of these securities. Accordingly, prices may not adjust as rapidly to new information as other securities. Stocks followed by few analysts and **stocks** not widely held by institutional investors generate superior risk-ad-

justed returns. Consistent with this neglected firm explanation, spun-off firms outperform the overall market over longer holding periods.

Other studies have examined the long-run performance of spun-off firms using accounting-based measures. The results indicate that performance of a spin-off does not necessarily improve after divestiture. The spun-off unit's relationship to the parent company and the relative size of the spin-off are associated with success. Nonrelated spin-offs are more likely to experience performance gains than related spin-offs, which have the same or similar types of customers, product lines, and production technology as their parent firms. In addition, smaller spin-offs consistently outperformed larger spin-offs on the basis of real sales growth, return on sales, and return on assets. In planning spin-offs, management should consider the costs and disruptions associated with the restructurings as well as the changes in organizational resources.

SEE ALSO: Corporate Downsizing

[Robert T. Kleiman]

FURTHER READING:

Hite, Galen, and James Owers. "Security Price Reactions around Corporate Spin-off Announcements." *Journal of Financial Economics*. 12, 1983, pp. 409-436.

Kleiman, Robert T., and Anandi P. Sahu. "The Performance of Corporate Spin-offs." *AAII Journal*. 12:7, 1990, pp. 8-11.

SPREADSHEETS

A spreadsheet, at its most basic level, is essentially a matrix of rows and columns, used to record amounts and perform calculations. Usually the entries across a given row will have something in common (e.g. sales dollars), while the entries filling a given column will have another dimension of commonality (e.g. the year 1994). Spreadsheets are used to present financial information and perform various ad-hoc analyses and calculations.

The manual form of the spreadsheet has been used in **accounting** for many years, and involved pencils, erasers, adding machines, tedium, and mistakes. Making a change used to be particularly painful when the item rippled through other sections or other spreadsheets. Today's electronic spreadsheets are created by widely available software that runs on personal computers. Interrelated spreadsheet calculations can be "linked" so that making a change will automatically update other derivative or related calculations. Making editorial changes has been made quick and painless.

Additionally, electronic spreadsheets provide a great deal of other functions that manual spreadsheets did not have (or made doing very difficult). Moving, copying, or deleting sections—by row(s), by column(s), or by sheet(s)—is now fast and easy. Multi-year calculations can quickly be programmed, and recalculated under a variety of different assumptions. Sensitivity, or "what-if" analyses have become enormously easier—and more ubiquitous—due to the advent of the electronic spreadsheet. This is facilitated by having the spreadsheet be "driven" by a number of input variables located in one section of the matrix. Once the spreadsheet model is set up, the variables can be quickly adjusted to gauge the impact of a particular percent change in a particular variable.

Business valuation using discounted **cash flow** analysis is one good example of a discipline assisted by the electronic spreadsheet. The basic cash flow model can be set up with variables established for revenue growth rate, market share, cost of goods sold, operating expenses, discount rate, the length of time to which to discount, etc. Any of the variables can then be modified, serially or concurrently, to quantify the effect on calculated value.

Electronic spreadsheets are especially useful, as compared to their manual predecessors, when doing complex calculations, such as certain statistical measures variances, regression coefficients of determination, confidence intervals for sample results, etc.). They are also most useful when dealing with large volumes of data. Most electronic spreadsheets provide three main types of functionality:

1. Mathematical calculations, in column and row format.

2. Database features, including filling a row or column with sequential numbers, sorting a table of data in a defined alpha or numeric order, and selecting items meeting certain criteria.

3. Graphic presentation of the data, in a variety of formats, including line, bar, and pie charts.

More recent versions of the electronic spreadsheets have incorporated a print enhancing capability whereby the user can set different font sizes and styles, boldface or underline selected items, create shaded areas for emphasis, and make other stylistic improvements to the hard copy output. The printing capabilities will compress large spreadsheets to fit on regular size paper, number sequential pages, add header or footer comments, and generally make the output look neat and professional. Some popular programs include Lotus 1-2-3, Borland's Quatro Pro, and Microsoft's Excel. Each of these spreadsheet programs has substantially similar functionality, with the key differences being style and protocol of commands.

[Christopher C. Barry]

STANDARD INDUSTRIAL CLASSIFICATION SYSTEM

The Standard Industrial Classification (SIC) system is a method of classifying all industries in the U.S., and thus is a useful tool for those conducting research on the industry level. The SIC system is a set of hierarchical numeric codes used to classify establishments based on their economic activity. This classification system was created by the U.S. government for use by various government agencies in formulating economic statistics. The system has also been adopted by nongovernmental organizations and private business for their own research.

An establishment is defined as an "economic unit that produces goods or services ... at a single physical location and is engaged in one, or predominantly one, type of economic activity." Thus an establishment may be identical to a company, but often is only part of a company. Federal statisticians are interested not in companies but in aggregate figures, such as sales and employment, for a specific product or service.

An Interdepartmental Committee on Industrial Classification was established in 1937 to develop a standard classification system for industries. It published its first classification of manufacturing industries in 1941, and nonmanufacturing industries in 1942. Revisions were made in 1958, 1963, 1967, 1972, 1977, and 1987. The next revision of the SIC codes is planned for 1997.

The Federal Office of Management and Budget heads the interdepartmental committee overseeing the SIC system and accepts proposals for changes, such as the addition or deletion of an industry. These changes must conform to the existing structure, reflect historical continuity, and represent industries of sufficient specialization, scope, and economic significance.

The SIC system consists of codes of one to four digits, whereby the first digit represent the broadest category and subsequent digits represent subcategories within the broader groupings. For example, the first digit in 3000 represents the division of manufacturing, 3700 is for manufacturing of transport equipment, 3710 is for motor vehicles and parts, and 3716 is for motor homes.

The major divisions, as designated by the first digit are as follows: 0 - agriculture, forestry, and fishing; 1 - mining and construction; 2 and 3 - manufacturing; 4 - transportation, communications, and utilities; 5 - wholesale and retail trade; 6 - finance, insurance, and real estate; 7 and 8 - services; and 9 - public administration. A description of each one of the approximately 1,000 classified industries can be found in the *Standard Industrial Classification*

Manual published by the Office of Management and Budget.

Various government departments and agencies, such as the U.S. Department of Agriculture, the Federal Trade Commission, and the U.S. Bureau of Labor Statistics, use the SIC system in preparing statistical studies of economic activity under their purview. The U.S. Bureau of the Census prepares a Census of Manufacturers and a Census of Service Industries every five years, which together cover every SIC classification. These statistical surveys and censuses are available to the public and are a valuable source to economic and business researchers.

Outside government, business research and publishing firms have applied the SIC system to their collected company data to facilitate their own research or that of their clients. Investment analysis firms use SIC codes when preparing financial analyses of industries. Company directories' publishers—such as Standard & Poor's, Dun & Bradstreet, and Gale Research assign SIC codes to each company they list. Firms that produce on-line and CD-ROM bibliographic databases of articles on companies or industries also assign SIC codes to citation entries as a search field.

Researchers can then obtain information by looking up the desired SIC codes. Market researchers create lists of potential client companies or survey market conditions within a given industry. Companies learn about their competition by searching for information limited to their own industry. Investors track the economic trends within given industries.

Despite the heavy reliance on the SIC system for all kinds of business research, the system is not without its drawbacks. There is much criticism in private industry that the SIC system goes out of date too quickly. The government, however, tries to maintain the same SIC version as long as it can in order to keep the meaning of the statistics consistent. The basic structure of the SIC system has also been challenged. There are problems classifying traditionally different industries which have begun offering the same services, or new types of establishments that offer a combination of products or services previously considered unrelated. Furthermore, the SIC system was not designed for company classification, but this is a major use outside government. When a company engages in more than one activity and is assigned more than one code, the relevance of each of the codes may be unclear. Finally, this SIC system is used only in the United States; other countries have their own systems. As business and industry becomes increasingly global, there is a greater need for adopting an international standard classification system.

[Heather Behn Hedden]

FURTHER READING:

Duncan, Joseph W. "Statistics Corner: Revising Classifications of Economic Activity." *Business Economics.* January, 1992, pp. 58-60.

Norwood, Janet L., and Deborah P. Klein. "Developing Statistics to Meet Society's Needs." *Monthly Labor Review.* October, 1989, pp. 14-19.

Ojala, Marydee. "Industry Searching by the Codes." *Online.* May, 1993, pp. 96-99.

Standard Industrial Classification Manual 1987. Executive Office of the President, Office of Management and Budget, pp. 3-18, pp. 699-703.

STANDARDIZATION

Standardization refers to the creation and use of guidelines for the production of uniform, interchangeable components, especially for use in mass production. It also refers to the establishment and adoption of guidelines for conduct. In global **marketing**, the term is used to describe the simplification of procurement and production to achieve economy.

The concept of standardization originated near the turn of the nineteenth century. Before that time, products were made individually, with unique, hand-fitted parts. Eli Whitney (1765-1825), inventor of the cotton gin, has been credited with developing the concept of standardization, which he first applied to rifle manufacture in 1797. Instead of hand-crafting each weapon, he produced components of uniform size in quantity, then assembled the parts into finished products. The concept saved time and money in production, and allowed for easy repair.

By the mid-1800s, standardization joined the division of labor and machine-assisted manufacturing as well-established principles of mass production, but they were not widely applied for decades to come. Twentieth century industrialist Henry Ford (1863-1947) was a great proponent and beneficiary of mass production. He organized the Ford Motor Co. around its principles, taking standardization to a high level. His plants only manufactured one type of car at a time. Each auto that came off the production lines was identical, even down to the color—black. Standardization not only saved on production costs, but also benefitted consumers, who no longer had to have replacement parts machined by hand.

Ford's success contributed to the proliferation of mass production principles, including standardization, throughout the developed world. The concept has promoted a dramatic increase in manufacturing productivity, which in turn improved living standards. The concept of standardization has been applied in many ways since.

In general, standardization determines and promulgates criteria to which objects or actions are expected to conform. Standardization for manufacturing may entail the creation of production standards, tolerances, and/or specifications. These can be expressed as formulas, drawings, measurements or definitions. They are the limits to within which products or components must fall in order to be useful. Components that do not adhere to such limits are "nonstandard" or, more commonly, "rejects." Virtually any aspect of a product or component can be standardized. Quality control and testing are used to measure achievement of standards. The use of such standards promotes clear communication within and among organizations. It can also lower the costs of labor, production, and repair. In the late twentieth century, businesses have demanded ever-increasing standardization from their suppliers as well as from their own production.

Individual industries may have distinct sets of standards that promote communication among participants and discourage duplication of effort. George Westinghouse (1846-1914), inventor of the air brake and founder of Westinghouse, was an early advocate of the standardization of railway equipment. In the world of scientific inquiry, for example, the metric system is the standard of measurement. In the American construction industry, architects, suppliers, and builders have established standards for prefabricated buildings and construction components.

Organizations and professions may also be held up to standards of practice or conduct, such as safety and ethical standards. For example, government agencies such as the U.S. Food and Drug Administration and the **U.S. Consumer Product Safety Commission** set and enforce safety standards in their respective fields. The Hippocratic oath is a well-known ethical standard that physicians follow.

National and international organizations have also evolved to synthesize the diverse standardization efforts of the individual groups and promote acceptance of and adherence to basic standards. In the United States, the American National Standards Institute (ANSI) has taken up this cause. Although this organization does not compose standards, it does compile national engineering, safety, and industrial standards. Since its 1946 establishment in Geneva, Switzerland, the International Organization for Standardization (ISO) has emerged as a powerful advocate of global standards for specifications, testing, approval and certification. Over 80 nations are counted among its membership. Companies large and small strive for certification by the ISO, which has helped provide a basis of comparison and cooperation among companies around the world, especially as global trade has become increasingly vital to success in the late twentieth century. The standards set by such

organizations often evolve with technological innovation.

Global marketing, in fact, has brought about a new definition and use of the term standardization. As companies have begun to compete on a global scale, they have sought out "standardized" suppliers— those that offer the most economical, convenient, and dependable service. Ford Motor Co., an early proponent of standardization for mass production, has been praised for its successful use of standardization as it applies to global manufacturing and marketing.

Although standardization tends to lead to inflexibility, it can also allow for customization. When basic elements of a product are standardized, other aspects can be more flexible. For example, autos on an assembly line may use the same standard of wheel attachment, but different size wheels. Micromanagement takes this theory to its ultimate end. This theory attempts to apply standardization to all aspects of an operation, be it manufacturing or service. It seeks to identify the smallest aspects of a function, make them as efficient as possible, and then apply them throughout the operation. Clearly, standardization in all its forms will continue to be applied in new ways in the future.

[April Dougal Gasbarre]

FURTHER READING:

International Organization for Standardization. *Access to Standards Information: How to Enquire or be Informed about Standards and Technical Regulations Worldwide.* International Organization for Standardization, c.1986.

Office of Technological Assessment, U.S. Congress. *Global Standards: Building Blocks for the Future.* Congress of the United States, Office of Technological Assessment, 1992.

Ricci, Patricia. *Standards: A Resource and Guide for Identification, Selection, and Acquisition.* Pat Ricci Enterprises, c.1992.

STATISTICAL ANALYSIS FOR MANAGEMENT

There are two broad types of business decision-making environments: **decision-making** under certainty and decision-making under uncertainty. In decision-making under certainty, one enumerates, at least conceptually, all possible choices and the consequences of each and attempts to find the choice which leads to the best possible consequence, as measured by some measure of effectiveness. Statistics deals with decision-making under uncertainty.

In decision-making under uncertainty, one must deal with random variables. A random variable is something that may take on one value at one time and another value on another occasion, and at the time a decision is made, there is no way to tell what value that variable will take. At the time the choice must be made, one does not know what value one or more random variables will assume. One must make the choice and then wait until later to see what value each of the random variables will take on. However, the degree of success or failure that will result from a particular choice will perhaps be different for each possible value the random variable can assume. Thus, at the time the decision must be made, it behooves the decision-maker to learn as much as possible about the random variable.

The most that can be learned about any random variable is its probability distribution—the various possible values that may occur and the relative likelihood of each. This is not to say that it is always possible to know the exact probability distribution, but only that it is impossible to know any more information about a random variable. Certainly, the value the random variable will assume on any given occasion cannot be known.

A probability distribution records the relative likelihood of each of the possible values that may occur. The various possibilities are recorded graphically in the horizontal direction and the likelihood of each is recorded in the vertical direction. Different probability distributions have different shapes. A very commonly encountered type is called the normal distribution. There are really an infinite number of normal distributions, but each has many things in common: they are all symmetric; they are all bell shaped; they are all the distribution of a continuous quantitative variable.

As a specific example of making a decision in this environment of uncertainty, consider the inventory decision that a businessman must make. For a particular item, it is easy to say conceptually how much inventory must be ordered. One should order an amount equal to demand. If one orders more than demand, capital is being tied-up in a sterile asset that will sit on the shelves and earn no return. Instead, the capital could be put into another product type that would sell and earn a return. Or, at the very least, the capital could be lent through some financial asset to someone else who has a use for it and is willing to pay to borrow it. Conversely, if one orders less than demand, customers will have to be turned away. These customers will go to the **competition**, and the decision-maker will not only lose the profit on the item that would have been sold, but probably some future profits on possible future sales to customers who get used to frequenting the competition.

Now that we have established that one wants to order just the right amount, the question becomes, "What is the right amount?" We know that the simple answer is: an amount exactly equal to demand. But, what is that? Demand is a random variable. It will

be one amount on one occasion and another amount on another occasion. At the time the inventory order decision must be made, there is no way to know what the level of demand would be for the period following the decision to order a given amount. One may then choose to order an amount which is most likely to be the right amount. Or, one may wish to order an amount that will be enough to cover at least 98 percent of the possible levels of demand. Whatever the decision strategy turns out to be, it is first necessary to determine as much as possible about the probability distribution of the random variable called demand.

To learn about a probability distribution there are two broad approaches. One is the probability approach and the other is the statistical approach. The probability approach involves enumerating equally likely fundamental outcomes and combining these outcomes into appropriate collections called events, and then deducing the probability of each of these events. The advantage of this approach is that it leads to exact results. The disadvantage is that it can be used only on the very simplest of random variables. One can figure the probability of a straight flush when playing poker, the probability of a black when spinning a roulette wheel, or the probability of a seven or an eleven when tossing a pair of dice. But when it comes to a more complicated and realistic random variable like demand, this method is not very successful.

The statistical method has the disadvantage that it will yield only approximate results, but the advantage is that it always works, no matter how complex the random variable might be. This method involves looking at how the random variable has behaved in the past and using that information to see how likely the various different possible events are. To use the statistical method to learn about a probability distribution, one divides the distribution up into various conceptual characteristics and then one uses the data to estimate each of these characteristics.

One set of characteristics which may be defined are called moments. There are many moments and each one tells something different about the data, but collectively they tell almost everything that can be said about the distribution. This is called the "method of moments". Let's begin by defining the technical term "moment."

In words, a moment is an average of deviations raised to some integer power. The "first moment about zero" is merely the mean of the data and measures a characteristic called central tendency, or the point of balance for the probability distribution. (Please be aware that the concept of moments, as well as other concepts discussed in this essay, can also be expressed as mathematical formulas. However, because these formulas are often extremely complex, we will limit this essay to just a general discussion of the concepts involved in statistical analysis.)

The second moment about the mean is called the "variance" and the symbol ~ is almost always used to represent the variance of the population. The characteristic which is measured by this moment is variability. If all of the values of the data are close to each other, the variance will be a relatively small number. If all of the values of the data are not close to each other (there is more spread between them) the variance will be a larger number for that data. This measure will play a most crucial role in the explanation to come later.

The third moment about the mean is a measure of the skewness of the distribution. If it is a positive number, it means that the distribution is skewed to the right. If it is a negative number, it means that the distribution is skewed to the left. If it is near zero, it means that the distribution is symmetric. Symmetry is the lack of skewness, or vice versa.

The fourth moment about the mean is a measure of the relative thickness of the tails—or the relative likelihood of the extreme values.

Again we note that each of these "moments" tell us something different about the distribution, but collectively, they tell us most of what we need to know to have a very good idea of what the distribution looks like.

To calculate any of these moments, we would need to have the entire population available to plug into the calculation. These moments are called parameters. Parameters are characteristics of the population. In practice, we usually only have a subset of the population available. If we plug the data from the sample into a similar formula, we get what is called a statistic. A statistic is a characteristic of a sample. The statistic will not, in most cases, end up being equal to the parameter. It is only an estimate of the parameter. Our concern is going to be with whether or not the estimate is a "good" estimate, and if not, how do we make it better?

The above moments are expressed as population parameters.It is rarely possible to calculate actual parameters. Instead we calculate sample statistics. There is a statistic which corresponds to each of the above parameters. Instead of using an upper-case N to stand for the size of the population when doing equations, statisticians instead use a lower-case n to stand for the size of the sample. Often statisticians write n<<N, which means the size of the sample is much, much less than the size of the population.

Any time one estimates a parameter, one has to stop to ponder the quality of the estimate. We want to be "pretty sure we are pretty close" when we calculate a statistic and use it as an estimate of the parameter. If we are not pretty sure that the statistic is pretty close to the parameter, we need to know that, so we can collect more data before using the statistic to estimate the parameter. Once we get enough data, we can be pretty sure that the statistic is pretty close to the parameter we are using it to estimate. There is a trade-off between three things when considering the quality of the estimate:

1. the amount of data we have (sample size)
2. the confidence we have in the estimate
3. the precision of the estimate.

If we choose any two of these, we can compute the third. That is, if we want to be pretty sure that we are pretty close, we can choose how sure we want to be (80, 90, 95, 98, or 99 percent sure) and how close we want to be (for example, within half an inch of the parameter, or within 100 dollars of the parameter), and then compute the size of the sample it would take to have achieve this level of confidence and precision. Or, if we choose the size of the sample and the amount of confidence we need, we can compute how much precision our estimate will have. Finally, if we choose the size of the sample and the amount of precision we have, we can compute how much confidence we have. It is not possible to choose all three. In summary, by choosing two of the three, the third is mathematically determined.

Anytime we compute a statistic to estimate a parameter that will ultimately be used to make an appropriate choice, an attempt is made to interpret the quality of that statistic. This is done by placing it in the context of all of the other values that would occur if we had selected samples other than the one we actually did select at random. It turns out that there is enough information in the sample that was used to compute a statistic to also evaluate the quality of that statistic for the purpose of making an estimate. To say that an estimate is a good one (i.e., we are pretty sure that our statistic is probably pretty close to the parameter that we are trying to estimate) one must learn about all of the samples that were not selected. Using mathematical formulas, it is possible to learn a tremendous amount about the samples that were not taken from the information within the sample that was taken.

If the statistic we are going to compute is the average of the sample and we wish to use it to estimate the parameter called the mean, there are four mathematical results and several definitions that must be understood to see how much or how little a sample of a given size will reveal about a parameter that we cannot hope to actually compute.

The critical concept necessary to understand this is the idea of a sampling distribution of the statistic. A sampling distribution is the probability distribution of all possible values of a statistic based upon all possible samples of some fixed size. If we were to take all possible random samples of size 100, and if we computed the average of each of these samples, we could see the relative frequency with which the average turned out to be various possible values. This display of relative frequencies would be the sampling distribution of all possible samples of size 100. There is a sampling distribution for every statistic, and it is different for each possible sample size. To compute this distribution empirically would take more effort than to just calculate the parameter we care to know about by looking at the entire population. So, of course, we would never try to compute the sampling distribution directly, except for arbitrary and artificially small populations used in classroom examples. However, just by imagining the existence of such a distribution, mathematical results can be developed that will illustrate how much or how little is known about the population parameters being estimated based upon the relatively small amount of data we probably have in any given actual case.

[Roger C. Gledhill]

FURTHER READING:

[*Editor's Note:* Those interested in a more advanced discussion of this topic (including detailed equations and graphs) may contact the author directly; his address may be found in the contributor's list in the front of this directory.]

STATISTICS

SEE: Financial Statistics; Statistical Analysis for Management; Statistical Office of the European Community; Statistical Process Control

STATISTICAL OFFICE OF THE EUROPEAN COMMUNITY

The Statistical Office of the European Union (Eurostat) is one of the Directorates-General of the European Union (the European Union is an economic and social union comprised of the **European Community**, the European Economic Community, the European Coal and Steel Community (ECSC), and the European Atomic Energy Community). The purpose of Eurostat is to collect, process, reconcile, and disseminate statistical information (largely of an economic nature) to its members. Eurostat and the European Union have a common membership: Belgium, Denmark, France, Germany, Great Britain, Greece, Ireland, Italy, Luxembourg, the Netherlands, Portugal, and Spain.

Eurostat is guided by the belief that productive negotiations between members of an economic union is dependent upon current and reliable statistical information. The information must also be in a format that can be justified between the various countries. At present, of the 12 national statistical systems from which information is gathered, there is a wide variance in terms of data quality and data uniformity. This is due to gathering techniques, budgetary restraints, confidentiality concerns, and differences in the way various countries view the utility of this information. An important task of Eurostat is to harmonize this data to make it uniformly meaningful.

Eurostat gathers and publishes macroeconomic statistical data for all 12 member nations. This includes social data as well as statistics on finance, balance of payments, foreign trade, industry, energy, and agriculture. Eurostat uses three databanks to disseminate this information. COMETEXT is the foreign trade databank that contains information on trade between European Union members and over 200 trading partners. REGIO stores macroeconomic data on various European regions and CRONOS contains information on most of the social, economic, and agricultural activities of the 12 member countries. Much of this data is available in an electronic format through CD-ROMs, on-line access, and magnetic tapes. Selective Eurostat data is also available in various other formats such as hard copy publications and microfiche.

Eurostat is headed by a director-general and a staff of various advisers and assistants. There are administrative units for agricultural accounts and structures, agricultural products and fisheries, planning and management of resources and environment. There are also five directorates: dissemination and computer processing; economic statistics and national accounts, prices, and coordination relating to a single market; international trade statistics; business statistics; and social and regional statistics.

[Michael Knes]

STATISTICAL PROCESS CONTROL

Traditional **quality control** is designed to prevent the production of products that do not meet certain acceptance criteria. This could be accomplished by performing inspection on products that, in many cases, have already been produced. Action could then be taken by rejecting those products. Some products would go on to be reworked, a process which is costly and time-consuming. In many cases, rework is more expensive than producing the product in the first

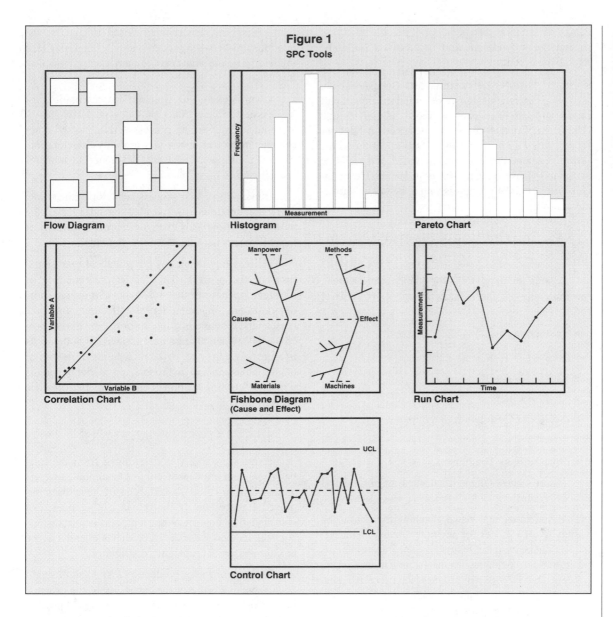

Figure 1
SPC Tools

Flow Diagram

Histogram

Pareto Chart

Correlation Chart

Fishbone Diagram
(Cause and Effect)

Run Chart

Control Chart

place. This situation often results in decreased **productivity**, customer dissatisfaction, loss of competitive position, and higher cost.

To avoid such results, quality must be built into the product and the processes. Statistical process control (SPC) involves the integration of quality control into each stage of producing the product. In fact, SPC is a powerful collection of tools that implement the concept of prevention as a shift from the traditional quality by inspection/correction.

SPC is a technique that employs statistical tools for controlling and improving processes. SPC is an important ingredient in continuous process improvement strategies. It uses simple statistical means to control, monitor, and improve processes. All SPC tools are graphical and simple to use and understand, as shown in Figure 1.

UNDERSTANDING VARIATION

The main objective of any SPC study is to reduce variation. Any process can be considered a transformation mechanism of different input factors into a product or service. Since inputs exhibit variation, the result is a combined effect of all variations. This, in turn, is translated into the product. The purpose of SPC is to isolate the natural variation in the process from other sources of variation that can be traced or whose causes may be identified. As follows, there are two different kinds of variation that affect the quality characteristics of products.

COMMON CAUSES OF VARIATION. Variation due to common causes are inherent in the process; they are inevitable and can be represented by a normal distribution. Common causes are also called chance causes of variation. A stable process exhibits only common causes of variation. The behavior of a stable process is predictable or consistent, and the process is said to be in statistical control.

SPECIAL CAUSES OF VARIATION. Special causes, also called assignable causes of variation, are not part of the process. The can be traced, identified, and eliminated. Control charts are designed to hunt for those causes as part of SPC efforts to improve the process. A process with the presence of special or assignable cause of variation is unpredictable or inconsistent, and the process is said to be out of statistical control.

STATISTICAL PROCESS CONTROL (SPC) TOOLS

Among the many tools for quality improvement, the following are the most commonly used tools of SPC:

- Histograms
- Cause and Effect Diagrams
- Pareto Diagrams
- Control Charts
- Scatter or Correlation diagrams
- Run Charts
- Process Flow Diagrams

Figure 1 shows the seven basic tools of statistical process control.

Histograms are visual displays that show the variability of a process or any other quality characteristic. It can be used to illustrate the specification limits on a product in relation to the natural limits for the process that is used to produce that product. Histograms can also be used to identify possible causes of a problem that is experienced by the process. It provides a powerful analytical tool to understand the process.

Pareto charts are another powerful tool for statistical process control and quality improvement. It focuses the attention on those few problems that cause trouble in a process. With Pareto charts, facts about the greatest improvement potential can be easily identified.

Cause and effect diagrams, also called Ishikawa diagrams or fishbone diagrams, provide a visual representation of the factors that most likely contribute to an observed problem or an effect on the process. The relationships between such factors can be clearly identified. Problems, therefore, may be identified and the root causes may be corrected.

Scatter diagrams, also called correlation charts, show the graphical representation of the relationship between two variables. In statistical process control,

scatter diagrams are normally used to explore the relationships between process variables and may lead to identifying possible ways to increased process performance.

Control charts are graphical representations of process performance. They provide a powerful analytical tool for monitoring process variability and other changes in process mean or variability deterioration. Control charts were basically developed to hunt for special causes of variation.

Run charts depicts process behavior against time. They are important in investigating changes in the process over time. Any changes in process stability or instability can be judged from a run chart.

Process flow diagrams are graphical representations of the process. They show the sequence of different operations that make up a process. Flow diagrams are important tool for documenting processes and communicating information about processes. They can also be used to identify bottlenecks in a process sequence, to identify points of rework or other phenomena in a process, or to define points where data or information about process performance need to be collected.

PROCESS CAPABILITY ANALYSIS

Process capability is determined from the total variations that are caused only by common causes of variation after all assignable causes have been removed. It represents the performance of a process that is in statistical control. When a process is in statistical control, its performance is predictable and can be represented by a probability distribution.

The proportion of production that is out of specification is a measure of the capability of the process. Such proportion may be determined using the process distribution. If the process maintains its status of being in statistical control, the proportion of defective or nonconforming production remains the same.

Before assessing the capability of the process, it must be brought first to a state of statistical control. There are several ways to measure the capability of the process:

USING CONTROL CHARTS. When the control chart indicates that the process is in a state of statistical control and when the control limits are stable and periodically reviewed, it can be used to assess the capability of the process and provide information to infer such capability.

USING HISTOGRAMS. If a histogram is available that shows measurements about a process or a quality characteristic of a process, the mean and standard deviation that are computed from the histogram can be used to estimate the process mean and process standard deviation. Histograms also show the relationship between process natural limits and specification limits.

RELATIONSHIP BETWEEN NATURAL TOLERANCE LIMITS & SPECIFICATION LIMITS. The natural tolerance limits of a process are normally these limits between which the process is capable of producing parts. Natural tolerance limits are expressed as the process mean $+$ z process standard deviation units. Unless otherwise stated, z is considered to be three standard deviation units. There are three situations to be considered that describe the relationship between process natural tolerance limits and specification limits.

In case one, specification limits are wider than the process natural tolerance limits. This situation represents a process that is capable of meeting specifications. Although not desirable, this situation accommodates, to a certain degree, some shift in the process mean or a change in process variability.

In case two, specification limits are equal to the process natural tolerance limits. This situation represents a critical process that is capable of meeting specifications only if no shift in the process mean or a change in process variability can take place. A shift in the process mean or a change in its variability will let the process produce nonconforming products. When dealing with a situation like this, care must be taken to avoid producing products that are not conforming to specifications.

In case three, specification limits are narrower than the process natural tolerance limits.

This situation guarantees the production of nonconforming products and not meeting the desired specifications. When dealing with this situation, action should be taken to widen the specification limits and change the design of the product, to control the process such that its variability is reduced. Another solution is to look for a different process.

[Ahmad K. Elshennawy]

STOCHASTIC PROCESSES

Stochastic processes involve experiments of random outcomes and are generally used in statistical analyses. Stochastic processes include one or more random variables observed in multiple steps, or iterations, whose outcomes are not independent. In other words, the outcomes, while random, are related and can indicate a pattern of behavior.

Stochastic processes are commonly found in game theory examples, polling, tracking, and statisti-

cal process control. In each case and at every step, an outcome may depend on any one of several random factors.

Because of the existence of at least one random variable, outcomes can never be determined accurately and consistently. But because of their ability to indicate patterns of behavior, stochastic processes can yield knowledge in the form of predictive capability; they can indicate parameters of likely outcomes.

For example, in a test involving the value of a security, a given variable A may be observed to increase value in 75 percent of past iterations. The variable B may be observed to decrease value in 75 percent of the cases. As a result, when A occurs in the function, the observer may assume a 75-percent likelihood that value will increase.

The solution is not certain, because there is still a 25-percent likelihood that value will decrease. But past iterations indicate a pattern of behavior suggesting that value is likely to increase when A is present in the function and decrease when B is present. Successive iterations may provide additional precision to the prediction, or identify the effects of other variables.

While multiple iterations can reduce the effects of stochastics in functions, they are amplified in single shot experiments. Consider, for example, shooting a projectile toward a target 800 yards away. Assumptions must be made about the weight of the projectile, amount of launch explosive, trajectory and direction of launch, wind direction and speeds, and even humidity.

If a single shot overshoots its target by 100 yards, adjustments must be made to gain accuracy. If additional shots are possible (because location is revealed to enemy mortars with every shot), variables such as trajectory, direction, and launch explosive may be adjusted to gain accuracy. The cycle is repeated on a third shot, then the fourth, until the target is hit.

Independent variables, such as atmospheric conditions, may change during the course of firings. They remain independent because changing wind speeds cannot be predicted with total accuracy. As a result, the projectile may be brought to land closer to the target, but unless conditions remain static, complete accuracy cannot be attained.

Stochastics in economics work in a similar fashion. If a sales strategy for a product fails to produce an intended outcome, dependent variables may be adjusted. But independent variables, governed by the actions of competitors, remain unpredictable. This is especially relevant because competitors may alter their own actions based on the results of the first strategy.

[John Simley]

FURTHER READING:

Chou, Ya-lun. *Statistical Analysis for Business and Economics.* Amsterdam: Elsevier Science Publishing, 1989, pp. 172-173.

Johnson, Robert R. *Elementary Statistics.* 3rd ed. North Scituate, MA: Duxbury Press, 1980.

STOCK INDEX FUTURES

A stock index future is a contract to buy or sell a stock index at a price based on the **index** level in a designated future month. Contract expiration dates may be as much as two or more years in the future, however most expire within one year. Usually, the expiration dates for stock index futures contracts are separated by two or three month intervals. Stock index futures may be used to either speculate on the market's general market performance or to hedge a stock portfolio against a decline in value. Furthermore, since a stock index cannot be delivered to an investor in a solid form, all settlements are in cash. To speculate in this way, investors usually have to meet liquidity or **income** requirements to show that they have money to cover their potential losses.

VALUING STOCK INDEX FUTURES

All stock index futures contracts have a value equal to their price multiplied by a specified dollar amount. To illustrate, the price of a stock index futures contract based on the New York Stock Exchange Composite Index is derived by multiplying the index level value by $500. This value results because each futures contract is equal to $500 times the quoted futures price. So, if the index level is determined to be 200, the corresponding stock index future would cost $100,000. The index level is marked-to-market, meaning that at the end of each day its value is adjusted to reflect changes in the day's share prices.

In stock index **futures contracts**, there are two parties directly involved. One party (the short position must deliver to a second party (the long position) an amount of cash equaling the contract's dollar multiplier multiplied by the difference between the spot price of a **stock market** index underlying the contract on the day of settlement (IP_{spot}) and the contract price on the date that the contract was entered (CP_0).

$$CASH = \text{Contract Dollar Multiplier} \times (IP_{spot} - CP_0)$$

If an investor sells a six-month NYSE Composite futures contract (with a multiplier of $500 per index point) at 444 and, six months later, the NYSE Composite Index closes at 445, the short party will receive $500 in cash from the long party.

$$CASH = \$500 (445 - 444) = \$500$$

Similarly, if an investor shorts a one-year futures contract at 442 and the index is 447 on the settlement day one year later (assuming that the multiplier is at $500), the short seller has to pay the long holder $2,500.

$$CASH = \$500 (447 - 442) = \$2,500$$

Thus, positive differences are paid by the seller and received by the buyer. Negative differences are paid by the buyer and received by the seller.

BUYING AND SELLING STOCK INDEX FUTURES

When an investor opens a futures position, he or she does not pay the entire amount of the equity underlying the futures contract. The investor is only required to put up a small percentage of the value of the contract as a margin. A margin is the amount of money required for the investor to give to his broker to maintain his futures contract. Unlike margins paid for stock purchases, margins paid for stock index futures are not purchases or sales of actual securities. Instead, they represent agreements to pay or receive the difference in price between the index underlying the contract on the day of settlement (IP_{spot}) and the contract price on the date that the contract was entered (CP_0). The exact amount of money needed to cover the margin is determined by two formulas. Both formulas are a function of the market price, the price of the index, and the strike price. The amount of money required for the margin is the greater result of the two formulas.

If the index moves against the seller, he will be required to add to the margin amount. Known as a maintenance or variation margin, it is the minimum level to which an investor's account equity can fall before he receives a margin call. When an investor's equity in a stock index futures account falls below the maintenance level, he receives a margin call for enough money to bring the account up to the initial margin level. This margin requirement mandates that holders of futures positions settle their realized and unrealized profits and losses in cash on a daily basis. These profits and losses are derived by comparing the trade price against the daily settlement price of the futures contract. The settlement price is broadcast by the exchanges soon after the markets close; it represents the pricing of the last thirty seconds of the day's trading.

USES OF STOCK INDEX FUTURES

Investors can use stock index futures to perform myriad tasks. Some common uses are: to speculate on changes in specific markets (see above examples); to change the weightings of portfolios; to separate market timing from market selection decisions; and to take part in index **arbitrage**, whereby the investors seek to gain profits whenever a futures contract is trading out-of-line with the fair price of the securities underlying it.

Investors commonly use stock index futures to change the weightings or risk exposures of their investment portfolios. A good example of this is an investor who holds equities from two or more countries. Suppose an investor has a portfolio invested in 60 percent U.S. equities and 40 percent Japanese equities and wants to increase his systematic risk to the U.S. market and reduce these risks to the Japanese market. He can do this by buying U.S. stock index futures contracts in the indexes underlying his holdings and selling Japanese contracts (in the Nikkei Index).

Stock index futures also allow investors to separate market timing from market selection decisions. For instance, an investor may want to take advantage of perceived immediate increases in an equity market but is not certain which securities to buy; he can do this by purchasing stock index futures. If the futures contracts are bought and the present value of the money used to buy them is invested in risk-free securities, the investor will have a risk exposure equal to that of the market. Similarly, the investor can adjust his portfolio holdings at a more leisurely pace. For example, assume an investor sees that he has several undesirable stocks but does not know what holdings to buy to replace them. He can sell the unwanted stocks and, at the same time, buy stock index futures to keep his exposure to the market. He can later sell the futures contracts when he has decided which specific stocks he wants to purchase.

Investors can also make money from stock index futures through index arbitrage, also referred to as program trading. Basically, arbitrage is the purchase of a security or commodity in one market and the simultaneous sale of an equal product in another market to profit from pricing differences. Investors taking part in stock index arbitrage seek to gain profits whenever a futures contract is trading out-of-line with the fair price of the securities underlying it. Thus, if a stock index futures contract is trading above its fair value, an investor could buy a basket of about 100 stocks composing the index in the correct proportion—such as a **mutual fund** comprised of stocks represented in the index—and then sell the expensively priced futures contract. Once the contract expires, the equities could then be sold and a net profit would result. While the investor can keep his arbitrage position until the futures contract expires, he is not required to. If the futures contract seems to be returning to fair market value before the expiration date, it may be prudent for the investor to sell early.

USING INDEXES TO HEDGE PORTFOLIO RISK

Aside from the above uses of indexes, investors often use stock index futures to hedge the value of their portfolios. To implement a hedge, the instruments in the cash and futures markets should have similar price movements. Also, the amount of money invested in the cash and futures markets should be the same. To illustrate, while investors owning well diversified investment portfolios are generally shielded from unsystematic risk (risk specific to particular firms), they are fully exposed to systematic risk (risk relating to overall market fluctuations). A cost-effective way for investors to reduce the exposure to systematic risk is to hedge with stock index futures, similar to the way that people hedge commodity holdings using commodity futures. Investors often use short hedges when they are in a long position in a stock portfolio and believe that there will be a temporary downturn in the overall stock market. **Hedging** transfers the price risk of owning the stock from a person unwilling to accept systematic risks to someone willing to take the risk.

To carry out a short hedge, the hedger sells a futures contract; thus, the short hedge is also called a "sell-hedge." For example, consider an investor who owns a portfolio of securities valued at $1.2 million with a dividend of 4 percent. The investor has been very successful with his stock picks. Therefore, while his portfolio's returns move up and down with the market, they consistently outperform the market by six percent. Thus, the portfolio would have a beta of 1.00 and an alpha of six percent. Say that the investor believes that the market is going to have a 15 percent decline, which would be offset by the one percent received from dividends. The net broad market return would be -14 percent but, since he consistently outperforms the market by six percent, his estimated return would be -8 percent. In this instance, the investor would like to cut his beta in half without necessarily cutting his alpha in half. He can achieve this by selling stock index futures. In this scenario, the S&P 500 index is at 240. The contract multiplier is $500, and therefore each contract represents a value of $120,000. Since the investor wants to simulate the sale of half of his $1.2 million portfolio, he must sell five contracts (5 × $120,000 = $600,000). Thus, his portfolio would only be affected by half of the market fluctuation. While the investor could protect his portfolio equally well by selling half of his shares of stock and buying them again a short time later, using a short hedge on stock index futures is much cheaper than paying the capital gains tax plus the broker commissions associated with buying and selling huge blocks of stock.

At the extreme, stock index futures can theoretically eliminate the effects of the broad market on a portfolio. Perfect hedges are very unusual because of the existence of basis risk. The basis is the difference between the existing price in the futures market and the cash price of the underlying securities. Basis risk occurs when changes in the economy and the financial situation have different impacts on the cash and futures markets.

TRANSACTION COSTS

Whenever an investor trades securities, he must pay transaction costs. Clearly, there is an explicit commission that the investor must give his broker for executing and clearing his trades. While the investor can negotiate the commissions paid for stock index futures transactions with his broker, generally, he will pay his broker around $25 per contract. (This commission varies somewhat with the investor's trading volume and the type of support he receives.) The commission usually covers the opening and the liquidation of the contracts and is paid at the time of their liquidation.

One of the largest attractions that trading stock index futures has is the relatively small transaction costs associated with them, especially when compared with other ways of attaining the same investment goals. For instance, the commissions paid to brokers for stock index futures transactions are much cheaper than the commissions paid for trading an equally large dollar amount of stocks underlying the index. Often, each futures contracts often represents more than $100,000 in stocks, and the associated commission would amount to about $25. For stocks, the commission paid on each share of stock would be about five cents. This could amount to hundreds of dollars commission depending on price per share.

LIMITS ON PRICE MOVEMENTS

For every contract, the exchange on which it is based establishes a limit on the amount the price can change. For each stock index futures contract the minimum price fluctuation, also called the "tick," is .05. So, a one point move in a futures contract means a gain or loss of one dollar times the dollar multiple of the specific contract, say $500. Therefore, the minimum amount that a price can change is .05 multiplied by the contract's dollar multiple, or .05 times $500 which is $25.

POPULAR STOCK INDEXES

Three of the most popular stock index for futures contracts are: The New York Stock Exchange Composite Index (traded on the New York Futures Exchange), the Value Line Composite Index (traded on the Kansas City Board of Trade), and the Standard & Poor's 500 Index (traded on the Chicago Mercantile Exchange). Furthermore, investors can also purchase

options on stock index futures; for instance, the Standard & Poor's 500 Stock Index futures options are traded on the Chicago Mercantile Exchange.

[Kathryn Snavely]

FURTHER READING:

Argenti, Paul A. *The Portable MBA Desk Reference*. New York: John Wiley & Sons, Inc. 1994.

Barron's Finance and Investment Handbook. 2nd ed. New York: Barron's, 1987.

Bodie, Zvi, Alex Kane, and Allan Marcus. *Investments*. Boston, MA: Irwin, 1989.

Fabozzi, Frank J., and Gregory M. Kipnis. *Stock Index Futures*. Homewood, IL: Dow Jones-Irwin, 1984.

Luskin, Donald L. *Index Options and Futures: A Complete Guide*. New York: John Wiley and Sons, 1987.

Millers, John. *Stock Index Options and Futures*. London: McGraw Hill Book Company, 1992.

Reilly, Frank K. *Investments*. 2nd ed. New York: The Dresden Press, 1986.

Reilly, Frank K. *Investment Analysis and Portfolio Management*. 2nd ed. New York: The Dresden Press, 1985.

Weiner, Neil S. *Stock Index Futures: A Guide for Traders, Investors, and Analysts*. New York: John Wiley and Sons, 1984.

STOCK MARKET

In financial terms the word "market" has a meaning that is conceptual, rather than physical: a market is the interaction of offers to buy ("bids") and offers to sell ("asks"). The critical component is the existence of the offers. A market maker is said to create a market in an item by simply standing ready to buy or sell the item. In the extreme, there are as many markets as market makers, but markets can be grouped in various ways. One common grouping is by the item traded. We will focus on the stock markets, as a part of the broader securities markets, using the plural to indicate that there are many trading mechanisms.

Philadelphia was originally the leading financial center of the United States, with New York and Boston representing less important locations. In New York, trading was conducted in an area near the site of the wall erected to separate the original Dutch colony from the indigenous inhabitants. Trading in financial instruments was sparse and haphazard, often occurring through personal contact in the area's coffee-houses. In the late 1700s, however, there was increased trading in the Continental and Colonial war bonds that had been issued to finance the War of Independence. Brokerage services were offered by some merchants as a secondary activity. On May 17, 1792, 24 New York brokers signed an agreement to trade a restricted list of securities among themselves, and to charge a fixed commission of 0.25 percent. This was referred to as the buttonwood agreement, as the designated meeting place was in the open near a buttonwood tree. The arrangement worked, and in the next year the association built the Tontine Coffee House and moved trading inside the building. Trading was conducted as a ''call'' market. Several times each day the brokers would gather, each in an assigned seat, and the names of the traded securities would be called out one at a time. As the name of a security was read, the brokers would orally exchange offers to buy and sell in an ''auction'' process, until a price was agreed on.

The buttonwood brokers faced considerable competition from other similar groups and were at times overshadowed. By the 1860s, 11 exchanges had evolved in New York from outdoor trading in the ''curb markets.'' These were outdoor markets where trading literally took place at the curbstones, with different stocks being traded at particular lampposts or other similar, agreed upon locations. In 1869, the original buttonwood association merged with the larger Open Board and adopted continuous auction trading, rather than the periodic call system originally used. The much-changed buttonwood association has endured, and still meets near the location of the buttonwood tree on Wall Street. It uses the name adopted in 1863: New York Stock Exchange, or NYSE. The NYSE is now the dominant U.S. stock exchange. The remaining New York curb markets went through various associations and combinations, eventually moving trading inside and merging into what is today the American Stock Exchange, or AMEX. The exchanges in Philadelphia and Boston continue, and a number of other regional exchanges have come into existence. Internationally, many exchanges were in existence before the beginning of U.S. markets. Some of the foreign exchanges are large, and compete with U.S. exchanges for international investments. The creation of new exchanges continues, particularly in emerging countries. There are also extensive informal markets outside the exchanges, both domestically and internationally. For some securities, such as **bonds**, these informal markets are the principal trading mechanism.

THE ROLE OF THE STOCK MARKETS

Securities markets may be classified by role into primary and secondary markets. The primary market is the process by which new securities are issued and marketed. After a securities issue has been sold to investors, the subsequent trading of the issue among investors is referred to as the secondary market.

THE PRIMARY MARKET. Capital for growth and new investments is the lifeblood of the firm. Large investors with the means to invest directly are scarce and difficult to attract. By issuing **securities**, a firm has access to a larger number of investors of varying means. This allows the firm to raise larger amounts of capital at less cost than through seeking **direct investment** by individuals or from bank loans. Without a primary securities market, new projects are difficult to finance, innovation slows, and economic development stagnates.

The process of selling stock to the general public for the first time is called an initial public offering (IPO). If the firm has previously issued stock to the general public, a new issue is called a seasoned new issue. Given the infrequency of a stock issue for a firm, and the unfamiliarity of the corporate financial officers with the complex process, it is logical for the firm to turn to an investment banker. The investment banker is an expert in public offerings who provides three functions for the firm. First, the investment banker knows the extensive legal requirements and other arrangements surrounding registration and sale of securities, and guides the firm through the process. The investment banker is familiar with the securities markets, and can help the firm choose the optimal form of security and design its terms. Second, the investment banker can market and distribute the issue to investors. The originating banker also provides price support or stabilization for the issue during the distribution phase, standing ready to buy the security to prevent or reduce price drops due to temporary imbalances. Notice of a **public offering** in the financial press is in the form of tombstones, so named because of the similarity in their appearances. The tombstone describes the security and lists the originating banker and the members of the syndicate.

While all of the services provided by investment bankers are important, the service which is of greatest appeal to the firm is the reduction of risk through the process of **underwriting**. A public offering is an important event in the evolution of a firm, and failure of the offering would be disastrous. In underwriting, the investment banker guarantees the success of the issue by simply buying the entire issue from the firm, accepting the risk that the security will not sell at the expected price. There are two reasons why the investment banker can accept the risk of underwriting. First, a syndicate, or temporary association of investment bankers, is formed to underwrite, market, and distribute the issue. The originating banker retains a larger portion of the issue and the accompanying risk than other syndicate members, but this is often a small fraction of the total. Second, although the firm has only one issue underway, the investment banker is able to diversify the risk by participating in many issues. In some cases the investment banker will not accept the risk of the offering by underwriting. If the investment banker does not underwrite the issue, it is called a best efforts offering.

In a secondary distribution the stock being sold is not issued by the firm, but is a large amount of previously issued stock held by an investor. The public offering may be accomplished more rapidly and perhaps at better prices than piecemeal selling. There are some variations on the issue process. Since 1982 firms have been permitted to register securities and then sell them gradually over a two-year period. This shelf registration, so called because the securities are "on the shelf" awaiting sale, is attractive because it is a ready source of capital. Shelf registration is also thought to have lower flotation costs, because the sale can be timed to take advantage of attractive market conditions, and small sales avoid the possible depression of prices associated with large offers. For bonds, an alternative to a public offering is private placement. In private placement, the issue is placed with a limited number of investors, usually institutions, instead of being offered to the general public. This alternative is sometimes attractive to the issuing firm because the security and its conditions can be negotiated, the issue can be accomplished in less time, and there are fewer disclosure requirements. Notices of private placements published in the financial press are in the nature of advertisements by investment bankers.

THE SECONDARY MARKET. The firm is not directly affected by trading in securities after issue, and only receives proceeds from the original issue of the security. As a result, it is sometimes thought that the secondary market is somewhat irrelevant, a place where investors gamble without any real economic impact. This view is absolutely wrong. The secondary markets provide the liquidity and price discovery that are necessary for the existence of an effective primary market.

Liquidity refers to the ability to convert **assets** to cash quickly at a price reflecting the fair (economically rational) value. Both conditions must be fulfilled, since any asset could be converted to cash quickly if offered at a low enough price. Liquidity in turn depends on three qualities. Depth is the presence of orders to trade at prices closely surrounding the market price, while breadth requires that the size of these orders be sufficient to prevent wide price swings, given trading volume. Resiliency refers to the speed with which prices due to temporary supply and demand imbalances call forth new orders. Lack of liquidity increases the risk of the buyer, since the asset may have to be sold at a low price. Under such conditions, investors are hesitant to invest, will demand a higher rate of return, and often require extensive safeguards. These conditions are often apparent in the **venture capital** market, in which firms that do not have access to the primary securities markets seek funding. In short, without secondary market liquidity a primary market for securities would not function

well. Even the venture capital market is aided by the secondary market, since one factor in investing is the likelihood that the firm will grow enough to accomplish a public offering, so that the stock will become liquid. The possibility of a secondary distribution or offering also encourages participation in public offerings by large investors. The liquidity provided by an effective secondary market not only supports, but indeed enables, an effective primary market. It is not surprising that developing countries establish securities markets to facilitate economic growth.

Price discovery is the **valuation** of assets. Through trading, an equilibrium price that represents the consensus of the markets is established. This price is the result of information entering the market, and it is also information in itself. It is a signal both to investors and to the firm's management as to the expected future of the firm. The secondary market controls access to the primary through the signals from price discovery. If a firm's securities are given a low value, signaling low expectations, the issue of new securities is difficult if not impossible. Even if a primary issue is possible, the cost of capital for the firm will be high, and the capital budget of the firm will be small, slowing growth. In essence, by deciding which firms will receive capital for new projects, the price discovery function of the secondary markets serves as the capital budgeting process of the economy, setting its goals, priorities, and future. Rather than being irrelevant gambling, secondary markets are a vital mechanism in the economy.

MARKET STRUCTURE

Another way of classifying securities markets is by the trading arrangements and rules. An organized exchange is characterized by a definite physical location and a restricted list of securities and traders. The over-the-counter (OTC) market, on the other hand, is simply a net of brokers and dealers who maintain contact and trade through various means of communication. A broker trades for the client as an agent without entering the trade as a principal, and is compensated by a commission. A dealer trades with the client as a principal. The dealer trades from inventory and receives no commission, compensation comes from trading gains and losses and the spread between the bid and ask prices. The distinction is by form of participation only. A given individual may function as both a dealer and a broker, but is not allowed to perform both functions in the same transaction.

ORGANIZED EXCHANGES. The NYSE and the AMEX are examples of organized exchanges. In terms of numbers of companies, the NYSE is small, listing over 2,000 stock issues of about 1,500 companies. These are large firms that meet the listing requirements, however, and in terms of value traded the

NYSE is huge, accounting for about 85 percent of the value traded on U.S. exchanges. The AMEX is national in scope but has less-stringent listing requirements, and the firms tend to be smaller than on the NYSE. Within the United States there are also regional stock exchanges that list firms that do not meet the listing requirements of the national exchanges. Trades made on the floor of an exchange are sometimes said to be the first market.

Both the NYSE and the AMEX provide continuous trading in an auction process. Each stock trades at a designated trading post on the trading floor. Only members, who are said to hold a seat on the exchange (the term arises from the original buttonwood association practice of call trading from assigned seats) are allowed to trade. The public has access to trading through commission brokers who represent brokerage houses, executing trades for the firm's clients. The commission brokers may be assisted by independent two-dollar brokers, the name arising from the amount once charged for this assistance. Two-dollar brokers may also be floor traders, trading for their own account, but they may not fill both roles in the same stock on the same day, to avoid **conflict of interest**. An exchange member called a specialist will be present at the designated trading spot. The specialist makes a market in the stock by providing firm bid and ask offers. Normally, there is only one specialist for a given issue, although there have been exceptions. The specialist also handles the several types of away-from-the-market or limit orders left by brokers, which specify trading at a price other than the immediate market price. To fill this role, the specialist maintains the order book. The order book, now a computer, is simply a listing of client's away-from-the-market orders left with the specialist by floor brokers. The specialist will execute these orders if and when the order flow permits. The execution of the orders preserves price priority, i.e., execution of highest bid or lowest offer to sell. The system does not necessarily preserve time priority, or execution in the order received, since order size is taken into account.

The specialist has the responsibility to maintain an orderly market, i.e., to avoid wide fluctuations in trading price. In order to do this, the specialist must stand ready to buy and sell on the firm's own account, and is subject to various trading rules to avoid conflict of interest. The possibility of large market movements makes market maintenance very risky, and the sharp market decline of 1987 caused large losses to specialists. Specialists must meet requirements to assure that they will have sufficient capital to maintain an orderly market. Despite the risks and limitations, being a specialist is rewarding. One source of specialist income is the commission on handling away-from-the-market orders. Perhaps more important, however, is the knowledge of investor intentions and of market depth and breadth provided by the order book. This information, known only to the specialist, helps the specialist to engage in profitable trades.

It must be noted that the specialist does not set or control the price. The trading edge comes only from superior information of probable price movements. Indeed, many trades do not involve the specialist but are instead the product of the simultaneous crowd trading. The crowd is the group of traders and brokers present at the trading post. New offers are announced publicly, and may be accepted or responded to by a member of the crowd independently of the specialist and the book. This may occur at a price inside the specialist's bid ask spread, although price priority must be maintained.

Block trades are transactions of over 10,000 shares, and account for about half of all transactions on the NYSE. Specialists are prohibited from soliciting orders in the stock in which they make a market. In order to maintain an orderly market in the face of such an order, the specialist would be forced to absorb much of the order into inventory. Understandably, specialists are reluctant to assume the risk of so large an inventory. As a result, block trades are not sent directly to the trading floor. Instead, a brokerage firm called a block house will undertake to find matching orders in what is sometimes called the upstairs market. The block and matched orders are then taken to the specialist and crossed, or executed, on the floor of the exchange.

Organized exchanges exist throughout the world, and compete with each other and with U.S. exchanges for international capital flows. Trading arrangements on these exchanges may differ from those used on domestic exchanges. The Tokyo Stock Exchange, for instance, is a pure agency market, in which the price is set by orders without exchange influence. Rather than using specialists, the order book is maintained by officials who may not trade in the stocks assigned to them. Trading on the Paris Bourse and the German and Austrian exchanges, are call markets. In call markets orders are accumulated over time and crossed or executed at intervals, as in the original NYSE buttonwood trading. Investors considering international investment on foreign exchanges must be careful to understand the differing exchange arrangements.

OVER-THE-COUNTER MARKETS. About 7,000 **stocks**, and almost all bonds, trade in the over-the-counter markets. The name originates from the time when stock trading was a sideline for merchants and bankers, and securities were literally sold over a counter. The OTC market is sometimes defined as any trade that does not take place on the organized exchanges. Stocks trading OTC tend to be smaller and younger firms, although there are exceptions. The quality of the securities varies widely. As indicated by the plural, the OTC is properly viewed as a group of submarkets sharing certain characteristics. One characteristic is that this market has no central meeting place. It is instead an informal network of brokers trading for clients and dealers who make a market in the securities. There may be multiple market makers for a given security, typically between 2 and 20. Brokers and dealers communicate and trade with each other by various means. Another distinction is that on the OTC the price of a trade is set by negotiation, rather than by the auction process of the NYSE. A broker receiving an order will contact the market makers and receive bid and ask quotations, and may choose the best offer or attempt to negotiate a better offer. There is no specialist or specific mechanism to maintain an orderly market, and price fluctuations depend on the breadth, depth, and resiliency of the market for the particular security. Trades executed over-the-counter for stocks not listed on an exchange are referred to as the second market. Stocks listed on an exchange may also be traded over-the-counter, and such trades are sometimes referred to as the third market.

One OTC subgroup consists of stocks listed on the **National Association of Securities Dealers Automated Quotations System (NASDAQ)**. This system provides an electronic display of dealer bids and asks, allowing the broker to obtain the best price. Listing on NASDAQ is restricted to about 3,500 of the more widely traded stocks that also meet other listing requirements. As with NYSE listings on the exchanges, the NASDAQ stocks are a minority in numbers but a majority in value and trading among OTC stocks. A step down from the NASDAQ stocks are those listed in the pink sheets. These are printed bid and ask quotations that are distributed daily, the name derives from the color of the paper used. The quotes also have some availability via computer. Unlike NASDAQ quotes, pink sheet quotes are more in the nature of workout quotes, or estimates, rather than firm quotes at which a trade can be executed. Although some large firms are included in this group, most are smaller firms. Trading in pink sheet stocks tends to be thin, or lacking in order depth and breadth, so that it is often difficult to move more than small amounts of stock without price concessions. Recently the fourth market has seen increased volume. This market consists of trading directly between institutions, without involving brokers.

MARKET EFFICIENCY

Among the first applications of **computers** was a search for the trends in stock prices postulated by the Dow theory. Various tests detected only very weak trends that were incapable of supporting investment strategies. Although the tests do not definitively disprove the existence of trends, the empirical observations led to the conclusion that stock prices are best described as a **random walk**, i.e., that changes in stock prices are random variables. The efficient markets hypothesis arose as an explanation of this empirical observation. The efficient markets hypothesis suggests that information is fully reflected in stock prices. If information is fully reflected, price changes will be the result of the arrival of new information. The arrival of new information will be random, since anything known would already be reflected in the price. This random arrival of information will result in random price fluctuations: informationally efficient markets will result in a random walk in stock prices. Two important possible misconceptions must be mentioned. The first misconception is that the random walk and the efficient markets hypotheses suggest that stock prices are random. The EMH suggests that information is fully and accurately reflected in prices, so that prices will be close estimates of true intrinsic value. The random walk refers to price changes, not to the prices themselves. The second misconception is that the hypotheses imply that nothing can be known about price changes. While price changes cannot be exactly predicted, it is still possible to describe the probability distribution of price changes

Market efficiency is closely related to both liquidity and price discovery. An efficient market is one in which price discovery is rapid and accurate, and the requirements for efficiency include the breadth, depth, and resiliency required for support of liquidity. Aside from the importance of efficiency for the capital budgeting role of the secondary markets, the question of market efficiency is important to investor strategy. If information is fully reflected in stock prices, that information cannot be used to generate excess returns, i.e., returns greater than could be expected without using the information. Definition of excess returns requires a definition of normal profits as a standard for comparison. A large number of tests of market efficiency have used the **capital asset pricing model (CAPM)** to establish a level of expected return on a risk-adjusted basis. In this approach, risk is defined as the beta or systematic, nondiversifiable variation. More recently, the CAPM has been found to be inadequate in several ways. Some researchers have instead used a multifactor approach based on the arbitrage pricing theory. Unfortunately, the factors are not defined by the theory, and there is no theoretically supported and generally accepted set of factors. While there is no entirely satisfactory theory to specify expected returns, this does not make testing impossible, merely less precise. The effect of information can be detected by testing not for excess but for unusual returns, where unusual returns are returns that differ from observed historical returns

The question of which information is reflected is treated by defining three levels of market efficiency based on the information set reflected. The lowest level of efficiency is called the weak-form. This form of the EMH holds that historical market trading data (such as prices and volume) cannot be used to increase returns over what would otherwise be expected. The next level of efficiency is the semi-strong form. This form applies to all publicly available data, such as **annual reports**, published brokerage reports, or newspaper articles, and all weak-form information. The highest level of efficiency is the strong form, which holds that all information, both public and private, is fully reflected in stock prices

Studies of the weak-form of the EMH include the original trend studies, and numerous tests of trading rules. The overwhelming majority of evidence to date supports weak form efficiency. This would seem to rule out **technical analysis** as an investment approach. Proponents of the approach argue, however, that the tests are inadequate and that application of mechanical rules without human judgment would of course be useless. Tests of the strong form have indicated that this extreme form is violated by exclusive information such as the specialist's knowledge of the order book. Finally, tests of the semi-strong form have provided mixed results, revealing the presence of anomalies, which indicate that at least some forms of public information are not fully reflected. The tests have several shortcomings. One problem is that they tend to use computer-accessible data that deals with the markets we would expect to be efficient. Another shortcoming is the time frame, with the majority of studies using daily or longer data.

The question of efficiency is best thought of as one of degree, rather than kind. Efficiency is not so much a matter of all stocks being correctly priced at all times, but of most stocks being close to intrinsic value most of the time. Markets are relatively efficient if mispricing is small, infrequent, and short-lived. Further, the question of efficiency depends on the market, the investor, and the time frame. The NYSE is relatively efficient, as is the AMEX. When we move to the OTC, we must consider the subgroup. For widely traded NASDAQ stocks, the markets are likely quite efficient. But the bond market is often described as less efficient, and market efficiency for low-volume pink sheet stocks can be expected to be below NASDAQ efficiency. This would indicate an indexing approach on the NYSE, but **fundamental analysis** might be more appropriate for pink sheet investors. Investor expertise and position in the information chain must also be considered. The market seems much more efficient for amateur investors in the countryside than for investment professionals on Wall Street. Finally, investors who are slow to act on information, or face trading delays, will find that information has already caused price adjustment. For these investors, the market is relatively efficient.

MARKET REGULATION

Given the importance of securities markets to the economy, and the spectacular profits that can be gained from abuse, regulation of securities markets is surprisingly recent and somewhat informal. There was little market regulation until 1911, when individual states began to enact blue-sky laws regulating securities. The name comes from a court ruling that noted that some investment schemes promised little more than a patch of blue sky. These state laws were insufficient, inadequately enforced, and easily circumvented. Pools, or small groups of investors cooperating in manipulation of stock prices, and other unethical practices were not unusual. Financial information was difficult to obtain. Although organized exchanges required the disclosure of some financial information for traded stocks, this information was not always reliable. Federal regulation did not appear until after the market fluctuations of 1929. The major regulatory framework was constructed by the **Securities Act of 1933** and the **Securities Exchange Act of 1934**. The 1933 act required that firms issuing new stock register and disclosure financial information about the issue, and included antifraud provisions. The 1934 act extended the disclosure requirements to publicly traded securities, and established the **Securities and Exchange Commission** (SEC) to administer and revise the securities regulations. The OTC market was not brought into the regulatory structure until the Maloney Act of 1938. The Securities Investor Protection Act of 1970 established the Securities Investor Protection Corporation (SIPC) to protect against the failure of brokerage firms, similar to protections against bank failure. It is important to note that SIPC does not protect against investment losses, only against losses due to failure of brokerage firms.

It is interesting to note that the disclosure requirements of the organized exchanges had an important impact on the field of public **accounting**, and that the 1933 and 1934 acts added the requirement that **financial statements** be audited by an independent accountant. The auditors opinion and the acceptance of registration of a securities issue by the SEC are similar in that neither is an endorsement of investment value. Instead, both simply indicate that all required information is included and presented according to accepted standards. Judgement of investment value is left to the informed investor. Registration of a new issue is automatic unless the SEC specifically rejects the statement within 20 days. The 1934 act granted the SEC approval of commission rate changes and power to change and formulate trading rules. It left the SEC out of some areas, granting control over minimum margin to the Federal Reserve Board and discipline of exchange members to the exchanges. The resulting structure is one which relies heavily on self-regulation by the exchanges, and by the National Association of

Securities Dealers (NASD) for the OTC market. Several professional organizations, such as the Institute of Chartered Financial Analysts, also set forth ethical codes governing those holding the designation.

Insider trading is an important issue that has not been satisfactorily resolved. Insider trading is trading on private information about a firm which has not been released to the general public. As a form of control, the SEC requires that insiders, such as corporate officers and directors of publicly held firms, report all transaction in the firm's stock. While some cases of insider trading are clear, such as buying by a corporate officer based on knowledge of unannounced increased earnings, there is no exact definition of insider trading. Present interpretations involve not only the nature of the information, but how and by whom it was obtained. Accidental acquisition of confidential information does not confer a fiduciary obligation, and the information can be used. Simply holding inside information does not preclude trading if the information is part of an overall mosaic of reasoning behind the trade, but was not by itself the primary reason for the trade.

THE FUTURE OF THE MARKETS

Since the days of buttonwood trading, the securities markets have been constantly changing. The introduction of the telegraph in the 1840s and the 1850s opened up trading on exchanges countrywide, and local newspapers began to list Wall Street price quotations. The 1870s saw the introduction of stock tickers and telephone. In 1883 a two-page leaflet called the Customer's Afternoon Letter started publication; in July 1889 the leaflet was expanded and the named changed to the *Wall Street Journal*. The assets traded also changed, from mining and railroad stocks to industrial issues. After the market crash of 1929, trading practices changed remarkably, although trading did not recover to its previous level until the 1960s.

Recent changes have been perhaps even more rapid. As trading volume expanded during the 1960s Wall Street experienced a back office crisis. A number of firms failed because they were unable to keep up with the paperwork. Trading by institutions began to increase, and these institution began to work outside the usual market procedures to avoid fixed commissions. In 1975 Congress passed the Securities Act Amendments. The amendments obligated the SEC to block anticompetitive exchange rules, precluded fixed commissions, and mandated the development of a National Market System (NMS). Although various steps have been taken that have resulted in closer integration of the markets, the controversy over how to achieve the NMS continues. The role of the specialist has been challenged by those who point to the OTC and to foreign markets such as the Tokyo exchange as proof that the specialist is an anachronism.

Regulation is only one source of pressure for change, however, and competition and technological innovation may be a bigger factor. Quotes from and execution on all of the U.S. exchanges are available. While for various reasons these arrangements are of low trading volume, the presence of the alternatives itself is a powerful force. Computerization and electronic communication makes trading on foreign exchanges not only feasible but easy and, for some purposes, preferable. While on a year-to-year basis change may seem slow, it is likely that the next decade will see major changes in trading mechanisms and practices.

[David E. Upton]

FURTHER READING:

Blume, Marshall E., Jeremy J. Siegel, and Dan Rottenberg. *Revolution on Wall Street: The Rise and Decline of the New York Stock Exchange*. W. W. Norton & Company.

Bodie, Zvi, Alex Kane, and Alan J. Marcus. *Investments*. 2nd ed. Irwin, 1993.

Ellis, Charles D. "The Loser's Game." *The Financial Analysts Journal*. July/August, 1975, pp. 19-26.

Fischer, Donald E., and Ronald J. Jordan. *Security Analysis and Portfolio Management*. 5th ed. Prentice-Hall.

Malkiel, Burton G. *A Random Walk Down Wall Street*. 4th ed. W.W. Norton & Company

Reilly, Frank K. *Investment Analysis and Portfolio Management*. 3rd ed. Chicago: Dryden Press, 1989.

Samuelson, Paul. "Proof That Properly Discounted Present Values Vibrate Randomly." *Bell Journal of Economics and Management Science*. Autumn, 1973, pp. 369-374.

Samuelson, Paul A. "Proof That Properly Anticipated Prices Fluctuate Randomly." *Industrial Management Review*. Spring, 1965, pp. 41-49.

Schwartz, Robert A. *Equity Markets: Structure, Trading, and Performance*. Harper & Row.

Teweles, Richard J., Edward S. Bradley, and Ted M. Teweles. *The Stock Market*. John Wiley & Sons.

STOCKS

An entrepreneur with a good idea can do nothing without capital to act on that idea. As a start, the entrepreneur can use personal resources to form a sole proprietorship. In this form the entrepreneur and the business are indistinguishable, and the amount of capital is limited to the personal wealth and borrowing power of the entrepreneur. The entrepreneur is personally liable for all obligations. If the business grows and prospers even more capital will be required, often rapidly outrunning the resources of the entrepreneur. Forming a partnership with other parties solves some of the problems by adding the personal resources of one or more partners. This form of organization dilutes the claim and authority of the entrepreneur. Partnerships may not work well if large amounts of capital are required. Potential investors with large amounts of capital are hard to find. Once found, they are reluctant to enter partnerships for two reasons. The first reason is that all partners are equally and totally responsible for the obligations of the partnership. This risk exposure may easily exceed the original investment. The second reason is that the partnership is a temporary alliance. Partners may withdraw at any time. Partnership interests are not liquid, and potential investors are reluctant to enter partnerships because of the difficulties of disposing of the investment and realizing a return. Many of these problems are avoided by the corporate form of ownership.

THE CORPORATE FORM

In the corporate form, a business is set up as legal entity that has the power to act as an individual, and for legal purposes is considered to be a real person. This entity by itself has no net legal value, as recognized in the basic accounting equation: ''Assets equals liabilities plus owners equity.'' What the firm owns as assets is owed to creditors and others as **liabilities**, and to the owners as equity. This creation of a legal person, however, separates the liabilities of the corporation from the liabilities of the owners. This results in ''limited liability'': should the firm fail, the obligations of the firm are not the obligations of the owners. The value of owning the firm may go to zero, but the investors' losses are limited to their original investment. Limited liability greatly reduces investor risk, so that investors are willing to consider more and riskier investments and will not require as great an anticipated return. This increased willingness to undertake new projects encourages innovation. Limited liability of investors has been an important factor encouraging economic growth. Another attraction of the corporate form is that ownership is subdivided into shares of stock. Shares may be sold to many investors, in varying amounts. This opens up a wider pool of investors. The shares are also transferable, so that the stockholder can liquidate and realize a return more easily than is possible with a partnership interest, further reducing investor risk. Given these advantages, it is not surprising that many business ventures choose the corporate form, either at first or after growth makes other forms overly cumbersome.

The corporate form does have some disadvantages. One disadvantage is double taxation of earnings. The earnings of a sole proprietorship are taxed once as the earnings of the proprietor. The firm is a legal entity, however, and its earnings are taxed. Any distribution of the already once-taxed earnings is considered income of the investor, and the earnings are taxed a second time. Another disadvantage is that as ownership becomes wider, it becomes more diverse. Entrepreneurs remaining as managers may be distracted more often by fellow owners and more formal requirements. A different style of **management** may be required. The corporate form also facilitates separation of ownership and management. This is a mixed blessing. On the one hand, it allows professional management and the application of expertise not yet developed by the entrepreneur. On the other it raises the agency, or control, problem. The professional manager is an agent of the stockholders, not necessarily part of the ownership, and may have different goals and agenda. Ownership may be diluted, and control limited to less direct, impersonal procedures.

Securities issued by a corporation are classified as **debt** or as equity, equity being an ownership claim. Under the corporate form, ownership may be complicated. The main types of equity claims are common and preferred stock. These equity claims may take many forms. There are related claims, such as rights, **warrants**, and convertible securities. The securities also may be divided into those which are publicly traded, and those which are not. Although the underlying securities are in the same class, public trading implies a much wider ownership and liquidity, and often a much different set of problems and considerations. Securities of firms that are closely held, or have few shareholders, look quite different from an investment viewpoint.

COMMON STOCK

A share of **common stock** is quite literally a share in the business, a partial claim to ownership of the firm. Owning a share of common stock provides a number of rights and privileges. These include sharing in the income of the firm, exercising a voice in the management of the firm, and holding a claim on the assets of the firm.

DIVIDENDS. Sharing in the income of the firm is generally in the form of a cash dividend. The firm is not obligated to pay **dividends**, which must be declared by the **board of directors**. The size and timing of the dividends is uncertain. In a strictly rational economic environment, dividends would be considered as a ''residual.'' In this view, the firm would weigh payment of dividends against other uses for the funds. Dividends would be paid only if the firm had no better use for the funds. In this case, declaring or increasing dividends would be a negative signal, since the firm would be admitting that it lacked possibilities for growth. For widely held, publicly traded firms there are a number of indications that this is not the case, and that shareholders and investors like dividends and dividend increases. The reason is that dividends are taken as a signal that the firm is healthy, and can afford to pay dividends. A decrease in dividends would indicate inability to maintain the level of dividends, signaling a decline in prospects. An increase would signal an improvement in prospects. The signal from a dividend decrease is strong because management will wish to give only positive signals by at least maintaining the dividend, making cuts only when absolutely necessary. The signal from a dividend increase is strong because management would be hesitant to increase dividends unless they could be maintained. The signaling nature of dividends is supported by cases in which the dividend is maintained in the face of declining earnings, sometimes even using borrowed funds. It is also supported by the occurrence of "extraordinary" or one-time-only dividends, a label by which management attempts to avoid increasing expectations.

This signaling approach is not applicable to **closely held firms**. In this situation, communication between management and shareholders is more direct and signals are not required. When owners are also the managers, sharing in earnings may take the indirect form of perks. In fact, shareholders in closely held firms may prefer that dividends be reinvested, even in relatively low return projects as a form of tax protection. The investment is on a pretax (before personal tax) basis for the investor, avoiding immediate double taxation and converting the income to **capital gains** that will be paid at a later date.

Dividends are declared for stockholders at a particular date, called the date of record. Since stock transactions ordinarily take five business days for completion, the stock goes "ex-dividend" four days before the date of record, unless special arrangement is made for immediate delivery. Since the dividend removes funds from the firm, it can be expected that the per share price will decrease by the amount of the dividend on the ex-dividend date.

Stock dividends are quite different in form and nature from cash dividends. In a stock dividend, the investor is given more shares in proportion to the number held. A stock split is similar, with a difference in accounting treatment and a greater increase in the number of shares. The use of the word "dividends" in stock dividends is actually a misuse of the word, since there is no flow of cash, and the proportional and absolute ownership of the investor is unchanged. The stockholder receives nothing more than a repackaging of ownership: the number of shares increases, but ceteris paribus share price will drop. There are, however, some arguments in favor of stock dividends. One of these is the argument that investors will avoid stocks of unusually high price, possibly due to required size of investment and round lot (100 share) trading. On the other hand, stocks with unusually low price are also avoided, perhaps perceived as "cheap." The price drop accompanying stock dividends can be used to adjust price. Stock dividends have also been suggested as a way to make cash dividends elective while also providing tax-advantaged reinvestment. With a cash dividend, an investor who wishes to reinvest must pay taxes and then reinvest the reduced amount. With a stock dividend, the entire amount is reinvested. Although taxes will ultimately be paid, in the interim a return is earned on the entire pretax amount. This is the same argument as that for low dividends in a closely held firm. Investors who wish cash dividends can simply sell the stock. Using stock dividends in this way faces restriction from the **Internal Revenue Service**.

CONTROL. The corporate form allows the separation of management and ownership, with the manager serving as the agent of the owner. Separation raises the problem of control, or what is termed the agency problem. Stockholders have only indirect control by voting for the directors. The directors in turn choose management and are responsible for monitoring and controlling management's conduct. In fact, the stockholders' ability to influence the conduct of the firm may be quite small, and management may have virtually total control within very broad limits.

Voting for the directors takes either of two forms. The first form is majority voting. In this form, each stockholder receives votes for each open position according to the number of shares held, and may cast those votes only for candidates for that position. The winning candidate is the candidate winning a majority of the votes cast. The second form is called cumulative voting. In this form, stockholders again receive votes for each open position according to the number of shares held, but may apportion the votes among the positions and candidates as desired. The candidates receiving the most votes are elected. Excluding minority stockholders from representation on the board is more difficult under cumulative voting. If there are four directors to be elected and 1 million shares eligible to vote at one vote per share, a stockholder with 500,001 shares would control the election. Under majority voting a dissident stockholder with 200,001 shares could cast only 200,001 votes apiece for candidates for each of the four positions, which would not be sufficient to ensure representation on the board. Under cumulative voting, a dissident stockholder with a minimum of 200,001 shares could be sure of representation by electing one candidate of choice, casting a cumulative 800,004 votes for that candidate. The remaining 799,999 shares could be sure of electing three chosen candidates, but could not command sufficient votes to exceed the cumulative dissident vote four times.

Although the board of directors is supposedly independent of management, the degree of independence is sometimes small. Typically, some members of the board are "insiders" drawn from management, while others are "outside" directors. Even the outside directors may not be completely independent of management for several reasons. One reason is that few shareholders can afford the time and expense to attend the annual meetings, so that voting is done through the mail. This usually takes the form of a ''proxy'' giving management the power to vote for the shareholder, as instructed. While the shareholder may instruct management on how to vote, the choices may be few and are controlled by management. Management will tend to nominate safe candidates for directorship, who will not be likely to challenge the status quo. As a result, directorship is at times an honor or sinecure, treated as having few real obligations. Dissidents may mount opposition and seek the proxy votes, but such opposition is liable to face legal challenges and must overcome both psychological barriers and shareholder apathy. Many shareholders do not vote or routinely vote for management. Further, dissidents must spend their own money, while management has the resources of the firm at its disposal. Another reason for a lack of independence on the part of directors is the practice of interlocking boards of directors, who are likely to reach a tacit agreement. Conventional wisdom on Wall Street has long been to sell the stock rather than oppose an entrenched management.

In addition to controlling the proxy system, managements have instituted a number of other defensive mechanisms in the face of takeover threats. It is not unusual to find several ''classes'' of stock with different voting power, some classes having no voting power at all. A number of firms have changed from cumulative to majority voting. Staggered boards, with only a portion of the board terms expiring in a given year, and supermajority voting for some questions have also been used. Takeover defenses include the **golden parachute**, or extremely generous severance compensation in the face of a takeover, and the **poison pill**, an action that is triggered by a takeover and has the effect of reducing the value of the firm. While Sidney Cottle, Rober F. Murray, and Frank E. Block may have gone too far in saying that ''The shareholder has become an ineffectual nuisance to be pacified by self-congratulatory reports and increasing dividends,'' it would appear that stockholder power has become more tenuous.

There has been some recent movement towards greater stockholder power. One factor in this movement is the increasing size of institutional investors such as pensions and mutual funds. This has led to a more activist stance, and a willingness to use the power of large stock positions to influence management. Another factor is a renewed emphasis on the duties of the directors, who may be personally liable for management's misconduct. At least part of this movement may be the result of the takeover activities of the 1980s. The takeover and breakup or consolidation of firms, with accompanying job loss, has been much criticized. This activity showed that challenging

management was possible, however, and encouraged dissident groups. It also sent a message to management that mediocre performance might not be tolerated. It has been suggested that the threat of takeover may have done much to reinforce the rights of stockholders. The use of defense mechanisms detrimental to the stockholder has called attention to managerial abuses. The appropriate level of salary and of management perks, such as use of the corporate jet and limousines, has come under scrutiny in the financial and popular press.

RESIDUAL OWNERSHIP. The common stockholder has a claim on the assets of the firm. This is an undifferentiated or general claim which does not apply to any specific asset. The claim cannot be exercised except at the breakup of the firm. The firm may be dissolved by a vote of the stockholders, or by bankruptcy. In either case, there is a well-defined priority in which the liabilities of the firm will be met. The common stockholders have the lowest priority, and receive a distribution only if prior claims are paid in full. For this reason the common stockholder is referred to as the residual owner of the firm.

PREEMPTIVE RIGHT. The corporate charter will often provide common stockholders with the right to maintain their proportional ownership in the firm, called the preemptive right. For example, if a stockholder owns 10 percent the stock outstanding and 100,000 new shares are to be issued, the stockholder has the right to purchase 10,000 shares (10 percent) of the new issue. This preemptive right can be honored in a rights offering. In a **rights** offering, each stockholder receives one right for each share held. Buying shares or subscribing to the issue then requires the surrender of a set number of rights, as well as payment of the offering price. The offering is often underpriced in order to assure the success of the offering. The rights are then valuable because possession of the rights allows subscription to the underpriced issue. The rights can be transferred, and are traded. Rights will be given to the owner of the stock on the date of record. During the time that a purchase will be completed before the date of record, the stock is said to be trading with rights or rights on. During this period the price of the stock reflects both the value of the stock and the value of the (to-be-issued) right. When purchase of the stock will not be completed until after the date of record, but before the offering, the stock is said to be trading ex-rights or rights off. Similar to the ex-dividend date, the ex-rights date will be four days before the date of record. At the ex-rights day the price of the stock will drop by the value of the right, since the stock purchase will not include the right.

A rights offering may be attractive to management because the stockholders, who thought enough of the firm to buy its stock, are a pre-sold group. The value of the preemptive right to the common stock-holders, however, is questionable. The preemptive right of proportional ownership is important only if proportional control is important to the stockholder. The stockholder may be quite willing to waive the preemptive right. If the funds are used properly, the price of the stock will increase, and all stockholders will benefit. Without buying part of the new issue, the stockholder may have a smaller proportional share, but the share will be worth more. While rights are usually valuable, this value arises from underpricing of the issue rather than from an inherent value of rights. The real question is whether the issue should be undertaken at all—i.e., what is to be done with the funds from the offering? If the funds are to be used in a way that the market perceives as having little value, the price of the stock will decline. If the funds are to be used in a way that the market perceives as having great value, the price of the stock will increase. The value of the rights ultimately depends on the use of the funds.

VALUATION. In investment practice, decisions are more often expressed and made in terms of the comparative expected rates of return, rather than on price. A number of models and techniques are used for valuation. A common approach to **valuation** of common stock is **present value**. This approach is based on an estimate of the future cash dividends. The present value is then the amount which, if invested at the required rate of return on the stock, could exactly recreate the estimated dividends. This required rate of return can be estimated from models such as the capital asset pricing model (CAPM), using the systematic risk of the stock, or from the estimated rate of return on stocks of similar risk. Another common approach is based on the **price-earnings ratios**, or P/E. In this approach, the estimated earnings of the firm are multiplied by the appropriate P/E to obtain the estimated price. This approach can be shown to be a special case of present value analysis, with restrictive assumptions. Since various models and minor differences in assumptions can produce widely different results, valuation is best applied as a comparative analysis.

In some cases, such as estate valuation, the dollar value of the stock must be estimated for legal purposes. For assets that are widely publicly traded, the market price is generally taken as an objective estimate of asset value for legal purposes, since this is sale value of the stock. For stock that is not widely traded, valuation is based on models such as present value, combined with a comparison with similar publicly traded stock. Often, however, a number of discounts are applied for various reasons. It is widely accepted that, compared to publicly traded stock, stock that is not publicly traded should be valued at a discount because of a lack of liquidity. This discount may be 60 percent or more. Another discount is ap-plied for a minority position in a closely held stock or a family firm, since the minority position would have no control This discount does not apply if the value is estimated from the value of publicly traded stock, because the market price of a stock is traded already the price of a minority position. There is an inverse effect for publicly traded stock in the form of a control premium. A large block of stock which would give control of the firm might be priced above market.

Finally, it should be noted that the **accounting** book value is only rarely more than tangentially relevant to market value. This is due to the use of accounting assumptions such as historic cost. While accounting information may be useful in a careful valuation study, accounting definitions of value differ sharply from economic value.

PREFERRED STOCK

Preferred stock is sometimes called a hybrid, since it has some of the properties of equity and some of the properties of debt. Like debt, the cash flows to be received are specified in advance. Unlike debt, these specified flows are in the form of promises rather than of legal obligations. It is not unusual for firms to have several issues of preferred stock outstanding, with differing characteristics. Other differences arise in the areas of control and claims on assets.

DIVIDENDS. Because the specified payments on preferred stock are not obligations, they are referred to as dividends. Preferred dividends are not tax-deductible expenses for the firm, and consequently the cost to the firm of raising capital from this source is higher than for debt. The firm is unlikely to skip, or fail to declare the dividend, however, for several reasons. One of the reasons is the dividends are typically (but not always) cumulative. Any skipped dividend remains due and payable by the firm, although no interest is due. One source of the preferred designation is that all preferred dividends in arrears must be paid before any dividend can be paid to common stockholders (although bond payments have priority over all dividends). Failure to declare preferred dividends may also trigger restrictive conditions of the issue. A very important consideration is that, just as for common dividends, preferred dividends are a signal to stockholders, both actual and potential. A skipped preferred dividend would indicate that common dividends will also be skipped, and would be a very negative signal that the firm was encountering problems. This would also close off access to the **capital markets**, and lenders would be wary.

There is also a form of preferred stock, called participating preferred stock, in which there may be a share in earnings above the specified dividends. Such participation would typically only occur if earnings or common dividends rose over some threshold, and might be limited in other ways. A more recent innovation is adjustable-rate preferred stock, with a variable dividend based on prevailing **interest rates**.

CONTROL

Under normal circumstances preferred stockholders do not have any voting power, resulting in little control over or direct influence on the conduct of the firm. Some minimal control would be provided by the indenture under which the stock was issued, and would be exercised passively, i.e., the trustees for the issue would be responsible for assuring that all conditions were observed. In some circumstances, the conditions of the issue could result in increased control on the part of the preferred stockholders. For instance, it is not unusual for the preferred stockholders to be given voting rights if more than a specified number of preferred dividends are skipped. Other provisions may restrict the payment of common dividends if certain conditions are not met. Preferred stockholders also may have a preemptive right.

CLAIM ON ASSETS AND OTHER FEATURES. Another source of the preferred designation is that preferred stock has a prior claim on assets over that of common stock. The claim of **bonds** is prior to that of the preferred stockholders. Although preferred stock typically has no maturity date, there is often some provision for retirement. One such provision is the call provision, under which the firm may buy back or recall the stock at a stated price. This price may vary over time, normally dropping as time passes. Another provision is the **sinking fund**, under which the firm will recall and retire a set number of shares each year. Alternately, the firm may repurchase the shares for retirement on the open market, and would prefer to do so if the market price of the preferred is below the call price. Preferred stock is sometimes convertible, i.e., it can be exchanged for common stock at the discretion of the holder. The conversion takes place at a set rate, but this rate may vary over time.

VALUATION. The par value of a preferred stock is not related to market value, except that it is often used to define the dividend. Since the cash flow of dividends to preferred stockholders is specified, valuation of preferred is much simpler than for common stock. The valuation techniques are actually more similar to those used for bonds, drawing heavily on the present value concept. The required rate of return on preferred stock is closely correlated with interest rates, but is above that of bonds because the bond payments are contractual obligations. As a result, preferred stock prices fluctuate with interest rates. The introduction of adjustable-rate preferred stock is an attempt to reduce this price sensitivity to interest rates.

FOREIGN STOCK

Purchases of foreign stock have greatly increased in recent years. One motivation behind this increase is that national economies are not perfectly correlated, so that greater diversification is possible than with a purely domestic portfolio. Another reason is that a number of foreign economies are growing, or are expected to grow, rapidly. Additionally, a number of developing countries have consciously promoted the development of secondary markets as an aid to economic development. Finally, developments in communications and an increasing familiarity with international affairs and opportunities has reduced the hesitance of investors to venture into what once was unfamiliar territory.

Foreign investment is not without problems. International communication is still more expensive and sometimes slower than domestic communication. Social and business customs often vary greatly between countries. Trading practices on some foreign exchanges are different than in the United States. Accounting differs not only in procedures, but often in degree of information disclosed. Although double taxation is generally avoided by international treaties, procedures are cumbersome. Political instability can be a consideration, particularly in developing countries. Finally, the investor faces exchange rate risk. A handsome gain in a foreign currency can be diminished, or even turned into a loss, by shifting exchange rates. These difficulties are felt less by professional managers of large institutions, and much of the foreign investment is through this channel.

An alternative vehicle for foreign investing is the American Depositary Receipt (ADR). This is simply a certificate of ownership of foreign stock that is deposited with a U.S. trustee. The depository institution also exchanges and distributes any dividends, and provides other administrative chores. ADRs are appealing to individual investors. It has also been suggested that the benefits of international investing can be obtained by investing in international firms.

INVESTMENT CHARACTERISTICS

As a class, common stock has provided the highest rate of return to investors. A study by Roger G. Ibbotsen and Rex A. Sinquefeld found that, over the period 1926-87, common stock provided an average annual return of 12 percent. This compares with an average annual return of 5.2% for long term corporate bonds, and 3.5 percent for Treasury bills (T-bills). Annual inflation over the period averaged 3 percent. Common stock also provided the highest risk, with returns having a standard deviation of 21.1 percent, as compared to 8.5 percent for long-term corporate bonds and 4.8 percent for Treasury bills. Although the data points out the desirability of common stock investment, these long-run averages must be interpreted carefully. Hidden within these averages were some extended loss periods, and some short periods of sharp losses. Also, the return on common stock was measured by the total return to the Standard & Poor's Composite Index, and reflect the effects of diversification. The historical returns of individual stocks or small portfolios could have quite different average returns, and would almost certainly exhibit greater risk. Finally, the disclaimer so frequently found in investment advertisements that future performance may differ from past performance is applicable.

While the above observations give a general idea of the comparative returns to stocks overall, stocks are diverse in nature and can be classified many ways for investment purposes. One class of stocks is composed of small cap stocks—that of smaller firms. Ibbotsen and Sinquefield found that, over the 1926-87 period, small cap stocks had an average annual return of 17.7 percent, but with a standard deviation of 35.9 percent. It must be noted that the sample used was the stocks in the lowest quintile of the New York Stock Exchange, when ranked on capitalization (shares outstanding times price per share). While small by comparison to the other quintiles, these firms are still sizable. Findings such as these have led to an investment strategy of purchasing such stocks to earn the historical higher return. Indicative of the problems of long-term averages, many such investors have been disappointed.

Stocks are also classified according to the level of risk. Thus risky stocks are sometime referred to as aggressive or speculative. They may also be growth stocks, which are expected to experience high rates of growth in size and earnings. If risk is measured by the beta (systematic or nondiversifiable risk), then the term applies to a stock with a beta greater than one. These stocks are quite sensitive to economic cycles, and are also called cyclical. Contrasted are the blue-chip stocks, high-quality stocks of major firms that have long and stable records of earnings and dividends. Stocks with low risk, or a beta of less than one, are referred to as defensive. One form of investment strategy, called timing, is to switch among cyclical and defensive stocks according to expected evolution of the economic cycle. This strategy is sometimes refined to movement among various types of stock or sectors of the economy. Another stock category is income stocks, stocks that have a long and stable record of comparatively high dividends.

Common stock has been suggested as a hedge against inflation. This suggestion arises from two lines of thought. The first is that stocks ultimately are claims to real assets and productivity, and the prices of such claims should rise with inflation. As pointed out by Lawrence J. Gitman and Michael D. Joehnk, however, in real terms the Dow Jones Industrial Average (DJIA) fell almost without interruption from 1965 to 1982. The second line of thought is that the total returns to common stock are high enough to overcome inflation (the DJIA measures only the capital gains or price change component of returns). While this is apparently true over longer periods, as shown in the Ibbotsen and Sinquefield study, it has not held true over shorter periods.

Preferred stock is generally not considered a desirable investment for individuals. While as noted the junior position of preferred stockholders as compared to bonds indicates that the required rate of return on preferred will be above that of bonds, observation indicates that the yield on bonds has generally been above that of preferred of similar quality. The reason for this is a provision of the tax codes that 70 percent of the preferred dividends received by a corporation are tax exempt. This provision is intended to avoid double taxation. Because of the tax exemption, the effective after-tax yield on preferreds is higher for corporations, and buying of preferreds by corporations drives the yields down. The resulting realized return for individuals, who cannot take advantage of this tax treatment, would generally be below acceptable levels.

[David E. Upton]

FURTHER READING:

Bodie, Zvi, Alex Kane, and Alan J. Marcus. *Investments*. 2nd ed. Irwin, 1993.

Cottle, Sidney, Roger F. Murray, and Frank E. Block. *Graham and Dodd's Security Analysis*. 5th ed. McGraw-Hill, 1988.

Gitman, Lawrence J., and Michael D. Joehnk. *Fundamentals of Investing*. 5th ed. HarperCollins, 1993.

Ibbotsen, Roger G., and Rex A. Sinquefield. *Stocks, Bonds, Bills, and Inflation: Historical Returns (1926-1987)*. The Research Foundation of The Institute of Chartered Financial Analysts/Dow Jones-Irwin, 1989.

Petty, J. William, Arthur J. Keown, David F Scott, Jr., and John D. Martin. *Basic Financial Management*. Prentice Hall, 1993.

Pinches, George E. *Essentials of Financial Management*. 4th ed. HarperCollins, 1992.

STRATEGIC PAY/NEW PAY

The terms "strategic pay" and the "new pay" became established through book titles–Edward Lawler's *Strategic Pay* in 1990, and J.R. Schuster and Patricia Zingheim's *The New Pay* in 1992. The concept of strategic pay looks at wages and benefits as one instrument through which an organization can meet its current business goals. Schuster and Zingheim provide the following definition of new pay: "Under new pay, . . . pay programs respond to specific business and human resource challenges. . . . New pay requires the use of all the possible 'communication' to hit the proper performance targets. . . . base pay, variable pay, indirect pay. . . . The centerpiece of new pay is variable pay (which) facilitates the employee-organization partnership by linking the fortunes of both parties in a positive manner.'' New pay programs specifically place portions of all employee pay ''at risk.'' If specified goals are met, all share in the gains; if not, all lose. This simple concept represents a paradigm shift in thinking about pay—from a cost to employers to an investment by employers.

For many years pay has been handled mechanically. Jobs were evaluated, and points were assigned for ''compensable factors'' in the job (such as responsibility, skill, mental effort, and working conditions). This approach is called the ''point-factor'' system. Pay was then related to the points in the job. Bands of jobs were developed in similar point ranges. Naturally, this system resulted in long lists of jobs at many companies (and in the federal government). Apart from the annual raise, one could only get more money by moving up in the point system. This ''pay the job'' approach had the obvious strengths of objectivity and impersonality. However, it did not really ask if anyone actually produced anything, and did not distinguish well between high- and low-performing persons. The concept of ''broad banding''—collapsing the long lists of jobs into broader ''bands''—was an attempt to address some of the difficulties of extensive job categories and provide a way around the potential lockstep of the point-factor system.

''Pay the person'' was an attempt to bring the person more directly into the pay equation. It did so by providing additional money for additional competencies learned on or through the job. ''Pay for knowledge'' and ''pay for skills'' systems allowed employees to earn more money if they acquired and demonstrated competence in additional skills. Employers liked this because employees became more broadly capable. However, difficulties arose because employees sometimes never got to use their new skills. These approaches lacked a focus on the results as well.

There were some other problems with the old pay system, aside from bureaucratization (pay the job) and disconnection between what people learned and what they could do (pay the person)—misalignment and annuitization. One problem with existing pay practices is that they tend to be unaligned with results. The rhetoric of linkage is used—as in the concept of ''merit raise''—but in many actual cases, there is no merit involved. Somehow, in some way, a raise is determined. This lack of alignment is one issue; annuitization is another. Conventional ''raises'' go into the base. Hence, employers are paying for past performance year after year.

In spite of the fact that compensation costs are a large fraction of most business operations, neither employees or employers thought of compensation as a total package. While the businessperson may have had a sense of total compensation costs, the employees lacked the idea of total compensation as something for which they worked. And both the business and the employees lacked the *idea* of total compensation (benefits especially were not seen as ''pay'' by employees). Rather, it was broken up into components. There was base pay, and indirect pay (fringe benefits), as well as a range of bonuses, overtime, perks, and allowances. Yet it was difficult to get all the numbers in one place.

These components were often administered by different parts of the organization. Frequently base salary was determined under one unit of the organization, using one theory, or a combination of theories. Benefits were often developed and administered under another department with different rationales and philosophies. Bonuses and special pay were often in yet another place. Something new was needed.

New pay begins with a view that one should think about compensation as a complete, ''total'' package. Total compensation includes base pay, variable pay (bonuses, etc.), indirect pay (fringe benefits), and also pay that comes to employees through ''perks'' (perks-pay), and ''works'' (works-pay). Works-pay reflects pay that defers the worker's ''costs of doing business''—a uniform or car allowance, for example. Assembling these components creates learning for employer and employee alike, as each sees the amount of money involved.

Base pay is what many think of as ''pay.'' It can be paid ''at market,'' below, or above market. In the future, base pay will likely become a smaller fraction of total compensation than it is now, and may be targeted at ''below market.'' Individuals and teams can add to their pay through increments in the variable pay area.

Variable pay is the portion of pay linked to results. A variety of types of performance goals—individual, team, unit, and total company—can become components of the variable pay amount. While such elements have been present—**profit sharing**, gain sharing, etc.–they have not usually been linked into a total compensation framework. Employees will be able to add a considerable amount to their ''pay,'' depending upon how they and the firm performs. The structuring of variable pay in this way means that ''the paycheck'' may vary a good bit more in the future than in the past. Also, variable pay does not go into the base; it is a year-by-year phenomenon.

Indirect pay–fringe benefits–has traditionally been viewed as an entitlement program within the company. In new pay, Schuester and Zingheim state the ''view of indirect pay is to contain indirect pay costs to free dollars to spend on direct pay, particularly variable pay.'' Defined contribution plans are becoming more popular than defined benefit plans in retirement programs; health-care costs are being closely examined. Rather than simply being willing to pick up additional costs, companies are defining the amount of money they wish to convey through indirect pay. This approach frees up dollars which, in previous years, might have gone to benefits automatically. It can now go into variable pay. Employees can purchase augmented benefits if they wish with variable pay dollars, but they can also do other things with the money.

Perks, as a component of pay, are declining. They tend to emphasize status distinctions in an era of more flattened, team-oriented firms. There has also been increased tax interest in perks. Works-pay is perhaps the most difficult area, as companies try to define what costs of business to employees should be considered for employee reimbursement.

The new pay emphasis requires that organizations define goals and review performance in a competent manner. Accomplishing these objectives is essential for organizational high performance today, regardless of the pay system. Companies could improve at objective setting and **performance appraisal**. Thus, initiating a new pay system is one way to usher in needed change. Nevertheless, achieving both these objectives is difficult, particularly the development of skills in performance appraisal within staff. Tales of appraisal avoidance, cursory reviews, and unhelpful comments aimed at the person of the employee rather than the employee's behavior abound. Without objectives and review, the total compensation idea will not work well.

If an employer or business is considering implementing a new pay system, there are several helpful tips. First, get information about the current system and the way it actually works. One needs to look carefully at the current practice, securing input from all levels of the organization. A consultant may be helpful, because securing information from the full range of employees is likely to be more accepted if it is done by an outside group. A company-wide committee of employees might also be helpful.

It is clear that communication with employees is a key element. Over-communication is usually needed in an organizational effort, and especially when issues of compensation are involved. Communication in a variety of media are helpful (video, print, oral, etc.). Candor in communication, as well as level and mode, is vital. Employees will think that employers are reducing their pay, rather than realigning it. Clarity about the total compensation package, and the ability of employees to affect some of their own compensation through variable pay is essential.

Step-by-step movement is important. Shifting from so-called merit raises to a variable pay raise system is a tough change. One method is to develop a strategy by which all increments to base and indirect pay are "market related" and anything else is variable, driven by year-to-year performance.

Employers might want to move step-by-step, however, by allowing some of the variable pay increment to go into base, especially as a transition to a more fully operating variable pay system. The approach below suggests an arrangement of the relation of base increments to variable pay to the employees' percentile position in the range ($\frac{1}{100}$ indicates the first percentile; $\frac{50}{100}$ the 50th, $\frac{100}{100}$, the top of the range). For employees at the bottom of the range ($\frac{1}{100}$), 99 percent of the raise goes in base, and one percent to bonus; for employees in the middle of the range, it is half and half; for employees at the top of the range ($\frac{100}{100}$), all is variable pay. Assume that a particular employee's raise is $2000. For the person in the tenth percentile, 90 percent of the money, or $1,800, would be an addition to base, while ten percent, or $200, would be bonus. For the person at the top of the range, it would all be bonus. Over time, the decision points could be adjusted to move more toward a completely variable pay system.

Finally, it is helpful to emphasize the flexibility of the new pay system. The company needs to be as efficient and effective with total compensation as with other expenditures.

Employees need to be motivated through pay. In theory, one does not worry how much staff are paid–what they produce is what counts. In speaking about the new mindset of organizations, Charles Handy refers to the $\frac{1}{2} \times 2 \times 3$ formula. It is ". . . shorthand for one executive's goal that in five years there will be half as many people in the core of the company, paid twice as well, and producing three times as much value." As Hal Lancaster wrote, new pay is part of a new social contract between employers and employees which includes "meaningful work, learning opportunities, career management skills, honest communications and no-fault exits."

SEE ALSO: Compensation Administration

[John E. Tropman]

FURTHER READING:

Handy, Charles. "The New Mind-Sets of Organizations." *Insights Quarterly*. Winter, 1992, pp. 69-70.

Henderson, Richard I. *Compensation Management: Rewarding Performance*. 6th ed. Englewood Cliffs, N.J.: Prentice Hall, 1994.

Lancaster, Hal. "A New Social Contract to Benefit Employer and Employee." *The Wall Street Journal*. November 24, 1994, p. B1.

Lawler, Edward E., III. *Strategic Pay*. San Francisco: Jossey Bass, 1990.

Lowman, Don. " 'New Pay': Compensation for People, Not Jobs." *Employment Relations Today*. 20, 1 Spring, 1993, pp. 37-445.

Schuster, J. R., and Patricia Zingheim. *The New Pay: Linking Employee and Organizational Performance.* New York: Lexington, 1992.

STRATEGY

Strategy has content and timing; each business unit's mission defines preferred customers to serve and product/technological parameters for satisfying demand. Assumptions about each competitive environment suggest whether early implementation of actions will be more advantageous than letting competitors take pioneering risks (whether a first-mover advantage exists).

Formulation of corporate strategy assigns a mission that is consistent with the organization's goals to each business unit. Each business unit's mission defines the timing of cash flows to be generated (or a responsibility to support other business units that generate cash). Because corporate-level strategy integrates the activities of its mix of businesses, it defines the firm's "personality" and risk-taking attitudes in its quest to create value for its stakeholders. Although corporate strategy has previously been focused on the timing of cash flows generated by astute investment in short-term projects, concerns about competitiveness and the challenge of managing people-based sources of competitive advantage have forced managers to fund longer-term projects, as well. Where business units once developed individual distinctive competencies appropriate to the unique opportunities and threats they faced, corporate managers now nurture the development and sharing of core competencies across organizational boundaries to cope with converging industry boundaries and to leverage the benefit of expenditures across several marketplaces.

Strategy (from *strategos*, the art of the general) has its roots in traditional military tactics and logistics such as those described in Sun Tzu's *Art of War.* Modern business practices have appropriated some of the tenets of the ancient military codes and applied them to business transactions in order to acquire a great market share, to improve efficiency, and to increase profit margins. Access to the vast computational power of mainframe computers in the late 1960s linked corporate strategy formulation issues inextricably with those of financial analyses, especially in matters of diversification where covariance terms were calculated to assess risk preferences. Promulgation of the 1970s strategic planning practices of General Electric Company popularized the use of strategic business units (SBUs), which assign "bottom line responsibility" to the use of resources within organizational units smaller than divisions (or with customer/technological responsibilities that transcend divisional boundaries). General Electric Company was also an early user of objective criteria, such as the growth/share matrix, to direct strategic investments. (Demand growth rates and relative market shares were typical criteria in such frameworks; low market-share businesses facing slow demand growth—dogs—were candidates for divestiture.) Troubled lines of business are candidates for turnarounds to improve liquidity; firms in turnarounds cut back in markets where they are overextended (retrenchment) and reduce noncontributing activities to improve their cash flows.

Strategy implementation issues have become inextricably linked with the design of effective **management information systems** and empowerment of organizational resources, particularly where corporate-level managers seek to manage their firm's ongoing mix of business units effectively (operating synergies) as well as pick the best businesses to invest in financial synergies. As strategic planning processes have sought to elicit support from personnel who must implement the firm's strategy, the power of strategic planners who once generated armchair analyses, complete with alternative scenarios that anticipate every contingency, has migrated to the "troops in the trenches" who must make the plan succeed. Line personnel in all aspects of operations have initiated suggestions for reengineering the process by which firms create value for their customers. Ongoing managers have voluntarily downsized their organizations to create value for shareholders, lest the managers be replaced by outsiders with the same mandate (the market for corporate control).

Each business-level strategy matches firms' discretionary investments to existing (and future) market conditions in light of competitors' strategies for serving chosen customers in anticipation of creating value for investors (competitive strategy). Some industries have greater profitability potential than others at a particular time in a particular country. The five-forces model, which considers whether an industry's structural traits support high profitability margins, suggests which lines of business to enter (or exit). Using the tools of **microeconomic** analysis, the model indicates that the most profitable industries will sustain high entry barriers, low supplier and customer bargaining power, no perfect substitute products, and little price competition. Forecasts of future industry conditions are critical to justify new (or continued) funding of business units when using the five-forces model because competition is dynamic. Business-unit managers must devise entry strategies appropriate to overcome the entry barriers in operation when products are introduced.

While corporate-level managers are charged with finding the best uses for resources, managers responsible for each business unit are charged with sustaining a basis for competitive advantage in serving the most attractive customers. Although cost-based strengths are fundamental to becoming a preferred vendor, the evolving requirements of sophisticated customers mean that competitive advantage is a constantly moving target and effective managers must anticipate how industry success requirements will change and make expenditures to preempt competitors from improving their relative positions vis-à-vis key customers. When industries seem attractive, cash is often reinvested to maximize market share (economies of scale). Implicit in such reinvestment policies is the expectation that postponed profits can be harvested later by surrendering market share. Because the "first to exit" liquidates more of its investment than firms that procrastinate, however, business-unit managers must also assess the changing costs of overcoming exit barriers when competitive conditions sour and declining demand no longer justifies continuing investment. In volatile markets, dominant market share is no longer a virtue.

Because corporate-level (headquarters) managerial activities (and overhead expenses) are justified by making particular combinations of business units more valuable than if each line of business were a separate company held in a financial portfolio, corporate strategy is centrally concerned with the *nature of relationships* between business units. Resource allocation among a multitude of business units is also a central concern of corporate-level strategy; corporate managers often proactively intervene in business-level decisions by deciding in which lines of business the firm should (1) enter; (2) exit; (3) expand (or shrink) by funding the capacity of a business unit's geographic plants; (4) encourage coordination among a business unit's geographic plants (or encourage autonomy among them instead); and/or (5) encourage coordination among the resources and facilities of related (but separate) business units more overtly than if decisions to share expenses, transfer knowledge, participate in each other's value-creation chains, or other relationships were left to chance. (In a "bottom-up" strategic planning process, these same decisions might surface when corporate-level managers arbitrate between competing uses of resources when resources are rationed.) Corporate strategy accounts for the differences between the two types of strategic planning processes (top-down versus bottom-up) with regard to which business unit initiates the need for headquarters to make trade-offs among competing uses of capital. Although business-unit managers typically compete across the firm for capital allocations, processes for enhancing the firm's core competencies increasingly make human resource allocations across business units a strategic concern that is coordinated by headquarters, as well.

Core competencies arising from an organization's accumulated technical knowledge and management systems can be shared more easily when its corporate strategy encourages intrafirm interactions (economies of scope) than when each business unit throughout a firm's international system of operations goes its own way. While business-unit managers often champion shorter-term interests that favor the market segments they have chosen to serve, product attributes they believe will best serve their customers, and technological postures that will develop competencies that best suit their respective lines of business, corporate-level managers champion "big-picture," corporate-wide interests and legitimize internal schemes of cross-subsidization by providing budgetary relief for activities that could enhance the longer-term priorities of the firm through the funding of (1) "corporate development" divisions, (2) strategic alliances that expose the firm to desired competencies without requiring equity ownership, or (3) other forms of corporate venturing.

Although business-unit managers are concerned with optimizing their internal value-creating chains of relationships (by forging effective competitive strategies), corporate-level managers are responsible for arranging (and monitoring) the best system of value-creating relationships among sister business units, as well as with outsiders—which may include international suppliers (and distributors), locally-competent suppliers (and distributors) within each site of international operations, competitors, local governments that build and support local infrastructures, and customers, among others. Doing so requires firms to maintain strategic flexibility since implementation may involve cross-licensing (or other forms of information exchange), **joint ventures** (or other forms of equity participation), or direct investments through acquisition.

Within flexible organizations, corporate-level strategy initiates and audits competitive advantages based on organizational attributes. In particular, effective vertical strategies require a continuous process of redesigning task responsibilities (in collaboration with suppliers and customers) to create more value-added opportunities internally while continually weeding-out activities (and customers) that do not fit the firm's choice regarding what businesses it wants to be in (vertical integration), hence what competencies it wants to develop to sustain its competitive advantage. Vertical relationships can be secured through contractual ties, strategic alliances, or equity ownership, depending upon the competitive environments where transactions must occur. Disinvestment (or the severing of vendor-customer relationships) must occur when necessary, even where both business units are owned by the same corporate parents. Thus corporate-level oversight is mandatory—especially where sister business units are linked in buyer-supplier relationships—to avoid perverting the firm's strategic vision.

Strategic flexibility requires organizations to gain new capabilities—through acquisition or internal development, depending upon the timing requirements of effective implementation—before competitors reach similar conclusions. Strategic flexibility may require firms to relocate stages of their value chain where national cost advantages in factors of production are short-lived. Where easy international flows of information make competitive imitation inevitable and timing advantages based on proprietary information are increasingly short-lived, flexible organizations need a corporate strategy that moves them from less competitive businesses to those where opportunities to prosper are greater and success requirements are more compatible with the strengths they have developed.

[Kathryn Rudie Harrigan]

FURTHER READING:

Harrigan, Kathryn Rudie. *Strategies for Synergy*, forthcoming

STRATEGY FORMULATION

Strategy formulation is vital to the well-being of a company or organization. It is the development of a plan whereby specific goals or objectives are achieved. There are two major types of strategy: (1) corporate strategy, in which companies decide which business to engage in; and (2) business strategy, which sets the framework for achieving success in that business.

ADVANTAGES TO SUPERIOR STRATEGY FORMULATION AND STEPS IN ITS DEVELOPMENT

The formulation of a sound strategy facilitates a number of actions and desired results that would be difficult otherwise. A strategic plan, when communicated to all members of an organization, provides employees with a clear vision of what the purposes and objectives of the firm are. The formulation of strategy forces organizations to examine the prospect of change in the foreseeable future and to prepare for change rather than to wait passively until market forces compel it. Strategic formulation allows the firm to plan its capital **budgeting**. Companies have limited monies to invest and must allocate capital funds where they will be most effective. Strategy allows the firm to be proactive in its decisions rather than reactive: that is, strategy gives the firm a direction in which all members of the organization have a framework for

making decisions so as to bring the firm closer to its strategic objectives. A firm without a strategic plan gives its decision makers no direction other than the maintenance of the status quo. The firm becomes purely reactive to external pressures and resistant to dealing effectively with change.

The formulation of sound strategy is commonly thought to have six important steps:

1. The company or organization must first choose the business in which it wishes to engage. (This is much more critical, and complex, than it appears.) This is corporate strategy.

2. The company or organization must then develop a "mission statement" consistent with its business definition.

3. Once the mission statement has been established, the company or organization must then be develop strategic objectives or goals and set performance objectives.

4. Next the company or organization must do an environmental analysis—i.e., identify opportunities and threats—as well as an internal analysis to identify strengths and weaknesses. With this information, the company can develop a business strategy describing how the company intends to compete in each of its businesses to achieve its goals.

5. The company or organization then executes its plan or implements the business strategy.

6. Finally, the company or organization reviews its strategy's effectiveness, measures its own performance, and possibly revises some or all of the above steps.

THE BEGINNING: "WHAT BUSINESS ARE WE IN?" AND "HOW BIG OR SMALL DO WE WANT TO BE?"

These are two key questions whose answers dictate much of the direction for the formulation of sound strategy. While these would on the surface appear to be simple questions that could be answered in a few minutes, the nuances in them are paramount in the formulation of successful strategy. Although a successful strategy is one that allows an organization to accomplish its objectives, many great strategies have been for naught as organizations discover upon accomplishment of their objectives that the original objectives sought and now achieved have not brought the expected and desired end results. These two questions, when thoughtfully and wisely answered, provide a solid foundation upon which to evaluate the worthiness of the various objectives and goals in the formulation of an organization's strategic plan.

DEFINING THE BUSINESS

While this would appear to be the easiest of the six steps listed above, the simplicity of this first step is deceptive. Businesses must be defined in terms of their customers. Without customers, there is no business. They are a firm's only real source of revenue and, hence, power. Successful businesses are those that create profitable customers. With this in mind, it makes sense to define any business in terms of its customers. Some companies achieve success by concentrating on product development, product quality, efficient production, and other product-related functions. However, it is important to remember that the success of these companies is entirely dependent upon customers valuing a firm's products above others, or being appreciative of the lower prices provided through the firm's abilities to produce at lower costs. One can not assume that customers always want to pay less for their goods and services: few perfume companies have been successful in pursuing the strategy of having the lowest priced perfume.

INDUSTRY DEFINITION BY END BENEFIT. Business scholars have long urged corporate leaders to define their institutions' business both in broad terms and in terms of the end benefit their customers receive from their products. Hence, ''oil companies'' should not view themselves as being in the ''oil business,'' but in terms of the broader category of ''energy'' when attempting to market oil as a fuel. Drivers of automobiles do not have a strong preference for exactly what fuels their vehicle. If ethanol could power their vehicle as conveniently as gasoline, the consumer would have little preference between the two systems. If ethanol were more convenient and less expensive than gasoline, consumers would buy ethanol and not gasoline. (Oil might then become more important as the raw input for plastics.) Drivers are not really buying gasoline when they visit a service station, because what they are buying is transportation. Transportation is another consumer benefit and a business in which many firms compete.

A broad example of an industry definition comes from Charles Revson (1906-1975), founder of Revlon cosmetics, who often said he was in the business of selling ''the promise of hope.'' This insightful business definition led Revson to concentrate his efforts on meticulously creating advertising depicting feminine images that were unrealistic to the vast majority of his customers but were perfectly consistent with their deepest hopes for themselves. Lotteries operate on the same principles. Few people expect to win, so the benefit is the hope of winning. Hope can be a very profitable business to be in even if it is difficult to imagine as an industry.

DEFINITION BY CUSTOMERS SERVED. Many successful companies have defined themselves in terms of their customers. A general store in a remote area would do well to define its business as serving the customers in its trading area. While such a business definition might lead the firm in directions that would be at the whim of the local clientele, that business should remain profitable as long as customers are happy. An example of such a business is L.L. Bean which was started when Mr. Bean developed a superior hunting boot well suited for his native Maine and sold it through the mail to a mailing list of Maine residents who had purchased hunting licenses. The mail order company grew by first serving the needs of hunters and later by expanding the concept to all wilderness activities. While this might seem to be a definition based upon an activity, careful examination of L.L. Bean shows that the firm has identified a psychographic market segment to which it continually caters. Many of its buyers really don't care for wilderness sports as much as they simply identify with the targeted market segment and wish to buy products that conform to the segment's norms.

DEFINITION BY TECHNOLOGY. Genentech Inc. is a firm engaged in the development of gene splicing technologies: it has defined itself as being in the gene engineering business. Business definition by technology leads to a very tumultuous corporate existence, as the business enterprise turns direction every time there's a new invention.

STRATEGIC MISSION

The strategic mission of an organization embodies a long-term view of what sort of organization it wishes to become. The value to management of having a lucid mission statement—the second step in strategy formulation—can be in rendering tangible the firm's long-term course and in guiding decisions toward a rational design.

STRATEGIC OBJECTIVES

Clearly stated strategic objectives, in the third step of strategy formulation, outline the position in the marketplace that the firm seeks. Performance targets state the measurable milestones that the firm needs to reach or obtain to achieve its strategic objectives.

Some strategic objectives relate to the positioning of goods and services in the competitive marketplace while others concern the structure of the company itself and how it plans to produce goods or manage its operations. Typical strategic objectives involve profitability, market share, return on investment, technological achievement, customer service level, size, and diversification.

In order to make strategic planning work, the goals, missions, objectives, performance targets, or other hopes of top management must some how be made real by others in more distant locations down the organizational chart. Merely communicating to each member of the business the vision that top management has for the firm is not sufficient. Strategic objectives and performance targets should penetrate every corner of the organizational chart. There should be a hierarchy of strategic formulation starting with the highest levels of the firm, from which it is consistently translated from level to level so that each department knows what its contribution to the overall mission of the firm is to be. This process should end with each individual in the firm having strategic objectives and performance targets tailored to their specific role in the firm.

ORGANIZATION-WIDE STRATEGY LEVEL. This is top management's plan for achieving its aims. These strategies are for the entire organization and should not concern the specific affairs of individual business units.

Organization-wide strategy requires schemes for overseeing the extent and combinations of companies' assorted actions in order to achieve a superior corporate performance. When numerous activities are being managed simultaneously, there are interactive effects in managing the group of activities as a whole. Such a group of activities is often referred to as the ''business portfolio.'' Proper management of the business portfolio demands actions and decisions about how and when the firm should enter new ventures and what areas the firm needs to exit. Further, in all management, timing is crucial. Top management needs to set the timetable for business entry, exit, growth, and downsizing. Often a sound strategy goes awry when management attempts to move too quickly, too slowly, or just fails to set any timetable for action allowing for little temporal coordination of the firm's efforts. Further, organization-wide strategy should address the balance of resources across the firm's various activities. These resources need to be allocated to direct the company's activities toward the strategic objectives of the organization. Through these activities at the corporate-wide level, decisions about balancing business risks can maximize security for the firm.

BUSINESS STRATEGY

The fourth step in strategy formulation requires development of business strategy. Business strategy refers to the strategy used in directing one business unit of the overall corporation. The most crucial question business strategy should address is how the unit plans to be competitive within its specific business market. Supportive issues to this crucial question in business strategy formulation are: (1) What role will each of the functional areas within the business unit play in creating this competitive advantage in the marketplace; (2) What are the potential responses to prospective changes in marketplace; and (3) How to allocate the business unit's resources between its various divisions.

Potential revision of business strategy should concentrate on a review of the current situation in three main aspects. The situation review should evaluate the strategic position of the firm with respect to events happening in their industry as a whole, the firm's position with respect to their competitors, and finally the factors internal to the firm.

INDUSTRY STRUCTURE. Factors critical in the review of the industry should include the structure of the industry, the forces compelling change within the industry, the cost and price economics of the industry, elements critical to success in the industry, and the imminent problems and issues in the industry. An industry structure review should consider: the size of the total market; the growth rate of the market; profitability of the firms in the industry; the capacity utilization rate on production facilities; the degree of difficulty new competitors would have in entering the market and the difficulties the firm would have in getting out of the business; the degree to which technological development is required to keep competitive in the market; capital requirements needed to keep competitive; and the degree to which products in the market are standardized rather than having unique designs or positionings. Factors that can compel change in an industry's structure may include: a fundamental change in the growth rate of the industry; a move towards product standardization within the industry; technological advancements in production; large firms entering or leaving the industry; product innovations; lapse of industry **patents**; regulatory and governmental influences; and basic change in the who, what, and why of the market's buying habits. Economics of industry costs and pricing should include an analysis of the balance of fixed cost to variable cost in product costs. Industries characterized by a high percentage of fixed costs are subject to extreme price wars during competitive times in the market. (Airlines are an example of a high fixed cost industry.) Industries with high variable costs tend to have smaller swings in their pricing structure. Production costs tend to decline over time in proportion to the total quantity of goods produced. This is due to two factors: learning and experience. Each has its own curve, the ''learning curve'' and the ''experience curve.'' While each of these effects was diagnosed separately, the end effect of both is the same: the firm that produces the most goods in the industry ends up having the lowest cost of production in the long term, which gives them long-term cost advantage in the industry for the life of the product. Being the low cost producer allows the firm to receive not only the greatest margin on its products when all firms in the market participate in an established price structure, but when price competition arises the low cost producer can make a profit or break even on its goods, while its competitors lose money. This is a key strategic advantage. It is for this reason that many firms in the development of a new and potentially large long-term market will forgo a profitable, small, prestige niche strategy for a less profitable market penetration strategy that demands heavy investment and expansion of production. This second strategy can yield a long term advantage in the industry by allowing the firm to gain from the "learning & experience" effects. Competitors are later unable to catch up since they lack the cumulative production experience of the pioneer in the industry.

COMPETITORS. Competitors first must be examined by their position in the industry. In other words, should competitors be classified by the type of goods they produce, their price, markets served, or channels of distribution used? Many industries have clear niching, with each firm or group of firms avoiding direct competition through some combination of product differentiation or **market segmentation**. Other industries are characterized by large-scale head-on **competition**. (Coke-a-Cola and Pepsi are such an example in the soft drink industry.) Not all future competition originates from present competitors, however.

New market entrants are most often found lurking on the sidelines of the firm. For example, suppliers are often looking to forward integrate into an industry. Suppliers of the raw materials that comprise a product may have a competitive cost advantage by forward integrating into the market. Suppliers are often motivated in such moves by the assurance of having a guaranteed market for their output. Cost advantages can make such forward integrations market entries successful.

On the flip side, customers may decide to backward integrate into business. Customers considering backward integration usually first attempt to establish their own "private labeled" product prior to integration. When customers put considerable time and effort into their private label version of a product, it may well be a sign of a growing intent to backward integrate.

Firms that produce either substitutes to a product, or complementary goods to a product may also be a competitor. These firms have experience in this market, and a competitor's product niche in the market represents a simple product line extension for their firm. Often the threat of competitive retaliation into

these firms' product areas is useful in deterring such moves.

Barriers to market entry are often responsible for setting the level of competition in an industry. Retail tends to be a competitive industry due to the relatively low costs of entry into the market. But compare retail to heavy industrial goods and one can readily see the differences substantial barriers to entry might make. American auto manufacturers probably worry very little about other American firms entering the market of passenger automobiles, because both the financial and regulatory barriers to entry are far too high. Not all barriers are financial. Drug firms enjoy oligopoly status due to their abilities to interface with the U.S. Food and Drug Administration in getting new drugs approved. New firms would have great difficulty in developing the same working relationships. Military suppliers also enjoy an **oligopoly** status due to political barriers to entering the market. Each firm must analyze what factors keep its competitors at bay when assessing the potential for others to want to share in their profits.

TACTICAL DEVELOPMENT & SYSTEM REVIEW

Strategies, to be effective, must be implemented and are done so at the fifth step of strategy formulation. The means of implementing strategies are called tactics. The tactical execution, while crucial to the success of any strategy, is not a traditional part of the formulation of that strategy. However, many firms have been successful in discovering successful tactics and building their strategies about "what works."

Strategy formulation should be done on a regular basis, as often as required by changes in the industry. Knowing that the review of strategic plans is a regular function, firms need to track the company's progress, or lack thereof, on the key goals and objectives outlined in the strategic plan. This evaluation and feedback of the strategy formulation, the final step, provides the foundation for successful future strategy formulation

[Bruce Buskirk]

FURTHER READING:

Andrews, Kenneth R. *The Concept of Corporate Strategy.* Burr Ridge, IL: Richard D. Irwin, 1980.

Ansoff, H. Igor. *Corporate Strategy.* New York: McGraw-Hill, 1965.

Carroll, Glenn R. "The Specialist Strategy," in *Strategy and Organization: A West Coast Perspective,* ed. Glenn Carroll and David Vogel. Marshfield, MA: Pitman Publishing, 1984, pp. 117-28.

Feldman, Lawrence P., and Albert L. Page. "Harvesting: The Misunderstood Market Exit Strategy," *Journal of Business Strategy.* Spring, 1985, pp. 79-85.

Ghemawat, Pankaj. "Building Strategy on the Experience Curve," *Harvard Business Review*. March-April, 1985, pp. 143-49.

Gluck, Frederick W. "A Fresh Look at Strategic Management," *Journal of Business Strategy*. Fall, 1985, pp. 4-21.

Harrigan, Kathryn R. *Strategic Flexibility*. New York: Lexington Books, 1985.

Harrigan, Kathryn R. "Formulating Vertical Integration Strategies," *Academy of Management Review*. October, 1984, pp. 638-52.

Hofer, Charles W. *Strategy Formulation: Analytical Concepts*. Eagan, MN: West Publishing, 1986.

Hofer, Charles W., and Dan Schendel. *Strategy Formulation: Analytical Concepts*. Eagan, MN: West Publishing, 1978.

Hout, Thomas et al. "How Global Companies Win Out." *Harvard Business Review*. September-October, 1982, pp. 98-108.

MacMillan, Ian C. "How Business Strategists Can Use Guerrilla Warfare Tactics," *Journal of Business Strategy*. Fall, 1980, pp. 63-65.

Peters, Thomas J., and Robert H. Waterman. *In Search of Excellence: Lessons from America's Best-Run Companies*. New York: Harper & Row, 1982.

Porter, Michael E. *Competitive Strategy: Techniques for Analyzing Industries and Competitors*. New York: Free Press, 1980.

Porter, Michael E. "How Competitive Forces Shape Strategy," *Harvard Business Review*. March-April, 1979, pp. 137-45.

Ross, Joel, and Michael Kami. *Corporate Management in Crisis: Why the Mighty Fall*. Englewood Cliffs, N.J.: Prentice-Hall, 1973.

Schnaars, Steven P. "When Entering Growth Markets, Are Pioneers Better than Poachers?" *Business Horizons*. March-April, 1986, pp. 27-36.

Thompson, Arthur A., Jr. "Strategies for Staying Cost Competitive," *Harvard Business Review*. January-February, 1984, pp. 110-117.

Vancil, Richard F. "Strategy Formulation in Complex Organizations," *Sloan Management Review*. Winter, 1976, pp. 1-18.

Vancil, Richard F., and Peter Lorange. "Strategic Planning in Diversified Companies," *Harvard Business Review*. January-February, 1975, pp. 81-90.

Wright, Peter. "The Strategic Options of Least-Cost, Differentiation, and Niche," *Business Horizons*. March-April, 1986, pp. 21-26.

Yip, George S. "Who Needs Strategic Planning?" *Journal of Business Strategy*. Fall, 1985, pp. 22-29.

STRESS IN THE WORKPLACE

In 1993, the New York-based Families and Work Institute published a study called "The Changing Workforce." Basing its results on a nationwide group of 3,400 corporate workers, the research project showed that few employees still boast a 40-hour week. Instead the average worker now spends 45 hours per week on the job, with commuting and overtime routinely included.

A workday as long as this inevitably leaves the average employee filled with tension. As a 1991 study of 600 workers by Northwestern National Insurance Company of Minneapolis noted, 34 percent felt their jobs were so stressful that they were thinking of quitting them.

Where is all this pressure coming from? One source is the global marketplace, which is demanding cutting-edge competitiveness from all companies interested in a share of the profits. In the past ten years most businesses have been giving themselves greater leverage by paring their operating costs more and more closely.

At the top of these trimming lists are usually the heaviest expenses—payrolls and health-care bills. So in the past decade the terms "layoff," "pink slip" and "early retirement incentives," have become more and more familiar to America's corporate employees.

Though many companies have indeed managed to bring their operating costs down, the victory has come with a stiff price-tag. The 1990s have seen a huge increase in the stress-related claims now winding their way through the courts. Also ever-present in news headlines are a lengthening catalog of harassment charges, plus a rising number of violent attacks from disgruntled ex-employees. While layoffs are responsible for a great deal of stress, they aren't the only tightrope-factor the employee must face. **Mergers and acquisitions**, by introducing replacement teams, produce fears of dismissal in a company's original workforce. If longtime workers survive the change, they suffer anxiety about changes in work methods, company goals and their office environment. This is why "The Changing Workforce" study revealed two other important results: that 80 percent of the 3,400-strong group felt they have to work very hard, and 65 percent feel they have to work very fast.

Far beyond the control of the individual employee, acquisitions, mergers and pink slips have blended into a predictable outcome. According to the National Institute of Occupational Health and Safety (NIOSH), by 1991 stress represented 11 percent of all **workers' compensation** claims—a percentage that ranked it among the top ten work-related illnesses and claimed between $150 and $200 billion of company money each year.

Just two years later stress claims had become so pervasive that the State California decided to take action. By the mid-1990s, instead of claiming 10 percent of stress as job-related, a claimant must prove 51 percent job-related stress before his case comes to court.

If all of these stress-producers from the wider economic environment have anything in common, it is that they emphasize a worker's lack of control over his own workload and workpace.

Also beyond individual control are changes within the company itself. Changes in benefit plans produce intense anxiety, especially if they exclude services that have previously been paid for by employers. The overwhelming avalanche of information cascading from data-bases produces feelings of inadequacy; a work-environment that discourages interaction leads to feelings of isolation. Supervisors promoted from the ranks and inadequately trained are frustrating to their former colleagues, and the increasingly popular strategy of worker surveillance by electronic devices may ensure that they do their jobs properly, but it is also degrading. In each of these everyday scenarios, tension hangs heavy in the air.

There are few ways in which the individual worker can fight back. Instead, feelings of helplessness are reflected in increased turnover, increased absenteeism, and reliance on drugs or alcohol—all blunt instruments that damage work quality, shatter loyalty to the company, and affect the bottom line.

Says Mary Ellen Gornick, president of Corporate Parenting Associates, a Des Plaines, Illinois employee assistance counseling firm: "There is now a large number of individuals looking forward to being *pushed* out—actually pushed out, because this is out of their control." In such cases, the fall of the axe is a relief, permitting the ex-employee to be loyal to his own goals at last.

Many sources mention that these stress-points, common to both sexes, are just part of the list for many women in the workforce. Joan Smith of Chicago-based Women Employed mentions just one of the frequently overlooked challenges women must face, "There is the safety issue. A woman who must work overtime often has a problem if she has to take a train at night, or walk through a dark, deserted parking garage to pick up her car."

The presence of stress in the workplace has been a given since Arthur Miller's Pulitzer Prize-winning play *Death of a Salesman* brought it to the public's attention in the 1940s. Though Miller emphasized that change was desperately needed and that the individual was unable to provide it, corporate tradition always downplayed the company's important role as the agent of change.

In the early 1980s, this perception began to evolve. Companies now saw their health-care bills for stress-related illnesses such as heart problems, ulcers, and depression escalating rapidly, and acknowledged that they would have to take the initiative if their operating costs were to be contained.

They began by offering courses aimed at improving the general health and well being of their employees. Fitness, weight-loss, and smoking cessation classes became more and more popular, as did in-house counseling programs to fight alcoholism and drug use. However, as the 1980s drew to a close, experts perceived that these aids to personal well being were simply not as effective.

Cathy McComas, director of corporate health promotion at Texas Instruments reflected in a 1993 interview with Paul Froiland, associate editor of *Training* magazine. "We gave people what we thought they needed—deep breathing and relaxation—and not what they wanted. Those things treat symptoms; they don't help identify the cause." A second expert agreed. Consulted by the same writer, San Francisco-based stress-research consultant Esther Orioli of Essi Systems Inc. pinpointed "personal power"—individual control over time, important information, resources, and workload—as the crucial factor in the ability to withstand pressure.

Control Data Corp.'s CYBER Systems took this maxim seriously. In 1989, after a major layoff, company leaders conducted an employee attitude survey. They were disturbed to find that their remaining workforce suffered from extreme anxiety. Noting that their engineering staff felt most tense about their own ability to find other employment, the company chose to offer them training in networking and job-hunting skills. This groundbreaking strategy brought a bottom-line bonus—a staff of engineers whose peace of mind allowed them to focus all their attention on their work.

While problems stemming from the workplace cause a great deal of concern, they fall short of the nagging worries most working parents in this two-paycheck era feel about both daytime childcare and night-time balancing acts between their own workplace priorities and their children's need for attention. This clash produces a particularly disturbing trend, Gornick observes. "Participants in my groups say that it's their families which have to make the accommodations for the worker to do the job at the price in the time specified."

Companies began to share some of this burden with their employees in the early 1980s. In 1982, for example, changes in the federal tax code allowed companies to let workers use pretax dollars to pay for child care—a benefit that saved them about 50 percent of the cost. Just two years later IBM became the first company to use a consulting firm to launch a service helping to provide child care. In the ten years since then child care has become one of the most favored of all staff benefits. It is now offered by 5,600 firms, whose help ranges from referral to cash subsidies. About 1,400 companies also provide on-site day care facilities.

By 1991, 188 *Fortune* 500 companies were using flextime, a work-schedule that can be adjusted to fill the requisite number of hours in time-blocks convenient to the worker. A privilege that allows for a parent's responsibilities, flextime quickly became one of working America's most sought-after staff benefits. A scant three years later it is a routine offering in most *Fortune* 500 companies.

Some firms are taking a different tack. According to one estimate, by 1991 an estimated 20,000 U.S. corporations were offering seminars in stress-reduction techniques of various types. Now they've begun to add seminars and support groups in parenting, elder-care, the crises of life.

If **corporate downsizing** has a plus, it lies in the stripping of management layers. Communication between workers and managers has become less stratified. Still, improved communication does not rule out the need to diagnose stress. The best way to head off an approaching problem, says the American Institute of Stress, is with a stress audit. Typically, this takes the form of a questionnaire listing potentially stressful situations, which is given to company employees to fill out anonymously. Their answers may point the way to a need for parenting seminars or other **employee assistance programs (EAP)**. If these are provided by the company, a second audit tells management whether their approach has been successful.

In "New Approaches to Job Stress" published in *Nation's Business*, May, 1994, writer Armin Brott notes that some companies are trying a team approach. Instead of instructions filtering down from above, workers are encouraged to work in groups, with each member making his own contribution. This gives each worker a degree of control over his own work and resources, thus lessening stress. While some companies use incentive plans to increase employee involvement and enthusiasm, not everyone agrees that this is a good idea. Says Brott, "By pitting people against one another . . . incentive programs make employees less likely to cooperate with one another." Not everyone agrees with this approach; privately-awarded bonuses as an incentive are widely accepted.

Also necessary nationwide, says the Northwestern National Life study, are plans to keep **employee benefits** steady; operating strategies to ensure that the amount of red tape necessary for project completion is kept at a minimum; and guidelines to lessen anxiety by allocating adequate budgets for each project. Not all responsibility for stress reduction can come from employers. Many companies provide sporting clubs—Apple Computer, Inc., for example, offers both running and ski clubs—but it is up to the employee to use them. Relaxation courses, massage and aromatherapy all have their followers, as do programs geared for instant tension release.

Other techniques any employee can use include lowering standards of personal performance and prioritizing tasks to be completed both at work and at home. Perfection should be dismissed as an unrealistic

goal in both places, say all management experts. Above all, they caution, the employee must recognize the symptoms of approaching burnout—exhaustion, boredom with the work, lack of new ideas, and lack of support.

[Gillian Wolf]

SUBSIDIARY

When one company acquires more than 50 percent of the voting stock of another company, thereby obtaining control of its operations, the acquired company becomes a subsidiary of the acquiring company. The acquiring company becomes the subsidiary's parent company. Together, the parent and the subsidiary form a corporate affiliation. Sometimes the parent company is organized expressly for the purpose of holding stock in other corporations; such parents are called **holding companies**. If the parent owns all of the voting stock of another company, that company is a wholly owned subsidiary of the parent company.

A company may become a subsidiary through acquisition, or it may be established as a subsidiary to begin with. Controlling interest in a company's stock may be obtained through purchasing the stock or exchanging it for shares of the parent company's stock. A company may establish a subsidiary by forming a new corporation and retaining all or part of its stock.

Company's choose to acquire or establish subsidiaries for a variety of financial and managerial reasons. From a management point of view, subsidiaries allow for the advantages of decentralized management, where each subsidiary has its own management team. Each subsidiary is responsible to the parent company on a profit and loss basis. Unprofitable subsidiaries can more easily be sold off than can divisions of a consolidated business. Subsidiaries retain their corporate identities, and the holding company benefits from any goodwill and recognition attached to the subsidiary's name.

Subsidiaries can be acquired or established with less investment than would be required in a merger or consolidation. Where a merger would require obtaining complete interest in another company, a subsidiary can be acquired with the purchase of only a controlling interest in the company. In deciding whether to establish a subsidiary or a separate operating division, the parent company often takes into account the funds that could be raised by selling some of the new subsidiary's stock.

There are also tax and other financial advantages to establishing or acquiring a subsidiary. Parent companies and their subsidiaries are considered separate legal entities, so that the assets of the parent company and the individual subsidiaries are protected against catastrophic and creditors' claims against one of the subsidiaries. Another advantage is that the stock in the subsidiary company is held as an asset on the books of the parent company and can be used as collateral for additional debt financing. In addition, one company can acquire stock in another company without approval of its stockholders; **mergers** and consolidations typically require stockholder approval.

Subsidiaries typically file financial reports on their operations with their parent companies. While subsidiaries and their parents are considered separate legal entities for the purpose of determining liability, they may be considered as a single economic entity for the purpose of filing financial statements. For tax purposes, the parent company must own at least 80 percent of the voting stock in another company in order to be able to file a consolidated tax return. In that case, the parent company and its subsidiaries are considered a single economic entity. The tax advantage here is that losses from one subsidiary can be used to offset profits from another subsidiary and reduce the overall taxable corporate income on the consolidated tax return. A significant disadvantage occurs when a company holds less than 80 percent of the subsidiary's voting stock; in that case separate tax returns must be filed for the parent and the subsidiary, and intercorporate **dividends** become subject to an additional tax.

[David Bianco]

SUBSIDIES

A subsidy is a government payment to individuals, businesses, other governments, and other domestic institutions and organizations. Unlike government purchases, for which the government receives goods or services, subsidies do not provide the government with any goods or services in return. The purpose of government subsidies is to ensure the availability of necessary goods and services.

A wide range of domestic businesses, individuals, and other organizations in the United States are eligible for government subsidies. A complete listing of all federal subsidies can be found in the government publication, *Catalog of Federal Domestic Assistance.* Among the areas receiving government subsidies are agriculture, maritime industries, and mass transportation.

A subsidy may take the form of direct payments from the government, as is the case in a variety of agricultural crop and livestock production programs. The purpose of direct payments to wheat, cotton,

wool, and other agricultural producers is to ensure adequate production to meet domestic and foreign demand and to protect or supplement the income of farmers.

A subsidy may also be in the form of a project grant. While direct payments may be used by the recipient for virtually any purpose, project grants usually carry stipulations regarding how the subsidy may be applied. The federal government provides project grants for a wide range of projects ranging from rural housing to urban mass transportation. Project grants and other federal subsidies that are given directly to state or local governments are also called grants-in-aid.

The federal government also subsidizes a range of services that its own agencies provide below cost to the public. When a government agency provides services to the public at a loss, the agency's income does not correspond to the value of the agency's output. Consequently, when calculating national income and gross national product, subsidies less surpluses of government enterprises are added to the value of output to arrive at national income.

In the area of international trade, export subsidies are government subsidies that are given to domestic producers of goods that will be exported. Export subsidies may take the form of a variety of government benefits, including direct payments, support prices, tax incentives, and funds for training. Export subsidies are given on the condition that the goods being produced will be exported. In the European Economic Community (EEC), export subsidies are called variable subsidies. Rules affecting variable subsidies of EEC countries are found in the Common Agricultural Policy of the EEC.

The **General Agreement on Tariffs and Trade (GATT)** contains restrictions on the use of export subsidies. Developed countries are forbidden to use subsidies to support the export of most manufactured goods, for example. Under GATT, less developed nations are permitted to subsidize manufactured goods that will be exported, provided the subsidies do not significantly damage the economies of developed countries. GATT also provides for remedies, such as countervailing duties, when it has been determined that one trading partner is unfairly using export subsidies.

[David Bianco]

SUGGESTION SYSTEMS

Suggestion systems are a form of employee-to-management communication that benefit employees as well as employers. They provide a two-way channel of communication between employees and **management**, with management accepting or rejecting employee suggestions and in some cases commenting on them. Suggestion systems give employees a voice and a role in determining company policies and operating procedures.

Employee suggestions can help increase efficiency, eliminate waste, improve safety, and improve the quality of a company's products and services. The company benefits not only in terms of cost savings realized as a result of employee suggestions, but also in terms of better employee morale. In many cases suggestion systems can help develop teamwork among employees. While the goal of a suggestion system is for cost savings to exceed expenses associated with the program, there are also intangible benefits to be realized from suggestion systems.

One of the first suggestion systems was started at General Electric in 1906. It consisted of a suggestion box in each department with a pad of blank paper on which employees were instructed to write practical suggestions for improving the company's manufacturing and other operations. The system was put into place only after an employee was fired for developing and proposing an idea for improving a manufacturing operation. Today, suggestion systems are common not only in manufacturing companies, but in businesses of all sizes and types.

A successful suggestion system must be promoted to the company's employees. Employees are typically given a handbook that explains the company's suggestion system. Such handbooks usually contain a statement of management support that encourages workers to ''speak up'' and make practical suggestions for improving operations. The handbook also spells out who is eligible for awards and what awards are given. In some companies certain levels of management are not eligible to receive awards for their suggestions. The handbook also defines what constitutes a suggestion, since some ''suggestions'' are simply considered part of doing one's job or routine maintenance and repair. Finally the handbook will usually contain one or more standardized forms on which suggestions can be submitted. Additional forms are usually made available in various ways to employees.

The administration of a suggestion system requires one or more plan administrators. A separate handbook may be prepared for company executives and supervisors, instructing them on their role in encouraging employees to participate in the suggestion system. In addition, each suggestion system requires certain individuals to be designated as suggestion evaluators. Usually the evaluator of a particular suggestion is someone with expertise in an area related to the suggestion. The evaluator's comments are then usually passed on to a committee who determines which suggestions will receive awards.

Suggestion systems typically provide some kind of reward to employees who have made suggestions that are adopted by the company. The rewards may be based on a percentage of cost savings realized as a result of the suggestion, or they may be a fixed amount with no relation to the savings involved. The awards may be given in cash or merchandise. The awards are usually heavily publicized within the company, and major awards are often publicized within the community. Such publicity serves as an incentive to other employees to come up with cost saving ideas and win awards on their own.

Suggestion systems may be continuous or conducted for a limited period of time. Some companies conduct annual suggestion contests that may last for a month. During that time, employees are encouraged to come up with as many suggestions as possible. In some cases employees may be divided into teams representing individual departments. Such teams compete against each other and try to produce the most suggestions. Prizes are then awarded to the teams making the most suggestions that can be used by the company. In the case of continuous suggestion systems, periodic contests can be used to stimulate employee interest in the existing program.

[David Bianco]

SUPERFUND

SEE: Comprehensive Environmental Response, Compensation and Liability Act (CERCLA) of 1980 (Superfund)

SUPERVISION

Supervision is a somewhat misunderstood term in business usage. Generally, supervision applies to **management** of first-level, or production, employees. Many people use it interchangeably with management. The terms are not always synonymous.

Supervision is managing others through **leadership** and personal influence. Management means simply getting things done, not necessarily through other people. Thus, an individual can be a good manager without ever dealing with people. A supervisor, however, exercises hands-on influence and leadership skills to guide others.

HISTORICAL OVERVIEW

Historically, supervisors were not trained to deal with subordinates. Rather, they managed by force and intimidation. It was not until the early part of the twentieth century that supervision became a subject of study among management theorists.

In the early 1900s, researchers like Frederick W. Taylor, Frank Gilbreth, and Chester Barnard began analyzing what motivated workers. Taylor, who is often called the "Father of Scientific Management," published two books, *Shop Management* (1903) and *Principles of Scientific Management* (1911), in which he said it was management's job to set up methods and standards of work and to provide incentives to workers to increase production. A few years later, Gilbreth began to concentrate on time and motion studies and the improvement of methods of work. Gilbreth's approach was to seek the best way to produce a certain product and then have managers teach all workers that best way. Barnard developed what is known as the acceptance theory, which suggested that if managers were to be effective, workers had to accept their authority.

THE THREE LEVELS OF MANAGEMENT

There are three levels of management: executive, middle, and supervisory. Technically speaking, management is the process by which an individual or group directs the use of resources, i.e., money, people, and things, toward common goals. Generally, the executive managers are responsible for overall planning, strategy, structure, etc. It is their role to oversee total operations, and usually they do not have much to do with the actual production process. They establish the company's mission and goals and leave the management of production to the next two levels.

Managers at the middle level manage other managers, i.e., the supervisors. They generally have less technical training than first-level supervisors. They are evaluated more on their managerial skills than their technical skills. Since they spend more of their time managing, that leaves the production supervision to the first-level managers, the supervisors.

THE SUPERVISOR'S ROLE AND FUNCTIONS

Supervisors play an important role in the business environment. Their primary job is to see that the work performed by employees is completed on time and at the highest level of quality. In order to complete this task, they must know the production process and have an understanding of human behavior. Theirs is a pressure-filled job.

Supervisors perform a wide range of functions, all of which are closely intertwined. For example, they must be excellent communicators. It is their job to write reports, letters, memos, performance appraisals, and the gamut of documents that businesses need to operate. They must be equally comfortable in communicating with chief executive officers and assembly line production workers. They must be able to run effective meetings. They must carefully monitor the organization's goals, strategies, tactics, and production schedules. They must be cognizant of union rules where applicable. They must be trainers, confidants, computer experts, goal setters . . . in short, supervisors must be well-rounded employees who are willing to accept the responsibilities required to keep a company running.

THE SUPERVISOR AS COMMUNICATOR

Supervisors are required to communicate with a variety of personnel in the course of their jobs. They must be able to write and speak concisely, clearly, consistently, and courteously with senior managers, production workers, customers, suppliers, and other people who have an interest in the organization's activities. It is the supervisor's responsibility to start the upward communication process to inform middle and senior managers about production problems, adherence to production schedules, budget variances, etc. Conversely, supervisors must be able to react to downward communications from senior managers in order to address problems as quickly and efficiently as possible.

The reporting mechanisms involve oral and written reports. They also include a variety of documents supervisors need to protect their workers, the organization, and themselves from legal actions. For instance, supervisors must know when and in what form to document problems with personnel, which regulatory forms must be completed, to whom they must be submitted, and how frequently they should be done. A large part of a supervisor's time is spent communicating. In fact, some estimates suggest that supervisors spend as much as 70 percent of their time communicating in one form or another. That does not leave much time for anything else.

THE SUPERVISOR AS TRAINER

An effective supervisor must be a polished trainer. It is part of the supervisor's responsibility to demonstrate to workers exactly how certain procedures are performed. That means that supervisors must also be excellent learners. Workers expect their supervisors to be doers, as well as teachers. Therefore, supervisors must be able to master the tasks that workers are assigned to perform. This ability is much more critical for first-line supervisors than those in middle and senior management, especially in the production process.

THE SUPERVISOR AS STUDENT

For supervisors, life is a learning process. Not only must they learn the rudiments of their subordinates' jobs, but they must also learn basic supervisory skills. They must take management courses, computer courses, communications courses, and other courses that will help them in their supervisory roles. If they do not continually update their skills, they will fail as supervisors, which is something neither they nor their organizations can afford.

THE SUPERVISOR AS GOAL SETTER

Supervisors are responsible for setting goals for themselves and their subordinates. In addition, they are charged with ensuring that unit and individual goals set by senior management are met. They must sit down with their subordinates and work together to set goals and monitor progress. This ties in with the supervisor's communications skills.

Supervisors cannot simply set goals and then ignore them. First, they must set realistic goals for themselves and their staff members. Then, they must establish communications channels through which they and their subordinates monitor progress. This involves constant feedback between supervisors and subordinates, without which supervisors cannot be effective.

THE SUPERVISOR AS EVALUATOR

It is the supervisor's job to evaluate workers on a regular basis. Workers appreciate feedback on their progress. Generally, they want honest and frequent appraisals of their work and suggestions from their supervisors on how to improve their performance.

THE SUPERVISOR AS HUMAN RESOURCES SPECIALIST

Supervisors need to be aware of the needs of their subordinates. For example, they must know how to motivate people, how to reward them, how and when to discipline them, and when and how to refer them to **employee assistance programs (EAP)**. They may have the assistance of **human resources** specialists in some of these areas, but the basic responsibility is the supervisor's.

THE SUPERVISOR AS COMPUTER EXPERT

In today's business environment, supervisors must be computer proficient. Many of today's management functions are tied closely to computers. For example, computers are used extensively in decision making., production scheduling, and product design. Supervisors are not responsible for many of the functions facilitated by computers, but they must have a working knowledge of how computers operate and their role in the production process.

In the production end of business, organizations are relying more and more on computer-integrated manufacturing (CIM). CIM comprises several types of systems, such as computer-aided design (CAD), computer-aided manufacturing (CAM), and flexible manufacturing systems (FMS) to aid in the manufacturing process. CAD uses computers to geometrically prepare, review, and evaluate product designs. CAM uses computers to design and control production processes. Finally, FMS is a manufacturing system that uses computers to control machines and the production process automatically so that different types of parts or product configurations can be handled on the same production line. It is essential that supervisors understand how these computerized systems work if they are to remain technologically current. First-level supervisors in particular must stay current in computerized production systems. They must also be in positions to advise senior management as to what computerized systems are applicable in particular environments and what are not.

THE SUPERVISOR AS PRODUCER

The supervisor is inextricably linked to the production of goods and services. First, supervisors must be knowledgeable about the production process they control. They are responsible for a large variety of simultaneous activities in the ongoing production process. For example, in large extent they control the production schedule. They staff their work units and train the members properly. They become involved in planning product design, simplification of work methods, the maintenance of equipment, and organizing tasks and activities while striving to keep workers relations as smooth as possible. While performing these tasks, they must keep the organization's goals in the forefront to assure they are being met.

The supervisor's tasks in the production process also include equipment and materials management, such as establishing guidelines for layout of the work being performed and selecting the right equipment for each job. Supervisors must schedule carefully to ensure that time is not wasted. It is a fact of business that idle time and workers are unproductive, costly, and a waste of capital investment. Thus, supervisors must be effective time managers and employee motivators. They must also keep an eye on technological developments, since innovative advancements in machinery and work performance techniques are never-ending.

Supervisors must keep one eye on the future when performing their tasks. For example, a punch machine in a factory may become outdated and need to be replaced. It is an axiom in the manufacturing world that what is right for a particular job today may be outdated tomorrow. Therefore, supervisors may not only need to recommend new equipment, but they might be required to do economic analyses to justify the purchase of new machinery. In some cases, they might also be asked to maintain machinery or upgrade computer software systems. At the least, they must be effective communicators who can persuade senior management of the need for upgraded machinery and the justification for capital expenditure outlays.

THE SUPERVISOR AS ADVISOR

This is one area in which supervisors must be particularly well-rounded. Supervisors who can advise senior managers, middle managers, and subordinates on topics that affect their work activities are valuable. The problem is to restrict advice only to those areas directly related to individuals' needs at a particular point in time. More often than not, the supervisor does not provide detailed advice on particular issues. Generally, the supervisor's role is to point employees toward qualified professionals who can be of assistance. That in itself requires that supervisors be aware of where the proper professionals can be found.

There is seemingly no end to the areas in which supervisors become advisors. In whatever area the advice is provided, it must be aimed at improving individuals' performances and organizational goals. Consider, for example, the supervisor as an advisor in staff members' personal lives as they relate to the organization's goals.

Many organizations today sponsor employee assistance programs (EAPs). These programs are constructive responses to employees' substance abuse, psychological, family-related, etc., problems. Through such programs, employers help employees overcome personal problems that adversely affect their performance and interfere with the organization's goals. Supervisors play an important role in EAP programs.

It is often the supervisor's responsibility to recognize problems manifested by employees that interfere with their work. Once they do, they refer the affected employees to EAP counselors or outside counselors who can assist in finding or providing treatment for the individuals' problems.

Another area in which the supervisor becomes an advisor is in skill development. Supervisors who do not encourage their subordinates to develop their personal and work-related skills are defeating their own

purposes, depriving the employees of valuable training and advancement opportunities, and interfering with the organization's goals. Supervisors must have a grasp of what training is available, how it relates specifically to individual employees' needs, and where such training can be completed.

It is imperative in the area of continuing development that supervisors work with their employees to set up individual training programs. To be able to do so, supervisors must know each employee's strengths and weaknesses and tie them to individual development. It is of no benefit to supervisor or employee to randomly select training courses that may be of no value to the individual or the organization. For example, sending a computer illiterate machine operator whose communications skills are weak to a spreadsheet training session is of no value. Supervisors must be able to assess which continuing training programs will benefit which individuals. This can only be done by supervisors who are themselves well-trained and active participants in continuing development programs. Again, supervisors are merely advisors in the continuing education process, but their advice can make or break individuals and the organization.

THE SUPERVISOR AS IDEA CHAMPION

An idea champion is an individual who generates a new idea or believes in the value of a new idea and supports it in the face of potential obstacles. Generally, idea champions are members of the lower supervisory levels. They typically are creative people who are willing to take risks. Consequently, they frequently have trouble convincing senior managers that a particular idea or system will be beneficial to the organization. Thus, idea champions must often coordinate their activities with sponsors, who are more often than not middle-level managers.

THE SUPERVISOR AS ENVIRONMENTAL WATCHDOG

Contemporary supervisors are the prototypical knowledge workers that the business world is beginning to demand. They must be knowledgeable about a wide range of environmental issues and workplace safety programs. Today's supervisors must be aware of public policy issues that were of no concern to their predecessors, but which are taking on added importance today.

Businesses today are corporate citizens. As such, their leaders must be aware of increased government intervention in business affairs and the increasing complexity of statutory and administrative law as it affects business. There are also upgraded ethical standards, changes in ideologies and values, and increasing involvement of the media in corporate affairs to consider. Finally, society's attitudes toward business have changed dramatically over the past few years. These changes have had a profound effect on supervisors from the highest level on down and have made their jobs more complex.

For example, supervisors at the first level must have a broader knowledge today of legislation affecting production. They must be careful to regulate the amount of air, water, and ground pollution released by the machinery they oversee. In particular, they must have some knowledge of the reporting mechanisms that provide governmental regulatory agencies with the information they need to ensure statutory compliance. It is the first-level supervisors who are closest to the production process. Therefore, it is primarily their responsibility to make sure the production process is safe for their workers and the public.

Government regulations in general have affected supervisors' roles dramatically in the past few years at every level. Supervisors must have some knowledge of federal regulations administered by the U.S. Food and Drug Administration, the **U.S. Environmental Protection Agency**, the **National Labor Relations Board (NLRB)**, **Equal Employment Opportunity Commission (EEOC)**, the **Consumer Product Safety Commission** . . . the list is a long one. It is virtually impossible for individual supervisors to familiarize themselves with all the governmental regulations affecting their jobs today. To compound matters, many supervisors are working in the international arena today as global competition expands. This requires them to widen their knowledge and experience even more.

THE SUPERVISOR AS INTERNATIONAL MANAGER

The emergence of large international businesses is creating a new demand for supervisors who can manage effectively in difficult circumstances. Contemporary supervisors are well-advised to learn new languages and become aware of cultural differences among workers. They must learn international trade laws and regulations and the differences in reward and punishment systems. They have to learn how to motivate workers in different countries and differentiate between what is ethical in one country but not in another. There is no doubt that acquiring the knowledge and experience to supervise on an international business is placing even more pressure on managers, but it is also opening new doors for supervisors.

THE NEW CHALLENGE FOR SUPERVISORS

The future holds much potential for supervisors. They have long been an important part of the business

world. It would be impossible to conduct business on any scale were it not for the presence of qualified supervisors who can lead production workers. Supervisors wear too many hats to be relegated to back seat positions in the business world. They are leaders, trainers, goal setters, environmental watchdogs, facilitators, communicators, and more. Simply put, they are the backbone of the business world—and will continue to be as long as there is business to conduct.

[Arthur G. Sharp]

FURTHER READING:

Chapman, Elwood N. *Supervisor's Survival Kit*. New York: Macmillan, 1990.

Daresh, John C. *Supervision as a Proactive Process*. Prospect Heights, IL: Waveland Press, 1991.

Eigen, Barry. *How to Think Like a Boss and Get Ahead at Work*. New York: Carol Publishing Group, 1990.

Fulmer, Robert M., and Stephen G. Franklin. *Supervision: Principles of Professional Management*. New York: Macmillan Publishing Co., 1982.

Giesecke, Joan, ed. *Practical Help for New Supervisors*. Chicago: American Library Association, 1992.

Lambert, Clark. *The Complete Book of Supervisory Training*. New York: John Wiley & Sons, 1984.

Lowery, Robert C. *Supervisory Management: Guides for Application*. Englewood Cliffs, NJ: Prentice-Hall, 1985.

Radde, Paul O. *Supervising: A Guide for All Levels*. Austin, TX: Learning Concepts. 1981.

Shulman, Lawrence. Skills *of Supervision and Staff Management*. Itasca, IL: F. E. Peacock Publishers, 1981.

Steinmetz, Lawrence L. *Supervision: First Line Management*. Homewood, IL: Irwin, 1992.

SUPPLY CHAIN MANAGEMENT

Supply chain management—a term that first appeared in the late 1980s—refers to the management of a distribution channel across organizations such that all the members of the channel, from suppliers to end users, coordinate their business activities and processes to minimize their total costs and maximize their effectiveness in the market. The goal is to achieve the coordination and continuity of a totally vertically integrated channel without centralized ownership of the entities comprising the channel. The firms in the channel form a long-term partnership or a strategic alliance to improve service to the end consumer, reduce the total costs of the channel, and to create a competitive advantage for the channel.

Supply chain management can be contrasted with a traditional distribution channel in which firms deal with one another on a short-term, arm's-length basis with each trying to maximize their gain from each transaction. The relationship between the firms lasts only from transaction to transaction. Most organizations in the traditional channel do not really see themselves as part of a channel. They only see themselves as independent businesses who buy from suppliers at the lowest possible price and sell to customers at the highest possible price. Diseconomies caused by redundancies, particularly of inventory, are common in a traditional channel. John B. Houlihan in his 1985 article "International Supply Chain Management" published in *International Journal of Physical Distribution and Materials Management* likened the buildup of excess inventories in distribution channels to snowdrifts by fences. The more fences there are, the more snow drifts and similarly the more independent organizations in a channel, the more piles of inventory. By looking across the entire channel, supply chain management tries to eliminate the redundancies.

There are a number of key characteristics of supply chain **management**. One of the most important is that the firms involved see themselves as part of the channel and understand that their future depends to a large extent on the success of the whole channel. The relationships are viewed as long term and the corporate philosophies, missions, and cultures are similar. There is joint planning, particularly of products and the locations and quantities of inventory to be kept in the system. There is also a great deal of sharing of information between firms in order to coordinate the efficient flow of goods through the channel. Modern computing and communication technology, such as **electronic data interchange (EDI)**, is used to rapidly move information to wherever in the channel it is needed. Cost advantages of individual members are exploited wherever possible. For example, the production of a product requiring a great deal of human labor would be produced by the member with the lowest labor costs.

SEE ALSO: Business Logistics; Physical Distribution Management (Transportation)

[George C. Jackson]

FURTHER READING:

Houlihan, John B. "International Supply Chain Management." *International Journal of Physical Distribution and Materials Management*. 15:1, 1985, pp. 22-38.

Jones, Thomas C., and Daniel W. Riley. "Using Inventory for Competitive Advantage through Supply Chain Management." *International Journal of Physical Distribution and Materials Management*. 15:5, pp. 16-26.

Cavinato, Joseph L. "Identifying Interfirm total Cost Advantages for Supply Chain Management." *Interntional Journal of Purchasing and Materials Management*. Fall, 1991, pp. 10-15.

Ellram, Lisa M., and Martha C. Cooper. "Supply Chain Management, Partnerships, and the Shipper-Third Party Relationship." *International Journal of Logistics Management*. 1:2, pp. 1-10.

SUSTAINABLE GROWTH

The concept of sustainable growth was originally developed by Robert C. Higgins. The sustainable growth rate (SGR) of a firm is the maximum rate of growth in sales that can be achieved, given the firm's profitability, asset utilization, and desired dividend payout and debt (financial leverage) ratios. The variables in the model include: (1) the net profit margin on new and existing revenues (P); (2) the asset turnover ratio, which is the ratio of sales revenues to total assets (A); (3) the assets to beginning of period equity ratio (T); and (4) the retention rate, which is defined as the fraction of earnings retained in the business (R).

To compute a firm's SGR, we multiply the four variables together, or, in other words, the SGR = PRAT. Alternatively, the SGR equals the retention ratio times the return on beginning of period equity. An examination of the SGR equation indicates that the SGR increases when the profit margin increases, the assets to beginning of period equity increases, asset turnover increases, or the retention rate increases.

The sustainable growth model assumes that the firm wants to: (1) maintain a target capital structure without issuing new equity; (2) maintain a target dividend payment ratio; and (3) increase sales as rapidly as market conditions allow. Since the asset to beginning of period equity ratio is constant and the firm's only source of new **equity** is retained earnings, sales and assets cannot grow any faster than the retained earnings plus the additional debt that the retained earnings can support. The SGR is consistent with the observed evidence that most corporations are reluctant to issue new equity. Over the last decade, the market value of shares extinguished through repurchase or acquisition for cash by American corporations far exceeded the value of shares issued. If, however, the firm is willing to issue additional equity, there is in principle, no financial constraint on its growth rate.

USING THE SUSTAINABLE GROWTH RATE

The concept of sustainable growth can be helpful for planning healthy corporate growth. This concept forces managers to consider the financial consequences of sales increases and to set sales growth goals that are consistent with the operating and financial policies of the firm. Often, a conflict can arise if growth objectives are not consistent with the value of the organization's sustainable growth.

If a company's sales expand at any rate other than the sustainable rate, one or some combination of the four ratios must change. If a company's actual growth rate temporarily exceeds its sustainable rate, the required cash can likely be borrowed. When actual growth exceeds sustainable growth for longer periods, management must formulate a financial strategy from among the following options: (1) sell new equity; (2) permanently increase financial leverage (i.e, the use of **debt**); (3) reduce **dividends**; (4) increase the **profit margin**; or (5) decrease the percentage of total assets to sales.

In practice, firms may be reluctant to undertake these measures. Firms are reluctant to issue equity because of high issue costs, possible dilution of earnings per share, and the unreliable nature of equity funding on terms favorable to the issuer. A firm can only increase financial leverage if there are assets that can be pledged and its debt/equity ratio is reasonable in relation its industry. The reduction of dividends typically has a negative impact on the company's stock price. Companies can attempt to liquidate marginal operations, increase prices, or enhance manufacturing and distribution efficiencies to improve the profit margin. In addition, firms can source more activities from outside vendors or rent production facilities and equipment, which has the effect of improving the asset turnover ratio. Increasing the profit margin is difficult, however, and large sustainable increases may not be possible. Therefore, it is possible for a firm to grow too rapidly resulting in reduced liquidity and the need to deplete financial resources.

The sustainable growth model is particularly helpful in the situation in which a borrower requests additional financing. The need for additional **loans** creates a potentially risky situation of too much debt and too little equity. Either additional equity must be raised or the borrower will have to reduce the rate of expansion to a level that can be sustained without an increase in financial leverage.

Mature firms often have actual growth rates that are less than the sustainable growth rate. In these cases, management's principal objective is finding productive uses for the cash flows in excess of their needs. Options are to return the money to shareholders through increased dividends or **common stock** repurchases, reduced debt, or increased lower earning liquid assets. Note that these actions serve to decrease the sustainable growth rate. Alternatively, these firms can attempt to enhance their actual growth rates through the acquisition of rapidly growing companies.

Growth can come from two sources: increased volume and **inflation**. The inflationary increase in assets must be financed as though it were real growth. Inflation increases the amount of external financing required and increases the debt-to-equity ratio when this ratio is measured on a historical cost basis. Thus, if creditors require that a firm's historical cost debt-to-equity ratio stay constant, inflation lowers the firm's sustainable growth rate.

[Robert T. Kleiman]

FURTHER READING:

Higgins, Robert C. ''How Much Growth Can the Firm Afford?'' *Financial Management*. Fall, 1977, pp. 7-16.

Moore, Darrell M. ''Growing Broke: Sustainable Growth as a Factor in Financial Analysis.'' *Business Credit*. September, 1988, pp. 49-51.

T

Tactical asset allocation is a contrarian investment strategy that involves evaluating asset classes—such as **stocks**, **bonds**, and **commodities**—and comparing their relative performance. Money managers evaluate the relative performance of each asset class, then adjust the exposure of their investment portfolios to each of the classes. Importantly, the performance of specific securities is not as critical as the performance of the entire class to which the security belongs. In making investment decisions, proponents of tactical asset allocation often buy securities in out-of-favor asset classes.

INVESTMENT STRATEGIES

An individual making investment decisions often arrives at a portfolio that consists of different asset classes. The security classes chosen and their proportions makeup the asset allocation mix. In the investment arena, individuals can put their money in stocks, bonds, commodities, money market instruments, government paper, or any combination of these assets.

In deciding the specific combination of investments to make, known as an investment portfolio, investors must assess their own aversion to risk and their required rate of return. Risk is the possibility of an investment losing or not gaining value. People who are risk averse seek securities offering the least amount of risk. Required rate of return is the percentage gain that an investment must produce for an investment to be made. Normally, an investment with low risk is an investment with a low return. The proportion of the portfolio in each kind of security reflects the expected risk and return of the money invested.

There are numerous methods for choosing and managing assets. Basically, portfolio management strategies are based on three fundamental tactics. First, investors can buy and hold assets. Under the buy and hold strategy, investors choose their desired level of risk and return. Any change to the mix of assets must produce a higher return for the same risk or a lower risk for the same return. A second way of managing a portfolio is through either technical analysis or fundamental. Known as active management strategies, these types of analysis seek to find individual securities that are undervalued; typically, fundamental and technical analysis strategies require frequent asset allocation changes. The third way to manage a portfolio is by **tactical asset allocation**. Briefly, investors using this strategy decide upon a particular asset allocation mix but vary the mix over time depending on comparative market conditions of each asset class.

TACTICAL ASSET ALLOCATION TECHNIQUES

Like other asset allocation strategies, tactical asset allocation seeks to determine the best mix of assets using the standard approach of getting the best rate of return given an investor's risk aversion. It involves determining the best places for an investor to put his or her funds when comparing the different investment options available for the various classes of assets. Adherents of tactical asset allocation believe that the broad asset class that is invested in is more important than the specific securities chosen. They believe, for example, that if the stock markets are having a general decline, the world's best money managers would have a difficult time profiting with a portfolio totally invested in stocks. In that situation, the investor would likely be better off in another asset class, such as bonds or commodities.

Unlike other asset allocation strategies, tactical asset allocation involves making investment decisions in the short term. This is due to an underlying assumption in this that markets are inefficient and overreact to information. Thus, this **strategy** is intended to take advantage of perceived short-term market inefficiencies relating to the prices and returns of investment instruments in different asset classes. Decisions made under this strategy are, therefore, driven by changes in predictions for the returns of the various asset classes.

Tactical asset allocation is said to be a value-oriented, contrarian strategy. In making investment decisions, managers analyze each asset class for expected return relative to the returns of other asset classes. Investors, therefore, are able to find and buy undervalued asset classes. Because of perceived short-term market inefficiencies, frequent adjustments to the asset mix are made as one class of assets becomes undervalued in comparison to the others.

Obviously, this strategy can make some investors very uncomfortable. While most investors tend to move away from out-of-favor asset classes, investors using tactical asset allocation tend to favor the unpopular markets. Thus, when an asset class's general price falls, its future expected return tends to rise, making it more likely to be included in the optimal asset mix. Similarly, when an asset class's price rises, its future expected return tends to fall, making it less likely to be included in an optimal asset mix. In a nutshell, the investor buys low and sells high.

Importantly, tactical asset allocation assumes that an investor's risk aversion is relatively stable for long periods and is in no way affected by small changes in the investor's net worth. This allocation strategy does acknowledge, however, that the conditions of the capital markets and the investor's expectations about his returns are linked. Thus, when asset prices change in the **capital markets**, the expected returns and risks of different asset mixes change—leading to a different optimal asset mix.

[Kathryn Snavely]

FURTHER READING:

Ehrhardt, Michael C., and John M. Wachowicz, Jr. "Tactical Asset Allocation." *Review of Business*. Winter, 1990, p. 9(6).

Elgin, Peggy R. "Tactical Asset Allocation Isn't for the Weak-Hearted." *Pension Management*. March, 1995, p. 26.

Jacques, William E. "Con: Tactical Asset Allocation: A Sure-Fire Investment Technique or Just a Fad?" *Financial Executive*. Vol. 5, no. 2 (March-April 1989): pp. 43(3).

Kinsley, Ralph L., Jr. "Pro: Tactical Asset Allocation: A Sure-Fire Investment Technique or Just a Fad?" *Financial Executive*. Vol. 5, no. 2 (March-April 1989): pp. 42(4).

Kohler, Eric L. *A Dictionary for Accountants*. 5th ed. Englewood Cliffs, NJ: 1975.

Lincoln, Sandy. "Asset Allocation and the Time Horizon Complete the Picture." *Pension Management*. March 1995): pp. 22 (5).

Solomon, Lanny M., Larry M. Walther, Richard J. Vargo. *Financial Accounting. 3rd ed.* New York: West Publishing Company, 1992.

Wise, Ray. "A Question of Timing." *Pension World*. July, 1994, pp.

THE TAFT-HARTLEY ACT

The Taft-Hartley Act was passed in 1947, and remains the cornerstone of United States labor law today. This act amended the Wagner Act of 1935. Commonly called the Labor Management Relations Act of 1947, this legislation reflects the attitudes of post-World War II America towards labor. Due to "national emergency" strikes during the war, post-war strikes, and the advantages given to unions by the Wagner Act, a Republican-controlled Congress passed the Act in an attempt to restore the balance of power between labor and management. The Act restricts the activities of unions in four ways by:

(1) prohibiting unfair labor practices by unions,

(2) listing the rights of employees who are union members,

(3) listing the rights of employers, and

(4) empowering the president of the United States to suspend labor strikes that may constitute a national emergency.

UNFAIR LABOR UNION PRACTICES

The Taft-Hartley Act prohibited several labor practices judged to be unfair. First, the Taft-Hartley Act made it illegal for unions to restrain employees from exercising their guaranteed bargaining rights. Therefore, a union cannot threaten the jobs of employees who voted against the union, once the union is recognized. Employees who criticize the union or testify against it in hearings or court cases cannot be punished. Second, the Act named as unfair any action by the union that would have employers discriminate against employees in order to encourage or discourage membership in a union. Exceptions to this include "closed" or "union" shop situations in which union membership is a prerequisite for employment. A closed shop is one in which the employer can hire only union members. Closed shops were outlawed in

1947, but still exist in some industries. A union shop is one in which the employer can hire non-union employees, but the employees must join the union within a certain period of time. If an employee does not join the union and pay dues, he or she can be terminated. In either situation, the union cannot force the employer to dismiss an employee for any other cause.

Third, the Taft-Hartley Act required unions to bargain ''in good faith'' with employers, and outlawed ''wildcat'' strikes (refusing to work while a valid contract exists). Bargaining in good faith requires both the union and management to communicate and counter proposals, and make every reasonable effort to reach an agreement. The parties are not required to make concessions, only to meet and to discuss proposals.

Finally, the Act made featherbedding illegal. Featherbedding is the practice of making employers pay salaries to individuals who perform no work.

RIGHTS OF EMPLOYEES

The Taft-Hartley Act also protected employees' rights against their unions. Closed shops that forced employees to join unions were considered to violate the individual right to freedom of association. Without the Taft-Hartley Act, states would not have been able to enact ''right-to-work'' legislation; this guarantees employees that they will not have to join a union as a condition of employment. Right-to-work laws prohibit closed shops. Many states in the southern United States have enacted such laws. In the North, however, where unions are strong, most states have not enacted right-to-work legislation.

RIGHTS OF EMPLOYERS

The Taft-Hartley Act also gave employers certain rights. Employers have the right to express their views and opinions concerning unions and the results of unionization. Employers may, in fact, say anything they wish about unions as long as they avoid threats, promises, coercion, and direct interference. For example, employers can say that unionization might result in a plant closing; but cannot say that the plant will be closed if the union is voted in.

NATIONAL EMERGENCY STRIKES

The Taft-Hartley Act gives the president of the United States the power to intervene when a strike becomes a ''national emergency strike.'' National emergency strikes are those that could endanger national health or safety. The president has the power to appoint a board of inquiry that would be charged with making a report of the situation. Based upon this report, the president could apply for an injunction

restraining the strike for 60 days. If there has been no resolution at the end of 60 days, the injunction can be extended for another 20 days. During this extended 20 day period, employees are polled in a secret ballot to determine their willingness to comply with the terms of their employer's last offer.

NATIONAL LABOR RELATIONS BOARD (NLRB)

The Taft-Hartley Act amended the Wagner Act of 1935. The Wagner Act was also commonly referred to as the National Labor Relations Act (NLRA). This Act created the **National Labor Relations Board (NLRB)**, whose function was to monitor the collective bargaining process.

The NLRB is composed of five members, all of whom are appointed to five-year terms by the president of the United States, with the consent of the U.S. Senate. The general counsel of the NLRB is also appointed by the president, but to only a four year term. The board is charged with running over fifty different offices throughout the United States.

The responsibilities of the NLRB include the following:

1. Preventing unfair labor practices, whether they involve employers, labor unions, or representatives.

2. Determining appropriate grouping for collective bargaining. (That is, should all company employees be represented by a single union, or should unionization be further divided by craft area or plant location).

3. Conducting secret ballot elections to determine a bargaining representative; also determining if employees want an agreement that requires union membership as a condition of employment.

The NLRB has the power to issue cease and desist orders for unfair labor practices. These orders are then enforced, upon appeal, by the U.S. Court System.

Any person or organization may file a charge of unfair labor practice with the NLRB. In addition, the NLRB accepts petitions to either certify or decertify an employee representative, with respect to collective bargaining issues. The NLRB will then conduct secret ballots of employees to determine the certification or decertification of a union.

LANDRUM-GRIFFIN ACT (1959)

Officially listed as the Labor Management Reporting and Disclosure Act of 1959, the Landrum-Griffin Act amended the Wagner Act (1935), and further enumerated unfair labor practices not named in the Taft-Hartley Act. The clear purpose of this Act was to further protect union members from possible wrongful acts on the part of their union leaders and officers. This legislation affords union employees with a number of rights within the framework of their union. The election processes were made more open through requirements that eliminated closed nomination systems. Union employees were assured of their right to sue their union for just damages without fear of retaliation. Union employees cannot be fined or suspended by the union without due process. Such due process includes a list of specific charges, a fair hearing, and time in which to prepare a defense. This Act also required unions to provide copies of the applicable collective bargaining agreement to all members working under that contract.

In addition, unions were banned from engaging in secondary boycotts, and from making agreements that forced employers to deal exclusively with other union shops or buy only union-made goods. Picketing an employer who had a valid collective bargaining contract with another union was also forbidden.

UNIONS AND THE LAW

The greatest period of growth for unions occurred between the Wagner Act of 1935 and the Taft-Hartley Act of 1947. During these twelve years, union membership increased from approximately 3.5 million to 15 million. It is clear that the Taft-Hartley Act slowed the growth of union membership in the years following its passage. The issue of the proper balance of power between employers and employees is one of the oldest and most controversial debates of this century.

SEE ALSO: Labor Laws & Legislation; Labor Unions

[Bruce D. Buskirk and John E. Oliver]

FURTHER READING:

Bayer, Richard O., and Herbert M. Morris. *Labor's Untold Story*. New York: United Electrical, Radio, and Machine Workers of America, 1955.

Jacoby, Sanford M., and Anil Verma. "Enterprises Unions in the United States." *Industrial Relations*, Vol. 31, Winter, 1992, pp. 137-58.

Kesler-Harris, Alice. "Trade Union Mirror Society in Conflict Between Collectivism and Individualism." *Monthly Labor Review*. August, 1987.

Kheel, Theodore. *Labor Law*. New York: Matthew Bender, 1988.

Lesnic, Howard. "The Supreme Court and Labor Law in the Fiftieth Year of the NLRA." *The Labor Lawyer*. Fall, 1985, pp. 703-19.

Morris, Charles J., ed. *The Developing Labor Law*. 2nd ed. Washington, D.C.: Bureau of National Affairs, 1983.

Neufeld, Maurice F. "The Persistence of Ideas in the American Labor Movement: The Heritage of the 1830s." *Industrial and Labor Relations Review*. January, 1982.

Rayback, Joseph. *A History of American Labor*. New York: Macmillan, 1959.

Somers, Gerald G., ed. *Collective Bargaining: Contemporary American Experience*. Madison, WI.: Industrial Relations Assoc., 1980.

Twomey, David P. *Labor Law and Legislation*. Cincinnati: South-Western, 1980.

TAGUCHI METHODS

There has been a great deal of controversy about Genichi Taguchi's methodology since it was first introduced in the United States. The controversy is about Taguchi's statistical methods, not about his philosophical concepts concerning quality or robust design. Furthermore, it is generally accepted that Taguchi's philosophy has promoted, on a worldwide scale, the design of experiments for quality improvement upstream, or at the product and process design stage.

Taguchi's philosophy and methods support, and are consistent with, the Japanese quality control approach which asserts that higher quality generally results in lower cost. This is in contrast to the dominant view in the United States which asserts that quality improvement is associated with higher cost. Furthermore, Taguchi's philosophy and methods support the Japanese approach to move quality improvement upstream. Taguchi's methods help design engineers build quality into products and processes. As George Box, Soren Bisgaard, and Conrad Fung observed: "Today the ultimate goal of quality improvement is to design quality into every product and process and to follow up at every stage from design to final manufacture and sale. An important element is the extensive and innovative use of statistically designed experiments."

TAGUCHI'S DEFINITION OF QUALITY

The old traditional definition of quality states quality is conformance to specifications. This definition was expanded by J. M. Jurann in 1974 and then by the American Society for Quality Control (ASQC) in 1983. Juran observed that "quality is fitness for use." The ASQC defined quality as "the totality of features and characteristics of a product or service that bear on its ability to satisfy given needs."

Taguchi presented another definition of quality. His definition stressed the losses associated with a product. Taguchi stated "quality is the loss a product causes to society after being shipped, other than losses caused by its intrinsic functions.'' Taguchi asserted that losses in his definition ''should be restricted to two categories: (1) loss caused by variability of function; and (2) loss caused by harmful side effects.'' Taguchi is saying that a product or service has good quality if it ''performs its intended functions without variability, and causes little loss through harmful side effects, including the cost of using it.''

It must be kept in mind here that ''society'' includes both the manufacturer and the customer. Loss associated with function variability include, for example, energy and time (problem fixing), and money (replacement cost of parts). Losses associated with harmful side effects could be market shares for the manufacturer and/or the physical effects, such as of the drug thalidomide, for the consumer.

Consequently, a company should provide products and services such that possible losses to society are minimized. Or, ''the purpose of quality improvement . . . is to discover innovative ways of designing products and processes that will give society more than they cost in the long run.'' The concept of reliability is not inappropriate here. The next section will clearly show that Taguchi's loss function yields an operational definition of the term ''loss to society'' in his definition of quality.

TAGUCHI'S LOSS FUNCTION

We have seen that Taguchi's quality philosophy strongly emphasizes losses or costs. W. H. Moore asserted that this is an ''enlightened approach'' which embodies ''three important premises: for every product quality characteristic there is a target value which results in the smallest loss; deviations from target value always results in increased loss to society; [and] loss should be measured in monetary units (dollars, pesos, francs, etc.).''

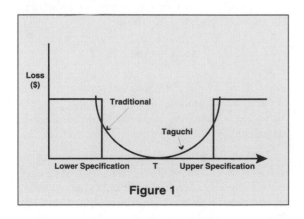

Figure 1

Figure 1 depicts Taguchi's typical loss function. The figure also contrasts Taguchi's function with the traditional view which states there is no loss if specifi-

cation are met. It can be seen that small deviations from the target value result in small losses. These losses, however, increase in a nonlinear fashion as deviations from the target value increase. The function shown is a simple quadratic equation which compares the measured value of a unit of output (Y) to the target (T):

$$L(Y) = k (Y - T)^2,$$

where L(Y) is the expected loss associated with the specific value of Y.

Essentially, this equation states that the loss is proportional to the square of the deviation of the measured value, Y, from the target value, T. This implies that any deviation from the target (based on customers' desires and needs) will diminish customer satisfaction. This is in contrast to the traditional definition of quality which states that quality is conformance to specifications. It should be recognized that the constant k can be determined if both the value of L(Y) and its associated Y value are known. Of course, under any circumstances a quadratic function is only a approximation.

Since Taguchi's loss function is presented in monetary terms, it provides a common language for all the departments or components within a company. Finally, the loss function can be used to define performance measures of a quality characteristic of a product or service. This property of Taguchi's loss function will be taken up in the next section. But to anticipate the discussion of this property, Taguchi's quadratic function can be converted to:

$$L(Y) = k[\sigma^2 + (\mu - T)^2].$$

This can be accomplished by assuming Y has some probability distribution with mean μ and variance σ^2. This second mathematical expression states that average or expected loss is due either to process variation or to being off target (called ''bias''), or both.

TAGUCHI, ROBUST DESIGN, AND THE DESIGN OF EXPERIMENTS

Taguchi asserted that the development of his methods of experimental design started in Japan about 1948. These methods were then refined over the next several decades. They were introduced in the United States around 1980. Although Taguchi's approach was built on traditional concepts of design of experiments (DOE), such as factorial and fractional factorial designs and orthogonal arrays, he created and promoted some new DOE techniques such as signal-to-noise ratios, robust designs, and parameter and tolerance designs. Some experts in the field have shown that some of these techniques, especially signal-to-noise ratios, are not optimal under certain conditions.

Nonetheless, Taguchi's ideas concerning robust design and the design of experiments will be now discussed.

DOE is a body of statistical techniques for the effective and efficient collection of data for a number of purposes. Two significant ones are the investigation of research hypotheses and the accurate relative determination of the effects of the many different factors which influence the quality of a product or process. DOE can be employed in both the product design phase and production phase.

A crucial component of quality is a product's ability to perform its tasks under a variety of conditions. Furthermore, the operating environmental conditions are usually beyond the control of the product designers, and, therefore, robust designs are essential. Robust designs are based on the use of DOE techniques for finding product parameter settings (such as temperature settings or drill speeds) which enable products to be resilient to changes and variations in working environments.

It is generally recognized that Taguchi deserves much of the credit for introducing the statistical study of robust design. We have seen how Taguchi's loss function sets variation reduction as a primary goal for quality improvement. Taguchi's DOE techniques employed the loss function concept to investigate both product parameters and key environmental factors. His DOE techniques were part of his philosophy of achieving economical quality design.

To achieve economical product quality design, Taguchi proposed three phases: system design, parameter design, and tolerance design. In the first phase, system design, design engineers use their practical experience, along with scientific and engineering principles, to create a viably functional design. To elaborate further, system design uses current technology, processed materials, and engineering methods to define and construct a new system. The system can be a new product or process or an improved modification of a existing product or process.

The parameter design phase determines the optimal settings for the product or process parameters. These parameters have been identified during the system design phase. DOE methods are applied here to determine the optimal parameter settings. Taguchi constructed a limited number of experimental designs, from which U.S. engineers have found it easy to select and apply in their manufacturing environments.

The goal of the parameter design is to design a robust product or process, which—as a result of minimizing performance variation—will minimize manufacturing and product lifetime costs. Robust design means that the performance of the product or process is insensitive to noise factors such as variation in environmental conditions, machine wear, or product-to-product variation due to raw material differences. Taguchi's DOE parameter design techniques are used to determine which controllable factors and which noise factors are the significant variables. The aim is to set the controllable factors at those levels that will result in a product or process being robust with respect to the noise factors.

In our previous discussion of Taguchi's loss function, two equations were discussed. It was observed that the second equation could be used to establish quality performance measures which permit the optimization of a given product's quality characteristic. In improving quality, both the average response of a quality and its variation are important. The second equation suggests that it may be advantageous to combine both the average response and variation into a single measure. And Taguchi did this with his signal-to-noise (S/N) ratios. Consequently, Taguchi's approach was to select design parameter levels that would maximize the appropriate S/N ratio.

These S/N ratios can be used to get closer to a given target value (such as tensile strength or baked tile dimensions), or to reduce variation in the product's quality characteristic(s). For example, one S/N ratio corresponds to what Taguchi called "nominal is best." Such a ratio is selected when a specific target value, such as tensile strength, is the design goal.

For the "nominal is best": case, Taguchi recommended finding an adjustment factor (some parameter setting) that will eliminate the bias discussed in the second equation. Sometimes a factor can be found which will control the average response without affecting the variance. If this is the case, our second equation tells us that the expected loss becomes

$$(k * \sigma^2).$$

Consequently, the aim now is to reduce the variation. Therefore, Taguchi's S/N ratio is:

$$S/N = -10 \log_{10} S^2,$$

where S^2 is the sample's standard deviation. In this formula, by minimizing S^2, $-10 \log_{10} S^2$ is maximized. Recall that all of Taguchi's S/N ratios are to be maximized.

Finally, a few brief comments concerning the tolerance design phase. This phase establishes tolerances, or specification limits, for either the product or process parameters that have been identified as critical during the second phase, the parameter design phase. The goal here is to establish tolerances wide enough to reduce manufacturing costs, while at the same time assuring that the product or process characteristics are within certain bounds.

As Thomas P. Ryan has stated, Taguchi at the very least has focused "our attention on new objectives in achieving quality improvement. The statistical tools for accomplishing these objectives will likely continue to be developed." Quality management "gurus," such as W. Edwards Deming and Kaoru Ishikawa, stressed the importance of continuous quality improvement by concentrating on processes upstream. This is a fundamental break with the traditional practice of relying on inspection downstream. Taguchi emphasized the importance of DOE in improving the quality of the engineering design of products and processes. Nevertheless, as previously mentioned, "his methods are frequently statistically inefficient and cumbersome."

SEE ALSO: Quality Control

[Peter B. Webb]

FURTHER READING:

Barker, T. B. "Quality Engineering by Design: Taguchi's Philosophy." *Quality Progress*. 19:12, 1986, pp. 32-42.

Box, G. E. P., R. N. Kackar, V. I. Nair, M. S. Phadke, A. C. Shoemaker, and C. F. Jeff Wu, "Quality Practices in Japan." *Quality Progress*. March, 1988, pp. 37-41.

Box, George, Soren Bisgaard, and Conrad Fung. "An Explanation and Critique of Taguchi's Contributions to Quality Engineering." *Quality and Reliability Engineering International*, Vol. 4, 1988, pp. 123-131.

Byrne, Diane M., and Shin Taguchi. "The Taguchi Approach to Parameter Design," *ASQC Quality Congress Transaction*. Anaheim, 1986, pp. 168-177.

Daniel, Cuthburt. *Applications of Statistics to Industrial Experimentation*. New York: John Wiley & Sons, 1976.

DeVor, Richard E., Tsong-how Change, and John W. Sutherland. *Statistical Quality Design and Control: Contemporary Concepts and Methods*. New York: Macmillan, 1992.

Kackar, R. N. "Off-Line Quality Control, Parameter Design, and the Taguchi Method." *Journal of Quality Technology*. 17:4, 1985, pp. 176-188.

Lochner, Robert H., and Joseph E. Matar. *Designing for Quality: An Introduction to the Best of Taguchi and Western Methods of Statistical Experimental Design*. Milwaukee, WI: ASQC Quality Press, 1990.

Mitra, Amitaua. *Fundamentals of Quality Control and Improvement*. New York: McMillan, 1993.

Phadke, M. S. *Quality Engineering Using Robust Design*. New York: Prentice Hall, 1989.

Quinlan, J. "Product Improvement by Application of Taguchi Methods." *Third Supplier Symposium on Taguchi Methods*. Dearborn, MI: American Supplier Institute, Inc., 1985.

Ross, P. J. *Taguchi Techniques for Quality Engineering*. New York: McGraw-Hill, 1988.

Ryan, T. P. "Taguchi's Approach to Experimental Design: Some Concerns." *Quality Progress*. May, 1988, pp. 34-36.

Ryan, Thomas P. *Statistical Methods for Quality Improvement*. New York, 1989.

Taguchi, Genichi. *Introduction to Quality Engineering*. White Plains, NY: Asia Productivity Organization, UNIPUB, 1986.

In the market for corporate control, **management teams** vie for the right to acquire and manage corporate assets and strategies. If an outside group acquires control of a target corporation, the transaction is termed a takeover. There are two basic methods of effecting a corporate acquisition: a friendly takeover and a hostile takeover. In a friendly takeover, the **board of directors** of the target firm is willing to agree to the acquisition. By contrast, a hostile takeover occurs when the board of directors is opposed to the acquisition. Friendly takeovers often involve firms with complementary skills and resources in growing industries. Hostile offers generally involve poorly performing firms in mature industries. In these cases, the suitor desires to replace the existing management team and sell off underperforming business units.

FRIENDLY TAKEOVERS

Friendly takeovers can either involve the acquisition of the assets of the company or the purchase of the stock of the target. There are several advantages associated with the purchase of assets. First, the acquiring firm can purchase only those assets that it desires. Second, the buyer avoids the assumption of any contingent **liabilities** of the target. Third, the purchase of assets is easier to negotiate since only the board of directors, and not the shareholders, need approve the acquisition.

The second type of friendly takeover involves the purchase of the stock of the target. In this instance, the acquiring firm does assume the liabilities of the target firm. The target firm continues to operate as an autonomous subsidiary or it may be merged into the operations of the acquiring firm. The approval of the target's shareholders is necessary for this type of acquisition.

HOSTILE TAKEOVERS

Hostile takeovers occur when the board of directors of the target is opposed to the sale of the company. In this instance, the acquiring firm has two options to proceed with the acquisition: a **tender offer** or a proxy fight. A tender offer represents an offer to buy the stock of the target firm either directly from the firm's shareholders or through the secondary market. This method tends to be an expensive way of acquiring the stock since the share price is bid up in anticipation of a takeover. Often, acquiring firms will first propose to the target company's board of directors an offer to buy the company's stock, with an indication that if the offer is turned down, it will then attempt a tender offer.

Federal securities regulations require the disclosure of the acquiring firm's intent with respect to the acquisition. Under the Williams Act, the acquiring firm must give 30 days notice to both the management of the target firm and the **Securities and Exchange Commission**. This enables the target firm to formulate a defensive strategy to maintain its independence.

In a proxy fight, the acquirer solicits the shareholders of the target firm in an attempt to obtain the right to vote their shares. The acquiring firm hopes to secure enough proxies to gain control of the board of directors and, in turn, replace the incumbent management. Proxy fights are expensive and difficult to win, since the incumbent management team can use the target's funds to pay all the costs of presenting their case and obtaining votes.

DEFENSIVE TACTICS. There are a number of maneuvers that can be used to ward off an unwanted suitor. These can be divided into two basic categories: preoffer tactics and postoffer tactics. Preoffer tactics are those that may employed prior to the receipt of a hostile bid. For example, private companies are almost invulnerable to takeovers since blocking stakes of more than 50 percent of the outstanding shares are held by an individual or an affiliated group. A high stock price will also fend off many potential acquirers since it will be difficult for the acquirer to earn a sufficiently high return on its investment in the target. In other cases, size alone may pose a valid defense. Also, high-tech firms in the defense industry may be immune to takeovers because of the political ramifications.

Target companies can also decrease the likelihood of a takeover though charter amendments. With the staggered board technique, the board of directors is classified into three groups, with only one group elected each year. Thus, a suitor cannot obtain control of the board immediately even though it may have acquired a majority ownership of the target via a tender offer. Under a supermajority amendment, a higher percentage than 50 percent, generally two-thirds or 80 percent is required to approve a merger. A fair price amendment, prohibits two-tier bids, where the first 80 percent of the shares tendered receive one price, whereas the last 20 percent receive a lower price for their stock.

Other preoffer tactics include **poison pills** and dual class recapitalizations. With poison pills, existing shareholders are issued rights which, if a bidder acquires a certain percentage of the outstanding shares, can be used to purchase additional shares at a bargain price, usually half the market price. Dual class recapitalizations distribute a new class of equity with superior voting rights. This enables the target firm's managers to obtain majority control even though they do not own a majority of the shares.

Postoffer tactics occur after an unsolicited offer is made to the target firm. The target may file suit against the bidder alleging violations of antitrust or securities laws. Alternatively, the target may engage in asset and liability restructuring to make it an unattractive target. With asset restructuring, the target purchases assets that the bidder does not want or that will create antitrust problems or sells off the "crown jewels," the assets that the suitor desires to obtain. Liability restructuring maneuvers include issuing shares to a friendly third party to dilute the bidder's ownership position or leveraging up the firm through a **leveraged recapitalization** making it difficult for the suitor to finance the transaction. Other postoffer tactics involve targeted share repurchases (often termed "**greenmail**" in which the target repurchases the shares of an unfriendly suitor at a premium over the current market price) and **golden parachute**s, which are lucrative supplemental compensation packages for the target firm's management. These packages are activated in the case of a takeover and the subsequent resignations of the senior executives.

SEE ALSO: Mergers and Acquisitions

[Robert T. Kleiman]

FURTHER READING:

Auerbach, Alan J. *Corporate Takeovers: Causes and Consequences.* Chicago, IL: University of Chicago Press, 1988.

Coffee, John C., Jr., Louis Lowenstein, and Susan Rose-Ackerman. *Knights, Raiders, and Targets: The Impact of the Hostile Takeover.* New York: Oxford University Press, 1988.

TARIFFS

SEE: Duty

TAXES AND TAXATION

To claim that taxes and taxation always have been unpopular is to state the obvious. Every American schoolchild learns about the Stamp Act of 1765 and how widespread resentment against "taxation without representation" precipitated the American Revolution. Few are aware of the fact that taxation with representation was just as unpopular: the Articles of Confederation of 1781 deprived the central government of the power of taxation. When a new constitution empowered Congress in 1791 to tax whiskey and other products, the Whiskey Rebellion ensued, nearly toppling the new government.

TAX HISTORY

Taxation—the raising of revenue—is about power, a subject that has excited much controversy throughout history. The Magna Carta of 1215, considered a watershed in the evolution of representative government, came about because of an English king's arbitrary imposition of taxes, without the consent of those being taxed. The issue was not about taxes themselves, but how they were being imposed. From then on, English rulers were deprived of the "power of the purse," which, for the most part, shifted to the taxpayers.

The concept of consent endured, elevated by English philosopher John Locke (1632-1704) into a constitutional principle. Locke maintained that government existed in order to protect liberty and the right of property; even so, it had no inherent right to tax without consent. Hence, since the Magna Carta the matter of taxation—the power to raise revenue—continued to buttress representative government. In 1689, the English "Bill of Rights" explicitly guaranteed the right of taxation only to parliament. This was a dramatic departure in the five thousand year history of taxation.

Another significant change has been the shared responsibility of all segments in society in the payment of taxes. In the United States, everybody from George Washington to the humble distiller of whiskey paid taxes. In medieval Europe and Russia, those least able to pay—the oppressed peasantry—carried most or all of the tax burden. Taxes were a social stigma. This changed with the evolution of the concept of taxation with representation, and its corollary: the responsibility of all to pay. In the early years of the American republic, so firmly entrenched was the idea that those who paid were those who ruled that the payment of property taxes (the only form of personal, individual tax in those days) became a more important voting criterion than mere citizenship.

Finally, the concept that those who are most able to afford to pay tax should pay the most—the "progressive" concept of taxation—is perhaps the most recent evolution in the history of taxation. It is nevertheless limited to the income tax, which in itself is the embodiment of the concept of everyone's responsibility to shoulder the tax burden.

Despite these changes over time, taxation is as old as recorded history. Today as in ancient times, all taxes fall into two broad categories: direct and indirect, internal and external. A direct tax is one that a person pays directly, as with income tax. An indirect tax is one that is usually figured into the price of a product, with the purchaser often unaware of its existence.

External taxes usually refer to tariffs, or taxes on imports, including food products. Internal taxes are those, such as excise taxes or sales taxes, added on to the price of a product produced or grown in this country (many foods are exempt from sales taxes).

Once the principle of taxation with representation was firmly established in the Constitution, which granted both the federal and state governments the right to tax, what becomes most notable in this country is the steady proliferation of taxes on the federal, state, and local level. This was not only in the number and types of taxes, but also in the numbers of those who paid them. Moreover, taxes that were meant to be temporary—such as income tax and sales taxes—ended up becoming permanent. Nowadays Americans sacrifice as much as, and sometimes more than, one-third of their income to taxes. How this came to be is the story of taxation in America.

There are roughly two periods of taxation in the United States: post-1913, which saw the adoption of the income tax (first by the federal government, then by the states) and the birth of Social Security, Medicare and the state sales tax; and the pre-1913 years, which is largely the story of the poll, property, tariff, and other non-income taxes.

POLL AND PROPERTY TAXES

In the pre-1913 period, while there were attempts to impose a personal income tax, taxes were non-income taxes. The oldest revenues, and the bedrock of local and state government, were poll and property taxes. These concepts were brought over from England, and were direct taxes. The poll tax was a fixed, regressive tax (everyone paid the same amount) that all adult males paid. It was this tax that the pacifist-minded Henry David Thoreau refused to pay, for which he was jailed. Because the poll tax had so many limitations and fell hardest on the poor, state after state discontinued it by the Civil War. Southern states revived it after 1870 in order to deprive newly-enfranchised African Americans of the right to vote (payment of poll taxes became a voting requirement). In 1964, the 24th amendment made this practice illegal, but did not outlaw the poll tax itself.

The largest share of revenue for state and local governments prior to 1913 derived from property taxes, which, before the Civil War, included not only land and buildings but also slaves and cattle. In those days of limited government expenditures, revenue from property went to the federal government as well. By the time of the "panic" of 1893, property revenues became inadequate for most states, and other sources of income had to be devised (the first business tax, followed in 1911 by the first mandatory income tax, inaugurated in Wisconsin). Nevertheless, property taxes continued to be a major source of revenue.

EXCISE TAXES

The most important sources of income for the federal government prior to 1913, with one or two exceptions, were excise taxes and above all, tariffs. Alexander Hamilton (1755-1804), the Treasury Secretary under George Washington, favored a rational system of taxation and effective collection of taxes. The result was the Revenue Act of 1791, which imposed a variety of excise taxes (i.e., sales taxes) on "luxury" products, such as distilled liquor, refined sugar, snuff (including tobacco), horse drawn carriages, and more. The very significant sum of $210,000 was collected by the 400 revenue collectors a year later, though these taxes were extremely unpopular. They were discontinued and the revenue officials dismissed from their jobs when Hamilton's nemesis, Thomas Jefferson, took the oath of office in 1801. Jefferson was a staunch proponent of little government and maximum freedom of the individual. Thereafter, excise taxes were most often used by the states to raise revenue and by the federal government before the Civil War only as an expedient. After 1865, the only excise taxes that continued in force were on alcohol and tobacco.

These days, excise taxes exist on a variety of "luxury" goods produced in this country; they are indirect taxes, that is, usually the consumer is unaware that he or she is paying them (unlike sales taxes). The producer or manufacturer adds the tax to the price of the product. Hence, while excise taxes have come and gone in American history, they have never disappeared.

TARIFFS

Excise taxes were not nearly as lucrative a source of federal revenue as tariffs. Particularly after 1816 the federal government raised much revenue on the taxes Congress imposed on imports, in opposition to free trade. Tariffs prevailed as the biggest source of federal revenue until the income tax appeared in 1913. After 1913, tariffs declined in importance, but never entirely disappeared.

Tariffs have had a long and stormy history down to the present day. As part of the federal government's revenue package in 1791, Congress added tariffs on a few imports. Alexander Hamilton wanted more, for he was strongly "protectionist," that is, favoring taxes on imports in order to protect fledgling American industries from too much foreign competition. Yet even then there was controversy over this view, with "free traders" opposed to any restraints on trade with

foreign nations, in the belief that they would retaliate against American goods. Hamilton was aware of the down side of his arguments, and therefore advocated temporary tariffs, only until American industry was on more solid competitive ground.

Because tariffs were so controversial, the initial ones were selective and limited. However, when the destructive Napoleonic Wars came to an end in 1815 and European industry threatened to recover rapidly, Congress gave in to pressure from northern business interests to pass a specific tariff act the following year.

The Tariff Act of 1816 called for moderate tariffs, but these were too few and too low to satisfy northern industrialists. However, southern cotton planters opposed any tariffs, which would raise prices on goods that they imported for their own use. When the Civil War resulted in a northern-controlled Congress, raising tariffs was a foregone conclusion. The Morrill Act of 1861 raised tariffs to the highest level in American history, followed by even higher rates during each successive year of the Civil War.

Even with the restoration of the southern states to the Union, northerners continued to control Congress. By the 1870s the federal budget was bloated with a huge surplus, far exceeding expenditures. Instead of lowering the high tariffs, Congressmen siphoned off the surplus to their own particular "pork barrels," with costly Civil War veterans' pensions on top of the list of every Congressman. Manufacturers as well as veterans were pleased. In the short run, the economy seemed to grow from high tariffs, and wealth appeared to be "trickling down" to the ordinary citizen.

At the same time, the downside of excessive protectionism was more and more in evidence. Prices rose precipitously on woolens and cottons, sugar, and sugar products, affecting mostly the poor. Monopolies gobbled up competition, and were themselves inefficient monoliths because of the absence of competition at home or abroad. By the time Democrat Grover Cleveland was reelected president in 1892, free trade was becoming an important issue. He persuaded Congress to slash tariffs by 40 percent. Before the benefits of a much lower tariff could be felt, a severe depression, the "panic" of 1893, struck, and four years later, the Republican Congress under William McKinley once again raised tariffs to an all-time high. Not until Woodrow Wilson was elected president in 1912 were tariffs once again lowered significantly. Nonetheless, they continued to zigzag from all-time lows, as during Wilson's two terms, to all-time highs, as during Calvin Coolidge's administrations in the 1920s. By then, international trade had all but shriveled up, as European countries enacted their own high tariffs in a belated revival of modern **mercantilism**. This only paved the way for the Great Depression to come.

What was becoming apparent in the first third of the twentieth century was the declining importance of tariffs as revenue, compared with personal and corporate incomes taxes. By 1920, income tax revenues totaled over $5 billion—ten times more than tariffs. Nonetheless, despite the warnings of over 1,000 economists, President Herbert Hoover satisfied powerful business interests by signing the Smoot-Hawley Tariff Act of 1930, considered to be the highest tariff in American history. Even when the Great Depression accelerated during Hoover's administration, Congress stubbornly refused to lower tariff rates. Economists and historians alike have cited the Smoot-Hawley Tariff Act as a major contributing factor to the country's swift economic decline in the 1930s.

The undeclared war between protectionists and free trade advocates eventually was won by the free traders with consequences that have reverberated down to the present time, with the passage of the **North American Free Trade Agreement** (NAFTA). Franklin D. Roosevelt, the first Democratic president in 12 years, took advantage of his enormous clout to get Congress to pass the Reciprocal Trade Agreements Act of 1934. **Reciprocity** was at the heart of this act: that is, if foreign governments would agree to lower their high tariffs, the United States would lower its tariffs accordingly. By the end of World War II, 29 countries had signed reciprocal trade agreements with the United States. This was enough to encourage the formation of a loose, free trade alliance in 1947 centered around GATT, the **General Agreement on Tariffs and Trade (GATT)**. Thereafter, more and more countries joined GATT, to the point where by 1990, 90 countries, accounting for 75 percent of the world's trade, had agreed to eliminate barriers to international trade.

GATT may be a final nail in the coffin of protectionism, but opponents of total **free trade** are still heard from. Farmers the world over resent international competition, as do automakers and computer chip producers. International competition opened the door to the virtual takeover of whole industries by the Japanese. Under pressure from U.S. automakers, GATT negotiations resulted in a trade pact in the early 1990s between the United States and Japan to limit the number of Japanese cars sold in the United States, and to enable more American cars to be sold in Japan. Vestiges of protective tariffs still exist, but these are disappearing in favor of regional free trade blocks, such as the European Union and NAFTA.

The history of tariffs as a tax on imported, foreign-made goods reveals how a tax, once considered indispensable, can decline in importance over time, and nearly disappear. As tariffs have lessened in importance during the twentieth century, income taxes have grown increasingly important and replaced revenue no longer generated from other sources.

INCOME TAXES

Income tax is unique in that it is one of the few major types of taxes that has philosophical underpinnings. Adam Smith (1723-1790), an eighteenth-century economic thinker whose modest treatise in 1776, *The Wealth of Nations*, has gone down in history as a work of genius, proposed the radical idea that income should be taxed regularly and permanently. Smith was of the same opinion as John Locke when it came to government: that it defended liberty and property rights; to Smith, government should be limited to those functions. Moreover, in order for the ''wealth of a nation'' to increase, government must spend only what it needed to run itself and nothing more. The revenue to run itself should be derived from a tax on income that must be fair and made clear to all well in advance of being levied.

Even before Smith's treatise was written, the colony of Massachusetts had been the first in the New World to impose an income tax in 1634, even though the property tax still remained the most important source of revenue. The idea had evolved, however, (and been taken for granted by Adam Smith's day) that wealth was more than just property consisting of land and buildings. That is, a person had certain skills and knowledge that could produce income, even if he had no concrete property. Hence in addition to the property tax, the colony imposed a tax on income of artisans, doctors, and so forth. The difficulty that the colony faced with income tax is an old one: taxpayers concealed their taxable income and paid as little as possible. How to collect income taxes efficiently became the chief problem, one that was not resolved until mandatory payroll deductions were introduced in the nineteenth century.

Hence the concept of an income tax and its philosophical justification were in place by the time the United States came into being. In addition, income tax is considered by tax historians and economists alike as the most advanced form of taxation in the long history of taxation. However, in the Articles of Confederation, the concept of taxation was surprisingly absent, and apparently had not caught on with the general public. The central government was all but deprived of any power to tax, while state governments taxed as little as possible. Property and poll taxes continued to hold sway, as did excise taxes on various goods.

Under the Constitution's explicit guarantee of the central government's power to tax in Article I, Section 8, a tax on income was not spelled out, though it was well known. In fact, the first U.S. Treasury Secretary, Alexander Hamilton, highly favored the idea. But in matters of taxation, Hamilton still is considered by twentieth-century historians as ahead of his times. The Revenue Act of 1791, Hamilton's brainchild, did not go down well with the public. What is noteworthy about this act, however, was its creation of the office of Commissioner of Revenue, forerunner of today's **Internal Revenue Service** (IRS). This, too, was Hamilton's idea. The Revenue Commissioner and his agents would administer the tax law, which mostly stipulated excise taxes and selected tariffs.

After Thomas Jefferson, who had led the opposition to the Revenue Act, became president in 1801, it was repealed and the Commissioner of Revenue Office was disbanded. Far from collapsing, the federal government grew wealthy on the lucrative revenues derived from tariffs, and the treasury recorded surpluses annually until the eve of the Civil War.

In July, 1862 President Lincoln signed the largest revenue bill in U.S. history up to that point. With $2 million a day going to fund the public debt incurred by war, the need for more revenue was desperate. The bill restored the office of Commissioner of Internal Revenue. The Commissioner was empowered to establish a system to collect a progressive income tax based on mandatory income withholding (a tax return form was duly created), as well as to collect numerous other internal taxes. For the first time, failure to comply with the tax laws could result in punishment—prosecution and confiscation of assets in the most extreme cases. Tax returns had to be signed under oath.

By the end of fiscal year 1863, the new revenue bureau took in, through its assessors and collectors, nearly $40 million. By war's end, the Bureau of Internal Revenue had grown from one employee to more than 4,000. Despite the huge sums garnered, the public deficit stood at an unprecedented $3 billion in 1865.

The income tax was discontinued after the Civil War, despite the large sums it had taken in. War time patriotism had ensured compliance with the income tax law, but public perception of the law was that it was a wartime exigency. Nevertheless, this time the Bureau of Internal Revenue was not dismantled, but was put in charge of collecting other taxes, notably the excise taxes on distilled liquor and tobacco.

The post-Civil War period, until 1913, witnessed the growth of the huge corporate monopoly and the stifling of competition. Radical populists and liberal Progressives criticized the lack of social responsibility on the part of the extremely wealthy, and lobbied on behalf of a graduated income tax, to ensure that the wealthy paid their dues. In 1894, Congress revived the income tax, only to see it struck down by the Supreme Court a year later. The problem lay in the vagueness of Article I, Section 8 of the Constitution which gave the federal government the right to tax; according to the Supreme Court decision in *Pollock v. Farmers Loan and Trust Co.*, such a tax would have to be apportioned among the states according to popula-

tion—and not just targeted to those with the most income. Since the intent of income tax proponents was to pressure those with the most income to pay the most, this decision was a resounding setback for their cause. Only an amendment to the Constitution could make income tax legal.

The Court's ruling precipitated a concerted movement towards adoption of an income tax amendment. Congress took the initiative in 1909, mainly in order to ensure the legality of its recently mandated one percent tax on corporate incomes over $5,000, which it disguised as an excise tax rather than as a tax on income. The amendment took nearly four years to acquire a three-quarters majority of the states' approval, but finally, in February, 1913, the 16th amendment was added to the Constitution. It quite simply invested Congress with authority to "lay and collect taxes on incomes, from whatever source derived, without apportionment among the several States, and without regard to any census or enumeration." The Bureau of Internal Revenue, a division of the U.S. Department of the Treasury, would administer and collect the new income tax, as it had during the Civil War. Nine years later, it established an Intelligence Division for the surveillance of possible income tax evaders.

The graduated income tax was hailed by the reform-minded everywhere as a sound blow to "special interests." On October 13, 1913, an income tax bill was passed, the first since the abortive 1894 bill. It stipulated that all incomes above $3,000 would be taxed. An annual salary of over $3,000 in those days was a generous middle class income; below that, no one paid income tax. Hence, fewer than one percent of working people would file tax returns. The new income tax bill repealed the 1909 excise tax on corporate incomes and levied a new corporate income tax on businesses. Mandatory withholding of income was reintroduced for the first time since the Civil War, but Congress repealed this measure in 1916 in favor of voluntary compliance.

The Revenue Act of 1916 raised income tax to new highs, and made more people eligible to file. A year later, incomes taxes were raised still more by the War Revenue Act of 1917. Nevertheless, as late as 1940 only 11 percent of working people were required to file, despite the huge cost of the preceding New Deal social legislation and the imposition of the Social Security Act of 1935.

The New Deal, however, had made deficit spending a respectable fiscal practice for the first time in American history. From then on, federal government spending would outstrip income, despite the increasing amounts of revenue derived from the income tax. In fact, mandatory payroll deductions, permanently enacted in 1943, increased revenue income tremendously: to $45 billion in 1945, from a mere $7.4 billion in 1941. However, unlike the Civil War period when payroll deductions were introduced for the first time only to be discontinued after the Civil War, mandatory payroll deductions remained in force after 1945. The additional categories of new taxpayers also were not discontinued after World War II, when virtually all working people filed income tax returns. Forty years later, revenue rose to almost one trillion dollars, still too inadequate to make a dent in the deficit, to fund the government overall, or to pay for the costly Cold War.

The story of internal revenue since World War II is one of increasingly higher taxes (despite tax cuts under Eisenhower), the expanding size and power of the Internal Revenue Service, and the growing deficit burden, in large part because of the need to finance the Cold War against the communist threat. By the end of the Cold War, the "peace dividend" had all but been swallowed up by the federal deficit, which amounted to hundreds of billions of dollars.

In 1952, Congress passed what it regarded as the most sweeping tax law since the 16th amendment inaugurated income tax. In retrospect, this new tax code reform did more to streamline and make the IRS more efficient (it changed its name from "Bureau of Internal Revenue" in 1953) than to alter personal income tax. Henceforth, all politically appointed posts within the bureau, except for commissioner and deputy commissioner, were replaced by civil service positions; the agency was significantly decentralized, with headquarters in Washington determining policy, while field offices were given wide latitude in decision making. In addition, electronic machines were introduced—predecessors of computers—to speed up processing of forms, which in turn were further simplified.

The consequence of decentralizing the IRS and giving decision making power to field offices has been a lack of uniformity in interpreting and enforcing tax laws: no two field offices are required to interpret the same tax law similarly, and there are often wide variations from field office to field office, for which the IRS is often criticized. The power of the IRS to enforce the tax laws has been increased. While in 1954 the IRS could inflict only 13 penalties on an errant taxpayer, by 1990, the number of penalties had escalated to 150, including seizure of a taxpayer's assets. The IRS made nearly three million such seizures in 1990 alone. Moreover, the IRS has the legal authority to request information from any bank, and to inquire into any type of vehicle registration or business activity. This uncovers a huge range of information on a business, individual, or married couple. The size of the IRS has grown to over 100,000 employees, making it the largest government agency in the world.

Ninety-five percent of Americans file tax returns. The federal government derives approximately 55 percent of its revenue from income tax, individual as well as corporate. In 1990, this revenue amounted to nearly one trillion dollars. Excise taxes, or "consumption" taxes, on fuel, cigarettes, alcohol, and selected luxury items account for another 4.4 percent. Despite these and other sources of income, the deficit in the national treasury has risen continuously; in 1994, it stood at over $250 billion. To pay for this, the government borrows money and must pay interest on the loans, which adds billions more to the deficit. The rising deficit more than offset the tax cuts of the Eisenhower and Reagan administrations.

Under President Ronald Reagan, tax reform became a high priority. The deficit was too big, taxes were too high, tax forms too complicated, and tax evasion too simple, Reagan concluded. In 1986, his tax reform package inaugurated the most sweeping changes in American income tax since 1913.

In essence, Reagan's tax measure slashed individual income taxes and drastically cut government spending, all in the hope of putting more money into the consumer's pocket. Individual tax brackets were reduced to two: all incomes up to $17,600 were taxed 15 percent; over that amount, 27 percent. Six million low-income working people were exempt from paying any federal income taxes. Dozens of deductions were eliminated. The reform package also ended "revenue sharing," a program introduced in President Richard Nixon's administration that involved the federal treasury "refunding" some federal tax monies to the states. While the bill slashed individual taxes and doubled the personal exemption, corporate taxes were raised, business exemptions were reduced, and loopholes were plugged. The business and corporate world would carry the tax burden, according to the 1986 tax reform bill, and not the individual.

Critics of Reagan's tax reform bill charged that the reduction in government spending was more than offset by the highest military expenditures in U.S. history; that the significant increase in corporate income tax was passed on to the consumer in the form of higher prices; and that the elimination of revenue sharing with the states forced states across-the-board to significantly raise state income taxes for individuals as well as for businesses.

Tax reform continues to bedevil presidents. Income taxes were raised under President George Bush, while in 1991 a deficit reduction plan was inaugurated that placed a ceiling on the deficit: automatic spending cuts would go into effect if this ceiling were exceeded. President Bill Clinton's deficit reduction plan, passed by Congress in August, 1993, seeks to reduce the federal deficit by $500 billion over a period of five years through a special 4.4 percent fuel tax and reduced government spending. In addition, his tax reform measure hiked taxes for the wealthy and corporations. Critics believed that the consequences of the Clinton tax bill would be higher consumer prices, a reduction in capital spending, and a reduction in the already low level of private savings.

SOCIAL SECURITY TAXES

Social Security taxes were the next major new tax after 1913 to follow income tax, deducted from payrolls simultaneously with income taxes. Meanwhile, like income tax, social security taxes have been steadily on the rise since they were first introduced in 1935.

Although income tax and social security taxes (which include Medicare) are both collected by the Internal Revenue Service, income tax monies make up general federal revenues, while social security taxes go straight into the Social Security Trust Fund. Social security taxes are the next biggest tax that individuals must pay annually, and for some of the 39 million self-employed, they may be higher than income tax.

The most enduring social legislation to emanate from the New Deal was social security. In 1935, the Social Security Act encompassed old age pensions, unemployment insurance, and aid to the handicapped as well as to dependent children. These benefits would be paid equally by the employer and the employee, making Social Security theoretically immune to the vicissitudes of the economy or to the size of budget deficits.

In 1950, Social Security benefits were extended to the self-employed, who, however, were compelled to pay not only their own share of the Social Security taxes but the employer's as well, all lumped into one tax called self-employment tax. In that same year, Congress raised the Social Security tax by an additional 2 percent (split between employer and employee) in order to fund disability medical insurance, which was added to Social Security benefits. Currently, Social Security taxes are 7.15 percent of gross annual income; for the self-employed, it is 15.3 percent.

Whatever is not paid out in the form of pensions from the Social Security fund is invested in government notes. This ''surplus'' has been growing steadily to the point where in 1994 alone, $56 billion was added to it.

In 1965, Medicare was inaugurated, providing government medical insurance mostly for the elderly; it does not cover all medical costs, however, such as prescription medicine and doctor's fees. The government docs cover these costs for the indigent elderly, although these costs are paid out of general federal revenue, rather than the Social Security trust fund.

STATE TAXES

While federal taxes, including Social Security and Medicare, ate up an average 28 percent of individual incomes in 1993, this did not include state income tax, local taxes, or property taxes. Forty-three states require everyone to file income tax returns. Reliance on state income tax for state treasuries increased dramatically after revenue sharing was discontinued under President Reagan, who correctly guessed that federal revenues would increase if a percentage were not returned to the states, as had been the practice. Hence state income tax also has become a sizable burden on the taxpayer. The rising cost of education and the expanding role of the state in funding education from grammar school through high school was the original impetus for state income tax. By the time most states required income tax returns, payroll deductions already were used by the federal government, a practice adopted by the states.

Most states also rely heavily on the sales tax, which Mississippi was the first to adopt in 1932. The Great Depression magnified the need for social services, and to finance these, state after state began to inaugurate sales taxes. Between 1933 and 1938, a total of 27 states had instituted a sales tax, that is, a tax on goods and services. Nowadays, 45 states have sales taxes, the highest sales tax being in the state of Connecticut. Half of a state's revenue derives from the sales tax in the states that have this tax.

Sales taxes vary: in some states, only luxuries are taxed, similar to an excise or consumption tax. Food items, except for food prepared for immediate consumption, rarely are taxed; some states exempt not only food but clothing from sales taxes. The reasons for this lack of uniformity in applying the sales tax is that it is a regressive tax, and hence falls hardest on those with the least income. So popular and necessary have sales taxes become that many cities have enacted sales taxes as well.

TAX EVASION AND AVOIDANCE

The willingness to risk not paying or underpaying taxes is prevalent today, despite vastly superior techniques of ferreting out the miscreant taxpayer. Of the two types of tax evasion, noncompliance (failure to submit a return or misrepresenting one's taxable income), is illegal, while ''tax avoidance'' is legal. Since the IRS audits only ten percent of the two hundred million tax returns it receives annually, many people are willing to risk noncompliance. Tax avoidance, on the other hand, is mainly the resort of middle and upper income Americans: for instance, tax shelters, such as foreign banks deposits, which are not taxed and have strict privacy laws; or deferral of income into the following year; or setting up business on an island that is a tax haven; or investing in a bankrupted business in order to claim the investment on one's tax return, are a few of the many ways that individuals and businesses avoid taxes.

Corporations and small businesses take yet another route in avoiding huge and burdensome taxes, especially employment taxes: hiring part-time rather than full-time employees, or resorting to temporary workers. To many observers, this has become a worrisome trend, since part-time and temporary workers usually receive no benefits or health insurance and are among the most insecure and vulnerable members in the American workforce.

Income tax, federal as well as state, Social Security taxes, and sales taxes have been the primary new taxes of the twentieth century in the United States, while taxes enforced in the nineteenth century have not disappeared (with the exception of the poll tax). The twentieth century, unlike the nineteenth, also has witnessed an unprecedented rise in taxes in many other countries.

SEE ALSO: Free Trade

[Sina Dubovoy]

FURTHER READING:

Bartlett, Donald L., and James B. Steele. *America: Who Really Pays the Taxes?* New York: Simon & Chuster, 1994.

Burnham, David. *A Law unto Itself, the IRS and the Abuse of Power.* New York: Vintage Books, 1989.

Doris, Lillian, ed. *The American Way in Taxation, Internal Revenue, 1862-1963.* Englewood Cliffs, NJ: Prentice Hall, 1963.

Webber, Carolyn, and Aaron Wildavsky. *A History of Taxation and Expenditure in the Western World.* New York: Simon & Schuster, 1986.

TEAMS

The concepts of teamwork and team building are taking on added importance in the business world. More and more businesses of all types are introducing or expanding teamwork as part of their production processes, with varying results. Organizational leaders are forming committees, assembling project teams, putting together temporary work groups. Whatever businesses call them, the groups are basically teams.

A team is best defined as a temporary or ongoing task group whose members are responsible for working together to identify problems, form consensuses about actions to be taken, and implement the most viable ones. Their purposes and goals often differ. For example, they may be formed to develop new products, act as liaisons between and among different departments within a corporation, or resolve problems. Teams are not, however, intended to be a panacea to all business problems. Nor do they always work smoothly.

Teams are not appropriate for all organizations or in all types of businesses. Behavioral scientists are still working to determine exactly when teams will be most effective, what motivates team members, what types of business can best benefit from the implementation of teams, etc. The study of the philosophy and psychology of teamwork is still in its infancy. But, as more and more businesses introduce the team concept, the wrinkles in the process are being ironed out and team popularity is growing. Teamwork may be the wave of the future in the business world.

THE TEAM PHILOSOPHY

The philosophy behind teamwork is simple: the goal is to mesh workers into cohesive groups in order to attain a common goal. The key word is "cohesive." If group members are not properly matched, they will be neither cohesive nor productive. A nonproductive team does not benefit the organization or the individuals. It becomes management's responsibility, then, to assure that teams are well managed and composed of individuals who manifest the necessary characteristics for group work.

Theoretically, if properly managed, people who work in groups will be more productive. That is the ideal. In reality, the teamwork approach does not always work well for a variety of reasons. One of them is that the right type of team may not be created. One of the keys to success in the team approach is to select the precise type of team best suited to accomplish the intended task. There is a wide variety of teams available from which to choose.

TYPES OF TEAMS

There exist many different types of teams in the business world. There are, for example, functional, task, project, ad hoc and standing committees; interest and friendship groups; autonomous, integrated, and entrepreneurial work teams; quality circles, and others. Often, people lose sight of the fact that some of these entities are actually teams. But, that is just what a committee is: it is a team put together for a specific purpose. Placed in that context, virtually every business uses one form of team or another.

Groups fall into two categories, formal and informal. Formal groups are those given legitimacy by the organization. Informal groups tend to be more social in nature. Nevertheless, they are sometimes sanctioned by the organization in order to stimulate innovation or increase employee morale. The type of group utilized by individual companies depends to a large extent on the business, the problems to be solved, and the level of participation (e.g., executive, managerial, supervisory, etc.). That is why it is so important that management choose from among the available categories the right team format.

FORMAL GROUPS

A *functional group*, also called a command group, is a formal group consisting of a manager and his/her subordinates, all of whom share a common specialty. For example, all the members of a functional group may be in the marketing department of an organization or the science department of a university. Functional groups tend to stay in existence for long periods of time. The type of organization which the functional group serves generally determines the group's objectives, interactions, interdependencies, and performance levels.

A *task group*, or project group, is a formal group created for a specific purpose, more often than not to identify and resolve problems. Task groups generally work toward a definite project completion date in accordance with well defined parameters and within set budgets. Usually, there exists a prepared master plan that governs their tasks and schedules.

Task groups supplement or replace work normally done by functional groups. They are frequently utilized in industries such as construction, petroleum, chemical, and aerospace, where workers tend to labor in teams assigned to complete specific projects. The teams might consist of a project manager, who oversees the team's activities, and specialists like engineers, research and development scientists, quality control technicians, etc., all of whom report to the project manager.

Closely related to the task group is the *task force*, also known as an ad hoc committee, which is a temporary team generally formed to address a specific issue. The task group does not actually perform the work required to resolve a problem. It is more an advisory group than anything else. The group makes recommendations on an issue, then disbands. It is a distant cousin of the *standing committee*, which is a permanent group responsible for handling recurring matters in a narrowly defined subject area over an indefinite, generally long, timeframe.

INFORMAL GROUPS

There are two categories of informal groups, both of which play an important role in business: *interest* and *friendship* groups. An interest group is one formed to facilitate employee pursuits of common concerns. A friendship group evolves mostly to meet employees' social needs. The leaders in both groups may differ from those appointed by the organization.

However, the characteristics of both formal and informal types of groups are basically the same.

The relationships among the members are based on some common characteristics, e.g., personal interests or political beliefs. Often, but not always, the group's goals may be the same as the organization's. There are times when either or both types of groups can be formal, i.e., legitimized by the organization. The legitimacy is bestowed by astute executives because they realize that informal groups play a vital role in employees' work lives by boosting morale and facilitating communication. These are also keys to the success of more legitimate groups such as autonomous and integrated teams.

THE GROWTH OF TEAMS

Generally, when the term teams is used in the business context, people think of formal groups such as work teams, integrated work teams, and autonomous work teams. That is because such formal work units are becoming more popular in the workplace today and receive more attention from researchers than do the more traditional teams.

A *work team* is simply a group of individuals who cooperate in completing a set of tasks. Work teams fall into one of two categories: integrated and autonomous.

An *integrated work team* is a group that accomplishes many tasks by making specific assignments to members and rotating jobs among them as the tasks require. The team decides the members' specific assignments and how and when to rotate jobs among them as the tasks require. An integrated team has an assigned supervisor who oversees its activities. Such teams are used frequently in business areas such as building maintenance and construction.

An *autonomous* (or *self-managing*) *work team* is a group that is given almost complete autonomy in determining how a task will be done. Autonomous work teams have a wider range of discretion than integrated teams. The organization provides the autonomous team with a goal. From that point on, the team members determine work assignments, rest periods, schedules, quality control procedures, and other matters associated with the job. Fully autonomous teams may decide who is hired, who is fired, and perform one another's evaluations. Often, there are no supervisors in autonomous teams. All members of the group share equal responsibility for the leadership.

Autonomous work teams have proven especially effective in auto manufacturing and associated industries. For example, Goodyear Tire and Rubber experienced success with them in its Lawton, Oklahoma radial-tire plant. The work force included 164 teams made up of 5 to 27 members. Each team set its own production schedule and goals and screened applicants to decide on new members. Goodyear's management discovered that by using the team concept, the plant doubled its daily volume of comparable-sized, traditionally designed plants. More importantly, it beat the cost of comparable tires made by its foreign competitors.

The idea of matching or exceeding foreign competition's prices is essential to the success of American businesses. In adopting the team concept, American businesses are simply borrowing a page from foreign companies, like Volvo, which apply the team approach with a great deal of success.

A. B. Volvo is perhaps the best known model when the team approach is discussed. Its plants in Sweden are designed to produce cars without using assembly lines. Volvo's new plant in Kamar, Sweden, uses autonomous work teams consisting of about 20 workers each. The members are responsible for constructing entire units of cars, e.g., the engine or the electric system. Each member performs a series of tasks in a few minutes, which differs a bit from the procedures American assembly line workers in auto plants carry out. American workers will more likely perform a single task in a few seconds. This is by no means the only difference between the American and Swedish workers involved in the assembly line process.

In the Volvo team environment, members learn several jobs to enable them to cover for sick or vacationing individuals. As smooth working as the system has become, it did not work well at first. There were problems in coordinating the team's multiple tasks, but constant refinements made the system work more effectively. During the last few years, it has enabled Volvo to reduce the labor hours involved in producing one car by 40 percent. The team approach has helped increase the inventory turnover from nine times per year to 22. Most importantly, it has sliced the number of defects by 40 percent, which is a tremendous cost saver for the company. Just how successful the autonomous team approach has been at Volvo is indicated by the fact that the company recently opened a new plant at Uddevalla, where work teams will perform an even larger variety of tasks.

Yet another type of team is the *entrepreneurial team*, which comprises a group of individuals with diverse expertise and backgrounds. The members are assembled to develop and implement innovative ideas aimed at creating new products or services or improving existing ones. One of the best examples of an entrepreneurial team's worth is the development of the Ford Taurus automobile.

During the 1980s, the Ford Motor Company was suffering from lagging auto sales and severe competition from foreign manufacturers. Company executives decided to capitalize on their foreign competitors' strengths. They formed an entrepreneurial group as one step in their new approach.

First, they sidestepped the normal five-year process involved in designing, building, and producing a new automobile. Ordinarily, product planners would start the process with a basic concept. Then, designers would develop the look. Their ideas would be translated by engineers into specifications. Next, suppliers and manufacturers would process the design. Each group worked in a vacuum. There was little, if any, contact among the various groups.

Ford's executives decided on a radical new approach to producing the Taurus. The company allocated $3 billion to fund a new group, called Team Taurus. The project involved a team approach in which representatives from all the participating functional departments, e.g., planning, designing, engineering, and manufacturing, cooperated. The team had the ultimate responsibility for developing the new auto. The advantages of the team approach became apparent immediately.

For one thing, any problems with the design could be resolved quickly, since each department involved in the process had representation on the team. And, the team could—and did—create sub-teams to perform investigative work. For example, one sub-team was responsible for designing comfortable, easy-to-use, seats. Another studied how to effectively reduce the number of parts used in the production process. The biggest contribution of the team, however, was in its approach to the workers who would actually build the cars.

Team members asked the assembly workers and suppliers for advice early in the design process. The workers were happy to participate. They suggested, for example, that the number of parts in a door panel be reduced from eight to two for easier handling and to ensure that all the bolts contained therein had the same size head. The idea was to eliminate the need for different-sized wrenches. Suppliers also presented some valuable ideas.

To date, Ford has been pleased with the results of the entrepreneurial team approach. In fact, the company has integrated it into the production of its other cars, e.g., Lincoln Continentals and Thunderbirds. The approach at Ford—as it is elsewhere—is still in the embryonic stage itself.

Quality circles are closely associated with the total quality management (TQM) process. TQM is a systematic approach to emphasizing organizationwide commitment, integration of quality improvement efforts with organizational goals, and inclusion of quality as a factor in performance appraisals. Quality circles represent one method toward achieving the goal of TQM.

Quality circles, also called quality improvement teams, comprise small groups of employees who work on solving specific problems related to quality and productivity, often with stated targets for improvement. Monsanto formed such a team several years ago in response to a problem reported to it by the Ford Motor Company.

Ford told Monsanto that a Monsanto product, Saflex, which was used to make laminated windshields, was experiencing problems. The dimensions of the materials somehow changed between the time the products left Monsanto's plants and arrived at Ford's facilities. Monsanto immediately assembled a quality control group. Within two months, the team traced the problem to packaging, designed a new prototype, tested it, and implemented a new packaging process. Monsanto's response satisfied Ford. The quick problem resolution was made possible in part because Monsanto's management adhered to one of the cardinal rules of team building: select the right people to perform the work. Achieving positive results is the ultimate goal for any team. It is paramount, then, if business executives hope to reach that goal, and any others for which they strive, that they exercise great care in forming their teams.

PUTTING THE TEAM TOGETHER

Simply put, forming a team involves a great deal more than just throwing several people together and assigning them a goal. Putting a team in place is a complex task comprising many crucial steps. For example, consideration must be given to motivation, conformity, rewards, intragroup relationships, and norms.

There are two basic types of groups: homogeneous and heterogeneous. Homogeneous groups comprise people who have similar needs, motives, and personalities. They are generally effective at handling simple, routine tasks. Their members' compatibility usually leads to high levels of cooperation and effective communications. The hallmark of the homogeneous group is the fact that the members have few interpersonal problems. Their group harmony is conducive to high group effectiveness—although that is not always the case. At times, the members of homogeneous groups tend to overconformity, which makes it difficult for them to deal effectively with nonroutine matters.

Heterogeneous groups, on the other hand, are most often effective at handling complex tasks, especially those requiring innovative approaches to problem solving. For the most part, the members possess different backgrounds and areas of specialization. What one member may lack in training and background, another one has. And, because they tend to have different types of personalities, they are not afraid to ask questions of one another or to differ on issues. They will challenge one another's conclusions, hypotheses, ideas, etc. Their willingness to confront other group members leads to a valuable exchange of ideas, which in turn leads to innovative solutions to problems. Of course, that is not always a positive thing. It can also lead to intra-group conflict, which is a barrier to productivity.

NORMS IN THE TEAM CONCEPT

Teams cannot work effectively to accomplish their goals if they do not establish norms by which they will operate, i.e., behavioral rules of conduct. Norms provide each individual in a group with guidelines on how to predict the behavior of the other members of the group.

Group norms are not designed to cover every conceivable situation in which a team might become involved. Rather, they address only those situations which are significant to the team. Similarly, not all norms apply to every team member. For example, all team members may have to adhere to norms regarding how much work they should do individually to help the group attain its goals. But, perhaps only one member would be responsible for alerting the others to starting and ending times for a group session. There are times, however, when team members may deviate from norms, which can create dissension among them.

Once teams set norms, it is expected that each member will adhere to them. However, not all team members are willing at all times to contribute 100 percent to the group's efforts. Some are free riders, who exert less effort when in groups than they do when working alone because they realize that when the team reaches its goal they will share in the glory and the rewards without regard to who actually completed the work.

Teams which include these free riders must develop procedures to discipline the individuals who do not perform their share of the work. Discipline can range from verbal warnings to firing or transferring the free rider. (Some teams, especially autonomous teams, have the power to hire and fire as they see fit without consulting with management. Thus, it is within their province to handle free riders without overwhelming bureaucratic intervention.) The key to success for a team, then, is to get individual members to conform to the norms as closely as possible.

CONFORMITY TO NORMS

Individuals conform to team norms for a variety of reasons. Among them are personal factors, ambiguity, situational factors, and intragroup relationships.

People generally feel more comfortable in groups whose members share some common personal factors, e.g., age and intelligence. However, most people in the American workplace tend to be nonconformists. It is important, then, that groups be assembled with conformity in mind if they are to accomplish their tasks.

Intelligence is also an important factor in group conformity, too. Researchers have determined that the more intelligent people are, the more inclined they will be to go their own way. This is closely tied to ambiguity in the team setting. If the more intelligent members of a team the instructions, alternatives, etc., involved in a group project, while other members see only ambiguity, then the latter faction will conform to the lead of those who seem to know what is going on. This can sway the power of balance among team members and lead to groupthink, i.e., social conformity to group ideas by members of the team. Groupthink can be hazardous for a team seeking diverse and innovative ideas to resolve a problem, create new products, etc.

Situational factors are also integral in the team concept. Such factors include the size of the group, unanimity of the majority, and structure. The people who form a group must consider carefully its optimum size in order to reduce friction as much as possible. They must also take into account the group's structure. Normally, the more decentralized a group is, the better it will perform. That is because contact and communications are limited to some extent, which lessens the possibility of groupthink. It is also essential that each member of a team knows his or her role within the group.

Everyone on a team is expected to act in a certain way. Those expectations constitute roles. Often, there is a direct connection between individual team members' functions and their roles. For instance, a marketing representative on a design team is expected to offer advice on how best to sell a new product. The quality control specialist is expected to oversee techniques designed to assure that the product is durable and performs as intended. That does not mean, though, that individuals' roles are limited to their particular areas of expertise. They are also expected to contribute in other ways, as devils' advocates for example.

In essence, every team member plays three roles: expected (the way he or she is expected to act), perceived (the activities or behaviors he or she believes are required), and enacted (the role he or she actually plays).

TEAM DEVELOPMENT

According to group researcher Bruce W. Tuckman, there are essentially five steps involved in the team development process. They are forming, storm-ing, norming, performing, and adjourning. Not all teams will go through all five stages. Some may pass through several and then regress. All teams do go through some of the stages, though.

Forming is the stage in which team members attempt to assess the ground rules that will apply to a task and to group interaction. Team members seek basic information about the group's goals and their roles in the project. They begin to test the extent to which their individual input will be assessed. Individuals may also try to analyze interpersonal behaviors within the group. Basically, forming is a feeling-out process in which the members try to make sense of the ground rules and assess one another's characteristics before carrying out the team's primary mission.

Once the forming stage is completed, the members go on to *storming*. This is the stage in which individuals initiate conflict with one another as they identify possible areas of disagreement. They also attempt to resolve differences of opinion regarding key issues. Areas of disagreement might include task requirements, possible resistance to them, and interpersonal relationships. The larger the team, the more likely are the chances of interpersonal conflicts. The storming stage is also the time in which leadership struggles begin. It is also during this stage that listening to one another and trying to find mutually acceptable resolutions to disagreements is vital. If issues cannot be resolved, the team's chances of achieving its goals diminish greatly. Once the sorting out process is completed, the third stage, norming, begins.

In *norming*, the team members begin to build cohesion and develop a consensus about norms for performing tasks and relating to one another. By this time, the team members are aware of individuals' idiosyncrasies and are better able to cope with them. They are also clear as to what individual members' roles are and exhibit a greater appreciation for problem solving techniques. Harmony is the watchword in the norming stage, which is the final step toward performing. Not all groups reach the performing stage, though.

It is during the *performing* stage that the team members actually channel their energy toward the completion of the group's task. If team members have not achieved the harmony necessary through the first three steps, they may either disband or regress until they do. Those that do reach the performing stage, however, apply the problem-solving solutions or innovative product ideas generated in the previous stages. By this time, the individual team members' roles have been clarified and the group exhibits positive synergy, i.e., the force that results when the combined gains from group interaction are greater than group process losses. Teams that reach this stage will most likely remain effective—as long as they continue to devote their energies toward completing the task and maintain harmonious interpersonal relationships. They may continue to do both until the inevitable fifth stage, adjournment, arrives.

Adjournment should be a happy stage, but it is not for some teams. It is the stage in which team members prepare for disengagement as the group nears successful completion of its goals. Members may be pleased with their efforts. However, they may feel some regrets at the team's imminent break-up. This, of course, depends on how long the team has been in operation. Adjournment is more often experienced by teams put together for short-term projects, e.g., ad hoc committees and temporary task groups. Nevertheless, adjournment is a part of the group development process—and often the most traumatic.

THE FUTURE OF TEAMS

Individual teams may adjourn, but teams in general will not. Teams have proven to be successful tools in the workplace, and no doubt will continue to be vital cogs in the future. More and more companies are resorting to teams as a way of resolving problems, designing innovative new products, or enhancing old ones. In many cases, teams lower companies' costs in accomplishing these goals. As long as teams have a positive impact on the bottom line, they will continue to be a part of the business environment.

[Arthur G. Sharp]

FURTHER READING:

Arnold, Hugh J. and Daniel C. Feldman. *Organizational Behavior.* McGraw-Hill, 1986.

Massie, Joseph L. and John Douglas. *Managing.* Prentice Hall, 1992.

Reitz, Joseph. *Behavior in Organizations.*, 3rd Ed. Irwin Publishers, 1987.

Shaw, Marvin E. *Group Dynamics—The Psychology of Small Group Behavior.*, 4th Ed. McGraw-Hill, 1985.

Stech, Ernest and Sharon A. Ratliffe. *Effective Group Communication.* National Textbook, 1985.

TECHNICAL ANALYSIS

Technical analysis, or chart theory, is research into the supply and demand of investments based on historic trade information, in terms of both price and volume. Technical analysts, also called chartists, believe that it is possible to detect the onset of a movement in stock or market value from one equilibrium condition to another. To do this, they use charts and computer programs of past stock, commodity, and market movements to identify trends that they believe will predict pricing movements. Chartists are not concerned about why conditions are changing, they only want to identify the beginning of the change to take advantage of short- and intermediate-term gains. While most of these analysts predict short and intermediate pricing trends, some also forecast long-term market cycles based on their data.

Like many professionals in the security industry, chartists believe that the value of the market is determined by supply and demand for stocks. Furthermore, like others, chartists think that the supply and demand is influenced by many factors—not always rational—which are weighed continuously and automatically by the market. Chart theory differs from other schools of security forecasting, however, in the timing of stock price changes. Chartists believe that **stocks** move in trends lasting over long periods and that astute investors can profit from these trends if they act when the trends first begin. This supposition is based on two beliefs. First, chartists contend that information about stocks leaks into the market over extended periods. Stock prices change gradually as information moves from industry insiders to analysts and finally to investors. Second, chartists believe that a further time lag occurs because investors do not unanimously agree about the validity of the information or its impact upon the security in question. The gradual nature of price changes gives investors time to act to take advantage of a trend.

Thus, it is the job of the technical analyst to develop a system that can detect the beginning of a movement from one equilibrium price to a new higher or lower price. It must be underscored that chartists are overwhelmingly concerned with detecting the onset of a change in the supply and demand of a stock (or other investment) so that they can benefit from the price changes associated with finding a new equilibrium.

HISTORY AND BACKGROUND

Technical analysis is, perhaps, the oldest form of security analysis. It is believed that the first technical analysis occurred in seventeenth century Japan, where analysts used charts to plot price changes in rice. Indeed, many present-day Japanese analysts still rely on technical analysis to forecast prices in their stock exchange, which is the second largest in the world. In the United States, technical analysis has been used for more than 100 years. This form of analysis was especially helpful at the turn of the century when financial statements were not commonly available to investors.

In recent years, the ever-increasing use of personal computers has led to substantial growth in technical analysis, and numerous **software** packages have been developed to meet these increased needs. Technical analysis can be applied to any pricing trend that is found in an efficient marketplace, such as an open auction. Thus, technical analysis can be applied not only to securities and their markets but also to **bonds**, **commodities**, fixed-income markets, industries within markets, and currencies. Moreover, one of the most popular uses of technical analysis is for futures derivatives.

TRADING RULES

Chartists rely on many rules—often using several at once—when deciding whether to buy, sell, or do nothing with an investment. Some of the best-known rules are contrary opinion rules, rules that follow sophisticated investors, and rules that follow the market prices and volume. As with other types of **forecasting**, however, these rules can be interpreted in a variety of ways, leading to a variety of forecasts using the same information.

The first type, contrary opinion rules, maintains that the majority of investors are incorrect about stock decisions most of the time, but especially at market highs and lows. Thus, when the majority of investors are very bearish, a chartist using this rule would say that it is a good time to buy; conversely, when the majority of investors are bullish, the contrary opinion rule would dictate that selling is the best course of action. A specific example of a contrary rule is the odd-lot theory. In this theory, analysts watch transactions involving amounts less than a round lot (usually 100 shares), called an odd lot. Because this theory contends that small investors are usually wrong in forecasting pricing peaks and troughs, analysts recommend doing the opposite of those actions taken by people purchasing odd lots.

In addition to contrary rules, some chartists follow the activities of investors that they consider to be smart and savvy. An indicator of such activities is Barron's confidence index, which is a bond index comparing Barron's average yield on ten high-grade corporate bonds to the average yield of 40 average bonds on the Dow Jones. This comparison results in a ratio that should never exceed 100 because the 10 high-grade bonds on the numerator should always a have lower average yield than the average bonds on the denominator. In bullish markets, investors tend to take increased risks and buy lower-quality bonds to reap the higher yields; doing this eventually decreases the low-quality yields and, thus, the ratio increases. Conversely, when investors are bearish, they buy safer, high-quality bonds which forces their yield still lower, and the ratio decreases. While this indicator has merit, it can give analysts false information because it is solely based on the demand for bonds and in no way accounts for fluctuations in their supply. If the bond supply suddenly changes, their subsequent yields will also change with little regard to investor preference.

In addition to using some of the above rules, chartists often take into account stock prices and trading volume when making their purchasing decisions. The Dow theory asserts that stock prices move in three different fashions: (1) major, longer-term trends; (2) intermediate trends; and (3) short-run movements. When analyzing stock prices, chartists try to discern which way the long-term pricing trends are heading, realizing that there will be short-lived trends in the opposite direction. In addition to having an interest in stock price changes, chartists are also interested in stocks' trading volumes relative to their normal trading volumes. While a change in stock price indicates the net effect of trading activity, it gives no information on how widespread the public interest is about the stock. Thus, if a stock price increases in an environment of heavy trading and then has a setback in lighter trading, chartists would probably still view it as a bullish stock, thinking that only a few investors were selling to make a profit.

Technical analysts also use the breadth of market measure to influence their decisions. This is a measure that compares the number of stocks that have increased in price, the number that have decreased, and the number that have remained stable. Similarly, the advance-decline series is an aggregated examination of the net stocks gaining and declining each day.

ADVANTAGES AND DISADVANTAGES

As stated earlier, technical analysts make decisions by examining market and security trends with little regard to the cause of those trends. Conversely, fundamental analysts make their decisions by relying on accurate information about companies and markets before it becomes available to the general public. Because technical analysts do not believe that it is possible to receive and process this information quickly enough, many of the advantages relating to technical analysis correspond directly with the disadvantages of **fundamental analysis**.

For example, to project risks and future returns, fundamental analysts depend a great deal on **financial statements** for information on a company's or industry's past performance. Technical analysts believe that there are inherent shortcomings in relying on these statements. First, the incredible variety of accounting methods makes it difficult to compare firms within the same industry and almost impossible to compare those in different industries. Second, financial statements do not contain all of the information that investors need to make sound decisions, such as information on sales of specific products or on the firm's customers. Finally, financial statements do not include any psychological aspects, such as goodwill, that influence stock prices. By observing patterns and information derived by the stock market itself, technical analysts avoid the trappings that often snare fundamental analysts.

The major disadvantage to technical analysis stems from the fact that market prices can change dramatically from seemingly random events. Furthermore, past pricing patterns are not always repeated in the future. Thus, while a forecasting technique can work for a time, it can later miss a major market turn. Another disadvantage of technical analysis is that pricing forecasts can be self-fulfilling prophesies. Thus, if a stock price is predicted to increase when it passes a given price, it sometimes will do so purely because people will buy the stock at the threshold price, expecting it to continue to increase. In this situation, the stock price often returns to its real equilibrium value at a later time. A final problem with chart theory is that there is a great deal of subjective judgment involved in making predictions. Two analysts can look at the same pricing history and arrive at very different pricing projections.

[Kathryn Snavely]

FURTHER READING:

Argenti, Paul A. *The Portable MBA Desk Reference*. NY: John Wiley & Sons, 1994.

DeMark, Thomas R. *The New Science of Technical Analysis*. NY: John Wiley & Sons, 1994.

Downes, John, and Jordan Elliot Goodman. *Barron's Finance and Investment Handbook*. 2nd ed. NY: Barron's, 1987.

Levine, Sumner N., ed. *Financial Analyst's Handbook*. 2nd ed. Homewood, IL: Dow Jones-Irwin, 1988.

Reilly, Frank K. *Investment Analysis and Portfolio Management*. 2nd ed. Drysden Press, 1985.

Reilly, Frank K. *Investments*. 2nd ed. Drysden Press, 1986.

TECHNOLOGY MANAGEMENT

TECHNOLOGY FOR BUSINESS APPLICATIONS

Technology has become the key strategic resource needed for the success, indeed the survival, of a business, corporation, or nation. The recent Persian Gulf War was won by **United Nations** forces in a short time (a ground attack lasting 100 hours in February, 1991), due to the technological sophistication of U.S. weapons and logistic support systems. However, the U.S. electronic optical consumer industry, with $8 billion in sales and 80,000 employees in the 1960's, has been practically destroyed by Japanese competition, because of the latter's continuous innovation in products and manufacturing processes, lower costs, and higher quality.

Technology is the body of knowledge, tools, and techniques derived from science and practical experience used in the development, design, production, and application of products, processes, systems, and services.

Technology is generally available in two forms: disembodied and embodied.

1) Disembodied technology is knowledge and practical expertise recorded in written and electronic form, such as technical papers, drawings, databases, **patents**, and trade secret. The value of disembodied technology depends upon its transferability from donor to recipient, and protection from unauthorized uses. An example of income from disembodied technology is royalties generated from patents.

2) Embodied technology is incorporated in new or improved products, processes, systems, and services, that are offered to the marketplace. The value of embodied technology depends upon the ability of its producer and marketer to obtain a sustainable advantage over competitors, thereby achieving higher share, sales, and profits.

The following four examples illustrate businesses that profited from embodied technology:

1. Incorporating advanced technology in new products. Texas Instruments developed the Speak and Spell toy to teach children and adults for whom English is a second language, the intricacies of English grammar. A simple product that sells in toy and retail stores for a few dollars, it has a sophisticated microchip and voice synthesizer that ''spells'' and ''speaks'' words from its very large dictionary. This proprietary technology was the unique advantage that made Speak and Spell user friendly, inexpensive, and very popular.

2. Incorporating new or improved technology into a manufacturing process. Italian sweaters, designed and knitted by hand, were very popular in the post-World War II era. At that time, the wages and benefits of Italian garment workers increased rapidly, becoming ten times higher than those of workers in Taiwan, the Philippines, and other Asian countries, where the Italian designs were quickly copied. Recently, Italian engineers mastered the techniques of designing new patterns on personal computers using **computer aided design** (CAD) programs, speeding up the design process. They then directly coupled the output of the CAD program to the input of the knitting ma-

chines using **Computer Aided Manufacturing (CAM)** programs. In the past, setting up the sweater-knitting robots to produce a new pattern was a lengthy and complicated process, requiring long runs of the same pattern to keep production costs down. Now the set up is done very rapidly by computer, producing one-of-a-kind patterns. Because many fashion-conscious customers are willing to pay premium prices for these exclusive patterns, the profitability of the producer is assured. In this case, proprietary-process technology was applied to a commodity in order to raise its value and gain a competitive advantage over lower-cost competitors.

3. Having new information systems immediately available wherever needed. Andorra is a small principality of 54,000 inhabitants located in a remote section of the Pyrenees mountains between France and Spain. Except for a small statistical tax on imported goods, it is virtually a tax-free market. In addition, its bank-secrecy laws make it a haven for money deposits. Andorra's principal bank offers competitive interest rates and a sophisticated computer system with up-to-the-minute information on interest and exchange rates worldwide. Taking advantage of such factors and the time zone differences between major exchanges such as New York, London, and Tokyo, short-term investment officers electronically move billions of dollars continously, resulting in profits for investors and banks.

4. Using new technologies to provide rapid, accurate, and securely advanced services, from legal expert systems to credit-card accounting. The General Electric tried in vain to enter the mainframe computer business in competition with IBM, and probably lost one billion dollars in the process from 1960-70. GE, however, was able to utilize its hardware and software to develop the worldwide GE Information System Business for international customers. The system consists of three large computer centers in the United States and Europe, connected by cable and satellite communications and accessible by local direct-dialing from 90 percent of the world's phones. Multinational corporations can use this system for on-line information retrieval, accounting, inventory control, and management information systems. This case illustrates GE's use of proprietary hardware and software to provide a high-value-added service worldwide.

TECHNOLOGY MANAGEMENT

Technology is a highly sophisticated and rapidly changing resource. The average life of a new PC product line is less than three years. As with any business resource, technology must be managed effectively and closely linked to corporate or national strategies and policies. This enables it to create wealth for a corporation or a nation; to improve the quality of life; to minimize physical, economic, and ecological ill effects; and to prevent disasters.

Technology management can be divided into the following categories:

1. Technology assessment (TA), planning, and **forecasting**.

2. Technology development (**Research and Development** and Engineering, R&D&E), acquisition, and integration.

3. **Technology transfer**, application, and sales.

4. Selection of the most appropriate technological strategies in relation to the specific environment, the capabilities and the competitive position of the organization.

TECHNOLOGY ASSESSMENT AND PLANNING

For meaningful and effective technology planning, a business or a corporation needs to evaluate the following:

1. its technological position in relation to competition (technology assessment)

2. the technologies required, in order of priority, to achieve its business objectives (technology planning)

3. the most appropriate technological strategies for achieving its business objectives in relation to trends in the environment, market, competition, government regulation, and the evolution of technology.

Technology assessment should address two questions: 1) Are we working on the ''right'' technologies for our business? 2) What is our competitive position?

TA should be a continuous effort by R & D & E personnel acting as ''technology gatekeepers,'' that is, following the evolution of technologies of interest to the business, as inferred from technical meetings and journals, new patents, new product announcements, and similar sources. Formal technology assessment should be conducted annually, during the preparation of the business's strategic plan, and should include five- to fifteen-year projections, depending on the industry.

Technology assessment should not be handled by R & D & E only, because of possible NIH (Not Invented Here) biases, and the need to be relate to other business functions. CEO's have the option of appointing a corporate multifunctional team. Team members would report directly to the CEO and be augmented by independent consultants who have no NIH bias and have access to information that may not be readily available to the corporation.

Technology assessment can be accomplished in three steps:

1) identification of core technologies,

2) construction of a product technology matrix,

3) and construction of a technology importance/competitiveness matrix.

STEP ONE: CORE TECHNOLOGIES. The core technologies of a business are those critical technologies necessary for advancing the key performance parameters of a company's products, processes, and services. Performance parameters establish a product's value to the customer, and, therefore, influence a company's position in the marketplace. For example, the key performance parameters of a commercial aircraft jet engine are: thrust, weight, fuel consumption, noise, and pollution. Aircraft engine R & D & E has established the following technologies as keys to producing jet engines with high thrust, low weight and acceptable fuel consumption: high temperature high-strength alloys, ceramic coatings to reduce corrosion, powder metallurgy, fluid flow, heat-transfer and noise abatement.

STEP TWO: PRODUCT/TECHNOLOGY MATRIX. Once the core technologies have been identified, the importance of each technology for each product line is established. In the case of aircraft engines, product lines might include military jet engines, commercial jet engines, helicopter engines, and stationary gas turbines that produce electric power from oil or natural gas. When ranking for example, noise abatement is not important for military aircraft engines, quite important for commercial aircraft engines, and less important for stationary gas turbines, which can be provided with baffles and surrounded by isolating walls.

Once the ratings of each core technology for each product line have been determined, they are then ranked according to the relative weight of each product line for the company, (as measured by sales, for example) to determine the rating of the technology for the company. Normally, four levels of importance are adequate: high, medium, low, or none.

STEP THREE: THE TECHNOLOGY IMPORTANCE/ COMPETITIVENESS MATRIX. Next, an assessment is made of the relative competitive position of the company in each core technology. This is done by comparing a company's key product-performance parameters to its competitor's. The business collects such data by talking to customers, manufacturers representatives, dealers, and consultants, and by relying on the "technology gatekeepers." Again, three rating levels are sufficient: the company leads, is equal to, or follows the competition in the specific technology.

We now have two ratings for each core technology: importance to the company, and relative competitive position. These ratings are plotted in Table 1, where the diameter of each circle is proportional to the amount of money budgeted for that specific technology. The aggregate position of the core technologies in the matrix of Table 1 shows the overall competitive standing of the company. A company with more circles in the upper left-hand corner (high-lead) is in a more competitive position than a company with circles scattered all over the matrix or bunched in the lower right-hand corner (low-follow).

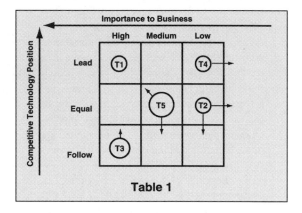

Table 1

The purpose of technology planning is to achieve company objectives through the proper allocation of limited technological, human, physical, and financial resources. In Table 1, the goal is to shift the circles towards the upper left-hand corner (high-lead) of the matrix, and to drop or starve technologies of lesser importance to the company. Examples, taken from the core technologies of GE Medical Systems, are listed here.

In the case of T1, the company leads in this technology, which has high importance for the business. The company's business plan should allocate sufficient effort to maintain this lead and strengthen the company's competitive position in the marketplace. An example of a high-lead technology is GE's Medical System MRI (Magnetic Resonance Imaging) product line.

T2 represents a technology of low importance for the company, although its competitive position is equal to competition. In this case, the company should sell the technology to a business where it is of high or medium importance; otherwise, it will die of starvation and drift out of the matrix. Except for this marketing effort, no further resources should be allocated to this technology. Such was the case of with GE's Ultrasound product line, which was transferred to a joint venture with the Japanese company Yokagawa Electric.

T3 represents a technology of high importance but in a noncompetitive market position. To meet this challenge, the company must focus its efforts in R & D, or acquire the means needed to make the technology competitive. This was the case at GE Medical Systems in 1974. At that time GE was the market leader in conventional X-ray equipment, which was being replaced by a new advanced technology, CAT (Computerized Axial Tomography), developed by the British firm EMI (Electrical and Musical Industries). Stung by a staggering loss of market share and the prospect of falling behind the competition, GE started a crash program in the Corporate R & D Center in order to overtake EMI's lead. Utilizing assets lacking at EMI—manufacturing, market, sales and service—GE Medical Systems met its goal in three years, making it a worldwide leader in CAT. EMI eventually sold what was left of its medical business to GE.

T4 depicts a company leading in a technology that is of low importance to the company. This company has two options: sell the technology or develop a new product line, which could generate substantial sales and profits. Technological superiority does not guarantee new product success (as happened in the case of EMI). The company must establish the manufacturing, marketing, and financial resources required for successfully launching a new product line. This was the situation at GE when its R & D Center developed MRI technology without the concurrence of GE Medical Systems management; eventually they adopted the technology.

Finally, T5 represents a technology whose value to the company is unclear. Both technical and strategic planning should be continued, in order to determine whether it warrants additional technical effort.

Up to now, the discussion of technology assessment and planning has been based on present core technologies. Each technology, however, has a limited life cycle, which could last only two or three years (for certain types of semiconductors) or as long as 40 years (for steam turbines). It is necessary, therefore, to include future core technologies in technology assessment and planning processes. These are the technologies that have a strong potential of displacing and replacing present core technologies. Computers, for example, initially used electro-mechanical relays, and later, vacuum tubes. These were replaced first by transistors, then by IC's (Integrated Circuits), currently by microchips, and in the future, possibly by super-conducting Josephson junctions or laser optics.

TECHNOLOGY APPLICATION AND SALES

As an asset, technology may be acquired or sold, stolen, wasted, made obsolete, or applied for company growth and profitability. Once technology has been developed or procured, it is part of a company's assets, and, as such, has value. Technology can be an intangible asset, hard to define, evaluate, or safeguard; therefore, it is difficult and risky to manage. Intellectual property, for example, can be lost if the holder leaves a company without transferring the technology to others. Thus, technology has no value for the company unless it is applied through embodiment in new or improved products, processes, systems, and services, or sold or transferred to other parties. In established companies, the originator of the technology, usually the R & D division, is separate from the user of the technology, usually the manufacturing and marketing departments. Therefore, the technology must be transferred across human, geographical, and organizational barriers, not a simple or smooth process.

Technology application is the practical utilization of technological assets to achieve customer satisfaction, to gain a competitive advantage in the market, and/or to improve the quality of life. In the past, the time span from technology development to application was lengthy. For example, it took 12 years for scientists to develop the first commercial application of the laser after its discovery in 1960. There is evidence that the time span between technology development and application is shortening, as evidenced by the Japanese electronic and electro-optical consumer industry and by the U.S. biotechnology industry.

Just as any company faces a make-or-buy alternative for obtaining technology, it also faces an apply-or-sell alternative for converting its technological assets into profits. Selling technology may be an attractive alternative for a company to cash in its technological assets, rather than go through the costly and risky process of technology application, and of new product, process, or service development. Following are factors to consider when making the apply-or-sell decision:

1. Strategic Fit. R & D may develop new valuable technologies that have no strategic fit with corporate objectives. For example, while working at the General Electric R & D center, Nobel laureate Ivar Giaever obtained several patents used in the detection of infectious diseases. As GE had no intention of competing with the pharmaceutical industry, it sold the patents to two new ventures for a limited amount of cash and a minority equity position.

2. Obsolescence. As a company develops improved technology, it must decide what to do with its older technology. The company has the option of selling the technology to a developing country with less sophisticated needs and lower production ex-

penses. GE, for example, sold its outmoded copper forming technology to Poland.

3. High Investments. Normally, R & D expenditures comprise 10 to 30 percent of the total cost of bringing a new product to market. Manufacturing investment, marketing/sales costs, advertising/sales promotion, and customer education usually constitute higher costs than R & D. If a company has difficulty raising additional financing, it may sell the technology to, or enter into a joint venture with, a large, well-established company with plenty of liquid assets. Many emerging biotechnology companies contribute only the technology to a joint-venture, with the established company providing cash and marketing expertise.

4. Closed Markets. For various reasons (trade barriers, for example), some markets may be closed to the company that developed the technology. For example, GE Power Systems developed heavy-duty gas turbines as an alternative to electricity, and had the leading market share in the United States. GE wanted to expand its market to Europe, where the demand for electricity was growing rapidly. However, in most European countries, power utilities are government-owned and, for political reasons, buy only from local suppliers. GE, therefore, had no choice but to enter into cooperative agreements with leading Italian, German and Spanish electrical-equipment manufacturers. The high-technology rotor was built in the United States and shipped to the customer site; the lower technology stator and housing were manufactured by local partners, who were also responsible for sales, installation, and maintenance. GE did not license its rotor technology and therefore, avoided possible leaks to European competitors. GE guaranteed the performance of the entire system, however.

5. Preempting Competitors. Once a proprietary technology has been developed, there is always the risk of a competitor developing an equal or better technology. To preempt the competitor, a company may sell the technology to the competitor at a reasonable price. The seller is at an advantage as the competitor will have increased production costs; may have to pay royalties, which can amount to a great percentage of sales; and may abandon the idea of developing a superior technology. In such agreements, there is often a cross-licensing clause, giving the licensor company direct access to any improvements made by the licensees, and the right to visit the buyer's plants and audit their books. For instance, GE developed and held a manufacturing-technology patent for, the first man-made industrial diamonds. Nonetheless, GE decided to license its main competitor, the South African diamond-mining company DeBeers, to preempt them, increase their costs, and, of course, make a profit.

6. Standards. As a product and an industry matures, rigid standards are established to facilitate interconnection of equipment and parts replacement, and to reduce operating costs. Various companies aggressively seek to have their specific technologies adopted as industry standards, at times giving away technology free to competitors in order to speed up the adoption process. Sun Microsystems, the leading producer of workstations, once sent engraved invitations to competitors to visit their display booths at trade fairs and obtain a free copy of the proposed standards. Sun wanted to convince competitors to adopt its standards, thereby expanding the market for compatible workstations and related software applications.

7. Multiple Sourcing. No company or organization is comfortable being dependant on a single supplier for vital components or products. Therefore, large buyers, such as the United States military or IBM, insist that their preferred supplier license other potential suppliers to ensure a steady flow of goods in cases of strikes, calamities, shortages of materials, and so forth. Having multiple sources also can prevent arbitrary price escalations by the initial supplier.

8. Cross-licensing. New technologies being developed by businesses may violate existing patents held by competitors. To avoid costly litigation and royalty payments, several large corporations may enter into cross-licensing agreements that exempt their core technologies. For many years GE, AT&T, and IBM had royalty-free cross-licensing agreements for patents not pertaining to core technologies. GE excluded new alloys for jet engines, and steam and gas turbines; AT&T, switching systems; and IBM, computer architecture.

9. Antitrust. While a patent is a legal monopoly for 17 years, the U.S. government contends that it cannot be used to violate antitrust laws. Therefore, if a company achieves a dominant market position because of its unique technology, it may be subject to antitrust investigations and litigation. For example, the U.S. Antitrust Division forced the Xerox Corp. to license its copier patents to its weaker U.S. competitors (this occured long before the Japanese moved in the U.S. copier market). As a result, many companies today prefer to license to their competitors, to avoid such a problem.

10. Joint ventures. In some cases, a company doesn't have the expertise needed to market a new technology. As a result, one company may contribute the technology; and a second, the marketing know-how, distribution channels, local sales and service, and so forth, creating a joint venture. GE Medical Systems entered into such an agreement with the Japanese company Yokagawa Electric, to develop the Japanese and Far Eastern Markets.

In conclusion, the main reasons for selling technology rather than incorporating it into new products are the desires to reduce exposure and risk, and to make a quick profit, even if the gain is less than one realized over a technology life cycle or patent validity.

TECHNOLOGICAL STRATEGIES

Technology is a valuable asset that a corporation can and should employ to gain a competitive advantage in the market. This can be achieved by utilizing business strategies in which technology is a major component. The choice of the most appropriate technological strategy for a business depends upon the environment, its strengths and weaknesses in relation to the competition, and the resources available—not only technological but also manufacturing, marketing, sales, distribution, and financial. Mixed strategies are utilized, but may cause organizational problems when implemented. Four basic technological strategies are:

(1) first to market;

(2) fast follower and overtaker;

(3) cost minimization;

(4) market niche or specialist.

FIRST TO MARKET. The first to market strategy is offensive, with a high risk and reward potential. This strategy is implemented after a radically innovative technology is discovered by chance or by design, and then is embodied in a product of high functional utility for the customer. It is often used by high-tech new ventures, such as the MapInfo company, for PC map displays; and by progressive, established firms with plenty of resources, such as GE, for man-made diamonds and engineering plastics. If the company's competitive advantage can be maintained, the company enjoys a temporary monopoly or quasi-monopoly that can be exploited to optimize sales and profits. This was the case for GE's man-made diamonds and its first engineering plastic, Lexan. Scientists discovered these products in GE's R & D Center while researching the behavior of simple elements, such as carbon, under high pressure and temperature; and a hard enamel for insulating copper wires. GE recognized the potential value of these inventions, devoted plenty of resources to their development and application, and waited patiently (ten years, in the case of Lexan) for the cash flow to become productive. Due to this strategy, GE Plastics, launched in 1957, is now a $5 billion business.

Long-term first-to-market strategy success requires more than a technology breakthrough. It is also necessary either to continue producing new products based on technological and market innovation, or to maintain market leadership through continuous price reduction, which in turn, depends upon cost reductions. This is not always easy, as shown by VisiCalc, the pioneer company that developed the first **spreadsheets** software program for personal computers. After the initial success, VisiCalc was not willing or able to develop an improved version or a second product; it was overtaken by Lotus Development Corporation, and is now bankrupt.

MapInfo is a case in contrast. It was founded by four Rensselaer Polytechnic Institute students who had developed, as part of their computer science project, the first program for displaying maps on a PC. They offered their first software package for only $750, making it affordable to the 30 million IBM-compatible PC owners worldwide. To stay ahead of competition, every few months, MapInfo introduces advanced versions of the first program, and new packages with additional functions. It has grown rapidly from $60,000 sales in 1987 to $34 million in 1994.

FAST FOLLOWER . . . AND OVERTAKER. After a pioneer has demonstrated that a technology actually works, and that the market is receptive to the innovation, a fast follower can move in rapidly, capture a large market share, and even overtake the first entrant. To succeed with this strategy, the fast follower should not duplicate the product of the pioneer and rely on lower production costs, as is practiced by some companies in the Pacific Rim. Rather, the fast follower should practice innovative imitation by offering a similar product that can be differentiated from the first entrant's offering. Fast followers capitalize on their existing complementary assets, such as production facilities, marketing channels, customer contacts, company image, and so forth, in order to achieve a substantial market share and even surpass the leader.

This was the case of with first IBM Personal Computer. Stung by the unexpected success of the Apple II, IBM started a crash program to develop its personal computer. Director Don Estridge was given a blank check to secure all the needed resources, make or buy the technology, and organize his project-team. In less than one year, his team developed the IBM PC, more or less equivalent in performance and price to Apple II. However, IBM's PC was painted "bright blue." That is, IBM relied on its strong image in the marketplace, and a large base of loyal customers, thereby commanding a market share equal to Apple's.

GE presents another example of a fast follower. In the field of Computerized Axial Tomography, GE differentiated its offerings from developer EMI's not only through improved performance, but also through its well respected trademark, extended warranties, application engineering, customer training, and endorsements by leading doctors and clinics.

COST MINIMIZATION. The cost minimization strategy is effective for mass-produced goods, where significant economies of scale can be realized through process innovation. This strategy has been successfully used by the Japanese and other Pacific Rim countries to gain dominant market share in consumer electronics, IBM-compatible PC clones, and even the fashion industry.

As a technology matures, products become standardized, functional differences between various brands decline in importance, personal selling is replaced by mass marketing, and price becomes the dominant factor in the customer's decision to buy. To minimize production costs, product innovation is gradually replaced by process innovation, utilizing the learning curve, which projects declining unit costs as volume increases. Similarly, marketing and distribution costs are reduced—for instance, by telemarketing, direct mail sales, and discount stores. Utilizing the cost minimization strategy, the company strives to become the lowest cost producer and, therefore, the price leader. By reducing selling price and production costs according to the learning curve, the company forces less efficient competitors to withdraw; the market stabilizes, and the company increases its market share and profits.

In some cases, the company can practice "forward pricing" below actual costs, in anticipation of the learning curve; this will "shake out" competition, but also, more importantly, discourages more powerful potential competitors from market entry. Because of possible antitrust litigation, this practice is more common in Japan than in the United States among computer manufacturers.

To succeed with cost minimization, a business needs superior process-engineering and value analysis skills. In addition, a company must strive to reduce its total costs, not just manufacturing costs, while maintaining a high level of quality. Most customers will not, however, trade lower costs for lower quality. Detroit discovered this when it produced compact cars after the first oil crisis, to compete with the Europeans and Japanese. While Detroit's prices were 15 to 20 percent lower than their foreign competitors, the quality of its cars—measured by the number of defects in a new car—was one-third to one-half of foreign competitors. As a result, American consumers were willing to pay premiums of $1,000 to $1,500 per car and wait several months for the Japanese models, while the American versions sat unsold in dealers' lots.

MARKET NICHE OR SPECIALIST. The market niche or specialist strategy is generally adopted by new high-tech ventures that are searching for "a place in the sun" in competition with established dominant suppliers. In the early days of the computer industry, Digital Equipment Corp., Wang, and Control Data Corp. all adopted this strategy to compete with IBM. Normally the selected market niche is initially of little or no interest to the dominant supplier, who is willing to let competitors develop it. For instance, IBM avoided serving the R & D laboratories, and university scientific computing and data acquisition markets, because of their limited size. In addition, laboratory researchers and university professors demanded special features, nonstandard components, and complex application engineering that IBM was unable or unwilling to provide. Digital Equipment Corp. (DEC) and Control Data were willing and able to provide specialist services for this small but rapidly growing market. Similarly, Wang developed the word processor market niche, a hybrid of electronic typewriters and small computers, and for a while, competed successfully with IBM and Olivetti.

To succeed, a market niche must be carefully selected and followed. If the market niche is too small, it will be saturated within a relatively short time, for the growth opportunity is limited. For example, Control Data Corp., to increase sales, was forced to abandon its original profitable but limited niche of data acquisition and control systems and compete directly with IBM in data processing, an area with low profits and fluctuations in market share.

Conversely, if the niche becomes too large, it becomes an attractive target for competitors. Cray Research illustrates this point. Cray was the original leader in the then-limited, but highly profitable market niche for supercomputers. Seymour Cray founded the company in 1972 with a mission "to design and build a larger more powerful computer than anyone now has." Initially the market niche was quite small, estimated at 80 users worldwide in 1976. The niche grew to a $1 billion market in 1990, with large companies, such as Control Data, IBM, Fujitsu, and Hitachi entering the market. Cray Research lost market share, encountered serious cash flow problems, and had to cut back on its advanced R & D efforts.

Another danger of the market niche strategy is that the niche may be detroyed by new technology. For instance, Wang's word processor market was eliminated by the rapid progress in micro-computer technology. While word processors are limited in their functions, the PC's features include computations, spread sheet calculations, graphics, and word processing, making them the preferred office tool.

To succeed with the market niche or specialist strategy, a company should be very selective in accepting orders that entail too much specialization. Such orders require excessive and expensive efforts in development and design engineering to meet the customer's unique specifications. A company can eventually becomes a "job shop," adapting its designs to serve various customers, but unable to reduce costs according to the learning curve. The secret is to have one or two basic designs that can be easily and rapidly adapted to meet customer requirements, while utilizing various factory and software operations.

In conclusion, the most important factor for effective technology management is the close coupling of technology and business strategies, and the cooperation of the R&D&E functions with the manufacturing, marketing, and financial functions.

[Pier A. Abetti]

FURTHER READING:

Abetti, Pier A. *Linking Technology and Business Strategy.* New York: American Management Association, 1989.

Betz, Frederick. *Strategic Technology Management.* New York: McGraw Hill, 1993.

Burgelman, Robert A. and Modesto A. Maidique. *Strategic Management of Technology and Innovation.* Homewood IL: Irwin, 1988.

Martin, Michael J.C. *Managing Technological Innovation and Entrepreneurship.* Reston VA: Reston, 1984.

TECHNOLOGY TRANSFER

Technology transfer refers to the use of a technology or a technological knowledge in a country or region other than that in which it originally developed. While technology is transferred across developed countries as well as across less developed countries (LDCs), technology transfer often refers specifically to transfers from the more advanced countries to LDCs. In this sense, technology transfer is central to the study of newly developing economies.

In his essay, "International Business and the Transborder Movement of Technology," Denis Simon defined three classes of technology transfer: material transfer, design transfer, and capacity transfer. Material transfer refers to physical goods ranging from product parts to fully operational plants. Design transfer refers to blueprints or other types of information used to build products or production facilities. Capacity transfer refers to education and training not only to operate existing plants but also to develop innovations in products and processes.

Technology transfer takes place through a number of different channels. Key among these are foreign **direct investment**, **licensing agreements**, joint ventures, research universities, and government-sponsored programs. Multinational corporations, particularly those based in the United States, Western Europe, and Japan, act as major transferrers of technology to LDCs. The newly industrialized countries of the Pacific Rim—including Taiwan, Hong Kong, South Korea, and Singapore—along with Brazil and India have recently emerged as significant sources of transferred technologies.

Japan is often referred to as a case of an advanced country that developed in large part through technology transfer. Previously developed capitalist countries such as England, the United States and Germany relied to a larger extent on domestically produced technologies. Japan's developmental success in the post war years provides a contrast with the patterns observed in many LDCs. In particular, many LDCs have depended heavily on exports of raw materials, the prices for which are often highly unstable in world markets, and have consequently run up large trade deficits and suffered from large debt burdens. Part of the appeal of technology transfer is that it creates the possibility for development that is less reliant on native sources of raw materials and more self-sustaining.

One of the central problems regarding technology transfer is whether the technology is "appropriate" for the recipient country. For example, technologies that are highly capital intensive may be transferred to a country in which there is substantial underemployment of labor. Transferred technologies may also require technically sophisticated workers and managers or natural resources that are in short supply in the recipient country. The problem of appropriate technologies suggests that substantial planning is generally required for technology transfer to be beneficial. At the same time, the problem highlights the potential conflicts between the interests of multinationals and the long-term development of recipient countries.

Education is a vital part of the technology transfer process and of the development process more generally. A gap often exists between the technical education levels in source and recipient countries. Employees must have sufficient training to efficiently operate and maintain machinery. More than that, **innovation** and **research and development** typically require highly educated technicians. LDCs often attempt to minimize their technical dependence on outside sources such that they are able to generate innovation from within, creating the possibility of a more self-sustaining development process.

The role of education becomes increasingly critical with the expansion of electronics-based and other medium- to high-tech goods. Accordingly, new product and process development generally requires a higher level of technical knowledge. At the same time, a larger share of all manufacturing production is beginning to be controlled by computers in highly integrated processes.

The viability of technology transfer is determined by the general level of industrial development in LDCs. New technologies are more readily able to be implemented if similar or complementary technologies have been previously established. Key among these considerations is the capacity of producers within an LDC to serve as suppliers of parts or services. Whether a transferred technology can be supported by suppliers within the country has a potentially large impact on the competitiveness of production, given the potentially higher costs of relying on parts from abroad as well as the greater lead times involved. In addition, toxin-producing industrial processes are potentially much more problematic in LDCs. These processes require pollution-abatement technologies in order to control environmental damage, technologies which are generally less well developed in LDCs.

Since the late 1970s, American universities have played an increasingly important role in the development and transfer of new technologies. Particularly important have been developments in electronics and biotechnology. Research expenditures have came primarily from the top 100 universities, which receive about 80 percent of research funding. The federal government has provided two-thirds of total university research funds, with private industry providing a relatively small though rapidly growing share.

The emphasis of the top U.S. research universities on the commercial applications of research had resulted from a widespread perception that the United State was losing out to its international competitors in both basic and applied research. This led government, industry, and university representatives to undertake initiatives to develop new linkages between companies and top research universities. Among these linkages were university ownership of **equity** in firms established on the basis of university research, liaison or technical assistance programs, research partnerships, and the establishment by universities of patent and technology licensing offices. Many top research universities in the United States took the route of equity ownership in start-up companies. It was argued that this method facilitated technology transfer, created the possibility of large financial gain for universities, and helped to attract and retain faculty.

Multinational firms engage in technology transfer through licensing arrangements with non-affiliated firms or through foreign direct investment with affiliated firms. These are sometimes referred to as external or internal technology transfer, respectively. Multinationals generally prefer internal technology transfer. In his essay, "Contractual Agreements and International Technology Transfer," Bernard Bonin described this preference as follows: "Foreign direct investment is normally preferred since the owner of the technology is thus in a position to capture all the rents attached to his technological advantage, while licensing is more risky in this regard. Contractual agreements will be entered into only when the potential benefit from intangible assets cannot be otherwise exploited."

There are a number of factors that impede technology transfer within a firm, making external transfer

more viable. Smaller firms may lack the resources to engage in direct investment. Firms may have inadequate managerial experience in overseas production and marketing. In other cases, the host country may restrict foreign direct investment, leaving licensing as the only option. More generally, firms are more inclined to license older products and processes, for which the relative technological advantage and profitability are generally less.

One of the contentious issues surrounding technology transfer is the means by which the success of such transfers should be evaluated. Traditionally the success of development has been measured in terms of the growth rate of **gross national product** (GNP) or per capita gross national product. This measure has been criticized on several grounds. For one, it does not take into account income distribution. In his *Strategic Planning in Technology Transfer to Less Developed Countries*, Christian Madu summarized other limitations of national income measures as follows: "Understanding the LDC's socio-economic structure and how it differs from that of the developed countries will help in the development of appropriate standards for measuring growth. For example, a major flaw of GNP is that it fails to take into account social costs due to industrial waste, crime, congestion, and different perceptions of the inhabitants about their changing environment in evaluating the nation's performance." New "quality of life" measures have been developed in recent years to complement GNP-based measures in evaluating technology transfer and other economic development policies.

The pace of technology transfer increased rapidly after the 1970s. This resulted from the growth of foreign direct investment by multinational corporations as well as by the increased use of outsourcing of product components in the international market. More generally, the growth of technology transfer reflects the increasingly international perspective of corporations. The growth in recent years was also an outcome of earlier technology transfers, in that these earlier transfers enabled a greater number of countries to act as important sources of technology. Technology transfer has been greatly facilitated by improvements in international transport and communications, enabling firms to more readily control operations across the globe. The growing transfer of technology was also facilitated by the establishment of free trade agreements within North America and Europe.

Government policy plays a large role in the issue of technology transfer. The advanced capitalist countries typically have policies that restrict the outflow of certain technologies. Among these are military equipment or technologies with potential military applications. **Exporting** technologies may also be restricted in an effort to protect competitive advantages in certain high-tech goods. Among these goods are supercomputers and superconductors. The government policies of LDCs vary widely in the extent to which they regulate technology transfers. While many LDCs compete with each other to accommodate multinational corporations, others restrict foreign ownership, **foreign investment**, and joint ventures.

U.S. government regulation of technology transfer in the postwar years was shaped in large part by the Cold War. The Export Control Act of 1949 authorized the president to regulate exports on the grounds of short supply and national security, as well as to achieve foreign policy objectives. In that same year, the United States and six European countries formed the **Coordinating Committee for Multilateral Export Control** (COCOM) in an effort to carry out strategic embargoes, particularly against China and the Soviet Union. COCOM was not strongly effective in these years since some of these European countries sought to increase trade with the Communist powers. Consequently the United States relied on the Export Controls Act to attach restrictions to technologies licensed to allied and neutral countries in an effort to control the reexport of these technologies. Congress extended the act in 1953.

Exports to the Warsaw Pact countries increased during the Nixon administration with the Export Administration Act of 1969 and with détente. With the Soviet invasion of Afghanistan in 1979 and the election of Ronald Reagan in 1980 came the move toward greater restriction of technology transfers. The U.S. Department of Commerce came to play a leading role in the regulation of nonmilitary exports, and the staff of the Export Administration unit of the department increased by fourfold through the 1980s. Similar expansions occurred in the export-control divisions of U.S. Customs and the departments of Defense and State. Many U.S. businesses complained that these regulations substantially hurt their sales and their capacity to develop new technologies. Restrictions on technology transfer were progressively loosened in trade legislation enacted after the mid-1980s. New laws and regulations sought to situate the issue of export controls in light of general trade considerations as well as national security interests. Entering the 1990s, the collapse of the Eastern Bloc and the expansion of trade to China created possibilities for substantial increases of technology transfer from the United States and other advanced capitalist countries.

[David Kucera]

FURTHER READING:

Agmon, Tamir, and Mary Ann von Glinow, eds. *Technology Transfer in International Business*. Oxford University Press, 1991.

Bonin, Bernard. "Contractual Agreements and International Technology Tranfers: the Empirical Studies." In *Multinationals, Governments, and International Technology Transfer*, edited by A. E. Safarian, and Gilles Bertin. St. Martin's Press, 1987.

Dakin, Karl J., and Jennifer Lindsay. *Technology Transfer: Financing and Commercializing the High Tech Product or Service: From Research to Roll Out*. Probus Publishing, 1991.

Gee, S. *Technology Transfer, Innovation and International Competitiveness*. John Wiley & Sons, 1981.

Guile, Bruce, and Harvey Brooks, eds. *Technology and Global Industry*. National Academy Press, 1987.

Madu, Christian N. *Strategic Planning in Technology Transfer to Less Developed Countries*. Quorum Books, 1992.

Mansfield, Edwin, and others. *Technology Transfer, Productivity and Economic Policy*. Norton, 1982.

Matkin, Gary W. *Technology Transfer and the University*. Macmillan Publishing Company, 1990.

Simon, Denis. "International Business and the Transborder Movement of Technology: A Dialectic Perspective." In *Technology Transfer in International Business*, edited by Tamir Agmon and Mary Ann von Glinow. Oxford University Press, 1991.

TELECOMMUNICATIONS

Telecommunications is a business tool, every bit as essential to an enterprise as personnel, capital, and marketing. To a manager, telecommunications is synonymous with access—access to capital, access to markets, access to information. It does this by enabling a manager to act as immediately as possible in making a decision. This is increasingly important as time becomes a greater competitive factor.

Telecommunications is by definition electronic and nearly universal. As a result, it enables communication to occur instantaneously with nearly three billion people—almost half the world's population—almost anywhere in the world.

But the applications go far beyond mere conversations, as important as those may be. Various forms of data are transmitted by means of telecommunication, from simple facsimiles, to on-line computer messages, to massive information downloads that might include financial, medical, or scientific data. The proliferation of ever more efficient networks, banded together to form one gigantic network, provide users as well as service providers with tremendous economies of scale. The result is a business resource that can establish agreements and contracts, maintain good relationships, and even provide products. As a result, good management of the telecommunications system is essential.

HISTORICAL DEVELOPMENT OF TELECOMMUNICATIONS

Telecommunications has its origin with telegraphy in 1844, when Samuel Morse (1791-1872) developed the capability to send pulses of electric current over wires that spanned distances farther than one could shout, walk, or ride. The mechanics involved a battery power source, a key switch to pass or interrupt the flow of current, wires to carry the signal to another location, and a receiving device that used current to operate a magnet that pulled on a metal armature to produce an audible click.

Morse developed the first application of discrete signals for telegraphy, using a lexicon of multiple long and short closures of the circuit to represent letters and numbers—known as Morse code. Telegraph operators used Morse code to send messages between stations located in different cities.

Due to the costs involved in setting up this network of operators linked by wires, the commercialization of telegraphy required that the service be offered at a price that only businesses could afford. Thus the first telecommunications network, using telegraphy, was largely a business-to-business enterprise whose dominant provider was the Western Union company.

Even with extremely fast key operators and massive networks consisting of hundreds of wires between locations, telegraph companies were unable to meet the rising demand for their services. This is because each wire could carry only one message at a time. In order to maximize the capacity of the wires already in place, several entrepreneurs tried to develop a system in which several messages could be sent over the same circuit using several harmonically discrete signals.

One of these experimenters was Alexander Graham Bell (1847-1922) who, in developing such a system, stumbled on the principle of telephony— transmission of a voice signal. When Bell's assistant Thomas Watson (1854-1934) flicked a telegraph armature to release it from its magnet, Bell heard the ring of the armature. This convinced him that sounds could be made to influence a magnetic field, and that these fluctuations in the magnetic force could be translated into an electrical signal that could operate a speaker.

In the celebrated event of his discovery, Bell set up his device, but spilled battery acid on his lap. He called for Watson, who was in a laboratory down the hallway. When Watson arrived, he reported that he had heard Bell's cry over the wires.

The two worked diligently to prepare a patent application, but in the oddest coincidence, filed their patent the very same day as Elisha Gray (1835-1901), another inventor who had developed a similar but slightly superior device. After an acrimonious 17-year legal battle, Bell was awarded the patent in 1876.

But Bell had tremendous difficulty selling his invention. He failed to interest Western Union, which maintained that there was no use for such a toy when key operators could communicate faster than people could talk. To raise money, Bell demonstrated his invention in sideshows, and eventually raised enough to set up the Bell Telephone Company with networks in Boston and New York, and even acquired Gray's rival Western Electric company.

As the telephone grew in popularity, it became obvious that Western Union had failed to appreciate the greatest asset of the telephone: *anyone*, not just skilled key operators, could use it. With the prospect of serving a thousand times as many accounts, Western Union scrambled to get in on the business and hired Thomas Edison to develop a superior telephone unrelated to Bell's patent. Bell sued and won, winning the right to acquire Western Union's telephone network and the patent rights on Edison's vastly improved telephone.

Bell's American Telephone & Telegraph Company (AT&T) unfairly muscled hundreds of other independent telephone companies into lopsided mergers. This invited U.S. Department Justice intervention in 1914, whereby AT&T was enjoined from further acquisitions and was declared a regulated monopoly.

During this time, a Kansas City undertaker named Almon Strowger noted a steady decline in his business. He suspected the culprit was the local operator, who was married to a competing mortician. Telephony was impractical as a strictly point-to-point system; it required operators to switch calls from one person to any number of others on the network. Strowger set out to develop an automatic switching system that used a dial on the telephone to mechanically switch calls without intervention from an operator. Thus, the automatic switch was born.

The telecommunications network remained basically unchanged for half a century. Due to its pre-1914 acquisitions, AT&T had monopolized the nation's largest markets and ran the only long distance network. During the 1960s, AT&T developed a touch-tone dialing system, using audible signaling tones, to replace the dial and its electromechanical switches.

More importantly, in 1968 the Carterfone company won the right to connect its own brand of equipment to the AT&T-dominated network. This cleared the way for other competing manufacturers to enter the market.

But also that year, an upstart company called MCI Communications Corp. established a long distance network separate from AT&T's, using microwave communications. Others followed, including GTE, which built another long distance network out of the Southern Pacific Railroad's sprawling private telephone system—an enterprise called Sprint.

In 1982, several decades of antitrust action against AT&T by the U.S. Department of Justice resulted in a consent decree in which AT&T agreed to divest its 22 local service Bell companies. The divestiture, which took place in 1984, created seven independent "Baby Bells" and left AT&T only with its long distance operations, its Bell Labs research group, and the Western Electric manufacturing division. It also cleared the way for competition in the long distance market.

TELECOMMUNICATIONS SYSTEMS AND COMPONENTS

The events since 1984 are difficult to chronicle because many issues related to organization and regulation remain to be settled. As a result, this section will deal with the mechanical and administrative aspects of the network, particularly as they relate to business.

In its simplest form, the telecommunications system is a network of terminal devices that are connected to switches by countless miles of wire. The terminal devices include telephones, fax machines, modems, computers, and other equipment. The switches are actually integrated systems that direct calls to another location and condition the signals for transmission. The connections between the caller, the switches, and the party called consist of copper wire, coaxial cable, fiber-optic cable, and even radio waves.

Each piece of terminal equipment is connected to the network with inside wire or building cable. This wire is connected to the public network at a terminal box, or "point of presence," where it meets telephone company wires that lead it to a central office or end office.

Each of these connections is called a local loop, because it consists of a single pair of wires. One sends current from the central office to the terminal equipment, and the other carries it back to the central office. The circuit is broken until a telephone is lifted off its switch hook. This allows current to flow through the circuit, signaling the central office switch that a request for service has been made.

The switch then provides dial tone, indicating that it is ready to receive instructions from the caller. These instructions are an address, or telephone number, which tell the switch where to send the call. If the call is to another number served by the same central office, the switch simply sets up a connection between the caller and the person being called.

If the call is to a number served by another central office, the switch sends the call over an interoffice trunk to the central office serving that number, and the switch at that location makes the final connection.

If the call is going a great distance, say to another state, it will direct the call over another type of trunk to a tandem toll office, which will send the call over long distance lines to a counterpart, and direct the call to another local office serving the party being called. This hierarchy of switching systems is necessary to support the immense number of telephone numbers that have been assigned.

Calls fall into roughly four billing categories, based on the mileage involved. Local calls generally run up to 8 miles, while zone calls cover distances up to 15 miles. Local long distance runs up to 40 miles or so, and distances beyond that are long distance calls. All but local calls are billed according to the duration of the call.

With the divestiture of the Bell System, the **Federal Communications Commission** established local access transport areas, or LATAs. These LATAs comprise the areas in which the Bell companies may complete calls alone. A call to someone in another LATA must be carried by a long distance company, or interexchange carrier (sometimes called an IXC).

LATAs were created to ensure that local Bell companies do not compete in the long distance market. But in addition to the Bell companies, several hundred independent telephone companies exist that are not bound by LATA restrictions because their presence is not nearly as ubiquitous. In most cases, they have no choice but to hand the call off to an IXC or another local telephone company.

The basic telephone circuit is engineered to carry a voice grade level of bandwidth, comprising 300 to 3300 Hertz. Several conversations may be carried over the same pair of wires through various forms of multiplexing.

Frequency division multiplexing literally stacks different conversations by changing their frequency, much like an FM radio signal. Filtering equipment can "tune in" to whichever conversation it is supposed to hear. Time division multiplexing gives each conversation one twenty-fourth of a given transmission period to pass over the wires. Sampling equipment can reconstruct all 24 conversations with completely adequate quality.

The wires used to transmit the calls are called facilities. An ordinary twisted wire pair can support several dozen voice grade conversations. Coaxial cable has greater bandwidth capacity, and can carry up to 10,800 different conversations. Fiber-optic cable, which operates on the concept of digital light pulses, rather than analog waveforms, has an even greater capacity, handling millions of signals simultaneously.

By and large, digital systems are more accurate than analog because they allow error correction. Over great distances, analog signals must be amplified. But in amplifying the conversation, intermediate transmission equipment also amplifies electrical "noise" that enters the circuit.

By contrast, digital signals are regenerated, meaning that transmission equipment hears the message being sent, but rather than amplifying it, it repeats what it has heard. Included in the stream of information are signals that ensure the transmission equipment has heard correctly. If it has not, the system will ask to hear it again and make adjustments, such as changing its timing, to correct the error. The result is a transmission of nearly perfect quality. This is why a long distance call from Hong Kong to Chicago can sound as clear as a call from next door.

Digital signals also are the common language of computer equipment. As a result, in order to be carried over the telephone network, digital computer signals do not have to be translated into analog signals and then turned back into digital signals to be understood.

However, most fax machines *do* work this way. In reading a piece of paper, the scanner in a fax machine signals where it sees black and where it does not. But in transmitting, the information is translated into a series of changes in an analog waveform. This complex signal can be sent over a voice grade line and give accurate instructions to another fax machine where to print black and where to print nothing. Newer generation fax machines use digital technology.

In handling a call, telephone switching equipment determines billing information by reading the identity of the line in use. As it switches the call to interoffice trunks, it provides that identity along with the number being dialed. This information is called automatic number identification, or ANI.

ANI allows every carrier associated in completing the call to properly assign charges. Recently, telephone companies have allowed consumers to use ANI by providing a service called Caller ID, that reveals the billing number on a small display device. Caller ID enables the called party to see the number, and in some cases the billing name, of the person calling even before he or she answers.

A more ominous use of ANI is made by inbound **telemarketing** organizations. By calling the telemarketer's 800 number, customers can reveal their ANI code. The company's computer can be instructed to match a customer record with the incoming call so that when an attendant answers, he or she already has the customer's purchasing and credit history on a computer screen.

These types of business systems are highly complex and always involve the use of private branch exchanges (PBXs). The PBX is a miniature telephone switch owned and operated by a company for its own use. It allows calls to be completed between offices without using telephone company facilities. PBXs can span several buildings and, with connections provided by telephone companies, can even link sites in different states or countries.

In some instances, a PBX will connect two different sites with a point-to-point connection that is not switched, called a dedicated circuit. These lines are constantly connected between the two points to ensure that access between the sites is always available. Dedicated circuits use telephone company facilities and are billed at a special rate.

Another type of service is the T-1, a collection of 24 circuits that are dedicated for special uses, such as connecting two PBXs in different locations. The T-1 also has special cost advantages, depending on how it is used.

Integrated services digital network, or ISDN, is an application of wire facilities that uses two wire pairs to handle broadband applications, including the simultaneous transmission of voice, computer data, and visual images. Telephone companies have been slow to provide ISDN because the development of applications for the service has been slow. And this slow development is due to the limited availability of ISDN services.

But ISDN is gaining acceptance and should become a popular business service before the year 2000. New generations of digital PBXs are being designed to handle ISDN applications, such as videoconferencing and on-line computer modeling.

For all practical purposes, PBXs, like telephone switches, are computers. Their job is to administer and complete requests for connections and monitor the system for trouble. They can assign billing to specific users—ending unauthorized use of the telephone for personal calls—and can be made to restrict certain types of calls, such as long distance or 900 numbers. PBXs can also be programmed to know which long distance company offers the lowest rate for a given destination and time, and automatically switch outgoing calls to that carrier.

But despite its cost-containment features, the PBX is primarily a tool for maximizing efficiency. An office of 100 people does not need 100 telephone lines, but perhaps the 24 offered by a T-1. This is because, depending on the employees' calling characteristics, no more than 15 or 20 people will be using a phone at any one time. The PBX can be used to match requests for service with available resources, with a minimum of waste. In addition, most PBXs are endowed with diagnostic features that allow the system operator to locate wiring faults and determine the nature of terminal equipment failures.

PBXs with an automated attendant feature can handle call answering tasks, greeting the caller and requesting an extension number to complete the call. If the called party does not answer, the PBX will switch the caller to a voice mail system to leave a message for that party. Automated attendant systems also handle routine menial tasks, such as providing hours of operation, a mailing address, fax number, or other frequently requested information.

For offices with a high amount of inbound calling, such as an order processing center, the PBX may be matched with an automatic call distributor, or ACD. These devices distribute incoming sales calls among a pool of operators, and may even direct calls to those who it knows are least busy. This ensures that operators share the workload evenly.

PBXs range in size from as few as 5 lines to as many as 10,000. Usually, the larger the system, the more sophisticated its capabilities.

Many offices today consist of multiple forms of terminal equipment at different workstations. The PBX is designed to handle voice communications and faxes, and in some cases data transfers between computer modems. But with the rapid decline in the cost of **computers**, PCs have become standard equipment on employees' desks.

Offices with as few as two or as many as several hundred computers may be networked so that each of these computers can communicate with any of the others. This allows all the computers to share processing power and storage capacity, in effect making each another type of terminal equipment. Networks that connect these computers, called **local area networks (LANs)**, are designed to handle computerized communication functions such as electronic mail and shared databases. LANs are software-driven applications that use building wire—including twisted wire pair, coaxial, and even fiber optic lines—to connect computers on the network.

Separate LANs in different locations may be connected to each other to form wide area networks (WANs). While newer PBXs can support these connections, most systems currently in place use bridge/routers to perform switching functions, linking LANS with dedicated circuits or dialing up a connection over the public switched network.

Other types of terminal equipment, specifically designed for the mobile market, are pagers and cellular phones. Pagers are radio receivers that are programmed to display simple messages, such as the telephone number of someone trying to reach them. Cellular phones are actual telephones, connected to the network not by wires, but by a radio signal. Each cellular phone operates off a host antenna located nearest to it. As the caller moves from one area, or "cell," to another, the system hands the call over to another antenna in an adjacent cell. This allows a caller to roam anywhere within a service area without losing the connection.

TELECOMMUNICATIONS TRENDS

Businesses are served by a single local telephone company that is authorized to provide service in a given area. All calls between the business and other parties on the network must be switched through this local exchange carrier, or LEC.

As discussed earlier, this type of monopoly no longer exists for long distance calls. A business may choose to route all its calls through a single long distance carrier, called a primary interexchange carrier, or PIC. All long distance calls originated by the company are automatically switched by the local telephone company to that long distance company.

When AT&T divested its Bell companies in 1984, all local telephone companies were ordered to provide equal access to any long distance company registered to do business. As a result, a company could choose any PIC it wanted, be it AT&T, MCI, Sprint, WilTel, LDDS, or any of the hundreds of others that have sprung up.

But competition will soon be extended to the local market. Local telephone companies face the loss of significant portions of market share to competing cellular telephone companies, digital wireless radio, bypass operators, and even cable television companies.

Bypass operators are the most ominous threat in the business market. They offer to establish alternate connections between a company's PBX and its long-distance carrier, completely bypassing the local telephone company. In practice, companies do not transfer all their communications traffic to a bypass operator, but choose to split it between them and the local telephone company to leverage each on price and service reliability.

In the consumer market, cable companies are best poised to provide competition. They have hundreds of miles of cable running through neighborhoods, are connected to millions of households and have armies of repair and installation workers. Perhaps most importantly, their wiring consists of coaxial cable, which can provide high-speed data and computer networking as well as television programs and telephone calls.

The manner in which competition will come to the local market, and how this might affect long distance and other services, has not yet been determined, pending settlement of numerous regulatory and legal questions.

As a result of the growing competition in the telecommunications industry and the complexity of applications, such as voice, data transfer, and video communications, management of the telecommunications system has become highly specialized. Where maintenance of such a system was once the duty of a building engineer, telecommunications management has become a vocation unto itself, requiring specialized training in computer science.

[John Simley]

FURTHER READING:

Brooks, John. *Telephone: The First Hundred Years*. New York: Harper & Row, 1976.

Green, Harry James. *The Business One Irwin Handbook of Telecommunications*. 2nd ed. Homewood, IL: Business One Irwin, 1991.

TELEMARKETING

In his book, *Strategic Telemarketing*, Richard L. Bencin defines telemarketing as simply: "A controllable and measurable method of professional marketing using **telecommunications** and **computers**. Its basic objective is to increase bottom-line profitability while reducing the cost of selling and improving market share."

A key part of the direct-marketing process, telemarketing can be either inbound or outbound in scope. Inbound telemarketing consists of handling incoming telephone calls—often generated by broadcast advertising, **direct mail**, or catalogs—and taking orders for a wide range of products. Representatives working in this type of telemarketing program normally do not need as much training or to be as sophisticated as outbound reps because the customer already has shown an interest by calling in.

Outbound telemarketing can be aimed directly at the end consumer—for example, a home repair business may call people in its community to search for prospects—or can be part of a business-to-business marketing program. Representatives working on this side of the industry generally are expected to require more training, as more actual selling is involved than with inbound operations.

Major applications of business-to-business telemarketing can include selling to existing accounts outbound new account development, inbound order processing and inquiry handling, customer service, and supporting the existing field **sales force**. With the cost of a field sales call continuing to escalate—from an average of $250 a call up to as much as $500 in high-technology fields—businesses are using telemarketing as a way to reduce the cost of selling and give more attention to marginal accounts.

One of the advantages telemarketing has over other direct marketing methods is that it involves human interaction. According to Robert J. McHatton in his book, *Total Telemarketing*: "Used correctly and by professionals, the telephone is the most cost-efficient, flexible and statistically accountable medium available. At the same time, the telephone is still very intimate and personal. It is individual to individual."

Although telemarketing has been the center of some controversies—ranging from scams run over the phone to a number of legal issues that have been the center of debate at both the state and national level—the industry continues to grow. In the early 1990s, telemarketing accounted for an estimated $435 billion in sales. The American Telemarketing Association estimated that nearly 481,000 companies sell by phone in the United States and that from 1981 to 1991, spending on telemarketing activities rose from $1 billion to $60 billion. In addition, one study projected that the telemarketing industry would account for eight million new jobs in the 1990s, although some in the industry view that as optimistic.

HISTORY AND BACKGROUND

The telemarketing industry dates back to the early part of the twentieth century, when the financial services industry used telephone marketing. Stock brokers have traditionally made extensive use of the phone, a practice that continues to this day. In the 1930s and 1940s, telemarketing units—commonly known as inside sales operations, because the sales reps remain "inside" the office—began to emerge in wholesale and distribution organizations. This trend accelerated during World War II as much of the nation's sales force was drafted into the service and travel was restricted domestically.

Magazine publishers began to use telemarketing extensively in the 1940s and 1950s, trying to sign up new subscribers as well as re-sign former subscribers. Reuben H. Donnelley in 1955 began what continues to be a major telemarketing success story when he started a telephone sales program to sell advertising in the Yellow Pages to small businesses. In 1985, the most profitable publishing entity in the state of California was the Pacific Telephone's Yellow Pages—and approximately 60 percent of the ads and one-third of the revenue was generated by phone.

The introduction in 1960 of the Wide Area Telephone Service (WATS) lines helped increase business use of the telephone. This opened the way for high-volume outbound calling at low cost, so it became cost-effective to have large regional or national call centers. Similarly, with the 1967 unveiling of 800 numbers, inbound WATS lines paved the way for direct response capability, where consumers could call in toll free.

Telemarketing programs can be either handled in-house by a company or farmed out to service bureaus. Operations range from extremely small to major corporations or service centers that have as many as 1,000 telephone stations.

TYPICAL TELEMARKETING USES

Although telemarketing can be used as a stand-alone operation, it often works best when part of an overall marketing effort. Companies considering the use of telemarketing have to look at such factors as which products and services are candidates to be sold by phone; whether telemarketing can be used to increase volume through upgrading the sale; how the process can help qualify prospects, define the market, and help service existing accounts; and whether telemarketing can help generate new business. Some of the roles telemarketing can be used to fulfill include:

SELLING. Telemarketing can be used to either supplement or replace face-to-face selling to existing accounts. It can complement the field sales effort by reaching new customer bases or geographic markets at relatively low cost.

The inside sales force can be used to replace direct contact for marginally profitable customers. A general rule of thumb in business says that 20 percent of customers account for 80 percent of sales, so conversely the remaining 80 percent of customers generate just 20 percent of sales. But businesses must keep in mind that marginal does not necessarily mean unprofitable. And the existing customer base is perhaps the most important asset in any business, as sales increases most often come from current accounts and it generally is less costly to maintain current customers than to gain new business.

Telemarketers, though, can give these customers the attention they deserve. The reps can phone as often as is needed, and determine the customers' purchasing cycles and contact them at appropriate reorder times.

In making such a consolidation between a direct and inside sales force, the company must be careful in determining which accounts stay with field sales and which are handled by telemarketing. Some businesses start their telemarketing operations with just small or inactive accounts, gradually increasing the size of accounts handled.

Telemarketing also can be used to sell goods and services independently, with no field sales force in place. This often is used for things such as repetitive supply purchases or readily identifiable products. It doesn't have to mean "low ticket item," though, as Xerox Corp. sells copiers by phone and one of the nation's leading Rolls-Royce dealers once generated 20 percent of his sales by phone.

LEAD GENERATION. Through telemarketing, a company can compile and update customer prospect leads and then go through these searching for sales leads. Telemarketing can be set up to screen the leads and qualify them according to priority, passing the best leads to the field sales force for immediate action. The inside sales force also can identify the decision maker with the buying power and set up appointments for the outside sales force.

GATHERING INFORMATION. Telemarkting can provide accurate information on advertising effectiveness, what customers are buying, from whom they're buying, and when they will buy again. It is also used in conducting surveys.

IMPROVING CUSTOMER SERVICE. Studies show it costs five times more to win over a new customer than to keep an existing one. By using telemarketing as a main facet of customer service, companies can go a long way toward keeping customers happy. General Electric (GE) is a leader in this field, as its Consumer Answer Center in Louisville, Kentucky, handles more than three million incoming calls annually.

SOME ADVANTAGES

Telemarketing offers the quickest and most direct method of reaching customers and prospects, also providing immediate feedback and a chance to overcome any objections as they occur. Many businesses also see it as a way to help keep costs down in an age where all companies, even the most successful, have to keep a close eye on the budget.

For example, businesses generally acknowledge that field sales calls cost at least $250 each and outside sales people make an average of four to six on-premise contacts a day. With time for travel and handling clerical work, one study claimed an average salesperson spends just 40 percent of his or her time selling. An outbound telemarketer, however, should make between 90 and 100 calls a day, and make between 35-50 complete product presentations, more than a traveling salesperson could make in a week. In addition, when used in conjunction with current computer technology, a telemarketing program can be analyzed for cost and benefit analysis, along with quantitative data on number of contacts, number of presentations, total sales, cost per sale, and income per sale.

But while telemarketing can be a stand-alone operation, it generally works best when used in connection with the other marketing and sales disciplines. Zacson Corp., a business-to-business marketing agency, teamed up with IBM to open an integrated teleservices center to manage IBM's northern California territory of more than 150,000 accounts. IBM wanted to elevate customer satisfaction ratings, reduce the cost of customer contacts, shorten the sales cycle, ensure high-caliber account coverage, and create a cost-effective telesales channel.

The center was organized into three groups: telesales to handle accounts for IBM products of medium complexity, customer service to handle anything from simple inquiries to complex problems, and direct marketing/lead generation to generate qualified leads and promote IBM events and educational seminars. The program helped reduce the cost of customer contact by nearly 97 percent, shortened field sales cycles by as much as 80 percent, and surpassed lead generation goals by 25 percent.

Countless other corporations make use of telemarketing to varying degrees. The *New York Times* sells 75 percent of its subscriptions over the phone. When Hewlett-Packard. started its first inbound telemarketing center in 1981, it had phones with ten lighted buttons across the top. Its phone now is a minicomputer that predicts staffing levels needed, routes calls based on call loads, and answers routine questions without sending them to a sales rep.

E.I. du Pont de Nemours & Co. has a 130-person, state-of-the-art Corporate Telemarketing Center which is trying to carve a wider role for itself in the $40 billion firm. The outbound portion handles the early stages of new account prospecting, as it may take from five to 12 interactions before a prospect buys a Du Pont product. If telemarketers handle four or five of these interactions, it helps the firm shorten its sales cycle time. Du Pont also has an inbound operation that handles 100,000 calls a month about such things as the company's Stainmaster carpet.

Of course, not all telemarketing programs are successful. Improper execution, unrealistic goals over a short time, oversimplification, and lack of top management support have caused the ultimate failure of more telephone sales programs than can be imagined.

ESTABLISHING A SUCCESSFUL PROGRAM

One magazine article about the ''myths'' of telemarketing, said the No. 2 myth is that to get started all you have to do is make a few calls and see how it goes. Like any marketing strategy, telemarketing takes time to plan and develop. It takes time to be able to predict bottom-line results, and it also takes time to gain confidence in the message and for weak areas to appear.

Most experts in the field agree that companies must be careful in forming goals and objectives, and should take the time to do it right. The most important factors for success include:

- developing a complete marketing plan with built-in criteria for accounting and analysis;

- writing scripts, sales outlines, and presentations to be performed;

- establishing training and hiring procedures for both supervisors and sales personnel;

- analyzing and evaluating campaigns, personnel, and cost effectiveness;

- having support and commitment from management for the telemarketing center's role in the overall marketing effort;

- establishing reachable goals;

- having continuous interaction between the telemarketing center and other departments;

- having a constant emphasis on follow-up.

The most common mistakes include not considering telemarketing as an option; not giving it a total commitment; not utilizing the proper expertise; failing to develop a proper database; improper human resource planning; lack of proper scripts and call guides; lack of quality control; and failing to understand the synergy with other direct marketing disciplines. As Bencin wrote in his book: ''Top management must understand and agree to the necessary personnel and financial resources, as well as the time required for program development and testing. Telemarketing and related direct marketing techniques can work astoundingly well. But they need a real chance to demonstrate that success. It doesn't happen over a couple of weekends.''

IN-HOUSE VS. OUTSIDE SERVICE BUREAU

When establishing a telemarketing program, a company has the option of setting up the operation in-house, or contracting it out to an outside service bureau. Both have advantages and disadvantages. In-house programs usually are better if products require extensive technical expertise. They also can be better for firms making a long-term commitment to telemarketing. Service bureaus can help firms that need around-the-clock coverage for inbound programs, are supporting television ad campaigns, or are running a seasonal marketing program.

SERVICE BUREAUS. These can likely offer lower costs on programs involving less than 100,000 calls a year. By grouping programs from several different companies, service bureaus can generate sufficient volume to reduce labor and telephone costs, which make up a majority of total costs. They can also get your program started more quickly because they have experienced telephone reps on staff along with necessary equipment.

When 24-hour coverage is needed on an inbound telemarketing program, it probably is more cost effective to go with a bureau. When setting up an outbound program, the experienced managers at a bureau can help a company avoid making mistakes and often can accurately project call volumes and sales per hour. Service bureaus also can help with testing new programs and have a greater ability to handle peaks.

On the downside, several companies must compete for attention, and for firms that share service with a broadcast advertiser whose response rates are underestimated, that can be a decided drawback. Stability of service bureaus has also been a problem at times.

IN-HOUSE OPERATIONS. The main reason for companies running their own campaign is maintaining total control over all facets, including hiring and firing, scripts and presentations, budgets, advertising, and compensation and incentive policies. By keeping programs in-house, phone reps have ready access to company databases, so they can confirm delivery, authorize credit, and suggest alternatives to out-of-stock items.

By training employees on individual product lines, in-house reps can handle highly technical calls no outside center likely would attempt. This also is an important part of maintaining effective customer service programs. It also is easier to have company loyalty from actual employees than people employed by an outside bureau, as well as to observe the program, monitor calls, and oversee the overall effort.

The biggest drawback to taking a program in-house is the large capital investment needed to get an in-house program started. It also involves hiring and training new personnel, and dealing with a process that isn't familiar to many in business.

GROWING USE OF TECHNOLOGY

Computers have been one important factor in the growth of telemarketing. Access to databases provides phone reps with account histories, stock status, order-taking formats, and other vital information. Besides analyzing data, computers are used for scheduling, scripting, and follow-ups.

Computers also can automatically dial phone numbers and connect the calls to telemarketers only if answered, screen out answering machines, and guide the phone rep through the telemarketing presentation. Automatic call distributors are common, as is cloning the best telesales person to provide quick access to appropriate responses to common questions and objections.

HUMAN RESOURCE ELEMENT

While technology plays a vital role in keeping telemarketing cost-effective, the human element is critical in making the effort successful. Unfortunately, many firms still see telemarketing positions as clerical-level jobs staffed by people with few skills, no training, and little understanding of the product or service being sold. Further, few opportunities exist to train managers; college courses are not readily available; and often there is little peer support, as the manager of the telemarketing operation often is the only person in an organization familiar with the discipline.

Some firms, though, have come to realize the importance of the telemarketers, as the firm's image is on the line with every call. They realize the position needs skilled, trained professionals who must be fairly compensated. GE, for example, puts reps at its Answer Center through a six- to seven-week training program that includes both computer and product training. Before they are allowed to answer a call, the reps learn 120 different product lines and 1,100 procedures. College graduates often use Answer Center positions as stepping stones to career track positions within GE.

For compensation most companies use a combination of salary, commission, and/or bonuses. Studies indicate that incentives generally aid in sales success, but it is important to link the inducements to the performance desired, be it total sales, calls completed, or presentations given. Some form of quotas also are common so sales reps know what is expected of them. Firms should be cautious in ensuring quotas are reasonable and achievable. If the goals are too high, the reps will become frustrated and, conversely, if they are too low, the reps may become overconfident and complacent about growth.

CONTROVERSIES

Because of its nature, telemarketing has been the catalyst for numerous scams over the year. Federal authorities estimate that con artists using the phone bilk people out of least $1 billion a year, with some contending the figure may be closer to $10 billion annually.

Operating out of offices known as "boiler rooms," these frauds have given the telemarketing industry much bad press. The scams often move from town to town, form one product to the next, and often involve getting people to disclose their credit card numbers over the phone.

All these cons have one thing in common: they promise big profits with little or no risk. Since they are often not easy to spot, embarrassed victims may shy away from filing complaints. Some scams last only a few weeks while others go on and on. One scheme involving the sale of desert land near Los Angeles lasted 17 years. Another fraud that lasted for years involved the sale of hundreds of thousands of fake Dali prints, netting more than $500 million.

California and Florida historically were home to many of these "boiler rooms." Those states passed legislation aimed at clamping down on those operations, but the crooked firms typically just moved to other states where the laws or enforcement were lax.

The firms are hard to catch because they tend to keep operations small; and to elude detection they usually solicit out-of-state targets.

LEGAL ISSUES

Legislators, both on the state and federal level, have debated a number of proposed laws that could affect telemarketing in the future. Some examples include:

REGISTRATION. These laws would require registration of telephone solicitors in a state. This often includes bonding requirements, submission of scripts and/or names of employees, and other administrative devices designed to create a paper trail to track fraudulent marketers.

ASTERISK BILLS. Such laws Would require the telephone company or state government to keep a list of people who object to receiving unsolicited phone sales calls. Marketers would be required to obtain the list and not call these people. A similar bill would mandate that marketers be allowed to call consumers on their calling lists, but remove the names of anyone requesting the marketer not contact him or her again.

HOURS. These seek to restrict hours, generally limiting calls to no later than nine p.m. local time.

CONTRACTS/CANCELLATION. Such laws would prohibit completion of some types of phone sales unless a written contract is signed and returned by consumer. The industry favors letting firms who offer consumers a right of examination and promise a refund to be exempt from such legislation.

RECORDING/MONITORING. Many states have considered legislation that would prohibit or restrict the practice of monitoring customer service employees who work over the phone. The industry considers monitoring vital to maintaining quality control and protecting consumers. They ask that employees sign a release in advance allowing such monitoring.

OUTLOOK

Despite the potential impact of such legislation, the future continues to look bright for telemarketing, particularly in the business-to-business arena. An ongoing study by Arthur Andersen & Co. showed that in 1970, contact with a field salesperson was the No. 1 thing vendors wanted from companies in 1970. By 1980 contact with the field salesperson had dropped to No. 3 and all the way to No. 8 in 1990.

Conversely, contact with an inside sales person, or telemarketer, was ranked as No. 5 in 1970, No. 4 in 1980, and then jumped to No. 1 in 1990. The same study also projected that inside sales reps eventually will account for two-thirds of all sales representatives.

SEE ALSO: Direct Marketing; Toll-Free Telephone Calls (800 Numbers)

[Bruce Meyer]

FURTHER READING:

Bencin, Richard L. *Strategic Telemarketing: How to Fit This New Medium into Your Marketing Plans.* Swansea Press, Inc., 1987.

Chesters, Sara. "Defusing the Demographic Time Bomb." *Direct Marketing.* May, 1991, p. 35.

Eisenhart, Tom. "Telemarketing Takes Quantum Leap." *Business Marketing.* September, 1993, p. 75.

Everett, Martin. "It's Jerry Hale on the Line." *Sales & Marketing Management,* December, 1993, p. 75.

Gottlieb, Mag. "Telemarketing and The Law." *Direct Marketing.* February, 1994, p. 22.

McHatton, Robert J. *Total Telemarketing.* John Wiley & Sons, Inc., 1988.

Moretti, Peggy. "Telemarketers Serve Clients." *Business Marketing.* April, 1994, p. 27.

Neff, Linda J. "Six Myths About Telemarketing." *Sales & Marketing Management.* p. 108.

Oetting, Rudy. "Telephone Marketing: Where We've Been and Where We Should Be Going." *Direct Marketing.* February, 1987, p. 86.

Stern, Aimee L. "Telemarketing Polished Its Image." *Sales & Marketing Management.* June, 1991, p. 107.

"Telefraud: They've Got Your Number." *Consumer Reports.* May, 1987, p. 289.

TEMPORARY EMPLOYMENT

Temporary employees typically work for firms for brief and often fixed periods, in contrast with permanent full- and part-time workers. Temporary employees are either hired directly or are provided to client firms by temporary employment firms (often referred to as temporary employment agencies). Entering the 1990s, 90 percent of U.S. businesses and 95 percent of Fortune 500 firms used some form of temporary employment. Among the areas of most rapid growth are the use of temporaries in the manufacturing sector and in professional occupations.

The first temporary employment firms began operations in the 1940s. It was not until the 1980s and 1990s, however, that temporary employment grew rapidly. Annual average temporary employment grew from 340,000 in 1978 to 695,000 by 1985, increasing three times faster than total service sector employment and eight times faster than total nonagricultural employment. Annual average temporary employment rose to 1.15 million workers by 1991 and to nearly 1.5 million by 1993, an annual growth rate of about 20 percent. The total number of workers performing temporary work in 1991 was six million, over five times greater than the annual average. As a share of the **workforce**, temporary employment rose from 0.4 percent in 1982 to 1.6 percent in 1993.

The growth of temporary employment was concurrent with so-called downsizing and restructuring, in which many corporations reduced the size of their core workforce. In the 1980s, for example, Fortune 500 firms cut three million jobs. Companies substitute temporary for permanent employees because temporaries receive hourly wages that average 75 percent of the wages of permanent employees, and generally receive fewer benefits. Temporary workers contracting directly with firms are generally not eligible for unemployment insurance or workers' compensation. In addition, temporary employees provided firms with a great deal of flexibility in the face of changing business conditions. The trend of substitution of temporary for permanent workers is reflected in the fact that the decline in temporary employment was substantially less in the recession of the early 1980s than in the recessions of the 1970s.

In the economic recovery of the early 1990s, 1.9 million jobs were added to the U.S. economy. Only 46 percent of these jobs were nontemporary private-sector jobs, however, and temporary agencies accounted for one-fourth of total job growth. The remaining share of temporary private sector jobs resulted from workers contracting directly with firms. Temporary and part-time employment made up a large proportion of what was referred to as the contingent workforce. One-fourth of the 1.9 million newly-created jobs were part-time, and three-fourths of these part-timers desired to work full time.

In his 1988 volume, *Alternative Staffing Strategies*, David Nye argued that the expanded use of temporary employment was likely to persist. He wrote: "The forces that gave rise to increased use of temporary workers as an alternative to permanent employment are generally expected to stay with us, if not accelerate. These forces include the shift from production of goods to processing of information and other service industries; employer reluctance to add permanent staff in the face of possible business downturns; increased technology that both requires special expertise and facilitates its deployment; and the availability of capable individuals who either must, or prefer to, enter the temporary labor market."

The manufacturing sector made up a growing proportion of the demand for temporary workers in recent years. A large number of manufacturers made increasing use of the just-in-time system, which minimized inventories. Temporary employment provided flexibility, which suited it to the conditions of the just-in-time production. The National Association of Temporary Services estimated that temporary agencies provided 348,000 temporary workers per day to the manufacturing sector in late 1992. An example was Nike's repackaging facility in Memphis. Nike employed 120 permanent employees, who received at least $13 per hour plus benefits. This core labor force worked alongside 60 to 225 temporaries provided by Norrell Services. Norrell received $8.50 per hour for each temporary, who in turn received $6.50 per hour. These temporaries did not receive health insurance, though Norrell did cover workers' compensation and Social Security.

The U.S. Department of Labor counts temporary workers as service-sector employees, even those who work in manufacturing. As a consequence, the department not only underestimated employment but also overestimated the growth of labor productivity in the manufacturing sector, a ratio of output per worker hour.

A study of the characteristics of temporary workers was published in the 1985 *Current Population Survey*, though it did not include temporary workers contracting directly with firms. The survey indicated that temporary workers were disproportionally female, young (particularly in the 16 to 24 age range), and black. For example, 64 percent of temporary workers were female, compared to 45 percent of all workers, and 20 percent of temporary workers were black, compared to 10 percent of all workers. Forty percent of temporary workers were part-time, twice that for all workers. Administrative support occupations made up the largest proportion of temporary workers, followed by factory workers. The Employee Benefit Research Institute estimated that in 1985, 30 percent of temporaries working for employment agencies did not have health insurance, whether through their job or spouse, and 63 percent were without an employer-provided pension plan.

The largest temporary employment firm in the United States in 1993 was Manpower Inc., with $2.8 billion in revenues. Manpower was founded in Milwaukee in 1948 and originally provided unskilled temporary workers for industrial employment. Soon the company diversified into providing temporary office workers. Manpower placed 640,000 employees in 1993, making it the largest employer in the United States—more employees than IBM and AT&T combined. About one-third of Manpower's workers receive permanent positions each year as a result of their temporary employment. As of the late 1980s, a third of Manpower's workers were assigned to factory jobs. The firm not only provides secretarial and factory workers, but also accountants and doctors. This is part of an overall trend in temporary employment in which professional occupations, including executives, lawyers, engineers and scientists, are among the fastest growing.

In terms of revenue, Manpower Inc. was followed by Kelly Services Inc., with $1.4 billion in revenues, and the Olsten Corporation, with $843 million, out of an industry total of over $10 billion. Temporary employment firms typically undertake hiring and firing decisions, issue paychecks, and also withhold payroll taxes and make contributions for unemployment insurance, workers' compensation, and Social Security. The industry is served by the National Association of Temporary Services, which has 1,000 members.

During the 1980s, an increasing number of firms made use of directly-hired temporary workers, eliminating the middleman role of the temporary agencies. A 1987 survey of 502 firms in the manufacturing and service sectors indicated that these firms were likely to increasingly rely on the direct hiring of temporaries. The two common types of directly-hired temporaries were workers belonging to ''on-call'' pools and those hired for a limited duration.

The use of on-call, limited duration, and agency-provided temporary workers varies widely by sector, according to a 1986 study by the U.S. Bureau of National Affairs. Among manufacturing firms surveyed, 57 percent used short-term hires, 49 percent used on-call workers, and 35 percent used agency-provided temporaries. For nonmanufacturing firms surveyed, 85 percent used short-term hires, 82 percent used on-call workers, and 100 percent used agency-provided temporaries. Among the large firms using directly-hired temporaries were Standard Oil, the Grumman Corporation, ARCO, Digital Corporation, Apple Computers Inc., Intel Corporation, Beatrice Foods, Hunt-Wesson, Hewlett-Packard, and AT&T. AT&T made use of 6,000 temporaries to operate long-distance stations during a 26-day strike in 1986.

The federal government is one of the largest employers of directly-hired temporary workers. In 1985, the Office of Personnel Management authorized the extension of temporary contracts from one to four years. As of 1986, 300,000 temporaries worked in federal government offices.

In his essay, ''Temporary Employment in the Eighties,'' Carre considered the issue of whether the increase in temporary employment was supply- or demand-led; that is, whether the increase resulted from changes in the labor force, among them the increasing number of working mothers, or whether the increase was primarily a cost-cutting strategy on the part of firms. Summarizing studies on this issue, Carre wrote: ''The research . . . suggests that changes in firm demand for labor rather than changes in workers' preference have driven the rapid growth of contingent employment during the 1980s. Reducing labor costs, adapting to variability in demand, and increasing flexibility in labor inputs are goals which have motivated much of the increase in firm demand for temporary help supply employment, and, most likely, for other forms of contingent employment.''

One area of concern for temporary workers is the extent to which they are protected by labor legislation. Temporary employment firms are required to abide by the **Fair Labor Standards Act of 1938**, the Equal Employment Opportunity Act of 1972, and the Occupational Safety and Health Act of 1970. Temporary workers are often ineligible for unemployment insurance. This results in part from their inability to meet the minimum earnings requirements specified in state laws. In addition, temporary employment firms may offer unemployed temporaries a one-day assignment just prior to their eligibility for unemployment benefits, thus minimizing firms' contribution to unemployment insurance.

The Employee Retirement Income Security Act of 1974 (ERISA) requires firms with pension plans to offer them to all employees working 1,000 or more hours per year. Firms can consequently minimize these costs by working temporaries a lesser number of hours. Labor legislation makes it difficult for short-term workers to engage in collective bargaining, and the **National Labor Relations Board (NLRB)** determines on a case-by-case basis whether temporaries can be included in bargaining units.

[David Kucera]

FURTHER READING:

''All about Temporary Workers: Filling the Gaps in the Post-Recession Workforce.'' *New York Times*. April 26, 1992.

Belous, Richard. *The Contingent Economy: The Growth of the Temporary, Part-Time and Subcontracted Workforce*. National Planning Association, 1989.

''Business and the Temp Temptation: A Permanent Situation.'' *Washington Post*. October 20, 1993.

''Business Gives in to Temptation.'' *US News and World Report*. July 4, 1994.

duRivage, Virginia, ed. *New Policies for the Part-Time and Contingent Workforce*. M. E. Sharpe, 1992.

Kilborn, Peter. ''New Jobs Lack the Old Security in a Time of 'Disposable Workers.' '' *New York Times*. March 15, 1993.

Nye, David. *Alternative Staffing Strategies*. The Bureau of National Affairs, 1988.

Parker, Robert. ''The Labor Force in Transition: The Growth of the Contingent Work Force in the United States.'' In *The Labor Process and Control of Labor: The Changing Nature of Work Relations in the Late Twentieth Century*, edited by Berch Berberoglu. Praeger, 1993.

Presley Noble, Barbara. ''At Work; Accounting for the Uncountable.'' *New York Times*. November 28, 1993.

Rowland, Mary. ''Your Own Account; Temporary Work: The New Career.'' *New York Times*. September 12, 1993.

Uchitelle, Louis. ''Temporary Workers Are on the Increase in Nation's Factories.'' *New York Times*. July 6, 1993.

Ward's Directory of U.S. Private and Public Companies. Gale Research Inc., 1993.

TENDER OFFERS

A tender offer asks the stockholders of a firm to submit, or tender, their shares for an established price. While tender offers may be made for any type of securities, they are usually made for common stock. A tender offer may be made by the firm that originally issued the stock, or by another company or group of investors. Tender offers are commonly used by issuing firms to repurchase a quantity of their stock. They are also used to acquire a controlling interest in a firm.

A tender offer must specify an offer price, the maximum number of shares that will be purchased, the beginning and expiration dates of the offer, and the last day when tendered stock can be withdrawn by shareholders. When a tender offer is made, it must remain open for a specified time period. During this time, shareholders have the right to withdraw shares they have already tendered. If the tender offer is oversubscribed—that is, more shares are tendered than are going to be purchased—then purchases must be made on a prorated basis. If the offer terms are amended to provide for a higher price, then shares already tendered automatically receive the higher price.

A tender offer that is made by the firm that originally issued the stock is known as a stock repurchase, or self tender offer. This often occurs when management believes the company's stock is undervalued on the market. While a self tender offer reduces the firm's liquidity—as it uses up some of its cash reserves—it also sends the message that management is confident of strong cash flows in the future. Consequently, a self tender offer often has the effect of increasing the value of the company's stock.

A tender offer may be used to acquire controlling interest in a company. When one company seeks to gain control over another, it will usually approach the target company's management with a merger proposal. If an agreement cannot be reached with management, then a takeover bid can be initiated by making a tender offer to the company's stockholders.

In a two-tier tender offer, the acquiring company will make a tender offer to obtain voting control of the target company. In a second stage or tier, the acquiring company votes its controlling interest to obtain merger approval at a shareholders' meeting. Typically, the target company's shareholders would receive higher compensation for their shares in the first tier (tender offer), than in the second tier (merger).

There are antitakeover measures a company may use to counter the threat of a two-tier tender offer. For example, a company may add fair price and super majority amendments to its corporate charter. A fair price amendment stipulates that an acquiring company must pay a fair price for all of the target company's shares that it purchases, which is usually the highest price the acquiring company has paid. A super majority amendment increases the necessary majority to approve an acquisition or merger from one-half to two-thirds. Companies may also attempt to thwart hostile takeovers by obtaining "marriage proposals," or more favorable tender offers, from other firms.

As a result of Congressional investigations, tender offers were placed under the jurisdiction of the Securities and Exchange Commission by the Williams Act of 1968, which also established disclosure rules and other requirements for tender offers. The acquiring firm must provide thirty days' notice of its intention to make an acquisition to the management of the target firm and to the SEC. Another requirement is that the beneficial owner of the stock, as well as the party financing the acquisition, must be disclosed when substantial amounts of stock are being acquired with the intent to gain control of a firm. In addition, anyone making a tender offer that would result in ownership of more than five percent of a class of securities is required to file a report with the SEC.

SEE ALSO: Takeovers

[David Bianco]

TERM STRUCTURE OF INTEREST RATES

The Term Structure of **interest rates** is the term used to describe the current situation with regard to yield to maturity (YTM) on securities which differ only in terms of time to maturity (TTM).

Treasury securities are generally used to map the term structure of interest rates (i.e., the yield curve) because they are virtually free of **default** risk.

The shape of the term structure may change from period to period, being either upward sloping (i.e., long-term rates higher than short-term rates), downward sloping (i.e., long-term rates lower than long-term rates), or flat (long-term rates equal to short-term rates). Most frequently, however, the term structure is upward sloping.

THREE THEORIES

Three theories have been developed to explain the shape of the term structure at a given point in time. They are the unbiased expectations theory, the liquidity preference theory, and the market segmentation theory.

UNBIASED EXPECTATIONS THEORY. The unbiased expectations theory contends that the long-term rate is the geometric mean of the intervening short-term rates. Further, it suggests that if the term structure is upward sloping, short-term interest rates are expected to rise in the future. If the term structure is downward sloping, short-term interest rates are expected to fall in the future.

LIQUIDITY PREFERENCE THEORY. The liquidity preference theory asserts that lenders anticipate the potential need to liquidate an investment earlier than expected. Since for a given change in interest rates, the price volatility of a short-term investment is lower than the price volatility of a long-term investment, investors prefer to lend short-term. Therefore, they must be offered a risk premium to induce them to lend long-term. Borrowers, on the other hand, often prefer long-term bonds because they eliminate the risk of having to refinance at higher interest rates in future periods. Furthermore, the fixed costs of frequent refinancing can be quite high. Therefore, borrowers are willing to pay the premium necessary to attract long-term financing.

The liquidity preference theory, in conjunction with the unbiased expectations theory, suggests that an upward sloping term structure would be expected to occur more often than a downward sloping term structure. In fact, as stated earlier, this is the most common situation.

MARKET SEGMENTATION THEORY. Market segmentation theory (MST) is also known as institutional **hedging** or habitat theory. This theory sees two separate maturity habitats or segments—one long and the other short. Each segment has a schedule of supply (lenders) and demand (borrowers) for loanable funds. The point at which the demand and supply intersect determines the prevailing rate for that sector.

MST recognizes that there are institutional restrictions on the asset side and hedging pressures on the liability side which allow for very little substitutability between **bonds** of different maturities. Some of these restrictions result from government regulation, company policy, **Securities and Exchange Commission** regulations, goals and objectives, and fiscal and operational considerations.

Commercial **banks** and nonfinancial corporations generally supply loans in the short-term segment of the market. Nonfinancial corporations invest (hedge) their excess liquidity until it is needed to meet cash distributions.

Life insurance companies, pension funds, and the like, supply the long-term segment in anticipation of a steady stream of income over the long haul. Their goals and objectives seem to differ completely from the short-term suppliers except that, for each to be successful over the long-term, they each must consistently operate within their predetermined habitat.

The flow of funds into these institutions, however, is not static. Customers make withdrawals, receive payments, and reallocate sources. As a result, the supply schedule in each market shifts among different institutions. Pensioners may place their monthly funds into commercial banks. The supply decreases in the long-term segment thus putting upward pressure on rates to attract more funds. The increase of capital in commercial banks increases the supply in the short-term, thus putting downward pressure on short-term rates.

The demand schedules for loanable funds also shifts with changes in the economic cycles. The demand for long-term funds increases when an upturn in the economy is perceived, putting upward pressure on rates. As a business cycle matures, the need to expand inventories creates upward pressures on short-term rates, thus attracting additional supply to the short segment.

The market segmentation model proposes that the spread between long- and short-term rates depends largely on the relative supply and demand for these instruments by transactors in their preferred habitats.

SEE ALSO: Valuation

[Roger J. AbiNader]

FURTHER READING:

Alexander, Gordon J., and Jack Clark Francis. *Portfolio Analysis*, 3rd ed. Prentice-Hall, 1986.

Dreman, David. *The New Contrarian Investment Strategy*. Random House, 1980.

Haugen, Robert A. *Introductory Investment Theory*. Prentice-Hall, 1987.

Kaufman, Henry. *Interest Rates, the Market, and the New Financial World*. Time Books, 1986.

Sharpe, William F., and Gordon J. Alexander. *Investments*. 4th ed. Prentice-Hall, 1990.

THAILAND, DOING BUSINESS IN

Thailand, formerly known as Siam, is a rapidly developing nation in Southeast Asia. At just under 200,000 square miles, Thailand is approximately three-fourths the size of Texas. Thailand has a population of approximately 57 million (or 3.3 times Texas's population). This makes Thailand among the world's most densely populated nations.

Thailand has long held a reputation as the world's leading rice exporter, and it still controls more than a third of all rice exports. Additionally, Thailand remains a major producer of tapioca (second in the world) as well as sugar, coconuts, and cotton. As a result, two-thirds of the nation's labor force still remains tied to agriculture. Still, it is in its manufacturing and service sectors that Thailand has received most attention.

Beginning in the 1960s and throughout the 1970s Thailand sustained an annual economic growth rate exceeding 7 percent. It was, however, during the 1980s, that Thailand emerged as one of the strongest developing economies in world trade. By 1990, its annual economic growth rate had reached 10 percent, with a growth in **gross domestic product** (GDP) of 18.2 percent over the four years closing the decade. While this growth rate had fallen to 8 percent during the political instability in the nation in 1991 and 1992, the economy has remained healthy. In less than a decade, Thailand's exports have more than doubled, making major inroads in the global marketplace in manufactured goods ranging from textiles to integrated circuitry. Even in agriculture, the nation has shown a shift from rice to processed food exports such as canned fruit and fish.

ETHNICITY

Thailand is not a homogeneous nation. Approximately 75 percent of Thailand's population are ethnic Thais. This group itself is not homogeneous—dividing into the dominant central Thais (or Siamese) of the Chao Phraya Delta and the nearly equally populous Thai-Lao of the northeastern part of the country near the border with Laos. The ethnic Thais also include the less numerous Northern Thais as well as several ethnically distinct Thai-speaking groups such as the Shan, the Phuan, and the Yaw peoples. Each of these groups has its own dialect and, to some extent, its own business behavior and cultural variations. Still the vast majority of interaction that the *farang*—foreigner—will have in business will be among the culturally and economically dominant central Thais.

THE ETHNIC CHINESE. Much more important for the *farang*—at least in terms of business—than the distinctions among Thai-speaking groups is Thailand's important Chinese minority. Between 12 percent and 14 percent of Thailand's population is comprised of ethnic Chinese. As with Thailand's neighbors in southeast Asia, the ethnic Chinese presence and influence in business far exceeds their numbers in the population. In distinct contrast to the Philippines, Malaysia, Indonesia, and other Asian nations where the Chinese play a significant economic role, however, Thailand has experienced very little ethnic tensions between the two groups, and ethnic Chinese groups have been harmoniously integrated into day-to-day life in Thailand.

Both of the nation's two major business cultures, the Thais and the ethnic Chinese, have their own customs, traditional dress, and usually distinctive names. It is, however, important to note that the ethnic Chinese in Thailand have assimilated into Thai culture at a level unequaled in anywhere else in Southeast Asia. In part this assimilation may be explained on the Thai side by the cultural value Thais place on tolerance of any *farangs*, not just the Chinese. Equally important are the two cultures' common ties to Buddhism. In part, assimilation may be explained on the Chinese side by the fact that the Chinese in Thailand never experienced prolonged persecution. Moreover, while the Chinese were traditionally prohibited from owning land or participating in government in Thailand, such bans are no longer practiced. In short, the Chinese may have assimilated more readily in Thailand than elsewhere in Southeast Asia simply because the ability to do so was open to them.

Indeed, intermarriage between Thais and ethnic Chinese is not uncommon and many leading Thai families have at least some Chinese ancestry. Even King Taksin, the eighteenth century Thai military leader (and later monarch), who was the avenger of the sack of Ayutthaya, had a Chinese mother. Such Chinese-Thai unions have made it more difficult (and arguably less important) to define clearly who is ethnically pure Thai or pure Chinese. Today, the two cultures live together harmoniously in Bangkok and other cities with large Chinese communities.

Despite harmonious ties and religious similarities with the ethnic Thai majority, Thailand's ethnic Chinese remain a distinctive group. Because of laws that were in force well into the twentieth century prohibiting ethnic Chinese land ownership and participation in government service, Thailand's Chinese gravitated toward trade and service industries, where they still play a force far disproportionate to their numbers.

Regardless of their position in society, the Chinese are not newcomers to Thailand. The Thais themselves came to Thailand in the tenth century AD from southwest China. Throughout the thirteenth through nineteenth centuries, Chinese had been present in small numbers in Thailand for trade purposes and as a counterbalance first to Burmese then later Portuguese threats.

It was not until 1824, however, that Chinese immigrants came in large numbers to Thailand. It was in that year that Rama III granted the Chinese tin-mining and sugar plantation rights to counterbalance British and U.S. colonial schemes in the region. While this laid the foundation for the Chinese presence in Thailand, the Chinese still entered Thailand from a position of strong home nation. By contrast, most Chinese emigration to Thailand came only after China's social and economic collapse that followed the European, Japanese, and U.S. colonial incursions there in the second half of the nineteenth century. This massive Chinese immigration to Thailand continued unabated throughout the nineteenth and early twentieth centuries and did not end until World War II and the closing of post-revolutionary China's borders.

The Chinese themselves are not a single ethnic group. Five major Chinese subcommunities exist in Thailand, each speaking mutually unintelligible dialects. These, in turn, form their own subcommunity ties and loyalties. The five major groups are Hokkien, Yueh or Cantonese, Hakka, Wu or Shanghaiese, and Hainanese. Additionally, many members of the other Chinese dialect groups are present in smaller numbers as well.

OTHER GROUPS IN THAILAND. An additional 3.5 percent of the population consists of ethnic Malays, most of whom are Muslims and most of whom live near Thailand's border with Malaysia. While numerous, Thailand's ethnic Malays have not played a major role in business and are regionally isolated, and so will not be addressed in this article. Their behavior follows that of ethnic Malays.

Another 5 percent of the population consists of small non-Thai-speaking communities. These consist of non-Thai regional groups such as the Semang, the Htin, the Khamu, and the Moken (or ''sea gypsies''— chao leh). This figure would also include the hundreds of thousands of refugees from Vietnam, Kampuchea (Cambodia), and Burma (Myanmar) to whom since 1975 Thailand has maintained an open-door policy of political asylum. For its provision of such asylum, Thailand has received widespread praise from numerous international humanitarian organizations. Moreover, these groups are of some marginal importance in regional trade, and may prove more so as the communist nations such as Vietnam enter more into the global trade arena.

Finally, just over 3 percent of the people consist of the members of the 20 or so hill tribes of the north such as the Hmong, the Akha, the Karen, the Lisu, the Lahu, and the Yao peoples. These groups are important in Thailand's growing tourism industry and in the manufacture of hand-crafted items, but aside from these two areas play little part in the business world. While each of these groups represent unique and important cultures, with different customs, languages and religions, they remain relatively unimportant in international trade and so are not addressed further in this article.

NAMES AND TITLES

THAI NAMES AND TITLES. As with English names, Thai names have a first name that is the individual's personal name and a second surname that is the family name. Unlike English names, however, Thai names attach the title to the first or personal name, not to the surname.

The standard Thai title is *Khun*. Unlike English titles, *Khun* applies equally to men or women. More-over, while Thai women do take on their husband's surnames, they will continue to be addressed by their first names. Thus, a woman named Rungludi Kasetsiri would be addressed as *Khun* Rungludi. Her husband Anand Kasetsiri would be addressed as *Khun* Anand.

Unlike the English titles of Mr. or Ms., however, *Khun* is not clearly an indicator of formality. One uses *Khun* when speaking of someone in the third person as a sign of respect and one uses *Khun* directly in conversation with another person when that person is a relative stranger. Thais quickly move to drop *Khun* when speaking with those they know well. In such cases, they use only the person's first or personal name. This use of the first name, however, does not have the same level of informality of first name use in English because *Khun* itself is always attached to the person's first name.

Additionally, *Khun* is not used when the individual addressed has a professional or academic title. Thus if a man named Prasert Pibulsonggram were a Ph.D. or M.D., he would be addressed as *Dokter* Prasert. If he were a military officer he would be *Muad'* Prasert, and so on. These titles, unlike *Khun*, do carry additional formality and respect and would be less likely to be dropped as quickly as *Khun* among those of lower status.

Many Thais, particularly in government, have royal titles. Preceding Thai royal names are (listed here in descending rank) the abbreviations M.C. (*Mom Chao*), M.R. (*Mom Rachawong*) and M.L. (*Mom Luang*). All of these royal titles are nonhereditary so that the child of one rank is born at the next lowest rank. Thus the child of someone with the title *Mom Rachawong* will have the next lowest title *Mom Luang*. The child of someone with the lowest title, in turn, will be born with no royal title at all.

Additionally, all Thais have nicknames. Unlike English, in which some people have nicknames and others do not, Thais without exception have a nickname. Also, unlike English, Thai nicknames are much less a sign of informality than English nicknames. English nicknames are used only among close friends and in relatively informal situations. Thai nicknames are used by even casual acquaintances and are used in all but the most formal settings. Thai nicknames mean something in Thai and some Thais will translate their names for use in English. This can be disquieting since the meanings often seem insulting in English, ranging as they do from animals (such as Pig or Cow) to physical features (such as Fat One or Shorty). Thai nicknames are, in general, shorter than Thai first names and so actually make names a bit simpler for *farangs* (foreigners).

When addressing *farangs*, Thais will usually use the foreigner's first name or *Khun* with the foreigner's first name. Thais well acquainted with English-speakers, however, may attempt to use English naming practice. This is particularly the case with Thais acquainted with *farangs* who do not come from the United States or Australia, where first name use is as common as in Thailand. Thus, a person named Ralph Griffiths would customarily be addressed as *Khun* Ralph or simply Ralph. As a sign of cross-cultural sensitivity, however, a Thai might address him as Mr. Griffiths. The Thai, would, in either case, still expect to be addressed in the Thai manner back, using his or her personal name. The *farang*, even if addressed by Mr. or Ms. and a last name, should address the Thai by his or her first (personal) name, probably preceded by *Khun*.

CHINESE NAMES AND TITLES. The large ethnic Chinese community of Thailand poses an additional naming problem for the foreigner. This is particularly so in the case of those in Thailand for business, in which the Chinese community plays so dominant a position.

Due to government pressure to make the ethnic Chinese adopt Thai names (by making a Thai name a prerequisite to obtaining government documents, scholarships, and so forth), many ethnic Chinese have adopted Thai names. Indeed, a number of Chinese and those of Chinese-Thai mixed ancestry may only have Thai names. As a result, unlike other ethnic Chinese communities in the rest of Southeast Asia, many Chinese in Thailand use the same address system as the rest of the country. Thus most ethnic Chinese use the Thai title *Khun* or professional titles in the same manner as the ethnic Thais.

Nevertheless, one title, *Aa-sia'*, is used in the Thai naming system specifically to show respect for important or powerful Chinese merchants. Thus an ethnic Thai merchant named Prasert Tantiyanon, even if important or powerful, would still be addressed as *Khun* Prasert while his or her Chinese counterpart even with the identical Thai name might likely be addressed as *Aa-sia'* Prasert.

It should not be assumed, however, that all ethnic Chinese have or even prefer Thai names. Many ethnic Chinese have two names. They are likely to have Thai names with which they conduct business with ethnic Thais and with foreigners and a second Chinese name that they use in the Chinese community. *Farang* business people may in fact achieve an advantage not readily open to ethnic Thais in using the Chinese name of such person. The Thai would be expected to use the Thai addressing system. *Farangs*, by contrast, can show a respect for their ethnic Chinese counterpart's traditions and community because they have chosen to use the Chinese address system. Finally, as with the rest of Southeast Asia, many ethnic Chinese do not follow the local naming system, and only have a Chinese name. In the Chinese naming system, the person using a Chinese name should be aware that the

individual's family name comes first. After this comes the generation name and the personal name, usually hyphenated when written in English. Thus, Wu Kwok-wen is Mr. Wu. Calling him Mr. Kwok-wen would be very insulting. Because Chinese traditionally are extremely reluctant to use personal names in any but the most intimate relationships, many ethnic Chinese have adopted additional Thai nicknames or—for foreigners—English names so that their ethnic Thai or U.S. counterparts can have the illusion of being on a first name basis without insulting anyone. Thus, Wu Kwok-wen may select the English name Ralph. His English-language card might even show the name as ''Ralph'' Wu Kwok-Wen. His U.S. business counterparts would then know to call him Ralph, *Khun* Ralph, or Mr. Wu as they felt appropriate.

Most Chinese women do not adopt the names of their husbands after marriage. Thus, Lee Mei-Ling could easily be the wife of Wu Kwok-Wen. For business purposes, with English-speakers, she may allow herself to be called Mrs. Wu, but most people will know her as Ms. Lee or by her Thai name.

THE ENVIRONMENT

ATTITUDES TOWARD TECHNOLOGY. The attitudes of both of Thailand's major ethnic groups regarding technology significantly differs from that of the United States. The United States is a control cultures, meaning that U.S. culture views technology as consistently positive and reinforces a belief that people can control their environment to conform to their needs. By contrast, both ethnic-Thai and ethnic-Chinese culture in Thailand are more accurately described as a harmonization culture. Here the emphasis is on one's integration into a natural order rather than one's control of that order. This is most evident in the Thai concept of spirit forces, ghosts, and the charms and rites used to placate or direct these forces. The Thai Buddhist concept of karma pervades Thai life as well and has within it the notion of a harmony between good and evil. This notion is summarized in the commonly used Thai proverb: ''Do good, get good; do evil, get evil.'' As a result, in Thai culture, the environment is not (as it is in U.S. culture) something to be conquered, but something to be kept in balance.

This harmonization orientation toward technology and the environment is even more clearly expressed by the ethnic Chinese following of *feng shui* (ancient geomancy dealing with the balance of spiritual forces). The importance of location, lucky or unlucky dates, and numerous other factors determined by *feng shui* experts guide most of Thailand's traditional Chinese community. For example, many Chinese would confer with a *feng shui* expert before deciding on an office location or signing an important agreement.

Considerations for maintaining good relations with spirits, balancing karma, and following *feng shui* are often looked down on by ethnocentric or religiously bigoted foreigners unfamiliar with them. Regardless of the foreigner's own beliefs, however, he or she should be aware that such practices are important to those who adhere to them. These practices should be accorded the same respect one would give to any Western religious practice, rather than be misinterpreted as the equivalent of minor superstition.

ENVIRONMENTAL ISSUES. Following World War II, approximately 70 percent of Thailand was covered in forest and woodlands. By the late 1980s, only 20 percent to no more than 30 percent could be considered forested. Deforestation had been conducted so haphazardly that in 1988 a major disaster occurred when hundreds of tons of cut lumber slid down hillsides cleared of their trees and buried several villages. Hundreds were killed and more were left homeless. In 1989, responding to the disaster, Thailand outlawed all logging and related industries. Timber imports are strictly monitored and the construction industry must even request government approval to use timber salvaged from existing structures.

SOCIAL ORGANIZATION

Social organizational factors in Thailand affecting business include the political structure and climate of the nation, the importance of the king, the role of Buddhism in all aspects of life, and the concept of the work ethic.

THE POLITICAL STRUCTURE AND CLIMATE. Thailand's political system has never been particularly stable since the 1932 coup d'etat that overthrew King Pokklao (Rama VII), Thailand's last absolute monarch. Since the advent of constitutional monarchy, Thailand has undergone ten successful coups, nine unsuccessful coup attempts, and a partial occupation by the Japanese (during World War II). Yet the stability of the Thai legal courts and the unifying respect for the monarchy—constitutionally limited or otherwise—have customarily sustained Thai economic stability and political consistency on the day-to-day level until fairly recent times.

On February 23, 1991, Thailand's longest modern period of stability was shaken when the government was overthrown by a bloodless military coup. In May 1992 antigovernment demonstrators demanded the military leader's resignation. The military killed dozens of the protesters and hundreds more were injured in the incident. These incidents have raised concerns among foreign investors and manufacturers regarding Thailand's political stability.

THE IMPORTANCE OF THE KING. The power of the absolute monarchy of the Thai king was ended with the forced abdication of King Pokklao in the 1932 pro-democracy coup. While theoretically, the king holds little direct power (he appoints the members of the Supreme Court and advises in a ceremonial capacity), in reality the monarchy is far stronger than any other constitutional monarchy in the world.

The king and the royal family are revered by the vast majority of Thailand's people, who view the monarch as a sort of demigod. Even the Thai constitution expressly indicates that the monarch be "enthroned in a position of revered worship." Not only is open criticism of the monarch and royal family illegal, but the vast majority of the Thai people will not tolerate even mildly negative comments regarding them. As a result, the foreigner conducting business in Thailand should avoid all negative comments regarding Thai royalty.

One side point to this is the unintentional insult many U.S. movie fans often make in referencing the unfortunate U.S. motion picture *The King and I.* This classic Hollywood musical depicts the Thai monarch Rama IV (King Mongkut the Great) as backward and naive, and needing to be educated to behave in a civilized manner by his Western tutor. Thais universally consider the film or reference to it to be an insult to the monarchy and Thailand.

Relatedly, Thais are highly patriotic. It is a serious offense to belittle the nation or insult shows of nationalism. For instance, the Thai national anthem is played each morning and each early evening through loudspeakers set up for the purpose in most Thai villages . Thais stop their activities and stand to show respect. For the foreigner, failure to stand may show lack of respect. While this widespread practice is not carried on in much of Bangkok, its counterpart exists when the anthem is played in movie theaters and other public gatherings.

THE ROLE OF BUDDHISM

Approximately 95 percent of Thailand's population—ethnic Thai, ethnic Chinese, and others—practice Buddhism. As Buddhism is a lifestyle as much as a religion, its near universal practice in Thailand has an effect on business as it does on all aspects of life. While Buddhism cannot adequately be summarized in a few paragraphs here, it is possible at least to point to areas where Buddhism will have an influence on business that would contrast with standard U.S. business practice.

First, the United States emphasizes to a large degree the importance of individual achievement. The average U.S. businessperson is motivated by a desire to succeed and a craving to get ahead. This a very foreign notion to Buddhism, which teaches that all desires result only in suffering. What one achieves is the sum total of one's meritorious and evil behavior in both this life and stored up from past life—this state of what happens to one is called karma. A Thai's success (or failure), therefore, is usually viewed as entirely apart from what one actually does—it is a function of good or bad karma. Thus, the North American notion of making one's own opportunities contrasts with the Thai notion of making the most of situations as (or if) they present themselves.

The Buddhist concept of the process of change also contrasts markedly with how change is viewed in the United States. Both Thai and U.S. cultures embrace change—but for entirely different reasons. The United States is a culture primarily of immigrants who believed in the positive nature of change. In the United States, however, change must be created; the average U.S. businessperson is—by Thai standards—almost obsessed with trying to change things as they are by force of will. For Thais, by contrast, change is inevitable. In Buddhism, change is the most fundamental principle—all things must change. As a result, Thais feel much less concerned than their U.S. counterparts precisely because change will occur regardless of one's efforts. To attempt to direct the change would be futile—whether that change is trying to stop the change of state from death to life or in any other event, including business.

Thailand and the United States are both nations with a strong emphasis on tolerance. This too, however, differs fundamentally between the two cultures. Those from the United States emphasize tolerance on the belief that all people are of equal importance. Thais do not share in the U.S. belief in equality. Instead, Thais emphasize tolerance based on the opposite rationale—the Buddhist precept that all things, including people, are essentially unimportant.

Finally, most Thai men, even fairly Westernized or relatively secularized Thais, will have spent a period as a monk. This explains the throngs of orange-robed monks one sees throughout the country from the most urban parts of Bangkok to the most rural northern villages. Again, while many monks *buat phra* (enter the monkhood—*sangha*) for a lifetime, it is the average people—not the exceptionally religious individuals—who make up the majority of the monks in the nation. Many Thais *buat phra* for only a few days, but the majority *buat phra* for at least three months, and many for considerably longer. One usually enters the monkhood just before marriage or before taking on a first major job. Monkhood is often seen as a sort of way to enter into the more responsible positions of work and family life. Nevertheless, Thais may enter the monkhood several times in their lives and for any number of reasons. The practice is so common that banks and government jobs are required to give leave for employees to make merit as monks, a practice followed by many Thai companies as well.

Leaves are taken for men to undergo the Buddhist monkhood to fulfill parental obligations, for *dukkha* (or mourning), and to give recognition for *kae bon* (to achieve goals in the Thai sense of the phrase).

THE WORK ETHIC IN THAILAND

The nature of the work ethic among ethnic Thais and ethnic Chinese differ from one another and both differ from that practiced generally in the United States.

ETHNIC-THAI WORK ETHIC. Most ethnic Thais are good and loyal workers. They are not, however, motivated, as are most people from the United States, by work itself as a prime object. For most North Americans, work in and of itself is considered to be a good thing. Most Americans identify themselves by their jobs and a common introductory question in North America is "What do you do?"—a rather un-Thai question.

Ethnic Thais see work as a part of life, but not an end in itself. Work per se is not good of its own accord. Work—as all things—must have an element of enjoyment in it. This need to have a good time—called *sanu'ke*—has almost the same attribute of being considered good in itself as North Americans tend to give the notion of work. In short, work without *sanu'ke* is unacceptable, while *sanu'ke* without work is acceptable. For Americans, work without fun is not only acceptable but arguably the norm and possibly even culturally preferable. A Thai, in short, must enjoy his or her job. The foreign manager must take this into account to manage a Thai **workforce** well.

ETHNIC-CHINESE WORK ETHIC. The ethnic Chinese do not share the ethnic-Thai drive for *sanu'ke*. Assuredly, the average Chinese will not eschew enjoyment in the workplace, but it is not a mandatory prerequisite there or in any other arena of life.

The ethnic Chinese, though Buddhist, are markedly influenced by the ethical principles of Confucianism. The Confucianist obligations to family and clan are strong in the workplace. These obligations tie family member to family member and clan member to clan member in a web of obligations known in Chinese as *guanxi*. This web of relationships motivates the ethnic Chinese to fulfill the needs of those to whom he or she is tied. *Guanxi*, also leads to a greater group identification than practiced among ethnic Thais and (even more so) than U.S. businesspeople. The Confucianist influence on Chinese life tends to lead the individual Chinese to see himself or herself first as a member of a larger kinship structure and only secondly as an individual. This is exactly the opposite notion of U.S. individualism, where the individual is always seen as primary and motivation is at its highest form in reaching self-actualization of one's individual goals. Such U.S.-style individualism is very foreign to most of Thailand's ethnic Chinese.

A second Confucianist notion differentiates ethnic Chinese behavior from ethnic Thai or U.S. behavior. This is the notion that one lives on in the memory of others after death, and that attachment to the memory of one's ancestors is good. In traditional Buddhism as practiced by ethnic Thais, any attachment is bad—including attachment to the memory of one's ancestors. In customary U.S. Judeo-Christian notions, one goes to heaven after one dies. One lives on in heaven, not in the memory of one's descendants. Being remembered after death is generally perceived as good in the United States, but it is not a religious precept. For the Confucianist-influenced Chinese, however, being remembered is one's afterlife. As a result, the traditional Chinese practice is to do as much as possible while alive so that one will be more likely to be remembered. The notion of overwork does not, per se, exist in the Chinese conception. One can work too much so that, by exhaustion, one becomes ill or one overlooks important obligations—but overwork as a state is not an understandable concept. By contrast, the U.S. notion of work rests on the Judeo-Christian notion of work as a punishment for sin in the Garden of Eden. Adam's punishment upon his banishment from Eden was work. When one works too much, in the United States, one is said to be a "glutton for punishment." Such notions traditionally have no counterpart in the ethnic-Chinese community.

CONTEXTING

Thailand is a high context society and the United States is a low context culture. This means that Thais are more likely to rely on implicit communication rather than on explicit messages. Thais as a result read more into what is said than the words themselves may actually mean. For most Thais, what is meant matters more than what is actually said.

In Thailand, meaning is usually communicated indirectly, especially in the delivery of bad news. As a result, Thais are likely to agree to things with which they disagree, allowing the context of the discussion or past relationship to convey their disagreement. This is clear to Thais but to those from low context cultures such as the United States, such indirect communication is often misread as dishonesty. Conversely, the direct style of communication practiced by most U.S. businesspeople in Thailand is perceived as rude and often causes others to lose face.

Thais, as a high context culture, place a strong value on value on face-saving, while most North Americans place little emphasis on face-saving. Most Thais are motivated by a desire to maintain surface harmony, even if disagreement brews beneath the surface. By contrast, low context U.S. business practice encourages individuals to say exactly what they think.

This also affects the U.S. and Thai approach to the law. U.S. business behavior is controlled by following the law and adherence to written agreements. In Thailand, one commonly holds to a contract to maintain harmony in the workplace rather than from fear of a lawsuit. The North American businessperson in Thailand is thus viewed as threatening to this carefully balanced harmony. Additionally, U.S. low context businesspeople are viewed as lacking tact (and therefore unpleasant to deal with), having no sense of face, and being needlessly litigious. The Thais in turn are viewed by their North American counterparts as dishonoring their promises and ignoring their own laws. In reality both perceptions are accurate when viewed through the contexting values of the other's culture.

Still, to succeed in business in Thailand, the foreigner will need to view contracts and other legally binding arrangements as ongoing rather than definitive. Moreover, the foreigner will have to be willing to allow some inconsistencies to stand at times to maintain appearance and avoid shaming the Thais who would otherwise terminate the business relationship.

TEMPORAL CONCEPTION

Thailand is a polychronic culture. Time is more fluid than in monochronic societies such as the United States. The Thais value friendship, personal commitments, and the completion of tasks at hand at the expense of preset schedules.

Time is seen as malleable. Appointment times are approximate. Work hours are variable. Consequently, the monochronic foreigner needs to adjust his or her concepts of scheduling, deadlines, and other time-linked activities in Thailand.

Additionally, most North Americans hold a short-term view of time. North American business practice is driven by a sense of urgency. In part, this is motivated by the needs for quarterly progress built into the system of stockholdership in the United States and Canada. In part, however, quarterly reports have little to do with this urgency—it is a cultural impatience for immediate gratification and the individual drive to bring about visible change.

By contrast, both of Thailand's major business ethnic groups hold a long-term view of time, although for different reasons. The ethnic-Chinese view of time is essentially Confucianist. Time is viewed in generational—not quarterly—terms. The ethnic Chinese view commitments and needs over a long-term view of actions spanning a lifetime as remembered by one's descendants. The ethnic-Thai view of time is equally long-term, but more Buddhist in motivation. Everything is in constant change as part of the endless life cycle that has always gone on before one was born and will continue to go on after one dies. Change is inevitable so one feels no need to force the change ahead of time. Generally Thais believe that things have a way of working out, so there is no need to pressure the end result. To do so would be presumptuous and probably disruptive.

SEE ALSO: Cross-Cultural/International Communication; Malaysia, Doing Business in

[David A. Victor]

FURTHER READING:

Cooper, Robert, and Nanthapa Cooper. *Culture Shock! Thailand*. Singapore: Times Books International, 1982.

Fieg, John Paul. *Thais and North Americans*. Yarmouth, ME: Intercultural Press, 1980.

Leppert, Paul. *Doing Business with the Thais*. Chula Vista, CA: Patton Pacific Press, 1992.

Moore, Frank J. *Thailand—Its People, Its Society, Its Culture*. NY: HRAF Press, 1974.

Olson, Grant A. *Looking to America to Solve Thailand's Problems*. Bangkok: Satirakoses-Nagapradipa Foundation, 1987.

O'Reilly, James, and Larry Habegger, eds. *Travelers' Tales: Thailand*. San Francisco: Travelers' Tales, 1993.

Schlossstein, Steve. *Asia's New Little Dragons: The Dynamic Emergence of Indonesia, Thailand & Malaysia*. Chicago: Contemporary Books, 1991.

Victor, David A. *International Business Communication*. New York: HarperCollins, 1992.

Wyatt, David K. *Thailand: A Short History*. New Haven, CT: Yale University Press, 1984.

THEORY OF CONSTRAINTS

Many challenges face business and industry today. Companies throughout the world are making the transition, or attempting to do so, from local, regional, or national companies, to global ones. For many businesses to survive, they can no longer isolate themselves from the rest of the world. Whether it be in exploiting global resources or entering more markets, to succeed and prosper in a global marketplace, a business must view itself as a global company. This new company view naturally implies increased global competition. To compete globally, companies must learn to accept a major challenge facing business and industry today: continuous, or ongoing improvement, and how to go about achieving it.

In order to work toward continuous improvement, a company must understand how to continuously improve itself. W. Edwards Deming (1900–) was credited with revolutionizing business in Japan by, effectively, introducing concepts of continuous improvement. Out of Deming's teachings, manage-

ment practices such as JIT (just-in-time) manufacturing, TQM (**total quality management**), SPC (statistical process control), and EI (employee involvement) were created. While each of these philosophies has merit, their actual benefits, as measured over time, have generally been less than what was originally assumed. This is because very few organizations that attempt to implement these various "improvement opportunities" correctly address the issues.

Companies should be asking the following critical questions of themselves (prior to implementing an "improvement opportunity"):

- What are the key areas within the organization for competitive improvement?
- What are the key technologies and techniques that will improve these key competitive areas at the least cost?
- How do these improvement and investment opportunities relate (i.e., how can they be applied in an integrated, supportive, and logical manner)?
- In what sequence should these opportunities be addressed?

Although Deming has passed on, the spirit of his work remains alive and well. TQM, JIT, EI, etc. are today being recast, according to a growing number of management experts, into a philosophy known as the "Theory of Constraints" (TOC).

TOC: A MANAGEMENT PHILOSOPHY

TOC, as a management philosophy, focuses on a company's most critical issues (obstacles or constraints) and the effects of those constraints on the rest of the system (company). TOC allows a company to use its constraints as leverages by which it can improve its subject system. A constraint is anything that limits a company's ability to achieve a higher level of performance.

TOC was developed by Israeli physicist Eliyahu M. Goldratt, of the Goldratt Institute in New Haven, Connecticut. Goldratt introduced TOC in his novel, *The Goal*. It is estimated that TOC is now being practiced in some form by 400 to 500 companies around the world. Some such companies include Procter and Gamble Co., Philip Morris Companies, Inc., Ford Motor Co., General Electric, and AT&T.

At its core, TOC accepts the reality that any company (or enterprise) is composed of a varying number of coupled subsystems. If each of these subsystems is optimized individually, overall company performance may actually be considered disappointing (because of the rule: you focus on everything and you end up focusing on nothing). Nevertheless, optimization of the entire system is appropriate, despite the fact that it could lead to subsystem "suboptimization." The company must identify its core problem(s) (or constraints) first. These constraints can involve:

- product quality
- product cost
- product engineering effectiveness
- materials procurement
- production planning and control

These constraints are most likely to directly affect the company's profitability and cash flow. This impact, or limitation, on profitability and cash flow serve as the platform for the TOC management philosophy.

TOC views an organization as a chain, composed of many links (resources). The contribution of a link in the chain is heavily dependent upon the performance of its other links. The organization must be successful in its effort to synchronize the various chain links it requires to satisfy the organization's predetermined purpose, whatever that purpose may be. In order for a company to improve its performance, to continuously improve, it must learn to identify and manage its weakest chain link. By doing this, the company has answered a critical question tied to performance improvement: What to change? Logically, the organization must then answer "to what should they change the constraint," and finally, "how to cause this change." This is accomplished by applying a five-step TOC process:

1. What: Identify the system's constraint(s)
2. To What: Decide how to exploit the constraint(s)
3. How To: Subordinate everything else to the constraint(s)
4. Elevate the system's constraint(s)
5. After breaking the constraint, Repeat the 5-step process

OVERLAP OF TOC PHILOSOPHY. TOC does in fact borrow from many of Deming's progressive management philosophies. TOC, however, goes well beyond Deming's approaches, and differs from them in many ways. This is what is making TOC a leading "contender" for the next generation of management theory for American business, and indeed the business world abroad. Areas of TOC that overlap with other management approaches include:

- It stresses ongoing, continuous improvement.
- It seeks employee involvement and empowerment.
- It stresses company-wide education and cultural transformation.

- It establishes clearly defined quality measurements.
- It breaks down departmental barriers, stressing global rather than local goals.
- It calls for shrinking the supplier base and reducing inventories.

Differences with TOC versus other management approaches include: (1) TOC focuses on identifying and exploiting constraints as the way to achieve ongoing improvement and increased profitability; and a major difference (2) it replaces cost accounting (which according to Goldratt, is "the number one enemy of productivity") with a new measurement system.

TOC maintains that cost-based management mentality invariably leads to: flawed decisions, focusing on artificial targets, and masking root causes of problems.

According to chief operating officer Larry Webb of Stanley Furniture, for a company dedicated to the implementation of TOC, the biggest difference between TOC and other philosophies is that "the others basically try to fix the whole company at once, which is a physical impossibility. By focusing on the constraint, everyone in the company is allocating resources in the right place. What TOC does in a succinct way is make sure you work on the right things rather than just doing things right."

MEASUREMENTS OF TOC

To understand TOC and to apply it effectively to an organization, one must completely understand the goal of the organization (for this essay, it is assumed that organization refers to a profit-seeking organization, as opposed to a nonprofit one). Goldratt, in *The Goal*, emphasized that the goal of any organization is to make money. It is important therefore to create a set of measurements that honestly and accurately allows an organization to monitor its performance as it relates to its goal. Professor James Cox of Georgia University contended that the traditional cost accounting system used by business for nearly 70 years, "doesn't lend itself to tracking the impact of decisions on revenues and profits."

With TOC, the "cost world" is replaced by the "throughput world," which is driven by these three key components:

1. Throughput: The rate at which the system generates new money through sales.
2. Inventory: Money the system has invested in things it intends to sell, which would include plant, property, and equipment.
3. Operating expense: The money spent to convert inventory into throughput.

Using these measurements in combination with TOC "scientific" problem-solving methods allows management to focus on critical issues and root causes rather than symptoms of problems.

A major difference in the cost world and the TOC throughput world is that the cost world focuses on reducing operating expenses as the primary means to improvement, whereas the throughput world views cutting operating expenses as the least important of the three key improvement measurements. The throughput world emphasizes increasing throughput, reducing inventory, and reducing operating expenses respectively.

Tradition in the cost world says to save money, or reduce costs, a company must explore laying people off as downturns occur. A TOC driven company, however, will not view layoffs as an option, as they would rather seek alternatives than to disrupt employee morale and loyalty.

TOC emphasizes reducing inventory as a way to expedite response time. In the throughput world, inventory is seen as a liability, not as an asset (as it is viewed in the cost world). Common-sense reasoning suggests that if a company reduces its inventories, the following occurs:

- Increased responsiveness to the market
- Improved "promise-date" performance
- Decreased obsolescence cost
- Increased quality

TYPES OF CONSTRAINTS

Constraints limit our ability to improve performance relative to throughput. In TOC, a constraint can take various forms. These include capacity constraint (bottleneck or physical), market constraint, policy constraint, logistical constraint, and behavioral constraint.

A capacity constraint is simply a situation where market demand for a product exceeds the amount of the product that the system is able to supply. Some general examples of capacity constraints include skewed investment policies towards a specific type of unit production process, "cost world" focus, traditional manning practices, and personnel hiring guidelines. The reverse of capacity constraint is considered a market constraint whereby an organization is capable and willing to sell more products than the market is willing to buy. Market constraints include pricing based upon product standard costs, sales commission policies, product technology development guidelines, and market segmentation practices. When a company issues a "no-overtime" policy, it is placing a policy constraint upon the system.

Perhaps the easiest constraint to illustrate is a physical constraint (bottleneck). Physical constraints are resources, either human or mechanical, whose capacity is less than or equal to the demand placed on them. The challenge therefore becomes to identify and utilize physical constraints to control the flow of product through the plant or store into the hands of the consumer. TOC proves that physical constraints control the pace of any system, so therefore an hour gained at the physical constraint is an hour gained for the entire system. An hour gained elsewhere, at a nonconstraint, is therefore meaningless.

TOC points out that investments made to support a nonconstraint are unwise. The TOC manager must ask himself or herself if an investment made will: (1) increase throughout; (2) Reduce inventory expense: (3) Reduce operating expense: and if the resource that may receive additional investment is a constraint.

EXAMPLES OF TOC IN MOTION

Of the 400-500 companies practicing TOC, their range of business involvement is quite varied. TOC is practiced in many different industries, which include: automotive, computers, telecommunications, furniture, cabinetry, retail food, consumer goods, and apparel.

The Warren-Featherbone Company in Gainesville, Georgia, an apparel business, has realized a 10 percent increase in gross margins (over industry averages) in the first one-year-plus of its TOC implementation. Kent-Moore Cabinets, Inc. of Bryan, Texas, has seen sales increase 15 percent, while its number of employees dropped nearly 20 percent, again in little over one-year's time.

Many other companies continue to see the benefits that the TOC management approach can provide. It is not considered an overnight process, although in certain manufacturing environments, quick, short-term results can be experienced. TOC is rather a long-term approach to how an organization, or a system, operates. As Deming's work revolutionized management practices, so too does the theory of constraints continue the transition.

[Art DuRivage]

FURTHER READING:

Sharcer, Kim D. *The Consumer Chase*. 1991.

THIRD WORLD, DOING BUSINESS IN THE

The term "third world" came to use in grouping countries by their economic status. The industrialized countries located mostly in the West are described as the "first world," the communist countries of the East are the "second world," and the rest of the developing countries are called the "third world." With the dismantling of the Soviet Union and the discarding of **communism** by the East European countries, the "second world" has lost its meaning, and the term "third world" has become a misnomer. The term is still being used as a synonym to describe the developing countries, but according to the **International Monetary Fund**, there are only two groupings of countries by their economic status—the 23 industrialized countries and the 138 developing countries. Force of habit still persists and the term "third world" is widely used even now. For the purposes of this article, third world countries are taken to be the same as developing countries as loosely grouped by the IMF.

HISTORICAL PERSPECTIVE

Most of the third world countries are former colonies of European powers. Most of them gained their independence after World War II. Colonialism was as much an economic domination as it was political. The main features of a colonial economy were twofold. First, the natural resources of the colonies were exploited and depleted by the colonial powers. Secondly, the colonies were used as the market for the finished goods of the colonial countries. In both ways the economic interests of the colonial countries prevailed.

When the colonies gained their independence, most of them faced this negative economic situation. When a country encounters an economy in this condition, many factors are necessary to turn things around. Economic discipline, good management, strategic planning, and above all, competent political leadership are some of those factors. Most newly independent countries sadly lacked these conditions.

A legacy of colonialism is mistrust of the colonial powers. The move for economic self-reliance on the part of many former colonies can be attributed to this mistrust. Protectionism is a by-product of a policy of self-reliance. Foreign investment is suspect. The fear of foreign profit draining the economy is real. The post-independent economic growth or lack of it in many countries can be traced back to this colonial past.

POLITICAL BACKGROUND

Politically most third world countries do not enjoy a democratic system. Dictatorships of one kind or other are a common feature of most countries. There are a few notable exceptions (such as India) that have managed to maintain an unbroken record of democratic leadership. In an undemocratic system, corruption thrives unchecked. Dictatorships often distort the

economic system. Efficiency and the need for quick decision making are reasons dictators give for seizing power. Dictatorships rarely live up to their promise. For a business to operate in a country, it needs political stability and consistent policies from the government. In the absence of these conditions in most third world countries, businesses have to be much more cautious. Doing business in many of these countries involves added political risk.

ECONOMIC CONDITIONS

Economically, a feature of most third world countries is their national debt. Often the economy of a country is based on a single commodity, meaning price fluctuations can cause serious damage. Even countries that have oil wealth have not been able to overcome economic problems because of poor management skills. The economies of these countries are in a vicious circle. To develop their economies these countries have to borrow the capital, increasing their debt. Servicing the debt becomes difficult if the country cannot export enough. The exports are primarily natural resources with their concomitant price fluctuations. When the price is low, exports do not generate enough surplus to service the debt.

To transform a colonial economy into a modern industrial economy, the third world countries need capital and skilled human resources. Again with some exceptions, most countries do not possess either of these. The internal savings are not adequate to mount an ambitious development program. Higher education has not progressed sufficiently, so skilled human resources at the technical and management level are lacking. With no political direction the problem becomes compounded. Poverty and economic drift are generally the consequence. As noted earlier, there is often a reluctance to invite foreign capital investment. Even when investment from abroad is welcomed, the economic conditions are often not good enough to attract such investment.

In recent years, increased globalization, a breakdown of protectionism, increased free trade, the collapse of the communist system, and the relative success of the free market economy, have allowed a group of third world countries to emerge as newly industrialized countries. These countries, in spite of their political systems, have embraced the capitalist path of development. In these countries, domestic savings and foreign investment have combined to provide the capital and the human resource skills are sufficiently developed to employ the capital toward productive enterprises. These countries are the more entrepreneurial among the developing countries. Hong Kong, South Korea, Taiwan, Singapore, Brazil, Chile, and Mexico, are examples of this.

Commensurate with the higher risks involved are the prospects of higher returns when doing business in third world countries, especially the newly industrializing countries. These countries provide cheaper labor that is skilled enough to perform many operations. As these countries become more prosperous, they also provide a growing market for goods and services; the high population in most of these countries means large potential markets as purchasing power increases. Many of these countries have started offering economic incentives to attract business and investment. It is in the interest of the industrialized countries to take advantage of this situation. In a highly competitive global economy, many industries can diversify manufacturing and keep costs to the minimum by moving to developing countries. Except where highly skilled labor is needed, diversification to at least some of the developing countries is a desirable alternative.

In many of the third world countries, the policy of nationalistic self-reliance is leading to the pragmatic approach of generating employment and prosperity even at the cost of profits being taken out of the country. The need of the industrialized countries to expand economically is consistent with the need of the developing countries to industrialize and improve the standard of living of the people. In this context the third world countries present a unique opportunity for the greater prosperity of both groups of countries.

BUSINESS ENVIRONMENT

It is not valid to generalize on the **business conditions** prevailing in all of the third world countries. As pointed out earlier, conditions vary greatly especially between the newly industrializing countries and the rest. However there are some common features. Political stability, especially when democratic roots are absent, is poor. Investment capital is scarce. Wages and benefits tend to be low. Availability of skilled workers is limited. Educational levels are low, especially for high technology business. Environmental regulations are few and not seriously enforced. The judicial system is likely to be difficult to utilize. It is often difficult to obtain permits to do business from the bureaucracy. Communication is a difficult process when dealing with a very different culture and value system. Misunderstandings are common. Lessons in the language and culture of the country are a prerequisite to doing business. **Infrastructure** necessary to operate a business such as communications system, transportation facilities, energy supplies etc. may not be fully available. These are the factors a business needs to examine before embarking on any business ventures in the third world. The nature of the business determines the varying degrees of importance of these factors. The risks and challenges are high, as is the potential for profit.

INFORMATION SOURCES

The United Nations Industrial Development Organization located in Vienna, Austria, is a major source of additional information on developing countries. It publishes the periodical *Industrial Development Abstracts* and the annual *Industry and Development Global Report*. The **World Bank** in Washington D.C. is another important source of information on developing countries. Its *World Debt Tables* is a two-volume annual publication that includes summary tables of external finance for developing countries, and country tables. Other publications from the World Bank that are particularly relevant to developing countries are: *African Development Indicators, Historically Planned Economies, Social Indicators of development, World Development Report, World Development Indicators* and the *World Tables*. It is possible to search by country in any of these publications and get statistical data on many of the variables described in this article. Most of the World Bank publications are also available in diskette form, making analysis easier.

The United Nations Economic Commission for Latin America and for Asia and the Pacific publish *Economic Survey of Latin America and the Caribbean* and *Economic Bulletin for Asia and the Pacific*. **Association of Southeast Asian Nations** (ASEAN) publishes annual surveys and statistical data on member countries. The *Asia Yearbook* published by the *Far Eastern Economic Weekly*, and *Latin America*, an annual published by Stryker-Post Publications in Washington D.C. are examples of private publications providing country-based information on their respective regions.

[Divakara K. (Dik) Varma]

TIME MANAGEMENT

The term "time management" refers to accomplishing maximum productivity within a set period— be it days, hours, weeks, or months. In business the principle of time management is to use the fixed amount of time available wisely, to work "smarter, not harder" in order to get more accomplished within that fixed period.

For centuries man used the general measurement of sun to sun in looking at accomplishments, but with the development of the clock, attention began to focus on the hours within a day as well. By the seventeenth century the clock had been perfected and so well-established in society that the philosopher Renè Descartes (1596-1650) used the clock as a model for humanity in his writings.

But it was with the Industrial Revolution that the clock really came of age. Frederick W. Taylor (1856-1915), an engineer, began to make time and motion studies. These put each aspect of the work process to a stopwatch measurement. Then, management studied the results to look for ways to reduce the number of steps needed to accomplish a particular task or job. This concept of time management as something that managers did for line workers proceeded until the 1930s when managers began to find their own tasks so overwhelming that they too sought a way to manage time.

In the 1930s, Ivy Lee, a management consultant initiated a simple "6-Step" process that became the watchword of managers. The Ivy Lee plan was simple. The manager needed to list the six most important things to be done that day, in order of importance, the most important being first. Then, the manager was to work on those items in order, not proceeding to item two until item one had been accomplished, and so on.

In the last half of the twentieth century the influence of time on activity became as precious as capital and was viewed in much the same terms. Time is spoken of as something to be spent or saved. "Time is money" is a commonly heard saying. Diana Scharf-Hunt and Pam Hart described time as a "commodity, a resource to be used, hoarded, traded, and exploited."

After World War II, studies of management began to broaden to look at time management in all aspects of life. Use of time became a strong focal area of management seminars in the 1960s and 1970s. In 1967 Peter Drucker proposed a chronological record-keeping method for managers; in 1972 that was further refined by Alec MacKenzie into an executive time directory. In 1973 Alan Lakein's book, *How to Get Control of Your Time and Your Life* reflected recognition by the business education sector of the general population's concern with time management. Some of the best-known resources on time management include *The One Minute Manager* by Dr. Kenneth H. Blanchard and Spencer Johnson, and its sequel by Blanchard and Robert Lorber, Putting the *One Minute Manager to Work*.

The essentials of time management involve recognition of goals and organization of one's efforts so that all steps taken follow a path toward that goal and are not wasted or diverted from that purpose. Many of the barriers to efficient time management are flaws of human nature—the desire to procrastinate, to pursue pleasure rather than purpose, perfectionism that will not accept a job as complete, and insecurity that does not allow a person to delegate tasks to others, trying to accomplish everything oneself. As such, a time management strategy often begins with an assessment of one's personal habits, including the ability to "just say no" to certain requests for demands upon your time that will not contribute to your basic goals. Alec

MacKenzie, in *The Time Trap*, said that time management is not just about the use of an abstract commodity—time. MacKenzie posited that time management is about what we can accomplish with time.

Good time management also reaches into other areas of good management—planning and goal setting, communication with others in order to effectively delegate, and assessment skills to determine if the goals were reached and how work can be done better in the future.

Will this view of time management continue? According to Diana Scharf-Hunt and Pam Hart, just as the clock—a mechanical tool in a mechanical age—led industry to respond to needs for time management in a mechanistic way with time and motion and lists and plans for steps to reach goals, the computer information age has broadened our understanding of time and created different needs to which management must respond.

Scharf-Hunt, a respected management consultant and specialist in time management, put forth the idea that as the twentieth century draws to a close, the seconds and minutes of a clock are no longer the final arbiters of time. The computer calculates in nanoseconds—a flash of light. Scharf-Hunt and Hart found "Just as the clock tolled hours, minutes and seconds for the Industrial age, now the computer measures intervals in fleeting blips of time so infinitesimal that we cannot experience, let alone absorb. As the clock once revolutionized work and society, the computer is revolutionizing how we work and live with time."

Scharf-Hunt and Hart formulated a time management style for the twenty-first century that involves a more thorough understanding of who we are, a more holistic approach to time that blends an outlook on work and life and the need to balance personal choices of all types—not just career choices—and philosophy with work. While appointments and meetings need to be viewed as relevant to the work goal, one needs also to consider their relevancy to total purpose. The broader basis for control is the belief that the mind is the ultimate control or site of management activity and the whole mind must be considered.

But while the foundation of time management may shift and go beyond the business setting to life as a whole, the premise remains that time management in business seeks to use time and structure it to enable managers to reach the goals of efficiency and effectiveness.

[Joan Leotta]

FURTHER READING:

Blanchard, Kenneth H., and Spencer Johnson. *The One Minute Manager*. New York: Berkley Books, 1982.

Blanchard, Kenneth H., and Robert Lorber. *Putting the One Minute Manager to Work*. New York: William Morrow and Company, 1984.

Drucker, Peter. *The Effective Executive*. New York: Harper, 1967.

Lakein, Alan. *How to Get Control of Your Time and Your Life*. PH Wyden. 1973.

MacKenzie, Alec. *The Time Trap*. New York: Amacon, 1990.

Mancini, Marc. *Time Management*. New York: Business One Irwin/Mirror Press, 1994.

Scharf-Hunt, Diana, and Pam Hart. *The Tao of Time*. New York: Simon and Schuster, 1990.

Weber, Rose A. *Time is Money*. New York: The Free Press, 1980.

TIME SERIES ANALYSIS

Time series analysis is a **forecasting** technique which relies on historic quantitative observations for predicting future values. A time series consists of a set of observations of a quantitative variable taken at successive points in time. Time series analysis attempts to relate the quantitative variable to the independent variable, time. Generally, the time series analysis models break the series down into separate components, each of which is then used to make the forecast. In this manner, greater accuracy is obtained because the separate influences of each of the components are given consideration.

COMPONENTS

The first component is trend, the variable which underlies the long-term growth or decline in the data. Trend data can form straight lines (linear relationships) or curves (nonlinear relationships) which reflect changes in either supply-side or demand-side factors. Such changes could be in demographics, technology, price levels, productivity, or tax laws.

The second component is seasonal variation. Seasonal fluctuations typically occur on a weekly, monthly, or quarterly basis and are dependent on such factors as consumer buying patterns, production times, or delivery schedules. These variations form patterns which recur regularly within a year's time, but not necessarily to the same extent.

The third, or cyclical component, produces wavelike fluctuations around the trend-line. However, the length of time of cyclical fluctuations is different than that of seasonal variations. These fluctuations are normally greater than one year's duration and are due to changing economic and business conditions.

The final component is the erratic component, which represents nonsystematic, or random, fluctuations in the data. This component produces variations in the data which cannot be explained by the other components. In the long-run, the erratic components tend to cancel each other out, (their statistical expectation is zero), therefore they are not used in the forecasting process.

As a hypothetical example, consider the sales of new motorcycles. The long-term trend is increasing as more models are available and advertising campaigns have heavily promoted their use. Sales of new motorcycles also contain a cyclical element due to the general level of business activity and therefore consumer income. Thirdly, there is a seasonal variation in new motorcycle sales: they are bought in greater numbers in the spring and summer months. Any variation in new motorcycle sales which cannot be explained by these factors are due to the erratic component.

MODELS

Many different models can be used to represent a time series. The relationship could be nonlinear (second degree, third degree, exponential, logarithmic, etc.) or linear. One of the most important tasks in time series analysis is to specify a model which best represents the underlying data. One of the most commonly used models for times series analysis is:

$$Y_t = T_t \times C_t \times S_t \times I_t$$

where:

$Y_t =$ the observed data of the series in period t,

$T_t =$ the trend component in period t,

$C_t =$ the cyclical component in period t,

$S_t =$ the seasonal component in period t,

$I_t =$ the random component in period t.

Implicit in this model is that the components interact in a multiplicative fashion and that percentage changes best describe the observed fluctuations in the data. Another commonly used model is the additive version of the above model where:

$$Y_t = T_t + C_t + S_t + I_t$$

Once a model has been specified, four general steps describe the time series analysis process. First, the seasonal component is determined and removed from the raw data. Secondly, the long-term trend effects are eliminated from the deseasonalized data. Next, the random component is calculated and eliminated from the remaining data. Lastly, the cyclical component is analyzed. Many methods are available to deseasonalize the data, isolate the trend and cyclical components, as well as eliminate the random component. A textbook on time series analysis, such as those listed in the Further Reading section of this essay, should be consulted to determine which method is most appropriate and how to use it.

Generally, the objective of time series analysis is for forecasting future values of the observed data. This is easily and accurately accomplished with the coefficients determined from the above four-step process.

[James A. Gerhardinger]

FURTHER READING:

Bails, Dale G., and Larry C. Peppers. *Business Fluctuations: Forecasting Techniques and Applications*. Prentice Hall, 1982.

Dauten, Carl A., and Lloyd M. Valentine. *Business Cycles and Forecasting*. 5th ed. South-Western Publishing Co., 1978.

Firth, Michael. *Forecasting Methods in Business Management*. Edward Arnold Publications Ltd., 1979.

Hanke, John E., and Arthur G. Reitsch. *Business Forecasting*. Allyn and Bacon, 1981.

Hoff, John C. *A Practical Guide to Box-Jenkins Forecasting*. Lifetime Learning Publications, 1983.

TOLL-FREE TELEPHONE CALLS (800 NUMBERS)

Toll-free numbers, which in the United States begin with the prefix 1-800, allow callers to call long distance free of charge. A monthly fee and a per minute fee are charged to the holder of the number.

AT&T introduced the first toll-free service in 1967. The first marketing campaign featuring a toll-free number was launched in 1969 by hotel giant Sheraton Corp., whose 1-800 numbers were generating over nine million calls a year by 1990.

Until 1985, when the **Federal Communications Commission** (FCC) ordered local phone companies to provide equal access for other carriers of toll-free service, the market had been a monopoly for AT&T. MCI Communications Corp. entered the market in 1987 and became AT&T's strongest competitor, with 70,000 customers in 1990, including the Social Security Administration. Market share was divided between No. 3 U.S. Sprint and many regional carriers, such as Telecom USA. AT&T continued to dominate 1-800 service after deregulation, particularly in the international arena. It handled nearly eight billion toll-free calls to its 930,000 1-800 numbers in more than 40 countries in 1989.

Toll-free numbers have been used to market a variety of products, from Cap'n Crunch cereal to Acura luxury automobiles. Through the alphabet printed on telephone keypads, the numbers themselves can provide a valuable mnemonic link to the product or company, and high prices have been paid for these numbers. MCI reportedly paid $200,000 to "buy" the number "1-800-COLLECT" from another user for its collect calling service. Lands' End, a catalog marketer of clothing, bought its number, "1-800-LANDSEND" for an undisclosed price. John M. Shanahan, founder of the "Hooked on Phonics" series of educational cassettes, bought his company's trademark number "1-800-ABCDEFG" for $10,000 and credited its use for much of the company's initial success. Technically, these sales violate federal law, although there has been little interest in prosecuting such offenses.

Toll-free numbers are also an important tool for maintaining contact with customers and gaining information about them; many customer service centers keep such statistics and have great success. Ideally, customer service representatives should be thoroughly trained in a company's products and procedures, and not merely thought of as low-level clerical workers, if the user is to get maximum benefits from customer support. WordPerfect Corp.'s huge success has been attributed by company officials to their use of toll-free numbers to maintain contact with customers. The company began toll-free customer support in 1984 with 17 employees taking 300 to 500 calls per day; this increased to 565 staffers handling 13,000 calls per day in 1990, when its monthly toll-free charges cost $475,000 per month and its annual revenues were $258 million.

By 1990, toll-free service had become affordable to consumers, who saw it as a alternative to expensive calling cards and collect calls. Small businesses sought the same cost savings for sales representatives and other personnel in the field. The numbers also made it relatively inexpensive for small businesses to implement national marketing efforts.

Many options are available with 1-800 service. The calls can be routed to regular phone lines for small business users or special high-capacity leased lines can be established. Call summaries and incoming phone number identification are other options. Special routing to alternate business numbers can help callers avoid busy signals. Average toll-free prices peaked at 32 cents a minute in 1983. By 1990, the figure had fallen to 20 cents.

[Frederick C. Ingram]

FURTHER READING:

Blake, Daniel. "1-800-SMALL-CO." *D&B Reports*. July/August, 1990, pp. 34-35, 46.

Fitzgerald, Kate. "Call It a Day: AT&T Hangs Up on 1-800-COLLECT Service." *Advertising Age*. April 4, 1994, p. 6.

Hoke, Henry R. "1-800-FLOWERS Blossoms as Premier Marketing Utility." *Direct Marketing*. March, 1993, pp. 28-30.

Lee, Chris. "1-800-TRAINING." *Training*. August, 1990, pp. 39-45.

Lefton, Terry. "1-800 May Day." *Brandweek*. March 29, 1993, p. 32.

Oliver, Suzanne. "1-800-GETCASH." *Forbes*. January 17, 1994, p. 55.

Rosen, M. Daniel. "Expanding Your Sales Operation? Just Dial 1-800 . . ." *Sales & Marketing Management*. July, 1990, pp. 82-88, 101.

Schulman, Scott C. "Teaching For Millions." *Success*. October, 1992, p. 10.

Sellers, Patricia. "Yes, Brands Can Still Work Magic." *Fortune*. February 7, 1994, pp. 133-134.

TOTAL QUALITY MANAGEMENT (TQM)

Total Quality Management (TQM) refers to management methods used to enhance quality and productivity in organizations, particularly businesses. In *Quality is Personal*, the authors provide a relatively concise interpretation of TQM as, "a people-focused management system that aims at continual increases in customer satisfaction at continually lower costs." That source further interprets TQM as a comprehensive system approach that works horizontally across an organization, involving all departments and employees and extending backward and forward to envelop both the supply and customer chains.

TQM is only one of many acronyms used to label management systems that focus on quality. Other acronyms that have been used to describe similar quality **management** philosophies and programs include CQI (continuous quality improvement), SQC (statistical quality control), QFD (quality function deployment), QIDW (quality in daily work), TQC (**total quality** control), etc. Despite the ambiguity of the popularized term, "TQM," that acronym is less important than the substance of the management ideology that underlies it. TQM provides a framework for implementing effective quality and productivity initiatives that can increase the profitability and competitiveness of organizations.

BACKGROUND

The roots of TQM concepts can be traced back to quality programs of the early 1900s, long before the TQM acronym was adopted. One of the first companies to implement an advanced quality program, in fact, was J.C. Penney. Its philosophy mirrored the foundation of modern TQM programs. In 1913 Penney adopted seven tenets on which the extremely successful organization was built during the 20th century. In summary, they were to:

1) serve the public to complete satisfaction;

2) expect a fair remuneration for rendered services, but not all the profit that can be extracted from the customers;

3) provide a high level of value, quality, and satisfaction;

4) engage in continual employee and associate training;

5) constantly improve the human factor in J.C. Penney's business activities;

6) reward workers through participation in what the business produces; and

7) hold every policy, method, and act up to this test: "Does it square with what is just and right?"

Although TQM techniques were adopted prior to World War II by a number of organizations, the creation of the Total Quality Management philosophy is generally attributed to Dr. W. Edwards Deming (1900–). In the late 1920s while working as a summer employee at Western Electric Company in Chicago, he found worker motivation systems to be degrading and economically unproductive; incentives were tied directly to quantity of output, and inefficient post-production inspection systems were used to find flawed goods.

Deming teamed up in the 1930s with Walter A. Shewhart, a Bell Telephone Company statistician. Shewhart's work convinced Deming that statistical control techniques could be used to supplant traditional management methods. Using Shewhart's theories, Deming devised a statistically controlled management process that provided managers with a means of determining when to intervene in an industrial process and when to leave it alone. Deming got a chance to put Shewhart's statistical-quality-control techniques, as well as his own management philosophies, to the test during World War Government managers found that his techniques could be easily taught to engineers and workers, and then quickly implemented in overburdened war production plants. One of Deming's clients, the U.S. State Department, sent him to Japan in 1947 as part of a national effort to revitalize the crumbling Japanese economy. It was in Japan that Deming found an enthusiastic reception for his management ideas. Deming introduced his **statistical process control**, or statistical quality control, programs into Japan's ailing manufacturing sector. Those techniques are credited with instilling a dedication to quality and productivity in the Japanese industrial and service sectors that allowed the country to become a dominant force in the global economy by the 1980s. In fact, Deming received the coveted Second Order Medal of Sacred Treasure from the Japanese emperor in 1960. Furthermore, Japanese scientists and engineers annually award the "Deming Prize" to companies that exhibit extraordinary contributions to quality.

While Japan's industrial sector embarked on a quality initiative during the middle 1900s, most American companies ignored Deming's successful war efforts and concentrated on producing mass quantities of goods using traditional management techniques. America prospered as war-ravaged European countries looked to the United States for manufactured goods. In addition, a domestic population boom resulted in surging U.S. markets. But the consequences of American manufacturers' indifference to quality began to surface in the 1970s. By that time, Japan and Europe had largely regained their production capabilities, and the rapid economic expansion in the United States had subsided. As a result of increasing economic globalization during the 1980s, made possible in part by advanced information technologies, the U.S. manufacturing sector fell prey to more competitive producers, particularly in Japan.

In response to massive market share gains achieved by Japanese companies during the late 1970s and 1980s, U.S. producers scrambled to adopt quality and productivity techniques that might restore their competitiveness. Indeed, Deming's philosophies and systems were finally recognized in the United States, and Deming himself became a highly-sought-after lecturer and author. The "Deming Management Method" became the model for many American corporations eager to improve. And Total Quality Management, the phrase applied to quality initiatives proffered by Deming and other management gurus, became a staple of American enterprise by the late 1980s. By the early 1990s, the U.S. manufacturing sector had achieved marked gains in quality and productivity, even surpassing the efficiency of many Japanese industrial segments that it had formerly lagged.

Specifics related to the framework and implementation of TQM vary between different management professionals and TQM program facilitators. Discussed below are the interpretations of TQM-related fundamentals of Deming, renowned quality management consultant Dr. Joseph M. Juran, and Joseph R. Jablonski, author of *Implementing TQM*.

JABLONSKI

Jablonski identifies three characteristics necessary for TQM to succeed within an organization: participative management; continuous process improvement; and the utilization of **teams**. Participative management refers to the intimate involvement of all members of a company in the management process, thus deemphasizing traditional top-down management methods. In other words, managers set policies and make key decisions only with the input and guidance of the subordinates that will have to implement and adhere to the directives. This technique improves upper management's grasp of operations and, more importantly, is an important motivator for workers who begin to feel like they have control and ownership of the process in which they participate.

Continuous process improvement, the second characteristic, entails the recognition of small, incremental gains toward the goal of total quality. Large gains are accomplished by small, sustainable improvements over a long term. This concept necessitates a long-term approach by managers and the willingness to invest today for gradual or future payoffs. A corollary of continuous improvement is that workers and management develop an appreciation for, and confidence in, TQM over a period of time.

Teamwork, the third necessary ingredient for the success of TQM, involves the organization of teams made up of a cross-section of members from different functions in a particular process, including: the individuals engaged in the process; the suppliers of resources into the process; and the consumers, or beneficiaries, of the process. This multidisciplinary team approach helps workers to identify problems and opportunities, derive a comprehensive understanding of their role in the overall process, and align their work goals with those of the organization.

In addition to the three necessary elements of any TQM system, Jablonski identifies six attributes of successful TQM programs. The first is customer focus, which includes an emphasis on serving customers both outside and inside the organization. An example of an inside customer relationship would be any division that was dependent on the accounting department for accurate and timely financial reports. The second attribute, a focus on process as well as results, entails creating an environment which is responsive to the complaints and negative reactions of customers. The negative feedback is used to change processes.

Prevention versus inspection, the third integral TQM characteristic, involves the development of a process that incorporates quality, rather than a process that attempts to achieve quality through inspection ("inspecting in" quality) after resources have already been consumed to produce the good or service. A company must be willing to make the investments necessary to create a high-quality process that ensures an acceptable, predictable degree of quality. The fourth attribute is mobilized work force expertise. This means that there are many ways to compensate employees, and that the work force embodies a great wealth of knowledge that can increase profits and reduce costs. This concept entails acknowledging workers' needs for recognition, importance, and control.

A fifth organizational attribute Jablonski deems critical to the success of TQM is fact-based **decision making**, which focuses on looking at problems as opportunities to improve, rather than emphasizing the placement of blame on those responsible for creating problems. The common goal of continual process improvement is stressed as a means of overcoming personality conflicts and biases. Fact-based decision making also entails the collection and comprehension of data on which problem-solving decisions are based. The sixth organizational virtue, feedback, allows the other five attributes to thrive. Feedback stresses open communication, encouraging employees to take chances, and rewarding worker input.

In addition to identifying three characteristics that need to be present in an organization and six attributes of successful TQM programs, Jablonski offers a five-phase guideline for implementing total quality management: preparation, planning, assessment, implementation, and diversification. Each phase is designed to be executed as part of a long-term goal of continually increasing quality and productivity. Jablonski's approach is one of many that has been applied to achieve TQM, but contains the key elements commonly associated with other popular total quality systems.

During preparation, the first phase, key executives determine whether or not they will consider the benefits of a TQM program. They undergo initial training, identify needs for outside consultants, develop a specific vision and goals, draft a corporate policy, commit the necessary resources, and communicate the goals throughout the organization. A ten-step process guides management through the preparation phase, which has a definite beginning and ending point, unlike the subsequent four phases.

In the planning stage, a detailed plan of implementation is drafted, the infrastructure that will support the program is established, and the resources necessary to begin the plan are earmarked and secured. A detailed, multi-step process guides management through this phase, which is the most complex and becomes a never-ending process. Highlights of the multiple steps include forming teams to implement aspects of the TQM plan, selecting and training TQM coordinators, bringing necessary support services and expertise into the company, and developing an implementation budget and schedule.

The six-step assessment stage includes:

1) quick assessment, whereby TQM facilitators consider questions about what they hope to gain from the TQM program;

2) self-assessment, which assesses the qualities and characteristics of individuals in the company and plays an important role in team-building efforts;

3) customer surveys, which give information to the company about problems, but also communicate a concern about service to customers;

4) organizational assessment, which entails understanding the relationship between individuals and the organization as a corporate entity;

5) TQM planning inventory, which is essentially a checklist that helps managers assess the progress of the five implementation stages; and

6) training feedback, which should provide insight into the perceived value of the program by trainees in the company.

Phase four, implementation, follows preparation, planning, and assessment activities. At this point, the organization can already begin to determine its return on its investment in TQM. It is during this phase that support personnel are chosen and trained, and managers and the work force are trained. Training entails raising workers' awareness of exactly what TQM involves and how it can help them and the company. It also explains each worker's role in the program and explains what is expected of all the workers. Next, process action teams (PATs) are formed. PATs are teams with four to eight members that are trained to address a specific process targeted for improved quality. They help form bonds between different functional areas within the company.

During the fifth phase, diversification, managers utilize their limited TQM experiences and successes to bring groups outside the organization into the quality process. Such groups will include suppliers, distributors, and other companies that have an impact on the company's overall quality, productivity, and customer service. Diversification activities include training, rewarding, supporting, and partnering with groups that are embraced by the organization's TQM initiatives.

DEMING

In his book, *Out of the Crisis*. Deming outlines the TQM-related philosophies that the U.S. industrial sector needs to implement in order to achieve a higher level of global competitiveness. Primary culprits of American malaise, Deming posits, are ''seven deadly diseases'' associated with outdated management practices:

1) lack of constancy or purpose, or having no long range goals;

2) emphasis on short term profits;

3) evaluation of workers by performance, merit rating, or annual review—all are practices which destroy teamwork, foster unhealthy rivalries, and create management defections;

4) mobility of management—job-hopping managers can't follow through on long term goals that are necessary for quality and productivity;

5) running a company on visible figures alone, or ignoring customers;

6) excessive employee health care costs; and

7) excessive warranty costs fueled by lawyers who work on the basis of contingency fees.

To eradicate the seven deadly diseases, Deming offers a 14-point cure that forms the foundation of his total quality philosophies. He stresses that every point must be implemented for a company to achieve a successful program of quality management. In summary, the points are:

1) create a constancy of purpose related to improvement of products and services, rather than simply striving to make money;

2) adopt the new philosophy and create an environment where mediocrity is unacceptable;

3) stop ''inspecting in'' quality, as explained earlier;

4) stop awarding business contracts based only on price;

5) establish systems of constant improvement over time;

6) institute proper training;

7) institute leadership, whereby managers lead rather than direct;

8) eliminate fear by encouraging employees to ask questions and to try new things without the threat of reprisal for failure;

9) break down barriers between departments, with multidisciplinary teams, for example;

10) eliminate slogans and other ineffective propaganda;

11) eliminate numerical quotas that stress quantity over quality;

12) remove barriers to pride of workmanship, such as faulty equipment and defective materials;

13) institute vigorous educational programs to teach new techniques, such as statistical analysis and teamwork; and

14) take decisive action to implement the first 13 points, particularly at the top management level.

Deming backs the 14-point philosophical foundation of his quality management methods with his system of statistical process control. Only through the use of statistics, Deming posits, can managers know exactly what their problems are, how to fix them, and whether or not they are achieving their quality and organizational objectives. Deming provides detailed statistical techniques that managers can use to implement his total quality initiatives. They can be organized into a general five-step process. First of all, managers must use data to identify problems. This is accomplished using quality control charts that have upper and lower control limits specifying the acceptable quality range for a product or process. Secondly, statistics should be used to classify the cause of the problem. The two primary types of problems are ''common cause,'' which are potentially company-wide in scope, and ''special cause,'' which are typically isolated difficulties. Deming provides numerous charting methods for cause classification.

Deming's third statistical control step is correction of the problem, whereby managers devise and implement a course of action that will correct the problem. Fourthly, managers should use statistical analysis, namely control charts, to continually boost performance. This can be accomplished by gradually narrowing the upper and lower control limits that specify various acceptable ranges of quality. Finally, an organization should implement a ''Plan-Do-Check-Act Cycle,'' a system which links the seven diseases, the fourteen points, and Deming's statistical techniques into a continuous process that has no starting or ending point. This last step ensures an ongoing quality-management process.

JURAN

Like Deming, Joseph M. Juran was educated in the early 1900s and worked in management for both government and private organizations. He was also sent to Japan after World War II to help rebuild the economy and received the Order of the Sacred Treasure for his development of quality control techniques. Juran's approach to TQM is generally less philosophical than Deming's and stresses specific shop-floor planning and quality control methods. His techniques focus on processes related to individual products and services. Juran believed that a company-wide orientation to quality would naturally follow the successful implementation of his quality programs.

Juran thought that America's competitiveness problems in the 1980s were the result of management's refusal to take full responsibility for poor quality. Indeed, many U.S. companies were actually planning poor quality into their products, he postulated. Furthermore, they failed to realize the huge gains that could be achieved through TQM. Juran felt that America's lack of attention to quality was a threat to society; it was tearing down the country's industrial sector, hurting its institutions, and diminishing the quality of life.

Juran defined quality as: "(1) product performance that results in customer satisfaction, and (2) freedom from product deficiencies, which avoids customer dissatisfaction." To achieve quality within an organization, Juran developed the "quality trilogy": quality planning, quality control, and quality improvements. Adoption of his trilogy program essentially forced an organization to redesign its product and service planning and control systems. Through his continuous improvement program, many companies have been able to permanently weed out the root causes of poor quality. The central theme of Juran's process was that a firm's planning systems should be guided by a universal thought process that eclipses subordinate production activities.

Juran's trilogy differs from other quality programs that stress planning, control, and improvements because his techniques combine the initiatives in a unique structure that reduces the cost of quality over time. During the quality planning stages, a company prepares to meet its established quality goals by establishing a dependable process. During the subsequent quality control phase, the entity designs control processes that will ensure that the goals set in the planning stage are actually being met during production. It is the planning and control activities that should result in a permeating quality culture within an organization.

The third phase of the trilogy, improvement, is also known as the "breakthrough sequence." It helps managers find quality-limiting problems ingrained in the company, and then fix those problems by going back and tweaking the planning and control processes. Juran's seven-step breakthrough sequence is designed to be administered both during and after the planning and control phases. The detailed seven-step process entails:

1) a breakthrough in attitudes and the creation of a change-oriented environment;

2) identification of vital projects using Pareto charts, or vertical bar charts that compare different problem types and causes;

3) organization of groups that analyze problems and implement solutions;

4) detailed analysis, which uncovers problems, tests theoretical solutions, and proposes action;

5) overcoming resistance to change, largely through participatory programs as opposed to logical arguments;

6) instituting change; and

7) instituting controls that monitor solutions and keep managers abreast of unforeseen developments.

Aside from Juran's trilogy, an integral component of his quality program is a cost-of-quality (COQ) accounting system, which he uses to keep the support of upper-level managers. COQ is effective in demonstrating the cost benefits derived from a shift to the quality management process and in guiding managers in determining how much effort to put into the program. COQ compares the cost of implementing Juran's system at different levels of intensity with the resultant savings at each level of implementation. Typically, in the initial stages of implementing the program, each dollar invested cuts costs by much more than one dollar. At higher levels of implementation, the law of diminishing marginal returns eventually negates the impact of increasing the scope of the system. In other words, the ideal quality level is slightly less than 100 percent.

THE MALCOLM BALDRIDGE AWARD

Among the many programs established in the United States to evaluate and award product and service quality in organizations, the Malcolm Baldridge National Quality Award is generally considered the most elite. The award was created by the Malcolm Baldridge National Quality Improvement Act (signed into law by President Reagan in 1987) to institute an annual U.S. national quality award. The stated purpose of the award is to promote quality awareness, recognize achievements of U.S. companies, and promote successful quality strategies. The award program also serves to: define and elevate quality standards; facilitate communication and sharing among organizations; and to serve as a tool that companies may use to plan, administer, and assess quality endeavors.

The goals of the award criteria, which closely mimic popular definitions of TQM, are to project key requirements for delivering ever-improving value to customers, while at the same time maximizing the overall productivity and effectiveness of the organization. Companies that apply for the award are evaluated in seven categories: leadership; information and analysis; strategic quality planning; human resource development and management; management of process quality; quality and operational results; and customer focus and satisfaction. Each category is assigned a number of points, for a combined total of 1,000. Customer satisfaction, the most important category, accounts for 300 of those points.

Though it is possible that no awards are presented in a given year, as many as two Baldridge Awards may be presented annually in each of three categories: 1) service companies or subsidiaries; 2) manufacturing companies or subsidiaries; and 3) small business (fewer than 500 employees). Only for-profit businesses are considered. At least four members of a board of examiners reviews each application, and the highest-scoring candidates are selected for site visits. Every entrant receives feedback indicating strengths and weaknesses, however. The awards are presented each year in November, and winners are allowed to publicize their award as long as they agree to share information about successful quality strategies with other companies.

One of the first companies to win a Baldridge Award was Motorola, Inc., a major producer and exporter of high-tech electronic and communications equipment primarily for commercial and defense applications. Although Motorola was extremely successful during the middle 1900s, particularly in consumer electronics markets, its competitiveness began to significantly lag in the 1970s. By the late 1970s, in fact, it was rapidly losing market share to Japanese competitors. In the early 1980s, Chairman Robert W. Galvin embarked on a mission to increase Motorola's quality ten-fold within five years. That strategy soon evolved into a quest for total quality that would propel the organization to the status of one of the most productive and innovative companies in the world.

Among Motorola's total quality initiatives was its participative management program (PMP), which sought to empower workers by giving them autonomy in their jobs and control over the processes in which they were involved. The PMP program included an emphasis on employee input and teamwork. Motorola also implemented a "Management by Measurement" plan. By establishing acceptable, measurable quality targets and regularly reviewing those targets, the company was able to instill an ideology of continuous improvement over time. Motorola eventually adopted a defect acceptance rate of 3.4 per million. The company backed its product quality achievements with proactive customer satisfaction programs, particularly cycle-time reduction efforts that, among other results, reduced the elapsed time between a customer placing an order and actually receiving a product.

An example of a smaller company that won a Baldridge Award is Wallace Company, Inc., a family-owned, Houston-based industrial distribution and construction company. Wallace was founded in 1942 and flourished both as a distributor of chemical and petroleum products and as an engineering and construction company. When the petroleum industry crashed in the early 1980s, Wallace skirted the short-term remedies adopted by many of its industry peers. Instead, management elected to pursue a long-term TQM strategy of continuous quality improvement. Despite sluggish markets, Wallace managed to thrive during the middle and late 1980s by increasing its market share through higher process quality and greater customer service. During the late 1980s, in fact, Wallace's share of its core markets leapt from about 10 percent to 18 percent its sales volume

climbed 69 percent, and its operating profits increased more than seven-fold.

Like Motorola, Wallace instituted a number of initiatives aimed at empowering workers, fostering teamwork and employee input, and improving customer service. Specifically, the company developed a 16-point strategic objective to guide all decisions in the organization. Wallace complemented those goals with detailed statistical processes. In fact, 12 statistical process control coordinators assist multidisciplinary decision-making teams by charting trends, analyzing problems, and evaluating the effects of decisions. The company eventually identified 72 processes on which it focused its planning, control, and improvement efforts. Reflective of Deming's system, Wallace requires its suppliers to meet the same standards of quality which it has set for itself, and ensures their cooperation by requiring statistical proof of product quality and delivery performance.

The first company to win a Malcom Baldridge National Quality Award in the service category was Federal Express Corporation, which achieved the honor in 1990. Federal Express started the air-express delivery industry in the early 1970s. Despite a plethora of new entrants into the industry, it continues to dominate its competitors through a long-practiced TQM philosophy that emphasizes people, services, and profit, in that order. The "people-service-profit" philosophy permeates the organization and guides decision-making at all levels. Backing that guiding philosophy, moreover, is a detailed statistical evaluation system called "Survey/Feedback/Action," or SFA. SFA is used to survey employees, analyze the success of team efforts, and help managers and their teams develop written action plans to become more effective.

Federal Express's TQM efforts particularly stress the importance of employees as the key to achieving excellent service and quality. For instance, the company emphasizes extensive training programs to keep its workers informed, and maintains a "no-layoff" philosophy to boost morale and instill loyalty. Low-level workers are offered the opportunity to participate in management training programs, and worker input is rewarded through established recognition programs. Another focal point of the company's total quality program is service quality indicators (SQI). SQIs are statistics that are used to determine customer's perception of service and then to identify and eliminate causes of problems, rather than place blame. Largely as a result of its lauded total quality initiatives, Federal Express rocketed its revenues to more than $7 billion in sales by 1990, representing a dominant market share of more than 40 percent.

SEE ALSO: Japan, Doing Business in

[Dave Mote]

FURTHER READING:

Deming, W. Edwards. *Out of the Crisis*. MIT Center for Advanced Engineering Study, 1982.

Hiam, Alexander. *Closing the Quality Gap: Lessons from America's Leading Companies*. Prentice Hall, Inc., 1992.

Hunt, V. Daniel. *Quality in America: How to Implement a Competitive Quality Program*. Business One Irwin, 1992.

Jablonski, Joseph R. *Implementing TQM*, 2nd ed. Technical Management Consortium, Inc., 1992.

Roberts, Harry V. and Bernard F. Sergesketter. *Quality is Personal: A Foundation for Total Quality Management*. The Free Press, 1993.

Walton, Mary. *The Deming Management Method*. Dodd, Mead, 1986.

TRADE BARRIERS

Trade barriers may occur in international trade when goods have to cross political boundaries. A trade barrier is a restriction on what would otherwise be **free trade**. The most common form of trade barriers are tariffs, or duties (the two words are often used interchangeably in the context of international trade), which are usually imposed on imports. There is also a category of nontariff barriers (NTBs), also known as nontariff measures (NTMs), which also serve to restrict global trade.

There are several different types of duties or tariffs. An export duty is a tax levied on goods leaving a country, while an import duty is charged on goods entering a country. A duty or tariff may be categorized according to how it is calculated. An *ad valorem* tariff is one that is calculated as a percentage of the value of the goods being imported or exported. For example, a 20 percent ad valorem duty means that a duty equal to 20 percent of the value of the goods in question must be paid. Duties that are calculated in other ways include a specific duty, which is based on the quantity, weight, or volume of goods, and a compound duty (also known as a mixed tariff), which is calculated as a combination of an ad valorem duty and a specific duty.

Duties and tariffs are also categorized according to their function or purpose. An antidumping duty is imposed on imports that are priced below fair market value and that would damage domestic producers. Antidumping duties are also called punitive tariffs. A countervailing duty, another type of punitive tariff, that is levied after there has been substantial or material damage done to domestic producers. A countervailing duty is specifically charged on imports that have been subsidized by the exporting country's government. The purpose of a countervailing duty is to offset the subsidy and increase the domestic price of the imported product.

A prohibitive tariff, also known as an exclusionary tariff, is designed to substantially reduce or stop altogether the importation of a particular product or commodity. It is typically used when the amount of an imported good exceeds a certain permitted level. It may be used to protect domestic producers. Another type of tariff is the end-use tariff, which is based on the use of an imported product. For example, the same product may be charged a different duty if it is intended for educational use as opposed to commercial use.

In addition to duties and tariffs, there are also nontariff barriers (NTBs) to international trade. These include quantitative restrictions, or quotas, that may be imposed by one country or as the result of agreements between two or more countries. Examples of quantitative restrictions include international commodity agreements, voluntary export restraints, and orderly marketing arrangements.

Administrative regulations constitute a second category of NTBs. These include a variety of requirements that must be met in order for trade to occur, including fees, licenses, permits, domestic content requirements, financial bonds and deposits, and government procurement practices. The third type of NTB covers technical regulations that apply to such areas as packaging, labeling, safety standards, and multilingual requirements.

In 1980 the Agreement on Technical Barriers to Trade, also known as the Standards Code, came into effect for the purpose of ensuring that administrative and technical practices do not act as trade barriers. By the end of 1988 the agreement had been signed by 39 countries. Additional work on promoting unified standards to eliminate these NTBs is being conducted by the **General Agreement on Tariffs and Trade (GATT)** Standards Committee.

Tariffs and other trade barriers have a definite effect on consumption and production. They serve to reduce consumption of the imported product, because the tariff raises the domestic price of the import. They also serve to stimulate domestic production of the product when that is possible, also because of the higher domestic price. Proponents of tariffs argue that such an increase in domestic production is desirable, while opponents argue that it is inefficient from an economic standpoint. The overall effect of tariffs and trade barriers on international trade is to reduce the volume of trade and to increase the prices of imports. Proponents of free trade argue that both of those results are undesirable, while proponents of protectionism argue that tariffs may be necessary for a variety of reasons.

There are several reasons advanced for imposing trade barriers. These include protecting domestic producers against foreign competitors (especially infant industries), improving a nation's terms of trade, reducing domestic unemployment, and improving a nation's balance-of-payments position. Those who would argue against imposing trade barriers point to the possibility of retaliation by other nations, leading to a trade war. The more trade barriers there are, the lower the volume of international trade and the higher the domestic prices of imported goods. As a result, global resources are less efficiently allocated and the level of world income and production is reduced. It has been the recognition of the negative effects of trade barriers on international trade that has led to international agreements, such as GATT, designed to reduce or eliminate them.

[David Bianco]

TRADE CREDIT

Trade credit refers to the **credit** that one business extends to another in the course of doing business with each other. Trade credit may be extended by a purchasing firm to its supplier, or vice versa. If prepayment is made, then the purchaser is extending trade credit to the seller. Where the seller allows a certain time period for payment to be made, then the seller is extending trade credit to the buyer.

Trade credit may either be long term or short term. Examples of long-term trade credit may be found in the automotive and petroleum industries, where it is common practice for manufacturers to extend long-term, low-interest **loans** to their dealers. Trade credit, however, is most commonly short term, anywhere from 30 to 120 days, and is typically extended by a seller to a buyer.

A seller typically extends trade credit to a buyer by offering the buyer a specified time to pay for the goods that were purchased. The trade credit may be offered on net terms, which means that no interest will be charged if payment is made within the specified period, usually 30, 60, 90, or 120 days. A two-part offer of trade credit adds a discount period during which the purchaser may take a discount if payment is made within an even shorter period. For example, a "2/10 Net 30" offer means that the buyer has the option of taking a 2 percent discount if payment is made within ten days. Otherwise, full payment is expected within 30 days.

Two-part trade credit offers have an implicit interest charge built in. That is, if the purchaser chooses the "Net 30" option over the "2/10" option and fails to take the trade discount offered, then the purchaser is in effect paying an interest charge on the 30 days of credit that has been extended. When annualized, the interest rate on most trade credit far exceeds that

offered by **banks** and other financial institutions. Consequently, some theorists hold that two-part trade credit offers provide sellers with information about the creditworthiness of their customers. It is argued that creditworthy customers would always take the trade discount, because they could find third-party financing at better rates than are offered by the two-part trade credit offer.

The actual credit terms of trade credit offers appear to be standardized within industries, although they may vary from industry to industry. They tend to remain constant and not be affected by supply and demand. The extending of trade credit can serve a business firm's informational and financial needs. In addition to providing sellers with information on the creditworthiness of their customers, trade credit offers can serve to bond relationships between buyers and sellers. Sellers who offer trade credit generally have a financial interest in maintaining a continuing relationship with their buyers. The extending of trade credit also gives the purchaser time to verify the quality of the goods purchased and evaluate the seller's performance.

Financially, the handling of trade credit offers and payments are part of a business firm's accounts receivable and accounts payable decisions. Financial decisions about extending two-part trade credit offers take into account the trade-off between offering a discount and receiving less money on the one hand, and receiving payment sooner and improving cash flow on the other. In terms of accounts payable, it is expected that all creditworthy firms would take advantage of trade discounts whenever possible. If no trade discount is offered, then simply being able to withhold payment for 30 to 120 days without paying interest improves the purchaser's cost of funds and provides greater control over cash flow.

[David Bianco]

TRADE DEFICIT

A trade deficit is a condition in the balance of trade between a country's exports and imports. If the value of a country's imports exceeds the value of its exports, then that country is said to have a trade deficit. When the value of a country's exports exceeds the value of its exports, then it has a trade surplus. Trade deficits and surpluses may be measured in terms of the international trade between two nations, or between one nation and the rest of the world.

For the United States, the balance of international transactions is reported on a regular basis in the monthly *Survey of Current Business* by the U.S. Bureau of Economic Analysis in the Economics and Statistics Administration of the U.S. Department of Commerce. The current account balance of U.S. international transactions consists of four types of transactions: merchandise, services, investment income, and unilateral transfers. When the current account balance is positive, the United States has a trade surplus. When it is negative, there is a trade deficit.

While the Bureau of Economic Analysis reports on the four major categories of international transactions to determine the current account balance for the United States, oftentimes discussions of the current U.S. trade deficit do not take all four categories of transactions into account. In some discussions, the trade deficit is cited only as the balance of trade in merchandise, or goods. In other cases, the trade deficit refers to the balance of international trade in goods and services.

Nevertheless, the current account balance as reported by the Bureau of Economic Analysis also includes international transactions in investment income and unilateral transfers. In this context investment income includes interest paid abroad to foreign investors and interest received by public and private sectors in the United States from foreign sources. Unilateral transfers include outflows for net U.S. purchases of foreign securities and inflows for net foreign purchases of U.S. securities, U.S. **banks'** claims against foreigners and **liabilities** to foreign sources, and net outflows for U.S. **direct investment** abroad and net inflows for foreign direct investment in the United States. All of these transactions affect the current account balance.

Looking at the recent history of the U.S. trade deficit in terms of all four categories of international transactions, the United States experienced a sharp increase in its trade deficit in the early 1990s. In 1991, for example, the current account balance showed a deficit of $8.3 billion. By 1992, that deficit had increased to $66.4 billion. In 1993 preliminary figures showed a deficit of $109.2 billion, and the trade deficit for 1994 promised to top $100 billion again.

In terms of international trade in goods and services only, the United States enjoyed a trade surplus in services and experienced a rising trade deficit in merchandise during the early 1990s. The merchandise trade balance went from a deficit of $73.8 billion in 1991 to $132.5 billion in 1993, while international trade in services showed a surplus of $45.9 billion in 1991 and $55.7 billion in 1993. Trade in services is now reported in seven categories, including travel, royalties and license fees, education, financial services, professional services, military sales, and telecommunications trade.

In terms of international merchandise trade with specific countries, the United States has a trade surplus with some countries and a trade deficit with others. From 1991 to 1993, the United States had an increasing trade deficit in goods with Canada, Germany, Japan, Asia (excluding Japan), and China. For the same period, the United States had a merchandise trade surplus with England, Latin America, and Mexico. Merchandise trade with Western Europe went from a surplus in 1991 and 1992 to a deficit in 1993.

A variety of factors determine the size of a country's trade deficit or surplus. Since the **balance of trade** is measured by the value of imports and exports, the quantity of trade as well as its price affects the size of a particular trade deficit or surplus. When a country's currency is weak, for example, exports are valued lower and imports cost more, thus tending to increase the size of a trade deficit and reduce the size of a trade surplus.

The strength of a country's economy as well as the condition of the international economy also affect trade deficits and surpluses. When there is a worldwide recession, with a weakening of many countries' economies, there is a reduced demand for a given country's exports. A lower international demand for exports tends to increase a country's trade deficit. When a country's domestic economy is expanding, then that economy's demand for exports tends to increase, also tending to increase a country's trade deficit. Thus, an increasing trade deficit could be the result of a growing domestic economy, a worldwide recession, or a weak currency.

[David Bianco]

TRADEMARK

SEE: Brands and Brand Names; Copyright; Patent Law/Patents

TRAINING AND DEVELOPMENT

Training and development represents the formal on-going efforts of corporations and other organizations to improve the performance and self-fulfillment of their employees through a variety of methods and programs. In the modern work place, these efforts have taken on a broad range of applications, from instruction in highly specific job skills to long-term professional development and are applicable to all sorts of employees ranging from line workers to the chief executive officer. In recent years, training and development has emerged as a formal corporate function, an integral element of corporate strategy, and a recognized profession with distinct theories and methodologies as companies increasingly acknowledge the fundamental importance of employee growth and development, as well as the necessity of a highly skilled **work force**, in order to improve the success and efficiency of their organizations.

The apprenticeship system emerged in ancient cultures to provide a formal framework for the training of the unskilled by master craftsmen and was marked by three distinct stages: the unskilled novice, the journeyman or yeoman, and finally, the master craftsman. Together, they formed an ''organic'' process whereby the novice ''grew'' into a master craftsman over a period of years.

With the onset of the Industrial Age, the training of the unskilled underwent a dramatic transformation in which vocational education and training emerged to replace the traditional apprentice system. The division of labor in an industrial factory resulted in specific job tasks that required equally specific training in a much shorter timespan. As training activities grew more methodical and focussed, the first recognizable modern training methods began to develop during the nineteenth century and early twentieth centuries: gaming simulations became an important tool in the Prussian military during the early 1800s; the case method was developed by Christopher Langdell for the Harvard Law School in the 1880s; pyschodrama and role playing were developed by Dr. J. L. Moreno of Vienna, Austria, in 1910.

The early twentieth century witnessed the emergence of training and development as a profession, resulting in the creation of training associations and societies; the advent of the **assembly line** requiring greater specificity in training; and the dramatic training requirements of the World Wars. Important groups forming during this period include the American Management Association in 1923 (began as the National Association of Corporation Schools in 1913), and the National Management Association in 1956 (began as the National Association of Foremen in 1925). At the same time, Henry Ford (1863-1947) introduced the assembly line at his Highland Park, MI plant. Because the assembly line created an even greater division of labor, along with an unprecedented need for precision and teamwork, job tasks and assignments required more highly specific and focussed training than ever before.

The enormous production needs of the First and Second World Wars created a heavy influx of new workers with little or no industrial education or skills to the work place thereby necessitating massive training efforts that were at once fast and effective. In particular, the heavy demand for shipping construction during World War I resulted in a tenfold increase in workers trained on-site by instructors who were

supervisors using a simple four-step method: show, tell, do, check. During World War II, large numbers of trained industrial workers left their jobs to enter the armed forces, severely limiting the organizational support normally provided by co-workers in training their replacements. Heavy demands were placed on foremen and supervisors, and the Training Within Industry Service (TWI) was formed to train supervisors as instructors. Job Instruction Training (JIT) was employed to train defense plant supervisors in instructing new employees in necessary job skills as quickly as possible. Other programs included Job Relations Training (JRT), Job Methods Training (JMT), and Job Safety Training (JST). During this time, the American Society for Training and Development (ASTD) was formed.

By the end of World War II, the importance of training and development as a fundamental organizational tool had been realized. Training functions that were developed in reaction to national crises had become established corporate activities with long-term strategies towards improving **employee performance**. In the mid 1950s, gaming simulations gained popularity. Trainers began giving serious consideration to the efficacy of their training programs, and interest in the evaluation of training programs grew. The 1960s witnessed an explosion of training methods as the number of corporations using **assessment centers** increased from one to 100 by the end of the decade. Government programs, to train young men for industrial jobs, such as the Job Development Program 1965, and the Job Corps, were initiated to improve the conditions of the economically disadvantaged. New methods included training laboratories, sensitivity training, programmed instruction, **performance appraisal** and evaluation, needs assessments, **management** training, and **organizational development**.

By the 1970s, a new sense of professionalism emerged in the training community. Training programs grew dramatically, and the ASTD produced the *Professional Development Manual for Trainers*. Government programs were aimed increasingly at minorities as a group and required corporations to increase their efforts to recruit minorities. With the rise of organizational development, the focus of training shifted away from the individual and toward the organization as a whole, hence the term human resource development. Technological advances in training programs included the use of video tapes, satellites, and **computers**.

The 1980s and early 90s witnessed important social, economic, and political changes that have had a profound effect on the way corporations do business. There is an ever increasing need for effective training. In a time of economic constraints coupled with increasing international **competition**, the training and development function has been required to respond more quickly and effectively to technological change. Increasing governmental regulations also require a greater breadth of training programs to reflect the greater diversity of employees.

For the most part, training and development are used together to describe the overall improvement and education of an organization's employees. However, while closely related, there are important differences between the terms that center around the scope of the application. In general, training programs have very specific and quantifiable goals, like operating a particular piece of machinery, understanding a specific process, or performing certain procedures with great precision. On the other hand, developmental programs concentrate on broader skills that are applicable to a wider variety of situations, such as **decision making**, **leadership** skills, and **goal setting**. In short, training programs are typically tied to a particular subject matter and are applicable to that subject only, while developmental programs center around developing methods. In the following sections, the fundamentals of designing training programs, as well as the process of instructional design, will be described, important training methods employed by organizations will be discussed; and finally distinctive training and development applications will be enumerated.

The design of training programs describes the core activity of the training and development function. Like the training function itself, the development of training programs has evolved into a profession which utilizes systematic models, methods, and processes of instructional systems design (ISD). In discussing the development of instructional systems methods and models, the influence of the behavioral sciences and the development of adult learning models deserve particular mention.

The behavioral sciences describe a loose group of social sciences concerned primarily with individual behavior, motivations, organizational dynamics, and interpersonal relationships. In the study of these phenomena, behavioral scientists have concentrated a great deal of study on business organizations. As a result, training methods have been modified to consider the needs, requirements, and limitations of employees. More importantly, the impact of the behavioral sciences on management styles has required managers and supervisors to become lay experts in psychology by understanding employee motivation, interpersonal relationships, and group dynamics as a means towards effective management.

Similarly, the development of a distinctive adult educational model has resulted in new instruction methods and practices focused exclusively on adults. Beginning with Eduard C. Linderman's The Meaning of Education in 1926, educators started to realize that a separate instructional model for the education and training of adults was necessary. By the late 1960s the term *andragogue* was being employed to connote the science of adult education, as distinct from pedagogy, the science of children's education. Because the learning experience of an adult differs so greatly from that of a child, educators have developed a different set of assumptions for the instruction and training of adults. Adults must understand the purpose of the learning experience and agree that the purpose or goal is valid. The *andragogue's* instructional approach differs greatly from that of a pedagogue who is primarily concerned with the transmission of knowledge. Unlike a *pedagogue*, who organizes his instruction and materials around the subject matter itself, an *andragogue's* instruction is primarily goal-oriented. In essence, an *andragogue* is far more concerned about what the student can do than what he knows. Given the goal-oriented needs of adult education, the design and development of instructional materials has taken on a much higher level of structure and methodology than traditional methods for instructional development.

Instructional systems design (ISD) describes the systematic design and development of instructional methods and materials to facilitate the process of training and development and ensure that training programs are necessary, valid, and effective. Although the instructional design process can take on variety of sequences, the process must include the collection of data on the tasks or skills to be learned or improved, the analysis of these skills and tasks, the development of methods and materials, delivery of the program, and finally the evaluation of the training's effectiveness. Table 1, on next page, describes the process in greater detail.

While new instructional methods are under continuous development, several training methods have proven highly effective and should be discussed in detail. They include the *case method, role playing, self-instruction, team building games and simulations, and computer-based training (CBT)*.

The *case method* is a non-directed method of study whereby students are provided with practical case reports to study and analyze. Dealing with practical problems using the case report, students develop independent thinking by discovering solutions and ideas for themselves, as opposed to relying upon the direction of an instructor. The case method is composed of three parts:

1. Case Report—A thorough description of a simulated or real-life situation.

2. Case Analysis—The analysis of problems and possible solutions of the case report.

3. Case Discussion—Open discussion with a group centering around their case analyses and the formulation of possible solutions.

Table 1

A TYPICAL INSTRUCTIONAL SYSTEMS DESIGN MODEL

STEP	DESCRIPTION
Needs analysis	Measuring the disparity between current and desired skill levels
Task assessment	Collection of data on job tasks and the subsequent identification of learning requirements and possible difficulties
Stating objectives	Creation of concise statement of objectives and purpose as a benchmark
Assessment/testing	Development of testing materials designed to measure the performance of the objectives
Development of materials	Selection of effective instructional strategies followed by the development of materials based on the chosen strategies
Pilot programs	Piloting the program to gauge the effectiveness of the materials as well as identify potential weaknesses through subsequent evaluation
Evaluation	Evaluation of the efficacy of the methods and materials

The main benefit of the case method is its use of a real-life situations. The multiplicity of problems and possible solutions provide the student with a practical learning experience rather than the collection of abstract knowledge and theories that may be difficult to apply to practical situations.

In *role playing*, students assume a role outside of themselves and play out that role within a group. A facilitator creates a scenario that is to be acted out by the participants and guided by the facilitator. While the situation might be contrived, the interpersonal relations are genuine. Furthermore, participants receive immediate feedback from the facilitator and the scenario itself allowing better understanding of their own behavior.

Self-Instruction describes an instructional method in which the students assume primary responsibility for their own learning. Unlike instructor- or facilitator-led instruction, students retain a greater degree of control regarding topics, the sequence of learning, and the pace of learning. Depending on the structure of the instructional materials, students can achieve a higher degree of customized learning. Forms of self-instruction include programmed learning, individualized instruction, personalized systems of instruction, learner-controlled instruction, and correspondence study. Benefits include a strong support system, immediate feedback, and systematization.

Team building is the active creation and maintenance of effective work groups with similar goals and objectives. Not to be confused with the informal, ad-hoc formation and use of **teams** in the work place, team building is a formal and methodological process of building work teams with objectives and goals, facilitated by a third-party consultant. Team building is commonly initiated to combat ineffectual group functioning which negatively impacts group dynamics, **labor-management relations**, quality, or productivity. By recognizing the problems and difficulties associated with the creation and development of work teams, team building provides a structured, guided process whose benefits include a greater ability to manage complex projects and processes, flexibility to respond to changing situations, and greater motivation among team members.

Games and simulations are structured competitions and operational models used as training situations to emulate real-life scenarios. The benefits of games and simulations include the improvement of **problem-solving** and decision-making skills, a greater understanding of the organizational whole, the ability to study actual problems, and the power to capture the student's interest.

Computer-Based Training (CBT) involves the use of **computers** and computer-based instructional materials as the primary medium of instruction. Computer-based training programs are designed to structure and present instructional materials and to facilitate the learning process for the student. Primary uses of CBT include instruction in computer hardware, software, and operational equipment. The last is of particular importance because CBT can provide the student with a simulated experience of operating a particular piece of equipment or machinery while eliminating the risk of damage to costly equipment by a trainee or even a novice user. At the same time, the actual equipment's operational use is maximized because it need not be utilized as a training tool. The use of computer-based training enables a training organization to reduce training **costs**, while improving the effectiveness of the training. Costs are reduced through a reduction in travel, training time, amount of operational hardware, equipment damage, and instructors. Effectiveness is improved through **standardization** and individualization. In recent years, videodisc and CD-ROM have been successfully integrated into PC-platforms allowing low cost personal computers to serve as multi-media machines, increasing the flexibility and possibilities of CBT.

While the applications of training and development are as various as the functions and skills required by the organization, several important applications can be distinguished, including *technical training, sales training, clerical training, computer training, communications training, organizational development, career development, supervisory development,* and *management development.*

Technical training describes a broad range of training programs varying greatly in application and difficulty. Technical training utilizes common training methods for instruction of technical concepts, factual information, procedures, as well as technical processes and principles.

Sales training concentrates on the education and training of individuals to communicate with customers in a persuasive manner. Sales training focusses on enhancing the employee's knowledge of the organization's products, improving his or her selling skills, instilling positive attitudes, and increasing the employee's self-confidence. Employees are taught to distinguish the needs and wants of the customer, and persuasively communicate the message that their products or services can effectively satisfy them.

Clerical training concentrates on the training of clerical and administrative support staffs, which have taken on an increasingly expanded role in the 20 years. With the increasing reliance on computers and computer applications, clerical training must be careful to distinguish basic skills from the ever-changing computer applications used to support these skills. To associate these skills with a particular system may limit the employees' ability to learn new systems. Clerical training increasingly must instill improved decision-making skills in these employees as they take on expanded roles and responsibilities.

Computer training teaches the effective use of the computer and its software applications, and often must address the basic fear of technology that most employees face and identify and minimize any resistance to change that might emerge. Furthermore, computer training must anticipate and overcome the long and steep learning curves that many employees will experience. To do so, such training is offered in longer uninterrupted modules to allow for greater concentration, and structured training is supplemented by hands-on practice.

Communications training concentrates on the improvement of interpersonal communication skills, including writing, oral presentation, listening, and reading. In order to be successful, any form of communications training should be focussed on the basic improvement of skills and not just on stylistic considerations. Furthermore, the training should serve to build on present skills rather than rebuilding from the ground up. Communications training can be taught separately or can be effectively integrated into other types of training, since it is fundamentally related to others disciplines.

Organizational development (OD) refers to the use of knowledge and techniques from the behavioral sciences to analyze existing organizational structure and implement changes in order to improve organizational effectiveness. OD is useful in such varied areas as the alignment of employee goals with those of the organization, communications, team functioning, and decision making. In short, it is a development process with an organizational focus to achieve the same goals as other training and development activities aimed at individuals. OD practitioners commonly practice what has been termed ''action research'' to effect an orderly change which has been carefully planned to minimize the occurrence of unpredicted or unforeseen events. Action research refers to a systematic analysis of an organization to acquire a better understanding of the nature of problems and forces within an organization.

Career development of employees represents the formal development of an employee's position within an organization by providing a long-term development strategy and training programs to implement this strategy and achieve individual goals. Career development represents a growing concern for employee welfare and their long-term needs. For the individual, it involves stating and describing career goals, the assessment of necessary action, and the choice and implementation of necessary actions. For the organization, career development represents the systematic development and improvement of employees. To remain effective, career development programs must allow individuals to articulate their desires. At the same time, the organization strives to meet those stated needs as much as possible by consistently following through on commitments and meeting the expectations of the employees raised by the program.

Management and supervisory development involves the training of managers and supervisors in basic leadership skills enabling them to effectively function in their positions. For managers this typically involves the development of the ability to balance the effective management of their employee resources, while striving to understand and achieve the strategies and goals of the organization. Management training typically involves individuals above the first two levels of supervision and below senior executive management. Managers learn to effectively develop their employees by helping employees learn and change, as well as by identifying and preparing them for future responsibilities. Management development may also include programs to teach decision-making skills, creating and managing successful work teams, allocating resources effectively, budgeting, communication skills, **business planning**, and goal setting.

Supervisory development addresses the unique situation of the supervisor as a link between the organization's management and work force. It must focus on enabling supervisors to deal with their responsibilities to both labor and management, as well as co-workers, and staff departments. Important considerations include the development of personal and interpersonal skills, understanding of the management process, and productivity and quality improvement.

Social, political, economic, and demographic conditions have a profound impact on the direction of training and development. The number of youths entering the work place is predicted to decreasing the applicant pool for entry-level positions and placing heavier demands on training organizations. At the same time, the work force will age, requiring training organizations to ensure that these employees are continually developing new skills to keep up with the ever increasing pace of technology. Our economy is undergoing a transformation from a **manufacturing** to a service-based economy with different training needs, along with the transition to a global economy which will result in an increased need for **cross-cultural** training. In short, corporate training and development functions are facing ever increasing demands that will dramatically affect the type and scope of training offered.

[Bradley T. Bernatek]

FURTHER READING:

Craig, Robert L., ed. *Training and Development Handbook: A Guide to Human Resource Development.* 3rd ed. McGraw-Hill Book Company, 1987.

Fallon, William K., ed. *AMA Management Handbook.* 2nd ed. AMACOM, 1983.

Goldstein, Irwin L., ed. *Training and Development in Organizations.* 2nd ed. Jossey-Bass Publishers, 1989.

TRANSACTION COSTS

In a widely used but limited sense, transaction costs refer to the cost of transferring ownership or property rights. Transaction costs are associated with buying and selling different kinds of property, including **real estate**, **stocks** and **bonds**, and currencies. Examples of such transaction costs include brokers's fees and salesperson's commissions, among others. In calculating the transaction costs of buying and selling any kind of property, both the costs to the seller and those of the buyer are considered.

In another sense, transaction costs as discussed in economic theory refer to the cost of anything that might be defined as a transaction. Whenever goods exchange hands, there are transaction costs. Broadly defined, transaction costs include that which would have been saved had the goods not exchanged hands. Many transaction cost studies have been conducted to determine their effect on different aspects of economic behavior and performance.

In a simple bilateral exchange, it is generally easy to quantify transaction costs. However, when there are complex contracts calling for exchanges among many different parties, transaction costs become so complex that it may be impossible to quantify them. Studies of such complex transactions often rely on a qualitative discussion of transaction costs.

Depending on the situation, transaction costs may be independent of the quantity or value of goods transferred. In other cases there may be pronounced economies of scale, where larger transactions incur relatively smaller transaction costs on a cost per unit basis. However, it is clear that the existence of transaction costs serves to reduce the overall volume of transactions in an economy. As the cost of transferring of goods increases, traders have a stronger incentive to minimize the number of their transactions.

Transaction costs have an interesting effect on currency trading. If there were no transaction costs in the foreign currency market, then each currency could be traded against any other currency using consistent rates. That is, the value of the dollar against the yen would equal the value of the yen against the British pound multiplied by the value of the British pound against the dollar. However, since there are transaction costs involved, it is not possible to calculate consistent rates among the many different currencies. That is, one cannot in practice calculate the value of the dollar against the yen by measuring the values of the dollar and the yen against a third currency.

Transaction costs also influence the structure of markets and the nature of intermediary networks. When transaction costs are low, a more complex intermediary network tends to arise. This is the case for financial assets such as securities, **foreign exchange**, commodity contracts, and gold, among others. The markets for these assets tend to move to where the transaction costs are lowest. As technological advances affect financial transactions and lower the transaction costs involved, it is anticipated that the financial system will become more elaborate, with greater specialization or division of labor and an increase in the number of transactions relative to the volume of traded assets.

It is also theorized that transaction costs determine what will be used as money, or a medium of exchange, in a particular economy. If one imagines that there are several commodities that could serve as a medium of exchange, the ones that will be chosen are those which involve the lowest transaction costs. The one that is selected as money, then, is the one with the lowest transaction cost (and holding cost). Thus, it can be seen that money serves to conserve resources that would otherwise disappear as transaction costs.

[David Bianco]

TRANSFER AGENT

The function of a transfer agent is to maintain up-to-date records of the ownership of a corporation's securities and to execute transfers of the corporation's stock and other securities. A transfer agent may be an officer or clerk of the corporation, or an outside individual, bank, or trust company. Larger corporations may have their own transfer departments. It is common practice for corporations to utilize the services of a bank's transfer department to fulfill the duties of a transfer agent.

A transfer agent is responsible for seeing that stock and other securities transfers are properly executed. When a corporation's stock is sold, the transfer agent re-registers the securities that are to be transferred. The securities that have been sold must be cancelled, and the transfer agent must establish the validity of the securities to be canceled. The transfer agent then cancels the old certificates and issues new certificates following transfer instructions. The transfer agent records the certificate numbers of the new stock, the new registration information, and the old certificate numbers and date of cancellation. At the end of each business day the transfer agent verifies all transactions by matching the number of shares canceled with the number of shares issued.

In the final step of a securities transfer, the transfer agent delivers the new securities according to instructions. The securities may be delivered to an indi-

vidual, a brokerage firm, a bank, or a depository institution. It normally takes four working days for a stock transfer to be completed following the transaction date.

State laws governing the activities of a transfer agent are based on the **Uniform Commercial Code**, Article 8, which covers investment securities. The UCC spells out the rights and **liabilities** of the buyer, seller, and transfer agent in transactions involving securities. In addition, transfer agents are regulated by the **Securities and Exchange Commission**. SEC regulations are designed to ensure that transfer agents act promptly and accurately. Transfer agents for corporations listed on the New York Stock Exchange (NYSE) must meet additional requirements of the NYSE, among which is the requirement to maintain an office on Manhattan in New York City.

[David Bianco]

TRANSFER PRICING

Transfer pricing is the value placed on goods and services exchanged between affiliates or divisions within a company. The transactions are not truly at arm's length, and therefore do not represent a market price for the goods or services provided. Because the organization may want to properly measure efficiency, productivity, or profitability at the division level, transfer prices must be established when one part of a company does business with another.

The need to track exchanges can occur for a variety of reasons. For example, a company might want to keep track of how its legal department's resources are consumed by various user groups. By charging other departments for use of the legal departments, the company can rationally allocate the cost to the area causing the expense. An obvious side effect of such a policy is that users may think twice about using the legal department, thereby limiting unnecessary demands. On the other hand, **management** may want to be sure that various decisions—hiring, firing, ad copy, contract terms, etc.—are approved by the legal staff before being completed, which may not happen if user groups restrict their use because of the charges incurred.

Beyond the question of staff department charge-backs are the issues of interdepartment or intercompany transfers of product or services that ultimately will be sold to third parties and the allocation of costs between **subsidiaries**. A common example is where one division manufactures product and another sells it. Although the parent company's goal may be to report true profitability at each level, the management teams responsible at the plant and at the sales office will have opposing agendas, with the former arguing for relatively high transfer prices and the latter lobbying for lower transfer prices. The best rule to follow is to let market prices be the guide; the factory would ''sell'' to the sales division at a price they could receive if selling to a third-party distributor. That way the manufacturing results are judged based on profits from market price transactions combined with their manufacturing efficiency and know-how, while the sales division is tracked on how well they are able to manage the interplay of market forces on demand and pricing.

Another important issue concerning transfer pricing arises with respect to income tax jurisdiction. Companies with international operations (or even interstate) will often have separate subsidiaries in each jurisdiction, sometimes for legal and/or political reasons. The affiliates will likely be subject to differential tax rates in the various jurisdictions they do business. In these cases, the transfer price issue becomes the concern of an interested third party—the tax authorities. Here the motivation might be to shift profits from a high tax-rate location to a lower one; this can be easily accomplished by manipulating the transfer prices. Obviously the **Internal Revenue Service** is aware of this practice, and will challenge inappropriate transfer prices in the course of audits. Section 482 of the Internal Revenue Code was written to set tax rules and guidelines for acceptable transfer pricing and cost allocations between affiliates.

SEE ALSO: Cost Accounting

[Christopher C. Barry]

TRAVEL

SEE: Business Travel

TREASURER

The treasurer is the person responsible for the custody and supervision of a business's funds. The office of the treasurer had its antecedent in English government which codified the organization, purposes, and general responsibilities of the business corporation during the seventeenth century when activities in worldwide colonization and trade exploded.

Corporate law, among other things, provided for a tripartite executive branch of president, secretary, and treasurer. States of the United States this model, modifying it as necessary. All fifty states require the inclusion of these three officers. The corporate

bylaws more specifically define their powers and responsibilities.

Ordinarily, the treasurer provides for the custody and supervision of all funds. Through a system of accounting controls and procedures, the treasurer tracks, in detail, the origin and utilization of funds. The treasurer employs, at a minimum, a series of standardized reports and analyses, integrating the dollars, volume of sales or production, number of employees, and financial costs into a series of ratios and percentages that assist management in evaluating progress and profitability.

Many businesses separate the reporting from the funds management functions. The resulting specialization has the **controller** performing tasks for the treasurer. The controller oversees the reporting and analysis of the sources and utilization of funds. Reporting directly to the treasurer, the controller is responsible for the accounting function. In this situation the treasurer manages the actual funds.

As an officer of the corporation, the treasurer has various corporate and accounting responsibilities. On the corporate level, the treasurer may transfer capital stock. The treasurer also maintains unissued (treasury) capital stock, performs **due diligence** (an evaluation) on financial and debt instruments, and records and transfers bonds on the company's books.

Accountable to the stockholders, the treasurer maintains capital stock records, signs checks for deposit, makes deposits, develops and maintains relations with financial and banking institutions, serves on the **board of directors**, and performs other duties that promote the profitability and objectives of the business. In conjunction with the other officers, the treasurer may transfer stock, sign checks for payment, borrow money, make long-term investments, sign contracts (e.g., employee benefits), repay debt, and distribute **dividends**.

In the capacity of chief accountant, the treasurer protects, from a ''book'' standpoint, the business assets by keeping track of their use and disposition. To prevent fraud and to ensure profit, the treasurer exercises a plethora of controls. These include the detail recording (**accounting**) of all financial activities, the discharging of all **liabilities** arising from debt, credit, and taxation, and the management of risk through an adequate insurance program. The treasurer also directs the tax accounting and the auditing functions. For budget and planning purposes the treasurer disseminates accounting and financial reports as appropriate.

As custodian, the treasurer supervises the collection and recording of cash receipts, manages the securing of credit, arranges debt financing and repayment, and invests excess funds. Through various planning and analytical tools, the treasurer ascertains cash balances, forecasts future needs, arranges for debt financing, invests excess funds, establishes the sales credit policy, and ensures the collection of receivables. In addition the treasurer signs and distributes the payroll.

An unincorporated business assigns concomitant duties to its treasurer where applicable. In either situation, the treasurer's office is the central processing area of the financial and personnel data required to construct intelligent budgets, to efficiently manage credit and excess funds, to establish long-term financial plans and strategies, and to identity the degree of operational productivity.

Because of the complexities of business and financial markets, classified advertisements look for a qualified employee with substantial experience as an accountant, preferably as a **certified public accountant** (CPA). In addition, even the smallest business needs a computer literate employee able to maintain computer accounting systems, perform **spreadsheet** analyses, create analytical models, and dabble in **desktop publishing**.

[Roger J. AbiNader]

TRUSTS AND TRUSTEES

A trust is a tool that an individual or institution uses to transfer property to a beneficiary. The party that grants the property is called the trustor. The trustor, in turn, gives the property to the trustee, who is charged with the task of disbursing the property to the beneficiary according to the instructions of the trustor. In the early 1990s, more than $1 trillion were held in U.S. trusts.

One important advantage that a trust has over a simple gift is that the trustor can exercise control over the dispersement of funds or property over time, even after his or her death (or dissolution, in the case of an institutional trustor). For example, a trustor may stipulate that funds periodically transferred to an all-male academy must be terminated if the school begins enrolling females. A second, and perhaps more important, advantage is that trusts can be used to minimize tax burdens incurred when transferring wealth.

The two main categories of trusts are non-charitable and charitable, they are differentiated from one another primarily by tax status. Charitable trusts are organized for non-profit beneficiaries, such as educational, religious, and charitable organizations. Beneficiaries of noncharitable trusts typically include individuals or groups—particularly relatives or employees of the trustor—or profit-seeking organizations.

Most trustees in the United States are banks' trust departments. However, other types of financial institutions act as trustees, and some companies specialize in trust management. Furthermore, a few trustees are separate entities that have been set up as foundations to manage large trust funds.

Trusts date back to about 4000 B.C. Egypt, when the equivalent of today's trust officers were charged with holding, managing, and caring for other people's property. Various prototypes of trust institutions were later developed in second-century Rome, some of which involved the use of property for charitable purposes. Trusts began to evolve into their present form during the eighth century, when English clergymen acted as executors of wills and trusts. Throughout the Middle Ages and into the seventeenth century, trusts developed under English common law to resemble their current legal structure.

Legalized trusts began in the United States in 1822, when Farmer's Fire Insurance and Loan Company of New York became the first institution chartered in the trust business. Corporate trusts developed in 1830 to help raise money for new business ventures. During the next half century, the number and types of institutions engaged in the trust business rose rapidly. Most of these entities maintained a separate department devoted exclusively to trust services.

In 1906, Congress enacted laws that allowed banks to act as trustees, resulting in approximately 1300 such institutions offering trust services by 1920. After the Great Depression, many trustees were prevented from conducting business by legislation that essentially restricted institutions other than banks and trust companies from serving as trustees. Legislation also established what became known as the ''Chinese Wall,'' which refers to measures that forbade bank trust departments from sharing customer credit or investment information.

The Depression also helped change American attitudes about saving and investing, and consequently, trusts. Employee benefit trusts, for example, became popular in the 1940s and proliferated so rapidly, that Congress enacted the **Employee Retirement Income Security Act of 1974 (ERISA)**, to define the responsibilities of trustees managing such funds. By 1980, more than 4000 banks, along with hundreds of trust companies, were managing $229 billion in employee benefit trusts. In 1986, employee benefit trusts represented over 40 percent of all U.S. trust assets.

Investments in individual and charitable trusts also escalated after the Depression. Wealthy individuals, in particular, increasingly used trusts as a way to invest their savings and to transfer wealth. Increases in tax benefits that allowed trustors to avoid estate and gift taxes boosted the utilization of trusts.

In the late 1970s and early 1980s, due to a number of economic and regulatory influences, trusts began to change. High interest rates and the deregulation of certain sectors of financial markets, for instance, prompted trust departments to invest their assets in a multitude of new instruments. Instead of traditional T-bills and commercial paper, trustees began investing money in **certificates of deposit**, money market funds, variable-rate notes, and other options many analysts deemed risky. In addition, a strong economy in the mid-1980s generated an influx of investment in trusts, much of which went into charitable trust funds. Between 1980 and 1986, the total amount of money invested in trusts jumped from $571 billion to $1.07 trillion.

Although assets under trustee management continued to climb through the mid-1980s, trustees faced a variety of setbacks in the late 1980s. The Tax Reform Act of 1986, for instance, increased costs and paperwork, and created some confusion for trustees, the end result of which was to discourage the use of trusts and estates as devices to accumulate and transfer wealth. Investment in trusts slowed in the late 1980s and early 1990s. Between 1987 and 1989, the number of trustees in the U.S. decreased from 6285 to 4283, and total employment by those trustees fell from 32,491 to 25,853. The use of trusts is expected to increase during the 1990s as a result of increased savings by the baby-boom generation.

TYPES OF TRUSTS

Several different kinds of charitable and noncharitable trusts are legally recognized. Generally, they all serve the same basic function, which is to transfer wealth from the trustor to the beneficiary(s) by means of a trustee. In addition to transferring wealth in the form of dollars, trusts may also include the following gifts: income-producing property, business inventory or equipment, securities, life insurance, works of art, real estate, or jewelry.

NONCHARITABLE TRUSTS

Noncharitable trust accounts that banks and trust companies manage are categorized as either individual or institutional (corporate). Individual accounts can be further classified into personal agencies or trusts. Personal agency accounts are different from ordinary trust accounts in that property does not actually change hands. Instead, the trust company simply manages assets under the direction of its client, often acting as a safekeeping agent, custodian, manager, or escrow agent. The company may provide complete investment management and reporting services as well.

In contrast to personal agencies, individual trust accounts involve a beneficiary. The trustor establishes an account with a trustee that manages, invests, and distributes the property. Income from the assets is then used to benefit dependents, organizations, or other parties. The trust may also be used to indirectly benefit the trustor. Many trust structures allow trustors various tax benefits and varying degrees of control over account assets.

Two types of individual trusts are guardianships and estate settlement accounts. In the first category, the trustee acts as a guardian to a minor or mentally incompetent individual, caring for the property that benefits that person. Estate settlements, on the other hand, involve securing and valuing a client's assets, distributing assets in accordance with a will, and representing the client's wishes at death.

Individual trusts are also classified as either revocable or irrevocable. Revocable trusts are used to distribute wealth while the grantor is alive, and can be amended at any time. In an irrevocable trust, the trustor relinquishes all control over account assets.

Like individual trusts, institutional (or corporate) trusts can be divided into agency and trust accounts. Institutional trusts, though, exist to raise capital for businesses, to reward employees, or to provide income for retired employees. The two most common types of corporate agencies are transfer agencies and registrarships. Trustees in agency relationships simply serve to transfer and register stocks and bonds.

In a corporate trust, the trust company acts as a trustee for a group of people who have lent money to a corporation through bonds or other obligatory instruments. Employee benefit accounts are another form of corporate trust. These trusts provide full custody services, compliance reporting, investment management, and special record keeping for each participating employee's interest in pension, profit-sharing, and other benefit accounts.

CHARITABLE TRUSTS

Donors may use a variety of trusts to transfer wealth to nonprofit causes. Each type of trust offers different advantages regarding the amount of control the trustor may exercise over the gift, various tax benefits that accrue to the trustor, and the method of compensation bestowed upon the beneficiary.

Charitable trusts, as opposed to all other forms of trusts, are usually enforced by the U.S. government. Furthermore, the entire trust industry is closely regulated by the U.S. government. For example, beneficiaries may reclaim property if trustees violate their fiduciary duty (or trust) by making unlawful or reckless investments.

The charitable remainder annuity trust (CRAT) periodically distributes a fixed amount of property to noncharitable parties—often the trust's grantor. After the recipient(s) die, the remainder of the CRAT passes to a charitable organization. Among other advantages, the CRAT allows the grantor charitable income tax deductions equal to the present value of the remaining interest that will ultimately be received by the charity. These deductions are used to offset income from the trust during the grantor's life.

The wealth replacement trust is used in conjunction with a charitable gift. This technically complex type of trust is used to replace assets given to a charity, while benefitting specific noncharitable parties—often the grantor's family members. The grantor may receive valuable tax benefits related to capital gains, gift, and estate taxes. Survivors of the grantor's estate typically benefit from reduced inheritance taxes.

Charitable lead trusts distribute income to philanthropic entities for a fixed term. At the end of the term, the remaining trust is transferred to a noncharitable beneficiary, such as a spouse or child. A benefit of a charitable lead trust is that the grantor avoids estate taxes on the value of assets that defaults to the beneficiaries.

A pooled income fund is a trust maintained by a charitable organization. Each donor who transfers income to the pool may be eligible to receive significant income-tax and gift-tax deductions, as well as estate tax benefits. Charitable gift annuities, which became popular in the 1980s, have similar donor benefits. This type of trust, however, is arranged so that grantors receive specified sum of money each year for the remainder of the donor's life.

Other charitable trusts include "bargain sales," in which donors sell property to charities for below market prices, and "charitable stock bailouts," in which a donor contributes closely held stock to a charity, thereby deriving various tax and/or business benefits.

TRUSTEES

Although trust companies and banks expect to profit in their role as trustee, they have a legal responsibility to act in the best interests of both the beneficiary and the trustor, and to conduct their activities with skill and care. Responsibilities include: protecting trust assets from attack by outside parties, dispensing property to beneficiaries, investing trust assets in a prudent manner, keeping accurate records, and being accountable to the beneficiary as specified by the trustor. Most importantly, the trustee is obliged to faithfully execute the wishes of the trustor. In return for their services, trustees are compensated by one of several methods. A common pricing schedule is a percentage of the market value of assets under management in a trust account. Under this arrangement, trustees typically charge from .1 to .5 percent, and in some cases as much as 1 percent per year of the total value of assets in the trust. For example, a $2 million trust fund might yield $5,000, or .25 percent, in annual fees.

Similarly, some trustees charge a "gross income receipts fee," which is a percentage of income collected from interest and dividends on the account. For instance, if the trustee earned interest and dividends of $50,000 by investing account assets for a period of one year, the trustee might receive five percent of those proceeds, or $2500 dollars. In addition to these charges, some trustees also charge minimum annual management fees or activity fees for special services.

For many financial institutions, fees from trust services are of vital importance. Mellon Bank, for example, one of the largest trustees in the United States, earned trusteeship fees of $279 million in 1990. Similarly, Citibank, the largest bank holding company in the United States, earned trust fees of $513 million in 1990.

EMPLOYMENT

Most trustees work for bank trust departments or trust companies, who typically hire trust officers and support staff to manage investments, to handle reporting and record-keeping, to market trust services to potential grantors, and to distribute benefits. In the early 1990s, trust officers at large banks earned $35,000 to $45,000 on average, while their counterparts at small and mid-size banks earned about $28,000 to $38,000. Trust support staff, earned $20,000 to $30,000 on average. Senior trust officers averaged approximately $100,000 per year, while subordinate trust investment officers averaged about $47,000.

[Dave Mote]

FURTHER READING:

Clarke, John M., Jack W. Zalaha and August Zinsser III. *The Trust Business*. Washington D.C.: American Bankers Association, 1988.

Esperti, Robert A., and Renno L. Patterson. *Protect Your Estate*. New York: McGraw Hill, 1993.

Haddock, Patricia. *Careers in Banking and Finance*. New York: The Rosen Publishing Group Inc., 1990.

Lochray, Paul J. *Charitable Giving Today: Taxes, Techniques, and Trusts*. Prentice-Hall, Inc., 1992.

Roussakis, Emmanuel N. *Commercial banking in an era of deregulation*. New York: Praeger Publishers, 1989.

TRW REPORTS

TRW, a highly-diversified company, issues reports on consumer and business credit worthiness through subsidiary credit bureaus and computer networks and directly to client companies. Information on companies' and individuals' histories of meeting obligations is maintained in databases which receive continuous updates from banks and lenders. TRW, along with Equifax and Trans Union, is one of the three major suppliers of consumer credit reports, while TRW and Dun & Bradstreet are the largest suppliers of credit reports on businesses. In 1988, TRW, which does not report its profits from credit reporting, earned an estimated $230 million from these services, according to one analyst (total revenues for the company were $7 billion).

In its beginnings the credit-reporting industry consisted of small, often nonprofit, agencies. As the industry developed into a profit-seeking oligarchy over time, it garnered the resentment of many in the banking community because of the rising cost of access to the data that they themselves helped to provide. Credit bureaus also began to sell information in credit reports for marketing purposes, often to competitors of their client banks.

In 1992 the **Federal Trade Commission** criticized the Big Three major credit reporting services for being unresponsive to complaints from consumers, who charged that credit histories had been unfairly tarnished by mistakes in data entry and that the sale of financial information to direct marketing companies constituted a violation of privacy. The credit-reporting services responded by installing toll-free complaint lines and refining their software to reduce mistakes; nevertheless, consumer dissatisfaction continued. In 1993 TRW agreed to stop selling consumer credit information to direct marketers.

Information on the payment habits of potential suppliers or customers is vital to businesses. Unlike a **balance sheet**, a credit report illustrates how promptly bills have been paid. Businesses can determine the financial health of suppliers, distributors, and licensees before completing purchases, sales, or agreements.

Besides payment information TRW's Business Credit Profiles also include information on the company's history. These are an important source of information on small, privately-owned companies. TRW also offers other services including statistical models that predict bankruptcy and delinquency and the Sherlock Service, which provides an individual's last known addresses and is used by collection agencies and police departments.

TRW's business reports offer more information about credit than those of Dun & Bradstreet, which primarily offer financial information. TRW's information comes from public records, legal filings, and telephone research on more than 13 million U.S. companies, including small companies and professional practices. Information on the 180 million individuals

in the United States over age 18 typically includes the number of loan applications made in the previous 120 days; the number of credit cards held; and information on delinquency, bankruptcy, and outstanding judgments.

Access to credit-reporting services' databases has traditionally been available only through annual agreements costing several thousand dollars per year. But in 1993 several on-line services began offering the reports on demand. Alternatives to on-line service include local credit bureaus affiliated with one of the national credit-reporting services.

[Frederick C. Ingram]

FURTHER READING:

"An Easier Way." *Small Business Reports*. January, 1993, pp. 6-7.

Basch, Reva. "Credit Reports: What You Need to Know." *Link-Up*. May/June, 1993, pp. 28, 35.

Betts, Mitch. "FTC Targets Credit Bureau Mailing Lists." *Computerworld*. January 18, 1993, p. 20.

Colacecchi, Mary Beth. "FTC Cracks Down on Credit Bureaus' List Prices." *Catalog Age*. March, 1993, p. 14.

Daly, James, and Thomas Hoffman. "Wiretap Snares Alleged Hackers." *Computerworld*. July 13, 1992, pp. 1, 14.

Garrett, Echo Montgomery. "Why You Still Can't Rely on Credit Bureaus." *Money*. March, 1993, pp. 17, 19.

Gaynor, Mark. "Consumer Credit Reporting." *Bank Administration*. May, 1989, pp. 44-47.

Haisten, Marilyn. "Making the Most of Credit Bureau Services." *Credit Union Management*. August, 1989, pp. 12-13.

Hulme, David C. "TRW: Credit Where Credit Is Due." *Tokyo Business Today*. May, 1993, pp. 54-55.

Maloney, Peter. "Credit Bureaus—An Oligopoly Raking in the Dollars." *United States Banker*. October, 1989, pp. 19-28.

Ojala, Marydee. "Business Credit Reports On-Line." *ONLINE*. July, 1991, pp. 83-86.

O'Leary, Mick. "NewsNet Responds to User Needs." *Link-Up*. July/August, 1992, pp. 9, 11.

Rothfeder, Jeffrey. "TRW's Troubled Credit-Data Network." *Credit Card Management*. November, 1991, pp. 22-29.

Schwartz, Evan I., Zachary Schiller, Walecia Konrad, and Stephanie Anderson Forest. "Credit Bureaus: Consumers Are Stewing—and Suing." *Business Week*. July 29, 1991, pp. 69-70.

Shermach, Kelly. "Speedy Loans Generated with Aid of Telemarketing." *Marketing News*. September 13, 1993, p. 45.

Smith, Robert Ellis. "TRW Sells Its Conscience for Cash." *Business & Society Review*. Fall, 1989, pp. 4-7.

Stewart, John. "Recovery Scoring with a Twist." *Credit Card Management*. September, 1992, pp. 16-9.

TURNOVER

SEE: Employee Turnover

U

UNDERGROUND ECONOMY

The term "underground economy" refers to the part of the economy that generates income but goes untaxed. According to Tibbett L. Speer, each year as much as $1 trillion of income goes unreported to the **Internal Revenue Service**. Moreover, the unreported amount appears to be growing, due in part to a rapid increase in small service companies and a large influx of illegal immigrants. Roughly 83 percent of the **taxes** Americans owe their government are paid voluntarily. Audits and other enforcement methods generate an additional 4 percent. The remaining 13 percent of potential tax revenue, however, slips through the cracks.

A number of hypotheses have been advanced to explain the increase in tax evasion. Some academic economists have studied the relationship between the tax rate itself and the tax revenue collected. Young H. Jung, Arthur Snow, and Gregory A. Trandel have suggested that, under certain assumptions regarding the risk-taking behavior of individuals, a rise in the tax rate increases the number of individuals avoid who taxes in the sectors of the economy in which tax evasion is possible. The level of the tax rate, consequently, also affects the total amount of tax evaded. Jung, Snow, and Trandel, thus, suggest that the design of tax policy itself sows the seeds of tax evasion. Therefore, tax policy makers need to carefully to craft a tax system that provides incentives to pay taxes and severely discourages the avoidance of tax payments.

Nevertheless, one cannot place all the blame for the underground economy on illegal immigrants or the design of the tax structure. The structure of the economy is itself to blame to a great extent. As mentioned, the rapid growth of small service companies has contributed to the growing size of the underground economy. Furthermore, some sections of the underground economy are truly "underground"—their activities are considered illegal. If one cannot admit to doing something, one cannot pay taxes on it. This illegal and hidden sector of the U.S. economy includes drug dealing, illegal prostitution, unlawful gambling, and other criminal activity. David Fettig has argued that while the amount of money involved in criminal activity, and the subsequent tax revenue that is lost, is of interest to economists and policy makers, it is largely considered unrecoverable. Thus, if one considers the underground economy to be comprised of legal and illegal segments, policy makers realize that they can recover taxes only from the legal segment of the underground economy. Therefore, policy makers' attention has focused more on the size of the underground economy as it relates to otherwise legal enterprises, such as off-the-books hiring or unrecorded retail sales. These activities normally appear above ground as part of normal business activities, but sometimes go unreported or unrecorded—most often, to avoid tax payments or the costs of meeting regulatory requirements. Fettig emphasized that the underground economy's impact on economic statistics and on government programs are foremost in policy makers' minds when they consider its signifcance because the goals of their new policies may be thwarted to some degree if they fail to take the underground economy into account.

SEE ALSO: Black Market (Trading)

[Anandi P. Sahu]

FURTHER READING:

Fettig, David. "You Can't Tax What You Can't See," *Fedgazette*. April, 1994, pp. 1, 3+.

Jung, Young H, Arthur Snow, and Gregory A. Trandel. "Tax Evasion and the Size of the Underground Economy," *Journal of Public Economics*. July, 1994, pp. 391-402.

Speer, Tibbett L. "Digging into the Underground Economy." *American Demographics*. February, 1995, pp. 15-16.

UNDERWRITING

Underwriting involves the orderly process of security registration for the financial sourcing of a **public offering** through the purchase of securities for resale to the public. The underwriting may be a firm commitment to purchase the entire amount of the company's securities regardless of the ability to resell them. The underwriting of such a low-priced initial public offering (IPO) and other less-well-known stock (e.g., OTC stock) may be done on a best-efforts basis where the underwriter acts only as an agent and accepts no financial **liabilities**.

A successful underwriting not only sells the securities, but does so at a fair price. In addition, underwriters maintain a stable, liquid aftermarket for the trading of securities.

Until the 1950s underwriting was the only function performed by a number of specialty houses. Thereafter, underwriters merged their talents with retail and institutional sales in order to bolster their sagging bottom lines. Today there is little distinction between wholesale underwriting, which serves institutional clients including broker-dealers, and retail underwriting which sells directly to individual investors.

Large underwriting firms assist the largest corporations with secondary offerings, and maintain a financial advisory role for the long term. As full-service houses, large firms need to handle IPOs in excess of $15.0 million for the fees to be profitable.

Medium size underwriting firms generally serve regional interests and handle offerings within the $5.0 to $15.0 million range. Although established companies, they lack the full range of services and number of personnel dedicated to underwriting and distribution. These firms are not likely to maintain a financial advisory capacity to their clients.

There are few remaining small underwriting firms. Some handle only small offerings called "penny stocks." Others specialize in a particular segment of the market. Offerings are usually under $7.0 million.

LETTER OF INTENT

A letter of intent (LOI) is an agreement to proceed with the registration of securities with the **Securities and Exchange Commission**. The contents of the LOI states, as clearly as possible, the duties and obligations of the parties.

A non-binding letter of intent requires a good-faith deposit from the company to demonstrate its financial capacity to complete the costly and cumbersome process of going public.

In a binding LOI the entrepreneur is responsible for payment of certain costs whether or not the securities are actually issued.

LOIs contain an adverse-change clause, allowing the underwriter to pull out if there are material adverse changes in the financial position of the company or business conditions.

UNDERWRITING AGREEMENT

The underwriting agreement finalizes the terms of the underwriting contract except for the final price of the security to be offered, and the amount of the security to be offered. The parties usually sign this agreement a day or two before the actual public offering.

For a firm commitment, the underwriting may include a "green shoe" provision which is an allotment option of up to 15 percent of additional stock for the account of the underwriter. When a public offering goes particularly well, the underwriter executes the green shoe to increase the amount of securities for sale.

Underwriting on a best-efforts basis uses a number of variable options to conclude the offering. An all-or-none offering will be canceled if all the securities are not sold. A mini-max offering establishes upper and lower acceptable ranges.

UNDERWRITING COSTS

Underwriters are paid commissions, securities or through a combination of fees and securities. In a firm commitment the price underwriters pay the company for the securities is expected to be less than the price offered to the public. This "underwriter's spread" compensates the underwriter for conducting the offering. The spread averages 10 percent or less and is dependent on the anticipated complexity and size of the offering. The maximum spread allowed by the National Association of Securities Dealers (NASD) is 10 percent.

There are certain "nonaccountable expenses" which cannot be construed as an integral part of the offering but which were necessitated by the preliminary steps to bring the company to the registration process. The NASD is the only exchange which requires accounting of these expenses.

UNDERWRITING SYNDICATES

When offerings are too large for one firm to digest, the lead underwriter forms a temporary syndicate of other underwriters and broker dealers to assist with the initial fund raising and the distribution of the securities. The participation of other firms in the underwriting minimizes the risks for all participants.

The originator of the offering is the managing underwriter and acts as the financial advisor to the syndicate. The managing underwriter keeps 30 percent of the underwriting spread, allowing 70 percent for the other participants.

At the time of the offering, a rectangular advertisement with a bold outline, called a ''tombstone ad,'' appears in the business pages announcing the offering, names the issues, describes the security offered, and lists all the participating firms.

[Roger J. AbiNader]

FURTHER READING:

Arkebauer, James B., with Ron Schultz. *The Entrepreneur's Guide to Going Public.* Upstart Publishing Company, Inc. 1994.

Malone, Michael S. *Going Public: MIPS Computer and the Entrepreneurial Dream.* Edward Burlingame Books, 1991.

Shillinglaw, Gordon and Philip E. Meyer. *Accounting: A Management Approach.* 7th ed. Richard D. Irwin, Inc., 1983.

Welsch, Glenn A., Robert N. Anthony, and Daniel G. Short. *Fundamentals of Financial Accounting.* 4th ed. Richard D. Irwin, Inc., 1984.

UNEMPLOYMENT

Unemployment is usually defined in percentage terms. The unemployment rate is defined as the percentage of labor force that is unemployed. The labor force is composed of individuals unemployed and employed. A person is considered unemployed if the person is out of work, but is actively seeking work. If a person is not working and is also not seeking work, then the person is voluntarily unemployed. A voluntarily unemployed person is not considered by the government as part of the labor force and is thus not counted as being truly unemployed.

The concept can be illustrated with the help of recent statistics. In 1993 a total of 129.5 million people were in the U.S. labor force, of which 8.7 million people were unemployed. These two numbers yielded the unemployment rate of 6.7 percent for *all workers.* It is customary to make a distinction between *civilian*

workers and *all workers.* The labor force in terms of all workers is made up of civilian workers and those in the U.S. armed forces. It is often considered that the civilian unemployment rate provides the truer picture of the underlying strength of the economy, as it captures the employment provided by market forces. As a result, the unemployment rate quoted in the popular and financial media is almost invariably the civilian unemployment rate. The 1993 U.S. unemployment rate for civilian workers was 6.8 percent. As is the case with the 1993 example, the difference between the unemployment rates for all workers and civilian workers is pretty small.

TYPES OF UNEMPLOYMENT

On the surface, full employment may appear to be equivalent to a zero unemployment rate. Official statistics, however, do not treat the full employment level in this manner. Full employment is officially defined as a 6 percent unemployment rate. The 6 percent is currently considered as the full employment rate of unemployment. The use of the 6 percent benchmark is based on the fact that it is not realistic to expect the unemployment rate to drop to zero even under best of circumstances—there will always be some unemployed people seeking jobs. One may appreciate this seemingly odd convention if one understands the different kinds of unemployment that may be prevalent at different points of time. There are mainly four kinds of unemployment.

SEASONAL UNEMPLOYMENT. Seasonal unemployment results from a variation in employment patterns from season to season. Thus, certain industries witness higher levels of unemployment during slack seasons whereas they may experience a labor shortage during peak seasons. For example, during harvesting season, employment in the agricultural sector increases drastically. Similarly, the construction industry experiences higher unemployment during winter and increased employment during summer. In cold weather regions, construction workers may be laid off for months at a time. So, why are these workers in such a high-risk industry? While the average unemployment rate in the construction industry is quite high, the industry attracts workers based on its high average wage rate. Agricultural workers are not so lucky. Wage rates for harvesting workers are quite low. As a result, often migrant workers from Latin America, enthusiastic to raise funds to take back home, end up with low-paying agricultural jobs.

It should be noted, however, that seasonal variations in unemployment can only occur if a region experiences a change in season. Thus, employment in the construction industry in California may not vary much across the year due to seasonal factors. While a particular region of the economy may be unaffected by seasonal factors, for the nation as a whole the seasonal employment pattern is easily detectable.

FRICTIONAL UNEMPLOYMENT. The U.S. labor market was made up of about 130 million individuals (as of 1993). The labor market is in a constant state of flux, even when the economy is in equilibrium. Millions of people are entering the labor force or leaving it at any time. Moreover, millions are seeking gainful employment at any time (roughly 9 million at the end of 1993).

The complexity of the labor force itself becomes a cause for temporary unemployment, known as the frictional unemployment. For example, a housewife sees that the economy is doing quite well and speculates that she may have a good chance of getting a decent job. She starts searching for a job actively, thereby entering the labor force for the first time. Now that she is part of the labor force and not yet employed, she will be counted in government statistics as being involuntarily unemployed. Let us assume that she finds an acceptable job after three months of being in the labor force. For these three months, she is a part of what is known as the frictionally unemployed labor force. Similarly, if a software programmer quits her current job due to inadequate pay or unsatisfactory work conditions, for example, and starts searching for a better job, she is also now part of the frictionally unemployed labor force. Similar norms apply to a worker who reenters the labor force. A new mother, for example, may leave her job to take care of her child for a few years and come back to look for a job when the child can go to preschool. When she reenters the labor force, she joins the group of frictionally unemployed workers.

One can thus summarize that frictional unemployment occurs during the normal job search process of individual workers. Since frictional unemployment occurs in the normal process of turnover in the labor market, it is also called turnover unemployment. While frictional unemployment for any one individual is a temporary phenomenon, for the economy as whole there are always a good number of people who are frictionally unemployed. Any economy is expected to have a modest amount of frictional unemployment. For a number of reasons, the United States seems to have a higher level of frictional unemployment than some other developed countries. The system of unemployment compensation in the United States may lead to higher frictional unemployment levels.

STRUCTURAL UNEMPLOYMENT. Structural unemployment occurs in the economy when it undergoes structural changes. These structural changes lead to a mismatch between skill requirements for existing jobs and the present skills of workers seeking jobs or between the geographic locations of these jobs and the geographic locations of unemployed workers. Since structural unemployment involves a mismatch between skills and/or locations, it is also called mismatch unemployment. There are number of factors that account for mismatches between skills, locations, or both.

Mismatches between current skills of workers and skill requirements of available jobs arise from the inability of workers to meet specific skill requirements of vacant jobs. If an office wants to hire a secretary who knows the filing system employed in that office, having general skills such as typing will not suffice. Sometimes the skill gap may be due to much higher technical skills required at emerging jobs. For example, openings for computer programmers can not be filled with workers who only know word processing.

Structural changes, often induced by technological changes, lead to job losses in some industries. For example, with a rise in wages and advancements in technology, the U.S. economy no longer has a comparative advantage in producing labor-intensive products. For instance, the U.S. steel industry has been losing a battle with steel manufacturers in less developed countries who possess the latest technology compared to the obsolete technology in U.S. steel plants. Workers who lose their jobs in the steel industry will most likely not find many steel industry jobs—they will have to find a job in another industry. This is a classic case of structural unemployment. Retraining to acquire new skills is the only remedy available for such workers.

It is also argued that job **discrimination** against women, minorities, teenagers, and others also cause structural unemployment. One can easily observe that most nurses, elementary school teachers, telephone operators, secretaries, and typists are women. Also, the majority of teenagers unemployed in the United States happen to be African Americans.

A mismatch of locations occurs when job vacancies and unemployed workers are distributed unequally across geographical regions. During the 1980s, while the New England economy was booming, the Texas went economy bust. The bursting of the economic bubble in Texas was blamed on a collapse in oil prices. Many oil industry and related jobs were lost. Meanwhile, the New England economy was booming due to increased demand for computer and financial services. With unemployed workers in Texas and plenty of jobs in New England, why did unemployed workers in Texas not move to New England? Texas workers were reluctant to move to New England because, first, job requirements for the two types of jobs were probably different, and, second, the preponderance of two-worker families meant that two jobs were often needed, not one. Thus, the potential move involved considerable risk.

Mismatch unemployment tends to last much longer than frictional unemployment, since it takes much longer to acquire new skills or to move to a new location to begin a job search. Several solutions have been suggested to deal with structural unemployment. Economists have suggested that the government should provide better public education, provide subsidies to firms that train workers, and initiate government-financed training programs to solve the problem of low skills. One of the suggestions to deal with the mismatch in locations is for the government to subsidize the cost of relocation. Another suggestion calls for the establishment of tax-incentive-based enterprise zones.

FULL EMPLOYMENT. As mentioned at the beginning, at the 6 percent rate of unemployment, the economy is considered to be at full employment. The 6 percent level is also called the benchmark unemployment or the natural rate of unemployment. This number is arrived at by adding the three components of unemployment discussed above—seasonal, frictional, and structural unemployment. The 6 percent level is the current estimate of these three components. With the increasing complexity in the U.S. labor market, this benchmark unemployment rate has been steadily revised upward over time—it was 4 percent during 1952-58, 4.5 percent in 1970, and 4.9 percent in 1977.

CYCLICAL UNEMPLOYMENT. Cyclical unemployment can be considered to be determined residually as the difference between the actual and natural rates of unemployment. Thus, if the current rate of unemployment is 7.5 percent, 1.5 percent (7.5 percent minus 6.0 percent) is attributable to cyclical unemployment. What causes cyclical unemployment?

Cyclical unemployment is the result of variations in the level of aggregate demand in the economy. If the aggregate demand level falls short of that necessary to maintain full employment, cyclical unemployment is the result and the unemployment rate goes above the 6 percent benchmark level. The higher the deficiency in aggregate demand, the higher the unemployment rate climbs above the 6 percent mark. Since fluctuations in aggregate demand are considered to be cyclical, unemployment caused by demand deficiency (i.e., those not attributable to "natural" factors) is called cyclical unemployment. It is cyclical unemployment that is the focus of government macroeconomic policies.

GOVERNMENT COLLECTION OF UNEMPLOYMENT DATA

Collection of unemployment data by the government on a continuous basis is of great importance for policy purposes, and is gathered every month. The government needs to know not only the prevailing unemployment rate at the national level, but also its geographic and demographic make up. Of course, collecting unemployment data every month by contacting everyone in the labor force would be a very time consuming and costly affair, as there are about 130 million people in the labor force. As a result, the government uses a cost-effective, but scientifically designed, alternative known as the survey method. Each month Census Bureau workers interview about 66,000 households regarding their employment status. In particular, they are asked if they are working for pay (full or part-time), are actively looking for jobs, are temporarily absent from work, or are on layoffs. Each month one-fourth of the households in the sample are replaced by new households in order to gradually update the sample.

FLAWS OF OFFICIAL UNEMPLOYMENT DATA

The official unemployment rate does not represent the true extent of unemployment in the economy. It suffers from several flaws that undermine its use as a gauge of labor market conditions. First, the unemployment rate does not capture the effects of discouraged workers dropping out of the labor force. For example, a female worker looks for a job for a year and does not find one. She is so discouraged about the prospect of landing a job that she quits searching. The moment she quits actively searching for a job, she is no longer considered a part of the labor force and is thus not counted among the unemployed in official statistics. As a result, if one envisions a lousy job market from which a lot of workers drop out, the official unemployment rate may actually go down. Suppose, for the purpose of illustration, that there are 100 people in the labor force, 10 of whom are unemployed, yielding an unemployment rate of 10 percent. Assume now that three discouraged workers drop out of the labor force—the labor force declines to 97 and the number of unemployed declines to 7. The official unemployment rate would drop from 10 percent to about 7 percent. One thus observes a rather perverse response of the unemployment rate in a discouraging labor market. An opposite phenomenon (and a second drawback) occurs when the economy is doing very well and the labor market shows a lot of promise to aspiring workers. People who are not yet in the labor market feel encouraged to enter the job market. Even if they find jobs ultimately, they raise the number of unemployed temporarily. This can result in a higher official unemployment rate even when the economy is doing better than before.

A third drawback of the unemployment statistic is that it does not distinguish between part-time and full-time employment. If working the 2:00 AM to

4:00 AM night shift at a distant 7–11 is not exactly the job a worker really wants, government statistics would count the person as being employed. This naturally inflates the extent of true employment in the economy.

Even if somebody is employed full time, he or she may have a minimum-wage job without fringe benefits or job security. Such a job may be unable to provide the worker with enough income to support a family. Workers employed in this manner have often been called the working poor.

GOVERNMENT POLICIES AND UNEMPLOYMENT

Unemployment of labor essentially amounts to a waste of productive labor resources of a nation. It also leads to a number of undesirable outcomes, such as lower incomes, lower standards of living, greater social tension, and greater welfare expenditures. Thus, we need to consider not only the economic costs (billions of dollars in lost output) but also the human costs associated with increased unemployment. With respect to economic costs, researchers have estimated that every percentage point increase in the unemployment rate above the natural rate leads to a loss in output equivalent to 2.5 percent of the year's **gross domestic product** (GDP). This implies that if the unemployment rate was 7 percent in 1993, it would have been equivalent to an output loss of about $625 billion in 1993 prices.

Researchers have also found that the human costs of unemployment are quite tragic. Estimates by the economists Bluestone and Harrison (in *The Deindustrialization of America*) suggest that for every 1 percent increase in the unemployment rate, 920 more people commit suicide, 650 more commit homicide, 500 more die from heart and kidney disease, 4,000 more are admitted to state mental hospitals, and an additional 3,300 individuals are sent to state prisons.

Both economic and human costs, in addition to political motivations, are the reasons behind the use of active government policies to reduce the unemployment rate to the full employment level. The government uses two sets of macroeconomic policies to reduce the unemployment rate—monetary and **fiscal policies**. These policies attempt to reduce unemployment by increasing aggregate demand for goods and services in the economy. Greater demand for goods and services leads to higher production that requires larger number of workers to be employed in the production process. This, generally, reduces the unemployment rate.

UNEMPLOYMENT AND INFLATION RATES. While reducing the unemployment rate sounds desirable, the process is not without complications. A lowering of the unemployment rate leads to higher **inflation**, especially when the economy is at or near full employment. Therefore, macroeconomic policies aim to strike a balance between acceptable unemployment and inflation rates. Normally, fiscal policy, conducted by the Congress and the White House in the United States, tends to have a pro-employment bias. Monetary policy, conducted by an independent **central bank** (the **Federal Reserve System** in the United States), on the other hand, tends to have an anti-inflation bias. In general, however, the purpose of both monetary and fiscal policies is to strive to achieve high employment consistent with low and stable inflation.

[Anandi P. Sahu]

FURTHER READING:

Bluestone, Barry, and Bennet Harrison. *The Deindustrialization of America.* Basic Books, 1984.

Branson, William H. *Macroeconomic Theory and Policy*, 2nd ed. Harper & Row Publishers, 1979.

Froyen, Richard T. *Macroeconomics: Theories and Policies.* 4th ed. Macmillan Publishing Company, 1993.

Gordon, Robert J. *Macroeconomics.* 6th ed. HarperCollins College Publishers, 1993.

Hall, Robert E. "Why Is the Unemployment Rate So High at Full Employment?" *Brookings Papers on Economic Activity.* Volume 3, 1970.

Sommers, Albert T. *The U.S. Economy Demystified.* Lexington Books, 1985.

UNIFORM COMMERCIAL CODE

The Uniform Commercial Code (UCC) is a collection of modernized, codified, and standardized laws that apply to all commercial transactions with the exception of real property. The UCC was developed under the direction of the National Conference of Commissioners on Uniform State Laws, the American Law Institute, and the American Bar Association (ABA). The purpose of the UCC was to introduce uniformity into state laws affecting business and commerce. To date, all 50 states (Louisiana has adopted Articles 1,3,4, and 5), the District of Columbia, and the U.S. Virgin Islands have adopted the UCC as state law.

The UCC has a permanent editorial board, and amendments to the UCC are added to cover new developments in commerce, such as electronic funds transfers and the leasing of personal property. Individual states then have the option of adopting the amendments and revisions to the UCC as state law.

The need for a UCC was recognized as early as 1940, and work on the UCC began in 1945. In 1952 a draft was approved by the National Conference of Commissioners on Uniform State Laws, the American Law Institute, and the American Bar Association (ABA). Pennsylvania became the first state to enact the UCC on April 6, 1953, effective July 1, 1954. The UCC editorial board issued a new code in 1957 in response to comments from various states and a special report by the Law Revision Commission of New York State. By 1966 48 states had enacted the code.

The UCC consists of ten articles. Article 10 provides for states to set the effective date of enactment and lists specific acts that should be repealed once the UCC has been enacted. Individual states may also add to the list of repealed acts. When enacted, the UCC replaces the following acts, which are listed in Article 10: Uniform Negotiable Instruments Act, Uniform Warehouse Receipts Act, Uniform Sales Act, Uniform Bills of Lading Act, Uniform Stock Transfer Act, Uniform Conditional Sales Act, and Uniform Trust Receipts Act. In addition Article 10 recommends repealing any acts regulating bank collections, bulk sales, chattel mortgages, conditional sales, factor's lien acts, farm storage of grain and similar acts, and assignment of accounts receivable. These are all areas covered in the UCC.

Article 1, General Provisions, gives principles of interpretation and general definitions that apply throughout the UCC. Article 2, Sales, superseded the Uniform Sales Act and covers areas such as sales contracts, performance, creditors, good faith purchasers, and remedies. Article 3, Commercial Paper, replaced the Uniform Negotiable Instruments Law and covers transfer and negotiation, rights of a holder, and liability of parties, among other areas. Article 4, Bank Deposits and Collections, incorporated much of the Bank Collection Code developed by the American Bankers Association and covers such areas as collections and deposits and customer relations.

Article 5 is devoted to letters of credit. Article 6 covers bulk transfers. Article 7 covers warehouse receipts, bills of lading, and other documents of title. Article 8, Investment Securities, replaced the Uniform Stock Transfer Act and covers the issuance, purchase, and registration of securities. Article 9 is devoted to secured transactions, sales of accounts, and chattel paper. It replaced the Uniform Trust Receipts Act, the Uniform Conditional Sales Act, the Uniform Chattel Mortgage Act, and a variety of other acts.

For up-to-date information on changes and interpretations of the Uniform Commercial Code, consult the *Business Lawyer*'s "Uniform Commercial Code Annual Survey."

[David Bianco]

UNIONS

SEE: Industrial Relations; Labor/Management Relations; Labor Unions; National Labor Relations Board (NLRB)

UNIT INVESTMENT TRUST

A unit investment trust (UIT) is a type of investment fund. A UIT consists of a portfolio of securities—usually **bonds**—that are fixed, meaning that they are not sold and that new securities are not added to the portfolio. Unlike other types of investment funds, such as open-end and closed-end **mutual funds**, the portfolio is not managed. Instead, it is established for a specified period—typically 20 to 30 years—and is placed in the trust of a trustee. After the trust is created, ownership shares, or units, that reflect the value of the underlying assets are sold to investors. The assets cannot be redeemed until maturity. Throughout the holding period, unit owners can sell their shares for whatever the market will bear.

Unlike managed funds, UITs do not have a **board of directors** or investment managers. The trustee simply collects the interest income and cash flow from the repayment of the bonds, and distributes the funds to the unit holders until all bonds mature or are called. Because the investments are not directed, annual fees charged to maintain the trust are sometimes lower than fees charged for managed funds. In addition to lower management fees, UITs may provide investors with a diversified portfolio of bonds that offer different maturity dates and an average holding period that complements their financial needs. Indeed, because most UIT assets are invested in bonds, UIT participants purchase shares with the expectation of earning a steady, monthly income and then receiving most of their principal back at expiration. Investors theoretically get the benefit of holding bonds until maturation without the volatility and risks inherent in short-term trading. Thus, unlike managed funds, UIT shareholders know exactly what they are buying.

Among the drawbacks of UITs are that their investment portfolios are unresponsive to changing market conditions. An individual investment that looks good when the trust is formed, for example, may sour soon afterward. Nevertheless, it cannot be removed from the trust. In addition to that trap, many UIT holders find that their shares are difficult to liquidate in the open market. Because no one tracks and compares the performance of the 12,000 UITs on the market (in 1993), moreover, investors may also have a difficult time comparing UIT alternatives. Finally, the UIT industry is characterized by a lack of standards for advertising and marketing, which dilutes the efficiency of UIT investing for many fund investors.

UITs usually charge a sales fee of 3 percent to 4 percent, although it can range from 1 percent to 5 percent. Shareholders may also pay a supervisory fee of $1.50 to $1.75 per $1,000 per month. These fees, which are high in comparison to competing no-load funds, have caused some analysts to consider UITs an unwise investment. Despite those detractions, UIT investments in the United States rose steadily during the late 1980s and early 1990s to about $200 billion by 1993. Some observers speculated that the high brokerage commissions offered by UIT companies were a major factor in their growth.

[Dave Mote]

FURTHER READING:

Black, Pam. "Unmanaged Stocks: Good Bet or Gimmick." *Business Week*. August 9, 1993.

Fredman, Albert J. *Investing in Closed-End Funds: Finding value and building wealth*. New York: Simon & Schuster, Inc., 1991.

Standard & Poor's Industry Corporate Descriptions. New York: Standard & Poor's Corporation, February 14, 1993.

"Unit Trusts Added $812 billion in November." *American Banker*. January 20, 1993.

UNITED NATIONS

The Charter of the United Nations was signed June 26, 1945 at San Francisco, California. This document was derived in part from deliberations held between the United States, the Soviet Union, China, and Great Britain, at the Dumbarton Oaks estate in Washington D.C., in 1944. These deliberations led to the United Nations Conference on International Organization which was held in San Francisco between April 25 and June 25, 1945. Representatives of 50 nations attended the conference. Poland did not send a delegation but shortly thereafter signed the Charter and is generally regarded as a founding member. China was until 1971 represented by the Nationalist government in Taiwan; however, the delegation from the People's Republic of China was seated in its stead in October of that year. On October 24 the United Nations (UN) became a viable entity with the Charter being ratified by the United States, China, France, the Soviet Union, Great Britain and most other signatories. (October 24 has since been declared United Nations day.) The name "United Nations" originated with President Franklin D. Roosevelt and was first used in the "Declaration by United Nations" issued during a 1942 meeting between 26 governments opposed to the World War II Axis powers. The United Nations succeeded the ill-fated League of Nations which was established following World War I.

The purpose of the United Nations is to promote international harmony, peace, and cooperation between the nations of the world. The UN is also involved in human rights issues as well as economic, cultural, health, and social issues. The guiding principles of the United Nations are set down in the Charter which also serves as the UN's constitution. The Charter enumerates four purposes and seven principles. The purposes deal with world peace and security, inter-member relations, and maintenance of the UN as a forum for achieving these goals. The principles are more specific and deal with equality of membership, member responsibilities, peaceful settlement of disputes, when force or various sanctions may or may not be used, responsibilities toward attaining the goals enumerated in the Charter, noninterference in the internal affairs of member states, and finally relations with and expectations concerning nonmember countries.

The United Nations is divided into six principal organs: the General Assembly, the Security Council, the International Court of Justice, the Economic and Social Council, the Trusteeship Council, and the Secretariat. All UN members belong to the General Assembly, which is the organization's deliberative body. The Assembly makes recommendations but cannot enforce them. The Security Council is responsible for the maintenance of peace through military action and economic sanctions. The Council has 15 members: The United States, Great Britain, France, Russia, and China are permanent members and constitute the so-called "Big Five." The 10 other members of the Council are elected for two-year terms by the General Assembly. The International Court of Justice is the only principal body of the UN not headquartered in New York. Residing at The Hague, the Netherlands, the Court seats 15 judges appointed to nine-year terms by the Assembly and Security Council. The Court issues advisory opinions and settles disputes between members within its limited jurisdiction. The Economic and Social Council has 54 members elected by the Assembly to three-year terms and issues advice and opinions related to social and economic issues. The Trusteeship Council administers non-self-governing territories going back to League of Nation mandates.

The United Nations Secretariat is headed by a secretary-general and is the organization's chief administrative body. The Secretariat is responsible for settling international disputes, carrying out peacekeeping activities, gathering information related to political and economic trends, and in general overseeing activities relating to the goals and aims of the

United Nations and directing the activities of the various UN special agencies.

These specialized agencies are many and varied. Some of the more notable ones are:

- The **International Monetary Fund** which stabilizes exchange rates between countries thus easing trade and balance of payments.

- The United Nations Educational, Scientific, and Cultural Organization (UNESCO) which encourages various projects in these fields thus increasing international cooperation and understanding.

- The **World Bank** (International Bank for Reconstruction and Development) which lends funds for infrastructure projects.

- The World Health Organization which deals with various health problems on both a global and local level.

- The Food and Agriculture Organization which combats world hunger by improving agriculture and fisheries.

There are also special bodies of the General Assembly including the United Nations Conference on Trade and Development, the United Nations Development Program, and the United Nations Environment Program. The best-known special body is the United Nations Children's Fund (UNICEF) which funds and administers child health and welfare programs in many areas of the world, especially developing countries.

One of the most controversial and often divisive roles of the United Nations is the deployment of peacekeeping forces by the Security Council. Since its inception the UN has sent such forces into India-Pakistan (1948, 1965), Korea (1950), Cyprus (1964), Israel-Syria (1974), Lebanon (1978), Angola (1988), Iraq-Kuwait (1991), Western Sahara (1991), and the former Yugoslavia (1993).

Funding for the United Nations and its activities comes from member assessments. Assessments are based on a sliding scale determined by the General Assembly. Criteria are per capita income, national income in relation to other members, and general ability to meet obligations. Any one member, however, may not pay more than 25 percent or less than .01 percent of expenses. For 1990-91 the UN budget was $1,974,634,000. In 1994 the United Nations had 184 members.

[Michael Knes]

FURTHER READING:

A Chronology and fact book of the United Nations. Oceana Publications.

Eichelberger, Clark M. *UN: The First Twenty-Five years*. St. Martin's Press, 1982.

Luard, Evan. *A History of the United Nations*. Harper & Row, 1970.

U.S.-CANADA FREE TRADE AGREEMENT OF 1989

The U.S.-Canada Free Trade Agreement of 1989 (FTA) represented a bilateral agreement between the world's largest trading partners. While many citizens of the United States may mistakenly believe that Japan is the United States's largest trading partner, the truth is that the United States and Canada have more trade between their nations than any other two countries on earth. At the time of the agreement, the United States and Canada traded roughly $150 billion worth of goods a year.

Negotiations on the FTA began in 1985 and the pact actually was agreed to on October 4, 1987. Following approval by the legislative bodies of both nations in 1988, the agreement officially took effect on January 1, 1989. The historic pact was the culmination of more than 100 years of on-again, off-again talk of **free trade** between the United States and its northern North American neighbor.

The issue actually caused much more of a stir in Canada than in the United States Polls taken at the time of the debate indicated that more than 40 percent of Americans were not even aware that the two nations had signed such an agreement, compared with just 3 percent of Canadians. In the United States, the FTA did not garner nearly as much press as did the **North American Free Trade Agreement** (NAFTA), the pact between the United States, Canada, and Mexico that came about five years later.

In Canada, however, the FTA was the subject of long and heated debate. The Liberal party in Canada even used the FTA to force an election—with free trade virtually the only subject of the campaign. The reason for the disparity in emotion on the issue is not that difficult to understand. For the United States, while trade with Canada is significant, it is not all that large when taken as a portion of the whole economy. From the Canadian standpoint, though, United States investment and trade was a fairly hefty percentage of the economy.

After all the talk and debate, the FTA was adopted and took effect on time—with the understanding that the agreement was an evolving document with mechanisms for changing and problem solving. What the FTA tried to do is put simply in the objectives agreed to by the two nations:

- eliminate barriers to trade in goods and services between the two countries;

- facilitate conditions of fair competition within the free trade area;

- significantly expand liberalization of conditions for cross-border investment;

- establish effective procedures for the joint administration of the agreement and the resolution of disputes; and

- lay the foundation for further bilateral and multilateral cooperation to expand and enhance the benefits of the agreement.

On the last point, the FTA apparently has been successful, as it helped lay the foundation for NAFTA, although certain differences do exist between the two agreements.

HISTORY AND BACKGROUND

When the FTA finally took effect in 1989, the issue of free trade talk had a history between the two nations that went back into the 1850s. In 1854, there actually was a reciprocal free trade agreement signed that lasted until 1866, when the United States terminated the pact.

That agreement actually was negotiated between the United States and Great Britain, because the five British colonial provinces that existed back then had not yet become nations. The agreement basically covered commodities such as natural resources and agricultural products. Although manufactured products were not part of the pact, about two-thirds of trade between the then-30 states in the United States and the Canadian provinces were covered.

There were attempts to make this agreement into a common market—where both areas would set unified tariffs for all third parties—but those efforts came to an end when the United States terminated the agreement in 1866. The United States appeared to take this action because of problems related to the Civil War, as protectionism began to develop in the United States during and after the war.

During the next 45 years, first Canada and then the United States tried to bring back the free trade agreement, but protectionism on one or the other's part stalled progress each time. An informal agreement that was never ratified came about in 1911 after a tariff war that took place in 1907. Canada started by adopting a three-tiered tariff system that greatly affected the United States, which retaliated in 1909.

An oral agreement on a free trade pact was reached in January 1911, put into a formal letter by the Canadian delegates, and then replied to formally by the United States Secretary of State, Philander Knox. But the Liberal party in Canada that negotiated the agreement was defeated in an election held because of the proposed free trade agreement, and the pact was never implemented.

The two nations held no further bilateral talks until 1935, when they agreed to what was termed a modest most-favored nation agreement. The two sides held negotiations again in 1948 but the Canadian government broke off the discussions.

Why the 1988 agreement succeeded where some of these earlier attempts did not is unclear, although a number of issues—including the globalization of the business world—no doubt had some impact. Some Canadians also wanted their nation protected from possible protectionist legislation they feared the United States might implement. Although most of the protectionist actions in the United States were aimed at Japan and the Far East, Canada thought it could be affected if the United States implemented emergency action under rules of the **General Agreement on Tariffs and Trade (GATT)**. Under GATT, all nations must be treated alike, and Canadians were afraid of the possibility of such measures from its largest trading partner.

DIFFERING OBJECTIVES

Leading up to the signing of the agreement, both the Canadian and American sides had objectives they wished to achieve. On one side, Canada had its high tariffs that encouraged foreign manufacturers to build plants in Canada for the Canadian market, as it would be too expensive to service the market with exports. During the 1950s and 1960s the Canadian economy grew extensively and the nation had few programs that influenced market conditions. But in the 1970s and 1980s, Canadians became more concerned about the extensive control and possible influence of the United States multinationals that had operations in Canada. The Canadian government began screening foreign direct investment and adopted policies aimed at making Canada less dependent on the United States and more competitive on its own. Although the ownership and control of the United States in Canada's industry did lessen, the United States share of Canada's trade remained high and Canadian competitiveness did not improve.

Canadians who favored free trade began to believe that Canada's resource products would no longer sustain the nation, so the country should focus on its competitiveness in the manufacturing arena. Canada's tariffs, following seven rounds of GATT talks, were no longer high enough to shield it from foreign competition. What was keeping Canada from being competitive were nontariff barriers in foreign nations, and the threat of further such barriers, particularly in the United States

According to, *Making Free Trade Work*, Canada had four main objectives heading into discussions on the FTA: access to the United States market by limiting the effects of United States trade laws; enhance access to the United States market by eliminating tariffs and achieving more liberal nontariff barriers; ensure any gains through a strong agreement with an effective dispute settlement mechanism; and maintain policy discretion in cultural industries and foreign investment in some sensitive sectors.

From the United States side, officials saw the FTA as beneficial in several ways. Limitations of the GATT agreement had affected United States access to foreign markets for United States high-technology products. Various things such as trade-related investment policies, subsidies, treatment of intellectual property rights, government procurement practices, and product standards had limited the United States in trade.

In addition the United States, by reaching this agreement with Canada, would be showing the **European Union**, Japan, and other nations that it was open to other trade possibilities if the ongoing Uruguay Round of the GATT talks did not bring substantial results.

The FTA also brought the United States a chance to eliminate the higher Canadian tariffs and to secure improvements made in the trade and investment climate. In nontariff barriers, the United States could get rid of or at least lessen discrimination of federal and provincial procurement practices along with barriers caused by technical standards and testing requirements.

BASIC TERMS

Over a ten-year period, the FTA will eliminate tariffs, duty drawbacks, and most import restrictions. The phase-in was aimed at allowing certain industries to get used to the realization of competition in a free market environment.

There were three options for tariff removal. As of January 1, 1989, duties were eliminated in full on about 15 percent of all dutiable goods traded between the two nations. Some of the industries and products included skis, whiskey, vending machines, needles, fur, and computers.

Products that covered another 35 percent of dutiable goods were placed on a five-year elimination program, with the tariffs reduced by 20 percent each year beginning January 1, 1989. Aftermarket auto parts, chemicals, furniture, explosives, paints, some meats, paper, subway cars, and telecommunication equipment were some of the covered products.

The final 50 percent of dutiable products were put on a ten-year tariff reduction path, with 10 percent of the duty taken off each year, with the process ending January 1, 1998. Those products included: most agricultural products, appliances, beef, pleasure craft, railcars, softwood plywood, steel, textiles and apparel, and tires. With regard to automotive products, tariffs are being phased out on vehicles that meet a 50-percent content rule, where half the content must come from the two nations.

The FTA also prohibits restrictions on exports, export taxes and subsidies, and the dual pricing of exports. There were, however, a few safeguards. During the ten-year phase-in period, duties could be restored for up to three years if domestic producers prove suffering because of the reductions.

Both nations also will give each other's subsidiaries what is known as "foreign treatment" with regards to foreign investment. Canada did reserve the right to screen direct purchases of its largest nonfinancial corporations and financial institutions. That nation's cultural industries were exempted from most provisions of the agreement.

For settling disputes, the FTA set up a five-person panel with two members from the United States, two from Canada, and one decided by the other four members or chosen at random from an approved list. Issues will be referred when either side feels the other has made an unfair judgment under trade laws. According to *Canadian-American Trade and Investment*, the dispute-settlement process was expected to develop a set of mutually-agreed rules about what constitutes dumping and subsidies, among other things.

GETTING IT APPROVED

In the United States the process was relatively quiet. President Reagan put the FTA on the fast-track process for congressional approval. That meant the Congress had so many days to debate it and then had to either accept it or reject it in total. They could not amend the agreement in any way. The United States House approved it July 9, 1988, while the Senate followed suit on September 9. Neither vote was close.

In Canada, however, there was no equivalent to the fast-track process. Under its parliamentary form of government, the House of Commons passed the matter easily because of the majority of seats held by the Progressive Conservative party that was led by Prime Minister Brian Mulroney.

But the Canadian Senate is not an elected body. Senators are appointed for life by the prime minister. Because the Liberal party had been in power for most of the 15 years prior to the FTA, that party had a majority of Senate seats and blocked passage. The Liberals used the debate to force a general election to break the impasse, and the election became an emotional debate on free trade and its impact on Canada. When the votes were counted, the conservatives still had a majority, although reduced, and the Liberal party did not oppose the voice of the people and allowed the FTA to go through.

Canadians were so aware of the debate because the impact on them was far greater than on United States citizens. Exports accounted for 28 percent of the Canadians' **gross national product**, compared with just 7 percent in the United States. And 80 percent of Canada's exports were destined to go to the United States

DIFFERENCES WITH NAFTA

Besides bringing Mexico into the arena for free trade, the North American Free Trade Agreement (NAFTA) also broadens the parameters of the FTA between United States and Canada in many respects. Areas where NAFTA either expounds upon or covers different ground than FTA include **intellectual property** rights, land transportation, the environment, and several others. Below is a summary of some of the differences:

MARKET ACCESS. NAFTA makes no changes in the three-stage phase-out of tariffs for items traded between the United States and Canada.

RULES-OF-ORIGIN. NAFTA clears up many of the questions regarding rules-of-origin in the FTA and also integrates the administration of the rules. It includes a provision that allows up to 7 percent of the value of North American products to originate outside the continent. It also mandates that cars and light trucks have 62.5 percent of costs come from North America to qualify for preferential treatment. For other vehicles, NAFTA specifies 60 percent North American content after a phase-in period.

NAFTA also makes the rules-of-origin simpler for certain electronics products and strengthens it for textiles. Fabric and yarn for garments must now come from North America, although there is a quota that allows a certain number of garments to qualify as North American in origin although they do not meet the rule.

CUSTOMS ISSUE. NAFTA extends by two years the deadline for elimination of duty drawback to January 1, 1996. Duty drawback is the refund of duties on imported inputs incorporated into products for export. NAFTA also allows trade and professional equipment duty-free treatment when brought in on a temporary basis by professionals covered by the provisions.

GOVERNMENT PROCUREMENT. NAFTA raises the guidelines on federal procurement of goods and services valued at over $50,000 ($25,000 on goods alone) and construction contracts that are valued at

over $6.5 million. The provisions also cover certain government-owned corporations for contracts over $250,000 on goods and services and $10 million on construction contracts. These items are intended to allow firms from all three countries to compete on equal footing for government contracts over the threshold. For example, under the FTA, firms from the United States won 535 Canadian contracts worth in excess of $20 million between January 1, 1989, and June 30, 1992.

SERVICES. Under NAFTA, the provisions covering services are expanded to most every service sector. The new agreement also eliminates federal and local restrictions on partner country access to services markets except in some instances. Also eliminates citizenship or permanent residency requirements on the licensing of professional service providers.

FINANCIAL SERVICES. NAFTA sets up a series of rules on trade and investment in financial services. It also ensures that United States firms in Canada can process financial data in the United States and gives access to NAFTA dispute settlement mechanisms for financial services firms.

INVESTMENT. NAFTA broadens guidelines regarding investors, so that the definition includes non-NAFTA individuals who operate in a NAFTA country. NAFTA also covers real estate, stocks, bonds, and certain contracts and technologies, and provides binding arbitration in disputes between investors and any of the three governments involved in NAFTA.

INTELLECTUAL PROPERTY RIGHTS. This area is not part of the FTA, NAFTA extends patent protection to a minimum of 20 years; provides **copyright** protection for products such as computer programs, sound recordings, motion pictures, and satellite signals; and bolsters trademark protection, service markets, trade secrets, and other intellectual property rights.

LAND TRANSPORTATION. Another area not covered by FTA. NAFTA makes certain that future Canadian laws and policies will not discriminate unfairly against land transportation service providers in the United States

ENVIRONMENT. Another new provision that was not in the FTA, it allows the three nations to keep their existing health, safety, and environmental standards and to impose new standards that can be scientifically justified and are not discriminatory.

[Bruce Meyer]

FURTHER READING:

Crookwell, Harold. *Canadian-American Trade and Investment under the Free Trade Agreement.* Quorum Books, 1990.
Morici, Peter, ed. *Making Free Trade Work: The Canada-United States Agreement.* Council on Foreign Relations Press, 1990.

UNITED STATES INTERNATIONAL TRADE COMMISSION

The International Trade Commission (ITC) of the United States is an independent bipartisan agency of the federal government and was established September 8, 1916. The Originally called the U.S. Tariff Commission, the ITC took its present name in 1974. The ITC is a quasi-adjudicative body that seeks to determine the effect of imports on American industries. The ITC also gathers information on international trade and disseminates this information to the office of the president, the U.S. Congress, the public, and various government agencies. The commission serves only in an advisory capacity to the government on trade issues and trade policy. It does not negotiate with foreign governments or set policy. The responsibilities and **duties** of the ITC are spelled out in numerous legislative acts including the Tariff Act of 1930; the Trade Expansion Act of 1962, the Trade Act of 1974, the Trade Agreements Act of 1979, and the Omnibus Trade and Competitiveness Act of 1988.

A tariff is a duty or **tax** imposed by a government on imports and occasionally exports. The purpose of a tariff is to protect home markets. In the United States, Congress is the sole authority for regulating commerce with foreign nations. Since its inception, the U.S. government had been under pressure at various times to create some sort of tariff commission. As the economy grew and trade expanded so did the pressure for such a commission. It was felt an independent agency could best provide the unbiased technical information needed by the government to make sound tariff and trade decisions. In 1882 Congress created a temporary trade commission and in 1888 legislation was introduced to make it permanent. The bill passed the Senate but failed in the House in 1889. During President Taft's team in office 1909-12, Taft created the Tariff Board, but like its predecessor, the board proved to be temporary. President Wilson, under pressure from the U.S. Chamber of Commerce, the American Federation of Laborand the Tariff Commission League, asked Congress to pass legislation creating a permanent tariff agency. The Tariff Commission was subsequently created in 1916. Under the Trade Act of 1974 it became the U.S. International Trade Commission with expanded powers and greater independence. The act removed the ITC's budget from the purview of the executive branch and gave the commission the power to review and issue remedies to trade infractions, subject to court review.

Two of the most important responsibilities of the ITC are determining whether or not the fair importation of foreign goods is hurting a domestic industry and whether or not dumping is taking place. A domestic industry could be damaged if competing foreign goods were imported into this country in overwhelming quantities. In such a case the ITC has the authority to recommend to the president a raise in the tariff or an adjustment in the import quota. Such an act would be protective of the home industry. Dumping involves the importation and sale of foreign goods at less than a fair market price or the unfair subsidization of an imported good by a foreign government. This action could result in home producers being driven out of business. In such a situation the U.S. Department of Commerce and the ITC would be involved in determining whether or not dumping is taking place and a home industry is being injured by the practice. In such a case increased duties equal to the dumping margin could be imposed. Complaints of unfair trade can be lodged by a home industry with the ITC. The commission has 30 days to decide whether or not to investigate; if it chooses to investigate it has one year to reach a decision. Complainants must show a relationship between the import and the injury and the relationship must be clearly documented. Such a complaint would be investigated by the commission's Unfair Import Investigation Division. The case could eventually be tried before an administrative law judge and appealed to a higher federal court. In such trials safeguards are often instituted to protect confidential technical information and marketing strategies.

The ITC is headed by six commissioners nominated by the president and confirmed with the advice and consent of the Senate. Commissioners serve nine-year terms and two are selected by the president to become chairman and vice-chairman. The chairman is responsible for the daily administration of the ITC but otherwise has no greater authority than other members of the commission. The chairman and vice-chairman cannot belong to the same political party and not more than three commissioners can belong to the same political party. This ensures the bipartisanship of the ITC.

[Michael Knes]

U.S. SECURITIES AND EXCHANGE COMMISSION

SEE: Securities and Exchange Commission, United States

U.S. TREASURY BILLS

To finance federal budget deficits, the U.S. Department of the Treasury issues both short-term and long-term debt obligations. Treasury bills (T-bills) are short-term money (money market) securities, maturing in a year or less. Known by their maturity date, the three-month bill matures in 13 weeks, the six-month bill matures in 26 weeks, and the one-year bill matures in 52 weeks.

Backed by the full faith and credit of the federal government, they are considered to be virtually free of default risk. In addition, a very active secondary market in T-bills provides high degree of liquidity. Another attractive feature of T-bills is that they may be purchased in denominations as low as $10,000, which is considerably smaller than the minimum denominations of other money-market instruments.

PRIMARY MARKET

The Treasury holds auctions for the 13-week and 26-week every Monday (or the next business day, when Monday is a holiday on which financial markets are closed). Auctions for the 52-week bill also occur on Monday, but only every fourth week. Prior to each auction the Treasury provides details concerning the total face value of each maturity it plans to issue. Investors submit bids on either a competitive or noncompetitive basis. Competitive bidders state the price they are willing to pay and noncompetitive bidders agree to accept the average price of all accepted bids. At the auction, the Treasury first accepts all noncompetitive bids then accepts competitive bids in descending order of price until the total face value of that maturity is sold. For example, if the Treasury wishes to issue $10 billion of 13-week bills and $6 billion of noncompetitive have been received, the first $4 million of competitive bids, beginning with the highest bid, will be accepted.

The price paid by the noncompetitive bidders is equal to the weighted average of the $4 million of accepted competitive bids. The results of each auction are summarized in the *Wall Street Journal* the next business day.

Treasury bills are sold at a discount, and prices are quoted as a percentage of the maturity value. The discount is the difference between the face value and the purchase price and represents the interest earned on the investment.

The rate referred to by market participants when buying and selling Treasury bills is calculated according to the bank-discount method as follows:

$$(M - P/M)(360/D)$$

where M = maturity date
P = purchase date
D = days to maturity

For example, the rate corresponding to the average price for the above auction is:

$$(\$100,000 - \$98,574/\$100,000)(360/91) = 5.64\%$$

When market participants are measuring rates of return, they refer to the coupon equivalent yield, which is calculated as follows:

$$(M - P)(365/D)$$

where M = maturity value
P = purchase price
D = days to maturity

For example, the coupon-equivalent yield corresponding to the average price for the above auction is:

$$(\$100,000 - \$98,574/\$98,574)(365/91) = 5.80\%$$

Money-center banks, securities dealers, and other institutional investors submit the majority of the competitive bids in any given T-bill auction. Individuals may purchase new issues of T-bills directly form one of 12 Federal Reserve banks or indirectly through a bank or broker.

SECONDARY MARKET

Government securities dealers are responsible for providing an active secondary market in all U.S. government securities, but especially in U.S. Treasury securities. The price at which dealers are willing to buy is called the bid price and the price at which they are willing to sell is called the asked price. The difference between these prices is called the spread, which is the dealer's compensation for arranging transactions between buyers and sellers.

Both the bid and the asked price are calculated using the bank-discount method as follows:

$$M - M(r)(D/360)$$

where M = maturity value
r = discount rate
D = days to maturity

For example, the bid for the Treasury bill maturing on August 24th is:

$$\$100,000 - \$100,000(5.65\%)(84/360) = \$98,682$$

and the asked price for the same Treasury bill is:

$$\$100,000 - \$100,000(5.63\%)(84/360) = \$98,686$$

Consequently, the dealer's spread on a transaction in this Treasury bill is $4.

The asked yield is calculated using the formula given above for the coupon equivalent yield but with P = the asked price.

[Roger AbiNader and Glenn Wolfe]

Table 1

Stated Interest Rate	Maturity Mo/Yr	Asked Price	Yield Based on Asked Price
8.50	07/97n	104:22	5.92%
6.375	07/99n	100:21	6.19
6.375	08/02n	99:29	6.39
6.5	05/05n	100:06	6.47

U.S. TREASURY NOTES

U. S. Treasury notes (T-notes) are **debts** with intermediate maturities of one to ten years issued by the U.S. Treasury Department. Prior to 1976, the maximum maturity was seven years. Today, the Treasury issues T-notes in minimum denominations of $5,000 for maturities of less than four years, and $1,000 for maturities of four to ten years. The maximum denomination is $1,000,000. Most T-notes (and **bonds**) are issued in book entry form which requires the Treasury to establish an account for the owner.

T-notes are issued on a rotational and "as needed" basis: (a) two-year notes, one week before month's end; (b) four-year notes, about the last month of every quarter; (c) five-year notes, mid-month of the second quarter; (d) three-year refunding notes, mid-quarter; and (e) seven and ten-year notes as options in quarterly refundings.

Treasury notes are sold at auction with both competitive and non-competitive bids accepted. Non-competitive bids are handled identically to **Treasury bills** auctions. However, unlike bill auctions where a rate of discount is indicated, bidders in T-note auctions indicate a yield to maturity. Given the average yield to maturity accepted at auction, the Treasury sets the stated interest rate on new notes at the nearest ⅛ percentage point that produces an average auction price slightly below par.

Unlike Treasury bills (T-bills) which have no coupon or stated rate of interest, Treasury notes (and bonds) do carry stated rates as determined at the time of sale; they also pay semi-annual interest. While T-bills will always sell at a discount, the market prices of T-notes will change in the same way as corporate bonds. Therefore, T-notes will sell at a discount or premium depending upon whether market interest rates move above, or below, the note's stated rate. All Treasury notes are non-callable.

There is also an extremely active market in T-note futures contracts. The Chicago Board of Trade began trading in Treasury note futures in June, 1979. The basic trading unit is $100,000 of face value.

PROS AND CONS OF T-NOTE INVESTING

Treasury Notes, like other U.S. Treasury debt, have several advantages. The interest received is exempt from state and local income taxes. In addition, except for longer maturities, T-notes have virtually no risk. T-notes also enjoy an extremely active secondary market, similar to other Treasury issues. Security firms and commercial depositories offer a wide-variety of notes in amounts and maturities to accommodate a broad range of investors. Government securities dealers are charged with maintaining the liquidity of this market.

Since T-notes are available in the secondary market in a wide variety of maturities, an investor can select a maturity (and yield) corresponding to the investor's requirements. Given the shape of the yield curve, the existence of T-notes frequently offers investors the opportunity to take advantage of intermediate term yields, which are just a few basis points lower than long-term rates. This provides the investor with the advantage of higher rates, without the price volatility associated with longer term maturities.

Treasury note rates are often used as bell-weather indicators for rates on home mortgages. Traditionally, changes in the ten year maturity T-note rates were the best indicators of changes in mortgage rates. Recently, however, with the dramatic increase in the pace of mortgage refinancing, yields on shorter term T-notes, usually around 3-5 year maturities, are thought to be better indicators.

TREASURY NOTE QUOTATIONS

T-note prices are reported daily in the *Wall Street Journal*, together with their yields to maturity. Since they are listed with Treasury bonds, most quotation sources use the letter "n" after the instrument's year of maturity to designate a note. T-notes trade in 32nds of a dollar. Hence, a price quotation of 98:16 (note the use of the colon to designate 32nds) equals $985.00. Table 1 presents the prices and yields of selected T-notes based on July 28, 1995 trades.

The yields to maturity are computed like any other debt instrument, being equal to that interest rate, which compares the present value of the remaining interest payments and the face amount of the note to the current price of the T-note.

STRIPS

To accommodate a huge market demand for risk free zero coupon bonds, the Treasury initiated Separate Trading of Registered Interest and Principal of Securities Notes (STRIPS). Depository institutions may request that the Treasury book the interest and principal separately to facilitate the timely payment of a wide variety of zero bond rates and maturities. Quotations for STRIPS appear with those for other Treasury instruments in the Wall Street Journal. Instruments which are stripped principal of T-notes are indicated by "np;" stripped interest is indicated by "ci."

FOREIGN-TARGETED NOTES

In October 1984, the Treasury instituted securities designed especially for foreign institutions and foreign branches of U.S. banks who certify that, on the day of issuance, they will place these notes only with non-U.S. citizens. After a 45-day period, foreign investors may exchange these notes for comparable domestic issues, or sell them to U.S. citizens. The Treasury sets the interest rate according to the results of the auction of the companion domestic issue and provides book-entry form during the 45-day waiting period. Afterwards, the Treasury makes registered notes available.

SEE ALSO: Credit; U.S. Treasury Bills

[Ronald M. Horwitz]

FURTHER READING:

Board of Governors of the Federal Reserve. *The Federal Reserve System: Purposes & Functions.* Washington, D.C., 1984.

Board of Governors of the Federal Reserve. *1989 Historical Chart Book.* Washington, D.C., 1990.

International Monetary Fund. *Government Finance Statistics Yearbook.* Vol. XVIII, 1994.

Kleege, Steven. "Does Treasury Know How to Make a Buck." *Business Week.* October 17, 1994.

Ricchiuto, Steve R. *The Rate Reference Guide to the U.S. Treasury Market.* Probus Publishing Co., 1990

Sullivan, Colleen. *The Money Market Fund Primer.* MacMillan Publishing Co., Inc., 1983.

UNIVERSAL PRODUCT CODE (UPC)

SEE: Bar Coding

UTILITARIANISM

Utilitarianism is a highly secular philosophy that originated in Great Britain in the late eighteenth century, but whose influence continues down to the present day. It is most often associated with Jeremy Bentham (1748-1832), James Mill (1773-1836), and his son, John Stuart Mill (1806-1873). Of the three, John Stuart Mill is considered the most brilliant exponent of utilitarianism, although he also is known for other significant contributions to nineteenth-century intellectual thought.

Jeremy Bentham finished his law studies at Oxford University in 1763 but never practiced law. His intellect was probing and highly analytical and concerned more with reforming injustices (such as the penal system and penal law) than with conforming to the status quo. In this respect he was typical of philosophers of the Enlightenment, which was at its zenith when Bentham began his singular career. Bentham's disciple, James Mill, did much to publicize his radical ideas in England.

Bentham was much influenced by the secularism of the age. Rejecting Christianity as too intuitive and untenable, he sought a material explanation for right and wrong, good and evil. He found his answers in the writings of such theorists as Scottish philosopher David Hume (1711-76) and French *philosophe* Claude-Adrien Helvètius (1715-71) , who posited that true justice was synonymous with the good of the whole. Bentham made this principle, dubbed the "greatest happiness" principle, a moral criterion and the basis for his philosophy of reform.

In *An Introduction to the Principles of Morals and Legislation* (1789), Bentham introduced his "utilitarian" doctrine: mankind has two masters, pleasure and pain; nothing is good except pleasure, or bad except pain. To advance pleasure is the aim of human nature, and therefore the goal of every person; it should be the goal of society as well. But since individual interests clash within every society, the aim of legislation and government should be to harmonize these clashing interests for the good of the whole.

In time Bentham's philosophy would be criticized (by none other than John Stuart Mill) for being excessively narrow, reducing human nature to almost instinctual pain and pleasure, and making no allowance for an individual's spiritual strivings or emotions. Therefore, although Bentham intended utilitarianism (a word he used only once) to be applicable to both the individual and to society, it seemed most persuasive as a social philosophy. In this respect, utilitarianism has had the most profound impact in the development of legal thought.

Bentham became convinced that the British government, controlled by a handful of leading families, was influenced solely by narrow self-interest. In time he came to advocate the abolition of the monarchy, universal male suffrage, and rule by parliament. In so doing he was not a promoter of democracy; rather, he viewed these changes (radical for his day and age) strictly from the perspective of utility, or what was best for the whole.

Bentham became the leader in England of a group of reform-minded radicals, including James Mill. A dissatisfied clergyman who came to abandon his religion, Mill became Bentham's ardent disciple and a rigid interpreter of "Benthamism." His unique contribution was *Analysis of the Phenomena of the Human Mind* (1829), in which Mill attempted to analyze the "pleasure principle," which many non-utilitarians rejected as hedonistic and selfish, a position he attempted to disprove. This unusual psychological study was saturated with "Benthamite" ideology—it was not original—but did much to disseminate Bentham's ideas.

James Mill's greatest contribution to the development of utilitarianism appears to have been his son, John Stuart Mill. The younger Mill became a rigid utilitarian in his teen years, but after suffering a nervous breakdown at age 20, he came to the conclusion that utilitarianism was a sterile, over-intellectualized moral theory that left no room for intuition or feelings.

John Stuart Mill never rejected the philosophy of his boyhood, but in his seminal work, *Utilitarianism* (1863), written in his middle years, he so revised the basic doctrine of Bentham that his book appeared to almost reject it. He proposed that goodness was not necessarily pleasurable; that quality of pleasure was more important than quantity; and that there were "lower" and "higher" pleasures, such as intellectual, spiritual, and emotional ones.

The most striking departure from traditional or classical utilitarianism was in John Stuart Mill's rejection of **laissez-faire** economics. While Jeremy Bentham advocated political and social reform rather than economic reform, a disciple of his, David Ricardo (1772-1823), expressed in 1817 the utilitarian view of economics in his *Principles of Political Economy.* Ricardo advocated free economic competition, without any legislative constraints, as leading to the greatest good for the greatest number. John Stuart Mill rejected this classic statement of laissez-faire economics. His readings of French socialist thinkers led him to question the sanctity of private property and to advocate a more equitable distribution of wealth and equal opportunity for all. Despite his considerable revision of classical utilitarianism, John Stuart Mill never abandoned this doctrine, which as a social and legal philosophy has remained influential to this day.

[Sina Dubovoy]

FURTHER READING:

Bluhm, William T. "Toward 1992: Utilitarianism as the Ideology of Europe." *History of European Ideas*. January, 1993, p. 487.

Brown, Kevin L. "On Human Nature: Utilitarianism and Darwin." *Social Science Information*. June, 1992, p. 239.

Ebenstein, Alan O. *The Greatest Happiness Principle: An Examination of Utilitarianism*. New York: Garland, 1991.

Jackson, Julius. *A Guided Tour of John Stuart Mill's Utilitarianism*. Mountain View, CA: Mayfield Publishing Co., 1993.

Majeed, J. "James Mill's 'The History of British India' and Utilitarianism as a Rhetoric of Reform." *Modern Asian Studies*. May, 1990, p. 2.

Mill, John Stuart. *On Liberty; and Utilitarianism*. Reprint. New York: Bantam Books, 1993.

Sprigge, T. L. S. "Utilitarianism and Respect for Human Life." *Utilitas*. May, 1989, p. 1.

V

VALUATION

Valuation involves putting a price on a piece of property, whether it be **real estate**, **intellectual property** (**patents**, copyrights, trademarks, and other intangibles), personal property, or a business. In the context of a business valuation the appraiser considers many factors, including financial attributes (e.g., sales and profitability trends, noncash expenses, capital expenditures, tangible and intangible assets, and the implications of long-term contracts, nonrecurring profit and loss statement items, related-party transactions, and contingent liabilities), marketing attributes (including location, competition, barriers to entry, distributor relationships) and macroeconomic attributes (regulatory constraints, labor relations, **interest rates**, general economic conditions, the state of the art for the company's products, and others). A thorough understanding of the subject company's background and circumstances is critical to the appraiser's ability to assess the reasonableness of various assumptions that will underlie the valuation.

VALUATION APPROACHES

There are many different valuation methodologies, some more suited to certain types of property than others. The main approaches include liquidation, asset value, market comparable, and discounted cash flow.

LIQUIDATION APPROACH. This method assumes a company will cease operations and that the value will simply be the sum of the individual assets that can be sold; no "goodwill" for the company's name, loca-

tion, customer base, or other accumulated experience is captured. This level is further divided into forced liquidations (as in a bankruptcy) and orderly liquidations, with values generally higher in the latter.

ASSET VALUE APPROACH. This approach starts with the company's book values per its balance sheet (at historical cost), and makes adjustments thereto to bring them in line with market values. For example, real estate acquired long ago is frequently worth more than its historical cost. Alternatively, some intangible assets may have no continuing value in certain situations, or may be worth much more than book value in others. This method is most often used in companies where much of the assets are commodity-like.

MARKET COMPARABLE APPROACH. This approach looks to comparable companies—in terms of industry, size, growth rates, capitalization, and other factors—for which a market value is known or observable (e.g., publicly traded companies) to establish a gauge. Then, a ratio of value is calculated for the comparable(s)—such as market to book, market to earnings, and market to cash flow—which is applied to the target company's parameters. In some cases a comparable private company may have recently changed hands under similar terms and circumstances. Here, the particular transaction may be useful as an indicator of value.

DISCOUNTED CASH FLOW (DCF) APPROACH. This method uses projections of future cash flows from operating the business or using the asset, and requires detailed assumptions about future operations, including volumes, pricing, costs, and other factors. DCF usually starts with forecast income, adding back non-cash expenses, deducting capital expenditures, and adjusting for working capital changes to arrive at ex-

expected cash flows. The appropriate **discount rate** must be determined and used to bring the future cash flows back to their present value at the as-of date of the valuation. DCF in its single period form is known as capitalization of earnings, which usually involves ''normalizing'' a recent measure of income or cash flow to reflect a steady-state or going forward amount that can be capitalized at the appropriate multiple.

VALUATION ISSUES AND STANDARDS

It is important to recognize and deal properly with certain subtleties and standards in the field of valuation. Issues and standards to be aware of include:

- Treatment of debt: if the methodology applied uses a pre-debt-service income measure, then debt must usually be subtracted from the resulting figure.

- Control premiums: if the methodology is based on price-earnings ratios of comparable public companies and the interest being valued is the entirety of a company, a control premium may be applicable. Conversely, if the starting point is from a controlling perspective and the interest being valued is ''minority,'' then a discount for lack of control may be indicated.

- Discount for lack of marketability: also known as the liquidity discount, this involves whether or not the property can be readily sold. For example, publicly traded companies are highly marketable, and their shares can be quickly turned into cash. Closely held companies, on the other hand, are more difficult (and in some cases by agreement, impossible) to sell. Depending on the reference point of the valuation, it may be necessary to subtract a discount for lack of marketability, or add a premium for the presence of marketability.

- The standard of value must be clearly defined. That is, whether the valuation is based on book value, fair market value, fair value, liquidating versus going concern value, investment value, or some other defined perspective of value. The distinction is important because of adjustments that are necessary under some, but not all, of these standards (e.g., control premiums, discounts for illiquidity).

- The as-of date must be specified and maintained. Values of property vary over time, and it is critical to state the date reference for any valuation. Further, the information used by the appraiser should be limited to that which would have been available at the as-of date; that is, subsequent information is generally excluded from the equation when doing valuations.

- The form of organization is important. Different legal forms of entity—corporations, **S corporation**, and partnerships—are subject to different tax rules, which affect the value of the enterprise.

- The focus of the valuation must be clearly identified. The portion of the enterprise being acquired, the type(s) of securities involved, whether the transaction is a stock purchase or an asset purchase deal, and how the transaction may affect existing relationships, such as related party transfers, can all affect the value.

[Christopher C. Barry]

FURTHER READING:

Pratt, Shannon P. *Valuing a Business*. Homewood, IL: Dow Jones-Irwin, 1989.

VALUE-ADDED TAX (VAT)

A value-added tax (VAT) is a **tax** levied on the value added to goods or services produced by businesses. Such a tax is collected in stages from each business that contributes to the final market value of goods and services. While VAT is paid by businesses, the actual tax burden is typically passed along to consumers. While sales tax is easily perceived by consumers, VAT is generally considered invisible to consumers because retailers add little value to the goods they sell, so there is little or no VAT charged to retailers. By the time goods reach the retail level, the VAT that has been charged along the way to companies in the manufacturing and distribution sectors has been incorporated into the selling price.

The concept of ''value added'' in manufacturing is used to measure the productive activity of a business. The tax base on which VAT is calculated is the difference between selling price of a firm's output and the purchase price for intermediate products. That difference is known as the value added by the firm. Value added consists of productive activity, such as labor done by workers and manufacturing operations performed by machines.

In countries that have a VAT, such as Canada and member states of the European Economic Community (EEC), the tax generally affects goods bought and sold within the country as well as imports into the country, while exports from the country receive a credit on the VATs that have been paid or assessed.

Goods that are exempt from the VAT are said to be zero-rated. In addition to exports, goods that may be zero-rated typically include food and other necessities. Countries may also charge a "luxury" rate on certain goods that is higher than their standard VAT.

In the European Economic Community, each country has a different VAT rate. Thus far, there has been little or no progress made on standardizing the different rates among the member countries, especially in terms of trade between member countries. As of 1992-93, the standard VAT rates varied from a low of 15 percent charged in Germany, Luxembourg, and Spain, to high rates of 21 percent in Ireland and 25 percent in Denmark. The United Kingdom was charging businesses a 17.5 percent VAT.

Canada adopted a national VAT in 1991, called the federal goods and services tax (GST). It replaced the federal manufacturers' sales tax (FMST), which was based on the total resale value of a manufacturer's goods, not just the value added.

The United States considered adding a VAT in the early 1980s as part of a general tax reform. It was argued that a VAT would result in balance-of-payments stability in international trade and that it would provide the government with enough revenue to reduce income taxes. The United States did not adopt a VAT, however, in part because it is considered a regressive tax that places a proportionally larger tax burden on lower-income consumers.

[David Bianco]

VARIABLE ANNUITY

Annuities are typically **contracts** sold by companies that provide series of payments for specified periods. For example, $100 paid each year for three years is a three-year annuity. While in a fixed annuity the payments are for a guaranteed amount, a variable annuity differs in that the amount of money paid out each period may vary. Typically, the payment changes in accordance with some outside influence, such as the return from an investment. For example, a three-year variable annuity may pay $70, $128, and $97 in years one, two, and three, respectively.

The term "annuity" is most commonly used to describe a contract between an insurance company and an individual or entity. Various annuity products proliferated in the insurance industry during the 1980s following increased competition for traditional life insurance dollars from investment vehicles such as **mutual funds** and **individual retirement accounts** (IRAs). Typically, an investor in an annuity gives a sum of money to an insurance company in return for

that insurer's promise to supply a series of payments for a fixed number of years during his or her lifetime. The person can elect to have the payments begin immediately (immediate annuity) or at some future date (deferred annuity). With an immediate annuity, payments start immediately after the initial payment of the premium by the individual. In contrast, disbursements for deferred annuity contracts start at least one year after the premium payment.

The most common type of annuities are deferred, because interest that accrues on the investment is not taxed until the money is disbursed. The advantage of such an arrangement is that the investor can time the payouts to reduce total **tax** liabilities. For example, a young investor in a high-income tax bracket could invest money in a deferred annuity with plans to withdraw the investment in the form of annual payments after retirement, when he or she would be in a lower-income tax bracket. Deferred annuities can be fixed or variable.

Investors in variable annuities can usually move their money around into different mutual funds offered by the insurance company—companies usually offer five to ten different funds, including bond, stock, and money market funds. A younger investor, for example, would have the option of gradually adopting a more conservative underlying investment portfolio as time passes. The arrangement is similar to investing in an IRA. The key difference is that the maximum amount of money one can invest in an IRA is limited by federal law and the initial IRA investment is tax-deductible. The amount that one can contribute to a deferred annuity, in contrast, is unlimited but not tax-deductible. Potential drawbacks of variable annuities include annual management fees, early-withdrawal penalties, and in some cases limited investment alternatives.

Variable annuities are often combined with life insurance products to form variable life insurance. Variable life insurance offers the advantages provided by variable annuities that are described above as well as the benefits of life insurance. Typically, an individual (the insured) pays a single premium or a series of premiums. The insured can then select from a number of options to convert the policy into an income stream, which entails a stated death benefit. The basic options include: (1) taking the market value of the investment as a lump-sum payment; (2) receiving a variable periodic payment; and (3) receiving a fixed annuity. Variable life insurance gives the insured more control over his or her investment than do other types of life insurance, and the surviving beneficiary is not subject to income tax on the death benefit.

Actuaries at insurance companies determine benefits and payments related to life annuities by consulting mortality tables. These tables of historical data show the probability for life expectancy for specific individuals. Using that information, the insurer effectively structures the variable annuity so that the insured bears the investment risk of the underlying investment portfolio. For example, assume that Jim retires at age 60 with $100,000 in his variable annuity contract. Mortality tables suggest that Jim, a motorcycle rider and heavy smoker, will likely die within five years. Assuming that the insurance company can expect to get an average investment return of 5 percent annually (the assumed investment return, or AIR), the insurer can calculate Jim's annual benefit payment with the following formula:

$$B_t = B_{t-1} [(1 + R_t)/(1 + .04)]$$

where B equals the benefit payment in each year t, and R_t is the actual return on Jim's portfolio in year t. The first payment is determined by simply calculating a constant payment that, over five years, would equal $100,000 given a discount rate equal to the AIR. In this case, the formula yields a first payment of $23,097 assuming a discount rate equal to the AIR of 5 percent. Thus, if Jim's portfolio returned 6 percent in the second year after his retirement, his annual payment would be $23,317, or $23,317 = $23,097[1.06/1.05].

Thus, each year's benefit is calculated by multiplying the previous year's benefit by a factor that reflects the actual investment performance of the portfolio. The formula guarantees that Jim will continue to receive a relatively substantial annual benefit throughout his life, regardless of how long he actually lives. If Jim lives 15 years the insurance company will obviously lose money on his annuity contract. Theoretically, however, the mortality tables will ensure that the company profits from the average performance of its large pool of annuity contracts—some insureds will die earlier than expected, and some will die later.

[Dave Mote]

FURTHER READING:

Bodie, Zvi, Alex Kane, and Alan J. Marcus. *Investments*. Homewood, IL: Irwin, 1989.

Garner, Robert J., Robert B. Coplan, Barbara J. Raasch, and Charles L. Ratner. *Ernst & Young's Personal Financial Planning Guide*. New York: John Wiley & Sons , 1994.

VENTURE CAPITAL

The term "venture capital" can apply to initial funding and capital for new and emerging enterprises. When individual entrepreneurs or very new businesses need funds or equity for further growth and expansion, they are said to be searching for venture capital to fuel the organizational activities. More and more, however, the term is used to refer to the professional organizations and institutions that specialize in backing new ventures or entrepreneurs. That is, the term has come to be applied to the organizations that provide the capital needed by new ventures in exchange for partial ownership of the business or interest on funds lent. Additionally, venture capital organizations provide the entrepreneur with **management** assistance and often become involved with the strategic planning of the new venture. While the venture capital organization may be affiliated with **banks** or other lending institutions, most are independent and privately managed. Their efforts are focused; business activity is limited to working with start-ups or young organizations. Venture capital organizations provide their clients with capital through direct equity investments, **loans**, or other financial arrangements. Due to the highly speculative nature of their investments, venture capital organizations are taking big risks by working with new ventures. In exchange for the high level of risk, venture capital organizations expect a high return on their investments.

All businesses need some financial resources to begin activity. The exchange between someone with a good idea (an entrepreneur) and someone with the resources to help make a business out of the idea (a banker, a rich uncle, or a venture capitalist) is as old as business itself. However, venture capital as a distinct form of business financing arose only recently. John Wilson, in his book *The New Ventures, Inside the High Stakes World of Venture Capital*, marks 1946 as the year the venture capital industry originated in the United States. J.H. Whitney brought together partners from the East Coast for the first venture capital fund, working with an initial capitalization of approximately $10 million. The structure of the first fund—a partnership between those contributing to the initial capitalization—was the model for a majority of venture capital organizations that followed as the industry grew.

One of the first venture capital funds was created by city leaders in Boston. The American Research and Development Corporation was headed by General George Doriot, one of the early leaders in the industry. The successful investments made by this group helped to legitimize the new form of financing. Burill and Norback, in their book *The Arthur Young Guide to Raising Venture Capital* argue that Doriot's leadership set the course for future venture capital organizations. "Doriot . . . is famous for instituting the ethos of the venture capital industry—the venture capitalist as one who guides and manages a growing company through times thick and thin." ADR, and Doriot, gained attention because of the success of one of their first clients, Digital Equipment Corp. (DEC). The American Research and Development Corporation's initial investment of $67,000 grew into more than $600 million.

The passage of the Small Business Investment Act of 1958 by the federal government was an important incentive for would-be venture capital organizations. The act provided venture capital firms organized as Small Business Investment Companies (SBICs) and Minority Enterprise Small Business Investment Companies (MESBICs) with an opportunity to increase the amount of funds available to entrepreneurs. The privately managed SBICs and MESBICs had access to federal money through the Small Business Administration which could then be leveraged four dollars to one against privately raised funds. The SBICs and MESBICs, in turn, made the financial resources available to new ventures and entrepreneurs in their communities.

In recent decades, the venture capital industry has become big business. According to the *U.S. Industrial Outlook 1994*, organizations engaged in venture capital disbursed approximately $2.55 billion in funds to new ventures and entrepreneurs. However, the industry has changed since its birth. Whereas the first venture capitalists provided money to organizations for start-up activities, the industry has shifted its focus somewhat as it matured. One of the characteristics of the industry in the 1990s is a tendency for venture capital organizations to shy away from early stage and start-up financing, preferring to invest in companies that are relatively established. Rather than provide the entrepreneur or new venture with money early on in the growth of the business (in the first year of business, for instance), venture capital firms in the 1990s more often provide funds for products and services with proven markets and a higher chance of success in the marketplace. Brand new businesses with financing needs are more often passed over in favor of those businesses with track records (albeit short) and a relatively clear path to profitability.

INSTITUTIONALIZATION

What may have started out as a relatively loose partnership of individuals with money to invest has become a set of organizations with formalized structures and business activities. Venture capital firms, or financial firms who disperse venture funds along with other financing options, have become accepted parts of the business world, finding their own niche as providers of capital for higher risk situations.

As the industry matures, two types of organizations predominate those disbursing venture capital. The structure of the venture organization usually dictates the means through which the organization makes a profit. Leveraged firms borrow money from other financial institutions, the government or private sources and, in turn, lend the funds to entrepreneurs and new ventures at a higher rate of interest. Leveraged firms make money by charging their clients a higher interest rate than they pay for the use of the funds. Because leveraged firms rely on interest income, they make most of the disbursements in the form of loans to new ventures.

Equity firms sell stock in the venture capital organization to individual or institutional investors and then use the proceeds from the sale to purchase equity in new ventures. Equity venture capital firms build "portfolios" of investments in companies. This kind of venture capital company tries to resell the stock of its portfolio businesses at a later date and for a profit. Whereas a leveraged firm can expect a relatively steady stream of interest income, an equity firm may not experience a return on their investment for years. The return usually comes as a result of the sale of their equity in the new venture. Venture capital organizations can either sell their equity back to the company itself or on the public stock exchanges (like the New York Stock Exchange) in an initial public offering (IPO).

Even though there are two primary forms of venture capital organizations, there are a variety of ownership schemes. David Gladstone, in his book *Venture Capital Handbook*, discusses the most common forms ownership. A few firms are publicly owned and are traded on the stock exchanges. Because of the nature of the ownership, these firms tend to be larger than most venture capital organizations. Gladstone notes that an overwhelming majority of firms are private companies. The firms may have been formed by families or small groups of investors. More often, they are limited partnerships formed by insurance companies or pension funds. These organizations generally form the venture capital organizations to achieve a greater rate of return than most of their other investments. Other firms are organized as bank subsidiaries as a way for the banks to own equity in small businesses. These organizations are independent of other bank activities. Some firms have been set up by corporations, though Gladstone notes these types of organizations are relatively rare. In other cases, corporations looking to gain high returns on their funds invest in existing venture capital limited partnerships where risk can be shared and **liabilities** are is limited.

Regardless of ownership, the professional managers who run the firms generally operate in the same manner. The strategy laid out by the firm's managers determines when and how much the firm will invest in entrepreneurial ventures. Venture capital organizations invest at different stages in the development of the enterprise. The managers of a venture capital firm may prefer to invest in brand new companies or their strategy may dictate investment in businesses that are much more developed. Because the business is unproven, early investments are inherently more risky and the firm can demand a higher return. Later investments are more stable and bring a more modest return. Most venture capital firms try to diversify their holdings by investing in a variety of enterprises at various stages of development.

When an entrepreneur solicits venture capital from a firm, the firm's managers, working with the entrepreneur, determines which stage the new venture is in. "Seed capital" is given to individuals or groups in the idea stage, the point at which there is a good idea for a business but no formal organization. At this stage, the entrepreneur is likely to use the money provided by a venture capital organization to conduct further **market research**, assemble a management team, or develop a prototype.

More often than not, those who look for seed capital are turned down by venture firms and must rely on their own resources to find the needed capital. However, after they have developed a prototype and proved their idea will be viable, new enterprises may approach a venture capital in order to gather funds needed to begin operations. In such cases, venture capital organizations provide "start-up," or "first round" financing that provide the growing business with capital sufficient to meet the demands of defining and developing customer base and creating solid relationships with suppliers. First round financing usually comes in the form of an equity investment. Venture firms will expect a higher rate of return for first round investments.

As a new venture prospers, it may require additional financing to meet the capital needs inherent in expansion. Venture firms can provide "second round" or "expansion-round financing" to their clients whose markets or sales are growing at such a rate that potential for profit looks good. At this point, the venture is usually heading towards success. Gladstone notes that those seeking expansion financing are in a better bargaining position than those seeking first round or seed money. Speaking as if to an entrepreneur or new venture he comments that such an entity "(w)ill not have to give up as much of the equity in your company if your venture has reached this stage in the life cycle."

If the expansion stage is successful, the new venture may begin a period of fast growth. At this point, the company may be making money, but not enough to finance the rapid expansion. Additional "growth stage" or "third round capital" may be solicited from venture capital firms. In other cases, the new venture may consider "going public," or offering equity on the public markets as a means of gaining a cash infusion.

In addition to financing different stages of growth, venture capital firms can be of service to entrepreneurs in other, related situations. Some venture firms will assist management in **leveraged buy outs** (LBOs) where the stock of a company is purchased by a management team or a group of other entrepreneurs with the help and financial support of the venture capital firm's managers. In such a case, the money used to purchase the business is loaned to the buy-out team by the venture capital firm. Another area of activity for some venture capital firms is "turnaround financing" for businesses that have suffered serious setbacks or are nearing bankruptcy. Funds provided by a venture capital firm are used to finance recovery efforts or launch new programs aimed at turning the business around. Although few firms undertake the risk inherent in financing a turnaround situation, most are willing to consider them as part of their business strategy.

Regardless of the amount or type of financing needed by a client, the venture capital firm must be sure the claims made by the entrepreneur are realistic and attainable. The venture capital firm must have confidence the investment will pay out according to the plans offered by the entrepreneur. Before a venture capital firm makes an investment, it thoroughly investigates the client and the client's business in a process called **due diligence**. Due diligence simply means extensive research into the industry, the entrepreneur's background and experience, and the accuracy of the financial projections supplied by the client. In addition, the due diligence process may include a visit to the client's place of business or questions about the client's personal history. By conducting research into the client, the venture capital firm tries to maximize its understanding of the opportunity and its potential risks and rewards. By accumulating information, the venture capital firm better prepares itself to make the best possible decision about the investment.

Alter the venture capital firm is confident in the abilities and claims of the entrepreneur, it must be certain that it understands the market in which the new venture will operate. The experience and specialties of the firm's management will dictate whether or not the firm will narrow the focus of their business. Some venture capital firms specialize in certain industries or specific technologies. There are firms that only invest in, for instance, computer network technology businesses. Other firms only work with businesses in the bio-technology field. Venture firms that have such specialties turn away those businesses that don't fit into their area of expertise.

What kind of businesses do venture capital firms finance? There are no hard and fast rules about the types of enterprises venture capital firms will invest in. Firms are looking for good investments where both they and the entrepreneur can make money. Experience has lead firms to look more favorably on some areas than others. For instance, almost no venture capital firm will back a retail venture unless the concept is a major innovation. In general, venture firms prefer businesses that sell products rather than those which provide services. Moreover, products that are technically advanced are more attractive than those that can be easily duplicated or improved upon by competitors. Those products which involve new technical advances or are based on proprietary technology have a competitive advantage. They impose a barrier to competitors and ensure the new venture a greater chance of success. Venture capital firms that back companies with innovative products stand to maximize return on their investment. The venture capital industry is a business like any other, looking for profits and wealth for the lowest price. Yet the business conducted by firms in the industry has a direct, positive affect on the economy. Venture capital is an important fuel for new business. The professional managers that direct the investments of the venture capital firms are major supporters of the new ventures that help drive innovation, technical advances and exploration. They help to make invention and creativity profitable. By helping entrepreneurs bring their new products and services to the national and international markets, venture firms foster competition within industry, rewarding those with the energy and vision to innovate and improve.

[Jim Cuene]

FURTHER READING:

Burrill, G. Steven and Craig T. Norback. *The Arthur Young Guide to Raising Venture Capital.* Liberty House, 1988.

Gladstone, David. *Venture Capital Handbook.* Prentice Hall, 1988.

Kosmetsky, George, Michael D. Gill, Jr., and Raymond W. Smilor. *Financing and Managing Fast Growth Companies: The Venture Capital Process.* Lexington Books, 1985.

Timmons, Jeffrey A. *Planning and Financing The New Venture.* Brick House Publishing Company, 1990.

VIRTUAL REALITY COMPUTER SIMULATION

EARLY HISTORY

Although the technology for computer simulation was not actually implemented until the early 1980s by Jaron Lanier in Foster City, California, the concept first received wide publicity in the novel *Brave New World* (1932) by Aldous Huxley. In this novel, set some 600 years in the future, mankind has built the perfect Utopia—complete with "Feelies," movies which give the viewer the ultimate sensation of interacting with the characters and events on the screen. This concept, however, remained just that until the 1960s, when Ivan Sutherland of Stanford University experimented with computer graphics and wrote a **software** program called SketchPad while working toward his doctoral degree. In an era when most people thought that **computers** were only for crunching numbers, Sutherland used clever software to make the computer manipulate engineering drawings. With SketchPad in the 1960s, Sutherland created the field of computer graphics and demonstrated an entirely new way of talking to the computer—interactive computing. In 1965, Sutherland realized that computers could conjure up powerful visual illusions, illusions that did not have to be confined to a flat, two-dimensional screen. He realized that computers held the key to a much richer kind of visualization and wondered what would happen if he could reach through the screen itself and surround himself in a simulated world. He then built an experimental helmet that gave the user the illusion of being inside a three-dimensional world. As the user moved his or her head, the pictures changed accordingly. But the technology was barely able to handle a simple geometrical world in those days.

More than two decades later, a group of scientists at the University of North Carolina, following Sutherland's academic theories, brought the art of simulation to a level where it could be demonstrated. A head-mounted display (HMD), consisting of a pair of small TV displays, was connected to a helmet and a small tracking system that allowed the computer to determine where the helmet was in position and orientation at every instant. Using these two technologies, scientists were able to program computers to impart to the individual wearing the helmet the feeling of being immersed in a computer-simulated environment. So, instead of looking at a computer-generated image on a standard television set on a table top, the user seemed to be inside that world. And, instead of walking through the world by knobs, buttons, and rotators, the user was able to walk through that world just by looking around. The effect was made all the more vivid because the user was performing those actions he was performing in everyday life.

Jaron Lanier first brought the commercial applications of virtual reality to the public's attention. He almost certainly was influenced by the work of the United States government in flight simulation for the training of astronauts in its aerospace program. Believing that people should be able to create their own media products through interactive computer networks, Lanier founded VPL Research, Inc., as a vehicle for his research into "virtual reality," a term he invented. Virtual reality used the appeal of the simulated experiences of computer games to "sell" its multi-sensory data that combined sight, sound, and touch and its interactive capabilities which gave the user greater control. Over the ensuing years, the company introduced many virtual-space hardware products, such as the Datasuit and the Dataglove.

Lanier expected the virtual reality industry to take off by the year 2000 and predicted that virtual reality applications in medicine would overshadow all others because the technology could be used for better visualization of diagnostic scans, for three-dimensional data bases, for analyzing wartime casualties, and for systems that would make remote surgery assistance possible.

APPLICATIONS OF VIRTUAL REALITY

Virtual reality, the computer interface that permits one to move through computer-generated images in three dimensions, is useful for those who need to view information in three dimensions or who need to interact with an environment as though it were real.

Basically, virtual reality consists of an enormous data base containing data representing practically anything a developer desires and a powerful graphics computer that can recreate the environment described by that data. Virtual reality worlds convey multiple sensory information. In some virtual reality systems, users wear a sensor-laden glove and headset, while in others, images are displayed on-screen for the user to manipulate with a joystick or mouse. In Autodesk, Inc.'s, virtual reality system, a rubber glove wired with fiber-optic cables connects through a microcomputer to a pair of goggles. Manipulating the glove changes the images projected on the television screens. Meanwhile, VPL has developed a fast, costlier virtual reality system for two people. Autodesk wants to link virtual reality technology to its computer-aided design software so that, for example, architects can tour buildings under design. The federal government is extremely interested in virtual reality, especially for its military applications. Private industry has also invested heavily in the technology to develop business applications, for virtual reality can be used to improve product design, speed products to market, boost productivity, and provide more cost-effective training.

In late 1993, virtual reality involving touch, christened haptics, was being researched by scientists at the Massachusetts Institute of Technology (MIT), and early commercial applications were being developed in such areas as industrial design and medicine. While early experiments have been promising, results are not expected until 2003, since not enough information is known about simulating the sense of touch.

Computer-generated sensations are similar to the sensations of viewing a scene through a pair of night binoculars, using a hearing aid, or wearing a pair of glasses, but these sensations offer a chance to view entirely new worlds rather than simply a new way to see an old, real world. Three types of computer-generated reality were identified in the book *Virtual Reality—Through the New Looking Glass* by Kenneth Pi-

mentel and Kevin Teixeira. They are total immersion, augmented reality, and projected reality. Total immersion attempts to put the user completely into a computer-generated world; augmented reality creates images and sounds intended to be merged with the user's perception of his or her real surroundings; and projected reality lets the user enter a computer-generated world while remaining solidly in the real world.

Telepresence allows users to create or recreate distant events by being part of the action. Through the user of virtual reality, telepresence can simulate objects, sounds, worlds, and people. The essence of the distant event is conveyed to the user via modem-to-modem links. Real objects and sound are output to a head-mounted display (HMD) from digital data bases, which minimize the amount of information that has to be sent to the user via the communications pipeline. As of 1993, telepresence equipment was both rare and expensive, starting at more than $100,000 per user. Some industry analysts believe that affordable telepresence equipment will hit the market in the next few years. Indeed, telepresence, via microscopic television cameras and fiber optics, is already being used to show doctors how to use virtual reality to perform microscopic surgery. In 1994, nonmilitary virtual reality had grown to be a $110 million business; it is expected to grow five times that much by 1997.

The main fields in which virtual reality is being used include aerodynamics, national defense, education, science (including all the social sciences), engineering, medicine, business, law, architecture, travel, and (predominantly) entertainment.

AERODYNAMIC APPLICATIONS. By May 1988, the Simmod (Simulation Module) Air Traffic Control System was helping American Airlines to rank at or near the top as far as on-time performance. Simmod was a microcomputer-based air traffic model that simulated landings, ground movements, and take-offs at any airport in the world. American Airlines was the first to test the Federal Aviation Administration's (FAA) project. At that time, the FAA planned to make the Simmod module available as public-domain software. American Airlines found that senior management believed that Simmod was a crucial planning tool to identify bottlenecks and to predict how factors affected flight schedules.

An area of aerodynamics in which virtual reality simulation has proven particularly significant is flight training. A helmet or goggles worn by a user trick him into feeling that he is in an alternate reality. Motion sickness affects many people who use virtual reality simulation, though, because visual cues depict movement but the other senses do not, which causes confusion in the nervous system. The federal government remains very interested in virtual reality because of its military applications.

EDUCATIONAL APPLICATIONS. One of the areas of greatest potential for virtual reality is education. With several companies developing interactive video education tools in 1994, young people do not have to be enticed or coerced into using interactive video. Not only do these new tools make learning fun, they also allow students to progress as rapidly as they possibly can. Using this new interactive, decentralized technology, a student can proceed ahead of his or her class, interacting with a teaching model that incorporates knowledge from the best teachers in America. In fact, the entrepreneurial, opportunistic firms that develop virtual reality usually do seek out the best teachers, actors, engineers, technicians, and artists for their products because they want to make learning so exhilarating and rewarding that parents would voluntarily pay for it. Soon, the entrepreneurs hope, every household in America with young children will be connected to one of these systems, generating hundreds of billions of dollars in revenue. Yet, with stakes so high, relatively few people even know about these firms.

SCIENTIFIC APPLICATIONS. Science has also benefitted from virtual reality. In 1992, Telepresence Research began providing services to customize virtual reality environments for specific scientific, business, and entertainment applications. That firm is working with the Matsushita Electronic Industrial Company on a project to enable users to look for products in virtual showrooms. The system, which is predicted to be fully developed in 1997, will utilize a viewing device from Fake Space Laboratories, a Telepresence strategic partner. Telepresence's goal is to promote practical applications of virtual reality technology.

ENGINEERING APPLICATIONS. Virtual reality can be used by design engineers which reduces costs associated with testing programs. In 1993, for example, manufacturers such as The Chrysler Corp. were utilizing virtual reality simulations instead of building expensive models of their products. Computer aided design (CAD) firm Autodesk, Inc., is a leading maker of simulators, and the United States Department of Defense is a leading user. The Ford Motor Co. is also exploring the utilization of virtual reality technology for designing and engineering its new cars. The virtual reality computer-aided-design (CAD) programs for **manufacturing** automobiles simulates three-dimensional objects, and automotive firms use them to create computerized ''mock-ups'' of new production systems that can be analyzed and revised before the companies buy the actual equipment.

MEDICAL APPLICATIONS. Although virtual reality technology was deficient in tactile control—haptics—until 1992, great strides were made in the technology that year as it related to medicine. For instance, one basic virtual reality system, invented in '92, manipulates abstract objects via a disembodied hand that floats in space. The hand's movements are then translated into commands that can control the visual display. For more complex applications, such as surgery, however, information obtained from tactile manipulation is essential for precise maneuvers. Virtual reality researchers are experimenting with various approaches to solve such tactile deficiencies. One approach utilizes tactors, or tiny switches (created from a ''shape memory'' nickel-titanium alloy) that are sensitive to touch.

Also in 1992, computer science professor Henry Fuchs and two graduate students superimposed ultrasonic images of a fetus onto a video image of a pregnant woman's abdomen to provide an accurate and unique perspective for guiding physicians as they inserted and manipulated probes in the body. In 1993, gastroenterologist Duncan Bell and his team of surgeons developed an imaging technique that allowed a physician to use computer-generated images of the patient's tissue to guide the performance of a colonoscopy.

This virtual reality technology, some doctors believe, might one day permit surgeons to perform procedures from remote sites, bringing specialized care to small communities and rural hospitals. In addition, virtual reality enables superior medical visualization, based on data from CAT imaging systems, and better visualization of diagnostic scans.

BUSINESS APPLICATIONS. One of the first substantial virtual reality applications with potential for business is Autodesk, Inc.'s, TRIX, an application-development tool launched in 1991 that is designed to create networked cyberspace environments where users can move and interact with other users and data in a world that exists only in the computer. Autodesk does not require unique hardware for its experimental systems, which utilize off-the-shelf Compaq, Macintosh, and Amiga microcomputers. TRIX is a ''nuts and bolts'' system designed to encourage developers to implement applications that corporations will find advantageous.

Since 1992, virtual reality has played an increasingly more important role in some online services. Three-dimensional technology, for instance, has been used to create innovative data presentations, such as 3-D versions of stock market data. Such presentations permit users to interact with data instead of merely scanning it for information. Not only can visual images enhance user thought processes, but users can react to audio and visual information instead of just reading data. Although virtual reality applications are still costly and involve custom programming, many business applications for the technology are expected to evolve as equipment and software prices fall.

LEGAL APPLICATIONS. The legal profession has benefitted from the technology's versatility, too. Law students investigating courtroom procedures and argumentation can vicariously interact with "individuals" in a fabricated courtroom. By travelling several avenues of debate on the same case, prospective attorneys can see beforehand the results of various approaches to a case. Also, virtual reality enables accident scenes to be reconstructed in the courtroom.

ARCHITECTURAL APPLICATIONS. Virtual reality applications used for architecture allow users to explore the interior of an unbuilt house. Although virtual reality systems can cost more than $30,000, architects feel they are well worth the cost because a client, wearing gloves and goggles, can feel as if she is walking through a simulated version of his or her own building.

ENTERTAINMENT APPLICATIONS. But of all the disciplines, entertainment stands to benefit the most financially from virtual reality technology. From movies and videos to games and amusement parks, from the golf course to the dance floor, from books to the stage, virtual reality is changing the way things are done. Market research firm 4th Wave predicts that entertainment ventures will account for 76 percent of virtual reality-generated applications between 1993 and 1997. Indeed, by 1993, 31 companies were already building virtual reality entertainment centers or creating home-video equipment that used virtual reality technology. Most companies investing in virtual reality entertainment were United-States-based, and most were independent and had fewer than 100 employees. Only two were publicly traded, and most had been in the business for 10 or fewer years. Virtual reality entertainment products were expected to reach $150 million in sales by 2000, while the total virtual reality market was predicted to bring in $575 million in sales by 1999.

[Virginia Barnstorff]

FURTHER READING:

Anzovin, Steven. "Cyberwocky," *Computer.* October, 1991, p. 97.

"Are New Realities More or Less Real? Fears and Optimism About Artificial Worlds," *U. S. News and World Report.* January 28, 1991, p. 59.

Aukstakalnis, Steve, and David Blatner. *Silicon Mirage: The Art and Science of Virtual Reality.* Peachpit Press.

Bacard, Andre. "Welcome to Virtual Reality," *The Humanist.* March-April, 1993, p. 42.

Barr, Christopher. "Virtual Reality Goes Mainstream," *PC Magazine.* April 28, 1992, p. 311.

Berger, Bob. "Fairway to Heaven," *Omni.* November, 1991, p. 33.

Berger, Warren. "Future Quest: Go Where No Real Estate Company Has Gone Before," *Real Estate Today.* January, 1994, p. 14.

Bertrand, Kate. "Virtual Reality on Marketing Horizon," *Business Marketing.* November, 1990, p. 14.

Bonner, William. *13 Breakthroughs and Breakdowns.* Agora, Inc.

Brunbaum, Rami. "Local Virtual Reality Firms Launch Real-World Ventures," *Puget Sound Business Journal.* November 20, 1992, p. 4.

Caneday, Lowell. "Outdoor Recreation: A Virtual Reality," *Parks & Recreation.* August, 1992, p. 48.

Carlsen, Clifford. "Virtual Reality: Walking Around Inside Software," *San Francisco Business Times.* June 4, 1990, p. 1.

Churbuck, David C. "Applied Reality," *Forbes.* September 14, 1992, p. 486.

"Computerized Tour Guides: Virtual Reality for Day Trippers," *Omni.* October 1990, p. 25.

Connell, Joan. "Computer Revolution Lacks Ethical Compass," *Star-Ledger* (Newark:NJ). November 21, 1993, sec. 3, p. 1.

Creedon, Jeremiah. "How Real Is Virtual Reality?" *Utne Reader.* November-December, 1992, p. 43.

Ditlea, Steve. "Another World: Inside Virtual Reality," *PC Computing.* November, 1989, p. 90.

Dolphin, Ric. "On the Edge of Reality: An Innovator Invents A New World," *Maclean's.* December 14, 1992, p. 48.

Dworstrzky, Tom. "Silence of the Rams," *Omni.* October 1993, p. 22.

Edwards, Larry M. "Virtual Reality Pushes Beyond Entertainment Field," *San Diego Business Journal.* February 8, 1993, p. 15.

Elmer-DeWitt, Philip. "(Mis)adventures in Cyberspace," *Time.* September 3, 1990, p. 74.

Englebardt, Stanley L. "Get Ready for Virtual Reality," *Reader's Digest.* December, 1993, p. 127.

Field, Roger. "Physicians Perform From a Remote Location: Virtual Reality Surgery May Bring Specialized Care to Every Small Community and Rural Hospital," *Medical World News.* February, 1993, p. 35.

Fisher, Scott, and Jane Morrill Tazelaar. "Living in a Virtual World," *Byte.* July, 1990, p. 215.

Glitman, Russell. "Bringing the Cyber Office to Corporate America," *PC Week.* January 14, 1991, p. 73.

Goldstein, Harry. "Virtual Reality Computers May Soon Allow Us to Experience Worlds We Cannot Enter," *Utne Reader.* March-April, 1990, p. 41.

Gomes, Lee. "Firms Flock to Explore Virtual Reality," *Journal of Commerce.* December 18, 1990, p. 10A.

Hamilton, Joan O'C. "Going Where No Minds Have Gone Before," *Business Week.* October 5, 1992, p. 104.

Helsel, Sandra K., and Judith Paris Roth, eds. *Virtual Reality: Theory, Practice, and Promise.* Meckler.

Hill, J. Dee. "A Walk on the Wild Side," *Dallas Business Journal.* July 10, 1992, p. 19.

Horn, John. "Movie Rides Join in the Mad Scramble for Oscar Glory," *Star-Ledger* (Newark:NJ). March 6, 1994, sec. 4, p. 11.

Huxley, Aldous. *Brave New World.* Perennial Library, Harper & Row, Publishers.

"Jaron Lanier Is Virtually Sure," *The New Yorker.* December 27, 1993, p. 59.

Jenish, D'Arcy, and Ric Dolphin. "Fantastic Voyages," *Maclean's.* December 14, 1992, p. 42.

Kellar, David. "Virtual Reality, Real Money," *Computerworld.* November 15, 1993, p. 70.

Lanier, Jaron. "Music from Inside Virtual Reality: The Sound of One Hand," *Whole Earth Review*. Summer, 1993, p. 30.

Laurel, Brenda. "Strange New Worlds of Entertainment," *Computer*. November, 1991, p. 102.

Lavroff, Nicholas. *Virtual Reality Playhouse: Explore Artificial Worlds on Your PC*. Waite Group Press.

Levis, Art. "Fly the Virtual Skies," *Video Magazine*. May, 1991, p. 6.

Levy, Steven. "Brave New World," *Rolling Stone*. June 14, 1990, p. 92.

Loh, Sandra Tsing. "Partying in Cyberspace," *Playboy*. April, 1992, p. 104.

Lowe, Walter, Jr. "Adventures in Cyberspace," *Playboy*. April, 1992, p. 104.

Lubove, Seth. "Fooling the Inner Ear: Amusement Park Simulators Based on Computer Technology," *Forbes*. February 18, 1991, p. 110.

Machlis, Sharon. "Computers Create a New Reality: After Years As a Laboratory Curiosity, the Field of Virtual Reality Is Poised to Spawn Useful Real-World Applications," *Design News*. October 26, 1992, p. 60.

McCullough, Michael. "Cyber-Present," *PC Business*. April, 1992, p. 35.

Meyer, Michael. "Get Ready, Set . . . Invest! Multimedia Technology," *Newsweek*. November 15, 1993, p. 47.

Mitchell, David H. "Being Here and There: Tele-Presence," *Byte*. March, 1993, p. 132.

Peterson, Ivars. "Looking-Glass World: Learning to Assemble the Machinery of Illusion," *Science News*. January 14, 1992, p. 8.

Pierson, John. "Virtual Reality Offers a View With a Room," *Wall Street Journal*. December 3, 1993, p. B1.

Piirto, Rebecca. "Virtual Unreality," *American Demographics*. November, 1993, p. 6.

Pimentel, Ken, and Kevin Teixeira. *Virtual Reality: Through the New Looking Glass*. Windcrest Books.

Porush, David. "Cyberspace: Portal to Transcendence?" *Omni*. April, 1993, p. 4.

Rheingold, Howard. "Cold Knowledge and Social Warmth," *Newsweek*. September 6, 1993, p. 49.

Rothma, Matt. " 'Voomies' or Bust?" *Variety*. December 14, 1992, p. 3.

Schroeder, Ralph. "Virtual Reality in the Real World: History, Applications, and Projections," *Futures*. November, 1993, p. 963.

Schuytema, Paul. "Inside A Virtual Robot," *Omni*. September, 1993, p. 27.

Sherman, Ted. "Mind Games," *Star-Ledger*. December 12, 1993, sec. 2, pp. 1, 7.

Snyder, Howard A. "The Cybergeneration," *Christianity Today*. December 13, 1993, p. 17.

Stedman, Nancy. "Fields of Dreams: Virtual Reality Systems Launch Video on a Daring New Quest for Total Immersion," *Video Magazine*. May, 1991, p. 30.

Stevens, Tim. "Virtual Reality: Is It Really Real?" *Industry Week*. May 17, 1993, p. 30.

Stix, Gary. "Reach Out: Touch Is Added to Virtual Reality Simulations," *Scientific American*. February, 1991, p. 134.

Stone, Robert J. "Virtual Reality and Cyberspace: From Science Fiction to Science Fact," *Information Services and Use*. September-November, 1991, p. 283.

Studt, Tim. "Virtual Reality: From Toys to Research Tools," *R & D*. March, 1993, p. 18.

"Trials of a Cyber-Celebrity," *Business Week*. February 22, 1993, p. 95.

"Virtual Vision: A View of Things to Come?" *Consumer Reports*. December, 1993, p. 763.

Welter, Theresa R. "The Artificial Tourist: Virtual Reality Promises New World for Industry," *Industry Week*. October 1, 1990, p. 66.

Wilder, Clinton. "Virtual Reality Seeks Practicality: Firm's Drive Toward Real-World Applications Shows Promise of Potentially Big Market," *Computerworld*. April 27, 1992, p. 26.

Wilson, J. R. "Virtual Reality Benefits May Prove Illusory," *Interavia Aerospace World*. April, 1993, p. 34.

Winter, Drew. "These Games Aren't for Kids," *Ward's Auto World*. December, 1993, p. 86.

"Wizard of Oz: Bringing Drama to Virtual Reality," *Science News*. December 19, 1992, p. 440.

Woolley, Benjamin. *Virtual Worlds: A Journal in Hype and Hyperreality*. Blackwell Publishers.

Yam, Philip. "Surreal Science: Virtual Reality Finds A Place in the Classroom," *Scientific American*. February, 1993, p. 103.

Zarley, Craig. "Air Traffic Model Aims to Get You There on Time," *PC Week*. May 10, 1988, p. 57.

VOCATIONAL EDUCATION

Vocational education is the training and retraining of individuals for particular businesses or trades. This instruction can take place at the secondary or post-secondary level, or as part of on-the-job training and retraining.

Vocational education in America can be traced back to the colonial era, when youngsters learned skilled trades through apprenticeship programs. Congressional support of vocational education as part of the public school system emerged in 1862, with the passage of the Morrill Tariff Act, which encouraged the establishment of land grant colleges to teach agricultural and mechanical skills. Vocational education began to filter down to the secondary level shortly thereafter, led by Professor Calvin Woodward (1837-1914) of St. Louis' Washington University. Woodward discovered that his engineering students were "woefully inept at the use of simple tools," and therefore urged secondary schools to add training in carpentry, printing, drafting, bricklaying, machine work, and home economics. Woodward hoped to arrive at a curriculum that balanced theoretical and practical knowledge, but the system actually evolved separately from academic schools in the form of manual training and trade schools.

In 1895 the National Association of Manufacturers was founded. This group promoted vocational education as a technique for making the United States globally competitive. The association's leaders based their logic on the performance of global economic leader of the time, Germany, which supported trade schools and apprenticeship programs. Labor leaders hoped that vocational education would keep children in school longer, thereby protecting them from harsh work environments and simultaneously shrinking the labor force, leading to wage increases. Agriculturists continued to encourage a curriculum that included scientific and technological courses that would help students advance in their field. Social reformers, largely proponents of the Progressive Movement, hoped that vocational education would imbue destitute people with the Protestant work ethic and help lift them from poverty. Educational leaders were often trapped in the midst of these diverse interests: many worried that vocational education would interfere with the public school ethic of "providing a common education for all students."

In the first decade of the twentieth century, forces in these diverse groups formed the National Society for the Promotion of Industrial Education. They lobbied for, and were successful in having Congress pass, legislation launching a public vocational education system in America. The Smith-Hughes Act of 1917 appropriated $1.7 million for secondary-level programs and established a Federal Board of Education. States that chose to participate in the federal vocational plan had to match federal contributions, appoint state directors and boards of vocational education, and formulate local guidelines for use of the funds.

Charles A. Prosser, the first federal administrator of vocational education, had a lasting influence on the program. Prosser maintained that courses at vocational high schools should be job specific, and that the enabling legislation limited training to the fields of agriculture, trade and industry, and home economics. Prosser also encouraged the division of vocational training programs from mainstream public education, thereby creating a system that vocational educator and author Charles Law later characterized as separate and unequal. (Vocational and academic teachers even had separate certification programs.) Over the ensuing six decades, secondary vocational programs grew separately and focused on specific skill training, with academics as an aside. By the late 1970s, combined federal, state and local expenditures on such programs totaled over $6.6 billion, and enrollment topped 19.5 million.

At this point, serious questions about the rationale behind, and effectiveness of, vocational education emerged. The U.S. Department of Health, Education and Welfare had released its critical *Work in America* report in 1972. The study charged that more than 50 percent of the graduates of secondary vocational education programs did not find employment related to their specialization, that unemployment statistics for program graduates were not significantly lower than those of traditional grads, that the programs cost from 50 to 75 percent more than traditional curricula, and that the skills taught in such programs were generally obsolete. After an initially defensive reaction, professionals in the field began to question their own practices and objectives.

The issue was thrust upon the general public when the National Commission on Excellence in Education published *A Nation at Risk* in 1983. The report criticized America's public education system (including vocational education) for "offering little or no direction or assistance" to the 50 percent of high school graduates who either dropped out or did not go on to college. Dubbed "forgotten youths," these students were characterized by: having poor basic skills (including communication, math, problem-solving and teamwork), the incapability to link theory and practice, the lack of participation and interest in school activities, and lack of movement from high school to college or the workplace.

Other factors, including military and corporate downsizing, a shrinking labor pool, intensifying global competition, and rising college tuition costs, have combined with a public sympathy for change, prompting reform efforts at all levels of education.

There have been three types of responses to the findings of *A Nation at Risk*: integration of academic and vocational high schools, renewed interest in apprenticeship programs and community and technical colleges, and a plethora of private initiatives across the country.

Integration of academic and vocational high schools was promoted by the Carl D. Perkins Vocational Education and Applied Technology Act of 1990. This legislation encouraged the combination of academic and vocational curricula so that students could obtain both academic and occupational knowledge and abilities. The objective of such programs reflect the goal established by Calvin Woodward for his nineteenth century manual-training schools: the union of the finest curricular and instructional practices of academic and vocational education into a single learning experience. Pilot integration programs funded by the Perkins Act generally have four themes in common: promotion of academic and generic skills through an engaging curricula, activity-based motivational and practical teaching methods, interdisciplinary cooperation, and a focus on skills and knowledge needed by students to make the transition to employment or college. Such programs have been undertaken in Ohio, Kentucky, California, Oregon, and Virginia.

Apprenticeships, which have existed in the United States since the colonial era, have also received increased attention among today's vocational educators. An apprenticeship is a contractual relationship between an employer and an employee that lasts a specific length of time during which the apprentice worker learns all aspects (including techniques and theory) of a trade. Apprenticeships range in length from one to six years, averaging four years, and may be cosponsored by trade unions. An apprentice's pay usually amounts to half that of an experienced journeyworker, and increases over the course of the program. Individuals who successfully complete one of over 830 federally registered apprenticeships receive certification. According to the *Occupational Outlook Quarterly* , "About 100,000 new apprentices are registered each year," most in construction.

Although a high school diploma or its equivalent is usually prerequisite to entry into an apprentice program, there are an increasing number of school-to-apprenticeship programs in which high school students split their days between academics and part-time apprenticeships. They graduate to full-time apprenticeships and eventually reach journeyworker status. In 1990, the U.S. Department of Labor inaugurated *Apprenticeship 2000*, a series of pilot school-to-work programs based on Germany's dual-educational system. The USDL also set up state and regional bureaus of apprenticeship and training around the country. These have expanded the application of the apprenticeship concept from traditional blue-collar fields such as plumbing and bricklaying, to areas including food services, healthcare and the hospitality industry.

The Boston Private Industry Council's "Project Protech" is an example of a school-to-apprenticeship program. The Council coordinates a program matching four urban high schools with some of the city's most renowned teaching hospitals. It was launched in 1991 with funding from the U.S. Department of Labor's Office of Work-Based Learning. The four-year program begins in a student's junior year, gradually phases in on-the-job training, and then segues into community college coursework after high school graduation. Participants who complete the program earn a community college associate degree and gain experience in areas such as nuclear medicine, ultrasound, and radiography. Participating hospitals benefit from a well-trained work force in this industry where labor shortages are predicted.

Community and technical colleges have also become important centers of preparatory and remedial vocational education. DeVry, Inc., for instance, was established in 1931 as an electronics trade school with two campuses, in Chicago and Toronto. It began a period of rapid expansion in the late 1960s, and by the early 1980s, the DeVry chain of schools boasted 30,000 students. Displacement of workers from the military and the defense industry, combined with rising tuition costs at liberal arts colleges have benefited community colleges like DeVry. In the early 1990s,

the chain responded to industries needs for remedial worker education with onsite training programs.

Some businesses have taken vocational education upon themselves to survive. For example, in the mid 1980s, the Will-Burt Co., a steel manufacturing and assembly concern in Orrville, Ohio was faced with a myriad of problems. Declining profits and sales, employee turnover of over 30 percent, and a product reject rate of 35 percent threatened the company's future. Remediating faulty work, in fact, consumed about 25,000 hours annually at the plant. In cooperation with Wayne College, a branch campus of the University of Akron, CEO Harry Featherstone developed a mandatory educational course that included practical applications of math, blueprint reading, geometry, and statistics. the program was undertaken on company time at full pay. Featherstone reflected on the project's success in a 1992 *D & B Reports* article, noting that within a few years, employee turnover was reduced to 2.5 percent, product rejects plummeted to 7 percent, and manufacturing efficiency increased over 95 percent. He estimated that the program cost $200,000.

The evolution of vocational education in America has created a patchwork of public and private initiatives that include vocational high schools, community and technical colleges, apprenticeships, and an array of private programs. As the twenty-first century looms, the federal government is seeking to establish a framework of standards that will link these diverse approaches.

[April Dougal Gasbarre]

FURTHER READING:

"Apprenticeship," *Occupational Outlook Quarterly* 35 (Winter 1991/1992): 26-40.

Byrne, Harlan S. "DeVry Inc." *Barron's* 73 (February 8, 1993): 36-38.

Klein, Easy. "Training Undereducated Workers," *D & B Reports* 40 (May/June 1992): 34-37.

Law, Charles J. Jr. *Tech Prep Education: A Total Quality Approach.* Lancaster, PA: Technomic Publishing Co., Inc., 1994.

Matthes, Karen. "Apprenticeships Can Support the 'Forgotten Youth,' " *HR Focus* 68 (December 1991): 19.

McClure, Arthur F., James Riley Chrisman, and Perry Mock. *Education for Work: The Historical Evolution of Vocational and Distributive Education in America.* Cranbury, NJ: Associated University Presses, 1985.

"Training and the Workplace: Smart Work," *Economist* 324 (August 22, 1992): 21-22.

VOCATIONAL REHABILITATION

Vocational rehabilitation refers to any programs that seek to restore handicapped individuals to their optimal physical, mental, social, vocational, and economic ability. Its roots in America can be traced to the diffuse development of disability-specific workshops in the early nineteenth century. The first of these was the Perkins Institute, incorporated in Boston in 1829 to train blind individuals for manufacturing jobs. Efforts such as this were few and far between, however, until turn-of-the-century Progressivism strengthened the impetus. Social justice was a key concern of the Progressive political movement, and many forward-looking vocational rehabilitation organizations were established during the era. Some programs, like Goodwill Industries, the Salvation Army, the Society of St. Vincent de Paul, and the Jewish Vocational Service Agencies, evolved under the sponsorship of religious organizations. Others, like the groundbreaking Sunbeam Circle (now known as Vocational Guidance and Rehabilitation Services) in Cleveland, Ohio, the National Society for Crippled Children and Adults (also known as the Easter Seals Society) in Elyria, Ohio, and the Red Cross Institution for Crippled and Disabled Men (ICD Rehabilitation and Research Center) in New York City, were the result of private altruism. All these programs have since expanded nationwide.

By far the greatest stimulus to vocational rehabilitation arose after World War I, when the influx of disabled veterans from overseas battlefields proved too much for private institutions to bear. There were philosophical and practical motives for inauguration of the public program of vocational rehabilitation. Soldiers had fulfilled their obligation to the country; the nation owed its disabled veterans the opportunity to return to work and productivity. In this pre-welfare era, private social support was simply not sufficient to support the millions of potential dependents. These factors compelled the passage of the Smith-Hughes Act of 1917, which created the Federal Board for Vocational Education of Veterans. The Soldier Rehabilitation Act of 1918 expanded Smith-Hughes to provide vocational training to disabled veterans. Ratification of the Vocational Rehabilitation (Smith-Fess) Act two years later extended services to disabled civilians. Vocational rehabilitation marked a significant landmark in the thirties, when the passage of the Social Security Act of 1935 established the first permanent base for the federal program.

These various pieces of legislation set up a federal/state cooperative whose budget was evenly shared. States that wanted to participate submitted a plan of action for federal approval and reported annually to the Federal Board for Vocational Education. The state agencies were prohibited from using funds for buildings, equipment, or physical restoration. A network of federal, state, and private agencies evolved through the passage of over a dozen pieces of legislation throughout the ensuing decades. These laws expanded the definition of eligibility and increased the amount of expenditures toward the program. By 1923, 36 states participated in the $1.3 million program. The federal government's role was to set administrative procedures and techniques; provide funding; and promote the program. Responsibility for actual programming fell to the states. In practice, state agencies usually evaluated client eligibility and potential for rehabilitation, provided counseling, and managed job placement. State agencies often contracted with private organizations for medical treatment, physical rehabilitation, and occupational training. In his text *Introduction to Rehabilitation*, James A. Bitter characterized the public-private vocational rehabilitation partnership as "perhaps the most successful human service program in the United States."

The public vocational rehabilitation program grew dramatically during the late 1950s and throughout the 1960s. Federal expenditures increased from $23 million in 1954 to $600 million by 1970. Funding for buildings, maintenance, and research was permitted, and definitions of eligibility were expanded during the period to include those developmentally disabled by epilepsy, cerebral palsy, and other neurological impairments.

Vocational rehabilitation came to the attention of the business community during the 1970s, when state governments, led by California, began to make it a mandatory part of the resolution of **workers' compensation** cases. A concurrent nationwide study of on-the-job injuries emphasized the failures of workers' compensation programs and spurred public and union pressure to make vocational rehabilitation part of disability management programs across America. Predictably, many employers resented and resisted vocational rehabilitation as yet another expensive bureaucracy. By the late 1980s, some states, including Georgia, Minnesota, and New Mexico, repealed the requirement. But two circumstances soon converged to make vocational rehabilitation more viable in the eyes of business leaders. By the early 1990s, abuse of the workers' compensation system had pushed annual national costs over $60 billion. Once again, California led the way: stress claims alone increased 700 percent from 1982 to 1992.

Perhaps the most important legislation affecting vocational rehabilitation since 1935 was the 1990 **Americans with Disabilities Act** (ADA). This mandate built upon the foundation laid by the Rehabilitation Act of 1973, which prohibited federal agencies, programs, and contractors from discriminating against people with disabilities. The ADA also incorporated the nondiscriminatory ideals of the Civil Rights Act of 1964, ruling that ". . . no employer shall discriminate against a qualified individual with a disability because of the disability of such individual in regard to job application procedures, the hiring or discharge of employees, employee compensation, advancement, job training, and other term and conditions of employment.'' The law requires that all employers, public and private, of over 25 people make ''reasonable accommodations'' (in terms of expense and degree of change) for disabled employees. The ADA also dramatically broadened the definition of disability to include any ''physical or mental impairment that substantially limits one or more of the major life activities,'' (including work) a history of having such an impairment, or even the perception of having an impairment.

The combined impact of skyrocketing workers' compensation costs and the legal requirements of the ADA compelled employers and insurers to turn to vocational rehabilitation as a cost containment technique. The alternative was the courtroom: from October 1992 to October 1993, approximately 3300 cases filed with the Equal Opportunity Commission were concerned with employers' failure to provide reasonable accommodation to disabled workers.

PRACTICAL APPLICATIONS OF VOCATIONAL REHABILITATION

Aside from the legal requirements of the ADA, there are many practical justifications for the application of vocational rehabilitation. In 1992, the President's Committee on Employment of the Handicapped estimated that there were 42 million disabled Americans. Of those, 58 percent of men and 80 percent of women (or an estimated two-thirds overall) were unemployed. The study surmised that most of them would like to work. What's more, a study released by Northwestern National Life in 1994 estimated that more than 25 percent of 25-year-old workers would be disabled for one year before they reached retirement age. In purely economic terms, these individuals represent hundreds of billions of dollars in welfare expenditures and lost productivity every year. In purely human terms, citizens of a democracy such as ours can claim ''an inherent right to earn a living,'' as asserted by James Bitter in *Introduction to Rehabilitation*. Since 1918, vocational rehabilitation has existed as a tool for both cost containment and empowerment.

In 1992, Peter C. Madega of General Rehabilitation Services Inc. cited returns of from $3 to $30 for every $1 invested in disability management. Two years later, Northwestern National Life's seven-year study of nearly 10,000 long-term disability cases found that rehabilitation and return to work saved employers and insurers $35 for every dollar spent. Those savings nearly triple to $96-to-$1 if workers can return to the job they left when injured. Businesses receive savings on direct costs through decreased expenditures on benefits and lowered work-

ers' compensation premiums, and indirect costs of replacing workers, losing productivity during training, increased supervision, and administrative burden. Weyerhaeuser Co., a lumber concern, credited vocational rehabilitation with saving almost $200 million on its workers' compensation expenses in just five years. The company's per-employee cost fell from $750 in 1984 to $300 in 1991.

Vocational rehabilitation can help solve other workplace dilemmas as well. Marriott Corporation, a food service company, turned to vocational rehabilitation as a solution to its problems of high turnover and a dwindling labor pool. The company tapped into the largely neglected supply of workers with disabilities through an in-house program called Pathways to Independence. Pathways incorporated job matching, social and occupational training, and ongoing support. Premier fast food chain McDonald's. initiated its McJobs program in 1981 for similar reasons. The six- to eight-week program recruits, trains, and employs an average of 900 mildly to severely disabled people annually. By 1992, it was implemented in 22 states, had graduated over 9,000 people, and employed 90 percent of them.

Technological innovations have further promoted placement of rehabilitated employees. IBM Corp.'s National Support Center for Persons With Disabilities, for example, opened in 1985. It features more than 800 devices and tools that can ease the transition to work, including voice synthesizers, adapters for people with impaired mobility, and voice-activated computers. Contrary to popular belief, disabled workers are not typically expensive or difficult to accommodate. A 1992 article in *Employment Relations Today* stated that 60 percent of workplace modifications cost less than $100, and 90 percent cost less than $1,000. Sears, Roebuck and Co. has noted that 90 percent of its accommodations have cost nothing.

In addition to the potential bottom-line benefits of vocational rehabilitation, such programs can promote positive employee relations. Communicating the benefits of the program, keeping in contact with workers on disability leave, and establishing light- and alternate-duty occupations can help show all employees that they are valued contributors to a business.

HOW VOCATIONAL REHAB WORKS

Vocational rehabilitation is a very individualized, goal-oriented process with the ultimate objective of employing its clientele. The delivery of this service is comprised of several steps, including diagnosis, compilation of an individualized written rehabilitation program (IWRP), counseling and guidance, physical and mental restoration, training, job placement, and post-employment services.

Diagnosis occurs at several levels. A preliminary diagnostic study determines a prospective client's eligibility for rehabilitation services in the public program. A medical evaluation identifies a client's disabilities and functional limitations. This very vital assessment may incorporate a physical examination as well as investigation of the client's medical and vocational history. A psychological evaluation of mental and emotional abilities and limitations, both historical and current, can also be included. A sociocultural evaluation includes compilation of identifying information; personal, family and home life histories; educational, and work histories; and assessment of personality, habits and economic situation. The vocational evaluation is an assessment of the client's occupational aptitudes and potential; work history, habits, interests, attitudes, and responsibilities; as well as the tenor of previous work relationships. Finally, the educational evaluation relates the client's skills to his vocational potential. It includes information on the level of education (including special areas of interest and achievement), as well as learning capacity and study habits. Clearly, many aspects of the diagnostic study overlap, just as the individual aspects of people's lives converge. The findings of these diagnoses are utilized in the next step, compilation of the individualized written rehabilitation program with the client.

The individualized written rehabilitation program (IWRP) is jointly developed by the rehabilitation counselor and the client (or his representative, in the case that the client is unable to contribute to the discussion). This ''plan of attack'' includes: a justification of the client's eligibility for treatment; a long-range employment goal; intermediate goals; identification of the services necessary to reach those goals; projected beginning dates for each service and the duration of each; and a procedure and schedule for the evaluation of the individual program.

Counseling and guidance are ongoing aspects of vocational rehabilitation. Called ''the synthesizing function of the rehabilitation process,'' counseling promotes the entire program. Physical and mental restoration works to alleviate the physical or mental conditions that impede a client's fullest potential functioning. This step may include medical, physical, and therapeutic treatment, prosthetics and/or orthotics, occupational or communication therapy, and psychiatry.

There are four types of training that a client of vocational rehabilitation may undergo: personal adjustment training, prevocational training, compensatory skill training, and vocational training. Personal adjustment training refers to the development of pro-work attitudes and habits like dependability, responsibility, and consistency. Prevocational training endows the background knowledge necessary to choose and prepare for occupational skill development. This may include tours of job sites, study of industries, and learning to fill out job applications and use public transportation. Compensatory skill training refers to the development of skills that make up for a disability, i.e., speech or lip reading for the hearing impaired and mobility training for the visually impaired. Vocational training alludes to the development of specific job skills, usually at trade and vocational schools, colleges and universities, rehabilitation facilities, sheltered workshops, apprenticeship programs, or on-the-job.

Job placement is the climax of the entire rehabilitation process. This complicated and underrated step matches client and job—two entities incorporating many variables. Just as no two work environments are exactly alike, no two vocational rehabilitation clients are exactly alike. Job placement often entails cooperation between the vocational rehabilitation agency and the potential employer, including modification of a job and/or the work environment. Computerization has helped facilitate the placement process. The Occupational Access System (OASYS) is an example of ''transferable skills analysis'' software. This job-matching software package based on the U.S. Department of Labor's *Dictionary of Occupational Titles*, can help mate a client's skills, work history, and interests with occupations. Databases of adaptive equipment can also facilitate a return to work.

Placement is not the end of the vocational rehabilitation story. Some clients require postemployment services such as continued counseling, supplementary training, health services, assistance with transportation, or other rehabilitation services.

[April Dougal Gasbarre]

FURTHER READING:

Bitter, James A. *Introduction to Rehabilitation.* C.V. Mosby Company, 1979.

Gice, Jon. ''The Relevance of the Americans with Disabilities Act to Workers Compensation,'' *CPCU Journal.* June 1992, pp. 79-83.

Heine, Alicia. ''Killing Two Birds with One Stone,'' *Business Insurance.* May 16, 1994, pp. 33-34.

Jones, David C. ''Co. Using Technology in Vocational Rehabilitation,'' *National Underwriter.* November 8, 1993, pp. 2, 13.

Madeja, Peter C. ''Return-to-Work Programs: Employers Should Re-Examine Vocational Rehabilitation,'' *Business Insurance.* September 28, 1992, pp. 47-48.

Mulcahy, Colleen. ''Rehab Saves $35 for Every $1 Spent, Study Finds,'' *National Underwriter* May 9, 1994, p. 17.

Obermann, C. Esco. *A History of Vocational Rehabilitation in America.* Arno Press, 1980.

Weiss, Joseph W. *The Management of Change: Administrative Logics and Actions.* Praeger Publishers, 1986.

Wiley, Carolyn. ''Programs That Lead the Way in Enabling People with Disabilities to Work,'' *Employment Relations Today.* Spring 1992, pp. 31-38.

W

WARRANTIES & GUARANTEES

A warranty or guarantee is given to the purchaser by a product manufacturer or provider of a service with the understanding that the manufacturer will replace or repair a defective product within a span of time. Popularized by national retailers and automobile manufacturers over the last few decades, written or implied warranties have become virtually standard and necessary to secure the trust of consumers. Few things are sold these days without some form of warranty—with the stereotypical exception of used cars where the original manufacturer's warranty has lapsed and the dealer has not chosen to offer one of his own.

New cars are a different story and the most visible use of warranties by manufacturers. Every television commercial for automobiles today touts the length of the warranty. In the 1960s Chrysler Corp. emphasized its generous warranty over the features of its cars, when it created a jarring jingle proclaiming that its cars were covered for "five long years or 50,000 miles—whichever comes first."

In the 1980s and 1990s, consumer activists pushed the boundaries of the car warranties with the passage of a "lemon law" in many state legislatures. These laws hold that automobiles should at least work reliably beyond the manufacturers' written warranties. If a consumer buys an automobile that undergoes continuous and unreasonable mechanical problems, lemon laws give the consumer the leverage to force the dealer to remedy the problems. Sometimes the simplest remedy for the dealer is to buy the vehicle back or offer the consumer a reduced price on a new car.

The manufacturers of high-cost electronic products such as computers have incorporated longer warranties as selling points against their competition, implying that any equipment sold with a shorter warranty must be of lesser quality. Often warranties can be extended for a full year for as little as $100, giving peace of mind to computer users while bringing in millions of dollars to computer manufacturers confident that their equipment will function well past the extended warranty date. One study estimated that nearly 40 percent of buyers of electronic products purchase extended warranties. More than half of car buyers also opt for.

While manufacturers would like consumers to think of warranties as something they provide as evidence of their faith in their products, the truth is that most warranties are covered by local, state and federal laws. The final judge in this country is the **Federal Trade Commission** that uses the Magnuson-Moss Warranty-Federal Trade Commission Improvement Act of 1975 as its guideline. This law requires stores to provide consumers copies of written warranties for products costing more than $15 if the customer requests them before purchase. The retailer should keep a binder or folder of warranties for all the products it carries.

States require that the manufacturer or seller of a product offer an implied warranty—some sort of guarantee that the product will work once it is out of the box and that it will work in the way that its manufacturer says it will. A wet vacuum that is supposed to suck up water from the garage floor has to perform that job, or the consumer has a legal right to return it for one that does. The length of time that these implied warranties are in effect varies from state to state.

There are two types of written warranties: full and limited. A manufacturer offering a full warranty must grant it for a specific length of time, must make repairs at no charge in a reasonable length of time, and cannot require the customer to jump through any hoops in order to invoke the warranty. Limited warranties, which must be labeled so in writing, limit the liability of the manufacturer. A limited warranty may offer to replace defective parts free while still levying high labor charges or require that the consumer ship the product to a manufacturer-approved service center. The distinctions between full and limited warranties and the obligations of manufacturers to honor them vary from state to state so it is up to the consumer to carefully read the literature and understand what is covered before the purchase. Fortunately for consumers manufacturers are required to follow any implied warranties created by local laws.

What some consumers wish would be part of a warranty might not be. The warranty might cover direct damages such as fixing a broken refrigerator but exclude indirect damages such as the cost of replacing ruined food that was in the refrigerator when it broke down. Some implied warranties exist that manufacturers leave up to consumers to discover on their own. One example is fixing paint on cars. Automobile manufacturers do not advertise that they can sometimes be persuaded that paint should not flake off a car after the warranty has expired. It may take persistence to get past the local dealer, but every year hundreds of dissatisfied car owners receive new paint jobs, sometimes after negotiations have failed and the car owners have threatened to publicize their cases or purchase competing models.

Extended warranties remain controversial. Manufacturers sell them betting that the extended warranty will not be needed or used, thereby resulting in profits. Consumers buy them for peace of mind, under the assumption that they are protecting their initial outlay of money. The controversy revolves around what the warranties cover. Some extended warranties are actually service agreements, resulting in higher charges than might be expected under a warranty. In other cases the fine print in the warranties exclude the very things that the consumer assumes would be covered. Automobile extended warranties usually require that consumers keep meticulous service records. For example, car owners who do not keep their receipts for oil and transmission fluid changes could find that they have invalidated the extended warranty purchased when the car was new.

Do consumers need extended warranties? One survey found only 38 percent of consumers who had bought extended warranties had ever had anything repaired under them. 62 percent of the manufacturers responding to the same survey reported offering extended warranties. But only 13 percent of the warranty work they performed was for a customer holding an extended warranty.

Small, local manufacturers and service providers who believe that adding warranties will make their sales pitches more attractive should carefully review local, state, and federal laws such as the Magnuson-Moss Act. Governments take the issuing of warranties very seriously as should any company that issues them.

[Clint Johnson]

WARRANTS (SECURITIES)

Warrants are **options** to purchase a fixed number of shares for a fixed price. Usually, warrants are sold with **bonds** as an equity sweetener. If the stock price rises substantially, the debt purchaser can exercise the warrants and participate in the equity growth. The warrant reduces the coupon's interest rate on the bond issue.

The intrinsic value of a warrant is equal to the market price of one share of common stock minus the exercise price of the warrant times the number of shares that can be purchased with each warrant. If the current market price per share of common stock is $10 and the warrant exercise price is $2, and if each warrant allows the investor to purchase two shares, the warrant has an intrinsic value of $16.

The actual **market value** of the warrant may be higher than the intrinsic value. The difference between the market value and the intrinsic value is the premium. The market value of the warrant can never be less than zero. The premium depends on the warrant's leverage effect, the time to maturity, and the volatility of the price of the underlying stock. The warrant's leverage depends on the difference between the market price of the underlying stock and the warrant exercise price; the greater the difference in price, the higher the leverage and the greater the potential for gain or loss. The longer the time to maturity, the higher the probability that the underlying stock will increase in price and increase the value of the warrant. The greater the volatility of the underlying stock, the higher the probability that the underlying stock will increase in price and increase the value of the warrant.

The warrant premium is a negative function of the cash dividend paid on the underlying stock. Since the owner of the warrant does not own the underlying stock, he/she is not entitled to the cash **dividend** paid. The larger the dividend that is paid on the underlying stock, the lower the premium on the warrant.

[Carl B. McGowan, Jr.]

FURTHER READING:

Reilly, Frank K. *Investment Analysis and Portfolio Management*. 3rd ed. Chicago: The Dryden Press, 1989.

WEALTH

The concept of wealth refers to the value of the total quantity of goods or assets in existence at a particular point in time. Private wealth, or the wealth of an individual, consists of the value of things owned, including money and other claims against goods and services such as **stocks** and **bonds**. In the case of national wealth, however, money and other claims against goods and services are not included as part of a country's wealth. Rather, national wealth consists of the goods in existence that are available for use. Thus, a distinction is made between private wealth and national wealth. If an individual destroys a $100 bill, that person loses wealth, but the national wealth remains unaffected.

Wealth is a measurement of a stock of goods at a point in time. Wealth is said to be a stock concept. In contrast, **income** and **gross national product** are flow concepts. That is, production and income measure the rate at which goods and services are produced over a period of time. While national wealth may be measured in terms of dollars, it is important to realize that national wealth consists of a supply of goods, not money or claims against goods.

Real or national wealth consists of two types of goods, natural wealth and produced wealth. Natural wealth includes the value of a country's natural resources, such as minerals, farm land, and construction sites. Produced wealth, or capital goods, consists of machinery, buildings, equipment, and inventories of raw materials and finished products. Capital goods, in turn, include both consumers' capital, producers' capital, and government capital. Consumers' capital includes such items as automobiles, appliances, and furniture. Producers' capital consists of buildings, productive equipment, inventory, and other goods that are owned by business firms. Government capital includes those goods owned by various governments, such as police and fire vehicles, highways, sewers, schools, and jails.

The capital stock portion of national wealth may be increased through investment. Gross private domestic investment is that part of the gross national product that is spent on nonresidential structures, producers' durable equipment, residential structures, and increases in business inventories. Gross investment includes the replacement of older equipment as well as additions to the total amount of capital goods. Net investment, or the net addition to the stock of capital goods, is calculated by subtracting capital consumption allowances from gross investment.

[David Bianco]

WHITE COLLAR CRIME

White-collar crime costs the United States approximately $4 billion per year, an amount ten times the annual cost of street crime. Today, business leaders and law enforcement personnel are focusing increasing attention on white-collar crime, but will be hard pressed to make a serious impact on its effects for a long time to come. More and more people, aided by computers and technology, are indulging in increasingly sophisticated schemes to bilk victims.

Rapid technological advances decrease the likelihood of criminals being caught. Consequently, society at large is being victimized more and more by sophisticated white-collar criminals. Indeed, no member of society is immune to white-collar crime. Victims range from school children to octogenarians to the **Internal Revenue Service** (IRS). Amazingly, the IRS is defrauded of up to $5 billion a year through electronic tampering with tax records, theft of Social Security numbers, and other schemes. Like other victims, such losses can be attributed in part to the IRS' lax approach to addressing the problem.

Often, people become victims due to their own greed and naivete. The best defense against white-collar crime is, in many instances, a heightened sense of awareness and a healthy suspicion.

WHAT IS WHITE-COLLAR CRIME?

White-collar crime includes offenses such as fraud or embezzlement committed by individuals working for a business, government, or not-for-profit organization. Perpetrators may also include professionals engaged in occupational activities. The list of crimes that fall into the white-collar category is almost endless. White-collar crimes may include innocuous activities like an employee taking home pencils and stationery for family members or major activities like insider trading or check kiting. The only real limit to the types and sophistication of white-collar crimes is the amount of imagination and inventiveness demonstrated by white-collar criminals.

AN HISTORICAL PERSPECTIVE

White-collar crime has existed in business since the first entrepreneur opened a store. Cases of fraud date back as far as 360 B.C., when Xenothemis and

Hegestratos, two residents of Syracuse, Sicily, then a Greek colony, conspired to bilk a buyer out of money through a clever scheme. They asked the unsuspecting buyer for an advance on a shipment of corn supposedly loaded on a vessel owned by Hegestratos. Their intention was to sink the vessel at sea and keep the money. However, passengers caught Hegestratos in the act of scuttling his ship. He panicked, jumped overboard, and drowned.

There was a time in U.S. history when white-collar crime was practically considered a normal part of doing business. For example, some of the best known "Captains of Industry" in the late-19th century were known to stretch business ethics at times. Among them were Jay Gould (1836-1885), Jim Fiske, Ulysses S. Grant's vice president Schuyler Colfax (1823-1885), and James A. Garfield, 20th president of the United States.

Colfax and Garfield were involved in the infamous Credit Mobilier scandal of the mid-1800s. Credit Mobilier was the construction company for the Union Pacific Railroad, constructed between December 1863 and May 1869. The United States government lent the company $16,000 per mile for the part of the railroad built on level ground, $32,000 per mile for that laid on somewhat more difficult terrain, and $48,000 per mile for rail placed in mountains. Credit Mobilier charged UP huge sums for its services, much of it for work that was never completed. The major stockholders owned shares in both corporations. They earned $23,000,000 in profits—much of it government money.

The *New York Sun* suspected corruption in the financial dealings, which it exposed in 1872. The *Sun* discovered that Oakes Ames, a member of the Pacific Railroad Committee in the House of Representatives, had "sold" stocks in Credit Mobilier to several congressmen, including future President Garfield, and then Vice President Colfax, in an effort to stave off any investigation into the matter. Ultimately, a senate investigating committee absolved the politicians of any wrongdoing and the matter was dropped.

Jay Gould and Jim Fiske were certainly no saints, either. In the 1870s they watered stock in the Erie Railroad by printing phony stock certificates, which they sold to Cornelius Vanderbilt (1794-1877), a railroad magnate who operated the New York Central Railroad—and a man who was no stranger to shady financial dealings himself. Their manipulations cost Vanderbilt millions of dollars and threw the Erie Railroad into bankruptcy in 1875. That was not the first time Fiske and Gould had created havoc in the United States through their financial wheeling and dealing—nor was it their last.

In 1869, the pair tried to corner the nation's available gold supply. President Grant had told them the government was not planning to sell gold on the open market. Fiske and Gould seized on that information to purchase large amounts of gold and drive the price up. That forced business owners who required gold to settle international transactions to sell stocks and bonds and call in debts to gather enough money to purchase gold. Grant reacted quickly and authorized the sale of $4,000,000 of the Treasury's gold supply. Somehow, Gould and Fiske learned about the sale before it occurred. They sold their gold first at a tremendous profit. These scandals had no adverse effect on Gould and Fiske, who brought white-collar crime to new heights in the late 1800s.

The 1900s have seen their share of white-collar crime as well. There was, for example, the savings and loan scandal in the 1980s in which Charles Keating, Jr., the director of a bank that violated federal banking regulations, cost its investors millions of dollars. Another famous case centered around insider trading information, which professional Wall Street trader Ivan Boesky used to reap millions of dollars in profits. Boesky conspired with an acquaintance, Dennis Levine, who worked for Drexel Burnham Lambert, an investment banking firm.

When Levine learned about an upcoming merger or acquisition, he would advise Boesky. He, in turn, bought and sold the appropriate stocks at favorable times and made huge profits in the process. Boesky shared the profits with Levine. In one outstanding case, Boesky capitalized on Levine's information about Nestle's plans to buy Carnation stock—and earn a profit of $28 million. Eventually, Boesky and Levine were caught. Both went to jail, unlike Gould and Fiske. That was due in part to changing times.

There began a growing emphasis on business ethics toward the end of the 20th century. Business people, government officials, and law enforcement administrators saw the potential for white-collar crime in virtually every aspect of society and began to concentrate more on the development of ethics programs, investigative techniques, and the creation of laws to make prosecution easier.

WHO COMMITS WHITE-COLLAR CRIMES?

White-collar crimes are committed by individuals ranging from company clerks to chief executive officers of multinational corporations and people working independently to rob their employers, co-workers, and private citizens. Crimes can also be perpetrated by corporations, through the actions of individuals or groups of employees. (More often than not, though, corporations are the targets of white-collar criminals, rather than the perpetrators of crimes.) The crimes can result in monetary losses of a few cents to millions of dollars, depending on their complexity and the expertise and intentions of the perpetrators. They can be committed by employees seeking only to embezzle a "few dollars" to executives siphoning off corporate funds under the guise of outlandish salaries.

TYPES OF WHITE-COLLAR CRIMES

White-collar crimes fall into two categories: those committed by individuals acting on their own behalf and those committed by corporate employees who often perpetrate crimes on behalf of their employers. White-collar crimes can be aimed at bilking one victim or groups of people on a one-time basis. At times they are committed by people who rob human or organizational victims out of large sums of money over a long period of time. The latter category often involves people employed by corporations who act either for self-enrichment or to benefit their companies. Their crimes may include such activities as improper financial management, check kiting, insider trading, misrepresentation, and parking cash.

IMPROPER FINANCIAL MANAGEMENT. Improper financial management may not always be considered a crime. It may simply be the intentional or unintentional mishandling of money. For example, executives may use huge amounts of a company's money to support lavish lifestyles. This is not necessarily illegal. Unfortunately, in many cases, it reduces the amount of money the company has to pay creditors and shareholders, neither of whom may have any recourse to payment or dividends. Shareholders can resort to tactics like forcing management changes, but that is sometimes self-defeating, since processes of this type can drive down the price of stock and adversely affect a company's reputation, neither of which appeal to shareholders.

CHECK KITING. This practice involves writing checks against money that has not yet arrived at the bank on which the check has been drawn. In a classic check kiting case during the 1980's, some E. F. Hutton & Company managers used as much as $250 million every day that did not belong to the firm. For example, managers would deposit $1 million worth of checks into a bank on a given day. Then, they would write checks against that money even though they knew the bank would not collect all of that total for several days. They also routinely transferred large sums of money between banks to take advantage of their delayed check collection procedures. Certainly, not all check kiting schemes involve millions of dollars, but combined they can cost unsuspecting victims large sums that can affect their finances dramatically.

INSIDER TRADING. As evidenced by the Boesky-Levine case, insider trading is the use of confidential information to gain from the purchase or sale of stock. Until recent years, it was not a criminal activity. However, the effects prompted laws rendering it illegal, since the use of inside information was deemed to destroy fairness for ordinary investors. Hence, anti-insider trading laws were passed to protect these ordinary investors from people like Boesky and Levine.

MISREPRESENTATION OF FINANCES. Executives sometimes practice financial trickery in order to magnify profits and attract investors. This is not a widespread practice, since most companies adhere to generally accepted accounting techniques in maintaining and reporting their financial statuses. However, companies are occasionally found legally guilty of misrepresenting their finances to outsiders. The bottom line is that they may pay fines and lose investors, which can be heavy financial blows for companies.

PARKING. Parking is the illegal and complex practice of shifting funds between countries in order to avoid taxes. The increase in the number of multinational companies may give rise to parking practices. For instance, a company may keep two sets of books, one "public" and the other "private," i.e., for certain managers only. These private funds allow select managers to keep close tabs on funds and transfer them when necessary to avoid paying taxes. This practice can be dangerous for companies, especially if whistleblowers, individuals who call attention to unethical, illegal, and/or socially irresponsible practices on the part of an organization, detect parking.

INDIVIDUAL WHITE-COLLAR CRIMES

Certainly, not all white-collar crime involves corporations. There are people who operate scams of various types designed to bilk corporations and private citizens alike of their money. There is a staggering variety of white-collar crimes designed to victimize people. They range from individuals robbing their employers to companies bilking potential customers.

For example, South Carolina authorities cracked down on real estate companies along the state's coast that bilked condominium owners out of millions of dollars in fees for promised sales. The brokers promised owners of time-share units that they had buyers to purchase their apartments. They solicited up-front fees for "processing" of the sales. Quite often, the brokers did not have buyers available. They simply used the money for their own purposes.

The money involved was not enough to break owners individually. The fees ranged from $295 to $395 per person. However, unscrupulous brokers collected such fees from as many as 2,000 owners, for a total of nearly $800,000. This is one of the hallmarks of white-collar crimes. Perpetrators often attempt to spread out their gains so individuals will not be unduly alarmed at their personal losses. The motto of white-collar thieves might be "A little at a time; a lot over time."

An example of this philosophy in action centers around credit cards, which are often tools used by white-collar thieves to bilk victims. Credit card fraud losses in the United States on just four major cards, Visa, MasterCard, Discover, and Optima, rose from $125 million in 1983 to $720 million in 1992. A typical credit card fraud case occurred in September, 1994, in Columbia Falls, Montana. City police reported a scheme in which someone in Connecticut obtained the credit card numbers of two local residents, called the card holders' credit card companies claiming to be the owners of the cards, and changed the owners' addresses to a post office box in Connecticut. Then, the thieves used the victims' names and new address to apply for other cards, on which they charged large sums of money which they never paid. Such scams cost individuals and credit card companies alike large sums of money. Unfortunately, crimes of this nature are growing in the United States.

Companies are often the victims of such scams. They also fall prey to other types of **embezzlement** at times. A bookkeeper for Star Silk and Woolen Company, in Hartford, Connecticut, embezzled $135,000 from her employer between 1989 and 1991. She simply pocketed some checks and altered others. While she was embezzling, the company's annual sales dropped from $10 million to $2.1 million and 18 of its 22 employees were laid off. Yet, the woman kept stealing the money. She was finally arrested and convicted. Although she was sentenced to six years in jail, she did not have to pay back any of the money.

In a similar case, a tax collector in nearby Chaplin embezzled $310,000 from the town between 1985 and 1992. A judge sentenced her to pay the town $210,000, the uninsured portion of the $310,000, plus $70,000 for legal and auditing costs. She received no prison time. The inconsistency in the sentences assessed to these two embezzlers points to the sometimes nonchalant legal approach to white-collar crimes over the years. Court officials, law enforcement administrators, and business executives tended to overlook the severity and the magnitude of the crimes. Often, companies would overlook white-collar crimes in order to protect their reputations and to prevent their shareholders and customers from learning that their security systems were somewhat lax. That is no longer the case.

There was a time, for example, when banks that detected embezzlers on their workforces would simply fire the perpetrators, often without notifying the police. However, employers are loathe to do that today except in cases which may involve tiny amounts of money, e.g., employees shoplifting small items from stores. Executives are more likely to pursue white-collar crime activities now, often with the assistance of law enforcement personnel. Still, according to an article published in the July 1994 edition of *Law and Order Magazine*, 42 percent of the respondents to a poll said that employers are still reluctant to report white-collar crimes to police. However, highly publicized recent successes enjoyed by law enforcement personnel in fighting white-collar crime may change that percentage.

FIGHTING WHITE-COLLAR CRIME

There is a growing effort to combat increasing white-collar crime. Law enforcement agencies are becoming more sophisticated in their approach to the problem. Police departments are hiring officers trained in areas such as embezzlement, fraud against the elderly, cellular phone theft . . . the list is growing.

Consider a 1994 case in Maryland in which two Baltimore men were sentenced to terms in federal prison for their parts in an elaborate cellular phone call scheme. The pair was part of a complex ''call-sell'' operation in which they copied a phone company mobile customer's cellular phone number and allowed other people to make calls on it in exchange for money. They felt safe from apprehension, since tracing problems like this was next to impossible until recently, much to the chagrin of phone companies. Cellular phone scams cost phone companies $1 million per day, which can be a drain on profits.

Phone company personnel developed new techniques to uncover cellular phone thieves and reduce their losses. In 1994 alone, Bell Atlantic Mobile technicians solved enough cases of fraud to have more than 65 swindlers arrested. The technicians comprise a 50-member full-time in-house Fraud Task Force, which pinpoints fraudulent calling activity. Once the sleuths identify the scheme, they request law enforcement officials to make arrests. In just four months, cellular phone fraud in the force's region dropped by 35 percent. Not only do the task force's members detect criminals themselves, but they also assist in training police officers in cellular phone fraud detection. By mid-1994, Bell Atlantic had trained over 350 officers in the specialty, and continues to train more. Such cooperation is effective in fighting white-collar crime, but it is only one of many methods.

Companies are developing and enforcing stringent codes of ethics to which their employees must adhere. Judges are assessing more severe penalties to white-collar criminals. Individuals and organizations of all types are increasing their efforts to detect white-collar crimes affecting their finances and insisting on more severe enforcement of the laws governing such activities. Authorities are relying more heavily on public awareness campaigns to educate potential victims of fraud on how to prevent it. For example, cellular phone companies advise their customers to protect their electronic serial and mobile numbers just as they would credit card numbers, report stolen phones to police immediately, or call their service providers if they are billed for calls they did not make. They encourage whistleblowers to report suspicious activities to company officials. And, they urge business owners and managers to tighten security to reduce the potential of white-collar crime.

Education plays a large part in fighting white-collar crime. Many managers are not aware of the possibility of white-collar crime being perpetrated in their offices or the costs incurred as a result. One bizarre case that demonstrates lax security occurred in Hartford, Connecticut, where an office worker embezzled nearly $150,000 in three years by removing about $200 per day from the cash register—even though the department's three supervisors sat only ten feet away. The embezzler was tripped up by a clerk in training who noticed an unusual transaction and reported it to the supervisors. Such cases point up the brazen attitude of white-collar thieves and the need for adequate security measures to deter them.

THE FUTURE OF WHITE-COLLAR CRIME

White-collar crime will not disappear any time soon. Criminals will continue to devise new and more elaborate schemes to take advantage of ever-changing technology in order to bilk victims. Executives, law enforcement officials, and other people will continue to develop sophisticated measure to detect the fraud and apprehend the criminals. White-collar crime did not begin with Xenothemis and Hegestratos, nor will it end any time soon. It has been a part of society since the dawn of business and will remain so. However, as more and more people become aware of its detrimental effects on individuals and society as a whole, the efforts to combat it will increase. That is the most effective way to combat the expensive problem.

[Arthur G. Sharp]

FURTHER READING:

Bequai, August. *White-Collar Crime: A Twentieth-Century Crisis*. Lexington, MA: D.C. Heath and Company, 1978.

Clarke, Michael. *Business Crime: Its Nature and Control*. New York: St. Martin's Press, 1990.

Clinard, M. B. *Corporate Ethics and Crime: The Role of Middle Management*. Beverly Hills, CA: Sage Publications, 1983.

Dudley, William, Ed. *Crime and Criminals: Opposing Viewpoints*. San Diego: Greenhaven Press, 1989.

Meier, Robert F. *Major Forms of Crime*. Beverly Hills, CA: Sage Publications, 1984.

WHOLESALING

Wholesalers represent one of the links in the chain along which most goods pass on their way to the marketplace. As intermediaries, wholesalers facilitate the transport, preparation of quantity, storage, and sale of articles destined for customers. Wholesalers may be defined as "those who generally purchase goods as close as possible to the place of production in field or factory and who carry them to the market where they are passed on to other marketers to sell to the public." (Babb, 1989)

Strictly speaking, although a wholesaler may own or control retail operations, wholesalers do not sell to end-customers. Indeed, many wholesale operations are themselves owned by retailers or manufacturers. Wholesalers are extremely important in a variety of industries, including automobiles, grocery products, plumbing supplies, electrical supplies, and raw farm produce. Latest estimates indicate that there are more than 460,000 wholesalers operating in the United States producing $2.5 trillion in sales.

Wholesaling involves that part of the **marketing** process in which intermediaries, i.e., those between the producer and end-consumer, buy and resell goods, making them available to an expanded buyer's market over an expanded geographical market area. According to Bromley (1984), the notion of trade, and therefore of wholesaling, is the movement of goods from one area to a market demand in another area. Wholesalers are frequently described as existing between producers and buyers, and are sometimes referred to as middle agents. As middle agents they are only effective when the price they charge for goods and services is less than the value placed by customers. By facilitating the transfer of title of goods, they are involved in the bulking and distributing of goods.

Wholesaling provides an expanded consumer market potential in terms of geographical locations and consumer purchasing power while at the same time providing a cash flow for the manufacturer. There are several major reasons for the importance of wholesaling. First, all goods and necessary supplies for their production pass through some form of middle agent and wholesaling system. For this reason, the effective functioning of wholesale linkages contributes directly to the economic well-being of a society.

Secondly, for most small producers, an immediate geographic location is typically insufficient to provide and maintain an on-going customer base for their operations. As a means to sell their goods, smaller producers must have avenues to develop market segments of potential customers and must make sure their goods are of the quality customers want at prices they are willing to pay. The role of wholesalers is to provide links to an expanded market base, i.e., to discover where customers are located and how best to reach them. In this sense, wholesaling uses time and place as it relates to information and availability. Wholesalers create utility through holding goods that can be drawn upon by buyers at a cost lower than direct exchange.

Finally, wholesalers act as distribution channels and interface with markets and producers within markets. Whereas wholesaling and retailing provide similar functions in that they receive, store, and distribute goods, the importance of wholesaling is in its ability to moderate supply and demand fluctuations and cope with larger transactions with less emphasis on selling techniques and services and product promotion. Wholesaling has the capability to adjust the distribution of goods from surplus to deficit areas.

Wholesalers are successful only if they are able to serve the needs of their customers, who may be retailers or other wholesalers. Some of the marketing functions provided by wholesalers to their buyers are:

- provide producer's goods in an appropriate quantity for resale by buyers
- provide wider geographical access and diversity in obtaining goods
- ensure and maintain a quality dimension with the goods that are being obtained and resold
- provide cost-effectiveness by reducing the number of producer contacts needed
- provide ready access to a supply of goods
- assemble and arrange goods of a compatible nature from a number of producers for resale
- minimize buyer transportation costs by buying goods in larger quantities and distributing them in smaller amounts for resale
- work with producers to understand and appreciate **consumerism** in their production process

Although there are a number of ways to classify wholesalers, the categories used by the Census of Wholesale Trade are employed most often. The three types of wholesalers are merchant wholesalers; agents, brokers, and commission merchants; and manufacturers' sales branches and offices.

Merchant wholesalers are firms engaged primarily in buying, taking title to, usually storing, and physically handling products in relatively large quantities and reselling the products in smaller quantities to retailers, industrial, commercial, or institutional concerns, and to other wholesalers. They go under many different names, such as wholesaler, jobber, distributor, industrial distributor, supply house, assembler, importer, exporter, and many others.

Agents, brokers, and commission merchants are also independent middlemen who do not (for the most part) take title to the goods in which they deal, but instead are actively involved in negotiatory functions of buying and selling while acting on behalf of their clients. They are usually compensated in the form of commissions on sales or purchases. Some of the more common types go under the names of manufacturers' agents, commission merchants, brokers, selling agents, and import and export agents.

Manufacturers' sales branches and offices are owned and operated by manufacturers but are physically separated from manufacturing plants. They are used primarily for the purpose of distributing the manufacturers' own products at wholesale. Some have warehousing facilities where inventories are maintained, while others are merely sales offices. Some of them also wholesale allied and supplementary products purchased from other manufacturers.

The future of wholesaling appears somewhat ambiguous. The major force affecting wholesaler activity is growth in the power of retail chain stores. The continued **mergers and acquisitions** taking place between similar regional chains since 1970 means that independent retailers will have a lesser need for wholesalers. However, there is a countervailing force at work in that retailing is becoming increasingly fragmented as more and more specialized retailers cater to specialized market niches. As this specialization continues, using wholesalers becomes the most cost-efficient way for manufacturers to cover fragmented retailer market segments. The wholesaler is able to bundle several manufacturers' items into combinations that can all be sold through the specialist outlet. In most cases, wholesalers will capitalize on market opportunities among specialized, independent retailers while they lose ground to chains buying directly from manufacturers. Many wholesalers have adopted nicely by becoming efficient importers, upgrading their operations with **computers**, improving inventory handling, and automating their warehouses. The key to success will be for the wholesalers to align themselves with retail specialists that offer solid, long-term growth prospects or to concentrate on merchandise categories where chains still must use wholesalers because of needed buying efficiencies.

[John Burnett]

FURTHER READING:

Babb, F. E. *Between Field and Cooking Pot: The Political Economy of Marketwomen in Peru*. Austin: University of Texas Press, 1989.

Bromley, R. "Market Centers, Market Policies and Agricultural Development." *Regional Development Dialogue*. vol. 5, no. 1, pp. 149-65, 1984.

WIDE AREA NETWORKS

A wide area network (WAN) is a **telecommunications** network, usually used for connecting **compu-**

ters, which spans a wide geographical area, such as between different cities, states, or even countries. WANs typically are used by corporations or organizations to facilitate the exchange of data between their computers in dispersed offices. Across all industries, most large corporations with facilities at multiple locations use WANs, and even small businesses with just two remote sites use increasingly WANs.

Although WANs serve a purpose similar to that of **local area networks (LANs)**, WANs are structured and operated quite differently. The user of a WAN usually does not own the communications lines that connect the remote computer systems but instead subscribes to a service through a telecommunications provider. Unlike LANs, WANs typically do not link individual computers, but rather are used to link LANs in what are known as internetworks, using devices called routers and remote bridges. WANs also transmit data at much slower speeds than LANs, most commonly at about 1.5 megabits per second (Mbps) or less, instead of the tens or hundreds of Mbps achieved by LANs. WANs are structurally similar to metropolitan area networks (MANs), but provide communications links for distances greater than 50 kilometers.

WANs have existed for decades, but new technologies, services, and applications have developed over the years. WANs were originally developed for digital leased-line services carrying only voice, rather than data. As such, they connected the private branch exchanges (PBXs) of remote offices of the same company. WANs are still used for voice services, but are used most heavily for data and recently also for images, such as for video conferencing. WAN usage is growing, as more companies have installed LANs and more kinds of affordable internetworking equipment has become available. According to International Data Corp., as cited in *PC Week*, 40 percent of the two million LANs worldwide that were not connected to WANs in 1994 were expected to make the connections by 1997 or 1998.

WANs are either point-to-point, involving a direct connection between two sites, or operate across packet-switched networks, in which data is transmitted in packets over shared circuits. Point-to-point WAN service may involve either analog dial-up lines, using a modem to connect the computer to the telephone line, or dedicated leased digital telephone lines, also known as "private lines." Analog lines, which may be either part of a public-switched telephone network or leased lines, are suitable for batch data transmissions, such as nonurgent order entry and point-of-sale transactions. Dedicated digital phone lines permit uninterrupted, secure data transmission at fixed costs.

A leading type of point-to-point WAN service in North America is T1, which is based on a method of dividing a digital line service with a rate of 1.544 Mbps into 24 channels of 64 kbps each. Other point-to-point services available include fractional T1, T3, dataphone digital services, switched 56 kbps, and integrated services digital network (ISDN). New technologies that promise greater speeds and reliability include asynchronous transfer mode (ATM) and Sonet. Point-to-point WAN service providers include both local telephone companies and long distance carriers, such as AT&T and MCI.

Packet-switched network services are typically chosen by organizations which have low volumes of data or numerous sites, for which multiple dedicated lines would be too expensive. Packet-switched network services include ACCUNET, Tymnet, CompuServe Network Services, GE Information Network Services, IBM Information Network, and Sprintnet. The most common kind of packet-switched network is used in conjunction with the X.25 data switching standard, providing speeds of 9.6 kbps to 64 kbps. Frame relay, which offers ten times the speed of X.25, began to be offered as a packet switching technology in the early 1990s.

Depending on the service, WANs can be used for almost any data sharing purpose for which LANs can be used, but slower transmission speeds may make some applications less practical. The most basic uses of WANs are for **electronic mail** and file transfer, but WANs can also permit users at remote sites to access and enter data on a central site's database, such as instantaneously updating accounting records. New types of network-based software that facilitate productivity and production tracking, such as groupware and work-flow automation software, can also be used over WANs. Using groupware, workers at dispersed locations can more easily collaborate on projects. WANs also give remote offices access to a central office's other data communications services, such as connections to on-line services and the Internet.

An example how a WAN improves efficiency is its use in order processing. Use of a WAN costs less than use of a fax or telephone, because only one person is needed instead of two—one to take the order at the remote end and one to enter it at the central location. Order processing on a WAN allows the remote operator to determine immediately and independently the availability of an inventory item, customer credit status, and other information. Relying on telephone and fax calls may require multiple calls for the same purpose. Line usage costs per page of data transmitted over WANs can even be lower than the costs of long-distance fax or telephone calls.

[Heather Behn Hedden]

FURTHER READING:

Chappell, Laura A., and Roger L. Spicer. *Novell's Guide to Multiprotocol Internetworking*. San Jose, CA: Novell Press, 1994.

Pecar, Joseph A., Roger J. O'Connor, and David A. Garbin. *The McGraw-Hill Telecommunications Factbook*. New York: McGraw-Hill, 1993.

Smith, Laura B. "Branch Office, Phone Home: Corporations Cast Nets to Remote Sites in an Internetworking Surge." *PC Week*, May 2, 1994, 80.

"Wide Area Networking Puts Remote Offices On-Line." *Managing Office Technology*, September, 1994, 49-50.

WOMEN IN BUSINESS

From the beginning of time, women have worked at home, as well as outside of the home to contribute to the greater economic well-being of family. Even in colonial America, characterized by rural and self-sufficient communities, women assumed roles in the manufacture and sale of goods. Beginning with the textile mills and the shoemaking industry of post-revolutionary America, the first real explosion of women into business appeared at the turn-of-the-century in secretarial and take-home work situations. By World War I, women were poised to enter the **workforce** in great numbers and spurred into the workplace by the absence of men at war. As men returned from the war and the economy gradually worsened into the Great Depression, women suffered displacement from the business world. World War II created a similar growth of women in business. Without a serious economic depression and as a result of changing societal norms, women's roles and functions in business have steadily increased in the years since World War II. In 1991, women represented 45 percent of the U.S. workforce.

Blue-collar workers traditionally evoke images of trades and manufacturing employees. White-collar employees hold positions of professional and managerial importance. Women in business, while represented in both, create a third category called pink-collar workers. Pink-collar workers are commonly associated with clerical, sales, and service positions. In each of these roles, women participate and create a presence. In the trade and manufacturing jobs particularly, the relationship between and women and labor unions has been noteworthy. In professional and managerial jobs, women directly interact with ideas and conceptions of power and control. And, in service jobs, women, as the dominant labor force, deal with effects of technology daily in a compelling way.

The sum total of this historical record and increasing participation in the workforce brings to light the controversial matter of a woman's work and worth. In particular, **sex discrimination** and pay inequity demonstrate the difficult transition of women into the business world. Protective legislation is one demonstration of governmental attempts to prevent and discourage sex discrimination on the job. Legal redress for salary inequities is another method of controlling pay discrimination. Other contributing concerns that women bring to business include issues about benefits. **Child care/elder care** needs accompany women into the business world as do preferences for flexible scheduling and **family leave**. These issues reflect the dual role that women hold in both the business world and the family/personal world. Married women, mothers, and older women benefit from workplace accommodations to individual needs and conflicting priorities when benefits are tailored accordingly.

HISTORY

In seventeenth- and eighteenth-century America, women worked at home with their husbands to contribute to the family's economic support. Employment opportunities for women were scarce. In this essentially self-supporting rural lifestyle, centers of commerce emerged as small towns and cities. Working out of necessity, women became shopkeepers, artisans, and merchants. The most frequent reason for working was widowhood. Examples of working women in colonial America are often associated with the clothing trade. Women printers, however, illustrate a particularly significant departure from textile-based employment. Women entrepreneurs such as Elizabeth Timothy and Cornelia Smith Bradford operated as independent printers and bookbinders in South Carolina and Boston in late eighteenth-century America. The employment of women in the printing trades was well-regarded and common at the time. Frequently, a woman would inherit her husband's printing business at the time of his death. As proprietors and purveyors of the printed word, women printers enjoyed a small but significant minority role in colonial America. The impending war with England created a demand for goods made in America, thus opening business opportunities to women engaged in the production of cloth and food. Even as women worked, however, they still worked out of necessity. The prevailing societal attitude projected the ideal woman as family oriented not business oriented.

As a logical conclusion, post-revolutionary America found women engaged in the business of working at home. Piecework or take-home work formed roots during this time that continue to modern day. In conjunction with increased industrialization, textile mills in the northeastern states sought women out as a source of cheap labor and the organized movement of women into the workforce first appeared. Combined with the endeavors of early women's rights activists such as Elizabeth Cady Stanton (1815-1902), the idea of women in the workplace began to gain approval. Yet, the outspoken cultural preference was still towards the ideal woman and ''spheres of influence.'' Spheres of influence refers to a prevailing theory that women belonged in the private sphere of family while men belonged in the public sphere of business. As cities grew and transportation improved, work and business were increasingly conducted from a centralized location. As a result, homework or piecework decreased. The influx of immigration from 1840 on increased the labor force. Society began to embrace the idea of the ideal woman and diminished the expectation for a woman's contribution to family financial health. Instead, men assumed the burden of sole provider while women stayed at home more and more frequently. With the advent of the Civil War, this model changed.

Clerical and teaching opportunities opened to women during the Civil War. Nursing began to assume a professional component due to the casualties of the war. As a result of the great many deaths in the Civil War, thousands of women were left to fend for themselves financially and economically. A conflict arose between the economic need for survival and the cultural expectations of family responsibility. Even among wealthy women, the move from private to public sphere accelerated in voluntary and charitable outlets.

By the turn of the nineteenth century, women altered the cultural landscape by creating the idea of a new woman to replace the ideal women. Changing ideas of women included the central role of woman as partner to the economic well-being of the family and society as a whole. By 1900, more than 20 percent of women worked for a wage. The range and variety of employment in the 1900 census indicates that women held jobs in law, journalism, dentistry, medicine, engineering, mining, and other typical occupations. Women were counted in 295 of the 305 occupations listed on the census. The increasing industrialization of the United States resulted in a surge in factory work. More than one million women worked in factories in 1900. Most of these women were young, single, and foreign-born. They worked for low wages and knew no job security. Factories were unsafe and dirty. As a result, the businesswoman's first association with labor unionism appeared. In the Uprising of the 20,000 in 1909, women banded together and struck to protest working conditions and wages in the clothing industry. Many other **labor unions** appeared that either solely represented or incorporated the female employee during the early 1900s.

Even as women worked in industry to fuel its growth, the outcome created new business opportunities for women in clerical jobs. Between 1900 and 1920, the number of women clerical workers grew from 187,000 to 1,421,000. Women entered professional and managerial jobs during this time, as well. Health, education, and caring professions emerged to alleviate suffering caused by industrialization while simultaneously expanding professional opportunities for women. During World War I, women assumed many of the roles and jobs of men during their absence. After the war, however, women were expected to return to familial pursuits. Still considered a secondary labor force, women were encouraged to engage in volunteer and charity work. Many who chose to remain in the workforce took lower-paying jobs as men returned from military service.

During World War II, women again entered the workforce in great numbers. In response to a need for new workers and new production, six million women went to work during the war. Society reflected approval of this phenomena with posters of Rosie the Riveter and other cultural signals. Magazines and movies and other media all reinforced a woman's patriotic duty to work. Again, however, at the end of the war, women were encouraged to leave the workplace and return to the family environment. While half the women in the workplace left between 1945 and 1946, by 1947 the employment rate of women had regained its wartime levels. And, by 1950, almost one-third of all women worked outside the home.

From the end of World War II to present, women continued to gain a significant presence in the work world. In the 1960s, the women's movement articulated a number of issues women employees including low pay, low status, and sexual discrimination. Gaining steam, women networked and organized and successfully lobbied for governmental protections such as the Equal Pay Act of 1963 and the Pregnancy Discrimination Act of 1978. Through a series of redress such as court decisions, laws, and **affirmative action**, women found new rights and opportunities in the workplace. During this time, married women and mothers continued to participate in employment outside the home in increasing numbers. Spurred by consumerism and the need to make more money to buy more things, married women composed almost two-thirds of the female labor force in the mid-1970s. And, as more women emerged as single parents, mothers also entered the workforce in increasing numbers as a matter of economic survival.

WORKING WOMEN

Women work in trades and labor jobs, in professional and managerial jobs, and in the **service industry**. Although women's work is as varied as the women themselves, these traditional categories of workplace employment serve as a useful framework to evaluate women in business. In trade and labor employment, women find themselves at particular odds with male-dominated occupational patterns. For example, blue-collar jobs are often associated with male-dominated unions. In professional and managerial jobs, women continue to enter business only to encounter a phenomena called the "**glass ceiling**." The glass ceiling documents the rise of women only to a certain point within a business (i.e., middle management) and points to sex discrimination as the cause of this limited advancement. As a result of more equal access to higher education and professional programs, women continue to advance themselves within the professional and managerial fields. In the service sector, women dominate business at the lowest levels. Almost 45 percent of all working women are employed within the low-paying and low-status jobs of the service sector.

TRADES AND UNIONS. Although women have joined labor unions since the early 1800s, their significant participation has been hampered for economic, cultural, and social reasons. Until wartime, women and their employers typically viewed the female workforce as temporary employees. These perceptions made women appear to be easily replaced, and diluted the effectiveness of any combined or unionized activities. Additionally, many of the unions strongest tactics, including the strike, were perceived by society and women workers as unfeminine and undesirable. In 1900 only about 2 percent of the female workforce were unionized. Nevertheless, the harsh conditions of early industrial America prevailed upon women to organize and unionize for better working conditions. One of the earliest, the International Ladies Garment Workers Union (ILGWU) represented women in the textile and garment industries. The 1909 Uprising of the 20,000 saw women flexing their union muscles and striking. Throughout the next several decades, women participated more frequently in unions including the American Federation of Labor (AFL) and Congress of Industrial Organizations (CIO). Of the two, the CIO is historically seen as more sympathetic to women. Fearful that low wages for women would decrease wages for men as well, both the AFL and CIO invited women to join and advocated equal pay. Mary Kenney was the first AFL woman organizer in 1891. The major unions, however, often exhibited ambivalent attitudes and actions towards women including refusal to take actions against affiliates that excluded women from membership.

PROFESSIONS AND MANAGEMENT. As women gained more equal access to education and professional programs, their presence began to be felt in the professional and managerial fields. Historically, graduate programs in business denied entry to women. In 1963, Harvard began to admit women into the Graduate School of Business Administration. By 1988-89, women received almost half the undergraduate degrees awarded in business nationally and almost a third of all M.B.A.s. Historically, women gained admittance to managerial and professional positions in traditionally female fields such as librarianship and human resource management. Other more male-dominated professions, however, such as law and medicine, more frequently reflect women's entrance and success. As early as 1869, Arabella Mansfield took and passed the Iowa bar exam. In 1981, Sandra Day O'Connor became the first female Supreme Court judge. In the interim century, women advanced in law and by 1989, 40 percent of all law degrees were awarded to women. Similarly, in medicine, women such as Elizabeth Blackwell (M.D., 1849) proved that women were competent and capable of performing within the professional fields. The American Medical Association began accepting women as members as early as 1876. Yet, until the 1970s, women were poorly represented in all medical fields except nursing. In 1990, women comprised 20 percent of all physicians. Today, women are present in accounting, architecture, engineering, medicine, journalism, psychology, and other professional endeavors. Yet, they remain stymied by a phenomena called the "glass ceiling."

The glass ceiling is a theory that attempts to explain why women do not advance into the uppermost professional and managerial jobs in business. For example, in medicine, only about 10 percent of women faculty members are full professors while almost a third of their male colleagues are full professors. Similar statistics in nearly every managerial or professional category points to the same inequity. In an apparent self-fulfilling pattern, productivity seems connected to the number of senior female positions within the company. Companies such as Motorola, Inc. programatically approach this problem by setting goals and structuring promotion and advancement opportunities that meet their goals. Like Deloitte and Touche, these and other companies recognize women's worth to the profession and competitive advance therein.

One result of the glass ceiling has been the rise of **women entrepreneurs**. By forming their own businesses, women entrepreneurs hope to avoid discriminatory factors and measures that impair their success in the traditionally male business world. Women form businesses at nearly twice the rate of men. And, in the United States, about 6.5 million businesses are owned or controlled by a woman. Some, such as Elizabeth Arden, Helena Rubinstein, and Estee Lauder Inc., made their fortunes in cosmetics while others, such as Olive Ann Mellor-Beech, inherited their businesses when their husbands died. Discrimination is not absent, however, in the entrepreneurial jobs. In 1992, only about 1 percent of all **government contracts** were awarded to women.

SERVICE INDUSTRY. The service industry, so thoroughly dominated by the female labor force, represents another category of employment frequently called the pink-collar jobs. These pink-collar jobs are characterized by low pay and low status. Clerical positions are perhaps the most widely recognized of these positions in the business world. With the advent of the typewriter in the late 1800s, women came forward to apply for and receive employment as typists. While previous male clerical workers had seen these entry level jobs as an effective means to move up within the organization, female workers soon discovered that management relied on breaking down clerical tasks so that workers would be interchangeable. In 1990, 80 percent of all clerical workers were women and more than 25 percent of all working women found themselves in clerical jobs. Retail sales workers account for another large segment of the service sector employment. Since the early 1900s, retail sales clerks have been transformed to cashiers with the restructuring of retail from full-service to self-service format.

WOMEN'S WORTH AND WORK

Early cultural consensus held that women and men enjoyed two different spheres of influence. Men moved within the public sphere of influence, including business and commerce, while women were confined to the private or family sphere of influence. More than any other factor, the issue of sex discrimination influences current promotion and pay practices within the workplace. Sex discrimination emerges from a strong past belief that women belonged in the home environment and not in the business environment. Two central tenants of sex discrimination hold that women do not need the money of employment since they will be supported by a man and that women are not as qualified as men. The Equal Pay Act of 1963 and the Civil Rights Act of 1964 provided protective legislation for women and enabled them to legally contest discriminatory practices in pay and promotion. As a result of these and other laws, bona fide occupational qualifications exist to define and determine the extent to which sex relates to ability to successfully complete a job. The **Equal Employment Opportunity Commission (EEOC)** is the watchdog governmental agency set up to deter sex discrimination in the workplace. Nevertheless, both historically and in current settings, women earn less than men for the same work. **Comparable worth**, or the principle that equal work deserves equal pay, continues to evoke considerable controversy since many fear that male wages will decline rather than women's wages increase.

Three factors account for the origins of the low pay of women. First, women workers were always seen as merely supplementing their husband's pay. Even unmarried women were perceived to be transitional and on their way to domestic life. Under these assumptions, women did not warrant the training or education to move to higher-paying jobs even if they had been available. Second, early professional positions in nursing, education, and librarianship were outgrowths of charitable and philanthropic work. Done for charity and "good works," the pay for these jobs reflected remuneration as an irrelevant part of employment. Finally, the historical involvement of women in domestic or housework-type employment (e.g., sewing, cleaning) tied women's employment to traditional household duties. These household duties, since they were unpaid in a familial situation, received low pay in a commercial situation.

WOMEN'S ISSUES IN BUSINESS

Married women, mothers, older women, and women of color are all present in the business world along with their single, white counterparts. In 1989 almost 30 million married women worked outside the home. In 1990, 65 percent of mothers with children under the age of 18 worked outside the home and 14 percent of women aged 65-69 years worked outside the home. In the coming years, women of color will compose the fastest-growing segment of the labor force. Because of their dual role in the home and at work, women bring to the job new and previously unconsidered issues in employment. Some of these issues include child care, elder care, scheduling, and financial considerations.

As more and more single female parents enter the business world, the need for child care increases. From a business perspective, this is imperative to ensure the continued supply of female workers. In the early nineteenth and twentieth century, women were normally left to their own devices to arrange for child care. Neighbors and relatives filled this need and, when unavailable, children were simply left home alone. At the turn of the century, women such as Josephine Dodge spearheaded philanthropic efforts to establish child-care centers for working mothers. Dormant until the 1970s, the lack of available child-care reflected society's preference for women to stay at home rather than work. Only during wartime did the government intervene with subsidized child-care arrangements to further the employment of women. With the advent of the 1960s, societal attention turned seriously to child-care efforts. And, in the 1970s, the White House Conference on Children addressed child-care issues by recommending federal funding. Rather than directly subsidizing child-care needs, federal tax reform in 1976 and 1978 offered tax relief for funds spent on child care. A relatively small number of businesses provide child-care arrangements as part of an employment package. Companies such as Boeing Corporation offer 24-hour hotline services and others, such as Apple Computer, Inc. offer onsite facilities. For small businesses, subsidization of child-care can be prohibitively expensive. In 1990, child care accounts for the fourth-largest expense in most working families.

As life expectancy increases, working women are often faced with a situation called "the sandwich generation." Caring for children and aging parents, female workers also bring to the workplace the issue of elder care. Similar in many ways—economically and socially—to child care, elder care is expensive and often requires specialized medical attendants. Almost three-quarters of all caregivers of aging relatives are women. The Family and Medical Leave Act of 1993 addresses both child and family needs by requiring 12 weeks of unpaid leave annually for the birth or adoption of a child or the serious illness of a family member.

As a result of conflicting family roles and responsibilities, women embrace the idea of flexible scheduling. Flexible scheduling allows women to set their own hours within limits set by corporate policy or practice. While companies must bear the costs of complicated schedules, they reap the benefits of increased productivity as women arrange schedules to meet their familial responsibilities. Almost 60 percent of all women would prefer a job with flexible hours. Other arrangements, such as job sharing1, allow women to share jobs with other women in order to accommodate home demands.

Pension plans that incorporate early vesting and portability accommodate women's more frequent entries and exits from the business world. Since women have not, however, typically received the same benefits, at retirement many women find themselves with considerably less financial security than their male counterparts. Pension plans that require women to pay more to participate than men are illegal since the 1978 Supreme Court ruling on *Los Angeles v. Manhart*.

[Tona Henderson]

FURTHER READING:

Amott, Teresa. *Caught in the Crisis: Women and the U.S. Economy Today*. New York: Monthly Review Press, 1993.

Amott, Teresa L., and Julie A. Matthaei. *Race, Gender & Work*. Boston: South End Press, 1991.

Baron, Ava, ed. *Work Engendered: Toward A New History of American Labor*. Ithaca: Cornell University Press, 1991.

Boris, Eileen. *Home To Work: Motherhood and the politics of industrial homework in the United States*. Cambridge: Cambridge University Press, 1994.

Bullock, Susan. *Women and Work*. London: Zed Books Ltd., 1994.

Chauvin, Keith W., and Ronald A. Ash. "Gender Earnings Differentials in Total Pay, Base Pay, and Contingent Pay." *Industrial Labor Relations & Review* July, 1994, pp. 634-639.

Cook, Alice H., Val R. Lorwin, and Arlene Kaplan Daniels. *The Most Difficult Revolution: Women and Trade Unions*. Ithaca, NY: Cornell University Press, 1992.

Coolidge, Leslie, and Danielle D'Angelo. "Family Issues to Shape the Profession's Future." *CPA Journal*. May, 1994, pp. 16-21.

"Dependent Care Is Valuable Support Tool for Employers, Employees." *Employee Benefit Plan Review* August, 1993, pp. 54-55.

Glazer, Nona Y. *Women's Paid and Unpaid Labor: The Work Transfer in Health Care and Retailing*. Philadelphia: Temple University Press, 1993.

Groneman, Carol, and Mary Beth Norton, eds. *To Toil the Livelong Day*. Ithaca: Cornell University Press, 1987.

Guteman, Roberta. "Changing the Face of Management." *Working Woman* November, 1994, pp. 21-23.

Hand, Shirley, and Robert A. Zawacki. "Family-Friendly Benefits: More Than A Frill." *HR Magazine* October, 1994, pp. 79-84.

Karsten, Margaret Foegen. *Management and Gender: Issues and Attitude*. Westport CN: Quorum Books, 1994.

Kassam, Shayde. "The Changing Face of the Workforce." *PEM: Plant Engineering & Maintenance*. Winter/Spring, 1994, p. 12.

Koziara, Karen Shallcross, Michael H. Mosckow, and Lucretia Tanner. *Working Women: Past, Present and Future*. Washington, D.C.: Bureau of National Affairs, 1987.

Kwolek-Folland, Angel. *Engendering Business: Men and Women in the Corporate Office 1870-1930*. Baltimore: Johns Hopkins University Press, 1994.

Nichols, Nancy A. "Whatever Happened to Rosie the Riveter?" *Harvard Business Review*. July/August, 1993, pp. 54-62.

Perkins, Anne G. "Women in the Workplace: The Ripple Effect." *Harvard Business Review*. November/December, 1994, page 15.

Schneider, Dorothy, and Carl Schneider. *Women in the Workplace*. Santa Barbara: ABL-CIO, 1993.

Waldrop, Judith. "What Do Working Women Want?" *American Demographics*. September, 1994, pp. 36-37.

Women's Action Coalition. *The Facts About Women*. New York: New Press, 1993.

Zellner, Wendy. "Women Entrepreneurs." *Business Week*. April 18, 1994 pp. 104-110.

WOMEN ENTREPRENEURS

Today there are over six million women business owners and by the year 2000, reports estimate over one half of all small businesses will be owned by women. The increasing role women are playing as business owners is part of the overall impact women are having on society today. Women in the media are bring new insights in reporting; women in the movies are featured in expanded roles beyond those wife, girlfriend, or mother; women in medicine are offering new dimensions to caring for patients and more research on women's health issues; women in law are seeking justice for crimes committed against women; and women in politics today represent the largest constituency in history.

While the trend of women owning businesses is growing, it is certainly not new. Women have owned and operated businesses since the beginnings of American history and much earlier in other parts of the world. They rarely were recognized, however, or given credit for their efforts. Often women were "invisible" as they worked side by side with their husband in business and may have only stepped into the leadership position when their husband died. Many recognizable businesses today are owned and operated by the wife or daughter of the founder. Two well-known examples are: Tootsie Roll which is controlled by a woman and her four daughters, and the *Playboy* empire, taken over by Hugh Hefner's daughter, Christie Hefner.

In other cases, women began a business on their own or they were the stimulus to begin one. Lila Bell Acheson Wallace helped to start *Reader's Digest*. Knox Gelatin was started by Mrs. Knox. Pepperidge Farms was started by a mother to create food products to help her asthmatic son. Josephine Dickson and her husband created Band-Aids. Susan Hoover, gave the name to Hoover Vacuum Sweepers. Elizabeth and Olivia Norris brought Procter and Gamble together and Alice Marriott ran a root beer stand with her husband Bill, which was the beginning of the Marriott hotel and food business. Eleanor Roosevelt operated her own school.

TRENDS IN INDUSTRIES

Most operated businesses in the service sector, which coincides with most new women-owned businesses being started today. Women tend to launch businesses in the industry where they have had direct experience, mostly in traditional fields. This explains the lack of women business owners in nontraditional fields such as manufacturing. However, this is slowly changing. From 1980 to 1989, women-owned sole proprietorships increased over 175% in mining, construction, manufacturing, and transportation.

Today 60 percent of women-owned businesses are concentrated in retail and service sectors and in traditional industries such as cosmetics, food, fashion, and personal care. Famous women business owners in these industries include: Mary Kay Ash, Mrs. Fields, Estée Lauder, and Donna Karan.

Unfortunately, U.S. Census Bureau statistics lag by several years and many questions about women entrepreneurs are still unanswered due to the lack of available data. Today, women-owned businesses are a vital economic force which, according to the National Association of Women Business Owners employ people more than the Fortune 500 firms. Also known is that most women conduct business as sole proprietor. In 1989, women owned 31.3 percent of all nonfarm sole proprietorships. Women own 83 percent of all social service firms and 61 percent of all educational firms.

More and more women are becoming role models each year. Today, numerous women own and manage billion dollar businesses in a variety industries with several thousand employees.

REASONS TO START

Women start businesses for different reasons than their male counterparts, and women tend to start bussinesses about ten years later then men. Motherhood, lack of management experience, and traditional socialization can all be reasons for delayed entry into a career as a business owner. Most women never plan to own a business or even consider business ownership as a career option. In fact, over 30 percent started a business due to some traumatic event, such as divorce, discrimination due to pregnancy or the corporate glass ceiling, the health of a family member, or economic reasons such as a layoff.

A new talent pool of women entrepreneurs today—is coming from those leaving corporate America to chart their own destiny. Many of these women have developed financial expertise and bring experience in manufacturing or nontraditional fields. Armed with more management experience and business savvy, these women, will be the trendsetters of tomorrow.

Family businesses may indeed be the best training ground for women entrepreneurs as 78 percent of women business owners recently polled mentioned some type of family business connection. While men start businesses for growth opportunities and profit potential, women most often found businesses for personal goals such as achievement, accomplishment, or stepping in to "help" their family. Women consider financial success as an external confirmation of their ability rather than as a primary goal or motivation to start a business. According to Joline Godfrey, author of Our Wildest Dreams, women gave the following reasons for start businesses:

- Happiness/Self Fulfillment: 38%
- Achievement/Challenge: 30%
- Helping Others: 20%
- Sales Growth/Profit: 12%

THE DEVELOPMENT OF A MANAGEMENT STYLE

Despite gains, women business owners still have many barriers to overcome before obtaining truly equal opportunities in the marketplace. Many of these challenges are rooted in childhood socialization which plays a critical role in the choices adults make throughout their lifetime. These early experiences are the beginnings of a management style developed by both males and females.

The realms of family and business have been separated since the Industrial Revolution. This has resulted in different gender roles and expectations based on different socialization experiences. Men and women in families and in business are still struggling with the results of these forces today because these roles carry deep-rooted emotions that are slow to change. Gender socialization has been described as the lifelong process of developing attitudes, skills, expectations, behaviors, and values. The study of gender focuses on people's perceptions and how males and females differ socially rather than biologically.

This process begins at birth when little girls are dressed in pink and boys in blue. Girls are described as cute and boys as strong. Girls are given baby dolls and household items and boys receive combat and sports items. Parents then begin to reward the ''right'' behavior and punish ''unacceptable'' behavior according to their preconceived ideas developed from society.

The management style people use as adults is developed at this early time in their lives. Girls begin to learn skills which are not conducive to today's business world. Females are taught to be sensitive and tactful; they learn to be ''helpless'' and to be dependent on their fathers, rather than to be self-assertive and self-reliant. They are taught to be economically dependent. Parents also protect their daughters rather than prepare them and are reluctant to give females much freedom to take risks.

During this early period, females learn to collaborate and work toward the good of the group, and they nurture and serve as peacemakers. They do not learn about winners and losers but rather they learn to feel responsible for the welfare of the group. Girls also attribute their own success to luck, effort, and ease of the task; whereas they attribute failure personally, ascribing it to their lack of ability. In March 1992, the American Association of University Women released a study titled, ''How Schools Shortchange Girls,'' documenting how girls are called on less, encouraged less, and overall get unequal treatment in the classroom setting.

Recent research revealed that many fathers' aim to protect their daughters rather than prepare them for the realities of today's world. Women business owners are succeeding despite the negative comments from their fathers such as: ''Don't worry your pretty little head about business,'' ''Business is not for women, marry a good businessman,'' ''Women should not be too smart or compete too much.''

In contrast, boys learn traits such as aggressiveness, competitiveness, and dominance—particularly when playing with war toys and sporting games. They learn strategy and tactics needed to win. And they learn that if they lose, there is always another opportunity. They are called on more in the classroom and guess more often.

Family, siblings, and peer groups have been identified as additional settings in which the unequal socialization takes place. Stereotypes are reinforced daily through television, magazines, and radio song lyrics. Families also set rules which are gender based; female roles are inside the house with cooking, cleaning, and laundry and the male roles are outside with grass cutting and taking out the trash.

Women organize their lives around the needs of the family, whereas men organize their lives around the demands of their work. Women's work roles have been second to executing the material, emotional, and social life of the family. It is not surprising then that women consider business ownership as a way to have more flexible time with their family.

CHALLENGES FACED BY WOMEN BUSINESS OWNERS

This lifelong socialization process provides a basis for most of the challenges women business owners face in the marketplace. The process does not provide most women with the skills and traits needed to compete as men do in today's business world and mores, nor does it educate most men about how the natural talents of women can be used to advantage in business. Until now, women have been to believe educated that they are the ones who need to cope and adjust to these issues. Since women business owners have gained an economic clout over the past 20 years, however, now businesses that have traditionally done business with males are beginning to recognize they should also make adjustments towards the needs of women.

Since this socialization process has taught women not to think big, to be risk adverse, and to fear financial issues, most are undercapitalized in their businesses and have limited access to resources such as financing know-how and the male network. It is not surprising then to learn that three out of four women-owned businesses started out with their own financing of less than $5,000. Today 38 percent still have no bank financing; 52 percent have used credit cards in their business as compared to 18 percent of all business owners.

Study after study confirms women business owners are not getting equal treatment at financial institutions. Sixty-seven percent of women business owners report difficulty in working with financial institutions as compared to 55 percent of all firms. Over one half of women business owners believed they faced gender discrimination when dealing with a loan officer; therefore, most women-owned businesses actually grow their businesses by reinvesting profits. This distressful scenario also carries over to the government sector where women-owned firms receive only 1.5 percent of the contracts of the total $200 billion which the federal government spends annually on goods and services.

Women often believed their professional advisers did not expect them to know a lot and spoke down to them, particularly when they were starting in business. The women felt an unjustified request was made on them when they were required to obtain their husband's guarantee in order to procure a bank loan. Women felt bankers were patronizing and this interfered with building relationship with their bankers. Many women said their personal ability to manage the venture was continually being questioned by male bankers. Women declared they wanted more details from their advisers, they wanted options and alternatives—not prescriptive advice, and not lectures.

Most women business owners do not have business degrees and most were never exposed in college to business ownership as a career option. Even today students have access to relatively few resources such as books, lectures, or role models of women business owners.

Furthermore, in business schools where most of the professional advisers today were trained, the male model of business is still being taught by an overwhelming majority of male professors. Examples of women entrepreneurs have been left out of textbooks, and rarely is ''she'' the business owner used as the example or case study. Neither the women nor the men students are learning about the natural abilities and talents women are using to succeed as business owners today. Unfortunately, without some very strong initiatives on the part of educators, the process will be slow to change.

One area where women business owners are getting shortchanged is in the area of procurement, or the selling of their goods and services to city, state, and federal governments. Fewer than five percent of the women-owned firms in the United States are certified to do business with their state government and only 1.5 percent of the billions of dollars in federal contracts go to women-owned firms.

If a company is 51 percent woman owned and controlled by a woman they can obtain certification and bid on government contracts. Many women, however, may have heard it is difficult to do business with the government or believe the government will not be interested in what they are selling. Another myth is that government contracts are too large for small businesses (especially women-owned businesses) and one needs to be a legal and contract expert to bid on government contracts. In actuality, many govern-

ments have created set-aside programs which specifically help women-owned businesses in the process.

STRENGTHS OF WOMEN BUSINESS OWNERS

Despite the many challenges women face, this early socialization has given women specific traits and abilities which define the female model of business ownership. This different management style can be an asset and one from which men can learn. The style can be described as more cooperative than the competitive male model which now serves as the model taught in business schools. This style is often further developed through volunteer activities in early adulthood.

The cooperative style naturally used by most women comes from their early experiences and focuses on the welfare of the group. Participation is shared among the employees with concerns given for their ideas and needs. The style often extends to social issues which are frequently driving forces within the company. The business strategy is formed through active listening and educational experiences and focuses on issues in addition to just the bottom line. Strengths in terms of building relationships are normally a asset with customers and suppliers, and in the international marketplace. In order to overcome the obstacles they face, women often come up with creative, out of the ordinary methods to help further their goal.

Dr. Gene Landrum researched male and female geniuses and defined them by the following variables:

	Female	**Male**
Brain Orientation	Generalized	Specialized
Ethical Values	Inter-relationships	Intra-relationships
Behavioral Styles	Attachments	Separations
Personal Needs	Relationships	Individually
Stress	Verbalize	Physical Aggression
Leadership	Nurture	Lecture
Decision Making	Feeling	Thinking
Communications	Negotiate	Intimidate
Emotional Needs	Respect	Ego Power

These variables help define the cooperative style that has developed from early socialization of females. Once aware of these traits they become more apparent to observation. This cooperative style is easier to recognize in women business owners where the women are not conforming to a culture set by males in a large corporation. This new, distinctive business is one that we all can learn from. The new model of business for the next century will combine the talents of this cooperative style used by women with the more traditional business approach.

THE FUTURE

With more and more women opening businesses every day the future for the next generation of business owners is bright. While the business world is normally slow to change, economic advantages of women-owned firms will help speed the process. As more young women see a wider range of women business owner role models they will be more encouraged. As mothers socialize their daughters to the business world during their preadolescent years, more are likely to choose business ownership as a career option.

RESOURCES

A number of resources now exist to support women entrepreneurs. In 1988 Congress authorized the Small Business Administration Office of Women's Business Ownership. They recently created a "Low-Doc" loan program which makes it easier for women entrepreneurs to obtain SBA financing. The SBA also has established a Women's Network for Entrepreneurial Training (WNET) which links women mentors with protegees. Small Business Development Centers (SBDC) are also co-sponsored by the SBA and operate in every state. They offer free and confidential counseling to anyone interested in small business.

Many states now have a Women's Business Advocate to promote women entrepreneurs within the state. These advocates are represented by an organization, the National Association of Women Business Advocates.

A number of trade associations now represent women entrepreneurs. The National Association of Women Business Owners is the largest group throughout the country. There are also some smaller regional groups which can be located through the Yellow Pages or local chambers of commerce. The American Business Women's Association provides leadership, networking, and educational support. The National Association of Female Executives makes women aware of the need to plan for career and financial success. In addition, approximately 25 Yellow Page directories throughout the country which list women-owned businesses.

SEE ALSO: Entrepreneurship

[Cynthia Ianarelli]

FURTHER READING:

Duff, Carolyn. When Women Work Together. Conari Press, 1993.

Godfrey, Joline. Our Wildest Dreams. Harper Business, 1992.

Harrison, Patricia. America's New Women Entrepreneurs, Acropolis Books, Washington, D.C. 1986.

Heim, Pat, and Susan Golant. Hardball for Women, Winning at the Game of Business. Penquin Publishing, 1992.

Helgesen, Sally. The Female Advantage. Doubleday, 1990.

Hisrich, Robert, and Candida Brush. The Women Entrepreneur; Starting, Financing and Managing a Successful New Business. Lexington Books, 1986.

Landrum, Gene. Female Genius. Prometheus Books, 1994.

Nierenberg, Juliet, and Irene Ross. Women and the Art of Negotiating. Fireside, 1985.

Ohio Women Business Leaders Directory, Ohio Department of Development, 1992.

Pinson, Linda, and Jerry Jinnett. Women Entrepreneurs, 33 Personal Stories of Success. Upstart Publishing, 1992.

Silver, A. David. Enterprising Women. Amacom, 1994.

Sinclair, Carole. When Women Retire. Crown Publishers, 1992.

Steel, Dawn. They Can Kill You, But They Can't Eat You, Lessons from the Front, Pocket Books, 1993.

White, Shelby. What Every Women Should Know About Her Husband's Money. Turtl Bay, 1992.

Zuckerman, Laurie. On Your Own: A Women's Guide to Building a Business. Upstart Publishing, 1990.

WORD PROCESSING

The use of **computers** in the composition, editing, storage, or printing of written language is referred to as word processing. The aim of word processors, the machines used to perform these tasks, has traditionally been the production of printed documents, although the resulting text can be disseminated through other media, particularly magnetic disks or CD-ROMs.

HISTORY OF WORD PROCESSING

The first machines able to record typed information for reuse were the automatic typewriters of the 1930s, which used rolls of paper tape to record keystrokes. IBM's MT/ST (Magnetic Tape/Selectric Typewriter), introduced in 1964, worked in a similar manner; however, its storage medium, magnetic tape, could store more information and could also be erased and reused. Limited text editing was possible with this device; however, corrections in the middle of the document had to fit into the same space on the tape as the characters they replaced. IBM later added a model replacing magnetic tape with magnetic cards (the Mag Card Selectric Typewriter, or MC/ST) which became the early standard for the word processing industry.

The industry developed swiftly during the 1970s as such companies as Wang Laboratories, Olivetti, and DEC entered the field. Technical developments such as cathode-ray tube monitors and microchips advanced the capabilities of word processors far beyond any kind of typewriter. The Xerox Bravo, introduced in the mid-1970s, allowed users to make font, formatting, and graphics changes easily using a mouse-controlled pointer (a Bravo innovation).

Large metropolitan newspapers were among the first to embrace word processors. Law and real estate offices, with their need to produce lengthy, largely standard contracts, were also enthusiastic. By 1992, 95 percent of all secretaries used word processing software, up from 71 percent in 1987. As experts had predicted, the use of word processors would become commonplace among not only secretaries and writers, but among all types of professionals, as well as students.

APPLICATIONS OF WORD PROCESSING

The production of printed documents before word processing was an arduous task. Standard contracts had to be typed individually. Minor corrections could require whole pages to be retyped. Word processing applications have allowed computers, which are well-suited to repetitive tasks, to relieve much of this tedium.

It has been estimated that a secretary supplied with a word processor has the potential of being at least three times more efficient than one using a typewriter. Ironically, the formation of centralized corporate word processing centers, justified by the high cost of early word processors, increased turnaround greatly for many managers. Even simple letters would sometimes require days to be completed and returned. After the price of word processing systems fell, aspects of the centralized system remained, partly due to the ease of monitoring clerical production (such as by keystroke counts). By then personal computers (and laptops) had found their way onto the desks (and into the laps) of managers and professionals themselves.

Besides typing letters and memos, word processors have other valuable applications. Most modern word processors can retrieve data from databases to create individualized mass mailings or address labels; graphics, charts, and tables can be imported from graphics or spreadsheet programs. With advances in formatting and graphics power, many word processors have become the equivalent of **desktop publishing** systems for creating books, brochures, booklets and other documents. The resulting products can be either printed or transmitted electronically via modem or fax.

Word processors have been described as "user seductive," encouraging deep involvement with the writing process, whether or not an improvement in writing occurs. Some studies assert that much experience is required with a word processor in order to match the writing quality and fluency of handwriting. Their results, however, do not account for an important difference in the quality of the end results: an essay written on paper usually must be typed before it can be disseminated in a business environment or submitted in a classroom.

It has also been asserted that the seductiveness and ease of making revisions encourages writers to linger over a document rather than moving on to the next one. An early study of word processing in business writing found that users of the machines tended to write longer communications. Nevertheless, word processing encourages a conversational style, making documents easier to read.

In another study, students using word processors to complete a writing assignment eagerly used built-in programs to check spelling and style while their counterparts writing by hand seldom consulted printed dictionaries at all. Although word processors are capable of inserting graphics into a document and in most cases displaying them on-screen, the students using them were less likely to use diagrams (e.g., boxes, arrows) to solve structural or conceptual problems than those writing by hand.

Some impediments to using a word processor include a lack of confidence in typing skills and a mistrust of computers or technology in general. Also, the practice of writing on paper is one which has survived for thousands of years; many people do not want to lose the simple tangibility of handwriting.

Other barriers are the health risks which have been associated with word processing, particularly in high-volume environments. Eyestrain is exacerbated by glare, which can be reduced by positioning monitor screens at right angles to windows and other light sources. The risk of carpal tunnel syndrome and other wrist injuries can be reduced by careful positioning of the keyboard and monitor or by using a wrist support.

Engineers have been quite active in developing alternate ways of interacting with computers. Speech recognition technology improves performance by registering commands in situations where the user's hands are not free. It also tends to reduce errors in entering commands. Speech recognition has other promising applications, including transcription of dictated speech. Other innovative aids to entering text include "reactive" programs (commonly used by disabled individuals) that present a menu of word choices after a few characters have been entered.

Another category of data input is "document capture," in which printed documents are optically scanned and converted into text files by optical character recognition (OCR) programs. A facsimile image can be similarly scanned and processed, and the resulting file of text used in word processing applications.

WORD PROCESSING FEATURES

All word processing systems share several common components. All have a keyboard similar to a typewriter's, with at least a few extra keys added. Like typewriters, they generally have some provision for printing characters on a page. Many different technologies—from the "golf ball" typing element of the Selectric to lasers—have been used for computer printers. Unlike typewriters, however, word processing systems have the ability to store text so that it can be reprinted or edited. The mechanism modern word processors use to store this information is the computer, hence the other components of the system: the central processing unit, the monitor (which the early memory typewriters lacked), and some type of storage device, such as a disk drive.

A word processing system's capability to enter changes in a file is performed by a component of the program called the editor, which also provides a means to undo changes in a document and to store backup copies. Search-and-replace functions are also provided by this part of the program. Editor/formatters or WYSIWYG (What You See Is What You Get) systems, such as most Windows- and Macintosh-based word processors, support the display of both graphics and text on-screen.

In order to control the appearance of documents, word processors insert certain codes, called "markup," into documents. These codes apply to four levels; two of which, the punctuational and the presentational, are part of the vocabulary of typing and even handwriting. Punctuational markup consists of the spaces and punctuation marks used to separate words, phrases, and sentences. Presentational markup adds spaces after headings and paragraphs, puts in page numbers and indents, adds bullets to lists of items, and handles other similar tasks.

Procedural markup consists of codes that instruct programs to perform certain functions, such as changing the font. These codes are inserted into a document by either specialized function keys (as in WordPerfect), selection of an option from a menu (as in MacWrite), or by a special series of characters called embedded commands, which are typed directly into the document (as in many older word processing systems). These codes and embedded commands are displayed on-screen but not in the printed document. Descriptive markup, the final level, describes the text logically. For example, a section of text may be marked as a footnote or a heading to be formatted by another level of the program: this provides the capability of electronically searching for footnotes, headings, or other sections of a document.

Automatic spell checking is favorite facility of word processors as manually proofreading for spelling can be tedious. An automated spelling checker compares words in a document with a list of reference words (its lexicon) and alerts the user to those words that are not on the list. Double words are another typing error easily overlooked by human eyes which most modern word processors can address quite easily.

Several programs have been developed for analyzing and correcting other elements of writing, such as diction, style, and grammar. Problems in diction can be found by searching for trite combinations of words. Style analysis is based on measurements of sentence length, word length, sentence types (e.g. simple, compound, complex), verb usage, and sentence beginnings. As these techniques are perfected, the effort continues to yoke computers to increasingly sophisticated text processing, such as producing abstracts and translations, and other tasks formerly the exclusive territory of people.

[Frederick C. Ingram]

FURTHER READING:

Arend, Mark. "Speech System Targets Manual Typing Jobs." *ABA Banking Journal.* October, 1993, pp. 64-66.

Blanchard, Carroll Henry. *The Early Word Processors.* Educators—Project IV.

Durand, Douglas E., Rex O. Bennett, and Samuel Betty. "What Does Information Technology 'Do' to Business Communications?: Two Empirical Studies." *Information & Management.* October, 1987, pp. 111-117.

"The Emergence of Electronic Publication Technology." *AT&T Technical Journal.* July/August, 1989, pp. 2-110.

Foster, Timothy R. V., and Alfred Glossbrenner. *Word Processing for Executives and Professionals.* Van Nostrand Reinhold.

Garson, Barbara. *The Electronic Sweatshop: How Computers Are Transforming the Office of the Future into the Factory of the Past.* Simon and Schuster.

Jaderstrom, Susan, Leonard Kruk, and Joanne Miller. *Professional Secretaries International Complete Office Handbook: The Secretary's Guide to Today's Electronic Office.* Random House.

Karl, Lewis R., Michael Pettey, and Ben Shneiderman. "Speech versus Mouse Commands for Word Processing: An Empirical Evaluation." *International Journal of Man-Machine Studies.* October, 1993, pp. 686-687.

Kellogg, Ronald T., and Suzanne Mueller. "Performance Amplification and Process Restructuring in Computer-Based Writing." *International Journal of Man-Machine Studies.* July, 1993, pp. 33-49.

Kurzweil, Raymond. "Voice-Activated Word Processing." *Byte.* April, 1992, p. 156.

Lee, Yvonne. "Pen Software Processes Handwritten Notes." *InfoWorld.* June 14, 1993, p. 8.

Major, Michael J. "Spelling, Grammar, and Style Go Electronic." *Managing Office Technology.* April, 1994, pp. 18-21.

Price, Jonathan, and Linda Pinneau Urban. *The Definitive Word Processing Book.* Penguin.

Roth, Stephen F. *The Computer Edge: Microcomputer Trends/Uses in Publishing.* R. R. Bowker Company.

Smith, Peter D. *An Introduction to Text Processing.* The MIT Press.

Unger, Sandra. "Why Patent Searchers (and Others) Need KEDIT When They Already Have a Word Processor." *Database*. August, 1994, pp. 63-67.

Waldrop, Judith. "More Than a Typist." *American Demographics*. April, 1994, p. 4.

Wolfe, Edward, Sandra Bolton, Brian Feltovich, and Catherine Welch. *A Comparison of Word-Processed and Handwritten Essays from a Standardized Writing Assignment*. ACT.

Yakal, Kathy. "Windows Word Processing: Power Costs." *Accounting Technology*. March, 1994, pp. 55-62.

Zinsser, William. *Writing with a Word Processor*. Harper & Row.

WORK SCHEDULES

SEE: Family Leave; Hours of Labor

WORKERS' COMPENSATION

Approximately every 19 seconds someone is injured in an on-the-job accident. But whether or not the injured individual has health insurance, if the injury occurred on the job it is very likely that the injury will be cared for and the worker's lost income replaced under the workers' compensation insurance system.

The workers' compensation system developed to provide medical coverage and/or income replacement for workers who were injured or became ill or died as a result of workplace conditions or accidents. These laws which require an employer to purchase insurance that provides care and income replacement were developed in the early industrial age. During that period machine industry workers were being injured at a high rate. Their only remedy for medical care and to replace income lost due to days off of work was to sue the employer in court for negligence. For many this was impossible and when it could happen, the cost to employers was very high. Both employers and employees found that a legal system of compensation whereby the employee gave up the right to sue, but was guaranteed legal protection and coverage for the injuries was preferable.

The first workers' compensation law was passed in Germany in 1883. The rest of industrialized Europe quickly followed suit. The first U.S. state law that passed and remained in force was in Wisconsin in 1911. By 1949 every state had a workers' compensation law.

In 1916, the U.S. Congress passed the Federal Employees Compensation Act providing protection to federal workers. The passage of this law, while it had no legal impact on any private, state or local workers, aided the cause of state workers' compensation laws by providing a national example of caring for employees. Today the federal government also administers the provisions of the Longshoremen's and Harbor Workers' Compensation Act, which provides benefits for longshoremen, and the Black Lung Act, which provides benefits for coal mine workers who suffer from Black Lung disease. Aside from these three exceptions, the rest of the more than 93.7 million wage and salary workers (as of 1989) are covered under the varying provisions of the 50 state laws and those of the District of Columbia.

Each State has its own workers' compensation law and administration. Although provisions of each State law differ greatly, the underlying principle is the same—that employers should assume the costs of injuries, illnesses, and deaths that occur on the job, without regard to fault, and partially replace wage income lost. While income replacement under workers' compensation is usually a percentage of the actual wage, is it counted as a transfer payment and, as such, is not subject to federal income tax.

Except for a few states, Coverage is compulsory for all private employers. Employers who reject coverage they also lose the common law defense for suits filed by employees for negligence. Some state laws exempt certain categories of employees from coverage. Those most likely to be excluded from coverage are domestics, agricultural workers, and manual laborers.

In 1989, employers paid almost $48 billion in premiums, approximately ten percent more than was paid in 1988. In that same year, $34.3 billion was paid out in benefits—approximately $20.9 billion in partial compensation for lost wages and $13.4 billion in medical expenses. This $34.3 billion in payments exceeded the 1988 level by about 11.7 percent. Employers pay all of the costs in workers' compensation.

Increasing costs have led employers to a deeper interest in on-the-job safety since insurance premiums for workers' compensation are often based on loss ratio. A loss ratio is defined by the Social Security Administration as the proportion of the premium dollar that is returned to the worker as cash or medical benefits.

Generally, there are three different methods available for employers to insure workers for the required workers' compensation protection. These are state insurance funds, private insurance, and self-insurance. The latter is seen as a cost saving method for many safety-oriented firms. Where states permit it, many large employers now self-insure and many small employers form groups to insure themselves and decrease the risks. Premiums paid out reflect the payment of benefits and the cost of administering the program, policy writing, claims investigations and adjustments, allocation of reserves for long-term accrued disabilities, and other administrative costs.

Changes to state workers' compensation laws are made by state legislatures. In 1993, changes mandated by states included measures to implement managed health care as a way to save money for employers, reduce fraud, and improve safety in the workplace.

Fraud is always a concern. But under the workers' compensation program there is also the question not only of legitimacy of the injury but of legitimacy of the place of injury. The system only covers injuries at the workplace injuries or related to workplace activity. If a worker injures his or her back over the weekend while doing yard work he or she is not covered, yet the injury may cost time from the job. The extension of workers' compensation into the full life of the worker and into caring for the family as a whole has been under study by many. In 1992, four states—Alabama, Georgia, California, and Maine—began to examine ways in which workers' compensation might be added to a health insurance plan for the general population. The federal Office of Workers' Compensation publishes a review of state workers' compensation legislative activity each year in the January issue of the *Monthly Labor Review*.

For more information on your responsibilities as an employer or your rights as an employee, contact your state office of workers' compensation for information on the state law.

[Joan Leotta]

FURTHER READING:

Nelson, William J., Jr. "Workers' Compensation, Coverage, Benefits, Costs, 1989." *Social Security Bulletin*. Spring, 1992, pp. 51-56.

WORKFORCE

Workforce is the total number of all workers and all workers available to a nation, project, industry, and the like. The U.S. Department of Labor (DOL) and U.S. industry also use this definition.

The U.S. Bureau of Labor Statistics (BLS), conceptualizes the workforce, called the "labor force," as "all employed and unemployed civilians." Children under age 16 are not included in the count. Other groups not included are those in school, engaged in housework, unable to work (due to illness or other cause), retired, or those who have left the workforce voluntarily, including discouraged workers.

The U.S. Bureau of the Census collects data that is analyzed and tabulated at BLS. These reports are published monthly by BLS in *Employment and Earnings*. In addition, each June issue of the magazine provides data on nearly 600 additional industries for which monthly data is not available. Many times, articles or even entire issues of the *Monthly Labor Review*, published by the U.S. DOL are devoted to workforce data. These articles compare the U.S. workforce to that of other countries, analyze the workforce in particular industries, and look at the workforce by education, race, age, or ethnic group to better understand the makeup of the workforce.

Workforce data is also reported by occupation. The Occupational Employment Statistics (OES) is a periodic survey mailed to a number of nonfarm establishments. On the survey, employee hours are reported by occupation for the actual number of hours worked. The occupations are categorized according to the **Standard Industrial Classification (SIC)** code or number for each type of workplace. The BLS *SIC Manual* is available in most public libraries.

Studies of the composition of the workforce benefit both industry and the individual. The current method of defining workforce was introduced in the 1930s. Before then there was no measurement of workforce available, only a count of the number of workers on an actual job. Industry needs to know how to reach workers, what skills they have, and how to plan for industry needs, something which today's measurements and forecasts allow.

The National Association of Manufacturers (NAM), joined with the U.S. DOL in November 1991 in a joint project known as "A Partnership in Work Force Readiness." The project's goal was to shape policies that help management and workers deal with predicted changes and aim toward making U.S. manufacturing more competitive globally. Then-president of NAM, Jerry Jasinowski, stated that the reports that came out of that project in 1992 discussed "the results of our current efforts to assist companies in meeting specific challenges to achieving high performance workplaces in America's manufacturing sector." The key elements noted in those reports were the need to keep pace with technological changes; to achieve higher productivity by being ready to reorganize work, training patterns, and education; and for flexibility in the workplace. The report also acknowledged the needs of workers, line managers, and upper management to understand, monitor, and enhance the skills of a culturally diverse workplace so that the United States will be competitive in a global marketplace.

Workforce 2000, a U.S. Department of Labor study undertaken to predict the workforce needs for the next century, showed that the greatest future demand will be for workers with technical skills. Other projections show that the one of the fastest-growing segments of the workforce is Hispanic males. The policy implications of these two predictions, that industry and educators need to train Hispanic males in technical skills, is one of the ways that workforce projections serve industry and the social fabric of the country.

Data revealing that more mothers with young children were remaining in the workforce, with projections of further increases in that segment of the population, underscored the need for child care facilities and helped substantiate arguments used to pass the Family and Medical Leave Act of 1993.

BLS predicts that there will be no dramatic increases in the workforce of the early twenty-first century. Growth in the workforce in the next century is predicted by BLS to come from immigration and population growth, rather than the transforming of another formerly nonparticipating segment (e.g., mothers with young children), into a participating one.

[Joan Leotta]

FURTHER READING:

Kolberg, William, and F. Smith. *Rebuilding America's Workforce.* Business One Irwin. Homewood, IL: 1992.

National Association of Manufacturers. *Workforce Readiness: How to Meet Our Greatest Competitive Challenges.*

National Association of Manufacturers. U.S. Department of Labor. *Workorce Readiness: A Manufacturing Perspective.*

WORKING CAPITAL

Working capital (WC) is the difference between current **assets** and current **liabilities** on a company's **balance sheet**. Current assets include such things as cash, accounts receivable, marketable securities, inventory, and prepaid expenses. Examples of current liabilities are accounts payable, accrued expenses, and the near-term portion of loan or lease payments due. "Current" is generally defined as those assets or liabilities that will be liquidated within the course of one business cycle, typically a year.

Working capital is one measure of liquidity; creditors will often be interested in a company's working capital as one indicator of the debtor's ability to make payments on a timely basis. The components of WC are used to calculate several **financial ratios**, including the current ratio, which is current assets divided by current liabilities. Banks will often write into their loan contracts covenants requiring the maintenance of prescribed levels of working capital or current ratio. The importance of these measures to credit analysts is what makes the determination of current versus noncurrent status so important on a company's balance sheet. Because of this, much thought goes into the classification of assets and liabilities.

Working capital is also of interest in the context of a business **valuation**, for at least two reasons. First, when using a discounted cash flow approach, the appraiser will often consider changes expected in working capital over the projected periods to convert income figures into cash flows. Second, an excess amount of working capital, particularly cash, is sometimes grounds for additional value being quantified, above and beyond that which would result from the income capitalization component of the valuation. This is because companies of a given SIC code, or industry type, are commonly thought of as requiring a certain level of working capital to operate under normal circumstances. Companies that vary significantly from the norm may be considered to have excess or inadequate WC, and therefore warrant an adjustment.

Working capital can be provided by several sources:

1. Net income, plus non-cash expenses;

2. Financing activities, including loans and equity infusions;

3. Decrease in noncurrent assets, e.g. the sale of fixed assets.

Most business activities affect WC, either consuming or generating it. Sales made at a positive margin increase WC, as they increase one current asset (accounts receivable or cash) more than they decrease another current asset (inventory). Starting up a new product line may require higher levels of WC, as inventory and receivables must be built up to some steady-state level. Changes in credit terms, either that the company gives on its receivables, or that it gets on its payables, will affect WC. For example, extending more favorable credit terms to one's customers will require higher amounts of WC, as accounts receivable will build without any compensating changes to make up the difference. The repayment of a long term debt (for example, bonds, capital leases, etc.) will result in a reduction, or use of working capital. This occurs as a current asset (cash) is used to reduce a noncurrent liability.

[Christopher Barry]

WORKS COUNCILS

German **labor-management relations** are referred to as a system of co-determination, in which both management and labor participate in **decision making**. The system is dualistic in that co-determination at the industry level is the province of industrial unions and at the workplace level the province of works councils (also called work councils). As with plant-level cooperation programs in Japan, German works councils became of great interest in the United States as a model for establishing less-antagonistic labor-management relations.

Works councils are legally required to be formally independent of industrial unions. In general, industrial unions deal with issues such as wages and working hours, while works councils deal with issues specific to a workplace or firm. Walther Mueller-Jentsch has described the functional separation of industrial unions and works councils as follows: "By collective agreements, the industrywide aggregation of wages and working time interests leads to a uniform branch-wide standardization of wage costs and working time in terms of minimum conditions. Using workshop negotiations, these minimum standards can be adapted in a flexible manner to the specific situation of the enterprise."

German industrial unions were legally recognized in 1918 and works councils in 1920 by the Works Councils Act. After World War II, the legal foundation for works councils was re-established by the Works Constitution Acts of 1952 and 1972. Depending on the size of the workplace, works councils have executive and economic committees, as provided for by the Works Constitution acts. The acts also provided for works councils to address recruiting and dismissal procedures as well as the organization of the labor process within the workplace.

Works councils may be established in any workplace with five or more permanent employees on the initiative of workers or unions representing workers. Works councils are representative bodies to which membership is attained through elections. Nonmanagerial employees 18 or over are eligible to vote. Works councilors are required to have been employed in the workplace they represent for six or more months. They hold three-year terms and cannot be dismissed from employment during their term.

The number of works council members varies from one in workplaces with 5 to 20 employees to 31 in workplaces with 7,001 to 9,000 employees, with two members added for every additional 3,000 employees beyond 9,000. Though works councilors are not paid for their Council service, they meet during regular working hours and continue to receive wages. In firms with 300 or more employees, works councilors are released from performing regular work. The Works Constitution acts require employers to pay for works council election expenses and to provide office space, equipment, and staff.

Works councils are established on a plant basis. When a firm comprises more than one plant, a central works council is established to coordinate works council affairs. Similarly, combine works councils are established to coordinate works councils across a firm's affiliates and subsidiaries. Employers and works councils hold joint meetings at least once a month.

Works councils have co-determination rights in specified areas, meaning that management cannot introduce changes without works council approval. These areas include plant operation, the use of employee monitoring devices, health and safety measures, and schedules for working hours, breaks, and pay. Cases of disagreement between works councils and management in these areas are settled by a conciliation panel consisting of an equal number of employer and works council representatives and a chairperson acceptable to both parties. When employers and works councils cannot agree on a chairperson, one is appointed by a labor court. In other areas, such as recruiting and transfers within the firm, employers have to meet the weaker condition of seeking the consent of works councils. For investment decisions and dismissals, management need only consult works councils.

Works councils set up economic committees in all firms with more than 100 regular employees. From three to seven economic committee members are appointed by works councils, depending on the firm's size. Economic committees meet monthly with the employer or the employer's representative. Employers are required to provide the committee with information regarding the firm's sales, financial situation, investment plans, marketing operations, possible slowdowns or shutdowns, and the introduction of new work methods. Works councils, on the other hand, are bound by confidentiality restrictions from divulging company information. In all firms with 300 or more employees, works council executive committees are established, with at least a chairperson and vice-chairperson.

In plants where there are five or more workers below the age of 18, youth representation committees are established. These committees are made up of workers below age 18 and address issues that pertain particularly to youths, such as vocational training. Youth representation committees are also established to ensure that young workers' interests are taken into account when works council consider general issues.

Volker R. Berghahn and Detlev Karsten have argued that work councils generally act to empower workers. They described the underlying process as follows: "Normally the management is well advised to seek the cooperation of the works council because the consent of the works council helps when it comes to the implementation of decisions. On the other hand, if the management tries to impose decisions which were taken against the advice of the works council, it can expect all kinds of trouble.''

Works councils focus on the interests of workers within their workplace, not on the more general interests of workers in the industry or the working class at large. As a result, conflicts occasionally arise between works councils and unions. In contractual conflicts, works councils are prohibited from lending support to workers or unions. Given that works councils have detailed information regarding their firm's economic situation, they often have a moderating influence in labor conflicts.

[David Kucera]

FURTHER READING:

Altmann, Norbert. "Company Performance Policies and the Role of the Works Council." In *Industrial Relations in Transition: The Cases of Japan and the Federal Republic of Germany*, edited by Tokunaga Shigeyoshi and Joachim Bergmann. University of Tokyo Press, 1984.

Berghahn, Volker R., and Detlev Karsten. *Industrial Relations in West Germany*. Berg Publishers, 1987.

"Company News; Opel Plans to Cut 2,000 Jobs, Union Official Says." *New York Times*. May 4, 1994.

Fukui, Haruhiro, et al., eds. *The Politics of Economic Change in Postwar Japan and West Germany: Volume 1: Macroeconomic Conditions and Policy Responses*. St. Martin's Press, 1993.

Mueller-Jentsch, Walther. "The Changing Balance between Workplace Representation and Industrywide Representation in West Germany." In *Industrial Relations in Transition: The Cases of Japan and the Federal Republic of Germany*, edited by Tokunaga Shigeyoshi and Joachim Bergmann. University of Tokyo Press, 1984.

Thelen, Kathleen. *Union of Parts: Labor Politics in Postwar Germany*. Cornell University Press, 1991.

WORLD BANK

The World Bank is more formally known as the International Bank for Reconstruction and Development (IBRD). The IBRD is affiliated with three other organizations: the International Development Association (IDA), the International Finance Corporation (IFC) and the Multilateral Investment Guarantee Agency (MIGA). Although "World Bank" and "IBRD" are often used interchangeably, the term "World Bank" more properly describes the organization jointly comprising the IBRD and the IDA. The World Bank Group is an umbrella organization comprised of the IBRD, the IDA, the IFC and the MIGA. The IBRD is also a designated "special agency" of the United Nations.

The IBRD and its sister institution the **International Monetary Fund** were established by the Bretton Woods held at Bretton Woods, New Hampshire in July of 1944. The purpose of the conference was to formulate a plan for post World War II international economic cooperation. President Franklin Roosevelt and U.S. Treasury Secretary Henry Morgenthau Jr. felt that a stabilized world economy would go a long way in preventing a reoccurrence of the 1930s depression and aiding future world peace. Establishment of the IBRD was an integral part of the plan.

The original purpose of the IBRD was to help stabilize and re-build war ravaged economies following World War II. It has since shifted its emphasis to aiding economic growth in developing nations. The IBRD makes loans directly to governments of member nations and to private development projects that are backed by guarantees of member nation governments. Loans to governments are generally made to ease balance of payment difficulties or to promote trade. Private loans are made for projects of high productivity and which benefit the citizens of a member nation. These loans are given at favorable interest rates. The IBRD, however, is often criticized by developing countries for imposing severe austerity measures on the borrowing country as a condition for granting a loan. IBRD capital is raised from member country's subscriptions to capital shares and net earnings and by borrowing from world capital markets. The subscription share for each member country is related to their International Monetary Fund quota.

The IBRD provides technical assistance to member countries and maintains a research staff which disseminates advice and information on economic policy. The IBRD's Operations Evaluation Department publishes the progress of various projects funded by the bank and often contains critiques for the enhancement of future projects and loans. In 1955 the IBRD established its Economic Development Institute which educates government employees in economic and project management techniques. In 1966 as part of the Convention of the Settlement of Investment Disputes between States and Nationals of Other States the IBRD founded its International Center for the Settlement of Investment Disputes (ICSID). The ICSID settles disputes arising between private investors and IBRD member countries. By providing a forum for the settlement of potential disputes, private investment is encouraged. However, not all IBRD members are signatories of the convention. The IBRD also sponsors the Consultative Group for International Agricultural Research which raises funds for research related to agriculture and animal husbandry. The IBRD also has an extensive publications program which includes: World Bank Catalog of Publications, World Bank News (weekly), World Bank Annual Report, World Development Report (both are annual), and the World Bank Economic Review which it issues once every three years.

The chief governing agency of the IBRD is the Board of Governors with one governor being appointed by each member country. The appointed Governor is usually a high finance official from the respective country. Daily operations of the IBRD are administered by 24 Executive Directors who represent the interests of their respective country and who oversee implementation of IBRD policy and project management. The IBRD has offices in New York at the United Nations, a European office in Paris, and regional missions in Eastern Africa (Nairobi), Western Africa (Abidjan, Ivory Coast), and Thailand (Bangkok). For further information: New York Office and World Bank Mission to the United Nations, 809 United Nations Plaza, 9th Floor, New York, New York 10017

SEE ALSO: Eurobond Market; European Bank for Reconstruction and Development

[Michael Knes]

FURTHER READING:

The World Bank. Bureau of Public Affairs, Dept. of State, 1989.

Wilson, Carol R. *The World Bank Group: A Guide to Information Sources*. Garland, 1991.

Z

ZERO ECONOMIC GROWTH

Zero economic growth is an economic condition that may be the result of a nation's public policy, or it may be caused by a recession. A number of factors may be used to measure a nation's economic growth. The largest overall measure of economic output is a country's **gross national product** (GNP), which is an annual measure of the goods and services produced in the country. When the GNP increases from year to year, economic growth is occurring. Should the GNP decrease, then there is said to be negative growth. Under zero economic growth, the GNP would remain constant over time.

As a matter of public policy, most nations strive for moderate economic growth from year to year. Two types of policies, monetary and fiscal, can be implemented to affect a country's economic performance. **Fiscal policy** refers to the use of government spending and taxation to affect the overall demand for goods and services. Increased government spending increases the size of the GNP. Higher tax rates reduce the amount of disposable personal income, with a corresponding reduction in demand. Using these two fiscal tools, a government can raise or lower the demand in the economy, with corresponding effects on the GNP and economic growth.

Monetary policy refers to the use of controls over **interest rates**, the **money supply**, and the ability of **banks** to make **loans**. In the United States monetary policy is established by the Federal Reserve Board. Monetary policies can help reduce **unemployment** and slow **inflation**. For example, when the Federal

Reserve Board makes it easier for banks to make loans, thus increasing the money supply, businesses are thereby encouraged to make more investments and hire more workers. By increasing the **discount rate**, on the other hand, the Federal Reserve Board can restrict the money supply and help reduce inflation. Restricting the money supply tends to reduce the size of the GNP, while measures to expand the money supply tend to increase the size of the GNP.

Zero economic growth may be an unwanted condition that a country experiences as the result of a recession or another set of economic circumstances. While fiscal and monetary policies can have some effect on economic performance, it is quite possible to experience unintended zero economic growth. Factors that could contribute to a flat or declining GNP might include high unemployment, inflation and higher prices, high interest rates and little business expansion, a general recession, and anything else that would lessen demand and business production.

Zero economic growth has been discussed in academic circles as a desirable goal of public policy. It is argued that an ever-expanding economy will sooner or later become too large for the finite world we live in. If the world's economies become too large, they will make too great a demand on our planet's finite resources. The ultimate effect of economic growth would thus be the collapse of the ecological, social, political, and economic systems as we know them.

The no-growth argument may be countered by pointing to the adaptability of existing social, economic, and political systems. As economic growth continues, new alternatives are likely to become available. Technological innovations may provide new solutions to the problems caused by economic growth.

While economic growth has its costs and benefits, public policy will likely continue to attempt to minimize the costs and maximize the benefits without abandoning the concept of stable economic growth as a policy objective.

[David Bianco]

Indexes

ENCYCLOPEDIA OF BUSINESS

Bold headings indicate major business disciplines; essays related to those disciplines are listed alphabetically under each heading. Essays that begin with the letters A through I are in Volume I; those that begin with letters J through Z are in Volume II.

A

Aggregate supply **I:** 121

Agreement on Technical Barriers to Trade **I:** 817, **II:** 1461

Agreement on the Regime for Central American Integration Industries **I:** 204

Agribusiness (*See Also* Commodities) **I: 30–31**

Agriculture **II:** 1312

AI Corp. **I:** 566

AICPA. *See* American Institute of Certified Public Accountants.

AIDS. *See* Acquired Immune Deficiency Syndrome.

AIDS in the Workplace **I: 31–33, II:** 1214

Aion Corp. **I:** 566

Airborne Express **II:** 956

Aktiengesellschaft, Bayer **II:** 997

Alaska Department of Commerce and Economic Development **I:** 402

Aldrich, Eastman & Waltch **I:** 712

Aldrich Plan **I:** 592

Aldrich Vreelad Act of 1908 **I:** 592

Aldus Company **I:** 407

Alexander, R.S. **I:** 560

Algorithms **I: 33,** 282

Aliens, Employment of **I: 34**

Alitalia Airline **I:** 331

All-or-none offering **II:** 1476

Allegis **I:** 330

Allende Gossens, Salvador **II:** 1349

Allied Command Atlantic **II:** 1082

Allied Command Channel **II:** 1082

Allied Command Europe **II:** 1082

Allocation **I:** 209

Allstate Insurance **II:** 1057

Almon, Copper **I:** 794

Alternative Control Systems Corporation **II:** 1336

Aluminum Company of America **I:** 260

Amalgamated Clothing and Textile Workers Union **I:** 681

America Online **I:** 275, 487

American Accounting Association **I:** 4, 6, 803, **II:** 953

American Airlines **II:** 1314, 1500

American Arbitration Association **I:** 53, 811, 813

American Association of University Women **II:** 1524

American Bankers Association (ABA) **II:** 1198, 1481

American Bar Association (ABA) **II:** 1197, 1256, 1480–81

American Business Women's Association **II:** 1526

American Cancer Society **II:** 1214

American Consultants League **I:** 296

American Depositary Receipt **II:** 1375

American Express Co. **I:** 29, 93, 99, 327, 339, 493, **II:** 858, 1297, 1314

American Express Travel Services **I:** 158

American Federation of Labor (AFL) **I:** 821, **II:** 887, 1487, 1520

American Federation of Labor-Congress of Industrial Organizations (AFL-CIO) **II:** 887, 889, 1080

American Federation of Musicians **II:** 918

American Federation of Teachers **II:** 890

American Federation of Television and Radio Artists **II:** 918

American Institute of Certified Public Accountants (AICPA) **I:** 2, 4, 5, 62–63, 207, 422, 600–01, 803, 809, **II:** 1181, 1197

American Institute of Management **II:** 949

American Institute of Stress **II:** 1387

American Iron and Steel Institute **II:** 1198

American Law Institute **I:** 234, 308, **II:** 1480–81

American Management Association **I:** 33, 133, 252, 254, **II:** 898, 1464

American Marketing Association **II:** 1284

American Medical Association **II:** 1197, 1520

American Motors Corp. **II:** 869

American National Standards Institute **I:** 778, **II:** 1086, 1355

American Railway Strike of 1894 **II:** 884

American Research and Development Corporation **II:** 1496

American Society for Quality Control (ASQC) **II:** 1220–21, 1400

American Society for Training and Development **II:** 1464

American Society of Composers, Authors, and Publishers (ASCAP) **II:** 918

American Society of Mechanical Engineers **I:** 778

American Standard Code of Information Interchange **I:** 271

American Steel Company v. Irving National Bank **II:** 907

American Stock Exchange **I:** 239, 424, 566, 754, **II:** 981, 1063, 1103, 1133, 1209, 1230, 1365

American Stores **I:** 330

American Technology Preeminence Act of 1991 **II:** 1066

American Telecast Corp. **I:** 781

American Telemarketing Association **II:** 1432

American Trading Companies **I:** 569, 571

Americans with Disabilities Act (ADA) (*See Also* Civil Rights Act of 1991) **I:** 16, 32, **34–36,** 222, 505–06, 509, 537, 540–43, 779, **II:** 1318, 1506

Ameritech **I:** 321–22, 514

AMF. *See* Arab Monetary Fund.

Amoco Corp. **I:** 229, 655, 790, **II:** 897

Amortization (*See Also* Intangible Assets) **I: 36–37,** 177, 752, **II:** 1130, 1185

Amortized loans **I:** 235

Amtrak **I:** 675

AMU. *See* Arab Maghreb Union.

Amway Corp. **II:** 1058

Analog computers **I:** 283

Analysis of variance **I:** 428

Andean Common Market **I:** 661

Andean Pact **II:** 1348–49

Andean Trade Initiative **II:** 1348

Andersen & Co., Arthur **I:** 4, **II:** 1436

Anheuser-Busch Companies **II:** 982, 1139, 1287

Ankuk Fire & Marine Insurance **II:** 874

Annual percentage rate **I:** 424, 798–99

Annual Reports **I: 37–40,** 266, 422–23, 615–16, 623, 633, **II:** 1213, 1369

Annuities **I:** 609–10

ANSI X12 **I:** 485

Ansonia Board of Education v. Philbrook **I:** 542

Antidumping duty **II:** 1461

Antipollution programs **II:** 1214

Antitrust **II:** 1246

Antitrust Acts and Laws **I: 40–43,** 152, 187, 260, 569, 596, 824, **II:** 865–66, 1250, 1343

Antitrust Division **I:** 596

Antitrust Improvement Act of 1976 **I:** 733

APB. *See* Accounting Principles Board.

APB Opinion No. 19, Reporting Changes in Financial Position **I:** 189

Apollo Computer **I:** 286

Apple Computer, Inc. **I:** 32, 99, 285, 407, 506, 696, 798, **II:** 982, 1245, 1247, 1387, 1521

Apple II **II:** 1423

Apple MacIntosh **II:** 1091, 1341

Apprenticeship Programs (*See Also* On-the-Job Training) **I: 43–44,** 182, **II:** 892, 1464, 1503–04

Apprenticeship system **II:** 1464

Apprenticeship 2000 **II:** 1505

Appropriation of retained earnings **I:** 193

Appropriations Act of 1977 **II:** 1087

Arab American Chamber of Commerce **I:** 51

Arab Common Market **I: 44**

Arab Information Centers **I:** 51

Arab League **I:** 44

Arab Maghreb Union (AMU) **II:** 935

Arab Monetary Fund (AMF) **I: 44–45**

Arab Trade Financing Program **I:** 45

Arab World, Doing Business in the **I: 45–51**

Arbitrage **I: 51–52,** 406, 800, **II:** 1107, 1216, 1363

Arbitrage opportunity **II:** 1217

Arbitrage pricing theory (APT) **I:** 51, **II:** 1166, 1368

Arbitrageur **I:** 406

Arbitration **I:** 589

Arbitration and Mediation **I: 52–54,** 774

Arbitron **I:** 837

Architectural Barriers Act of 1968 **I:** 35

ARCO **I:** 334

ARCO Foundation **I:** 334

Arden, Elizabeth **II:** 1520

Army Corps of Engineers **I:** 265, 532

Articles of Confederation **I:** 806

Articles of incorporation **I:** 334, **II:** 1160

Artificial Intelligence **I: 54–57**, 269, 564, 566

Artzt, Edwin L. **I:** 11

ASCAP. *See* American Society of Composers, Authors, and Publishers.

ASEAN. *See* Association of South East Asian Nations.

ASEAN Free Trade Area **I:** 61

ASEAN-Washington Committee **I:** 60

Asian-Pacific Economic Cooperation Forum (APEC) **I:** 61, 570

Asian-rate options **I:** 606

Asian Tigers. *See* Five Tigers.

Ask price **II:** 1134

Asked price **II:** 1488

ASQC. *See* American Society for Quality Control.

Assembly line **II:** 1464

Assembly Line Methods **I: 58–59**, 628

Assessment center evaluation **II:** 1152

Assessment Centers **I: 59–60**, **II:** 1464

Asset **I:** 603, **II:** 1303

Asset allocation **II:** 1397

Asset allocation funds **II:** 871

Asset management services **II:** 1206

Asset trades **I:** 321

Assets (*See Also* Financial Statements) **I:** 36, 42, 51, 73–75, 80, 94, 147, 163, 165, 171, 206, 234, 245, 280, 315, 318, 333, 351, 361–62, 386, 388, 397, 403–04, 413, 423–24, 477, 490, 511, 513, 547, 576, 597–98, 601, 604, 611–12, 614–17, 624, 652, 691–92, 705, 709, 712, 733, 750, 796, 800, 806, 849, 851, **II:** 870, 905, 914–16, 924, 949, 981, 993, 1009–12, 1047, 1104, 1107, 1132, 1153, 1159, 1164–65, 1180, 1183, 1199, 1206, 1229, 1232, 1241, 1256–57, 1291, 1300, 1304–05, 1329, 1351, 1366, 1370–71, 1373–74, 1376, 1388, 1394–95, 1403, 1469, 1472, 1481, 1531

Assignable causes of variation **II:** 1360

Associated Advertising Clubs of the World **I:** 91

Associated Spring **I:** 303

Association for Computing Machinery **II:** 1028

Association for Investment Management and Research **I:** 293

Association of South East Asian Nations (ASEAN) **I: 60–61**, 675

Association of Southeast Asian Nations **II:** 1451

Associations. *See* Professional and Trade Associations.

Assumption of risk **II:** 1069

AST Research **I:** 286

Asterisk bills **II:** 1436

Asynchronous transfer mode **II:** 1517

AT&T **I:** 43, 278, 321–23, 327, 335, 402, 478, 482, 506, 754, 765, 768, 781, **II:** 897, 926, 1028, 1057, 1133, 1235, 1294, 1313, 1351, 1422, 1428, 1431, 1437–38, 1447, 1454, 1517

AT&T EasyLink **I:** 487

At the money **II:** 1105

Atanasoff, John V. **I:** 284

Atlanta (Georgia) Gas Company **I:** 556

ATMs **I:** 82, 366, 609

Attar Software **I:** 566

Attest audit **I:** 61

Audit **I:** 66, 93, 156, 691, 734, 801, 803, **II:** 948

Audit and Investigations Office **I:** 27

Audit program **I:** 62

Audit trail **I:** 62

Auditing (*See Also* Accounting; Balance Sheet; Financial Statements; Income Statement) **I: 61–63**, **II:** 1240

Audits **I:** 587

Australia, Doing Business in **I: 63–66**

Australia Group **I:** 312

Australian Options Market **I:** 238

Austrian Futures and Options Exchange **I:** 238

Autodesk, Inc. **II:** 1501

Automated attendant systems **II:** 1430

Automated Clearing House (ACH) **I:** 483

Automated guided vehicle systems (AGVS) **I:** 626, 629

Automated Office Security (*See Also* Data Security) **I: 66–69**

Automated résumé banks **II:** 1258

Automated storage and retrieval systems (ASRS) **I:** 629

Automated Teller Machines (ATMs) **I: 69–70**, 82, **II:** 1212

Automatic call distributor **II:** 1431

Automatic Identification Systems **I: 70–71**

Automation **I: 71–72**, 337, 626, 838

Automobile Information Council **II:** 1214

Automotive Industry Action Group (AIAG) **I:** 85

Autonomation **II:** 863

Average cost **I:** 479, 481, **II:** 959, 1031

Average fixed cost **I:** 479, **II:** 959

Average-rate options **I:** 606

Average revenue **II:** 960, 1031

Average variable cost **I:** 479, **II:** 959

Averits, Robert **II:** 880

Avis **I:** 331

Ayer & Son, N.W. **I:** 10

Ayer, Francis Wayland **I:** 10

B

B.F. Goodrich Company **I:** 270, 561, 738

Babbage, Charles **I:** 55, 284

Babeuf, Gracchus **II:** 1338

Back pay **II:** 1318

Backward integration **II:** 1384

Backward vertical integration **I:** 42

Bacon, Francis **I:** 54

Balance of payments **I:** 828

Balance of Trade **I: 75–79**, 795, 828, **II:** 1463

Balance Sheet (*See Also* Accounting; Auditing; Income Statement) **I: 73–75**, 95, 106, 144, 149, 171, 189, 234, 245, 363, 423, 439, 442, 601, 612, 614, 616, 618, 633, 846, **II:** 994, 1010, 1135, 1182, 1184, 1474, 1531

Baltic Futures Exchange **I:** 239

Banana Republic **I: 79–80**

Bangkok Declaration **I:** 60

Bank Collection Code **II:** 1481

Bank-discount method **II:** 1488

Bank float **I:** 193

Bank investment contracts (BICs) **I:** 710

Bank of America **I:** 32, 323, 569, 837, **II:** 1214

Bank of England **I:** 81

Bank subsidiaries **II:** 1497

BankAmerica Corp. **I:** 607

Banker's acceptances **II:** 1304

Bankers Trust **I:** 710

Banking **I:** 276, 360, 399, 409, 654, 677, **II:** 1098, 1232, 1312

Banking Act of 1933 **I: 80–81**, 594

Bankruptcies **I:** 291

Bankruptcy (*See Also* Business Failure) **I:** 128, 171, 234, 360, 395, 397, 527, 587, 599, **II:** 915, 950, 1205, 1302–04, 1373

Bankruptcy Reform Act of 1978 **II:** 1299

Banks and Banking (*See Also* Savings and Loan Associations) **I:** 69, 80, **81–82**, 146, 175, 245, 280, 313–14, 320, 324, 326, 360, 384, 424, 548, 586, 597, 601, 647, 708, 796, 817, **II:** 904, 924, 1045, 1054, 1126, 1173, 1177, 1232, 1256–57, 1440, 1462–63, 1496, 1535

Bar Coding **I:** 70, **82–86**, 359, **II:** 1230

Bargain lease **II:** 906

Bargain sales **II:** 1473

Barnard, Chester **I:** 554, **II:** 1390

Barnes Group **I:** 303

Barre Plan **I:** 550

Barrier options **I:** 606

Bartering **I: 86–87**, 321, 356, 358, 360, 570, **II:** 1046

Basel Convention **II:** 1254

Basis **I:** 168–69, 730

Basis risk **II:** 1364

Battelle Memorial Institute **II:** 1246

Battle Act of 1951 **I:** 311

Baumol Model **I:** 193

Bayer World **II:** 997

Bayes Rule **I:** 430

Bean, L.L. **I:** 195, 414, 418, **II:** 937, 1382

Bearer bonds **I:** 94, 548

Bebel, August **II:** 1340
Bechtel Group **II:** 1213
Becker, Gary **II:** 880
Beech Aircraft **I:** 228
Beer, Michael **I:** 740
Beginning inventory budget **I:** 107
Behavioral management **II:** 942
Behaviorally anchored rating scales **II:** 1151
Belgian Futures and Options Exchange **I:** 238
Belgium-Luxembourg Economic Union **I:** 88
Bell Atlantic **I:** 321
Bell Atlantic Mobile **II:** 1514
Bell Canada **I:** 49, 401, 790
Bell, Daniel **I:** 725
Bell Telephone Company **I:** 554, **II:** 1428, 1455
Bell Telephone Laboratories **II:** 1221
BellSouth **I:** 321
Below-investment-grade **II:** 869
Ben and Jerry's **I:** 328
Benchmark jobs **I:** 254
Benchmarking (*See Also* Competition) **I:** **87-88**, 522
Bendata Management Systems **I:** 566
Beneficiary **II:** 1471
Benefits **I:** 510
Benefits Quarterly **I:** 712
Benelux **I:** **88-89**, 550
Benelux Economic Union (BEU) **I:** 88
Benelux Interparliamentary Consultative Council **I:** 89
Benelux Treaty of Economic Union **I:** 88
Benini **I:** 454
Benneton **I:** 580
Bennigan's Tavern **I:** 329
Bentham, Jeremy **I:** 545, **II:** 879, 1490
Berenson, Conrad **I:** 560
Beretta **I:** 580
Bergen Brunswig Drug Company **I:** 485
Bernays, Edward L. **II:** 1211
Berne Convention **I:** **89-90**, 312
Berne Convention Implementation Act **I:** 90
Best efforts **II:** 1365
Best efforts basis **II:** 1476
Best linear unbiased estimator (BLUE) **II:** 906
Better Business Bureau (BBB) **I:** **91**, 297
Bharat Heavy Electricals, Ltd. **I:** 402
Bhopol **I:** 332
Bias **I:** 59
Bid price **II:** 1134, 1488
Biddle, Nicholas **I:** 591
Bids **I:** 238
BIFFEX **I:** 239
Big Board **II:** 1133
Big Brothers/Big Sisters **II:** 1212
Big Six **I:** 4
Bill of exchange **II:** 1071
Binary digits **I:** 284
Binding LOI **II:** 1476

Biometric technology **I:** 67-68
Biometrics **I:** 280
Bios Lite Diet **II:** 1060
Bird-in-hand **I:** 438
Bits **I:** 284
Black & Decker Corp. **I:** 789
Black Lung Act **II:** 1529
Black market **I:** 206
Black Market (Trading) **I:** **92**
Black-Scholes Option Pricing Model **I:** 160, **II:** 1107
Black's Law Dictionary **I:** 291
Blake, R.R. **I:** 294
Blanchard, Kenneth H. **II:** 1452
Blanqui, August **II:** 1338
Block house **II:** 1367
Block trades **II:** 1367
Blockbuster Entertainment **I:** 338, **II:** 976
BLS **II:** 1531
"Blue Angel" program **I:** 701
Blue-chip stocks **I:** 620, **II:** 1376
Blue Cross Blue Shield **I:** 114
Blue-Sky Laws **II:** 1209
BMI Music Performance Agreement for Colleges and Universities **II:** 918
Board of Contract Appeals **I:** 677
Board of Directors **I:** **92-94**, 141, 156, 210, 238, 263, 314, 318, 324-25, 334, 439, 802, **II:** 856, 889, 1012, 1061, 1201, 1215, 1229, 1299, 1301, 1343, 1371-72, 1403, 1470, 1481
Board of governors **I:** 205
Boards of trade **I:** 208
Boatright, John R. **I:** 291
The Body Shop **I:** 328
Boeing Corporation **I:** 270, 558, 827, **II:** 890, 951, 1521
Boesky, Ivan **II:** 1512
Boiler rooms **II:** 1435
Bolsa de Mercadorias & Futuros **I:** 238
Bolsa de Mercadorias de Sao Paulo **I:** 238
Bolsa Mercantil & de Futuros **I:** 238
Bona fide occupational qualification **II:** 1318, 1322, 1521
Bond indenture **I:** 94, 315, 439, **II:** 1328
Bond index fund **II:** 1140
Bond price index **I:** 754
Bond ratings **I:** 397
Bond trustee **II:** 1237
Bonds **I:** 9, 52, 80, **94-95**, 171, 219, 245, 315, 362, 386-87, 397, 422, 424, 426, 522, 548, 599, 601, 604, 611, 621, 751, 760, 801, 835, 844-45, 849-50, 852, **II:** 925, 934, 981, 1009, 1047, 1054, 1061, 1129, 1133, 1140, 1173, 1206, 1208, 1237, 1243, 1264, 1301-02, 1305, 1329, 1365, 1367, 1375-76, 1397, 1417, 1440, 1468, 1481, 1489, 1510-11
Bookbinder's Restaurant **II:** 1315
Bookkeeping **I:** 3, **95-96**, 350
Booz, Allen, and Hamilton **II:** 1202
Border Environmental Cooperation Commission **II:** 1080

Bosch GMBH, Robert **I:** 329
Boston Consulting Group **I:** 188
Boston Private Industry Council **II:** 1505
Boston Tropical Fruit Trading Company **I:** 79
Bottom-up approach **I:** 845
Bottom-up communication **I:** 246
Bottom-up Forecasting **II:** 1275
Botwinick, Howard **II:** 881
Bounty payments **I:** 65
Boutwell, George S. **I:** 807
Boycott, Charles **I:** 96
Boycotts **I:** 41, **96-97**, 206, 297, 437, 508, 571, **II:** 1256
Boyd, Jr., Harper W. **II:** 991
Brand advertising **II:** 999
Brand loyalty **I:** 14
Brandeis, Louis D. **II:** 1262
Brands and Brand Names **I:** **97-100**, 300, 528, **II:** 1000, 1007-08, 1344
Braverman, Harry **II:** 880
Breadth **II:** 1366
Breadth analysis **I:** 847
Breadth index **I:** 847
Break-Even Analysis **I:** **100**
Bretton Woods **I:** 455, 675, **II:** 1533
Brezhnev Doctrine **II:** 1147
Bribery **I:** **100-02**, 291, **II:** 859
Bridgestone/Firestone Inc. **I:** 778
Briggs & Stratton **I:** 478
Briggs v. City of Madison **I:** 249-50
Bristol-Meyers Squibb **II:** 897
British Airways **I:** 323, **II:** 1297
British Commonwealth Development Bank **I:** 186
British East India Company **I:** 436, **II:** 1002-03, 1344
British Petroleum Exploration **I:** 368
Broadcast Music, Inc. **II:** 918
Broadway Stores **I:** 331
Broker-dealers **II:** 1476
Brokers **II:** 1366, 1516
Brown Consulting Group **I:** 681
Browner, Carol **I:** 536
BRTA. *See* Business Responds to AIDS.
Buckley Amendment of 1974 **I:** 741
Budget and Accounting Act of 1921 **I:** 674
Budgeted balance sheet **I:** 111
Budgeted statement of cash flows **I:** 111
Budgeted statement of financial position **I:** 111
Budgeting (*See Also* Capital Budget; Sales Forecasting) **I:** **102-12**, 139, 168, 308, 343, 352, 355, 396, 611, **II:** 948, 954, 1205, 1279, 1381, 1468
Buick **I:** 87
Building permits **I:** 461
Building Trades Department of the AFL-CIO **II:** 894
Bulkeley, Eliphalet Adams **I:** 554
Bull market **II:** 870

Cash dividend **II:** 1371–72

Cash flow **I:** 336, 433, **II:** 871, 1353

Cash Flow Statement **I:** 37, 144, **189–93**, 363, 611, 614, 618

Cash forward contracts **I:** 238

Cash Management **I: 193–94**

Cash method **I:** 337

Cash receipts and disbursements method **I:** 337

Cass Logistics, Inc. **I:** 134

Casualty loss **I:** 168

Catalina Marketing **I:** 359

Catalog Marketing **I: 194–98**

Catalog showrooms **I:** 196–97

Catalyst **I:** 679

Categorical variable **I:** 428

Caterpillar **II:** 890

Cause marketing **I:** 338, 340

Cause-related marketing **I:** 335

CBI. *See* Caribbean Basin Initiative.

CBS Inc. **I:** 341

CBW Automation Inc. **II:** 1267

CD-ROM **I:** 288

CDC. *See* Centers for Disease Control.

CEFTA. *See* Central European Free Trade Agreement.

Cell manufacturing **I:** 58

Cellar, Emanuel **I:** 649

Census Data **I: 198–200**

Census of Manufacturers of 1958 **I:** 792

Census of Wholesale Trade **II:** 1516

Center for Auto Safety **I:** 297

Center for Creative Leadership **I:** 679

Center for the Study of American Business **I:** 267

Center for the Study of Responsive Law **I:** 155, 297

Center for the Utilization of Federal Technology **II:** 1066

Center for Work Performance Problems **I:** 32

Centers for Disease Control (CDC) **I:** 31–32, 532

Central America, Doing Business in **I: 200–03**

Central American Agreement on the Equalization of Import Duties and Charges **I:** 204

Central American Clearing House **I:** 204

Central American Common Market (CACM) **I:** 200–02, **203–04**, **II:** 1348

Central American Economic Integration Program **I:** 203

Central American Isthmus **I:** 203

Central American Monetary Council **I:** 204

Central American Parliament **I:** 204

Central Banks **I:** 64, 81, **204–05**, 550, 552, 647, **II:** 1480

Central European Free Trade Agreement (CEFTA) **I:** 244

Central Intelligence Agency **I:** 768

Central processing unit (CPU) **I:** 283, 285, 287, **II:** 1026

Centrally Planned Economy **I: 205–06**

Centre for Cooperation with European Economies in Transition **II:** 1111

Centre for Educational Research and Innovation **II:** 1111

Cents-off deals **II:** 1286

Century 21 **II:** 1229

CEO. *See* Chief Executive Officer.

Certificate of Accrual on Treasury Securities **II:** 1129

Certificate of Origin **I: 206–07**

Certificates of deposit **I:** 364, 366, 607, 708, 760, 835, 844, **II:** 871, 1045, 1049, 1071, 1108, 1167, 1173, 1472

Certification. *See* Licensing and Certification, Occupational.

Certified Financial Planner **I:** 612, **II:** 1307

Certified Management Accountant (CMA) **II:** 955

Certified Public Accountants (CPAs) **I:** 4, **207**, 293, 600, 619, **II:** 955, 1471

Cessna Aircraft **II:** 1036

CETA. *See* Comprehensive Employment and Training Act.

CFO. *See* Chief Financial Officer.

CFP **I:** 612

chaebols **II:** 874

Chains of command **I:** 19

Challenger, Gray & Christmas **I:** 502

Chamber of Commerce **I:** 206, **208–09**

Chamber of Commerce of the U.S. **I:** 208

Championing **I:** 788

Chance causes of variation **II:** 1359

Chance fork **I:** 396

Change Masters **I:** 558

Channel management **I:** 209

Channels of Distribution (*See Also* Physical Distribution Management; Retail Trade; Wholesaling) **I: 209–10**, **II:** 1001

Chapter 7 **I:** 128, 130

Chapter 11 **I:** 128–29, 331, **II:** 1299

Chapter 13 **I:** 128–30

Charismatic Leadership **II:** 902

Charitable gift annuities **II:** 1473

Charitable lead trusts **II:** 1473

Charitable remainder annuity trust (CRAT) **II:** 1472

Charitable stock bailouts **II:** 1473

Charitable trusts **II:** 1471–72

Chart theory **II:** 1416, 1418

Chartered financial analyst **I:** 293, **II:** 1307

Chase Manhattan Bank **I:** 292

Chase, Stuart **II:** 1195

Chattel mortgages **II:** 1481

Check kiting **II:** 1513

Chemical Manufacturers Association (CMA) **I:** 157, 266, 703

Chemical Release Forms **I:** 266

Chemical Workers Association **II:** 1220

Chesebrough-Pond's USA **II:** 1212

Chicago Board of Exchange **I:** 424

Chicago Board of Options Exchange **I:** 239, **II:** 1103–04

Chicago Board of Options Trading **II:** 981

Chicago Board of Trade (CBOT) **I:** 237–39, 664, 729, **II:** 1133, 1489

Chicago Mercantile Exchange **I:** 239, 818, 835, **II:** 1364

Chicago Tribune Co. Inc. **I:** 338

Chief Executive Officer (CEO) **I:** 20, 37, 92, 141, 156, **210–11**, 212, 246, 231, 253, 324–25, 334, 423, 487, 504–05, 559, 605, 682, 692, **II:** 951, 964

Chief financial **I:** 141

Chief Financial Officer (CFO) **I: 211–12**, 308, 599, 692, **II:** 955

Chief Information Officer (CIO) **I: 212–13**, 263, 782, **II:** 1208

Child care **I:** 178, 252, 255, 494, 500, 735, **II:** 1056, 1308

Child Care and Development Programs **I:** 677

Child Care/Elder Care **I: 213–14**, **II:** 1518

Child Labor **I:** 25, 43, **214**, 253–54

China, Doing Business in (*See Also* Socialism & Communism) **I: 214–20**

Chinese Communist Party (CCP) **I:** 217

Chinese Wall **II:** 1471

Chori **II:** 1346

Christensen, Ward **I:** 112, 271

Christian Copyright Licensing International **II:** 917

Chrysler Corp. **I:** 32, 93, 334, 442, 486, 837, **II:** 869, 1200, 1214, 1267, 1501, 1509

Cincinnati Milacron **II:** 1267

CIO. *See* Chief Information Officer *or* Congress of Industrial Organizations.

Ciompa, Paweł **I:** 454

Circulation mobility **II:** 1083

CIRRUS **I:** 69

Citibank **I:** 114, **II:** 1049, 1349, 1473

Citicorp **I:** 323, 607

Civil bonds **I:** 94

Civil Rights Act of 1964 **I:** 14, 35–36, 155, 221–22, 248, 435, 509–10, 537, 539, 541–42, 741, 765, 824, **II:** 886, 1316, 1318, 1322, 1521

Civil Rights Act of 1991 **I:** 14, 16, **220–24**, 510, 537, 539, 541–43, 679–80, 741, **II:** 1318, 1321

Civil rights legislation **II:** 882

Civil Rights Reformation Act of 1987 **I:** 539

Civil Service Act of 1883 **II:** 1072

Civil Service Reform Act of 1978 **I:** 588

Civilian Agency Acquisition Council **I:** 677

Civilian chief (United Nations) **II:** 1082

Clark, John Bates **II:** 879

Classic Coke **II:** 987

Classical economics **I:** 468–69, 474, **II:** 934–35

Classical management **II:** 941, 1117

Classical political economy **II:** 878

Data Processing Manager's Association **II:** 1028

Data Security (*See Also* Automated Office Security; Computer Security) **I:** **381–82**

Data storage **II:** 1089

Database management **II:** 1027, 1342

Database management programs **I:** 784

Database Management Systems **I:** 287, **382–84**, 737

Database Marketing **I:** **384–85**, 421

Databases **II:** 950

Datapoint **I:** 285

Date of record **II:** 1372–73

Davis-Bacon Act of 1931 **I:** 741

Day Care. *See* Child/Elder Care.

Days Inn **I:** 506

Dayton Hudson Corporation **I:** 229, 334

De Gaulle, Charles **II:** 1082

De Wolff, Peter **II:** 1030

Dealer **II:** 1366

Dealer's spread **II:** 1134

Dear, Joseph **I:** 779

DeBeers **II:** 1422

Debenture bond **II:** 925

Debentures **I:** 316, 387, **II:** 1303

Debs, Eugene **II:** 884

Debt (*See Also* Eurobond Market; Mortgages/Mortgage-Backed Securities) **I:** 94, 147, 171, 219, 320, 324, 356, 361, **386–88**, 397, 409, 424, 477–78, 590, 601, 611, 613, 751, 846, 850, **II:** 908, 913–15, 1010–11, 1013, 1022, 1126, 1129, 1159, 1183, 1232, 1237, 1256, 1328, 1371, 1374, 1395

Debt burden **II:** 905

Debt capital **II:** 1335

Debt financing **I:** 171

Debt/equity ratio **I:** 427, 613, **II:** 1395

Debts **I:** 360, **II:** 1489

DEC. *See* Digital Equipment Corp.

Decision audit **I:** 391

Decision fork **I:** 396

Decision Making (*See Also* Management Science; Operations Management) **I:** 20, 33, 94, 123, 139, 147, 166, 303, 334, 343, **388–93**, 478, 512, 565, 631, 667, 672, 706–08, 808–09, **II:** 860, 889, 913, 948, 956, 958, 962, 964, 990, 1053, 1060, 1098, 1127, 1149, 1152, 1181, 1456, 1465, 1532

Decision-making under certainty **II:** 1355

Decision-making under uncertainty **II:** 1355

Decision matrix **I:** 389

Decision mosaic **I:** 390

Decision Support System (DSS) **I:** **393–96**, 566, **II:** 1027–28

Decision Tree **I:** **396–97**, **II:** 1187–89

Dedicated circuit **II:** 1430

Dedication **II:** 1141

Deductible **I:** 728

Deductions **I:** 337

Default (*See Also* Interest Rate Risk) **I:** 235, **397–99**, 576, 647, **II:** 1045, 1053, 1103, 1439

Default risk **II:** 1265

Defense Contract Audit Agency (DCAA) **I:** 262

Defense Planning Committee **II:** 1082

Deferred annuity **II:** 1495

Deferred barter **I:** 356

Deferred call **II:** 1237

Deferred expense **I:** 190

Deferred income plans **I:** 709

Deficit Reduction Act of 1984 (DEFRA) **I:** 651, 692

Deficit spending **II:** 1064

Defined benefit **I:** 650, **II:** 1260

Defined benefit plans **I:** 652

Defined contribution plans **I:** 255, 650, 652, 709, **II:** 1260

Deflation **I:** 780

Degaussing **I:** 283

The Deindustrialization of America **II:** 1480

Delaney, Robert V. **I:** 134

Delegation. *See* Organization Theory; Organizational Behavior.

Deloitte and Touche **I:** 4, 506, **II:** 1520

The Delphi Technique **I:** 393, **399–03**, 641, **II:** 1275

Demarketing **I:** 699

Deming Prize **II:** 1221

Deming, W. Edwards **I:** 545, 558, **II:** 855, 861, 1121, 1219, 1221, 1403, 1447, 1455

Democratic National Committee **II:** 886

Demographic economics **II:** 877

Demographics. *See* Organization Theory; Organizational Behavior.

Denim Council **II:** 1212

Denny's **I:** 655

Dentsu **II:** 857

Dependent variable **I:** 428, 743

Depletion **I:** 177

Depository Institutions Deregulation and Monetary Control Act of 1980 **I:** 609, **II:** 1293

Depreciation **I:** 36, 169, 177, 190, 341, 345, 350, 355, **403–04**, 409, 424, 614, 624, 705, 749, 752, 847, **II:** 871, 905, 933, 953, 994, 1009, 1011, 1134, 1183, 1185, 1199, 1291, 1329

Depression **I:** 119

Depth **II:** 1366

Deregulation **I:** 65

Derivative securities **I:** 52, **404–07**, 424, 601, 603, 851–52, **II:** 1134, 1263, 1304

DeSantis, Carl **II:** 1060

Design for Manufacturing and Assembly **II:** 1098

Desktop Publishing **I:** **407–09**, **II:** 1471, 1527

Deutsche Bundesbank **I:** 678

Deutsche Terminboerse **I:** 238

Devaluation (Money) **I:** **409–11**

Development Banks **I:** 202, **411–12**

Development capital **I:** 411

Development cycles **II:** 1204

Development Diversified **II:** 1229

Development stage company **I:** 618

DeVry, Inc. **II:** 1505

Dewey Decimal System **I:** 717

Dewing, Arthur Stone **II:** 872

Dexter Manufacturing **I:** 719

Dial Corporation **I:** 327

Dialectical materialism **II:** 1338–40

DIALOG Information Services **I:** 384

Dickson, William J. **I:** 724

Dictionary of Occupational Titles **I:** 180, 252–53

Dies Committee **II:** 886

Differential cost **I:** 346

DigiCash BV **I:** 837

Digital computers **I:** 283

Digital Equipment Corp. (DEC) **I:** 32, 285, 564, **II:** 897, 926, 1424, 1496, 1526

Digital Plant **I:** 837

Digital Software **II:** 920

Dill-White Radio Act of 1927 **I:** 585

Diminishing returns **I:** 209, **II:** 1175

Direct costs **I:** 345, 354

Direct debits **I:** 483

Direct deposit **I:** 483

Direct finance **I:** 606

Direct Investment **I:** 87, **412–13**, 649, 814–15, 817, 826, **II:** 1006, 1300, 1365, 1425–26, 1463

Direct labor **I:** 108

Direct Mail (*See Also* Database Marketing) **I:** 195, 209, **414–17**, **II:** 936, 1271, 1277, 1279, 1286, 1432

Direct Marketing **I:** 9, 194, 198, 384, 414, **417–21**, 837, **II:** 858, 936, 938, 1000, 1279

Direct Marketing Association **I:** 195, 417, **II:** 936, 938

Direct method of cash flow statement presentation **I:** 190

Direct numerical control **I:** 268

Direct premiums **II:** 1287

Direct response advertising **II:** 938

Direct Selling Association **II:** 1157

Directive leadership **II:** 901

Directors. *See* Board of Directors.

Disbursement **I:** 193

Disclaimer of opinion **I:** 63

Disclosure **II:** 1300

Disclosure Laws and Regulations **I:** **422–24**

Discontinued operations **I:** 751

Discount bond **I:** 316, 386

Discount Broker (*See Also* Commodities; Futures/Futures Contracts; Hedging; Options/Options Contracts; Stock Market) **I:** **424–25**

Discount Rate **I:** 176, **425–26**, 427, 438, 587, 592–94, **II:** 1012, 1052, 1167, 1494, 1535

Discounted Cash Flow **I:** 110, 167, **426–27**, **II:** 1305, 1493

Discounted loan **I:** 235

Equity **I:** 94, 147, 176, 218, 245, 254, 315, 324, 356, 361, 386, 424, 438, 477–78, 523, 590, 611, 615, 709, 750, 846, 850, **II:** 870, 913–14, 950, 993, 1010, 1012, 1237, 1270, 1362, 1371, 1374, 1394–95, 1404, 1426, 1496
Equity accounts **I:** 192
Equity capital **II:** 1335
Equity carve-outs **II:** 1351
Equity firms **II:** 1497
Equity funding **I:** 365
Equity investments **II:** 1496
Equity REITs **II:** 1230
Equity related bonds **I:** 387
Equity warrant **I:** 317
Equivalence principle **I:** 670
Ergonomic disorders **I:** 544
Ergonomics **I: 544**
Erie Railroad **II:** 941, 1512
ERISA. *See* Employee Retirement Income Security Act.
Erlang, A.K. **II:** 1225
Ernst & Young **I:** 4
Ernst & Young's Center for Information Technology and Strategy **I:** 212
Erratic component **II:** 1453
Error Analysis **I: 544–46**
Escalator Clauses **I: 546–47**
Espionage **I:** 280
Esprit Corporation **I:** 700
Essi Systems Inc. **II:** 1386
Estate Planning **I:** 582
Estate settlement accounts **II:** 1472
Estate Taxes **I: 547**, 611, 806
Estee Lauder Inc. **I:** 580, **II:** 1520
Estridge, Don **II:** 1423
Ethernet **II:** 926
Ethical business practices audit **I:** 805
Ethics. *See* Business Ethics.
EU. *See* European Union.
Euro-commercial paper **I:** 317
Eurobond Market (*See Also* Capital Markets) **I: 548**
Eurobonds **I:** 317, 387
Eurodollar **I:** 169, 835, **II:** 1050, 1304
Eurodollar bond **I:** 317
Eurodollar CDs **II:** 1045, 1304
European Article Number **I:** 84
European Atomic Energy Community **I:** 236, 242, 550–51, **II:** 931, 1358
European Bank for Reconstruction and Development **I: 548–49**
European Central Bank **I:** 551
European Coal and Steel Community (ECSC) **I:** 236, 242, 550–51, 684, **II:** 931, 1358
European Common Market **I:** 88, 201, 481, **II:** 931
European Community **I:** 235, 550–51, 568, 659, 685, 822–23, **II:** 931, 1358
European Council **I:** 550
European Court of Justice **I:** 236, 242
European Currency Unit (ECU) **I:** 243, 550
European Economic Area **I:** 550

European Economic Community (*See Also* European Union) **I:** 38, 88, 236, 241, 458, 548–51, 570, 684, **II:** 931, 1358, 1388, 1494
European Economic Community Treaty of 1957 **II:** 935
European Economic Space **I:** 550
European Free Trade Association (EFTA) (*See Also* European Union) **I: 549–50**, 684
European Investment Bank **I:** 450
European Monetary Institute **I:** 244
European Monetary System **I:** 243, **550–51**
European Options Exchange **I:** 238
European Parliament **I:** 243, **II:** 931
European Union (EU) **I:** 157, 241, 452, 550, **551–52**, 659, 661, 675, 703, 785, 814, 817, 826, 831, **II:** 931, 935–36, 1347, 1485
European unit of account **I:** 550
Ex-dividend date **I:** 439, **II:** 1372–73
Excess Profits Tax **I:** 334, **552–53**
Exchange rate **I:** 550, 647
Exchange rate mechanism (ERM) **I:** 550
Excise Tax **I: 553–54**, **II:** 1290
Excise taxes, **I:** 302
Exclusionary tariff **II:** 1461
Executive Development **I: 554–60**
Executive Life **I:** 709
Executive Order 8802 **I:** 537
Executive Order 10925 **I:** 155
Executive Order 11246 **II:** 1316
Executive Order 11478 **I:** 537
Executors **I:** 597
Exercise price **I:** 159, 405, 606, 664, 851, **II:** 1103–04, 1108
Eximbank **I:** 202
Exit Strategies **I: 560–61**
Expanded Presence Program **I:** 538
Expansion **I:** 119
Expansion-round financing **II:** 1498
Expectations theory **I:** 800
Expected Value **I: 561–63**
Expense Accounts **I: 563**, **II:** 1155
Expenses **I:** 750
Expenses for Business Use of Your Home (IRS form 8829) **I:** 734
Experience and Learning Curves **I: 563–64**
Expert Systems (*See Also* Management Information Systems) **I:** 269, 287, **564–67**, **II:** 950, 1027–28
Exponential smoothing **II:** 1276
Export **I:** 207
Export Administration Act of 1969 **I:** 311, 823, **II:** 1427
Export commission house **I:** 569
Export Control Act of 1949 **I:** 311, **II:** 1427
Export duty **II:** 1461
Export-Import Bank of the United States **I:** 452, 647
Export management company (EMC) **I:** 568, 687
Export revenues **I:** 48

Export trading companies (ETCs) **I:** 569
Export Trading Company Act of 1982 **I:** 569
Exporting (*See Also* Global Strategy) **I:** 76, 96, 120, 296, 409, 445, 489, **567–571**, 649, 683, 815, 817, **II:** 1426
Expropriation **I:** 828
External Auditing **I:** 802, 804
External labor markets **II:** 877
External review **II:** 948
External tariff **II:** 1008
Externalities **I:** 168, **571**
Extortion **I:** 367
Extraordinary dividend **II:** 1302
Extraordinary gains or losses **I:** 751
Exxon Corporation **I:** 329
Exxon International **I:** 367
Exxon Research and Engineering Company **I:** 539
Exxon Valdez **I:** 332, 367, 701
EzBase **II:** 1066

F

Facility Management **I: 573–74**
Facsimile transmission **II:** 1090
Factor Analysis **I: 574–76**
Factor income **I:** 704
Factor loadings **I:** 575
Factor score coefficients **I:** 576
Factoring **I:** 235, **576–77**
Fair Credit Billing Act **I:** 595
Fair Credit Reporting Act **I:** 301, 365, 596, 741
Fair Debt Collection Practices Act **I:** 365
Fair Employment Practice (FEP) Act **I:** 155
Fair Employment Practices Committee (FEPC) **I:** 537
Fair Labor Standards Act of 1938 (FLSA) (*See Also* Child Labor; Compensation Administration; Sex Discrimination) **I:** 25, 214, 254–55, 505, 508, 510, 540, **577–578**, 735, 741, **II:** 883, 1438
Fair Packaging and Labeling Act of 1966 **I:** 596, **II:** 1138, 1283
Fair use **I:** 312
Fairfax Hospital **I:** 682
Fake Space Laboratories **II:** 1501
False disclosures **I:** 65
Families and Work Institute **II:** 1385
Family and Medical Leave Act of 1993 **I:** 178, 213, 510, 539, 541, 578, **II:** 886, 1522, 1531
Family business consultant **I:** 583
Family Leave **I:** 178, **578–79**, **II:** 1518
Family-Owned Businesses **I: 580–84**, **II:** 1072
Famous Amos **I:** 654
Fannie Mae. *See* Federal National Mortgage Association.
Farmer's Fire Insurance and Loan Company of New York **II:** 1471

FASB. *See* Financial Accounting Standards Board

Fascism **I: 584–85**

Fayol, Henri **II:** 941, 1113

FCC. *See* Federal Communications Commission.

FCPA. *See* Foreign Corrupt Practices Act.

FDA. *See* U.S. Food and Drug Administration.

FDIC Improvement Act of 1991 **I:** 587

Federal Acquisition Institute **I:** 677

Federal Acquisition Regulation **I:** 676, 695

Federal Advisory Council **I:** 594

Federal agency bonds **II:** 1141

Federal agency securities **I:** 590

Federal Arbitration Act **II:** 1321

Federal Aviation Administration **I:** 566, 674, **II:** 923, 1500

Federal Board for Vocational Education of Veterans **II:** 1506

Federal Board of Education **II:** 1504

Federal Bureau of Investigation **I:** 280

Federal Cigarette Labeling and Advertising Act **I:** 299

Federal Classification Act of 1923 **I:** 251

Federal Communications Commission (FCC) **I:** 13, 17, 262, 443, **585–86**, **II:** 1145, 1429, 1454

Federal deposit insurance **II:** 1232

Federal Deposit Insurance Corporation (FDIC) **I:** 80, 82, **586–87**, 607, 609, 709

Federal Dispute Resolution Conference **I:** 538

Federal Employees Compensation Act **II:** 1529

Federal Energy Regulatory Commission **I:** 262, 532, 840

Federal Express Corporation **II:** 956, 1460

Federal Food and Drugs Act of 1906 **I:** 299

Federal goods and services tax **II:** 1495

Federal Hazardous Substances Act **II:** 1196

Federal Home Loan Bank Board **I:** 587

Federal Home Loan Mortgage Corporation **I: 587–88**, 590, **II:** 1054

Federal Home Loan Mortgage Corporation Act **I:** 587

Federal Housing Administration (FHA) **II:** 1054

Federal Housing Enterprises Financial Safety and Soundness Act **I:** 588

Federal Information Center Program **I:** 677

Federal Insecticide, Fungicide, and Rodenticide Act (FIFRA) **I:** 533

Federal Labor Relations Authority **I: 588–89**

Federal manufacturers' sales tax **II:** 1495

Federal Maritime Commission **I:** 262, 532

Federal Meat Inspection Act (1907) **II:** 1195

Federal Mediation & Conciliation Service (FMCS) (*See Also* Arbitration & Mediation) **I:** 53–54, **589**

Federal National Mortgage Association **I:** 364, 387, 588, **589–90**, 710, **II:** 1054

Federal Open Market Committee **I:** 591–92, 594

Federal Organized Crime Strike Force **I:** 275

Federal Procurement Data System **I:** 677

Federal Property and Administrative Services Act **I:** 676

Federal Radio Commission **I:** 585

Federal Reserve Act **I:** 205, 208, 592, 594

Federal Reserve Bank **I:** 122, 409, 469–70, 483, 593–94, 607, 754, 759, **II:** 1040

Federal Reserve Board **I:** 298, 592, **II:** 1104, 1173, 1304, 1369, 1535

The Federal Reserve Bulletin **I:** 592

Federal Reserve System **I:** 80, 113, 123, 205, 426, 519, 587, **590–95**, 607, 733, 795, 799, **II:** 1044, 1047–48, 1208, 1242, 1480

Federal Savings and Loan Insurance Corporation (FSLIC) **I:** 587, **II:** 1293

Federal Savings Bank **I:** 327

Federal Service Labor-Management Statute **I:** 588

Federal Trade Commission Act of 1914 **I:** 41, 187, 567, 595, **II:** 1195

Federal Trade Commission (FTC) **I:** 41, 187, 234, 262, 300, 365, **595–97**, 655, 657, 701, 733, 802, **II:** 938, 1145, 1283, 1299, 1354, 1474, 1509

Federal Water Pollution Control Act (FWPCA) **I:** 182, 225

Federally insured mortgages **I:** 590

FedWire **I:** 483

Feigenbaum, Armand V. **II:** 1221

Feng shui **II:** 939

Ferkauf, Eugene **II:** 987

Ferranti **I:** 440

Feuerbach, Ludwig **II:** 1339

Fiber optic **I:** 272

Fiduciary Capital Management **I:** 711

Fiduciary Duty (*See Also* Employee Benefits) **I: 597–99**, **II:** 913

Field review appraisal **II:** 1151

FIFO. *See* First in, First out.

Finance **I:** 148, 172, 410, **599–600**, 788, **II:** 860, 952, 1098

Financial accounting **I:** 350, 355

Financial Accounting Foundation (FAF) **I:** 5, 600, 695

Financial Accounting Standards Advisory Council **I:** 6, 600

Financial Accounting Standards Board (FASB) **I:** 5, 189, 422, 424, **600–01**,

614–15, 633, 695, 750, 810, **II:** 1183

Financial Accounting Standards No. 95—Statement of Cash Flows **I:** 189

Financial analysis **I:** 364, 627

Financial Analysts Federation **I:** 6

Financial auditing **I:** 802, **II:** 948

Financial disclosure regulations **I:** 66

Financial due diligence **I:** 440

Financial EDI **I:** 483

Financial Engineering **I: 601–06**, **II:** 1104, 1108, 1301

Financial Executives Institute **I:** 5, 189, 803

Financial Executives Research Foundation **I:** 189

Financial flexibility **I:** 750

Financial institutions **I:** 276, 337, **606–11**

Financial Institutions Reform, Recovery and Enforcement Act (FIRREA) **II:** 1293, 1251

Financial instruments **I:** 599

Financial intermediation **I:** 363

Financial leases **II:** 906

Financial leverage **II:** 908, 912

Financial markets **I:** 754

Financial Planning (*See Also* Investment Management; Securities and Investments) **I:** 255, 354, **611–12**

Financial Ratios **I: 612–13**, 622, 846, **II:** 1531

Financial reports **II:** 1388

Financial risk management **II:** 1263

Financial service institutions **I:** 384

Financial statement audit **I:** 61

Financial Statements (*See Also* Audits and Auditing) **I:** 37, 74, 343, 404, 422–24, 448, 477, 600–11, **613–19**, 622, 634, 691, 803, 805, 840, 846, 851, **II:** 916, 948, 1009, 1135, 1181, 1210, 1241, 1257, 1298, 1369, 1417

Financial Statistics **I: 619–22**

Financial Times 100 **I:** 602

Financiele Termijnmarkt Amsterdam N.V **I:** 238

Financing activity **I:** 190

Finnish Options Exchange, Ltd., **I:** 238

Firewall **I:** 282

Firm commitment **II:** 1476

FIRREA **II:** 1293

First Bank of the United States **I:** 205, 591

First Brands Corp. **I:** 321

First Chicago Corporation **II:** 1095

First in, first out method (FIFO) **I:** 841

First round financing **II:** 1498

First Virtual Holdings Inc. **I:** 837

Fiscal policy **I:** 122, 230, 467, 469, 845, **II:** 934, 949, 1037–38, 1041, 1043, 1045, 1064, 1232, 1480, 1535

Fiscal Year (*See Also* Inventory Accounting) **I:** 141, **623**, 807

Fishbone diagrams **II:** 1360

Fisher effect **I:** 819

Fiske, Jim **II:** 1512

Fitch Consultants **I:** 327

Integrated project management **II:** 1202
Integrated services digital network **II:** 928, 1430, 1517
Intel Corp. **II:** 926, 909, 946, 1133, 1139
Intellectual capital **I:** 736
Intellectual Property **I:** 90, 218, 676, 796, **797–98**, 823, **II:** 919, 921, 1141, 1486, 1493
Inter-American Commercial Arbitration Association (IACAC) **I:** 811
Inter-American Treaty of Reciprocal Assistance **II:** 1109
Inter-market spread swap **I:** 9
Inter-regional investment **II:** 1008
Interactive advertising **I:** 10
Interbrand Group, plc. of London **I:** 99
Interest **I:** 318, 613, **II:** 915, 924
Interest income **I:** 705
Interest-only loans **II:** 924
Interest rate parity **I:** 52
Interest rate risk **II:** 1141, 1265
Interest rate swaps **I:** 405, 605
Interest Rates **I:** 9, 52, 75, 81, 95, 135, 170, 205, 235, 298, 317, 360, 362–63, 366, 386, 397, 405, 426, 444, 460, 470, 474, 512, 588, 601, 607, 620, 648, 709, **798–801**, 817, 819, 845, 850, **II:** 870, 905, 925, 933, 1006, 1038, 1043, 1053, 1104, 1107, 1129, 1131, 1171, 1173, 1178, 1229–30, 1263, 1307, 1329, 1375, 1439, 1493, 1535
Interest reinvestment rate **II:** 1141
Interface **II:** 1342
Interim financial statements **I:** 614
Interim financing **II:** 925
Intermarket spreads **I:** 239
Internal Auditing (*See Also* Compliance Auditing) **I:** 276, 308, **801–06**, **II:** 948
Internal controls **I:** 490
Internal Information Systems Management Service **I:** 677
Internal labor markets **II:** 877
Internal rate of return **I:** 167
Internal Revenue Code **I:** 202, 663, 692, **II:** 1269, 1351
Internal Revenue Service (IRS) **I:** 6, 262–63, 274, 292, 304–05, 337, 513, 563, 650, 663, 734, **806–09**, **II:** 1131, 1154, 1201, 1229, 1231, 1241, 1310–11, 1328, 1333, 1372, 1408–10, 1470, 1475, 1511
International Accounting Standards Committee (IASC) **I:** 809–10
International Arbitration **I:** 810–14
International Association for Financial Planning **I:** 612
International Association for Labor Legislation (IALL) **I:** 821
International Association of Business Communicators (IABC) **I:** 504
International Bank for Reconstruction and Development (IBRD) **I:** 64, **II:** 1533–34

International Benchmarking Clearinghouse **I:** 88
International Board of Standards and Practices for Certified Financial Planners, Inc. **I:** 612
International bond **I:** 387
International business **I:** 434
International Business Machines Corp. (IBM) **I:** 29, 55, 43, 93, 99, 113, 282, 284–85, 304, 314, 323, 327, 329, 336, 387, 402, 500, 506, 694, 696–98, 754, 765, 781, 789, 826, 830, **II:** 897, 920, 982, 1026, 1057, 1133, 1234, 1245, 1386, 1419, 1422–24, 1433, 1437, 1526
International Center for the Settlement of Investment Disputes (ICSID) **I:** 811–12, **II:** 1533
International Chamber of Commerce **I:** 101, 208, 811, 825
International commerce **I:** 208
International Communication. *See* Cross-Cultural/International Communication.
International Communication Agency. **I:** 589
International Competition **I:** 336, **814–17**
International Convention for the Protection of Industrial Property **I:** 797
International Convention for the Protection of Literary and Artistic Works **I:** 89
International Cooperative Alliance (ICA) **I:** 309
International Court of Justice **I:** 822
International Data Corp. **II:** 1517
International Development Association **II:** 1533
International Disaster Assistance Program **I:** 28
International Emergency Economic Powers Act **I:** 823
International Energy Agency **II:** 1111
International Events Group **I:** 338, **II:** 1287
International Exchange Rate **I:** **817–18**
International Federation of Accountants (IFAC) **I:** 809
International Finance **I:** **818–21**
International Finance Corporation **II:** 1533
International Franchise Association (IFA) **I:** 653, 655
International Harvester **I:** 331
International Labor Organization (ILO) **I:** **821–22**
International Labour Conference **I:** 822
International Law **I:** 413, **822–25**
International Management (*See Also* Global Strategy) **I:** 303, **825–30**
International Marketing (*See Also* Africa, Doing Business in; China, Doing Business in; Eastern Europe, Doing Business in; Indonesia, Doing Business in; Japan, Doing Business in; Korea, Doing Business in the Re-

public of; Malaysia, Doing Business in; Mexico, Doing Business in; South America, Doing Business in) **I:** **830–34**
International Monetary Fund (IMF) **I:** 64, 117, 217, 409, 450, 455, 570, 659, 831, **834–35**, **II:** 1109, 1163, 1450, 1483, 1533
International Monetary Market **I:** 239, **835**
International Organization for Standardization (ISO) **II:** 1355
International Organization of Consumers Unions **I:** 297
International Petroleum Exchange of London Ltd. **I:** 239
International Reciprocal Trade Association **I:** 87
International Signal & Control **I:** 440
International Tin Council **I:** 187
International trade **II:** 1097
International Trade Administration (ITA) **I:** 118, 233
International Trade Commission **I:** 661
International Trade Organization (ITO) **I:** 675, 831, 823
International Union of Operating Engineers **II:** 1096
Internet **I:** 13, 131, 271, 282, 487–88, 837, **II:** 858, 917, 1089, 1517
Internet (Business Applications) **I:** **835–38**
Internet Profiles Corp. **I:** 837
Internships **I:** 123, 181, **838–39**
Interstate commerce **I:** 589
Interstate Commerce Act **I:** 152, 839, **II:** 1298
Interstate Commerce Commission (ICC) **I:** 152, 262, 547, 733, **839–40**
Intertemporal modeling **I:** 165
Interventions **II:** 1121, 1123
Intra-firm finance **I:** 310
Intra-regional trade **I:** 457
Intramarket spreads **I:** 239
Intrinsic value **II:** 1305
Introducing Broker (IB) **I:** 425
Inventory **I:** 58, 235, 337, 461, 613, **II:** 916
Inventory Accounting **I:** **840–42**
Inventory and receivables management **I:** 613
Inventory control **II:** 1158, 1207, 1259
Inventory Control Systems (*See Also* Bar Coding; Electronic Data Interchange) **I:** **842–43**
Inventory cycles **I:** 122
Inventory holding period **I:** 613
Inventory to assets ratio **I:** 613
Inventory tracking **II:** 905
Investing activity **I:** 190
Investment **I:** 58, 705, **II:** 1101
Investment Advisers Act of 1940 **I:** **844–45**, **II:** 1299–300
Investment Analysis (*See Also* Valuation) **I:** **845–49**
Investment banker **I:** 170, **II:** 1210, 1365

Investment Company Act of 1940 **I:** 802, **II:** 1062, 1299–300
Investment grades **I:** 388
Investment income **II:** 1463
Investment Management (*See Also* Diversification in Investments; Stock Market) **I:** 599, **849–53, II:** 1307
Investment plan **I:** 141
Investment properties **II:** 1206
Investment spending **I:** 121
Investments **I:** 634
"Invisible Hand" **II:** 895, 1005, 1097
Iowa State University **I:** 284
IPO. *See* Initial public offering.
Irish Futures & Options Exchange **I:** 238
Irish Land League **I:** 96
Irrevocable trust **II:** 1472
IRS. *See* Internal Revenue Service.
Isaacs, Rufus **I:** 668
Isard-Kuene method **I:** 795
ISD. *See* Instructional systems design.
Ishikawa diagrams **II:** 1360
Ishikawa, Kaoru **II:** 1221, 1403
ISO. *See* International Organization for Standardization.
Isoquants **I:** 794
ITA. *See* International Trade Administration.
ITESM. *See* Instituto Tecnologico y Estudios Superiores de Monterrey.
ITO. *See* International Trade Organization.
Itoh, C. **II:** 1346
Itoman **II:** 1346
ITT Automotive **I:** 839
ITT Corporation **I:** 839
ITT Hartford Life Insurance **I:** 712

J

J.O.B.S. **I:** 653
Jablonski, Joseph R. **II:** 1456
Jacquard, Joseph-Marie **I:** 284
Jaguar **I:** 332
James River Corp. **II:** 1236
Japan, Doing Business in **II: 855–59**
Japan Human Relations Association **II:** 861, 1220
Japanese Association of Suggestion Systems **II:** 861, 1220
Japanese Industrial Robot Association **II:** 1266
Japanese Information Center of Science and Technology's On-Line Information System **II:** 1066
Japanese Management and Coordination Agency **II:** 858
Japanese management and manufacturing techniques **II:** 1219
Japanese Management Techniques (*See Also* Japanese Manufacturing Techniques) **I:** 558, **II: 859–62**
Japanese Manufacturing Techniques (*See Also* Japanese Management Techniques) **II: 862–65**
Jardine Matheson **II:** 1344

Jaures, Jean **II:** 1340
Jaycees **I:** 208
Jefferson, Thomas **II:** 895
Jenson v. Eveleth Taconite Co. **I:** 223
Jevons, William Stanley **II:** 879
Jewish Vocational Service Agencies **II:** 1506
Job analysis **I:** 59
Job Corps **II:** 1464
Job costing **I:** 355
Job description **I:** 505
Job Development Program **II:** 1464
Job Instruction Training (JIT) **II:** 1464
Job market **II:** 1257
Job Methods Training (JMT) **II:** 1464
Job Relations Training (JRT) **II:** 1464
Job rotation **I:** 558
Job Safety Training (JST) **II:** 1464
Job satisfaction **I:** 575
Job segration **I:** 249
Job sharing **I:** 501, 506, 578, **II:** 1522
Job-specific skill training **II:** 880
Job specification **I:** 505
Job training **I:** 672
Job Training Partnership Act **I:** 507, **II:** 1083–84, 1094
Jobbers **I:** 570
Jobs, Steve **II:** 1247
John Deere **II:** 890
John Hancock Mutual Life Insurance Co. **I:** 340
Johns Manville **I:** 127
Johnson and Johnson **I:** 332, 506, **II:** 897
Johnson Box **II:** 1278
Johnson, Fred **II:** 1278
Johnson, Spencer **II:** 1452
Joint and several liability **I:** 703
Joint costs **I:** 345
Joint Operating Agreement **II: 865–66**
Joint Ventures **I:** 215, 218–19, 357, 464, 826, 832, **II:** 857, 865, **866–69**, 1125, 1182, 1380
The Jungle **II:** 1195
Junk Bonds **I:** 172, 316, 398, 427, 610, 709, 801, **II: 869–72**, 1129
Juran, Joseph M. **II:** 861, 1121, 1221, 1456, 1458
JUSE **II:** 1221
Just-in-time **I:** 58, 139, **II:** 862, 1028, 1437, 1447
Just-in-time costing **I:** 344
Just-in-time inventory systems **I:** 85, 108
Justice Department **I:** 321
JVC **I:** 327

K

Kahn, R. S. **I:** 794
Kaiser Aluminum and Chemical Corporation **I:** 779
Kaiser, Henry J. **I:** 727
Kaizen technology **II:** 1222
Kanban **II:** 864
Kanematsu-Gosho **II:** 1346
Kansas City Board of Trade **II:** 1364

Kant, Immanuel **I:** 127, 399
Kanter, Rosabeth Moss **I:** 558
Kearns, David **I:** 747
Keating, Jr, Charles **II:** 1512
Keidanren **II:** 1344
Keiretsu **II:** 856, 874
Keith, Minor **I:** 79
Kellogg Co. **I:** 99
Kelly Services **II:** 1438
Kemper Insurance **II:** 1287
Kent-Moore Cabinets, Inc. **II:** 1449
Keogh plans **II:** 1131, 1260
Kepner, Charles H. **II:** 1189
Kepner-Tregoe **II:** 1188
Ketchum Communications **I:** 781
Kevlar **II:** 1244
Key Escrow chip **I:** 282
Keynes, John Maynard **I:** 175, 468, 791, 834, **II:** 879, 1006, 1030, 1039
Keynesian economics **I:** 470, 474, 791
Kimberly-Clark **I:** 32
Kimo Realty **II:** 1229
King, Gregory **I:** 454
Kingsley, Charles **II:** 1338
Kinnear, Thomas C. **I:** 698
Kinship obligations **I:** 18
Kleiman-Sahu study **I:** 711
Kmart Corp. **I:** 29, 135, 314, **II:** 987, 1008, 1258
Knight Ridder's Dialog service **I:** 838
Knights of Labor **II:** 890
Kobe Raw Silk Exchange **I:** 238
Kobe Rubber Exchange **I:** 238
Korea, Doing Business in the Republic of **I:** 491, **II: 873–76**
Korean-American Business Institute (KABI) **II:** 876
Korean Chamber of Commerce and Industry **II:** 876
Korean Trade Promotion **II:** 876
Korvette **II:** 987
Kotler, Philip **I:** 560, **II:** 1154
KPMG Peat Marwick **I:** 4
Kraft General Foods Inc. **I:** 97–98, 340
Kresge, S. S. **I:** 314
Kroc, Ray **I:** 654–55
Kuala Lumpur Commodity Exchange **I:** 238
Kubota **II:** 1346
Kuhn, Harold **I:** 668

L

La Salle University **II:** 1023
Labeling (*See Also* Packaging) **I:** 234, 596, **II:** 1138
LaBoon, Joe T. **I:** 556
Labor **I:** 457–58
Labor advocacy groups **I:** 96
Labor and Monopoly Capital **II:** 880
Labor bargaining **I:** 667
Labor Economics **I:** 774, **II: 877–82**
Labor Force. *See* Human Capital; Multicultural Work Force; Workforce.
Labor Law and Legislation **II: 882–86**
Labor laws **I:** 510, **II:** 1078

Mitsubishi Foods **I:** 229
Mitsui **II:** 1344, 1346
Mixed costs **I:** 346, 354
Mixed Economy **II: 1037–38**
Mixed strategies **I:** 669
Mixed tariff **II:** 1461
Mixed-use development **II:** 1207
Mobil **I:** 655, **II:** 897
Modeling **II:** 1060
Modeling technique **I:** 667
Modem **I:** 271
Modern portfolio management **II:** 1306
Modified accelerated cost recovery system (MACRS) **I:** 404
Modigliani, F. **I:** 438
Molins Machine Tool Company **I:** 629
Moments **II:** 1356
Monaghan, Tom S. **II:** 986
Mondale, Walter **II:** 898
Monetarism **I:** 470, 474–75, **II:** 934, **1038–45**
Monetary Control Act of 1980 **I:** 593–94
Monetary policy **I:** 122–23, 455, 457, 469–70, 550, 590, 592–94, 834, **II:** 934, 1038–39, 1043, 1061, 1173, 1232, 1480, 1535
Money aggregate **II:** 1046
Money-center banks **II:** 1488
Money income **I:** 749–50
Money market **I:** 169, 316, 366, 386, 426, **II:** 1049
Money market deposit accounts **II:** 1049
Money market funds **II:** 871, 1472
Money Market Instruments **I:** 94, **II:** **1045–46**, 1241
Money market mutual funds **I:** 610
Money market securities **II:** 1304, 1307
Money supply **I:** 205, 454, 594, 743, 845, **II:** 934, 1038, 1040, 1042–43, **1046–53**, 1535
Monochronic time **I:** 50
Monopolist **II:** 961
Monopolistic Competition **I:** 256, 258, 471, **II:** 960, 1032
Monopoly **I:** 40, 65, 152, 256, 471, 473, 480, 596, 796, **II:** 895, 960, 962, 1032–033
Monopsony **I:** 206
Monrovia Group **II:** 1108
Monte Carlo Method **II: 1053**
Montgomery Ward **I:** 194, 196, 493, **II:** 937
Montreal Exchange **I:** 238
Moody's **II:** 1045
Moody's Investors Service **I:** 95, 315, 388, 397, 801, 845, **II:** 869
Moody's Municipal Bond Guide **II:** 1130
Moore, Geoffrey **II:** 904
Moore, Henry **I:** 454
Moore-Peterson approach **I:** 795
Morgan, J.P. **I:** 152, 710
Morgenstern, Oskar **I:** 669
Morrill Tariff Act **I:** 446, **II:** 1406, 1503

Morrison, Ann **I:** 679
Mortality risk **I:** 711
Mortgage-backed bonds **II:** 1054, 1141
Mortgage bonds **I:** 315, **II:** 925, 1303
Mortgage loans **I:** 362, **II:** 925
Mortgage pass-through securities **II:** 1054
Mortgage pay-through bonds **II:** 1054
Mortgage REITs **II:** 1230
Mortgages **I:** 590, 800, **II:** 916, 1171, 1206, 1238
Mortgages/Mortgage-Backed Securities **I:** 590, **II: 1053–55**, 1304
Morton International **I:** 321
Most Favored Nation (MFN) **I:** 567, 659, 823, **II: 1055**, 1233
Motivation. *See* Employee Motivation.
Motor Carrier Act of 1980 **I:** 840
Motor Vehicle and Aircraft Emissions Standards **I:** 224
Motorola, Inc. **I:** 182, 278, 323, 747, **II:** 857, 1095, 1460, 1520
Motorola/Quasar **I:** 323
Mouton, J.S. **I:** 294
Moving averages **I:** 643, **II:** 1276
MSDS. *See* Material Safety Data Sheets.
Muckrakers **I:** 297
Muckraking Era **II:** 1194
Multicultural Workforce **II: 1055–58**
Multilateral Investment Guarantee Agency (MIGA) **I:** 452, **II:** 1533
Multilateral Treaty of Central American Free Trade/Economic Integration **I:** 204
Multilevel Marketing **II: 1058–60**
Multimedia computer systems **I:** 288
Multinational corporations (MNC) **I:** 826
Multiple Awards Schedule Program **I:** 677
Multivariate Analysis **II: 1060–61**
Municipal bonds **I:** 169, 387, 607, 609, 801, **II:** 1129, 1141, 1302
Municipal over bond (MOB) spread **I:** 240
Münsterberg, Hugo **I:** 764
Mutual Benefit Life **I:** 709
Mutual Funds **I:** 82, 424, 601, 610, 621, 652, 709, 760, 796, 847, 852, **II:** 870, 1045, 1049, 1054, **1061–62**, 1177, 1230, 1261, 1299, 1304, 1363, 1481, 1495
Mutual of Omaha **II:** 1213
Mutual savings banks **I:** 608
Myers-Briggs Type Indicator **I:** 180

N

NAA. *See* National Academy of Arbitrators *or* National Association of Accountants.
Nabisco, RJR **I:** 32
Nader, Ralph **I:** 155, 297, **II:** 1195
NAFTA. *See* North American Free Trade Agreement.
Nagano, Shigeto **II:** 859

Nagoya Stock Exchange **I:** 238
Nagoya Textile Exchange **I:** 238
Naive diversification **I:** 433
Naked options **I:** 160, **II:** 1106
NASA. *See* National Aeronautics and Space Administration.
NASDAQ. *See* National Association of Securities Dealers Automated Quotations System.
NASDAQ National Market System **II:** 1230
Nash equilibrium **I:** 669
Nash, John **I:** 669
A Nation at Risk **II:** 1504
National Academy of Arbitrators (NAA) **I:** 53
National Academy of Sciences **I:** 723
National Administrative Office (NAO) **II:** 1078
National Aeronautics and Space Administration (NASA) **I:** 56, 515, 674, **II:** 995, 1189
National Ambient Air Quality Standards (NAAQS) **I:** 224, **II:** 1020
National Association for the Advancement of Colored People (NAACP) **I:** 522, 653
National Association of Accountants (NAA) **I:** 803, **II:** 952, 955
National Association of Corporate Directors **I:** 94
National Association of Corporation Schools **II:** 1464
National Association of Female Executives **II:** 1526
National Association of Foremen **II:** 1464
National Association of Insurance Commissioners **II:** 871
National Association of Manufacturers **II:** 893, 1198, 1214, 1503, 1530
National Association of Realtors **II:** 1229
National Association of Securities Dealers **II:** 1063, 1299, 1370
National Association of Securities Dealers Automated Quotations System (NASDAQ) **I:** 754, **II:** 981, **II:** **1063–64**, 1133, 1368
National Association of Securities Dealers (NASD) **I:** 424, **II:** 1476
National Association of Security **II:** 1307
National Association of State Auditors **I:** 6
National Association of Stock Car Auto Racing **I:** 339
National Association of Temporary Services **II:** 1437–38
National Association of Women Business Advocates **II:** 1526
National Association of Women Business Owners **II:** 1523, 1526
National Banking Act of 1863 **I:** 591
National Black Chamber of Commerce (NBCC) **II:** 1036

National Bureau of Economic Research **I:** 619, 793, **II:** 1274, 1276

National Business Incubation Association **I:** 753

National Cash Register **I:** 738, **II:** 1154

National check clearing system **I:** 586

National City Bank **I:** 292

National Coalition On Television Violence **I:** 97

National Commission on Excellence in Education **II:** 1504

National Commission on Product Safety **I:** 299

National Committee on Governmental Accounting (NCGA) **I:** 695

National Computer Center **I:** 809

National Conference of Commissioners on Uniform State Laws **I:** 234, 308, **II:** 1480–81

National Cooperative Research Act of 1984 (NCRA) **II:** 1250

National Credit Union Association **I:** 367, 608

National Credit Union Share Insurance Fund **I:** 608

National Debt **II: 1064**, 1208

National Education Association **II:** 890

National Emission Standards for Hazardous Air Pollutants (NESHAP) **I:** 224

National Employer Supported Child Care Project **I:** 213

National Employment Priorities Act **II:** 898

National Environmental Policy Act (NEPA) **I:** 530, 532, 534–35

National Fire Protection Association **I:** 778, **II:** 1086

National Futures Association **I:** 241, 425

National Hero Awards Program **II:** 1212

National Highway Traffic Safety Administration (NHTSA) **I:** 154

National Hot Rod Association **I:** 341

National Housing Act of 1938 **I:** 590

National income **I:** 459, 749–50, **II:** 933

National Industrial Recovery Act of 1933 (NIRA) **II:** 887, 1065

National Infomercial Marketing Association **I:** 781

National Institute of Occupational Safety and Health (NIOSH) **I:** 510, 532, 778–79, **II:** 1086, 1385

National Institute of Standards and Technology **I:** 382

National Institute of Standards and Technology Authorization Act **II:** 1066

National Labor Board **II:** 887

National Labor-Management Conference of 1945 **I:** 53

National Labor Relations Act (NLRA) of 1935 **I:** 505, 508, 742, 776, 778, **II:** 883, 885, 887, 890, 1065

National Labor Relations Act of 1947 **II:** 887

National Labor Relations Board (NLRB) (*See Also* Labor Unions) **I:** 508, **II:** 883, 886–87, 891, **1065**, 1220, 1393, 1399, 1438

National Labor Relations Board vs. Jones Laughlin Steel Corporation **II:** 887

National Leadership Coalition on AIDS **I:** 32

National Management Association **II:** 1464

National Market System **II:** 1064, 1370

National Minority Business Council **II:** 1035

National Monetary Commission **I:** 592

National Mortgage Corporation **I:** 590

National Oceanic and Atmospheric Administration **I:** 535

National Paint and Coatings Association **II:** 1214

National Park Service **I:** 532

National People's Congress (NPC) **I:** 217

National Priority List **I:** 265

National Quotation Bureau **II:** 1063

National Research Council (NRC) **I:** 723

National Retail Federation **II:** 1258

National Science Foundation **I:** 836

National Securities Dealers Association **I:** 754

National Security Agency **I:** 282

National Society for the Promotion of Industrial Education **II:** 1504

National Support Center for Persons With Disabilities **II:** 1507

National Technical Information Act of 1988 **II:** 1066

National Technical Information Service **II: 1065–66**

National Traffic and Motor Vehicle Safety Act **I:** 299

National Transportation Safety Board (NTSB) **II: 1066–67**

National Underwriter **I:** 712

National Urban League **I:** 506, 522

National Vigilante Commission **I:** 91

National War Labor Board **I:** 53

National Wildlife Federation **I:** 157

National Workplace Literacy Program **I:** 747

Nationwide Insurance **I:** 506

NATO **I:** 242, **II:** 931

Natural limits **II:** 1361

Natural monopoly **I:** 260, **II:** 962, 1032

Natural rate of unemployment **I:** 518

Natural variation **II:** 1359

Navistar **I:** 331

NCR **I:** 278

Near-money **II:** 1048

NEC **I:** 286, **II:** 856

Necessary expenditure **I:** 427

Negative covenants **II:** 1257

Negative growth **I:** 459

Negative net worth **I:** 613

Negligence (*See Also* Product Liability) **I:** 777, **II: 1067–71**

Negotiable CDs **II:** 1304

Negotiable Instruments **I:** 237, **II: 1071–72**

Negotiable Instruments Act **I:** 234

Negotiations. *See* Arbitration and Mediation; Federal Mediation and Conciliation Service; Industrial Relations; International Arbitration; Labor/Management Relations.

Neoclassical economic theory **II:** 878

Neoclassical economics **I:** 791, **II:** 934, 1006

Neoclassical political economy **II:** 878

Neoclassical school of labor economics **II:** 878

Neoclassical theory **I:** 794

NEPA. *See* National Environmental Policy Act.

Nepotism (*See Also* Career and Family) **I:** 22, 48, 373, 762, **II:** 1023, **1072–73**

Nestle Foods Corp. **II:** 1095, 1512

Net asset value **II:** 1062

Net exports **I:** 704–05

Net income **I:** 109, 177, 336, 612, 750

Net leases **II:** 906

Net national product (NNP) **I:** 459, **II:** 933

Net present value **I:** 167, 438, **II:** 1011–12

Net profit **II:** 1198

Net profitability **I:** 612

Net realizable value **I:** 74

Net reliable value **I:** 614

Net Sales **I:** 612

Net working capital **I:** 632

NetScape Communications Corp. **I:** 837

NetWare **II:** 1342

Network marketing **II:** 1058

Network model **I:** 729

Network operating systems **II:** 1342

Network topology **I:** 272

Networks **I:** 282

Neural networks **I:** 280

New Deal **I:** 175, 577, 807, **II:** 1408

New factory orders **I:** 461

New Pay. *See* Strategic Pay/New Pay.

New to Export policies **I:** 647

New United Motor Manufacturing (NUMMI) **II:** 888

New York Central Railroad **I:** 151, **II:** 1512

New York Convention **I:** 811, 813, 825

New York Cotton Exchange **I:** 239

New York Futures Exchange **I:** 239, **II:** 1364

New York Mercantile Exchange **I:** 239

New York State School of Industrial and Labor Relations, Cornell University **I:** 774

New York Stock Exchange Composite **I:** 620

New York Stock Exchange Composite Index **II:** 1362, 1364

New York Stock Exchange (NYSE) **I:** 170, 239, 367, 424, 590, 600, 610, 621, 754, 849, **II:** 981, 1063, 1133, 1209, 1230, 1365, 1376, 1469, 1497
New York Times **II:** 1434
New York Times Company **I:** 681
New Zealand Futures & Options Exchange Ltd. **I:** 238
Newsletters **I:** 503
Newspaper advertising **I:** 420
Newspaper Association of America **I:** 12
Newspaper Preservation Act **II:** 865
Niche product **I:** 143
Nichimen **II:** 1346
Niching **II:** 1384
Nielsen Company, A.C. **II:** 975
Nike **I:** 32, **II:** 1437
Nikkei 225 **I:** 602, 620
Nikkei Index **II:** 856, 1363
1986 Superfund Amendments and Re-authorization Act (SARA) **I:** 265
NIOSH. *See* National Institute of Occupational Health and Safety.
Nippon Telegraph & Telephone Corp. **II:** 856–57
Nissho-Iwai **II:** 1346
NLRA. *See* National Labor Relations Act.
NLRB. *See* National Labor Relations Board.
NNP. *See* Net national product.
No-brain advertising **II:** 999
No-load funds **II:** 1062
No-waste advertising **II:** 999
Nokyo **I:** 188
Nominal group technique **I:** 401
Nominal income **II:** 1040–41
Nominal interest rate **I:** 460, 462
Non-binding letter of intent **II:** 1476
Non-price competition **I:** 256
Nonaccountable expenses **II:** 1476
Nonaccountable plans **I:** 563
Noncallable bonds **II:** 1303
Noncharitable trusts **II:** 1471–72
Noncompetitive bids **II:** 1302, 1489
Noncooperative strategies **II:** 1176
Noncurrent liabilities **II:** 916
Nondiversifiable risks **II:** 1306
Nondurable Goods **I:** 443, **II: 1073**
Noninvestment-grade **II:** 869
Nonleveraged ESOP **I:** 512
Nonparametric Statistics **II: 1073–75**
Nonproduction overhead **II:** 1134
Nonprofit corporation **I:** 333
Nonqualified stock options **I:** 513
Nonsystematic risk **II:** 1307
Nontariff **I:** 570
Nontariff barriers **II:** 1461
Nontariff measures **II:** 1461
Nonverbal behavior **I:** 50
Nordson Corporation **II:** 1028
Nordstrom's **I:** 378
Normas Oficiales Mexicanos **II:** 1020
Norrell Services **II:** 1437
Norris-LaGuardia Act of 1932 **I:** 508, 742, 786, **II:** 885

North American Advertising Agency Network **I:** 13
North American Agreement on Environmental Cooperation **II:** 1077
North American Agreement on Labor Cooperation **II:** 1078
North American Development Bank (NADBank) **I:** 411, **II:** 1080
North American Free Trade Agreement (NAFTA) **I:** 38, 79, 161–62, 185, 201, 230, 244, 411, 533, 570, 648, 659, 661, 675, 684, 814, 817, 823, 826, 831, **II:** 890, 1002, 1009, 1014, 1016–17, 1021, **1075–81**, 1100, 1313, 1347, 1407, 1483, 1486
North Atlantic Council **II:** 1082
North Atlantic Treaty Organization **II: 1081–82**
Northrop **II:** 1220
Northwest Airlines **II:** 1294
Northwestern National Insurance Company **II:** 1385, 1387
Not in my backyard (NIMBY) Syndrome **II:** 1253
Note issuance facilities **I:** 317
Notes payable **I:** 234, **II:** 920, 1027, 1342
NTIS Bibliographic Database **II:** 1066
Nuclear Agency **II:** 1111
Nuclear Non-Proliferation Treaty **I:** 312
Nuclear Regulatory Commission **I:** 532
Nuclear Waste Policy Act (NWPA) **I:** 534
Numeric variable **I:** 428
Numerical control (NC) **I:** 268, 625
Numerically controlled machine tool (NCMT) **I:** 625
Nutrilite Products Inc. **II:** 1058
Nutrition Labeling and Education Act of 1990 **II:** 1139
Nynex **I:** 321, **II:** 897

O

Objective criteria **II:** 1379
Objective function **I:** 429
OCC. *See* Options Clearing Corporation.
Occidental Petroleum Corp. **I:** 530
Occupational Access System (OASYS) **II:** 1508
Occupational illnesses **I:** 544
Occupational Licensing and Certification. *See* Licensing and Certification, Occupational.
Occupational Mobility and Retraining **II: 1083–85**
Occupational Outlook Handbook **I:** 180, **II:** 1259
Occupational Outlook Quarterly **II:** 1505
Occupational Safety **I:** 777, 822
Occupational Safety and Health Act of 1970 **I:** 32, 154, 303, 509–10, 738, 741, 778, **II:** 882–83, 886, 1088, 1438

Occupational Safety and Health Administration (OSHA) **I:** 32, 154, 266, 331, 510, 530–31, 533, 544, 740–41, 778, **II: 1085–88**
Occupational Safety and Health Review Commission (*See Also* Occupational Safety and Health Administration (OSHA)) **II: 1088–89**
Oceaneering Techologies **I:** 182
Odd-lot indices **I:** 848
Odd-lot theory **I:** 848
OECS. *See* Organization of Eastern Caribbean States.
OFCCP. *See* Office of Federal Contract Compliance.
Office Automation **II: 1089–91**
Office Management **II: 1091–92**
Office of Acquisition Policy **I:** 676–77
Office of Arbitration Services **I:** 589
Office of Business, Industry and Governmental Affairs **I:** 676
Office of Compliance and Consumer Assistance **I:** 840
Office of Federal Contract Compliance Programs (OFCCP) **I:** 15–16, 510, 540, 542–43, 680–82, **II:** 1317.
Office of Federal Housing Enterprise Oversight (OFHEO) **I:** 590
Office of Management and Budget **I:** 675, **II:** 1013, 1353
Office of Minority Business Enterprises (OMBE) **II:** 1034
Office of Personnel Management **I:** 766, **II:** 1438
Office of Small and Disadvantaged Business Utilization **I:** 677
Office of Strategic Services **I:** 768
Office of Technical Services **I:** 589
Office of the Controller of the Currency **I:** 490
Office of the Inspector General **I:** 27, 262
Office of Thrift Supervision **I:** 586, 608, **II:** 1251
Office of Workers' Compensation **II:** 1530
Offsets **I:** 357
Offsetting trade **II:** 1107
Oil Pollution Act of 1924 **I:** 225
Okura **II:** 1346
Oligopoly **I:** 256, 260, 442, 471–72, 480, **II:** 960–61, 1032, **1092–93**, 1384
Olive Garden **I:** 655
Olivetti **I:** 331, **II:** 1526
Olsten Corporation **II:** 1438
Olympics **II:** 1287
OM London Ltd. **I:** 239
OM Stockholm AS **I:** 239
Omnibus Trade and Competitiveness Act of 1988 **I:** 101, **II:** 1066, 1487
On-the-Job Training **I:** 537, 735, **II: 1093–97**
One-Minute Manager **I:** 132
One-stop capital shops **I:** 523
Ono and Shimada **II:** 1344
Ontario Securities Commission **I:** 162

Q

Quaker Oats **I:** 478
Qualified opinion **I:** 63
Qualified option **I:** 424
Qualified plans **I:** 651–52
Qualitative research **I:** 638
Qualitative restrictions **I:** 686
Quality by inspection/correction **II:** 1359
Quality Circles **I:** 500, 557–58, **II:** 861, 1095, 1119, **1219–20**
Quality Control (*See Also* Taguchi Methods) **I:** 511, **II:** 1132, **1220–23**, 1267, 1358
Quality Function Deployment (QFD) **II:** 1098, 1221, 1455
Quality in daily work **II:** 1455
Quantitative analysis **I:** 667
Quantitative management **II:** 942
Quantitative research **I:** 638
Quantity indexes **I:** 755, 759
Quantity theory of money **II:** 1005–06, 1041–42
Quasi-public corporations **I:** 333
Queens University **II:** 948
Quesnay, Francois **I:** 792–93
Queuing Theory **II:** **1224–26**
Quick assets **I:** 613
Quick ratio **I:** 613
quid pro quo sexual harassment **II:** 1319, 1323
Quotas **I:** 688
QVC Home Shopping **II:** 1260

R

Racial discrimination **II:** 877
Racketeer Influenced and Corrupt Organizations Act of 1970 (RICO) **I:** 618
Radiation Control for Health and Safety Act of 1968 **I:** 299
Radio Act of 1912 **I:** 585
Radio Act of 1927 **I:** 585
Radio emissions **I:** 282
Radio frequency (RF) **I:** 70
Railroad Cost Adjustment Factor (RCAF) **I:** 547
Railroad Cost Recovery (RCR) Index **I:** 547
Railroad Revitalization and Regulatory Reform Act of 1976 **I:** 840
Railway Labor Act of 1926 **I:** 508, **II:** 1065
Ralston Purina Company **II:** 1140
Rand Corporation **I:** 399, 401
Rand Institute for Civil Justice **I:** 267
Random Access Memory **I:** 284, **II:** 1242
Random component **II:** 1453
Random factors **II:** 1361
Random variable **II:** 1355, 1361
Random Walk Theory **I:** 848, **II:** **1227–28**, 1368
Rank Organization **I:** 688
Ranking **I:** 253, 256, **II:** 1151, **1228**
RAS Commodity Exchange **I:** 239
Rate of profit **II:** 1198

Rate of Return **I:** 438, 599, 601, 620, 851, **II:** 1164, 1167, 1198, 1366, 1374, 1376
The Rational Manager: A Systematic Approach to Problem-solving and Decision Making **II:** 1189
Ratios. *See* Financial Ratios; Price/Earnings (P/E) Ratio.
Raymond Corporation **II:** 1028
RCA **I:** 323
RCRA. *See* Resource Conservation and Recovery Act.
Re Max **II:** 1229
Real disposable income **I:** 645, **II:** 963
Real Estate **I:** 64, 315, 324, 362, 384, 477, 587, 611, 849, **II:** 905, 924, 981, 1047, 1098, 1203, 1205, **1228–29**, 1237, 1468, 1493
Real Estate Investment Trust Act of 1960 **II:** 1229
Real Estate Investment Trusts (REITs) (*See Also* Banks and Banking; Dividends; Mortgages/Mortgage-Backed Securities; Stocks; Taxes and Taxation; Trusts and Trustees) **II:** 1185, 1206, **1229–30**
Real estate management **II:** 1205
Real estate mortgage investment conduits (REMICs) **II:** 1054
Real estate owned properties (REOs) **II:** 1206
Real gross domestic output **I:** 462
Real gross domestic product **I:** 459, 642
Real income **I:** 749–50
Real interest rate **I:** 460
Real property **II:** 1228
Reauthorization Act of 1986 **I:** 778
Rebates **II:** **1230–31**, 1286
Receipts **I:** 563
Recession **I:** 119, 318, 459, **II:** 904, 1230, **1231–32**
Reciprocal trade agreements **II:** 1055
Reciprocal Trade Agreements Act of 1934 **I:** 446, 567, 823, **II:** 1407
Reciprocal Trade Agreements Program **II:** 1233
Reciprocity (Commercial Policy) **I:** 675, **II:** 1055, **1232–33**, 1407
Recognition programs **II:** 1460
Reconstruction Finance Corporation **I:** 589
Recruiting. *See* Employee Recruiting.
Recycling **I:** 265
Recycling Programs **II:** **1233–37**
Red herring **II:** 1210
Redemption agreements **I:** 232
Reductions in Force (RIF) **I:** 498
Refinancing **I:** 362, **II:** 870, **1237–38**
Refrigerator Safety Act of 1956 **I:** 154, 299, **II:** 1195
Refund **II:** 1230, 1237, 1286
Regents of the University of California v. Bakke **I:** 16
REGIO **II:** 1358
Regional Shipping Council **I:** 184

Regional Tariff Preference (RTP) **II:** 896
Register of Copyrights **I:** 312–13
Registered offering **II:** 924
Registered representative stockbroker **II:** 1307
Registrarships **II:** 1472
Registration statement **II:** 1297
Registry of Financial Planning Practitioners **I:** 612
Regression **I:** 395, **II:** 906, 1060, 1239
Regression Analysis **I:** 428, 644–45, **II:** 906, 963, **1239–40**, 1276, 1351
Regression lines **II:** 906
Regressive tax **II:** 1405, 1410
Regulation Z **I:** 424
Regulatory compliance **I:** 504
Rehabilitation **I:** 255
Rehabilitation Act of 1972 **I:** 540–41
Rehabilitation Act of 1973 **I:** 35, 537, 542, **II:** 1506
Rehnborg, Carl **II:** 1058
Reich, Robert **II:** 888, 1094
Reilly, William K. **I:** 536
Reis Machine **II:** 1267
Relationship investing **I:** 325
Relative frequency histogram **I:** 731
Relevant cost **I:** 346
Reliability **I:** 347, **II:** **1240–41**
Religious Belief Exemption **I:** 509
REMIC **II:** 1054
Remington Rand **I:** 284
Remote connections **I:** 280
Rensselaer Polytechnic Institute **II:** 1423
Reorganization Plan No. 2 of 1978 (Federal Labor Relations Authority) **I:** 588
Repetitive motion disorders **I:** 544
Repetitive motion syndrome **II:** 1091
Replacement Cost **II:** **1241**
Repos (securities) **II:** 1304
Repurchase Agreements **II:** 1050, **1241–42**
Request for Proposal **II:** **1242–43**
Required rate of return **II:** 1305, 1397
Resale **I:** 295
Research and Development **I:** 65, 103, 109, 141, 156, 477, 618, 649, 753, 836, 846, **II:** 856, 858, 869, 914, 948, 1066, 1126, 1182, **1244–50**, 1250, 1268, 1273, 1419, 1425
Research and Development Consortia **II:** **1250–51**
Research Center for Group Dynamics **II:** 1120
Reserve Bank Organization Committee **I:** 592
Reserve requirement ratio **II:** 1051
Residential mortgages **I:** 709
Resiliency **II:** 1366
Resolution Trust Corporation (RTC) (*See Also* Banks and Banking; Savings and Loan Associations) **II:** **1251–52**, 1293–94

Society of Consumer Affairs Professionals in Business **I:** 378
Society of St. Vincent de Paul **II:** 1506
Software **I:** 161, 281–82, 284, 303, 382, 393, 396, 407, 526, 564, 627, 715, 733, 784, 836–37, **II:** 920–21, 927, 950, 991, 1027, 1102, 1242, 1267, **1341–43**, 1416, 1499
Sogo Shosha **II:** **1343–47**
Soldier Rehabilitation Act of 1918 **II:** 1506
Sole proprietorship **I:** 28, 333, **II:** 1331, 1370
Solid Waste Disposal Act **II:** 1234, 1252
Solomon Brothers **I:** 681
Solomon Brothers Bond Indexes **I:** 602
Solution concepts **I:** 669
Sonet **II:** 1517
Sony Corporation **I:** 99, 327, **II:** 856, 858, 1031, 1244, 1346
South African Futures Exchange **I:** 239
South America, Doing Business in **II:** **1347–50**
South Shore Bank **I:** 412
Southern Cone Common Market **II:** 1348
Southern Pacific Rail Corporation **I:** 304, **II:** 1428
Southland Corporation **I:** 653, 657
Southwest Airlines **I:** 328
Southwestern Bell **I:** 321, 746
Speakers bureaus **II:** 1215
Special Drawing Rights **I:** 834
Specialist (AMEX, NYSE) **II:** 1367, 1369
Specialized Small Business Investment Company (SSBIC) **I:** 523
Specialty houses **II:** 1476
Specie-flow mechanism **II:** 1005
Specific duty **II:** 1461
Specific Identification Method **I:** 840–41
Specification limits **II:** 1361
Spectral Analysis **II:** **1350–51**
Speculation **I:** 550
Speculative-grade **II:** 869
Speculative stocks **II:** 1265
Speech recognition technology **II:** 1527
Sperry Vickers **II:** 1220
Spiegel **I:** 196
Spiffs **II:** 1289
Spikes **I:** 281
Spin-offs (*See Also* Corporate Downsizing) **I:** 146, 321, 561, **II:** **1351–52**
Spinelli, Altiero **I:** 243
Split-off point **I:** 345
Split-offs **II:** 1351
Split-ups **II:** 1351
Spot market **I:** 406, 835
Spot price **II:** 1105
Spot rates **I:** 818
Spread **I:** 170, **II:** 1488
Spreadsheets **I:** 287, 383, 720, 784, 1342, **1352–53**, 1423, 1471
Sprint **II:** 1428, 1431

SprintMail **I:** 113, 487
SRI International **II:** 1246
Ssangyong **II:** 1346
Stable histogram **I:** 731
Stable value funds **I:** 712
Staff arrangement **I:** 729
Stagflation **I:** 550, **II:** 1037
Staggers Rail Act of 1980 **I:** 840
Stained Glass Overlay **II:** 867
Stalin, Joseph **II:** 1341
Stamp Act **I:** 96
Standard & Poor's **I:** 95, 315, 388, 397, 754, 801, 845, 848, **II:** 869, 1045, 1167, 1259, 1306, 1352, 1354, 1364
Standard & Poor's 100 **I:** 754
Standard & Poor's 500 **I:** 164, 333, 602, 604, 620, 754
Standard & Poor's Composite Index **II:** 1376
Standard & Poor's Industry Survey **II:** 1229
Standard & Poor's Register of Corporations, Directors and Executives **I:** 180
Standard costs **I:** 343
Standard deduction **I:** 808
Standard deviation **II:** 962
Standard Industrial Classification System (SIC) **I:** 415, **II:** 1066, **1353–54**, 1530
Standard of living **I:** 427
Standard Oil Trust **I:** 350
Standardization **II:** 1151, **1354–55**, 1467
Standards Code **I:** 817, **II:** 1461
Stanford Research Institute **II:** 998
Stanley Furniture **II:** 1448
Stanley Herz & Co **I:** 503
Stanley Works **I:** 539
Start-up financing **II:** 1497
State Emergency Planning Response Commission **I:** 266
State of statistical control **II:** 1360
Statement of cash flow **I:** 633
Statement of Changes in Financial Position (SCFP) **I:** 632–34, 636
Statement of Concepts No. 6 **I:** 750
Statement of retained earnings **I:** 189
Statement of Sources and Applications of Funds **I:** 632
Statement of Sources and Uses of Funds **I:** 632
Statements of Financial Accounting Standards **I:** 5
Static budget **I:** 105
Statistical analysis **I:** 453
Statistical Analysis for Management **II:** **1355–58**
Statistical approach **II:** 1356
Statistical integration **I:** 59
Statistical Navigator **I:** 396
Statistical Office of the European Community **II:** **1358**
Statistical Package for the Social Sciences **I:** 575

Statistical Process Control **II:** **1358–61**, 1447, 1455, 1458, 1460
Statistical quality control **II:** 1455
Statistics (*See Also* Financial Statistics; Statistical Analysis for Management; Statistical Office of the European Community; Statistical Process Control) **II:** 1060, 1355
Statute of Frauds **II:** 1270
Statutory audits **I:** 61
Steers, Richard M. **II:** 874
Steffens, Lincoln **I:** 297
Stern-Stewart & Co **I:** 476
Stochastic Processes **II:** **1361–62**
Stock brokerages **I:** 384
Stock dividends **I:** 193, **II:** 1372
Stock index **I:** 405, **II:** 1362
Stock Index Futures **II:** **1362–64**
Stock issues **I:** 590
Stock Market **I:** 80, 169, 177, **II:** 981, 1232, 1362, **1364–70**
Stock portfolio **II:** 1362
Stock Price Change **I:** 613
Stock Price Paid **I:** 613
Stock splits **I:** 193
Stocks **I:** 80, 237, 245, 275, 404, 422, 424, 433, 437, 439, 477, 511, 590, 599, 601, 604, 606, 609, 611, 646, 692, 711, 731, 760, 844–45, 846, 849, **II:** 911, 908, 958, 1009, 1047, 1061, 1103, 1105, 1126, 1133, 1169, 1177, 1215–16, 1264, 1301, 1334, 1352, 1367, **1370–76**, 1387, 1397, 1416, 1439, 1468, 1495, 1511
Stone Model **I:** 193
Straddle **I:** 406, **II:** 1106
Straight bonds **I:** 317, 387
Straight-line depreciation **I:** 404
Straight-line method **II:** 1291
Straps **II:** 1106
Strategic advantage **II:** 1384
Strategic business units **II:** 1379
Strategic marketing **I:** 335
Strategic Pay/New Pay (*See Also* Compensation Administration) **II:** **1376–79**
Strategic philanthropy **I:** 335
Strategic planning **I:** 141, 156, 388, **II:** 1496
Strategy **I:** 40, 92, 324, 326, 328, 335, 337, 431–32, 504, 560, 667, **II:** 867, 948, 967, 988, 1127, 1173, **1379–81**, 1398
Strategy Formulation **II:** **1381–85**
Stress in the Workplace **I:** 492, **II:** **1385–87**
Strike price **I:** 159, **II:** 1104
Strikes **I:** 96, 664, 851
Strips **II:** 1106
Strowger, Almon **II:** 1428
Structrual mobility **II:** 1083
Structural analysis **I:** 846
Structural unemployment **I:** 517, **II:** 1478–79
Structured Query Language (SQL) **I:** 383
Subchapter S corporation **II:** 1269

Turnover unemployment **I:** 517, **II:** 1478

TWA **I:** 93, **II:** 956

The Twentieth Century Fund **I:** 292

Two-dollar brokers **II:** 1367

Two-Plus-Four Treaty on the Final Settlement with Respect to Germany **I:** 678

2-2-2 rule **II:** 1238

Tylenol **I:** 332, 367

U

U-Haul **I:** 580

UAW. *See* United Auto Workers.

UCC. *See* Uniform Commercial Code.

Umbrella policies **I:** 647

Unbiased expectations theory **II:** 1439

UNCITRAL **I:** 812

Uncontrollable costs **I:** 346, 354–55

Underground Economy (*See Also* Black Market (Trading)) **I:** 808, **II:** **1475–76**

Underinvestment **I:** 310

Underlying security **I:** 159

Underwood Tariff Act of 1913 **I:** 446

Underwriters Laboratories **I:** 278

Underwriting **I:** 364, **II:** 1365, **1476–77**

Unearned revenue **I:** 190

Unemployment (*See Also* Employment) **I:** 78, 117, 119, 252, 255, 410, 458–59, 473, 494, 496, 515, 522, 620, 791, **II:** 904, 932–33, 1030, 1037, 1232, 1349, **1477–80**, 1535

Unemployment Relief Act **I:** 539

UNESCO. *See* United Nations Educational, Scientific and Cultural Organization.

UNESCO Universal Copyright Convention **I:** 312

Unfair labor practices **I:** 508

Ungson, Gerardo R. **II:** 874

UNICEF **II:** 1483

Unification Treaty **I:** 678

Uniform Bills of Lading Act **I:** 234, **II:** 1481

Uniform Chattel Mortgage Act **II:** 1481

Uniform Commercial Code (UCC) **I:** 234, 295, 305, 307–08, **II:** 908, 1071, 1194, 1270, 1469, **1480–81**

Uniform Conditional Sales Act **II:** 1481

Uniform Customs and Practices for Documentary Credits (UCP) **II:** 908

Uniform Fiduciary Act **I:** 597

Uniform Guidelines on Employee Selection Procedures **I:** 16, 541, **II:** 1319–20

Uniform Negotiable Instruments Act **II:** 1481

Uniform Product Liability Act **II:** 1192

Uniform Sales Act **I:** 234, **II:** 1481

Uniform Stock Transfer Act **I:** 234, **II:** 1481

Uniform Trust Receipts Act **II:** 1481

Uniform Trustees' Powers Act **I:** 597

Uniform Warehouse Receipts Act **I:** 234, **II:** 1481

Unilateral transfers **II:** 1463

Unilever **I:** 827

Unimation, Inc. **II:** 1267

Union Bank of Switzerland **I:** 275

Union Carbide **I:** 266, 321, 332, 367, 689, 790

Union of Japanese Scientists and Engineers **II:** 1219, 1221

Union Pacific Railroad **I:** 137, **II:** 1512

Unions. *See* Industrial Relations; Labor/Management Relations; Labor Unions; National Labor Relations Board (NLRB).

Unisys Corp. **I:** 765

Unit Investment Trust **II:** **1481–82**

United Airlines **I:** 87, 330, **II:** 951

United Artists Cable Systems **II:** 1028

United Auto Workers **I:** 310, **II:** 890, 1085

United Food and Commercial Workers (UFCW) **II:** 892

United Fruit Company **I:** 79

United Marketing Services (UMS) **II:** 1231

United Mine Workers **II:** 884, 894

United Nations **I:** 90, 97, 117, 242, 485, 489, 659, 693, 745, 794, 821–22, 831, 834, **II:** 1109, 1270, 1292, 1316, 1418, **1482–83**, 1533

United Nations Commission on International Trade Law **I:** 812

United Nations Convention on the Recognition and Enforcement of Arbitral Awards **I:** 811

United Nations Development Programme (UNDP) **I:** 118

United Nations Economic Commission for Latin America **II:** 896, 1451

United Nations Educational, Scientific and Cultural Organization (UNESCO) **I:** 90, **II:** 1109, 1483

United Nations Industrial Development Organization **II:** 1451

United Nations Monetary and Financial Conference **I:** 455

United Nations Security Council **II:** 859

United Parcel Service **II:** 956

United Shoe Machinery Company **I:** 260

U.S. Antitrust Division **II:** 1422

U.S. Army Corps of Engineers **I:** 227

U.S. Army Research Institute **I:** 766

United States-ASEAN Council for Business and Technology **I:** 60

U.S. Bureau of Alcohol, Tobacco and Firearms **I:** 808

U.S. Bureau of Economic Analysis **I:** 117, 337, 704–05, **II:** 1463

U.S. Bureau of Export **I:** 311

U.S. Bureau of Internal Revenue **I:** 806–07, **II:** 1153, 1408

U.S. Bureau of Labor Statistics (BLS) **I:** 1, 180, 254, 298, 546, 726, 735,

757–58, 779, 791, **II:** 1083, 1171, 1354, 1530

U.S. Bureau of National Affairs **I:** 53, 130, **II:** 897, 1438

U.S. Bureau of Salesmanship Research **I:** 764

U.S. Bureau of the Census **I:** 1, 117, 198, 284, 427, **II:** 1013, 1094, 1199, 1354, 1530

U.S.-Canada Free Trade Agreement of 1989 **I:** 206, 230, 815, **II:** **1483–86**

U.S. Census of Manufacturers **I:** 793

U.S. Centers for Disease Control **I:** 31

U.S. Chamber of Commerce (*See Also* Chamber of Commerce) **I:** 452, **II:** 1200, 1330

U.S. Civil Service Commission **I:** 537, 539, **II:** 1319

U.S. Coast Guard **I:** 535, **II:** 923, 1067

United States Code Annotated **I:** 312

U.S. Congress **I:** 519, 645

U.S. Congressional Budget Office **I:** 785

U.S. Consolidated Omnibus Budget Reconciliation Act of 1986 **I:** 32

U.S. Constitution **I:** 291, **II:** 883

U.S. Copyright Act of 1976 **II:** 917

U.S. Council for Automotive Research **II:** 1250

U.S. Court of International Trade **I:** 442

U.S. Department of Agriculture **I:** 240, **II:** 1354

U.S. Department of Commerce **I:** 99, 113, 117, 186, 199, 202, 233, 311, 358, 442–43, 452, 490, 625, 656, 658, 705, 754, **II:** 904, 918, 1013, 1066, 1073, 1098, 1314, 1331, 1427, 1463, 1487

U.S. Department of Defense **I:** 265, 277, 382, 693, 792, **II:** 1085

U.S. Department of Defense's Advanced Research Project Agency (ARPA) **I:** 836

U.S. Department of Education **I:** 745

U.S. Department of Energy **I:** 265, 674

U.S. Department of Health and Human **I:** 524

U.S. Department of Health, Education, and Welfare **I:** 225, **II:** 1504

U.S. Department of Housing and Urban Development (HUD) **I:** 522–24, 587, 590

U.S. Department of Justice **I:** 16, 42–43, 102, 241, 596, 618, 733, 807, **II:** 865, 1160, 1250, 1317, 1319, 1428

U.S. Department of Labor **I:** 15, 177, 213–14, 427, 509–10, 515, 540, 544, 577–78, 652, 679, 734, 745, 754, **II:** 883, 1085, 1094, 1096, 1317, 1319, 1437, 1505, 1508, 1530

U.S. Department of Labor, Bureau of Apprenticeship and Training **I:** 43

U.S. Department of Labor, Office of Work-Based Learning **II:** 1505

War Labor Board **II:** 878

War Revenue Act of 1917 **I:** 807, **II:** 1408

Ward, Aaron Montgomery **I:** 195, 414, 417, **II:** 937

Wards Cove Packing Company v. Antonio **I:** 16, 221, 541

Warner, W. Lloyd **I:** 724

Warranties **I:** 596, **II:** 1184

Warranties & Guarantees **II: 1509–10**

Warrants (Securities) **I:** 404, 751, **II:** 1108, 1371, **1510–11**

Warren-Featherbone Company **II:** 1449

Warren, Samuel D. **II:** 1262

Warsaw Pact **II:** 1081

Wash sales **II:** 1299

Water Pollution Act of 1956 **I:** 225

Water Pollution Control Act of 1948 **I:** 225

Water Pollution Control Administration **I:** 225

Water Power Act **II:** 1195

Water Quality Act of 1965 **I:** 225

Water Quality Improvement Act of 1970 **I:** 182, 225

WATS line **II:** 936

Watson, Sr., Thomas **I:** 500

Wealth **I:** 361, 623, **II:** 1100, 1231, **1511**

The Wealth of Nations **I:** 126, 173, 658, 684, **II:** 895, 1097

Wealth replacement trust **II:** 1473

Webb-Pomerene Associations (Webb-Pomerene Export Trade Act of 1918) **I:** 569

Weber, Max **I:** 175, **II:** 994, 1113

WEFA Group **I:** 195

Weichart Realtors **II:** 1229

Weighted aggregate price index **I:** 759

Weighted average cost of capital **I:** 167, 477

Weighted Average Method **I:** 841

Welfare economics **I:** 389

Wells Fargo **I:** 837

Wendy's **I:** 655, **II:** 1335

Werner Report **I:** 550

Western Electric Company **I:** 722–23, 764, **II:** 1113, 1428, 1455

Western Electric Hawthorne Works **I:** 723

Western Union **II:** 1428

Westinghouse **I:** 688, **II:** 865, 897, 1220, 1267, 1355

Westinghouse Electric Corp. **I:** 32

Westinghouse, George **II:** 1355

Wetlands-protection laws **I:** 537

Weyerhaeuser Co. **II:** 1507

Wharton School of Business **I:** 581

What you see is what you get (WYSIWYG) **II:** 1528

White Collar Crime **I:** 274, **II:** **1511–15**

White, Harry Dexter **I:** 834

White lists **I:** 96

Whitney, Eli **II:** 1354

Whitney, J.H. **II:** 1496

Wholesaling **I:** 753, **II: 1515–16**

Wholesome Meat Act **I:** 299

Wide Area Networks (WANs) **I:** 227, 288, 737, 836, **II:** 928, 950, 1029, **1516–18**, 1431

Wide Area Telephone Service **II:** 1432

Wiggins, Albert **I:** 292

Wiley, Harvey W. **I:** 300

Wiley Pure Food and Drug Act **I:** 299

Wilks lambda **I:** 429

Will-Burt Co. **II:** 1505

Williams Act of 1968 **II:** 1160, 1404, 1439

Williams, John Skelton **I:** 592

Williams-Steiger Occupational Safety and Health Act of 1970 **II:** 1085

Williamson, D.T.N. **I:** 629

Willis, H. Parker **I:** 592

Wills **I:** 611

Wilshire 5000 **I:** '164, 754

WilTel **II:** 1431

Windows **I:** 272, 697

Winterbottom v. Wright **II:** 1192

Wireless Ship Act of 1910 **I:** 585

Wm. Wrigley Jr. Co. **I:** 99

Women Entrepreneurs (*See Also* Entrepreneurship) **II:** 1520, **1522–26**

Women in Business **I:** 677, **II: 1518–22**

Women in Nationwide Sales (WINS) **I:** 506

Women's Bureau **I:** 213

Women's Business Advocate **II:** 1526

Women's National Democratic Club **I:** 681

Women's Network for Entrepreneurial Training **II:** 1526

Women's Wear Daily **II:** 1259

Woodward, Calvin **II:** 1503

Wool Products Labeling Act of 1939 **I:** 596, **II:** 1195

Word processing **I:** 383, 408, 784, **II:** 1342, **1526–29**

WordPerfect Corp. **I:** 114, 682, **II:** 1454

Work breakdown structure **II:** 1204

Work ethic **II:** 1504

Work-for-hire **I:** 663

Work in America **II:** 1504

Work in process budget **I:** 107

Work Schedules. *See* Family Leave; Hours of Labor.

Worker Adjustment and Retraining Notification Act **I:** 510, **II:** 898

Worker retraining **II:** 877

Worker Right to Know (RTK) **I:** 533

Worker surveillance **II:** 1386

Worker turnover **I:** 310

Workers' Compensation **I:** 252, 255, 333, 494–95, 508, 510, 544, 742, 777, **II:** 1308, 1385, 1506, **1529–30**

Workforce **I:** 147, 178, 323, 433, 501, 514, 519, 541, 726, 774, 827, 838, **II:** 858, 897, 1056, 1099, 1149, 1180–181, 1200, 1437, 1445, 1464, 1518, **1530–31**

Working Capital **I:** 74, 81, 143, 351, 360, 635, **II:** 915–16, 925, 1011, 1199, 1257, 1272, **1531**

Working conditions **I:** 509

working hours. *See* Hours of Labor.

Workplace Fairness Act **I:** 510, **II:** 886

Workplace safety **I:** 508

Works Constitution Acts of 1952 and 1972 **II:** 1532

Works Councils **I:** 326, **II: 1531–33**

Workstations **I:** 286, 625

World Bank (*See Also* Eurobond Market; European Bank for Reconstruction and Development) **I:** 118, 217, 452–53, 455, 463, 676, 822, 831, 835, **II:** 1109, 1181, 1451, 1483, **1533–34**

World Health Organization **I:** 31, **II:** 1483

World Intellectual Property Organization (WIPO) **I:** 90

World Trade Organization (WTO) **I:** 659–61, 823, **II:** 1292

World War II **I:** 225, **II:** 1081

World Wide Web **I:** 836

World Wildlife Fund **I:** 536

Worms **I:** 281

WTO. *See* World Trade Organization.

WYSIWYG. *See* What you see is what you get.

X

X/Open Co., Ltd. **II:** 920

Xerox Corporation **I:** 87–88, 281, 329, 688, 747, 829, **II:** 897, 926, 1141, 1245, 1422, 1433

Xerox PARC **II:** 1247

Y

Yankee CD **II:** 1045

Yankee Group **I:** 304

Yaskawa Electric Company **II:** 1223

Yasuda **II:** 1344

Yellow dog contract **II:** 884

Yellowstone National Park **I:** 227

Yeltsin, Boris **II:** 1147

Yield **I:** 799, 801

Yield curve **I:** 387, 620, 800

Yield spread **I:** 318

Yield to call **I:** 317

Yield to maturity **I:** 317, **II:** 1439, 1489

Yokagawa Electric **II:** 1421

Young & Rubicam Inc. **I:** 101

Your Money's Worth **II:** 1195

Z

Zacson Corp. **II:** 1433

Zenith Electronics Corporation **I:** 323, 482

Zermelo **I:** 668

Zero coupon bonds **I:** 95, 316, 386, 851, **II:** 1108, 1129, 1303

Zero Economic Growth **I:** 459, **II:** **1535–36**